William Wordsworth

IF thou indeed derive thy light from Heaven,
Then, to the measure of that heaven-born light,
Shine, Poet! in thy place, and be content:—
The stars pre-eminent in magnitude,
And they that from the zenith dart their beams,
(Visible though they be to half the earth,
Though half a sphere be conscious of their brightness)
Are yet of no diviner origin,
No purer essence, than the one that burns,
Like an untended watch-fire, on the ridge
Of some dark mountain; or than those which seem
Humbly to hang, like twinkling winter lamps,
Among the branches of the leafless trees;
All are the undying offspring of one Sire:
Then, to the measure of the light vouchsafed,
Shine, Poet! in thy place, and be content.

The Works of
William Wordsworth

with an Introduction and Bibliography

The Wordsworth Poetry Library

This edition published 1994 by Wordsworth Editions Ltd,
Cumberland House, Crib Street, Ware, Hertfordshire.

Copyright © Wordsworth Editions Ltd 1994.

ISBN 1-85326-401-6

Printed and bound in Denmark by Nørhaven.

Introduction

PARADOXICALLY, Wordsworth, who notoriously strove to avoid the highfaluting and artificial 'poetic diction' of his predecessors and to address his readers in 'the very language of men', is, in spite of his unpretentious and accessible style, surprisingly difficult for modern readers to 'get into'. This is partly because he *is* so understandable that we read him quickly, without pausing to reflect on the significance of certain terms. And it's because almost all of us have 'done' Wordsworth at school, and find it difficult to bring a fresh approach, or even real enthusiasm, to his work. There must be few people in the English-speaking world who don't make associations with daffodils, the Lake District, and Nature as a Good Thing on hearing Wordsworth's name. And that's another of the problems: all of us have come to think of 'Nature' as a Good Thing, without any very clear idea of what 'Nature' is. We are not only heirs to, even participators in, the Romantic tradition (often seen as opening with Wordsworth's and Coleridge's Preface to the 1800 edition of the *Lyrical Ballads*) but inhabitants of a world increasingly threatened by man-made devastation. This vague consensus makes it difficult to appreciate the sheer force and acuity of Wordsworth's response to 'the beautiful and permanent forms of nature'.

His early poem, 'Tintern Abbey', is a powerful declaration of how he perceives

> In nature and the language of the sense,
> The anchor of my purest thoughts, the nurse,
> The guide, the guardian of my heart, and soul
> Of all my moral being.

This long poem in blank verse records his return to the already renowned beauty spot on the Wye in 1798 with his sister, Dorothy, five years after his first visit. It describes the scene with lyrical fervour and, as he reflects on the difference between his feelings during each visit, we learn how

> nature then . . .
> To me was all in all. – I cannot paint
> What then I was. The sounding cataract
> Haunted me like a passion: the tall rock,
> The mountain, and the deep and gloomy wood,
> Their colours and their forms, were then to me
> An appetite.

In what he described as 'the impassioned music of the versification', he pursues the maturing of his feelings, his perceptions of the moral and philosophical lessons to be learned when

> with an eye made quiet by the power
> Of harmony, and the deep power of joy,
> We see into the life of things.

His style here, though never difficult, is consciously elevated. He did, however, often use the deliberately ingenuous ballad form and, in a poem of about the same date, condensed his philosophy into a single stanza:

> One impulse from a vernal wood
> May teach you more of man,
> Of moral evil and of good,
> Than all the sages can.

It is this view of nature as having palpable moral significance which sets Wordsworth apart not only from other poets who are thought of as belonging to the Romantic Movement (though Coleridge did share it to some extent) but from earlier poets who extolled the beauties of the natural world. And, even more, it is a real mysticism which gives his nature poetry such profound and piercing power. This mysticism, and the sense of an almost platonic world of more perfect reality, informs the slightly later ode, 'Intimations of Immortality from Recollections of Early Childhood'. Here he explores the significance of childhood's intense responses to the natural world, noting how this intensity fades, and that 'Shades of the prison house begin to close/Upon the growing boy'. 'Our birth', he suggests, 'is but a sleep and a forgetting', though we can catch a glimpse of 'that immortal sea/Which brought us hither'. Whilst much of the tone is that of loss, the poet is able to affirm his faith in the power of the human mind, and the poem is imbued with rhapsodic feeling.

Although the dignifying and validation of childhood and its experiences was an important part of the Romantic programme (with William Blake its chief prophet) it does appear that Wordsworth's youthful sensations were peculiarly intense. He was born in 1770 at Cockermouth, Cumberland, the son of a lawyer. His sister, Dorothy, was born the following year, and three brothers succeeded them. Their mother died in 1778, his father only five years later, something which may account for his closeness to Dorothy, who was to become his lifelong companion, even after his marriage in 1802 to Mary Hutchinson. His long autobiographical poem, *The Prelude*, tells us of his unhappiness at Cambridge, his walking tour in the Alps and his time in France, where he was overwhelmed by the republican ideals of the French Revolution.

He records only vaguely his love affair with Annette Vallon, which produced a daughter. On his return to England he started publishing. In 1795 a legacy gave him the freedom to devote his life to writing, and to set up home with Dorothy, first in Dorset, then, in order to be near his friend Coleridge, in Somerset, where they collaborated on the *Lyrical Ballads*. In 1799 Wordsworth and Dorothy settled at Grasmere in Cumberland, where three years later the payment of an old debt made his marriage possible. This was still a time of intense creativity and increasing renown. But his real fame was to come much later in life, at a time when, to modern readers, his poetry shows a distinct falling off and his political views had shifted from those of youthful radical to a pretty crusted conservatism.

On the whole, therefore, readers embarking on or coming afresh to Wordsworth's poetry would be well advised to concentrate on his earlier work. The great poems mentioned above, when read with that relaxed concentration which furnishes the necessary responsiveness, make a good entry point and, with patience, *The Prelude*, particularly Books I and II which were published on their own in 1799 when Wordsworth was at the height of his powers, yields similar rewards. In the poems recording and celebrating the lives of individuals, like 'The Old Cumberland Beggar', 'Goody Blake and Simon Gill', 'The Idiot Boy' or 'Peter Bell', Wordsworth in the deliberately simple style which was often to scandalise contemporary critics and which even today requires a willingness to respect his methods, brings a tender reverence to even the humblest human existence. The poems in ballad form, too, like 'We are Seven' which tells of a child's (to Wordsworth appropriate) inability to see her dead siblings as anything but a part of the living family, require the modern reader to enter into the poet's intentions with the respect he accorded his subjects. It is 'the still, sad music of humanity' which sounds in such poems, and, with a grave beauty, in 'Resolution and Independence' where 'the great and simple affections' of humankind are observed and celebrated together with the impact of the natural world.

Not that Wordsworth was in any way a naïve poet. In spite of this highly-crafted simplicity he was a sophisticated and literary writer. This is most readily perceived in his accomplished prosody: contemporary readers would have recognised his use of the Pindaric ode form in 'Intimations of Immortality' and he employs a knowing mock heroic (like Pope's in *The Rape of the Lock*) in Book III of *The Prelude*. His assured handling of verse forms is probably most familiar in his use of the sonnet, of which 'Composed Upon Westminster Bridge' is probably the best known. Of the many others, the one written to Toussaint L'Ouverture (the leader of a rebellion of West Indian slaves) is a noble tribute to Toussaint's bravery and 'exultations, agonies,/And love, and Man's unconquerable mind'.

The 'Lucy' poems, ('A slumber did my spirit seal', 'She dwelt among th'untrodden ways', 'Strange fits of passion I have known', 'Three years she grew in sun and shower' and 'I travelled among unknown Men'), so apparently simple, are Wordsworth's most enigmatic statements. It is thought unlikely that they reflect actual historical 'facts', but many commentators believe that the seemingly coded emotion which breathes through these short lyrics owes much to the profundity of his feelings for an intense relationship with Dorothy. (An enjoyable exercise in practical criticism is to compare Wordsworth's poem, 'I wandered lonely as a Cloud' with his sister's journal entry about seeing the 'host of golden daffodils'.) In most of them he uses his well-loved ballad form, with its connotations of folk song and populism, and the vocabulary is, when examined closely, startlingly simple. The majority of his words are monosyllabic, with the occasional disyllable. Thus the employment of a word which is longer and more 'literary' can impart astonishing power:

> No motion has she now, no force;
> She neither hears nor sees,
> Rolled round in earth's diurnal course
> With rocks and stones and trees.

This use of the almost-scientific 'diurnal' brings a cosmic dimension to the dead girl, and the natural world in which she is buried, linking her extinguished humanity not only with Wordsworth's loved landscape but with the eternal silences of infinite space. It is this mastery of both the transcendent and the immanent, the majestic and the most mundane simplicity, which justifies Wordsworth's place among the greatest English poets.

FURTHER READING

Journals of Dorothy Wordsworth, ed. Mary Moorman, (Oxford, 1971)

Mary Moorman, *William Wordsworth: A Biography. The Early Years* (Oxford, 1957); *The Later Years* (Oxford, 1965).

Geoffrey Durrant, *William Wordsworth* (Cambridge, 1969)

David Perkins, *Wordsworth and the Poetry of Sincerity*, (Cambridge, Mass., 1964)

Christopher Salveson, *The Landscape of Memory* (London, 1965)

Jonathan Wordsworth, *The Music of Humanity* (London, 1969)

Jonathan Wordsworth, *William Wordsworth: The Borders of Vision* (Oxford, 1982)

Basil Willey, *The Eighteenth Century Background* (London, 1940)

Marilyn Butler, *Romantics, Rebels and Reactionaries: English Literature and its Background 1760-1830* (Oxford, 1981)

Contents

---+---

MISCELLANEOUS SONNETS.

PART I.

PART II.

Contents.

Contents.

Contents.

MEMORIALS OF A TOUR ON THE CONTINENT, 1820.

MEMORIALS OF A TOUR IN ITALY, 1837.

Contents.

YARROW REVISITED,

AND OTHER POEMS.

Composed (two excepted) during a Tour in Scotland, and on the English Border, in the Autumn of 1831.

THE WHITE DOE OF RYLSTONE;

OR, THE FATE OF THE NORTONS.

—◆—

POEMS OF SENTIMENT AND REFLECTION.

—◆—

SONNETS DEDICATED TO LIBERTY AND ORDER.

—◆—

SONNETS UPON THE PUNISH- MENT OF DEATH.

PAGE

PAGE

THE EXCURSION.

POEMS

BY

WILLIAM WORDSWORTH

POEMS WRITTEN IN YOUTH

Of the Poems in this class, "The Evening Walk" and "Descriptive Sketches" were first published in 1793. They are reprinted with some alterations that were chiefly made very soon after their publication.

． ． ． ． ． ．

This notice, which was written some time ago, scarcely applies to the Poem, "Descriptive Sketches," as it now stands. The corrections, though numerous, are not, however, such as to prevent its retaining with propriety a place in the class of Juvenile Pieces[1].

1836.

I.

EXTRACT.

FROM THE CONCLUSION OF A POEM, COM-
POSED IN ANTICIPATION OF LEAVING
SCHOOL.

[Composed 1786.—Published 1815.]

DEAR native regions, I foretell,
From what I feel at this farewell,
That, wheresoe'er my steps may tend,
And whensoe'er my course shall end,
If in that hour a single tie   5
Survive of local sympathy,
My soul will cast the backward view,
The longing look alone on you.

Thus, while the Sun sinks down to rest
Far in the regions of the west,   10
Though to the vale no parting beam
Be given, not one memorial gleam,
A lingering light he fondly throws
On the dear hills where first he rose.

II.

WRITTEN IN VERY EARLY YOUTH.

[Composed 1786 (?).—Published *Morning Post*
February 13, 1802; ed. 1807.]

CALM is all nature as a resting wheel.
The kine are couched upon the dewy
grass;
The horse alone, seen dimly as I pass,
Is cropping audibly his later meal:
Dark is the ground; a slumber seems to
steal   5
O'er vale, and mountain, and the starless
sky.
Now, in this blank of things, a har-
mony,
Home-felt, and home-created, comes to
heal
That grief for which the senses still
supply
Fresh food; for only then, when me-
mory   10

---

[1] See APPENDIX: *Poems of* 1793, pp. 591-617.

Is hushed, am I at rest. My Friends!
restrain
Those busy cares that would allay my
pain;
Oh! leave me to myself, nor let me feel
The officious touch that makes me droop
again.

III.

AN EVENING WALK[1].

ADDRESSED TO A YOUNG LADY.

[Composed 1787-89.—Published 1793.]

General Sketch of the Lakes—Author's regret of
his Youth which was passed amongst them—
Short description of Noon—Cascade—Noon-
tide Retreat—Precipice and sloping Lights—
Face of Nature as the Sun declines—Moun-
tain-farm, and the Cock—Slate-quarry—Sun-
set—Superstition of the Country connected
with that moment—Swans—Female Beggar—
Twilight-sounds—Western Lights—Spirits—
Night — Moonlight — Hope — Night-sounds —
Conclusion.

FAR from my dearest Friend, 'tis mine to
rove
Through bare grey dell, high wood, and
pastoral cove;
Where Derwent rests, and listens to the
roar
That stuns the tremulous cliffs of high
Lodore;
Where peace to Grasmere's lonely island
leads, 5
To willowy hedge-rows, and to emerald
meads;
Leads to her bridge, rude church, and
cottaged grounds,
Her rocky sheepwalks, and her woodland
bounds;
Where, undisturbed by winds, Winander[2]
sleeps;
'Mid clustering isles, and holly-sprinkled
steeps; 10

Where twilight glens endear my Esth-
waite's shore,
And memory of departed pleasures, more.

Fair scenes, erewhile, I taught, a happy
child,
The echoes of your rocks my carols wild:
The spirit sought not then, in cherished
sadness, 15
A cloudy substitute for failing gladness.
In youth's keen eye the livelong day was
bright,
The sun at morning, and the stars at night,
Alike, when first the bittern's hollow bill
Was heard, or woodcocks[3] roamed the
moonlight hill. 20

In thoughtless gaiety I coursed the
plain,
And hope itself was all I knew of pain;
For then the inexperienced heart would
beat
At times, while young Content forsook
her seat,
And wild Impatience, pointing upward,
showed, 25
Through passes yet unreached, a brighter
road.
Alas! the idle tale of man is found
Depicted in the dial's moral round;
Hope with reflection blends her social
rays
To gild the total tablet of his days; 30
Yet still, the sport of some malignant
power,
He knows but from its shade the present
hour.

But why, ungrateful, dwell on idle pain?
To show what pleasures yet to me remain,
Say, will my Friend, with unreluctant
ear, 35
The history of a poet's evening hear?

When, in the south, the wan noon,
brooding still,
Breathed a pale steam around the glar-
ing hill,

---

[1] So many and so important changes have been
made in this Poem since its first appearance, that
it has been thought well to reprint the original
text of 1793. See Appendix, page 591.—ED.

[2] These lines are only applicable to the middle
part of that lake.

[3] In the beginning of winter these mountains
are frequented by woodcocks, which in dark
nights retire into the woods.

And shades of deep-embattled clouds were
  seen,
Spotting the northern cliffs with lights
  between;   40
When crowding cattle, checked by rails
  that make
A fence far stretched into the shallow
  lake,
Lashed the cool water with their restless
  tails,
Or from high points of rock looked out
  for fanning gales;
When school-boys stretched their length
  upon the green;   45
And round the broad-spread oak, a glim-
  mering scene,
In the rough fern-clad park, the herded
  deer
Shook the still-twinkling tail and glanc-
  ing ear;
When horses in the sunburnt intake[1]
  stood,
And vainly eyed below the tempting
  flood,   50
Or tracked the passenger, in mute distress,
With forward neck the closing gate to
  press—
Then, while I wandered where the hud-
  dling rill
Brightens with water-breaks the hollow
  ghyll[2]
As by enchantment, an obscure retreat
Opened at once, and stayed my devious
  feet.   56
While thick above the rill the branches
  close,
In rocky basin its wild waves repose,
Inverted shrubs, and moss of gloomy
  green,
Cling from the rocks, with pale wood-
  weeds between;   60
And its own twilight softens the whole
  scene,
Save where aloft the subtle sunbeams
  shine

On withered briars that o'er the crags
  recline;
Save where, with sparkling foam, a small
  cascade
Illumines, from within, the leafy shade;
Beyond, along the vista of the brook,   66
Where antique roots its bustling course
  o'erlook,
The eye reposes on a secret bridge,[3]
Half grey, half shagged with ivy to its
  ridge;
There, bending o'er the stream, the listless
  swain   70
Lingers behind his disappearing wain.
—Did Sabine grace adorn my living line,
Bandusia's praise, wild stream, should
  yield to thine !
Never shall ruthless minister of death
'Mid thy soft glooms the glittering steel
  unsheath;   75
No goblets shall, for thee, be crowned
  with flowers,
No kid with piteous outcry thrill thy
  bowers;
The mystic shapes that by thy margin rove
A more benignant sacrifice approve—
A mind that, in a calm angelic mood   80
Of happy wisdom, meditating good,
Beholds, of all from her high powers
  required,
Much done, and much designed, and more
  desired,—
Harmonious thoughts, a soul by truth
  refined,
Entire affection for all human kind.   85

Dear Brook, farewell ! To-morrow's
  noon again
Shall hide me, wooing long thy wildwood
  strain;
But now the sun has gained his western
  road,
And eve's mild hour invites my steps
  abroad.

While, near the midway cliff, the sil-
  vered kite   90

---

[1] The word *intake* is local, and signifies a
mountain-inclosure.
[2] Ghyll is also, I believe, a term confined to
this country: ghyll and dingle have the same
meaning.

[3] The reader, who has made the tour of this
country, will recognise, in this description, the
features which characterise the lower waterfall
in the grounds of Rydal.

In many a whistling circle wheels her
flight;
Slant watery lights, from parting clouds,
apace
Travel along the precipice's base;
Cheering its naked waste of scattered
stone,
By lichens grey, and scanty moss, o'er-
grown;   95
Where scarce the foxglove peeps, or
thistle's beard;
And restless stone-chat, all day long, is
heard.

How pleasant, as the sun declines, to
view
The spacious landscape change in form
and hue!
Here, vanish, as in mist, before a flood 100
Of bright obscurity, hill, lawn, and
wood;
There, objects, by the searching beams
betrayed,
Come forth, and here retire in purple
shade;
Even the white stems of birch, the cottage
white
Soften their glare before the mellow
light;   105
The skiffs, at anchor where with umbrage
wide
Yon chestnuts half the latticed boat-house
hide,
Shed from their sides, that face the sun's
slant beam,
Strong flakes of radiance on the tremulous
stream:
Raised by yon travelling flock, a dusty
cloud   110
Mounts from the road, and spreads its
moving shroud;
The shepherd, all involved in wreaths of
fire,
Now shows a shadowy speck, and now is
lost entire.

Into a gradual calm the breezes sink,
A blue rim borders all the lake's still
brink;   115
There doth the twinkling aspen's foliage
sleep,

And insects clothe, like dust, the glassy
deep:
And now, on every side, the surface
breaks
Into blue spots, and slowly lengthening
streaks;
Here, plots of sparkling water tremble
bright   120
With thousand thousand twinkling points
of light;
There, waves that, hardly weltering, die
away,
Tip their smooth ridges with a softer ray;
And now the whole wide lake in deep
repose
Is hushed, and like a burnished mirror
glows,   125
Save where, along the shady western
marge,
Coasts, with industrious oar, the charcoal
barge.

Their panniered train a group of potters
goad,
Winding from side to side up the steep
road;
The peasant, from yon cliff of fearful edge
Shot, down the headlong path darts with
his sledge;   131
Bright beams the lonely mountain-horse
illume
Feeding 'mid purple heath, "green
rings,"[1] and broom;
While the sharp slope the slackened team
confounds,
Downward the ponderous timber-wain re-
sounds;   135
In foamy breaks the rill, with merry song,
Dashed o'er the rough rock, lightly leaps
along;
From lonesome chapel at the mountain's
feet
Three humble bells their rustic chime re-
peat;
Sounds from the water-side the hammer-
ed boat;   140
And *blasted* quarry thunders, heard re-
mote!

---

1 "Vivid rings of green."—GREENWOOD'S *Poem
on Shooting.*

Even here, amid the sweep of endless
woods,
Blue pomp of lakes, high cliffs and falling
floods,
Not undelightful are the simplest charms,
Found by the grassy door of mountain-
farms.   145

Sweetly ferocious,[1] round his native
walks,
Pride of his sister-wives, the monarch
stalks;
Spur-clad his nervous feet, and firm his
tread;
A crest of purple tops the warrior's head.
Bright sparks his black and rolling eye-
ball hurls   150
Afar, his tail he closes and unfurls;
On tiptoe reared, he strains his clarion
throat,
Threatened by faintly-answering farms
remote:
Again with his shrill voice the mountain
rings,
While, flapped with conscious pride, re-
sound his wings!   155

Where, mixed with graceful birch, the
sombrous pine
And yew-tree o'er the silver rocks recline,
I love to mark the quarry's moving trains,
Dwarf panniered steeds, and men, and
numerous wains: 159
How busy all the enormous hive within,
While Echo dallies with its various din!
Some (hear you not their chisels' clinking
sound?)
Toil, small as pygmies in the gulf pro-
found;
Some, dim between the lofty cliffs de-
scried,
O'erwalk the slender plank from side to
side;   165
These, by the pale-blue rocks that cease-
less ring,
In airy baskets hanging, work and sing.

Just where a cloud above the mountain
rears
An edge all flame, the broadening sun
appears;
A long blue bar its ægis orb divides,   170
And breaks the spreading of its golden
tides;
And now that orb has touched the purple
steep,
Whose softened image penetrates the deep.
'Cross the calm lake's blue shades the
cliffs aspire,
With towers and woods, a "prospect all
on fire;"   175
While coves and secret hollows, through
a ray
Of fainter gold, a purple gleam betray.
Each slip of lawn the broken rocks
between
Shines in the light with more than earthly
green:
Deep yellow beams the scattered stems
illume,   180
Far in the level forest's central gloom:
Waving his hat, the shepherd, from the
vale,
Directs his winding dog the cliffs to
scale,—
The dog, loud barking, 'mid the glittering
rocks,
Hunts, where his master points, the inter-
cepted flocks.   185
Where oaks o'erhang the road the radiance
shoots
On tawny earth, wild weeds, and twisted
roots;
The druid-stones a brightened ring unfold;
And all the babbling brooks are liquid
gold;
Sunk to a curve, the day-star lessens
still,   190
Gives one bright glance, and drops behind
the hill.[2]

In these secluded vales, if village fame,
Confirmed by hoary hairs, belief may
claim;
When up the hills, as now, retired the
light,

[1] "Dolcemente feroce."—TASSO.—In this de-
scription of the cock, I remembered a spirited one
of the same animal in L'Agriculture, ou Les Gé-
orgiques Françoises, of M. Rossuet.

[2] From Thomson.

Strange apparitions mocked the shep-
    herd's sight.   195

The form appears of one that spurs his
    steed
Midway along the hill with desperate
    speed;
Unhurt pursues his lengthened flight,
    while all
Attend, at every stretch, his headlong fall.
Anon, appears a brave, a gorgeous show
Of horsemen-shadows moving to and fro;
At intervals imperial banners stream,
And now the van reflects the solar beam;
The rear through iron brown betrays a
    sullen gleam.
While silent stands the admiring crowd
    below,   205
Silent the visionary warriors go,
Winding in ordered pomp their upward
    way,[1]
Till the last banner of their long array
Has disappeared, and every trace is fled
Of splendour—save the beacon's spiry
    head   210
Tipt with eve's latest gleam of burning
    red.

Now, while the solemn evening sha-
    dows sail,
On slowly-waving pinions, down the vale;
And, fronting the bright west, yon oak
    entwines
Its darkening boughs and leaves in
    stronger lines;   215
'Tis pleasant near the tranquil lake to
    stray
Where, winding on along some secret bay,
The swan uplifts his chest, and backward
    flings
His neck, a varying arch, between his
    towering wings:
The eye that marks the gliding creature
    sees   220
How graceful, pride can be, and how
    majestic, ease.

---

[1] See a description of an appearance of this kind
in Clark's Survey of the Lakes, accompanied by
vouchers of its veracity, that may amuse the
reader.

While tender cares and mild domestic
    loves
With furtive watch pursue her as she
    moves,
The female with a meeker charm suc-
    ceeds,
And her brown little-ones around her
    leads,   225
Nibbling the water lilies as they pass,
Or playing wanton with the floating grass.
She, in a mother's care, her beauty's pride
Forgetting, calls the wearied to her side;
Alternately they mount her back, and
    rest   230
Close by her mantling wings' embraces
    prest.

Long may they float upon this flood
    serene;
Theirs be these holms untrodden, still,
    and green,
Where leafy shades fence off the bluster-
    ing gale,
And breathes in peace the lily of the
    vale!   235
Yon isle, which feels not even the milk-
    maid's feet,
Yet hears her song, "by distance made
    more sweet,"
Yon isle conceals their home, their hut-
    like bower;
Green water-rushes overspread the
    floor;
Long grass and willows form the woven
    wall,   240
And swings above the roof the poplar tall.
Thence issuing often with unwieldy stalk,
They crush with broad black feet their
    flowery walk;
Or, from the neighbouring water, hear at
    morn
The hound, the horse's tread, and mellow
    horn;   245
Involve their serpent-necks in changeful
    rings,
Rolled wantonly between their slippery
    wings,
Or, starting up with noise and rude de-
    light,
Force half upon the wave their cumbrous
    flight.

Fair Swan! by all a mother's joys
    caressed,   250
Haply some wretch has eyed, and called
    thee blessed;
When with her infants, from some shady
    seat
By the lake's edge, she rose—to face the
    noontide heat;
Or taught their limbs along the dusty
    road
A few short steps to totter with their
    load.   255

I see her now, denied to lay her head,
On cold blue nights, in hut or straw-built
    shed,
Turn to a silent smile their sleepy cry,
By pointing to the gliding moon on high.
—When low-hung clouds each star of
    summer hide,   260
And fireless are the valleys far and wide,
Where the brook brawls along the public
    road
Dark with bat-haunted ashes stretching
    broad,
Oft has she taught them on her lap to lay
The shining glow-worm; or, in heedless
    play,   265
Toss it from hand to hand, disquieted;
While others, not unseen, are free to shed
Green unmolested light upon their mossy
    bed.

Oh! when the sleety showers her path
    assail,
And like a torrent roars the headstrong
    gale;   270
No more her breath can thaw their fingers
    cold,
Their frozen arms her neck no more can
    fold;
Weak roof a cowering form two babes to
    shield,
And faint the fire a dying heart can
    yield!
Press the sad kiss, fond mother! vainly
    fears   275
Thy flooded cheek to wet them with its
    tears;
No tears can chill them, and no bosom
    warms,

Thy breast their death-bed, coffined in
    thine arms!

Sweet are the sounds that mingle from
    afar,
Heard by calm lakes, as peeps the folding
    star,   280
Where the duck dabbles 'mid the rustling
    sedge,
And feeding pike starts from the water's
    edge,
Or the swan stirs the reeds, his neck and
    bill
Wetting, that drip upon the water still;
And heron, as resounds the trodden
    shore,   285
Shoots upward, darting his long neck
    before.

Now, with religious awe, the farewell
    light
Blends with the solemn colouring of
    night;
'Mid groves of clouds that crest the moun-
    tain's brow,
And round the west's proud lodge their
    shadows throw,   290
Like Una shining on her gloomy way,
The half-seen form of Twilight roams
    astray;
Shedding, through paly loop-holes mild
    and small,
Gleams that upon the lake's still bosom
    fall;
Soft o'er the surface creep those lustres
    pale   295
Tracking the motions of the fitful gale.
With restless interchange at once the
    bright
Wins on the shade, the shade upon the
    light.
No favoured eye was e'er allowed to
    gaze
On lovelier spectacle in faery days;   300
When gentle Spirits urged a sportive
    chase,
Brushing with lucid wands the water's face:
While music, stealing round the glimmer-
    ing deeps,
Charmed the tall circle of the enchanted
    steeps.

—The lights are vanished from the watery
    plains: 305
No wreck of all the pageantry remains.
Unheeded night has overcome the vales:
On the dark earth the wearied vision
    fails;
The latest lingerer of the forest train,
The lone black fir, forsakes the faded
    plain;   310
Last evening sight, the cottage smoke, no
    more,
Lost in the thickened darkness, glimmers
    hoar;
And, towering from the sullen dark-brown
    mere,
Like a black wall, the mountain-steeps
    appear.
—Now o'er the soothed accordant heart
    we feel   315
A sympathetic twilight slowly steal,
And ever, as we fondly muse, we find
The soft gloom deepening on the tranquil
    mind.
Stay! pensive, sadly-pleasing visions,
    stay!
Ah no! as fades the vale, they fade
    away: 320
Yet still the tender, vacant gloom re-
    mains;
Still the cold cheek its shuddering tear
    retains.

The bird, who ceased, with fading light,
    to thread
Silent the hedge or steamy rivulet's bed,
From his grey re-appearing tower shall
    soon   325
Salute with gladsome note the rising
    moon,
While with a hoary light she frosts the
    ground,
And pours a deeper blue to Æther's
    bound;
Pleased, as she moves, her pomp of clouds
    to fold
In robes of azure, fleecy-white, and gold.

Above yon eastern hill, where darkness
    broods   331
O'er all its vanished dells, and lawns, and
    woods;

Where but a mass of shade the sight can
    trace,
Even now she shows, half-veiled, her love-
    ly face:
Across the gloomy valley flings her
    light,   335
Far to the western slopes with hamlets
    white;
And gives, where woods the chequered
    upland strew,
To the green corn of summer, autumn's
    hue.

Thus Hope, first pouring from her bless-
    ed horn
Her dawn, far lovelier than the moon's
    own morn,   340
Till higher mounted, strives in vain to
    cheer
The weary hills, impervious, blackening
    near;
Yet does she still, undaunted, throw the
    while
On darling spots remote her tempting
    smile.

Even now she decks for me a distant
    scene,   345
(For dark and broad the gulf of time be-
    tween)
Gilding that cottage with her fondest ray,
(Sole bourn, sole wish, sole object of my
    way;
How fair its lawns and sheltering woods
    appear!
How sweet its streamlet murmurs in
    mine ear!)   350
Where we, my Friend, to happy days
    shall rise,
Till our small share of hardly-paining
    sighs
(For sighs will ever trouble human breath)
Creep hushed into the tranquil breast of
    death.

But now the clear bright Moon her
    zenith gains,   355
And, rimy without speck, extend the
    plains:
The deepest cleft the mountain's front
    displays

Scarce hides a shadow from her searching
rays;
From the dark-blue faint silvery threads
divide
The hills, while gleams below the azure
tide; 360
Time softly treads; throughout the land-
scape breathes
A peace enlivened, not disturbed, by
wreaths
Of charcoal-smoke, that, o'er the fallen
wood,
Steal down the hill, and spread along the
flood.

The song of mountain-streams, unheard
by day, 365
Now hardly heard, beguiles my home-
ward way.
Air listens, like the sleeping water, still,
To catch the spiritual music of the hill,
Broke only by the slow clock tolling deep,
Or shout that wakes the ferry-man from
sleep, 370
The echoed hoof nearing the distant
shore,
The boat's first motion—made with dash-
ing oar;
Sound of closed gate, across the water
borne,
Hurrying the timid hare through rustling
corn; 374
The sportive outcry of the mocking owl;
And at long intervals the mill-dog's howl;
The distant forge's swinging thump pro-
found;
Or yell, in the deep woods, of lonely
hound.

IV.

LINES

WRITTEN WHILE SAILING IN A BOAT AT
EVENING.

[Composed 1789.—Published 1798.]

How richly glows the water's breast
Before us, tinged with evening hues,
While, facing thus the crimson west,
The boat her silent course pursues!
And see how dark the backward stream!
A little moment past so smiling! 6

And still, perhaps, with faithless gleam,
Some other loiterers beguiling.

Such views the youthful Bard allure;
But, heedless of the following gloom, 10
He deems their colours shall endure
Till peace go with him to the tomb.
—And let him nurse his fond deceit,
And what if he must die in sorrow!
Who would not cherish dreams so sweet,
Though grief and pain may come to-
morrow? 16

V.

REMEMBRANCE OF COLLINS,

COMPOSED UPON THE THAMES NEAR
RICHMOND.

[Composed 1789.—Published 1798.]

GLIDE gently, thus for ever glide,
O Thames! that other bards may see
As lovely visions by thy side
As now, fair river! come to me.
O glide, fair stream! for ever so, 5
Thy quiet soul on all bestowing,
Till all our minds for ever flow
As thy deep waters now are flowing.

Vain thought!—Yet be as now thou art,
That in thy waters may be seen 10
The image of a poet's heart,
How bright, how solemn, how serene!
Such as did once the Poet bless,
Who, murmuring here a later [1] ditty,
Could find no refuge from distress 15
But in the milder grief of pity.

Now let us, as we float along,
For *him* suspend the dashing oar;
And pray that never child of song
May know that Poet's sorrows more. 20
How calm! how still! the only sound,
The dripping of the oar suspended!
—The evening darkness gathers round
By virtue's holiest Powers attended.

---

[1] Collins' Ode on the death of Thomson, the
last written, I believe, of the poems which were
published during his life-time. This Ode is also
alluded to in the next stanza.

VI.

DESCRIPTIVE SKETCHES[1]

TAKEN DURING A PEDESTRIAN TOUR AMONG
THE ALPS.

[Composed 1791-92.—Published 1793.]

TO

THE REV. ROBERT JONES,

FELLOW OF ST. JOHN'S COLLEGE,
CAMBRIDGE.

DEAR SIR,

However desirous I might have been of
giving you proofs of the high place you hold in
my esteem, I should have been cautious of
wounding your delicacy by thus publicly address-
ing you, had not the circumstance of our having
been companions among the Alps seemed to give
this dedication a propriety sufficient to do away
any scruples which your modesty might otherwise
have suggested.

In inscribing this little work to you I consult
my heart. You know well how great is the differ-
ence between two companions lolling in a post-
chaise and two travellers plodding slowly along
the road, side by side, each with his little knap-
sack of necessaries upon his shoulders. How
much more of heart between the two latter!

I am happy in being conscious that I shall have
one reader who will approach the conclusion of
these few pages with regret. You they must cer-
tainly interest, in reminding you of moments to
which you can hardly look back without a pleasure
not the less dear from a shade of melancholy.
You will meet with few images without recollect-
ing the spot where we observed them together;
consequently, whatever is feeble in my design, or
spiritless in my colouring, will be amply supplied
by your own memory.

With still greater propriety I might have in-
scribed to you a description of some of the fea-
tures of your native mountains, through which
we have wandered together, in the same manner,
with so much pleasure. But the sea-sunsets,
which give such splendour to the vale of Clwyd,
Snowdon, the chair of Idris, the quiet village of

Bethgelert, Menai and her Druids, the Alpine
steeps of the Conway, and the still more interest-
ing windings of the wizard stream of the Dee,
remain yet untouched. Apprehensive that my
pencil may never be exercised on these subjects,
I cannot let slip this opportunity of thus publicly
assuring you with how much affection and esteem,
I am, dear Sir,

Most sincerely yours,

London, 1793.   W. WORDSWORTH.

Happiness (if she had been to be found on earth)
among the charms of Nature—Pleasures of the
pedestrian Traveller—Author crosses France
to the Alps—Present state of the Grande
Chartreuse—Lake of Como—Time, Sunset—
Same Scene, Twilight—Same Scene, Morning;
its voluptuous Character; Old man and forest-
cottage music—River Tusa—Via Mala and
Grison Gipsy—Sckellenen-thal—Lake of Uri—
Stormy sunset—Chapel of William Tell—Force
of local emotion—Chamois-chaser—View of the
higher Alps—Manner of life of a Swiss moun-
taineer, interspersed with views of the higher
Alps—Golden age of the Alps—Life and views
continued—Ranz des Vaches, famous Swiss
Air—Abbey of Einsiedlen and its pilgrims—
Valley of Chamouny—Mont Blanc—Slavery of
Savoy—Influence of liberty on cottage-happi-
ness—France—Wish for the Extirpation of
slavery—Conclusion.

WERE there, below, a spot of holy ground
Where from distress a refuge might be
      found,
And solitude prepare the soul for heaven;
Sure, nature's God that spot to man had
      given
Where falls the purple morning far and
      wide   5
In flakes of light upon the mountain-side;
Where with loud voice the power of water
      shakes
The leafy wood, or sleeps in quiet lakes.

Yet not unrecompensed the man shall
      roam,
Who at the call of summer quits his
      home,   10
And plods through some wide realm o'er
      vale and height,
Though seeking only holiday delight;
At least, not owning to himself an aim
To which the sage would give a prouder
      name.

---

[1] The original (1793) text of this Poem will be
found in the Appendix, pp. 601-617. It differs in
many important particulars from the finally re-
vised text here given.—ED.

No gains too cheaply earned his fancy
cloy,   15
Though every passing zephyr whispers joy;
Brisk toil, alternating with ready ease,
Feeds the clear current of his sympathies.
For him sod-seats the cottage-door adorn;
And peeps the far-off spire, his evening
bourn !   20
Dear is the forest frowning o'er his head,
And dear the velvet green-sward to his
tread :
Moves there a cloud o'er mid-day's flam-
ing eye?
Upward he looks—"and calls it luxury:"
Kind Nature's charities his steps at-
tend ;   25
In every babbling brook he finds a friend;
While chastening thoughts of sweetest
use, bestowed
By wisdom, moralise his pensive road.
Host of his welcome inn, the noon-tide
bower,
To his spare meal he calls the passing
poor ;   30
He views the sun uplift his golden fire,
Or sink, with heart alive like Memnon's
lyre ; [1]
Blesses the moon that comes with kindly
ray,
To light him shaken by his rugged way.
Back from his sight no bashful children
steal ;   35
He sits a brother at the cottage-meal ;
His humble looks no shy restraint impart ;
Around him plays at will the virgin heart.
While unsuspended wheels the village
dance,
The maidens eye him with enquiring
glance,   40
Much wondering by what fit of crazing
care,
Or desperate love, bewildered, he came
there.

A hope, that prudence could not then
approve,
That clung to Nature with a truant's love,

O'er Gallia's wastes of corn my footsteps
led ;   45
Her files of road-elms, high above my head
In long-drawn vista, rustling in the
breeze ;
Or where her pathways straggle as they
please
By lonely farms and secret villages.
But lo! the Alps, ascending white in
air,   50
Toy with the sun and glitter from afar.

And now, emerging from the forest's
gloom,
I greet thee, Chartreuse, while I mourn
thy doom.
Whither is fled that Power whose frown
severe
Awed sober Reason till she crouched in
fear?   55
That Silence, once in deathlike fetters
bound,
Chains that were loosened only by the
sound
Of holy rites chanted in measured round?
—The voice of blasphemy the fane alarms,
The cloister startles at the gleam of
arms.   60
The thundering tube the aged angler
hears,
Bent o'er the groaning flood that sweeps
away his tears.
Cloud-piercing pine-trees nod their trou-
bled heads,
Spires, rocks, and lawns a browner night
o'erspreads ;
Strong terror checks the female peasant's
sighs,   65
And start the astonished shades at female
eyes.
From Bruno's forest screams the affright-
ed jay,
And slow the insulted eagle wheels away.
A viewless flight of laughing Demons
mock
The Cross, by angels planted [2] on the
aerial rock.   70

---

[1] The lyre of Memnon is reported to have
emitted melancholy or cheerful tones, as it was
touched by the sun's evening or morning rays.

[2] Alluding to crosses seen on the tops of the
spiry rocks of Chartreuse, which have every ap-
pearance of being inaccessible.

The "parting Genius" sighs with hollow
    breath
Along the mystic streams of Life and
    Death.[1]
Swelling the outcry dull, that long re-
    sounds
Portentous through her old woods' track-
    less bounds,
Vallombre,[2] 'mid her falling fanes, de-
    plores,   75
For ever broke, the sabbath of her bowers.

More pleased, my foot the hidden mar-
    gin roves
Of Como, bosomed deep in chestnut
    groves.
No meadows thrown between, the giddy
    steeps
Tower, bare or sylvan, from the narrow
    deeps.   80
—To towns, whose shades of no rude
    noise complain,
From ringing team apart and grating
    wain—
To flat-roofed towns, that touch the wa-
    ter's bound,
Or lurk in woody sunless glens profound,
Or, from the bending rocks, obtrusive
    cling,   85
And o'er the whitened wave their sha-
    dows fling—
The pathway leads, as round the steeps
    it twines;
And Silence loves its purple roof of vines.
The loitering traveller hence, at evening,
    sees
From rock-hewn steps the sail between
    the trees ;   90
Or marks, 'mid opening cliffs, fair dark-
    eyed maids
Tend the small harvest of their garden
    glades ;
Or stops the solemn mountain-shades to
    view
Stretch o'er the pictured mirror broad
    and blue,
And track the yellow lights from steep
    to steep,   95

As up the opposing hills they slowly
    creep.
Aloft, here, half a village shines, arrayed
In golden light; half hides itself in
    shade:
While, from amid the darkened roofs, the
    spire,
Restlessly flashing, seems to mount like
    fire :   100
There, all unshaded, blazing forests throw
Rich golden verdure on the lake below.
Slow glides the sail along the illumined
    shore,
And steals into the shade the lazy oar ;
Soft bosoms breathe around contagious
    sighs,   105
And amorous music on the water dies.

How blest, delicious scene! the eye that
    greets
Thy open beauties, or thy lone retreats ;
Beholds the unwearied sweep of wood
    that scales
Thy cliffs ; the endless waters of thy
    vales ;   110
Thy lowly cots that sprinkle all the shore,
Each with its household boat beside the
    door :
Thy torrents shooting from the clear-blue
    sky ;
Thy towns that cleave, like swallows'
    nests, on high ;
That glimmer hoar in eve's last light,
    descried   115
Dim from the twilight water's shaggy side,
Whence lutes and voices down the en-
    chanted woods
Steal, and compose the oar-forgotten
    floods ;
—Thy lake that, streaked or dappled,
    blue or grey,
'Mid smoking woods gleams hid from
    morning's ray   120
Slow-travelling down the western hills,
    to enfold
Its green-tinged margin in a blaze of
    gold ;
Thy glittering steeples, whence the matin
    bell
Calls forth the woodman from his desert
    cell,

---

[1] Names of rivers at the Chartreuse.
[2] Name of one of the valleys of the Chartreuse.

And quickens the blithe sound of oars
that pass   125
Along the steaming lake, to early mass.
But now farewell to each and all—adieu
To every charm, and last and chief to
you,
Ye lovely maidens that in noontide shade
Rest near your little plots of wheaten
glade;   130
To all that binds the soul in powerless
trance,
Lip-dewing song, and ringlet-tossing
dance; ·
Where sparkling eyes and breaking smiles
illume
The sylvan cabin's lute-enlivened gloom.
—Alas! the very murmur of the streams
Breathes o'er the failing soul voluptuous
dreams,   136
While Slavery, forcing the sunk mind to
dwell
On joys that might disgrace the captive's
cell,
Her shameless timbrel shakes on Como's
marge,
And lures from bay to bay the vocal
barge.   140

Yet are thy softer arts with power in-
dued
To soothe and cheer the poor man's soli-
tude.
By silent cottage-doors, the peasant's
home
Left vacant for the day, I loved to roam.
But once I pierced the mazes of a wood
In which a cabin undeserted stood;   146
There an old man an olden measure
scanned
On a rude viol touched with withered
hand.
As lambs or fawns in April clustering lie
Under a hoary oak's thin canopy,   150
Stretched at his feet, with steadfast up-
ward eye,
His children's children listened to the
sound;
—A Hermit with his family around!

But let us hence; for fair Locarno
smiles

Embowered in walnut slopes and citron
isles: 155
Or seek at eve the banks of Tusa's stream,
Where, 'mid dim towers and woods, her [1]
waters gleam.
From the bright wave, in solemn gloom,
retire
The dull-red steeps, and, darkening still,
aspire
To where afar rich orange lustres glow
Round undistinguished clouds, and rocks,
and snow: 161
Or, led where Via Mala's chasms confine
The indignant waters of the infant Rhine,
Hang o'er the abyss, whose else imper-
vious gloom
His burning eyes with fearful light il-
lume.   165

The mind condemned, without reprieve,
to go
O'er life's long deserts with its charge of
woe,
With sad congratulation joins the train
Where beasts and men together o'er the
plain
Move on—a mighty caravan of pain: 170
Hope, strength, and courage, social suf-
fering brings,
Freshening the wilderness with shades
and springs.
—There be whose lot far otherwise is
cast:
Sole human tenant of the piny waste,
By choice or doom a gipsy wanders here,
A nursling babe her only comforter;   176
Lo, where she sits beneath yon shaggy
rock,
A cowering shape half hid in curling
smoke!

When lightning among clouds and
mountain-snows
Predominates, and darkness comes and
goes,   180
And the fierce torrent at the flashes broad
Starts, like a horse, beside the glaring
road—

---

[1] The river along whose banks you descend in
crossing the Alps by the Simplon Pass.

She seeks a covert from the battering
shower
In the roofed bridge;[1] the bridge, in that
dread hour,
Itself all trembling at the torrent's power.

Nor is she more at ease on some *still*
night,   186
When not a star supplies the comfort of
its light;
Only the waning moon hangs dull and red
Above a melancholy mountain's head,
Then sets. In total gloom the Vagrant
sighs,   190
Stoops her sick head, and shuts her weary
eyes;
Or on her fingers counts the distant clock,
Or to the drowsy crow of midnight cock
Listens, or quakes while from the forest's
gulf
Howls near and nearer yet the famished
wolf.   195

From the green vale of Urseren smooth
and wide
Descend we now, the maddened Reuss
our guide;
By rocks that, shutting out the blessed
day,
Cling tremblingly to rocks as loose as
they;
By cells[2] upon whose image, while he
prays,   200
The kneeling peasant scarcely dares to
gaze;
By many a votive death-cross[3] planted
near,
And watered duly with the pious tear,
That faded silent from the upward eye
Unmoved with each rude form of peril
nigh;   205

Fixed on the anchor left by Him who saves
Alike in whelming snows and roaring
waves.

But soon a peopled region on the sight
Opens—a little world of calm delight;
Where mists, suspended on the expiring
gale,   210
Spread rooflike o'er the deep secluded vale,
And beams of evening, slipping in be-
tween,
Gently illuminate a sober scene:—
Here, on the brown wood-cottages[4] they
sleep,   214
There, over rock or sloping pasture creep.
On as we journey, in clear view displayed,
The still vale lengthens underneath its
shade
Of low-hung vapour: on the freshened
mead
The green light sparkles;—the dim bowers
recede.
While pastoral pipes and streams the
landscape lull,   220
And bells of passing mules that tinkle
dull,
In solemn shapes before the admiring eye
Dilated hang the misty pines on high,
Huge convent domes with pinnacles and
towers,
And antique castles seen through gleamy
showers.   225

From such romantic dreams, my soul,
awake
To sterner pleasure, where, by Uri's lake,
In Nature's pristine majesty outspread,
Winds neither road nor path for foot to
tread:
The rocks rise naked as a wall, or stretch
Far o'er the water, hung with groves of
beech;   231
Aerial pines from loftier steeps ascend,
Nor stop but where creation seems to end.
Yet here and there, if 'mid the savage
scene   234
Appears a scanty plot of smiling green,
Up from the lake a zigzag path will creep

---

[1] Most of the bridges among the Alps are of
wood, and covered: these bridges have a heavy
appearance, and rather injure the effect of the
scenery in some places.

[2] The Catholic religion prevails here: these
cells are, as is well known, very common in the
Catholic countries, planted, like the Roman
tombs, along the road side.

[3] Crosses, commemorative of the deaths of
travellers, by the fall of snow and other accidents,
are very common along this dreadful road.

[4] The houses in the more retired Swiss valleys
are all built of wood.

To reach a small wood-hut hung boldly
    on the steep.
—Before those thresholds (never can they
    know
The face of traveller passing to and fro,)
No peasant leans upon his pole, to tell 240
For whom at morning tolled the funeral
    bell;
Their watch-dog ne'er his angry bark for-
    goes,
Touched by the beggar's moan of human
    woes;
The shady porch ne'er offered a cool seat
To pilgrims overcome by summer's heat.
Yet thither the world's business finds its
    way   246
At times, and tales unsought beguile the
    day,
And *there* are those fond thoughts which
    Solitude,
However stern, is powerless to exclude.
There doth the maiden watch her lover's
    sail   250
Approaching, and upbraid the tardy gale;
At midnight listens till his parting oar,
And its last echo, can be heard no more.

And what if ospreys, cormorants, herons
    cry,   254
Amid tempestuous vapours driving by,
Or hovering over wastes too bleak to rear
That common growth of earth, the food-
    ful ear;
Where the green apple shrivels on the
    spray,
And pines the unripened pear in sum-
    mer's kindliest ray;
Contentment shares the desolate domain
With Independence, child of high Dis-
    dain.   261
Exulting 'mid the winter of the skies,
Shy as the jealous chamois, Freedom flies,
And grasps by fits her sword, and often
    eyes;
And sometimes, as from rock to rock she
    bounds,   265
The Patriot nymph starts at imagined
    sounds,
And, wildly pausing, oft she hangs aghast,
Whether some old Swiss air hath checked
    her haste,

Or thrill of Spartan fife is caught between
    the blast.

Swoln with incessant rains from hour
    to hour,   270
All day the floods a deepening murmur
    pour:
The sky is veiled, and every cheerful
    sight:
Dark is the region as with coming night;
But what a sudden burst of overpowering
    light!
Triumphant on the bosom of the storm,
Glances the wheeling eagle's glorious
    form!   276
Eastward, in long perspective glittering,
    shine
The wood-crowned cliffs that o'er the lake
    recline;
Those lofty cliffs a hundred streams un-
    fold,
At once to pillars turned that flame with
    gold: 280
Behind his sail the peasant shrinks, to
    shun
The *west*, that burns like one dilated sun,
A crucible of mighty compass, felt
By mountains, glowing till they seem to
    melt.   284

But, lo! the boatman, overawed, before
The pictured fane of Tell suspends his oar;
Confused the Marathonian tale appears,
While his eyes sparkle with heroic tears.
And who, that walks where men of an-
    cient days
Have wrought with godlike arm the deeds
    of praise,   290
Feels not the spirit of the place control,
Or rouse and agitate his labouring soul?
Say, who, by thinking on Canadian hills,
Or wild Aosta lulled by Alpine rills,
On Zutphen's plain, or on that highland
    dell,   295
Through which rough Garry cleaves his
    way, can tell
What high resolves exalt the tenderest
    thought
Of him whom passion rivets to the spot,
Where breathed the gale that caught
    Wolfe's happiest sigh,

And the last sunbeam fell on Bayard's
eye;   300
Where bleeding Sidney from the cup re-
tired,
And glad Dundee in "faint huzzas" ex-
pired?

But now with other mind I stand alone
Upon the summit of this naked cone,
And watch the fearless chamóis-hunter
chase   305
His prey, through tracts abrupt of deso-
late space,
[1] Through vacant worlds where Nature
never gave
A brook to murmur or a bough to wave,
Which unsubstantial Phantoms sacred
keep;
Thro' worlds where Life, and Voice, and
Motion sleep;   310
Where silent Hours their death-like sway
extend,
Save when the avalanche breaks loose, to
rend
Its way with uproar, till the ruin, drowned
In some dense wood or gulf of snow pro-
found,
Mocks the dull ear of Time with deaf
abortive sound.   315
—'Tis his, while wandering on from
height to height,
To see a planet's pomp and steady light
In the least star of scarce-appearing night;
While the pale moon moves near him, on
the bound   319
Of ether, shining with diminished round,
And far and wide the icy summits blaze,
Rejoicing in the glory of her rays:
To him the day-star glitters small and
bright,   323
Shorn of its beams, insufferably white,
And he can look beyond the sun, and view
Those fast-receding depths of sable blue
Flying till vision can no more pursue!
—At once bewildering mists around him
close,   328
And cold and hunger are his least of woes;

The Demon of the snow, with angry roar
Descending, shuts for aye his prison door.
Soon with despair's whole weight his spi-
rits sink;   332
Bread has he none, the snow must be his
drink;
And, ere his eyes can close upon the day,
The eagle of the Alps o'ershades her prey.

Now couch thyself where, heard with
fear afar,   336
Thunders through echoing pines the head-
long Aar;
Or rather stay to taste the mild delights
Of pensive Underwalden's [2] pastoral
heights.
—Is there who 'mid these awful wilds
has seen   340
The native Genii walk the mountain
green?
Or heard, while other worlds their charms
reveal,
Soft music o'er the aerial summit steal?
While o'er the desert, answering every
close,
Rich steam of sweetest perfume comes
and goes.   345
And sure there is a secret Power that
reigns
Here, where no trace of man the spot
profanes,
Nought but the *chalets*,[3] flat and bare, on
high
Suspended 'mid the quiet of the sky;
Or distant herds that pasturing upward
creep,   350
And, not untended, climb the dangerous
steep.
How still! no irreligious sound or sight
Rouses the soul from her severe delight.
An idle voice the sabbath region fills
Of Deep that calls to Deep across the hills,
And with that voice accords the soothing
sound   356

---

[1] For most of the images in the next sixteen
verses, I am indebted to M. Raymond's interesting
observations, annexed to his translation of Coxe's
Tour in Switzerland.

[2] The people of this Canton are supposed to be
of a more melancholy disposition than the other
inhabitants of the Alps; this, if true, may pro-
ceed from their living more secluded.

[3] This picture is from the middle region of the
Alps. *Chalets* are summer huts for the Swiss
herdsmen.

Of drowsy bells, for ever tinkling round;
Faint wail of eagle melting into blue
Beneath the cliffs, and pine-wood's steady
    sugh ;[1]
The solitary heifer's deepened low;   360
Or rumbling, heard remote, of falling
    snow.
All motions, sounds, and voices, far and
    nigh,
Blend in a music of tranquillity ;
Save when, a stranger seen below, the
    boy
Shouts from the echoing hills with savage
    joy.   365

    When, from the sunny breast of open
        seas,
And bays with myrtle fringed, the
    southern breeze
Comes on to gladden April with the
    sight
Of green isles widening on each snow-
    clad height ;
When shouts and lowing herds the valley
    fill,   370
And louder torrents stun the noon-tide
    hill,
The pastoral Swiss begin the cliffs to
    scale,
Leaving to silence the deserted vale ;
And, like the Patriarchs in their simple
    age,
Move, as the verdure leads, from stage
    to stage ;   375
High and more high in summer's heat
    they go,
And hear the rattling thunder far below ;
Or steal beneath the mountains, half-
    deterred,
Where huge rocks tremble to the bellow-
    ing herd.

    One I behold who, 'cross the foaming
        flood,   380
Leaps with a bound of graceful hardi-
    hood;
Another high on that green ledge ;—he
    gained

The tempting spot with every sinew
    strained ;
And downward thence a knot of grass
    he throws,
Food for his beasts in time of winter
    snows.   385
—Far different life from what Tradition
    hoar
Transmits of happier lot in times of yore !
Then Summer lingered long ; and honey
    flowed
From out the rocks, the wild bees' safe
    abode :
Continual waters welling cheered the
    waste,   390
And plants were wholesome, now of
    deadly taste :
Nor Winter yet his frozen stores had
    piled,
Usurping where the fairest herbage
    smiled :
Nor Hunger driven the herds from pas-
    tures bare,
To climb the treacherous cliffs for scanty
    fare.   395
Then the milk-thistle flourished through
    the land,
And forced the full-swoln udder to de-
    mand,
Thrice every day, the pail and welcome
    hand.
Thus does the father to his children tell
Of banished bliss, by fancy loved too
    well.   400
Alas ! that human guilt provoked the rod
Of angry Nature to avenge her God.
Still, Nature, ever just, to him imparts
Joys only given to uncorrupted hearts.

    'Tis morn : with gold the verdant moun-
        tain glows ;   405
More high, the snowy peaks with hues
    of rose.
Far stretched beneath the many-tinted
    hills,
A mighty waste of mist the valley fills,
A solemn sea ! whose billows wide around
Stand motionless, · to awful silence
    bound :   410
Pines, on the coast, through mist their
    tops uprear,

[1] Sugh, a Scotch word expressive of the sound of the wind through the trees.

That like to leaning masts of stranded
ships appear.
A single chasm, a gulf of gloomy blue,
Gapes in the centre of the sea—and,
through
That dark mysterious gulf ascending,
sound   415
Innumerable streams with roar profound.
Mount through the nearer vapours notes
of birds,
And merry flageolet; the low of herds,
The bark of dogs, the heifer's tinkling bell,
Talk, laughter, and perchance a church-
tower knell: 420
Think not the peasant from aloft has
gazed
And heard with heart unmoved, with soul
unraised:
Nor is his spirit less enrapt, nor less
Alive to independent happiness,
Then, when he lies, out-stretched, at
even-tide   425
Upon the fragrant mountain's purple
side:
For as the pleasures of his simple day
Beyond his native valley seldom stray,
Nought round its darling precincts can
he find
But brings some past enjoyment to his
mind;   430
While Hope, reclining upon Pleasure's
urn,
Binds her wild wreaths, and whispers his
return.

Once, Man entirely free, alone and wild,
Was blest as free—for he was Nature's
child.
He, all superior but his God disdain-
ed,   435
Walked none restraining, and by none
restrained:
Confessed no law but what his reason
taught,
Did all he wished, and wished but what
he ought.
As man in his primeval dower arrayed
The image of his glorious Sire dis-
played,   440
Even so, by faithful Nature guarded,
here

The traces of primeval Man appear;
The simple dignity no forms debase;
The eye sublime, and surly lion-grace:
The slave of none, of beasts alone the
lord,   445
His book he prizes, nor neglects his
sword;
—Well taught by that to feel his rights,
prepared
With this "the blessings he enjoys to
guard."

And as his native hills encircle ground
For many a marvellous victory renown-
ed,   450
The work of Freedom daring to oppose,
With few in arms,[1] innumerable foes,
When to those famous fields his steps are
led,
An unknown power connects him with
the dead:
For images of other worlds are there; 455
Awful the light, and holy is the air.
Fitfully, and in flashes, through his soul,
Like sun-lit tempests, troubled trans-
ports roll;
His bosom heaves, his Spirit towers a-
main,
Beyond the senses and their little
reign.   460

And oft, when that dread vision hath
past by,
He holds with God himself communion
high,
There where the peal of swelling torrents
fills
The sky-roofed temple of the eternal hills;
Or, when upon the mountain's silent
brow   465

---

[1] Alluding to several battles which the Swiss
in very small numbers have gained over their
oppressors, the House of Austria; and, in par-
ticular, to one fought at Næffels near Glarus,
where three hundred and thirty men are said to
have defeated an army of between fifteen and
twenty thousand Austrians. Scattered over the
valley are to be found eleven stones, with this
inscription, 1388, the year the battle was fought,
marking out, as I was told upon the spot, the
several places where the Austrians, attempting to
make a stand, were repulsed anew.

Reclined, he sees, above him and below,
Bright stars of ice and azure fields of
    snow;
While needle peaks of granite shooting
    bare
Tremble in ever-varying tints of air.
And when a gathering weight of shadows
    brown   470
Falls on the valleys as the sun goes
    down;
And Pikes, of darkness named and fear
    and storms,[1]
Uplift in quiet their illumined forms,
In sea-like reach of prospect round him
    spread,
Tinged like an angel's smile all rosy
    red—   475
Awe in his breast with holiest love unites,
And the near heavens impart their own
    delights.

When downward to his winter hut he
    goes,
Dear and more dear the lessening circle
    grows;
That hut which on the hills so oft em-
    ploys   480
His thoughts, the central point of all his
    joys.
And as a swallow, at the hour of rest,
Peeps often ere she darts into her nest,
So to the homestead, where the grandsire
    tends
A little prattling child, he oft descends,
To glance a look upon the well-matched
    pair;   486
Till storm and driving ice blockade him
    there.
There, safely guarded by the woods be-
    hind,
He hears the chiding of the baffled wind,
Hears Winter calling all his terrors
    round,   490
And, blest within himself, he shrinks not
    from the sound.

Through Nature's vale his homely plea-
    sures glide,

Unstained by envy, discontent, and
    pride;
The bound of all his vanity, to deck,
With one bright bell a favourite heifer's
    neck;   495
Well pleased upon some simple annual
    feast,
Remembered half the year and hoped the
    rest,
If dairy-produce, from his inner hoard,
Of thrice ten summers dignify the board.
—Alas! in every clime a flying ray   500
Is all we have to cheer our wintry way;
And here the unwilling mind may more
    than trace
The general sorrows of the human race:
The churlish gales of penury, that blow
Cold as the north-wind o'er a waste of
    snow,   505
To them the gentle groups of bliss deny
That on the noon-day bank of leisure lie.
Yet more;—compelled by Powers which
    only deign
That *solitary* man disturb their reign,
Powers that support an unremitting strife
With all the tender charities of life,   511
Full oft the father, when his sons have
    grown
To manhood, seems their title to disown;
And from his nest amid the storms of
    heaven
Drives, eagle-like, those sons as he was
    driven;   515
With stern composure watches to the
    plain—
And never, eagle-like, beholds again!

When long familiar joys are all re-
    signed,
Why does their sad remembrance haunt
    the mind?
Lo! where through flat Batavia's willowy
    groves,   520
Or by the lazy Seine, the exile roves;
O'er the curled waters Alpine measures
    swell,
And search the affections to their inmost
    cell;
Sweet poison spreads along the listener's
    veins,
Turning past pleasures into mortal pains;

---

[1] As Schreck-Horn, the pike of terror; Wetter-Horn, the pike of storms, &c., &c.

Poison, which not a frame of steel can
    brave,   526
Bows his young head with sorrow to the
    grave.[1]

Gay lark of hope, thy silent song re-
    sume!
Ye flattering eastern lights, once more
    the hills illume!
Fresh gales and dews of life's delicious
    morn,   530
And thou, lost fragrance of the heart,
    return!
Alas! the little joy to man allowed
Fades like the lustre of an evening cloud;
Or like the beauty in a flower installed,
Whose season was, and cannot be re-
    called.   535
Yet, when opprest by sickness, grief, or
    care,
And taught that pain is pleasure's natural
    heir,
We still confide in more than we can
    know;
Death would be else the favourite friend
    of woe.

'Mid savage rocks, and seas of snow
    that shine,   540
Between interminable tracts of pine,
Within a temple stands an awful shrine,
By an uncertain light revealed, that falls
On the mute Image and the troubled
    walls.
Oh! give not me that eye of hard dis-
    dain   545
That views, undimmed, Einsiedlen's[2]
    wretched fane.
While ghastly faces through the gloom
    appear,
Abortive joy, and hope that works in
    fear;
While prayer contends with silenced
    agony,

Surely in other thoughts contempt may
    die.   550
If the sad grave of human ignorance bear
One flower of hope—oh, pass and leave it
    there!

The tall sun, pausing on an Alpine
    spire,
Flings o'er the wilderness a stream of fire:
Now meet we other pilgrims ere the
    day   555
Close on the remnant of their weary way;
While they are drawing toward the sacred
    floor
Where, so they fondly think, the worm
    shall gnaw no more.
How gaily murmur and how sweetly
    taste
The fountains[3] reared for them amid the
    waste!   560
Their thirst they slake:—they wash their
    toil-worn feet,
And some with tears of joy each other
    greet.
Yes, I must see you when ye first behold
Those holy turrets tipped with evening
    gold,
In that glad moment will for you a
    sigh   565
Be heaved of charitable sympathy;
In that glad moment when your hands
    are prest
In mute devotion on the thankful breast!

Last, let us turn to Chamouny that
    shields
With rocks and gloomy woods her fertile
    fields: 570
Five streams of ice amid her cots de-
    scend,
And with wild flowers and blooming
    orchards blend;—
A scene more fair than what the Grecian
    feigns
Of purple lights and ever-vernal plains;
Here all the seasons revel hand in
    hand: 575

---

[1] The well-known effect of the famous air, called in French Ranz des Vaches, upon the Swiss troops.

[2] This shrine is resorted to, from a hope of relief, by multitudes, from every corner of the Catholic world, labouring under mental or bodily afflictions.

[3] Rude fountains built and covered with sheds for the accommodation of the Pilgrims, in their ascent of the mountain.

'Mid lawns and shades by breezy rivulets
    fanned,
They sport beneath that mountain's
    matchless height
That holds no commerce with the sum-
    mer night.
From age to age, throughout his lonely
    bounds
The crash of ruin fitfully resounds;   580
Appalling havoc! but serene his brow,
Where daylight lingers on perpetual
    snow;
Glitter the stars above, and all is black
    below.

What marvel then if many a Wanderer
    sigh,   584
While roars the sullen Arve in anger by,
That not for thy reward, unrivall'd Vale!
Waves the ripe harvest in the autumnal
    gale;
That thou, the slave of slaves, art doomed
    to pine
And droop, while no Italian arts are
    thine,
To soothe or cheer, to soften or refine. 590

Hail Freedom! whether it was mine to
    stray,
With shrill winds whistling round my
    lonely way,
On the bleak sides of Cumbria's heath-
    clad moors,
Or where dank sea-weed lashes Scotland's
    shores;
To scent the sweets of Piedmont's breath-
    ing rose,   595
And orange gale that o'er Lugano blows;
Still have I found, where Tyranny pre-
    vails,
That virtue languishes and pleasure fails,
While the remotest hamlets blessings share
In thy loved presence known, and only
    there;   600
Heart-blessings—outward treasures too
    which the eye
Of the sun peeping through the clouds
    can spy,
And every passing breeze will testify.
There, to the porch, belike with jasmine
    bound

Or woodbine wreaths, a smoother path is
    wound;   605
The housewife there a brighter garden
    sees,
Where hum on busier wing her happy
    bees;
On infant cheeks there fresher roses blow;
And grey-haired men look up with livelier
    brow,—
To greet the traveller needing food and
    rest;   610
Housed for the night, or but a half-hour's
    guest.

And oh, fair France! though now the
    traveller sees
Thy three-striped banner fluctuate on the
    breeze;
Though martial songs have banished songs
    of love,
And nightingales desert the village grove,
Scared by the fife and rumbling drum's
    alarms,   616
And the short thunder, and the flash of
    arms;
That cease not till night falls, when far
    and nigh,
Sole sound, the Sourd[1] prolongs his
    mournful cry;
—Yet hast thou found that Freedom
    spreads her power   620
Beyond the cottage hearth, the cottage-
    door:
All nature smiles, and owns beneath her
    eyes
Her fields peculiar, and peculiar skies.
Yes, as I roamed where Loiret's waters
    glide
Through rustling aspens heard from side
    to side,   625
When from October clouds a milder light
Fell where the blue flood rippled into
    white;
Methought from every cot the watchful
    bird
Crowed with ear-piercing power till then
    unheard;

---

[1] An insect so called, which emits a short,
melancholy cry, heard at the close of the sum-
mer evenings, on the banks of the Loire.

Each clacking mill, that broke the mur-
    muring streams,   630
Rocked the charmed thought in more
    delightful dreams;
Chasing those pleasant dreams, the fall-
    ing leaf
Awoke a fainter sense of moral grief;
The measured echo of the distant flail
Wound in more welcome cadence down
    the vale;   635
With more majestic course[1] the water
    rolled,
And ripening foliage shone with richer
    gold.
—But foes are gathering—Liberty must
    raise
Red on the hills her beacon's far-seen
    blaze;
Must bid the tocsin ring from tower to
    tower!—   640
Nearer and nearer comes the trying hour!
Rejoice, brave Land, though pride's per-
    verted ire
Rouse hell's own aid, and wrap thy fields
    in fire:
Lo, from the flames a great and glorious
    birth;
As if a new-made heaven were hailing a
    new earth!   645
—All cannot be: the promise is too fair
For creatures doomed to breathe terres-
    trial air:
Yet not for this will sober reason frown
Upon that promise, nor the hope dis-
    own;
She knows that only from high aims
    ensue   650
Rich guerdons, and to them alone are
    due.

Great God! by whom the strifes of men
    are weighed
In an impartial balance, give thine aid
To the just cause; and, oh! do thou pre-
    side
Over the mighty stream now spreading
    wide: 655

---

[1] The duties upon many parts of the French
rivers were so exorbitant, that the poorer people,
deprived of the benefit of water carriage, were
obliged to transport their goods by land.

So shall its waters, from the heavens
    supplied
In copious showers, from earth by whole-
    some springs,
Brood o'er the long-parched lands with
    Nile-like wings!
And grant that every sceptred child of
    clay
Who cries presumptuous, "Here the flood
    shall stay,"   660
May in its progress see thy guiding hand,
And cease the acknowledged purpose to
    withstand;
Or, swept in anger from the insulted
    shore,
Sink with his servile bands, to rise no
    more!

To-night, my Friend, within this hum-
    ble cot   665
Be scorn and fear and hope alike forgot
In timely sleep; and when, at break of
    day,
On the tall peaks the glistening sunbeams
    play,
With a light heart our course we may
    renew,
The first whose footsteps brush the moun-
    tain dew.   670

VII.

LINES

Left upon a Seat in a Yew-tree, which stands
near the lake of Esthwaite, on a desolate part
of the shore, commanding a beautiful prospect.

[Begun 1787.—Completed 1795.—Published 1798.]

NAY, Traveller! rest. This lonely Yew-
    tree stands
Far from all human dwelling: what if
    here
No sparkling rivulet spread the verdant
    herb?
What if the bee love not these barren
    boughs?
Yet, if the wind breathe soft, the curling
    waves,   5
That break against the shore, shall lull
    thy mind
By one soft impulse saved from vacancy.
           —————Who he was

That piled these stones and with the
  mossy sod
First covered, and here taught this aged
  Tree   10
With its dark arms to form a circling
  bower,
I well remember.—He was one who owned
No common soul. In youth by science
  nursed,
And led by nature into a wild scene
Of lofty hopes, he to the world went
  forth   15
A favoured Being, knowing no desire
Which genius did not hallow; 'gainst the
  taint
Of dissolute tongues, and jealousy, and
  hate,
And scorn,—against all enemies prepared,
All but neglect. The world, for so it
  thought,   20
Owed him no service; wherefore he at once
With indignation turned himself away,
And with the food of pride sustained his
  soul
In solitude.—Stranger! these gloomy
  boughs
Had charms for him; and here he loved
  to sit,   25
His only visitants a straggling sheep,
The stone-chat, or the glancing sand-
  piper:
And on these barren rocks, with fern and
  heath,
And juniper and thistle, sprinkled o'er,
Fixing his downcast eye, he many an
  hour   30
A morbid pleasure nourished, tracing here
An emblem of his own unfruitful life:
And, lifting up his head, he then would
  gaze
On the more distant scene,—how lovely
  'tis
Thou seest,—and he would gaze till it
  became   35
Far lovelier, and his heart could not
  sustain
The beauty, still more beauteous! Nor,
  that time,
When nature had subdued him to herself,
Would he forget those Beings to whose
  minds

Warm from the labours of benevolence   40
The world, and human life, appeared a
  scene
Of kindred loveliness: then he would sigh,
Inly disturbed, to think that others felt
What he must never feel: and so, lost
  Man!
On visionary views would fancy feed,   45
Till his eye streamed with tears. In this
  deep vale
He died,—this seat his only monument.

If Thou be one whose heart the holy
  forms
Of young imagination have kept pure,
Stranger! henceforth be warned; and
  know that pride,   50
Howe'er disguised in its own majesty,
Is littleness; that he who feels contempt
For any living thing, hath faculties
Which he has never used; that thought
  with him
Is in its infancy. The man whose eye   55
Is ever on himself doth look on one,
The least of Nature's works, one who
  might move
The wise man to that scorn which wisdom
  holds
Unlawful, ever. O be wiser, Thou!
Instructed that true knowledge leads to
  love;   60
True dignity abides with him alone
Who, in the silent hour of inward thought,
Can still suspect, and still revere himself,
In lowliness of heart.

VIII.

GUILT AND SORROW;

OR,

INCIDENTS UPON SALISBURY PLAIN.

[Begun 1791-92.—Completed 1793-94.—Pub-
lished 1842.]

ADVERTISEMENT,

PREFIXED TO THE FIRST EDITION OF THIS
POEM, PUBLISHED IN 1842.

Not less than one-third of the following poem,
though it has from time to time been altered in
the expression, was published so far back as the

year 1798, under the title of "The Female Vagrant." The extract is of such length that an apology seems to be required for reprinting it here: but it was necessary to restore it to its original position, or the rest would have been unintelligible. The whole was written before the close of the year 1794, and I will detail, rather as matter of literary biography than for any other reason, the circumstances under which it was produced.

During the latter part of the summer of 1793, having passed a month in the Isle of Wight, in view of the fleet which was then preparing for sea off Portsmouth at the commencement of the war, I left the place with melancholy forebodings. The American war was still fresh in memory. The struggle which was beginning, and which many thought would be brought to a speedy close by the irresistible arms of Great Britain being added to those of the Allies, I was assured in my own mind would be of long continuance, and productive of distress and misery beyond all possible calculation. This conviction was pressed upon me by having been a witness, during a long residence in revolutionary France, of the spirit which prevailed in that country. After leaving the Isle of Wight, I spent two days in wandering on foot over Salisbury Plain, which, though cultivation was then widely spread through parts of it, had upon the whole a still more impressive appearance than it now retains.

The monuments and traces of antiquity, scattered in abundance over that region, led me unavoidably to compare what we know or guess of those remote times with certain aspects of modern society, and with calamities, principally those consequent upon war, to which, more than other classes of men, the poor are subject. In those reflections, joined with particular facts that had come to my knowledge, the following stanzas originated.

In conclusion, to obviate some distraction in the minds of those who are well acquainted with Salisbury Plain, it may be proper to say that, of the features described as belonging to it, one or two are taken from other desolate parts of England.

I.

A TRAVELLER on the skirt of Sarum's
    Plain
Pursued his vagrant way, with feet half
    bare;
Stooping his gait, but not as if to gain
Help from the staff he bore; for mien
    and air

Were hardy, though his cheek seemed
    worn with care   5
Both of the time to come, and time long
    fled:
Down fell in straggling locks his thin grey
    hair;
A coat he wore of military red
But faded, and stuck o'er with many a
    patch and shred.

II.

While thus he journeyed, step by step
    led on,   10
He saw and passed a stately inn, full sure
That welcome in such house for him was
    none.
No board inscribed the needy to allure
Hung there, no bush proclaimed to old
    and poor
And desolate, "Here you will find a
    friend!"   15
The pendent grapes glittered above the
    door;—
On he must pace, perchance till night
    descend,
Where'er the dreary roads their bare
    white lines extend.

III.

The gathering clouds grew red with
    stormy fire,
In streaks diverging wide and mounting
    high;   20
That inn he long had passed; the distant
    spire,
Which oft as he looked back had fixed his
    eye,
Was lost, though still he looked, in the
    blank sky.
Perplexed and comfortless he gazed
    around,
And scarce could any trace of man descry,
Save cornfields stretched and stretching
    without bound;   26
But where the sower dwelt was nowhere
    to be found.

IV.

No tree was there, no meadow's pleasant
    green,
No brook to wet his lip or soothe his ear;

Long files of corn-stacks here and there
　　were seen, 　　　　　　　　　30
But not one dwelling-place his heart to
　　cheer.
Some labourer, thought he, may per-
　　chance be near;
And so he sent a feeble shout—in vain;
No voice made answer, he could only hear
Winds rustling over plots of unripe grain,
Or whistling thro' thin grass along the
　　unfurrowed plain. 　　　　　　36

V.

Long had he fancied each successive slope
Concealed some cottage, whither he might
　　turn
And rest; but now along heaven's dark-
　　ening cope
The crows rushed by in eddies, homeward
　　borne. 　　　　　　　　　　40
Thus warned he sought some shepherd's
　　spreading thorn
Or hovel from the storm to shield his head,
But sought in vain; for now, all wild,
　　forlorn,
And vacant, a huge waste around him
　　spread;
The wet cold ground, he feared, must be
　　his only bed. 　　　　　　　45

VI.

And be it so—for to the chill night shower
And the sharp wind his head he oft hath
　　bared;
A Sailor he, who many a wretched hour
Hath told; for, landing after labour hard,
Full long endured in hope of just reward,
He to an armèd fleet was forced away 51
By seamen, who perhaps themselves had
　　shared
Like fate; was hurried off, a helpless prey,
'Gainst all that in *his* heart, or theirs
　　perhaps, said nay.

VII.

For years the work of carnage did not
　　cease, 　　　　　　　　　　55
And death's dire aspect daily he surveyed,
Death's minister; then came his glad re-
　　lease,
And hope returned, and pleasure fondly
　　made

Her dwelling in his dreams. By Fancy's
　　aid
The happy husband flies, his arms to
　　throw 　　　　　　　　　　60
Round his wife's neck; the prize of victory
　　laid
In her full lap, he sees such sweet tears
　　flow
As if thenceforth nor pain nor trouble she
　　could know.

VIII.

Vain hope! for fraud took all that he had
　　earned.
The lion roars and gluts his tawny brood
Even in the desert's heart; but he, re-
　　turned, 　　　　　　　　　　66
Bears not to those he loves their needful
　　food.
His home approaching, but in such a mood
That from his sight his children might
　　have run,
He met a traveller, robbed him, shed his
　　blood; 　　　　　　　　　　70
And when the miserable work was done
He fled, a vagrant since, the murderer's
　　fate to shun.

IX.

From that day forth no place to him
　　could be
So lonely, but that thence might come a
　　pang 　　　　　　　　　　74
Brought from without to inward misery.
Now, as he plodded on, with sullen clang
A sound of chains along the desert rang;
He looked, and saw upon a gibbet high
A human body that in irons swang,
Uplifted by the tempest whirling by; 80
And, hovering, round it often did a raven
　　fly.

X.

It was a spectacle which none might view,
In spot so savage, but with shuddering
　　pain;
Nor only did for him at once renew
All he had feared from man, but roused
　　a train 　　　　　　　　　　85
Of the mind's phantoms, horrible as vain.
The stones, as if to cover him from day,
Rolled at his back along the living plain;

He fell, and without sense or motion lay;
But, when the trance was gone, feebly
    pursued his way.   90

XI.

As one whose brain habitual frenzy fires
Owes to the fit in which his soul hath
    tossed
Profounder quiet, when the fit retires,
Even so the dire phantasma which had
    crossed
His sense, in sudden vacancy quite lost,
Left his mind still as a deep evening
    stream.   96
Nor, if accosted now, in thought en-
    grossed,
Moody, or inly troubled, would he seem
To traveller who might talk of any casual
    theme.

XII.

Hurtle the clouds in deeper darkness
    piled,   100
Gone is the raven timely rest to seek;
He seemed the only creature in the wild
On whom the elements their rage might
    wreak;
Save that the bustard, of those regions
    bleak
Shy tenant, seeing by the uncertain light
A man there wandering, gave a mournful
    shriek,   106
And half upon the ground, with strange
    affright,
Forced hard against the wind a thick
    unwieldy flight.

XIII.

All, all was cheerless to the horizon's
    bound;
The weary eye—which, wheresoe'er it
    strays,   110
Marks nothing but the red sun's setting
    round,
Or on the earth strange lines, in former
    days
Left by gigantic arms—at length surveys
What seems an antique castle spreading
    wide;
Hoary and naked are its walls, and raise
Their brow sublime: in shelter there to
    bide   116

He turned, while rain poured down
    smoking on every side.

XIV.

Pile of Stone-henge! so proud to hint yet
    keep
Thy secrets, thou that lov'st to stand and
    hear
The Plain resounding to the whirlwind's
    sweep,   120
Inmate of lonesome Nature's endless year;
Even if thou saw'st the giant wicker rear
For sacrifice its throngs of living men,
Before thy face did ever wretch appear,
Who in his heart had groaned with dead-
    lier pain   125
Than he who, tempest-driven, thy shelter
    now would gain?

XV.

Within that fabric of mysterious form
Winds met in conflict, each by turns
    supreme;
And, from the perilous ground dislodged,
    through storm
And rain he wildered on, no moon to
    stream   130
From gulf of parting clouds one friendly
    beam,
Nor any friendly sound his footsteps led;
Once did the lightning's faint disastrous
    gleam
Disclose a naked guide-post's double head,
Sight which, tho' lost at once, a gleam of
    pleasure shed.   135

XVI.

No swinging sign-board creaked from cot-
    tage elm
To stay his steps with faintness over-
    come;
'Twas dark and void as ocean's watery
    realm
Roaring with storms beneath night's star-
    less gloom;
No gipsy cower'd o'er fire of furze or
    broom;   140
No labourer watched his red kiln glaring
    bright,
Nor taper glimmered dim from sick man's
    room;

Along the waste no line of mournful light
From lamp of lonely toll-gate streamed
     athwart the night.

XVII.

At length, though hid in clouds, the moon
     arose; 145
The downs were visible—and now revealed
A structure stands, which two bare slopes
     enclose.
It was a spot where, ancient vows fulfilled,
Kind pious hands did to the Virgin build
A lonely Spital, the belated swain 150
From the night terrors of that waste to
     shield:
But there no human being could remain,
And now the walls are named the "Dead
     House" of the plain.

XVIII.

Though he had little cause to love the
     abode
Of man, or covet sight of mortal face, 155
Yet when faint beams of light that ruin
     showed,
How glad he was at length to find some
     trace
Of human shelter in that dreary place.
Till to his flock the early shepherd goes,
Here shall much-needed sleep his frame
     embrace. 160
In a dry nook where fern the floor be-
     strows
He lays his stiffened limbs,—his eyes be-
     gin to close;

XIX.

When hearing a deep sigh, that seemed
     to come
From one who mourned in sleep, he raised
     his head,
And saw a woman in the naked room 165
Outstretched, and turning on a restless
     bed:
The moon a wan dead light around her
     shed.
He waked her—spake in tone that would
     not fail,
He hoped, to calm her mind; but ill he
     sped,

For of that ruin she had heard a tale 170
Which now with freezing thoughts did all
     her powers assail;

XX.

Had heard of one who, forced from storms
     to shroud,
Felt the loose walls of this decayed
     Retreat
Rock to incessant neighings shrill and
     loud,
While his horse pawed the floor with
     furious heat; 175
Till on a stone, that sparkled to his feet,
Struck, and still struck again, the trou-
     bled horse:
The man half raised the stone with pain
     and sweat,
Half raised, for well his arm might lose
     its force
Disclosing the grim head of a late mur-
     dered corse. 180

XXI.

Such tale of this lone mansion she had
     learned,
And when that shape, with eyes in sleep
     half drowned,
By the moon's sullen lamp she first dis-
     cerned,
Cold stony horror all her senses bound.
Her he addressed in words of cheering
     sound; 185
Recovering heart, like answer did she
     make;
And well it was that of the corse there
     found
In converse that ensued she nothing
     spake;
She knew not what dire pangs in him
     such tale could wake.

XXII.

But soon his voice and words of kind
     intent 190
Banished that dismal thought; and now
     the wind
In fainter howlings told its *rage* was
     spent:
Meanwhile discourse ensued of various
     kind,

Which by degrees a confidence of mind
And mutual interest failed not to create.
And, to a natural sympathy resigned,   196
In that forsaken building where they sate
The Woman thus retraced her own un-
    toward fate.

XXIII.

"By Derwent's side my father dwelt—a
    man
Of virtuous life, by pious parents bred;
And I believe that, soon as I began   201
To lisp, he made me kneel beside my bed,
And in his hearing there my prayers I
    said:
And afterwards, by my good father
    taught,
I read, and loved the books in which I
    read;   205
For books in every neighbouring house
    I sought,
And nothing to my mind a sweeter plea-
    sure brought.

XXIV.

"A little croft we owned—a plot of corn,
A garden stored with peas, and mint, and
    thyme,
And flowers for posies, oft on Sunday
    morn   210
Plucked while the church bells rang their
    earliest chime.
Can I forget our freaks at shearing time!
My hen's rich nest through long grass
    scarce espied;
The cowslip-gathering in June's dewy
    prime;
The swans that with white chests up-
    reared in pride   215
Rushing and racing came to meet me at
    the waterside!

XXV.

"The staff I well remember which upbore
The bending body of my active sire;
His seat beneath the honied sycamore
Where the bees hummed, and chair by
    winter fire;   220
When market-morning came, the neat
    attire
With which, though bent on haste, myself
    I decked;

Our watchful house-dog, that would tease
    and tire
The stranger till its barking-fit I checked;
The red-breast, known for years, which
    at my casement pecked.   225

XXVI.

"The suns of twenty summers danced
    along,—
Too little marked how fast they rolled
    away:
But, through severe mischance and cruel
    wrong,
My father's substance fell into decay:
We toiled and struggled, hoping for a day
When Fortune might put on a kinder
    look;   231
But vain were wishes, efforts vain as they;
He from his old hereditary nook
Must part; the summons came;—our final
    leave we took.

XXVII.

"It was indeed a miserable hour   235
When, from the last hill-top, my sire sur-
    veyed,
Peering above the trees, the steeple tower
That on his marriage day sweet music
    made!
Till then he hoped his bones might there
    be laid
Close by my mother in their native
    bowers: 240
Bidding me trust in God, he stood and
    prayed;—
I could not pray:—through tears that fell
    in showers
Glimmered our dear-loved home, alas! no
    longer ours!

XXVIII.

"There was a Youth whom I had loved
    so long,
That when I loved him not I cannot say:
'Mid the green mountains many a thought-
    less song   246
We two had sung, like gladsome birds in
    May;
When we began to tire of childish play,
We seemed still more and more to prize
    each other;

We talked of marriage and our marriage
   day ;   250
And I in truth did love him like a brother,
For never could I hope to meet with such
   another.

XXIX.

"Two years were passed since to a distant
   town
He had repaired to ply a gainful trade :
What tears of bitter grief, till then un-
   known,   255
What tender vows our last sad kiss de-
   layed !
To him we turned :—we had no other aid :
Like one revived, upon his neck I wept ;
And her whom he had loved in joy, he
   said,
He well could love in grief ; his faith he
   kept ;   260
And in a quiet home once more my father
   slept.

XXX.

"We lived in peace and comfort ; and
   were blest
With daily bread, by constant toil sup-
   plied.
Three lovely babes had lain upon my
   breast ;
And often, viewing their sweet smiles, I
   sighed,   265
And knew not why. My happy father
   died,
When threatened war reduced the chil-
   dren's meal :
Thrice happy ! that for him the grave
   could hide
The empty loom, cold hearth, and silent
   wheel,
And tears which flowed for ills which
   patience might not heal.   270

XXXI.

"'Twas a hard change ; an evil time was
   come ;
We had no hope, and no relief could gain :
But soon, with proud parade, the noisy
   drum
Beat round to clear the streets of want
   and pain.

My husband's arms now only served to
   strain   275
Me and his children hungering in his view ;
In such dismay my prayers and tears
   were vain :
To join those miserable men he flew,
And now to the sea-coast, with numbers
   more, we drew.

XXXII.

"There were we long neglected, and we
   bore   280
Much sorrow ere the fleet its anchor
   weighed ;
Green fields before us, and our native
   shore,
We breathed a pestilential air, that made
Ravage for which no knell was heard.
   We prayed
For our departure ; wished and wished—
   nor knew,   285
'Mid that long sickness and those hopes
   delayed,
That happier days we never more must
   view.
The parting signal streamed—at last the
   land withdrew.

XXXIII.

"But the calm summer season now was
   past.
On as we drove, the equinoctial deep 290
Ran mountains high before the howling
   blast,
And many perished in the whirlwind's
   sweep.
We gazed with terror on their gloomy
   sleep,
Untaught that soon such anguish must
   ensue,
Our hopes such harvest of affliction reap,
That we the mercy of the waves should
   rue :   296
We reached the western world, a poor
   devoted crew.

XXXIV.

"The pains and plagues that on our heads
   came down,
Disease and famine, agony and fear, 299
In wood or wilderness, in camp or town,

It would unman the firmest heart to
    hear.
All perished—all in one remorseless year,
Husband and children! one by one, by
    sword
And ravenous plague, all perished: every
    tear
Dried up, despairing, desolate, on board
A British ship I waked, as from a trance
    restored."   306

XXXV.

Here paused she, of all present thought
    forlorn,
Nor voice, nor sound, that moment's pain
    expressed,
Yet Nature, with excess of grief o'er-
    borne,
From her full eyes their watery load re-
    leased.   310
He too was mute: and, ere her weeping
    ceased,
He rose, and to the ruin's portal went,
And saw the dawn opening the silvery
    east
With rays of promise, north and south-
    ward sent ;
And soon with crimson fire kindled the
    firmament.   315

XXXVI.

"O come," he cried, "come, after weary
    night
Of such rough storm, this happy change
    to view."
So forth she came, and eastward looked ;
    the sight
Over her brow like dawn of gladness
    threw ;
Upon her cheek, to which its youthful
    hue   320
Seemed to return, dried the last lingering
    tear,
And from her grateful heart a fresh one
    drew :
The whilst her comrade to her pensive
    cheer
Tempered fit words of hope ; and the lark
    warbled near.

XXXVII.

They looked and saw a lengthening road,
    and wain   325
That rang down a bare slope not far re-
    mote :
The barrows glistered bright with drops
    of rain,
Whistled the waggoner with merry note,
The cock far off sounded his clarion
    throat ;
But town, or farm, or hamlet, none they
    viewed,   330
Only were told there stood a lonely cot
A long mile thence. While thither they
    pursued
Their way, the Woman thus her mournful
    tale renewed.

XXXVIII.

"Peaceful as this immeasurable plain
Is now, by beams of dawning light im-
    prest,   335
In the calm sunshine slept the glittering
    main ;
The very ocean hath its hour of rest.
I too forgot the heavings of my breast.
How quiet 'round me ship and ocean were !
As quiet all within me. I was blest,   340
And looked, and fed upon the silent air
Until it seemed to bring a joy to my de-
    spair.

XXXIX.

"Ah! how unlike those late terrific sleeps,
And groans that rage of racking famine
    spoke ;
The unburied dead that lay in festering
    heaps,   345
The breathing pestilence that rose like
    smoke,
The shriek that from the distant battle
    broke,
The mine's dire earthquake, and the
    pallid host.
Driven by the bomb's incessant thunder-
    stroke
To loathsome vaults, where heart-sick an-
    guish tossed,   350
Hope died, and fear itself in agony was
    lost !

XL.

"Some mighty gulf of separation passed,
I seemed transported to another world;
A thought resigned with pain, when from
the mast
The impatient mariner the sail unfurled,
And, whistling, called the wind that
hardly curled 356
The silent sea. From the sweet thoughts
of home
And from all hope I was for ever hurled.
For me—farthest from earthly port to
roam
Was best, could I but shun the spot where
man might come. 360

XLI.

"And oft I thought (my fancy was so
strong)
That I, at last, a resting-place had found;
'Here will I dwell,' said I, 'my whole life
long,
Roaming the illimitable waters round;
Here will I live, of all but heaven dis-
owned, 365
And end my days upon the peaceful
flood.'—
To break my dream the vessel reached its
bound;
And homeless near a thousand homes I
stood,
And near a thousand tables pined and
wanted food.

XLII.

"No help I sought; in sorrow turned
adrift, 370
Was hopeless, as if cast on some bare
rock;
Nor morsel to my mouth that day did lift,
Nor raised my hand at any door to knock.
I lay where, with his drowsy mates, the
cock
From the cross-timber of an outhouse
hung: 375
Dismally tolled, that night, the city clock!
At morn my sick heart hunger scarcely
stung,
Nor to the beggar's language could I fit
my tongue.

XLIII.

"So passed a second day; and, when the
third
Was come, I tried in vain the crowd's
resort. 380
—In deep despair, by frightful wishes
stirred,
Near the sea-side I reached a ruined fort;
There, pains which nature could no more
support,
With blindness linked, did on my vitals
fall;
And, after many interruptions short 385
Of hideous sense, I sank, nor step could
crawl:
Unsought for was the help that did my
life recall.

XLIV.

"Borne to a hospital, I lay with brain
Drowsy and weak, and shattered memory;
I heard my neighbours in their beds com-
plain 390
Of many things which never troubled me—
Of feet still bustling round with busy
glee,
Of looks where common kindness had no
part,
Of service done with cold formality,
Fretting the fever round the languid
heart, 395
And groans which, as they said, might
make a dead man start.

XLV.

"These things just served to stir the slum-
bering sense,
Nor pain nor pity in my bosom raised.
With strength did memory return; and,
thence
Dismissed, again on open day I gazed, 400
At houses, men, and common light, a-
mazed.
The lanes I sought, and, as the sun retired,
Came where beneath the trees a faggot
blazed;
The travellers saw me weep, my fate in-
quired,
And gave me food—and rest, more wel-
come, more desired. 405

XLVI.

"Rough potters seemed they, trading so-
    berly
With panniered asses driven from door to
    door;
But life of happier sort set forth to me,
And other joys my fancy to allure—
The bag-pipe dinning on the midnight
    moor   410
In barn uplighted; and companions boon,
Well met from far with revelry secure
Among the forest glades, while jocund
    June
Rolled fast along the sky his warm and
    genial moon.

XLVII.

"But ill they suited me—those journeys
    dark   415
O'er moor and mountain, midnight theft
    to hatch!
To charm the surly house-dog's faithful
    bark,
Or hang on tip-toe at the lifted latch.
The gloomy lantern, and the dim blue
    match,
The black disguise, the warning whistle
    shrill,   420
And ear still busy on its nightly watch,
Were not for me, brought up in nothing
    ill:
Besides, on griefs so fresh my thoughts
    were brooding still.

XLVIII.

"What could I do, unaided and unblest?
My father! gone was every friend of
    thine: 425
And kindred of dead husband are at best
Small help; and, after marriage such as
    mine,
With little kindness would to me in-
    cline.
Nor was I then for toil or service fit;
My deep-drawn sighs no effort could con-
    fine;   430
In open air forgetful would I sit
Whole hours, with idle arms in moping
    sorrow knit.

XLIX.

"The roads I paced, I loitered through
    the fields;
Contentedly, yet sometimes self-accused,
Trusted my life to what chance bounty
    yields,   435
Now coldly given, now utterly refused.
The ground I for my bed have often used:
But what afflicts my peace with keenest
    ruth,
Is that I have my inner self abused,
Forgone the home delight of constant
    truth,   440
And clear and open soul, so prized in
    fearless youth.

L.

"Through tears the rising sun I oft have
    viewed,
Through tears have seen him towards that
    world descend
Where my poor heart lost all its fortitude:
Three years a wanderer now my course I
    bend—   445
Oh! tell me whither—for no earthly friend
Have I."—She ceased, and weeping turned
    away;
As if because her tale was at an end,
She wept; because she had no more to say
Of that perpetual weight which on her
    spirit lay.   450

LI.

True sympathy the Sailor's looks ex-
    pressed,
His looks—for pondering he was mute the
    while.
Of social Order's care for wretchedness,
Of Time's sure help to calm and reconcile,
Joy's second spring and Hope's long-
    treasured smile,   455
'Twas not for *him* to speak—a man so
    tried.
Yet, to relieve her heart, in friendly style
Proverbial words of comfort he applied,
And not in vain, while they went pacing
    side by side.

LII.

Ere long, from heaps of turf, before their
    sight,   460

Together smoking in the sun's slant beam,
Rise various wreaths that into one unite
Which high and higher mounts with
    silver gleam:
Fair spectacle,—but instantly a scream
Thence bursting shrill did all remark pre-
    vent;   465
They paused, and heard a hoarser voice
    blaspheme,
And female cries. Their course they
    thither bent,
And met a man who foamed with anger
    vehement.

LIII.

A woman stood with quivering lips and
    pale,
And, pointing to a little child that lay 470
Stretched on the ground, began a piteous
    tale;
How in a simple freak of thoughtless play
He had provoked his father, who straight-
    way,
As if each blow were deadlier than the
    last,
Struck the poor innocent. Pallid with
    dismay   475
The Soldier's Widow heard and stood
    aghast;
And stern looks on the man her grey-
    haired Comrade cast.

LIV.

His voice with indignation rising high
Such further deed in manhood's name
    forbade;
The peasant, wild in passion, made reply
With bitter insult and revilings sad; 481
Asked him in scorn what business there
    he had;
What kind of plunder he was hunting
    now;
The gallows would one day of him be
    glad;—
Though inward anguish damped the
    Sailor's brow,   485
Yet calm he seemed as thoughts so
    poignant would allow.

LV.

Softly he stroked the child, who lay out-
    stretched

With face to earth; and, as the boy turn-
    ed round
His battered head, a groan the Sailor
    fetched
As if he saw—there and upon that ground—
Strange repetition of the deadly wound
He had himself inflicted. Through his
    brain   492
At once the griding iron passage found;
Deluge of tender thoughts then rushed
    amain,
Nor could his sunken eyes the starting
    tear restrain.   495

LVI.

Within himself he said—What hearts
    have we!
The blessing this a father gives his child!
Yet happy thou, poor boy! compared with
    me,
Suffering not doing ill—fate far more mild.
The stranger's looks and tears of wrath
    beguiled   500
The father, and relenting thoughts awoke;
He kissed his son—so all was reconciled.
Then, with a voice which inward trouble
    broke
Ere to his lips it came, the Sailor them
    bespoke.

LVII.

"Bad is the world, and hard is the world's
    law   505
Even for the man who wears the warmest
    fleece;
Much need have ye that time more closely
    draw
The bond of nature, all unkindness cease,
And that among so few there still be
    peace:
Else can ye hope but with such numerous
    foes   510
Your pains shall ever with your years
    increase?"—
While from his heart the appropriate
    lesson flows,
A correspondent calm stole gently o'er his
    woes.

LVIII.

Forthwith the pair passed on; and down
    they look

Into a narrow valley's pleasant scene   515
Where wreaths of vapour tracked a wind-
     ing brook,
That babbled on through groves and
     meadows green ;
A low-roofed house peeped out the trees
     between ;
The dripping groves resound with cheerful
     lays,
And melancholy lowings intervene   520
Of scattered herds, that in the meadow
     graze,
Some amid lingering shade, some touched
     by the sun's rays.

LIX.

They saw and heard, and, winding with
     the road
Down a thick wood, they dropt into the
     vale ;
Comfort by prouder mansions unbestowed
Their wearied frames, she hoped, would
     soon regale.   526
Ere long they reached that cottage in the
     dale :
It was a rustic inn ;—the board was
     spread,
The milk maid followed with her brimming
     pail,
And lustily the master carved the bread,
Kindly the housewife pressed, and they in
     comfort fed.   531

LX.

Their breakfast done, the pair, though
     loth, must part ;
Wanderers whose course no longer now
     agrees.
She rose and bade farewell ! and, while
     her heart
Struggled with tears nor could its sorrow
     ease,   535
She left him there ; for, clustering round
     his knees,
With his oak-staff the cottage children
     played ;
And soon she reached a spot o'erhung with
     trees
And banks of ragged earth ; beneath the
     shade
Across the pebbly road a little runnel
     strayed.   540

LXI.

A cart and horse beside the rivulet stood ;
Chequering the canvas roof the sunbeams
     shone.
She saw the carman bend to scoop the
     flood
As the wain fronted her,—wherein lay one,
A pale-faced Woman, in disease far gone.
The carman wet her lips as well behoved ;
Bed under her lean body there was none,
Though even to die near one she most had
     loved
She could not of herself those wasted
     limbs have moved.

LXII.

The Soldier's Widow learned with honest
     pain   550
And homefelt force of sympathy sincere,
Why thus that worn-out wretch must
     there sustain
The jolting road and morning air severe.
The wain pursued its way ; and following
     near
In pure compassion she her steps re-
     traced   555
Far as the cottage. "A sad sight is here,"
She cried aloud ; and forth ran out in haste
The friends whom she had left but a few
     minutes past.

LXIII.

While to the door with eager speed they
     ran,
From her bare straw the Woman half
     upraised   560
Her bony visage—gaunt and deadly wan ;
No pity asking, on the group she gazed
With a dim eye, distracted and amazed ;
Then sank upon her straw with feeble
     moan.
Fervently cried the housewife—"God be
     praised,   565
I have a house that I can call my own ;
Nor shall she perish there, untended and
     alone ! "

LXIV.

So in they bear her to the chimney seat,
And busily, though yet with fear, untie
Her garments, and, to warm her icy feet
And chafe her temples, careful hands
     apply.   571

Nature reviving, with a deep-drawn sigh
She strove, and not in vain, her head to
rear;
Then said—"I thank you all; if I must
die,
The God in heaven my prayers for you
will hear;   575
Till now I did not think my end had been
so near.

LXV.

"Barred every comfort labour could pro-
cure,
Suffering what no endurance could as-
suage,
I was compelled to seek my father's door,
Though loth to be a burthen on his age.
But sickness stopped me in an early stage
Of my sad journey; and within the wain
They placed me—there to end life's pil-
grimage,
Unless beneath your roof I may remain:
For I shall never see my father's door
again.   585

LXVI.

"My life, Heaven knows, hath long been
burthensome;
But, if I have not meekly suffered, meek
May my end be! Soon will this voice be
dumb:
Should child of mine e'er wander hither,
speak
Of me, say that the worm is on my
cheek.—   590
Torn from our hut, that stood beside the
sea
Near Portland lighthouse in a lonesome
creek,
My husband served in sad captivity
On shipboard, bound till peace or death
should set him free.

LXVII.

"A sailor's wife I knew a widow's cares,
Yet two sweet little ones partook my bed;
Hope cheered my dreams, and to my
daily prayers   597
Our heavenly Father granted each day's
bread;
Till one was found by stroke of violence
dead,

Whose body near our cottage chanced to
lie;   600
A dire suspicion drove us from our shed;
In vain to find a friendly face we try,
Nor could we live together those poor
boys and I;

LXVIII.

"For evil tongues made oath how on that
day
My husband lurked about the neighbour-
hood;   605
Now he had fled, and whither none could
say,
And *he* had done the deed in the dark
wood—
Near his own home!—but he was mild
and good;
Never on earth was gentler creature seen;
He'd not have robbed the raven of its
food.   610
My husband's loving kindness stood be-
tween
Me and all worldly harms and wrongs
however keen."

LXIX.

Alas! the thing she told with labouring
breath
The Sailor knew too well. That wicked-
ness
His hand had wrought; and when, in the
hour of death,   615
He saw his Wife's lips move his name to
bless
With her last words, unable to suppress
His anguish, with his heart he ceased to
strive;
And, weeping loud in this extreme dis-
tress,
He cried—"Do pity me! That thou
shouldst live   620
I neither ask nor wish—forgive me, but
forgive!"

LXX.

To tell the change that Voice within her
wrought
Nature by sign or sound made no essay;
A sudden joy surprised expiring thought,
And every mortal pang dissolved away.

Borne gently to a bed, in death she lay;
Yet still, while over her the husband bent,
A look was in her face which seemed to say,
"Be blest: by sight of thee from heaven
    was sent
Peace to my parting soul, the fulness of
    content."   630

LXXI.

She slept in peace,—his pulses throbbed
    and stopped,
Breathless he gazed upon her face,—then
    took
Her hand in his, and raised it, but both
    dropped,
When on his own he cast a rueful look.
His ears were never silent; sleep forsook
His burning eyelids stretched and stiff as
    lead;   636
All night from time to time under him
    shook
The floor as he lay shuddering on his bed;
And oft he groaned aloud, "O God, that
    I were dead!"

LXXII.

The Soldier's Widow lingered in the cot;
And, when he rose, he thanked her pious
    care   641
Through which his Wife, to that kind
    shelter brought,
Died in his arms; and with those thanks
    a prayer
He breathed for her, and for that mer-
    ciful pair.
The corse interred, not one hour he re-
    mained   645

Beneath their roof, but to the open air
A burthen, now with fortitude sustained,
He bore within a breast where dreadful
    quiet reigned.

LXXIII.

Confirmed of purpose, fearlessly prepared
For act and suffering, to the city straight
He journeyed, and forthwith his crime
    declared: 651
"And from your doom," he added, "now
    I wait,
Nor let it linger long, the murderer's fate."
Not ineffectual was that piteous claim:
"O welcome sentence which will end
    though late,"   655
He said, "the pangs that to my conscience
    came
Out of that deed. My trust, Saviour! is
    in thy name!"

LXXIV.

His fate was pitied. Him in iron case
(Reader, forgive the intolerable thought)
They hung not:—no one on *his* form or
    face   660
Could gaze, as on a show by idlers sought;
No kindred sufferer, to his death place
    brought
By lawless curiosity or chance,
When into storm the evening sky is
    wrought,
Upon his swinging corse an eye can
    glance,   665
And drop, as he once dropped, in misera-
    ble trance.

The Borderers

A TRAGEDY.

[Composed 1795-96. — Published 1842.]

DRAMATIS PERSONÆ.

MARMADUKE. ⎫
OSWALD. ⎪
WALLACE. ⎬ Of the Band of
LACY. ⎪ Borderers.
LENNOX. ⎭
HERBERT.
WILFRED, Servant to MARMADUKE.
Host.

Forester.
ELDRED, a Peasant.
Peasant, Pilgrims, &c.

IDONEA.
Female Beggar.
ELEANOR, Wife of ELDRED.

SCENE, *Borders of England and Scotland.*

TIME, *The Reign of Henry III.*

READERS already acquainted with my Poems will recognise, in the following composition, some eight or ten lines, which I have not scrupled to retain in the places where they originally stood. It is proper however to add that they would not have been used elsewhere, if I had foreseen the time when I might be induced to publish this Tragedy.

February 28, 1842.

ACT I.

SCENE, *Road in a Wood.*

WALLACE and LACY.

Lacy. The Troop will be impatient; let us hie
Back to our post, and strip the Scottish Foray
Of their rich Spoil, ere they recross the Border.
—Pity that our young Chief will have no part
In this good service.
Wal.   Rather let us grieve 5
That, in the undertaking which has caused
His absence, he hath sought, whate'er his aim,
Companionship with One of crooked ways,
From whose perverted soul can come no good
To our confiding, open-hearted, Leader. 10

Lacy. True; and, remembering how the Band have proved
That Oswald finds small favour in our sight,
Well may we wonder he has gained such power
Over our much-loved Captain.
Wal.   I have heard
Of some dark deed to which in early life
His passion drove him—then a Voyager
Upon the midland Sea. You knew his bearing 17
In Palestine?
Lacy.   Where he despised alike
Mohammedan and Christian. But enough;
Let us begone—the Band may else be foiled.   [*Exeunt.*

Enter MARMADUKE *and* WILFRED.

Wil. Be cautious, my dear Master!
Mar.   I perceive

That fear is like a cloak which old men
    huddle
About their love, as if to keep it warm.
    Wil. Nay, but I grieve that we should
    part. This Stranger,   24
For such he is—
    Mar.   Your busy fancies, Wilfred,
Might tempt me to a smile; but what of
    him?
    Wil. You know that you have saved
    his life.
    Mar.   I know it.
    Wil. And that he hates you!—Pardon
    me, perhaps
That word was hasty.
    Mar.   Fy! no more of it.
    Wil. Dear Master! gratitude's a heavy
    burden   30
To a proud Soul.—Nobody loves this
    Oswald—
Yourself, you do not love him.
    Mar.   I do more,
I honour him. Strong feelings to his heart
Are natural; and from no one can be learnt
More of man's thoughts and ways than
    his experience   35
Has given him power to teach: and then
    for courage
And enterprise—what perils hath he
    shunned?
What obstacles hath he failed to over-
    come?
Answer these questions, from our common
    knowledge,   39
And be at rest.
    Wil.   Oh, Sir!
    Mar.   Peace, my good Wilfred;
Repair to Liddesdale, and tell the Band
I shall be with them in two days at
    farthest.
    Wil. May He whose eye is over all
    protect you!   [*Exit.*

Enter OSWALD (*a bunch of plants in
    his hand*).

    Osw. This wood is rich in plants and
    curious simples.   44
    Mar. (*looking at them*). The wild rose,
    and the poppy, and the nightshade:
Which is your favourite, Oswald?
    Osw.   That which, while it is

Strong to destroy, is also strong to heal—
                [*Looking forward.*
Not yet in sight!—We'll saunter here
    awhile;
They cannot mount the hill, by us unseen.
    Mar. (*a letter in his hand*). It is no com-
    mon thing when one like you   50
Performs these delicate services, and
    therefore
I feel myself much bounden to you,
    Oswald;
'Tis a strange letter this!—You saw her
    write it?
    Osw. And saw the tears with which she
    blotted it.
    Mar. And nothing less would satisfy
    him?
    Osw.   No less;   55
For that another in his Child's affection
Should hold a place, as if 'twere robbery,
He seemed to quarrel with the very
    thought.
Besides, I know not what strange prejudice
Is rooted in his mind; this Band of ours,
Which you've collected for the noblest
    ends,   61
Along the confines of the Esk and Tweed
To guard the Innocent he calls us
    "Outlaws;"
And, for yourself, in plain terms he asserts
This garb was taken up that indolence 65
Might want no cover, and rapacity
Be better fed.
    Mar.   Ne'er may I own the heart
That cannot feel for one, helpless as he is.
    Osw. Thou know'st me for a Man not
    easily moved,
Yet was I grievously provoked to think 70
Of what I witnessed.
    Mar.   This day will suffice
To end her wrongs.
    Osw.   But if the blind Man's tale
Should *yet* be true?
    Mar.   Would it were possible!
Did not the Soldier tell thee that himself,
And others who survived the wreck,
    beheld   75
The Baron Herbert perish in the waves
Upon the coast of Cyprus?
    Osw.   Yes, even so,
And I had heard the like before: in sooth

The tale of this his quondam Barony
Is cunningly devised; and, on the back 80
Of his forlorn appearance, could not fail
To make the proud and vain his tributa-
ries,
And stir the pulse of lazy charity.
The seignories of Herbert are in Devon;
We, neighbours of the Esk and Tweed:
'tis much   85
The Arch-impostor——
   Mar.   Treat him gently, Oswald;
Though I have never seen his face,
methinks,
There cannot come a day when I shall
cease
To love him. I remember, when a Boy
Of scarcely seven years' growth, beneath
the Elm   90
That casts its shade over our village school,
'Twas my delight to sit and hear Idonea
Repeat her Father's terrible adventures,
Till all the band of playmates wept to-
gether;
And that was the beginning of my love. 95
And, through all converse of our later
years,
An image of this old Man still was present,
When I had been most happy. Pardon me
If this be idly spoken.
   Osw.   See, they come, 99
Two Travellers!
   Mar. (points). The woman is Idonea.
   Osw. And leading Herbert.
   Mar.   We must let them pass—
This thicket will conceal us.
                          [*They step aside.*

Enter IDONEA, *leading* HERBERT *blind.*
   Idon. Dear Father, you sigh deeply;
ever since
We left the willow shade by the brook-
side,
Your natural breathing has been troubled.
   Her.   Nay, 105
You are too fearful; yet must I confess,
Our march of yesterday had better suited
A firmer step than mine.
   Idon.   That dismal Moor—
In spite of all the larks that cheered our
path,
I never can forgive it: but how steadily

You paced along, when the bewildering
moonlight   111
Mocked me with many a strange fantastic
shape!—
I thought the Convent never would
appear;
It seemed to move away from us: and yet
That you are thus the fault is mine; for
the air   115
Was soft and warm, no dew lay on the
grass,
And midway on the waste ere night had
fallen
I spied a Covert walled and roofed with
sods—
A miniature; belike some Shepherd-boy,
Who might have found a nothing-doing
hour   120
Heavier than work, raised it: within that
hut
We might have made a kindly bed of
heath,
And thankfully there rested side by side
Wrapped in our cloaks, and, with re-
cruited strength,
Have hailed the morning sun. But
cheerily, Father,—   125
That staff of yours, I could almost have
heart
To fling 't away from you: you make no
use
Of me, or of my strength;—come, let me
feel
That you do press upon me. There—
indeed
You are quite exhausted. Let us rest
awhile   130
On this green bank.   [*He sits down.*
   Her. (after some time). Idonea, you are
silent,
And I divine the cause.
   Idon.   Do not reproach me:
I pondered patiently your wish and will
When I gave way to your request; and
now,
When I behold the ruins of that face, 135
Those eyeballs dark—dark beyond hope
of light,
And think that they were blasted for my
sake,
The name of Marmaduke is blown away:

Father, I would not change that sacred feeling
For all this world can give.
    Her.   Nay, be composed : 140
Few minutes gone a faintness overspread
My frame, and I bethought me of two things.
I ne'er had heart to separate—my grave,
And thee, my Child !
    Idon.   Believe me, honoured Sire !
'Tis weariness that breeds these gloomy fancies,   145
And you mistake the cause : you hear the woods
Resound with music, could you see the sun,
And look upon the pleasant face of Nature——
    Her. I comprehend thee—I should be as cheerful
As if we two were twins ; two songsters bred   150
In the same nest, my spring-time one with thine.
My fancies, fancies if they be, are such
As come, dear Child ! from a far deeper source
Than bodily weariness. While here we sit
I feel my strength returning. · The bequest   155
Of thy kind Patroness, which to receive
We have thus far adventured, will suffice
To save thee from the extreme of penury ;
But when thy Father must lie down and die,
How wilt thou stand alone?
    Idon.   Is he not strong? 160
Is he not valiant?
    Her.   Am I then so soon
Forgotten? have my warnings passed so quickly
Out of thy mind? My dear, my only, Child ;
Thou wouldst be leaning on a broken reed—
This Marmaduke——
    Idon.   O could you hear his voice : 165
Alas ! you do not know him. He is one
(I wot not what ill tongue has wronged him with you)

All gentleness and love. His face bespeaks
A deep and simple meekness : and that Soul,
Which with the motion of a virtuous act
Flashes a look of terror upon guilt,   171
Is, after conflict, quiet as the ocean,
By a miraculous finger stilled at once.
    Her. Unhappy Woman !
    Idon.   Nay, it was my duty
Thus much to speak ; but think not I forget—   175
Dear Father ! how *could* I forget and live ?—
You and the story of that doleful night
When, Antioch blazing to her topmost towers,
You rushed into the murderous flames, returned
Blind as the grave, but, as you oft have told me,   180
Clasping your infant Daughter to your heart.
    Her. Thy Mother too !—scarce had I gained the door,
I caught her voice ; she threw herself upon me,
I felt thy infant brother in her arms ;
She saw my blasted face—a tide of soldiers   185
That instant rushed between us, and I heard
Her last death-shriek, distinct among a thousand.
    Idon. Nay, Father, stop not ; let me hear it all,
    Her. Dear Daughter ! precious relic of that time—
For my old age, it doth remain with thee
To make it what thou wilt. Thou hast been told,   191
That when, on our return from Palestine,
I found how my domains had been usurped,
I took thee in my arms, and we began
Our wanderings together. Providence 195
At length conducted us to Rossland,—there,
Our melancholy story moved a Stranger
To take thee to her home—and for myself,

Soon after, the good Abbot of St. Cuthbert's
Supplied my helplessness with food and
    raiment,   200
And, as thou know'st, gave me that
    humble Cot
Where now we dwell.—For many years I
    bore
Thy absence, till old age and fresh infirmities .
Exacted thy return, and our reunion.
I did not think that, during that long
    absence,   205
My Child, forgetful of the name of
    Herbert,
Had given her love to a wild Freebooter,
Who here, upon the borders of the Tweed,
Doth prey alike on two distracted Countries,   209
Traitor to both.
    Idon.   Oh, could you hear his voice!
I will not call on Heaven to vouch for me,
But let this kiss speak what is in my heart.

Enter a Peasant.

    Pea. Good morrow, Strangers! If you
    want a Guide,
Let me have leave to serve you!
    Idon.   My Companion
Hath need of rest; the sight of Hut or
    Hostel   215
Would be most welcome.
    Pea.   Yon white hawthorn gained,
You will look down into a dell, and there
Will see an ash from which a sign-board
    hangs;
The house is hidden by the shade. Old
    Man,
You seem worn out with travel—shall I
    support you?   220
    Her. I thank you; but, a resting-place
    so near,
'Twere wrong to trouble you.
    Pea.   God speed you both.
                        [*Exit* Peasant.
    Her. Idonea, we must part. Be not
    alarmed—
'Tis but for a few days—a thought has
    struck me.
    Idon. That I should leave you at this
    house, and thence   225

Proceed alone. It shall be so; for strength
Would fail you ere our journey's end be
    reached.
        [*Exit* HERBERT *supported by* IDONEA.

Re-enter MARMADUKE *and* OSWALD.

    Mar. This instant will we stop him——
    Osw.   Be not hasty,
For sometimes, in despite of my conviction,
He tempted me to think the Story true;
'Tis plain he loves the Maid, and what he
    said   231
That savoured of aversion to thy name
Appeared the genuine colour of his soul—
Anxiety lest mischief should befall her
After his death.
    Mar.   I have been much deceived.
    Osw. But sure he loves the Maiden, and
    never love   236
Could find delight to nurse itself so
    strangely,
Thus to torment her with *inventions!*—
    death——
There must be truth in this.
    Mar.   Truth in his story!
He must have felt it then, known what it
    was,   240
And in such wise to rack her gentle heart
Had been a tenfold cruelty.
    Osw.   Strange pleasures
Do we poor mortals cater for ourselves!
To see him thus provoke her tenderness
With tales of weakness and infirmity! 245
I'd wager on his life for twenty years.
    Mar. We will not waste an hour in
    such a cause.
    Osw. Why, this is noble! shake her off
    at once.
    Mar. Her virtues are his instruments.
    —A Man
Who has so practised on the world's cold
    sense,   250
May well deceive his Child—What! leave
    her thus,
A prey to a deceiver?—no—no—no—
'Tis but a word and then——
    Osw.   Something is here
More than we see, or whence this strong
    aversion?
Marmaduke! I suspect unworthy tales

Have reached his ear—you have had
 enemies.   256
Mar. Enemies !—of his own coinage.
Osw.   That may be,
But wherefore slight protection such as
 you
Have power to yield? perhaps he looks
 elsewhere.—
I am perplexed.
 Mar. What hast thou heard or seen?
 Osw. No—no—the thing stands clear
 of mystery;   261
(As you have said) he coins himself the
 slander
With which he taints her ear;—for a
 plain reason ;
He dreads the presence of a virtuous
 man
Like you; he knows your eye would
 search his heart,   265
Your justice stamp upon his evil deeds
The punishment they merit. All is plain :
It cannot be——
 Mar. What cannot be?
 Osw.   Yet that a Father
Should in his love admit no rivalship,
And torture thus the heart of his own
 Child   270
 Mar. Nay, you abuse my friendship !
 Osw.   Heaven forbid !—
There was a circumstance, trifling in-
 deed—
It struck me at the time—yet I believe
I never should have thought of it again
But for the scene which we by chance
 have witnessed.   275
 Mar. What is your meaning?
 Osw. Two days gone I saw,
Though at a distance and he was dis-
 guised,
Hovering round Herbert's door, a man
 whose figure
Resembled much that cold voluptuary,
The villain, Clifford. He hates you, and
 he knows   280
Where he can stab you deepest.
 Mar.   Clifford never
Would stoop to skulk about a Cottage
 door—
It could not be.
 Osw. And yet I now remember

That, when your praise was warm upon
 my tongue,
And the blind Man was told how you had
 rescued   285
A maiden from the ruffian violence
Of this same Clifford, he became im-
 patient
And would not hear me.
 Mar.   No—it cannot be—
I dare not trust myself with such a
 thought—
Yet whence this strange aversion? You
 are a man   290
Not used to rash conjectures——
 Osw.   If you deem it
A thing worth further notice, we must act
With caution, sift the matter artfully.
   [*Exeunt* Marmaduke *and* Oswald.

SCENE, *The door of the Hostel.*

Herbert, Idonea, *and* Host.

 Her. (*seated*). As I am dear to you, re-
 member, Child !
This last request.
 Idon. You know me, Sire ; farewell !
 Her. And are you going then? Come,
 come, Idonea,   296
We must not part,—I have measured
 many a league
When these old limbs had need of rest,—
 and now
I will not play the sluggard.
 Idon.   Nay, sit down.
     [*Turning to* Host.
Good Host, such tendance as you would
 expect   300
From your own Children, if yourself were
 sick,
Let this old Man find at your hands;
 poor Leader, [*Looking at the dog.*
We soon shall meet again. If thou neglect
This charge of thine, then ill befall thee !
 —Look,
The little fool is loth to stay behind. 305
Sir Host ! by all the love you bear to
 courtesy,
Take care of him, and feed the truant
 well.
 Host. Fear not, I will obey you ;—but
 One so young,

And One so fair, it goes against my heart
That you should travel unattended, Lady!—
I have a palfrey and a groom : the lad 311
Shall squire you, (would it not be better,
     Sir?)
And for less fee than I would let him run
For any lady I have seen this twelve-
     month.
  Idon. You know, Sir, I have been too
     long your guard   315
Not to have learnt to laugh at little fears.
Why, if a wolf should leap from out a
     thicket,
A look of mine would send him scouring
     back,
Unless I differ from the thing I am 319
When you are by my side.
  Her.   Idonea, wolves
Are not the enemies that move my fears.
  Idon. No more, I pray, of this. Three
     days at farthest
Will bring me back—protect him, Saints
     —farewell!   [*Exit* IDONEA.
  Host. 'Tis never drought with us—
     St. Cuthbert and his Pilgrims,
Thanks to them, are to us a stream of
     comfort :   325
Pity the Maiden did not wait a while ;
She could not, Sir, have failed of company.
  Her. Now she is gone, I fain would
     call her back.
  Host. (*calling*). Holla !
  Her. No, no, the business must be
     done.—
What means this riotous noise?
  Host.   The villagers
Are flocking in—a wedding festival— 331
That's all—God save you, Sir.

Enter OSWALD.

  Osw.   Ha ! as I live,
The Baron Herbert.
  Host.   Mercy, the Baron Herbert !
  Osw. So far into your journey ! on my
     life,
You are a lusty Traveller. But how fare
     you?   335
  Her. Well as the wreck I am permits.
     And you, Sir?
  Osw. I do not see Idonea.
  Her.   Dutiful Girl,

She is gone before, to spare my weariness.
But what has brought you hither?
  Osw.   A slight affair,
That will be soon despatched.
  Her.   Did Marmaduke 340
Receive that letter?
  Osw.   Be at peace.—The tie
Is broken, you will hear no more of *him.*
  Her. This is true comfort, thanks a
     thousand times !—
That noise !—would I had gone with her
     as far
As the Lord Clifford's Castle : I have
     heard   345
That, in his milder moods, he has ex-
     pressed
Compassion for me. His influence is great
With Henry, our good King ;—the Baron
     might
Have heard my suit, and urged my plea
     at Court.
No matter—he's a dangerous Man.—That
     noise !—   350
'Tis too disorderly for sleep or rest.
Idonea would have fears for me,—the
     Convent
Will give me quiet lodging. You have
     a boy, good Host,
And he must lead me back.
  Osw.   You are most lucky ;
I have been waiting in the wood hard by
For a companion—here he comes ; our
     journey   356

Enter MARMADUKE.

Lies on your way ; accept us as your
     Guides.
  Her. Alas ! I creep so slowly.
  Osw.   Never fear ;
We'll not complain of that.
  Her.   My limbs are stiff
And need repose. Could you but wait
     an hour?   360
  Osw. Most willingly !—Come, let me
     lead you in,
And, while you take your rest, think not
     of us ;
We'll stroll into the wood ; lean on my
     arm.
          [*Conducts* HERBERT *into the house.*
               Exit MARMADUKE.

Enter Villagers.

Osw. (*to himself coming out of the Hostel*).
    I have prepared a most apt Instru-
      ment—
The Vagrant must, no doubt, be loitering
    somewhere   365
About this ground; she hath a tongue
    well skilled,
By mingling natural matter of her own
With all the daring fictions I have taught
    her,
To win belief, such as my plot requires.
                     [*Exit* Oswald.

Enter more Villagers, *a* Musician *among
    them.*

    Host (*to them*). Into the court, my
      Friend, and perch yourself   370
Aloft upon the elm-tree. Pretty Maids,
Garlands and flowers, and cakes and
    merry thoughts,
Are here, to send the sun into the west
More speedily than you belike would
    wish.

Scene *changes to the Wood adjoining the
    Hostel*—Marmaduke *and* Oswald *enter-
    ing.*

    Mar. I would fain hope that we deceive
      ourselves: 375
When first I saw him sitting there, alone,
It struck upon my heart I know not how.
    Osw. To-day will clear up all.—You
      marked a Cottage,
That ragged Dwelling, close beneath a
    rock
By the brook-side: it is the abode of One,
A Maiden innocent till ensnared by
    Clifford,   381
Who soon grew weary of her; but, alas!
What she had seen and suffered turned
    her brain.
Cast off by her Betrayer, she dwells alone,
Nor moves her hands to any needful
    work: 385
She eats her food which every day the
    peasants
Bring to her hut; and so the Wretch has
    lived
Ten years; and no one ever heard her
    voice;

But every night at the first stroke of twelve
She quits her house and, in the neigh-
    bouring Churchyard   390
Upon the self-same spot, in rain or storm,
She paces out the hour 'twixt twelve and
    one—
She paces round and round an Infant's
    grave,
And in the Churchyard sod her feet have
    worn
A hollow ring; they say it is knee-
    deep——   395
Ah! what is here?
        [*A female* Beggar *rises up, rub-
          bing her eyes as if in sleep—a
          Child in her arms.*

    Beg.   Oh! Gentlemen, I thank you;
I've had the saddest dream that ever
    troubled
The heart of living creature.—My poor
    Babe
Was crying, as I thought, crying for
    bread
When I had none to give him; where-
    upon   400
I put a slip of foxglove in his hand,
Which pleased him so, that he was
    hushed at once;
When into one of those same spotted bells
A bee came darting, which the Child with
    joy   404
Imprisoned there, and held it to his ear,
And suddenly grew black, as he would die.
    Mar. We have no time for this, my
      babbling Gossip;
Here's what will comfort you.
                [*Gives her money.*
    Beg.   The Saints reward you
For this good deed!—Well, Sirs, this
    passed away;   409
And afterwards I fancied, a strange dog,
Trotting alone along the beaten road,
Came to my child as by my side he slept,
And, fondling, licked his face, then on a
    sudden
Snapped fierce to make a morsel of his
    head:
But here he is, [*kissing the Child*] it must
    have been a dream.   415
    Osw. When next inclined to sleep,
    take my advice

And put your head, good Woman, under
  cover.
    Beg. Oh, Sir, you would not talk thus,
    if you knew
What life is this of ours, how sleep will
  master
The weary-worn.—You gentlefolk have
  got   420
Warm chambers to your wish. I'd rather
  be
A stone than what I am.—But two nights
  gone,
The darkness overtook me—wind and rain
Beat hard upon my head—and yet I saw
A glow-worm, through the covert of the
  furze,   425
Shine calmly as if nothing ailed the sky:
At which I half accused the God in
  Heaven.—
You must forgive me.
    Osw.   Ay, and if you think
The Fairies are to blame, and you should
  chide
Your favourite saint—no matter—this
  good day   430
Has made amends.
    Beg.   Thanks to you both; but,
    Oh Sir!
How would you like to travel on whole
  hours
As I have done, my eyes upon the
  ground,
Expecting still, I knew not how, to find
A piece of money glittering through the
  dust?   435
    Mar. This woman is a prater. Pray,
    good Lady!
Do you tell fortunes?
    Beg.   Oh Sir, you are like the rest.
This Little-one—it cuts me to the heart—
Well! they might turn a beggar from
  their doors,
But there are Mothers who can see the
  Babe   440
Here at my breast, and ask me where I
  bought it:
This they can do, and look upon my face—
But you, Sir, should be kinder.
    Mar.   Come hither, Fathers,
And learn what nature is from this poor
  Wretch!

    Beg. Ay, Sir, there's nobody that feels
    for us.   445
Why now—but yesterday I overtook
A blind old Greybeard and accosted him,
I' th' name of all the Saints, and by the
  Mass
He should have used me better!—Charity!
If you can melt a rock, he is your man;
But I'll be even with him—here again   451
Have I been waiting for him.
    Osw.   Well, but softly,
Who is it that hath wronged you?
    Beg.   Mark you me;
I'll point him out;—a Maiden is his guide,
Lovely as Spring's first rose; a little dog,
Tied by a woollen cord, moves on before
With look as sad as he were dumb; the
  cur,   457
I owe him no ill will, but in good sooth
He does his Master credit.
    Mar.   As I live,
'Tis Herbert and no other!
    Beg.   'Tis a feast to see him,
Lank as a ghost and tall, his shoulders
  bent,   461
And long beard white with age—yet
  evermore,
As if he were the only Saint on earth,
He turns his face to heaven.
    Osw.   But why so violent
Against this venerable Man?
    Beg.   I'll tell you: 465
He has the very hardest heart on earth;
I had as lief turn to the Friar's school
And knock for entrance, in mid holiday.
    Mar. But to your story.
    Beg.   I was saying, Sir—
Well!—he has often spurned me like a
  toad,   470
But yesterday was worse than all; at
  last
I overtook him, Sirs, my Babe and I,
And begged a little aid for charity:
But he was snappish as a cottage cur.
Well then, says I—I'll out with it; at
  which   475
I cast a look upon the Girl, and felt
As if my heart would burst; and so I left
  him.
    Osw. I think, good Woman, you are the
    very person

Whom, but some few days past, I saw in
     Eskdale,   479
At Herbert's door.

Beg.   Ay ; and if truth were known
I have good business there.

Osw.   I met you at the threshold,
And he seemed angry.

Beg.   Angry ! well he might ;
And long as I can stir I'll dog him.—
Yesterday,
To serve me so, and knowing that he owes
The best of all he has to me and mine. 485
But 'tis all over now. That good old
     Lady
Has left a power of riches ; and I say it,
If there's a lawyer in the land, the knave
Shall give me half.

Osw. What's this?—I fear, good Woman,
You have been insolent.

Beg.   And there's the Baron,
I spied him skulking in his peasant's
     dress.   491

Osw. How say you? in disguise?—

Mar.   But what's your business
With Herbert or his Daughter?

Beg.   Daughter ! truly—
But how's the day?—I fear, my little
     Boy,
We've overslept ourselves.—Sirs, have
     you seen him?   [*Offers to go.*

Mar. I must have more of this ;—you
     shall not stir   496
An inch, till I am answered. Know you
     aught
That doth concern this Herbert?

Beg.   You are provoked,
And will misuse me, Sir !

Mar.   No trifling, Woman !—

Osw. You are as safe as in a sanctuary ; 500
Speak.

Mar. Speak !

Beg. He is a most hard-hearted Man.

Mar. Your life is at my mercy.

Beg.   Do not harm me,
And I will tell you all !—You know not,
     Sir,
What strong temptations press upon the
     Poor.

Osw. Speak out.

Beg.   Oh, Sir, I've been a wicked
     Woman.   505

Osw. Nay, but speak out !

Beg.   He flattered me, and said
What harvest it would bring us both ;
     and so
I parted with the Child.

Mar.   Parted with whom?

Beg. Idonea, as he calls her ; but the Girl
Is mine.

Mar. Yours, Woman ! are you Her-
     bert's wife?   510

Beg. Wife, Sir ! his wife—not I ; my
     husband, Sir,
Was of Kirkoswald—many a snowy
     winter
We've weathered out together. My poor
     Gilfred !
He has been two years in his grave.

Mar.   Enough.

Osw. We've solved the riddle—Mis-
     creant !

Mar. Do you,   515
Good Dame, repair to Liddesdale and
     wait
For my return ; be sure you shall have
     justice.

Osw. A lucky woman !—go, you have
     done good service.   [*Aside.*

Mar. (*to himself*) Eternal praises on the
     power that saved her !—   519

Osw. (*gives her money*). Here's for your
     little boy, and when you christen him
I'll be his Godfather.

Beg. Oh Sir, you are merry with me.
In grange or farm this Hundred scarcely
     owns
A dog that does not know me.—These
     good Folks,—
For love of God I must not pass their
     doors ;
But I'll be back with my best speed : for
     you—   525
God bless and thank you both, my gentle
     Masters.   [*Exit Beggar.*

Mar. (*to himself*). The cruel Viper !—
     Poor devoted Maid,
Now I *do* love thee.

Osw.   I am thunderstruck.

Mar. Where is she—holla !
     [*Calling to the* Beggar, *who returns ;*
     he looks at her stedfastly.
     You are Idonea's Mother ?—

Nay, be not terrified—it does me good 530
To look upon you.

   Osw. (*interrupting*). In a peasant's
    dress
You saw, who was it?

   Beg.   Nay, I dare not speak ;
He is a man, if it should come to his
    ears
I never shall be heard of more.

   Osw.   Lord Clifford?

   Beg. What can I do? believe me, gentle
    Sirs,
                        535
I love her, though I dare not call her
    daughter.

   Osw. Lord Clifford—did you see him
    talk with Herbert?

   Beg. Yes, to my sorrow—under the
    great oak
At Herbert's door—and when he stood
    beside
The blind Man—at the silent Girl he
    looked
                        540
With such a look—it makes me tremble,
    Sir,
To think of it.

   Osw.   Enough ! you may depart.

   Mar. (*to himself*) Father !—to God him-
    self we cannot give   543
A holier name ; and, under such a mask,
To lead a Spirit, spotless as the blessed,
To that abhorrèd den of brutish vice !—
Oswald, the firm foundation of my life
Is going from under me ; these strange
    discoveries—
Looked at from every point of fear or
    hope,
Duty, or love—involve, I feel, my ruin. 550

ACT II.

Scene, *A Chamber in the Hostel*—Oswald
  *alone, rising from a Table on which he
  had been writing.*

   Osw. They chose *him* for their Chief !—
    what covert part
He in the preference, modest Youth,
    might take,
I neither know nor care. The insult bred
More of contempt than hatred ; both are
    flown ;

That either e'er existed is my shame : 555
'Twas a dull spark—a most unnatural fire
That died the moment the air breathed
    upon it.
—These fools of feeling are mere birds of
    winter
That haunt some barren island of the
    north,
Where, if a famishing man stretch forth
    his hand,   560
They think it is to feed them. I have left
    him
To solitary meditation ;—now
For a few swelling phrases, and a flash
Of truth, enough to dazzle and to blind,
And he is mine for ever—here he comes.

        Enter Marmaduke.

   Mar. These ten years she has moved
    her lips all day   566
And never speaks !

   Osw.   Who is it?

   Mar.   I have seen her.

   Osw. Oh ! the poor tenant of that
    ragged homestead,
Her whom the Monster, Clifford, drove to
    madness.

   Mar. I met a peasant near the spot ; he
    told me,   570
These ten years she had sate all day alone
Within those empty walls.

   Osw.   I too have seen her ;
Chancing to pass this way some six
    months gone,
At midnight, I betook me to the Church-
    yard :
The moon shone clear, the air was still,
    so still   575
The trees were silent as the graves be-
    neath them.
Long did I watch, and saw her pacing
    round
Upon the self-same spot, still round and
    round,
Her lips for ever moving.

   Mar.   At her door
Rooted I stood ; for, looking at the
    woman,   580
I thought I saw the skeleton of Idonea.

   Osw. But the pretended Father——

   Mar.   Earthly law

Measures not crimes like his.

Osw.   *We* rank not, happily,
With those who take the spirit of their
    rule
From that soft class of devotees who feel
Reverence for life so deeply, that they
    spare   586
The verminous brood, and cherish what
    they spare
While feeding on their bodies. Would
    that Idonea
Were present, to the end that we might
    hear
What she can urge in his defence; she
    loves him.   590
    Mar. Yes, loves him; 'tis a truth that
    multiplies
His guilt a thousand-fold.

Osw.   'Tis most perplexing:
What must be done?

    Mar.   We will conduct her hither;
These walls shall witness it—from first
    to last
He shall reveal himself.

Osw.   Happy are we, 595
Who live in these disputed tracts, that own
No law but what each man makes for
    himself ;
Here justice has indeed a field of triumph.

    Mar. Let us begone and bring her
    hither ;—here
The truth shall be laid open, his guilt
    proved   600
Before her face. The rest be left to me.

    Osw. You will be firm: but though we
    well may trust
The issue to the justice of the cause,
Caution must not be flung aside; re-
    member,
Yours is no common life. Self-stationed
    here,   605
Upon these savage confines, we have
    seen you
Stand like an isthmus 'twixt two stormy
    seas
That oft have checked their fury at your
    bidding.
'Mid the deep holds of Solway's mossy
    waste,
Your single virtue has transformed a
    Band   610

Of fierce barbarians into Ministers
Of peace and order. Aged men with tears
Have blessed their steps, the fatherless
    retire   613
For shelter to their banners. But it is,
As you must needs have deeply felt, it is
In darkness and in tempest that we seek
The majesty of Him who rules the world.
Benevolence, that has not heart to use
The wholesome ministry of pain and evil,
Becomes at last weak and contemptible.
Your generous qualities have won due
    praise,   621
But vigorous Spirits look for something
    more
Than Youth's spontaneous products; and
    to-day
You will not disappoint them; and here-
    after——

    Mar. You are wasting words; hear me
    then once for all: 625
You are a Man—and therefore, if com-
    passion,
Which to our kind is natural as life,
Be known unto you, you will love this
    Woman,
Even as I do; but I should loathe the
    light,
If I could think one weak or partial
    feeling——   630

    Osw. You will forgive me——

    Mar.   If I ever knew
My heart, could penetrate its inmost
    core,
'Tis at this moment.—Oswald, I have
    loved
To be the friend and father of the
    oppressed,
A comforter of sorrow ;—there is some-
    thing   635
Which looks like a transition in my soul,
And yet it is not.—Let us lead him
    hither.

    Osw. Stoop for a moment; 'tis an act
    of justice ;
And where's the triumph if the delegate
Must fall in the execution of his office? 640
The deed is done—if you will have it so—
Here where we stand—that tribe of vul-
    gar wretches
(You saw them gathering for the festival)

Rush in—the villains seize us——
Mar.   Seize !
· *Osw.*   Yes, they—
Men who are little given to sift and
  weigh—   645
Would wreak on us the passion of the
  moment.
Mar. The cloud will soon disperse—
  farewell—but stay,
Thou wilt relate the story.
Osw.   Am I neither
To bear a part in this Man's punishment,
Nor be its witness?
Mar.   I had many hopes 650
That were most dear to me, and some
  will bear
To be transferred to thee.
Osw.   When I'm dishonoured !
Mar. I would preserve thee. How may
  this be done?
Osw. By showing that you look beyond
  the instant.
A few leagues hence we shall have open
  ground,   655
And nowhere upon earth is place so fit
To look upon the deed. Before we enter
The barren Moor, hangs from a beetling
  rock
The shattered Castle in which Clifford
  oft
Has held infernal orgies—with the gloom,
And very superstition of the place,   661
Seasoning his wickedness. The Debauchee
Would there perhaps have gathered the
  first fruits
Of this mock Father's guilt.

Enter Host *conducting* HERBERT.

Host.   The Baron Herbert
Attends your pleasure.
Osw. (*to* Host).   We are ready—
                      (*to* HERBERT) Sir ! 665
I hope you are refreshed.—I have just
  written
A notice for your Daughter, that she may
  know
What is become of you.—You'll sit down
  and sign it ;
'Twill glad her heart to see her father's
  signature.
            [*Gives the letter he had written.*

Her. Thanks for your care.
            [*Sits down and writes. Exit* Host.
Osw. (*aside to* MARMADUKE). Perhaps it
  would be useful   670
That you too should subscribe your name.
            [MARMADUKE *overlooks* HERBERT
                —*then writes—examines the let-
                ter eagerly.*
Mar. I cannot leave this paper.
            [*He puts it up, agitated.*
Osw. (*aside*).   Dastard ! Come.
            [MARMADUKE *goes towards* HER-
                BERT *and supports him*—MAR-
                MADUKE *tremblingly beckons*
                OSWALD *to take his place.*
Mar. (*as he quits* HERBERT). There is a
  palsy in his limbs—he shakes.
            [*Exeunt* OSWALD *and* HERBERT—
                MARMADUKE *following.*

SCENE *changes to a Wood—a Group of*
  Pilgrims *and* IDONEA *with them.*

First Pil. A grove of darker and more
  lofty shade
I never saw.
Sec. Pil. The music of the birds. 675
Drops deadened from a roof so thick with
  leaves.
Old Pil. This news ! it made my heart
  leap up with joy.
Idon. I scarcely can believe it.
Old Pil.   Myself, I heard
The Sheriff read, in open Court, a letter
Which purported it was the royal plea-
  sure   680
The Baron Herbert, who, as was supposed,
Had taken refuge in this neighbourhood,
Should be forthwith restored. The hear-
  ing, Lady,
Filled my dim eyes with tears. When
  I returned
From Palestine, and brought with me a
  heart,   685
Though rich in heavenly, poor in earthly,
  comfort,
I met your Father, then a wandering
  Outcast :
He had a Guide, a Shepherd's boy ; but
  grieved
He was that One so young should pass
  his youth

In such sad service; and he parted with
    him.   690
We joined our tales of wretchedness
    together,
And begged our daily bread from door
    to door.
I talk familiarly to you, sweet Lady!
For once you loved me.
    Idon.   You shall back with me
And see your Friend again. The good old
    Man   695
Will be rejoiced to greet you.
    Old Pil.   It seems but yesterday
That a fierce storm o'ertook us, worn with
    travel,
In a deep wood remote from any town.
A cave that opened to the road presented
A friendly shelter, and we entered in. 700
    Idon. And I was with you?
    Old Pil.   If indeed 'twas you—
But you were then a tottering Little-
    one—
We sate us down. The sky grew dark
    and darker:
I struck my flint, and built up a small
    fire
With rotten boughs and leaves, such as
    the winds   705
Of many autumns in the cave had piled.
Meanwhile the storm fell heavy on the
    woods;
Our little fire sent forth a cheering
    warmth
And we were comforted, and talked of
    comfort;
But 'twas an angry night, and o'er our
    heads   710
The thunder rolled in peals that would
    have made
A sleeping man uneasy in his bed.
O Lady, you have need to love your
    Father.
His voice—methinks I hear it now, his
    voice
When, after a broad flash that filled the
    cave,   715
He said to me, that he had seen his
    Child,
A face (no cherub's face more beautiful)
Revealed by lustre brought with it from
    heaven;

And it was you, dear Lady!
    Idon.   God be praised,
That I have been his comforter till now!
And will be so through every change of
    fortune   721
And every sacrifice his peace requires.—
Let us begone with speed, that he may
    hear
These joyful tidings from no lips but
    mine.   724
            [*Exeunt* IDONEA *and* Pilgrims.

SCENE, *The Area of a half-ruined Castle—
    on one side the entrance to a dungeon—*
    OSWALD *and* MARMADUKE *pacing back-
    wards and forwards.*

    Mar. 'Tis a wild night.
    Osw.   I'd give my cloak and bonnet
For sight of a warm fire.
    Mar.   The wind blows keen;
My hands are numb.
    Osw.   Ha! ha! 'tis nipping cold.
                        [*Blowing his fingers.*
I long for news of our brave Comrades;
    Lacy
Would drive those Scottish Rovers to
    their dens
If once they blew a horn this side the
    Tweed.   730
    Mar. I think I see a second range of
    Towers;
This castle has another Area—come,
Let us examine it.
    Osw.   'Tis a bitter night;
I hope Idonea is well housed. That
    horseman,
Who at full speed swept by us where the
    wood   735
Roared in the tempest, was within an ace
Of sending to his grave our precious
    Charge:
That would have been a vile mischance.
    Mar.   It would.
    Osw. Justice had been most cruelly
    defrauded.
    Mar. Most cruelly.
    Osw.   As up the steep we clomb,
I saw a distant fire in the north-east; 741
I took it for the blaze of Cheviot Beacon:
With proper speed our quarters may be
    gained

To-morrow evening.

[*Looks restlessly towards the mouth
of the dungeon.*

Mar.   When, upon the plank,
I had led him 'cross the torrent, his voice
    blessed me: 745
You could not hear, for the foam beat the
    rocks
With deafening noise,—the benediction
    fell
Back on himself; but changed into a
    curse.

Osw. As well indeed it might.

Mar.   And this you deem
The fittest place?

Osw. (*aside*). He is growing pitiful. 750

Mar. (*listening*). What an odd moan-
    ing that is!—

Osw.   Mighty odd
The wind should pipe a little, while we
    stand
Cooling our heels in this way!—I'll begin
And count the stars.

Mar. (*still listening*). That dog of his,
    you are sure,
Could not come after us—he *must* have
    perished;   755
The torrent would have dashed an oak to
    splinters.
You said you did not like his looks—
    that he
Would trouble us; if he were here again,
I swear the sight of him would quail me
    more
Than twenty armies.

Osw.   How?

Mar.   The old blind Man,
When you had told him the mischance,
    was troubled   761
Even to the shedding of some natural tears
Into the torrent over which he hung,
Listening in vain.

Osw.   He has a tender heart!

[Oswald *offers to go down into the
                            dungeon.*

Mar. How now, what mean you?

Osw.   Truly, I was going
To waken our stray Baron. Were there
    not   766
A farm or dwelling-house within five
    leagues,

We should deserve to wear a cap and
    bells,
Three good round years, for playing the
    fool here
In such a night as this.

Mar.   Stop, stop.

Osw.   Perhaps, 770
You'd better like we should descend
    together,
And lie down by his side—what say you
    to it?
Three of us—we should keep each other
    warm:
I'll answer for it that our four-legged
    friend
Shall not disturb us; further I'll not
    engage;   775
Come, come, for manhood's sake!

Mar.   These drowsy shiverings,
This mortal stupor which is creeping over
    me,
What do they mean? were this my single
    body
Opposed to armies, not a nerve would
    tremble:
Why do I tremble now?—Is not the
    depth   780
Of this Man's crimes beyond the reach of
    thought?
And yet, in plumbing the abyss for
    judgment,
Something I strike upon which turns my
    mind
Back on herself, I think, again—my
    breast   784
Concentres all the terrors of the Universe:
I look at him and tremble like a child.

Osw. Is it possible?

Mar.   One thing you noticed not:
Just as we left the glen a clap of thunder
Burst on the mountains with hell-rousing
    force.
This is a time, said he, when guilt may
    shudder;   790
But there's a Providence for them who
    walk
In helplessness, when innocence is with
    them.
At this audacious blasphemy, I thought
The spirit of vengeance seemed to ride
    the air.

Osw. Why are you not the man you
were that moment?   795
    [*He draws* MARMADUKE *to the
dungeon.*

Mar. You say he was asleep,—look at
this arm,
And tell me if 'tis fit for such a work.

Oswald, Oswald!   [*Leans upon* OSWALD.

Osw.   This is some sudden seizure!

Mar. A most strange faintness,—will
you hunt me out
A draught of water?

Osw.   Nay, to see you thus 800
Moves me beyond my bearing.—I will try
To gain the torrent's brink. [*Exit* OSWALD.

Mar. (*after a pause*).   It seems an age
Since that Man left me.—No, I am not
lost.

Her. (*at the mouth of the dungeon*). Give
me your hand; where are you,
Friends? and tell me
How goes the night.

Mar.   'Tis hard to measure time
In such a weary night, and such a
place.   805

Her. I do not hear the voice of my friend
Oswald.

Mar. A minute past he went to fetch
a draught
Of water from the torrent. 'Tis, you'll say,
A cheerless beverage.

Her.   How good it was in you
To stay behind!—Hearing at first no
answer,   811
I was alarmed.

Mar.   No wonder; this is a place
That well may put some fears into *your*
heart.

Her. Why so? a roofless rock had been
a comfort,
Storm-beaten and bewildered as we
were;   815
And in a night like this to lend your
cloaks
To make a bed for me!—My Girl will weep
When she is told of it.

Mar.   This Daughter of yours
Is very dear to you.

Her.   Oh! but you are young;
Over your head twice twenty years must
roll,   820

With all their natural weight of sorrow
and pain,
Ere can be known to you how much a
Father
May love his Child.

Mar.   Thank you, old Man, for this!
    [*Aside.*

Her. Fallen am I, and worn out, a
useless Man;
Kindly have you protected me to-
night,   825
And no return have I to make but
prayers;
May you in age be blest with such a
daughter!—
When from the Holy Land I had re-
turned
Sightless, and from my heritage was
driven,
A wretched Outcast—but this strain of
thought   830
Would lead me to talk fondly.

Mar.   Do not fear;
Your words are precious to my ears;
go on.

Her. You will forgive me, but my heart
runs over.
When my old Leader slipped into the
flood
And perished, what a piercing outcry
you   835
Sent after him. I have loved you ever
since.
You start—where are we?

Mar.   Oh, there is no danger;
The cold blast struck me.

Her.   'Twas a foolish question.

Mar. But when you were an Outcast?—
Heaven is just;
Your piety would not miss its due re-
ward;   840
The little Orphan then would be your
succour,
And do good service, though she knew it
not.

Her. I turned me from the dwellings
of my Fathers,
Where none but those who trampled on
my rights
Seemed to remember me. To the wide
world   845

I bore her in my arms; her looks won
pity;
She was my Raven in the wilderness,
And brought me food. Have I not cause
to love her?

Mar. Yes.

Her.   More than ever Parent
loved a Child?   849

Mar. Yes, yes.

Her. I will not murmur, merciful God!
I will not murmur; blasted as I have been,
Thou hast left me ears to hear my Daugh-
ter's voice,
And arms to fold her to my heart. Sub-
missively   853
Thee I adore, and find my rest in faith.

Enter OSWALD.

Osw. Herbert!—confusion! (*aside*). Here
it is, my Friend, [*Presents the Horn.*
A charming beverage for you to carouse
This bitter night.

Her. Ha! Oswald! ten bright crosses
I would have given, not many minutes
gone,
To have heard your voice.

Osw. Your couch, I fear, good Baron,
Has been but comfortless; and yet that
place,   860
When the tempestuous wind first drove
us hither,
Felt warm as a wren's nest. You'd better
turn
And under covert rest till break of day,
Or till the storm abate.
(*To* MARMADUKE *aside.*) He has restored
you,
No doubt you have been nobly enter-
tained?   865
But soft!—how came he forth? The Night-
mare Conscience
Has driven him out of harbour?

Mar.   I believe
You have guessed right.

Her.   The trees renew their murmur:
Come, let us house together.

[OSWALD *conducts him to the dungeon.*

Osw. (*returns*).   Had I not
Esteemed you worthy to conduct the af-
fair   870
To its most fit conclusion, do you think

I would so long have struggled with my
Nature,
And smothered all that's man in me?—
away!—
[*Looking towards the dungeon.*
This man's the property of him who best
Can feel his crimes. I have resigned a
privilege;   875
It now becomes my duty to resume it.

Mar. Touch not a finger——

Osw.   What then must be done?

Mar. Which way soe'er I turn, I am
perplexed.

Osw. Now, on my life, I grieve for you.
The misery
Of doubt is insupportable. Pity, the facts
Did not admit of stronger evidence;   881
Twelve honest men, plain men, would set
us right;
Their verdict would abolish these weak
scruples.

Mar. Weak! I am weak—there does
my torment lie,
Feeding itself.

Osw.   Verily, when he said   885
How his old heart would leap to hear her
steps,
You thought his voice the echo of Idonea's.

Mar. And never heard a sound so ter-
rible.

Osw. Perchance you think so now?

Mar.   I cannot do it:
Twice did I spring to grasp his withered
throat,   890
When such a sudden weakness fell upon
me,
I could have dropped asleep upon his
breast.

Osw. Justice—is there not thunder in
the word?
Shall it be law to stab the petty robber
Who aims but at our purse; and shall
this Parricide—   895
Worse is he far, far worse (if foul dis-
honour
Be worse than death) to that confiding
Creature
Whom he to more than filial love and duty
Hath falsely trained—shall he fulfil his
purpose?
But you are fallen.

Mar.   Fallen should I be indeed— 900
Murder—perhaps asleep, blind, old, alone,
Betrayed, in darkness! Here to strike the
blow—
Away! away!——[*Flings away his sword.*
Osw.   Nay, I have done with you:
We'll lead him to the Convent. He shall
live,
And she shall love him. With unquestion-
ed title   905
He shall be seated in his Barony,
And we too chant the praise of his good
deeds.
I now perceive we do mistake our mas-
ters,
And most despise the men who best can
teach us:
Henceforth it shall be said that bad men
only   910
Are brave: Clifford is brave; and that
old Man
Is brave.
          [*Taking* MARMADUKE'S *sword and
                    giving it to him.*
To Clifford's arms he would have led
His Victim—haply to this desolate house.
Mar. (*advancing to the dungeon*). It
must be ended!—

Osw.   Softly; do not rouse him;
He will deny it to the last. He lies   915
Within the Vault, a spear's length to the
left.
          [MARMADUKE *descends to the dungeon.*
(*Alone*). The Villains rose in mutiny to
destroy me;
I could have quelled the Cowards, but this
Stripling
Must needs step in, and save my life. The
look
With which he gave the boon—I see it
now!   920
The same that tempted me to loathe the
gift.—
For this old venerable Grey-beard—faith
'Tis his own fault if he hath got a face
Which doth play tricks with them that
look on it:
'Twas this that put it in my thoughts—
that countenance—   925
His staff—his figure—Murder!—what, of
whom?

We kill a worn-out horse, and who but
women
Sigh at the deed? Hew down a withered
tree,
And none look grave but dotards. He
may live
To thank me for this service. Rainbow
arches,   930
Highways of dreaming passion, have too
long,
Young as he is, diverted wish and hope
From the unpretending ground we mortals
tread;—
Then shatter the delusion, break it up
And set him free. What follows? I have
learned   935
That things will work to ends the slaves
o' the world
Do never dream of. I *have* been what he—
This Boy—when he comes forth with
bloody hands—
Might envy, and am now,—but he shall
know
What I am now—
          [*Goes and listens at the dungeon.*
          Praying or parleying?—tut! 940
Is he not eyeless? He has been half-dead
These fifteen years——

Enter female Beggar *with two or three of
her Companions.*

(*Turning abruptly*). Ha! speak—what
Thing art thou?
(*Recognises her*). Heavens! my good
Friend!   [*To her.*
Beg.   Forgive me, gracious Sir!—
Osw. (*to her companions*). Begone, ye
Slaves, or I will raise a whirlwind
And send ye dancing to the clouds, like
leaves.   [*They retire affrighted.*
Beg. Indeed we meant no harm; we
lodge sometimes   946
In this deserted Castle—I repent me.
          [OSWALD *goes to the dungeon—
               listens—returns to the* Beggar.
Osw. Woman, thou hast a helpless In-
fant—keep
Thy secret for its sake, or verily
That wretched life of thine shall be the
forfeit.   950
Beg. I *do* repent me, Sir; I fear the curse

Of that blind Man. 'Twas not your mo-
ney, Sir,——

Osw. Begone!

Beg. (*going*). There is some wicked deed
in hand: [*Aside.*
Would I could find the old Man and his
Daughter.   [*Exit* Beggar.

MARMADUKE *re-enters from the dungeon.*

Osw. It is all over then;—your foolish
fears   955
Are hushed to sleep, by your own act and
deed,
Made quiet as he is.

Mar.   Why came you down?
And when I felt your hand upon my arm
And spake to you, why did you give no
answer?
Feared you to waken him? he must have
been   960
In a deep sleep. I whispered to him thrice.
There are the strangest echoes in that
place!

Osw. Tut! let them gabble till the day
of doom.

Mar. Scarcely, by groping, had I reach-
ed the Spot,
When round my wrist I felt a cord drawn
tight,   965
As if the blind Man's dog were pulling
at it.

Osw. But after that?

Mar.   The features of Idonea
Lurked in his face——

Osw.   Pshaw! Never to these eyes
Will retribution show itself again   969
With aspect so inviting. Why forbid me
To share your triumph?

Mar.   Yes, her very look,
Smiling in sleep——

Osw.   A pretty feat of Fancy!

Mar. Though but a glimpse, it sent me
to my prayers.

Osw. Is he alive?

Mar.   What mean you? who alive?

Osw. Herbert! since you will have it,
Baron Herbert;   975
He who will gain his Seignory when
Idonea
Hath become Clifford's harlot—is *he* liv-
ing?

Mar. The old Man in that dungeon *is*
alive.

Osw. Henceforth, then, will I never in
camp or field
Obey you more. Your weakness, to the
Band,   980
Shall be proclaimed: brave Men, they all
shall hear it.
You a protector of humanity!
Avenger you of outraged innocence!

Mar. 'Twas dark—dark as the grave;
yet did I see,
Saw him—his face turned toward me; and
I tell thee   985
Idonea's filial countenance was there
To baffle me—it put me to my prayers.
Upwards I cast my eyes, and, through a
crevice,
Beheld a star twinkling above my head,
And, by the living God, I could not do it.
                    [*Sinks exhausted.*

Osw. (*to himself*). Now may I perish if
this turn do more   991
Than make me change my course.

(*To* MARMADUKE).   Dear Marmaduke,
My words were rashly spoken; I recall
them:
I feel my error; shedding human blood
Is a most serious thing.

Mar.   Not I alone,   995
Thou too art deep in guilt.

Osw.   We have indeed
Been most presumptuous. There *is* guilt
in this,
Else could so strong a mind have ever
known
These trepidations? Plain it is that Hea-
ven
Has marked out this foul Wretch as one
whose crimes   1000
Must never come before a mortal judg-
ment-seat,
Or be chastised by mortal instruments.

Mar. A thought that's worth a thou-
sand worlds!
                    [*Goes towards the dungeon.*

Osw.   I grieve
That, in my zeal, I have caused you so
much pain.

Mar. Think not of that! 'tis over—we
are safe.   1005

Osw. (*as if to himself, yet speaking aloud*).
The truth is hideous, but how stifle it?
        [*Turning to* MARMADUKE.
Give me your sword—nay, here are stones
    and fragments,
The least of which would beat out a man's
    brains;
Or you might drive your head against
    that wall.   1009
No! this is not the place to hear the tale:
It should be told you pinioned in your
    bed,
Or on some vast and solitary plain
Blown to you from a trumpet.
  Mar.   Why talk thus?
Whate'er the monster brooding in your
    breast
I care not: fear I have none, and cannot
    fear——   1015
    [*The sound of a horn is heard.*
That horn again—'Tis some one of our
    Troop;
What do they here? Listen!
  Osw.   What; dogged like thieves!

Enter WALLACE *and* LACY, &c.

  Lacy. You are found at last, thanks to
the vagrant Troop
For not misleading us.
  Osw. (*looking at* WALLACE). That subtle
    Grey-beard—   1019
I'd rather see my father's ghost.
  Lacy (*to* MARMADUKE).   My Captain,
We come by order of the Band. Belike
You have not heard that Henry has at last
Dissolved the Barons' League, and sent
    abroad
His Sheriffs with fit force to reinstate
The genuine owners of such Lands and
    Baronies   1025
As, in these long commotions, have been
    seized.
His Power is this way tending. It befits
    us
To stand upon our guard, and with our
    swords
Defend the innocent.
  Mar.   Lacy! we look   1029
But at the surfaces of things; we hear
Of towns in flames, fields ravaged, young
    and old

Driven out in troops to want and naked-
    ness;
Then grasp our swords and rush upon a
    cure
That flatters us, because it asks not
    thought:
The deeper malady is better hid;   1035
The world is poisoned at the heart.
  Lacy.   What mean you?
  Wal. (*whose eye has been fixed suspici-
    ously upon* OSWALD). Ay, what is
    it you mean?
  Mar.   Harkee, my Friends;—
    [*Appearing gay.*
Were there a Man who, being weak and
    helpless
And most forlorn, should bribe a Mother,
    pressed   1039
By penury, to yield him up her Daughter,
A little Infant, and instruct the Babe,
Prattling upon his knee, to call him Fa-
    ther——
  Lacy. Why, if his heart be tender, that
    offence
I could forgive him.
  Mar. (*going on*). And should he make
    the Child
An instrument of falsehood, should he
    teach her   1043
To stretch her arms, and dim the glad-
    some light
Of infant playfulness with piteous looks
Of misery that was not——
  Lacy.   Troth, 'tis hard—
But in a world like ours——
  Mar. (*changing his tone*). This self-
    same Man—
Even while he printed kisses on the cheek
Of this poor Babe, and taught its innocent
    tongue   1051
To lisp the name of Father—could he look
To the unnatural harvest of that time
When he should give her up, a Woman
    grown,   1054
To him who bid the highest in the market
Of foul pollution——
  Lacy.   The whole visible world
Contains not such a Monster!
  Mar.   For this purpose
Should he resolve to taint her Soul by
    means

Which bathe the limbs in sweat to think
   of them;
Should he, by tales which would draw
   tears from iron,   1060
Work on her nature, and so turn com-
   passion
And gratitude to ministers of vice,
And make the spotless spirit of filial love
Prime mover in a plot to damn his Victim
Both soul and body— —
  Wal.   'Tis too horrible; 1065
Oswald, what say you to it?
  Lacy.   Hew him down,
And fling him to the ravens.
  Mar.   But his aspect,
It is so meek, his countenance so vene-
   rable.
  Wal. (*with an appearance of mistrust*).
   But how, what say you, Oswald?
  Lacy (*at the same moment*). Stab him,
   were it
Before the Altar.
  Mar.   What, if he were sick, 1070
Tottering upon the very verge of life,
And old, and blind——
  Lacy.   Blind, say you?
  Osw. (*coming forward*).   Are we Men,
Or own we baby Spirits? Genuine courage
Is not an accidental quality,
A thing dependent for its casual birth
On opposition and impediment.   1076
Wisdom, if Justice speak the word, beats
   down
The giant's strength; and, at the voice of
   Justice,
Spares not the worm. The giant and the
   worm—
She weighs them in one scale. The wiles
   of woman,   1080
And craft of age, seducing reason, first
Made weakness a protection, and obscured
The moral shapes of things. His tender
   cries
And helpless innocence—do they protect
The infant lamb? and shall the infirmi-
   ties,   1085
Which have enabled this enormous Culprit
To perpetrate his crimes, serve as a Sanc-
   tuary
To cover him from punishment? Shame!—
   Justice,

Admitting no resistance, bends alike
The feeble and the strong. She needs not
   here   1090
Her bonds and chains, which make the
   mighty feeble.
—We recognise in this old Man a victim
Prepared already for the sacrifice.
  Lacy. By heaven, his words are reason !
  Osw.   Yes, my Friends,
His countenance is meek and vener-
   able;   1095
And, by the Mass, to see him at his
   prayers !—
I am of flesh and blood, and may I perish
When my heart does not ache to think
   of it !—
Poor Victim ! not a virtue under heaven
But what was made an engine to ensnare
   thee ;   1100
But yet I trust, Idonea, thou art safe.
  Lacy. Idonea !
  Wal.   How ! what? your Idonea?
              [*To* MARMADUKE.
  Mar.   *Mine;*
But now no longer mine. You know
   Lord Clifford;
He is the Man to whom the Maiden—pure
As beautiful, and gentle and benign, 1105
And in her ample heart loving even me —
Was to be yielded up.
  Lacy.   Now, by the head
Of my own child, this Man must die ; my
   hand,
A worthier wanting, shall itself entwine
In his grey hairs !—
  Mar. (*to* LACY). I love the Father in
   thee.   1110
You know me, Friends ; I have a heart
   to feel,
And I have felt, more than perhaps be-
   comes me
Or duty sanctions.
  Lacy.   We will have ample justice.
Who are we, Friends ? Do we not live on
   ground
Where Souls are self-defended, free to
   grow   1115
Like mountain oaks rocked by the stormy
   wind.
Mark the Almighty Wisdom, which de-
   creed

This monstrous crime to be laid open—
    here,
Where Reason has an eye that she can
    use,
And Men alone are Umpires. To the
    Camp   1120
He shall be led, and there, the Country
    round
All gathered to the spot, in open day
Shall Nature be avenged.
    Osw.   'Tis nobly thought;
His death will be a monument for ages.
    Mar. (*to* LACY). I thank you for that
        hint. He shall be brought   1125
Before the Camp, and would that best
        and wisest
Of every country might be present. There
His crime shall be proclaimed; and for
        the rest
It shall be done as Wisdom shall decide:
Meanwhile, do you two hasten back and
        see   1130
That all is well prepared.
    Wal.   We will obey you.
(*Aside*). But softly! we must look a little
    nearer.
    Mar. 'Tell where you found us. At
    some future time
I will explain the cause.   [*Exeunt.*

ACT III.

SCENE, *The door of the Hostel, a group of*
Pilgrims *as before;* IDONEA *and the*
Host *among them.*

    Host. Lady, you'll find your Father at
        the Convent   1135
As I have told you: He left us yesterday
With two Companions; one of them, as
        seemed,
His most familiar Friend. (*Going.*) There
        was a letter
Of which I heard them speak, but that I
        fancy
Has been forgotten.
    Idon. (*to* Host). Farewell!
    Host.   Gentle pilgrims,
St. Cuthbert speed you on your holy
        errand.   1141
            [*Exeunt* IDONEA *and* Pilgrims.

SCENE, *A desolate Moor.*
OSWALD (*alone*).

    Osw. Carry him to the Camp! Yes, to
        the Camp.
Oh, Wisdom! a most wise resolve! and
    then,
That half a word should blow it to the
    winds!
This last device must end my work.—
        Methinks   1145
It were a pleasant pastime to construct
A scale and table of belief—as thus—
Two columns, one for passion, one for
    proof;
Each rises as the other falls: and first,
Passion a unit and *against* us—proof—
Nay, we must travel in another path, 1151
Or we're stuck fast for ever;—passion,
    then,
Shall be a unit *for* us; proof—no, passion!
We'll not insult thy majesty by time,
Person, and place—the where, the when,
    the how,   1155
And all particulars that dull brains re-
    quire
To constitute the spiritless shape of Fact,
They lay to, calling the idol, Demonstra-
    tion.
A whipping to the Moralists who preach
That misery is a sacred thing: for me,
I know no cheaper engine to degrade a
    man,   1161
Nor any half so sure. This Stripling's
    mind
Is shaken till the dregs float on the sur-
    face;
And, in the storm and anguish of the
    heart,
He talks of a transition in his Soul, 1165
And dreams that he is happy. We dis-
    sect
The senseless body, and why not the
    mind?—
These are strange sights—the mind of
    man, upturned,
Is in all natures a strange spectacle;
In some a hideous one—hem! shall I
    stop?   1170
No.—Thoughts and feelings will sink
    deep, but then

They have no substance. Pass but a few
  minutes,
And something shall be done which
  Memory
May touch, whene'er her Vassals are at
  work.

Enter MARMADUKE, *from behind.*

  Osw. (*turning to meet him*). But listen,
    for my peace——
  Mar.   Why, I *believe* you.
  Osw. But hear the proofs——
  Mar.   Ay, prove that when two peas
Lie snugly in a pod, the pod must
  then   1177
Be larger than the peas—prove this—
  'twere matter
Worthy the hearing. Fool was I to
  dream
It ever could be otherwise!
  Osw.   Last night, 1180
When I returned with water from the
  brook,
I overheard the Villains—every word
Like red-hot iron burnt into my heart.
Said one, "It is agreed on. The blind
  Man
Shall feign a sudden illness, and the
  Girl,   1185
Who on her journey must prcceed alone,
Under pretence of violence, be seized.
She is," continued the detested Slave,
"She is right willing—strange if she were
  not !—
They say Lord Clifford is a savage
  man ;   1190
But, faith, to see him in his silken tunic,
Fitting his low voice to the minstrel's
  harp,
There's witchery in't. I never knew a
  maid
That could withstand it. True," con-
  tinued he,
"When we arranged the affair, she wept
  a little   1195
(Not the less welcome to my Lord for
  that)
And said, 'My Father he will have
  it so.'"
  Mar. I am your hearer.
  Osw.   This I caught, and more

That may not be retold to any ear.
The obstinate bolt of a small iron door
Detained them near the gateway of the
  Castle.   1201
By a dim lantern's light I saw that
  wreaths
Of flowers were in their hands, as if de-
  signed
For festive decoration ; and they said,
With brutal laughter and most foul allu-
  sion,   1205
That they should share the banquet with
  their Lord
And his new Favorite.
  Mar.   Misery !—
  Osw.   I knew
How you would be disturbed by this dire
  news,
And therefore chose this solitary Moor,
Here to impart the tale, of which, last
  night,   1210
I strove to ease my mind, when our two
  Comrades,
Commissioned by the Band, burst in
  upon us.
  Mar. Last night, when moved to lift
    the avenging steel,
I did believe all things were shadows—
  yea,
Living or dead all things were bodi-
  less,   1215
All but the mutual mockeries of body,
Till that same star summoned me back
  again.
Now I could laugh till my ribs ached.
  Oh, Fool !
To let a creed, built in the heart of
  things,
Dissolve before a twinkling atom !—Os-
  wald,   1220
I could fetch lessons out of wiser schools
Than you have entered, were it worth the
  pains.
Young as I am, I might go forth a
  teacher,
And you should see how deeply I could
  reason
Of love in all its shapes, beginnings,
  ends ;   1225
Of moral qualities in their diverse as-
  pects ;

Of actions, and their laws and tendencies.
  Osw. You take it as it merits——
  Mar.   One a King,
General or Cham, Sultan or Emperor,
Strews twenty acres of good meadow-
    ground   1230
With carcasses, in lineament and shape
And substance, nothing differing from his
    own,
But that they cannot stand up of them-
    selves;
Another sits i' th' sun, and by the hour
Floats kingcups in the brook—a Hero one
We call, and scorn the other as Time's
    spendthrift;   1236
But have they not a world of common
    ground
To occupy—both fools, or wise alike,
Each in his way?
  Osw.   Troth, I begin to think so.
  Mar. Now for the corner-stone of my
    philosophy: 1240
I would not give a denier for the man
Who, on such provocation as this earth
Yields, could not chuck his babe beneath
    the chin,
And send it with a fillip to its grave.
  Osw. Nay, you leave me behind.
  Mar.   That such a One,
So pious in demeanour! in his look   1246
So saintly and so pure!——Harkee, my
    Friend,
I'll plant myself before Lord Clifford's
    Castle,
A surly mastiff kennels at the gate,
And he shall howl and I will laugh, a
    medley   1250
Most tunable.
  Osw.   In faith, a pleasant scheme;
But take your sword along with you, for
    that
Might in such neighbourhood find seemly
    use.—
But first, how wash our hands of this old
    Man?
  Mar. Oh yes, that mole, that viper in
    the path;   1255
Plague on my memory, him I had for-
    gotten.
  Osw. You know we left him sitting—
    see him yonder.

  Mar. Ha! ha!—
  Osw.   As 'twill be but a moment's
    work,
I will stroll on; you follow when 'tis done.
                         [*Exeunt.*

SCENE *changes to another part of the Moor
  at a short distance—*HERBERT *is dis-
  covered seated on a stone.*

  Her. A sound of laughter, too!—'tis
    well—I feared   1260
The Stranger had some pitiable sorrow
Pressing upon his solitary heart.
Hush!—'tis the feeble and earth-loving
    wind
That creeps along the bells of the crisp
    heather.
Alas! 'tis cold—I shiver in the sun-
    shine—   1265
What can this mean? There is a psalm
    that speaks
Of God's parental mercies—with Idonea
I used to sing it.—Listen!—what foot is
    there?

         Enter MARMADUKE.

  Mar. (*aside—looking at* HERBERT). And
    I have loved this Man! and she hath
    loved him!
And I loved her, and she loves the Lord
    Clifford!   1270
And there it ends;—if this be not enough
To make mankind merry for evermore,
Then plain it is as day that eyes were
    made
For a wise purpose—verily to weep with!
                 [*Looking round.*
A pretty prospect this, a masterpiece 1275
Of Nature, finished with most curious
    skill!
(*To* HERBERT). Good Baron, have you
    ever practised tillage?
Pray tell me what this land is worth by
    the acre.
  Her. How glad I am to hear your voice!
    I know not   1279
Wherein I have offended you;—last night
I found in you the kindest of Protectors;
This morning, when I spoke of weariness,
You from my shoulder took my scrip and
    threw it

About your own; but for these two hours
    past
Once only have you spoken, when the
    lark   1285
Whirred from among the fern beneath our
    feet,
And I, no coward in my better days,
Was almost terrified.

Mar.   That's excellent!—
So you bethought you of the many ways
In which a man may come to his end,
    whose crimes   1290
Have roused all Nature up against him—
    pshaw!—

Her. For mercy's sake, is nobody in
    sight?
No traveller, peasant, herdsman?

Mar.   Not a soul:
Here is a tree, ragged, and bent, and
    bare,
That turns its goat's-beard flakes of pea-
    green moss   1295
From the stern breathing of the rough
    sea-wind;
This have we, but no other company:
Commend me to the place. If a man
    should die
And leave his body here, it were all one
As he were twenty fathoms underground.

Her. Where is our common Friend?

Mar.   A ghost, methinks—
The Spirit of a murdered man, for in-
    stance—
Might have fine room to ramble about
    here,
A grand domain to squeak and gibber in.

Her. Lost Man! if thou have any close-
    pent guilt   1305
Pressing upon thy heart, and this the
    hour
Of visitation——

Mar.   A bold word from *you!*

Her. Restore him, Heaven!

Mar.   The desperate
    Wretch!—A Flower,
Fairest of all flowers, was she once, but
    now
They have snapped her from the stem—
    Poh! let her lie   1310
Besoiled with mire, and let the houseless
    snail

Feed on her leaves. You knew her well—
    ay, there,
Old Man! you were a very Lynx, you
    knew
The worm was in her——

Her.   Mercy! Sir, what mean you?

Mar. You have a Daughter!

Her.   Oh that she were here!—
She hath an eye that sinks into all
    hearts,   1316
And if I have in aught offended you,
Soon would her gentle voice make peace
    between us.

Mar. (aside). I do believe he weeps—
    I could weep too—
There is a vein of her voice that runs
    through his: 1320
Even such a Man my fancy bodied forth
From the first moment that I loved the
    Maid;
And for his sake I loved her more: these
    tears—
I did not think that aught was left in me
Of what I have been—yes, I thank thee,
    Heaven!   1325
One happy thought has passed across my
    mind.
—It may not be—I am cut off from man;
No more shall I be man—no more shall I
Have human feelings!—(*To* HERBERT)—
    Now, for a little more
About your Daughter!

Her.   Troops of armed men,
Met in the roads, would bless us; little
    children,   1331
Rushing along in the full tide of play,
Stood silent as we passed them! I have
    heard
The boisterous carman, in the miry road,
Check his loud whip and hail us with
    mild voice,   1335
And speak with milder voice to his poor
    beasts.

Mar. And whither were you going?

Her.   Learn, young Man,—
To fear the virtuous, and reverence misery,
Whether too much for patience, or, like
    mine,
Softened till it becomes a gift of mercy.

Mar. Now, this is as it should be!

Her.   I am weak!— 1341

My Daughter does not know how weak
    I am;
And, as thou see'st, under the arch of
    heaven
Here do I stand, alone, to helplessness,
By the good God, our common Father,
    doomed!—   1345
But I had once a spirit and an arm——
  Mar. Now, for a word about your
    Barony:
I fancy when you left the Holy Land,
And came to—what's your title—eh?
    your claims
Were undisputed!
  Her.   Like a mendicant, 1350
Whom no one comes to meet, I stood
    alone;—
I murmured—but, remembering Him who
    feeds
The pelican and ostrich of the desert,
From my own threshold I looked up to
    Heaven
And did not want glimmerings of quiet
    hope.   1355
So from the court I passed, and down the
    brook,
Led by its murmur, to the ancient oak
I came; and when I felt its cooling shade,
I sate me down, and cannot but believe—
While in my lap I held my little Babe
And clasped her to my heart, my heart
    that ached   1361
More with delight than grief—I heard a
    voice
Such as by Cherith on Elijah called;
It said, "I will be with thee." A little
    boy,
A shepherd-lad, ere yet my trance was
    gone,   1365
Hailed us as if he had been sent from
    heaven,
And said, with tears, that he would be
    our guide:
I had a better guide—that innocent
    Babe—
Her, who hath saved me, to this hour,
    from harm,
From cold, from hunger, penury, and
    death;   1370
To whom I owe the best of all the
    good

I have, or wish for, upon earth—and more
And higher far than lies within earth's
    bounds:
Therefore I bless her: when I think of
    Man,
I bless her with sad spirit,—when of
    God,   1375
I bless her in the fulness of my joy!
  Mar. The name of daughter in his
    mouth, he prays!
With nerves so steady, that the very flies
Sit unmolested on his staff.—Innocent!
If he were innocent—then he would
    tremble   1380
And be disturbed, as I am. (*Turning
    aside*). I have read
In Story, what men now alive have wit-
    nessed,
How, when the People's mind was racked
    with doubt,
Appeal was made to the great Judge: the
    Accused
With naked feet walked over burning
    ploughshares.   1385
Here is a Man by Nature's hand prepared
For a like trial, but more merciful.
Why else have I been led to this bleak
    Waste?
Bare is it, without house or track, and
    destitute
Of obvious shelter, as a shipless sea. 1390
Here will I leave him—here—All-seeing
    God!
Such as *he* is, and sore perplexed as I am,
I will commit him to this final *Ordeal!*—
He heard a voice—a shepherd-lad came to
    him
And was his guide; if once, why not
    again,   1395
And in this desert? If never—then the
    whole
Of what he says, and looks, and does,
    and is,
Makes up one damning falsehood. Leave
    him here
To cold and hunger!—Pain is of the
    heart,
And what are a few throes of bodily
    suffering   1400
If they can waken one pang of remorse?
        [*Goes up to* HERBERT.

Old Man! my wrath is as a flame burnt
    out,
It cannot be rekindled. Thou art here
Led by my hand to save thee from per-
    dition;
Thou wilt have time to breathe and
    think——
    Her.   Oh, Mercy!
    Mar. I know the need that all men
        have of mercy,   1406
And therefore leave thee to a righteous
    judgment.
    Her. My Child, my blessèd Child!·
    Mar.   No more of that;
Thou wilt have many guides if thou art
    innocent;
Yea, from the utmost corners of the
    earth,   1410
That Woman will come o'er this Waste
    to save thee.
    [*He pauses and looks at* HERBERT'S *staff.*
Ha! what is here? and carved by her
    own hand!   [*Reads upon the staff.*
"I am eyes to the blind, saith the Lord.
He that puts his trust in me shall not
    fail!"
Yes, be it so;—repent and be forgiven—
God and that staff are now thy only
    guides.   1416
        [*He leaves* HERBERT *on the Moor.*

    SCENE, *An eminence, a Beacon on the
            summit.*

    LACY, WALLACE, LENNOX, &c. &c.

Several of the Band (confusedly). But
    patience!
One of the Band. Curses on that Traitor,
    Oswald!—
Our Captain made a prey to foul device!—
    Len. (to WALLACE). His tool, the wander-
        ing Beggar, made last night
A plain confession, such as leaves no
    doubt,   1420
Knowing what otherwise we know too
    well,
That she revealed the truth. Stand by
    me now;
For rather would I have a nest of vipers
Between my breast-plate and my skin
    than make
Oswald my special enemy, if you   1425

Deny me your support.
    Lacy.   We have been fooled—
But for the motive?
    Wal.   Natures such as his
Spin motives out of their own bowels,
    Lacy!
I learn'd this when I was a Confessor.
I know him well; there needs no other
    motive   1430
Than that most strange incontinence in
    crime
Which haunts this Oswald. Power is life
    to him
And breath and being; where he cannot
    govern,
He will destroy.
    Lacy.   To have been trapped like
    moles!—
Yes, you are right, we need not hunt for
    motives: 1435
There is no crime from which this man
    would shrink;
He recks not human law; and I have
    noticed
That often, when the name of God is
    uttered,
A sudden blankness overspreads his face.
    Len. Yet, reasoner as he is, his pride
        has built   1440
Some uncouth superstition of its own.
    Wal. I have seen traces of it.
    Len.   Once he headed
A band of Pirates in the Norway seas;
And when the King of Denmark sum-
    moned him
To the oath of fealty, I well remember,
'Twas a strange answer that he made; he
    said,   1446
"I hold of Spirits, and the Sun in hea-
    · ven."
    Lacy. He is no madman.
    Wal.   A most subtle doctor
Were that man, who could draw the line
    that parts
Pride and her daughter, Cruelty, from
    Madness,   1450
That should be scourged, not pitied.
    Restless Minds,
Such Minds as find amid their fellow-men
No heart that loves them, none that they
    can love,

Will turn perforce and seek for sympathy
In dim relation to imagined Beings. 1455
   One of the Band. What if he mean to
offer up our Captain
An expiation and a sacrifice
To those infernal fiends!
   Wal.   Now, if the event
Should be as Lennox has foretold, then
swear,
My Friends, his heart shall have as many
wounds   1460
As there are daggers here.
   Lacy.   What need of swearing!
   One of the Band. Let us away!
   Another.   Away!
   A third.   Hark! how the horns
Of those Scotch Rovers echo through the
vale.
   Lacy. Stay you behind; and, when
the sun is down,
Light up this beacon.
   One of the Band. You shall be obeyed.
               [*They go out together.*

SCENE, *The Wood on the edge of the Moor.*
       MARMADUKE (*alone*).

   Mar. Deep, deep and vast, vast be-
yond human thought,
Yet calm.—I could believe that there
was here
The only quiet heart on earth. In terror,
Remembered terror, there is peace and
rest.   1469

       Enter OSWALD.

   Osw. Ha! my dear Captain.
   Mar.   A later meeting, Oswald,
Would have been better timed.
   Osw.   Alone, I see;
You have done your duty. I had hopes,
which now
I feel that you will justify.
   Mar.   I had fears,
From which I have freed myself—but 'tis
my wish
To be alone, and therefore we must part.
   Osw. Nay, then — I am mistaken.
There's a weakness   1476
About you still; you talk of solitude—
I am your friend.
   Mar.   What need of this assurance

At any time? and why given now?
   Osw.   Because
You are now in truth my Master; you
have taught me   1480
What there is not another living man
Had strength to teach;—and therefore
gratitude
Is bold, and would relieve itself by praise.
   Mar. Wherefore press this on me?
   Osw.   Because I feel
That you have shown, and by a signal
instance,   1485
How they who would be just must seek
the rule
By diving for it into their own bosoms.
To-day you have thrown off a tyranny
That lives but in the torpid acquiescence
Of our emasculated souls, the tyranny
Of the world's masters, with the musty
rules   1491
By which they uphold their craft from
age to age:
You have obeyed the only law that sense
Submits to recognise; the immediate law,
From the clear light of circumstances,
flashed   1495
Upon an independent Intellect.
Henceforth new prospects open on your
path;
Your faculties should grow with the
demand;
I still will be your friend, will cleave to
you
Through good and evil, obloquy and
scorn,   1500
Oft as they dare to follow on your steps.
   Mar. I would be left alone.
   Osw. (*exultingly*). I know your motives!
I am not of the world's presumptuous
judges,
Who damn where they can neither see
nor feel,
With a hard-hearted ignorance; your
struggles   1505
I witness'd, and now hail your victory.
   Mar. Spare me awhile that greeting.
   Osw.   It may be
That some there are, squeamish half-
thinking cowards,
Who will turn pale upon you, call you
murderer,

And you will walk in solitude among
    them.   1510
A mighty evil for a strong-built mind!—
Join twenty tapers of unequal height
And light them joined, and you will see
    the less
How 'twill burn down the taller; and
    they all   1514
Shall prey upon the tallest. Solitude!—
The Eagle lives in Solitude!

  Mar.   Even so,
The Sparrow so on the house-top, and I,
The weakest of God's creatures, stand
    resolved
To abide the issue of my act, alone.

  Osw. Now would you? and for ever?—
    My young Friend,   1520
As time advances either we become
The prey or masters of our own past
    deeds.
Fellowship we *must* have, willing or no;
And if good Angels fail, slack in their
    duty,
Substitutes, turn our faces where we may,
Are still forthcoming; some which, though
    they bear   1526
Ill names, can render no ill services,
In recompense for what themselves re-
    quired.
So meet extremes in this mysterious
    world,
And opposites thus melt into each other.

  Mar. Time, since Man first drew breath,
    has never moved   1531
With such a weight upon his wings as
    now;
But they will soon be lightened.

  Osw.   Ay, look up—
Cast round you your mind's eye, and you
    will learn
Fortitude is the child of Enterprise: 1535
Great actions move our admiration, chiefly
Because they carry in themselves an
    earnest
That we can suffer greatly.

  Mar.   Very true.

  Osw. Action is transitory—a step, a
    blow,
The motion of a muscle—this way or
    that—   1540
'Tis done, and in the after-vacancy

We wonder at ourselves like men be-
    trayed:
Suffering is permanent, obscure and dark,
And shares the nature of infinity.

  Mar. Truth—and I feel it.

  Osw.   What! if you had bid
Eternal farewell to unmingled joy   1546
And the light dancing of the thoughtless
    heart;
It is the toy of fools, and little fit
For such a world as this. The wise ab-
    jure
All thoughts whose idle composition lives
In the entire forgetfulness of pain.   1551
—I see I have disturbed you.

  Mar.   By no means.

  Osw. Compassion!—pity!—pride can
    do without them;
And what if you should never know them
    more!—
He is a puny soul who, feeling pain, 1555
Finds ease because another feels it too.
If e'er I open out this heart of mine
It shall be for a nobler end—to teach
And not to purchase puling sympathy.
—Nay, you are pale.

  Mar.   It may be so.

  Osw.   Remorse—
It cannot live with thought; think on,
    think on,   1561
And it will die. What! in this universe,
Where the least things control the great-
    est, where
The faintest breath that breathes can
    move a world;
What! feel remorse, where, if a cat had
    sneezed,   1565
A leaf had fallen, the thing had never
    been
Whose very shadow gnaws us to the
    vitals.

  Mar. Now, whither are you wandering?
    That a man,
So used to suit his language to the time,
Should thus so widely differ from him-
    self—   1570
It is most strange.

  Osw. Murder!—what's in the word!—
I have no cases by me ready made
To fit all deeds. Carry him to the Camp!—
A shallow project;—you of late have seen

More deeply, taught us that the insti-
tutes   1575
Of Nature, by a cunning usurpation
Banished from human intercourse, exist
Only in our relations to the brutes
That make the fields their dwelling. If a
snake
Crawl from beneath our feet we do not ask
A license to destroy him: our good gover-
nors   1581
Hedge in the life of every pest and plague
That bears the shape of man; and for
what purpose,
But to protect themselves from extirpa-
tion?—
This flimsy barrier you have overleaped.
  Mar. My Office is fulfilled—the Man is
now   1586
Delivered to the Judge of all things.
  Osw.   Dead !
  Mar. I have borne my burthen to its
destined end.
  Osw. This instant we'll return to our
Companions—
Oh how I long to see their faces again !

Enter IDONEA *with* Pilgrims *who continue
their journey.*

  Idon. (*after some time*). What, Marma-
duke ! now thou art mine for ever.
And Oswald, too ! (*To* MARMADUKE.) On
will we to my Father   1592
With the glad tidings which this day
hath brought;
We'll go together, and, such proof received
Of his own rights restored, his gratitude
To God above will make him feel for ours.
  Osw. I interrupt you?
  Idon.   Think not so.
  Mar.   Idonea,
That I should ever live to see this mo-
ment !
  Idon. Forgive me.—Oswald knows it
all—he knows,
Each word of that unhappy letter fell 1600
As a blood-drop from my heart.
  Osw.   'Twas even so.
  Mar. I have much to say, but for
whose ear?—not thine.
  Idon. Ill can I bear that look—Plead
for me, Oswald !

You are my Father's Friend.
  (*To* MARMADUKE). Alas, you know not,
And never *can* you know, how much he
loved me.   1605
Twice had he been to me a father, twice
Had given me breath, and was I not to be
His daughter, once his daughter? could I
withstand
His pleading face, and feel his clasping
arms,
And hear his prayer that I would not for-
sake him   1610
In his old age——   [*Hides her face.*
  Mar.   Patience—Heaven grant
me patience !—
She weeps, she weeps—*my* brain shall
burn for hours
Ere *I* can shed a tear.
  Idon.   I was a woman ;
And, balancing the hopes that are the
dearest
To womankind with duty to my Father,
I yielded up those precious hopes, which
nought   1616
On earth could else have wrested from
me ;—if erring,
Oh let me be forgiven !
  Mar.   I *do* forgive thee.
  Idon. But take me to your arms thin
breast, alas !
It throbs, and you have a heart that does
not feel it.   1620
  Mar. (*exultingly*). She is innocent.
                          [*He embraces her.*
  Osw. (*aside*).   Were I a Moralist,
I should make wondrous revolution here ;
It were a quaint experiment to show
The beauty of truth— [*Addressing them.*
                    I see I interrupt you ;
I shall have business with you, Marma-
duke ;   1625
Follow me to the Hostel. [*Exit* OSWALD.
  Idon.   Marmaduke,
This is a happy day. My Father soon
Shall sun himself before his native doors ;
The lame, the hungry, will be welcome
there.
No more shall he complain of wasted
strength,   1630
Of thoughts that fail, and a decaying
heart;

His good works will be balm and life to
him.
　Mar. This is most strange !—I know
　　not what it was,
But there was something which most
　　plainly said　　　　　　　　　1634
That thou wert innocent.
　Idon.　　　　　　How innocent !—
Oh heavens ! you 've been deceived.
　Mar.　　　　　　Thou art a Woman
To bring perdition on the universe.
　Idon. Already I've been punished to
　　the height
Of my offence.　　[*Smiling affectionately.*
　　　　　I see you love me still,
The labours of my hand are still your joy ;
Bethink you of the hour when on your
　　shoulder　　　　　　　　　　1641
I hung this belt.
　　[*Pointing to the belt on which was
　　　　suspended* HERBERT'S *scrip.*
　Mar. Mercy of Heaven !　　　[*Sinks.*
　Idon. What ails you !　[*Distractedly.*
　Mar. The scrip that held his food, and
　　I forgot
To give it back again !
　Idon.　　　　What mean your words ?
　Mar. I know not what I said—all may
　　be well.　　　　　　　　　　1645
　Idon. That smile hath life in it !
　Mar.　　　　　This road is perilous ;
I will attend you to a Hut that stands
Near the wood's edge—rest there to-night,
　I pray you:
For me, I have business, as you heard,
　　with Oswald,　　　　　　　1649
But will return to you by break of day.
　　　　　　　　　　　　　　[*Exeunt.*

ACT IV.

SCENE, *A desolate prospect—a ridge of
rooks—a Chapel on the summit of one—
Moon behind the rocks—night stormy—
irregular sound of a bell—*HERBERT
enters exhausted.

　Her. That Chapel-bell in mercy seemed
　　to guide me,
But now it mocks my steps; its fitful
　　stroke
Can scarcely be the work of human hands.
Hear me, ye Men upon the cliffs, if such

There be who pray nightly before the
　　Altar.　　　　　　　　　　1655
Oh that I had but strength to reach the
　　place !
My Child — my Child — dark — dark — I
　　faint — this wind —
These stifling blasts—God help me !

　　　　　Enter ELDRED.

　Eld.　　　　Better this bare rock,
Though it were tottering over a man's
　　head,
Than a tight case of dungeon walls for
　　shelter　　　　　　　　　　1660
From such rough dealing.
　　　　　[*A moaning voice is heard.*
　　　　　　Ha ! what sound is that ?
Trees creaking in the wind (but none are
　　here)
Send forth such noises—and that weary
　　bell !
Surely some evil Spirit abroad to-night
Is ringing it—'twould stop a Saint in
　　prayer,　　　　　　　　　　1665
And that—what is it ? never was sound
　　so like
A human groan. Ha ! what is here ?
　　Poor Man—
Murdered ! alas ! speak—speak, I am your
　　friend !
No answer—hush—lost wretch, he lifts
　　his hand
And lays it to his heart—(*Kneels to him*).
　　I pray you speak !　　　　　1670
What has befallen you ?
　Her. (*feebly*). A stranger has done this,
And in the arms of a stranger I must die.
　Eld. Nay, think not so: come, let me
　　raise you up:　　　[*Raises him.*
This is a dismal place—well—that is
　　well—　　　　　　　　　　1674
I was too fearful—take me for your guide
And your support—my hut is not far off.
　　　　　[*Draws him gently off the stage.*

SCENE, *A room in the Hostel—*MARMADUKE
　　　　　and OSWALD.

　Mar. But for Idonea !—I have cause to
　　think
That she is innocent.
　Osw.　　　　Leave that thought awhile

As one of those beliefs which in their
    hearts
Lovers lock up as pearls, though oft no
    better   1680
Than feathers clinging to their points of
    passion.
This day's event has laid on me the duty
Of opening out my story; you must hear
    it,
And without further preface.—In my
    youth,
Except for that abatement which is paid
By envy as a tribute to desert,   1686
I was the pleasure of all hearts, the dar-
    ling
Of every tongue—as you are now. You've
    heard
That I embarked for Syria. On our
    voyage
Was hatched among the crew a foul Con-
    spiracy   1690
Against my honour, in the which our
    Captain
Was, I believed, prime Agent. The wind
    fell ;
We lay becalmed week after week, until
The water of the vessel was exhausted ;
I felt a double fever in my veins,   1695
Yet rage suppressed itself ;—to a deep
    stillness
Did my pride tame my pride ;—for many
    days,
On a dead sea under a burning sky,
I brooded o'er my injuries, deserted
By man and nature ;—if a breeze had
    blown,   1700
It might have found its way into my
    heart,
And I had been—no matter—do you
    mark me?
    Mar. Quick—to the point—if any un-
        told crime
Doth haunt your memory,
    Osw.   Patience, hear me further !—
One day in silence did we drift at
    noon   1705
By a bare rock, narrow, and white, and
    bare ;
No food was there, no drink, no grass, no
    shade,
No tree, nor jutting eminence, nor form

Inanimate large as the body of man,
Nor any living thing whose lot of life 1710
Might stretch beyond the measure of one
    moon.
To dig for water on the spot, the Cap-
    tain
Landed with a small troop, myself being
    one :
There I reproached him with his trea-
    chery.
Imperious at all times, his temper rose ;
He struck me ; and that instant had I
    killed him,   1716
And put an end to his insolence, but my
    Comrades
Rushed in between us : then did I insist
(All hated him, and I was stung to mad-
    ness)
That we should leave him there, alive !—
    we did so.   1720
    Mar. And he was famished?
    Osw.   Naked was the spot ;
Methinks I see it now—how in the sun
Its stony surface glittered like a shield ;
And in that miserable place we left him,
Alone but for a swarm of minute crea-
    tures   1725
Not one of which could help him while
    alive,
Or mourn him dead.
    Mar.   A man by men cast off,
Left without burial ! nay, not dead nor
    dying,
But standing, walking, stretching forth
    his arms,
In all things like ourselves but in the
    agony   1730
With which he called for mercy ; and—
    even so—
He was forsaken?
    Osw.   There is a power in sounds :
The cries he uttered might have stopped
    the boat
That bore us through the water——
    Mar.   You returned
Upon that dismal hearing—did you not?
    Osw. Some scoffed at him with hellish
        mockery,   1736
And laughed so loud it seemed that the
    smooth sea
Did from some distant region echo us.

Mar. We all are of one blood, our veins
   are filled
At the same poisonous fountain !
Osw.   'Twas an island
Only by sufferance of the winds and
   waves,   1741
Which with their foam could cover it at
   will.
I know not how he perished; but the
   calm,
The same dead calm, continued many
   days.
   Mar. But his own crime had brought
   on him this doom,   1745
His wickedness prepared it; these expe-
   dients
Are terrible, yet ours is not the fault.
   Osw. The man was famished, and was
     innocent !
Mar. Impossible !
Osw. The man had never wronged me.
Mar. Banish the thought, crush it, and
   be at peace.   1750
His guilt was marked—these things could
   never be
Were there not eyes that see, and for
   good ends,
Where ours are baffled.
   Osw.   I had been deceived.
   Mar. And from that hour the miser-
   able man   1754
No more was heard of?
   Osw.   I had been betrayed.
   Mar. And he found no deliverance !
   Osw.   The Crew
Gave me a hearty welcome; they had laid
The plot to rid themselves, at any cost,
Of a tyrannic Master whom they loathed.
So we pursued our voyage: when we
   landed,   1760
The tale was spread abroad; my power
   at once
Shrunk from me; plans and schemes, and
   lofty hopes—
All vanished. I gave way—do you attend?
   Mar. The Crew deceived you?
   Osw.   Nay, command yourself.
   Mar. It is a dismal night—how the
   wind howls!   1765
   Osw. I hid my head within a Convent,
   there

Lay passive as a dormouse in mid winter.
That was no life for me—I was o'er-
   thrown,
But not destroyed.
   Mar.   The proofs—you ought
   to have seen
The guilt—have touched it—felt it at
   your heart—   1770
As I have done.
   Osw.   A fresh tide of Crusaders
Drove by the place of my retreat: three
   nights
Did constant meditation dry my blood;
Three sleepless nights I passed in sound-
   ing on,
Through words and things, a dim and
   perilous way;   1775
And, wheresoe'er I turned me, I beheld
A slavery compared to which the dungeon
And clanking chains are perfect liberty.
You understand me—I was comforted;
I saw that every possible shape of ac-
   tion   1780
Might lead to good—I saw it and burst
   forth,
Thirsting for some of those exploits that
   fill
The earth for sure redemption of lost
   peace.
      [*Marking* Marmaduke's *countenance.*
Nay, you have had the worst. Ferocity
Subsided in a moment, like a wind 1785
That drops down dead out of a sky it
   vexed.
And yet I had within me evermore
A salient spring of energy ; I mounted
From action up to action with a mind
That never rested—without meat or
   drink   1790
Have I lived many days—my sleep was
   bound
To purposes of reason—not a dream
But had a continuity and substance
That waking life had never power to
   give.
   Mar. O wretched Human-kind!—Until
   the mystery   1795
Of all this world is solved, well may we
   envy
The worm, that, underneath a stone whose
   weight

Would crush the lion's paw with mortal
   anguish,
Doth lodge, and feed, and coil, and sleep,
   in safety.
Fell not the wrath of Heaven upon those
   traitors?   1800
   Osw. Give not to them a thought. From
   Palestine
We marched to Syria: oft I left the
   Camp,
When all that multitude of hearts was
   still,
And followed on, through woods of gloomy
   cedar,
Into deep chasms troubled by roaring
   streams;   1805
Or from the top of Lebanon surveyed
The moonlight desert, and the moonlight
   sea:
In these my lonely wanderings I per-
   ceived
What mighty objects do impress their
   forms
To elevate our intellectual being;   1810
And felt, if ought on earth deserves a
   curse,
'Tis that worst principle of ill which
   dooms
A thing so great to perish self-consumed.
—So much for my remorse!
   Mar.   Unhappy Man!
   Osw. When from these forms I turned
   to contemplate   1815
The World's opinions and her usages,
I seemed a Being who had passed alone
Into a region of futurity,
Whose natural element was freedom——
   Mar.   Stop—
I may not, cannot, follow thee.
   Osw.   You must.   1820
I had been nourished by the sickly food
Of popular applause. I now perceived
That we are praised, only as men in us
Do recognise some image of themselves,
An abject counterpart of what they are,
Or the empty thing that they would wish
   to be.   1826
I felt that merit has no surer test
Than obloquy; that, if we wish to serve
The world in substance, not deceive by
   show,

We must become obnoxious to its hate,
Or fear disguised in simulated scorn. 1831
   Mar. I pity, can forgive, you; but
   those wretches—
That monstrous perfidy!
   Osw.   Keep down your wrath.
False Shame discarded, spurious Fame
   despised,
Twin sisters both of Ignorance, I found
Life stretched before me smooth as some
   broad way   1836
Cleared for a monarch's progress. Priests
   might spin
Their veil, but not for me—'twas in fit
   place
Among its kindred cobwebs. I had been,
And in that dream had left my native
   land,   1840
One of Love's simple bondsmen—the soft
   chain
Was off for ever; and the men, from
   whom
This liberation came, you would destroy:
Join me in thanks for their blind services.
   Mar. 'Tis a strange aching that, when
   we would curse   1845
And cannot. You have betrayed me—I
   have done—
I am content—I know that he is guilt-
   less—
That both are guiltless, without spot or
   stain,
Mutually consecrated. Poor old Man!
And I had heart for this, because thou
   lovedst   1850
Her who from very infancy had been
Light to thy path, warmth to thy blood!—
   Together   [*Turning to* OSWALD.
We propped his steps, he leaned upon us
   both.
   Osw. Ay, we are coupled by a chain of
   adamant;
Let us be fellow-labourers, then, to en-
   large   1855
Man's intellectual empire. We subsist
In slavery; all is slavery; we receive
Laws, but we ask not whence those laws
   have come;
We need an inward sting to goad us on.
   Mar. Have you betrayed me? Speak
   to that.

Osw. The mask, 1860
Which for a season I have stooped to
wear,
Must be cast off.—Know then that I was
urged,
(For other impulse let it pass) was driven,
To seek for sympathy, because I saw
In you a mirror of my youthful self; 1865
I would have made us equal once again,
But that was a vain hope. You have
struck home,
With a few drops of blood cut short the
business;
Therein for ever you must yield to me.
But what is done will save you from the
blank 1870
Of living without knowledge that you
live:
Now you are suffering—for the future
day,
'Tis his who will command it.—Think of
my story—
Herbert is *innocent*.
    Mar. (*in a faint voice, and doubtingly*).
        You do but echo
My own wild words?
    Osw. Young Man, the seed must lie
Hid in the earth, or there can be no
harvest; 1876
'Tis Nature's law. What I have done in
darkness
I will avow before the face of day.
Herbert *is* innocent.
    Mar. What fiend could prompt
This action? Innocent!—oh breaking
heart!— 1880
Alive or dead, I'll find him. [*Exit.*
    Osw. Alive—perdition! [*Exit.*

SCENE, *The inside of a poor Cottage.*

ELEANOR *and* IDONEA *seated.*

Idon. The storm beats hard—Mercy for
poor or rich,
Whose heads are shelterless in such a
night!
    A Voice without. Holla! to bed, good
Folks, within!
    Elea. O save us! 1884
    Idon. What can this mean?
    Elea. Alas, for my poor husband!—

We'll have a counting of our flocks to-
morrow;
The wolf keeps festival these stormy
nights:
Be calm, sweet Lady, they are wassailers
    [*The voices die away in the distance.*
Returning from their Feast—my heart
beats so—
A noise at midnight does *so* frighten me.
    Idon. Hush! [*Listening.*
    Elea. They are gone. On such
        a night my husband, 1891
Dragged from his bed, was cast into a
dungeon,
Where, hid from me, he counted many
years,
A criminal in no one's eyes but theirs—
Not even in theirs—whose brutal vio-
lence 1895
So dealt with him.
    Idon. I have a noble Friend
First among youths of knightly breeding,
One
Who lives but to protect the weak or in-
jured.
There again! [*Listening.*
    Elea. 'Tis my husband's foot.
        Good Eldred 1899
Has a kind heart; but his imprisonment
Has made him fearful, and he'll never be
The man he was.
    Idon. I will retire;—good night!
        [*She goes within.*

Enter ELDRED (*hides a bundle*).

Eld. Not yet in bed, Eleanor!—there
are stains in that frock which must be
washed out. 1905
    Elea. What has befallen you?
    Eld. I am belated, and you must know
the cause—(*speaking low*) that is the blood
of an unhappy Man.
    Elea. Oh! we are undone for ever. 1910
    Eld. Heaven forbid that I should lift
my hand against any man. Eleanor, I
have shed tears to-night, and it comforts
me to think of it.
    Elea. Where, where is he? 1915
    Eld. I have done him no harm, but—it
will be forgiven me; it would not have
been so once.

Elea. You have not *buried* anything? You are no richer than when you left me?

Eld. Be at peace; I am innocent.   1921

Elea. Then God be thanked ——

[*A short pause; she falls upon his neck.*

Eld. To-night I met with an old Man lying stretched upon the ground—a sad spectacle: I raised him up with the hope that we might shelter and restore him.

Elea. (*as if ready to run*). Where is he? You were not able to bring him *all* the way with you; let us return, I can help you.   1930

[*ELDRED shakes his head.*

Eld. He did not seem to wish for life: as I was struggling on, by the light of the moon I saw the stains of blood upon my clothes—he waved his hand, as if it were all useless; and I let him sink again to the ground.   1936

Elea. Oh that I had been by your side!

Eld. I tell you his hands and his body were cold—how could I disturb his last moments? he strove to turn from me as if he wished to settle into sleep.   1941

Elea. But, for the stains of blood ——

Eld. He must have fallen, I fancy, for his head was cut; but I think his malady was cold and hunger.   1945

Elea. Oh, Eldred, I shall never be able to look up at this roof in storm or fair but I shall tremble.

Eld. Is it not enough that my ill stars have kept me abroad to-night till this hour? I come home, and this is my comfort!   1952

Elea. But did he say nothing which might have set you at ease?

Eld. I thought he grasped my hand while he was muttering something about his Child—his Daughter—(*starting as if he heard a noise*). What is that?   1958

Elea. Eldred, you are a father.

Eld. God knows what was in my heart, and will not curse my son for my sake.

Elea. But you prayed by him? you waited the hour of his release?   1964

Eld. The night was wasting fast; I have no friend; I am spited by the world—his wound terrified me—if I had

brought him along with me, and he had died in my arms! —— I am sure I heard something breathing—and this chair!   1970

Elea. Oh, Eldred, you will die alone. You will have nobody to close your eyes—no hand to grasp your dying hand—I shall be in my grave. A curse will attend us all.   1975

Eld. Have you forgot your own troubles when I was in the dungeon?

Elea. And you left him alive?

Eld. Alive!—the damps of death were upon him—he could not have survived an hour.   1981

Elea. In the cold, cold night.

Eld. (*in a savage tone*). Ay, and his head was bare; I suppose you would have had me lend my bonnet to cover it.—You will never rest till I am brought to a felon's end.   1987

Elea. Is there nothing to be done? cannot we go to the Convent?

Eld. Ay, and say at once that I murdered him!   1991

Elea. Eldred, I know that ours is the only house upon the Waste; let us take heart; this Man may be rich, and could he be saved by our means, his gratitude may reward us.   1996

Eld. 'Tis all in vain.

Elea. But let us make the attempt. This old Man may have a wife, and he may have children—let us return to the spot; we may restore him, and his eyes may yet open upon those that love him.   2003

Eld. He will never open them more; even when he spoke to me, he kept them firmly sealed, as if he had been blind.

Idon. (*rushing out*). It is, it is, my Father—

Eld. We are betrayed!

[*Looking at* IDONEA.

Elea. His Daughter!—God have mercy!

[*Turning to* IDONEA.

Idon. (*sinking down*). Oh! lift me up and carry me to the place.   2010 You are safe; the whole world shall not harm you.

Elea. This Lady is his Daughter.

Eld. (*moved*). I'll lead you to the spot.

Idon. (*springing up*). Alive! you heard
　　him breathe? quick, quick—
　　　　　　　　　　　　　[*Exeunt.*

ACT V.

SCENE, *A Wood on the edge of the Waste.*

Enter OSWALD *and a* Forester.

For. He leaned upon the bridge that
　　spans the glen,　　　　　　　2015
And down into the bottom cast his eye,
That fastened there, as it would check
　　the current.
Osw. He listened too; did you not say
　　he listened?
For. As if there came such moaning from
　　the flood　　　　　　　　　2019
As is heard often after stormy nights.
Osw. But did he utter nothing?
For. 　　　　　　　　　See him there!

MARMADUKE *appearing.*

Mar. Buzz, buzz, ye black and winged
　　freebooters;
That is no substance which ye settle on!
For. His senses play him false; and
　　see, his arms
Outspread, as if to save himself from
　　falling!—　　　　　　　　2025
Some terrible phantom I believe is now
Passing before him, such as God will
　　not
Permit to visit any but a man　　2028
Who has been guilty of some horrid crime.
　　　　　　　　[MARMADUKE *disappears.*
Osw. The game is up!—
For. 　　　　　If it be needful, Sir,　2030
I will assist you to lay hands upon him.
Osw. No, no, my Friend, you may pur-
　　sue your business—
'Tis a poor wretch of an unsettled mind,
Who has a trick of straying from his
　　keepers;
We must be gentle. Leave him to my
　　care.　　　　　　[*Exit.* Forester.
If his own eyes play false with him, these
　　freaks　　　　　　　　　2036
Of fancy shall be quickly tamed by mine;
The goal is reached. My Master shall
　　become
A shadow of myself—made by myself.

SCENE, *The edge of the Moor.*

MARMADUKE *and* ELDRED *enter from
opposite sides.*

Mar. (*raising his eyes and perceiving*
　　ELDRED). In any corner of this
　　savage Waste　　　　　　　2040
Have you, good Peasant, seen a blind old
　　Man?
Eld. I heard——
Mar. 　　　You heard him, where? when
　　heard him?
Eld. 　　　　　　　As you know,
The first hours of last night were rough
　　with storm:
I had been out in search of a stray heifer;
Returning late, I heard a moaning sound;
Then, thinking that my fancy had de-
　　ceived me,　　　　　　　2046
I hurried on, when straight a second moan,
A human voice distinct, struck on my ear
So guided, distant a few steps, I found
An aged Man, and such as you describe.
Mar. You heard!—he called you to
　　him? Of all men　　　　　2051
The best and kindest!—but where is he?
　　guide me,
That I may see him.
Eld. 　　　　　　On a ridge of rocks
A lonesome Chapel stands, deserted now:
The bell is left, which no one dares re-
　　move;　　　　　　　　　2055
And, when the stormy wind blows o'er
　　the peak,
It rings, as if a human hand were there
To pull the cord. I guess he must have
　　heard it;
And it had led him towards the precipice,
To climb up to the spot whence the sound
　　came;　　　　　　　　　2060
But he had failed through weakness. From
　　his hand
His staff had dropped, and close upon the
　　brink
Of a small pool of water he was laid,
As if he had stooped to drink, and so
　　remained　　　　　　　　2064
Without the strength to rise.
Mar. 　　　　　　Well, well, he lives,
And all is safe: what said he?
Eld. 　　　　　　　　But few words:

He only spake to me of a dear Daughter,
Who, so he feared, would never see him
    more;
And of a Stranger to him, One by whom
He had been sore misused; but he forgave
The wrong and the wrong-doer. You are
    troubled—   2071
Perhaps you are his son?

Mar.   The All-seeing knows,
I did not think he had a living Child.—
But whither did you carry him?

Eld.   He was torn,
His head was bruised, and there was blood
    about him——   2075

Mar. That was no work of mine.

Eld.   Nor was it mine.

Mar. But had he strength to walk? I
    could have borne him
A thousand miles.

Eld.   I am in poverty,
And know how busy are the tongues of
    men;
My heart was willing, Sir, but I am one
Whose good deeds will not stand by their
    own light;   2081
And, though it smote me more than words
    can tell,
I left him.

Mar. I believe that there are phantoms,
That in the shape of man do cross our path
On evil instigation, to make sport   2085
Of our distress—and thou art one of them!
But things substantial have so pressed on
    me——

Eld. My wife and children came into
    my mind.

Mar. Oh Monster! Monster! there are
    three of us,
And we shall howl together.

    [*After a pause and in a feeble voice.*
         I am deserted
At my worst need, my crimes have in a
    net   2091
(*Pointing to* ELDRED) Entangled this poor
    man? Where was it? where?
         [*Dragging him along.*

Eld. 'Tis needless; spare your violence.
    His Daughter——

Mar. Ay, in the word a thousand scor-
    pions lodge:
This old man *had* a Daughter.

Eld.   To the spot   2095
I hurried back with her.—Oh save me, Sir,
From such a journey!——there was a
    black tree,
A single tree; she thought it was her
    Father.—
Oh Sir, I would not see that hour again
For twenty lives. The daylight dawned,
    and now—   2100
Nay; hear my tale, 'tis fit that you should
    hear it—
As we approached, a solitary crow
Rose from the spot;—the Daughter clap-
    ped her hands,
And then I heard a shriek so terrible
         [MARMADUKE *shrinks back.*
The startled bird quivered upon the wing.

Mar. Dead, dead!—

Eld. (*after a pause*). A dismal matter,
    Sir, for me,   2106
And seems the like for you; if 'tis your
    wish,
I'll lead you to his Daughter; but 'twere
    best
That she should be prepared; I'll go be-
    fore.

Mar. There will be need of preparation.
         [Eldred goes off

Elea. (*enters*).   Master!
Your limbs sink under you, shall I sup-
    port you?   2111

Mar. (*taking her arm*). Woman, I've
    lent my body to the service
Which now thou tak'st upon thee. God
    forbid
That thou shouldst ever meet a like oc-
    casion
With such a purpose in thine heart as
    mine was.   2115

Elea. Oh, why have I to do with things
    like these?   [*Exeunt.*

SCENE *changes to the door of* ELDRED'S
*cottage—*IDONEA *seated—enter* ELDRED.

Eld. Your Father, Lady, from a wilful
    hand
Has met unkindness; so indeed he told
    me,
And you remember such was my report:
From what has just befallen me I have
    cause   2120

To fear the very worst.

Idon.   My Father is dead;
Why dost thou come to me with words
like these?

Eld. A wicked Man should answer for
his crimes.

Idon. Thou seest me what I am.

Eld.   It was most heinous,
And doth call out for vengeance.

Idon.   Do not add,
I prithee, to the harm thou 'st done al-
ready.   2126

Eld. Hereafter you will thank me for
this service.

Hard by a Man I met, who, from plain
proofs
Of interfering Heaven, I have no doubt,
Laid hands upon your Father. Fit it were
You should prepare to meet him.

Idon.   I have nothing   2131
To do with others; help me to my Father—
          [*She turns and sees* MARMADUKE
          leaning on ELEANOR—*throws
          herself upon his neck, and after
          some time,*
In joy I met thee, but a few hours past;
And thus we meet again; one human stay
Is left me still in thee. Nay, shake not so.

Mar. In such a wilderness—to see no
thing,   2136
No, not the pitying moon!

Idon.   And perish so.

Mar. Without a dog to moan for him.

Idon.   Think not of it,
But enter there and see him how he sleeps,
Tranquil as he had died in his own bed.

Mar. Tranquil—why not?

Idon.   Oh, peace!

Mar.   He is at peace; 2141
His body is at rest: there was a plot,
A hideous plot, against the soul of man:
It took effect—and yet I baffled it,
In *some* degree.

Idon.   Between us stood, I thought,
A cup of consolation, filled from Heaven
For both our needs; must I, and in thy
presence,   2147
Alone partake of it?—Belovèd Marma-
duke!

Mar. Give me a reason why the wisest
thing

That the earth owns shall never choose to
die,   2150
But some one must be near to count his
groans.
The wounded deer retires to solitude,
And dies in solitude: all things but man,
All die in solitude.
          [*Moving towards the cottage door.*
          Mysterious God,
If she had never lived I had not done it!—

Idon. Alas, the thought of such a cruel
death   2156
Has overwhelmed him.—I must follow.

Eld.   Lady!
You will do well; (*she goes*) unjust sus-
picion may
Cleave to this Stranger: if, upon his
entering,
The dead Man heave a groan, or from his
side   2160
Uplift his hand—that would be evidence.

Elea. Shame! Eldred, shame!

Mar. (*both returning*). The dead have
but one face. (*To himself.*)
And such a Man—so meek and unoffend-
ing—
Helpless and harmless as a babe: a Man
By obvious signal to the world's pro-
tection   2165
Solemnly dedicated—to decoy him!—

Idon. Oh, had you seen him living!—

Mar.   I (so filled
With horror is this world) am unto thee
The thing most precious that it now con-
tains:
Therefore through me alone must be re-
vealed   2170
By whom thy Parent was destroyed,
Idonea!
I have the proofs!—

Idon.   O miserable Father!
Thou didst command me to bless all man-
kind;
Nor to this moment have I ever wished
Evil to any living thing; but hear me,
Hear me, ye Heavens!—(*kneeling*)—may
vengeance haunt the fiend   2176
For this most cruel murder: let him live
And move in terror of the elements;
The thunder send him on his knees to
prayer

In the open streets, and let him think he
     sees,   2180
If e'er he entereth the house of God,
The roof, self-moved, unsettling o'er his
     head;
And let him, when he would lie down at
     night,
Point to his wife the blood-drops on his
     pillow!
Mar. My voice was silent, but my heart
     hath joined thee.   2185
Idon. (*leaning on* MARMADUKE). Left
     to the mercy of that savage Man!
How could he call upon his Child!—O
     Friend!   [*Turns to* MARMADUKE.
My faithful true and only Comforter.
Mar. Ay, come to me and weep.
            (*He kisses her.*)
    (*To* ELDRED). Yes, Varlet, look,
The devils at such sights do clap their
     hands.   [ELDRED *retires alarmed.*
Idon. Thy vest is torn, thy cheek is
     deadly pale;   2191
Hast thou pursued the monster?
Mar.   I have found him.—
Oh! would that thou hadst perished in
     the flames!
Idon. Here art thou, then can I be
     desolate?
Mar. There was a time, when this
     protecting hand   2195
Availed against the mighty; never more
Shall blessings wait upon a deed of mine.
Idon. Wild words for me to hear, for
     me, an orphan,
Committed to thy guardianship by Hea-
     ven;   2199
And, if thou hast forgiven me, let me hope,
In this deep sorrow, trust, that I am thine
For closer care;—here, is no malady.
            [*Taking his arm.*
Mar. There, *is* a malady—
(*Striking his heart and forehead.*) And
     here, and here,
A mortal malady. I am accurst:
All nature curses me, and in my heart
Thy curse is fixed; the truth must be laid
     bare.   2206
It must be told, and borne. I am the man,
(Abused, betrayed, but how it matters not)
Presumptuous above all that ever breathed,

Who, casting as I thought a guilty Person
Upon Heaven's righteous judgment, did
     become   2211
An instrument of Fiends. Through me,
     through me,
Thy Father perished.
    Idon. Perished—by what mischance?
    Mar. Belovèd! if I dared, so would I
     call thee—
Conflict must cease, and, in thy frozen
     heart,   2215
The extremes of suffering meet in absolute
     peace.   [*He gives her a letter.*
Idon. (*reads*) "Be not surprised if you
hear that some signal judgment has be-
fallen the man who calls himself your
father; he is now with me, as his signa-
ture will show: abstain from conjecture
till you see me.

         "HERBERT.

         "MARMADUKE."

The writing Oswald's; the signature my
     Father's: 2225
(*Looks steadily at the paper*) And here is
     yours,—or do my eyes deceive me?
You have then seen my Father?
    Mar.   He has leaned
Upon this arm.
    Idon. You led him towards the Convent?
    Mar. That Convent was Stone-Arthur
     Castle. Thither
We were his guides. I on that night re-
     solved   2230
That he should wait thy coming till the day
Of resurrection.
    Idon.   Miserable Woman,
Too quickly moved, too easily giving way,
I put denial on thy suit, and hence,   2234
With the disastrous issue of last night,
Thy perturbation, and these frantic words.
Be calm, I pray thee!
    Mar.   Oswald—
    Idon.   Name him not.

       Enter female Beggar.

Beg. And he is dead!—that Moor—
     how shall I cross it?
By night, by day, never shall I be able
To travel half a mile alone.—Good Lady!
Forgive me!—Saints forgive me. Had I
     thought   2241

It would have come to this!—

Idon. What brings you hither? speak!

Beg. (*pointing to* MARMADUKE). This
innocent Gentleman. Sweet hea-
vens! I told him
Such tales of your dead Father!—God is
my judge,
I thought there was no harm: but that
bad Man,　　　　2245
He bribed me with his gold, and looked
so fierce.
Mercy! I said I know not what—oh pity
me—
I said, sweet Lady, you were not his
Daughter—
Pity me, I am haunted;—thrice this day
My conscience made me wish to be struck
blind;　　　　2250
And then I would have prayed, and had
no voice.

Idon. (*to* MARMADUKE). Was it my Fa-
ther?—no, no, no, for he
Was meek and patient, feeble, old and blind,
Helpless, and loved me dearer than his life.
—But hear me. For *one* question, I have
a heart　　　　2255
That will sustain me. Did you murder
him?

Mar. No, not by stroke of arm. But
learn the process:
Proof after proof was pressed upon me;
guilt
Made evident, as seemed, by blacker guilt,
Whose impious folds enwrapped even
thee; and truth　　　　2260
And innocence, embodied in his looks,
His words and tones and gestures, did
but serve
With me to aggravate his crimes, and
heaped
Ruin upon the cause for which they
pleaded.
Then pity crossed the path of my resolve:
Confounded, I looked up to Heaven, and
cast,　　　　2266
Idonea! thy blind Father on the Ordeal
Of the bleak Waste—left him—and so he
died!

[IDONEA *sinks senseless;* Beggar,
ELEANOR, &c., *crowd round, and
bear her off.*

Why may we speak these things, and do
no more;
Why should a thrust of the arm have
such a power,　　　　2270
And words that tell these things be heard
in vain?
She is not dead. Why!—if I loved this
Woman,
I would take care she never woke again;
But she WILL wake, and she will weep for
me,
And say no blame was mine—and so, poor
fool,　　　　2275
Will waste her curses on another name.

[*He walks about distractedly.*

Enter OSWALD.

OSWALD (*to himself*). Strong to o'erturn,
strong also to build up.

[*To* MARMADUKE.

The starts and sallies of our last encounter
Were natural enough; but that, I trust,
Is all gone by. You have cast off the
chains　　　　2280
That fettered your nobility of mind—
Delivered heart and head!

Let us to Palestine;
This is a paltry field for enterprise.

Mar. Ay, what shall we encounter next?
This issue—
'Twas nothing more than darkness deepen-
ing darkness,　　　　2285
And weakness crowned with the impo-
tence of death!—
Your pupil is, you see, an apt proficient
(*ironically*).
Start not!—Here is another face hard by;
Come, let us take a peep at both together,
And, with a voice at which the dead will
quake,　　　　2290
Resound the praise of your morality—
Of this too much.

[*Drawing* OSWALD *towards the Cot-
tage—stops short at the door.*

Men are there, millions, Oswald,
Who with bare hands would have plucked
out thy heart
And flung it to the dogs: but I am raised
Above, or sunk below, all further sense
Of provocation. Leave me, with the weight
Of that old Man's forgiveness on thy heart,

Pressing as heavily as it doth on mine.
Coward I have been; know, there lies not
    now,   2299
Within the compass of a mortal thought,
A deed that I would shrink from;—but
    to endure,
That is my destiny. May it be thine:
Thy office, thy ambition, be henceforth
To feed remorse, to welcome every sting
Of penitential anguish, yea with tears.
When seas and continents shall lie be-
    tween us—   2306
The wider space the better—we may find
In such a course fit links of sympathy,
An incommunicable rivalship
Maintained, for peaceful ends beyond our
    view.   2310

    [*Confused voices—several of the
    band enter—rush upon* OSWALD
    and seize him.

  One of them. I would have dogged him
    to the jaws of hell—
  Osw. Ha! is it so!—That vagrant
    Hag!—this comes
Of having left a thing like her alive!
                  [*Aside.*

  Several voices. Despatch him!
  Osw.   If I pass beneath a rock
And shout, and, with the echo of my voice,
Bring down a heap of rubbish, and it
    crush me,   2316
I die without dishonour. Famished,
    starved,
A Fool and Coward blended to my wish!
    [*Smiles scornfully and exultingly
    at* MARMADUKE.

  Wal. 'Tis done! (*stabs him*).
  Another of the band. The ruthless traitor!
  Mar.   A rash deed!—
With that reproof I do resign a station
Of which I have been proud.
  Wil. (*approaching* MARMADUKE). O my
    poor Master!   2321
  Mar. Discerning Monitor, my faithful
    Wilfred,
Why art thou here? [*Turning to* WALLACE.
    Wallace, upon these Borders,

Many there be whose eyes will not want
    cause
To weep that I am gone. Brothers in
    arms!   2325
Raise on that dreary Waste a monument
That may record my story: nor let words—
Few must they be, and delicate in their
    touch
As light itself—be there withheld from Her
Who, through most wicked arts, was made
    an orphan   2330
By One who would have died a thousand
    times
To shield her from a moment's harm. To
    you,
Wallace and Wilfred, I commend the
    Lady,
By lowly nature reared, as if to make her
In all things worthier of that noble birth,
Whose long-suspended rights are now on
    the eve   2336
Of restoration: with your tenderest care
Watch over her, I pray—sustain her——
  Several of the band (*eagerly*). Captain!
  Mar. No more of that; in silence hear
    my doom:
A hermitage has furnished fit relief 2340
To some offenders; other penitents,
Less patient in their wretchedness, have
    fallen,
Like the old Roman, on their own sword's
    point.
They had their choice: a wanderer *must
    I* go,
The Spectre of that innocent Man, my
    guide.   2345
No human ear shall ever hear me speak;
No human dwelling ever give me food,
Or sleep, or rest: but over waste and wild,
In search of nothing that this earth can
    give,
But expiation, will I wander on—   2350
A Man by pain and thought compelled to
    live,
Yet loathing life—till anger is appeased
In Heaven, and Mercy gives me leave to
    die.

POEMS REFERRING TO THE PERIOD OF CHILDHOOD.

—⁍—

I.

[Composed March 26, 1802.—Published 1807.]

MY heart leaps up when I behold
   A rainbow in the sky:
So was it when my life began;
So is it now I am a man;
So be it when I shall grow old,   5
   Or let me die!
The Child is father of the Man;
And I could wish my days to be
Bound each to each by natural piety.

II.

TO A BUTTERFLY.

[Composed March 14, 1802.—Published 1807.]

STAY near me—do not take thy flight!
A little longer stay in sight!
Much converse do I find in thee,
Historian of my infancy!
Float near me; do not yet depart!   5
Dead times revive in thee:
Thou bring'st, gay creature as thou art!
A solemn image to my heart,
My father's family!

Oh! pleasant, pleasant were the days,   10
The time, when in our childish plays,
My sister Emmeline[1] and I
Together chased the butterfly!
A very hunter did I rush
Upon the prey;—with leaps and springs 15
I followed on from brake to bush;
But she, God love her! feared to brush
The dust from off its wings.

III.

THE SPARROW'S NEST.

[Composed 1801.—Published 1807.]

BEHOLD, within the leafy shade,
Those bright blue eggs together laid!
On me the chance-discovered sight
Gleamed like a vision of delight.

I started—seeming to espy   5
The home and sheltered bed,
The Sparrow's dwelling, which, hard by
My Father's house, in wet or dry
My sister Emmeline[1] and I
   Together visited.   10

She looked at it and seemed to fear it;
Dreading, tho' wishing, to be near it:
Such heart was in her, being then
A little Prattler among men.
The Blessing of my later years   15
Was with me when a boy:
She gave me eyes, she gave me ears;
And humble cares, and delicate fears;
A heart, the fountain of sweet tears;
   And love, and thought, and joy. 20

IV.

FORESIGHT.

[Composed April 28, 1802.—Published 1807.]

THAT is work of waste and ruin—
Do as Charles and I are doing!
Strawberry-blossoms, one and all,
We must spare them—here are many:
Look at it—the flower is small,   5
Small and low, though fair as any:
Do not touch it! summers two
I am older, Anne, than you.

Pull the primrose, sister Anne!
Pull as many as you can.   10
—Here are daisies, take your fill;
Pansies, and the cuckoo-flower:
Of the lofty daffodil
Make your bed, or make your bower;
Fill your lap and fill your bosom;   15
Only spare the strawberry-blossom!

Primroses, the Spring may love them—
Summer knows but little of them:
Violets, a barren kind,
Withered on the ground must lie;   20

[1] See Editor's Note, p. 897.

Daisies leave no fruit behind
When the pretty flowerets die;
Pluck them, and another year
As many will be blowing here.

God has given a kindlier power   25
To the favoured strawberry-flower.
Hither soon as spring is fled
You and Charles and I will walk;
Lurking berries, ripe and red,
Then will hang on every stalk,   30
Each within its leafy bower;
And for that promise spare the flower!

V.

CHARACTERISTICS OF A CHILD
THREE YEARS OLD.

[Composed 1811.—Published 1815.]

LOVING she is, and tractable, though wild;
And Innocence hath privilege in her
To dignify arch looks and laughing eyes;
And feats of cunning; and the pretty
    round
Of trespasses, affected to provoke   5
Mock-chastisement and partnership in
    play.
And, as a faggot sparkles on the hearth,
Not less if unattended and alone
Than when both young and old sit ga-
    thered round
And take delight in its activity;   10
Even so this happy Creature of herself
Is all-sufficient; solitude to her
Is blithe society, who fills the air
With gladness and involuntary songs.
Light are her sallies as the tripping
    fawn's   15
Forth-startled from the fern where she
    lay couched;
Unthought-of, unexpected, as the stir
Of the soft breeze ruffling the meadow-
    flowers,
Or from before it chasing wantonly
The many-coloured images imprest   20
Upon the bosom of a placid lake.

VI.

ADDRESS TO A CHILD,

DURING A BOISTEROUS WINTER EVENING.
BY MY SISTER.

[Composed 1806.—Published 1815.]

WHAT way does the Wind come? What
    way does he go?
He rides over the water, and over the
    snow,
Through wood, and through vale; and
    o'er rocky height,
Which the goat cannot climb, takes his
    sounding flight;
He tosses about in every bare tree,   5
As, if you look up, you plainly may see;
But how he will come, and whither he
    goes,
There's never a scholar in England knows.

He will suddenly stop in a cunning nook,
And ring a sharp 'larum;—but, if you
    should look,   10
There's nothing to see but a cushion of
    snow,
Round as a pillow, and whiter than milk,
And softer than if it were covered with
    silk.
Sometimes he'll hide in the cave of a rock,
Then whistle as shrill as the buzzard cock;
—Yet seek him,—and what shall you find
    in the place?   16
Nothing but silence and empty space;
Save, in a corner, a heap of dry leaves,
That he's left, for a bed, to beggars or
    thieves!

As soon as 'tis daylight to-morrow, with
    me   20
You shall go to the orchard, and then you
    will see
That he has been there, and made a great
    rout,
And cracked the branches, and strewn
    them about;
Heaven grant that he spare but that one
    upright twig
That looked up at the sky so proud and
    big   25
All last summer, as well you know,
Studded with apples, a beautiful show!

Hark! over the roof he makes a pause,
And growls as if he would fix his claws
Right in the slates, and with a huge
rattle   30
Drive them down, like men in a battle:
—But let him range round; he does us no
harm,
We build up the fire, we're snug and
warm;
Untouched by his breath see the candle
shines bright,
And burns with a clear and steady light;
Books have we to read,—but that half-
stifled knell,   36
Alas! 'tis the sound of the eight o'clock
bell.
—Come now we'll to bed! and when we
are there
He may work his own will, and what
shall we care?
He may knock at the door,—we'll not let
him in;   40
May drive at the windows,—we'll laugh
at his din;
Let him seek his own home wherever it be;
Here's a *cozie* warm house for Edward[1]
and me.

VII.

THE MOTHER'S RETURN.

BY THE SAME.

[Composed April or May, 1807.—Published 1815.]

A MONTH, sweet Little-ones, is past
Since your dear Mother went away,—
And she to-morrow will return;
To-morrow is the happy day.

O blessèd tidings! thought of joy!   5
The eldest heard with steady glee;
Silent he stood; then laughed amain,—
And shouted, "Mother, come to me!"

Louder and louder did he shout,
With witless hope to bring her near!—   10
"Nay, patience! patience, little boy;
Your tender mother cannot hear."

---

[1] Edward = Johnnie, the household name of
Wordsworth's eldest son. See note on *To a
Butterfly*, p. 897.—Ed.

I told of hills, and far-off towns,
And long, long vales to travel through;
He listens, puzzled, sore perplexed,   15
But he submits; what can he do?

No strife disturbs his sister's breast;
She wars not with the mystery
Of time and distance, night and day;
The bonds of our humanity.   20

Her joy is like an instinct, joy
Of kitten, bird, or summer fly;
She dances, runs without an aim,
She chatters in her ecstasy.

Her brother now takes up the note,   25
And echoes back his sister's glee;
They hug the infant in my arms,
As if to force his sympathy.

Then, settling into fond discourse,
We rested in the garden bower;   30
While sweetly shone the evening sun
In his departing hour.

We told o'er all that we had done,—
Our rambles by the swift brook's side
Far as the willow-skirted pool,   35
Where two fair swans together glide.

We talked of change, of winter gone,
Of green leaves on the hawthorn spray,
Of birds that build their nests and sing,
And all "since Mother went away!"   40

To her these tales they will repeat,
To her our new-born tribes will show,
The goslings green, the ass's colt,
The lambs that in the meadow go.

—But see, the evening star comes forth!
To bed the children must depart;   46
A moment's heaviness they feel,
A sadness at the heart:

'Tis gone—and in a merry fit
They run up stairs in gamesome race;   50
I, too, infected by their mood,
I could have joined the wanton chase.

Five minutes past—and, O the change!
Asleep upon their beds they lie;
Their busy limbs in perfect rest,   55
And closed the sparkling eye.

VIII.
ALICE FELL;
OR, POVERTY.

[Composed March 12, 13, 1802.—Published 1807.]

THE post-boy drove with fierce career,
For threatening clouds the moon had
      drowned;
When, as we hurried on, my ear
Was smitten with a startling sound.

As if the wind blew many ways,   5
I heard the sound,—and more and more;
It seemed to follow with the chaise,
And still I heard it as before.

At length I to the boy called out;
He stopped his horses at the word,   10
But neither cry, nor voice, nor shout,
Nor aught else like it, could be heard.

The boy then smacked his whip, and fast
The horses scampered through the rain;
But, hearing soon upon the blast   15
The cry, I bade him halt again.

Forthwith alighting on the ground,
"Whence comes," said I, "this piteous
      moan?"
And there a little Girl I found,
Sitting behind the chaise, alone.   20

"My cloak!" no other word she spake,
But loud and bitterly she wept,
As if her innocent heart would break;
And down from off her seat she leapt.

"What ails you, child?"—she sobbed,
      "Look here!"   25
I saw it in the wheel entangled,
A weather-beaten rag as e'er
From any garden scare-crow dangled.

There, twisted between nave and spoke,
It hung, nor could at once be freed;   30
But our joint pains unloosed the cloak,
A miserable rag indeed!

"And whither are you going, child,
To-night along these lonesome ways?"
"To Durham," answered she, half wild—
"Then come with me into the chaise."   36

Insensible to all relief
Sat the poor girl, and forth did send
Sob after sob, as if her grief
Could never, never have an end.   40

"My child, in Durham do you dwell?"
She checked herself in her distress,
And said, "My name is Alice Fell;
I'm fatherless and motherless.

"And I to Durham, Sir, belong."   45
Again, as if the thought would choke
Her very heart, her grief grew strong;
And all was for her tattered cloak!

The chaise drove on; our journey's end
Was nigh; and, sitting by my side,   50
As if she had lost her only friend
She wept, nor would be pacified.

Up to the tavern-door we post;
Of Alice and her grief I told;
And I gave money to the host,   55
To buy a new cloak for the old.

"And let it be of duffil grey,
As warm a cloak as man can sell!"
Proud creature was she the next day,
The little orphan, Alice Fell!   60

IX.
LUCY GRAY;
OR, SOLITUDE.

[Composed 1799.—Published 1800.]

OFT I had heard of Lucy Gray:
And, when I crossed the wild,
I chanced to see at break of day
The solitary child.

No mate, no comrade Lucy knew;   5
She dwelt on a wide moor,
—The sweetest thing that ever grew
Beside a human door!

You yet may spy the fawn at play,
The hare upon the green;   10
But the sweet face of Lucy Gray
Will never more be seen.

"To-night will be a stormy night—
You to the town must go;
And take a lantern, Child, to light   15
Your mother through the snow."

"That, Father! will I gladly do:
'Tis scarcely afternoon—
The minster-clock has just struck two,
And yonder is the moon!"   20

At this the Father raised his hook,
And snapped a faggot-band;
He plied his work;—and Lucy took
The lantern in her hand.

Not blither is the mountain roe: 25
With many a wanton stroke
Her feet disperse the powdery snow,
That rises up like smoke.

The storm came on before its time:
She wandered up and down;   30
And many a hill did Lucy climb:
But never reached the town.

The wretched parents all that night
Went shouting far and wide;
But there was neither sound nor sight   35
To serve them for a guide.

At day-break on a hill they stood
That overlooked the moor;
And thence they saw the bridge of wood,
A furlong from their door.   40

They wept—and, turning homeward, cried,
"In heaven we all shall meet;"
—When in the snow the mother spied
The print of Lucy's feet.

Then downwards from the steep hill's
       edge   45
They tracked the footmarks small;
And through the broken hawthorn hedge,
And by the long stone-wall;

And then an open field they crossed:
The marks were still the same;   50
They tracked them on, nor ever lost;
And to the bridge they came.

They followed from the snowy bank
Those footmarks, one by one,
Into the middle of the plank;   55
And further there were none!

—Yet some maintain that to this day
She is a living child;
That you may see sweet Lucy Gray
Upon the lonesome wild.   60

O'er rough and smooth she trips along,
And never looks behind;
And sings a solitary song
That whistles in the wind.

X.

WE ARE SEVEN.

[Composed 1798.—Published 1800.]

——A SIMPLE Child,
That lightly draws its breath,
And feels its life in every limb,
What should it know of death?

I met a little cottage Girl: 5
She was eight years old, she said;
Her hair was thick with many a curl
That clustered round her head.

She had a rustic, woodland air,
And she was wildly clad: 10
Her eyes were fair, and very fair;
—Her beauty made me glad.

"Sisters and brothers, little maid,
How many may you be?"
"How many? Seven in all," she said,   15
And wondering looked at me.

"And where are they? I pray you tell."
She answered, "Seven are we;
And two of us at Conway dwell,
And two are gone to sea.   20

"Two of us in the church-yard lie,
My sister and my brother;
And, in the church-yard cottage, I
Dwell near them with my mother."

"You say that two at Conway dwell,   25
And two are gone to sea,
Yet ye are seven! I pray you tell,
Sweet Maid, how this may be."

Then did the little Maid reply,
"Seven boys and girls are we;   30
Two of us in the church-yard lie,
Beneath the church-yard tree."

"You run about, my little Maid,
Your limbs they are alive;
If two are in the church-yard laid,   35
Then ye are only five."

"Their graves are green, they may be
        seen,"
The little Maid replied,
"Twelve steps or more from my mother's
        door,
And they are side by side.   40

"My stockings there I often knit,
My kerchief there I hem;
And there upon the ground I sit,
And sing a song to them.

"And often after sun-set, Sir,   45
When it is light and fair,
I take my little porringer,
And eat my supper there.

"The first that died was sister Jane;
In bed she moaning lay,   50
Till God released her of her pain;
And then she went away.

"So in the church-yard she was laid;
And, when the grass was dry,
Together round her grave we played,   55
My brother John and I.

"And when the ground was white with
        snow,
And I could run and slide,
My brother John was forced to go,
And he lies by her side."   60

"How many are you, then," said I,
"If they two are in heaven?"
Quick was the little Maid's reply,
"O Master! we are seven."

"But they are dead; those two are dead!
Their spirits are in heaven!"   66
'Twas throwing words away; for still
The little Maid would have her will,
And said, "Nay, we are seven!"

XI.

THE IDLE SHEPHERD-BOYS;

OR, DUNGEON-GHYLL FORCE.[1]

A PASTORAL.

[Composed 1800.—Published 1800.]

THE valley rings with mirth and joy;
Among the hills the echoes play
A never never ending song,
To welcome in the May.
The magpie chatters with delight;   5
The mountain raven's youngling brood
Have left the mother and the nest;
And they go rambling east and west
In search of their own food;
Or through the glittering vapours dart   10
In very wantonness of heart.

Beneath a rock, upon the grass,
Two boys are sitting in the sun;
Their work, if any work they have,
Is out of mind—or done.   15
On pipes of sycamore they play
The fragments of a Christmas hymn;
Or with that plant which in our dale
We call stag-horn, or fox's tail,
Their rusty hats they trim: 20
And thus, as happy as the day,
Those Shepherds wear the time away.

Along the river's stony marge
The sand-lark chants a joyous song;
The thrush is busy in the wood,   25
And carols loud and strong.
A thousand lambs are on the rocks,
All newly born! both earth and sky
Keep jubilee, and, more than all,
Those boys with their green coronal;   30
They never hear the cry,

---

[1] *Ghyll*, in the dialect of Cumberland and Westmoreland, is a short and, for the most part, a steep narrow valley, with a stream running through it. *Force* is the word universally employed in these dialects for waterfall.

That plaintive cry! which up the hill
Comes from the depth of Dungeon-Ghyll.

Said Walter, leaping from the ground,
"Down to the stump of yon old yew   35
We'll for our whistles run a race."
——Away the shepherds flew;
They leapt—they ran—and when they
       came
Right opposite to Dungeon-Ghyll,
Seeing that he should lose the prize,   40
"Stop!" to his comrade Walter cries—
James stopped with no good will:
Said Walter then, exulting; "Here
You'll find a task for half a year.   44

"Cross, if you dare, where I shall cross—
Come on, and tread where I shall tread."
The other took him at his word,
And followed as he led.
It was a spot which you may see
If ever you to Langdale go;   50
Into a chasm a mighty block
Hath fallen, and made a bridge of rock:
The gulf is deep below;
And, in a basin black and small,
Receives a lofty waterfall.   55

With staff in hand across the cleft
The challenger pursued his march;
And now, all eyes and feet, hath gained
The middle of the arch.
When list! he hears a piteous moan—   60
Again!—his heart within him dies—
His pulse is stopped, his breath is lost,
He totters, pallid as a ghost,
And, looking down, espies
A lamb, that in the pool is pent   65
Within that black and frightful rent.

The lamb had slipped into the stream,
And safe without a bruise or wound
The cataract had borne him down
Into the gulf profound.   70
His dam had seen him when he fell,
She saw him down the torrent borne;
And, while with all a mother's love
She from the lofty rocks above
Sent forth a cry forlorn,   75
The lamb, still swimming round and
       round,
Made answer to that plaintive sound.

When he had learnt what thing it was,
That sent this rueful cry, I ween
The Boy recovered heart, and told   80
The sight which he had seen.
Both gladly now deferred their task;
Nor was there wanting other aid—
A Poet, one who loves the brooks
Far better than the sages' books,   85
By chance had thither strayed;
And there the helpless lamb he found
By those huge rocks encompassed round.

He drew it from the troubled pool,
And brought it forth into the light: 90
The Shepherds met him with his charge,
An unexpected sight!
Into their arms the lamb they took,
Whose life and limbs the flood had spared;
Then up the steep ascent they hied,   95
And placed him at his mother's side;
And gently did the Bard
Those idle Shepherd-boys upbraid,
And bade them better mind their trade.

XII.

ANECDOTE FOR FATHERS.

"Retine vim istam, falsa enim dicam, si coges."
                                    EUSEBIUS.

[Composed 1798.—Published 1798.]

I HAVE a boy of five years old;
His face is fair and fresh to see;
His limbs are cast in beauty's mould,
And dearly he loves me.

One morn we strolled on our dry walk,   5
Our quiet home all full in view,
And held such intermitted talk
As we are wont to do.

My thoughts on former pleasures ran;
I thought of Kilve's delightful shore,   10
Our pleasant home when spring began,
A long, long year before.

A day it was when I could bear
Some fond regrets to entertain;
With so much happiness to spare,   15
I could not feel a pain.

The green earth echoed to the feet
Of lambs that bounded through the glade,
From shade to sunshine, and as fleet
From sunshine back to shade.   20

Birds warbled round me—and each
        trace
Of inward sadness had its charm;
Kilve, thought I, was a favoured place,
And so is Liswyn farm.

My boy beside me tripped, so slim   25
And graceful in his rustic dress!
And, as we talked, I questioned him,
In very idleness.

"Now tell me, had you rather be,"
I said, and took him by the arm,   30
"On Kilve's smooth shore, by the green
        sea,
Or here at Liswyn farm?"

In careless mood he looked at me,
While still I held him by the arm,
And said, "At Kilve I'd rather be   35
Than here at Liswyn farm."

"Now, little Edward, say why so:
My little Edward, tell me why."—
"I cannot tell, I do not know."—
"Why, this is strange," said I;   40

"For here are woods, hills smooth and
        warm:
There surely must some reason be
Why you would change sweet Liswyn
        farm
For Kilve by the green sea."

At this my boy hung down his head,   45
He blushed with shame, nor made
        reply;
And three times to the child I said,
"Why, Edward, tell me why?"

His head he raised—there was in sight,
It caught his eye, he saw it plain—   50
Upon the house-top, glittering bright,
A broad and gilded vane.

Then did the boy his tongue unlock,
And eased his mind with this reply:
"At Kilve there was no weather-cock;   55
And that's the reason why."

O dearest, dearest boy! my heart
For better lore would seldom yearn,
Could I but teach the hundredth part
Of what from thee I learn.   60

XIII.
RURAL ARCHITECTURE.
[Composed (probably) 1800.—Published 1800.]

THERE's George Fisher, Charles Fleming,
        and Reginald Shore,
Three rosy-cheeked school-boys, the high-
        est not more
Than the height of a counsellor's bag;
To the top of GREAT HOW [1] did it please
        them to climb:
And there they built up, without mortar
        or lime,   5
A Man on the peak of the Crag.

They built him of stones gathered up as
        they lay:
They built him and christened him all in
        one day,
An urchin both vigorous and hale;
And so without scruple they called him
        Ralph Jones.   10
Now Ralph is renowned for the length of
        his bones;
The Magog of Legberthwaite dale.

Just half a week after, the wind sallied
        forth,
And, in anger or merriment, out of the
        north,
Coming on with a terrible pother,   15
From the peak of the crag blew the giant
        away.
And what did these school-boys? The
        very next day
They went and they built up another.

—Some little I've seen of blind boisterous
        works
By Christian disturbers more savage than
        Turks,   20
Spirits busy to do and undo:
At remembrance whereof my blood some-
        times will flag;
Then, light-hearted Boys, to the top of
        the crag;
And I'll build up a giant with you.

[1] GREAT HOW is a single and conspicuous hill,
which rises towards the foot of Thirlmere, on the
western side of the beautiful dale of Legber-
thwaite, along the high road between Keswick
and Ambleside.

XIV.

THE PET-LAMB.

A PASTORAL.

[Composed 1800.—Published 1800.]

THE dew was falling fast, the stars began
　to blink;
I heard a voice; it said, "Drink, pretty
　creature, drink!"
And, looking o'er the hedge, before me
　I espied
A snow-white mountain-lamb with a
　Maiden at its side.

Nor sheep nor kine were near; the lamb
　was all alone,　　　　　　　　　　5
And by a slender cord was tethered to a
　stone;
With one knee on the grass did the little
　Maiden kneel,
While to that mountain-lamb she gave
　its evening meal.

The lamb, while from her hand he thus
　his supper took,
Seemed to feast with head and ears; and
　his tail with pleasure shook.　　　10
"Drink, pretty creature, drink," she said
　in such a tone
That I almost received her heart into my
　own.

'Twas little Barbara Lewthwaite, a child
　of beauty rare!
I watched them with delight, they were
　a lovely pair.
Now with her empty can the Maiden
　turned away:　　　　　　　　　　15
But ere ten yards were gone her foot-
　steps did she stay.

Right towards the lamb she looked; and
　from a shady place
I unobserved could see the workings of
　her face:
If Nature to her tongue could measured
　numbers bring,
Thus, thought I, to her lamb that little
　Maid might sing:　　　　　　　　20

"What ails thee, young One? what? Why
　pull so at thy cord?
Is it not well with thee? well both for bed
　and board?
Thy plot of grass is soft, and green as
　grass can be;
Rest, little young One, rest; what is 't
　that aileth thee?

"What is it thou wouldst seek? What is
　wanting to thy heart?　　　　　　25
Thy limbs, are they not strong? And
　beautiful thou art:
This grass is tender grass; these flowers
　they have no peers;
And that green corn all day is rustling
　in thy ears!

"If the sun be shining hot, do but stretch
　thy woollen chain,
This beech is standing by, its covert thou
　canst gain;　　　　　　　　　　30
For rain and mountain-storms! the like
　thou need'st not fear,
The rain and storm are things that
　scarcely can come here.

"Rest, little young One, rest; thou hast
　forgot the day
When my father found thee first in places
　far away;
Many flocks were on the hills, but thou
　wert owned by none,　　　　　　35
And thy mother from thy side for ever-
　more was gone.

"He took thee in his arms, and in pity
　brought thee home:
A blessèd day for thee! then whither
　wouldst thou roam?
A faithful nurse thou hast; the dam that
　did thee yean
Upon the mountain-tops no kinder could
　have been.　　　　　　　　　　40

"Thou know'st that twice a day I have
　brought thee in this can
Fresh water from the brook, as clear as
　ever ran;
And twice in the day, when the ground
　is wet with dew,
I bring thee draughts of milk, warm
　milk it is and new.

"Thy limbs will shortly be twice as stout
　　as they are now,　　　　　　45
Then I'll yoke thee to my cart like a pony
　　in the plough;
My playmate thou shalt be; and when
　　the wind is cold
Our hearth shall be thy bed, our house
　　shall be thy fold.

"It will not, will not rest!—Poor creature,
　　can it be
That 'tis thy mother's heart which is
　　working so in thee?　　　　50
Things that I know not of belike to thee
　　are dear,
And dreams of things which thou canst
　　neither see nor hear.

"Alas, the mountain-tops that look so
　　green and fair!
I've heard of fearful winds and darkness
　　that come there;
The little brooks that seem all pastime
　　and all play,　　　　　　55
When they are angry, roar like lions for
　　their prey.

"Here thou need'st not dread the raven in
　　the sky;
Night and day thou art safe,—our cottage
　　is hard by.
Why bleat so after me? Why pull so at
　　thy chain?
Sleep—and at break of day I will come
　　to thee again!"　　　　　60

—As homeward through the lane I went
　　with lazy feet,
This song to myself did I oftentimes
　　repeat;
And it seemed, as I retraced the ballad
　　line by line,
That but half of it was hers, and one half
　　of it was *mine*.

Again, and once again, did I repeat the
　　song;　　　　　　　65
"Nay," said I, "more than half to the
　　damsel must belong,
For she looked with such a look, and she
　　spake with such a tone,
That I almost received her heart into my
　　own."

XV.

TO H. C.

SIX YEARS OLD.

[Composed 1802.—Published 1807.]

O THOU! whose fancies from afar are
　　brought;
Who of thy words dost make a mock
　　apparel,
And fittest to unutterable thought
The breeze-like motion and the self-born
　　carol;
Thou faery voyager! that dost float　　5
In such clear water, that thy boat
May rather seem
To brood on air than on an earthly
　　stream;
Suspended in a stream as clear as sky,
Where earth and heaven do make one
　　imagery;　　　　　　10
O blessèd vision! happy child!
Thou art so exquisitely wild,
I think of thee with many fears
For what may be thy lot in future years.

I thought of times when Pain might
　　be thy guest,　　　　　15
Lord of thy house and hospitality;
And Grief, uneasy lover! never rest
But when she sate within the touch of
　　thee.
O too industrious folly!
O vain and causeless melancholy!　　20
Nature will either end thee quite;
Or, lengthening out thy season of delight,
Preserve for thee, by individual right,
A young lamb's heart among the full-
　　grown flocks.
What hast thou to do with sorrow,　　25
Or the injuries of to-morrow?
Thou art a dew-drop, which the morn
　　brings forth,
Ill fitted to sustain unkindly shocks,
Or to be trailed along the soiling earth;
A gem that glitters while it lives,　　30
And no forewarning gives;
But, at the touch of wrong, without a
　　strife
Slips in a moment out of life.

XVI.

INFLUENCE OF NATURAL OBJECTS

IN CALLING FORTH AND STRENGTHENING
THE IMAGINATION IN BOYHOOD AND
EARLY YOUTH.

[Composed 1798-9.—Published in *The Friend*,
Dec. 28, 1809; ed. 1815.]

FROM AN UNPUBLISHED POEM.

[This extract is reprinted from *The Friend*.]

WISDOM and Spirit of the universe!
Thou Soul, that art the Eternity of
   thought!
And giv'st to forms and images a breath
And everlasting motion! not in vain,
By day or star-light, thus from my first
   dawn   5
Of childhood didst thou intertwine for me
The passions that build up our human
   soul;
Not with the mean and vulgar works
   of Man;
But with high objects, with enduring
   things,
With life and nature; purifying thus   10
The elements of feeling and of thought,
And sanctifying by such discipline
Both pain and fear,—until we recognise
A grandeur in the beatings of the heart.

Nor was this fellowship vouchsafed
   to me   15
With stinted kindness. In November
   days,
When vapours rolling down the valleys
   made
A lonely scene more lonesome; among
   woods
At noon; and 'mid the calm of summer
   nights,
When, by the margin of the trembling
   lake,   20
Beneath the gloomy hills, homeward I
   went
In solitude, such intercourse was mine:
Mine was it in the fields both day and
   night,
And by the waters, all the summer long.

And in the frosty season, when the sun 25
Was set, and, visible for many a mile,
The cottage-windows through the twilight
   blazed,
I heeded not the summons: happy time
It was indeed for all of us; for me
It was a time of rapture! Clear and
   loud
The village-clock tolled six—I wheeled
   about,   31
Proud and exulting like an untired horse
That cares not for his home.—All shod
   with steel
We hissed along the polished ice, in
   games
Confederate, imitative of the chase   35
And woodland pleasures,—the resound-
   ing horn,
The pack loud-chiming, and the hunted
   hare.
So through the darkness and the cold we
   flew,
And not a voice was idle: with the din
Smitten, the precipices rang aloud;   40
The leafless trees and every icy crag
Tinkled like iron; while far-distant hills
Into the tumult sent an alien sound
Of melancholy, not unnoticed while the
   stars,
Eastward, were sparkling clear, and in
   the west   45
The orange sky of evening died away.

Not seldom from the uproar I retired
Into a silent bay, or sportively
Glanced sideway, leaving the tumultuous
   throng,
To cut across the reflex of a star;   50
Image that, flying still before me, gleamed
Upon the glassy plain: and oftentimes,
When we had given our bodies to the
   wind,
And all the shadowy banks on either side
Came sweeping through the darkness,
   spinning still   55
The rapid line of motion, then at once
Have I, reclining back upon my heels,
Stopped short; yet still the solitary cliffs
Wheeled by me—even as if the earth had
   rolled
With visible motion her diurnal round! 60

Behind me did they stretch in solemn
    train,
Feebler and feebler, and I stood and
    watched
Till all was tranquil as a summer sea.

XVII.

THE LONGEST DAY.

ADDRESSED TO MY DAUGHTER, DORA.

[Composed 1817.—Published 1820.]

LET us quit the leafy arbour,
And the torrent murmuring by ;
For the sun is in his harbour,
Weary of the open sky.

Evening now unbinds the fetters   5
Fashioned by the glowing light ;
All that breathe are thankful debtors
To the harbinger of night.

Yet by some grave thoughts attended
Eve renews her calm career ;   10
For the day that now is ended
Is the longest of the year.

Dora ! sport, as now thou sportest,
On this platform, light and free ;
Take thy bliss, while longest, shortest,   15
Are indifferent to thee !

Who would check the happy feeling
That inspires the linnet's song ?
Who would stop the swallow, wheeling
On her pinions swift and strong ?   20

Yet, at this impressive season,
Words which tenderness can speak
From the truths of homely reason
Might exalt the loveliest cheek ;

And, while shades to shades succeeding   25
Steal the landscape from the sight,
I would urge this moral pleading,
Last forerunner of "Good night !"

SUMMER ebbs ;—each day that follows
Is a reflux from on high,   30
Tending to the darksome hollows
Where the frosts of winter lie.

He who governs the creation,
In his providence, assigned
Such a gradual declination   35
To the life of human kind.

Yet we mark it not ;—fruits redden,
Fresh flowers blow as flowers have blown,
And the heart is loth to deaden
Hopes that she so long hath known.   40

Be thou wiser, youthful Maiden !
And when thy decline shall come,
Let not flowers, or boughs fruit-laden,
Hide the knowledge of thy doom.

Now, even now, ere wrapped in slumber,
Fix thine eyes upon the sea   46
That absorbs time, space, and number ;
Look thou to Eternity !

Follow thou the flowing river
On whose breast are thither borne   50
All deceived, and each deceiver,
Through the gates of night and morn ;

Through the year's successive portals ;
Through the bounds which many a star
Marks, not mindless of frail mortals,   55
When his light returns from far.

Thus when thou with Time hast travelled
Toward the mighty gulf of things,
And the mazy stream unravelled
With thy best imaginings ;   60

Think, if thou on beauty leanest,
Think how pitiful that stay,
Did not virtue give the meanest
Charms superior to decay.

Duty, like a strict preceptor,   65
Sometimes frowns, or seems to frown ;
Choose her thistle for thy sceptre,
While youth's roses are thy crown.

Grasp it,—if thou shrink and tremble,
Fairest damsel of the green,   70
Thou wilt lack the only symbol
That proclaims a genuine queen ;

And ensures those palms of honour
Which selected spirits wear,
Bending low before the Donor,   75
Lord of heaven's unchanging year !

XVIII.

THE NORMAN BOY.

[Composed ?.—Published 1842.]

HIGH on a broad unfertile tract of forest-
    skirted Down,
Nor kept by Nature for herself, nor made
    by man his own,
From home and company remote and
    every playful joy,
Served, tending a few sheep and goats,
    a ragged Norman Boy.

Him never saw I, nor the spot; but from
    an English Dame,   5
Stranger to me and yet my friend, a
    simple notice came,
With suit that I would speak in verse of
    that sequestered child
Whom, one bleak winter's day, she met
    upon the dreary Wild.

His flock, along the woodland's edge with
    relics sprinkled o'er
Of last night's snow, beneath a sky threat-
    ening the fall of more,   10
Where tufts of herbage tempted each,
    were busy at their feed,
And the poor Boy was busier still, with
    work of anxious heed.

There *was* he, where of branches rent and
    withered and decayed,
For covert from the keen north wind, his
    hands a hut had made.
A tiny tenement, forsooth, and frail, as
    needs must be   15
A thing of such materials framed, by a
    builder such as he.

The hut stood finished by his pains, nor
    seemingly lacked aught
That skill or means of his could add, but
    the architect had wrought
Some limber twigs into a Cross, well-
    shaped with fingers nice,
To be engrafted on the top of his small
    edifice.   20

That Cross he now was fastening there,
    as the surest power and best
For supplying all deficiencies, all wants
    of the rude nest
In which, from burning heat, or tempest
    driving far and wide,
The innocent Boy, else shelterless, his
    lonely head must hide.

That Cross belike he also raised as a
    standard for the true   25
And faithful service of his heart in the
    worst that might ensue
Of hardship and distressful fear, amid the
    houseless waste
Where he, in his poor self so weak, by
    Providence was placed.

—Here, Lady! might I cease; but nay,
    let *us* before we part
With this dear holy shepherd-boy breathe
    a prayer of earnest heart,   30
That unto him, where'er shall lie his life's
    appointed way,
The Cross, fixed in his soul, may prove an
    all-sufficing stay.

XIX.

THE POET'S DREAM.

SEQUEL TO "THE NORMAN BOY."

[Composed ?.—Published 1842.]

JUST as those final words were penned,
    the sun broke out in power,
And gladdened all things; but, as chanced,
    within that very hour,
Air blackened, thunder growled, fire
    flashed from clouds that hid the
    sky,
And for the Subject of my Verse I heaved
    a pensive sigh.

Nor could my heart by second thoughts
    from heaviness be cleared,   5
For bodied forth before my eyes the cross-
    crowned hut appeared;
And while around it storm as fierce
    seemed troubling earth and air,
I saw, within, the Norman Boy kneeling
    alone in prayer.

The Child, as if the thunder's voice spake
   with articulate call,
Bowed meekly in submissive fear, before
   the Lord of All;   10
His lips were moving; and his eyes, up-
   raised to sue for grace,
With soft illumination cheered the dim-
   ness of that place.

How beautiful is holiness!—what wonder
   if the sight,
Almost as vivid as a dream, produced a
   dream at night?
It came with sleep and showed the Boy,
   no cherub, not transformed,   15
But the poor ragged Thing whose ways
   my human heart had warmed.

Me had the dream equipped with wings,
   so I took him in my arms,
And lifted from the grassy floor, stilling
   his faint alarms,
And bore him high through yielding air
   my debt of love to pay,
By giving him, for both our sakes, an
   hour of holiday.   20

I whispered, "Yet a little while, dear
   Child! thou art my own,
To show thee some delightful thing, in
   country or in town.
What shall it be? a mirthful throng? or
   that holy place and calm
St. Denis, filled with royal tombs, or the
   Church of Notre Dame?

"St. Ouen's golden Shrine? Or choose
   what else would please thee most
Of any wonder Normandy, or all proud
   France, can boast!"   26
"My Mother," said the Boy, "was born
   near to a blessèd Tree,
The Chapel Oak of Allonville; good
   Angel, show it me!"

On wings from broad and steadfast poise
   let loose by this reply,
For Allonville, o'er down and dale, away
   then did we fly;   30
O'er town and tower we fled, and fields
   in May's fresh verdure drest;
The wings they did not flag; the Child,
   though grave, was not deprest.

But who shall show, to waking sense, the
   gleam of light that broke
Forth from his eyes, when first the Boy
   looked down on that huge oak,
For length of days so much revered, so
   famous where it stands   35
For twofold hallowing—Nature's care,
   and work of human hands?

Strong as an Eagle with my charge I
   glided round and round
The wide-spread boughs, for view of door,
   window, and stair that wound
Gracefully up the gnarled trunk; nor
   left we unsurveyed
The pointed steeple peering forth from
   the centre of the shade.   40

I lighted—opened with soft touch the
   chapel's iron door,
Past softly, leading in the Boy; and
   while from roof to floor,
From floor to roof, all round his eyes the
   Child with wonder cast,
Pleasure on pleasure crowded in, each
   livelier than the last.

For, deftly framed within the trunk, the
   sanctuary showed,   45
By light of lamp and precious stones,
   that glimmered here, there glowed,
Shrine, Altar, Image, Offerings hung in
   sign of gratitude;
Sight that inspired accordant thoughts;
   and speech I thus renewed:

"Hither the Afflicted come, as thou hast
   heard thy Mother say,
And, kneeling, supplication make to our
   Lady de la Paix;   50
What mournful sighs have here been
   heard, and, when the voice was stopt
By sudden pangs; what bitter tears have
   on this pavement dropt!

"Poor Shepherd of the naked Down, a
   favoured lot is thine,
Far happier lot, dear Boy, than brings
   full many to this shrine;
From body pains and pains of soul thou
   needest no release,   55
Thy hours as they flow on are spent, if
   not in joy in peace.

"Then offer up thy heart to God in
    thankfulness and praise,
Give to Him prayers, and many thoughts,
    in thy most busy days;
And in His sight the fragile Cross, on thy
    small hut, will be
Holy as that which long hath crowned
    the Chapel of this Tree;   60
"Holy as that far seen which crowns the
    sumptuous Church in Rome
Where thousands meet to worship God
    under a mighty Dome;
He sees the bending multitude, He hears
    the choral rites,
Yet, not the less, in children's hymns
    and lonely prayer delights.

"God for His service needeth not proud
    work of human skill;   65
They please Him best who labour most
    to do in peace His will:
So let us strive to live, and to our Spirits
    will be given
Such wings as, when our Saviour calls,
    shall bear us up to heaven."

The Boy no answer made by words, but,
    so earnest was his look,
Sleep fled, and with it fled the dream—
    recorded in this book,   70
Lest all that passed should melt away in
    silence from my mind,
As visions still more bright have done,
    and left no trace behind.

But oh! that Country-man of thine,
    whose eye, loved Child, can see
A pledge of endless bliss in acts of early
    piety,
In verse, which to thy ear might come,
    would treat this simple theme,   75
Nor leave untold our happy flight in that
    adventurous dream.

Alas the dream, to thee, poor Boy! to
    thee from whom it flowed,
Was nothing, scarcely can be aught, yet
    'twas bounteously bestowed,
If I may dare to cherish hope that gentle
    eyes will read
Not loth, and listening Little-ones, heart-
    touched, their fancies feed[1].   80

[1] See Note, p. 897

XX.

THE WESTMORELAND GIRL.

TO MY GRANDCHILDREN.

[Composed June 6, 1845.—Published 1845.]

PART I.

Seek who will delight in fable,
I shall tell you truth. A Lamb
Leapt from this steep bank to follow
'Cross the brook its thoughtless dam.

Far and wide on hill and valley   5
Rain had fallen, unceasing rain,
And the bleating mother's Young-one
Struggled with the flood in vain:

But, as chanced, a Cottage-maiden
(Ten years scarcely had she told)   10
Seeing, plunged into the torrent,
Clasped the Lamb and kept her hold.

Whirled adown the rocky channel,
Sinking, rising, on they go,
Peace and rest, as seems, before them   15
Only in the lake below.

Oh! it was a frightful current
Whose fierce wrath the Girl had braved;
Clap your hands with joy my Hearers,
Shout in triumph, both are saved;   20

Saved by courage that with danger
Grew, by strength the gift of love,
And belike a guardian angel
Came with succour from above.

PART II.

Now, to a maturer Audience,   25
Let me speak of this brave Child
Left among her native mountains
With wild Nature to run wild.

So, unwatched by love maternal,
Mother's care no more her guide,   30
Fared this little bright-eyed Orphan
Even while at her father's side.

Spare your blame,—remembrance makes
    him
Loth to rule by strict command;
Still upon her cheek are living   35
Touches of her infant hand,

Dear caresses given in pity,
Sympathy that soothed his grief,
As the dying mother witnessed
To her thankful mind's relief.   40

Time passed on ; the Child was happy,
Like a Spirit of air she moved,
Wayward, yet by all who knew her
For her tender heart beloved.

Scarcely less than sacred passions,   45
Bred in house, in grove, and field,
Link her with the inferior creatures,
Urge her powers their rights to shield.

Anglers, bent on reckless pastime,
Learn how she can feel alike   50
Both for tiny harmless minnow
And the fierce sharp-toothed pike.

Merciful protectress, kindling
Into anger or disdain ;
Many a captive hath she rescued,   55
Others saved from lingering pain.

Listen yet awhile ;—with patience
Hear the homely truths I tell,
She in Grasmere's old church-steeple
Tolled this day the passing bell.   60

Now, the wild Girl of the mountains
To their echoes gave the sound,
Notice punctual as the minute,
Warning solemn and profound.

She, fulfilling her sire's office,   65
Rang alone the far-heard knell,
Tribute, by her hand, in sorrow,
Paid to One who loved her well.

When his spirit was departed,
On that service she went forth ;   70
Nor will fail the like to render
When his corse is laid in earth.

What then wants the Child to temper,
In her breast, unruly fire,
To control the froward impulse   75
And restrain the vague desire ?

Easily a pious training
And a steadfast outward power
Would supplant the weeds, and cherish
In their stead each opening flower.   80

Thus the fearless Lamb-deliv'rer,
Woman-grown, meek-hearted, sage,
May become a blest example
For her sex, of every age.

Watchful as a wheeling eagle,   85
Constant as a soaring lark,
Should the country need a heroine,
She might prove our Maid of Arc.

Leave that thought ; and here be uttered
Prayer that Grace divine may raise   90
Her humane courageous spirit
Up to heaven, thro' peaceful ways.

POEMS FOUNDED ON THE AFFECTIONS.

I.

THE BROTHERS.

[Composed (in or about) February, 1800.—Published 1800.]

"THESE Tourists, heaven preserve us!
needs must live
A profitable life: some glance along,
Rapid and gay, as if the earth were air,
And they were butterflies to wheel about
Long as the summer lasted: some, as
wise,   5
Perched on the forehead of a jutting crag,
Pencil in hand and book upon the knee,
Will look and scribble, scribble on and
look,
Until a man might travel twelve stout
miles,
Or reap an acre of his neighbour's corn. 10
But, for that moping Son of Idleness,
Why can he tarry *yonder?*—In our church-
yard
Is neither epitaph nor monument,
Tombstone nor name—only the turf we
tread
And a few natural graves."

                        To Jane, his wife,
Thus spake the homely Priest of Enner-
dale.   16
It was a July evening; and he sate
Upon the long stone-seat beneath the
eaves
Of his old cottage,—as it chanced, that
day,
Employed in winter's work. Upon the
stone   20
His wife sate near him, teasing matted
wool,
While, from the twin cards toothed with
glittering wire,

He fed the spindle of his youngest child,
Who, in the open air, with due accord
Of busy hands and back-and-forward
steps,   25
Her large round wheel was turning. To-
wards the field
In which the Parish Chapel stood alone,
Girt round with a bare ring of mossy
wall,
While half an hour went by, the Priest
had sent
Many a long look of wonder: and at last,
Risen from his seat, beside the snow-white
ridge   31
Of carded wool which the old man had
piled
He laid his implements with gentle care,
Each in the other locked; and down the
path,
That from his cottage to the church-yard
led,   35
He took his way, impatient to accost
The Stranger, whom he saw still lingering
there.

'Twas one well known to him in former
days,
A Shepherd-lad; who ere his sixteenth
year
Had left that calling, tempted to entrust
His expectations to the fickle winds   41
And perilous waters; with the mariners
A fellow-mariner; and so had fared
Through twenty seasons; but he had been
reared   44
Among the mountains, and he in his heart
Was half a shepherd on the stormy seas.
Oft in the piping shrouds had Leonard
heard
The tones of waterfalls, and inland sounds
Of caves and trees:—and when the regular
wind

Between the tropics filled the steady
    sail,
And blew with the same breath through
    days and weeks,   51
Lengthening invisibly its weary line
Along the cloudless Main, he, in those
    hours
Of tiresome indolence, would often hang
Over the vessel's side, and gaze and
    gaze ;
And, while the broad blue wave and
    sparkling foam   56
Flashed round him images and hues that
    wrought
In union with the employment of his
    heart,
He, thus by feverish passion overcome,
Even with the organs of his bodily eye,
Below him, in the bosom of the deep,   61
Saw mountains ; saw the forms of sheep
    that grazed
On verdant hills—with dwellings among
    trees,
And shepherds clad in the same country
    grey
Which he himself had worn.[1]

             And now, at last,
From perils manifold, with some small
    wealth   66
Acquired by traffic 'mid the Indian
    Isles,
To his paternal home he is returned,
With a determined purpose to resume
The life he had lived there ; both for the
    sake   70
Of many darling pleasures, and the love
Which to an only brother he has borne
In all his hardships, since that happy
    time
When, whether it blew foul or fair, they
    two
Were brother-shepherds on their native
    hills.   75
—They were the last of all their race :
    and now,

[1] This description of the Calenture is sketched
from an imperfect recollection of an admirable
one in prose, by Mr. Gilbert, author of the *Hurricane*.

When Leonard had approached his home,
    his heart
Failed in him ; and, not venturing to
    enquire
Tidings of one so long and dearly loved,
He to the solitary church-yard turned ; 80
That, as he knew in what particular
    spot
His family were laid, he thence might
    learn
If still his Brother lived, or to the file
Another grave was added.—He had found
Another grave,—near which a full half-
    hour   85
He had remained ; but, as he gazed, there
    grew
Such a confusion in his memory,
That he began to doubt ; and even to
    hope
That he had seen this heap of turf be-
    fore,—
That it was not another grave ; but one 90
He had forgotten. He had lost his
    path,
As up the vale, that afternoon, he walked
Through fields which once had been well
    known to him ;
And oh what joy this recollection now
Sent to his heart ! he lifted up his eyes, 95
And, looking round, imagined that he
    saw
Strange alteration wrought on every
    side
Among the woods and fields, and that the
    rocks,
And everlasting hills themselves were
    changed.

By this the Priest, who down the field
    had come,   100
Unseen by Leonard, at the church yard
    gate
Stopped short,—and thence, at leisure,
    limb by limb
Perused him with a gay complacency.
Ay, thought the Vicar, smiling to him-
    self,
'Tis one of those who needs must leave
    the path   105
Of the world's business to go wild alone :
His arms have a perpetual holiday ;

The happy man will creep about the
fields,
Following his fancies by the hour, to
bring
Tears down his cheek, or solitary smiles
Into his face, until the setting sun   111
Write fool upon his forehead.—Planted
thus
Beneath a shed that over-arched the gate
Of this rude church-yard, till the stars
appeared
The good Man might have communed
with himself,   115
But that the Stranger, who had left the
grave,
Approached; he recognised the Priest at
once,
And, after greetings interchanged, and
given
By Leonard to the Vicar as to one
Unknown.to him, this dialogue ensued.
    Leonard. You live, Sir, in these dales,
a quiet life :   121
Your years make up one peaceful family ;
And who would grieve and fret, if, wel-
come come
And welcome gone, they are so like each
other,
They cannot be remembered? Scarce a
funeral   125
Comes to this church-yard once in eighteen
months ;
And yet, some changes must take place
among you :
And you, who dwell here, even among
these rocks,
Can trace the finger of mortality,
And see, that with our threescore years
and ten   130
We are not all that perish.——I re-
member,
(For many years ago I passed this road)
There was a foot-way all along the fields
By the brook-side—'tis gone—and that
dark cleft !
To me it does not seem to wear the
face   135
Which then it had !
    Priest.   Nay, Sir, for aught I know,
That chasm is much the same—
    Leonard.   But, surely, yonder—

    Priest. Ay, there, indeed, your memory
is a friend
That does not play you false.—On that
tall pike
(It is the loneliest place of all these
hills)   140
There were two springs which bubbled
side by side,
As if they had been made that they
might be
Companions for each other : the huge
crag
Was rent with lightning—one hath dis-
appeared ;
The other, left behind, is flowing still. 145
For accidents and changes such as these,
We want not store of them ;—a water-
spout
Will bring down half a mountain ; what
a feast
For folks that wander up and down like
you,
To see an acre's breadth of that wide
cliff   150
One roaring cataract ! a sharp May-
storm
Will come with loads of January snow,
And in one night send twenty score of
sheep
To feed the ravens ; or a shepherd
dies
By some untoward death among the
rocks :   155
The ice breaks up and sweeps away a
bridge ;
A wood is felled :—and then for our own
homes !
A child is born or christened, a field
ploughed,
A daughter sent to service, a web
spun,
The old house-clock is decked with a new
face ;   160
And hence, so far from wanting facts or
dates
To chronicle the time, we all have here
A pair of diaries,—one serving, Sir,
For the whole dale, and one for each
fire-side—
Yours was a stranger's judgment : for
historians,   165

Commend me to these valleys!

Leonard. Yet your Church-yard
Seems, if such freedom may be used with
you,
To say that you are heedless of the past:
An orphan could not find his mother's
grave:
Here's neither head nor foot-stone, plate
of brass,   170
Cross-bones nor skull,—type of our earthly
state
Nor emblem of our hopes: the dead man's
home
Is but a fellow to that pasture-field.

Priest. Why, there, Sir, is a thought
that's new to me!
The stone-cutters, 'tis true, might beg
their bread   175
If every English church-yard were like
ours;
Yet your conclusion wanders from the
truth:
We have no need of names and epitaphs;
We talk about the dead by our fire-sides.
And then, for our immortal part! *we*
want   180
No symbols, Sir, to tell us that plain tale:
The thought of death sits easy on the man
Who has been born and dies among the
mountains.

Leonard. Your Dalesmen, then, do in
each other's thoughts
Possess a kind of second life: no doubt 185
You, Sir, could help me to the history
Of half these graves?

Priest. For eight-score winters past,
With what I've witnessed, and with what
I've heard,
Perhaps I might; and, on a winter-
evening,
If you were seated at my chimney's nook,
By turning o'er these hillocks one by one,
We two could travel, Sir, through a
strange round;   192
Yet all in the broad highway of the world.
Now there's a grave—your foot is half
upon it,—
It looks just like the rest; and yet that
man   195
Died broken-hearted.

Leonard. 'Tis a common case.

We'll take another: who is he that lies
Beneath yon ridge, the last of those three
graves?
It touches on that piece of native rock
Left in the church-yard wall.

Priest. That's Walter Ewbank. 200
He had as white a head and fresh a cheek
As ever were produced by youth and age
Engendering in the blood of hale four-
score.
Through five long generations had the
heart
Of Walter's forefathers o'erflowed the
bounds   205
Of their inheritance, that single cottage—
You see it yonder! and those few green
fields.
They toiled and wrought, and still, from
sire to son,
Each struggled, and each yielded as be-
fore
A little—yet a little,—and old Walter, 210
They left to him the family heart, and
land
With other burthens than the crop it
bore.
Year after year the old man still kept up
A cheerful mind,—and buffeted with bond,
Interest, and mortgages; at last he
sank,   215
And went into his grave before his time.
Poor Walter! whether it was care that
spurred him
God only knows, but to the very last
He had the lightest foot in Ennerdale:
His pace was never that of an old
man: 220
I almost see him tripping down the path
With his two grandsons after him:—but
you,
Unless our Landlord be your host to-
night,
Have far to travel,—and on these rough
paths   224
Even in the longest day of midsummer—

Leonard. But those two Orphans!

Priest. Orphans!—Such they were—
Yet not while Walter lived:—for, though
their parents
Lay buried side by side as now they lie,
The old man was a father to the boys,

Two fathers in one father: and if tears,
Shed when he talked of them where they
    were not,   231
And hauntings from the infirmity of love,
Are aught of what makes up a mother's
    heart,
This old Man, in the day of his old age,
Was half a mother to them.—If you weep,
    Sir,   235
To hear a stranger talking about strangers,
Heaven bless you when you are among
    your kindred !
Ay—you may turn that way—it is a grave
Which will bear looking at.
    Leonard.   These boys—I hope
They loved this good old Man?—
    Priest.   They did—and truly : 240
But that was what we almost overlooked,
They were such darlings of each other.
    Yes,
Though from the cradle they had lived
    with Walter,
The only kinsman near them, and though he
Inclined to both by reason of his age, 245
With a more fond, familiar, tenderness ;
They, notwithstanding, had much love to
    spare,
And it all went into each other's hearts.
Leonard, the elder by just eighteen
    months,
Was two years taller : 'twas a joy to see,
To hear, to meet them !—From their house
    the school   251
Is distant three short miles, and in the
    time
Of storm and thaw, when every water-
    course
And unbridged stream, such as you may
    have noticed
Crossing our roads at every hundred steps,
Was swoln into a noisy rivulet,   256
Would Leonard then, when elder boys
    remained
At home, go staggering through the slip-
    pery fords,
Bearing his brother on his back. I have
    seen him,
On windy days, in one of those stray
    brooks,   260
Ay, more than once I have seen him, mid-
    leg deep,

Their two books lying both on a dry stone,
Upon the hither side : and once I said,
As I remember, looking round these rocks
And hills on which we all of us were
    born,   265
That God who made the great book of the
    world
Would bless such piety—
    Leonard.   It may be then—
    Priest. Never did worthier lads break
    English bread ;
The very brightest Sunday Autumn saw,
With all its mealy clusters of ripe nuts,
Could never keep those boys away from
    church,   271
Or tempt them to an hour of sabbath
    breach.
Leonard and James ! I warrant, every
    corner
Among these rocks, and every hollow
    place
That venturous foot could reach, to one or
    both   275
Was known as well as to the flowers that
    grow there.
Like roe-bucks they went bounding o'er
    the hills ;
They played like two young ravens on the
    crags :
Then they could write, ay, and speak too,
    as well
As many of their betters—and for Leonard!
The very night before he went away, 281
In my own house I put into his hand
A Bible, and I'd wager house and field
That, if he be alive, he has it yet.
    Leonard. It seems, these Brothers have
    not lived to be   285
A comfort to each other—
    Priest.   That they might
Live to such end is what both old and
    young
In this our valley all of us have wished,
And what, for my part, I have often
    prayed :
But Leonard—
    Leonard.   Then James still is left
    among you !   290
    Priest. 'Tis of the elder brother I am
    speaking :
They had an uncle ;—he was at that time

A thriving man, and trafficked on the
  seas:
And, but for that same uncle, to this hour
Leonard had never handled rope or
  shroud: 295
For the boy loved the life which we lead
  here;
And though of unripe years, a stripling
  only,
His soul was knit to this his native soil.
But, as I said, old Walter was too weak
To strive with such a torrent; when he
  died,   300
The estate and house were sold; and all
  their sheep,
A pretty flock, and which, for aught I
  know,
Had clothed the Ewbanks for a thousand
  years:—
Well—all was gone, and they were desti-
  tute,
And Leonard, chiefly for his Brother's
  sake,   305
Resolved to try his fortune on the seas.
Twelve years are past since we had tid-
  ings from him.
If there were one among us who had heard
That Leonard Ewbank was come home
  again,
From the Great Gavel,[1] down by Leeza's
  banks,   310
And down the Enna, far as Egremont,
The day would be a joyous festival;
And those two bells of ours, which there
  you see—
Hanging in the open air—but, O good Sir!
This is sad talk—they 'll never sound for
  him—   315
Living or dead.—When last we heard of
  him,
He was in slavery among the Moors

---

[1] The Great Gavel, so called, I imagine, from
its resemblance to the gable end of a house, is
one of the highest of the Cumberland mountains.
It stands at the head of the several vales of
Ennerdale, Wastdale, and Borrowdale.

  The Leeza is a river which flows into the Lake
of Ennerdale: on issuing from the Lake, it
changes its name, and is called the End, Eyne,
or Enna. It falls into the sea a little below
Egremont.

Upon the Barbary coast.—'Twas not a
  little
That would bring down his spirit; and no
  doubt,
Before it ended in his death, the Youth 320
Was sadly crossed.—Poor Leonard! when
  we parted,
He took me by the hand, and said to me,
If e'er he should grow rich, he would
  return,
To live in peace upon his father's land,
And lay his bones among us.
  Leonard.   If that day 325
Should come, 'twould needs be a glad day
  for him;
He would himself, no doubt, be happy then
As any that should meet him—
  Priest.   Happy! Sir—
  Leonard. You said his kindred all were
  in their graves,
And that he had one Brother—
  Priest.   That is but 330
A fellow-tale of sorrow. From his youth
James, though not sickly, yet was delicate;
And Leonard being always by his side
Had done so many offices about him,
That, though he was not of a timid
  nature,   335
Yet still the spirit of a mountain-boy
In him was somewhat checked; and, when
  his Brother
Was gone to sea, and he was left alone,
The little colour that he had was soon
Stolen from his cheek; he drooped, and
  pined, and pined—   340
  Leonard. But these are all the graves of
  full-grown men!
  Priest. Ay, Sir, that passed away: we
  took him to us;
He was the child of all the dale—he lived
Three months with one, and six months
  with another;
And wanted neither food, nor clothes,
  nor love: 345
And many, many happy days were his.
But, whether blithe or sad, 'tis my belief
His absent Brother still was at his heart.
And, when he dwelt beneath our roof, we
  found
(A practice till this time unknown to
  him)   350

That often, rising from his bed at night,
He in his sleep would walk about, and
   sleeping
He sought his brother Leonard.—You are
   moved!
Forgive me, Sir: before I spoke to you,
I judged you most unkindly.
  Leonard.   But this Youth, 355
How did he die at last?
  Priest.   One sweet May-morning,
(It will be twelve years since when Spring
   returns)
He had gone forth among the new-dropped
   lambs,
With two or three companions, whom
   their course   359
Of occupation led from height to height
Under a cloudless sun—till he, at length,
Through weariness, or, haply, to indulge
The humour of the moment, lagged be-
   hind.
You see yon precipice;—it wears the shape
Of a vast building made of many crags;
And in the midst is one particular
   rock   366
That rises like a column from the vale,
Whence by our shepherds it is called THE
   PILLAR.
Upon its aëry summit crowned with
   heath,
The loiterer, not unnoticed by his com-
   rades,   370
Lay stretched at ease; but, passing by
   the place
On their return, they found that he was
   gone.
No ill was feared; till one of them by
   chance
Entering, when evening was far spent, the
   house
Which at that time was James's home,
   there learned   375
That nobody had seen him all that day:
The morning came, and still he was un-
   heard of:
The neighbours were alarmed, and to the
   brook
Some hastened; some ran to the lake:
   ere noón
They found him at the foot of that same
   rock   380

Dead, and with mangled limbs. The third
   day after
I buried him, poor Youth, and there he
   lies!
  Leonard. And that then *is* his grave!—
   Before his death
You say that he saw many happy years?
  Priest. Ay, that he did—
  Leonard. And all went well with him?—
  Priest. If he had one, the Youth had
   twenty homes.   386
  Leonard. And you believe, then, that
   his mind was easy?—
  Priest. Yes, long before he died, he
   found that time
Is a true friend to sorrow; and, unless
His thoughts were turned on Leonard's
   luckless fortune,   390
He talked about him with a cheerful love.
  Leonard. He could not come to an un-
   hallowed end!
  Priest. Nay, God forbid!—You recollect
   I mentioned
A habit which disquietude and grief
Had brought upon him; and we all con-
   jectured   395
That, as the day was warm, he had lain
   down
On the soft heath,—and, waiting for his
   comrades,
He there had fallen asleep; that in his
   sleep
He to the margin of the precipice
Had walked, and from the summit had
   fallen headlong: 400
And so no doubt he perished. When the
   Youth
Fell, in his hand he must have grasped,
   we think,
His shepherd's staff; for on that Pillar of
   rock
It had been caught mid-way; and there
   for years
It hung;—and mouldered there.

             The Priest here ended—
The Stranger would have thanked him,
   but he felt   406
A gushing from his heart, that took away
The power of speech. Both left the spot
   in silence;

And Leonard, when they reached the
   church-yard gate,
As the Priest lifted up the latch, turned
   round,—   410
And, looking at the grave, he said, "My
   Brother!"
The Vicar did not hear the words: and
   now
He pointed towards his dwelling-place,
   entreating
That Leonard would partake his homely
   fare:
The other thanked him with an earnest
   voice;   415
But added, that, the evening being calm,
He would pursue his journey. So they
   parted.

  It was not long ere Leonard reached a
   grove
That overhung the road: he there stopped
   short,
And, sitting down beneath the trees,
   reviewed   420
All that the Priest had said: his early
   years
Were with him:—his long absence, che-
   rished hopes,
And thoughts which had been his an hour
   before,
All pressed on him with such a weight,
   that now,
This vale, where he had been so happy,
   seemed   425
A place in which he could not bear to
   live:
So he relinquished all his purposes.
He travelled back to Egremont: and
   thence,
That night, he wrote a letter to the
   Priest,
Reminding him of what had passed be-
   tween them;   430
And adding, with a hope to be forgiven,
That it was from the weakness of his
   heart
He had not dared to tell him who he
   was.
This done, he went on shipboard, and is
   now
A seaman, a grey-headed Mariner.   435

II.

ARTEGAL AND ELIDURE.

(SEE THE CHRONICLE OF GEOFFREY OF
MONMOUTH, AND MILTON'S HISTORY
OF ENGLAND.)

[Composed 1815.—Published 1820.]

WHERE be the temples which in Britain's
   Isle,
For his paternal Gods, the Trojan raised?
Gone like a morning dream, or like a pile
Of clouds that in cerulean ether blazed!
Ere Julius landed on her white-cliffed
   shore,   5
  They sank, delivered o'er
To fatal dissolution; and, I ween,
No vestige then was left that such had
   ever been.

Nathless, a British record (long concealed
In old Armorica, whose secret springs 10
No Gothic conqueror ever drank) revealed
The marvellous current of forgotten things;
How Brutus came, by oracles impelled,
  And Albion's giants quelled,
A brood whom no civility could melt, 15
"Who never tasted grace, and goodness
   ne'er had felt."

By brave Corineus aided, he subdued,
And rooted out the intolerable kind;
And this too-long-polluted land imbued
With goodly arts and usages refined; 20
Whence golden harvests, cities, warlike
   towers,
  And pleasure's sumptuous bowers;
Whence all the fixed delights of house
   and home,
Friendships that will not break, and love
   that cannot roam.

O, happy Britain! region all too fair 25
For self-delighting fancy to endure
That silence only should inhabit there,
Wild beasts, or uncouth savages impure!
But, intermingled with the generous seed,
  Grew many a poisonous weed; 30
Thus fares it still with all that takes its
   birth
From human care, or grows upon the
   breast of earth.

Hence, and how soon! that war of ven-
geance waged
By Guendolen against her faithless lord;
Till she, in jealous fury unassuaged, 35
Had slain his paramour with ruthless
sword:
Then into Severn hideously defiled,
  She flung her blameless child,
Sabrina,—vowing that the stream should
bear
That name through every age, her hatred
to declare. 40

So speaks the Chronicle, and tells of Lear
By his ungrateful daughters turned adrift.
Ye lightnings, hear his voice!—they can-
not hear,
Nor can the winds restore his simple gift.
But One there is, a Child of nature meek,
  Who comes her Sire to seek; 46
And he, recovering sense, upon her breast
Leans smilingly, and sinks into a perfect
rest.

There too we read of Spenser's fairy
themes,
And those that Milton loved in youthful
years; 50
The sage enchanter Merlin's subtle schemes;
The feats of Arthur and his knightly peers;
Of Arthur,—who, to upper light restored,
  With that terrific sword
Which yet he brandishes for future war,
Shall lift his country's fame above the
polar star! 56

What wonder, then, if in such ample field
Of old tradition, one particular flower
Doth seemingly in vain its fragrance yield,
And bloom unnoticed even to this late hour?
Now, gentle Muses, your assistance grant,
  While I this flower transplant 62
Into a garden stored with Poesy;
Where flowers and herbs unite, and haply
some weeds be,
That, wanting not wild grace, are from
all mischief free! 65

A KING more worthy of respect and love
Than wise Gorbonian ruled not in his day;
And grateful Britain prospered far above
All neighbouring countries through his
righteous sway;

He poured rewards and honours on the
good; 70
  The oppressor he withstood;
And while he served the Gods with reve-
rence due,
Fields smiled, and temples rose, and towns
and cities grew.

He died, whom Artegal succeeds—his son;
But how unworthy of that sire was he! 75
A hopeful reign, auspiciously begun,
Was darkened soon by foul iniquity.
From crime to crime he mounted, till at
length
  The nobles leagued their strength
With a vexed people, and the tyrant
chased; 80
And on the vacant throne his worthier
Brother placed.

From realm to realm the humbled Exile
went,
Suppliant for aid his kingdom to regain;
In many a court, and many a warrior's
tent,
He urged his persevering suit in vain. 85
Him, in whose wretched heart ambition
failed,
  Dire poverty assailed;
And, tired with slights his pride no more
could brook,
He towards his native country cast a
longing look.

Fair blew the wished-for wind—the voyage
sped; 90
He landed; and by many dangers scared,
"Poorly provided, poorly followèd,"
To Calaterium's forest he repaired.
How changed from him who, born to
highest place,
  Had swayed the royal mace, 95
Flattered and feared, despised yet deified,
In Troynovant, his seat by silver Thames's
side!

From that wild region where the crown-
less king
Lay in concealment with his scanty train,
Supporting life by water from the spring,
And such chance food as outlaws can
obtain, 101

Unto the few whom he esteems his friends
   A messenger he sends;
And from their secret loyalty requires
Shelter and daily bread,—the sum of his
   desires.   105

While he the issue waits, at early morn
Wandering by stealth abroad, he chanced
   to hear
A startling outcry made by hound and
   horn,
From which the tusky wild boar flies in
   fear;
And, scouring toward him o'er the grassy
   plain,   110
   Behold the hunter train!
He bids his little company advance
With seeming unconcern and steady coun-
   tenance.

The royal Elidure, who leads the chase,
Hath checked his foaming courser:—can
   it be!   115
Methinks that I should recognise that face,
Though much disguised by long adversity!
He gazed rejoicing, and again he gazed,
   Confounded and amazed—
"It is the king, my brother!" and, by
   sound   120
Of his own voice confirmed, he leaps upon
   the ground.

Long, strict, and tender was the embrace
   he gave,
Feebly returned by daunted Artegal;
Whose natural affection doubts enslave,
And apprehensions dark and criminal. 125
Loth to restrain the moving interview,
   The attendant lords withdrew;
And, while they stood upon the plain apart,
Thus Elidure, by words, relieved his
   struggling heart.

"By heavenly Powers conducted, we have
   met;   130
—O Brother! to my knowledge lost so long,
But neither lost to love, nor to regret,
Nor to my wishes lost;—forgive the wrong,
(Such it may seem) if I thy crown have
   borne,
   Thy royal mantle worn: 135

I was their natural guardian; and 'tis just
That now I should restore what hath been
   held in trust."

A while the astonished Artegal stood mute,
Then thus exclaimed: "To me, of titles
   shorn,
And stripped of power! me, feeble, desti-
   tute,   140
To me a kingdom! spare the bitter scorn:
If justice ruled the breast of foreign kings,
   Then, on the wide-spread wings
Of war, had I returned to claim my right;
This will I here avow, not dreading thy
   despite."   145

"I do not blame thee," Elidure replied;
"But, if my looks did with my words
   agree,
I should at once be trusted, not defied,
And thou from all disquietude be free.
May the unsullied Goddess of the chase,
   Who to this blessed place   151
At this blest moment led me, if I speak
With insincere intent, on me her ven-
   geance wreak!

"Were this same spear, which in my hand
   I grasp,
The British sceptre, here would I to thee
The symbol yield; and would undo this
   clasp,   156
If it confined the robe of sovereignty.
Odious to me the pomp of regal court,
   And joyless sylvan sport,
While thou art roving, wretched and
   forlorn,   160
Thy couch the dewy earth, thy roof the
   forest thorn!"

Then Artegal thus spake: "I only sought
Within this realm a place of safe retreat;
Beware of rousing an ambitious thought;
Beware of kindling hopes for me un-
   meet!   165
Thou art reputed wise, but in my mind
   Art pitiably blind:
Full soon this generous purpose thou
   may'st rue,
When that which has been done no wishes
   can undo.

"Who, when a crown is fixed upon his head,
Would balance claim with claim, and right
 with right?   171
But thou—I know not how inspired, how
 led—
Wouldst change the course of things in
 all men's sight!
And this for one who cannot imitate
 Thy virtue, who may hate: 175
For, if, by such strange sacrifice restored,
He reign, thou still must be his king, and
 sovereign lord;

"Lifted in magnanimity above
Aught that my feeble nature could perform,
Or even conceive; surpassing me in love
Far as in power the eagle doth the worm:
I, Brother! only should be king in name,
 And govern to my shame;
A shadow in a hated land, while all
Of glad or willing service to thy share
 would fall."   185

"Believe it not," said Elidure; "respect
Awaits on virtuous life, and ever most
Attends on goodness with dominion
 decked,
Which stands the universal empire's boast;
This can thy own experience testify: 190
 Nor shall thy foes deny
That, in the gracious opening of thy reign,
Our father's spirit seemed in thee to
 breathe again.

"And what if o'er that bright unbosoming
Clouds of disgrace and envious fortune
 past!   195
Have we not seen the glories of the spring
By veil of noontide darkness overcast?
The frith that glittered like a warrior's
 shield,
 The sky, the gay green field,
Are vanished; gladness ceases in the
 groves,   200
And trepidation strikes the blackened
 mountain-coves.

"But is that gloom dissolved? how pass-
 ing clear
Seems the wide world, far brighter than
 before!
Even so thy latent worth will re-appear,

Gladdening the people's heart from shore
 to shore;   205
For youthful faults ripe virtues shall atone;
 Re-seated on thy throne,
Proof shalt thou furnish that misfortune,
 pain,
And sorrow, have confirmed thy native
 right to reign.

"But, not to overlook what thou may'st
 know,   210
Thy enemies are neither weak nor few;
And circumspect must be our course, and
 slow,
Or from my purpose ruin may ensue.
Dismiss thy followers;—let them calmly
 wait
 Such change in thy estate   215
As I already have in thought devised;
And which, with caution due, may soon
 be realized."

The Story tells what courses were pursued,
Until king Elidure, with full consent
Of all his peers, before the multitude, 220
Rose,—and, to consummate this just in-
 tent,
Did place upon his brother's head the
 crown,
 Relinquished by his own;
Then to his people cried, "Receive your
 lord,
Gorbonian's first-born son, your rightful
 king restored!"   225

The people answered with a loud acclaim:
Yet more;—heart-smitten by the heroic
 deed,
The reinstated Artegal became
Earth's noblest penitent; from bondage
 freed
Of vice—thenceforth unable to subvert
 Or shake his high desert.   231
Long did he reign; and, when he died,
 the tear
Of universal grief bedewed his honoured
 bier.

Thus was a Brother by a Brother saved;
With whom a crown (temptation that
 hath set   235
Discord in hearts of men till they have
 braved

Their nearest kin with deadly purpose met)
'Gainst duty weighed, and faithful love,
　　did seem
　A thing of no esteem ;
And, from this triumph of affection pure,
He bore the lasting name of "pious Eli-
　　dure !"　　　　　　　　　　　　241

III.

TO A BUTTERFLY.

[Composed April 20, 1802.—Published 1807.]

I 've watched you now a full half-hour,
Self-poised upon that yellow flower ;
And, little Butterfly ! indeed
I know not if you sleep or feed.
How motionless !—not frozen seas　　5
More motionless ! and then
What joy awaits you, when the breeze
Hath found you out among the trees,
And calls you forth again !

This plot of orchard-ground is ours ;　　10
My trees they are, my Sister's flowers ;
Here rest your wings when they are weary ;
Here lodge as in a sanctuary !
Come often to us, fear no wrong ;
Sit near us on the bough !　　　　　15
We 'll talk of sunshine and of song,
And summer days, when we were young;
Sweet childish days, that were as long
As twenty days are now.

IV.

A FAREWELL.

[Finished May 29, 1802.—Published 1815.]

FAREWELL, thou little Nook of mountain-
　　ground,
Thou rocky corner in the lowest stair
Of that magnificent temple which doth
　　bound
One side of our whole vale with grandeur
　　rare ;
Sweet garden-orchard, eminently fair,　　5
The loveliest spot that man hath ever
　　found,
Farewell !—we leave thee to Heaven's
　　peaceful care,
Thee, and the Cottage which thou dost
　　surround.

Our boat is safely anchored by the shore,
And there will safely ride when we are
　　gone ;　　　　　　　　　　　　10
The flowering shrubs that deck our hum-
　　ble door
Will prosper, though untended and alone :
Fields, goods, and far-off chattels we have
　　none :
These narrow bounds contain our private
　　store
Of things earth makes, and sun doth shine
　　upon ;　　　　　　　　　　　15
Here are they in our sight—we have no
　　more.

Sunshine and shower be with you, bud
　　and bell !
For two months now in vain we shall be
　　sought ;
We leave you here in solitude to dwell
With these our latest gifts of tender
　　thought ;　　　　　　　　　　20
Thou, like the morning, in thy saffron
　　coat,
Bright gowan, and marsh-marigold, fare-
　　well !
Whom from the borders of the Lake we
　　brought,
And placed together near our rocky Well.

We go for One to whom ye will be dear ;
And she will prize this Bower, this Indian
　　shed,　　　　　　　　　　　　26
Our own contrivance, Building without
　　peer !
—A gentle Maid, whose heart is lowly
　　bred,
Whose pleasures are in wild fields gathered,
With joyousness, and with a thoughtful
　　cheer,　　　　　　　　　　　30
Will come to you ; to you herself will wed ;
And love the blessed life that we lead
　　here.

Dear Spot ! which we have watched with
　　tender heed,
Bringing thee chosen plants and blossoms
　　blown
Among the distant mountains, flower and
　　weed,　　　　　　　　　　　35
Which thou hast taken to thee as thy
　　own,

Making all kindness registered and known;
Thou for our sakes, though Nature's child
indeed,
Fair in thyself and beautiful alone,
Hast taken gifts which thou dost little
need.   40

And O most constant, yet most fickle
Place,
That hast thy wayward moods, as thou
dost show
To them who look not daily on thy face;
Who, being loved, in love no bounds dost
know,
And say'st, when we forsake thee, "Let
them go!"   45
Thou easy-hearted Thing, with thy wild
race
Of weeds and flowers, till we return be
slow,
And travel with the year at a soft pace.

Help us to tell Her tales of years gone
by,
And this sweet spring, the best beloved
and best;   50
Joy will be flown in its mortality;
Something must stay to tell us of the
rest.
Here, thronged with primroses, the steep
rock's breast
Glittered at evening like a starry sky;
And in this bush our sparrow built her
nest,   55
Of which I sang one song that will not
die.

O happy Garden! whose seclusion deep
Hath been so friendly to industrious
hours;
And to soft slumbers, that did gently
steep
Our spirits, carrying with them dreams of
flowers,   60
And wild notes warbled among leafy
bowers;
Two burning months let summer over-
leap,
And, coming back with Her who will be
ours,
Into thy bosom we again shall creep.

V.

STANZAS

WRITTEN IN MY POCKET-COPY OF THOMSON'S
"CASTLE OF INDOLENCE."

[Composed May 9-11, 1802.—Published 1815.]

WITHIN our happy Castle there dwelt
One
Whom without blame I may not over-
look;
For never sun on living creature shone
Who more devout enjoyment with us
took:
Here on his hours he hung as on a book, 5
On his own time here would he float
away,
As doth a fly upon a summer brook;
But go to-morrow, or belike to-day,
Seek for him,—he is fled; and whither
none can say.

Thus often would he leave our peaceful
home,   10
And find elsewhere his business or de-
light;
Out of our Valley's limits did he roam:
Full many a time, upon a stormy night,
His voice came to us from the neighbour-
ing height:
Oft could we see him driving full in view
At mid-day when the sun was shining
bright;   16
What ill was on him, what he had to do,
A mighty wonder bred among our quiet
crew.

Ah! piteous sight it was to see this Man
When he came back to us, a withered
flower,—   20
Or like a sinful creature, pale and wan.
Down would he sit; and without strength
or power
Look at the common grass from hour to
hour:
And oftentimes, how long I fear to say,
Where apple-trees in blossom made a
bower,   25
Retired in that sunshiny shade he lay;
And, like a naked Indian, slept himself
away.

Great wonder to our gentle tribe it was
Whenever from our Valley he withdrew;
For happier soul no living creature has   30
Than he had, being here the long day
   through.
Some thought he was a lover, and did
   woo:
Some thought far worse of him, and
   judged him wrong;
But verse was what he had been wedded
   to;
And his own mind did like a tempest
   strong   35
Come to him thus, and drove the weary
   Wight along.

With him there often walked in friendly
   guise,
Or lay upon the moss by brook or tree,
A noticeable Man with large grey eyes,
And a pale face that seemed undoubt-
   edly   40
As if a blooming face it ought to be;
Heavy his low-hung lip did oft appear,
Deprest by weight of musing Phantasy;
Profound his forehead was, though not
   severe;
Yet some did think that he had little
   business here: 45

Sweet heaven forefend! his was a lawful
   right;
Noisy he was, and gamesome as a boy;
His limbs would toss about him with
   delight,
Like branches when strong winds the
   trees annoy.   49
Nor lacked his calmer hours device or toy
To banish listlessness and irksome care;
He would have taught you how you might
   employ
Yourself; and many did to him repair,—
And certes not in vain; he had inven-
   tions rare.

Expedients, too, of simplest sort he tried:
Long blades of grass, plucked round him
   as he lay,   56
Made, to his ear attentively applied,
A pipe on which the wind would deftly
   play;

Glasses he had, that little things display,
The beetle panoplied in gems and gold,   60
A mailèd angel on a battle-day;
The mysteries that cups of flowers enfold,
And all the gorgeous sights which fairies
   do behold.

He would entice that other Man to hear
His music, and to view his imagery: 65
And, sooth, these two were each to the
   other dear:
No livelier love in such a place could be:
There did they dwell—from earthly labour
   free,
As happy spirits as were ever seen;
If but a bird, to keep them company,   70
Or butterfly sate down, they were, I ween,
As pleased as if the same had been a
   Maiden-queen.

VI.

LOUISA[1].

AFTER ACCOMPANYING HER ON A MOUN-
TAIN EXCURSION.

[Composed (probably) 1801.—Published 1807.]

I MET Louisa in the shade,
And, having seen that lovely Maid,
Why should I fear to say
That, nymph-like, she is fleet and strong,
And down the rocks can leap along   5
Like rivulets in May?

[And she hath smiles to earth unknown;
Smiles, that with motion of their own
Do spread, and sink, and rise;
That come and go with endless play,
And ever, as they pass away,
Are hidden in her eyes.[2]]

She loves her fire, her cottage-home;
Yet o'er the moorland will she roam
In weather rough and bleak;   9
And, when against the wind she strains,
Oh! might I kiss the mountain rains
That sparkle on her cheek.

---

[1] On the question of the identity of *Louisa*,
see Editor's note on *To a Butterfly*, p. 897.—ED.

[2] This stanza came second in all edd. from
1807 to 1843. It was most unfortunately omitted
—for some reason unknown to us—in edd. 1845
and 1849.—ED.

Take all that's mine "beneath the moon,"
If I with her but half a noon
May sit beneath the walls   15
Of some old cave, or mossy nook,
When up she winds along the brook
To hunt the waterfalls.

VII.

[Composed 1799.—Published 1800.]

STRANGE fits of passion have I known:
And I will dare to tell,
But in the Lover's ear alone,
What once to me befell.

When she I loved looked every day   5
Fresh as a rose in June,
I to her cottage bent my way,
Beneath an evening-moon.

Upon the moon I fixed my eye,
All over the wide lea;   10
With quickening pace my horse drew nigh
Those paths so dear to me.

And now we reached the orchard-plot;
And, as we climbed the hill,
The sinking moon to Lucy's cot   15
Came near, and nearer still.

In one of those sweet dreams I slept,
Kind Nature's gentlest boon!
And all the while my eyes I kept
On the descending moon.   20

My horse moved on; hoof after hoof
He raised, and never stopped:
When down behind the cottage roof,
At once, the bright moon dropped.

What fond and wayward thoughts will
        slide   25
Into a Lover's head!
"O mercy!" to myself I cried,
"If Lucy should be dead!"

VIII.

[Composed 1799.—Published 1800.]

SHE dwelt among the untrodden ways
    Beside the springs of Dove,
A Maid whom there were none to praise
    And very few to love:

A violet by a mossy stone   5
    Half hidden from the eye!
—Fair as a star, when only one
    Is shining in the sky.

She lived unknown, and few could know
    When Lucy ceased to be;   10
But she is in her grave, and, oh,
    The difference to me!

IX.

[Composed 1801.—Published 1807.]

I TRAVELLED among unknown men,
    In lands beyond the sea;
Nor, England! did I know till then
    What love I bore to thee.

'Tis past, that melancholy dream!   5
    Nor will I quit thy shore
A second time; for still I seem
    To love thee more and more.

Among thy mountains did I feel
    The joy of my desire;   10
And she I cherished turned her wheel
    Beside an English fire.

Thy mornings showed, thy nights con-
        cealed,
    The bowers where Lucy played;
And thine too is the last green field   15
    That Lucy's eyes surveyed.

X.

[Composed 1826.—Published 1827.]

ERE with cold beads of midnight dew
    Had mingled tears of thine,
I grieved, fond Youth! that thou shouldst
        sue
    To haughty Geraldine.

Immoveable by generous sighs,   5
    She glories in a train
Who drag, beneath our native skies,
    An Oriental chain.

Pine not like them with arms across,
    Forgetting in thy care   10
How the fast-rooted trees can toss
    Their branches in mid air.

The humblest rivulet will take
  Its own wild liberties;
And every day the imprisoned lake   15
  Is flowing in the breeze.

Then crouch no more on suppliant knee,
  But scorn with scorn outbrave;
A Briton, even in love, should be
  A subject, not a slave!   20

XI.

TO ——

[Composed 1824.—Published 1827.]

LOOK at the fate of summer flowers,
Which blow at daybreak, droop ere even-
    song;
And, grieved for their brief date, confess
    that ours,
Measured by what we are and ought to be,
Measured by all that, trembling, we fore-
    see,
  Is not so long!   5

If human Life do pass away,
Perishing not more swiftly than the flower,
If we are creatures of a *winter's* day;
What space hath Virgin's beauty to dis-
    close   10
Her sweets, and triumph o'er the breath-
    ing rose?
  Not even an hour!

The deepest grove whose foliage hid
The happiest lovers Arcady might boast,
Could not the entrance of this thought
    forbid: 15
O be thou wise as they, soul-gifted Maid!
Nor rate too high what must so quickly
    fade,
  So soon be lost.

Then shall love teach some virtuous Youth
"To draw, out of the object of his eyes,"   20
The while on thee they gaze in simple
    truth,
Hues more exalted, "a refinèd Form,"
That dreads not age, nor suffers from the
    worm,
  And never dies.

XII.

THE FORSAKEN.

[Dated 1804 (W.).—Probably composed earlier.—
    Published 1842.]

THE peace which others seek they find;
The heaviest storms not longest last;
Heaven grants even to the guiltiest mind
An amnesty for what is past;
When will my sentence be reversed?   5
I only pray to know the worst;
And wish, as if my heart would burst.

O weary struggle! silent years
Tell seemingly no doubtful tale;
And yet they leave it short, and fears   10
And hopes are strong and will prevail.
My calmest faith escapes not pain;
And, feeling that the hope is vain,
I think that he will come again.

XIII.

[Composed 1800.—Published 1800.]

'TIS said that some have died for love:
And here and there a church-yard grave
    is found
In the cold north's unhallowed ground,
Because the wretched man himself had
    slain,
His love was such a grievous pain.   5
And there is one whom I five years have
    known;
He dwells alone
Upon Helvellyn's side:
He loved—the pretty Barbara died;
And thus he makes his moan: 10
Three years had Barbara in her grave
    been laid
When thus his moan he made:

"Oh, move, thou Cottage, from behind
    that oak!
Or let the aged tree uprooted lie,
That in some other way yon smoke   15
May mount into the sky!
The clouds pass on; they from the hea-
    vens depart:
I look—the sky is empty space;
I know not what I trace;
But when I cease to look, my hand is on
    my heart.   20

"O! what a weight is in these shades!
    Ye leaves,
That murmur once so dear, when will it
    cease?
Your sound my heart of rest bereaves,
It robs my heart of peace.
Thou Thrush, that singest loud—and loud
    and free,   25
Into yon row of willows flit,
Upon that alder sit;
Or sing another song, or choose another
    tree.

"Roll back, sweet Rill! back to thy
    mountain-bounds,   29
And there for ever be thy waters chained!
For thou dost haunt the air with sounds
That cannot be sustained;
If still beneath that pine-tree's ragged
    bough
Headlong yon waterfall must come,
Oh let it then be dumb!   35
Be anything, sweet Rill, but that which
    thou art now.

"Thou Eglantine, so bright with sunny
    showers,
Proud as a rainbow spanning half the
    vale,
Thou one fair shrub, oh! shed thy flowers,
And stir not in the gale.   40
For thus to see thee nodding in the air,
To see thy arch thus stretch and bend,
Thus rise and thus descend,—
Disturbs me till the sight is more than I
    can bear."

The Man who makes this feverish com-
    plaint   45
Is one of giant stature, who could dance
Equipped from head to foot in iron
    mail.
Ah gentle Love! if ever thought was
    thine
To store up kindred hours for me, thy
    face
Turn from me, gentle Love! nor let me
    walk   50
Within the sound of Emma's voice, nor
    know
Such happiness as I have known to-day.

XIV.

A COMPLAINT.

[Composed 1806.—Published 1807.]

THERE is a change—and I am poor;
Your love hath been, nor long ago,
A fountain at my fond heart's door,
Whose only business was to flow;
And flow it did; not taking heed   5
Of its own bounty, or my need.

What happy moments did I count!
Blest was I then all bliss above!
Now, for that consecrated fount
Of murmuring, sparkling, living love,   10
What have I? shall I dare to tell?
A comfortless and hidden well.

A well of love—it may be deep—
I trust it is,—and never dry:
What matter? if the waters sleep   15
In silence and obscurity.
—Such change, and at the very door
Of my fond heart, hath made me poor.

XV.

TO ——

[Composed 1824.—Published 1827.]

LET other bards of angels sing,
    Bright suns without a spot;
But thou art no such perfect thing:
    Rejoice that thou art not!

Heed not tho' none should call thee fair;
    So, Mary, let it be   6
If nought in loveliness compare
    With what thou art to me.

True beauty dwells in deep retreats,
    Whose veil is unremoved   10
Till heart with heart in concord beats,
    And the lover is beloved.

XVI.

[Composed ?.—Published 1845.]

YES! thou art fair, yet be not moved
    To scorn the declaration,
That sometimes I in thee have loved
    My fancy's own creation.

Imagination needs must stir;   5
  Dear Maid, this truth believe,
Minds that have nothing to confer
  Find little to perceive.

Be pleased that nature made thee fit
  To feed my heart's devotion,   10
By laws to which all Forms submit
  In sky, air, earth, and ocean.

XVII.

[Composed 1824.—Published 1827.]

How rich that forehead's calm expanse!
How bright that heaven-directed glance!
—Waft her to glory, wingèd Powers,
  Ere sorrow be renewed,
And intercourse with mortal hours   5
  Bring back a humbler mood!
So looked Cecilia when she drew
  An Angel from his station;
So looked; not ceasing to pursue
  Her tuneful adoration!   10

But hand and voice alike are still;
No sound here sweeps away the will
That gave it birth: in service meek
One upright arm sustains the cheek,
And one across the bosom lies—   15
That rose, and now forgets to rise,
Subdued by breathless harmonies
Of meditative feeling;
Mute strains from worlds beyond the
    skies,
Through the pure light of female eyes   20
Their sanctity revealing!

XVIII.

[Composed ?.—Published 1845.]

What heavenly smiles! O Lady mine,
Through my very heart they shine;
And, if my brow gives back their light,
Do thou look gladly on the sight;
As the clear Moon with modest pride   5
  Beholds her own bright beams
Reflected from the mountain's side
  And from the headlong streams.

XIX.
TO ——

[Composed 1824.—Published 1827.]

O DEARER far than light and life are
    dear,
Full oft our human foresight I deplore;
Trembling, through my unworthiness,
    with fear
That friends, by death disjoined, may
    meet no more!

Misgivings, hard to vanquish or control, 5
Mix with the day, and cross the hour of
    rest;
While all the future, for thy purer soul,
With "sober certainties" of love is blest.

That sigh of thine, not meant for human
    ear,
Tells that these words thy humbleness
    offend;   10
Yet bear me up—else faltering in the rear
Of a steep march: support me to the end.

Peace settles where the intellect is meek,
And Love is dutiful in thought and deed;
Through Thee communion with that Love
    I seek: 15
The faith Heaven strengthens where he
    moulds the Creed.

XX.
LAMENT OF MARY QUEEN OF SCOTS

ON THE EVE OF A NEW YEAR.

[Composed 1817.—Published 1820.]

I.

SMILE of the Moon!—for so I name
That silent greeting from above;
A gentle flash of light that came
From her whom drooping captives love;
Or art thou of still higher birth?   5
Thou that didst part the clouds of earth
My torpor to reprove!

II.

Bright boon of pitying Heaven!—alas,
I may not trust thy placid cheer!
Pondering that Time to-night will pass   10
The threshold of another year;

For years to me are sad and dull;
My very moments are too full
Of hopelessness and fear.

III.

And yet the soul-awakening gleam, 15
That struck perchance the farthest cone
Of Scotland's rocky wilds, did seem
To visit me, and me alone;
Me, unapproached by any friend,
Save those who to my sorrows lend 20
Tears due unto their own.

IV.

To-night the church-tower bells will ring
Through these wide realms a festive peal;
To the new year a welcoming;
A tuneful offering for the weal 25
Of happy millions lulled in sleep;
While I am forced to watch and weep,
By wounds that may not heal.

V.

Born all too high, by wedlock raised
Still higher—to be cast thus low! 30
Would that mine eyes had never gazed
On aught of more ambitious show
Than the sweet flowerets of the fields!
—It is my royal state that yields
This bitterness of woe. 35

VI.

Yet how?—for I, if there be truth
In the world's voice, was passing fair;
And beauty, for confiding youth,
Those shocks of passion can prepare
That kill the bloom before its time; 40
And blanch, without the owner's crime,
The most resplendent hair.

VII.

Unblest distinction! showered on me
To bind a lingering life in chains:
All that could quit my grasp, or flee, 45
Is gone;—but not the subtle stains
Fixed in the spirit; for even here
Can I be proud that jealous fear
Of what I was remains.

VIII.

A Woman rules my prison's key; 50
A sister Queen, against the bent
Of law and holiest sympathy,

Detains me, doubtful of the event;
Great God, who feel'st for my distress,
My thoughts are all that I possess, 55
O keep them innocent!

IX.

Farewell desire of human aid,
Which abject mortals vainly court!
By friends deceived, by foes betrayed,
Of fears the prey, of hopes the sport; 60
Nought but the world-redeeming Cross
Is able to supply my loss,
My burthen to support.

X.

Hark! the death-note of the year
Sounded by the castle-clock! 65
From her sunk eyes a stagnant tear
Stole forth, unsettled by the shock;
But oft the woods renewed their green,
Ere the tired head of Scotland's Queen
Reposed upon the block! 70

XXI.

THE COMPLAINT

OF A FORSAKEN INDIAN WOMAN.

[Composed 1798.—Published 1798.]

[When a Northern Indian, from sickness, is un-
able to continue his journey with his com-
panions, he is left behind, covered over with
deer-skins, and is supplied with water, food,
and fuel, if the situation of the place will afford
it. He is informed of the track which his com-
panions intend to pursue, and if he be unable
to follow, or overtake them, he perishes alone
in the desert, unless he should have the good
fortune to fall in with some other tribes of
Indians. The females are equally, or still more,
exposed to the same fate. See that very in-
teresting work Hearne's "Journey from Hud-
son's Bay to the Northern Ocean." In the high
northern latitudes, as the same writer informs
us, when the northern lights vary their position
in the air, they make a rustling and a crackling
noise, as alluded to in the following poem.]

I.

BEFORE I see another day,
Oh let my body die away!
In sleep I heard the northern gleams;
The stars, they were among my dreams;

In rustling conflict through the skies, 5
I heard, I saw the flashes drive,
And yet they are upon my eyes,
And yet I am alive;
Before I see another day,
Oh let my body die away! 10

II.

My fire is dead: it knew no pain;
Yet is it dead, and I remain:
All stiff with ice the ashes lie;
And they are dead, and I will die.
When I was well, I wished to live, 15
For clothes, for warmth, for food, and fire;
But they to me no joy can give,
No pleasure now, and no desire.
Then here contented will I lie!
Alone, I cannot fear to die. 20

III.

Alas! ye might have dragged me on
Another day, a single one!
Too soon I yielded to despair;
Why did ye listen to my prayer?
When ye were gone my limbs were
　　stronger; 25
And ye how grievously I rue
That, afterwards, a little longer,
My friends, I did not follow you!
For strong and without pain I lay,
Dear friends, when ye were gone away. 30

IV.

My Child! they gave thee to another,
A woman who was not thy mother.
When from my arms my Babe they took,
On me how strangely did he look!
Through his whole body something ran,
A most strange working did I see; 36
—As if he strove to be a man,
That he might pull the sledge for me:
And then he stretched his arms, how wild!
Oh mercy! like a helpless child. 40

V.

My little joy! my little pride!
In two days more I must have died.
Then do not weep and grieve for me;
I feel I must have died with thee.
O wind, that o'er my head art flying 45

The way my friends their course did bend,
I should not feel the pain of dying,
Could I with thee a message send;
Too soon, my friends, ye went away;
For I had many things to say. 50

VI.

I'll follow you across the snow;
Ye travel heavily and slow;
In spite of all my weary pain
I'll look upon your tents again.
—My fire is dead, and snowy white 55
The water which beside it stood:
The wolf has come to me to-night,
And he has stolen away my food.
For ever left alone am I;
Then wherefore should I fear to die? 60

VII.

Young as I am, my course is run,
I shall not see another sun;
I cannot lift my limbs to know
If they have any life or no.
My poor forsaken Child, if I 65
For once could have thee close to me,
With happy heart I then would die,
And my last thought would happy be;
But thou, dear Babe, art far away,
Nor shall I see another day. 70

XXII.

THE LAST OF THE FLOCK.

[Composed 1798.—Published 1798.]

I.

In distant countries have I been,
And yet I have not often seen
A healthy man, a man full grown,
Weep in the public roads, alone.
But such a one, on English ground, 5
And in the broad highway, I met;
Along the broad highway he came,
His cheeks with tears were wet:
Sturdy he seemed, though he was sad;
And in his arms a Lamb he had. 10

II.

He saw me, and he turned aside,
As if he wished himself to hide:
And with his coat did then essay
To wipe those briny tears away.

I followed him, and said, "My friend,   15
What ails you? wherefore weep you so?"
—"Shame on me, Sir! this lusty Lamb,
He makes my tears to flow.
To-day I fetched him from the rock;
He is the last of all my flock.   20

III.

"When I was young, a single man,
And after youthful follies ran,
Though little given to care and thought,
Yet, so it was, an ewe I bought;
And other sheep from her I raised,   25
As healthy sheep as you might see;
And then I married, and was rich
As I could wish to be;
Of sheep I numbered a full score,
And every year increased my store.   30

IV.

"Year after year my stock it grew;
And from this one, this single ewe,
Full fifty comely sheep I raised,
As fine a flock as ever grazed!
Upon the Quantock hills they fed;   35
They throve, and we at home did thrive:
—This lusty Lamb of all my store
Is all that is alive;
And now I care not if we die,
And perish all of poverty.   40

V.

"Six Children, Sir! had I to feed;
Hard labour in a time of need!
My pride was tamed, and in our grief
I of the Parish asked relief.
They said, I was a wealthy man;   45
My sheep upon the uplands fed,
And it was fit that thence I took
Whereof to buy us bread.
'Do this: how can we give to you,'
They cried, 'what to the poor is due?'   50

VI.

"I sold a sheep, as they had said,
And bought my little children bread,
And they were healthy with their food;
For me—it never did me good.
A woeful time it was for me,   55

To see the end of all my gains,
The pretty flock which I had reared
With all my care and pains,
To see it melt like snow away—
For me it was a woeful day.   60

VII.

"Another still! and still another!
A little lamb, and then its mother!
It was a vein that never stopped—
Like blood-drops from my heart they
    dropped.
Till thirty were not left alive   65
They dwindled, dwindled, one by one;
And I may say, that many a time
I wished they all were gone—
Reckless of what might come at last
Were but the bitter struggle past.   70

VIII.

"To wicked deeds I was inclined,
And wicked fancies crossed my mind;
And every man I chanced to see,
I thought he knew some ill of me:
No peace, no comfort could I find,   75
No ease, within doors or without;
And crazily and wearily
I went my work about;
And oft was moved to flee from home,
And hide my head where wild beasts
    roam.   80

IX.

"Sir! 'twas a precious flock to me,
As dear as my own children be;
For daily with my growing store
I loved my children more and more.
Alas! it was an evil time;   85
God cursed me in my sore distress;
I prayed, yet every day I thought
I loved my children less;
And every week, and every day,
My flock it seemed to melt away.   90

X.

"They dwindled, Sir, sad sight to see!
From ten to five, from five to three,
A lamb, a wether, and a ewe;—
And then at last from three to two;
And, of my fifty, yesterday   95

I had but only one:
And here it lies upon my arm,
Alas! and I have none;—
To-day I fetched it from the rock;
It is the last of all my flock."   100

XXIII.

REPENTANCE.

A PASTORAL BALLAD.

[Composed 1804.—Published 1820.]

THE fields which with covetous spirit we
    sold,
Those beautiful fields, the delight of the
    day,
Would have brought us more good than a
    burthen of gold,
Could we but have been as contented as
    they.

When the troublesome Tempter beset us,
    said I,   5
"Let him come, with his purse proudly
    grasped in his hand;
But, Allan, be true to me, Allan,—we'll
    die
Before he shall go with an inch of the
    land!"

There dwelt we, as happy as birds in their
    bowers;
Unfettered as bees that in gardens abide;
We could do what we liked with the land,
    it was ours;   11
And for us the brook murmured that ran
    by its side.

But now we are strangers, go early or
    late;
And often, like one overburthened with
    sin,
With my hand on the latch of the half-
    opened gate,   15
I look at the fields, but I cannot go in!

When I walk by the hedge on a bright
    summer's day,
Or sit in the shade of my grandfather's
    tree,
A stern face it puts on, as if ready to say,
"What ails you, that you must come
    creeping to me!"   20

With our pastures about us, we could not
    be sad;
Our comfort was near if we ever were
    crost;
But the comfort, the blessings, and wealth
    that we had,
We slighted them all,—and our birth-
    right was lost.

Oh, ill-judging sire of an innocent son   25
Who must now be a wanderer! but peace
    to that strain!
Think of evening's repose when our labour
    was done,
The sabbath's return; and its leisure's
    soft chain!

And in sickness, if night had been sparing
    of sleep,
How cheerful, at sunrise, the hill where I
    stood,   30
Looking down on the kine, and our trea-
    sure of sheep
That besprinkled the field; 'twas like
    youth in my blood!

Now I cleave to the house, and am dull as
    a snail;
And, oftentimes, hear the church-bell
    with a sigh,
That follows the thought—We've no land
    in the vale,   35
Save six feet of earth where our fore-
    fathers lie!

XXIV.

THE

AFFLICTION OF MARGARET——.

[Dated 1804 (W.).—Probably composed earlier
(1801?).—Published 1807.]

I.

WHERE art thou, my beloved Son,
Where art thou, worse to me than dead?
Oh find me, prosperous or undone!
Or, if the grave be now thy bed,
Why am I ignorant of the same   5
That I may rest; and neither blame
Nor sorrow may attend thy name?

II.

Seven years, alas! to have received
No tidings of an only child;
To have despaired, have hoped, believed,
And been for evermore beguiled;   11
Sometimes with thoughts of very bliss!
I catch at them, and then I miss;
Was ever darkness like to this?

III.

He was among the prime in worth,   15
An object beauteous to behold;
Well born, well bred; I sent him forth
Ingenuous, innocent, and bold:
If things ensued that wanted grace,
As hath been said, they were not base; 20
And never blush was on my face.

IV.

Ah! little doth the young-one dream,
When full of play and childish cares,
What power is in his wildest scream,
Heard by his mother unawares!   25
He knows it not, he cannot guess:
Years to a mother bring distress;
But do not make her love the less.

V.

Neglect me! no, I suffered long
From that ill thought; and, being blind,
Said, "Pride shall help me in my wrong:
Kind mother have I been, as kind   32
As ever breathed:" and that is true;
I've wet my path with tears like dew,
Weeping for him when no one knew.   35

VI.

My Son, if thou be humbled, poor,
Hopeless of honour and of gain,
Oh! do not dread thy mother's door;
Think not of me with grief and pain:
I now can see with better eyes;   40
And worldly grandeur I despise,
And fortune with her gifts and lies.

VII.

Alas! the fowls of heaven have wings,
And blasts of heaven will aid their flight;
They mount—how short a voyage brings
The wanderers back to their delight!   46

Chains tie us down by land and sea;
And wishes, vain as mine, may be
All that is left to comfort thee.

VIII.

Perhaps some dungeon hears thee groan,
Maimed, mangled by inhuman men;   51
Or thou upon a desert thrown
Inheritest the lion's den;
Or hast been summoned to the deep,
Thou, thou and all thy mates, to keep 55
An incommunicable sleep.

IX.

I look for ghosts; but none will force
Their way to me: 'tis falsely said
That there was ever intercourse
Between the living and the dead;   60
For, surely, then I should have sight
Of him I wait for day and night,
With love and longings infinite.

X.

My apprehensions come in crowds;
I dread the rustling of the grass;   65
The very shadows of the clouds
Have power to shake me as they pass:
I question things and do not find
One that will answer to my mind;
And all the world appears unkind.   70

XI.

Beyond participation lie
My troubles, and beyond relief:
If any chance to heave a sigh,
They pity me, and not my grief.
Then come to me, my Son, or send   75
Some tidings that my woes may end;
I have no other earthly friend!

XXV.

THE COTTAGER TO HER INFANT.

BY MY SISTER.

[Composed 1805.—Published 1815.]

THE days are cold, the nights are long,
The north-wind sings a doleful song;
Then hush again upon my breast;
All merry things are now at rest,
　　Save thee, my pretty Love!   5

The kitten sleeps upon the hearth,
The crickets long have ceased their mirth ;
There 's nothing stirring in the house
Save one *wee*, hungry, nibbling mouse,
    Then why so busy thou ?   10

Nay ! start not at that sparkling light ;
'Tis but the moon that shines so bright
On the window pane bedropped with
    rain :
Then little Darling ! sleep again,
    And wake when it is day.   15

XXVI.

MATERNAL GRIEF.

[Composed 1810 (?).—Published 1842.]

DEPARTED Child ! I could forget thee once
Though at my bosom nursed ; this woeful
    gain
Thy dissolution brings, that in my soul
Is present and perpetually abides
A shadow, never, never to be displaced 5
By the returning substance, seen or
    touched,
Seen by mine eyes, or clasped in my
    embrace,
Absence and death how differ they ! and
    how
Shall I admit that nothing can restore 9
·What one short sigh so easily removed ?—
Death, life, and sleep, reality and thought,
Assist me, God, their boundaries to
    know,
O teach me calm submission to thy Will !

The Child she mourned had overstepped
    the pale
Of Infancy, but still did breathe the air 15
That sanctifies its confines, and partook
Reflected beams of that celestial light
To all the Little-ones on sinful earth
Not unvouchsafed—a light that warmed
    and cheered
Those several qualities of heart and mind
Which, in her own blest nature, rooted
    deep,   21
Daily before the Mother's watchful eye,
And not hers only, their peculiar charms
Unfolded,—beauty, for its present self,
And for its promises to future years, 25
With not unfrequent rapture fondly hailed.

Have you espied upon a dewy lawn
A pair of Leverets each provoking each
To a continuance of their fearless sport,
Two separate Creatures in their several
    gifts   30
Abounding, but so fashioned that, in all
That Nature prompts them to display,
    their looks,
Their starts of motion and their fits of
    rest,
An undistinguishable style appears
And character of gladness, as if Spring 35
Lodged in their innocent bosoms, and the
    spirit
Of the rejoicing morning were their own ?

Such union, in the lovely Girl main-
    tained
And her twin Brother, had the parent
    seen,
Ere, pouncing like a ravenous bird of
    prey,   40
Death in a moment parted them, and left
The Mother, in her turns of anguish,
    worse
Than desolate ; for oft-times from the
    sound
Of the survivor's sweetest voice (dear
    child,
He knew it not) and from his happiest
    looks,   45
Did she extract the food of self-reproach,
As one that lived ungrateful for the stay
By Heaven afforded to uphold her maimed
And tottering spirit. And full oft the Boy,
Now first acquainted with distress and
    grief,   50
Shrunk from his Mother's presence, shun-
    ned with fear
Her sad approach, and stole away to find,
In his known haunts of joy where'er he
    might,
A more congenial object. But, as time
Softened her pangs, and reconciled the
    child   55
To what he saw, he gradually returned,
Like a scared Bird encouraged to renew
A broken intercourse ; and, while his eyes
Were yet with pensive fear and gentle
    awe
Turned upon her who bore him, she
    would stoop   60

To imprint a kiss that lacked not power
to spread
Faint colour over both their pallid cheeks,
And stilled his tremulous lip. Thus they
were calmed
And cheered; and now together breathe
fresh air
In open fields; and when the glare of
day   65
Is gone, and twilight to the Mother's
wish
Befriends the observance, readily they
join
In walks whose boundary is the lost One's
grave,
Which he with flowers hath planted,
finding there
Amusement, where the Mother does not
miss   70
Dear consolation, kneeling on the turf
In prayer, yet blending with that solemn
rite
Of pious faith the vanities of grief;
For such, by pitying Angels and by
Spirits
Transferred to regions upon which the
clouds   75
Of our weak nature rest not, must be
deemed
Those willing tears, and unforbidden
sighs,
And all those tokens of a cherished sor-
row,
Which, soothed and sweetened by the
grace of Heaven   79
As now it is, seems to her own fond heart
Immortal as the love that gave it being.

XXVII.

THE SAILOR'S MOTHER.

[Composed March 11, 12, 1802.—Published 1807.]

ONE morning (raw it was and wet—
A foggy day in winter time)
A Woman on the road I met,
Not old, though something past her
prime:
Majestic in her person, tall and straight;
And like a Roman matron's was her mien
and gait.   6

The ancient spirit is not dead;
Old times, thought I, are breathing
there;
Proud was I that my country bred
Such strength, a dignity so fair: 10
She begged an alms, like one in poor
estate;
I looked at her again, nor did my pride
abate.

When from these lofty thoughts I woke,
"What is it," said I, "that you bear,
Beneath the covert of your Cloak,   15
Protected from this cold damp air?"
She answered, soon as she the question
heard,
"A simple burthen, Sir, a little Singing-
bird."

And, thus continuing, she said,
"I had a Son, who many a day   20
Sailed on the seas, but he is dead;
In Denmark he was cast away:
And I have travelled weary miles to see
If aught which he had owned might still
remain for me.

"The bird and cage they both were his:
'Twas my Son's bird; and neat and
trim   26
He kept it: many voyages
The singing-bird had gone with him;
When last he sailed, he left the bird
behind;
From bodings, as might be, that hung
upon his mind.   30

"He to a fellow-lodger's care
Had left it, to be watched and fed,
And pipe its song in safety;—there
I found it when my Son was dead;
And now, God help me for my little
wit!   35
I bear it with me, Sir;—he took so much
delight in it."

XXVIII.

THE CHILDLESS FATHER.

[Composed 1800.—Published 1800.]

"UP, Timothy, up with your staff and
away!
Not a soul in the village this morning will
stay;

The hare has just started from Hamilton's
grounds,
And Skiddaw is glad with the cry of the
hounds."

—Of coats and of jackets grey, scarlet,
and green,   5
On the slopes of the pastures all colours
were seen;
With their comely blue aprons, and caps
white as snow,
The girls on the hills made a holiday show.

Fresh sprigs of green box-wood, not six
months before,
Filled the funeral basin[1] at Timothy's
door;   10
A coffin through Timothy's threshold had
past;
One Child did it bear, and that Child
was his last.

Now fast up the dell came the noise and
the fray,
The horse, and the horn, and the hark!
hark away!
Old Timothy took up his staff, and he shut
With a leisurely motion the door of his hut.

Perhaps to himself at that moment he said;
"The key I must take, for my Ellen is
dead."
But of this in my ears not a word did he
speak;
And he went to the chase with a tear on
his cheek.   20

XXIX.

THE EMIGRANT MOTHER.

[Composed March 16, 17, 1802.—Published 1807.]

ONCE in a lonely hamlet I sojourned
In which a Lady driven from France did
dwell;
The big and lesser griefs with which she
mourned
In friendship she to me would often tell.

---

[1] In several parts of the North of England,
when a funeral takes place, a basin full of sprigs
of box-wood is placed at the door of the house
from which the coffin is taken up, and each
person who attends the funeral ordinarily takes
a sprig of this box-wood, and throws it into the
grave of the deceased.

This Lady, dwelling upon British ground,
Where she was childless, daily would
repair   6
To a poor neighbouring cottage; as I
found,
For sake of a young Child whose home
was there.

Once having seen her clasp with fond
embrace
This Child, I chanted to myself a lay,   10
Endeavouring, in our English tongue, to
trace
Such things as she unto the Babe might
say;
And thus, from what I heard and knew,
or guessed,
My song the workings of her heart
expressed.

I.

"Dear Babe, thou daughter of another, 15
One moment let me be thy mother!
An infant's face and looks are thine
And sure a mother's heart is mine:
Thy own dear mother's far away,
At labour in the harvest field: 20
Thy little sister is at play;—
What warmth, what comfort would it
yield
To my poor heart, if thou wouldst be
One little hour a child to me!

II.

"Across the waters I am come,   25
And I have left a babe at home:
A long, long way of land and sea!
Come to me—I'm no enemy:
I am the same who at thy side
Sate yesterday, and made a nest   30
For thee, sweet Baby!—thou hast tried,
Thou know'st the pillow of my breast;
Good, good art thou:—alas! to me
Far more than I can be to thee.

III.

"Here, little Darling, dost thou lie;   35
An infant thou, a mother I!
Mine wilt thou be, thou hast no fears;
Mine art thou—spite of these my tears.

Alas! before I left the spot,
My baby and its dwelling-place, 40
The nurse said to me, 'Tears should not
Be shed upon an infant's face,
It was unlucky'—no, no, no;
No truth is in them who say so!

IV.

"My own dear Little-one will sigh, 45
Sweet Babe! and they will let him die.
'He pines,' they'll say, 'it is his doom,
And you may see his hour is come.'
Oh! had he but thy cheerful smiles,
Limbs stout as thine, and lips as gay, 50
Thy looks, thy cunning, and thy wiles,
And countenance like a summer's day,
They would have hopes of him;—and then
I should behold his face again!

V.

"'Tis gone—like dreams that we forget;
There was a smile or two—yet—yet 56
I can remember them, I see
The smiles, worth all the world to me.
Dear Baby! I must lay thee down; 59
Thou troublest me with strange alarms;
Smiles hast thou, bright ones of thy own;
I cannot keep thee in my arms;
For they confound me;—where—where is
That last, that sweetest smile of his?

VI.

"Oh! how I love thee!—we will stay 65
Together here this one half day.
My sister's child, who bears my name,
From France to sheltering England came;
She with her mother crossed the sea;
The babe and mother near me dwell: 70
Yet does my yearning heart to thee
Turn rather, though I love her well:
Rest, little Stranger, rest thee here!
Never was any child more dear!

VII.

"—I cannot help it; ill intent 75
I've none, my pretty Innocent!
I weep—I know they do thee wrong,
These tears—and my poor idle tongue.

Oh, what a kiss was that! my cheek
How cold it is! but thou art good; 80
Thine eyes are on me—they would speak,
I think, to help me if they could.
Blessings upon that soft, warm face,
My heart again is in its place!

VIII.

"While thou art mine, my little Love, 85
This cannot be a sorrowful grove;
Contentment, hope, and mother's glee,
I seem to find them all in thee:
Here's grass to play with, here are flowers;
I'll call thee by my darling's name; 90
Thou hast, I think, a look of ours,
Thy features seem to me the same;
His little sister thou shalt be;
And, when once more my home I see,
I'll tell him many tales of Thee." 95

XXX.

VAUDRACOUR AND JULIA.

[Composed probably 1804.—Published 1820.]

The following tale was written as an Episode, in a work from which its length may perhaps exclude it. The facts are true; no invention as to these has been exercised, as none was needed.

O HAPPY time of youthful lovers (thus
My story may begin) O balmy time,
In which a love-knot on a lady's brow
Is fairer than the fairest star in heaven!
To such inheritance of blessed fancy 5
(Fancy that sports more desperately with minds
Than ever fortune hath been known to do)
The high-born Vaudracour was brought, by years
Whose progress had a little overstepped
His stripling prime. A town of small repute, 10
Among the vine-clad mountains of Auvergne,
Was the Youth's birth-place. There he wooed a Maid
Who heard the heart-felt music of his suit
With answering vows. Plebeian was the stock,
Plebeian, though ingenuous, the stock, 15

From which her graces and her honours
    sprung:
And hence the father of the enamoured
    Youth,
With haughty indignation, spurned the
    thought
Of such alliance.—From their cradles up,
With but a step between their several
    homes,   20
Twins had they been in pleasure; after
    strife
And petty quarrels, had grown fond again;
Each other's advocate, each other's stay;
And, in their happiest moments, not
    content,
If more divided than a sportive pair   25
Of sea-fowl, conscious both that they are
    hovering
Within the eddy of a common blast,
Or hidden only by the concave depth
Of neighbouring billows from each other's
    sight.

Thus, not without concurrence of an age
Unknown to memory, was an earnest
    given   31
By ready nature for a life of love,
For endless constancy, and placid truth;
But whatsoe'er of such rare treasure lay
Reserved, had fate permitted, for sup-
    port   35
Of their maturer years, his present mind
Was under fascination ;—he beheld
A vision, and adored the thing he saw.
Arabian fiction never filled the world
With half the wonders that were wrought
    for him.   40
Earth breathed in one great presence of
    the spring ;
Life turned the meanest of her imple-
    ments,
Before his eyes, to price above all gold ;
The house she dwelt in was a sainted
    shrine ;
Her chamber-window did surpass in glory
The portals of the dawn ; all Paradise 46
Could, by the simple opening of a door,
Let itself in upon him :—pathways, walks,
Swarmed with enchantment, till his spirit
    sank,
Surcharged, within him, overblest to move

Beneath a sun that wakes a weary world
To its dull round of ordinary cares ;   52
A man too happy for mortality !

So passed the time, till, whether through
    effect
Of some unguarded moment that dis-
    solved   55
Virtuous restraint—ah, speak it, think it,
    not !
Deem rather that the fervent Youth, who
    saw
So many bars between his present state
And the dear haven where he wished
    to be
In honourable wedlock with his Love,   60
Was in his judgment tempted to decline
To perilous weakness, and entrust his
    cause
To nature for a happy end of all ;
Deem that by such fond hope the Youth
    was swayed,
And bear with their transgression, when
    I add   65
That Julia, wanting yet the name of wife,
Carried about her for a secret grief
The promise of a mother.
                          To conceal
The threatened shame, the parents of the
    Maid
Found means to hurry her away by night,
And unforewarned, that in some distant
    spot   71
She might remain shrouded in privacy,
Until the babe was born. When morning
    came,
The Lover, thus bereft, stung with his loss,
And all uncertain whither he should turn,
Chafed like a wild beast in the toils ; but
    soon   76
Discovering traces of the fugitives,
Their steps he followed to the Maid's
    retreat.
Easily may the sequel be divined—
Walks to and fro—watchings at every
    hour ;   80
And the fair Captive, who, whene'er she
    may,
Is busy at her casement as the swallow
Fluttering its pinions, almost within
    reach,

About the pendent nest, did thus espy
Her Lover!—thence a stolen interview, 85
Accomplished under friendly shade of
night.

I pass the raptures of the pair;—such
theme
Is, by innumerable poets, touched
In more delightful verse than skill of
mine
Could fashion; chiefly by that darling
bard   90
Who told of Juliet and her Romeo,
And of the lark's note heard before its
time,
And of the streaks that laced the severing
clouds
In the unrelenting east.—Through all her
courts
The vacant city slept; the busy winds, 95
That keep no certain intervals of rest,
Moved not; meanwhile the galaxy dis-
played
Her fires, that like mysterious pulses beat
Aloft;—momentous but uneasy bliss!
To their full hearts the universe seemed
hung   100
On that brief meeting's slender filament!

They parted; and the generous Vau-
dracour
Reached speedily the native threshold,
bent
On making (so the Lovers had agreed)
A sacrifice of birthright to attain   105
A final portion from his father's hand;
Which granted, Bride and Bridegroom
then would flee
To some remote and solitary place,
Shady as night, and beautiful as heaven,
Where they may live, with no one to
behold   110
Their happiness, or to disturb their love.
But *now* of this no whisper; not the less,
If ever an obtrusive word were dropped
Touching the matter of his passion, still,
In his stern father's hearing, Vaudracour
Persisted openly that death alone   116
Should abrogate his human privilege
Divine, of swearing everlasting truth,
Upon the altar, to the Maid he loved.

"You shall be baffled in your mad in-
tent   120
If there be justice in the court of France,"
Muttered the Father.—From these words
the Youth
Conceived a terror; and, by night or day
Stirred nowhere without weapons, that
full soon   124
Found dreadful provocation: for at night,
When to his chamber he retired, attempt
Was made to seize him by three armèd
men,
Acting, in furtherance of the Father's will,
Under a private signet of the State.
One the rash Youth's ungovernable hand
Slew, and as quickly to a second gave 131
A perilous wound—he shuddered to behold
The breathless corse; then peacefully re-
signed
His person to the law, was lodged in
prison,
And wore the fetters of a criminal.   135

Have you observed a tuft of wingèd seed
That, from the dandelion's naked stalk,
Mounted aloft, is suffered not to use
Its natural gifts for purposes of rest,
Driven by the autumnal whirlwind to
and fro   140
Through the wide element? or have you
marked
The heavier substance of a leaf-clad bough,
Within the vortex of a foaming flood,
Tormented? by such aid you may conceive
The perturbation that ensued;—ah, no!
Desperate the Maid—the Youth is stained
with blood;   146
Unmatchable on earth is their disquiet!
Yet as the troubled seed and tortured
bough
Is man, subjected to despotic sway.

For him, by private influence with the
Court,   150
Was pardon gained, and liberty procured;
But not without exaction of a pledge,
Which liberty and love dispersed in air.
He flew to her from whom they would
divide him—
He clove to her who could not give him
peace—   155

Yea, his first word of greeting was,—"All
　　right
Is gone from me; my lately-towering
　　hopes,
To the least fibre of their lowest root,
Are withered; thou no longer canst be
　　mine,
I thine—the conscience-stricken must
　　not woo　　　　　　　　　　　　160
The unruffled Innocent,—I see thy face,
Behold thee, and my misery is complete!"

"One, are we not?" exclaimed the
　　Maiden—"One,
For innocence and youth, for weal and
　　woe?"
Then with the father's name she coupled
　　words　　　　　　　　　　　　165
Of vehement indignation; but the Youth
Checked her with filial meekness; for no
　　thought
Uncharitable crossed his mind, no sense
Of hasty anger, rising in the eclipse
Of true domestic loyalty, did e'er　170
Find place within his bosom.—Once again
The persevering wedge of tyranny
Achieved their separation: and once more
Were they united,—to be yet again
Disparted, pitiable lot! But here　175
A portion of the tale may well be left
In silence, though my memory could add
Much how the Youth, in scanty space of
　　time,
Was traversed from without; much, too,
　　of thoughts
That occupied his days in solitude　180
Under privation and restraint; and what,
Through dark and shapeless fear of things
　　to come,
And what, through strong compunction
　　for the past,
He suffered—breaking down in heart and
　　mind!

Doomed to a third and last captivity,
His freedom he recovered on the eve　186
Of Julia's travail. When the babe was
　　born,
Its presence tempted him to cherish
　　schemes
Of future happiness. "You shall return,

Julia," said he, "and to your father's
　　house　　　　　　　　　　　　190
Go with the child.—You have been
　　wretched; yet
The silver shower, whose reckless burthen
　　weighs
Too heavily upon the lily's head,
Oft leaves a saving moisture at its root.
Malice, beholding you, will melt away. 195
Go!—'tis a town where both of us were
　　born;
None will reproach you, for our truth is
　　known;
And if, amid those once-bright bowers,
　　our fate
Remain unpitied, pity is not in man.
With ornaments—the prettiest, nature
　　yields　　　　　　　　　　　　200
Or art can fashion, shall you deck our boy,
And feed his countenance with your own
　　sweet looks,
Till no one can resist him.—Now, even
　　now,
I see him sporting on the sunny lawn;
My father from the window sees him
　　too;　　　　　　　　　　　　205
Startled, as if some new created thing
Enriched the earth, or Faery of the woods
Bounded before him;—but the unweeting
　　Child
Shall by his beauty win his grandsire's
　　heart,
So that it shall be softened, and our loves
End happily, as they began!"
　　　　　　　　　　　　These gleams
Appeared but seldom; oftener was he
　　seen　　　　　　　　　　　　212
Propping a pale and melancholy face
Upon the Mother's bosom; resting thus
His head upon one breast, while from the
　　other　　　　　　　　　　　　215
The Babe was drawing in its quiet food.
—That pillow is no longer to be thine,
Fond Youth! that mournful solace now
　　must pass
Into the list of things that cannot be!
Unwedded Julia, terror-smitten, hears
The sentence, by her mother's lip pro-
　　nounced,　　　　　　　　　　221
That dooms her to a convent.—Who shall
　　tell,

Who dares report, the tidings to the lord
Of her affections? so they blindly asked
Who knew not to what quiet depths a
    weight   225
Of agony had pressed the Sufferer down:
The word, by others dreaded, he can hear
Composed and silent, without visible sign
Of even the least emotion. Noting this,
When the impatient object of his love 230
Upbraided him with slackness, he re-
    turned
No answer, only took the mother's hand
And kissed it; seemingly devoid of pain,
Or care, that what so tenderly he pressed
Was a dependant on the obdurate heart
Of one who came to disunite their lives 236
For ever—sad alternative! preferred,
By the unbending Parents of the Maid,
To secret 'spousals meanly disavowed.
—So be it!

    In the city he remained   240
A season after Julia had withdrawn
To those religious walls. He, too, de-
    parts—
Who with him?—even the senseless Little-
    one.
With that sole charge he passed the city-
    gates,
For the last time, attendant by the side
Of a close chair, a litter, or sedan,   246
In which the Babe was carried. To a hill,
That rose a brief league distant from the
    town,
The dwellers in that house where he had
    lodged
Accompanied his steps, by anxious love
Impelled;—they parted from him there,
    and stood   251
Watching below till he had disappeared
On the hill top. His eyes he scarcely took,
Throughout that journey, from the vehicle
(Slow-moving ark of all his hopes!) that
    veiled   255
The tender infant: and at every inn,
And under every hospitable tree
At which the bearers halted or reposed,
Laid him with timid care upon his knees,
And looked, as mothers ne'er were known
    to look,   260
Upon the nursling which his arms em-
    braced.

This was the manner in which Vau-
    dracour
Departed with his infant; and thus
    reached
His father's house, where to the innocent
    child
Admittance was denied. The young man
    spake   265
No word of indignation or reproof,
But of his father begged, a last request,
That a retreat might be assigned to him,
Where in forgotten quiet he might dwell,
With such allowance as his wants re-
    quired;   270
For wishes he had none. To a lodge that
    stood
Deep in a forest, with leave given, at
    the age
Of four-and-twenty summers he withdrew;
And thither took with him his motherless
    Babe,
And one domestic for their common
    needs,   275
An aged woman. It consoled him here
To attend upon the orphan, and perform
Obsequious service to the precious child,
Which, after a short time, by some mis-
    take
Or indiscretion of the Father, died.— 280
The Tale I follow to its last recess
Of suffering or of peace, I know not
    which:
Theirs be the blame who caused the woe,
    not mine!

From this time forth he never shared a
    smile
With mortal creature. An Inhabitant 285
Of that same town, in which the pair
    had left
So lively a remembrance of their griefs,
By chance of business coming within
    reach
Of his retirement, to the forest lodge
Repaired, but only found the matron
    there,   290
Who told him that his pains were thrown
    away,
For that her Master never uttered word
To living thing—not even to her.—Be-
    hold!

While they were speaking, Vaudracour
    approached;
But seeing some one near, as on the latch
Of the garden-gate his hand was laid, he
    shrunk—   296
And, like a shadow, glided out of view.
Shocked at his savage aspect, from the place
The visitor retired.
                Thus lived the Youth
Cut off from all intelligence with man, 300
And shunning even the light of common
    day;
Nor could the voice of Freedom, which
    through France
Full speedily resounded, public hope,
Or personal memory of his own deep
    wrongs,
Rouse him: but in those solitary shades
His days he wasted, an imbecile mind! 306

XXXI.

THE IDIOT BOY.

[Composed 1798.—Published 1798.]

'Tis eight o'clock,—a clear March night,
The moon is up,—the sky is blue,
The owlet, in the moonlight air,
[Shouts from nobody knows where;]
He lengthens out his lonely shout,   5
Halloo! halloo! a long halloo!

—Why bustle thus about your door,
What means this bustle, Betty Foy?
Why are you in this mighty fret?
And why on horseback have you set   10
Him whom you love, your Idiot Boy?

Scarcely a soul is out of bed;
Good Betty, put him down again;
His lips with joy they burr at you;
But, Betty! what has he to do   15
With stirrup, saddle, or with rein?

But Betty's bent on her intent;
For her good neighbour Susan Gale,
Old Susan, she who dwells alone,
Is sick, and makes a piteous moan,   20
As if her very life would fail.

There's not a house within a mile,
No hand to help them in distress;
Old Susan lies a-bed in pain,
And sorely puzzled are the twain,   25
For what she ails they cannot guess.

And Betty's husband's at the wood,
Where by the week he doth abide,
A woodman in the distant vale;
There's none to help poor Susan Gale; 30
What must be done? what will betide?

And Betty from the lane has fetched
Her Pony, that is mild and good;
Whether he be in joy or pain,
Feeding at will along the lane,   35
Or bringing fagots from the wood.

And he is all in travelling trim,—
And, by the moonlight, Betty Foy
Has on the well-girt saddle set
(The like was never heard of yet)   40
Him whom she loves, her Idiot Boy.

And he must post without delay
Across the bridge and through the dale,
And by the church, and o'er the down,
To bring a Doctor from the town,   45
Or she will die, old Susan Gale.

There is no need of boot or spur,
There is no need of whip or wand;
For Johnny has his holly-bough,
And with a *hurly burly* now   50
He shakes the green bough in his hand.

And Betty o'er and o'er has told
The Boy, who is her best delight,
Both what to follow, what to shun,
What do, and what to leave undone,   55
How turn to left, and how to right.

And Betty's most especial charge,
Was, "Johnny! Johnny! mind that you
Come home again, nor stop at all,—
Come home again, whate'er befall,   60
My Johnny, do, I pray you, do."

To this did Johnny answer make,
Both with his head and with his hand,
And proudly shook the bridle too;
And then! his words were not a few,   65
Which Betty well could understand.

And now that Johnny is just going,
Though Betty's in a mighty flurry,
She gently pats the Pony's side,
On which her Idiot Boy must ride,   70
And seems no longer in a hurry.

But when the Pony moved his legs,
Oh! then for the poor Idiot Boy!
For joy he cannot hold the bridle,
For joy his head and heels are idle,   75
He's idle all for very joy.

And, while the Pony moves his legs,
In Johnny's left hand you may see
The green bough motionless and dead:
The Moon that shines above his head   80
Is not more still and mute than he.

His heart it was so full of glee
That, till full fifty yards were gone,
He quite forgot his holly whip,
And all his skill in horsemanship: 85
Oh! happy, happy, happy John.

And while the Mother, at the door,
Stands fixed, her face with joy o'erflows,
Proud of herself, and proud of him,
She sees him in his travelling trim,   90
How quietly her Johnny goes.

The silence of her Idiot Boy,
What hopes it sends to Betty's heart!
He's at the guide-post—he turns right;
She watches till he's out of sight,   95
And Betty will not then depart.

Burr, burr—now Johnny's lips they burr,
As loud as any mill, or near it;
Meek as a lamb the Pony moves,
And Johnny makes the noise he loves,
And Betty listens, glad to hear it.   101

Away she hies to Susan Gale:
Her Messenger's in merry tune;
The owlets hoot, the owlets curr,
And Johnny's lips they burr, burr, burr,
As on he goes beneath the moon.   106

His steed and he right well agree;
For of this Pony there's a rumour
That, should he lose his eyes and ears,
And should he live a thousand years,   110
He never will be out of humour.

But then he is a horse that thinks!
And, when he thinks, his pace is slack;
Now, though he knows poor Johnny well,
Yet, for his life, he cannot tell   115
What he has got upon his back.

So through the moonlight lanes they go,
And far into the moonlight dale,
And by the church, and o'er the down,
To bring a Doctor from the town,   120
To comfort poor old Susan Gale.

And Betty, now at Susan's side,
Is in the middle of her story,
What speedy help her Boy will bring,
With many a most diverting thing,   125
Of Johnny's wit, and Johnny's glory.

And Betty, still at Susan's side,
By this time is not quite so flurried:
Demure with porringer and plate
She sits, as if in Susan's fate   130
Her life and soul were buried.

But Betty, poor good woman! she,
You plainly in her face may read it,
Could lend out of that moment's store
Five years of happiness or more   135
To any that might need it.

But yet I guess that now and then
With Betty all was not so well;
And to the road she turns her ears,
And thence full many a sound she hears,
Which she to Susan will not tell.   141

Poor Susan moans, poor Susan groans;
"As sure as there's a moon in heaven,"
Cries Betty, "he'll be back again;
They'll both be here—'tis almost ten—145
Both will be here before eleven."

Poor Susan moans, poor Susan groans;
The clock gives warning for eleven;
'Tis on the stroke—"He must be near,"
Quoth Betty, "and will soon be here, 150
As sure as there's a moon in heaven."

The clock is on the stroke of twelve,
And Johnny is not yet in sight:
—The Moon's in heaven, as Betty sees,
But Betty is not quite at ease;   155
And Susan has a dreadful night.

And Betty, half an hour ago,
On Johnny vile reflections cast:
"A little idle sauntering Thing!"
With other names, an endless string; 160
But now that time is gone and past.

And Betty's drooping at the heart,
That happy time all past and gone,
"How can it be he is so late?
The Doctor, he has made him wait;   165
Susan! they'll both be here anon."

And Susan's growing worse and worse,
And Betty's in a sad *quandary;*
And then there's nobody to say
If she must go, or she must stay!   170
—She's in a sad *quandary.*

The clock is on the stroke of one;
But neither Doctor nor his Guide
Appears along the moonlight road;
There's neither horse nor man abroad, 175
And Betty's still at Susan's side

And Susan now begins to fear
Of sad mischances not a few,
That Johnny may perhaps be drowned;
Or lost, perhaps, and never found;   180
Which they must both for ever rue.

She prefaced half a hint of this
With, "God forbid it should be true!"
At the first word that Susan said
Cried Betty, rising from the bed,   185
"Susan, I'd gladly stay with you

"I must be gone, I must away:
Consider, Johnny's but half-wise;
Susan, we must take care of him,
If he is hurt in life or limb"—   190
"Oh God forbid!" poor Susan cries.

"What can I do?" says Betty, going,
"What can I do to ease your pain?
Good Susan tell me, and I'll stay;
I fear you're in a dreadful way,   195
But I shall soon be back again."

"Nay, Betty, go! good Betty, go!
There's nothing that can ease my pain."
Then off she hies; but with a prayer,
That God poor Susan's life would spare,
Till she comes back again.   201

So, through the moonlight lane she goes,
And far into the moonlight dale;
And how she ran, and how she walked,
And all that to herself she talked,   205
Would surely be a tedious tale.

In high and low, above, below,
In great and small, in round and square,
In tree and tower was Johnny seen,
In bush and brake, in black and green;
'Twas Johnny, Johnny, everywhere.   211

And while she crossed the bridge, there
    came
A thought with which her heart is sore—
Johnny perhaps his horse forsook,
To hunt the moon within the brook,   215
And never will be heard of more.

Now is she high upon the down,
Alone amid a prospect wide;
There's neither Johnny nor his Horse
Among the fern or in the gorse;   220
There's neither Doctor nor his Guide.

"Oh saints! what is become of him?
Perhaps he's climbed into an oak,
Where he will stay till he is dead;
Or sadly he has been misled,   225
And joined the wandering gipsy-folk.

"Or him that wicked Pony's carried
To the dark cave, the goblin's hall;
Or in the castle he's pursuing
Among the ghosts his own undoing;   230
Or playing with the waterfall."

At poor old Susan then she railed,
While to the town she posts away;
"If Susan had not been so ill,
Alas! I should have had him still,   235
My Johnny, till my dying day."

Poor Betty, in this sad distemper,
The Doctor's self could hardly spare:
Unworthy things she talked, and wild;
Even he, of cattle the most mild,   240
The Pony had his share.

But now she's fairly in the town,
And to the Doctor's door she hies;
'Tis silence all on every side;
The town so long, the town so wide,   245
Is silent as the skies.

And now she's at the Doctor's door,
She lifts the knocker, rap, rap, rap;
The Doctor at the casement shows
His glimmering eyes that peep and doze!
And one hand rubs his old night-cap.   251

"Oh Doctor! Doctor! where's my
    Johnny?"
"I'm here, what is't you want with me?"
"Oh Sir! you know I'm Betty Foy,
And I have lost my poor dear Boy,   255
You know him—him you often see;

He's not so wise as some folks be:"
"The devil take his wisdom!" said
The Doctor, looking somewhat grim,
"What, Woman! should I know of him?"
And, grumbling, he went back to bed! 261

"O woe is me! O woe is me!
Here will I die; here will I die;
I thought to find my lost one here,
But he is neither far nor near,   265
Oh! what a wretched Mother I!"

She stops, she stands, she looks about;
Which way to turn she cannot tell.
Poor Betty! it would ease her pain
If she had heart to knock again;   270
—The clock strikes three—a dismal knell!

Then up along the town she hies,
No wonder if her senses fail;
This piteous news so much it shocked her,
She quite forgot to send the Doctor,   275
To comfort poor old Susan Gale.

And now she's high upon the down,
And she can see a mile of road:
"O cruel! I'm almost threescore;
Such night as this was ne'er before,   280
There's not a single soul abroad."

She listens, but she cannot hear
The foot of horse, the voice of man;
The streams with softest sound are flowing,
The grass you almost hear it growing,
You hear it now, if e'er you can.   286

The owlets through the long blue night
Are shouting to each other still:
Fond lovers! yet not quite hob nob,
They lengthen out the tremulous sob,   290
That echoes far from hill to hill.

Poor Betty now has lost all hope,
Her thoughts are bent on deadly sin,
A green-grown pond she just has past,
And from the brink she hurries fast,   295
Lest she should drown herself therein.

And now she sits her down and weeps;
Such tears she never shed before;
"Oh dear, dear Pony! my sweet joy!
Oh carry back my Idiot Boy!   300
And we will ne'er o'erload thee more."

A thought is come into her head:
The Pony he is mild and good,
And we have always used him well;
Perhaps he's gone along the dell,   305
And carried Johnny to the wood.

Then up she springs as if on wings;
She thinks no more of deadly sin;
If Betty fifty ponds should see,
The last of all her thoughts would be   310
To drown herself therein.

Oh Reader! now that I might tell
What Johnny and his Horse are doing!
What they've been doing all this time,
Oh could I put it into rhyme,   315
A most delightful tale pursuing!

Perhaps, and no unlikely thought!
He with his Pony now doth roam
The cliffs and peaks so high that are,
To lay his hands upon a star,   320
And in his pocket bring it home.

Perhaps he's turned himself about,
His face unto his horse's tail,
And, still and mute, in wonder lost,
All silent as a horseman-ghost,   325
He travels slowly down the vale.

And now, perhaps, is hunting sheep,
A fierce and dreadful hunter he;
Yon valley, now so trim and green,
In five months' time, should he be seen,
A desert wilderness will be!   331

Perhaps, with head and heels on fire,
And like the very soul of evil,
He's galloping away, away,
And so will gallop on for aye,   335
The bane of all that dread the devil!

I to the Muses have been bound
These fourteen years, by strong inden-
    tures:
O gentle Muses! let me tell
But half of what to him befell;   340
He surely met with strange adventures.

O gentle Muses! is this kind?
Why will ye thus my suit repel?
Why of your further aid bereave me?
And can ye thus unfriended leave me;   345
Ye Muses! whom I love so well?

Who's yon, that, near the waterfall,
Which thunders down with headlong force,
Beneath the moon, yet shining fair,
As careless as if nothing were,   350
Sits upright on a feeding horse?

Unto his horse—there feeding free,
He seems, I think, the rein to give;
Of moon or stars he takes no heed;
Of such we in romances read: 355
—'Tis Johnny! Johnny! as I live.

And that's the very Pony, too!
Where is she, where is Betty Foy?
She hardly can sustain her fears;
The roaring waterfall she hears,   360
And cannot find her Idiot Boy.

Your Pony's worth his weight in gold:
Then calm your terrors, Betty Foy!
She's coming from among the trees,
And now all full in view she sees   365
Him whom she loves, her Idiot Boy.

And Betty sees the Pony too:
Why stand you thus, good Betty Foy?
It is no goblin, 'tis no ghost,
'Tis he whom you so long have lost,   370
He whom you love, your Idiot Boy.

She looks again—her arms are up—
She screams—she cannot move for joy;
She darts, as with a torrent's force,
She almost has o'erturned the Horse,   375
And fast she holds her Idiot Boy.

And Johnny burrs, and laughs aloud;
Whether in cunning or in joy
I cannot tell; but, while he laughs,
Betty a drunken pleasure quaffs   380
To hear again her Idiot Boy.

And now she's at the Pony's tail,
And now is at the Pony's head,—
On that side now, and now on this;
And, almost stifled with her bliss,   385
A few sad tears does Betty shed.

She kisses o'er and o'er again
Him whom she loves, her Idiot Boy;
She's happy here, is happy there,
She is uneasy everywhere;   390
Her limbs are all alive with joy.

She pats the Pony, where or when
She knows not, happy Betty Foy!
The little Pony glad may be,
But he is milder far than she,   395
You hardly can perceive his joy.

"Oh! Johnny, never mind the Doctor;
You've done your best, and that is all:"
She took the reins, when this was said,
And gently turned the Pony's head   400
From the loud waterfall.

By this the stars were almost gone,
The moon was setting on the hill,
So pale you scarcely looked at her:
The little birds began to stir,   405
Though yet their tongues were still.

The Pony, Betty, and her Boy,
Wind slowly through the woody dale;
And who is she, betimes abroad,
That hobbles up the steep rough road?
Who is it, but old Susan Gale?   411

Long time lay Susan lost in thought;
And many dreadful fears beset her,
Both for her Messenger and Nurse;
And, as her mind grew worse and worse,
Her body—it grew better.   416

She turned, she tossed herself in bed,
On all sides doubts and terrors met her;
Point after point did she discuss;
And, while her mind was fighting thus,
Her body still grew better.   421

"Alas! what is become of them?
These fears can never be endured;
I'll to the wood."—The word scarce said,
Did Susan rise up from her bed,   425
As if by magic cured.

Away she goes up hill and down,
And to the wood at length is come;
She spies her Friends, she shouts a greet-
    ing;
Oh me! it is a merry meeting   430
As ever was in Christendom.

The owls have hardly sung their last,
While our four travellers homeward wend;
The owls have hooted all night long,
And with the owls began my song,   435
And with the owls must end.

For, while they all were travelling home,
Cried Betty, "Tell us, Johnny, do,
Whére all this long night you have been,
What you have heard, what you have seen:
And, Johnny, mind you tell us true."   441

Now Johnny all night long had heard
The owls in tuneful concert strive;
No doubt too he the moon had seen;
For in the moonlight he had been   445
From eight o'clock till five.

And thus, to Betty's question, he
Made answer, like a traveller bold,
(His very words I give to you,)
"The cocks did crow to-whoo, to-whoo,
And the sun did shine so cold!"   451
—Thus answered Johnny in his glory,
And that was all his travel's story.

XXXII.

MICHAEL.

A PASTORAL POEM.

[Composed October 11–December 9, 1800.—
Published 1800.]

If from the public way you turn your steps
Up the tumultuous brook of Green-head
     Ghyll,
You will suppose that with an upright
     path
Your feet must struggle; in such bold
     ascent
The pastoral mountains front you, face to
     face.   5
But, courage! for around that boisterous
     brook
The mountains have all opened out them-
     selves,
And made a hidden valley of their own.
No habitation can be seen; but they
Who journey thither find themselves
     alone   10
With a few sheep, with rocks and stones,
     and kites
That overhead are sailing in the sky.
It is in truth an utter solitude;

Nor should I have made mention of this
     Dell
But for one object which you might
     pass by,   15
Might see and notice not. Beside the
     brook
Appears a straggling heap of unhewn
     stones!
And to that simple object appertains
A story—unenriched with strange events,
Yet not unfit, I deem, for the fireside,   20
Or for the summer shade. It was the first
Of those domestic tales that spake to me
Of Shepherds, dwellers in the valleys,
     men
Whom I already loved;—not verily
For their own sakes, but for the fields
     and hills   25
Where was their occupation and abode.
And hence this Tale, while I was yet a
     Boy
Careless of books, yet having felt the
     power
Of Nature, by the gentle agency
Of natural objects, led me on to feel   30
For passions that were not my own, and
     think
(At random and imperfectly indeed)
On man, the heart of man, and human life.
Therefore, although it be a history
Homely and rude, I will relate the same   35
For the delight of a few natural hearts;
And, with yet fonder feeling, for the sake
Of youthful Poets, who among these hills
Will be my second self when I am gone.

Upon the forest-side in Grasmere Vale
There dwelt a Shepherd, Michael was his
     name;   41
An old man, stout of heart, and strong of
     limb.
His bodily frame had been from youth to
     age
Of an unusual strength: his mind was
     keen,
Intense, and frugal, apt for all affairs,   45
And in his shepherd's calling he was
     prompt
And watchful more than ordinary men.
Hence had he learned the meaning of all
     winds,

Of blasts of every tone; and oftentimes,
When others heeded not, He heard the
    South   50
Make subterranean music, like the noise
Of bagpipers on distant Highland hills.
The Shepherd, at such warning, of his
    flock
Bethought him, and he to himself would
    say,
"The winds are now devising work for
    me!"   55
And, truly, at all times, the storm, that
    drives
The traveller to a shelter, summoned him
Up to the mountains: he had been alone
Amid the heart of many thousand mists,
That came to him, and left him, on the
    heights.   60
So lived he till his eightieth year was
    past.
And grossly that man errs, who should
    suppose
That the green valleys, and the streams
    and rocks,
Were things indifferent to the Shepherd's
    thoughts.
Fields, where with cheerful spirits he had
    breathed   65
The common air; hills, which with vigor-
    ous step
He had so often climbed; which had
    impressed
So many incidents upon his mind
Of hardship, skill or courage, joy or fear;
Which, like a book, preserved the
    memory   70
Of the dumb animals, whom he had
    saved,
Had fed or sheltered, linking to such
    acts
The certainty of honourable gain;
Those fields, those hills—what could they
    less? had laid
Strong hold on his affections, were to
    him   75
A pleasurable feeling of blind love,
The pleasure which there is in life itself.

His days had not been passed in single-
    ness.
His Helpmate was a comely matron, old—

Though younger than himself full twenty
    years.   80
She was a woman of a stirring life,
Whose heart was in her house: two wheels
    she had
Of antique form; this large, for spinning
    wool;
That small, for flax; and, if one wheel
    had rest,
It was because the other was at work.   85
The Pair had but one inmate in their
    house,
An only Child, who had been born to them
When Michael, telling o'er his years,
    began
To deem that he was old,—in shepherd's
    phrase,
With one foot in the grave. This only
    Son,   90
With two brave sheep-dogs tried in many
    a storm,
The one of an inestimable worth,
Made all their household. I may truly
    say,
That they were as a proverb in the vale
For endless industry. When day was
    gone,   95
And from their occupations out of doors
The Son and Father were come home,
    even then,
Their labour did not cease; unless when
    all
Turned to the cleanly supper-board, and
    there,
Each with a mess of pottage and skimmed
    milk,   100
Sat round the basket piled with oaten
    cakes,
And their plain home-made cheese. Yet
    when the meal
Was ended, Luke (for so the Son was
    named)
And his old Father both betook them-
    selves
To such convenient work as might employ
Their hands by the fire-side; perhaps to
    card   105
Wool for the Housewife's spindle, or
    repair
Some injury done to sickle, flail, or scythe,
Or other implement of house or field.

Down from the ceiling, by the chim-
ney's edge,   110
That in our ancient uncouth country style
With huge and black projection over-
browed
Large space beneath, as duly as the light
Of day grew dim the Housewife hung a
lamp ;
An aged utensil, which had performed 115
Service beyond all others of its kind.
Early at evening did it burn—and late,
Surviving comrade of uncounted hours,
Which, going by from year to year, had
found,
And left, the couple neither gay perhaps
Nor cheerful, yet with objects and with
hopes,   121
Living a life of eager industry.
And now, when Luke had reached his
eighteenth year,
There by the light of this old lamp they
sate,
Father and Son, while far into the night
The Housewife plied her own peculiar
work,   126
Making the cottage through the silent
hours
Murmur as with the sound of summer flies.
This light was famous in its neighbour-
hood,
And was a public symbol of the life   130
That thrifty Pair had lived. For, as it
chanced,
Their cottage on a plot of rising ground
Stood single, with large prospect, north
and south,
High into Easedale, up to Dunmail-Raise,
And westward to the village near the
lake ;   135
And from this constant light, so regular,
And so far seen, the House itself, by all
Who dwelt within the limits of the vale,
Both old and young, was named THE
EVENING STAR.

Thus living on through such a length of
years,   140
The Shepherd, if he loved himself, must
needs
Have loved his Helpmate ; but to Mi-
chael's heart

This son of his old age was yet more
dear—
Less from instinctive tenderness, the same
Fond spirit that blindly works in the
blood of all—   145
Than that a child, more than all other
gifts
That earth can offer to declining man,
Brings hope with it, and forward-looking
thoughts,
And stirrings of inquietude, when they
By tendency of nature needs must fail. 150
Exceeding was the love he bare to him,
His heart and his heart's joy ! For often-
times
Old Michael, while he was a babe in arms,
Had done him female service, not alone
For pastime and delight, as is the use 155
Of fathers, but with patient mind enforced
To acts of tenderness ; and he had rocked
His cradle, as with a woman's gentle hand.

And in a later time, ere yet the Boy
Had put on boy's attire, did Michael
love,   160
Albeit of a stern unbending mind,
To have the Young-one in his sight,
when he
Wrought in the field, or on his shepherd's
stool
Sate with a fettered sheep before him
stretched
Under the large old oak, that near his
door   165
Stood single, and, from matchless depth
of shade,
Chosen for the Shearer's covert from the
sun,
Thence in our rustic dialect was called
The CLIPPING TREE,[1] a name which yet it
bears.
There, while they two were sitting in the
shade,   170
With others round them, earnest all and
blithe,
Would Michael exercise his heart with
looks
Of fond correction and reproof bestowed

---

[1] Clipping is the word used in the North of
England for shearing.

Upon the Child, if he disturbed the sheep
By catching at their legs, or with his
    shouts   175
Scared them, while they lay still beneath
    the shears.

And when by Heaven's good grace the
    boy grew up
A healthy Lad, and carried in his cheek
Two steady roses that were five years old;
Then Michael from a winter coppice cut
With his own hand a sapling, which he
    hooped   181
With iron, making it throughout in all
Due requisites a perfect shepherd's staff,
And gave it to the Boy; wherewith equipt
He as a watchman oftentimes was placed
At gate or gap, to stem or turn the flock;
And, to his office prematurely called, 187
There stood the urchin, as you will divine,
Something between a hindrance and a
    help;
And for this cause not always, I believe,
Receiving from his Father hire of praise;
Though nought was left undone which
    staff, or voice,
Or looks, or threatening gestures, could
    perform

But soon as Luke, full ten years old,
    could stand
Against the mountain blasts; and to the
    heights,   195
Not fearing toil, nor length of weary ways,
He with his Father daily went, and they
Were as companions, why should I relate
That objects which the Shepherd loved
    before
Were dearer now? that from the Boy
    there came   200
Feelings and emanations—things which
    were
Light to the sun and music to the wind;
And that the old Man's heart seemed
    born again?

Thus in his Father's sight the Boy
    grew up:
And now, when he had reached his eigh-
    teenth year,   205
He was his comfort and his daily hope.

While in this sort the simple household
    lived
From day to day, to Michael's ear there
    came
Distressful tidings. Long before the time
Of which I speak, the Shepherd had been
    bound   210
In surety for his brother's son, a man
Of an industrious life, and ample means;
But unforeseen misfortunes suddenly
Had prest upon him; and old Michael
    now
Was summoned to discharge the for-
    feiture,   215
A grievous penalty, but little less
Than half his substance. This unlooked-
    for claim,
At the first hearing, for a moment took
More hope out of his life than he sup-
    posed
That any old man ever could have lost. 220
As soon as he had armed himself with
    strength
To look his trouble in the face, it seemed
The Shepherd's sole resource to sell at
    once
A portion of his patrimonial fields.
Such was his first resolve; he thought
    again,   225
And his heart failed him. "Isabel," said
    he,
Two evenings after he had heard the
    news,
"I have been toiling more than seventy
    years,
And in the open sunshine of God's love
Have we all lived; yet, if these fields
    of ours   230
Should pass into a stranger's hand, I think
That I could not lie quiet in my grave.
Our lot is a hard lot; the sun himself
Has scarcely been more diligent than I;
And I have lived to be a fool at last 235
To my own family. An evil man
That was, and made an evil choice, if he
Were false to us; and, if he were not false,
There are ten thousand to whom loss like
    this
Had been no sorrow. I forgive him;—
    but   240
'Twere better to be dumb than to talk thus.

When I began, my purpose was to
    speak
Of remedies and of a cheerful hope.
Our Luke shall leave us, Isabel; the land
Shall not go from us, and it shall be
    free;   245
He shall possess it, free as is the wind
That passes over it. We have, thou
    know'st,
Another kinsman—he will be our friend
In this distress. He is a prosperous man,
Thriving in trade—and Luke to him
    shall go,   250
And with his kinsman's help and his own
    thrift
He quickly will repair this loss, and then
He may return to us. If here he stay,
What can be done? Where every one is
    poor,
What can be gained?"
        At this the old Man paused, 255
And Isabel sat silent, for her mind
Was busy, looking back into past times.
There's Richard Bateman, thought she to
    herself,
He was a parish-boy—at the church-door
They made a gathering for him, shillings,
    pence,   260
And halfpennies, wherewith the neigh-
    bours bought
A basket, which they filled with pedlar's
    wares;
And, with this basket on his arm, the lad
Went up to London, found a master there,
Who, out of many, chose the trusty boy
To go and overlook his merchandise 266
Beyond the seas; where he grew won-
    drous rich,
And left estates and monies to the poor,
And, at his birth-place, built a chapel
    floored
With marble, which he sent from foreign
    lands.   270
These thoughts, and many others of like
    sort,
Passed quickly through the mind of
    Isabel,
And her face brightened. The old Man
    was glad,
And thus resumed:—"Well, Isabel! this
    scheme

These two days has been meat and drink
    to me.   275
Far more than we have lost is left us yet.
We have enough—I wish indeed that I
Were younger;—but this hope is a good
    hope.
Make ready Luke's best garments, of the
    best
Buy for him more, and let us send him
    forth   280
To-morrow, or the next day, or to-night:
    If he *could* go, the Boy should go to-
    night."

    Here Michael ceased, and to the fields
    went forth
With a light heart. The Housewife for
    five days
Was restless morn and night, and all day
    long   285
Wrought on with her best fingers to
    prepare
Things needful for the journey of her son.
But Isabel was glad when Sunday came
To stop her in her work: for, when she lay
By Michael's side, she through the last
    two nights   290
Heard him, how he was troubled in his
    sleep:
And when they rose at morning she
    could see
That all his hopes were gone. That day
    at noon
She said to Luke, while they two by
    themselves
Were sitting at the door, "Thou must
    not go: 295
We have no other Child but thee to lose,
None to remember—do not go away,
For if thou leave thy Father he will die."
The Youth made answer with a jocund
    voice;
And Isabel, when she had told her fears,
Recovered heart. That evening her best
    fare   301
Did she bring forth, and all together sat
Like happy people round a Christmas fire.

    With daylight Isabel resumed her work;
And all the ensuing week the house
    appeared   305

As cheerful as a grove in Spring: at length
The expected letter from their kinsman
   came,
With kind assurances that he would do
His utmost for the welfare of the Boy;
To which, requests were added, that
   forthwith   310
He might be sent to him. Ten times or
   more
The letter was read over; Isabel
Went forth to show it to the neighbours
   round;
Nor was there at that time on English land
A prouder heart than Luke's. When
   Isabel   315
Had to her house returned, the old Man
   said,
"He shall depart to-morrow." To this
   word
The Housewife answered, talking much
   of things
Which, if at such short notice he should go,
Would surely be forgotten. But at length
She gave consent, and Michael was at
   ease.   321

Near the tumultuous brook of Green-
   head Ghyll,
In that deep valley, Michael had designed
To build a Sheep-fold; and, before he
   heard
The tidings of his melancholy loss,   325
For this same purpose he had gathered up
A heap of stones, which by the streamlet's
   edge
Lay thrown together, ready for the work.
With Luke that evening thitherward he
   walked:
And soon as they had reached the place
   he stopped,   330
And thus the old Man spake to him:—
   "My son,
To-morrow thou wilt leave me: with full
   heart
I look upon thee, for thou art the same
That wert a promise to me ere thy birth,
And all thy life hast been my daily joy.
I will relate to thee some little part   336
Of our two histories; 'twill do thee good
When thou art from me, even if I should
   touch

On things thou canst not know of.——
   After thou
First cam'st into the world—as oft befalls
To new-born infants—thou didst sleep
   away   341
Two days, and blessings from thy Father's
   tongue
Then fell upon thee. Day by day passed
   on,
And still I loved thee with increasing
   love.
Never to living ear came sweeter sounds
Than when I heard thee by our own fire-
   side   346
First uttering, without words, a natural
   tune;
While thou, a feeding babe, didst in thy
   joy
Sing at thy Mother's breast. Month
   followed month,
And in the open fields my life was passed
And on the mountains; else I think that
   thou   351
Hadst been brought up upon thy Father's
   knees.
But we were playmates, Luke: among
   these hills,
As well thou knowest, in us the old and
   young
Have played together, nor with me didst
   thou   355
Lack any pleasure which a boy can know."
Luke had a manly heart; but at these
   words
He sobbed aloud. The old Man grasped
   his hand,
And said, "Nay, do not take it so—I see
That these are things of which I need not
   speak.   360
—Even to the utmost I have been to thee
A kind and a good Father: and herein
I but repay a gift which I myself
Received at others' hands; for, though
   now old
Beyond the common life of man, I still 365
Remember them who loved me in my
   youth.
Both of them sleep together: here they
   lived,
As all their Forefathers had done; and,
   when

At length their time was come, they were
  not loth
To give their bodies to the family mould.
I wished that thou shouldst live the life
  they lived, 371
But 'tis a long time to look back, my
  Son,
And see so little gain from threescore
  years.
These fields were burthened when they
  came to me;
Till I was forty years of age, not more 375
Than half of my inheritance was mine.
I toiled and toiled; God blessed me in
  my work,
And till these three weeks past the land
  was free.
—It looks as if it never could endure
Another Master. Heaven forgive me,
  Luke, 380
If I judge ill for thee, but it seems good
That thou shouldst go."
              At this the old Man paused;
Then, pointing to the stones near which
  they stood,
Thus, after a short silence, he resumed:
"This was a work for us; and now, my
  Son, 385
It is a work for me. But, lay one stone—
Here, lay it for me, Luke, with thine own
  hands.
Nay, Boy, be of good hope;—we both
  may live
To see a better day. At eighty-four
I still am strong and hale;—do thou thy
  part; 390
I will do mine.—I will begin again
With many tasks that were resigned to
  thee:
Up to the heights, and in among the
  storms,
Will I without thee go again, and do 394
All works which I was wont to do alone,
Before I knew thy face.—Heaven bless
  thee, Boy!
Thy heart these two weeks has been beat-
  ing fast
With many hopes; it should be so—yes—
  yes—
I knew that thou couldst never have a
  wish

To leave me, Luke: thou hast been bound
  to me 400
Only by links of love: when thou art
  gone,
What will be left to us!—But I forget
My purposes. Lay now the corner-stone,
As I requested; and hereafter, Luke,
When thou art gone away, should evil
  men 405
Be thy companions, think of me, my Son,
And of this moment; hither turn thy
  thoughts,
And God will strengthen thee: amid all
  fear
And all temptation, Luke, I pray that
  thou
May'st bear in mind the life thy Fathers
  lived, 410
Who, being innocent, did for that cause
Bestir them in good deeds. Now, fare
  thee well—
When thou return'st, thou in this place
  wilt see
A work which is not here: a covenant 414
'Twill be between us; but, whatever fate
Befall thee, I shall love thee to the last,
And bear thy memory with me to the
  grave."

  The Shepherd ended here; and Luke
  stooped down,
And, as his Father had requested, laid
The first stone of the Sheep-fold. At the
  sight 420
The old Man's grief broke from him; to
  his heart
He pressed his Son, he kissèd him and
  wept;
And to the house together they returned.
—Hushed was that House in peace, or
  seeming peace,
Ere the night fell:—with morrow's dawn
  the Boy 425
Began his journey, and, when he had
  reached
The public way, he put on a bold face;
And all the neighbours, as he passed their
  doors,
Came forth with wishes and with farewell
  prayers, 429
That followed him till he was out of sight.

A good report did from their Kinsman
   come,
Of Luke and his well-doing: and the Boy
Wrote loving letters, full of wondrous
   news,
Which, as the Housewife phrased it, were
   throughout   434
"The prettiest letters that were ever seen."
Both parents read them with rejoicing
   hearts.
So, many months passed on: and once
   again
The Shepherd went about his daily work
With confident and cheerful thoughts;
   and now
Sometimes when he could find a leisure
   hour   440
He to that valley took his way, and there
Wrought at the Sheep-fold. Meantime
   Luke began
To slacken in his duty; and, at length,
He in the dissolute city gave himself
To evil courses: ignominy and shame 445
Fell on him, so that he was driven at last
To seek a hiding-place beyond the seas.

There is a comfort in the strength of
   love,
'Twill make a thing endurable, which else
Would overset the brain, or break the
   heart: 450
I have conversed with more than one who
   well
Remember the old Man, and what he was
Years after he had heard this heavy news.
His bodily frame had been from youth to
   age
Of an unusual strength. Among the rocks
He went, and still looked up to sun and
   cloud,   456
And listened to the wind; and, as before,
Performed all kinds of labour for his
   sheep,
And for the land, his small inheritance.
And to that hollow dell from time to
   time   460
Did he repair, to build the Fold of which
His flock had need. 'Tis not forgotten
   yet
The pity which was then in every heart
For the old Man—and 'tis believed by all

That many and many a day he thither went,
And never lifted up a single stone.   466

There, by the Sheep-fold, sometimes
   was he seen
Sitting alone, or with his faithful Dog,
Then old, beside him, lying at his feet.
The length of full seven years, from time
   to time,   470
He at the building of this Sheep-fold
   wrought,
And left the work unfinished when he
   died.
Three years, or little more, did Isabel
Survive her Husband: at her death the
   estate
Was sold, and went into a stranger's
   hand.   475
The Cottage which was named the EVEN-
   ING STAR
Is gone—the ploughshare has been through
   the ground
On which it stood; great changes have
   been wrought
In all the neighbourhood:—yet the oak
   is left
That grew beside their door; and the
   remains   480
Of the unfinished Sheep-fold may be seen
Beside the boisterous brook of Green-
   head Ghyll.

XXXIII.

THE WIDOW ON WINDERMERE SIDE.

[Composed 1837 (?).—Published 1842.]

I.

How beautiful when up a lofty height
Honour ascends among the humblest
   poor,
And feeling sinks as deep! See there the
   door
Of One, a Widow, left beneath a weight
Of blameless debt. On evil Fortune's
   spite   5
She wasted no complaint, but strove to
   make
A just repayment, both for conscience-
   sake
And that herself and hers should stand
   upright

In the world's eye. Her work when day-
light failed
Paused not, and through the depth of
night she kept   10
Such earnest vigils, that belief prevailed
With some, the noble Creature never
slept;
But, one by one, the hand of death as-
sailed
Her children from her inmost heart be-
wept.

II.

The Mother mourned, nor ceased her
tears to flow,   15
Till a winter's noon-day placed her buried
Son
Before her eyes, last child of many gone—
His raiment of angelic white, and lo!
His very feet bright as the dazzling snow
Which they are touching; yea far brighter,
even   20
As that which comes, or seems to come,
from heaven,
Surpasses aught these elements can show.
Much she rejoiced, trusting that from
that hour
Whate'er befell she could not grieve or
pine;
But the Transfigured, in and out of season,
Appeared, and spiritual presence gained
a power   26
Over material forms that mastered reason.
Oh, gracious Heaven, in pity make her
thine!

III.

But why that prayer? as if to her could
come
No good but by the way that leads to
bliss   30
Through Death,—so judging we should
judge amiss.
Since reason failed want is her threatened
doom,
Yet frequent transports mitigate the
gloom:
Nor of those maniacs is she one that kiss
The air or laugh upon a precipice;   35
No, passing through strange sufferings
toward the tomb,

She smiles as if a martyr's crown were
won:
Oft, when light breaks through clouds or
waving trees,
With outspread arms and fallen upon her
knees
The Mother hails in her descending Son
An Angel, and in earthly ecstasies   41
Her own angelic glory seems begun.

XXXIV.

THE ARMENIAN LADY'S LOVE.

[Composed 1830.—Published 1835.]

[The subject of the following poem is from the
Orlandus of the author's friend, Kenelm Henry
Digby: and the liberty is taken of inscribing it
to him as an acknowledgment, however unwor-
thy, of pleasure and instruction derived from his
numerous and valuable writings, illustrative of
the piety and chivalry of the olden time.]

I.

You have heard "a Spanish Lady
How she wooed an English man;"[1]
Hear now of a fair Armenian,
Daughter of the proud Soldàn;
How she loved a Christian Slave, and
told her pain   5
By word, look, deed, with hope that he
might love again.

II.

"Pluck that rose, it moves my liking,"
Said she, lifting up her veil;
"Pluck it for me, gentle gardener,
Ere it wither and grow pale."   10
"Princess fair, I till the ground, but may
not take
From twig or bed an humbler flower, even
for your sake!"

III.

"Grieved am I, submissive Christian!
To behold thy captive state;
Women, in your land, may pity   15
(May they not?) the unfortunate."

[1] See in Percy's Reliques that fine old ballad,
"The Spanish Lady's Love;" from which Poem
the form of stanza, as suitable to dialogue, is
adopted.

"Yes, kind Lady! otherwise man could
   not bear
Life, which to every one that breathes is
   full of care."

IV.

"Worse than idle is compassion
   If it end in tears and sighs;   20
Thee from bondage would I rescue
   And from vile indignities;
Nurtured, as thy mien bespeaks, in high
   degree,
Look up—and help a hand that longs to
   set thee free."

V.

'Lady! dread the wish, nor venture 25
   In such peril to engage;
Think how it would stir against you
   Your most loving father's rage:
Sad deliverance would it be, and yoked
   with shame,
Should troubles overflow on her from
   whom it came."   30

VI.

"Generous Frank! the just in effort
   Are of inward peace secure;
Hardships for the brave encountered
   Even the feeblest may endure:
If almighty grace through me thy chains
   unbind,   35
My father for slave's work may seek a
   slave in mind."

VII.

"Princess, at this burst of goodness,
   My long-frozen heart grows warm!"
"Yet you make all courage fruitless,
   Me to save from chance of harm: 40
Leading such companion I that gilded
   dome,
Yon minarets, would gladly leave for his
   worst home."

VIII.

"Feeling tunes your voice, fair Princess!
   And your brow is free from scorn,
Else these words would come like
   mockery,   45
   Sharper than the pointed thorn."

"Whence the undeserved mistrust? Too
   wide apart
Our faith hath been,—O would that eyes
   could see the heart!"

IX.

"Tempt me not, I pray; my doom is
   These base implements to wield;   50
Rusty lance, I ne'er shall grasp thee,
   Ne'er assoil my cobwebbed shield!
Never see my native land, nor castle
   towers,
Nor Her who thinking of me there counts
   widowed hours."

X.

"Prisoner! pardon youthful fancies, 55
   Wedded? If you *can*, say no!
Blessed is and be your consort;
   Hopes I cherished—let them go!
Handmaid's privilege would leave my
   purpose free,
Without another link to my felicity."   60

XI.

"Wedded love with loyal Christians,
   Lady, is a mystery rare;
Body, heart, and soul in union,
   Make one being of a pair."
"Humble love in me would look for no
   return,   65
Soft as a guiding star that cheers, but
   cannot burn."

XII.

"Gracious Allah! by such title
   Do I dare to thank the God,
Him who thus exalts thy spirit,
   Flower of an unchristian sod!   70
Or hast thou put off wings which thou in
   heaven dost wear?
What have I seen, and heard, or dreamt?
   where am I? where?"

XIII.

Here broke off the dangerous converse:
   Less impassioned words might tell
How the pair escaped together,   75
   Tears not wanting, nor a knell
Of sorrow in her heart while through her
   father's door,
And from her narrow world, she passed
   for evermore.

XIV.

But affections higher, holier,
  Urged her steps; she shrunk from
    trust   80
In a sensual creed that trampled
  Woman's birthright into dust.
Little be the wonder then, the blame be
    none,
If she, a timid Maid, hath put such bold-
    ness on.

XV.

Judge both Fugitives with knowledge:
  In those old romantic days   86
Mighty were the soul's commandments
  To support, restrain, or raise.
Foes might hang upon their path, snakes
    rustle near,
But nothing from their inward selves had
    they to fear.   90

XVI.

Thought infirm ne'er came between
  them,
  Whether printing desert sands
With accordant steps, or gathering
  Forest-fruit with social hands;
Or whispering like two reeds that in the
    cold moonbeam   95
Bend with the breeze their heads, beside
  a crystal stream.

XVII.

On a friendly deck reposing
  They at length for Venice steer;
There, when they had closed their
    voyage,
  One, who daily on the pier   100
Watched for tidings from the East, be-
    held his Lord,
Fell down and clasped his knees for joy,
  not uttering word.

XVIII.

Mutual was the sudden transport;
  Breathless questions followed fast,
Years contracting to a moment,   105
  Each word greedier than the last;
"Hie thee to the Countess, friend! return
  with speed,
And of this Stranger speak by whom her
  lord was freed.

XIX.

"Say that I, who might have languished,
  Drooped and pined till life was spent,
Now before the gates of Stolberg   111
  My Deliverer would present
For a crowning recompense, the precious
    grace
Of her who in my heart still holds her
    ancient place.

XX.

"Make it known that my Companion 115
  Is of royal eastern blood,
Thirsting after all perfection,
  Innocent, and meek, and good,
Though with misbelievers bred; but that
    dark night
Will holy Church disperse by beams of
    gospel-light."   120

XXI.

Swiftly went that grey-haired Servant,
  Soon returned a trusty Page
Charged with greetings, benedictions,
  Thanks and praises, each a gage
For a sunny thought to cheer the Stran-
    ger's way,   125
Her virtuous scruples to remove, her fears
  allay.

XXII.

And how blest the Reunited,
  While beneath their castle-walls
Runs a deafening noise of welcome!—
  Blest, though every tear that falls 130
Doth in its silence of past sorrow tell,
And makes a meeting seem most like a
  dear farewell.

XXIII.

Through a haze of human nature,
  Glorified by heavenly light,
Looked the beautiful Deliverer   135
  On that overpowering sight,
While across her virgin cheek pure blushes
  strayed,
For every tender sacrifice her heart had
  made.

XXIV.

On the ground the weeping Countess
  Knelt and kissed the Stranger's hand;
Act of soul-devoted homage,   141
  Pledge of an eternal band:
Nor did aught of future days that kiss
  belie,
Which, with a generous shout, the crowd
  did ratify.

XXV.

Constant to the fair Armenian,   145
  Gentle pleasures round her moved,
Like a tutelary spirit
  Reverenced, like a sister loved.
Christian meekness smoothed for all the
  path of life,
Who, loving most, should wiseliest love,
  their only strife.   150

XXVI.

Mute memento of that union
  In a Saxon church survives,
Where a cross-legged Knight lies sculp-
  tured
  As between two wedded Wives—
Figures with armorial signs of race and
  birth,   155
And the vain rank the pilgrims bore
  while yet on earth.

XXXV.

LOVING AND LIKING:

IRREGULAR VERSES

ADDRESSED TO A CHILD.

(BY MY SISTER.)

[Composed 1832.—Published 1835.]

THERE'S more in words than I can teach:
Yet listen, Child!—I would not preach;
But only give some plain directions
To guide your speech and your affections.
Say not you *love* a roasted fowl   5
But you may love a screaming owl,
And, if you can, the unwieldy toad
That crawls from his secure abode
Within the mossy garden wall
When evening dews begin to fall.   10

Oh! mark the beauty of his eye:
What wonders in that circle lie!
So clear, so bright, our fathers said
He wears a jewel in his head!
And when, upon some showery day,   15
Into a path or public way
A frog leaps out from bordering grass,
Startling the timid as they pass,
Do you observe him, and endeavour
To take the intruder into favour;   20
Learning from him to find a reason
For a light heart in a dull season.
And you may love him in the pool,
That is for him a happy school,
In which he swims as taught by nature, 25
Fit pattern for a human creature,
Glancing amid the water bright,
And sending upward sparkling light.

Nor blush if o'er your heart be stealing
A love for things that have no feeling: 30
The spring's first rose by you espied,
May fill your breast with joyful pride;
And you may love the strawberry-flower,
And love the strawberry in its bower;
But when the fruit, so often praised   35
For beauty, to your lip is raised,
Say not you *love* the delicate treat,
But *like* it, enjoy it, and thankfully eat.

Long may you love your pensioner
  mouse,
Though one of a tribe that torment the
  house: 40
Nor dislike for her cruel sport the cat
Deadly foe both of mouse and rat;
Remember she follows the law of her kind,
And Instinct is neither wayward nor
  blind.
Then think of her beautiful gliding form,
Her tread that would scarcely crush a
  worm,   46
And her soothing song by the winter fire,
Soft as the dying throb of the lyre.

I would not circumscribe your love:
It may soar with the eagle and brood with
  the dove,   50
May pierce the earth with the patient
  mole,
Or track the hedgehog to his hole.
Loving and liking are the solace of life,

Rock the cradle of joy, smooth the death-
bed of strife.
You love your father and your mother, 55
Your grown-up and your baby brother;
You love your sister and your friends,
And countless blessings which God sends:
And while these right affections play,
You *live* each moment of your day;   60
They lead you on to full content,
And likings fresh and innocent,
That store the mind, the memory feed,
And prompt to many a gentle deed:
But *likings* come, and pass away;   65
'Tis *love* that remains till our latest day:
Our heavenward guide is holy love,
And will be our bliss with saints above.

XXXVI.

FAREWELL LINES.

[Composed 1828 (?).—Published 1842.]

"HIGH bliss is only for a higher state,"
But, surely, if severe afflictions borne
With patience merit the reward of peace,
Peace ye deserve; and may the solid good,
Sought by a wise though late exchange,
and here   5
With bounteous hand beneath a cottage-
roof
To you accorded, never be withdrawn,
Nor for the world's best promises re-
nounced.
Most soothing was it for a welcome
Friend,
Fresh from the crowded city, to behold 10
That lonely union, privacy so deep,
Such calm employments, such entire con-
tent.
So when the rain is over, the storm laid,
A pair of herons oft-times have I seen,
Upon a rocky islet, side by side,   15
Drying their feathers in the sun, at ease;
And so, when night with grateful gloom
had fallen,
Two glow-worms in such nearness that
they shared,
As seemed, their soft self-satisfying light,
Each with the other, on the dewy ground,
Where He that made them blesses their
repose.—   21

When wandering among lakes and hills
I note,
Once more, those creatures thus by nature
paired,
And guarded in their tranquil state of
life,
Even, as your happy presence to my mind
Their union brought, will they repay the
debt,   26
And send a thankful spirit back to you,
With hope that we, dear Friends! shall
meet again.

XXXVII.

THE REDBREAST.

(SUGGESTED IN A WESTMORELAND COTTAGE.)

[Composed 1834.—Published 1835.]

DRIVEN in by Autumn's sharpening air
From half-stripped woods and pastures
bare,
Brisk Robin seeks a kindlier home:
Not like a beggar is he come,
But enters as a looked-for guest,   5
Confiding in his ruddy breast,
As if it were a natural shield
Charged with a blazon on the field,
Due to that good and pious deed
Of which we in the Ballad read.   10
But pensive fancies putting by,
And wild-wood sorrows, speedily
He plays the expert ventriloquist;
And, caught by glimpses now—now
missed,
Puzzles the listener with a doubt   15
If the soft voice he throws about
Comes from within doors or without!
Was ever such a sweet confusion,
Sustained by delicate illusion?
He's at your elbow—to your feeling   20
The notes are from the floor or ceiling;
And there's a riddle to be guessed,
Till you have marked his heaving chest,
And busy throat whose sink and swell
Betray the Elf that loves to dwell   25
In Robin's bosom, as a chosen cell.

Heart-pleased we smile upon the Bird
If seen, and with like pleasure stirred
Commend him, when he's only heard.
But small and fugitive our gain   30

Compared with *hers* who long hath lain,
With languid limbs and patient head
Reposing on a lone sick-bed;
Where now she daily hears a strain
That cheats her of too busy cares,   35
Eases her pain, and helps her prayers.
And who but this dear Bird beguiled
The fever of that pale-faced Child;
Now cooling, with his passing wing,
Her forehead, like a breeze of Spring;   40
Recalling now, with descant soft
Shed round her pillow from aloft,
Sweet thoughts of angels hovering nigh,
And the invisible sympathy
Of "Matthew, Mark, and Luke, and
     John,   45
Blessing the bed she lies upon?"[1]
And sometimes, just as listening ends
In slumber, with the cadence blends
A dream of that low-warbled hymn
Which old folk, fondly pleased to trim   50
Lamps of faith, now burning dim,
Say that the Cherubs carved in stone,
When clouds gave way at dead of night
And the ancient church was filled with
     light,
Used to sing in heavenly tone,   55
Above and round the sacred places
They guard, with wingèd baby-faces.

Thrice happy Creature! in all lands
Nurtured by hospitable hands:
Free entrance to this cot has he,   60
Entrance and exit both *yet* free;
And when the keen unruffled weather,
That thus brings man and bird together,
Shall with its pleasantness be past,
And casement closed and door made fast,
To keep at bay the howling blast,   66
He needs not fear the season's rage,
For the whole house is Robin's cage.
Whether the bird flit here or there,
O'er table *lilt*, or perch on chair,   70
Though some may frown and make a
     stir,

---

[1] The words—
     "Matthew, Mark, and Luke, and John,
       Bless the bed that I lie on,"
are part of a child's prayer, still in general use
through the northern counties.

To scare him as a trespasser,
And he belike will flinch or start,
Good friends he has to take his part;
One chiefly, who with voice and look   75
Pleads for him from the chimney-nook,
Where sits the Dame, and wears away
Her long and vacant holiday;
With images about her heart,
Reflected from the years gone by,   80
On human nature's second infancy.

XXXVIII.

HER EYES ARE WILD.

[Composed 1798.—Published 1798.]

I.

Her eyes are wild, her head is bare,
The sun has burnt her coal-black hair;
Her eyebrows have a rusty stain,
And she came far from over the main.
She has a baby on her arm,   5
Or else she were alone:
And underneath the hay-stack warm,
And on the greenwood stone,
She talked and sung the woods among,
And it was in the English tongue.   10

II.

"Sweet babe! they say that I am mad,
But nay, my heart is far too glad;
And I am happy when I sing
Full many a sad and doleful thing:
Then, lovely baby, do not fear!   15
I pray thee have no fear of me;
But safe as in a cradle, here
My lovely baby! thou shalt be:
To thee I know too much I owe;
I cannot work thee any woe.   20

III.

"A fire was once within my brain;
And in my head a dull, dull pain;
And fiendish faces, one, two, three,
Hung at my breast, and pulled at me;
But then there came a sight of joy;   25
It came at once to do me good;
I waked, and saw my little boy,
My little boy of flesh and blood;

Oh joy for me that sight to see!
For he was here, and only he. 30

IV.

"Suck, little babe, oh suck again!
It cools my blood; it cools my brain;
Thy lips I feel them, baby! they
Draw from my heart the pain away.
Oh! press me with thy little hand; 35
It loosens something at my chest;
About that tight and deadly band
I feel thy little fingers prest.
The breeze I see is in the tree:
It comes to cool my babe and me. 40

V.

"Oh! love me, love me, little boy!
Thou art thy mother's only joy;
And do not dread the waves below,
When o'er the sea-rock's edge we go;
The high crag cannot work me harm, 45
Nor leaping torrents when they howl;
The babe I carry on my arm,
He saves for me my precious soul;
Then happy lie; for blest am I;
Without me my sweet babe would die. 50

VI.

"Then do not fear, my boy! for thee
Bold as a lion will I be;
And I will always be thy guide,
Through hollow snows and rivers wide.
I'll build an Indian bower; I know 55
The leaves that make the softest bed:
And if from me thou wilt not go,
But still be true till I am dead,
My pretty thing! then thou shalt sing
As merry as the birds in spring. 60

VII.

"Thy father cares not for my breast,
'Tis thine, sweet baby, there to rest;
'Tis all thine own!—and if its hue
Be changed, that was so fair to view,

'Tis fair enough for thee, my dove! 65
My beauty, little child, is flown,
But thou wilt live with me in love;
And what if my poor cheek be brown?
'Tis well for me thou canst not see
How pale and wan it else would be. 70

VIII.

"Dread not their taunts, my little Life;
I am thy father's wedded wife;
And underneath the spreading tree
We two will live in honesty.
If his sweet boy he could forsake, 75
With me he never would have stayed:
From him no harm my babe can take;
But he, poor man! is wretched made;
And every day we two will pray
For him that's gone and far away 80

IX.

"I'll teach my boy the sweetest things:
I'll teach him how the owlet sings.
My little babe! thy lips are still,
And thou hast almost sucked thy fill.
—Where art thou gone, my own dear
    child? 85
What wicked looks are those I see?
Alas! Alas! that look so wild,
It never, never came from me:
If thou art mad, my pretty lad,
Then I must be for ever sad. 90

X.

"Oh! smile on me, my little lamb!
For I thy own dear mother am:
My love for thee has well been tried:
I've sought thy father far and wide.
I know the poisons of the shade; 95
I know the earth-nuts fit for food:
Then, pretty dear, be not afraid:
We'll find thy father in the wood.
Now laugh and be gay, to the woods
    away!
And there, my babe, we'll live for
    aye." 100

POEMS ON THE NAMING OF PLACES.

ADVERTISEMENT.

By persons resident in the country, and attached to rural objects, many places will be found unnamed or of unknown names, where little Incidents must have occurred, or feelings been experienced, which will have given to such places a private and peculiar interest. From a wish to give some sort of record to such Incidents, and renew the gratification of such feelings, Names have been given to Places by the Author and some of his Friends, and the following Poems written in consequence.

I.

[Composed 1800.—Published 1800.]

It was an April morning: fresh and clear
The Rivulet, delighting in its strength,
Ran with a young man's speed; and yet the voice
Of waters which the winter had supplied
Was softened down into a vernal tone. 5
The spirit of enjoyment and desire,
And hopes and wishes, from all living things
Went circling, like a multitude of sounds.
The budding groves seemed eager to urge on
The steps of June; as if their various hues
Were only hindrances that stood between
Them and their object: but, meanwhile, prevailed 12
Such an entire contentment in the air
That every naked ash, and tardy tree
Yet leafless, showed as if the countenance
With which it looked on this delightful day 16
Were native to the summer.—Up the brook
I roamed in the confusion of my heart,
Alive to all things and forgetting all.
At length I to a sudden turning came 20
In this continuous glen, where down a rock
The Stream, so ardent in its course before,
Sent forth such sallies of glad sound, that all
Which I till then had heard appeared the voice
Of common pleasure: beast and bird, the lamb, 25

The shepherd's dog, the linnet and the thrush,
Vied with this waterfall, and made a song
Which, while I listened, seemed like the wild growth
Or like some natural produce of the air,
That could not cease to be. Green leaves were here; 30
But 'twas the foliage of the rocks—the birch,
The yew, the holly, and the bright green thorn,
With hanging islands of resplendent furze:
And on a summit, distant a short space,
By any who should look beyond the dell 35
A single mountain-cottage might be seen.
I gazed and gazed, and to myself I said,
"Our thoughts at least are ours; and this wild nook,
My Emma[1], I will dedicate to thee."
—— Soon did the spot become my other home, 40
My dwelling, and my out-of-doors abode.
And of the Shepherds who have seen me there,
To whom I sometimes in our idle talk
Have told this fancy, two or three, perhaps,
Years after we are gone and in our graves,
When they have cause to speak of this wild place, 46
May call it by the name of Emma's Dell.

[1] Emma: the poet's sister Dorothy: Emmeline is elsewhere used as a pseudonym for her. See editor's note on To a Butterfly, p. 897.—Ed.

II.

TO JOANNA.

[Composed August, 1800.—Published 1800.]

AMID the smoke of cities did you pass
The time of early youth; and there you
    learned,
From years of quiet industry, to love
The living Beings by your own fire-side,
With such a strong devotion, that your
    heart   5
Is slow to meet the sympathies of them
Who look upon the hills with tenderness,
And make dear friendships with the
    streams and groves.
Yet we, who are transgressors in this kind,
Dwelling retired in our simplicity   10
Among the woods and fields, we love you
    well,
Joanna! and I guess, since you have been
So distant from us now for two long years,
That you will gladly listen to discourse
However trivial, if you thence be taught
That they, with whom you once were
    happy, talk   16
Familiarly of you and of old times.

While I was seated, now some ten days
    past,
Beneath those lofty firs, that overtop
Their ancient neighbour, the old steeple-
    tower,   20
The Vicar from his gloomy house hard by
Came forth to greet me; and, when he
    had asked,
"How fares Joanna, that wild-hearted
    Maid!
And when will she return to us?" he
    paused;
And, after short exchange of village news,
He with grave looks demanded for what
    cause,   26
Reviving obsolete idolatry,
I, like a Runic Priest, in characters
Of formidable size had chiselled out
Some uncouth name upon the native rock,
Above the Rotha, by the forest-side.   31
—Now, by those dear immunities of heart
Engendered between malice and true love,
I was not loth to be so catechised,
And this was my reply:—"As it befell,

One summer morning we had walked
    abroad   36
At break of day, Joanna and myself.
—'Twas that delightful season when the
    broom,
Full-flowered, and visible on every steep,
Along the copses runs in veins of gold. 40
Our pathway led us on to Rotha's banks;
And, when we came in front of that tall
    rock
That eastward looks, I there stopped short
    —and stood
Tracing the lofty barrier with my eye
From base to summit; such delight I
    found   45
To note in shrub and tree, in stone and
    flower,
That intermixture of delicious hues,
Along so vast a surface, all at once,
In one impression, by connecting force
Of their own beauty, imaged in the heart.
—When I had gazed perhaps two minutes'
    space,   51
Joanna, looking in my eyes, beheld
That ravishment of mine, and laughed
    aloud.
The Rock, like something starting from a
    sleep,
Took up the Lady's voice, and laughed
    again;   55
That ancient Woman seated on Helm-crag
Was ready with her cavern; Hammar-scar,
And the tall Steep of Silver-how, sent forth
A noise of laughter; southern Loughrigg
    heard,
And Fairfield answered with a mountain
    tone;   60
Helvellyn far into the clear blue sky
Carried the Lady's voice,—old Skiddaw
    blew
His speaking-trumpet;—back out of the
    clouds
Of Glaramara southward came the voice;
And Kirkstone tossed it from his misty
    head.   65
—Now whether (said I to our cordial
    Friend,
Who in the hey-day of astonishment
Smiled in my face) this were in simple
    truth
A work accomplished by the brotherhood

Of ancient mountains, or my ear was
   touched   70
With dreams and visionary impulses
To me alone imparted, sure I am
That there was a loud uproar in tho hills.
And, while we both were listening, to my
   side
The fair Joanna drew, as if she wished 75
To shelter from some object of her fear.
—And hence, long afterwards, when eigh-
   teen moons
Were wasted, as I chanced to walk alone
Beneath this rock, at sunrise, on a calm
And silent morning, I sat down, and there,
In memory of affections old and true, 81
I chiselled out in those rude characters
Joanna's name deep in the living stone:—
And I, and all who dwell by my fireside,
Have called the lovely rock, JOANNA'S
   ROCK."   85

    NOTE.—In Cumberland and Westmoreland are
several Inscriptions, upon the native rock, which,
from the wasting of time, and the rudeness of the
workmanship, have been mistaken for Runic.
They are, without doubt, Roman.
    The Rotha, mentioned in this poem, is the
River which, flowing through the lakes of Gras-
mere and Rydal, falls into Winandermere. On
Helm-crag, that impressive single mountain at
the head of the Vale of Grasmere, is a rock which
from most points of view bears a striking resem-
blance to an old Woman cowering. Close by this
rock is one of those fissures or caverns, which in
the language of the country are called dungeons.
Most of the mountains here mentioned imme-
diately surround the Vale of Grasmere; of the
others, some are at a considerable distance, but
they belong to the same cluster.

III.

[Composed 1800.—Published 1800.]

THERE is an Eminence,—of these our hills
The last that parleys with the setting sun;
We can behold it from our orchard seat;
And, when at evening we pursue our walk
Along the public way, this Peak, so high
Above us, and so distant in its height, 6
Is visible; and often seems to send
Its own deep quiet to restore our hearts.
The meteors make of it a favourite haunt:
The star of Jove, so beautiful and large
In the mid heavens, is never half so fair

As when he shines above it. 'Tis in truth
The loneliest place we have among the
   clouds.
And She who dwells with me, whom I
   have loved
With such communion that no place on
   earth   15
Can ever be a solitude to me,
Hath to this lonely Summit given my
   Name.

IV.

[Composed October 10, 1800.—Published 1800.]

A NARROW girdle of rough stones and crags,
A rude and natural causeway, interposed
Between the water and a winding slope
Of copse and thicket, leaves the eastern
   shore
Of Grasmere safe in its own privacy: 5
And there myself and two beloved Friends,
One calm September morning, ere the mist
Had altogether yielded to the sun,
Sauntered on this retired and difficult way.
—Ill suits the road with one in haste;
   but we   10
Played with our time; and, as we strolled
   along,
It was our occupation to observe
Such objects as the waves had tossed
   ashore—
Feather, or leaf, or weed, or withered
   bough,
Each on the other heaped, along the line
Of the dry wreck. And, in our vacant
   mood,   16
Not seldom did we stop to watch some tuft
Of dandelion seed or thistle's beard,
That skimmed the surface of the dead
   calm lake,
Suddenly halting now—a lifeless stand!
And starting off again with freak as sudden;
In all its sportive wanderings, all the while,
Making report of an invisible breeze
That was its wings, its chariot, and its
   horse,
Its playmate, rather say, its moving soul.
—And often, trifling with a privilege 26
Alike indulged to all, we paused, one now,
And now the other, to point out, perchance
To pluck, some flower or water-weed, too
   fair

Either to be divided from the place 30
On which it grew, or to be left alone
To its own beauty. Many such there are,
Fair ferns and flowers, and chiefly that
    tall fern,
So stately, of the Queen Osmunda named;
Plant lovelier, in its own retired abode 35
On Grasmere's beach, than Naiad by the
    side
Of Grecian brook, or Lady of the Mere,
Sole-sitting by the shores of old romance.
—So fared we that bright morning: from
    the fields,
Meanwhile, a noise was heard, the busy
    mirth 40
Of reapers, men and women, boys and girls.
Delighted much to listen to those sounds,
And feeding thus our fancies, we advanced
Along the indented shore; when suddenly,
Through a thin veil of glittering haze was
    seen 45
Before us, on a point of jutting land,
The tall and upright figure of a Man
Attired in peasant's garb, who stood alone,
Angling beside the margin of the lake.
"Improvident and reckless," we exclaimed,
"The Man must be, who thus can lose a
    day 51
Of the mid harvest, when the labourer's
    hire
Is ample, and some little might be stored
Wherewith to cheer him in the winter
    time."
Thus talking of that Peasant, we ap-
    proached 55
Close to the spot where with his rod and
    line
He stood alone; whereat he turned his
    head
To greet us—and we saw a Man worn down
By sickness, gaunt and lean, with sunken
    cheeks
And wasted limbs, his legs so long and lean
That for my single self I looked at them,
Forgetful of the body they sustained.— 62
Too weak to labour in the harvest field,
The Man was using his best skill to gain
A pittance from the dead unfeeling lake
That knew not of his wants. I will not say
What thoughts immediately were ours,
    nor how 67

The happy idleness of that sweet morn,
With all its lovely images, was changed
To serious musing and to self-reproach. 70
Nor did we fail to see within ourselves
What need there is to be reserved in speech,
And temper all our thoughts with charity.
—Therefore, unwilling to forget that day,
My Friend, Myself, and She who then
    received 75
The same admonishment, have called the
    place
By a memorial name, uncouth indeed
As e'er by mariner was given to bay
Or foreland, on a new-discovered coast;
And POINT RASH-JUDGMENT is the Name
    it bears. 80

V.

TO M. H.

[Composed after December 21, and before
December 23, 1799.—Published 1800.]

OUR walk was far among the ancient trees:
There was no road, nor any woodman's
    path;
But a thick umbrage—checking the wild
    growth
Of weed and sapling, along soft green turf
Beneath the branches—of itself had made
A track, that brought us to a slip of lawn,
And a small bed of water in the woods. 7
All round this pool both flocks and herds
    might drink
On its firm margin, even as from a well,
Or some stone-basin which the herdsman's
    hand 10
Had shaped for their refreshment; nor
    did sun,
Or wind from any quarter, ever come,
But as a blessing to this calm recess,
This glade of water and this one green
    field.
The spot was made by Nature for herself;
The travellers know it not, and 'twill
    remain 16
Unknown to them; but it is beautiful;
And if a man should plant his cottage near,
Should sleep beneath the shelter of its trees,
And blend its waters with his daily meal,
He would so love it, that in his death-hour
Its image would survive among his
    thoughts: 22

And therefore, my sweet MARY, this still
  Nook,
With all its beeches, we have named from
  You!

VI.

[Begun August 29, 30, 1800.—Finished 1802.—
Published 1815.]

WHEN, to the attractions of the busy world
Preferring studious leisure, I had chosen
A habitation in this peaceful Vale,
Sharp season followed of continual storm
In deepest winter; and, from week to
  week,   5
Pathway, and lane, and public road, were
  clogged
With frequent showers of snow. Upon a
  hill,
At a short distance from my cottage, stands
A stately Fir-grove, whither I was wont
To hasten, for I found, beneath the roof 10
Of that perennial shade, a cloistral place
Of refuge, with an unincumbered floor.
Here, in safe covert, on the shallow snow,
And sometimes on a speck of visible earth,
The redbreast near me hopped; nor was
  I loth   15
To sympathize with vulgar coppice birds
That, for protection from the nipping blast,
Hither repaired.—A single beech-tree grew
Within this grove of firs! and, on the fork
Of that one beech, appeared a thrush's nest;
A last year's nest, conspicuously built 21
At such small elevation from the ground
As gave sure sign that they, who in that
  house
Of nature and of love had made their home
Amid the fir-trees, all the summer long 25
Dwelt in a tranquil spot. And oftentimes
A few sheep, stragglers from some moun-
  tain-flock,
Would watch my motions with suspicious
  stare,
From the remotest outskirts of the grove,—
Some nook where they had made their
  final stand,   30
Huddling together from two fears—the
  fear
Of me and of the storm. Full many an
  hour
Here did I lose. But in this grove the trees

Had been so thickly planted and had
  thriven
In such perplexed and intricate array, 35
That vainly did I seek beneath their stems
A length of open space, where to and fro
My feet might move without concern or
  care;
And, baffled thus, though earth from day
  to day
Was fettered, and the air by storm dis-
  turbed,   40
I ceased the shelter to frequent,—and
  prized,
Less than I wished to prize, that calm
  recess.

The snows dissolved, and genial Spring
  returned
To clothe the fields with verdure. Other
  haunts
Meanwhile were mine; till one bright
  April day,   45
By chance retiring from the glare of noon
To this forsaken covert, there I found
A hoary pathway traced between the trees,
And winding on with such an easy line
Along a natural opening, that I stood 50
Much wondering how I could have sought
  in vain
For what was now so obvious. To abide,
For an allotted interval of ease,
Under my cottage-roof, had gladly come
From the wild sea a cherished Visitant;
And with the sight of this same path—
  begun,   56
Begun and ended, in the shady grove,
Pleasant conviction flashed upon my mind
That, to this opportune recess allured,
He had surveyed it with a finer eye, 60
A heart more wakeful; and had worn the
  track
By pacing here, unwearied and alone,
In that habitual restlessness of foot
That haunts the Sailor, measuring o'er
  and o'er
His short domain upon the vessel's deck, 65
While she pursues her course through the
  dreary sea.

When thou hadst quitted Esthwaite's
  pleasant shore,

And taken thy first leave of those green
    hills
And rocks that were the play-ground of
    thy youth,
Year followed year, my Brother! and we
    two,   70
Conversing not, knew little in what mould
Each other's mind was fashioned; and at
    length,
When once again we met in Grasmere
    Vale,
Between us there was little other bond
Than common feelings of fraternal love.
But thou, a School-boy, to the sea hadst
    carried   76
Undying recollections; Nature there
Was with thee; she, who loved us both,
    she still
Was with thee; and even so didst thou
    become
A *silent* Poet; from the solitude   80
Of the vast sea didst bring a watchful heart
Still couchant, an inevitable ear,
And an eye practised like a blind man's
    touch.[1]
—Back to the joyless Ocean thou art gone;
Nor from this vestige of thy musing hours
Could I withhold thy honoured name,—
    and now   86
I love the fir-grove with a perfect love.
Thither do I withdraw when cloudless suns
Shine hot, or wind blows troublesome
    and strong;
And there I sit at evening, when the steep
Of Silver-how, and Grasmere's peaceful
    lake   91
And one green island, gleam between the
    stems
Of the dark firs, a visionary scene!
And while I gaze upon the spectacle
Of clouded splendour, on this dream-like
    sight   95
Of solemn loveliness, I think on thee,

[1] Lines 1–83 were probably written on August
29, 30, 1800; the remainder in 1802, while John W.
was absent on the voyage to China from which
he returned in September of that year. Can this
be the *Silver How Poem* to which (Dorothy W.
tells us) William wrote a conclusion on March 26,
1802? See Knight's "Life of W. W.," vol. I.
pp. 302-3.—ED.

My Brother, and on all which thou hast
    lost.
Nor seldom, if I rightly guess, while Thou,
Muttering the verses which I muttered
    first
Among the mountains, through the mid-
    night watch   100
Art pacing thoughtfully the vessel's deck
In some far region, here, while o'er my
    head,
At every impulse of the moving breeze,
The fir-grove murmurs with a sea-like
    sound,
Alone I tread this path;—for aught I know,
Timing my steps to thine; and, with a
    store   106
Of undistinguishable sympathies,
Mingling most earnest wishes for the day
When we, and others whom we love, shall
    meet   109
A second time, in Grasmere's happy Vale.

NOTE.—This wish was not granted; the la-
mented Person not long after perished by ship-
wreck, in discharge of his duty as Commander of
the Honourable East India Company's Vessel,
the Earl of Abergavenny.

VII.

[Composed 1845.—Published 1845.]

FORTH from a jutting ridge, around whose
    base
Winds our deep Vale, two heath-clad
    Rocks ascend
In fellowship, the loftiest of the pair
Rising to no ambitious height; yet both,
O'er lake and stream, mountain and flowery
    mead,   5
Unfolding prospects fair as human eyes
Ever beheld. Up-led with mutual help,
To one or other brow of those twin Peaks
Were two adventurous Sisters wont to
    climb,
And took no note of the hour while thence
    they gazed,   10
The blooming heath their couch, gazed
    side by side,
In speechless admiration. I, a witness
And frequent sharer of their calm delight
With thankful heart, to either Eminence
Gave the baptismal name each Sister bore.

Now are they parted, far as Death's cold
   hand   16
Hath power to part the Spirits of those
   who love
As they did love. Ye kindred Pinnacles—
That, while the generations of mankind
Follow each other to their hiding-place 20
In time's abyss, are privileged to endure
Beautiful in yourselves, and richly graced

With like command of beauty—grant your
   aid
For MARY's humble, SARAH's silent claim,[1]
That their pure joy in nature may survive
From age to age in blended memory.   26

---

[1] MARY, the poet's wife; SARAH, her sister, who died at Rydal Mount on June 23, 1835. See *Miscellaneous Sonnets*, I. XXIX.—ED.

POEMS OF THE FANCY.

I.

A MORNING EXERCISE.

[Composed 1828.—Published 1832.]

FANCY, who leads the pastimes of the glad,
Full oft is pleased a wayward dart to
throw;
Sending sad shadows after things not sad,
Peopling the harmless fields with signs of
woe:
Beneath her sway, a simple forest cry   5
Becomes an echo of man's misery.

Blithe ravens croak of death; and when
the owl
Tries his two voices for a favourite strain—
Tu-whit—Tu-whoo! the unsuspecting fowl
Forebodes mishap or seems but to com-
plain;   10
Fancy, intent to harass and annoy,
Can thus pervert the evidence of joy.

Through border wilds where naked
Indians stray,
Myriads of notes attest her subtle skill;
A feathered task-master cries, "WORK
AWAY!"   15
And in thy iteration, "WHIP POOR
WILL!"[1]
Is heard the spirit of a toil-worn slave,
Lashed out of life, not quiet in the grave.

What wonder? at her bidding, ancient
lays   19
Steeped in dire grief the voice of Philomel;
And that fleet messenger of summer days,
The Swallow, twittered subject to like
spell;
But ne'er could Fancy bend the buoyant
Lark
To melancholy service—hark! O hark!

The daisy sleeps upon the dewy lawn, 25
Not lifting yet the head that evening
bowed;
But *He* is risen, a later star of dawn,
Glittering and twinkling near yon rosy
cloud;
Bright gem instinct with music, vocal
spark;
The happiest bird that sprang out of the
Ark!   30

Hail, blest above all kinds!—Supremely
skilled
Restless with fixed to balance, high with
low,
Thou leav'st the halcyon free her hopes to
build
On such forbearance as the deep may
show;   34
Perpetual flight, unchecked by earthly ties,
Leav'st to the wandering bird of paradise.

Faithful, though swift as lightning, the
meek dove;
Yet more hath Nature reconciled in thee;
So constant with thy downward eye of
love,
Yet, in aërial singleness, so free;   40
So humble, yet so ready to rejoice
In power of wing and never-wearied voice.

To the last point of vision, and beyond,
Mount, daring warbler!—that love-
prompted strain,
('Twixt thee and thine a never-failing
bond),   45
Thrills not the less the bosom of the plain:
Yet might'st thou seem, proud privilege!
to sing
All independent of the leafy spring.[2]

---

[1] See Waterton's "Wanderings in South
America."

[2] This stanza was transferred in 1845 to its
present place from the poem (composed 1825;
published 1827) *To a Skylark*, beginning,
"Ethereal minstrel! pilgrim of the sky."—ED.

How would it please old Ocean to partake,
With sailors longing for a breeze in vain,
The harmony thy notes most gladly make
Where earth resembles most his own
    domain!
Urania's self might welcome with pleased
    ear
These matins mounting towards her na-
    tive sphere.

Chanter by heaven attracted, whom no
    bars   55
To daylight known deter from that pur-
    suit,
'Tis well that some sage instinct, when
    the stars
Come forth at evening, keeps Thee still
    and mute;
For not an eyelid could to sleep incline
Wert thou among them, singing as they
    shine!   60

II.

A FLOWER GARDEN

AT COLEORTON HALL, LEICESTERSHIRE.

[Composed 1824.—Published 1827.]

TELL me, ye Zephyrs! that unfold,
While fluttering o'er this gay Recess,
Pinions that fanned the teeming mould
Of Eden's blissful wilderness,
Did only softly-stealing hours   5
There close the peaceful lives of flowers?

Say, when the *moving* creatures saw
All kinds commingled without fear,
Prevailed a like indulgent law
For the still growths that prosper here?
Did wanton fawn and kid forbear   11
The half-blown rose, the lily spare?

Or peeped they often from their beds,
And prematurely disappeared,
Devoured like pleasure ere it spreads   15
A bosom to the sun endeared?
If such their harsh untimely doom,
It falls not *here* on bud or bloom.

All summer-long the happy Eve
Of this fair Spot her flowers may bind, 20
Nor e'er, with ruffled fancy, grieve,
From the next glance she casts, to find
That love for little things by Fate
Is rendered vain as love for great.

Yet, where the guardian fence is wound, 25
So subtly are our eyes beguiled,
We see not nor suspect a bound,
No more than in some forest wild;
The sight is free as air—or crost
Only by art in nature lost.   30

And though the jealous turf refuse
By random footsteps to be prest,
And feed on never-sullied dews,
Ye, gentle breezes from the west,
With all the ministers of hope   35
Are tempted to this sunny slope!

And hither throngs of birds resort;
Some, inmates lodged in shady nests,
Some, perched on stems of stately port
That nod to welcome transient guests;   40
While hare and leveret, seen at play,
Appear not more shut out than they.

Apt emblem (for reproof of pride)
This delicate Enclosure shows
Of modest kindness, that would hide   45
The firm protection she bestows;
Of manners, like its viewless fence,
Ensuring peace to innocence.

Thus spake the moral Muse—her wing
Abruptly spreading to depart,   50
She left that farewell offering,
Memento for some docile heart;
That may respect the good old age
When Fancy was Truth's willing Page;
And Truth would skim the flowery glade,
Though entering but as Fancy's Shade.   56

III.

[Composed March 18, 1798.—Published 1800.]

A WHIRL-BLAST from behind the hill
Rushed o'er the wood with startling
    sound;
Then—all at once the air was still,
And showers of hailstones pattered round.
Where leafless oaks towered high above, 5
I sat within an undergrove
Of tallest hollies, tall and green;
A fairer bower was never seen.
From year to year the spacious floor
With withered leaves is covered o'er,   10
And all the year the bower is green.

But see! where'er the hailstones drop
The withered leaves all skip and hop;
There's not a breeze—no breath of air—
Yet here, and there, and every where   15
Along the floor, beneath the shade
By those embowering hollies made,
The leaves in myriads jump and spring,
As if with pipes and music rare
Some Robin Good-fellow were there,   20
And all those leaves, in festive glee,
Were dancing to the minstrelsy.

IV.

THE WATERFALL AND THE EGLANTINE.

[Composed 1800.—Published 1800.]

I.

"BEGONE, thou fond presumptuous Elf,"
Exclaimed an angry Voice,
"Nor dare to thrust thy foolish self
Between me and my choice!"
A small Cascade fresh swoln with snows 5
Thus threatened a poor Briar-rose,
That, all bespattered with his foam,
And dancing high and dancing low,
Was living, as a child might know,
In an unhappy home.   10

II.

"Dost thou presume my course to block?
Off, off! or, puny Thing!
I'll hurl thee headlong with the rock
To which thy fibres cling."
The Flood was tyrannous and strong;   15
The patient Briar suffered long,
Nor did he utter groan or sigh,
Hoping the danger would be past;
But, seeing no relief, at last
He ventured to reply.   20

III.

"Ah!" said the Briar, "blame me not;
Why should we dwell in strife?
We who in this sequestered spot
Once lived a happy life?
You stirred me on my rocky bed—   25
What pleasure through my veins you
   spread

The summer long, from day to day,
My leaves you freshened and bedewed;
Nor was it common gratitude
That did your cares repay.   30

IV.

"When spring came on with bud and bell,
Among these rocks did I
Before you hang my wreaths to tell
That gentle days were nigh!
And in the sultry summer hours   35
I sheltered you with leaves and flowers;
And in my leaves—now shed and gone,
The linnet lodged, and for us two
Chanted his pretty songs, when you
Had little voice or none.   40

V.

"But now proud thoughts are in your
   breast—
What grief is mine you see,
Ah! would you think, even yet how blest
Together we might be!
Though of both leaf and flower bereft,   45
Some ornaments to me are left—
Rich store of scarlet hips is mine,
With which I, in my humble way,
Would deck you many a winter day,
A happy Eglantine!"   50

VI.

What more he said I cannot tell,
The Torrent down the rocky dell
Came thundering loud and fast;
I listened, nor aught else could hear;
The Briar quaked—and much I fear   55
Those accents were his last.

V.

THE OAK AND THE BROOM.

A PASTORAL.

[Composed 1800.—Published 1800.]

I.

HIS simple truths did Andrew glean
Beside the babbling rills;
A careful student he had been
Among the woods and hills.
One winter's night, when through the
   trees   5
The wind was roaring, on his knees

His youngest born did Andrew hold:
And while the rest, a ruddy quire,
Were seated round their blazing fire,
This Tale the Shepherd told.   10

II.

"I saw a crag, a lofty stone
As ever tempest beat!
Out of its head an Oak had grown,
A Broom out of its feet.
The time was March, a cheerful noon—   15
The thaw-wind, with the breath of June,
Breathed gently from the warm south-
      west:
When, in a voice sedate with age,
This Oak, a giant and a sage,
His neighbour thus addressed:—   20

III.

"'Eight weary weeks, through rock and
      clay,
Along this mountain's edge,
The Frost hath wrought both night and
      day,
Wedge driving after wedge.
Look up! and think, above your head   25
What trouble, surely, will be bred;
T̶ᴀ̶s̶t̶ ̶n̶i̶g̶h̶t̶ ̶I̶ ̶h̶e̶a̶r̶d̶ ̶a̶ ̶c̶r̶a̶s̶h̶—̶'̶t̶i̶s̶ ̶t̶r̶u̶e̶
The splinters took another road—
I see them yonder—what a load
For such a Thing as you!   30

IV.

"'You are preparing as before,
To deck your slender shape;
And yet, just three years back—no more—
You had a strange escape:
Down from yon cliff a fragment broke; 35
It thundered down, with fire and smoke,
And hitherward pursued its way;
This ponderous block was caught by me,
And o'er your head, as you may see,
'Tis hanging to this day!   40

V.

"'If breeze or bird to this rough steep
Your kind's first seed did bear;
The breeze had better been asleep,
The bird caught in a snare:
For you and your green twigs decoy   45
The little witless shepherd-boy

To come and slumber in your bower;
And trust me, on some sultry noon,
Both you and he, Heaven knows how
      soon!
Will perish in one hour.   50

VI.

"'From me this friendly warning take'—
The Broom began to doze,
And thus, to keep herself awake,
Did gently interpose:
'My thanks for your discourse are due;
That more than what you say is true   56
I know, and I have known it long;
Frail is the bond by which we hold
Our being, whether young or old,
Wise, foolish, weak, or strong.   60

VII.

"'Disasters, do the best we can,
Will reach both great and small;
And he is oft the wisest man,
Who is not wise at all.
For me, why should I wish to roam?   65
This spot is my paternal home,
It is my pleasant heritage;
My father many a happy year
Spread here his careless blossoms, here
A̶t̶t̶a̶i̶n̶e̶d̶ ̶a̶ ̶g̶o̶o̶d̶ ̶o̶l̶d̶ ̶a̶g̶e̶.̶   70

VIII.

"'Even such as his may be my lot.
What cause have I to haunt
My heart with terrors? Am I not
In truth a favoured plant!
On me such bounty Summer pours,   75
That I am covered o'er with flowers;
And when the Frost is in the sky,
My branches are so fresh and gay
That you might look at me and say,
This Plant can never die.   80

IX.

"'The butterfly, all green and gold,
To me hath often flown,
Here in my blossoms to behold
Wings lovely as his own.
When grass is chill with rain or dew, 85
Beneath my shade the mother-ewe
Lies with her infant lamb; I see
The love they to each other make,
And the sweet joy which they partake,
It is a joy to me.'   90

X.

"Her voice was blithe, her heart was light;
The Broom might have pursued
Her speech, until the stars of night
Their journey had renewed;
But in the branches of the oak   95
Two ravens now began to croak
Their nuptial song, a gladsome air;
And to her own green bower the breeze
That instant brought two stripling bees
To rest, or murmur there.   100

XI.

"One night, my Children! from the north
There came a furious blast;
At break of day I ventured forth,
And near the cliff I passed.
The storm had fallen upon the Oak,   105
And struck him with a mighty stroke,
And whirled, and whirled him far away;
And, in one hospitable cleft,
The little careless Broom was left
To live for many a day."   110

VI.

TO A SEXTON.

[Composed 1799.—Published 1800.]

LET thy wheel-barrow alone—
Wherefore, Sexton, piling still
In thy bone-house bone on bone?
'Tis already like a hill
In a field of battle made,   5
Where three thousand skulls are laid;
These died in peace each with the other,—
Father, sister, friend, and brother.

Mark the spot to which I point!
From this platform, eight feet square,   10
Take not even a finger-joint:
Andrew's whole fire-side is there.
Here, alone, before thine eyes,
Simon's sickly daughter lies,
From weakness now and pain defended,
Whom he twenty winters tended.   16

Look but at the gardener's pride—
How he glories, when he sees
Roses, lilies, side by side,
Violets in families!   20

By the heart of Man, his tears,
By his hopes and by his fears,
Thou, too heedless, art the Warden
Of a far superior garden.

Thus then, each to other dear,   25
Let them all in quiet lie,
Andrew there, and Susan here,
Neighbours in mortality,
And should I live through sun and rain
Seven widowed years without my Jane,
O Sexton, do not then remove her,   31
Let one grave hold the Loved and Lover!

VII.

TO THE DAISY.

[Composed 1802—Published 1807.]

" Her[1] divine skill taught me this,
That from every thing I saw
I could some instruction draw,
And raise pleasure to the height
Through the meanest object's sight.
By the murmur of a spring,
Or the least bough's rustelling;
By a Daisy whose leaves spread
Shut when Titan goes to bed;
Or a shady bush or tree;
She could more infuse in me
Than all Nature's beauties can
In some other wiser man."

              G. WITHER.

IN youth from rock to rock I went,
From hill to hill in discontent
Of pleasure high and turbulent,
  Most pleased when most uneasy;
But now my own delights I make,—   5
My thirst at every rill can slake,
And gladly Nature's love partake
  Of Thee, sweet Daisy!

Thee Winter in the garland wears
That thinly decks his few grey hairs;   10
Spring parts the clouds with softest airs,
  That she may sun thee;
Whole Summer-fields are thine by right;
And Autumn, melancholy Wight!
Doth in thy crimson head delight   15
  When rains are on thee.

---

[1] His Muse.

In shoals and bands, a morrice train,
Thou greet'st the traveller in the lane;
Pleased at his greeting thee again;
    Yet nothing daunted,   20
Nor grieved if thou be set at nought:
And oft alone in nooks remote
We meet thee, like a pleasant thought,
    When such are wanted.

Be violets in their secret mews   25
The flowers the wanton Zephyrs choose;
Proud be the rose, with rains and dews
    Her head impearling,
Thou liv'st with less ambitious aim,
Yet hast not gone without thy fame;   30
Thou art indeed by many a claim
    The Poet's darling.

If to a rock from rains he fly,
Or, some bright day of April sky,
Imprisoned by hot sunshine lie   35
    Near the green holly,
And wearily at length should fare;
He needs but look about, and there
Thou art!—a friend at hand, to scare
    His melancholy.   40

A hundred times, by rock or bower,
Ere thus I have lain couched an hour,
Have I derived from thy sweet power
    Some apprehension;
Some steady love; some brief delight;   45
Some memory that had taken flight;
Some chime of fancy wrong or right;
    Or stray invention.

If stately passions in me burn,
And one chance look to Thee should turn,
I drink out of an humbler urn   51
    A lowlier pleasure;
The homely sympathy that heeds
The common life our nature breeds;
A wisdom fitted to the needs   55
    Of hearts at leisure.

Fresh-smitten by the morning ray,
When thou art up, alert and gay,
Then, cheerful Flower! my spirits play
    With kindred gladness: 60
And when, at dusk, by dews opprest
Thou sink'st, the image of thy rest
Hath often eased my pensive breast
    Of careful sadness.

And all day long I number yet,   65
All seasons through, another debt,
Which I, wherever thou art met,
    To thee am owing;
An instinct call it, a blind sense;
A happy, genial influence,   70
Coming one knows not how, nor whence,
    Nor whither going.

Child of the Year! that round dost run
Thy pleasant course,—when day's begun
As ready to salute the sun   75
    As lark or leveret,
Thy long-lost praise thou shalt regain;
Nor be less dear to future men
Than in old time;—thou not in vain
    Art Nature's favourite.[1]   80

VIII.

TO THE SAME FLOWER.

[Composed 1802.—Published 1807.]

WITH little here to do or see
Of things that in the great world be,
Daisy! again I talk to thee,
    For thou art worthy,
Thou unassuming Common-place   5
Of Nature, with that homely face,
And yet with something of a grace
    Which love makes for thee!

Oft on the dappled turf at ease
I sit, and play with similes,   10
Loose types of things through all degrees,
    Thoughts of thy raising;
And many a fond and idle name
I give to thee, for praise or blame,
As is the humour of the game,   15
    While I am gazing.

A nun demure of lowly port;
Or sprightly maiden, of Love's court,
In thy simplicity the sport
    Of all temptations;   20
A queen in crown of rubies drest;
A starveling in a scanty vest;
Are all, as seems to suit thee best,
    Thy appellations.

[1] See, in Chaucer and the elder Poets, the
honours formerly paid to this flower.

A little Cyclops with one eye   25
Staring to threaten and defy,
That thought comes next—and instantly
    The freak is over,
The shape will vanish—and behold
A silver shield with boss of gold,   30
That spreads itself, some faery bold
    In fight to cover!

I see thee glittering from afar—
And then thou art a pretty star;
Not quite so fair as many are   35
    In heaven above thee!
Yet like a star, with glittering crest,
Self-poised in air thou seem'st to rest;—
May peace come never to his nest,
    Who shall reprove thee!   40

Bright *Flower!* for by that name at last,
When all my reveries are past,
I call thee, and to that cleave fast,
    Sweet silent creature!
That breath'st with me in sun and air,   45
Do thou, as thou art wont, repair
My heart with gladness, and a share
    Of thy meek nature!

IX.

THE GREEN LINNET.

[Composed 1803.—Published 1807.]

BENEATH these fruit-tree boughs that shed
Their snow-white blossoms on my head,
With brightest sunshine round me spread
    Of spring's unclouded weather,
In this sequestered nook how sweet   5
To sit upon my orchard-seat!
And birds and flowers once more to greet,
    My last year's friends together.

One have I marked, the happiest guest
In all this covert of the blest: 10
Hail to Thee, far above the rest
    In joy of voice and pinion!
Thou, Linnet! in thy green array,
Presiding Spirit here to-day,
Dost lead the revels of the May;   15
    And this is thy dominion.

While birds, and butterflies, and flowers,
Make all one band of paramours,
Thou, ranging up and down the bowers,
    Art sole in thy employment: 20

A Life, a Presence like the Air,
Scattering thy gladness without care,
Too blest with any one to pair;
    Thyself thy own enjoyment.

Amid yon tuft of hazel trees,   25
That twinkle to the gusty breeze,
Behold him perched in ecstasies,
    Yet seeming still to hover;
There! where the flutter of his wings
Upon his back and body flings   30
Shadows and sunny glimmerings,
    That cover him all over.

My dazzled sight he oft deceives,
A Brother of the dancing leaves;
Then flits, and from the cottage eaves   35
    Pours forth his song in gushes;
As if by that exulting strain
He mocked and treated with disdain
The voiceless Form he chose to feign,
    While fluttering in the bushes.   40

X.

TO A SKY-LARK.

[Composed 1805.—Published 1807.]

UP with me! up with me into the clouds!
    For thy song, Lark, is strong;
Up with me, up with me into the clouds!
    Singing, singing,
With clouds and sky about thee ringing,   5
Lift me, guide me, till I find
That spot which seems so to thy mind!

I have walked through wildernesses
    dreary,
And to-day my heart is weary;
Had I now the wings of a Faery,   10
Up to thee would I fly.
There is madness about thee, and joy
    divine
In that song of thine;
Lift me, guide me, high and high
To thy banqueting place in the sky.   15

    Joyous as morning,
    Thou art laughing and scorning;
    Thou hast a nest for thy love and thy
        rest,
    And, though little troubled with sloth,
    Drunken Lark! thou wouldst be loth

To be such a traveller as I.   21
Happy, happy Liver,
With a soul as strong as a mountain
    river
Pouring out praise to the almighty
    Giver,
Joy and jollity be with us both !   25

Alas ! my journey, rugged and uneven,
Through prickly moors or dusty ways
    must wind ;
But hearing thee, or others of thy kind,
As full of gladness and as free of heaven,
I, with my fate contented, will plod on, 30
And hope for higher raptures, when life's
    day is done.

XI.

TO THE SMALL CELANDINE.[1]

[Composed April 30, 1802.—Published 1807.]

PANSIES, lilies, kingcups, daisies,
Let them live upon their praises ;
Long as there's a sun that sets,
Primroses will have their glory ;
Long as there are violets,   5
They will have a place in story ;
There's a flower that shall be mine,
'Tis the little Celandine.

Eyes of some men travel far
For the finding of a star ;   10
Up and down the heavens they go,
Men that keep a mighty rout !
I'm as great as they, I trow,
Since the day I found thee out,
Little Flower—I'll make a stir,   15
Like a sage astronomer.

Modest, yet withal an Elf
Bold, and lavish of thyself ;
Since we needs must first have met
I have seen thee, high and low,   20
Thirty years or more, and yet
'Twas a face I did not know ;
Thou hast now, go where I may,
Fifty greetings in a day.

Ere a leaf is on a bush,   25
In the time before the thrush

---

[1] Common Pilewort.

Has a thought about her nest,
Thou wilt come with half a call,
Spreading out thy glossy breast
Like a careless Prodigal ;   30
Telling tales about the sun,
When we've little warmth, or none.

Poets, vain men in their mood !
Travel with the multitude :
Never heed them ; I aver   35
That they all are wanton wooers ;
But the thrifty cottager,
Who stirs little out of doors,
Joys to spy thee near her home ;
Spring is coming, Thou art come !   40

Comfort have thou of thy merit,
Kindly, unassuming Spirit !
Careless of thy neighbourhood,
Thou dost show thy pleasant face
On the moor, and in the wood,   45
In the lane ;—there's not a place,
Howsoever mean it be,
But 'tis good enough for thee.

Ill befall the yellow flowers,
Children of the flaring hours !   50
Buttercups, that will be seen,
Whether we will see or no ;
Others, too, of lofty mien ;
They have done as worldlings do,
Taken praise that should be thine,   55
Little, humble Celandine.

Prophet of delight and mirth,
Ill-requited upon earth ;
Herald of a mighty band,
Of a joyous train ensuing,   60
Serving at my heart's command,
Tasks that are no tasks renewing,
I will sing, as doth behove,
Hymns in praise of what I love !

XII.

TO THE SAME FLOWER.

[Composed May 1, 1802.—Published 1807.]

PLEASURES newly found are sweet
When they lie about our feet :
February last, my heart
First at sight of thee was glad ;

All unheard of as thou art,   5
Thou must needs, I think, have had,
Celandine! and long ago,
Praise of which I nothing know.

I have not a doubt but he,
Whosoe'er the man might be,   10
Who the first with pointed rays
(Workman worthy to be sainted)
Set the sign-board in a blaze,
When the rising sun he painted,
Took the fancy from a glance   15
At thy glittering countenance.

Soon as gentle breezes bring
News of winter's vanishing,
And the children build their bowers,
Sticking 'kerchief-plots of mould   20
All about with full-blown flowers,
Thick as sheep in shepherd's fold!
With the proudest thou art there,
Mantling in the tiny square.

Often have I sighed to measure   25
By myself a lonely pleasure,
Sighed to think I read a book
Only read, perhaps, by me;
Yet I long could overlook
Thy bright coronet and Thee,   30
And thy arch and wily ways,
And thy store of other praise.

Blithe of heart, from week to week
Thou dost play at hide-and-seek;
While the patient primrose sits   35
Like a beggar in the cold,
Thou, a flower of wiser wits,
Slip'st into thy sheltering hold;
Liveliest of the vernal train
When ye all are out again.   40

Drawn by what peculiar spell,
By what charm of sight or smell,
Does the dim-eyed curious Bee,
Labouring for her waxen cells,
Fondly settle upon Thee   45
Prized above all buds and bells
Opening daily at thy side,
By the season multiplied?[1]

[1] This stanza originally came after line 40 of the preceding poem (No. XI.). It was placed here in 1845.—ED.

Thou art not beyond the moon,
But a thing "beneath our shoon:"   50
Let the bold Discoverer thrid
In his bark the polar sea;
Rear who will a pyramid;
Praise it is enough for me,
If there be but three or four   55
Who will love my little Flower.

XIII.

THE SEVEN SISTERS;

OR,

THE SOLITUDE OF BINNORIE.

[Composed before August 17, 1800.—Published 1807.]

SEVEN Daughters had Lord Archibald,
All children of one mother:
You could not say in one short day
What love they bore each other.
A garland of seven lilies wrought!   5
Seven Sisters that together dwell;
But he, bold Knight as ever fought,
Their Father, took of them no thought,
He loved the wars so well.
Sing, mournfully, oh! mournfully,   10
The solitude of Binnorie!

II.

Fresh blows the wind, a western wind,
And from the shores of Erin,
Across the wave, a Rover brave
To Binnorie is steering: 15
Right onward to the Scottish strand
The gallant ship is borne;
The warriors leap upon the land,
And hark! the Leader of the band
Hath blown his bugle horn.   20
Sing, mournfully, oh! mournfully,
The solitude of Binnorie.

III.

Beside a grotto of their own,
With boughs above them closing,
The Seven are laid, and in the shade   25
They lie like fawns reposing.
But now, upstarting with affright
At noise of man and steed,
Away they fly to left, to right—
Of your fair household, Father-knight,   30
Methinks you take small heed!

Sing, mournfully, oh! mournfully,
The solitude of Binnorie.

IV.

Away the seven fair Campbells fly,
And over hill and hollow,   35
With menace proud, and insult loud,
The youthful Rovers follow.
Cried they, "Your Father loves to roam:
Enough for him to find
The empty house when he comes home; 40
For us your yellow ringlets comb,
For us be fair and kind!"
Sing, mournfully, oh! mournfully,
The solitude of Binnorie.

V.

Some close behind, some side by side, 45
Like clouds in stormy weather;
They run, and cry, "Nay, let us die,
And let us die together."
A lake was near; the shore was steep;
There never foot had been;   50
They ran, and with a desperate leap
Together plunged into the deep,
Nor ever more were seen.
Sing, mournfully, oh! mournfully,
The solitude of Binnorie.

VI.

The stream that flows out of the lake,
As through the glen it rambles,
Repeats a moan o'er moss and stone,
For those seven lovely Campbells.
Seven little Islands, green and bare, 60
Have risen from out the deep:
The fishers say, those sisters fair
By faeries all are buried there,
And there together sleep.
Sing, mournfully, oh! mournfully,   65
The solitude of Binnorie.

XIV.

[Composed 1803.—Published 1807.]

WHO fancied what a pretty sight
This Rock would be if edged around
With living snow-drops! circlet bright!
How glorious to this orchard-ground!
Who loved the little Rock, and set   5
Upon its head this coronet?

Was it the humour of a child?
Or rather of some gentle maid,
Whose brows, the day that she was styled
The shepherd-queen, were thus arrayed? 10
Of man mature, or matron sage?
Or old man toying with his age?

I asked—'twas whispered; The device
To each and all might well belong:
It is the Spirit of Paradise   15
That prompts such work, a Spirit strong,
That gives to all the self-same bent
Where life is wise and innocent.

XV.

THE REDBREAST CHASING THE BUTTERFLY.

[Composed April 18, 1802.—Published 1807.]

ART thou the bird whom Man loves best,
The pious bird with the scarlet breast,
    Our little English Robin;
The bird that comes about our doors
When Autumn-winds are sobbing?   5
Art thou the Peter of Norway Boors?
    Their Thomas in Finland,
    And Russia far inland?
The bird that by some name or other
All men who know thee call their brother, 10
The darling of children and men?
Could Father Adam[1] open his eyes
And see this sight beneath the skies,
He'd wish to close them again.
—If the Butterfly knew but his friend, 15
Hither his flight he would bend;
And find his way to me,
Under the branches of the tree:
In and out, he darts about;
Can this be the bird, to man so good,   20
That, after their bewildering,
Covered with leaves the little children,
    So painfully in the wood?

What ailed thee, Robin, that thou couldst
    pursue
    A beautiful creature,   25
That is gentle by nature?

---

[1] See "Paradise Lost," Book XI., where Adam
points out to Eve the ominous sign of the Eagle
chasing "two Birds of gayest plume," and the
gentle Hart and Hind pursued by their enemy.

Beneath the summer sky
From flower to flower let him fly;
'Tis all that he wishes to do.
The cheerer Thou of our in-door sadness, 30
He is the friend of our summer gladness:
What hinders, then, that ye should be
Playmates in the sunny weather,
And fly about in the air together!
His beautiful wings in crimson are drest, 35
A crimson as bright as thine own:
Wouldst thou be happy in thy nest,
O pious Bird! whom man loves best,
Love him, or leave him alone!

XVI.

SONG FOR THE SPINNING WHEEL.

FOUNDED UPON A BELIEF PREVALENT AMONG
THE PASTORAL VALES OF WESTMORELAND.

[Composed 1812.—Published 1820.]

SWIFTLY turn the murmuring wheel!
Night has brought the welcome hour,
When the weary fingers feel
Help, as if from faery power;
Dewy night o'ershades the ground; 5
Turn the swift wheel round and round!

Now, beneath the starry sky,
Couch the widely-scattered sheep;—
Ply the pleasant labour, ply!
For the spindle, while they sleep, 10
Runs with speed more smooth and fine,
Gathering up a trustier line.

Short-lived likings may be bred
By a glance from fickle eyes;
But true love is like the thread 15
Which the kindly wool supplies,
When the flocks are all at rest,
Sleeping on the mountain's breast.

XVII.

HINT FROM THE MOUNTAINS

FOR CERTAIN POLITICAL PRETENDERS.

[Composed 1817.—Published 1820.]

"WHO but hails the sight with pleasure
When the wings of genius rise,
Their ability to measure
With great enterprise;

But in man was ne'er such daring 5
As yon Hawk exhibits, pairing
His brave spirit with the war in
The stormy skies!

"Mark him, how his power he uses,
Lays it by, at will resumes! 10
Mark, ere for his haunt he chooses
Clouds and utter glooms!
There he wheels in downward mazes;
Sunward now his flight he raises,
Catches fire, as seems, and blazes 15
With uninjured plumes!"

ANSWER.

"Stranger, 'tis no act of courage
Which aloft thou dost discern;
No bold *bird* gone forth to forage
'Mid the tempest stern; 20
But such mockery as the nations
See, when public perturbations
Lift men from their native stations,
Like yon TUFT OF FERN;

"Such it is; the aspiring creature 25
Soaring on undaunted wing,
(So you fancied) is by nature
A dull helpless thing,
Dry and withered, light and yellow;—
That to be the tempest's fellow! 30
Wait—and you shall see how hollow
Its endeavouring!"

XVIII.

ON SEEING A NEEDLECASE IN THE FORM OF A HARP.

THE WORK OF E. M. S.

[Composed 1827.—Published 1827.]

FROWNS are on every Muse's face,
Reproaches from their lips are sent,
That mimicry should thus disgrace
The noble Instrument.

A very Harp in all but size! 5
Needles for strings in apt gradation!
Minerva's self would stigmatize
The unclassic profanation.

Even her *own* needle that subdued
Arachne's rival spirit, 10
Though wrought in Vulcan's happiest mood,
Such honour could not merit.

And this too from the Laureate's Child,
  A living lord of melody!
How will her Sire be reconciled   15
  To the refined indignity?

I spake, when whispered a low voice,
  "Bard! moderate your ire;
Spirits of all degrees rejoice
  In presence of the lyre.   20

"The Minstrels of Pygmean bands,
  Dwarf Genii, moonlight-loving Fays,
Have shells to fit their tiny hands
  And suit their slender lays.

"Some, still more delicate of ear,   25
  Have lutes (believe my words)
Whose framework is of gossamer,
  While sunbeams are the chords.

"Gay Sylphs this miniature will court,
  Made vocal by their brushing wings,   30
And sullen Gnomes will learn to sport
  Around its polished strings;

"Whence strains to love-sick maiden dear,
  While in her lonely bower she tries
To cheat the thought she cannot cheer,   35
  By fanciful embroideries.

"Trust, angry Bard! a knowing Sprite,
  Nor think the Harp her lot deplores;
Though 'mid the stars the Lyre shine bright,
  Love stoops as fondly as he soars."   40

XIX.

TO A LADY,

IN ANSWER TO A REQUEST THAT I WOULD
WRITE HER A POEM UPON SOME DRAWINGS
THAT SHE HAD MADE OF FLOWERS IN THE
ISLAND OF MADEIRA.

[Composed 1845 (?).—Published 1845.]

FAIR Lady! can I sing of flowers
  That in Madeira bloom and fade,
I who ne'er sate within their bowers,
  Nor through their sunny lawns have
    strayed?
How they in sprightly dance are worn   5
  By Shepherd-groom or May-day queen,
Or holy festal pomps adorn,
  These eyes have never seen.

Yet tho' to me the pencil's art
  No like remembrances can give,   10
Your portraits still may reach the heart
  And there for gentle pleasure live;
While Fancy ranging with free scope
  Shall on some lovely Alien set
A name with us endeared to hope,   15
  To peace, or fond regret.

Still as we look with nicer care,
  Some new resemblance we may trace
A Heart's-ease will perhaps be there,
  A Speedwell may not want its place.   20
And so may we, with charmèd mind
  Beholding what your skill has wrought,
Another Star-of-Bethlehem find,
  A new Forget-me-not.

From earth to heaven with motion fleet   25
  From heaven to earth our thoughts will
    pass,
A Holy-thistle here we meet
  And there a Shepherd's weather-glass;
And haply some familiar name
  Shall grace the fairest, sweetest, plant   30
Whose presence cheers the drooping frame
  Of English Emigrant.

Gazing she feels its power beguile
  Sad thoughts, and breathes with easier
    breath;
Alas! that meek that tender smile   35
  Is but a harbinger of death:
And pointing with a feeble hand
  She says, in faint words by sighs broken,
Bear for me to my native land
  This precious Flower, true love's last
    token.   40

XX.

[Composed 1845 (?).—Published 1845.]

GLAD sight wherever new with old
Is joined through some dear homeborn
    tie;
The life of all that we behold
Depends upon that mystery.
Vain is the glory of the sky,   5
The beauty vain of field and grove,
Unless, while with admiring eye
We gaze, we also learn to love.

XXI.

THE CONTRAST.

THE PARROT AND THE WREN.

[Composed 1825.—Published 1827.]

I.

WITHIN her gilded cage confined
I saw a dazzling Belle,
A Parrot of that famous kind
Whose name is NON-PAREIL.

Like beads of glossy jet her eyes;   5
And, smoothed by Nature's skill,
With pearl or gleaming agate vies
Her finely-curvèd bill.

Her plumy mantle's living hues,
In mass opposed to mass,   10
Outshine the splendour that imbues
The robes of pictured glass.

And, sooth to say, an apter Mate
Did never tempt the choice
Of feathered Thing most delicate   15
In figure and in voice.

But, exiled from Australian bowers,
And singleness her lot,
She trills her song with tutored powers,
Or mocks each casual note.   20

No more of pity for regrets
With which she may have striven!
Now but in wantonness she frets,
Or spite, if cause be given;

Arch, volatile, a sportive bird   25
By social glee inspired;
Ambitious to be seen or heard,
And pleased to be admired!

II.

THIS moss-lined shed, green, soft, and dry,
Harbours a self-contented Wren,   30
Not shunning man's abode, though shy,
Almost as thought itself, of human ken.

Strange places, coverts unendeared,
She never tried; the very nest
In which this Child of Spring was reared
Is warmed thro' winter by her feathery
breast.   36

To the bleak winds she sometimes gives
A slender unexpected strain;
Proof that the hermitess still lives,
Though she appear not, and be sought in
vain.   40

Say, Dora! tell me, by yon placid moon,
If called to choose between the favoured
pair,
Which would you be,—the bird of the
saloon,
By lady-fingers tended with nice care,
Caressed, applauded, upon dainties fed,   45
Or Nature's DARKLING of this mossy shed?

XXII.

THE DANISH BOY.

A FRAGMENT.

[Composed 1799.—Published 1800.]

I.

BETWEEN two sister moorland rills
There is a spot that seems to lie
Sacred to flowerets of the hills,
And sacred to the sky.
And in this smooth and open dell   5
There is a tempest-stricken tree;
A corner-stone by lightning cut,
The last stone of a lonely hut;
And in this dell you see
A thing no storm can e'er destroy,   10
The shadow of a Danish Boy.

II.

In clouds above, the lark is heard,
But drops not here to earth for rest;
Within this lonesome nook the bird
Did never build her nest.   15
No beast, no bird, hath here his home;
Bees, wafted on the breezy air,
Pass high above those fragrant bells
To other flowers:—to other dells
Their burdens do they bear;   20
The Danish Boy walks here alone:
The lovely dell is all his own.

III.

A Spirit of noon-day is he;
Yet seems a form of flesh and blood;
Nor piping shepherd shall he be,   25
Nor herd-boy of the wood.

A regal vest of fur he wears,
In colour like a raven's wing;
It fears not rain, nor wind, nor dew;
But in the storm 'tis fresh and blue   30
As budding pines in spring;
His helmet has a vernal grace,
Fresh as the bloom upon his face.

IV.

A harp is from his shoulder slung;
Resting the harp upon his knee,   35
To words of a forgotten tongue
He suits its melody.
Of flocks upon the neighbouring hill
He is the darling and the joy;
And often, when no cause appears,   40
The mountain-ponies prick their ears,
—They hear the Danish Boy,
While in the dell he sings alone
Beside the tree and corner-stone.

V.

There sits he; in his face you spy   45
No trace of a ferocious air,
Nor ever was a cloudless sky
So steady or so fair.
The lovely Danish Boy is blest
And happy in his flowery cove: 50
From bloody deeds his thoughts are far;
And yet he warbles songs of war,
That seem like songs of love,
For calm and gentle is his mien;
Like a dead Boy he is serene.   55

XXIII.

SONG

FOR THE WANDERING JEW.

[Composed 1800.—Published 1800.]

Though the torrents from their fountains
Roar down many a craggy steep,
Yet they find among the mountains
Resting-places calm and deep.

Clouds that love through air to hasten,   5
Ere the storm its fury stills,
Helmet-like themselves will fasten
On the heads of towering hills.

What if through the frozen centre
Of the Alps the Chamois bound,   10
Yet he has a home to enter
In some nook of chosen ground:

And the Sea-horse, though the ocean
Yield him no domestic cave,
Slumbers without sense of motion,   15
Couched upon the rocking wave.

If on windy days the Raven
Gambol like a dancing skiff,
Not the less she loves her haven
In the bosom of the cliff.   20

The fleet Ostrich, till day closes,
Vagrant over desert sands,
Brooding on her eggs reposes
When chill night that care demands.

Day and night my toils redouble,   25
Never nearer to the goal;
Night and day, I feel the trouble
Of the Wanderer in my soul.

XXIV.

STRAY PLEASURES.

[Composed 1806.—Published 1807.]

"——*Pleasure is spread through the earth*
In stray gifts to be claimed by whoever shall
find."

By their floating mill,
That lies dead and still,
Behold yon Prisoners three,
The Miller with two Dames, on the breast
of the Thames!
The platform is small, but gives room for
them all;   5
And they're dancing merrily.

From the shore come the notes
To their mill where it floats,
To their house and their mill tethered
fast:
To the small wooden isle where, their
work to beguile,   10
They from morning to even take what-
ever is given;—
And many a blithe day they have past.

In sight of the spires,
All alive with the fires
Of the sun going down to his rest,   15
In the broad open eye of the solitary sky,
They dance,—there are three, as jocund
as free,
While they dance on the calm river's
breast.

Man and Maidens wheel,
They themselves make the reel, 20
And their music's a prey which they
    seize;
It plays not for them,—what matter? 'tis
    theirs;
And if they had care, it has scattered
    their cares
While they dance, crying, "Long as ye
    please!"

They dance not for me, 25
    Yet mine is their glee!
Thus pleasure is spread through the earth
In stray gifts to be claimed by whoever
    shall find;
Thus a rich loving-kindness, redundantly
    kind,
Moves all nature to gladness and mirth.

The showers of the spring 31
    Rouse the birds, and they sing;
If the wind do but stir for his proper
    delight,
Each leaf, that and this, his neighbour
    will kiss;
Each wave, one and t'other, speeds after
    his brother; 35
They are happy, for that is their right!

XXV.

THE PILGRIM'S DREAM;

OR, THE STAR AND THE GLOW-WORM.

[Composed 1818.—Published 1820.]

A PILGRIM, when the summer day
Had closed upon his weary way,
A lodging begged beneath a castle's roof;
But him the haughty Warder spurned;
And from the gate the Pilgrim turned, 5
To seek such covert as the field
Or heath-besprinkled copse might yield,
Or lofty wood, shower-proof.

He paced along; and pensively,
Halting beneath a shady tree, 10
Whose moss-grown root might serve for
    couch or seat,
Fixed on a Star his upward eye;

Then from the tenant of the sky
He turned, and watched with kindred
    look
A Glow-worm, in a dusky nook, 15
Apparent at his feet.

The murmur of a neighbouring stream
Induced a soft and slumbrous dream,
A pregnant dream, within whose shadowy
    bounds
He recognised the earth-born Star, 20
And *That* which glittered from afar;
And (strange to witness!) from the frame
Of the ethereal Orb there came
Intelligible sounds.

Much did it taunt the humble Light 25
That now, when day was fled, and night
Hushed the dark earth, fast closing weary
    eyes,
A very reptile could presume
To show her taper in the gloom,
As if in rivalship with One 30
Who sat a ruler on his throne
Erected in the skies.

"Exalted Star!" the Worm replied,
"Abate this unbecoming pride,
Or with a less uneasy lustre shine; 35
Thou shrink'st as momently thy rays
Are mastered by the breathing haze;
While neither mist, nor thickest cloud
That shapes in heaven its murky shroud,
Hath power to injure mine. 40

"But not for this do I aspire
To match the spark of local fire,
That at my will burns on the dewy lawn,
With thy acknowledged glories;—No!
Yet, thus upbraided, I may show 45
What favours do attend me here,
Till, like thyself, I disappear
Before the purple dawn."

When this in modest guise was said,
Across the welkin seemed to spread 50
A boding sound—for aught but sleep
    unfit!
Hills quaked, the rivers backward ran;
That Star, so proud of late, looked wan;
And reeled with visionary stir
In the blue depth, like Lucifer 55
Cast headlong to the pit!

Fire raged: and, when the spangled floor
Of ancient ether was no more,
New heavens succeeded, by the dream
   brought forth:
And all the happy Souls that rode   60
Transfigured through that fresh abode
Had heretofore, in humble trust,
Shone meekly 'mid their native dust,
   The Glow-worms of the earth!

This knowledge, from an Angel's voice 65
Proceeding, made the heart rejoice
Of Him who slept upon the open lea:
Waking at morn he murmured not;
And, till life's journey closed, the spot
Was to the Pilgrim's soul endeared,   70
Where by that dream he had been cheered
   Beneath the shady tree.

XXVI.

THE POET AND THE CAGED TURTLEDOVE.

[Composed 1830.—Published 1835.]

As often as I murmur here
   My half-formed melodies,
Straight from her osier mansion near
   The Turtledove replies:
Though silent as a leaf before,   5
   The captive promptly coos;
Is it to teach her own soft lore,
   Or second my weak Muse?

I rather think the gentle Dove
   Is murmuring a reproof,   10
Displeased that I from lays of love
   Have dared to keep aloof;
That I, a Bard of hill and dale,
   Have carolled, fancy free,
As if nor dove nor nightingale   15
   Had heart or voice for me.

If such thy meaning, O forbear,
   Sweet Bird! to do me wrong;
Love, blessed Love, is everywhere
   The spirit of my song: 20
'Mid grove, and by the calm fireside,
   Love animates my lyre—
That coo again!—'tis not to chide,
   I feel, but to inspire.

XXVII.

A WREN'S NEST.

[Composed 1833.—Published 1835.]

AMONG the dwellings framed by birds
   In field or forest with nice care,
Is none that with the little Wren's
   In snugness may compare.

No door the tenement requires,   5
   And seldom needs a laboured roof;
Yet is it to the fiercest sun
   Impervious, and storm-proof.

So warm, so beautiful withal,
   In perfect fitness for its aim,   10
That to the Kind by special grace
   Their instinct surely came.

And when for their abodes they seek
   An opportune recess,
The hermit has no finer eye   15
   For shadowy quietness.

These find, 'mid ivied abbey-walls,
   A canopy in some still nook;
Others are pent-housed by a brae
   That overhangs a brook.   20

There to the brooding bird her mate
   Warbles by fits his low clear song;
And by the busy streamlet both
   Are sung to all day long.

Or in sequestered lanes they build,   25
   Where, till the flitting bird's return,
Her eggs within the nest repose,
   Like relics in an urn.

But still, where general choice is good,
   There is a better and a best;   30
And, among fairest objects, some
   Are fairer than the rest;

This, one of those small builders proved
   In a green covert, where, from out
The forehead of a pollard oak,   35
   The leafy antlers sprout;

For She who planned the mossy lodge,
   Mistrusting her evasive skill,
Had to a Primrose looked for aid
   Her wishes to fulfil.   40

High on the trunk's projecting brow,
  And fixed an infant's span above
The budding flowers, peeped forth the
    nest
  The prettiest of the grove!

The treasure proudly did I show   45
  To some whose minds without disdain
Can turn to little things; but once
  Looked up for it in vain:

'Tis gone—a ruthless spoiler's prey,
  Who heeds not beauty, love, or song, 50
'Tis gone! (so seemed it) and we grieved
  Indignant at the wrong.

Just three days after, passing by
  In clearer light the moss-built cell
I saw, espied its shaded mouth;   55
  And felt that all was well.

The Primrose for a veil had spread
  The largest of her upright leaves;
And thus, for purposes benign,
  A simple flower deceives.   60

Concealed from friends who might disturb
  Thy quiet with no ill intent,
Secure from evil eyes and hands
  On barbarous plunder bent,   64

Rest, Mother-bird! and when thy young
  Take flight, and thou art free to roam,
When withered is the guardian Flower,
  And empty thy late home,

Think how ye prospered, thou and thine,
  Amid the unviolated grove   70
Housed near the growing Primrose-tuft
  In foresight, or in love.

XXVIII.

LOVE LIES BLEEDING.

[Composed 1842 (?).—Published 1842.]

You call it, "Love lies bleeding,"—so you
    may,
Though the red Flower, not prostrate,
    only droops,
As we have seen it here from day to day,
From month to month, life passing not
    away:
A flower how rich in sadness! Even thus
    stoops,   5

(Sentient by Grecian sculpture's mar-
    vellous power),
Thus leans, with hanging brow and body
    bent
Earthward in uncomplaining languish-
    ment,
The dying Gladiator. So, sad Flower!
('Tis Fancy guides me willing to be led, 10
Though by a slender thread,)
So drooped Adonis, bathed in sanguine
    dew
Of his death-wound, when he from in-
    nocent air
The gentlest breath of resignation drew;
While Venus in a passion of despair   15
Rent, weeping over him, her golden hair
Spangled with drops of that celestial
    shower.
She suffered, as Immortals sometimes do;
But pangs more lasting far *that* Lover
    knew
Who first, weighed down by scorn, in
    some lone bower   20
Did press this semblance of unpitied
    smart
Into the service of his constant heart,
His own dejection, downcast Flower!
    could share
With thine, and gave the mournful name
    which thou wilt ever bear.   24

XXIX.

COMPANION TO THE FOREGOING.

[Composed 1842 (?).—Published 1842.]

Never enlivened with the liveliest ray
That fosters growth or checks or cheers
    decay,
Nor by the heaviest rain-drops more
    deprest,
This Flower, that first appeared as sum-
    mer's guest,
Preserves her beauty 'mid autumnal
    leaves,   5
And to her mournful habits fondly
    cleaves.
When files of stateliest plants have ceased
    to bloom,
One after one submitting to their doom,

When her coevals each and all are fled,
What keeps her thus reclined upon her
    lonesome bed?   10

  The old mythologists, more impressed
    than we
Of this late day by character in tree
Or herb that claimed peculiar sympathy,
Or by the silent lapse of fountain clear,
Or with the language of the viewless air 15
By bird or beast made vocal, sought a
    cause
To solve the mystery, not in Nature's laws
But in Man's fortunes. Hence a thousand
    tales
Sung to the plaintive lyre in Grecian vales.
Nor doubt that something of their spirit
    swayed   20
The fancy-stricken Youth or heart-sick
    Maid,
Who, while each stood companionless and
    eyed
This undeparting Flower in crimson dyed,
Thought of a wound which death is slow
    to cure,   24
A fate that has endured and will endure,
And, patience coveting yet passion feeding,
Called the dejected Lingerer *Love lies
Bleeding.*

XXX.

RURAL ILLUSIONS.

[Composed 1832.—Published 1835.]

SYLPH was it? or a Bird more bright
  Than those of fabulous stock?
A second darted by;—and lo!
  Another of the flock,
Through sunshine flitting from the bough
  To nestle in the rock.   6

Transient deception! a gay freak
  Of April's mimicries!
Those brilliant strangers, hailed with joy
  Among the budding trees,   10
Proved last year's leaves, pushed from the
    spray
  To frolic on the breeze.

Maternal Flora! show thy face,
  And let thy hand be seen,

Thy hand here sprinkling tiny flowers, 15
  That, as they touch the green,
Take root (so seems it) and look up
  In honour of their Queen.
Yet, sooth, those little starry specks,
  That not in vain aspired   20
To be confounded with live growths,
  Most dainty, most admired,
Were only blossoms dropped from twigs
  Of their own offspring tired.

Not such the World's illusive shows; 25
  Her wingless flutterings,
Her blossoms which, though shed, out-
    brave
  The floweret as it springs,
For the undeceived, smile as they may,
  Are melancholy things: 30
But gentle Nature plays her part
  With ever-varying wiles,
And transient feignings with plain truth
  So well she reconciles,
That those fond Idlers most are pleased 35
  Whom oftenest she beguiles.

XXXI.

THE KITTEN AND FALLING LEAVES.

[Composed 1804.—Published 1807.]

THAT way look, my Infant, lo!
What a pretty baby-show!
See the Kitten on the wall,
Sporting with the leaves that fall,
Withered leaves—one—two—and three— 5
From the lofty elder-tree!
Through the calm and frosty air
Of this morning bright and fair,
Eddying round and round they sink
Softly, slowly: one might think,   10
From the motions that are made,
Every little leaf conveyed
Sylph or Faery hither tending,—
To this lower world descending,
Each invisible and mute,   15
In his wavering parachute.
——But the Kitten, how she starts,
Crouches, stretches, paws, and darts!
First at one, and then its fellow,
Just as light and just as yellow;   20
There are many now—now one—
Now they stop and there are none:

What intenseness of desire
In her upward eye of fire !
With a tiger-leap half-way   25
Now she meets the coming prey,
Lets it go as fast, and then
Has it in her power again :
Now she works with three or four,
Like an Indian conjurer ;   30
Quick as he in feats of art,
Far beyond in joy of heart.
Were her antics played in the eye
Of a thousand standers-by,
Clapping hands with shout and stare,   35
What would little Tabby care
For the plaudits of the crowd ?
Over happy to be proud,
Over wealthy in the treasure
Of her own exceeding pleasure !   40

'Tis a pretty baby-treat ;
Nor, I deem, for me unmeet ;
Here, for neither Babe nor me,
Other playmate can I see.
Of the countless living things,   45
That with stir of feet and wings
(In the sun or under shade,
Upon bough or grassy blade)
And with busy revellings,
Chirp and song, and murmurings,   50
Made this orchard's narrow space,
And this vale, so blithe a place ;
Multitudes are swept away
Never more to breathe the day :
Some are sleeping ; some in bands   55
Travelled into distant lands ;
Others slunk to moor and wood,
Far from human neighbourhood ;
And among the Kinds that keep
With us closer fellowship,   60
With us openly abide,
All have laid their mirth aside.

Where is he that giddy Sprite,
Blue-cap, with his colours bright,
Who was blest as bird could be,   65
Feeding in the apple-tree ;
Made such wanton spoil and rout,
Turning blossoms inside out ;
Hung—head pointing towards the ground—
Fluttered, perched, into a round   70
Bound himself, and then unbound ;

Lithest, gaudiest Harlequin !
Prettiest Tumbler ever seen !
Light of heart and light of limb ;
What is now become of Him ?   75
Lambs, that through the mountains
            went
Frisking, bleating merriment,
When the year was in its prime,
They are sobered by this time.
If you look to vale or hill,   80
If you listen, all is still,
Save a little neighbouring rill,
That from out the rocky ground
Strikes a solitary sound.
Vainly glitter hill and plain,   85
And the air is calm in vain ;
Vainly Morning spreads the lure
Of a sky serene and pure ;
Creature none can she decoy
Into open sign of joy :   90
Is it that they have a fear
Of the dreary season near ?
Or that other pleasures be
Sweeter even than gaiety ?

        Yet, whate'er enjoyments dwell   95
In the impenetrable cell
Of the silent heart which Nature
Furnishes to every creature ;
Whatsoe'er we feel and know
Too sedate for outward show,   100
Such a light of gladness breaks,
Pretty Kitten ! from thy freaks,—
Spreads with such a living grace
O'er my little Dora's face ;
Yes, the sight so stirs and charms   105
Thee, Baby, laughing in my arms,
That almost I could repine
That your transports are not mine,
That I do not wholly fare
Even as ye do, thoughtless pair !   110
And I will have my careless season
Spite of melancholy reason,
Will walk through life in such a way
That, when time brings on decay,
Now and then I may possess   115
Hours of perfect gladsomeness.
—Pleased by any random toy ;
By a kitten's busy joy,
Or an infant's laughing eye
Sharing in the ecstasy ;   120

I would fare like that or this,
Find my wisdom in my bliss;
Keep the sprightly soul awake,
And have faculties to take,
Even from things by sorrow wrought, 125
Matter for a jocund thought,
Spite of care, and spite of grief,
To gambol with Life's falling Leaf.

XXXII.

ADDRESS TO MY INFANT DAUGHTER, DORA,

ON BEING REMINDED THAT SHE WAS A , MONTH OLD THAT DAY, SEPTEMBER 16.

[Composed September 16, 1804.—Published 1815.]

————Hast thou then survived—
Mild Offspring of infirm humanity,
Meek Infant! among all forlornest things
The most forlorn—one life of that bright
    star,
The second glory of the Heavens?—Thou
    hast;   5
Already hast survived that great decay,
That transformation through the wide
    earth felt,
And by all nations. In that Being's might
From whom the Race of human kind
    proceed,
A thousand years are but as yesterday; 10
And one day's narrow circuit is to Him
Not less capacious than a thousand years.
But what is time? What outward glory?
    Neither
A measure is of Thee, whose claims extend
Through "heaven's eternal year."—Yet
    hail to Thee,   15
Frail, feeble, Monthling!—by that name,
    methinks,
Thy scanty breathing-time is portioned
    out
Not idly.—Hadst thou been of Indian
    birth,
Couched on a casual bed of moss and
    leaves,
And rudely canopied by leafy boughs, 20
Or to the churlish elements exposed
On the blank plains,—the coldness of the
    night,
Or the night's darkness, or its cheerful face

Of beauty, by the changing moon adorned,
Would, with imperious admonition, then
Have scored thine age, and punctually
    timed   26
Thine infant history, on the minds of
    those
Who might have wandered with thee.—
    Mother's love,
Nor less than mother's love in other
    breasts,
Will, among us warm-clad and warmly
    housed,   30
Do for thee what the finger of the heavens
Doth all too often harshly execute
For thy unblest coevals, amid wilds
Where fancy hath small liberty to grace
The affections, to exalt them or refine; 35
And the maternal sympathy itself,
Though strong, is, in the main, a joyless
    tie
Of naked instinct, wound about the heart.
Happier, far happier is thy lot and ours!
Even now—to solemnise thy helpless
    state,   40
And to enliven in the mind's regard
Thy passive beauty—parallels have risen,
Resemblances, or contrasts, that connect,
Within the region of a father's thoughts,
Thee and thy mate and sister of the sky.
And first;—thy sinless progress, through
    a world   46
By sorrow darkened and by care dis-
    turbed,
Apt likeness bears to hers, through
    gathered clouds
Moving untouched in silver purity,
And cheering oft-times their reluctant
    gloom.   50
Fair are ye both, and both are free from
    stain:
But thou, how leisurely thou fill'st thy
    horn
With brightness! leaving her to post
    along,
And range about, disquieted in change,
And still impatient of the shape she
    wears.   55
Once up, once down the hill, one journey,
    Babe,
That will suffice thee; and it seems that
    now

Thou hast foreknowledge that such task
  is thine;
Thou travellest so contentedly, and
  sleep'st   59
In such a heedless peace. Alas! full soon
Hath this conception, grateful to behold,
Changed countenance, like an object
  sullied o'er
By breathing mist; and thine appears
  to be
A mournful labour, while to her is given
Hope, and a renovation without end. 65
—That smile forbids the thought; for on
  thy face
Smiles are beginning, like the beams of
  dawn,
To shoot and circulate; smiles have there
  been seen;
Tranquil assurances that Heaven supports
The feeble motions of thy life, and cheers
Thy loneliness: or shall those smiles be
  called   71
Feelers of love, put forth as if to explore
This untried world, and to prepare thy
  way
Through a strait passage intricate and
  dim?
Such are they; and the same are tokens,
  signs,   75
Which, when the appointed season hath
  arrived,
Joy, as her holiest language, shall adopt;
And Reason's godlike Power be proud to
  own.

XXXIII.

THE WAGGONER.

[Composed 1805.—Published 1819.]

> "In Cairo's crowded streets
> The impatient Merchant, wondering, waits in vain,
> And Mecca saddens at the long delay."
> THOMSON.

TO CHARLES LAMB, ESQ.

MY DEAR FRIEND,
    When I sent you, a few weeks ago, the
Tale of Peter Bell, you asked "why THE
WAGGONER was not added?"—To say the truth,
—from the higher tone of imagination, and
the deeper touches of passion aimed at in the
former, I apprehended this little Piece could not

accompany it without disadvantage. In the
year 1806, if I am not mistaken, THE WAG-
GONER was read to you in manuscript, and, as
you have remembered it for so long a time, I
am the more encouraged to hope that, since
the localities on which the Poem partly depends
did not prevent its being interesting to you, it
may prove acceptable to others. Being there-
fore in some measure the cause of its present
appearance, you must allow me the gratification
of inscribing it to you; in acknowledgment of
the pleasure I have derived from your Writings,
and of the high esteem with which

        I am very truly yours,

      WILLIAM WORDSWORTH.

RYDAL MOUNT, *May* 20, 1819.

Canto First.

'Tis spent—this burning day of June!
Soft darkness o'er its latest gleams is
  stealing;
The buzzing dor-hawk, round and round,
  is wheeling,—
That solitary bird
Is all that can be heard   5
In silence deeper far than that of deepest
  noon!

Confiding Glow-worms, 'tis a night
Propitious to your earth-born light!
But where the scattered stars are seen
In hazy straits the clouds between, 10
Each, in his station twinkling not,
Seems changed into a pallid spot.
The mountains against heaven's grave
  weight
Rise up, and grow to wondrous height.
The air, as in a lion's den,   15
Is close and hot;—and now and then
Comes a tired and sultry breeze
With a haunting and a panting,
Like the stifling of disease;
But the dews allay the heat,   20
And the silence makes it sweet.

Hush, there is some one on the stir!
'Tis Benjamin the Waggoner;
Who long hath trod this toilsome way,
Companion of the night and day. 25
That far-off tinkling's drowsy cheer,
Mixed with a faint yet grating sound
In a moment lost and found.

The Wain announces—by whose side
Along the banks of Rydal Mere   30
He paces on, a trusty Guide,—
Listen! you can scarcely hear!
Hither he his course is bending;—
Now he leaves the lower ground,
And up the craggy hill ascending   35
Many a stop and stay he makes,
Many a breathing-fit he takes;
Steep the way and wearisome,
Yet all the while his whip is dumb!

The Horses have worked with right
        good-will,   40
And so have gained the top of the hill;
He was patient, they were strong,
And now they smoothly glide along,
Recovering breath, and pleased to win
The praises of mild Benjamin.   45
Heaven shield him from mishap and
        snare!
But why so early with this prayer?—
Is it for threatenings in the sky?
Or for some other danger nigh?
No; none is near him yet, though he   50
Be one of much infirmity;
For at the bottom of the brow,
Where once the Dove and Olive-bough
Offered a greeting of good ale
To all who entered Grasmere Vale;   55
And called on him who must depart
To leave it with a jovial heart;
There, where the Dove and Olive-bough
Once hung, a Poet harbours now,
A simple water-drinking Bard;   60
Why need our Hero then (though frail
His best resolves) be on his guard?
He marches by, secure and bold;
Yet, while he thinks on times of old,
It seems that all looks wondrous cold;   65
He shrugs his shoulders, shakes his head,
And, for the honest folk within,
It is a doubt with Benjamin
Whether they be alive or dead!

Here is no danger,—none at all!   70
Beyond his wish he walks secure;
But pass a mile—and *then* for trial,—
Then for the pride of self-denial;
If he resist that tempting door,
Which with such friendly voice will call;

If he resist those casement panes,   76
And that bright gleam which thence will
        fall
Upon his Leaders' bells and manes,
Inviting him with cheerful lure:
For still, though all be dark elsewhere,   80
Some shining notice will be *there*,
Of open house and ready fare.

The place to Benjamin right well
Is known, and by as strong a spell
As used to be that sign of love   85
And hope—the Olive-bough and Dove;
He knows it to his cost, good Man!
Who does not know the famous Swan?
Object uncouth! and yet our boast,
For it was painted by the Host;   90
His own conceit the figure planned,
'Twas coloured all by his own hand;
And that frail Child of thirsty clay,
Of whom I sing this rustic lay,
Could tell with self-dissatisfaction   95
Quaint stories of the bird's attraction![1]

Well! that is past—and in despite
Of open door and shining light.
And now the conqueror essays
The long ascent of Dunmail-raise;   100
And with his team is gentle here
As when he clomb from Rydal Mere;
His whip they do not dread—his voice
They only hear it to rejoice.
To stand or go is at *their* pleasure;   105
Their efforts and their time they measure
By generous pride within the breast;
And while they strain, and while they rest,
He thus pursues his thoughts at leisure.

Now am I fairly safe to-night—   110
And with proud cause my heart is light:
I trespassed lately worse than ever—
But Heaven has blest a good endeavour;
And, to my soul's content, I find
The evil One is left behind.   115
Yes, let my master fume and fret,
Here am I—with my horses yet!
My jolly team, he finds that ye
Will work for nobody but me!

---

[1] This rude piece of self-taught art (such is the progress of refinement) has been supplanted by a professional production.

Full proof of this the Country gained; 120
It knows how ye were vexed and strained,
And forced unworthy stripes to bear,
When trusted to another's care.
Here was it—on this rugged slope,
Which now ye climb with heart and
    hope, 125
I saw you, between rage and fear,
Plunge, and fling back a spiteful ear,
And ever more and more confused,
As ye were more and more abused:
As chance would have it, passing by 130
I saw you in that jeopardy:
A word from me was like a charm;
Ye pulled together with one mind;
And your huge burthen, safe from harm,
Moved like a vessel in the wind! 135
—Yes, without me, up hills so high
'Tis vain to strive for mastery.
Then grieve not, jolly team! though
    tough
The road we travel, steep, and rough;
Though Rydal-heights and Dunmail-raise,
And all their fellow banks and braes, 141
Full often make you stretch and strain,
And halt for breath and halt again,
Yet to their sturdiness 'tis owing
That side by side we still are going! 145

While Benjamin in earnest mood
His meditations thus pursued,
A storm, which had been smothered long,
Was growing inwardly more strong;
And, in its struggles to get free, 150
Was busily employed as he.
The thunder had begun to growl—
He heard not, too intent of soul;
The air was now without a breath—
He marked not that 'twas still as death.
But soon large rain-drops on his head 156
Fell with the weight of drops of lead;—
He starts—and takes, at the admonition,
A sage survey of his condition.
The road is black before his eyes, 160
Glimmering faintly where it lies;
Black is the sky—and every hill,
Up to the sky, is blacker still—
Sky, hill, and dale, one dismal room,
Hung round and overhung with gloom;
Save that above a single height 166
Is to be seen a lurid light,

Above Helm-crag [1]—a streak half dead,
A burning of portentous red;
And near that lurid light, full well 170
The Astrologer, sage Sidrophel,
Where at his desk and book he sits,
Puzzling aloft his curious wits;
He whose domain is held in common
With no one but the Ancient Woman, 175
Cowering beside her rifted cell,
As if intent on magic spell;—
Dread pair that, spite of wind and wea-
    ther,
Still sit upon Helm-crag together!

The Astrologer was not unseen 180
By solitary Benjamin;
But total darkness came anon,
And he and every thing was gone:
And suddenly a ruffling breeze,
(That would have rocked the sounding
    trees, 185
Had aught of sylvan growth been there),
Swept through the Hollow long and bare:
The rain rushed down—the road was
    battered,
As with the force of billows shattered;
The horses are dismayed, nor know 190
Whether they should stand or go;
And Benjamin is groping near them,
Sees nothing, and can scarcely hear them.
He is astounded,—wonder not,—
With such a charge in such a spot; 195
Astounded in the mountain gap
With thunder-peals, clap after clap,
Close-treading on the silent flashes—
And somewhere, as he thinks, by crashes
Among the rocks; with weight of rain,
And sullen motions long and slow, 201
That to a dreary distance go—
Till, breaking in upon the dying strain,
A rending o'er his head begins the fray
    again.

Meanwhile, uncertain what to do, 205
And oftentimes compelled to halt,
The horses cautiously pursue
Their way, without mishap or fault;

---

[1] A mountain of Grasmere, the broken summit
of which presents two figures, full as distinctly
shaped as that of the famous Cobbler near Ar-
roquhar in Scotland.

And now have reached that pile of stones,
Heaped over brave King Dunmail's bones,
He who had once supreme command, 211
Last king of rocky Cumberland;
His bones, and those of all his Power,
Slain here in a disastrous hour!

When, passing through this narrow
   strait, 215
Stony, and dark, and desolate,
Benjamin can faintly hear
A voice that comes from some one near,
A female voice:—"Whoe'er you be,
Stop," it exclaimed, "and pity me!" 220
And less in pity than in wonder,
Amid the darkness and the thunder,
The Waggoner, with prompt command,
Summons his horses to a stand.

While, with increasing agitation, 225
The Woman urged her supplication,
In rueful words, with sobs between—
The voice of tears that fell unseen;
There came a flash—a startling glare,
And all Seat-Sandal was laid bare! 230
'Tis not a time for nice suggestion,
And Benjamin, without a question,
Taking her for some way worn rover,
Said, "Mount, and get you under cover!"

Another voice, in tone as hoarse 235
As a swoln brook with rugged course,
Cried out, "Good brother, why so fast?
I've had a glimpse of you—avast!
Or, since it suits you to be civil,
Take her at once—for good and evil!" 240

"It is my Husband," softly said
The Woman, as if half afraid:
By this time she was snug within,
Through help of honest Benjamin;
She and her Babe, which to her breast 245
With thankfulness the Mother pressed;
And now the same strong voice more near
Said cordially, "My Friend, what cheer?
Rough doings these! as God's my judge,
The sky owes somebody a grudge! 250
We've had in half an hour or less
A twelvemonth's terror and distress!"

Then Benjamin entreats the Man
Would mount, too, quickly as he can:
The Sailor—Sailor now no more, 255
But such he had been heretofore—

To courteous Benjamin replied,
"Go you your way, and mind not me;
For I must have, whate'er betide,
My Ass and fifty things beside,— 260
Go, and I'll follow speedily!"

The Waggon moves—and with its load
Descends along the sloping road;
And the rough Sailor instantly
Turns to a little tent hard by: 265
For when, at closing-in of day,
The family had come that way,
Green pasture and the soft warm air
Tempted them to settle there.—
Green is the grass for beast to graze, 270
Around the stones of Dunmail-raise!

The Sailor gathers up his bed,
Takes down the canvas overhead;
And after farewell to the place,
A parting word—though not of grace, 275
Pursues, with Ass and all his store,
The way the Waggon went before.

Canto Second.

If Wytheburne's modest House of prayer,
As lowly as the lowliest dwelling,
Had, with its belfry's humble stock,
A little pair that hang in air,
Been mistress also of a clock, 5
(And one, too, not in crazy plight),
Twelve strokes that clock would have
      been telling
Under the brow of old Helvellyn—
Its bead-roll of midnight,
Then, when the Hero of my tale 10
Was passing by, and, down the vale
(The vale now silent, hushed, I ween,
As if a storm had never been)
Proceeding with a mind at ease;
While the old Familiar of the seas, 15
Intent to use his utmost haste,
Gained ground upon the Waggon fast,
And gives another lusty cheer;
For, spite of rumbling of the wheels,
A welcome greeting he can hear;— 20
It is a fiddle in its glee
Dinning from the CHERRY TREE!

Thence the sound—the light is there—
As Benjamin is now aware,
Who, to his inward thoughts confined, 25

Had almost reached the festive door,
When, startled by the Sailor's roar,
He hears a sound and sees the light,
And in a moment calls to mind
That 'tis the village MERRY-NIGHT![1]   30

Although before in no dejection,
At this insidious recollection
His heart with sudden joy is filled,—
His ears are by the music thrilled,
His eyes take pleasure in the road   35
Glittering before him bright and broad;
And Benjamin is wet and cold,
And there are reasons manifold
That make the good, tow'rds which he's
    yearning,
Look fairly like a lawful earning.   40

Nor has thought time to come and go,
To vibrate between yes and no;
For, cries the Sailor, "Glorious chance
That blew us hither!—let him dance,
Who can or will!—my honest soul,   45
Our treat shall be a friendly bowl!"
He draws him to the door—"Come in,
Come, come," cries he to Benjamin!
And Benjamin—ah, woe is me!
Gave the word—the horses heard   50
And halted, though reluctantly.

"Blithe souls and lightsome hearts have
    we
Feasting at the CHERRY TREE!"
This was the outside proclamation,
This was the inside salutation;   55
What bustling—jostling—high and low!
A universal overflow!
What tankards foaming from the tap!
What store of cakes in every lap!
What thumping—stumping—overhead!
The thunder had not been more busy:
With such a stir you would have said,   62
This little place may well be dizzy!
'Tis who can dance with greatest vigour—
'Tis what can be most prompt and eager;
As if it heard the fiddle's call,   66
The pewter clatters on the wall;
The very bacon shows its feeling,
Swinging from the smoky ceiling!

A steaming bowl, a blazing fire,   70
What greater good can heart desire?
'Twere worth a wise man's while to try
The utmost anger of the sky:
To *seek* for thoughts of a gloomy cast,
If such the bright amends at last.   75
Now should you say I judge amiss,
The CHERRY TREE shows proof of this;
For soon, of all the happy there,
Our Travellers are the happiest pair;
All care with Benjamin is gone—   80
A Cæsar past the Rubicon!
He thinks not of his long, long, strife;—
The Sailor, Man by nature gay,
Hath no resolves to throw away;
And he hath now forgot his Wife,   85
Hath quite forgotten her—or may be
Thinks her the luckiest soul on earth,
Within that warm and peaceful berth,
        Under cover,
        Terror over,   90
Sleeping by her sleeping Baby.

With bowl that sped from hand to hand,
The gladdest of the gladsome band,
Amid their own delight and fun,
They hear—when every dance is done,   95
When every whirling bout is o'er—
The fiddle's *squeak*[2]—that call to bliss,
Ever followed by a kiss;
They envy not the happy lot,
But enjoy their own the more!   100

While thus our jocund Travellers fare,
Up springs the Sailor from his chair—
Limps (for I might have told before
That he was lame) across the floor—
Is gone—returns—and with a prize;   105
With what?—a Ship of lusty size;
A gallant stately Man-of-war,
Fixed on a smoothly-sliding car.
Surprise to all, but most surprise
To Benjamin, who rubs his eyes,   110
Not knowing that he had befriended
A Man so gloriously attended!

"This," cries the Sailor, "a Third-rate
    is—
Stand back, and you shall see her gratis!

---

[1] A term well known in the North of England,
and applied to rural Festivals where young per-
sons meet in the evening for the purpose of
dancing.

[2] At the close of each strathspey, or jig, a
particular note from the fiddle summons the Rus-
tic to the agreeable duty of saluting his partner.

This was the Flag-ship at the Nile,   115
The VANGUARD—you may smirk and
    smile,
But, pretty Maid, if you look near,
You'll find you've much in little here !
A nobler ship did never swim,
And you shall see her in full trim :   120
I'll set, my friends, to do you honour,
Set every inch of sail upon her."
So said, so done ; and masts, sails, yards,
He names them all ; and interlards
His speech with uncouth terms of art,   125
Accomplished in the showman's part ;
And then, as from a sudden check,
Cries out—"'Tis there, the quarter-deck
On which brave Admiral Nelson stood—
A sight that would have roused your
    blood !   130
One eye he had, which, bright as ten,
Burned like a fire among his men ;
Let this be land, and that be sea,
Here lay the French—and *thus* came we !"

Hushed was by this the fiddle's sound,
The dancers all were gathered round,   136
And such the stillness of the house,
You might have heard a nibbling mouse ;
While, borrowing helps where'er he may,
The Sailor through the story runs   140
Of ships to ships and guns to guns ;
And does his utmost to display
The dismal conflict, and the might
And terror of that marvellous night !
"A bowl, a bowl of double measure,"   145
Cries Benjamin, "a draught of length !
To Nelson, England's pride and treasure,
Her bulwark and her tower of strength !"
When Benjamin had seized the bowl,
The mastiff, from beneath the waggon,
Where he lay, watchful as a dragon,   151
Rattled his chain ;—'twas all in vain,
For Benjamin, triumphant soul !
He heard the monitory growl ;
Heard—and in opposition quaffed   155
A deep, determined, desperate draught !
Nor did the battered Tar forget,
Or flinch from what he deemed his debt :
Then, like a hero crowned with laurel,
Back to her place the ship he led ;   160
Wheeled her back in full apparel ;
And so, flag flying at mast head,

Re-yoked her to the Ass :—anon
Cries Benjamin, "We must be gone."
Thus, after two hours' hearty stay,   165
Again behold them on their way !

Canto Third.

RIGHT gladly had the horses stirred,
When they the wished-for greeting heard,
The whip's loud notice from the door,
That they were free to move once more.
You think, those doings must have bred 5
In them disheartening doubts and dread ;
No, not a horse of all the eight,
Although it be a moonless night,
Fears either for himself or freight ;
For this they know (and let it hide,   10
In part, the offences of their guide)
That Benjamin, with clouded brains,
Is worth the best with all their pains ;
And, if they had a prayer to make,
The prayer would be that they may take
With him whatever comes in course,   16
The better fortune or the worse ;
That no one else may have business near
    them,
And, drunk or sober, he may steer them.

So forth in dauntless mood they fare, 20
And with them goes the guardian pair.

Now, heroes, for the true commotion,
The triumph of your late devotion !
Can aught on earth impede delight,
Still mounting to a higher height ;   25
And higher still—a greedy flight !
Can any low-born care pursue her,
Can any mortal clog come to her ?
No notion have they—not a thought,
That is from joyless regions brought !   30
And, while they coast the silent lake,
Their inspiration I partake ;
Share their empyreal spirits—yea,
With their enraptured vision see—
O fancy—what a jubilee !   35
What shifting pictures—clad in gleams
Of colour bright as feverish dreams !
Earth, spangled sky, and lake serene,
Involved and restless all—a scene
Pregnant with mutual exaltation,   40
Rich change, and multiplied creation !
This sight to me the Muse imparts ;—
And then, what kindness in their hearts !

What tears of rapture, what vow-making,
Profound entreaties, and hand-shaking!
What solemn, vacant, interlacing,   46
As if they'd fall asleep embracing!
Then, in the turbulence of glee,
And in the excess of amity,
Says Benjamin, "That Ass of thine,   50
He spoils thy sport, and hinders mine:
If he were tethered to the waggon,
He'd drag as well what he is dragging;
And we, as brother should with brother,
Might trudge it alongside each other!"   55

Forthwith, obedient to command,
The horses made a quiet stand;
And to the waggon's skirts was tied
The Creature, by the Mastiff's side,
The Mastiff wondering, and perplext   60
With dread of what will happen next;
And thinking it but sorry cheer
To have such company so near!

This new arrangement made, the Wain
Through the still night proceeds again;
No moon hath risen her light to lend;   66
But indistinctly may be kenned
The VANGUARD, following close behind,
Sails spread, as if to catch the wind!

"Thy wife and child are snug and
    warm,   70
Thy ship will travel without harm;
I like," said Benjamin, "her shape and
    stature:
And this of mine—this bulky creature
Of which I have the steering—this,
Seen fairly, is not much amiss!   75
We want your streamers, friend, you
    know;
But, altogether as we go,
We make a kind of handsome show!
Among these hills, from first to last,
We've weathered many a furious blast;
Hard passage forcing on, with head   81
Against the storm, and canvas spread.
I hate a boaster; but to thee
Will say't, who know'st both land and
    sea,
The unluckiest hulk that stems the brine
Is hardly worse beset than mine,   86
When cross-winds on her quarter beat;
And, fairly lifted from my feet,

I stagger onward—heaven knows how;
But not so pleasantly as now: 90
Poor pilot I, by snows confounded,
And many a foundrous pit surrounded!
Yet here we are, by night and day
Grinding through rough and smooth our
    way;   94
Through foul and fair our task fulfilling;
And long shall be so yet—God willing!"

"Ay," said the Tar, "through fair and
    foul—
But save us from yon screeching owl!"
That instant was begun a fray
Which called their thoughts another way:
The Mastiff, ill-conditioned carl!   101
What must he do but growl and snarl,
Still more and more dissatisfied
With the meek comrade at his side!
Till, not incensed though put to proof,   105
The Ass, uplifting a hind hoof,
Salutes the Mastiff on the head;
And so were better manners bred,
And all was calmed and quieted.

"Yon screech-owl," says the Sailor,
    turning   110
Back to his former cause of mourning,
"Yon owl!—pray God that all be well!
'Tis worse than any funeral bell;
As sure as I've the gift of sight,
We shall be meeting ghosts to-night!"   115
—Said Benjamin, "This whip shall lay
A thousand, if they cross our way.
I know that Wanton's noisy station,
I know him and his occupation;
The jolly bird hath learned his cheer   120
Upon the banks of Windermere;
Where a tribe of them make merry,
Mocking the Man that keeps the ferry;
Hallooing from an open throat,
Like travellers shouting for a boat.   125
—The tricks he learned at Windermere
This vagrant owl is playing here—
That is the worst of his employment:
He's at the top of his enjoyment!"

This explanation stilled the alarm,   130
Cured the foreboder like a charm;
This, and the manner, and the voice,
Summoned the Sailor to rejoice;
His heart is up—he fears no evil
From life or death, from man or devil;

He wheels—and, making many stops, 136
Brandished his crutch against the moun-
    tain tops;
And, while he talked of blows and scars,
Benjamin, among the stars,
Beheld a dancing—and a glancing;   140
Such retreating and advancing
As, I ween, was never seen
In bloodiest battle since the days of Mars!

Canto Fourth.

THUS they, with freaks of proud delight,
Beguile the remnant of the night;
And many a snatch of jovial song
Regales them as they wind along;
While to the music, from on high,   5
The echoes make a glad reply.—
But the sage Muse the revel heeds
No farther than her story needs;
Nor will she servilely attend
The loitering journey to its end.   10
—Blithe spirits of her own impel
The Muse, who scents the morning air,
To take of this transported pair
A brief and unreproved farewell;
To quit the slow-paced waggon's side,   15
And wander down yon hawthorn dell,
With murmuring Greta for her guide.
—There doth she ken the awful form
Of Raven-crag—black as a storm—
Glimmering through the twilight pale;   20
And Ghimmer-crag,[1] his tall twin brother,
Each peering forth to meet the other:—
And, while she roves through St. John's
    Vale,
Along the smooth unpathwayed plain,
By sheep-track or through cottage lane,   25
Where no disturbance comes to intrude
Upon the pensive solitude,
Her unsuspecting eye, perchance,
With the rude shepherd's favoured glance,
Beholds the faeries in array,   30
Whose party-coloured garments gay
The silent company betray:
Red, green, and blue; a moment's sight!
For Skiddaw-top with rosy light
Is touched—and all the band take flight.
—Fly also, Muse! and from the dell   36
Mount to the ridge of Nathdale Fell;

[1] The crag of the ewe lamb.

Thence look thou forth o'er wood and
    lawn
Hoar with the frost-like dews of dawn;
Across yon meadowy bottom look,   40
Where close fogs hide their parent brook;
And see, beyond that hamlet small
The ruined towers of Threlkeld-hall,
Lurking in a double shade,
By trees and lingering twilight made!   45
There, at Blencathara's rugged feet,
Sir Lancelot gave a safe retreat
To noble Clifford; from annoy
Concealed the persecuted boy,
Well pleased in rustic garb to feed   50
His flock, and pipe on shepherd's reed
Among this multitude of hills,
Crags, woodlands, waterfalls, and rills;
Which soon the morning shall enfold,
From east to west, in ample vest   55
Of massy gloom and radiance bold.

The mists, that o'er the streamlet's bed
Hung low, begin to rise and spread;
Even while I speak, their skirts of grey
Are smitten by a silver ray;   60
And, lo!—up Castrigg's naked steep
(Where, smoothly urged, the vapours
    sweep
Along—and scatter and divide,
Like fleecy clouds self-multiplied)
The stately waggon is ascending,   65
With faithful Benjamin attending,
Apparent now beside his team—
Now lost amid a glittering steam:
And with him goes his Sailor-friend,
By this time near their journey's end;   70
And, after their high-minded riot,
Sickening into thoughtful quiet;
As if the morning's pleasant hour
Had for their joys a killing power.
And sooth for Benjamin a vein   75
Is opened of still deeper pain,
As if his heart by notes were stung
From out the lowly hedge-rows flung;
As if the warbler lost in light
Reproved his soarings of the night,   80
In strains of rapture pure and holy
Upbraided his distempered folly.

Drooping is he, his step is dull;
But the horses stretch and pull;

With increasing vigour climb, 85
Eager to repair lost time;
Whether, by their own desert,
Knowing what cause there is for shame,
They are labouring to avert
As much as may be of the blame, 90
Which, they foresee, must soon alight
Upon *his* head, whom, in despite
Of all his failings, they love best;
Whether for him they are distrest;
Or, by length of fasting roused, 95
Are impatient to be housed:
Up against the hill they strain
Tugging at the iron chain,
Tugging all with might and main,
Last and foremost, every horse 100
To the utmost of his force!
And the smoke and respiration,
Rising like an exhalation,
Blend with the mist—a moving shroud
To form, an undissolving cloud; 105
Which, with slant ray, the merry sun
Takes delight to play upon.
Never golden-haired Apollo,
Pleased some favourite chief to follow
Through accidents of peace or war, 110
In a perilous moment threw
Around the object of his care
Veil of such celestial hue;
Interposed so bright a screen—
Him and his enemies between! 115

Alas! what boots it?—who can hide,
When the malicious Fates are bent
On working out an ill intent?
Can destiny be turned aside?
No—sad progress of my story! 120
Benjamin, this outward glory
Cannot shield thee from thy Master,
Who from Keswick has pricked forth,
Sour and surly as the north;
And, in fear of some disaster, 125
Comes to give what help he may,
And to hear what thou canst say;
If, as needs he must forbode,
Thou hast been loitering on the road!
His fears, his doubts, may now take flight— 130
The wished-for object is in sight;
Yet, trust the Muse, it rather hath
Stirred him up to livelier wrath;

Which he stifles, moody man!
With all the patience that he can; 135
To the end that, at your meeting,
He may give thee decent greeting.

There he is—resolved to stop,
Till the waggon gains the top;
But stop he cannot—must advance: 140
Him Benjamin, with lucky glance,
Espies—and instantly is ready,
Self-collected, poised, and steady:
And, to be the better seen,
Issues from his radiant shroud, 145
From his close-attending cloud,
With careless air and open mien.
Erect his port, and firm his going;
So struts yon cock that now is crowing;
And the morning light in grace 150
Strikes upon his lifted face,
Hurrying the pallid hue away
That might his trespasses betray.
But what can all avail to clear him,
Or what need of explanation, 155
Parley or interrogation?
For the Master sees, alas!
That unhappy Figure near him,
Limping o'er the dewy grass,
Where the road it fringes, sweet, 160
Soft and cool to way-worn feet;
And, O indignity! an Ass,
By his noble Mastiff's side,
Tethered to the waggon's tail:
And the ship, in all her pride, 165
Following after in full sail!
Not to speak of babe and mother;
Who, contented with each other,
And snug as birds in leafy arbour,
Find, within, a blessed harbour! 170

With eager eyes the Master pries;
Looks in and out, and through and through;
Says nothing—till at last he spies
A wound upon the Mastiff's head,
A wound where plainly might be read 175
What feats an Ass's hoof can do!
But drop the rest:—this aggravation,
This complicated provocation,
A hoard of grievances unsealed;
All past forgiveness it repealed; 180
And thus, and through distempered blood
On both sides, Benjamin the good,

The patient, and the tender-hearted,
Was from his team and waggon parted;
When duty of that day was o'er,   185
Laid down his whip—and served no more.—
Nor could the waggon long survive,
Which Benjamin had ceased to drive:
It lingered on;—guide after guide
Ambitiously the office tried;   190
But each unmanageable hill
Called for *his* patience and *his* skill;—
And sure it is that through this night,
And what the morning brought to light,
Two losses had we to sustain,   195
We lost both WAGGONER and WAIN!

Accept, O Friend, for praise or blame,
The gift of this adventurous song;
A record which I dared to frame,   199
Though timid scruples checked me long;
They checked me—and I left the theme
Untouched;—in spite of many a gleam
Of fancy which thereon was shed,
Like pleasant sunbeams shifting still
Upon the side of a distant hill: 205
But Nature might not be gainsaid;
For what I have and what I miss
I sing of these;—it makes my bliss!
Nor is it I who play the part,
But a shy spirit in my heart,   210
That comes and goes—will sometimes leap
From hiding-places ten years deep;
Or haunts me with familiar face,
Returning, like a ghost unlaid,
Until the debt I owe be paid.   215
Forgive me then; for I had been
On friendly terms with this Machine:
In him, while he was wont to trace
Our roads, through many a long year's
    space,
A living almanack had we;   220
We had a speaking diary,
That in this uneventful place,
Gave to the days a mark and name
By which we knew them when they came.

—Yes, I, and all about me here,   225
Through all the changes of the year,
Had seen him through the mountains go,
In pomp of mist or pomp of snow,
Majestically huge and slow:
Or with a milder grace adorning   230
The landscape of a summer's morning;
While Grasmere smoothed her liquid
    plain
The moving image to detain;
And mighty Fairfield, with a chime
Of echoes, to his march kept time;   235
When little other business stirred,
And little other sound was heard;
In that delicious hour of balm,
Stillness, solitude, and calm,
While yet the valley is arrayed,   240
On this side with a sober shade;
On that is prodigally bright—
Crag, lawn, and wood—with rosy light.
—But most of all, thou lordly Wain!
I wish to have thee here again,   245
When windows flap and chimney roars,
And all is dismal out of doors;
And, sitting by my fire, I see
Eight sorry carts, no less a train!
Unworthy successors of thee,   250
Come straggling through the wind and
    rain:
And oft, as they pass slowly on,
Beneath my windows, one by one,
See, perched upon the naked height
The summit of a cumbrous freight,   255
A single traveller—and there
Another; then perhaps a pair—
The lame, the sickly, and the old;
Men, women, heartless with the cold;
And babes in wet and starveling plight;
Which once, be weather as it might,   261
Had still a nest within a nest,
Thy shelter—and their mother's breast!
Then most of all, then far the most,
Do I regret what we have lost;   265
Am grieved for that unhappy sin
Which robbed us of good Benjamin;—
And of his stately Charge, which none
Could keep alive when He was gone!

POEMS OF THE IMAGINATION.

I.

THERE WAS A BOY.

[Composed November or December, 1798.
Published 1800.]

THERE was a Boy; ye knew him well, ye
    cliffs
And islands of Winander!—many a time,
At evening, when the earliest stars began
To move along the edges of the hills,
Rising or setting, would he stand alone, 5
Beneath the trees, or by the glimmering
    lake;
And there, with fingers interwoven, both
    hands
Pressed closely palm to palm and to his
    mouth
Uplifted, he, as through an instrument,
Blew mimic hootings to the silent owls, 10
That they might answer him.—And they
    would shout
Across the watery vale, and shout again,
Responsive to his call,—with quivering
    peals,
And long halloos, and screams, and echoes
    loud
Redoubled and redoubled; concourse
    wild   15
Of jocund din! And, when there came a
    pause
Of silence such as baffled his best skill:
Then sometimes, in that silence, while he
    hung
Listening, a gentle shock of mild surprise
Has carried far into his heart the voice 20
Of mountain-torrents; or the visible scene
Would enter unawares into his mind
With all its solemn imagery, its rocks,
Its woods, and that uncertain heaven
    received
Into the bosom of the steady lake.   25

This boy was taken from his mates, and
    died
In childhood, ere he was full twelve years
    old.
Pre-eminent in beauty is the vale
Where he was born and bred: the church-
    yard hangs
Upon a slope above the village-school; 30
And through that churchyard when my
    way has led
On summer-evenings, I believe that there
A long half-hour together I have stood
Mute—looking at the grave in which he
    lies!

II.

TO THE CUCKOO.

[Composed March 23-26, 1802.—Published 1807.]

O BLITHE New-comer! I have heard,
I hear thee and rejoice.
O Cuckoo! shall I call thee Bird,
Or but a wandering Voice?

While I am lying on the grass   5
Thy twofold shout I hear;
From hill to hill it seems to pass
At once far off, and near.

Though babbling only to the Vale,
Of sunshine and of flowers,   10
Thou bringest unto me a tale
Of visionary hours.

Thrice welcome, darling of the Spring!
Even yet thou art to me
No bird, but an invisible thing,   15
A voice, a mystery;

The same whom in my schoolboy days
I listened to; that Cry
Which made me look a thousand ways
In bush, and tree, and sky.   20

To seek thee did I often rove
Through woods and on the green;
And thou wert still a hope, a love;
Still longed for, never seen.

And I can listen to thee yet;   25
Can lie upon the plain
And listen, till I do beget
That golden time again.

O blessèd Bird! the earth we pace
Again appears to be   30
An unsubstantial, faery place;
That is fit home for Thee!

III.

A NIGHT-PIECE.

[Composed January 25, 1798.—Published 1815.]

————The sky is overcast
With a continuous cloud of texture close,
Heavy and wan, all whitened by the
     Moon,
Which through that veil is indistinctly
     seen,
A dull, contracted circle, yielding light   5
So feebly spread that not a shadow falls,
Chequering the ground—from rock, plant,
     tree, or tower.
At length a pleasant instantaneous gleam
Startles the pensive traveller while he
     treads
His lonesome path, with unobserving eye
Bent earthwards; he looks up—the clouds
     are split   11
Asunder,—and above his head he sees
The clear Moon, and the glory of the
     heavens.
There in a black-blue vault she sails along,
Followed by multitudes of stars, that, small
And sharp, and bright, along the dark
     abyss   16
Drive as she drives: how fast they wheel
     away,
Yet vanish not!—the wind is in the tree,
But they are silent;—still they roll along
Immeasurably distant; and the vault,   20
Built round by those white clouds, enor-
     mous clouds,
Still deepens its unfathomable depth.
At length the Vision closes; and the mind,

Not undisturbed by the delight it feels,
Which slowly settles into peaceful calm,
Is left to muse upon the solemn scene.   26

IV.

AIREY-FORCE VALLEY.

[Composed ? — Published 1842.]

————NOT a breath of air
Ruffles the bosom of this leafy glen.
From the brook's margin, wide around,
     the trees
Are steadfast as the rocks; the brook itself,
Old as the hills that feed it from afar,   5
Doth rather deepen than disturb the calm
Where all things else are still and motion-
     less.
And yet, even now, a little breeze, per-
     chance
Escaped from boisterous winds that rage
     without,
Has entered, by the sturdy oaks unfelt,   10
But to its gentle touch how sensitive
Is the light ash! that, pendent from the
     brow
Of yon dim cave, in seeming silence makes
A soft eye-music of slow-waving boughs,
Powerful almost as vocal harmony   15
To stay the wanderer's steps and soothe
     his thoughts.

V.

YEW-TREES.

[Composed 1803.—Published 1815.]

THERE is a Yew-tree, pride of Lorton Vale,
Which to this day stands single, in the
     midst
Of its own darkness, as it stood of yore:
Not loth to furnish weapons for the bands
Of Umfraville or Percy ere they marched
To Scotland's heaths; or those that
     crossed the sea   6
And drew their sounding bows at Azin-
     cour,
Perhaps at earlier Crecy, or Poictiers.
Of vast circumference and gloom profound
This solitary Tree! a living thing   10
Produced too slowly ever to decay;
Of form and aspect too magnificent
To be destroyed. But worthier still of note

Are those fraternal Four of Borrowdale,
Joined in one solemn and capacious grove;
Huge trunks! and each particular trunk
  a growth   16
Of intertwisted fibres serpentine
Up-coiling, and inveterately convolved;
Nor uninformed with Phantasy, and looks
That threaten the profane; a pillared
  shade,   20
Upon whose grassless floor of red-brown
  hue,
By sheddings from the pining umbrage
  tinged
Perennially—beneath whose sable roof
Of boughs, as if for festal purpose decked
With unrejoicing berries—ghostly Shapes
May meet at noontide; Fear and trem-
  bling Hope,   26
Silence and Foresight; Death the Skeleton
And Time the Shadow;—there to celebrate,
As in a natural temple scattered o'er
With altars undisturbed of mossy stone,
United worship; or in mute repose   31
To lie, and listen to the mountain flood
Murmuring from Glaramara's inmost
  caves.

VI.

NUTTING.

[Composed 1798-9.—Published 1800.]

—————————It seems a day
(I speak of one from many singled out)
One of those heavenly days that cannot die;
When, in the eagerness of boyish hope,
I left our cottage-threshold, sallying forth
With a huge wallet o'er my shoulders slung,
A nutting-crook in hand; and turned my
  steps   7
Tow'rd some far-distant wood, a Figure
  quaint,
Tricked out in proud disguise of cast-off
  weeds
Which for that service had been hus-
  banded,   10
By exhortation of my frugal Dame—
Motley accoutrement, of power to smile
At thorns, and brakes, and brambles,—
  and in truth
More ragged than need was! O'er path-
  less rocks,

Through beds of matted fern, and tangled
  thickets,   15
Forcing my way, I came to one dear nook
Unvisited, where not a broken bough
Drooped with its withered leaves, un-
  gracious sign
Of devastation; but the hazels rose
Tall and erect, with tempting clusters
  hung,   20
A virgin scene!—A little while I stood,
Breathing with such suppression of the
  heart
As joy delights in; and with wise restraint
Voluptuous, fearless of a rival, eyed
The banquet;—or beneath the trees I sate
Among the flowers, and with the flowers
  I played;   26
A temper known to those who, after long
And weary expectation, have been blest
With sudden happiness beyond all hope.
Perhaps it was a bower beneath whose
  leaves   30
The violets of five seasons re-appear
And fade, unseen by any human eye;
Where fairy water-breaks do murmur on
For ever; and I saw the sparkling foam,
And—with my cheek on one of those green
  stones   35
That, fleeced with moss, under the shady
  trees,
Lay round me, scattered like a flock of
  sheep—
I heard the murmur and the murmuring
  sound,
In that sweet mood when pleasure loves
  to pay
Tribute to ease; and, of its joy secure, 40
The heart luxuriates with indifferent
  things,
Wasting its kindliness on stocks and stones,
And on the vacant air. Then up I rose,
And dragged to earth both branch and
  bough, with crash   44
And merciless ravage: and the shady nook
Of hazels, and the green and mossy bower,
Deformed and sullied, patiently gave up
Their quiet being: and unless I now
Confound my present feelings with the
  past,
Ere from the mutilated bower I turned 50
Exulting, rich beyond the wealth of kings,

I felt a sense of pain when I beheld
The silent trees, and saw the intruding
  sky.—
Then, dearest Maiden, move along these
  shades   54
In gentleness of heart; with gentle hand
Touch—for there is a spirit in the woods.

VII.

THE SIMPLON PASS.

[Composed 1799? (certainly not later than 1803).—
Published 1845.]

————Brook and road
Were fellow-travellers in this gloomy Pass,
And with them did we journey several
  hours
At a slow step. The immeasurable height
Of woods decaying, never to be decayed,   5
The stationary blasts of waterfalls,
And in the narrow rent, at every turn,
Winds thwarting winds bewildered and
  forlorn,
The torrents shooting from the clear blue
  sky,
The rocks that muttered close upon our
  ears,   10
Black drizzling crags that spake by the
  wayside
As if a voice were in them, the sick sight
And giddy prospect of the raving stream,
The unfettered clouds and region of the
  heavens,
Tumult and peace, the darkness and the
  light—   15
Were all like workings of one mind, the
  features
Of the same face, blossoms upon one tree,
Characters of the great Apocalypse,
The types and symbols of Eternity,
Of first, and last, and midst, and without
  end.   20

VIII.

[Composed 1804.—Published 1807.]

She was a Phantom of delight
When first she gleamed upon my sight;
A lovely Apparition, sent
To be a moment's ornament;
Her eyes as stars of Twilight fair;   5
Like Twilight's, too, her dusky hair;

But all things else about her drawn
From May-time and the cheerful Dawn;
A dancing Shape, an Image gay,
To haunt, to startle, and way-lay.   10
I saw her upon nearer view,
A Spirit, yet a Woman too!
Her household motions light and free,
And steps of virgin-liberty;
A countenance in which did meet   15
Sweet records, promises as sweet;
A Creature not too bright or good
For human nature's daily food;
For transient sorrows, simple wiles,
Praise, blame, love, kisses, tears, and
  smiles.   20
And now I see with eye serene
The very pulse of the machine;
A Being breathing thoughtful breath,
A Traveller between life and death;
The reason firm, the temperate will,   25
Endurance, foresight, strength, and skill;
A perfect Woman, nobly planned,
To warn, to comfort, and command;
And yet a Spirit still, and bright
With something of angelic light.   30

IX

[Composed 1806.—Published 1807.]

O Nightingale! thou surely art
A creature of a "fiery heart":—
These notes of thine—they pierce and
  pierce;
Tumultuous harmony and fierce!
Thou sing'st as if the God of wine   5
Had helped thee to a Valentine;
A song in mockery and despite
Of shades, and dews, and silent night;
And steady bliss, and all the loves
Now sleeping in these peaceful groves.   10
I heard a Stock-dove sing or say
His homely tale, this very day;
His voice was buried among trees,
Yet to be come-at by the breeze:
He did not cease; but cooed—and cooed;
And somewhat pensively he wooed: 16
He sang of love, with quiet blending,
Slow to begin, and never ending;
Of serious faith, and inward glee;
That was the song—the song for me!   20

X.

[Composed 1799.—Published 1800.]

THREE years she grew in sun and shower,
Then Nature said, "A lovelier flower
On earth was never sown;
This Child I to myself will take;
She shall be mine, and I will make   5
A Lady of my own.

"Myself will to my darling be
Both law and impulse: and with me
The Girl, in rock and plain,
In earth and heaven, in glade and bower,
Shall feel an overseeing power   11
To kindle or restrain.

"She shall be sportive as the fawn
That wild with glee across the lawn
Or up the mountain springs;   15
And hers shall be the breathing balm,
And hers the silence and the calm
Of mute insensate things.

"The floating clouds their state shall
   lend
To her; for her the willow bend;   20
Nor shall she fail to see
Even in the motions of the Storm
Grace that shall mould the Maiden's
   form
By silent sympathy.

"The stars of midnight shall be dear   25
To her; and she shall lean her ear
In many a secret place
Where rivulets dance their wayward round,
And beauty born of murmuring sound
Shall pass into her face.   30

"And vital feelings of delight
Shall rear her form to stately height,
Her virgin bosom swell;
Such thoughts to Lucy I will give
While she and I together live   35
Here in this happy dell."

Thus Nature spake—The work was done—
How soon my Lucy's race was run!
She died, and left to me
This heath, this calm, and quiet scene; 40
The memory of what has been,
And never more will be.

XI.

[Composed 1799.—Published 1800.]

A SLUMBER did my spirit seal;
  I had no human fears:
She seemed a thing that could not feel
  The touch of earthly years.

No motion has she now, no force;   5
  She neither hears nor sees;
Rolled round in earth's diurnal course,
  With rocks, and stones, and trees.

XII.

[Composed 1804.—Published 1807.]

I WANDERED lonely as a cloud
That floats on high o'er vales and hills,
When all at once I saw a crowd,
A host, of golden daffodils;
Beside the lake, beneath the trees,   5
Fluttering and dancing in the breeze.

Continuous as the stars that shine
And twinkle on the milky way,
They stretched in never-ending line
Along the margin of a bay: 10
Ten thousand saw I at a glance,
Tossing their heads in sprightly dance.

The waves beside them danced; but they
Out-did the sparkling waves in glee:
A poet could not but be gay,   15
In such a jocund company:
I gazed—and gazed—but little thought
What wealth the show to me had brought:

For oft, when on my couch I lie
In vacant or in pensive mood,   20
They flash upon that inward eye
Which is the bliss of solitude;
And then my heart with pleasure fills,
And dances with the daffodils.

XIII.

THE REVERIE OF POOR SUSAN.

[Composed 1797.—Published 1800.]

AT the corner of Wood Street, when day-
  light appears,
Hangs a Thrush that sings loud, it has
  sung for three years:

Poor Susan has passed by the spot, and
    has heard
In the silence of morning the song of the
    Bird.

'Tis a note of enchantment; what ails
    her? She sees   5
A mountain ascending, a vision of trees;
Bright volumes of vapour through Loth-
    bury glide,
And a river flows on through the vale of
    Cheapside.

Green pastures she views in the midst of
    the dale,
Down which she so often has tripped with
    her pail;   10
And a single small cottage, a nest like a
    dove's,
The one only dwelling on earth that she
    loves.

She looks, and her heart is in heaven:
    but they fade,
The mist and the river, the hill and the
    shade:
The stream will not flow, and the hill will
    not rise,   15
And the colours have all passed away
    from her eyes!

XIV.

POWER OF MUSIC.

[Composed 1806.—Published 1807.]

AN Orpheus! an Orpheus! yes, Faith
    may grow bold,
And take to herself all the wonders of
    old;—
Near the stately Pantheon you'll meet
    with the same
In the street that from Oxford hath bor-
    rowed its name.

His station is there; and he works on the
    crowd,   5
He sways them with harmony merry and
    loud;
He fills with his power all their hearts to
    the brim—
Was aught ever heard like his fiddle and
    him?

What an eager assembly! what an empire
    is this!
The weary have life, and the hungry have
    bliss;   10
The mourner is cheered, and the anxious
    have rest;
And the guilt-burthened soul is no longer
    opprest.

As the Moon brightens round her the
    clouds of the night,
So He, where he stands, is a centre of light;
It gleams on the face, there, of dusky-
    browed Jack,   15
And the pale-visaged Baker's, with basket
    on back.

That errand-bound 'Prentice was passing
    in haste—
What matter! he's caught—and his time
    runs to waste;
The Newsman is stopped, though he stops
    on the fret;
And the half-breathless Lamplighter—
    he's in the net!   20

The Porter sits down on the weight which
    he bore;
The Lass with her barrow wheels hither
    her store;—
If a thief could be here he might pilfer at
    ease;
She sees the Musician, 'tis all that she sees!

He stands, backed by the wall;—he abates
    not his din;   25
His hat gives him vigour, with boons
    dropping in,
From the old and the young, from the
    poorest; and there!
The one-pennied Boy has his penny to
    spare.

O blest are the hearers, and proud be the
    hand
Of the pleasure it spreads through so
    thankful a band;   30
I am glad for him, blind as he is!—all the
    while
If they speak 'tis to praise, and they
    praise with a smile.

That tall Man, a giant in bulk and in
  height,
Not an inch of his body is free from
  delight;
Can he keep himself still, if he would?
  oh, not he!   35
The music stirs in him like wind through
  a tree.

Mark that Cripple who leans on his
  crutch; like a tower
That long has leaned forward, leans hour
  after hour!—
That Mother, whose spirit in fetters is
  bound,
While she dandles the Babe in her arms
  to the sound.   40

Now, coaches and chariots! roar on like a
  stream;
Here are twenty souls happy as souls in
  a dream:
They are deaf to your murmurs—they
  care not for you,
Nor what ye are flying, nor what ye
  pursue!

XV.

STAR-GAZERS.

[Composed 1806.—Published 1807.]

WHAT crowd is this? what have we here!
  we must not pass it by;
A Telescope upon its frame, and pointed
  to the sky:
Long is it as a barber's pole, or mast of
  little boat,
Some little pleasure-skiff, that doth on
  Thames's waters float.

The Showman chooses well his place, 'tis
  Leicester's busy Square;   5
And is as happy in his night, for the
  heavens are blue and fair;
Calm, though impatient, is the crowd;
  each stands ready with the fee,
And envies him that's looking;—what an
  insight must it be!

Yet, Showman, where can lie the cause?
  Shall thy Implement have blame,

A boaster that, when he is tried, fails, and
  is put to shame?   10
Or is it good as others are, and be their
  eyes in fault?
Their eyes, or minds? or, finally, is yon
  resplendent vault?

Is nothing of that radiant pomp so good
  as we have here?
Or gives a thing but small delight that
  never can be dear?
The silver moon with all her vales, and
  hills of mightiest fame,   15
Doth she betray us when they're seen? or
  are they but a name?

Or is it rather that Conceit rapacious is
  and strong,
And bounty never yields so much but it
  seems to do her wrong?
Or is it that, when human Souls a journey
  long have had
And are returned into themselves, they
  cannot but be sad?   20

Or must we be constrained to think that
  these Spectators rude,
Poor in estate, of manners base, men of
  the multitude,
Have souls which never yet have risen,
  and therefore prostrate lie?
No, no, this cannot be;—men thirst for
  power and majesty!

Does, then, a deep and earnest thought
  the blissful mind employ   25
Of him who gazes, or has gazed? a grave
  and steady joy,
That doth reject all show of pride, admits
  no outward sign,
Because not of this noisy world, but silent
  and divine!

Whatever be the cause, 'tis sure that they
  who pry and pore
Seem to meet with little gain, seem less
  happy than before: 30
One after One they take their turn, nor
  have I one espied
That doth not slackly go away, as if dis-
  satisfied.

XVI.

WRITTEN IN MARCH,

WHILE RESTING ON THE BRIDGE AT THE
FOOT OF BROTHER'S WATER.

[Composed April 16, 1802.—Published 1807.]

THE Cock is crowing,
The stream is flowing,
The small birds twitter,
The lake doth glitter,
The green field sleeps in the sun;   5
   The oldest and youngest
   Are at work with the strongest;
The cattle are grazing,
Their heads never raising;
There are forty feeding like one!   10

Like an army defeated
The snow hath retreated,
And now doth fare ill
On the top of the bare hill;
The Ploughboy is whooping—anon—anon:
   There's joy in the mountains;   16
   There's life in the fountains;
Small clouds are sailing,
Blue sky prevailing;
The rain is over and gone!   20

XVII.

[Composed ?.—Published 1842.]

LYRE! though such power do in thy magic
     live
   As might from India's farthest plain
   Recall the not unwilling Maid,
     Assist me to detain
       The lovely Fugitive: 5
Check with thy notes the impulse which,
     betrayed
By her sweet farewell looks, I longed to
     aid.

Here let me gaze enrapt upon that eye,
The impregnable and awe-inspiring fort
Of contemplation, the calm port   10
By reason fenced from winds that sigh
Among the restless sails of vanity.
But if no wish be hers that we should
     part,
A humbler bliss would satisfy my heart.
     Where all things are so fair,   15

Enough by her dear side to breathe the
     air
   Of this Elysian weather;
And on or in, or near, the brook, espy
   Shade upon the sunshine lying
     Faint and somewhat pensively;
   And downward Image gaily vying   21
     With its upright living tree
'Mid silver clouds, and openings of blue
     sky
As soft almost and deep as her cerulean
     eye.

Nor less the joy with many a glance   25
Cast up the Stream or down at her be-
     seeching,
To mark its eddying foam-balls prettily
     distrest
By ever-changing shape and want of rest;
     Or watch, with mutual teaching,
     The current as it plays   30
     In flashing leaps and stealthy
       creeps
     Adown a rocky maze;
Or note (translucent summer's happiest
     chance!)
In the slope-channel floored with pebbles
     bright,
Stones of all hues, gem emulous of gem,
So vivid that they take from keenest
     sight   36
The liquid veil that seeks not to hide
     them.

XVIII.

BEGGARS.

[Composed March 13, 14, 1802.—Published 1807.]

SHE had a tall man's height or more;
Her face from summer's noontide heat
No bonnet shaded, but she wore
A mantle, to her very feet
Descending with a graceful flow,   5
And on her head a cap as white as new-
     fallen snow.

Her skin was of Egyptian brown:
Haughty, as if her eye had seen
Its own light to a distance thrown,
She towered, fit person for a Queen   10
To lead those ancient Amazonian files;
Or ruling Bandit's wife among the Grecian
     isles.

Advancing, forth she stretched her hand
And begged an alms with doleful plea
That ceased not; on our English land   15
Such woes, I knew, could never be;
And yet a boon I gave her, for the
    creature
Was beautiful to see—a weed of glorious
    feature.

I left her, and pursued my way;
And soon before me did espy   20
A pair of little Boys at play,
Chasing a crimson butterfly;
The taller followed with his hat in hand,
Wreathed round with yellow flowers the
    gayest of the land.

The other wore a rimless crown   25
With leaves of laurel stuck about;
And while both followed up and down,
Each whooping with a merry shout,
In their fraternal features I could trace
Unquestionable lines of that wild Sup-
    pliant's face.   30

Yet *they*, so blithe of heart, seemed fit
For finest tasks of earth or air:
Wings let them have, and they might flit
Precursors to Aurora's car,
Scattering fresh flowers; though happier
    far, I ween,   35
To hunt their fluttering game o'er rock
    and level green.

They dart across my path—but lo,
Each ready with a plaintive whine!
Said I, "not half an hour ago
Your Mother has had alms of mine."   40
"That cannot be," one answered—"she is
    dead:"—
I looked reproof—they saw—but neither
    hung his head.

"She has been dead, Sir, many a day."—
"Hush, boys! you're telling me a lie;
It was your Mother, as I say!"   45
And, in the twinkling of an eye,
"Come! come!" cried one, and without
    more ado
Off to some other play the joyous Vagrants
    flew!

XIX.

SEQUEL TO THE FOREGOING.

COMPOSED MANY YEARS AFTER.

[Composed 1817.—Published 1827.]

WHERE are they now, those wanton Boys?
For whose free range the dædal earth
Was filled with animated toys,
And implements of frolic mirth;
With tools for ready wit to guide;   5
And ornaments of seemlier pride,
More fresh, more bright, than princes
    wear;
For what one moment flung aside,
Another could repair;
What good or evil have they seen   10
Since I their pastime witnessed here,
Their daring wiles, their sportive cheer?
I ask—but all is dark between!

    They met me in a genial hour,
When universal nature breathed   15
As with the breath of one sweet flower,—
A time to overrule the power
Of discontent, and check the birth
Of thoughts with better thoughts at strife,
The most familiar bane of life   20
Since parting Innocence bequeathed
Mortality to Earth!
Soft clouds, the whitest of the year,
Sailed through the sky—the brooks ran
    clear;
The lambs from rock to rock were bound-
    ing;   25
With songs the budded groves resound-
    ing;
And to my heart are still endeared
The thoughts with which it then was
    cheered;
The faith which saw that gladsome pair
Walk through the fire with unsinged hair.
Or, if such faith must needs deceive—   31
Then, Spirits of beauty and of grace,
Associates in that eager chase;
Ye, who within the blameless mind
Your favourite seat of empire find—   35
Kind Spirits! may we not believe
That they, so happy and so fair
Through your sweet influence, and the
    care

Of pitying Heaven, at least were free
From touch of *deadly* injury? 40
Destined, whate'er their earthly doom,
For mercy and immortal bloom?

XX.
GIPSIES.

[Composed 1807.—Published 1807.]

YET are they here the same unbroken
knot
Of human Beings, in the self-same spot!
   Men, women, children, yea the frame
   Of the whole spectacle the same!
Only their fire seems bolder, yielding
   light, 5
Now deep and red, the colouring of night;
   That on their Gipsy-faces falls,
   Their bed of straw and blanket-walls,
—Twelve hours, twelve bounteous hours
   are gone, while I
Have been a traveller under open sky, 10
   Much witnessing of change and cheer,
   Yet as I left I find them here!
The weary Sun betook himself to rest;—
Then issued Vesper from the fulgent west,
   Outshining like a visible God 15
   The glorious path in which he trod.
And now, ascending, after one dark hour
And one night's diminution of her power,
   Behold the mighty Moon! this way
   She looks as if at them—but they 20
Regard not her:—oh, better wrong and
   strife
(By nature transient) than this torpid
   life;
   Life which the very stars reprove
   As on their silent tasks they move!
Yet, witness all that stirs in heaven or
   earth! 25
In scorn I speak not;—they are what their
   birth
   And breeding suffer them to be;
   Wild outcasts of society!

XXI.
RUTH.

[Composed 1799.—Published 1800.]

WHEN Ruth was left half desolate,
Her Father took another Mate;

And Ruth, not seven years old,
A slighted child, at her own will
Went wandering over dale and hill, 5
In thoughtless freedom, bold.

And she had made a pipe of straw,
And music from that pipe could draw
Like sounds of winds and floods;
Had built a bower upon the green, 10
As if she from her birth had been
An infant of the woods.

Beneath her father's roof, alone
She seemed to live; her thoughts her
   own;
Herself her own delight; 15
Pleased with herself, nor sad, nor gay;
And, passing thus the live-long day,
She grew to woman's height.

There came a Youth from Georgia's
   shore—
A military casque he wore, 20
With splendid feathers drest;
He brought them from the Cherokees;
The feathers nodded in the breeze,
And made a gallant crest.

From Indian blood you deem him sprung:
But no! he spoke the English tongue, 26
And bore a soldier's name;
And, when America was free
From battle and from jeopardy,
He 'cross the ocean came. 30

With hues of genius on his cheek
In finest tones the Youth could speak:
—While he was yet a boy,
The moon, the glory of the sun,
And streams that murmur as they run, 35
Had been his dearest joy.

He was a lovely Youth! I guess
The panther in the wilderness
Was not so fair as he;
And, when he chose to sport and play, 40
No dolphin ever was so gay
Upon the tropic sea.

Among the Indians he had fought,
And with him many tales he brought
Of pleasure and of fear; 45
Such tales as told to any maid
By such a Youth, in the green shade,
Were perilous to hear.

He told of girls—a happy rout!
Who quit their fold with dance and shout,
Their pleasant Indian town,   51
To gather strawberries all day long;
Returning with a choral song
When daylight is gone down.

He spake of plants that hourly change 55
Their blossoms, through a boundless range
Of intermingling hues;
With budding, fading, faded flowers
They stand the wonder of the bowers
From morn to evening dews.   60

He told of the magnolia, spread
High as a cloud, high over head!
The cypress and her spire;
—Of flowers that with one scarlet gleam
Cover a hundred leagues, and seem   65
To set the hills on fire.

The Youth of green savannahs spake,
And many an endless, endless lake,
With all its fairy crowds
Of islands, that together lie   70
As quietly as spots of sky
Among the evening clouds.

"How pleasant," then he said, "it were
A fisher or a hunter there,
In sunshine or in shade   75
To wander with an easy mind;
And build a household fire, and find
A home in every glade!

"What days and what bright years! Ah
 me!
Our life were life indeed, with thee 80
So passed in quiet bliss,
And all the while," said he, "to know
That we were in a world of woe,
On such an earth as this!"

And then he sometimes interwove   85
Fond thoughts about a father's love:
"For there," said he, "are spun
Around the heart such tender ties,
That our own children to our eyes
Are dearer than the sun.   90

"Sweet Ruth! and could you go with me
My helpmate in the woods to be,
Our shed at night to rear;
Or run, my own adopted bride,
A sylvan huntress at my side,   95
And drive the flying deer!

"Beloved Ruth!"—No more he said.
The wakeful Ruth at midnight shed
A solitary tear:
She thought again—and did agree   100
With him to sail across the sea,
And drive the flying deer.

"And now, as fitting is and right,
We in the church our faith will plight,
A husband and a wife."   105
Even so they did; and I may say
That to sweet Ruth that happy day
Was more than human life.

Through dream and vision did she sink,
Delighted all the while to think   110
That on those lonesome floods,
And green savannahs, she should share
His board with lawful joy, and bear
His name in the wild woods.

But, as you have before been told, 115
This Stripling, sportive, gay, and bold,
And, with his dancing crest,
So beautiful, through savage lands
Had roamed about, with vagrant bands
Of Indians in the West.   120

The wind, the tempest roaring high,
The tumult of a tropic sky,
Might well be dangerous food
For him, a Youth to whom was given
So much of earth—so much of heaven, 125
And such impetuous blood.

Whatever in those climes he found
Irregular in sight or sound
Did to his mind impart
A kindred impulse, seemed allied   130
To his own powers, and justified
The workings of his heart.

Nor less, to feed voluptuous thought,
The beauteous forms of nature wrought,
Fair trees and gorgeous flowers;   135
The breezes their own languor lent;
The stars had feelings, which they sent
Into those favoured bowers.

Yet, in his worst pursuits I ween
That sometimes there did intervene 140
Pure hopes of high intent:
For passions linked to forms so fair
And stately needs must have their share
Of noble sentiment.

But ill he lived, much evil saw, 145
With men to whom no better law
Nor better life was known;
Deliberately, and undeceived,
Those wild men's vices he received,
And gave them back his own. 150

His genius and his moral frame
Were thus impaired, and he became
The slave of low desires:
A Man who without self-control
Would seek what the degraded soul 155
Unworthily admires.

And yet he with no feigned delight
Had wooed the Maiden, day and night
Had loved her, night and morn:
What could he less than love a Maid 160
Whose heart with so much nature played?
So kind and so forlorn!

Sometimes, most earnestly, he said,
"O Ruth! I have been worse than dead;
False thoughts, thoughts bold and vain,
Encompassed me on every side 166
When I, in confidence and pride,
Had crossed the Atlantic main.

"Before me shone a glorious world—
Fresh as a banner bright, unfurled 170
To music suddenly:
I looked upon those hills and plains,
And seemed as if let loose from chains,
To live at liberty.

"No more of this; for now, by thee 175
Dear Ruth! more happily set free
With nobler zeal I burn;
My soul from darkness is released,
Like the whole sky when to the east
The morning doth return." 180

Full soon that better mind was gone:
No hope, no wish remained, not one,—
They stirred him now no more;
New objects did new pleasure give,
And once again he wished to live 185
As lawless as before.

Meanwhile, as thus with him it fared,
They for the voyage were prepared,
And went to the sea-shore,
But, when they thither came, the Youth
Deserted his poor Bride, and Ruth 191
Could never find him more.

God help thee, Ruth!—Such pains she had,
That she in half a year was mad,
And in a prison housed; 195
And there, with many a doleful song
Made of wild words, her cup of wrong
She fearfully caroused.

Yet sometimes milder hours she knew,
Nor wanted sun, nor rain, nor dew, 200
Nor pastimes of the May;
—They all were with her in her cell;
And a clear brook with cheerful knell
Did o'er the pebbles play.

When Ruth three seasons thus had lain,
There came a respite to her pain; 206
She from her prison fled;
But of the Vagrant none took thought;
And where it liked her best she sought
Her shelter and her bread. 210

Among the fields she breathed again:
The master-current of her brain
Ran permanent and free;
And, coming to the Banks of Tone,
There did she rest; and dwell alone 215
Under the greenwood tree.

The engines of her pain, the tools
That shaped her sorrow, rocks and pools,
And airs that gently stir
The vernal leaves—she loved them still;
Nor ever taxed them with the ill 221
Which had been done to her.

A Barn her *winter* bed supplies;
But, till the warmth of summer skies
And summer days is gone, 225
(And all do in this tale agree)
She sleeps beneath the greenwood tree,
And other home hath none.

An innocent life, yet far astray!
And Ruth will, long before her day, 230
Be broken down and old:
Sore aches she needs must have! but less
Of mind than body's wretchedness,
From damp, and rain, and cold.

If she is prest by want of food, 235
She from her dwelling in the wood
Repairs to a road-side;
And there she begs at one steep place
Where up and down with easy pace
The horsemen-travellers ride. 240

That oaten pipe of hers is mute,
Or thrown away; but with a flute
Her loneliness she cheers:
This flute, made of a hemlock stalk,
At evening in his homeward walk   245
The Quantock woodman hears.

I, too, have passed her on the hills
Setting her little water-mills
By spouts and fountains wild—
Such small machinery as she turned   250
Ere she had wept, ere she had mourned,
A young and happy Child!

Farewell! and when thy days are told,
Ill-fated Ruth, in hallowed mould
Thy corpse shall buried be,   255
For thee a funeral bell shall ring,
And all the congregation sing
A Christian psalm for thee.

XXII.

RESOLUTION AND INDEPENDENCE.

Composed May 3–July 4, 1802.—Published 1807.

I.

THERE was a roaring in the wind all
          night;
The rain came heavily and fell in floods;
But now the sun is rising calm and bright;
The birds are singing in the distant woods;
Over his own sweet voice the Stock-dove
          broods;   5
The Jay makes answer as the Magpie
          chatters;
And all the air is filled with pleasant
          noise of waters.

II.

All things that love the sun are out of
          doors;
The sky rejoices in the morning's birth;
The grass is bright with rain-drops;—on
          the moors   10
The hare is running races in her mirth;
And with her feet she from the plashy
          earth
Raises a mist; that, glittering in the sun,
Runs with her all the way, wherever she
          doth run.

III.

I was a Traveller then upon the moor; 15
I saw the hare that raced about with joy;
I heard the woods and distant waters roar;
Or heard them not, as happy as a boy:
The pleasant season did my heart employ:
My old remembrances went from me
          wholly;   20
And all the ways of men, so vain and
          melancholy.

IV.

But, as it sometimes chanceth, from the
          might
Of joy in minds that can no further go,
As high as we have mounted in delight
In our dejection do we sink as low;   25
To me that morning did it happen so;
And fears and fancies thick upon me came;
Dim sadness—and blind thoughts, I knew
          not, nor could name.

V.

I heard the sky-lark warbling in the sky;
And I bethought me of the playful
          hare: 30
Even such a happy Child of earth am I;
Even as these blissful creatures do I fare;
Far from the world I walk, and from all
          care;
But there may come another day to me—
Solitude, pain of heart, distress, and po-
          verty.   35

VI.

My whole life I have lived in pleasant
          thought,
As if life's business were a summer mood;
As if all needful things would come un-
          sought
To genial faith, still rich in genial good;
But how can He expect that others should
Build for him, sow for him, and at his
          call   41
Love him, who for himself will take no
          heed at all?

VII.

I thought of Chatterton, the marvellous
          Boy,
The sleepless Soul that perished in his
          pride;

Of Him who walked in glory and in joy   45
Following his plough, along the moun-
    tain-side:
By our own spirits are we deified:
We Poets in our youth begin in gladness;
But thereof come in the end despondency
    and madness.

VIII.

Now, whether it were by peculiar grace,   50
A leading from above, a something given,
Yet it befell that, in this lonely place,
When I with these untoward thoughts
    had striven,
Beside a pool bare to the eye of heaven
I saw a Man before me unawares: 55
The oldest man he seemed that ever wore
    grey hairs.

IX.

As a huge stone is sometimes seen to lie
Couched on the bald top of an eminence;
Wonder to all who do the same espy,
By what means it could thither come,
    and whence;   60
So that it seems a thing endued with
    sense:
Like a sea-beast crawled forth, that on a
    shelf
Of rock or sand reposeth, there to sun
    itself;

X.

Such seemed this Man, not all alive nor
    dead,
Nor all asleep—in his extreme old age: 65
His body was bent double, feet and head
Coming together in life's pilgrimage;
As if some dire constraint of pain, or rage
Of sickness felt by him in times long past,
A more than human weight upon his
    frame had cast.   70

XI.

Himself he propped, limbs, body, and
    pale face,
Upon a long grey staff of shaven wood:
And, still as I drew near with gentle pace,
Upon the margin of that moorish flood
Motionless as a cloud the old Man stood,

That heareth not the loud winds when
    they call;   76
And moveth all together, if it move at all.

XII.

At length, himself unsettling, he the pond
Stirred with his staff, and fixedly did look
Upon the muddy water, which he conned,
As if he had been reading in a book: 81
And now a stranger's privilege I took;
And, drawing to his side, to him did say,
"This morning gives us promise of a
    glorious day."

XIII.

A gentle answer did the old Man make,
In courteous speech which forth he slowly
    drew: 86
And him with further words I thus be-
    spake,
"What occupation do you there pursue?
This is a lonesome place for one like you."
Ere he replied, a flash of mild surprise   90
Broke from the sable orbs of his yet-vivid
    eyes.

XIV.

His words came feebly, from a feeble
    chest,
But each in solemn order followed each,
With something of a lofty utterance
    drest—
Choice word and measured phrase, above
    the reach   95
Of ordinary men; a stately speech;
Such as grave Livers do in Scotland use,
Religious men, who give to God and man
    their dues.

XV.

He told, that to these waters he had come
To gather leeches, being old and poor: 100
Employment hazardous and wearisome!
And he had many hardships to endure:
From pond to pond he roamed, from moor
    to moor;
Housing, with God's good help, by choice
    or chance;
And in this way he gained an honest
    maintenance.   105

XVI.

The old Man still stood talking by my
    side;
But now his voice to me was like a stream
Scarce heard; nor word from word could
    I divide;
And the whole body of the Man did seem
Like one whom I had met with in a
    dream;   110
Or like a man from some far region sent,
To give me human strength, by apt ad-
    monishment.

XVII.

My former thoughts returned: the fear
    that kills;
And hope that is unwilling to be fed;
Cold, pain, and labour, and all fleshly
    ills;   115
And mighty Poets in their misery dead.
—Perplexed, and longing to be comforted,
My question eagerly did I renew,
"How is it that you live, and what is it
    you do?"

XVIII.

He with a smile did then his words repeat;
And said that, gathering leeches, far and
    wide   121
He travelled; stirring thus about his feet
The waters of the pools where they abide.
"Once I could meet with them on every
    side;
But they have dwindled long by slow
    decay;   125
Yet still I persevere, and find them where
    I may."

XIX.

While he was talking thus, the lonely
    place,
The old Man's shape, and speech—all
    troubled me:
In my mind's eye I seemed to see him pace
About the weary moors continually,   130
Wandering about alone and silently.
While I these thoughts within myself
    pursued,
He, having made a pause, the same dis-
    course renewed.

XX.

And soon with this he other matter
    blended,
Cheerfully uttered, with demeanour kind,
But stately in the main; and, when he
    ended,   136
I could have laughed myself to scorn to
    find
In that decrepit Man so firm a mind.
"God," said I, "be my help and stay
    secure;
I'll think of the Leech-gatherer on the
    lonely moor!"   140

XXIII.
THE THORN.

Composed 1798.—Published 1798.

I.

"THERE is a Thorn—it looks so old,
In truth, you'd find it hard to say
How it could ever have been young,
It looks so old and grey.
Not higher than a two years' child   5
It stands erect, this aged Thorn;
No leaves it has, no prickly points;
It is a mass of knotted joints,
A wretched thing forlorn.
It stands erect, and like a stone   10
With lichens is it overgrown.

II.

"Like rock or stone, it is o'ergrown,
With lichens to the very top,
And hung with heavy tufts of moss,
A melancholy crop: 15
Up from the earth these mosses creep,
And this poor Thorn they clasp it round
So close, you'd say that they are bent
With plain and manifest intent
To drag it to the ground;   20
And all have joined in one endeavour
To bury this poor Thorn for ever.

III.

"High on a mountain's highest ridge,
Where oft the stormy winter gale
Cuts like a scythe, while through the
    clouds   25
It sweeps from vale to vale;

Not five yards from the mountain path,
This Thorn you on your left espy;
And to the left, three yards beyond,
You see a little muddy pond   30
Of water—never dry,
Though but of compass small, and bare
To thirsty suns and parching air.

IV.

"And, close beside this aged Thorn,
There is a fresh and lovely sight,   35
A beauteous heap, a hill of moss,
Just half a foot in height.
All lovely colours there you see,
All colours that were ever seen;
And mossy network too is there,   40
As if by hand of lady fair
The work had woven been;
And cups, the darlings of the eye,
So deep is their vermilion dye.

V.

"Ah me! what lovely tints are there   45
Of olive green and scarlet bright,
In spikes, in branches, and in stars,
Green, red, and pearly white!
This heap of earth o'ergrown with moss,
Which close beside the Thorn you
    see,   50
So fresh in all its beauteous dyes,
Is like an infant's grave in size,
As like as like can be:
But never, never any where,
An infant's grave was half so fair.   55

VI.

"Now would you see this aged Thorn,
This pond, and beauteous hill of moss,
You must take care and choose your
    time
The mountain when to cross.
For oft there sits between the heap,   60
So like an infant's grave in size,
And that same pond of which I spoke,
A Woman in a scarlet cloak,
And to herself she cries,
'Oh misery! oh misery!   65
Oh woe is me! oh misery!'

VII.

"At all times of the day and night
This wretched Woman thither goes;
And she is known to every star,
And every wind that blows;   70
And there, beside the Thorn, she sits
When the blue daylight's in the skies,
And when the whirlwind's on the hill,
Or frosty air is keen and still,
And to herself she cries,   75
'Oh misery! oh misery!
Oh woe is me! oh misery!'"

VIII.

"Now wherefore, thus, by day and night,
In rain, in tempest, and in snow,
Thus to the dreary mountain-top   80
Does this poor Woman go?
And why sits she beside the Thorn
When the blue daylight's in the sky
Or when the whirlwind's on the hill,
Or frosty air is keen and still,   85
And wherefore does she cry?—
O wherefore? wherefore? tell me why
Does she repeat that doleful cry?"

IX.

"I cannot tell; I wish I could;
For the true reason no one knows: 90
But would you gladly view the spot,
The spot to which she goes;
The hillock like an infant's grave,
The pond—and Thorn, so old and grey;
Pass by her door—'tis seldom shut—   95
And if you see her in her hut—
Then to the spot away!
I never heard of such as dare
Approach the spot when she is there."

X.

"But wherefore to the mountain-top   100
Can this unhappy Woman go,
Whatever star is in the skies,
Whatever wind may blow?"
"Full twenty years are past and gone
Since she (her name is Martha Ray)   105
Gave with a maiden's true good-will
Her company to Stephen Hill;
And she was blithe and gay,
While friends and kindred all approved
Of him whom tenderly she loved.   110

XI.

"And they had fixed the wedding day,
The morning that must wed them both;
But Stephen to another Maid
Had sworn another oath;
And, with this other Maid, to church   115
Unthinking Stephen went—
Poor Martha! on that woeful day
A pang of pitiless dismay
Into her soul was sent;
A fire was kindled in her breast,   120
Which might not burn itself to rest.

XII.

"They say, full six months after this,
While yet the summer leaves were green,
She to the mountain-top would go,
And there was often seen.   125
What could she seek?—or wish to hide?
Her state to any eye was plain;
She was with child, and she was mad;
Yet often was she sober sad
From her exceeding pain.   130
O guilty Father—would that death
Had saved him from that breach of faith!

XIII.

"Sad case for such a brain to hold
Communion with a stirring child!
Sad case, as you may think, for one   135
Who had a brain so wild!
Last Christmas-eve we talked of this,
And grey-haired Wilfred of the glen
Held that the unborn infant wrought
About its mother's heart, and brought   140
Her senses back again:
And, when at last her time drew near,
Her looks were calm, her senses clear.

XIV.

"More know I not, I wish I did,
And it should all be told to you;   145
For what became of this poor child
No mortal ever knew;
Nay—if a child to her was born
No earthly tongue could ever tell;
And if 'twas born alive or dead,   150
Far less could this with proof be said;
But some remember well
That Martha Ray about this time
Would up the mountain often climb.

XV.

"And all that winter, when at night   155
The wind blew from the mountain-peak,
'Twas worth your while, though in the
   dark,
The churchyard path to seek:
For many a time and oft were heard
Cries coming from the mountain head: 160
Some plainly living voices were;
And others, I've heard many swear,
Were voices of the dead:
I cannot think, whate'er they say,
They had to do with Martha Ray.   165

XVI.

"But that she goes to this old Thorn,
The Thorn which I described to you,
And there sits in a scarlet cloak,
I will be sworn is true.
For one day with my telescope,   170
To view the ocean wide and bright,
When to this country first I came,
Ere I had heard of Martha's name,
I climbed the mountain's height:—
A storm came on, and I could see   175
No object higher than my knee.

XVII.

"'Twas mist and rain, and storm and
   rain:
No screen, no fence could I discover;
And then the wind! in sooth, it was
A wind full ten times over.   180
I looked around, I thought I saw
A jutting crag,—and off I ran,
Head-foremost, through the driving rain,
The shelter of the crag to gain;
And, as I am a man,   185
Instead of jutting crag I found
A Woman seated on the ground.

XVIII.

"I did not speak—I saw her face;
Her face!—it was enough for me;
I turned about and heard her cry,   190
'Oh misery! oh misery!'
And there she sits, until the moon
Through half the clear blue sky will go;
And when the little breezes make
The waters of the pond to shake,   195
As all the country know,

She shudders, and you hear her cry,
'Oh misery! oh misery!'"

XIX.

"But what's the Thorn? and what the
       pond?
And what the hill of moss to her?   200
And what the creeping breeze that comes
The little pond to stir?".
"I cannot tell; but some will say
She hanged her baby on the tree;
Some say she drowned it in the pond,   205
Which is a little step beyond:
But all and each agree,
The little Babe was buried there,
Beneath that hill of moss so fair.

XX.

"I've heard, the moss is spotted red   210
With drops of that poor infant's blood;
But kill a new-born infant thus,
I do not think she could!
Some say if to the pond you go,
And fix on it a steady view,   215
The shadow of a babe you trace,
A baby and a baby's face,
And that it looks at you;
Whene'er you look on it, 'tis plain
The baby looks at you again.   220

XXI.

"And some had sworn an oath that she
Should be to public justice brought;
And for the little infant's bones
With spades they would have sought.
But instantly the hill of moss   225
Before their eyes began to stir!
And, for full fifty yards around,
The grass—it shook upon the ground!
Yet all do still aver
The little Babe lies buried there,   230
Beneath that hill of moss so fair.

XXII.

"I cannot tell how this may be,
But plain it is the Thorn is bound
With heavy tufts of moss that strive
To drag it to the ground;   235
And this I know, full many a time,
When she was on the mountain high,

By day, and in the silent night,
When all the stars shone clear and bright,
That I have heard her cry,   240
'Oh misery! oh misery!
Oh woe is me! oh misery!'"

XXIV.
HART-LEAP WELL.

[Composed January or February, 1800.—Pub-
       lished 1800.]

Hart-Leap Well is a small spring of water, about
five miles from Richmond in Yorkshire, and
near the side of the road that leads from Rich-
mond to Askrigg. Its name is derived from a
remarkable Chase, the memory of which is
preserved by the monuments spoken of in
the second Part of the following Poem, which
monuments do now exist as I have there de-
scribed them.

THE Knight had ridden down from Wen-
       sley Moor
With the slow motion of a summer's
       cloud,
And now, as he approached a vassal's
       door,
"Bring forth another horse!" he cried
       aloud.

"Another horse!"—That shout the vassal
       heard   5
And saddled his best Steed, a comely
       grey;
Sir Walter mounted him; he was the third
Which he had mounted on that glorious
       day.

Joy sparkled in the prancing courser's
       eyes;
The horse and horseman are a happy
       pair;   10
But, though Sir Walter like a falcon flies,
There is a doleful silence in the air.

A rout this morning left Sir Walter's Hall,
That as they galloped made the echoes
       roar;
But horse and man are vanished, one and
       all;   15
Such race, I think, was never seen before.

Sir Walter, restless as a veering wind,
Calls to the few tired dogs that yet re-
       main:

Blanch, Swift, and Music, noblest of their
kind,
Follow, and up the weary mountain
strain. 20

The Knight hallooed, he cheered and chid
them on
With suppliant gestures and upbraidings
stern;
But breath and eyesight fail; and, one
by one,
The dogs are stretched among the moun-
tain fern.

Where is the throng, the tumult of the
race? 25
The bugles that so joyfully were blown?
—This chase it looks not like an earthly
chase;
Sir Walter and the Hart are left alone.

The poor Hart toils along the mountain-
side;
I will not stop to tell how far he fled, 30
Nor will I mention by what death he died;
But now the Knight beholds him lying
dead.

Dismounting, then, he leaned against a
thorn;
He had no follower, dog, nor man, nor
boy:
He neither cracked his whip, nor blew his
horn, 35
But gazed upon the spoil with silent joy.

Close to the thorn on which Sir Walter
leaned
Stood his dumb partner in this glorious
feat;
Weak as a lamb the hour that it is yeaned;
And white with foam as if with cleaving
sleet. 40

Upon his side the Hart was lying
stretched:
His nostril touched a spring beneath a
hill,
And with the last deep groan his breath
had fetched
The waters of the spring were trembling
still.

And now, too happy for repose or rest, 45
(Never had living man such joyful lot!)
Sir Walter walked all round, north, south,
and west,
And gazed and gazed upon that darling
spot.

And climbing up the hill—(it was at least
Four roods of sheer ascent) Sir Walter
found 50
Three several hoof-marks which the hunt-
ed Beast
Had left imprinted on the grassy ground.

Sir Walter wiped his face, and cried,
"Till now
Such sight was never seen by human eyes:
Three leaps have borne him from this
lofty brow 55
Down to the very fountain where he lies.

"I'll build a pleasure-house upon this
spot,
And a small arbour, made for rural joy;
'Twill be the traveller's shed, the pilgrim's
cot,
A place of love for damsels that are coy. 60

"A cunning artist will I have to frame
A basin for that fountain in the dell!
And they who do make mention of the
same,
From this day forth, shall call it HART-
LEAP WELL.

"And, gallant Stag! to make thy praises
known, 65
Another monument shall here be raised;
Three several pillars, each a rough-hewn
stone,
And planted where thy hoofs the turf
have grazed.

"And in the summer-time, when days are
long,
I will come hither with my Paramour; 70
And with the dancers and the minstrel's
song
We will make merry in that pleasant
bower.

"Till the foundations of the mountains
fail
My mansion with its arbour shall endure;—

The joy of them who till the fields of
　Swale,　　　　　　　　　　　　　　75
And them who dwell among the woods
　of Ure !"

Then home he went, and left the Hart
　stone-dead,
With breathless nostrils stretched above
　the spring.
—Soon did the Knight perform what he
　had said ;
And far and wide the fame thereof did
　ring.　　　　　　　　　　　　　　80

Ere thrice the Moon into her port had
　steered,
A cup of stone received the living well ;
Three pillars of rude stone Sir Walter
　reared,
And built a house of pleasure in the dell.

And, near the fountain, flowers of stature
　tall　　　　　　　　　　　　　　　85
With trailing plants and trees were inter-
　twined,—
Which soon composed a little sylvan hall,
A leafy shelter from the sun and wind.

And thither, when the summer days were
　long,　　　　　　　　　　　　　　90
Sir Walter led his wondering Paramour ;
And with the dancers and the minstrel's
　song
Made merriment within that pleasant
　bower.

The Knight, Sir Walter, died in course of
　time,
And his bones lie in his paternal vale.—
But there is matter for a second rhyme, 95
And I to this would add another tale.

PART SECOND.

The moving accident is not my trade ;
To freeze the blood I have no ready arts :
'Tis my delight, alone in summer shade, 99
To pipe a simple song for thinking hearts.

As I from Hawes to Richmond did repair,
It chanced that I saw standing in a dell
Three aspens at three corners of a square ;
And one, not four yards distant, near a
　well.

What this imported I could ill divine: 105
And, pulling now the rein my horse to
　stop,
I saw three pillars standing in a line,—
The last stone-pillar on a dark hill-top.

The trees were grey, with neither arms
　nor head ;
Half wasted the square mound of tawny
　green ;　　　　　　　　　　　　110
So that you just might say, as then I said,
"Here in old time the hand of man hath
　been."

I looked upon the hill both far and near,
More doleful place did never eye survey ;
It seemed as if the spring-time came not
　here,　　　　　　　　　　　　　115
And Nature here were willing to decay.

I stood in various thoughts and fancies lost,
When one, who was in shepherd's garb
　attired,
Came up the hollow :—him did I accost,
And what this place might be I then en-
　quired.　　　　　　　　　　　　120

The Shepherd stopped, and that same
　story told
Which in my former rhyme I have re-
　hearsed,
"A jolly place," said he, "in times of old !
But something ails it now: the spot is
　curst.

"You see these lifeless stumps of aspen
　wood—　　　　　　　　　　　　125
Some say that they are beeches, others
　elms—
These were the bower; and here a man-
　sion stood,
The finest palace of a hundred realms !

"The arbour does its own condition tell ;
You see the stones, the fountain, and the
　stream ;　　　　　　　　　　　　130
But as to the great Lodge ! you might as
　well
Hunt half a day for a forgotten dream.

"There's neither dog nor heifer, horse nor
　sheep,
Will wet his lips within that cup of stone ;
And oftentimes, when all are fast asleep,
This water doth send forth a dolorous
　groan.　　　　　　　　　　　　136

"Some say that here a murder has been done,
And blood cries out for blood: but, for my part,
I've guessed, when I've been sitting in the sun,
That it was all for that unhappy Hart.

"What thoughts must through the creature's brain have past !   141
Even from the topmost stone, upon the steep,
Are but three bounds—and look, Sir, at this last—
O Master ! it has been a cruel leap.

"For thirteen hours he ran a desperate race ;   145
And in my simple mind we cannot tell
What cause the Hart might have to love this place,
And come and make his death-bed near the well.

"Here on the grass perhaps asleep he sank,
Lulled by the fountain in the summer-tide ;   150
This water was perhaps the first he drank
When he had wandered from his mother's side.

"In April here beneath the flowering thorn
He heard the birds their morning carols sing ;
And he perhaps, for aught we know, was born   155
Not half a furlong from that self-same spring.

"Now, here is neither grass nor pleasant shade ;
The sun on drearier hollow never shone ;
So will it be, as I have often said,
Till trees, and stones, and fountain, all are gone."   160

"Grey-headed Shepherd, thou hast spoken well ;
Small difference lies between thy creed and mine :
This Beast not unobserved by Nature fell ;
His death was mourned by sympathy divine.

"The Being that is in the clouds and air,
That is in the green leaves among the groves,   166
Maintains a deep and reverential care
For the unoffending creatures whom he loves.

"The pleasure-house is dust :—behind, before,
This is no common waste, no common gloom ;   170
But Nature, in due course of time, once more
Shall here put on her beauty and her bloom.

"She leaves these objects to a slow decay,
That what we are, and have been, may be known ;
But at the coming of the milder day   175
These monuments shall all be overgrown.

"One lesson, Shepherd, let us two divide,
Taught both by what she shows, and what conceals ;
Never to blend our pleasure or our pride
With sorrow of the meanest thing that feels."   180

XXV.

SONG AT THE FEAST OF BROUGHAM CASTLE,

UPON THE RESTORATION OF LORD CLIFFORD, THE SHEPHERD, TO THE ESTATES AND HONOURS OF HIS ANCESTORS.

Composed 1807.—Published 1807.

HIGH in the breathless Hall the Minstrel sate,
And Emont's murmur mingled with the Song.—
The words of ancient time I thus translate,
A festal strain that hath been silent long :—

"From town to town, from tower to tower,
The red rose is a gladsome flower.   6
Her thirty years of winter past,
The red rose is revived at last ;
She lifts her head for endless spring,
For everlasting blossoming :   10

Both roses flourish, red and white:
In love and sisterly delight
The two that were at strife are blended,
And all old troubles now are ended.—
Joy! joy to both! but most to her   15
Who is the flower of Lancaster!
Behold her how She smiles to-day
On this great throng, this bright array!
Fair greeting doth she send to all
From every corner of the hall;   20
But chiefly from above the board
Where sits in state our rightful Lord,
A Clifford to his own restored!

"They came with banner, spear, and
    shield;
And it was proved in Bosworth-field.   25
Not long the Avenger was withstood—
Earth helped him with the cry of blood:
St. George was for us, and the might
Of blessed Angels crowned the right.
Loud voice the Land has uttered forth,   30
We loudest in the faithful north:
Our fields rejoice, our mountains ring,
Our streams proclaim a welcoming;
Our strong-abodes and castles see
The glory of their loyalty.   35

"How glad is Skipton at this hour—
Though lonely, a deserted Tower;
Knight, squire, and yeoman, page and
    groom:
We have them at the feast of Brough'm.
How glad Pendragon—though the sleep
Of years be on her!—She shall reap   41
A taste of this great pleasure, viewing
As in a dream her own renewing.
Rejoiced is Brough, right glad, I deem,
Beside her little humble stream;   45
And she that keepeth watch and ward
Her statelier Eden's course to guard;
They both are happy at this hour,
Though each is but a lonely Tower:—
But here is perfect joy and pride   50
For one fair House by Emont's side,
This day, distinguished without peer,
To see her Master and to cheer—
Him, and his Lady-mother dear!

"Oh! it was a time forlorn   55
When the fatherless was born—
Give her wings that she may fly,

Or she sees her infant die!
Swords that are with slaughter wild
Hunt the Mother and the Child.   60
Who will take them from the light?
—Yonder is a man in sight—
Yonder is a house—but where?
No, they must not enter there.
To the caves, and to the brooks,   65
To the clouds of heaven she looks;
She is speechless, but her eyes
Pray in ghostly agonies.
Blissful Mary, Mother mild,
Maid and Mother undefiled,   70
Save a Mother and her Child!

"Now Who is he that bounds with joy
On Carrock's side, a Shepherd-boy?
No thoughts hath he but thoughts that
    pass
Light as the wind along the grass.   75
Can this be He who hither came
In secret, like a smothered flame?
O'er whom such thankful tears were shed
For shelter, and a poor man's bread!   79
God loves the Child; and God hath willed
That those dear words should be fulfilled,
The Lady's words, when forced away
The last she to her Babe did say:
'My own, my own, thy Fellow-guest
I may not be; but rest thee, rest,   85
For lowly shepherd's life is best!'

"Alas! when evil men are strong
No life is good, no pleasure long.
The Boy must part from Mosedale's groves,
And leave Blencathara's rugged coves,   90
And quit the flowers that summer brings
To Glenderamakin's lofty springs;
Must vanish, and his careless cheer
Be turned to heaviness and fear.
—Give Sir Lancelot Threlkeld praise!   95
Hear it, good man, old in days!
Thou tree of covert and of rest
For this young Bird that is distrest;
Among thy branches safe he lay,
And he was free to sport and play,   100
When falcons were abroad for prey.

"A recreant harp, that sings of fear
And heaviness in Clifford's ear!
I said, when evil men are strong,
No life is good, no pleasure long,   105

A weak and cowardly untruth!
Our Clifford was a happy Youth,
And thankful through a weary time,
That brought him up to manhood's prime.
—Again he wanders forth at will,   110
And tends a flock from hill to hill:
His garb is humble; ne'er was seen
Such garb with such a noble mien;
Among the shepherd-grooms no mate
Hath he, a Child of strength and state!
Yet lacks not friends for simple glee,   116
Nor yet for higher sympathy.
To his side the fallow-deer
Came, and rested without fear;
The eagle, lord of land and sea,   120
Stooped down to pay him fealty;
And both the undying fish that swim
Through Bowscale-tarn did wait on him;
The pair were servants of his eye
In their immortality;   125
And glancing, gleaming, dark or bright,
Moved to and fro, for his delight.
He knew the rocks which Angels haunt
Upon the mountains visitant;
He hath kenned them taking wing: 130
And into caves where Faeries sing
He hath entered; and been told
By Voices how men lived of old.
Among the heavens his eye can see
The face of thing that is to be;   135
And, if that men report him right,
His tongue could whisper words of might.
—Now another day is come,
Fitter hope, and nobler doom;
He hath thrown aside his crook,   140
And hath buried deep his book;
Armour rusting in his halls
On the blood of Clifford calls;—
'Quell the Scot,' exclaims the Lance—
Bear me to the heart of France,   145
Is the longing of the Shield—
Tell thy name, thou trembling Field;
Field of death, where'er thou be,
Groan thou with our victory!
Happy day, and mighty hour,   150
When our Shepherd in his power,
Mailed and horsed, with lance and sword,
To his ancestors restored
Like a re-appearing Star,
Like a glory from afar,   155
First shall head the flock of war!"

Alas! the impassioned minstrel did not
    know
How, by Heaven's grace, this Clifford's
    heart was framed:
How he, long forced in humble walks to go,
Was softened into feeling, soothed, and
    tamed.   160

Love had he found in huts where poor men
    lie;
His daily teachers had been woods and
    rills,
The silence that is in the starry sky,
The sleep that is among the lonely hills.

In him the savage virtue of the Race,   165
Revenge, and all ferocious thoughts were
    dead:
Nor did he change; but kept in lofty place
The wisdom which adversity had bred.

Glad were the vales, and every cottage-
    hearth;
The Shepherd-lord was honoured more
    and more;   170
And, ages after he was laid in earth,
"The good Lord Clifford" was the name
    he bore.

XXVI.

LINES

COMPOSED A FEW MILES ABOVE TINTERN
ABBEY, ON REVISITING THE BANKS OF
THE WYE DURING A TOUR. JULY 13, 1798.

[Composed July 13, 1798.—Published 1798.]

FIVE years have past; five summers, with
    the length
Of five long winters! and again I hear
These waters, rolling from their mountain-
    springs
With a soft inland murmur.[1]—Once again
Do I behold these steep and lofty cliffs, 5
That on a wild secluded scene impress
Thoughts of more deep seclusion; and
    connect
The landscape with the quiet of the sky.
The day is come when I again repose
Here, under this dark sycamore, and view

---

[1] The river is not affected by the tides a few
miles above Tintern.

These plots of cottage-ground, these orch-
  ard-tufts,   11
Which at this season, with their unripe
  fruits,
Are clad in one green hue, and lose them-
  selves
'Mid groves and copses. Once again I see
These hedge-rows, hardly hedge-rows, lit-
  tle lines   15
Of sportive wood run wild: these pastoral
  farms,
Green to the very door; and wreaths of
  smoke
Sent up, in silence, from among the trees!
With some uncertain notice, as might seem
Of vagrant dwellers in the houseless
  woods,   20
Or of some Hermit's cave, where by his fire
The Hermit sits alone.

                      These beauteous forms,
Through a long absence, have not been to
  me
As is a landscape to a blind man's eye:
But oft, in lonely rooms, and 'mid the din
Of towns and cities, I have owed to them,
In hours of weariness, sensations sweet,
Felt in the blood, and felt along the heart;
And passing even into my purer mind,   29
With tranquil restoration:—feelings too
Of unremembered pleasure: such, perhaps,
As have no slight or trivial influence
On that best portion of a good man's life,
His little, nameless, unremembered, acts
Of kindness and of love. Nor less, I trust,
To them I may have owed another gift,   36
Of aspect more sublime; that blessed
  mood,
In which the burthen of the mystery,
In which the heavy and the weary weight
Of all this unintelligible world,   40
Is lightened:—that serene and blessed
  mood,
In which the affections gently lead us on,—
Until, the breath of this corporeal frame
And even the motion of our human blood
Almost suspended, we are laid asleep   45
In body, and become a living soul:
While with an eye made quiet by the
  power
Of harmony, and the deep power of joy,

We see into the life of things.
                                If this
Be but a vain belief, yet, oh! how oft— 50
In darkness and amid the many shapes
Of joyless daylight; when the fretful stir
Unprofitable, and the fever of the world,
Have hung upon the beatings of my heart—
How oft, in spirit, have I turned to thee,
O sylvan Wye! thou wanderer thro' the
  woods,   56
How often has my spirit turned to thee!

And now, with gleams of half-extin-
  guished thought,
With many recognitions dim and faint,
And somewhat of a sad perplexity,   60
The picture of the mind revives again:
While here I stand, not only with the sense
Of present pleasure, but with pleasing
  thoughts
That in this moment there is life and food
For future years. And so I dare to hope,
Though changed, no doubt, from what I
  was when first   66
I came among these hills; when like a roe
I bounded o'er the mountains, by the sides
Of the deep rivers, and the lonely streams,
Wherever nature led: more like a man
Flying from something that he dreads
  than one
Who sought the thing he loved. For na-
  ture then
(The coarser pleasures of my boyish days,
And their glad animal movements all gone
  by)
To me was all in all.—I cannot paint   75
What then I was. The sounding cataract
Haunted me like a passion: the tall rock,
The mountain, and the deep and gloomy
  wood,
Their colours and their forms, were then
  to me
An appetite; a feeling and a love,   80
That had no need of a remoter charm,
By thought supplied, nor any interest
Unborrowed from the eye.—That time is
  past,
And all its aching joys are now no more,
And all its dizzy raptures. Not for this 85
Faint I, nor mourn nor murmur; other
  gifts

Have followed; for such loss, I would
  believe,
Abundant recompense. For I have learned
To look on nature, not as in the hour
Of thoughtless youth; but hearing often-
  times   90
The still, sad music of humanity,
Nor harsh nor grating, though of ample
  power
To chasten and subdue. And I have felt
A presence that disturbs me with the joy
Of elevated thoughts; a sense sublime   95
Of something far more deeply interfused,
Whose dwelling is the light of setting suns,
And the round ocean and the living air,
And the blue sky, and in the mind of man:
A motion and a spirit, that impels   100
All thinking things, all objects of all
  thought,
And rolls through all things. Therefore
  am I still
A lover of the meadows and the woods,
And mountains; and of all that we behold
From this green earth; of all the mighty
  world   105
Of eye, and ear,—both what they half
  create,[1]
And what perceive; well pleased to re-
  cognise
In nature and the language of the sense
The anchor of my purest thoughts, the
  nurse,
The guide, the guardian of my heart, and
  soul   110
Of all my moral being.
                        Nor perchance,
If I were not thus taught, should I the
  more
Suffer my genial spirits to decay:
For thou art with me here upon the banks
Of this fair river; thou my dearest Friend,
My dear, dear Friend; and in thy voice I
  catch   116
The language of my former heart, and read
My former pleasures in the shooting lights
Of thy wild eyes. Oh! yet a little while
May I behold in thee what I was once,

My dear, dear Sister! and this prayer I
  make,   121
Knowing that Nature never did betray
The heart that loved her; 'tis her privilege,
Through all the years of this our life, to lead
From joy to joy: for she can so inform   125
The mind that is within us, so impress
With quietness and beauty, and so feed
With lofty thoughts, that neither evil
  tongues,
Rash judgments, nor the sneers of selfish
  men,
Nor greetings where no kindness is, nor all
The dreary intercourse of daily life,   131
Shall e'er prevail against us, or disturb
Our cheerful faith, that all which we behold
Is full of blessings. Therefore let the
  moon
Shine on thee in thy solitary walk;   135
And let the misty mountain-winds be free
To blow against thee: and, in after years,
When these wild ecstasies shall be matured
Into a sober pleasure; when thy mind
Shall be a mansion for all lovely forms, 140
Thy memory be as a dwelling-place
For all sweet sounds and harmonies; oh!
  then,
If solitude, or fear, or pain, or grief,
Should be thy portion, with what healing
  thoughts
Of tender joy wilt thou remember me,   145
And these my exhortations! Nor, per-
  chance—
If I should be where I no more can hear
Thy voice, nor catch from thy wild eyes
  these gleams
Of past existence—wilt thou then forget
That on the banks of this delightful stream
We stood together; and that I, so long
A worshipper of Nature, hither came   152
Unwearied in that service: rather say
With warmer love—oh! with far deeper
  zeal
Of holier love. Nor wilt thou then forget
That after many wanderings, many years
Of absence, these steep woods and lofty
  cliffs,   157
And this green pastoral landscape, were
  to me
More dear, both for themselves and for
  thy sake!

[1] This line has a close resemblance to an
admirable line of Young's, the exact expression
of which I do not recollect.

XXVII.

[Composed 1803.—Published 1807.]

It is no Spirit who from heaven hath
flown,
And is descending on his embassy;
Nor Traveller gone from earth the heavens
to espy!
'Tis Hesperus—there he stands with glit-
tering crown,
First admonition that the sun is down! 5
For yet it is broad day-light: clouds
pass by;
A few are near him still—and now the sky,
He hath it to himself—'tis all his own.
O most ambitious Star! an inquest
wrought
Within me when I recognised thy light;
A moment I was startled at the sight: 11
And, while I gazed, there came to me a
thought
That I might step beyond my natural race
As thou seem'st now to do; might one day
trace
Some ground not mine; and, strong her
strength above, 15
My Soul, an Apparition in the place,
Tread there with steps that no one shall
reprove!

XXVIII.

FRENCH REVOLUTION,

AS IT APPEARED TO ENTHUSIASTS AT ITS
COMMENCEMENT.[1] REPRINTED FROM
"THE FRIEND."

[Composed 1804.—Published October 26, 1809 (*The
Friend*); ed. 1815.]

Oh! pleasant exercise of hope and joy!
For mighty were the auxiliars which then
stood
Upon our side, we who were strong in love!
Bliss was it in that dawn to be alive,
But to be young was very heaven!—Oh!
times, 5
In which the meagre, stale, forbidding ways

[1] This and the Extract, page 89, and the first
Piece of this Class, are from the unpublished
Poem of which some account is given in the
Preface to THE EXCURSION.

Of custom, law, and statute, took at once
The attraction of a country in romance;
When Reason seemed the most to assert
her rights,
When most intent on making of herself 10
A prime Enchantress—to assist the work
Which then was going forward in her
name!
Not favoured spots alone, but the whole
earth,
The beauty wore of promise, that which
sets
(As at some moment might not be unfelt
Among the bowers of paradise itself) 16
The budding rose above the rose full
blown.
What temper at the prospect did not wake
To happiness unthought of? The inert
Were roused, and lively natures rapt away!
They who had fed their childhood upon
dreams, 21
The playfellows of fancy, who had made
All powers of swiftness, subtilty, and
strength
Their ministers,—who in lordly wise had
stirred
Among the grandest objects of the sense,
And dealt with whatsoever they found
there 26
As if they had within some lurking right
To wield it;—they, too, who, of gentle
mood,
Had watched all gentle motions, and to
these
Had fitted their own thoughts, schemers
more mild, 30
And in the region of their peaceful
selves;—
Now was it that both found, the meek and
lofty
Did both find, helpers to their heart's
desire,
And stuff at hand, plastic as they could
wish;
Were called upon to exercise their skill, 35
Not in Utopia, subterranean fields,
Or some secreted island, Heaven knows
where!
But in the very world, which is the world
Of all of us,—the place where in the end
We find our happiness, or not at all! 40

XXIX.

[Composed 1806.—Published 1807.]

YES, it was the mountain Echo,
Solitary, clear, profound,
Answering to the shouting Cuckoo,
Giving to her sound for sound!

Unsolicited reply 5
To a babbling wanderer sent;
Like her ordinary cry,
Like—but oh, how different!

Hears not also mortal Life?
Hear not we, unthinking Creatures! 10
Slaves of folly, love, or strife—
Voices of two different natures?

Have not *we* too?—yes, we have
Answers, and we know not whence;
Echoes from beyond the grave, 15
Recognised intelligence!

Such rebounds our inward ear
Catches sometimes from afar—
Listen, ponder, hold them dear;
For of God,—of God they are. 20

XXX.

TO A SKYLARK[1].

[Composed 1825.—Published 1827.]

ETHEREAL minstrel! pilgrim of the sky!
Dost thou despise the earth where cares
    abound?
Or, while the wings aspire, are heart and
    eye
Both with thy nest upon the dewy
    ground?
Thy nest which thou canst drop into at
    will, 5
Those quivering wings composed, that
    music still!

Leave to the nightingale her shady wood;
A privacy of glorious light is thine;
Whence thou dost pour upon the world a
    flood
Of harmony, with instinct more divine; 10

[1] For Stanza ii. of this poem, omitted in 1845
and 1849-50, see note 2, page 153.—ED.

Type of the wise who soar, but never
    roam;
True to the kindred points of Heaven and
    Home!

XXXI.

LAODAMIA.

[Composed 1814.—Published 1815.]

"WITH sacrifice before the rising morn
Vows have I made by fruitless hope in-
    spired;
And from the infernal Gods, 'mid shades
    forlorn
Of night, my slaughtered Lord have I
    required:
Celestial pity I again implore;— 5
Restore him to my sight—great Jove,
    restore!"

So speaking, and by fervent love endowed
With faith, the Suppliant heavenward
    lifts her hands;
While, like the sun emerging from a
    cloud,
Her countenance brightens—and her eye
    expands; 10
Her bosom heaves and spreads, her stature
    grows;
And she expects the issue in repose.

O terror! what hath she perceived?—O
    joy!
What doth she look on?—whom doth she
    behold?
Her Hero slain upon the beach of Troy? 15
His vital presence? his corporeal mould?
It is—if sense deceive her not—'tis He!
And a God leads him, wingèd Mercury!

Mild Hermes spake—and touched her
    with his wand
That calms all fear; "Such grace hath
    crowned thy prayer, 20
Laodamía! that at Jove's command
Thy Husband walks the paths of upper
    air:
He comes to tarry with thee three hours'
    space;
Accept the gift, behold him face to face!"

Forth sprang the impassioned Queen her
    Lord to clasp;   25
Again that consummation she essayed;
But unsubstantial Form eludes her grasp
As often as that eager grasp was made.
The Phantom parts—but parts to re-unite,
And re-assume his place before her sight.

"Protesiláus, lo! thy guide is gone!   31
Confirm, I pray, the vision with thy voice:
This is our palace,—yonder is thy throne;
Speak, and the floor thou tread'st on will
    rejoice.
Not to appal me have the gods bestowed
This precious boon; and blest a sad
    abode."   36

"Great Jove, Laodamía! doth not leave
His gifts imperfect:—Spectre though I be,
I am not sent to scare thee or deceive;
But in reward of thy fidelity.   40
And something also did my worth obtain;
For fearless virtue bringeth boundless gain.

"Thou knowest, the Delphic oracle fore-
    told
That the first Greek who touched the
    Trojan strand
Should die; but me the threat could not
    withhold.   45
A generous cause a victim did demand;
And forth I leapt upon the sandy plain;
A self-devoted chief—by Hector slain."

"Supreme of Heroes—bravest, noblest,
    best!
Thy matchless courage I bewail no more,
Which then, when tens of thousands were
    deprest   51
By doubt, propelled thee to the fatal shore;
Thou found'st—and I forgive thee—here
    thou art—
A nobler counsellor than my poor heart.

"But thou, though capable of sternest
    deed,   55
Wert kind as resolute, and good as brave;
And he, whose power restores thee, hath
    decreed
Thou shouldst elude the malice of the
    grave:
Redundant are thy locks, thy lips as fair
As when their breath enriched Thessalian
    air.   60

"No Spectre greets me,—no vain Shadow
    this;
Come, blooming Hero, place thee by my
    side!
Give, on this well-known couch, one nup-
    tial kiss
To me, this day, a second time thy bride!"
Jove frowned in heaven: the conscious
    Parcæ threw   65
Upon those roseate lips a Stygian hue.

"This visage tells thee that my doom is
    past:
Nor should the change be mourned, even
    if the joys
Of sense were able to return as fast
And surely as they vanish. Earth de-
    stroys   70
Those raptures duly—Erebus disdains:
Calm pleasures there abide—majestic
    pains.

"Be taught, O faithful Consort, to control
Rebellious passion: for the Gods approve
The depth, and not the tumult, of the
    soul;   75
A fervent, not ungovernable, love.
Thy transports moderate; and meekly
    mourn
When I depart, for brief is my sojourn—"

"Ah wherefore?—Did not Hercules by
    force
Wrest from the guardian Monster of the
    tomb   80
Alcestis, a reanimated corse,
Given back to dwell on earth in vernal
    bloom?
Medea's spells dispersed the weight of
    years,
And Æson stood a youth 'mid youthful
    peers.   84

"The Gods to us are merciful—and they
Yet further may relent: for mightier far
Than strength of nerve and sinew, or the
    sway
Of magic potent over sun and star,
Is love, though oft to agony distrest,
And though his favourite seat be feeble
    woman's breast.   90

"But if thou goest, I follow—" "Peace!"
  he said,—
She looked upon him and was calmed and
  cheered;
The ghastly colour from his lips had fled;
In his deportment, shape, and mien,
  appeared
Elysian beauty, melancholy grace,   95
Brought from a pensive though a happy
  place.

He spake of love, such love as Spirits feel
In worlds whose course is equable and
  pure;
No fears to beat away—no strife to heal—
The past unsighed for, and the future
  sure;   100
Spake of heroic arts in graver mood
Revived, with finer harmony pursued;

Of all that is most beauteous—imaged
  there
In happier beauty; more pellucid streams,
An ampler ether, a diviner air,   105
And fields invested with purpureal gleams;
Climes which the sun, who sheds the
  brightest day
Earth knows, is all unworthy to survey.

Yet there the Soul shall enter which hath
  earned
That privilege by virtue.—"Ill," said he,
" The end of man's existence I discerned,
Who from ignoble games and revelry
Could draw, when we had parted, vain
  delight,
While tears were thy best pastime, day
  and night;

"And while my youthful peers before my
  eyes   115
(Each hero following his peculiar bent)
Prepared themselves for glorious enterprise
By martial sports,—or, seated in the tent,
Chieftains and kings in council were de-
  tained;
What time the fleet at Aulis lay enchained.

"The wished-for wind was given:—I then
  revolved   121
The oracle, upon the silent sea;
And, if no worthier led the way, resolved
That, of a thousand vessels, mine should be

The foremost prow in pressing to the
  strand,—   125
Mine the first blood that tinged the Trojan
  sand.

"Yet bitter, oft-times bitter, was the pang
When of thy loss I thought, belovèd Wife!
On thee too fondly did my memory hang,
And on the joys we shared in mortal life,—
The paths which we had trod—these foun-
  tains, flowers;   131
My new-planned cities, and unfinished
  towers.

"But should suspense permit the Foe to
  cry,
'Behold they tremble!—haughty their
  array,
Yet of their number no one dares to die?'
In soul I swept the indignity away: 136
Old frailties then recurred:—but lofty
  thought,
In act embodied, my deliverance wrought.

"And Thou, though strong in love, art all
  too weak
In reason, in self-government too slow;
I counsel thee by fortitude to seek   141
Our blest re-union in the shades below.
The invisible world with thee hath sym-
  pathised;
Be thy affections raised and solemnised.

"Learn, by a mortal yearning, to ascend—
Seeking a higher object. Love was given,
Encouraged, sanctioned, chiefly for that
  end;   147
For this the passion to excess was driven—
That self might be annulled: her bondage
  prove
The fetters of a dream opposed to love."—

Aloud she shrieked! for Hermes re-
  appears!   151
Round the dear Shade she would have
  clung—'tis vain:
The hours are past—too brief had they
  been years;
And him no mortal effort can detain:
Swift, toward the realms that know not
  earthly day,   155
He through the portal takes his silent way,
And on the palace-floor a lifeless corse She
  lay.

Thus, all in vain exhorted and reproved,
She perished; and, as for a wilful crime,
By the just Gods whom no weak pity
  moved,   160
Was doomed to wear out her appointed
  time,
Apart from happy Ghosts, that gather
  flowers
Of blissful quiet 'mid unfading bowers.[1]

—Yet tears to human suffering are due;
And mortal hopes defeated and o'erthrown
Are mourned by man, and not by man
  alone,   166
As fondly he believes.—Upon the side
Of Hellespont (such faith was entertained)
A knot of spiry trees for ages grew
From out the tomb of him for whom she
  died;   170
And ever, when such stature they had
  gained
That Ilium's walls were subject to their
  view,
The trees' tall summits withered at the
  sight;
A constant interchange of growth and
  blight![2]

XXXII.

DION.

[Composed 1816.—Published 1820.]

(SEE PLUTARCH.)

[I.]

[FAIR is the Swan, whose majesty, pre-
  vailing
O'er breezeless water, on Locarno's lake,
Bears him on while proudly sailing
He leaves behind a moon-illumined wake:
Behold! the mantling spirit of reserve 5
Fashions his neck into a goodly curve;

[1] For an account of the important changes—
material as well as formal—introduced from time
to time into this stanza, see Editor's note,
p. 901.—ED.

[2] For the account of these long-lived trees, see
Pliny's "Natural History," lib. xvi. cap. 44; and
for the features in the character of Protesilaus,
see the "Iphigenia in Aulis" of Euripides. Virgil
places the Shade of Laodamia in a mournful
region, among unhappy Lovers,

    —— His Laodamia
    It comes.——

An arch thrown back between luxuriant
  wings
Of whitest garniture, like fir-tree boughs
To which, on some unruffled morning,
  clings
A flaky weight of winter's purest snows!
—Behold!—as with a gushing impulse
  heaves   11
That downy prow, and softly cleaves
The mirror of the crystal flood,
Vanish inverted hill, and shadowy wood,
And pendent rocks, where'er, in gliding
  state,   15
Winds the mute Creature without visible
  Mate
Or Rival, save the Queen of night
Showering down a silver light,
From heaven, upon her chosen Favourite!]

[II.]

[So pure, so bright, so fitted to embrace
Where'er he turned, a natural grace 20
Of haughtiness without pretence,
    &c. &c. &c. (Edd. 1820, 1827, 1832).]

I.

SERENE, and fitted to embrace,
Where'er he turned, a swan-like grace
Of haughtiness without pretence,
And to unfold a still magnificence,
Was princely Dion, in the power 5
And beauty of his happier hour.
And what pure homage *then* did wait
On Dion's virtues, while the lunar beam
Of Plato's genius, from its lofty sphere,
Fell round him in the grove of Academe,
Softening their inbred dignity austere—
  That he, not too elate
  With self-sufficing solitude,
But with majestic lowliness endued,
Might in the universal bosom reign, 15
And from affectionate observance gain
Help, under every change of adverse fate.

II.

Five thousand warriors—O the rapturous
  day!
Each crowned with flowers, and armed
  with spear and shield,
Or ruder weapon which their course might
  yield,   20
To Syracuse advance in bright array.

Who leads them on?—The anxious people
see
Long-exiled Dion marching at their head,
He also crowned with flowers of Sicily,
And in a white, far-beaming, corselet clad!
Pure transport undisturbed by doubt or
fear   26
The gazers feel; and, rushing to the plain,
Salute those strangers as a holy train
Or blest procession (to the Immortals
dear)
That brought their precious liberty again.
Lo! when the gates are entered, on each
hand,   31
Down the long street, rich goblets filled
with wine
    In seemly order stand,
On tables set, as if for rites divine;—
And, as the great Deliverer marches by,
He looks on festal ground with fruits
bestrown;   36
And flowers are on his person thrown
    In boundless prodigality;
Nor doth the general voice abstain from
prayer,
Invoking Dion's tutelary care,   40
As if a very Deity he were!

III.

Mourn, hills and groves of Attica! and
mourn
Ilissus, bending o'er thy classic urn!
Mourn, and lament for him whose spirit
dreads
Your once sweet memory, studious walks
and shades!   45
For him who to divinity aspired,
Not on the breath of popular applause,
But through dependence on the sacred
laws
Framed in the schools where Wisdom
dwelt retired,
Intent to trace the ideal path of right   50
(More fair than heaven's broad causeway
paved with stars)
Which Dion learned to measure with
sublime delight;—
But He hath overleaped the eternal bars;
And, following guides whose craft holds
no consent

With aught that breathes the ethereal
element,   55
Hath stained the robes of civil power
with blood,
Unjustly shed, though for the public
good.
Whence doubts that came too late, and
wishes vain,
Hollow excuses, and triumphant pain;
And oft his cogitations sink as low   60
As, through the abysses of a joyless heart,
The heaviest plummet of despair can go—
But whence that sudden check? that
fearful start!
    He hears an uncouth sound—
    Anon his lifted eyes   65
Saw, at a long-drawn gallery's dusky
bound,
A Shape of more than mortal size
And hideous aspect, stalking round and
round!
    A woman's garb the Phantom wore,
    And fiercely swept the marble floor,—
    Like Auster whirling to and fro,   71
    His force on Caspian foam to try;
Or Boreas when he scours the snow
That skins the plains of Thessaly,
Or when aloft on Mænalus he stops   75
His flight, 'mid eddying pine-tree tops!

IV.

So, but from toil less sign of profit
reaping,
The sullen Spectre to her purpose bowed,
    Sweeping—vehemently sweeping—
No pause admitted, no design avowed! 80
"Avaunt, inexplicable Guest!—avaunt,"
Exclaimed the Chieftain—"let me rather
see
The coronal that coiling vipers make;
The torch that flames with many a lurid
flake,
And the long train of doleful pageantry 85
Which they behold, whom vengeful Furies
haunt;
Who, while they struggle from the scourge
to flee,
Move where the blasted soil is not
unworn,
And, in their anguish, bear what other
minds have borne!"

v.

But Shapes, that come not at an earthly
  call,   90
Will not depart when mortal voices bid ;
Lords of the visionary eye whose lid,
Once raised, remains aghast, and will not
  fall !
Ye Gods, thought He, that servile Im-
  plement
  Obeys a mystical intent !   95
Your Minister would brush away
The spots that to my soul adhere ;
But should she labour night and day,
They will not, cannot disappear ;
Whence angry perturbations,—and that
  look   100
Which no philosophy can brook !

vi.

Ill-fated Chief ! there are whose hopes are
  built
Upon the ruins of thy glorious name ;
Who, through the portal of one moment's
  guilt,
Pursue thee with their deadly aim !   105
O matchless perfidy ! portentous lust
Of monstrous crime !—that horror striking
  blade,
Drawn in defiance of the Gods, hath laid
The noble Syracusan low in dust !
Shuddered the walls—the marble city
  wept—   110
And sylvan places heaved a pensive sigh ;
But in calm peace the appointed Victim
  slept,
As he had fallen in magnanimity ;
Of spirit too capacious to require
That Destiny her course should change ;
  too just   115
To his own native greatness to desire
That wretched boon, days lengthened by
  mistrust.
So were the hopeless troubles, that in-
  volved
The soul of Dion, instantly dissolved.
Released from life and cares of princely
  state,   120
He left this moral grafted on his Fate ;
"Him only pleasure leads, and peace
  attends,

Him, only him, the shield of Jove de-
  fends,
Whose means are fair and spotless as his
  ends."

XXXIII.

THE PASS OF KIRKSTONE.

[Composed 1817.—Published 1820.]

I.

WITHIN the mind strong fancies work,
A deep delight the bosom thrills,
Oft as I pass along the fork
Of these fraternal hills :
Where, save the rugged road, we find   5
No appanage of human kind,
Nor hint of man ; if stone or rock
Seem not his handy-work to mock
By something cognizably shaped ;
Mockery—or model roughly hewn,   10
And left as if by earthquake strewn,
Or from the Flood escaped :
Altars for Druid service fit ;
(But where no fire was ever lit,
Unless the glow-worm to the skies   15
Thence offer nightly sacrifice)
Wrinkled Egyptian monument ;
Green moss-grown tower ; or hoary tent ;
Tents of a camp that never shall be
  razed—
On which four thousand years have
  gazed !   20

II.

Ye ploughshares sparkling on the slopes !
Ye snow-white lambs that trip
Imprisoned 'mid the formal props
Of restless ownership !
Ye trees, that may to-morrow fall   25
To feed the insatiate Prodigal !
Lawns, houses, chattels, groves, and
  fields,
All that the fertile valley shields ;
Wages of folly—baits of crime,
Of life's uneasy game the stake,   30
Playthings that keep the eyes awake
Of drowsy, dotard Time ;—
O care ! O guilt !—O vales and plains,
Here, 'mid his own unvexed domains,
A Genius dwells, that can subdue   35
At once all memory of You,—

Most potent when mists veil the sky,
Mists that distort and magnify,
While the coarse rushes, to the sweeping
   breeze,
Sigh forth their ancient melodies!   40

III.

List to those shriller notes!—*that* march
Perchance was on the blast,
When, through this Height's inverted
   arch,
Rome's earliest legion passed!
—They saw, adventurously impelled,   45
And older eyes than theirs beheld,
This block—and yon, whose church-like
   frame
Gives to this savage Pass its name.
Aspiring Road! that lov'st to hide
Thy daring in a vapoury bourn,   50
Not seldom may the hour return
When thou shalt be my guide:
And I (as all men may find cause,
When life is at a weary pause,
And they have panted up the hill   55
Of duty with reluctant will)
Be thankful, even though tired and faint,
For the rich bounties of constraint;
Whence oft invigorating transports flow
That choice lacked courage to bestow!   60

IV.

My Soul was grateful for delight
That wore a threatening brow;
A veil is lifted—can she slight
The scene that opens now?
Though habitation none appear,   65
The greenness tells, man must be there;
The shelter—that the perspective
Is of the clime in which we live;
Where Toil pursues his daily round;
Where Pity sheds sweet tears—and Love,
In woodbine bower or birchen grove,   71
Inflicts his tender wound.
—Who comes not hither ne'er shall know
How beautiful the world below;
Nor can he guess how lightly leaps   75
The brook adown the rocky steeps.
Farewell, thou desolate Domain!
Hope, pointing to the cultured plain,
Carols like a shepherd-boy;
And who is she?—Can that be Joy!   80

Who, with a sunbeam for her guide,
Smoothly skims the meadows wide;
While Faith, from yonder opening cloud,
To hill and vale proclaims aloud,
"Whate'er the weak may dread, the
   wicked dare,   85
Thy lot, O Man, is good, thy portion
   fair!"

XXXIV.

TO ENTERPRISE.

[Composed 1820 (?).—Published 1822.]

KEEP for the Young the impassioned
   smile
Shed from thy countenance, as I see thee
   stand
High on that chalky cliff of Britain's
   Isle,
A slender volume grasping in thy hand—
(Perchance the pages that relate   5
The various turns of Crusoe's fate)—
Ah, spare the exulting smile,
And drop thy pointing finger bright
As the first flash of beacon light;
But neither veil thy head in shadows dim,
Nor turn thy face away   11
From One who, in the evening of his day,
To thee would offer no presumptuous
   hymn!

I.

Bold Spirit! who art free to rove
Among the starry courts of Jove,   15
And oft in splendour dost appear
Embodied to poetic eyes,
While traversing this nether sphere,
Where Mortals call thee ENTERPRISE.
Daughter of Hope! her favourite Child,
Whom she to young Ambition bore,   21
When hunter's arrow first defiled
The grove, and stained the turf with gore;
Thee wingèd Fancy took, and nursed
On broad Euphrates' palmy shore,   25
And where the mightier Waters burst
From caves of Indian mountains hoar!
She wrapped thee in a panther's skin;
And Thou, thy favourite food to win,
The flame-eyed eagle oft wouldst scare   30
From her rock-fortress in mid air,

With infant shout; and often sweep,
Paired with the ostrich, o'er the plain;
Or, tired with sport, wouldst sink asleep
Upon the couchant lion's mane !   35
With rolling years thy strength increased;
And, far beyond thy native East,
To thee, by varying titles known
As variously thy power was shown,
Did incense-bearing altars rise,   40
Which caught the blaze of sacrifice,
From suppliants panting for the skies !

II.

What though this ancient Earth be trod
No more by step of Demi-god
Mounting from glorious deed to deed   45
As thou from clime to clime didst lead ;
Yet still the bosom beating high,
And the hushed farewell of an eye
Where no procrastinating gaze
A last infirmity betrays,   50
Prove that thy heaven-descended sway
Shall ne'er submit to cold decay.
By thy divinity impelled,
The Stripling seeks the tented field ;
The aspiring Virgin kneels ; and, pale 55
With awe, receives the hallowed veil,
A soft and tender Heroine
Vowed to severer discipline ;
Inflamed by thee, the blooming Boy
Makes of the whistling shrouds a toy, 60
And of the ocean's dismal breast
A play-ground,—or a couch of rest ;
'Mid the blank world of snow and ice,
Thou to his dangers dost enchain
The Chamois-chaser awed in vain   65
By chasm or dizzy precipice ;
And hast Thou not with triumph seen
How soaring Mortals glide between
Or through the clouds, and brave the light
With bolder than Icarian flight ?   70
How they, in bells of crystal, dive—
Where winds and waters cease to strive—
For no unholy visitings,
Among the monsters of the Deep ;
And all the sad and precious things 75
Which there in ghastly silence sleep?
Or adverse tides and currents headed,
And breathless calms no longer dreaded,
In never-slackening voyage go
Straight as an arrow from the bow ; 80

And, slighting sails and scorning oars,
Keep faith with Time on distant shores?
—Within our fearless reach are placed
The secrets of the burning Waste ;
Egyptian tombs unlock their dead,   85
Nile trembles at his fountain head ;
Thou speak'st—and lo ! the polar Seas
Unbosom their last mysteries.
—But oh ! what transports, what sublime
    reward,
Won from the world of mind, dost thou
    prepare   90
For philosophic Sage; or high-souled
    Bard
Who, for thy service trained in lonely
    woods,
Hath fed on pageants floating through
    the air,
Or calentured in depth of limpid floods ;
Nor grieves—tho' doomed thro' silent
    night to bear   95
The domination of his glorious themes,
Or struggle in the net-work of thy dreams !

III.

If there be movements in the Patriot's soul,
From source still deeper, and of higher
    worth,
'Tis thine the quickening impulse to
    control,   100
And in due season send the mandate
    forth ;
Thy call a prostrate Nation can restore,
When but a single Mind resolves to
    crouch no more.

IV.

Dread Minister of wrath !
Who to their destined punishment dost
    urge   105
The Pharaohs of the earth, the men of
    hardened heart !
Not unassisted by the flattering stars,
Thou strew'st temptation o'er the path
When they in pomp depart
With trampling horses and refulgent
    cars—   110
Soon to be swallowed by the briny surge ;
Or cast, for lingering death, on unknown
    strands ;
Or caught amid a whirl of desert sands—

An Army now, and now a living hill
That a brief while heaves with convulsive
    throes—   115
Then all is still;
Or, to forget their madness and their woes,
Wrapt in a winding-sheet of spotless
    snows!

V.

Back flows the willing current of my Song:
If to provoke such doom the Impious
    dare,   120
Why should it daunt a blameless prayer?
—Bold Goddess! range our Youth among;
Nor let thy genuine impulse fail to beat
In hearts no longer young;
Still may a veteran Few have pride   125
In thoughts whose sternness makes them
    sweet;
In fixed resolves by Reason justified;
That to their object cleave like sleet
Whitening a pine tree's northern side,
When fields are naked far and wide,   130
And withered leaves, from earth's cold
    breast
Up-caught in whirlwinds, nowhere can
    find rest.

VI.

But if such homage thou disdain
As doth with mellowing years agree,
One rarely absent from thy train   135
More humble favours may obtain
For thy contented Votary.
She who incites the frolic lambs
In presence of their heedless dams,
And to the solitary fawn   140
Vouchsafes her lessons, bounteous Nymph
That wakes the breeze, the sparkling
    lymph
Doth hurry to the lawn;
She who inspires that strain of joyance
    holy
Which the sweet Bird, misnamed the
    melancholy,   145
Pours forth in shady groves, shall plead
    for me;
And vernal mornings opening bright
With views of undefined delight,
And cheerful songs, and suns that shine
On busy days, with thankful nights, be
    mine.   150

VII.

But thou, O Goddess! in thy favourite Isle
(Freedom's impregnable redoubt,
The wide earth's storehouse fenced about
With breakers roaring to the gales
That stretch a thousand thousand sails) 155
Quicken the slothful, and exalt the vile!—
Thy impulse is the life of Fame;
Glad Hope would almost cease to be
If torn from thy society;
And Love, when worthiest of his name, 160
Is proud to walk the earth with Thee!

XXXV.

TO —,

ON HER FIRST ASCENT TO THE SUMMIT OF
HELVELLYN.

[Composed 1816.—Published 1820.]

INMATE of a mountain-dwelling,
Thou hast clomb aloft, and gazed
From the watch-towers of Helvellyn;
Awed, delighted, and amazed!

Potent was the spell that bound thee   5
Not unwilling to obey;
For blue Ether's arms, flung round thee,
Stilled the pantings of dismay.

Lo! the dwindled woods and meadows;
What a vast abyss is there!   10
Lo! the clouds, the solemn shadows,
And the glistenings—heavenly fair!

And a record of commotion
Which a thousand ridges yield;
Ridge, and gulf, and distant ocean   15
Gleaming like a silver shield!

Maiden! now take flight;—inherit
Alps or Andes—they are thine!
With the morning's roseate Spirit
Sweep their length of snowy line;   20

Or survey their bright dominions
In the gorgeous colours drest
Flung from off the purple pinions,
Evening spreads throughout the west!

Thine are all the choral[1] fountains   25
Warbling in each sparry vault
Of the untrodden lunar mountains;
Listen to their songs!—or halt,

---

[1] "Choral", edd. 1820, 1827; "coral", 1832–
1849.—ED.

To Niphates' top invited,
Whither spiteful Satan steered ;   30
Or descend where the ark alighted,
When the green earth re-appeared ;

For the power of hills is on thee,
As was witnessed through thine eye
Then, when old Helvellyn won thee   35
To confess their majesty !

XXXVI.

TO A YOUNG LADY,

WHO HAD BEEN REPROACHED FOR TAKING
LONG WALKS IN THE COUNTRY.

[Composed 1801 (?).—Published *Morning Post*,
February 11, 1802 ; ed. 1807.]

DEAR Child of Nature, let them rail !
—There is a nest in a green dale,
A harbour and a hold ;
Where thou, a Wife and Friend, shalt see
Thy own heart-stirring days, and be   5
A light to young and old.

There, healthy as a shepherd boy,
And treading among flowers of joy
Which at no season fade,
Thou, while thy babes around thee cling, 10
Shalt show us how divine a thing
A Woman may be made.

Thy thoughts and feelings shall not die,
Nor leave thee, when grey hairs are nigh,
A melancholy slave ;   15
But an old age serene and bright,
And lovely as a Lapland night,
Shall lead thee to thy grave.

XXXVII.

WATER FOWL.

[Composed 1812 (?) [1].—Published 1823 ; ed. 1827.]

" Let me be allowed the aid of verse to describe
the evolutions which these visitants sometimes
perform, on a fine day towards the close of
winter."—*Extract from the Author's Book on
the Lakes* (*edition of* 1823.—ED.).

[1] These lines form portion of *The Recluse,
Book I.*, much of which was undoubtedly com-
posed in 1800. In 1836 Wordsworth assigned them
to the year 1812 ; but his memory on such mat-
ters was treacherous, and it is quite possible that
they were written as far back as 1800.—ED.

MARK how the feathered tenants of the
flood,
With grace of motion that might scarcely
seem
Inferior to angelical, prolong
Their curious pastime ! shaping in mid air
(And sometimes with ambitious wing that
soars   5
High as the level of the mountain-tops)
A circuit ampler than the lake beneath—
Their own domain ; but ever, while intent
On tracing and retracing that large round,
Their jubilant activity evolves   10
Hundreds of curves and circlets, to and fro,
Upward and downward, progress intricate
Yet unperplexed, as if one spirit swayed
Their indefatigable flight.   'Tis done—
Ten times, or more, I fancied it had ceased ;
But lo ! the vanished company again   16
Ascending ; they approach—I hear their
wings,
Faint, faint at first ; and then an eager
sound,
Past in a moment—and as faint again !
They tempt the sun to sport amid their
plumes ;   20
They tempt the water, or the gleaming ice,
To show them a fair image ; 'tis themselves,
Their own fair forms, upon the glimmer-
ing plain,
Painted more soft and fair as they descend
Almost to touch ;—then up again aloft, 25
Up with a sally and a flash of speed,
As if they scorned both resting-place and
rest !

XXXVIII.

VIEW FROM THE TOP OF BLACK
COMB [2].

[Composed 1813.—Published 1815.]

THIS Height a ministering Angel might
select :
For from the, summit of BLACK COMB
(dread name

[2] Black Comb stands at the southern extremity
of Cumberland : its base covers a much greater
extent of ground than any other mountain in
those parts ; and, from its situation, the summit
commands a more extensive view than any other
point in Britain.

Derived from clouds and storms!) the
  amplest range
Of unobstructed prospect may be seen
That British ground commands:—low
  dusky tracts,   5
Where Trent is nursed, far southward!
  Cambrian hills
To the south-west, a multitudinous show;
And, in a line of eye-sight linked with
  these,
The hoary peaks of Scotland that give
  birth
To Tiviot's stream, to Annan, Tweed, and
  Clyde:—   10
Crowding the quarter whence the sun
  comes forth
Gigantic mountains rough with crags;
  beneath,
Right at the imperial station's western
  base,
Main ocean, breaking audibly, and
  stretched
Far into silent regions blue and pale;—
And visibly engirding Mona's Isle   16
That, as we left the plain, before our
  sight
Stood like a lofty mount, uplifting
  slowly
(Above the convex of the watery globe)
Into clear view the cultured fields that
  streak   20
Her habitable shores, but now appears
A dwindled object, and submits to lie
At the spectator's feet.—Yon azure ridge,
Is it a perishable cloud? Or there
Do we behold the line of Erin's coast? 25
Land sometimes by the roving shepherd-
  swain
(Like the bright confines of another
  world)
Not doubtfully perceived.—Look home-
  ward now!
In depth, in height, in circuit, how
  serene
The spectacle, how pure!—Of Nature's
  works,   30
In earth, and air, and earth-embracing
  sea,
A revelation infinite it seems;
Display august of man's inheritance,
Of Britain's calm felicity and power!

XXXIX.

THE HAUNTED TREE.

TO ——.

[Composed 1819.—Published 1820.]

THOSE silver clouds collected round the
  sun
His mid-day warmth abate not, seeming
  less
To overshade than multiply his beams
By soft reflection—grateful to the sky,
To rocks, fields, woods. Nor doth our
  human sense   5
Ask, for its pleasure, screen or canopy
More ample than the time-dismantled Oak
Spreads o'er this tuft of heath, which now,
  attired
In the whole fulness of its bloom, affords
Couch beautiful as e'er for earthly use 10
Was fashioned; whether by the hand of
  Art,
That eastern Sultan, amid flowers en-
  wrought
On silken tissue, might diffuse his limbs
In languor; or by Nature, for repose
Of panting Wood-nymph, wearied with
  the chase.   15
O Lady! fairer in thy Poet's sight
Than fairest spiritual creature of the
  groves,
Approach;—and, thus invited, crown with
  rest
The noon-tide hour: though truly some
  there are
Whose footsteps superstitiously avoid 20
This venerable Tree; for, when the wind
Blows keenly, it sends forth a creaking
  sound
(Above the general roar of woods and
  crags)
Distinctly heard from far—a doleful note!
As if (so Grecian shepherds would have
  deemed)   25
The Hamadryad, pent within, bewailed
Some bitter wrong. Nor is it unbelieved,
By ruder fancy, that a troubled ghost
Haunts the old trunk; lamenting deeds
  of which
The flowery ground is conscious. But no
  wind   30

Sweeps now along this elevated ridge;
Not even a zephyr stirs ;—the obnoxious
    Tree
Is mute; and, in his silence, would look
    down,
O lovely Wanderer of the trackless hills,
On thy reclining form with more delight 35
Than his coevals in the sheltered vale
Seem to participate, the while they view
Their own far-stretching arms and leafy
    heads
Vividly pictured in some glassy pool,
That, for a brief space, checks the hurrying
    stream !   40

XL.

THE TRIAD.

[Composed 1828.—Published 1829 (*The Keepsake*);
            ed. 1832.]

SHOW me the noblest Youth of present
    time,
Whose trembling fancy would to love
    give birth ;
Some God or Hero, from the Olympian
    clime
Returned, to seek a Consort upon earth ;
Or, in no doubtful prospect, let me see
The brightest star of ages yet to be,
And I will mate and match him blissfully.

I will not fetch a Naiad from a flood
Pure as herself—(song lacks not mightier
    power)
Nor leaf-crowned Dryad from a pathless
    wood,   10
Nor Sea-nymph glistening from her coral
    bower ;
Mere Mortals, bodied forth in vision still,
Shall with Mount Ida's triple lustre fill
The chaster coverts of a British hill.

  "Appear !—obey my lyre's command ! 15
Come, like the Graces, hand in hand !
For ye, though not by birth allied,
Are Sisters in the bond of love ;
Nor shall the tongue of envious pride
Presume those interweavings to reprove 20
In you, which that fair progeny of Jove
Learned from the tuneful spheres that
    glide
In endless union, earth and sea above."

—I sing in vain ;—the pines have hushed
    their waving :
A peerless Youth expectant at my side, 25
Breathless as they, with unabated craving
Looks to the earth, and to the vacant air ;
And, with a wandering eye that seems to
    chide,
Asks of the clouds what occupants they
    hide :—
But why solicit more than sight could
    bear,   30
By casting on a moment all we dare ?
Invoke we those bright Beings one by
    one !
And what was boldly promised, truly
    shall be done.

  "Fear not a constraining measure !
—Yielding to this gentle spell,   35
Lucida ! from domes of pleasure,
Or from cottage-sprinkled dell,
Come to regions solitary,
Where the eagle builds her aery,
Above the hermit's long-forsaken cell !" 40
—She comes !—behold
That Figure, like a ship with snow-white
    sail !
Nearer she draws ; a breeze uplifts her
    veil,
Upon her coming wait
As pure a sunshine and as soft a gale 45
As e'er, on herbage covering earthly mould,
Tempted the bird of Juno to unfold
His richest splendour—when his veering
    gait
And every motion of his starry train
Seem governed by a strain   50
Of music, audible to him alone.

  "O Lady, worthy of earth's proudest
    throne !
Nor less, by excellence of nature, fit
Beside an unambitious hearth to sit
Domestic queen, where grandeur is un-
    known ;   55
What living man could fear
The worst of Fortune's malice, wert Thou
    near,
Humbling that lily-stem, thy sceptre meek,
That its fair flowers may from his cheek
Brush the too happy tear ?   60

——Queen, and handmaid lowly!
Whose skill can speed the day with lively
    cares,
And banish melancholy
By all that mind invents or hand prepares;
O Thou, against whose lip, without its
    smile   65
And in its silence even, no heart is proof;
Whose goodness, sinking deep, would
    reconcile
The softest Nursling of a gorgeous palace
To the bare life beneath the hawthorn-roof
Of Sherwood's Archer, or in caves of
    Wallace—   70
Who that hath seen thy beauty could
    content
His soul with but a *glimpse* of heavenly
    day?
Who that hath loved thee, but would lay
His strong hand on the wind, if it were
    bent
To take thee in thy majesty away?   75
—Pass onward (even the glancing deer
Till we depart intrude not here;)
That mossy slope, o'er which the wood-
    bine throws
A canopy, is smoothed for thy repose!"

Glad moment is it when the throng   80
Of warblers in full concert strong
Strive, and not vainly strive, to rout
The lagging shower, and force coy Phœbus
    out,
Met by the rainbow's form divine,
Issuing from her cloudy shrine;—   85
So may the thrillings of the lyre
Prevail to further our desire,
While to these shades a sister Nymph I
    call.

"Come, if the notes thine ear may pierce,
Come, youngest of the lovely Three,   90
Submissive to the might of verse
And the dear voice of harmony,
By none more deeply felt than Thee!"
—I sang; and lo! from pastimes virginal
She hastens to the tents   95
Of nature, and the lonely elements.
Air sparkles round her with a dazzling
    sheen;
But mark her glowing cheek, her vesture
    green!

And, as if wishful to disarm
Or to repay the potent Charm,   100
She bears the stringèd lute of old romance,
That cheered the trellised arbour's privacy,
And soothed war-wearied knights in raft-
    ered hall.
How vivid, yet how delicate, her glee!
So tripped the Muse, inventress of the
    dance;   105
So, truant in waste woods, the blithe
    Euphrosyne!

But the ringlets of that head
Why are they ungarlanded?
Why bedeck her temples less
Than the simplest shepherdess?   110
Is it not a brow inviting
Choicest flowers that ever breathed,
Which the myrtle would delight in
With Idalian rose enwreathed?
But her humility is well content   115
With *one* wild floweret (call it not forlorn)
FLOWER OF THE WINDS, beneath her bosom
    worn—
Yet more for love than ornament.

Open, ye thickets! let her fly,
Swift as a Thracian Nymph o'er field and
    height!   120
For She, to all but those who love her, shy,
Would gladly vanish from a Stranger's
    sight;
Though, where she is beloved and loves,
Light as the wheeling butterfly she moves,
Her happy spirit as a bird is free,   125
That rifles blossoms on a tree,
Turning them inside out with arch
    audacity.
Alas! how little can a moment show
Of an eye where feeling plays
In ten thousand dewy rays;   130
A face o'er which a thousand shadows go!
—She stops—is fastened to that rivulet's
    side;
And there (while, with sedater mien,
O'er timid waters that have scarcely left
Their birthplace in the rocky cleft   135
She bends) at leisure may be seen
Features to old ideal grace allied,
Amid their smiles and dimples dignified—
Fit countenance for the soul of primal truth;
The bland composure of eternal youth!

What more changeful than the sea? 141
But over his great tides
Fidelity presides;
And this light-hearted Maiden constant
is as he.
High is her aim as heaven above, 145
And wide as ether her good-will;
And, like the lowly reed, her love
Can drink its nurture from the scantiest
rill:
Insight as keen as frosty star
Is to *her* charity no bar, 150
Nor interrupts her frolic graces
When she is, far from these wild places,
Encircled by familiar faces.

O the charm that manners draw,
Nature, from thy genuine law! 155
If from what her hand would do,
Her voice would utter, aught ensue
Untoward or unfit;
She, in benign affections pure,
In self-forgetfulness secure, 160
Sheds round the transient harm or vague
mischance
A light unknown to tutored elegance:
Hers is not a cheek shame-stricken,
But her blushes are joy flushed;
And the fault (if fault it be) 165
Only ministers to quicken
Laughter-loving gaiety,
And kindle sportive wit—
Leaving this Daughter of the mountains
free,
As if she knew that Oberon king of Faery
Had crossed her purpose with some quaint
vagary, 171
And heard his viewless bands
Over their mirthful triumph clapping
hands.

"Last of the Three, though eldest born,
Reveal thyself, like pensive Morn 175
Touched by the skylark's earliest note,
Ere humbler gladness be afloat.
But whether in the semblance drest
Of Dawn—or Eve, fair vision of the west,
Come with each anxious hope subdued
By woman's gentle fortitude, 181
Each grief, through meekness, settling
into rest.

—Or I would hail thee when some high-
wrought page
Of a closed volume lingering in thy hand
Has raised thy spirit to a peaceful stand
Among the glories of a happier age." 186

Her brow hath opened on me—see it
there,
Brightening the umbrage of her hair;
So gleams the crescent moon, that loves
To be descried through shady groves. 190
Tenderest bloom is on her cheek;
Wish not for a richer streak;
Nor dread the depth of meditative eye;
But let thy love, upon that azure field
Of thoughtfulness and beauty, yield 195
Its homage offered up in purity.
What wouldst thou more? In sunny glade,
Or under leaves of thickest shade,
Was such a stillness e'er diffused
Since earth grew calm while angels
mused? 200
Softly she treads, as if her foot were loth
To crush the mountain dew-drops—soon
to melt
On the flower's breast; as if she felt
That flowers themselves, whate'er their
hue,
With all their fragrance, all their glisten-
ing, 205
Call to the heart for inward listening—
And though for bridal wreaths and tokens
true
Welcomed wisely; though a growth
Which the careless shepherd sleeps on,
As fitly spring from turf the mourner
weeps on— 210
And without wrong are cropped the mar-
ble tomb to strew.
The Charm is over; the mute Phantoms
gone,
Nor will return—but droop not, favoured
Youth;
The apparition that before thee shone
Obeyed a summons covetous of truth. 215
From these wild rocks thy footsteps I
will guide
To bowers in which thy fortune may be
tried,
And one of the bright Three become thy
happy Bride.

XLI.

THE WISHING-GATE.

[Composed 1828.—Published 1829 (*The Keepsake*); ed. 1832.]

In the vale of Grasmere, by the side of the old highway, leading to Ambleside, is a gate, which, time out of mind, has been called the Wishing-gate, from a belief that wishes formed or indulged there have a favourable issue.

HOPE rules a land for ever green:
All powers that serve the bright-eyed Queen
   Are confident and gay;
Clouds at her bidding disappear;
Points she to aught?—the bliss draws near,
   And Fancy smooths the way. 6

Not such the land of Wishes—there
Dwell fruitless day-dreams, lawless prayer,
   And thoughts with things at strife;
Yet how forlorn, should *ye* depart, 10
Ye superstitions of the *heart*,
   How poor, were human life!

When magic lore abjured its might,
Ye did not forfeit one dear right,
   One tender claim abate; 15
Witness this symbol of your sway,
Surviving near the public way,
   The rustic Wishing-gate!

Enquire not if the faery race
Shed kindly influence on the place, 20
   Ere northward they retired;
If here a warrior left a spell,
Panting for glory as he fell;
   Or here a saint expired.

Enough that all around is fair, 25
Composed with Nature's finest care,
   And in her fondest love—
Peace to embosom and content—
To overawe the turbulent,
   The selfish to reprove. 30

Yea! even the Stranger from afar,
Reclining on this moss-grown bar,
   Unknowing, and unknown,
The infection of the ground partakes,
Longing for his Beloved—who makes 35
   All happiness her own.

Then why should conscious Spirits fear
The mystic stirrings that are here,
   The ancient faith disclaim?
The local Genius ne'er befriends 40
Desires whose course in folly ends,
   Whose just reward is shame.

Smile if thou wilt, but not in scorn,
If some, by ceaseless pains outworn,
   Here crave an easier lot; 45
If some have thirsted to renew
A broken vow, or bind a true,
   With firmer, holier knot.

And not in vain, when thoughts are cast
Upon the irrevocable past, 50
   Some Penitent sincere
May for a worthier future sigh,
While trickles from his downcast eye
   No unavailing tear.

The Worldling, pining to be freed 55
From turmoil, who would turn or speed
   The current of his fate,
Might stop before this favoured scene,
At Nature's call, nor blush to lean
   Upon the Wishing-gate. 60

The Sage, who feels how blind, how weak
Is man, though loth such help to *seek*,
   Yet, passing, here might pause,
And thirst for insight to allay
Misgiving, while the crimson day 65
   In quietness withdraws;

Or when the church-clock's knell profound
To Time's first step across the bound
   Of midnight makes reply;
Time pressing on with starry crest 70
To filial sleep upon the breast
   Of dread eternity.

XLII.

THE WISHING-GATE DESTROYED.

[Composed ?.—Published 1842.]

'TIS gone—with old belief and dream
That round it clung, and tempting scheme
   Released from fear and doubt;
And the bright landscape too must lie,
By this blank wall, from every eye, 5
   Relentlessly shut out.

Bear witness ye who seldom passed
That opening—but a look ye cast
　　Upon the lake below,
What spirit-stirring power it gained　　10
From faith which here was entertained,
　　Though reason might say no.

Blest is that ground, where, o'er the springs
Of history, Glory claps her wings,
　　Fame sheds the exulting tear;　　15
Yet earth is wide, and many a nook
Unheard of is, like this, a book
　　For modest meanings dear.

It was in sooth a happy thought
That grafted, on so fair a spot,　　20
　　So confident a token
Of coming good;—the charm is fled;
Indulgent centuries spun a thread,
　　Which one harsh day has broken.

Alas! for him who gave the word;　　25
Could he no sympathy afford,
　　Derived from earth or heaven,
To hearts so oft by hope betrayed;
Their very wishes wanted aid
　　Which here was freely given?　　30

Where, for the love-lorn maiden's wound,
Will now so readily be found
　　A balm of expectation?
Anxious for far-off children, where
Shall mothers breathe a like sweet air　　35
　　Of home-felt consolation?

And not unfelt will prove the loss
'Mid trivial care and petty cross
　　And each day's shallow grief;
Though the most easily beguiled　　40
Were oft among the first that smiled
　　At their own fond belief.

If still the reckless change we mourn,
A reconciling thought may turn
　　To harm that might lurk here,　　45
Ere judgment prompted from within
Fit aims, with courage to begin,
　　And strength to persevere.

Not Fortune's slave is Man: our state
Enjoins, while firm resolves await　　50
　　On wishes just and wise,
That strenuous action follow both,
And life be one perpetual growth
　　Of heaven-ward enterprise.

So taught, so trained, we boldly face　　55
All accidents of time and place;
　　Whatever props may fail,
Trust in that sovereign law can spread
New glory o'er the mountain's head,
　　Fresh beauty through the vale.　　60

That truth informing mind and heart,
The simplest cottager may part,
　　Ungrieved, with charm and spell;
And yet, lost Wishing-gate, to thee
The voice of grateful memory　　65
　　Shall bid a kind farewell![1]

XLIII.

THE PRIMROSE OF THE ROCK.

[Composed 1831.—Published 1835.]

A Rock there is whose homely front
　　The passing traveller slights;
Yet there the glow-worms hang their lamps,
　　Like stars, at various heights;
And one coy Primrose to that Rock　　5
　　The vernal breeze invites.

What hideous warfare hath been waged,
　　What kingdoms overthrown,
Since first I spied that Primrose-tuft
　　And marked it for my own;　　10
A lasting link in Nature's chain
　　From highest heaven let down!

The flowers, still faithful to the stems,
　　Their fellowship renew;
The stems are faithful to the root,　　15
　　That worketh out of view;
And to the rock the root adheres
　　In every fibre true.

Close clings to earth the living rock,
　　Though threatening still to fall;　　20
The earth is constant to her sphere;
　　And God upholds them all:
So blooms this lonely Plant, nor dreads
　　Her annual funeral.

．　　．　　．　　．　　．

Here closed the meditative strain;　　25
　　But air breathed soft that day,
The hoary mountain-heights were cheered,
　　The sunny vale looked gay;
And to the Primrose of the Rock
　　I gave this after-lay.　　30

----

[1] See Note, p. 901.

I sang—Let myriads of bright flowers,
  Like Thee, in field and grove
Revive unenvied ;—mightier far,
  Than tremblings that reprove
Our vernal tendencies to hope,   35
  Is God's redeeming love ;

That love which changed—for wan disease,
  For sorrow that had bent
O'er hopeless dust, for withered age—
  Their moral element,   40
And turned the thistles of a curse
  To types beneficent.

Sin-blighted though we are, we too,
  The reasoning Sons of Men,
From one oblivious winter called   45
  Shall rise, and breathe again ;
And in eternal summer lose
  Our threescore years and ten.

To humbleness of heart descends
  This prescience from on high,   50
The faith that elevates the just,
  Before and when they die ;
And makes each soul a separate heaven,
  A court for Deity.

XLIV.

PRESENTIMENTS.

[Composed 1830.—Published 1835.]

PRESENTIMENTS ! they judge not right
Who deem that ye from open light
  Retire in fear of shame ;
All *heaven-born* Instincts shun the touch
Of vulgar sense,—and, being such,   5
  Such privilege ye claim.

The tear whose source I could not guess,
The deep sigh that seemed fatherless,
  Were mine in early days ;
And now, unforced by time to part   10
With fancy, I obey my heart,
  And venture on your praise.

What though some busy foes to good,
Too potent over nerve and blood,
  Lurk near you—and combine   15
To taint the health which ye infuse ;
This hides not from the moral Muse
  Your origin divine.

How oft from you, derided Powers !
Comes Faith that in auspicious hours 20
  Builds castles, not of air :
Bodings unsanctioned by the will
Flow from your visionary skill,
  And teach us to beware.

The bosom-weight, your stubborn gift, 25
That no philosophy can lift,
  Shall vanish, if ye please,
Like morning mist : and, where it lay,
The spirits at your bidding play
  In gaiety and ease.   30

Star-guided contemplations move
Through space, though calm, not raised
    above
  Prognostics that ye rule ;
The naked Indian of the wild,
And haply too the cradled Child,   35
  Are pupils of your school.

But who can fathom your intents,
Number their signs or instruments ?
  A rainbow, a sunbeam,
A subtle smell that Spring unbinds,   40
Dead pause abrupt of midnight winds,
  An echo, or a dream.

The laughter of the Christmas hearth
With sighs of self-exhausted mirth
  Ye feelingly reprove ;   45
And daily, in the conscious breast,
Your visitations are a test
  And exercise of love.

When some great change gives boundless
    scope
To an exulting Nation's hope   50
  Oft, startled and made wise
By your low-breathed interpretings,
The simply-meek foretaste the springs
  Of bitter contraries.

Ye daunt the proud array of war,   55
Pervade the lonely ocean far
  As sail hath been unfurled ;
For dancers in the festive hall
What ghastly partners hath your call
  Fetched from the shadowy world.   60

'Tis said that warnings ye dispense,
Emboldened by a keener sense ;

That men have lived for whom,
With dread precision, ye made clear
The hour that in a distant year   65
    Shculd knell them to the tomb.

Unwelcome insight! Yet there are
Blest times when mystery is laid bare,
Truth shows a glorious face,
While on that isthmus which commands
The councils of both worlds she stands,
    Sage Spirits! by your grace.

God, who instructs the brutes to scent
All changes of the element,
    Whose wisdom fixed the scale   75
Of natures, for our wants provides
By higher, sometimes humbler, guides,
    When lights of reason fail.

XLV.

VERNAL ODE.

[Composed 1817.—Published 1820.]

"Rerum Natura tota est nusquam magis quam
in minimis."   PLIN. *Nat. Hist.*

I.

Beneath the concave of an April sky,
When all the fields with freshest green
    were dight,
Appeared, in presence of the spiritual eye
That aids or supersedes our grosser sight,
The form and rich habiliments of One   5
Whose countenance bore resemblance to
    the sun,
When it reveals, in evening majesty,
Features half lost amid their own pure
    light.
Poised like a weary cloud, in middle air
He hung,—then floated with angelic ease
(Softening that bright effulgence by de-
    grees)   11
Till he had reached a summit sharp and
    bare,
Where oft the venturous heifer drinks the
    noontide breeze.
Upon the apex of that lofty cone
Alighted, there the Stranger stood alone;
Fair as a gorgeous Fabric of the east   16
Suddenly raised by some enchanter's
    power,

Where nothing was; and firm as some old
    Tower
Of Britain's realm, whose leafy crest
Waves high, embellished by a gleaming
    shower!   20

II.

Beneath the shadow of his purple wings
Rested a golden harp;—he touched the
    strings;
And, after prelude of unearthly sound
Poured through the echoing hills around,
He sang—
            "No wintry desolations,   25
Scorching blight or noxious dew,
Affect my native habitations;
Buried in glory, far beyond the scope
Of man's enquiring gaze, but to his hope
Imaged, though faintly, in the hue   30
Profound of night's ethereal blue;
And in the aspect of each radiant orb;—
Some fixed, some wandering with no
    timid curb;
But wandering star and fixed, to mortal
    eye,
Blended in absolute serenity,   35
And free from semblance of decline;—
Fresh as if Evening brought their natal
    hour,
Her darkness splendour gave, her silence
    power,
To testify of Love and Grace divine.

III.

"What if those bright fires   40
Shine subject to decay,
Sons haply of extinguished sires,
Themselves to lose their light, or pass
    away
Like clouds before the wind,
Be thanks poured out to Him whose hand
    bestows,   45
Nightly, on human kind
That vision of endurance and repose.
—And though to every draught of vital
    breath,
Renewed throughout the bounds of earth
    or ocean,
The melancholy gates of Death   50
Respond with sympathetic motion;

Though all that feeds on nether air
Howe'er magnificent or fair,
Grows but to perish, and entrust
Its ruins to their kindred dust;   55
Yet, by the Almighty's ever-during care,
Her procreant vigils Nature keeps
Amid the unfathomable deeps;
And saves the peopled fields of earth
From dread of emptiness or dearth.   60
Thus, in their stations, lifting tow'rd the
    sky
The foliaged head in cloud-like majesty,
The shadow-casting race of trees survive:
Thus, in the train of Spring, arrive
Sweet flowers;—what living eye hath
    viewed   65
Their myriads?—endlessly renewed,
Wherever strikes the sun's glad ray;
Where'er the subtle waters stray;
Wherever sportive breezes bend
Their course, or genial showers descend!
Mortals, rejoice! the very Angels quit 71
Their mansions unsusceptible of change,
Amid your pleasant bowers to sit,
And through your sweet vicissitudes to
    range!"

IV.

O, nursed at happy distance from the
    cares   75
Of a too-anxious world, mild pastoral
    Muse!
That to the sparkling crown -Urania
    wears,
And to her sister Clio's laurel wreath,
Preferr'st a garland culled from purple
    heath,
Or blooming thicket moist with morning
    dews;   80
Was such bright Spectacle vouchsafed
    to me?
And was it granted to the simple ear
Of thy contented Votary
Such melody to hear!
Him rather suits it, side by side with
    thee,   85
Wrapped in a fit of pleasing indolence,
While thy tired lute hangs on the haw-
    thorn-tree,
To lie and listen—till o'er-drowsèd sense
Sinks, hardly conscious of the influence—

To the soft murmur of the vagrant Bee. 90
—A slender sound! yet hoary Time
Doth to the *Soul* exalt it with the chime
Of all his years;—a company
Of ages coming, ages gone;
(Nations from before them sweeping,   95
Regions in destruction steeping,)
But every awful note in unison
With that faint utterance, which tells
Of treasure sucked from buds and bells,
For the pure keeping of those waxen
    cells;   100
Where She—a statist prudent to confer
Upon the common weal; a warrior bold,
Radiant all over with unburnished gold,
And armed with living spear for mortal
    fight;
    A cunning forager   105
That spreads no waste; a social builder;
    one
In whom all busy offices unite
With all fine functions that afford de-
    light—
Safe through the winter storm in quiet
    dwells!

V.

And is She brought within the power 110
Of vision?—o'er this tempting flower
Hovering until the petals stay
Her flight, and take its voice away!—
Observe each wing!—a tiny van!
The structure of her laden thigh,   115
How fragile! yet of ancestry
Mysteriously remote and high;
High as the imperial front of man;
The roseate bloom on woman's cheek;
The soaring eagle's curvèd beak;   120
The white plumes of the floating swan;
Old as the tiger's paw, the lion's mane
Ere shaken by that mood of stern disdain
At which the desert trembles.—Humming
    Bee!
Thy sting was needless then, perchance
    unknown,   125
The seeds of malice were not sown;
All creatures met in peace, from fierceness
    free,
And no pride blended with their dignity.
—Tears had not broken from their source;
Nor Anguish strayed from her Tartarean
    den;   130

The golden years maintained a course
Not undiversified though smooth and
    even;
We were not mocked with glimpse and
    shadow then,
Bright Seraphs mixed familiarly with
    men;
And earth and stars composed a universal
    heaven!   135

XLVI.

DEVOTIONAL INCITEMENTS.

[Composed 1832.—Published 1835.]

      "Not to the earth confined,
Ascend to heaven."

WHERE will they stop, those breathing
    Powers,
The Spirits of the new-born flowers?
They wander with the breeze, they wind
Where'er the streams a passage find;
Up from their native ground they rise   5
In mute aerial harmonies;
From humble violet—modest thyme—
Exhaled, the essential odours climb,
As if no space below the sky
Their subtle flight could satisfy: 10
Heaven will not tax our thoughts with
    pride
If like ambition be *their* guide.

Roused by this kindliest of May-
    showers,
The spirit-quickener of the flowers,
That with moist virtue softly cleaves   15
The buds, and freshens the young leaves,
The birds pour forth their souls in notes
Of rapture from a thousand throats—
Here checked by too impetuous haste,
While there the music runs to waste,   20
With bounty more and more enlarged,
Till the whole air is overcharged;
Give ear, O Man! to their appeal,
And thirst for no inferior zeal,
Thou, who canst *think*, as well as feel. 25

Mount from the earth; aspire! aspire!
So pleads the town's cathedral quire,
In strains that from their solemn height
Sink, to attain a loftier flight;

While incense from the altar breathes   30
Rich fragrance in embodied wreaths;
Or, flung from swinging censer, shrouds
The taper-lights, and curls in clouds
Around angelic Forms, the still
Creation of the painter's skill,   35
That on the service wait concealed
One moment, and the next revealed.
—Cast off your bonds, awake, arise,
And for no transient ecstasies!
What else can mean the visual plea   40
Of still or moving imagery—
The iterated summons loud,
Not wasted on the attendant crowd,
Nor wholly lost upon the throng
Hurrying the busy streets along?   45

Alas! the sanctities combined
By art to unsensualise the mind
Decay and languish; or, as creeds
And humours change, are spurned like
    weeds:
The priests are from their altars thrust;
Temples are levelled with the dust;   51
And solemn rites and awful forms
Founder amid fanatic storms.
Yet evermore, through years renewed
In undisturbed vicissitude   55
Of seasons balancing their flight
On the swift wings of day and night,
Kind Nature keeps a heavenly door
Wide open for the scattered Poor.
Where - flower-breathed incense to the
    skies   60
Is wafted in mute harmonies;
And ground fresh-cloven by the plough
Is fragrant with a humbler vow;
Where birds and brooks from leafy dells
Chime forth unwearied canticles,   65
And vapours magnify and spread
The glory of the sun's bright head—
Still constant in her worship, still
Conforming to the eternal Will,
Whether men sow or reap the fields,   70
Divine monition Nature yields,
That not by bread alone we live,
Or what a hand of flesh can give;
That every day should leave some part
Free for a sabbath of the heart: 75
So shall the seventh be truly blest,
From morn to eve, with hallowed rest.

XLVII.

THE CUCKOO-CLOCK.

[Composed ?.— Published 1842.]

WOULDST thou be taught, when sleep has
    taken flight,
By a sure voice that can most sweetly tell,
How far off yet a glimpse of morning
    light,
And if to lure the truant back be well,
Forbear to covet a Repeater's stroke,   5
That, answering to thy touch, will sound
    the hour;
Better provide thee with a Cuckoo-clock,
For service hung behind thy chamber-
    door;
And in due time the soft spontaneous
    shock,
The double note, as if with living power,
Will to composure lead—or make thee
    blithe as bird in bower.   11

List, Cuckoo—Cuckoo!—oft tho' tempests
    howl,
Or nipping frost remind thee trees are
    bare,
How cattle pine, and droop the shivering
    fowl,
Thy spirits will seem to feed on balmy air:
I speak with knowledge,—by that Voice
    beguiled,   16
Thou wilt salute old memories as they
    throng
Into thy heart; and fancies, running wild
Through fresh green fields, and budding
    groves among,
Will make thee happy, happy as a child;
Of sunshine wilt thou think, and flowers,
    and song,   21
And breathe as in a world where nothing
    can go wrong.

And know—that, even for him who shuns
    the day
And nightly tosses on a bed of pain;
Whose joys, from all but memory swept
    away,   25
Must come unhoped for, if they come
    again;
Know—that, for him whose waking
    thoughts, severe

As his distress is sharp, would scorn my
    theme,
The mimic notes, striking upon his ear
In sleep, and intermingling with his
    dream,   30
Could from sad regions send him to a dear
Delightful land of verdure, shower and
    gleam,
To mock the *wandering* Voice beside some
    haunted stream.

O bounty without measure! while the
    grace
Of Heaven doth in such wise, from hum-
    blest springs,   35
Pour pleasure forth, and solaces that trace
A mazy course along familiar things,
Well may our hearts have faith that
    blessings come,
Streaming from founts above the starry
    sky,
With angels when their own untroubled
    home   40
They leave, and speed on nightly embassy
To visit earthly chambers,—and for
    whom?
Yea, both for souls who God's forbear-
    ance try,
And those that seek his help, and for his
    mercy sigh.

XLVIII.

TO THE CLOUDS.

[Composed ?.—Published 1842.]

ARMY of Clouds! ye wingèd Host in troops
Ascending from behind the motionless
    brow
Of that tall rock, as from a hidden world,
Oh whither with such eagerness of speed?
What seek ye, or what shun ye? of the gale
Companions, fear ye to be left behind,   6
Or racing o'er your blue ethereal field
Contend ye with each other? of the sea
Children, thus post ye over vale and
    height
To sink upon your mother's lap—and
    rest?   10
Or were ye rightlier hailed, when first
    mine eyes
Beheld in your impetuous march the
    likeness

Of a wide army pressing on to meet
Or overtake some unknown enemy?—
But your smooth motions suit a peaceful
    aim;   15
And Fancy, not less aptly pleased, com-
    pares
Your squadrons to an endless flight of
    birds
Aerial, upon due migration bound
To milder climes; or rather do ye urge
In caravan your hasty pilgrimage   20
To pause at last on more aspiring heights
Than these, and utter your devotion there
With thunderous voice? Or are ye jubi-
    lant,
And would ye, tracking your proud lord
    the Sun,
Be present at his setting; or the pomp 25
Of Persian mornings would ye fill, and
    stand
Poising your splendours high above the
    heads
Of worshippers kneeling to their up-risen
    God?
Whence, whence, ye Clouds! this eager-
    ness of speed?
Speak, silent creatures.—They are gone,
    are fled,   30
Buried together in yon gloomy mass
That loads the middle heaven; and clear
    and bright
And vacant doth the region which they
    thronged
Appear; a calm descent of sky conducting
Down to the unapproachable abyss,   35
Down to that hidden gulf from which
    they rose
To vanish—fleet as days and months and
    years,
Fleet as the generations of mankind,
Power, glory, empire, as the world itself,
The lingering world, when time hath
    ceased to be.   40
But the winds roar, shaking the rooted
    trees,
And see! a bright precursor to a train
Perchance as numerous, overpeers the rock
That sullenly refuses to partake
Of the wild impulse. From a fount of
    life   45
Invisible, the long procession moves

Luminous or gloomy, welcome to the vale
Which they are entering, welcome to
    mine eye
That sees them, to my soul that owns in
    them,
And in the bosom of the firmament   50
O'er which they move, wherein they are
    contained,
A type of her capacious self and all
Her restless progeny.
            A humble walk
Here is my body doomed to tread, this
    path,
A little hoary line and faintly traced,   55
Work, shall we call it, of the shepherd's
    foot
Or of his flock?—joint vestige of them
    both.
I pace it unrepining, for my thoughts
Admit no bondage and my words have
    wings.
Where is the Orphean lyre, or Druid
    harp,   60
To accompany the verse? The mountain
    blast
Shall be our *hand* of music; he shall
    sweep
The rocks, and quivering trees, and bil-
    lowy lake,
And search the fibres of the caves, and
    they
Shall answer, for our song is of the
    Clouds,   65
And the wind loves them; and the gentle
    gales—
Which by their aid re-clothe the naked
    lawn
With annual verdure, and revive the
    woods,
And moisten the parched lips of thirsty
    flowers—
Love them; and every idle breeze of air
Bends to the favourite burthen. Moon
    and stars   71
Keep their most solemn vigils when the
    Clouds
Watch also, shifting peaceably their place
Like bands of ministering Spirits, or
    when they lie,
As if some Protean art the change had
    wrought,   75

In listless quiet o'er the ethereal deep
Scattered, a Cyclades of various shapes
And all degrees of beauty. O ye Light-
    nings!
Ye are their perilous offspring; and the
    Sun—
Source inexhaustible of life and joy,   80
And type of man's far-darting reason,
    therefore
In old time worshipped as the god of verse,
A blazing intellectual deity-
Loves his own glory in their looks, and
    showers
Upon that unsubstantial brotherhood 85
Visions with all but beatific light
Enriched—too transient, were they not
    renewed
From age to age, and did not, while we
    gaze
In silent rapture, credulous desire
Nourish the hope that memory lacks not
    power   90
To keep the treasure unimpaired. Vain
    thought!
Yet why repine, created as we are
For joy and rest, albeit to find them only
Lodged in the bosom of eternal things?

XLIX.

SUGGESTED BY A PICTURE OF THE BIRD OF PARADISE.

[Composed ?.—Published 1842.]

THE gentlest Poet, with free thoughts
    endowed,
And a true master of the glowing strain,
Might scan the narrow province with
    disdain
That to the Painter's skill is here allowed.
This, this the Bird of Paradise! disclaim
The daring thought, forget the name; 6
This the Sun's Bird, whom Glendoveers
    might own
As no unworthy Partner in their flight
Through seas of ether, where the ruffling
    sway
Of nether air's rude billows is unknown;
Whom Sylphs, if e'er for casual pastime
    they   11
Through India's spicy regions wing their
    way,

Might bow to as their Lord. What
    character,
O sovereign Nature! I appeal to thee,
Of all thy feathered progeny   15
Is so unearthly, and what shape so fair?
So richly decked in variegated down,
Green, sable, shining yellow, shadowy
    brown,
Tints softly with each other blended,
Hues doubtfully begun and ended; 20
Or intershooting, and to sight
Lost and recovered, as the rays of light
Glance on the conscious plumes touched
    here and there?
Full surely, when with such proud gifts
    of life
Began the pencil's strife,   25
O'erweening Art was caught as in a snare.

A sense of seemingly presumptuous
    wrong
Gave the first impulse to the Poet's song;
But, of his scorn repenting soon, he drew
A juster judgment from a calmer view; 30
And, with a spirit freed from discontent,
Thankfully took an effort that was meant
Not with God's bounty, Nature's love,
    to vie,
Or made with hope to please that inward
    eye   34
Which ever strives in vain itself to satisfy,
But to recall the truth by some faint trace
Of power ethereal and celestial grace,
That in the living Creature find on earth
    a place.

L.

A JEWISH FAMILY.

(IN A SMALL VALLEY OPPOSITE ST. GOAR,
UPON THE RHINE.)

[Composed 1828.—Published 1835.]

GENIUS of Raphael! if thy wings
    Might bear thee to this glen,
With faithful memory left of things
    To pencil dear and pen,
Thou wouldst forego the neighbouring
    Rhine,   5
    And all his majesty—
A studious forehead to incline
    O'er this poor family.

The Mother—her thou must have seen,
   In spirit, ere she came   10
To dwell these rifted rocks between,
   Or found on earth a name;
An image, too, of that sweet Boy,
   Thy inspirations give—
Of playfulness, and love, and joy,   15
   Predestined here to live.

Downcast, or shooting glances far,
   How beautiful his eyes,
That blend the nature of the star
   With that of summer skies!   20
I speak as if of sense beguiled;
   Uncounted months are gone,
Yet am I with the Jewish Child,
   That exquisite Saint John.

I see the dark-brown curls, the brow,   25
   The smooth transparent skin,
Refined, as with intent to show
   The holiness within;
The grace of parting Infancy
   By blushes yet untamed;   30
Age faithful to the mother's knee,
   Nor of her arms ashamed.

Two lovely Sisters, still and sweet
   As flowers, stand side by side;
Their soul-subduing looks might cheat   35
   The Christian of his pride:
Such beauty hath the Eternal poured
   Upon them not forlorn,
Though of a lineage once abhorred,
   Nor yet redeemed from scorn.   40

Mysterious safeguard, that, in spite
   Of poverty and wrong,
Doth here preserve a living light,
   From Hebrew fountains sprung;
That gives this ragged group to cast   45
   Around the dell a gleam
Of Palestine, of glory past,
   And proud Jerusalem!

LI.

ON THE POWER OF SOUND.

[Composed 1828.—Published 1835.]

ARGUMENT.

The Ear addressed, as occupied by a spiritual functionary, in communion with sounds, individual, or combined in studied harmony.— Sources and effects of those sounds (to the close of 6th Stanza).—The power of music, whence proceeding, exemplified in the idiot.— Origin of music, and its effect in early ages— how produced (to the middle of 10th Stanza).— The mind recalled to sounds acting casually and severally.—Wish uttered (11th Stanza) that these could be united into a scheme or system for moral interests and intellectual contemplation.—(Stanza 12th.)—The Pythagorean theory of numbers and music, with their supposed power over the motions of the universe—imaginations consonant with such a theory.—Wish expressed (in 11th Stanza) realized, in some degree, by the representation of all sounds under the form of thanksgiving to the Creator. —(Last Stanza) the destruction of earth and the planetary system—the survival of audible harmony, and its support in the Divine Nature, as revealed in Holy Writ.

I.

THY functions are ethereal,
As if within thee dwelt a glancing mind,
Organ of vision! And a Spirit aërial
Informs the cell of Hearing, dark and blind;
Intricate labyrinth, more dread for thought
To enter than oracular cave;   6
Strict passage, through which sighs are
     brought,
And whispers for the heart, their slave;
And shrieks, that revel in abuse
Of shivering flesh; and warbled air,   10
Whose piercing sweetness can unloose
The chains of frenzy, or entice a smile
Into the ambush of despair;
Hosannas pealing down the long-drawn
     aisle,
And requiems answered by the pulse that
     beats   15
Devoutly, in life's last retreats!

II.

The headlong streams and fountains
Serve Thee, invisible Spirit, with untired
     powers;
Cheering the wakeful tent on Syrian
     mountains,
They lull perchance ten thousand thousand flowers.
That roar, the prowling lion's *Here I am*,   20
How fearful to the desert wide!
That bleat, how tender! of the dam
Calling a straggler to her side.

Shout, cuckoo!—let the vernal soul   25
Go with thee to the frozen zone;
Toll from thy loftiest perch, lone bell-
   bird, toll!
At the still hour to Mercy dear,
Mercy from her twilight throne
Listening to nun's faint throb of holy
   fear,   30
To sailor's prayer breathed from a darken-
   ing sea,
Or widow's cottage-lullaby.

III.

Ye Voices, and ye Shadows
And Images of voice—to hound and horn
From rocky steep and rock-bestudded
   meadows   35
Flung back, and, in the sky's blue caves,
   reborn—
On with your pastime! till the church-
   tower bells
A greeting give of measured glee;
And milder echoes from their cells
Repeat the bridal symphony.   40
Then, or far earlier, let us rove
Where mists are breaking up or gone,
And from aloft look down into a cove
Besprinkled with a careless quire,
Happy milk-maids, one by one   45
Scattering a ditty each to her desire,
A liquid concert matchless by nice Art,
A stream as if from one full heart.

IV.

Blest be the song that brightens
The blind man's gloom, exalts the vete-
   ran's mirth;   50
Unscorned the peasant's whistling breath,
   that lightens
His duteous toil of furrowing the green
   earth.
For the tired slave, Song lifts the languid
   oar,
And bids it aptly fall, with chime
That beautifies the fairest shore,   55
And mitigates the harshest clime.
Yon pilgrims see—in lagging file
They move; but soon the appointed way
A choral *Ave Marie* shall beguile,
And to their hope the distant shrine   60

Glisten with a livelier ray:
Nor friendless he, the prisoner of the
   mine,
Who from the well-spring of his own
   clear breast
Can draw, and sing his griefs to rest.

V.

When civic renovation   65
Dawns on a kingdom, and for needful
   haste
Best eloquence avails not, Inspiration
Mounts with a tune, that travels like a
   blast
Piping through cave and battlemented
   tower;
Then starts the sluggard, pleased to meet
That voice of Freedom, in its power   71
Of promises, shrill, wild, and sweet!
Who, from a martial *pageant*, spreads
Incitements of a battle-day,
Thrilling the unweaponed crowd with
   plumeless heads?—   75
Even She whose Lydian airs inspire
Peaceful striving, gentle play
Of timid hope and innocent desire
Shot from the dancing Graces, as they
   move
Fanned by the plausive wings of Love. 80

VI.

How oft along thy mazes,
Regent of sound, have dangerous Passions
   trod!
O Thou, through whom the temple rings
   with praises,
And blackening clouds in thunder speak
   of God,
Betray not by the cozenage of sense   85
Thy votaries, wooingly resigned
To a voluptuous influence
That taints the purer, better, mind;
But lead sick Fancy to a harp
That hath in noble tasks been tried;   90
And, if the virtuous feel a pang too sharp,
Soothe it into patience—stay
The uplifted arm of Suicide;
And let some mood of thine in firm array
Knit every thought the impending issue
   needs,   95
Ere martyr burns, or patriot bleeds!

VII.

As Conscience, to the centre
Of being, smites with irresistible pain,
So shall a solemn cadence, if it enter
The mouldy vaults of the dull idiot's
brain,   100
Transmute him to a wretch from quiet
hurled—
Convulsed as by a jarring din;
And then aghast, as at the world
Of reason partially let in
By concords winding with a sway   105
Terrible for sense and soul!
Or awed he weeps, struggling to quell
dismay.
Point not these mysteries to an Art
Lodged above the starry pole;
Pure modulations flowing from the heart
Of divine Love, where Wisdom, Beauty,
Truth   111
With Order dwell, in endless youth?

VIII.

Oblivion may not cover
All treasures hoarded by the miser, Time.
Orphean Insight! truth's undaunted
lover,   115
To the first leagues of tutored passion
climb,
When Music deigned within this grosser
sphere
Her subtle essence to enfold,
And voice and shell drew forth a tear
Softer than Nature's self could mould. 120
Yet strenuous was the infant Age:
Art, daring because souls could feel,
Stirred nowhere but an urgent equipage
Of rapt imagination sped her march
Through the realms of woe and weal: 125
Hell to the lyre bowed low; the upper
arch
Rejoiced that clamorous spell and magic
verse
Her wan disasters could disperse.

IX.

The GIFT to king Amphion
That walled a city with its melody   130
Was for belief no dream:—thy skill,
Arion!

Could humanize the creatures of the sea,
Where men were monsters.   A last grace
he craves,
Leave for one chant;—the dulcet sound
Steals from the deck o'er willing waves,
And listening dolphins gather round. 136
Self-cast, as with a desperate course,
'Mid that strange audience, he bestrides
A proud One docile as a managed horse;
And singing, while the accordant hand
Sweeps his harp, the Master rides;   141
So shall he touch at length a friendly
strand,
And he, with his preserver, shine star-
bright
In memory, through silent night.

X.

The pipe of Pan, to shepherds   145
Couched in the shadow of Mænalian
pines,
Was passing sweet; the eyeballs of the
leopards,
That in high triumph drew the Lord of
vines,
How did they sparkle to the cymbal's
clang!
While Fauns and Satyrs beat the ground
In cadence,—and Silenus swang   151
This way and that, with wild-flowers
crowned.
To life, to life give back thine ear:
Ye who are longing to be rid
Of fable, though to truth subservient,
hear   155
The little sprinkling of cold earth that fell
Echoed from the coffin-lid;
The convict's summons in the steeple's
knell;
"The vain distress-gun," from a leeward
shore,
Repeated—heard, and heard no more! 160

XI.

For terror, joy, or pity,
Vast is the compass and the swell of
notes:
From the babe's first cry to voice of regal
city,
Rolling a solemn sea-like bass, that floats

Far as the woodlands—with the trill to
    blend   165
Of that shy songstress, whose love-tale
Might tempt an angel to descend,
While hovering o'er the moonlight vale.
Ye wandering Utterances, has earth no
    scheme,
No scale of moral music—to unite   170
Powers that survive but in the faintest
    dream
Of memory?—O that ye might stoop to bear
Chains, such precious chains of sight
As laboured minstrelsies through ages
    wear!
O for a balance fit the truth to tell   175
Of the Unsubstantial, pondered well!

XII.

By one pervading spirit
Of tones and numbers all things are con-
    trolled,
As sages taught, where faith was found
    to merit
Initiation in that mystery old.   180
The heavens, whose aspect makes our
    minds as still
As they themselves appear to be,
Innumerable voices fill
With everlasting harmony;
The towering headlands, crowned with
    mist,   185
Their feet among the billows, know
That Ocean is a mighty harmonist;
Thy pinions, universal Air,
Ever waving to and fro,
Are delegates of harmony, and bear   190
Strains that support the Seasons in their
    round;
Stern Winter loves a dirge-like sound.

XIII.

Break forth into thanksgiving,
Ye banded instruments of wind and
    chords;

Unite, to magnify the Ever-living,   195
Your inarticulate notes with the voice of
    words!
Nor hushed be service from the lowing
    mead,
Nor mute the forest hum of noon;
Thou too be heard, lone eagle! freed
From snowy peak and cloud, attune   200
Thy hungry barkings to the hymn
Of joy, that from her utmost walls
The six-days' Work by flaming Sera-
    phim
Transmits to Heaven! As Deep to Deep
Shouting through one valley calls,   205
All worlds, all natures, mood and mea-
    sure keep
For praise and ceaseless gratulation,
    poured
Into the ear of God, their Lord!

XIV.

A Voice to Light gave Being;
To Time, and Man his earth-born chro-
    nicler;   210
A Voice shall finish doubt and dim fore-
    seeing,
And sweep away life's visionary stir;
The trumpet (we, intoxicate with pride,
Arm at its blast for deadly wars)
To archangelic lips applied,   215
The grave shall open, quench the stars.
O Silence! are Man's noisy years
No more than moments of thy life?
Is Harmony, blest queen of smiles and
    tears,
With her smooth tones and discords just,
Tempered into rapturous strife,   221
Thy destined bond-slave? No! though
    earth be dust
And vanish, though the heavens dissolve,
    her stay
Is in the WORD, that shall not pass
    away.

Peter Bell,

A TALE.

[Composed 1798.—Published 1819.]

"What's in a *Name?*"
"Brutus will start a Spirit as soon as Cæsar!"

TO ROBERT SOUTHEY, Esq., P.L.,
ETC., ETC.

MY DEAR FRIEND,

The Tale of Peter Bell, which I now introduce to your notice, and to that of the Public, has, in its Manuscript state, nearly survived its *minority*:—for it first saw the light in the summer of 1798. During this long interval, pains have been taken at different times to make the production less unworthy of a favourable reception; or rather to fit it for filling *permanently* a station, however humble, in the Literature of our Country. This has, indeed, been the aim of all my endeavours in Poetry, which, you know, have been sufficiently laborious to prove that I deem the Art not lightly to be approached; and that the attainment of excellence in it may laudably be made the principal object of intellectual pursuit by any man, who, with reasonable consideration of circumstances, has faith in his own impulses.

The Poem of Peter Bell, as the Prologue will show, was composed under a belief that the Imagination not only does not require for its exercise the intervention of supernatural agency, but that, though such agency be excluded, the faculty may be called forth as imperiously, and for kindred results of pleasure, by incidents within the compass of poetic probability, in the humblest departments of daily life. Since that Prologue was written, *you* have exhibited most splendid effects of judicious daring in the opposite and usual course. Let this acknowledgment make my peace with the lovers of the supernatural; and I am persuaded it will be admitted that to you, as a Master in that province of the art, the following Tale, whether from contrast or congruity, is not an unappropriate offering. Accept it, then, as a public testimony of affectionate admiration from one with whose name yours has been often coupled (to use your own words) for evil and for good; and believe me to be, with earnest wishes that life and health may be granted you to complete the many important works in which you are engaged, and with high respect,

Most faithfully yours,

WILLIAM WORDSWORTH.

RYDAL MOUNT,
April 7, 1819.

PROLOGUE.

THERE'S something in a flying horse,
There's something in a huge balloon;
But through the clouds I'll never float
Until I have a little Boat,
Shaped like the crescent-moon.   5

And now I *have* a little Boat,
In shape a very crescent-moon:
Fast through the clouds my Boat can sail;
But if perchance your faith should fail,
Look up—and you shall see me soon!   10

The woods, my Friends, are round you roaring,
Rocking and roaring like a sea;
The noise of danger's in your ears,
And ye have all a thousand fears
Both for my little Boat and me!   15

Meanwhile untroubled I admire
The pointed horns of my canoe;
And, did not pity touch my breast
To see how ye are all distrest,
Till my ribs ached I'd laugh at you!   20

Away we go, my Boat and I—
Frail man ne'er sate in such another;
Whether among the winds we strive,
Or deep into the clouds we dive,
Each is contented with the other.   25

Away we go—and what care we
For treasons, tumults, and for wars?
We are as calm in our delight
As is the crescent-moon so bright
Among the scattered stars.   30

Up goes my Boat among the stars
Through many a breathless field of light,
Through many a long blue field of ether,
Leaving ten thousand stars beneath her:
Up goes my little Boat so bright!   35

The Crab, the Scorpion, and the Bull—
We pry among them all; have shot

High o'er the red-haired race of Mars,
Covered from top to toe with scars;
Such company I like it not! 40

The towns in Saturn are decayed,
And melancholy Spectres throng them;—
The Pleiads, that appear to kiss
Each other in the vast abyss,
With joy I sail among them. 45

Swift Mercury resounds with mirth,
Great Jove is full of stately bowers;
But these, and all that they contain,
What are they to that tiny grain,
That little Earth of ours? 50

Then back to Earth, the dear green Earth:—
Whole ages if I here should roam,
The world for my remarks and me
Would not a whit the better be;
I've left my heart at home. 55

See! there she is, the matchless Earth!
There spreads the famed Pacific Ocean!
Old Andes thrusts yon craggy spear
Through the grey clouds; the Alps are here,
Like waters in commotion! 60

Yon tawny slip is Libya's sands;
That silver thread the river Dnieper;
And look, where clothed in brightest green
Is a sweet Isle, of isles the Queen;
Ye fairies, from all evil keep her! 65

And see the town where I was born!
Around those happy fields we span
In boyish gambols;—I was lost
Where I have been, but on this coast
I feel I am a man. 70

Never did fifty things at once
Appear so lovely, never, never;—
How tunefully the forests ring!
To hear the earth's soft murmuring
Thus could I hang for ever! 75

"Shame on you!" cried my little Boat,
"Was ever such a homesick Loon,
Within a living Boat to sit,
And make no better use of it;
A Boat twin-sister of the crescent-moon!

"Ne'er in the breast of full-grown Poet
Fluttered so faint a heart before;—
Was it the music of the spheres
That overpowered your mortal ears?
—Such din shall trouble them no more. 85

"These nether precincts do not lack
Charms of their own;—then come with
me,
I want a comrade, and for you
There's nothing that I would not do;
Nought is there that you shall not see. 90

"Haste! and above Siberian snows
We'll sport amid the boreal morning;
Will mingle with her lustres gliding
Among the stars, the stars now hiding,
And now the stars adorning. 95

"I know the secrets of a land
Where human foot did never stray;
Fair is that land as evening skies,
And cool, though in the depth it lies
Of burning Africa. 100

"Or we'll into the realm of Faery,
Among the lovely shades of things;
The shadowy forms of mountains bare,
And streams, and bowers, and ladies fair,
The shades of palaces and kings! 105

"Or, if you thirst with hardy zeal
Less quiet regions to explore,
Prompt voyage shall to you reveal
How earth and heaven are taught to feel
The might of magic lore!" 110

"My little vagrant Form of light,
My gay and beautiful Canoe,
Well have you played your friendly part;
As kindly take what from my heart
Experience forces—then adieu! 115

"Temptation lurks among your words;
But, while these pleasures you're pur-
suing
Without impediment or let,
No wonder if you quite forget
What on the earth is doing. 120

"There was a time when all mankind
Did listen with a faith sincere
To tuneful tongues in mystery versed;
Then Poets fearlessly rehearsed
The wonders of a wild career. 125

"Go—(but the world's a sleepy world,
And 'tis, I fear, an age too late)
Take with you some ambitious Youth!
For, restless Wanderer! I, in truth,
Am all unfit to be your mate. 130

"Long have I loved what I behold,
The night that calms, the day that cheers;
The common growth of mother-earth
Suffices me—her tears, her mirth,
Her humblest mirth and tears.   135

"The dragon's wing, the magic ring,
I shall not covet for my dower,
If I along that lowly way
With sympathetic heart may stray,
And with a soul of power.   140

"These given, what more need I desire
To stir, to soothe, or elevate?
What nobler marvels than the mind
May in life's daily prospect find,
May find or there create?   145

" A potent wand doth Sorrow wield;
What spell so strong as guilty Fear!
Repentance is a tender Sprite;
If aught on earth have heavenly might,
'Tis lodged within her silent tear.   150

"But grant my wishes,—let us now
Descend from this ethereal height;
Then take thy way, adventurous Skiff,
More daring far than Hippogriff,
And be thy own delight!   155

"To the stone-table in my garden,
Loved haunt of many a summer hour,
The Squire is come: his daughter Bess
Beside him in the cool recess
Sits blooming like a flower.   160

"With these are many more convened;
They know not I have been so far;—
I see them there, in number nine,
Beneath the spreading Weymouth-pine!
I see them—there they are!   165

" There sits the Vicar and his Dame;
And there my good friend, Stephen Otter;
And, ere the light of evening fail,
To them I must relate the Tale
Of Peter Bell the Potter."   170

Off flew the Boat—away she flees,
Spurning her freight with indignation!
And I, as well as I was able,
On two poor legs, toward my stone-table
Limped on with sore vexation.   175

"O, here he is!" cried little Bess—
She saw me at the garden-door;
"We've waited anxiously and long,"
They cried, and all around me throng,
Full nine of them or more!   180

"Reproach me not—your fears be still—
Be thankful we again have met;—
Resume, my Friends! within the shade
Your seats, and quickly shall be paid
The well-remembered debt."   185

I spake with faltering voice, like one
Not wholly rescued from the pale
Of a wild dream, or worse illusion;
But straight, to cover my confusion,
Began the promised Tale.   190

PART FIRST.

ALL by the moonlight river-side
Groaned the poor Beast—alas! in vain;
The staff was raised to loftier height,
And the blows fell with heavier weight
As Peter struck—and struck again.   195

"Hold!" cried the Squire, "against the
    rules
Of common sense you're surely sinning;
This leap is for us all too bold;
Who Peter was, let that be told,
And start from the beginning."   200

——"A Potter,[1] Sir, he was by trade,"
Said I, becoming quite collected;
"And wheresoever he appeared,
Full twenty times was Peter feared
For once that Peter was respected.   205

"He, two-and-thirty years or more,
Had been a wild and woodland rover;
Had heard the Atlantic surges roar
On farthest Cornwall's rocky shore,
And trod the cliffs of Dover.   210

"And he had seen Caernarvon's towers,
And well he knew the spire of Sarum;
And he had been where Lincoln bell
Flings o'er the fen that ponderous knell—
A far-renowned alarum!   215

---

[1] In the dialect of the North, a hawker of earthenware is thus designated.

"At Doncaster, at York, and Leeds,
And merry Carlisle had he been;
And all along the Lowlands fair,
All through the bonny shire of Ayr;
And far as Aberdeen.   220

"And he had been at Inverness;
And Peter, by the mountain-rills,
Had danced his round with Highland
          lasses;
And he had lain beside his asses
On lofty Cheviot Hills: 225

"And he had trudged through Yorkshire
          dales,
Among the rocks and winding *scars;*
Where deep and low the hamlets lie
Beneath their little patch of sky
And little lot of stars: 230

"And all along the indented coast,
Bespattered with the salt-sea foam;
Where'er a knot of houses lay
On headland, or in hollow bay;—
Sure never man like him did roam!   235

"As well might Peter in the Fleet
Have been fast bound, a begging debtor;—
He travelled here, he travelled there;—
But not the value of a hair
Was heart or head the better.   240

"He roved among the vales and streams,
In the green wood and hollow dell;
They were his dwellings night and day,—
But nature ne'er could find the way
Into the heart of Peter Bell.   245

"In vain, through every changeful year,
Did Nature lead him as before;
A primrose by a river's brim
A yellow primrose was to him,
And it was nothing more.   250

"Small change it made in Peter's heart
To see his gentle panniered train
With more than vernal pleasure feeding,
Where'er the tender grass was leading
Its earliest green along the lane.   255

"In vain, through water, earth, and air,
The soul of happy sound was spread,
When Peter on some April morn,
Beneath the broom or budding thorn,
Made the warm earth his lazy bed.   260

"At noon, when, by the forest's edge
He lay beneath the branches high,
The soft blue sky did never melt
Into his heart; he never felt
The witchery of the soft blue sky!   265

"On a fair prospect some have looked
And felt, as I have heard them say,
As if the moving time had been
A thing as steadfast as the scene
On which they gazed themselves away.

"Within the breast of Peter Bell   271
These silent raptures found no place;
He was a Carl as wild and rude
As ever hue-and-cry pursued,
As ever ran a felon's race.   275

"Of all that lead a lawless life,
Of all that love their lawless lives,
In city or in village small,
He was the wildest far of all;—
He had a dozen wedded wives.   280

"Nay, start not!—wedded wives—and
          twelve!
But how one wife could e'er come near him,
In simple truth I cannot tell;
For, be it said of Peter Bell,
To see him was to fear him.   285

"Though Nature could not touch his heart
By lovely forms, and silent weather,
And tender sounds, yet you might see
At once that Peter Bell and she
Had often been together.   290

"A savage wildness round him hung
As of a dweller out of doors;
In his whole figure and his mien
A savage character was seen
Of mountains and of dreary moors.   295

"To all the unshaped half-human thoughts
Which solitary Nature feeds
'Mid summer storms or winter's ice,
Had Peter joined whatever vice
The cruel city breeds.   300

"His face was keen as is the wind
That cuts along the hawthorn-fence;
Of courage you saw little there,
But, in its stead, a medley air
Of cunning and of impudence.   305

"He had a dark and sidelong walk,
And long and slouching was his gait;
Beneath his looks so bare and bold,
You might perceive, his spirit cold
Was playing with some inward bait. 310

"His forehead wrinkled was and furred;
A work, one half of which was done
By thinking of his 'whens' and 'hows;'
And half, by knitting of his brows
Beneath the glaring sun. 315

"There was a hardness in his cheek,
There was a hardness in his eye,
As if the man had fixed his face,
In many a solitary place,
Against the wind and open sky!" 320

———

ONE NIGHT, (and now, my little Bess!
We've reached at last the promised Tale;)
One beautiful November night,
When the full moon was shining bright
Upon the rapid river Swale, 325

Along the river's winding banks
Peter was travelling all alone;—
Whether to buy or sell, or led
By pleasure running in his head,
To me was never known 770

He trudged along through copse and
    brake
He trudged along o'er hill and dale;
Nor for the moon cared he a tittle,
And for the stars he cared as little,
And for the murmuring river Swale. 335

But, chancing to espy a path
That promised to cut short the way;
As many a wiser man hath done,
He left a trusty guide for one
That might his steps betray. 340

To a thick wood he soon is brought
Where cheerily his course he weaves,
And whistling loud may yet be heard,
Though often buried like a bird
Darkling, among the boughs and leaves.

But quickly Peter's mood is changed, 346
And on he drives with cheeks that burn
In downright fury and in wrath;—
There's little sign the treacherous path
Will to the road return! 350

The path grows dim, and dimmer still;
Now up, now down, the Rover wends,
With all the sail that he can carry,
Till brought to a deserted quarry—
And there the pathway ends. 355

He paused—for shadows of strange shape,
Massy and black, before him lay;
But through the dark, and through the
    cold,
And through the yawning fissures old,
Did Peter boldly press his way 360

Right through the quarry;—and behold
A scene of soft and lovely hue!
Where blue and grey, and tender green,
Together make as sweet a scene
As ever human eye did view. 365

Beneath the clear blue sky he saw
A little field of meadow ground;
But field or meadow name it not;
Call it of earth a small green plot,
With rocks encompassed round. 370

The Swale flowed under the grey rocks,
But he flowed quiet and unseen:—
You need a strong and stormy gale
To bring the noises of the Swale
To that green spot, so calm and green!

And is there no one dwelling here, 376
No hermit with his beads and glass?
And does no little cottage look
Upon this soft and fertile nook?
Does no one live near this green grass?

Across the deep and quiet spot 381
Is Peter driving through the grass—
And now has reached the skirting trees;
When, turning round his head, he sees
A solitary Ass. 385

"A prize!" cries Peter—but he first
Must spy about him far and near:
There's not a single house in sight,
No woodman's hut, no cottage light—
Peter, you need not fear! 390

There's nothing to be seen but woods,
And rocks that spread a hoary gleam,
And this one Beast, that from the bed
Of the green meadow hangs his head
Over the silent stream. 395

His head is with a halter bound;
The halter seizing, Peter leapt
Upon the Creature's back, and plied
With ready heels his shaggy side;
But still the Ass his station kept.   400

Then Peter gave a sudden jerk,
A jerk that from a dungeon-floor
Would have pulled up an iron ring;
But still the heavy-headed Thing
Stood just as he had stood before!   405

Quoth Peter, leaping from his seat,
"There is some plot against me laid;"
Once more the little meadow-ground
And all the hoary cliffs around
He cautiously surveyed.   410

All, all is silent—rocks and woods,
All still and silent—far and near!
Only the Ass, with motion dull,
Upon the pivot of his skull
Turns round his long left ear.   415

Thought Peter, What can mean all this?
Some ugly witchcraft must be here!
—Once more the Ass, with motion dull,
Upon the pivot of his skull
Turned round his long left ear.   420

Suspicion ripened into dread;
Yet, with deliberate action slow,
His staff high-raising, in the pride
Of skill, upon the sounding hide
He dealt a sturdy blow.   425

The poor Ass staggered with the shock;
And then, as if to take his ease,
In quiet uncomplaining mood,
Upon the spot where he had stood,
Dropped gently down upon his knees;   430

As gently on his side he fell;
And by the river's brink did lie;
And, while he lay like one that mourned,
The patient Beast on Peter turned
His shining hazel eye.   435

'Twas but one mild, reproachful look,
A look more tender than severe;
And straight in sorrow, not in dread,
He turned the eye-ball in his head
Towards the smooth river deep and
          clear.   440

Upon the Beast the sapling rings;
His lank sides heaved, his limbs they
          stirred;
He gave a groan, and then another,
Of that which went before the brother,
And then he gave a third.   445

All by the moonlight river side
He gave three miserable groans;
And not till now hath Peter seen
How gaunt the Creature is,—how lean
And sharp his staring bones!   450

With legs stretched out and stiff he lay:—
No word of kind commiseration
Fell at the sight from Peter's tongue;
With hard contempt his heart was wrung,
With hatred and vexation.   455

The meagre beast lay still as death;
And Peter's lips with fury quiver;
Quoth he, "You little mulish dog,
I'll fling your carcass like a log
Head-foremost down the river!"   460

An impious oath confirmed the threat—
Whereat from the earth on which he lay
To all the echoes, south and north,
And east and west, the Ass sent forth
A long and clamorous bray!   465

This outcry, on the heart of Peter,
Seems like a note of joy to strike,—
Joy at the heart of Peter knocks;
But in the echo of the rocks
Was something Peter did not like.   470

Whether to cheer his coward breast,
Or that he could not break the chain,
In this serene and solemn hour,
Twined round him by demoniac power,
To the blind work he turned again.   475

Among the rocks and winding crags;
Among the mountains far away;
Once more the Ass did lengthen out
More ruefully a deep-drawn shout,
The hard dry see-saw of his horrible bray!

What is there now in Peter's heart!   481
Or whence the might of this strange sound?
The moon uneasy looked and dimmer,
The broad blue heavens appeared to
          glimmer,
And the rocks staggered all around—   485

From Peter's hand the sapling dropped!
Threat has he none to execute;
"If any one should come and see
That I am here, they'll think," quoth he,
"I'm helping this poor dying brute." 490

He scans the Ass from limb to limb,
And ventures now to uplift his eyes;
More steady looks the moon, and clear,
More like themselves the rocks appear
And touch more quiet skies. 495

His scorn returns—his hate revives;
He stoops the Ass's neck to seize
With malice—that again takes flight;
For in the pool a startling sight
Meets him, among the inverted trees. 500

Is it the moon's distorted face?
The ghost-like image of a cloud?
Is it a gallows there portrayed?
Is Peter of himself afraid?
Is it a coffin,—or a shroud? 505

A grisly idol hewn in stone?
Or imp from witch's lap let fall?
Perhaps a ring of shining fairies?
Such as pursue their feared vagaries
In sylvan bower, or haunted hall? 510

Is it a fiend that to a stake
Of fire his desperate self is tethering?
Or stubborn spirit doomed to yell
In solitary ward or cell,
Ten thousand miles from all his brethren?

Never did pulse so quickly throb, 516
And never heart so loudly panted;
He looks, he cannot choose but look;
Like some one reading in a book—
A book that is enchanted. 520

Ah, well-a-day for Peter Bell!
He will be turned to iron soon,
Meet Statue for the court of Fear!
His hat is up—and every hair
Bristles, and whitens in the moon! 525

He looks, he ponders, looks again;
He sees a motion—hears a groan;
His eyes will burst—his heart will break—
He gives a loud and frightful shriek,
And back he falls, as if his life were flown!

PART SECOND.

We left our Hero in a trance, 531
Beneath the alders, near the river;
The Ass is by the river-side,
And, where the feeble breezes glide,
Upon the stream the moonbeams quiver.

A happy respite! but at length 536
He feels the glimmering of the moon;
Wakes with glazed eye, and feebly
sighing—
To sink, perhaps, where he is lying,
Into a second swoon! 540

He lifts his head, he sees his staff;
He touches—'tis to him a treasure!
Faint recollection seems to tell
That he is yet where mortals dwell—
A thought received with languid pleasure!

His head upon his elbow propped, 546
Becoming less and less perplexed,
Sky-ward he looks—to rock and wood—
And then—upon the glassy flood
His wandering eye is fixed. 550

Thought he, that is the face of one
In his last sleep securely bound!
So toward the stream his head he bent,
And downward thrust his staff, intent
The river's depth to sound. 555

Now—like a tempest-shattered bark,
That overwhelmed and prostrate lies,
And in a moment to the verge
Is lifted of a foaming surge—
Full suddenly the Ass doth rise! 560

His staring bones all shake with joy,
And close by Peter's side he stands:
While Peter o'er the river bends,
The little Ass his neck extends,
And fondly licks his hands. 565

Such life is in the Ass's eyes,
Such life is in his limbs and ears;
That Peter Bell, if he had been
The veriest coward ever seen,
Must now have thrown aside his fears. 570

The Ass looks on—and to his work
Is Peter quietly resigned;
He touches here—he touches there—
And now among the dead man's hair
His sapling Peter has entwined. 575

He pulls—and looks—and pulls again;
And he whom the poor Ass had lost,
The man who had been four days dead,
Head-foremost from the river's bed
Uprises like a ghost!   580

And Peter draws him to dry land;
And through the brain of Peter pass
Some poignant twitches, fast and faster;
"No doubt," quoth he, "he is the Master
Of this poor miserable Ass!"   585

The meagre shadow that looks on—
What would he now? what is he doing?
His sudden fit of joy is flown,—
He on his knees hath laid him down,
As if he were his grief renewing;   590

But no—that Peter on his back
Must mount, he shows well as he can:
Thought Peter then, come weal or woe,
I'll do what he would have me do,
In pity to this poor drowned man.   595

With that resolve he boldly mounts
Upon the pleased and thankful Ass;
And then, without a moment's stay,
That earnest Creature turned away,
Leaving the body on the grass.   600

Intent upon his faithful watch,
The Beast four days and nights had past;
A sweeter meadow ne'er was seen,
And there the Ass four days had been,
Nor ever once did break his fast: 605

Yet firm his step, and stout his heart;
The mead is crossed—the quarry's mouth
Is reached; but there the trusty guide
Into a thicket turns aside,
And deftly ambles towards the south. 610

When hark a burst of doleful sound!
And Peter honestly might say,
The like came never to his ears,
Though he has been, full thirty years,
A rover—night and day!   615

'Tis not a plover of the moors,
'Tis not a bittern of the fen;
Nor can it be a barking fox,
Nor night-bird chambered in the rocks,
Nor wild-cat in a woody glen!   620

The Ass is startled—and stops short
Right in the middle of the thicket;
And Peter, wont to whistle loud
Whether alone or in a crowd,
Is silent as a silent cricket.   625

What ails you now, my little Bess?
Well may you tremble and look grave!
This cry—that rings along the wood,
This cry—that floats adown the flood,
Comes from the entrance of a cave: 630

I see a blooming Wood-boy there,
And if I had the power to say
How sorrowful the wanderer is,
Your heart would be as sad as his
Till you had kissed his tears away!   635

Grasping a hawthorn branch in hand,
All bright with berries ripe and red,
Into the cavern's mouth he peeps;
Thence back into the moonlight creeps;
Whom seeks he—whom?—the silent
    dead: 640

His father!—Him doth he require—
Him hath he sought with fruitless pains,
Among the rocks, behind the trees;
Now creeping on his hands and knees,
Now running o'er the open plains.   645

And hither is he come at last,
When he through such a day has gone,
By this dark cave to be distrest
Like a poor bird—her plundered nest
Hovering around with dolorous moan! 650

Of that intense and piercing cry
The listening Ass conjectures well;
Wild as it is, he there can read
Some intermingled notes that plead
With touches irresistible.   655

But Peter—when he saw the Ass
Not only stop but turn, and change
The cherished tenor of his pace
That lamentable cry to chase—
It wrought in him conviction strange; 660

A faith that for the dead man's sake,
And this poor slave who loved him well,
Vengeance upon his head will fall,
Some visitation worse than all
Which ever till this night befell.   665

Meanwhile the Ass to reach his home
Is striving stoutly as he may ;
But, while he climbs the woody hill,
The cry grows weak—and weaker still ;
And now at last it dies away. 670

So with his freight the Creature turns
Into a gloomy grove of beech,
Along the shade with footsteps true
Descending slowly, till the two
The open moonlight reach. 675

And there, along the narrow dell,
A fair smooth pathway you discern,
A length of green and open road—
As if it from a fountain flowed—
Winding away between the fern. 680

The rocks that tower on either side
Build up a wild fantastic scene ;
Temples like those among the Hindoos,
And mosques, and spires, and abbey-win-
  dows,
And castles all with ivy green ! 685

And while the Ass pursues his way
Along this solitary dell,
As pensively his steps advance,
The mosques and spires change counte-
  nance,
And look at Peter Bell ! 690

That unintelligible cry
Hath left him high in preparation,—
Convinced that he, or soon or late,
This very night will meet his fate—
And so he sits in expectation ! 695

The strenuous Animal hath clomb
With the green path ; and now he wends
Where, shining like the smoothest sea,
In undisturbed immensity
A level plain extends. 700

But whence this faintly-rustling sound
By which the journeying pair are chased?
—A withered leaf is close behind,
Light plaything for the sportive wind
Upon that solitary waste. 705

When Peter spied the moving thing,
It only doubled his distress ;
"Where there is not a bush or tree,
The very leaves they follow me—
So huge hath been my wickedness !" 710

To a close lane they now are come,
Where, as before, the enduring Ass
Moves on without a moment's stop,
Nor once turns round his head to crop
A bramble-leaf or blade of grass. 715

Between the hedges as they go,
The white dust sleeps upon the lane ;
And Peter, ever and anon
Back-looking, sees, upon a stone,
Or in the dust, a crimson stain. 720

A stain—as of a drop of blood
By moonlight made more faint and wan ;
Ha ! why these sinkings of despair ?
He knows not how the blood comes there—
And Peter is a wicked man. 725

At length he spies a bleeding wound,
Where he had struck the Ass's head ;
He sees the blood, knows what it is,—
A glimpse of sudden joy was his,
But then it quickly fled ; 730

Of him whom sudden death had seized
He thought,—of thee, O faithful Ass !
And once again those ghastly pains,
Shoot to and fro through heart and reins,
And through his brain like lightning
  pass. 735

PART THIRD.

I 've heard of one, a gentle Soul,
Though given to sadness and to gloom,
And for the fact will vouch,—one night
It chanced that by a taper's light
This man was reading in his room ; 740

Bending, as you or I might bend
At night o'er any pious book,
When sudden blackness overspread
The snow-white page on which he read,
And made the good man round him look.

The chamber walls were dark all round,—
And to his book he turned again ;
—The light had left the lonely taper,
And formed itself upon the paper
Into large letters—bright and plain ! 750

The godly book was in his hand—
And on the page, more black than coal,
Appeared, set forth in strange array,
A *word*—which to his dying day
Perplexed the good man's gentle soul. 755

The ghostly word, thus plainly seen,
Did never from his lips depart;
But he hath said, poor gentle wight!
It brought full many a sin to light
Out of the bottom of his heart.   760

Dread Spirits! to confound the meek
Why wander from your course so far,
Disordering colour, form, and stature!
—Let good men feel the soul of nature,
And see things as they are.   765

Yet, potent Spirits! well I know,
How ye, that play with soul and sense,
Are not unused to trouble friends
Of goodness, for most gracious ends—
And this I speak in reverence!   770

But might I give advice to you,
Whom in my fear I love so well;
From men of pensive virtue go,
Dread Beings! and your empire show
On hearts like that of Peter Bell.   775

Your presence often have I felt
In darkness and the stormy night;
And with like force, if need there be,
Ye can put forth your agency   779
When earth is calm, and heaven is bright.

Then coming from the wayward world,
That powerful world in which ye dwell,
Come, Spirits of the Mind! and try,
To-night, beneath the moonlight sky,
What may be done with Peter Bell!   785

—O, would that some more skilful voice
My further labour might prevent!
Kind Listeners, that around me sit,
I feel that I am all unfit
For such high argument.   790

I've played, I've danced, with my nar-
ration;
I loitered long ere I began:
Ye waited then on my good pleasure;
Pour out indulgence still, in measure
As liberal as ye can!   795

Our Travellers, ye remember well,
Are thridding a sequestered lane;

And Peter many tricks is trying,
And many anodynes applying,
To ease his conscience of its pain.   800

By this his heart is lighter far;
And, finding that he can account
So snugly for that crimson stain,
His evil spirit up again
Does like an empty bucket mount.   805

And Peter is a deep logician
Who hath no lack of wit mercurial;
"Blood drops—leaves rustle—yet," quoth
he,
"This poor man never but for me
Could have had Christian burial.   810

"And, say the best you can, 'tis plain,
That here has been some wicked dealing;
No doubt the devil in me wrought;
I'm not the man who could have thought
An Ass like this was worth the steal-
ing!"   815

So from his pocket Peter takes
His shining horn tobacco-box;
And in a light and careless way,
As men who with their purpose play,
Upon the lid he knocks.   820

Let them whose voice can stop the clouds,
Whose cunning eye can see the wind,
Tell to a curious world the cause
Why, making here a sudden pause,
The Ass turned round his head and *grin-
ned.*   825

Appalling process! I have marked
The like on heath, in lonely wood;
And, verily, have seldom met
A spectacle more hideous—yet
It suited Peter's present mood.   830

And, grinning in his turn, his teeth
He in jocose defiance showed—
When, to upset his spiteful mirth,
A murmur, pent within the earth,
In the dead earth beneath the road,   835

Rolled audibly!—it swept along,
A muffled noise—a rumbling sound!—
'Twas by a troop of miners made,
Plying with gunpowder their trade,
Some twenty fathoms under ground.   840

Small cause of dire effect! for, surely,
If ever mortal, King or Cotter,
Believed that earth was charged to quake
And yawn for his unworthy sake,
'Twas Peter Bell the Potter.   845

But as an oak in breathless air
Will stand though to the centre hewn;
Or as the weakest things, if frost
Have stiffened them, maintain their post;
So he, beneath the gazing moon!—   850

The Beast bestriding thus, he reached
A spot where, in a sheltering cove,
A little chapel stands alone,
With greenest ivy overgrown,
And tufted with an ivy grove;   855

Dying insensibly away
From human thoughts and purposes,
It seemed—wall, window, roof and tower—
To bow to some transforming power,
And blend with the surrounding trees. 860

As ruinous a place it was,
Thought Peter, in the shire of Fife
That served my turn, when following still
From land to land a reckless will
I married my sixth wife!   865

The unheeding Ass moves slowly on,
And now is passing by an inn
Brim-full of a carousing crew,
That make, with curses not a few,
An uproar and a drunken din.   870

I cannot well express the thoughts
Which Peter in those noises found;—
A stifling power compressed his frame,
While-as a swimming darkness came
Over that dull and dreary sound.   875

For well did Peter know the sound;
The language of those drunken joys
To him, a jovial soul, I ween,
But a few hours ago, had been
A gladsome and a welcome noise.   880

Now, turned adrift into the past,
He finds no solace in his course;
Like planet-stricken men of yore,
He trembles, smitten to the core
By strong compunction and remorse.   885

But, more than all, his heart is stung
To think of one, almost a child;
A sweet and playful Highland girl,
As light and beauteous as a squirrel,
As beauteous and as wild!   890

Her dwelling was a lonely house,
A cottage in a heathy dell;
And she put on her gown of green,
And left her mother at sixteen,
And followed Peter Bell.   895

But many good and pious thoughts
Had she; and, in the kirk to pray,
Two long Scotch miles, through rain or
      snow,
To kirk she had been used to go,
Twice every Sabbath-day.   900

And, when she followed Peter Bell,
It was to lead an honest life;
For he, with tongue not used to falter,
Had pledged his troth before the altar
To love her as his wedded wife.   905

A mother's hope is hers;—but soon
She drooped and pined like one forlorn;
From Scripture she a name did borrow;
Benoni, or the child of sorrow,
She called her babe unborn.   910

For she had learned how Peter lived,
And took it in most grievous part;
She to the very bone was worn,
And, ere that little child was born,
Died of a broken heart.   915

And now the Spirits of the Mind
Are busy with poor Peter Bell;
Upon the rights of visual sense
Usurping, with a prevalence
More terrible than magic spell.   920

Close by a brake of flowering furze
(Above it shivering aspens play)
He sees an unsubstantial creature,
His very self in form and feature,   924
Not four yards from the broad highway:

And stretched beneath the furze he sees
The Highland girl—it is no other;
And hears her crying as she cried,
The very moment that she died,
"My mother! oh my mother!"   930

The sweat pours down from Peter's face,
So grievous is his heart's contrition;
With agony his eye-balls ache
While he beholds by the furze-brake
This miserable vision!   935

Calm is the well-deserving brute,
His peace hath no offence betrayed;
But now, while down that slope he wends,
A voice to Peter's ear ascends,
Resounding from the woody glade: 940

The voice, though clamorous as a horn
Re-echoed by a naked rock,
Comes from that tabernacle—List!
Within, a fervent Methodist
Is preaching to no heedless flock!   945

"Repent! repent!" he cries aloud,
"While yet ye may find mercy;—strive
To love the Lord with all your might;
Turn to him, seek him day and night,
And save your souls alive!   950

"Repent! repent! though ye have gone,
Through paths of wickedness and woe,
After the Babylonian harlot;
And though your sins be red as scarlet,
They shall be white as snow!"   955

Even as he passed the door, these words
Did plainly come to Peter's ears;
And they such joyful tidings were,
The joy was more than he could bear!—
He melted into tears.   960

Sweet tears of hope and tenderness!
And fast they fell, a plenteous shower!
His nerves, his sinews seemed to melt;
Through all his iron frame was felt
A gentle, a relaxing, power!   965

Each fibre of his frame was weak;
Weak all the animal within;
But, in its helplessness, grew mild
And gentle as an infant child,
An infant that has known no sin.   970

'Tis said, meek Beast! that, through Hea-
        ven's grace,
He not unmoved did notice now
The cross upon thy shoulder scored,
For lasting impress, by the Lord
To whom all human-kind shall bow;   975

Memorial of his touch—that day
When Jesus humbly deigned to ride,
Entering the proud Jerusalem,
By an immeasurable stream
Of shouting people deified!   980

Meanwhile the persevering Ass
Turned towards a gate that hung in view
Across a shady lane; his chest
Against the yielding gate he pressed
And quietly passed through.   985

And up the stony lane he goes;
No ghost more softly ever trod;
Among the stones and pebbles he
Sets down his hoofs inaudibly,
As if with felt his hoofs were shod.   990

Along the lane the trusty Ass
Went twice two hundred yards or more,
And no one could have guessed his aim,—
Till to a lonely house he came,
And stopped beside the door.   995

Thought Peter, 'tis the poor man's home
He listens—not a sound is heard
Save from the trickling household rill;
But, stepping o'er the cottage-sill,
Forthwith a little Girl appeared.   1000

She to the Meeting-house was bound
In hopes some tidings there to gather:
No glimpse it is, no doubtful gleam;
She saw—and uttered with a scream,
"My father! here's my father!"   1005

The very word was plainly heard,
Heard plainly by the wretched Mother—
Her joy was like a deep affright:
And forth she rushed into the light,
And saw it was another!   1010

And instantly upon the earth,
Beneath the full moon shining bright,
Close to the Ass's feet she fell;
At the same moment Peter Bell
Dismounts in most unhappy plight.   1015

As he beheld the Woman lie
Breathless and motionless, the mind
Of Peter sadly was confused;
But, though to such demands unused,
And helpless almost as the blind,   1020

He raised her up; and while he held
Her body propped against his knee,
The Woman waked—and when she spied
The poor Ass standing by her side,
She moaned most bitterly.   1025

"Oh! God be praised—my heart's at
          ease—
For he is dead—I know it well!"
—At this she wept a bitter flood;
And, in the best way that he could,
His tale did Peter tell.   1030

He trembles—he is pale as death;
His voice is weak with perturbation;
He turns aside his head, he pauses;
Poor Peter from a thousand causes
Is crippled sore in his narration.   1035

At length she learned how he espied
The Ass in that small meadow-ground;
And that her Husband now lay dead,
Beside that luckless river's bed
In which he had been drowned.   1040

A piercing look the Widow cast
Upon the Beast that near her stands;
She sees 'tis he, that 'tis the same;
She calls the poor Ass by his name,
And wrings, and wrings her hands.   1045

"O wretched loss—untimely stroke!
If he had died upon his bed!
He knew not one forewarning pain;
He never will come home again—
Is dead, for ever dead!"   1050

Beside the Woman Peter stands;
His heart is opening more and more;
A holy sense pervades his mind;
He feels what he for human-kind
Has never felt before.   1055

At length, by Peter's arm sustained,
The Woman rises from the ground—
"Oh, mercy! something must be done,
My little Rachel, you must run,—
Some willing neighbour must be found.

"Make haste—my little Rachel—do, 1061
The first you meet with—bid him come,
Ask him to lend his horse to-night,
And this good Man whom Heaven requite,
Will help to bring the body home."   1065

Away goes Rachel weeping loud;—
An Infant, waked by her distress,
Makes in the house a piteous cry;
And Peter hears the Mother sigh,
"Seven are they, and all fatherless!"   1070

And now is Peter taught to feel
That man's heart is a holy thing;
And Nature, through a world of death,
Breathes into him a second breath,
More searching than the breath of spring.

Upon a stone the Woman sits   1076
In agony of silent grief—
From his own thoughts did Peter start;
He longs to press her to his heart,
From love that cannot find relief.   1080

But roused, as if through every limb
Had past a sudden shock of dread,
The Mother o'er the threshold flies,
And up the cottage stairs she hies,
And on the pillow lays her burning
          head.   1085

And Peter turns his steps aside
Into a shade of darksome trees,
Where he sits down, he knows not how,
With his hands pressed against his brow,
His elbows on his tremulous knees.   1090

There, self-involved, does Peter sit
Until no sign of life he makes,
As if his mind were sinking deep
Through years that have been long asleep!
The trance is passed away—he wakes;

He lifts his head—and sees the Ass   1096
Yet standing in the clear moonshine;
"When shall I be as good as thou?
Oh! would, poor beast, that I had now
A heart but half as good as thine!"   1100

But *He*—who deviously hath sought
His Father through the lonesome woods,
Hath sought, proclaiming to the ear
Of night his grief and sorrowful fear—
He comes, escaped from fields and
 floods;—   1105

With weary pace is drawing nigh;
He sees the Ass—and nothing living
Had ever such a fit of joy
As hath this little orphan Boy,
For he has no misgiving! 1110

Forth to the gentle Ass he springs,
And up about his neck he climbs;
In loving words he talks to him,
He kisses, kisses face and limb,—
He kisses him a thousand times! 1115

This Peter sees, while in the shade
He stood beside the cottage-door;

And Peter Bell, the ruffian wild,
Sobs loud, he sobs even like a child,
"Oh! God, I can endure no more!" 1120

—Here ends my Tale: for in a trice
Arrived a neighbour with his horse;
Peter went forth with him straightway;
And, with due care, ere break of day,
Together they brought back the Corse.

And many years did this poor Ass, 1126
Whom once it was my luck to see
Cropping the shrubs of Leming-Lane,
Help by his labour to maintain
The Widow and her family. 1130

And Peter Bell, who, till that night,
Had been the wildest of his clan,
Forsook his crimes, renounced his folly,
And, after ten months' melancholy,
Became a good and honest man. 1135

MISCELLANEOUS SONNETS.

DEDICATION.

TO ——.

[Composed 1826 (?).—Published 1827.]

HAPPY the feeling from the bosom thrown
In perfect shape (whose beauty Time shall spare
Though a breath made it) like a bubble blown
For summer pastime into wanton air;
Happy the thought best likened to a stone   5
Of the sea-beach, when, polished with nice care,
Veins it discovers exquisite and rare,
Which for the loss of that moist gleam atone
That tempted first to gather it.   That here,
O chief of Friends! such feelings I present   10
To thy regard, with thoughts so fortunate,
Were a vain notion; but the hope is dear
That thou, if not with partial joy elate,
Wilt smile upon this gift with more than mild
content!

PART I.

I.

[Composed ?.—Published 1807.]

NUNS fret not at their convent's narrow
room;
And hermits are contented with their
cells;
And students with their pensive citadels;
Maids at the wheel, the weaver at his
loom,
Sit blithe and happy; bees that soar for
bloom,   5
High as the highest Peak of Furness-fells,
Will murmur by the hour in foxglove
bells:
In truth the prison, unto which we doom
Ourselves, no prison is: and hence for me,
In sundry moods, 'twas pastime to be
bound   10
Within the Sonnet's scanty plot of ground;
Pleased if some Souls (for such there needs
must be)

Who have felt the weight of too much
liberty,
Should find brief solace there, as I have
found.

II.

ADMONITION.

Intended more particularly for the perusal of
those who may have happened to be enamoured
of some beautiful place of Retreat, in the Coun-
try of the Lakes.

[Composed ?.—Published 1807.]

WELL may'st thou halt—and gaze with
brightening eye!
The lovely Cottage in the guardian nook
Hath stirred thee deeply; with its own
dear brook,
Its own small pasture, almost its own sky!
But covet not the Abode; forbear to
sigh,   5
As many do, repining while they look;
Intruders—who would tear from Nature's
book
This precious leaf, with harsh impiety.
Think what the Home must be if it were
thine,
Even thine, though few thy wants!—Roof,
window, door,   10
The very flowers are sacred to the Poor,
The roses to the porch which they entwine:
Yea, all, that now enchants thee, from
the day
On which it should be touched, would
melt away.

III.

[Composed ?.—Published 1807.]

"BELOVED Vale!" I said, "when I shall
con
Those many records of my childish years,
Remembrance of myself and of my peers

Will press me down : to think of what is
    gone
Will be an awful thought, if life have
    one."   5
But, when into the Vale I came, no fears
Distressed me ; from mine eyes escaped
    no tears ;
Deep thought, or dread remembrance, had
    I none.
By doubts and thousand petty fancies crost
I stood, of simple shame the blushing
    Thrall ;   10
So narrow seemed the brooks, the fields
    so small !
A Juggler's balls old Time about him
    tossed ;
I looked, I stared, I smiled, I laughed ;
    and all
The weight of sadness was in wonder lost.

IV.

AT APPLETHWAITE, NEAR KESWICK.

[Composed 1804.—Published 1842.]

BEAUMONT ! it was thy wish that I should
    rear
A seemly Cottage in this sunny Dell,
On favoured ground, thy gift, where I
    might dwell
In neighbourhood with One to me most
    dear,
That undivided we from year to year   5
Might work in our high Calling—a bright
    hope
To which our fancies, mingling, gave free
    scope
Till checked by some necessities severe.
And should these slacken, honoured
    BEAUMONT ! still
Even then we may perhaps in vain
    implore   10
Leave of our fate thy wishes to fulfil.
Whether this boon be granted us or not,
Old Skiddaw will look down upon the Spot
With pride, the Muses love it evermore.

V.

[Composed 1801.—Published 1815.]

PELION and Ossa flourish side by side,
Together in immortal books enrolled :
His ancient dower Olympus hath not sold ;

And that inspiring Hill, which "did
    divide
Into two ample horns his forehead wide," 5
Shines with poetic radiance as of old ;
While not an English Mountain we behold
By the celestial Muses glorified.
Yet round our sea-girt shore they rise in
    crowds :
What was the great Parnassus' self to
    Thee,   10
Mount Skiddaw ? In his natural so-
    vereignty
Our British Hill is nobler far ; he shrouds
His double front among Atlantic clouds,
And pours forth streams more sweet than
    Castaly.

VI.

[Composed 1801.—Published 1820.]

THERE is a little unpretending Rill
Of limpid water, humbler far than aught
That ever among Men or Naiads sought
Notice or name !—It quivers down the
    hill,
Furrowing its shallow way with dubious
    will ;   5
Yet to my mind this scanty Stream is
    brought
Oftener than Ganges or the Nile ; a
    thought
Of private recollection sweet and still !
Months perish with their moons ; year
    treads on year ;
But, faithful Emma ! thou with me canst
    say   10
That, while ten thousand pleasures dis-
    appear,
And flies their memory fast almost as they ;
The immortal Spirit of one happy day
Lingers beside that Rill, in vision clear.

VII.

[Composed ?.—Published 1827.]

HER only pilot the soft breeze, the boat
Lingers, but Fancy is well satisfied ;
With keen-eyed Hope, with Memory, at
    her side,
And the glad Muse at liberty to note
All that to each is precious, as we float   5

Gently along; regardless who shall chide
If the heavens smile, and leave us free to
    glide,
Happy Associates breathing air remote
From trivial cares. But, Fancy and the
    Muse,
Why have I crowded this small bark with
    you   10
And others of your kind, ideal crew!
While here sits One whose brightness
    owes its hues
To flesh and blood; no Goddess from
    above,
No fleeting Spirit, but my own true Love?

VIII.

[Composed ?.—Published 1815.]

THE fairest, brightest, hues of ether fade;
The sweetest notes must terminate and
    die;
O Friend! thy flute has breathed a
    harmony
Softly resounded through this rocky glade;
Such strains of rapture as [1] the Genius
    played   5
In his still haunt on Bagdad's summit
    high;
He who stood visible to Mirza's eye,
Never before to human sight betrayed.
Lo, in the vale, the mists of evening
    spread!
The visionary Arches are not there,   10
Nor the green Islands, nor the shining
    Seas;
Yet sacred is to me this Mountain's head,
Whence I have risen, uplifted on the
    breeze
Of harmony, above all earthly care.

IX.

UPON THE SIGHT OF A BEAUTIFUL PICTURE,
Painted by Sir G. H. Beaumont, Bart.

[Composed August, 1811.—Published 1815.]

PRAISED be the Art whose subtle power
    could stay
Yon cloud, and fix it in that glorious
    shape;

----

[1] See the "Vision of Mirza" in the "Spectator."

Nor would permit the thin smoke to
    escape,
Nor those bright sunbeams to forsake the
    day;
Which stopped that band of travellers on
    their way,   5
Ere they were lost within the shady
    wood;
And showed the Bark upon the glassy
    flood
For ever anchored in her sheltering
    bay.
Soul-soothing Art! whom Morning, Noon-
    tide, Even,
Do serve with all their changeful
    pageantry;   10
Thou, with ambition modest yet sublime,
Here, for the sight of mortal man, hast
    given
To one brief moment caught from fleeting
    time
The appropriate calm of blest eternity.

X.

[Composed ?.—Published 1827.]

"WHY, Minstrel, these untuneful mur-
    murings—
Dull, flagging notes that with each other
    jar?"
"Think, gentle Lady, of a Harp so far
From its own country, and forgive the
    strings."
A simple answer! but even so forth
    springs,   5
From the Castalian fountain of the heart,
The Poetry of Life, and all *that*
    Art
Divine of words quickening insensate
    things.
From the submissive necks of guiltless
    men
Stretched on the block the glittering axe
    recoils;   10
Sun, moon, and stars, all struggle in the
    toils
Of mortal sympathy; what wonder then
That the poor Harp distempered music
    yields
To its sad Lord, far from his native
    fields?

XI.

[Composed ?.—Published 1819[1].]

AERIAL Rock—whose solitary brow
From this low threshold daily meets my
        sight;
When I step forth to hail the morning
        light;
Or quit the stars with a lingering fare-
        well—how
Shall Fancy pay to thee a grateful vow? 5
How, with the Muse's aid, her love attest?
—By planting on thy naked head the crest
Of an imperial Castle, which the plough
Of ruin shall not touch. Innocent scheme!
That doth presume no more than to sup-
        ply   10
A grace the sinuous vale and roaring
        stream
Want, through neglect of hoar Antiquity.
Rise, then, ye votive Towers! and catch a
        gleam
Of golden sunset, ere it fade and die.

XII.

TO SLEEP.

[Composed ?.—Published 1807.]

O GENTLE Sleep! do they belong to thee,
These twinklings of oblivion? Thou dost
        love
To sit in meekness, like the brooding
        Dove,
A captive never wishing to be free.
This tiresome night, O Sleep! thou art
        to me   5
A Fly, that up and down himself doth
        shove
Upon a fretful rivulet, now above,
Now on the water vexed with mockery.
I have no pain that calls for patience, no;
Hence am I cross and peevish as a
        child: 10
Am pleased by fits to have thee for my
        foe,
Yet ever willing to be reconciled:

---

[1] This, and eleven other Sonnets here marked
simply "1819," appeared in the vol. containing
The Waggoner, which was published in the
summer of 1819 shortly after *Peter Bell.*—ED.

O gentle Creature! do not use me so,
But once and deeply let me be beguiled.

XIII.

TO SLEEP.

[Composed ?.—Published 1807.]

FOND words have oft been spoken to thee,
        Sleep!
And thou hast had thy store of tenderest
        names;
The very sweetest Fancy culls or frames,
When thankfulness of heart is strong and
        deep!
Dear Bosom-child we call thee, that dost
        steep   5
In rich reward all suffering; Balm that
        tames
All anguish; Saint that evil thoughts and
        aims
Takest away, and into souls dost creep,
Like to a breeze from heaven. Shall I
        alone,
I surely not a man ungently made,   10
Call thee worst Tyrant by which Flesh is
        crost?
Perverse, self-willed to own and to disown,
Mere slave of them who never for thee
        prayed,
Still last to come where thou art wanted
        most!

XIV.

TO SLEEP.

[Composed ?.—Published 1807.]

A FLOCK of sheep that leisurely pass by,
One after one; the sound of rain, and bees
Murmuring; the fall of rivers, winds and
        seas,
Smooth fields, white sheets of water, and
        pure sky;
I have thought of all by turns, and yet
        do lie   5
Sleepless! and soon the small birds'
        melodies
Must hear, first uttered from my orchard
        trees;
And the first cuckoo's melancholy cry.
Even thus last night, and two nights
        more, I lay

And could not win thee, Sleep ! by any
    stealth: 10
So do not let me wear to-night away :
Without Thee what is all the morning's
    wealth?
Come, blessed barrier between day and day,
Dear mother of fresh thoughts and joyous
    health !

XV.

THE WILD DUCK'S NEST.

[Composed ?.—Published 1819.]

THE imperial Consort of the Fairy-king
Owns not a sylvan bower; or gorgeous cell
With emerald floored, and with purpureal
    shell
Ceilinged and roofed; that is so fair a
    thing
As this low structure, for the tasks of
    Spring   5
Prepared by one who loves the buoyant
    swell
Of the brisk waves, yet here consents to
    dwell ;
And spreads in steadfast peace her brood-
    ing wing.
Words cannot paint the o'ershadowing
    your tree bough,
And dimly-gleaming Nest,—a hollow
    crown   10
Of golden leaves inlaid with silver down,
Fine as the mother's softest plumes allow:
I gazed—and, self-accused while gazing,
    sighed
For human-kind, weak slaves of cumbrous
    pride !

XVI.

WRITTEN UPON A BLANK LEAF IN "THE
COMPLETE ANGLER."

[Composed ?.—Published 1819.]

WHILE flowing rivers yield a blameless
    sport,
Shall live the name of Walton: Sage
    benign !
Whose pen, the mysteries of the rod and
    line
Unfolding, did not fruitlessly exhort   4
To reverend watching of each still report
That Nature utters from her rural shrine.
Meek, nobly versed in simple discipline—

He found the longest summer day too
    short,
To his loved pastime given by sedgy Lee,
Or down the tempting maze of Shawford
    brook—   10
Fairer than life itself, in this sweet Book,
The cowslip-bank and shady willow-tree ;
And the fresh meads—where flowed, from
    every nook
Of his full bosom, gladsome Piety !

XVII.

TO THE POET, JOHN DYER.

[Composed 1811.—Published 1820.]

BARD of the Fleece, whose skilful genius
    made
That work a living landscape fair and
    bright ;
Nor hallowed less with musical delight
Than those soft scenes through which thy
    childhood strayed,
Those southern tracts of Cambria, "deep
    embayed,   5
With green hills fenced, with ocean's mur-
    mur lulled ;"
Though hasty Fame hath many a chaplet
    culled
For worthless brows, while in the pensive
    shade
Of cold neglect she leaves thy head un-
    graced,
Yet pure and powerful minds, hearts
    meek and still,   10
A grateful few, shall love thy modest Lay,
Long as the shepherd's bleating flock
    shall stray
O'er naked Snowdon's wide aerial waste ;
Long as the thrush shall pipe on Gron-
    gar Hill !

XVIII.

ON THE DETRACTION WHICH FOLLOWED THE
PUBLICATION OF A CERTAIN POEM.

[Composed 1820.—Published 1820.]

See Milton's Sonnet, beginning, "A Book was
    writ of late called 'Tetrachordon.'"

A BOOK came forth of late, called PETER
    BELL ;
Not negligent, the style ;—the matter?—
    good

As aught that song records of Robin
   Hood;
Or Roy, renowned through many a Scot-
   tish dell;
But some (who brook those hackneyed
   themes full well,   5
Nor heat, at Tam o' Shanter's name, their
   blood)
Waxed wroth, and with foul claws, a
   harpy brood,
On Bard and Hero clamorously fell.
Heed not, wild Rover once through heath
   and glen,
Who mad'st at length the better life thy
   choice,   10
Heed not such onset! nay, if praise of
   men
To thee appear not an unmeaning
   voice,
Lift up that grey-haired forehead, and
   rejoice
In the just tribute of thy Poet's pen!

XIX.

[Composed ?.—Published 1819.]

GRIEF, thou hast lost an ever-ready
   friend
Now that the cottage Spinning-wheel is
   mute;
And Care—a comforter that best could
   suit
Her froward mood, and softliest repre-
   hend;
And Love—a charmer's voice, that used
   to lend,   5
More efficaciously than aught that
   flows
From harp or lute, kind influence to
   compose
The throbbing pulse—else troubled with-
   out end:
Even Joy could tell, Joy craving truce
   and rest
From her own overflow, what power
   sedate   10
On those revolving motions did await
Assiduously—to soothe her aching breast;
And, to a point of just relief, abate
The mantling triumphs of a day too
   blest.

XX.

TO S. H.

[Composed ?.—Published 1827.]

EXCUSE is needless when with love sincere
Of occupation, not by fashion led,
Thou turn'st the Wheel that slept with
   dust o'erspread;
My nerves from no such murmur shrink,—
   tho' near,
Soft as the Dorhawk's to a distant ear,   5
When twilight shades darken the moun-
   tain's head.
Even She who toils to spin our vital
   thread
Might smile on work, O Lady, once so
   dear
To household virtues. Venerable Art,
Torn from the Poor! yet shall kind Hea-
   ven protect   10
Its own; though Rulers, with undue
   respect,
Trusting to crowded factory and mart
And proud discoveries of the intellect,
Heed not the pillage of man's ancient
   heart.

XXI.

COMPOSED IN ONE OF THE VALLEYS OF WESTMORELAND, ON EASTER SUNDAY.

[Composed ?.—Published 1819.]

WITH each recurrence of this glorious
   morn
That saw the Saviour in his human frame
Rise from the dead, erewhile the Cottage-
   dame
Put on fresh raiment—till that hour un-
   worn:
Domestic hands the home-bred wool had
   shorn,   5
And she who span it culled the daintiest
   fleece,
In thoughtful reverence to the Prince of
   Peace,
Whose temples bled beneath the platted
   thorn.
A blest estate when piety sublime
These humble props disdained not! O
   green dales!   10

Sad may *I* be who heard your sabbath chime
When Art's abused inventions were unknown;
Kind Nature's various wealth was all your own;
And benefits were weighed in Reason's scales!

XXII.

DECAY OF PIETY.

[Composed ?.—Published 1827.]

Oft have I seen, ere Time had ploughed my cheek,
Matrons and Sires—who, punctual to the call
Of their loved Church, on fast or festival
Through the long year the House of Prayer would seek:
By Christmas snows, by visitation bleak 5
Of Easter winds, unscared, from hut or hall
They came to lowly bench or sculptured stall,
But with one fervour of devotion meek.
I see the places where they once were known,
And ask, surrounded even by kneeling crowds, 10
Is ancient Piety for ever flown?
Alas! even then they seemed like fleecy clouds
That, struggling through the western sky, have won
Their pensive light from a departed sun!

XXIII.

COMPOSED ON THE EVE OF THE MARRIAGE OF A FRIEND[1] IN THE VALE OF GRASMERE, 1812.

[Composed 1812.—Published 1815.]

What need of clamorous bells, or ribands gay,
These humble nuptials to proclaim or grace?
Angels of love, look down upon the place;

[1] The poet's wife's brother, Thomas Hutchinson, who married Mary Monkhouse, November 1, 1812.—Ed.

Shed on the chosen vale a sun-bright day!
Yet no proud gladness would the Bride display 5
Even for such promise:—serious is her face,
Modest her mien; and she, whose thoughts keep pace
With gentleness, in that becoming way
Will thank you. Faultless does the Maid appear;
No disproportion in her soul, no strife: 10
But, when the closer view of wedded life
Hath shown that nothing human can be clear
From frailty, for that insight may the Wife
To her indulgent Lord become more dear.

XXIV.

FROM THE ITALIAN OF MICHAEL ANGELO.

I.

[Composed 1805.—Published 1807.]

Yes! hope may with my strong desire keep pace,
And I be undeluded, unbetrayed;
For if of our affections none finds grace
In sight of Heaven, then, wherefore hath God made 4
The world which we inhabit? Better plea
Love cannot have than that in loving thee
Glory to that eternal Peace is paid,
Who such divinity to thee imparts
As hallows and makes pure all gentle hearts. 9
His hope is treacherous only whose love dies
With beauty, which is varying every hour;
But in chaste hearts, uninfluenced by the power
Of outward change, there blooms a deathless flower,
That breathes on earth the air of paradise.

XXV.

FROM THE SAME.

II.

[Composed probably 1805.—Published 1807.]

No mortal object did these eyes behold
When first they met the placid light of thine,
And my Soul felt her destiny divine,

And hope of endless peace in me grew
    bold:
Heaven-born, the Soul a heavenward
    course must hold;   5
Beyond the visible world she soars to seek
(For what delights the sense is false and
    weak)
Ideal Form, the universal mould.
The wise man, I affirm, can find no rest
In that which perishes: nor will he lend
His heart to aught which doth on time
    depend.   11
'Tis sense, unbridled will, and not true
    love,
That kills the soul: love betters what
    is best,
Even here below, but more in heaven
    above.

XXVI.

FROM THE SAME. TO THE SUPREME BEING.

III.

[Composed 1805.—Published 1807.]

THE prayers I make will then be sweet
    indeed
If Thou the spirit give by which I pray:
My unassisted heart is barren clay,
That of its native self can nothing feed:
Of good and pious works Thou art the seed,
That quickens only where Thou say'st
    it may: 6
Unless Thou show to us thine own true
    way
No man can find it: Father! Thou must
    lead.
Do Thou, then, breathe those thoughts
    into my mind   9
By which such virtue may in me be bred
That in thy holy footsteps I may tread;
The fetters of my tongue do Thou un-
    bind,
That I may have the power to sing of
    Thee,
And sound thy praises everlastingly.

XXVII.

[Composed later than June, 1812.—Published
1815.]

SURPRISED by joy—impatient as the Wind
I turned to share the transport—Oh! with
    whom

But Thee[1], deep buried in the silent tomb,
That spot which no vicissitude can find?
Love, faithful love, recalled thee to my
    mind—   5
But how could I forget thee? Through
    what power,
Even for the least division of an hour,
Have I been so beguiled as to be blind
To my most grievous loss!—That thought's
    return   9
Was the worst pang that sorrow ever
    bore,
Save one, one only, when I stood for-
    lorn,
Knowing my heart's best treasure was no
    more;
That neither present time, nor years un-
    born
Could to my sight that heavenly face
    restore.

XXVIII.

I.

[Composed ?.—Published 1807.]

METHOUGHT I saw the footsteps of a
    throne
Which mists and vapours from mine eyes
    did shroud—
Nor view of who might sit thereon al-
    lowed;
But all the steps and ground about were
    strown
With sights the ruefullest that flesh and
    bone   5
Ever put on; a miserable crowd,
Sick, hale, old, young, who cried before
    that cloud,
"Thou art our king, O Death! to thee we
    groan."
Those steps I clomb; the mists before me
    gave
Smooth way; and I beheld the face of one
Sleeping alone within a mossy cave,   11
With her face up to heaven; that seemed
    to have

---

[1] Catherine, the poet's second daughter, born
September 6, 1808, died June 5, 1812. See the
poem, *Characteristics of a Child Three Years
Old*, page 80.—ED.

Pleasing remembrance of a thought fore-
gone ;
A lovely Beauty in a summer grave !

XXIX.

NOVEMBER, 1836.

II.

[Composed November, 1836.—Published 1837.]

EVEN so for me a Vision sanctified
The sway of Death ; long ere mine eyes
had seen
Thy countenance—the still rapture of thy
mien—
When thou, dear Sister ! wert become
Death's Bride :
No trace of pain or languor could abide 5
That change :—age on thy brow was
smoothed—thy cold
Wan cheek at once was privileged to
unfold
A loveliness to living youth denied.
Oh ! if within me hope should e'er decline,
The lamp of faith, lost Friend ! too faintly
burn ;   10
Then may that heaven-revealing smile of
thine,
The bright assurance, visibly return :
And let my spirit in that power divine
Rejoice, as, through that power, it ceased
to mourn.

XXX.

[Composed August, 1802.—Published 1807.]

IT is a beauteous evening, calm and free,
The holy time is quiet as a Nun
Breathless with adoration ; the broad sun
Is sinking down in its tranquillity ;
The gentleness of heaven broods o'er the
Sea :   5
Listen ! the mighty Being is awake,
And doth with his eternal motion make
A sound like thunder—everlastingly.
Dear Child ! dear Girl ! that walkest with
me here,
If thou appear untouched by solemn
thought,   10
Thy nature is not therefore less divine :
Thou liest in Abraham's bosom all the
year ;

And worshipp'st at the Temple's inner
shrine,
God being with thee when we know it not.

XXXI.

[Composed ?.—Published 1807.]

WHERE lies the Land to which yon Ship
must go ?
Fresh as a lark mounting at break of day,
Festively she puts forth in trim array ;
Is she for tropic suns, or polar snow ?
What boots the enquiry ?—Neither friend
nor foe   5
She cares for ; let her travel where she
may,
She finds familiar names, a beaten way
Ever before her, and a wind to blow.
Yet still I ask, what haven is her mark ?
And, almost as it was when ships were
rare,   10
(From time to time, like Pilgrims, here
and there
Crossing the waters) doubt, and some-
thing dark,
Of the old Sea some reverential fear,
Is with me at thy farewell, joyous Bark !

XXXII.

[Composed ?.—Published 1807.]

WITH Ships the sea was sprinkled far
and nigh,
Like stars in heaven, and joyously it
showed ;
Some lying fast at anchor in the road,
Some veering up and down, one knew
not why.
A goodly Vessel did I then espy   5
Come like a giant from a haven broad ;
And lustily along the bay she strode,
Her tackling rich, and of apparel high.
This Ship was nought to me, nor I to her,
Yet I pursued her with a Lover's look ; 10
This Ship to all the rest did I prefer :
When will she turn, and whither ? She
will brook
No tarrying ; where She comes the winds
must stir :
On went She, and due north her journey
took.

XXXIII.

[Composed ?.—Published 1807.]

THE world is too much with us; late and
    soon,
Getting and spending, we lay waste our
    powers:
Little we see in Nature that is ours;
We have given our hearts away, a sordid
    boon!
This Sea that bares her bosom to the
    moon;   5
The winds that will be howling at all
    hours,
And are up-gathered now like sleeping
    flowers;
For this, for everything, we are out of
    tune;
It moves us not.—Great God! I'd rather
    be
A Pagan suckled in a creed outworn;   10
So might I, standing on this pleasant lea,
Have glimpses that would make me less
    forlorn;
Have sight of Proteus rising from the sea;
Or hear old Triton blow his wreathèd
    horn.

XXXIV.

[Composed ?.—Published 1823 (Joanna Baillie's
    Poetic Miscellanies); ed. 1827.]

A VOLANT Tribe of Bards on earth are
    found,
Who, while the flattering Zephyrs round
    them play,
On "coignes of vantage" hang their nests
    of clay;
How quickly from that aery hold un-
    bound,
Dust for oblivion! To the solid ground   5
Of nature trusts the Mind that builds
    for aye;
Convinced that there, there only, she can
    lay
Secure foundations. As the year runs
    round,
Apart she toils within the chosen ring;
While the stars shine, or while day's
    purple eye   10
Is gently closing with the flowers of
    spring;

Where even the motion of an Angel's
    wing
Would interrupt the intense tranquillity
Of silent hills, and more than silent sky.

XXXV.

[Composed probably 1815.—Published 1815.]

"WEAK is the will of Man, his judgment
    blind;
Remembrance persecutes, and Hope be-
    trays;
Heavy is woe;—and joy, for human-kind,
A mournful thing, so transient is the
    blaze!"
Thus might *he* paint our lot of mortal
    days   5
Who wants the glorious faculty assigned
To elevate the more-than-reasoning Mind,
And colour life's dark cloud with orient
    rays.
Imagination is that sacred power,
Imagination lofty and refined: 10
'Tis hers to pluck the amaranthine flower
Of Faith, and round the sufferer's temples
    bind
Wreaths that endure affliction's heaviest
    shower,
And do not shrink from sorrow's keenest
    wind.

XXXVI.

TO THE MEMORY OF RAISLEY CALVERT.

[Composed ?.—Published 1807.]

CALVERT! it must not be unheard by
    them
Who may respect my name that I to thee
Owed many years of early liberty.
This care was thine when sickness did
    condemn
Thy youth to hopeless wasting, root and
    stem—   5
That I, if frugal and severe, might stray
Where'er I liked; and finally array
My temples with the Muse's diadem.
Hence, if in freedom I have loved the
    truth;
If there be aught of pure, or good, or
    great,   10
In my past verse; or shall be, in the lays
Of higher mood, which now I meditate;—

It gladdens me, O worthy, short-lived,
Youth!
To think how much of this will be thy
praise.

PART II.

I.

[Composed ?.—Published 1827.]

Scorn not the Sonnet; Critic, you have
frowned,
Mindless of its just honours; with this
key
Shakspeare unlocked his heart; the
melody
Of this small lute gave ease to Petrarch's
wound;
A thousand times this pipe did Tasso
sound;   5
With it Camöens soothed an exile's grief;
The Sonnet glittered a gay myrtle leaf
Amid the cypress with which Dante
crowned
His visionary brow: a glow-worm lamp,
It cheered mild Spenser, called from
Faery-land   10
To struggle through dark ways; and
when a damp
Fell round the path of Milton, in his
hand
The Thing became a trumpet; whence he
blew
Soul-animating strains—alas, too few!

II.

[Composed December 1806.—Published 1807.]

How sweet it is, when mother Fancy
rocks
The wayward brain, to saunter through a
wood!
An old place, full of many a lovely brood,
Tall trees, green arbours, and ground-
flowers in flocks;
And wild rose tip-toe upon hawthorn
stocks,   5
Like a bold Girl, who plays her agile
pranks
At Wakes and Fairs with wandering
Mountebanks,—
When she stands cresting the Clown's
head, and mocks
The crowd beneath her. Verily I think,

Such place to me is sometimes like a
dream   10
Or map of the whole world: thoughts,
link by link,
Enter through ears and eyesight, with
such gleam
Of all things, that at last in fear I shrink,
And leap at once from the delicious
stream.

III.

TO B. R. HAYDON.

[Composed December 1815.—Published February
4, 1816 (*The Champion*); March 31, 1816 (*The
Examiner*); vol. of 1816.

High is our calling, Friend!—Creative
Art
(Whether the instrument of words she
use,
Or pencil pregnant with ethereal hues,)
Demands the service of a mind and heart,
Though sensitive, yet, in their weakest
part,   5
Heroically fashioned——to infuse
Faith in the whispers of the lonely Muse,
While the whole world seems adverse to
desert.
And, oh! when Nature sinks, as oft she
may,
Through long-lived pressure of obscure
distress,   10
Still to be strenuous for the bright re-
ward,
And in the soul admit of no decay,
Brook no continuance of weak-minded-
ness—
Great is the glory, for the strife is hard!

IV.

[Composed 1814.—Published 1815.]

From the dark chambers of dejection
freed,
Spurning the unprofitable yoke of care,
Rise, Gillies, rise: the gales of youth
shall bear
Thy genius forward like a wingèd steed.
Though bold Bellerophon (so Jove de-
creed   5
In wrath) fell headlong from the fields of
air,

Yet a rich guerdon waits on minds that
    dare,
If aught be in them of immortal seed,
And reason govern that audacious flight
Which heavenward they direct.—Then
    droop not thou,   10
Erroneously renewing a sad vow
In the low dell 'mid Roslin's faded grove:
A cheerful life is what the Muses love,
A soaring spirit is their prime delight.

V.

[Composed ?.—Published 1827].

FAIR Prime of life! were it enough to gild
With ready sunbeams every straggling
    shower;
And, if an unexpected cloud should lower,
Swiftly thereon a rainbow arch to build
For Fancy's errands,—then, from fields
    half-tilled   5
Gathering green weeds to mix with poppy
    flower,
Thee might thy Minions crown, and chant
    thy power,
Unpitied by the wise, all censure stilled.
Ah! show that worthier honours are thy
    due;
Fair Prime of life! arouse the deeper
    heart;   10
Confirm the Spirit glorying to pursue
Some path of steep ascent and lofty aim;
And, if there be a joy that slights the
    claim
Of grateful memory, bid that joy depart.

VI.

[Composed ?.—Published 1819.]

I WATCH, and long have watched, with
    calm regret
Yon slowly-sinking star—immortal Sire
(So might he seem) of all the glittering
    quire!
Blue ether still surrounds him—yet—and
    yet;
But now the horizon's rocky parapet   5
Is reached, where, forfeiting his bright
    attire,
He burns—transmuted to a dusky fire—
Then pays submissively the appointed
    debt

To the flying moments, and is seen no
    more.
Angels and gods! We struggle with our
    fate,   10
While health, power, glory, from their
    height decline,
Depressed; and then extinguished: and
    our state,
In this, how different, lost Star, from
    thine,
That no to-morrow shall our beams re-
    store!

VII.

[Composed ?.—Published 1819.]

I HEARD (alas! 'twas only in a dream)
Strains—which, as sage Antiquity be-
    lieved,
By waking ears have sometimes been
    received
Wafted adown the wind from lake or
    stream;
A most melodious requiem, a supreme   5
And perfect harmony of notes, achieved
By a fair Swan on drowsy billows heaved,
O'er which her pinions shed a silver gleam.
For is she not the votary of Apollo?
And knows she not, singing as he in-
    spires,   10
That bliss awaits her which the ungenial
    Hollow[1]
Of the dull earth partakes not, nor de-
    sires?
Mount, tuneful Bird, and join the im-
    mortal quires!
She soared—and I awoke, struggling in
    vain to follow.

VIII.

RETIREMENT.

[Composed ?.—Published 1827.]

IF the whole weight of what we think and
    feel,
Save only far as thought and feeling
    blend
With action, were as nothing, patriot
    Friend!

[1] See the "Phædo" of Plato, by which this
Sonnet was suggested.

From thy remonstrance would be no
  appeal;
But to promote and fortify the weal   5
Of her own Being is her paramount end;
A truth which they alone shall compre-
  hend
Who shun the mischief which they cannot
  heal.
Peace in these feverish times is sovereign
  bliss:
Here, with no thirst but what the stream
  can slake,   10
And startled only by the rustling brake,
Cool air I breathe; while the unincum-
  bered Mind,
By some weak aims at services assigned
To gentle Natures, thanks not Heaven
  amiss.

IX.

[Composed ?.—Published 1823 (Joanna Baillie's
Poetic Miscellanies); ed. 1827.]

NOT Love, not War, nor the tumultuous
  swell
Of civil conflict, nor the wrecks of change,
Nor Duty struggling with afflictions
  strange—
Not these *alone* inspire the tuneful shell;
But where untroubled peace and concord
  dwell,   5
There also is the Muse not loth to range,
Watching the twilight smoke of cot or
  grange,
Skyward ascending from a woody dell.
Meek aspirations please her, lone endea-
  vour,
And sage content, and placid melancholy;
She loves to gaze upon a crystal river—11
Diaphanous because it travels slowly;
Soft is the music that would charm for
  ever;
The flower of sweetest smell is shy and
  lowly.

X.

[Composed ?.—Published 1815.]

MARK the concentred hazels that en-
  close
Yon old grey Stone, protected from the
  ray

Of noontide suns:—and even the beams
  that play
And glance, while wantonly the rough
  wind blows,
Are seldom free to touch the moss that
  grows   5
Upon that roof, amid embowering gloom,
The very image framing of a Tomb,
In which some ancient Chieftain finds
  repose
Among the lonely mountains.—Live, ye
  trees!
And thou, grey Stone, the pensive like-
  ness keep   10
Of a dark chamber where the Mighty
  sleep:
For more than Fancy to the influence
  bends
When solitary Nature condescends
To mimic Time's forlorn humanities.

XI.

COMPOSED AFTER A JOURNEY ACROSS THE
HAMBLETON HILLS, YORKSHIRE.

[Composed October 4, 1802.—Published 1807.]

DARK and more dark the shades of even-
  ing fell;
The wished-for point was reached—but at
  an hour
When little could be gained from that
  rich dower
Of prospect, whereof many thousands
  tell.
Yet did the glowing west with marvellous
  power   5
Salute us; there stood Indian citadel,
Temple of Greece, and minster with its
  tower
Substantially expressed—a place for bell
Or clock to toll from! Many a tempting
  isle,
With groves that never were imagined,
  lay
'Mid seas how steadfast! objects all for
  the eye   11
Of silent rapture; but we felt the while
We should forget them; they are of the
  sky,
And from our earthly memory fade away.

XII.

[Composed ?.—Published 1807.]

—— "they are of the sky,
And from our earthly memory fade away."

THOSE words were uttered as in pensive
  mood
We turned, departing from that solemn
  sight:
A contrast and reproach to gross delight,
And life's unspiritual pleasures daily
  wooed!
But now upon this thought I cannot
  brood;   5
It is unstable as a dream of night;
Nor will I praise a cloud, however bright,
Disparaging Man's gifts, and proper food.
Grove, isle, with every shape of sky-built
  dome,
Though clad in colours beautiful and
  pure,   10
Find in the heart of man no natural
  home:
The immortal Mind craves objects that
  endure:
These cleave to it; from these it cannot
  roam,
Nor they from it: their fellowship is
  secure.

XIII.

SEPTEMBER, 1815.

[Composed December, 1815.—Published February
  11, 1816 (*The Examiner*); vol. of 1816.]

WHILE not a leaf seems faded; while the
  fields,
With ripening harvest prodigally fair,
In brightest sunshine bask; this nipping
  air,
Sent from some distant clime where
  Winter wields
His icy scimitar, a foretaste yields   5
Of bitter change, and bids the flowers
  beware;
And whispers to the silent birds, "Pre-
  pare
Against the threatening foe your trustiest
  shields."
For me, who under kindlier laws belong

To Nature's tuneful quire, this rustling dry
Through leaves yet green, and yon crystal-
  line sky,   11
Announce a season potent to renew,
'Mid frost and snow, the instinctive joys
  of song,
And nobler cares than listless summer
  knew.

XIV.

NOVEMBER I.

[Composed December, 1815.—Published January
  28, 1816 (*The Examiner*); vol. of 1816.]

How clear, how keen, how marvellously
  bright
The effluence from yon distant mountain's
  head,
Which, strewn with snow smooth as the
  sky can shed,
Shines like another sun—on mortal sight
Uprisen, as if to check approaching Night,
And all her twinkling stars. Who now
  would tread,   6
If so he might, yon mountain's glittering
  head—
Terrestrial, but a surface, by the flight
Of sad mortality's earth-sullying wing,
Unswept, unstained? Nor shall the aerial
  Powers   10
Dissolve that beauty, destined to endure,
White, radiant, spotless, exquisitely pure,
Through all vicissitudes, till genial Spring
Has filled the laughing vales with wel-
  come flowers.

XV.

COMPOSED DURING A STORM.

[Composed February, 1819.—Published in *Peter
  Bell* vol., 1819.]

ONE who was suffering tumult in his soul
Yet failed to seek the sure relief of prayer,
Went forth—his course surrendering to
  the care
Of the fierce wind, while mid-day light-
  'nings prowl
Insidiously, untimely thunders growl;   5
While trees, dim-seen, in frenzied num-
  bers, tear
The lingering remnant of their yellow hair,

And shivering wolves, surprised with
   darkness, howl
As if the sun were not. He raised his eye
Soul-smitten; for, that instant did appear
Large space ('mid dreadful clouds) of
   purest sky,   11
An azure disc—shield of Tranquillity;
Invisible, unlooked-for, minister
Of providential goodness ever nigh!

XVI.

TO A SNOWDROP.

[Composed ?.—Published 1819.]

LONE Flower, hemmed in with snows,
   and white as they
But hardier far, once more I see thee bend
Thy forehead as if fearful to offend,
Like an unbidden guest. Though day
   by day
Storms, sallying from the mountain-tops,
   waylay   5
The rising sun, and on the plains descend;
Yet art thou welcome, welcome as a
   friend
Whose zeal outruns his promise! Blue-
   eyed May
Shall soon behold this border thickly set
With bright jonquils, their odours lavish-
   ing   10
On the soft west-wind and his frolic
   peers;
Nor will I then thy modest grace forget,
Chaste Snowdrop, venturous harbinger
   of Spring,
And pensive monitor of fleeting years!

XVII.

TO THE LADY MARY LOWTHER.

With a selection from the Poems of Anne, Coun-
tess of Winchilsea; and extracts of similar cha-
racter from other Writers; transcribed by a
female friend.

[Composed ?.—Published 1820.]

LADY! I rifled a Parnassian Cave
(But seldom trod) of mildly-gleaming ore;
And culled, from sundry beds a lucid
   store

Of genuine crystals, pure as those that
   pave
The azure brooks, where Dian joys to
   lave   5
Her spotless limbs; and ventured to
   explore
Dim shades—for reliques, upon Lethe's
   shore,
Cast up at random by the sullen wave.
To female hands the treasures were re-
   signed;
And lo this Work!—a grotto bright and
   clear   10
From stain or taint; in which thy blame-
   less mind
May feed on thoughts though pensive not
   austere;
Or, if thy deeper spirit be inclined
To holy musing, it may enter here.

XVIII.

TO LADY BEAUMONT.

[Composed January or February, 1807.—Pub-
lished 1807.]

LADY! the songs of Spring were in the
   grove
While I was shaping beds for winter
   flowers;
While I was planting green unfading
   bowers,
And shrubs—to hang upon the warm
   alcove,
And sheltering wall; and still, as Fancy
   wove   5
The dream, to time and nature's blended
   powers
I gave this paradise for winter hours,
A labyrinth, Lady! which your feet shall
   rove.
Yes! when the sun of life more feebly
   shines,
Becoming thoughts, I trust, of solemn
   gloom   10
Or of high gladness you shall hither
   bring;
And these perennial bowers and murmur-
   ing pines
Be gracious as the music and the bloom
And all the mighty ravishment of spring.

XIX.

[Composed ?.—Published 1827.]

THERE is a pleasure in poetic pains
Which only Poets know ;—'t was rightly
  said ;
Whom could the Muses else allure to
  tread
Their smoothest paths, to wear their
  lightest chains ?
When happiest Fancy has inspired the
  strains,   5
How oft the malice of one luckless word
Pursues the Enthusiast to the social
  board,
Haunts him belated on the silent plains !
Yet he repines not, if his thought stand
  clear,
At last, of hindrance and obscurity,   10
Fresh as the star that crowns the brow of
  morn ;
Bright, speckless, as a softly-moulded tear
The moment it has left the virgin's eye,
Or rain-drop lingering on the pointed
  thorn.

XX.

[Composed ?.—Published 1815].

THE Shepherd, looking eastward, softly
  said,
"Bright is thy veil, O Moon, as thou art
  bright !"
Forthwith that little cloud, in ether
  spread
And penetrated all with tender light,
She cast away, and showed her fulgent
  head   5
Uncovered ; dazzling the Beholder's sight
As if to vindicate her beauty's right,
Her beauty thoughtlessly disparaged.
Meanwhile that veil, removed or thrown
  aside,
Went floating from her, darkening as it
  went ;   10
And a huge mass, to bury or to hide,
Approached this glory of the firmament ;
Who meekly yields, and is obscured—
  content
With one calm triumph of a modest
  pride.

XXI.

[Composed not later than 1819.—Published 1820.]

WHEN haughty expectations prostrate lie,
And grandeur crouches like a guilty
  thing,
Oft shall the lowly weak, till nature bring
Mature release, in fair society
Survive, and Fortune's utmost anger
  try ;   5
Like these frail snowdrops that together
  cling,
And nod their helmets, smitten by the
  wing
Of many a furious whirl-blast sweeping by.
Observe the faithful flowers ! if small to
  great
May lead the thoughts, thus struggling
  used to stand   10
The Emathian phalanx, nobly obstinate ;
And so the bright immortal Theban band,
Whom onset, fiercely urged at Jove's
  command,
Might overwhelm, but could not separate !

XXII.

[Composed ?.—Published 1815.]

HAIL, Twilight, sovereign of one peaceful
  hour !
Not dull art Thou as undiscerning Night ;
But studious only to remove from sight
Day's mutable distinctions.—Ancient
  Power !
Thus did the waters gleam, the moun-
  tains lower,   5
To the rude Briton, when, in wolf-skin vest
Here roving wild, he laid him down to
  rest
On the bare rock, or through a leafy
  bower
Looked ere his eyes were closed. By him
  was seen
The self-same Vision which we now behold,
At thy meek bidding, shadowy Power !
  brought forth ;   11
These mighty barriers, and the gulf be-
  tween ;
The flood, the stars,—a spectacle as old
As the beginning of the heavens and
  earth !

XXIII[1].

[Composed perhaps 1802.—Published 1807.]

"With how sad steps, O Moon, thou
climb'st the sky,
How silently, and with how wan a
face!"
Where art thou? Thou so often seen on
high
Running among the clouds a Wood-
nymph's race!
Unhappy Nuns, whose common breath's
a sigh   5
Which they would stifle, move at such a
pace!
The northern Wind, to call thee to the
chase,
Must blow to-night his bugle horn. Had I
The power of Merlin, Goddess! this
should be:
And all the stars, fast as the clouds were
riven,   10
Should sally forth, to keep thee company,
Hurrying and sparkling through the clear
blue heaven;
But, Cynthia! should to thee the palm
be given,
Queen both for beauty and for majesty

XXIV.

[Composed ?.—Published 1815.]

Even as a dragon's eye that feels the
stress
Of a bedimming sleep, or as a lamp
Sullenly [2] glaring through sepulchral
damp,
So burns yon Taper 'mid a black recess

---

[1] This poem originally consisted of fifteen lines:
it was shortened and classed as a Sonnet in ed.
1820. See *Supplement*, page 629.—Ed.

[2] The collective edd. of the Poems from 1827
to 1849 read "suddenly"; edd. 1815, 1820, and
the Sonnet-vol. of 1838 read "sullenly." The
latter is undoubtedly the word intended by
Wordsworth. Cf. "sullen fire," *Misc. Son.* II. vi.
l. 7 (edd. 1819, 1820, 1827); "sullen star," *Excur-
sion* IV. 487; and the "sullen light," i.e. the
faintly glowing wick of an extinguished candle,
spoken of in Wordsworth's reply to the letter of
Mathetes (*The Friend*, iii. 48, ed. 1818).—Ed.

Of mountains, silent, dreary, motionless:
The lake below reflects it not; the sky
Muffled in clouds, affords no company
To mitigate and cheer its loneliness.
Yet, round the body of that joyless Thing
Which sends so far its melancholy light,
Perhaps are seated in domestic ring   11
A gay society with faces bright,
Conversing, reading, laughing;—or they
sing,
While hearts and voices in the song unite.

XXV.

[Composed ?.—Published 1820.]

The stars are mansions built by Nature's
hand,
And, haply, there the spirits of the blest
Dwell, clothed in radiance, their im-
mortal vest;
Huge Ocean shows, within his yellow
strand,
A habitation marvellously planned,   5
For life to occupy in love and rest;
All that we see—is dome, or vault, or
nest,
Or fortress, reared at Nature's sage com-
mand.
Glad thought for every season! but the
Spring
Gave it while cares were weighing on my
heart,   10
'Mid song of birds, and insects murmur-
ing;
And while the youthful year's prolific
art—
Of bud, leaf, blade, and flower—was
fashioning
Abodes where self-disturbance hath no
part.

XXVI.

[Composed ?.—Published 1835.]

Desponding Father! mark this altered
bough,
So beautiful of late, with sunshine
warmed,
Or moist with dews; what more un-
sightly now,
Its blossoms shrivelled, and its fruit, if
formed,

Invisible? yet Spring her genial brow   5
Knits not o'er that discolouring and decay
As false to expectation. Nor fret thou
At like unlovely process in the May
Of human life: a Stripling's graces blow,
Fade and are shed, that from their timely
    fall   10
(Misdeem it not a cankerous change) may
    grow
Rich mellow bearings, that for thanks
    shall call:
In all men, sinful is it to be slow
To hope—in Parents, sinful above all.

XXVII.

CAPTIVITY.—MARY QUEEN OF SCOTS.

[Composed ?.—Published 1819.]

"As the cold aspect of a sunless way
Strikes through the Traveller's frame
    with deadlier chill,
Oft as appears a grove, or obvious hill,
Glistening with unparticipated ray,
Or shining slope where he must never
    stray;   5
So joys, remembered without wish or will,
Sharpen the keenest edge of present
    ill,—
On the crushed heart a heavier burthen
    lay.
Just Heaven, contract the compass of
    my mind
To fit proportion with my altered state!
Quench those felicities whose light I find
Reflected in my bosom all too late!—   12
O be my spirit, like my thraldom, strait;
And, like mine eyes that stream with
    sorrow, blind!"

XXVIII.

ST. CATHERINE OF LEDBURY.

[Composed ?.—Published 1835.]

WHEN human touch (as monkish books
    attest)
Nor was applied nor could be, Ledbury
    bells
Broke forth in concert flung adown the
    dells,

And upward, high as Malvern's cloudy
    crest;
Sweet tones, and caught by a noble Lady
    blest   5
To rapture! Mabel listened at the side
Of her loved mistress: soon the music
    died,
And Catherine said, *Here I set up my
    rest.*
Warned in a dream, the Wanderer long
    had sought
A home that by such miracle of sound   10
Must be revealed:—she heard it now,
    or felt
The deep, deep joy of a confiding
    thought;
And there, a saintly Anchoress, she
    dwelt
Till she exchanged for heaven that happy
    ground.

XXIX.

[Composed probably 1807.—Published 1807.]

—— "gives to airy nothing
A local habitation and a name."

THOUGH narrow be that old Man's cares,
    and near,
The poor old Man is greater than he
    seems:
For he hath waking empire, wide as
    dreams;
An ample sovereignty of eye and ear.
Rich are his walks with supernatural
    cheer;   5
The region of his inner spirit teems
With vital sounds and monitory gleams
Of high astonishment and pleasing fear.
He the seven birds hath seen, that never
    part,
Seen the SEVEN WHISTLERS in their
    nightly rounds,   10
And counted them: and oftentimes will
    start—
For overhead are sweeping GABRIEL'S
    HOUNDS
Doomed, with their impious Lord, the
    flying Hart
To chase for ever, on aerial grounds!

XXX.

[Composed ?.—Published 1835.]

FOUR fiery steeds impatient of the rein
Whirled us o'er sunless ground beneath
    a sky
As void of sunshine, when, from that
    wide plain,
Clear tops of far-off mountains we descry,
Like a Sierra of cerulean Spain,   5
All light and lustre. Did no heart reply?
Yes, there was One;—for One, asunder
    fly
The thousand links of that ethereal chain;
And green vales open out, with grove and
    field,
And the fair front of many a happy
    Home;   10
Such tempting spots as into vision come
While Soldiers, weary of the arms they
    wield,
And sick at heart of strifeful Christendom,
Gaze on the moon by parting clouds re-
    vealed.

XXXI.

[Composed 1806.—Published 1815.]

BROOK! whose society the Poet seeks,
Intent his wasted spirits to renew;
And whom the curious Painter doth
    pursue
Through rocky passes, among flowery
    creeks,
And tracks thee dancing down thy water-
    breaks;   5
If wish were mine some type of thee to
    view,
Thee, and not thee thyself, I would not do
Like Grecian Artists, give thee human
    cheeks,
Channels for tears; no Naiad shouldst
    thou be,—
Have neither limbs, feet, feathers, joints,
    nor hairs: 10
It seems the Eternal Soul is clothed in
    thee
With purer robes than those of flesh and
    blood,
And hath bestowed on thee a safer good;
Unwearied joy, and life without its cares.

XXXII.

COMPOSED ON THE BANKS OF A ROCKY
STREAM.

[Composed ?.—Published 1820.]

DOGMATIC Teachers, of the snow-white
    fur!
Ye wrangling Schoolmen, of the scarlet
    hood!
Who, with a keenness not to be with-
    stood,
Press the point home, or falter and
    demur,
Checked in your course by many a teas-
    ing burr;   5
These natural council-seats your acrid
    blood
Might cool;—and, as the Genius of the
    flood
Stoops willingly to animate and spur
Each lighter function slumbering in the
    brain,
Yon eddying balls of foam, these arrowy
    gleams   10
That o'er the pavement of the surging
    streams
Welter and flash, a synod might detain
With subtle speculations, haply vain,
But surely less so than your far-fetched
    themes!

XXXIII.

THIS AND THE TWO FOLLOWING WERE
SUGGESTED BY MR. W. WESTALL'S VIEWS
OF THE CAVES, ETC., IN YORKSHIRE.

[Composed 1818.—Published January, 1819 (*Black-
wood's Magazine*); *Peter Bell* vol., 1819.]

PURE element of waters! wheresoe'er
Thou dost forsake thy subterranean
    haunts,
Green herbs, bright flowers, and berry-
    bearing plants,
Rise into life and in thy train appear:
And, through the sunny portion of the year,
Swift insects shine, thy hovering pursui-
    vants: 6
And, if thy bounty fail, the forest pants;
And hart and hind and hunter with his
    spear
Languish and droop together. Nor unfelt

In man's perturbèd soul thy sway benign;
And, haply, far within the marble belt 11
Of central earth, where tortured Spirits
    pine
For grace and goodness lost, thy mur-
    murs melt
Their anguish,—and they blend sweet
    songs with thine[1].

XXXIV.

MALHAM COVE.

[Composed 1818.—Published January 1819 (*Black-wood's Magazine*); *Peter Bell* vol., 1819.]

WAS the aim frustrated by force or guile,
When giants scooped from out the rocky
    ground,
Tier under tier, this semicirque profound?
(Giants—the same who built in Erin's isle
That Causeway with incomparable toil!)—
Oh, had this vast theatric structure wound
With finished sweep into a perfect round,
No mightier work had gained the plausive
    smile
Of all-beholding Phœbus! But, alas,
Vain earth! false world! Foundations
    must be laid   10
In Heaven; for, 'mid the wreck of IS and
    WAS,
Things incomplete and purposes betrayed
Make sadder transits o'er thought's optic
    glass
Than noblest objects utterly decayed.

XXXV.

GORDALE.

[Composed 1818.—Published January, 1819 (*Black-wood's Magazine*); *Peter Bell* vol., 1819.]

AT early dawn, or rather when the air
Glimmers with fading light, and shadowy
    Eve
Is busiest to confer and to bereave;
Then, pensive Votary! let thy feet repair
To Gordale-chasm, terrific as the lair   5
Where the young lions couch; for so, by
    leave

[1] Waters (as Mr. Westall informs us in the letterpress prefixed to his admirable views) are invariably found to flow through these caverns.

Of the propitious hour, thou may'st per-
    ceive
The local Deity, with oozy hair
And mineral crown, beside his jagged
    urn,
Recumbent: Him thou may'st behold,
    who hides   10
His lineaments by day, yet there presides,
Teaching the docile waters how to turn,
Or (if need be) impediment to spurn,
And force their passage to the salt-sea
    tides!

XXXVI.

COMPOSED UPON WESTMINSTER BRIDGE, SEPTEMBER 3, 1802.

[Composed July 31, 1802.—Published 1807.]

EARTH has not anything to show more
    fair:
Dull would he be of soul who could
    pass by
A sight so touching in its majesty:
This City now doth, like a garment, wear
The beauty of the morning; silent, bare,
Ships, towers, domes, theatres, and tem-
    ples lie   6
Open unto the fields, and to the sky;
All bright and glittering in the smokeless
    air.
Never did sun more beautifully steep
In his first splendour, valley, rock, or
    hill;   10
Ne'er saw I, never felt, a calm so deep!
The river glideth at his own sweet will:
Dear God! the very houses seem asleep;
And all that mighty heart is lying still!

XXXVII.

CONCLUSION.

TO ——

[Composed probably 1827.—Published 1827.]

IF these brief Records, by the Muses' art
Produced as lonely Nature or the strife
That animates the scenes of public life[2]
Inspired, may in thy leisure claim a part;
And if these Transcripts of the private
    heart   5

[2] This line alludes to Sonnets which will be found in another Class.

Have gained a sanction from thy falling
 tears;
Then I repent not. But my soul hath fears
Breathed from eternity; for, as a dart
Cleaves the blank air, Life flies: now
 every day
Is but a glimmering spoke in the swift
 wheel   10
Of the revolving week. Away, away,
All fitful cares, all transitory zeal!
So timely Grace the immortal wing may
 heal,
And honour rest upon the senseless clay.

PART III.
I.

[Composed ?.—Published 1842.]

THOUGH the bold wings of Poesy affect
The clouds, and wheel around the moun-
 tain tops
Rejoicing, from her loftiest height she
 drops
Well pleased to skim the plain with wild
 flowers deckt,
Or muse in solemn grove whose shades
 protect   5
The lingering dew—there steals along, or
 stops
Watching the least small bird that round
 her hops,
Or creeping worm, with sensitive respect.
Her functions are they therefore less
 divine,
Her thoughts less deep, or void of grave
 intent   10
Her simplest fancies? Should that fear
 be thine,
Aspiring Votary, ere thy hand present
One offering, kneel before her modest
 shrine,
With brow in penitential sorrow bent!

II.
OXFORD, MAY 30, 1820.

[Composed 1820.—Published 1820.]

YE sacred Nurseries of blooming Youth!
In whose collegiate shelter England's
 Flowers
Expand, enjoying through their vernal
 hours

The air of liberty, the light of truth;
Much have ye suffered from Time's gnaw-
 ing tooth: 5
Yet, O ye spires of Oxford! domes and
 towers!
Gardens and groves! your presence over-
 powers
The soberness of reason; till, in sooth,
Transformed, and rushing on a bold
 exchange   9
I slight my own beloved Cam, to range
Where silver Isis leads my stripling feet;
Pace the long avenue, or glide adown
The stream-like windings of that glorious
 street—
An eager Novice robed in fluttering gown!

III.
OXFORD, MAY 30, 1820.

[Composed 1820.—Published 1820.]

SHAME on this faithless heart! that could
 allow
Such transport, though but for a mo-
 ment's space;
Not while—to aid the spirit of the place—
The crescent moon clove with its glitter-
 ing prow
The clouds, or night-bird sang from shady
 bough;   5
But in plain daylight:——She, too, at my
 side,
Who, with her heart's experience satisfied,
Maintains inviolate its slightest vow!
Sweet Fancy! other gifts must I receive;
Proofs of a higher sovereignty I claim; 10
Take from *her* brow the withering flowers
 of eve,
And to that brow life's morning wreath
 restore;
Let *her* be comprehended in the frame
Of these illusions, or they please no more.

IV.
RECOLLECTION OF THE PORTRAIT OF KING
HENRY THE EIGHTH, TRINITY LODGE,
CAMBRIDGE.

[Composed ?.—Published 1827.]

THE imperial Stature, the colossal stride,
Are yet before me; yet do I behold
The broad full visage, chest of amplest
 mould,

The vestments 'broidered with barbaric
　　pride:
And lo! a poniard, at the Monarch's
　　side,　　　　　　　　　　5
Hangs ready to be grasped in sympathy
With the keen threatenings of that ful-
　　gent eye,
Below the white-rimmed bonnet, far-
　　descried.
Who trembles now at thy capricious
　　mood?
'Mid those surrounding Worthies, haughty
　　King,　　　　　　　　　　10
We rather think, with grateful mind
　　sedate,
How Providence educeth, from the spring
Of lawless will, unlooked-for streams of
　　good,
Which neither force shall check nor time
　　abate!

V.

ON THE DEATH OF HIS MAJESTY (GEORGE
THE THIRD).

(Composed 1820.—Published 1820.

WARD of the Law!—dread Shadow of a
　　King!
Whose realm had dwindled to one stately
　　room;
Whose universe was gloom immersed in
　　gloom,
Darkness as thick as life o'er life could
　　fling,
Save haply for some feeble glimmering　5
Of Faith and Hope—if thou, by nature's
　　doom,
Gently hast sunk into the quiet tomb,
Why should we bend in grief, to sorrow
　　cling,
When thankfulness were best?—Fresh-
　　flowing tears,
Or, where tears flow not, sigh succeeding
　　sigh,　　　　　　　　　　10
Yield to such after-thought the sole
　　reply
Which justly it can claim. The Nation
　　hears
In this deep knell, silent for threescore
　　years,
An unexampled voice of awful memory!

VI.

JUNE, 1820.

[Composed 1820.—Published 1820.]

FAME tells of groves—from England far
　　away—
Groves[1] that inspire the Nightingale to
　　trill
And modulate, with subtle reach of skill
Elsewhere unmatched, her ever-varying
　　lay;
Such bold report I venture to gainsay:　5
For I have heard the quire of Richmond
　　hill
Chanting with indefatigable bill,
Strains that recalled to mind a distant
　　day;
When, haply under shade of that same
　　wood,
And scarcely conscious of the dashing
　　oars　　　　　　　　　　10
Plied steadily between those willowy
　　shores,
The sweet-souled Poet of the Seasons
　　stood—
Listening, and listening long, in raptur-
　　ous mood,
Ye heavenly Birds! to your Progenitors.

VII.

A PARSONAGE IN OXFORDSHIRE.

[Composed 1820.—Published 1822 (*Ecclesiastical
Sketches*, note, p. 121); ed. 1827.]

WHERE holy ground begins, unhallowed
　　ends,
Is marked by no distinguishable line;
The turf unites, the pathways intertwine;
And, wheresoe'er the stealing footstep
　　tends,
Garden, and that Domain where kindred,
　　friends,　　　　　　　　　　5
And neighbours rest together, here con-
　　found
Their several features, mingled like the
　　sound
Of many waters, or as evening blends
With shady night. Soft airs, from shrub
　　and flower,

---

[1] Wallachia is the country alluded to.

Waft fragrant greetings to each silent
   grave; 10
And while those lofty poplars gently wave
Their tops, between them comes and goes
   a sky
Bright as the glimpses of eternity,
To saints accorded in their mortal hour.

VIII.

COMPOSED AMONG THE RUINS OF A CASTLE
IN NORTH WALES.

[Composed probably September, 1824.—Published
1827.]

THROUGH shattered galleries, 'mid roof-
   less halls,
Wandering with timid footsteps oft be-
   trayed,
The Stranger sighs, nor scruples to up-
   braid
Old Time, though he, gentlest among the
   Thralls 4
Of Destiny, upon these wounds hath laid
His lenient touches, soft as light that falls,
From the wan Moon, upon the towers
   and walls,
Light deepening the profoundest sleep
   of shade.
Relic of Kings! Wreck of forgotten wars,
To winds abandoned and the prying stars,
Time *loves* Thee! at his call the Seasons
   twine 11
Luxuriant wreaths around thy forehead
   hoar;
And, though past pomp no changes can
   restore,
A soothing recompense, his gift, is thine!

IX.

TO THE LADY E. B. AND THE HON. MISS P.

[Composed September, 1824.—Published 1827.]

Composed in the Grounds of Plass Newidd, near
Llangollen, 1824.

A STREAM, to mingle with your favourite
   Dee,
Along the VALE OF MEDITATION [1] flows;
So styled by those fierce Britons, pleased
   to see

---

[1] Glyn Myrvr.

In Nature's face the expression of repose;
Or haply there some pious hermit chose 5
To live and die, the peace of heaven his
   aim;
To whom the wild sequestered region owes,
At this late day, its sanctifying name.
GLYN CAFAILLGAROCH, in the Cambrian
   tongue,
In ours, the VALE OF FRIENDSHIP, let
   this spot 10
Be named; where, faithful to a low-
   roofed Cot,
On Deva's banks, ye have abode so long;
Sisters in love, a love allowed to climb,
Even on this earth, above the reach of
   Time!

X.

TO THE TORRENT AT THE DEVIL'S BRIDGE,
NORTH WALES, 1824.

[Composed September, 1824.—Published 1827.]

How art thou named? In search of what
   strange land,
From what huge height, descending?
   Can such force
Of waters issue from a British source,
Or hath not Pindus fed thee, where the band
Of Patriots scoop their freedom out, unth
   hand 5
Desperate as thine? Or come the in-
   cessant shocks
From that young Stream, that smites the
   throbbing rocks,
Of Viamala? There I seem to stand,
As in life's morn; permitted to behold,
From the dread chasm, woods climbing
   above woods, 10
In pomp that fades not; everlasting snows;
And skies that ne'er relinquish their
   repose;
Such power possess the family of floods
Over the minds of Poets, young or old!

XI.

IN THE WOODS OF RYDAL.

[Composed ?.—Published 1827.]

WILD Redbreast! hadst thou at Je-
   mima's lip
Pecked, as at mine, thus boldly, Love
   might say,

A half-blown rose had tempted thee
 to sip
Its glistening dews; but hallowed is
 the clay
Which the Muse warms; and I, whose
 head is grey,   5
Am not unworthy of thy fellowship;
Nor could I let one thought—one mo-
 tion—slip
That might thy sylvan confidence betray.
For are we not all His without whose
 care
Vouchsafed no sparrow falleth to the
 ground?   10
Who gives his Angels wings to speed
 through air,
And rolls the planets through the blue
 profound;
Then peck or perch, fond Flutterer! nor
 forbear
To trust a Poet in still musings bound.

XII.

[Composed ?.—Published 1827.]

WHEN Philoctetes in the Lemnian isle
Like a Form sculptured on a monument
Lay couched; on him or his dread bow
 unbent
Some wild Bird oft might settle and
 beguile
The rigid features of a transient smile,   5
Disperse the tear, or to the sigh give
 vent,
Slackening the pains of ruthless banish-
 ment
From his loved home, and from heroic
 toil.
And trust that spiritual Creatures round
 us move,
Griefs to allay which Reason cannot
 heal;   10
Yea, veriest reptiles have sufficed to
 prove
To fettered wretchedness that no Bas-
 tille
Is deep enough to exclude the light of
 love,
Though man for brother man has ceased
 to feel.

XIII.

[Composed ?.—Published 1827.]

WHILE Anna's peers and early play-
 mates tread,
In freedom, mountain-turf and river's
 marge;
Or float with music in the festal barge;
Rein the proud steed, or through the
 dance are led;
Her doom it is to press a weary bed—   5
Till oft her guardian Angel, to some
 charge
More urgent called, will stretch his wings
 at large,
And friends too rarely prop the languid
 head.
Yet, helped by Genius—untired com-
 forter,
The presence even of a stuffed Owl for
 her   10
Can cheat the time; sending her fancy out
To ivied castles and to moonlight skies,
Though he can neither stir a plume, nor
 shout;
Nor veil, with restless film, his staring
 eyes.

XIV.

TO THE CUCKOO.

[Composed ?.—Published 1827.]

NOT the whole warbling grove in concert
 heard
When sunshine follows shower, the breast
 can thrill
Like the first summons, Cuckoo! of thy
 bill,
With its twin notes inseparably paired.
The captive 'mid damp vaults unsunned,
 unaired,   5
Measuring the periods of his lonely doom,
That cry can reach; and to the sick
 man's room
Sends gladness, by no languid smile
 declared.
The lordly eagle-race through hostile
 search
May perish; time may come when never
 more   10
The wilderness shall hear the lion roar;

But, long as cock shall crow from house-
hold perch
To rouse the dawn, soft gales shall speed
thy wing,
And thy erratic voice be faithful to the
Spring !

XV.

TO ——

[Composed ?.—Published 1835.]

" Miss not the occasion: by the forelock take
That subtle Power, the never-halting Time,
Lest a mere moment's putting-off should make
Mischance almost as heavy as a crime."

" WAIT, prithee, wait !" this answer Les-
bia threw
Forth to her Dove, and took no further
heed.
Her eye was busy, while her fingers flew
Across the harp, with soul-engrossing
speed ;
But from that bondage when her thoughts
were freed   5
She rose, and toward the close-shut case-
ment drew,
Whence the poor unregarded Favourite,
true
To old affections, had been heard to plead
With flapping wing for entrance. What
a shriek
Forced from that voice so lately tuned
to a strain   10
Of harmony !—a shriek of terror, pain,
And self-reproach ! for, from aloft, a Kite
Pounced,—and the Dove, which from its
ruthless beak
She could not rescue, perished in her
sight !

XVI.

THE INFANT M—— M——.

[Composed ?.—Published 1827.]

UNQUIET Childhood here by special grace
Forgets her nature, opening like a flower
That neither feeds nor wastes its vital
power
In painful struggles. Months each other
chase,
And nought untunes that Infant's voice ;
no trace   5

Of fretful temper sullies her pure cheek ;
Prompt, lively, self-sufficing, yet so meek
That one enrapt with gazing on her face
(Which even the placid innocence of death
Could scarcely make more placid, heaven
more bright)   10
Might learn to picture, for the eye of
faith,
The Virgin, as she shone with kindred
light ;
A nursling couched upon her mother's
knee,
Beneath some shady palm of Galilee.

XVII.

TO ——, IN HER SEVENTIETH YEAR.

[Composed 1824.—Published 1827.].

SUCH age how beautiful ! O Lady bright,
Whose mortal lineaments seem all refined
By favouring Nature and a saintly Mind
To something purer and more exquisite
Than flesh and blood ; whene'er thou
meet'st my sight,   5
When I behold thy blanched unwithered
cheek,
Thy temples fringed with locks of gleam-
ing white,
And head that droops because the soul
is meek,
Thee with the welcome Snowdrop I com-
pare ;
That child of winter, prompting thoughts
that climb   10
From desolation toward the genial prime;
Or with the Moon conquering earth's
misty air,
And filling more and more with crystal
light
As pensive Evening deepens into night.

XVIII.

TO ROTHA Q——.

[Composed some years after 1822.—Published
1827.]

ROTHA, my Spiritual Child ! this head
was grey
When at the sacred font for thee I stood ;
Pledged till thou reach the verge of
womanhood,

And shalt become thy own sufficient stay:
Too late, I feel, sweet Orphan! was the
    day   5
For steadfast hope the contract to fulfil;
Yet shall my blessing hover o'er thee still,
Embodied in the music of this Lay,
Breathed forth beside the peaceful moun-
    tain Stream [1]
Whose murmur soothed thy languid Mo-
    ther's ear   10
After her throes, this Stream of name
    more dear
Since thou dost bear it,—a memorial
    theme
For others; for thy future self, a spell
To summon fancies out of Time's dark
    cell.

XIX.

A GRAVESTONE UPON THE FLOOR IN THE
CLOISTERS OF WORCESTER CATHEDRAL.

[Composed probably 1828.—Published 1829 (*The
Keepsake*); ed. 1832.]

"*MISERRIMUS!*" and neither name nor
    date,
Prayer, text, or symbol, graven upon
    the stone;
Nought but that word assigned to the
    unknown,
That solitary word—to separate
From all, and cast a cloud around the fate
Of him who lies beneath. Most wretched
    one,   6
Who chose his epitaph?—Himself alone
Could thus have dared the grave to
    agitate,
And claim, among the dead, this awful
    crown;
Nor doubt that He marked also for his
    own   10
Close to these cloistral steps a burial-
    place,
That every foot might fall with heavier
    tread,
Trampling upon his vileness. Stranger,
    pass
Softly!—To save the contrite, Jesus bled.

[1] The river Rotha, that flows into Windermere
from the Lakes of Grasmere and Rydal.

XX.

ROMAN ANTIQUITIES DISCOVERED AT
BISHOPSTONE, HEREFORDSHIRE.

[Composed ?.—Published 1835.]

WHILE poring Antiquarians search the
    ground
Upturned with curious pains, the Bard,
    a Seer,
Takes fire:—The men that have been
    reappear;
Romans for travel girt, for business
    gowned;
And some recline on couches, myrtle-
    crowned,   5
In festal glee: why not? For fresh and
    clear,
As if its hues were of the passing year,
Dawns this time-buried pavement. From
    that mound
Hoards may come forth of Trajans, Maxi-
    mins,
Shrunk into coins with all their warlike
    toil: 10
Or a fierce impress issues with its foil
Of tenderness—the Wolf, whose suckling
    Twins
The unlettered ploughboy pities when
    he wins
The casual treasure from the furrowed soil.

XXI.
1830.

[Composed November, 1830.—Published 1835.]

CHATSWORTH! thy stately mansion, and
    the pride
Of thy domain, strange contrast do present
To house and home in many a craggy rent
Of the wild Peak; where new-born waters
    glide
Through fields whose thrifty occupants
    abide   5
As in a dear and chosen banishment,
With every semblance of entire content;
So kind is simple Nature, fairly tried!
Yet He whose heart in childhood gave
    her troth
To pastoral dales, thin-set with modest
    farms,   10
May learn, if judgment strengthen with
    his growth,

That, not for Fancy only, pomp hath
    charms;
And, strenuous to protect from lawless
    harms
The extremes of favoured life, may honour
    both.

XXII.

A TRADITION OF OKER HILL IN DARLEY
DALE, DERBYSHIRE.

[Composed probably 1828.—Published 1829 (*The
    Keepsake*); ed. 1832.]

'TIS said that to the brow of yon fair
    hill
Two Brothers clomb, and, turning face
    from face,
Nor one look more exchanging, grief to
    still
Or feed, each planted on that lofty place
A chosen Tree; then, eager to fulfil   5
Their courses, like two new-born rivers,
    they
In opposite directions urged their way
Down from the far-seen mount. No blast
    might kill
Or blight that fond memorial;—the trees
    grew,
And now entwine their arms; but ne'er
    again   10
Embraced those Brothers upon earth's
    wide plain;
Nor aught of mutual joy or sorrow knew
Until their spirits mingled in the sea
That to itself takes all, Eternity.

XXIII.

FILIAL PIETY [1].

[Composed probably 1828.—Published 1829 (*The
    Casket*); ed. 1832.]

On the Wayside between Preston and Liverpool.

UNTOUCHED through all severity of cold;
Inviolate, whate'er the cottage hearth

---

[1] Thomas Scarisbrick was killed by a stroke
of lightning while building a turf-stack between
Ormskirk and Preston in 1779. His son James
finished the stack, and while he lived kept it
in constant repair in memory of the father.
James died in 1824, leaving to his grandchildren
goblets and decanters cut with a turf-stack
between two trees. (See Mr. J. Bromley's letter
to the *Athenæum*, May 17, 1890.)—ED.

Might need for comfort, or for festal
    mirth;
That Pile of Turf is half a century old:
Yes, Traveller! fifty winters have been
    told   5
Since suddenly the dart of death went
    forth
'Gainst him who raised it,—his last work
    on earth:
Thence has it, with the Son, so strong
    a hold
Upon his Father's memory, that his
    hands,
Through reverence, touch it only to re-
    pair   10
Its waste.—Though crumbling with each
    breath of air,
In annual renovation thus it stands—
Rude Mausoleum! but wrens nestle there,
And red-breasts warble when sweet sounds
    are rare.

XXIV.

TO THE AUTHOR'S PORTRAIT.

Painted at Rydal Mount, by W. Pickersgill, Esq.,
for St. John's College, Cambridge.]

[Composed probably 1832. Published 1835.]

Go, faithful Portrait! and where long
    hath knelt
Margaret, the saintly Foundress, take
    thy place;
And, if Time spare the colours for the
    grace
Which to the work surpassing skill hath
    dealt,
Thou, on thy rock reclined, though king-
    doms melt   5
And states be torn up by the roots, wilt
    seem
To breathe in rural peace, to hear the
    stream,
And think and feel as once the Poet
    felt.
Whate'er thy fate, those features have
    not grown
Unrecognised through many a household
    tear   10
More prompt, more glad, to fall than
    drops of dew

By morning shed around a flower half-
blown;
Tears of delight, that testified how true
To life thou art, and, in thy truth, how
dear!

XXV.

[Composed 1832 or 1833.—Published 1835.]

WHY art thou silent! Is thy love a plant
Of such weak fibre that the treacherous
air
Of absence withers what was once so fair?
Is there no debt to pay, no boon to grant?
Yet have my thoughts for thee been
vigilant—   5
Bound to thy service with unceasing care,
The mind's least generous wish a mendi-
cant
For nought but what thy happiness could
spare.
Speak—though this soft warm heart, once
free to hold
A thousand tender pleasures, thine and
mine,   10
Be left more desolate, more dreary cold
Than a forsaken bird's-nest filled with
snow
'Mid its own bush of leafless eglantine—
Speak, that my torturing doubts their end
may know!

XXVI.

TO B. R. HAYDON, ON SEEING HIS PICTURE
OF NAPOLEON BUONAPARTE ON THE
ISLAND OF ST. HELENA.

[Composed June 11, 1831.—Published 1832.]

HAYDON! let worthier judges praise the
skill
Here by thy pencil shown in truth of
lines
And charm of colours; *I* applaud those
signs
Of thought, that give the true poetic
thrill;
That unencumbered whole of blank and
still,   5
Sky without cloud—ocean without a
wave;
And the one Man that laboured to en-
slave

The World, sole-standing high on the
bare hill—
Back turned, arms folded, the unapparent
face
Tinged, we may fancy, in this dreary
place   10
With light reflected from the invisible
sun
Set, like his fortunes; but not set for
aye
Like them. The unguilty Power pursues
his way,
And before *him* doth dawn perpetual run.

XXVII.

[Composed ?.—Published: vol. of 1842.]

A POET!—He hath put his heart to
school,
Nor dares to move unpropped upon the
staff
Which Art hath lodged within his hand
—must laugh
By precept only, and shed tears by rule.
Thy Art be Nature; the live current
quaff,   5
And let the groveller sip his stagnant
pool,
In fear that else, when Critics grave and
cool
Have killed him, Scorn should write his
epitaph.
How does the Meadow-flower its bloom
unfold?
Because the lovely little flower is free   10
Down to its root, and, in that freedom,
bold;
And so the grandeur of the Forest-tree
Comes not by casting in a formal mould,
But from its *own* divine vitality.

XXVIII.

[Composed ?.—Published: vol. of 1842.]

THE most alluring clouds that mount the
sky
Owe to a troubled element their forms,
Their hues to sunset. If with raptured
eye
We watch their splendour, shall we covet
storms,
And wish the Lord of day his slow de-
cline   5

Would hasten, that such pomp may float
    on high?
Behold, already they forget to shine,
Dissolve—and leave to him who gazed a
    sigh.
Not loth to thank each moment for its boon
Of pure delight, come whensoe'er it may,
Peace let us seek,—to steadfast things
    attune   11
Calm expectations, leaving to the gay
And volatile their love of transient
    bowers,
The house that cannot pass away be ours.

XXIX.

ON A PORTRAIT OF THE DUKE OF WELLING-
TON UPON THE FIELD OF WATERLOO, BY
HAYDON.

[Composed August 31, 1840.—Published: vol. of
1842.]

BY Art's bold privilege Warrior and War-
    horse stand
On ground yet strewn with their last
    battle's wreck ;
Let the Steed glory while his Master's hand
Lies fixed for ages on his conscious neck ;
But by the Chieftain's look, though at his
    side   5
Hangs that day's treasured sword, how
    firm a check
Is given to triumph and all human pride !
Yon trophied Mound shrinks to a sha-
    dowy speck
In his calm presence ! Him the mighty deed
Elates not, brought far nearer the grave's
    rest,   10
As shows that time-worn face, for he such
    seed
Has sown as yields, we trust, the fruit of
    fame
In Heaven ; hence no one blushes for thy
    name,
Conqueror, 'mid some sad thoughts, di-
    vinely blest !

XXX.

COMPOSED ON A MAY MORNING, 1838.

[Composed May, 1838.—Published: Sonnet-vol.
of 1838.]

LIFE with yon Lambs, like day, is just
    begun,
Yet Nature seems to them a heavenly guide.

Does joy approach? they meet the coming
    tide;
And sullenness avoid, as now they
    shun
Pale twilight's lingering glooms,—and in
    the sun   5
Couch near their dams, with quiet satis-
    fied ;
Or gambol—each with his shadow at his
    side,
Varying its shape wherever he may
    run.
As they from turf yet hoar with sleepy
    dew
All turn, and court the shining and the
    green,   10
Where herbs look up, and opening flowers
    are seen ;
Why to God's goodness cannot We be
    true,
And so, His gifts and promises between,
Feed to the last on pleasures ever new?

XXXI.

[Composed ?.—Published: vol. of 1842.]

Lo ! where she stands fixed in a quiet like
    trance,
One upward hand, as if she needed rest
From rapture, lying softly on her breast !
Nor wants her eyeball an ethereal glance ;
But not the less—nay more—that counte-
    nance,   5
While thus illumined, tells of painful
    strife
For a sick heart made weary of this life
By love, long crossed with adverse circum-
    stance.
—Would She were now as when she hoped
    to pass
At God's appointed hour to them who
    tread   10
Heaven's sapphire pavement, yet breathed
    well content,
Well pleased, her foot should print earth's
    common grass,
Lived thankful for day's light, for daily
    bread,
For health, and time in obvious duty
    spent.

XXXII.

TO A PAINTER.

[Composed 1840.—Published: vol. of 1842.]

ALL praise the Likeness by thy skill
   portrayed ;
But 'tis a fruitless task to paint for me,
Who, yielding not to changes Time has
   made,
By the habitual light of memory see
Eyes unbedimmed, see bloom that cannot
   fade,   5
And smiles that from their birthplace
   ne'er shall flee
Into the land where ghosts and phantoms
   be ;
And, seeing this, own nothing in its stead.
Couldst thou go back into far-distant
   years,
Or share with me, fond thought ! that
   inward eye,   10
Then, and then only, Painter ! could thy
   Art
The visual powers of Nature satisfy,
Which hold, whate'er to common sight
   appears,
Their sovereign empire in a faithful
   heart.

XXXIII.

ON THE SAME SUBJECT.

[Composed 1840.—Published: vol. of 1842.]

THOUGH I beheld at first with blank sur-
   prise
This Work, I now have gazed on it so
   long
I see its truth with unreluctant eyes ;
O, my Belovèd ! I have done thee wrong,
Conscious of blessedness, but, whence it
   sprung,   5
Ever too heedless, as I now perceive :
Morn into noon did pass, noon into eve,
And the old day was welcome as the
   young,
As welcome, and as beautiful—in sooth
More beautiful, as being a thing more
   holy :   10
Thanks to thy virtues, to the eternal
   youth

Of all thy goodness, never melancholy ;
To thy large heart and humble mind, that
   cast
Into one vision, future, present, past.

XXXIV.

[Composed 1838.—Published: Sonnet-vol. of 1838.]

HARK ! 'tis the Thrush, undaunted, unde-
   prest,
By twilight premature of cloud and rain ;
Nor does that roaring wind deaden his
   strain
Who carols thinking of his Love and nest,
And seems, as more incited, still more
   blest.   5
Thanks ; thou hast snapped a fireside
   Prisoner's chain,
Exulting Warbler ! eased a fretted brain,
And in a moment charmed my cares to rest.
Yes, I will forth, bold Bird ! and front
   the blast,
That we may sing together, if thou wilt,
So loud, so clear, my Partner through
   life's day,   11
Mute in her nest love-chosen, if not love-
   built
Like thine, shall gladden, as in seasons
   past,
Thrilled by loose snatches of the social
   Lay.

XXXV.

[Composed 1838.—Published: Sonnet-vol. of 1838.]

'TIS He whose yester-evening's high dis-
   dain
Beat back the roaring storm—but how
   subdued
His day-break note, a sad vicissitude !
Does the hour's drowsy weight his glee
   restrain ?
Or, like the nightingale, her joyous vein   5
Pleased to renounce, does this dear Thrush
   attune
His voice to suit the temper of yon Moon
Doubly depressed, setting, and in her
   wane ?
Rise, tardy Sun ! and let the Songster
   prove
(The balance trembling between night
   and morn   10

No longer) with what ecstasy upborne
He can pour forth his spirit.   In heaven
above,
And earth below, they best can serve true
gladness
Who meet most feelingly the calls of
sadness.

XXXVI.

[Composed 1837.—Published: Sonnet-vol. of 1838.]

OH what a Wreck ! how changed in mien
and speech !
Yet—though dread Powers, that work in
mystery, spin
Entanglings of the brain ; though shadows
stretch
O'er the chilled heart—reflect ; far, far
within
Hers is a holy Being, freed from Sin.   5
She is not what she seems, a forlorn
wretch,
But delegated Spirits comforts fetch
To Her from heights that Reason may
not win.
Like Children, She is privileged to hold
Divine communion ; both do live and
move,   10
Whate'er to shallow Faith their ways
unfold,
Inly illumined by Heaven's pitying love ;
Love pitying innocence, not long to last,
In them—in Her our sins and sorrows
past.

XXXVII.

[Composed March 8, 1842.—Published: vol. of 1842.]

INTENT on gathering wool from hedge
and brake
Yon busy Little-ones rejoice that soon
A poor old Dame will bless them for the
boon :
Great is their glee while flake they add to
flake
With rival earnestness ; far other strife   5
Than will hereafter move them, if they
make
Pastime their idol, give their day of life
To pleasure snatched for reckless plea-
sure's sake.

Can pomp and show allay one heart-born
grief ?
Pains which the World inflicts can she
requite ?   10
Not for an interval however brief ;
The silent thoughts that search for stead-
fast light,
Love from her depths, and Duty in her
might,
And Faith—these only yield secure relief.

XXXVIII.

A PLEA FOR AUTHORS.

[Composed May, 1838.—Published: Sonnet-vol. of
1838.]

FAILING impartial measure to dispense
To every suitor, Equity is lame ;
And social Justice, stript of reverence
For natural rights, a mockery and a
shame ;
Law but a servile dupe of false pretence,
If, guarding grossest things from common
claim   6
Now and for ever, She, to works that
came
From mind and spirit, grudge a short-
lived fence.
"What ! lengthened privilege, a lineal tie,
For *Books !*" Yes, heartless Ones, or be it
proved   10
That 'tis a fault in Us to have lived and
loved
Like others, with like temporal hopes to die ;
No public harm that Genius from her
course
Be turned ; and streams of truth dried
up, even at their source !

XXXIX.

VALEDICTORY SONNET.

Closing the Volume of Sonnets published in 1838.

[Composed 1838.—Published: Sonnet-vol. of 1838.]

SERVING no haughty Muse, my hands
have here
Disposed some cultured Flowerets (drawn
from spots
Where they bloomed singly, or in scat-
tered knots,)

Each kind in several beds of one par-
terre;
Both to allure the casual Loiterer,   5
And that, so placed, my Nurslings may
requite
Studious regard with opportune delight,
Nor be unthanked, unless I fondly err.
But metaphor dismissed, and thanks
apart,
Reader, farewell! My last words let them
be—   10
If in this book Fancy and Truth agree;
If simple Nature trained by careful Art
Through It have won a passage to thy
heart;
Grant me thy love, I crave no other fee!

XL.

TO THE REV. CHRISTOPHER WORDSWORTH,
D.D., MASTER OF HARROW SCHOOL,

After the perusal of his "Theophilus Anglicanus,"
recently published.

[Composed December 11, 1843.—Published 1845.]

ENLIGHTENED Teacher, gladly from thy
hand
Have I received this proof of pains be-
stowed
By Thee to guide thy Pupils on the
road
That, in our native isle, and every land,
The Church, when trusting in divine
command   5
And in her Catholic attributes, hath trod:
O may these lessons be with profit scanned
To thy heart's wish, thy labour blest by
God!
So the bright faces of the young and
gay
Shall look more bright—the happy,
happier still;   10
Catch, in the pauses of their keenest
play,
Motions of thought which elevate the
will
And, like the Spire that from your classic
Hill
Points heavenward, indicate the end and
way.

XLI.

TO THE PLANET VENUS,

Upon its approximation (as an Evening Star) to
the Earth, January, 1838.

[Composed January, 1838.—Published: Sonnet-
vol. of 1838.]

WHAT strong allurement draws, what
spirit guides,
Thee, Vesper! brightening still, as if the
nearer
Thou com'st to man's abode the spot grew
dearer
Night after night? True is it Nature
hides
Her treasures less and less.—Man now
presides   5
In power, where once he trembled in his
weakness;
Science advances with gigantic strides;
But are we aught enriched in love and
meekness?
Aught dost thou see, bright Star! of pure
and wise
More than in humbler times graced human
story;   10
That makes our hearts more apt to sym-
pathize
With heaven, our souls more fit for future
glory,
When earth shall vanish from our closing
eyes,
Ere we lie down in our last dormitory?

XLII.

[Composed December 24, 1842.—Published 1845.]

WANSFELL![1] this Household has a fa-
voured lot,
Living with liberty on thee to gaze,
To watch while Morn first crowns thee
with her rays,
Or when along thy breast serenely float
Evening's angelic clouds. Yet ne'er a
note   5
Hath sounded (shame upon the Bard!)
thy praise
For all that thou, as if from heaven, hast
brought

---

[1] The Hill that rises to the south-east, above
Ambleside.

Of glory lavished on our quiet days.
Bountiful Son of Earth! when we are
    gone
From every object dear to mortal sight, 10
As soon we shall be, may these words
    attest
How oft, to elevate our spirits, shone
Thy visionary majesties of light,
How in thy pensive glooms our hearts
    found rest.

XLIII.

[Composed January 1, 1843.—Published 1845.]

WHILE beams of orient light shoot wide
    and high,
Deep in the vale a little rural Town[1]
Breathes forth a cloud-like creature of its
    own,
That mounts not toward the radiant
    morning sky,
But, with a less ambitious sympathy,   5
Hangs o'er its Parent waking to the cares
Troubles and toils that every day pre-
    pares.
So Fancy, to the musing Poet's eye,
Endears that Lingerer. And how blest
    her sway,
(Like influence never may my soul reject),
If the calm Heaven, now to its zenith
    decked   11
With glorious forms in numberless array,
To the lone shepherd on the hills disclose
Gleams from a world in which the saints
    repose.

XLIV.

[Composed ?.—Published 1827.]

IN my mind's eye a Temple, like a cloud
Slowly surmounting some invidious hill,
Rose out of darkness: the bright Work
    stood still;
And might of its own beauty have been
    proud,
But it was fashioned and to God was
    vowed   5
By Virtues that diffused, in every part,
Spirit divine through forms of human art:

---

[1] Ambleside.

Faith had her arch—her arch, when winds
    blow loud,
Into the consciousness of safety thrilled;
And Love her towers of dread foundation
    laid   10
Under the grave of things; Hope had her
    spire
Star-high, and pointing still to some-
    thing higher;
Trembling I gazed, but heard a voice—it
    said,
"Hell-gates are powerless Phantoms
    when *we* build."

XLV.

ON THE PROJECTED KENDAL AND
WINDERMERE RAILWAY.

[Composed October 12, 1844.—Published in pam-
phlet *Kendal and Windermere Railway*, 1844;
ed. 1845.]

IS then no nook of English ground secure
From rash assault?[2] Schemes of retire-
    ment sown
In youth, and 'mid the busy world kept
    pure
As when their earliest flowers of hope
    were blown,
Must perish;—how can they this blight
    endure?   5
And must he too the ruthless change be-
    moan
Who scorns a false utilitarian lure
'Mid his paternal fields at random thrown?
Baffle the threat, bright Scene, from Or-
    rest-head
Given to the pausing traveller's rapturous
    glance: 10
Plead for thy peace, thou beautiful ro-
    mance

---

[2] The degree and kind of attachment which
many of the yeomanry feel to their small in-
heritances can scarcely be over-rated. Near the
house of one of them stands a magnificent tree,
which a neighbour of the owner advised him to
fell for profit's sake. "Fell it!" exclaimed the
yeoman, "I had rather fall on my knees and
worship it." It happens, I believe, that the in-
tended railway would pass through this little
property, and I hope that an apology for the
answer will not be thought necessary by one
who enters into the strength of the feeling.

Of nature; and, if human hearts be dead,
Speak, passing winds; ye torrents, with
   your strong
And constant voice, protest against the
   wrong.

XLVI.

[Composed 1844.—Published along with XLV.]

PROUD were ye, Mountains, when, in times
   of old,
Your patriot sons, to stem invasive war,
Intrenched your brows; ye gloried in each
   scar:
Now, for your shame, a Power, the Thirst
   of Gold,
That rules o'er Britain like a baneful star,
Wills that your peace, your beauty, shall
   be sold, 6
And clear way made for her triumphal car
Through the beloved retreats your arms
   enfold!
Hear YE that Whistle? As her long-linked
   Train
Swept onwards, did the vision cross your
   view? 10
Yes, ye were startled;—and, in balance
   true,
Weighing the mischief with the promised
   gain,
Mountains, and Vales, and Floods, I call
   on you
To share the passion of a just disdain.

XLVII.

AT FURNESS ABBEY.

[Composed probably 1845.—Published 1845.]

HERE, where, of havoc tired and rash
   undoing,
Man left this Structure to become Time's
   prey,
A soothing spirit follows in the way
That Nature takes, her counter-work pur-
   suing.
See how her ivy clasps the sacred Ruin, 5

Fall to prevent or beautify decay;
And, on the mouldered walls, how bright,
   how gay,
The flowers in pearly dews their bloom
   renewing!
Thanks to the place, blessings upon the
   hour;
Even as I speak the rising Sun's first
   smile 10
Gleams on the grass-crowned top of yon
   tall Tower,
Whose cawing occupants with joy pro-
   claim
Prescriptive title to the shattered pile,
Where, Cavendish, *thine* seems nothing
   but a name!

XLVIII.

AT FURNESS ABBEY.

[Composed June 21, 1845.—Published 1845.]

WELL have yon Railway Labourers to
   THIS ground
Withdrawn for noontide rest. They sit,
   they walk
Among the Ruins, but no idle talk
Is heard; to grave demeanour all are
   bound;
And from one voice a Hymn with tuneful
   sound 5
Hallows once more the long-deserted
   Quire
And thrills the old sepulchral earth, a-
   round.
Others look up, and with fixed eyes ad-
   mire
That wide-spanned arch, wondering how
   it was raised,
To keep, so high in air, its strength and
   grace: 10
All seem to feel the spirit of the place,
And by the general reverence God is
   praised:
Profane Despoilers, stand ye not reproved,
While thus these simple-hearted men are
   moved?

MEMORIALS OF A TOUR IN SCOTLAND, 1803.

I.

DEPARTURE

FROM THE VALE OF GRASMERE. AUGUST,
1803.

[Composed 1811[1].—Published 1827.]

THE gentlest Shade that walked Elysian
    plains
Might sometimes covet dissoluble chains;
Even for the tenants of the zone that lies
Beyond the stars, celestial Paradise,
Methinks 'twould heighten joy, to over-
    leap   5
At will the crystal battlements, and peep
Into some other region, though less fair,
To see how things are made and managed
    there.
Change for the worse might please, in-
    cursion bold
Into the tracts of darkness and of cold; 10
O'er Limbo lake with aery flight to steer,
And on the verge of Chaos hang in fear.
Such animation often do I find,
Power in my breast, wings growing in my
    mind,
Then, when some rock or hill is overpast,
Perchance without one look behind me
    cast,   16
Some barrier with which Nature, from
    the birth
Of things, has fenced this fairest spot on
    earth.
O pleasant transit, Grasmere! to resign
Such happy fields, abodes so calm as thine;
Not like an outcast with himself at strife;
The slave of business, time, or care for life,

[1] Originally the opening lines of the *Epistle
to Sir George Beaumont.* See p. 521.—ED.

But moved by choice; or, if constrained
    in part,
Yet still with Nature's freedom at the
    heart;—   24
To cull contentment upon wildest shores,
And luxuries extract from bleakest moors;
With prompt embrace all beauty to enfold,
And having rights in all that we behold.
—Then why these lingering steps?—A
    bright adieu,   29
For a brief absence, proves that love is true;
Ne'er can the way be irksome or forlorn
That winds into itself for sweet return.

II.

AT THE GRAVE OF BURNS.
1803.

SEVEN YEARS AFTER HIS DEATH.

[Composed partly before 1807.—Published: vol.
of 1842.]

I SHIVER, Spirit fierce and bold,
At thought of what I now behold:
As vapours breathed from dungeons cold
    Strike pleasure dead,
So sadness comes from out the mould   5
    Where Burns is laid.

And have I then thy bones so near,
And thou forbidden to appear?
As if it were thyself that's here
    I shrink with pain;   10
And both my wishes and my fear
    Alike are vain.

Off weight—nor press on weight!—away
Dark thoughts!—they came, but not to
    stay;
With chastened feelings would I pay   15
    The tribute due
To him, and aught that hides his clay
    From mortal view.

Fresh as the flower, whose modest worth
He sang, his genius "glinted" forth,   20
Rose like a star that touching earth,
   For so it seems,
Doth glorify its humble birth
   With matchless beams.

The piercing eye, the thoughtful brow,   25
The struggling heart, where be they now?—
Full soon the Aspirant of the plough,
   The prompt, the brave,
Slept, with the obscurest, in the low
   And silent grave.   30

I mourned with thousands, but as one
More deeply grieved, for He was gone
Whose light I hailed when first it shone,
   And showed my youth   34
How Verse may build a princely throne
   On humble truth.

Alas! where'er the current tends,
Regret pursues and with it blends,—
Huge Criffel's hoary top ascends
   By Skiddaw seen,—   40
Neighbours we were, and loving friends
   We might have been;

True friends though diversely inclined;
But heart with heart and mind with mind,
Where the main fibres are entwined,   45
   Through Nature's skill,
May even by contraries be joined
   More closely still.

The tear will start, and let it flow;
Thou "poor Inhabitant below,"   50
At this dread moment—even so—
   Might we together
Have sate and talked where gowans blow,
   Or on wild heather.

What treasures would have then been
   placed   55
Within my reach; of knowledge graced
By fancy what a rich repast!
   But why go on?—
Oh! spare to sweep, thou mournful blast,
   His grave grass-grown.   60

There, too, a Son, his joy and pride,
(Not three weeks past the Stripling died,)
Lies gathered to his Father's side,

   Soul-moving sight!
Yet one to which is not denied   65
   Some sad delight.

For *he* is safe, a quiet bed
Hath early found among the dead,
Harboured where none can be misled,
   Wronged, or distrest;   70
And surely here it may be said
   That such are blest.

And oh for Thee, by pitying grace
Checked oft-times in a devious race,
May He, who halloweth the place   75
   Where Man is laid,
Receive thy Spirit in the embrace
   For which it prayed!

Sighing I turned away; but ere
Night fell I heard, or seemed to hear,   80
Music that sorrow comes not near,
   A ritual hymn,
Chanted in love that casts out fear
   By Seraphim.

III.

THOUGHTS

SUGGESTED THE DAY FOLLOWING, ON THE
BANKS OF NITH, NEAR THE POET'S
RESIDENCE.

[Finished 1839.—Published: vol. of 1842.]

Too frail to keep the lofty vow
That must have followed when his brow
Was wreathed—"The Vision" tells us
   how—
   With holly spray,
He faltered, drifted to and fro,   5
   And passed away.

Well might such thoughts, dear Sister,
   throng
Our minds when, lingering all too long,
Over the grave of Burns we hung
   In social grief—   10
Indulged as if it were a wrong
   To seek relief.

But, leaving each unquiet theme
Where gentlest judgments may misdeem,
And prompt to welcome every gleam   15
   Of good and fair,
Let us beside the limpid Stream
   Breathe hopeful air.

Enough of sorrow, wreck, and blight;
Think rather of those moments bright   20
When to the consciousness of right
    His course was true,
When Wisdom prospered in his sight
    And virtue grew.

Yes, freely let our hearts expand,   25
Freely as in youth's season bland,
When side by side, his Book in hand,
    We wont to stray,
Our pleasure varying at command
    Of each sweet Lay.   30

How oft inspired must he have trod
These pathways, yon far-stretching road!
There lurks his home; in that Abode,
    With mirth elate,
Or in his nobly-pensive mood,   35
    The Rustic sate.

Proud thoughts that Image overawes,
Before it humbly let us pause,
And ask of Nature from what cause
    And by what rules   40
She trained her Burns to win applause
    That shames the Schools.

Through busiest street and loneliest glen
Are felt the flashes of his pen;
He rules 'mid winter snows, and when   45
    Bees fill their hives;
Deep in the general heart of men
    His power survives.

What need of fields in some far clime
Where Heroes, Sages, Bards sublime,   50
And all that fetched the flowing rhyme
    From genuine springs,
Shall dwell together till old Time
    Folds up his wings?

Sweet Mercy! to the gates of Heaven   55
This Minstrel lead, his sins forgiven;
The rueful conflict, the heart riven
    With vain endeavour,
And memory of Earth's bitter leaven,
    Effaced for ever.   60

But why to Him confine the prayer,
When kindred thoughts and yearnings
    bear
On the frail heart the purest share

    With all that live?—
The best of what we do and are,   65
    Just God, forgive![1]

IV.

TO THE SONS OF BURNS,

AFTER VISITING THE GRAVE OF THEIR
FATHER.

[Composed partly between June 1805 and
Feb. 1806.—Published 1807[2].]

"The Poet's grave is in a corner of the churchyard.
We looked at it with melancholy and painful re-
flections, repeating to each other his own verses—
"'Is there a man whose judgment clear,' etc."
    —*Extract from the Journal of
    my Fellow-traveller.*

'MID crowded obelisks and urns
I sought the untimely grave of Burns;
Sons of the Bard, my heart still mourns
    With sorrow true;
And more would grieve, but that it turns
    Trembling to you!   6

Through twilight shades of good and ill
Ye now are panting up life's hill,
And more than common strength and skill
    Must ye display;   10
If ye would give the better will
    Its lawful sway.

Hath Nature strung your nerves to bear
Intemperance with less harm, beware!
But if the Poet's wit ye share,   15
    Like him can speed
The social hour—of tenfold care
    There will be need;

For honest men delight will take
To spare your failings for his sake,   20
Will flatter you,—and fool and rake
    Your steps pursue;
And of your Father's name will make
    A snare for you.

Far from their noisy haunts retire,   25
And add your voices to the quire
That sanctify the cottage fire
    With service meet;
There seek the genius of your Sire,
    His spirit greet;   30

---

[1] See Note, p. 902.
[2] Stanzas ii., iii., iv., viii., published in 1807;
stanzas i., v., vi., vii., published in 1827.—ED

Or where 'mid "lonely heights and hows,"
He paid to Nature tuneful vows;
Or wiped his honourable brows
    Bedewed with toil,
While reapers strove, or busy ploughs 35
    Upturned the soil;

His judgment with benignant ray
Shall guide, his fancy cheer, your way;
But ne'er to a seductive lay
    Let faith be given;   40
Nor deem that "light which leads astray
    Is light from Heaven."

Let no mean hope your souls enslave;
Be independent, generous, brave;
Your Father such example gave,   45
    And such revere;
But be admonished by his grave,
    And think, and fear!

V.

ELLEN IRWIN:

OR,

THE BRAES OF KIRTLE [1].

[Composed probably 1799 or 1800.—Published 1800.]

FAIR Ellen Irwin, when she sate
Upon the braes of Kirtle,
Was lovely as a Grecian maid
Adorned with wreaths of myrtle;
Young Adam Bruce beside her lay,   5
And there did they beguile the day
With love and gentle speeches,
Beneath the budding beeches.

From many knights and many squires
The Bruce had been selected;   10
And Gordon, fairest of them all,
By Ellen was rejected.
Sad tidings to that noble Youth!
For it may be proclaimed with truth,
If Bruce hath loved sincerely,   15
That Gordon loves as dearly.

But what are Gordon's form and face,
His shattered hopes and crosses,

----

[1] The Kirtle is a river in the southern part of
Scotland, on the banks of which the events here
related took place.

To them, 'mid Kirtle's pleasant braes,
Reclined on flowers and mosses?   20
Alas that ever he was born!
The Gordon, couched behind a thorn,
Sees them and their caressing;
Beholds them blest and blessing.

Proud Gordon, maddened by the thoughts
That through his brain are travelling,   26
Rushed forth, and at the heart of Bruce
He launched a deadly javelin!
Fair Ellen saw it as it came,
And, starting up to meet the same,   30
Did with her body cover
The Youth, her chosen lover.

And, falling into Bruce's arms,
Thus died the beauteous Ellen,
Thus, from the heart of her True-love, 35
The mortal spear repelling.
And Bruce, as soon as he had slain
The Gordon, sailed away to Spain;
And fought with rage incessant
Against the Moorish crescent.   40

But many days, and many months,
And many years ensuing,
This wretched Knight did vainly seek
The death that he was wooing.
So, coming his last help to crave,   45
Heart-broken, upon Ellen's grave
His body he extended,
And there his sorrow ended.

Now ye, who willingly have heard
The tale I have been telling,   50
May in Kirkconnell churchyard view
The grave of lovely Ellen:
By Ellen's side the Bruce is laid;
And, for the stone upon his head,
May no rude hand deface it,   55
And its forlorn 𝕳𝕚𝕔 𝕛𝕒𝕮𝕖𝕥!

VI.

TO A HIGHLAND GIRL,

AT INVERSNEYDE, UPON LOCH LOMOND.

[Composed 1803.—Published 1807.]

SWEET Highland Girl, a very shower
Of beauty is thy earthly dower!
Twice seven consenting years have shed
Their utmost bounty on thy head:

And these grey rocks; that household
   lawn;   5
Those trees, a veil just half withdrawn;
This fall of water that doth make
A murmur near the silent lake;
This little bay; a quiet road
That holds in shelter thy Abode—   10
In truth together do ye seem
Like something fashioned in a dream;
Such Forms as from their covert peep
When earthly cares are laid asleep!
But, O fair Creature! in the light   15
Of common day, so heavenly bright,
I bless Thee, Vision as thou art,
I bless thee with a human heart;
God shield thee to thy latest years!
Thee, neither know I, nor thy peers;   20
And yet my eyes are filled with tears.

With earnest feeling I shall pray
For thee when I am far away:
For never saw I mien, or face,
In which more plainly I could trace   25
Benignity and home-bred sense
Ripening in perfect innocence.
Here scattered, like a random seed,
Remote from men, Thou dost not need
The embarrassed look of shy distress,   30
And maidenly shamefacedness:
Thou wear'st upon thy forehead clear
The freedom of a Mountaineer:
A face with gladness overspread!
Soft smiles, by human kindness bred!   35
And seemliness complete, that sways
Thy courtesies, about thee plays;
With no restraint, but such as springs
From quick and eager visitings
Of thoughts that lie beyond the reach   40
Of thy few words of English speech:
A bondage sweetly brooked, a strife
That gives thy gestures grace and life!
So have I, not unmoved in mind,
Seen birds of tempest-loving kind—   45
Thus beating up against the wind.

What hand but would a garland cull
For thee who art so beautiful?
O happy pleasure! here to dwell
Beside thee in some heathy dell;   50
Adopt your homely ways, and dress,
A Shepherd, thou a Shepherdess!

But I could frame a wish for thee
More like a grave reality:
Thou art to me but as a wave   55
Of the wild sea; and I would have
Some claim upon thee, if I could,
Though but of common neighbourhood.
What joy to hear thee, and to see!
Thy elder Brother I would be,   60
Thy Father—anything to thee!

Now thanks to Heaven! that of its
   grace
Hath led me to this lonely place.
Joy have I had; and going hence
I bear away my recompense.   65
In spots like these it is we prize
Our Memory, feel that she hath eyes:
Then, why should I be loth to stir?
I feel this place was made for her;
To give new pleasure like the past,   70
Continued long as life shall last.
Nor am I loth, though pleased at heart,
Sweet Highland Girl! from thee to part;
For I, methinks, till I grow old,
As fair before me shall behold,   75
As I do now, the cabin small,
The lake, the bay, the waterfall;
And Thee, the Spirit of them all!

VII.

GLEN ALMAIN;

OR, THE NARROW GLEN.

[Composed probably 1803.--Published 1807.]

IN this still place, remote from men,
Sleeps Ossian, in the NARROW GLEN;
In this still place, where murmurs on
But one meek streamlet, only one:
He sang of battles, and the breath   5
Of stormy war, and violent death;
And should, methinks, when all was past,
Have rightfully been laid at last
Where rocks were rudely heaped, and
   rent
As by a spirit turbulent;   10
Where sights were rough, and sounds
   were wild,
And everything unreconciled;
In some complaining, dim retreat,
For fear and melancholy meet;

But this is calm; there cannot be   15
A more entire tranquillity.

Does then the Bard sleep here indeed?
Or is it but a groundless creed?
What matters it?—I blame them not
Whose Fancy in this lonely Spot   20
Was moved; and in such way expressed
Their notion of its perfect rest.
A convent, even a hermit's cell,
Would break the silence of this Dell:
It is not quiet, is not ease;   25
But something deeper far than these:
The separation that is here
Is of the grave; and of austere
Yet happy feelings of the dead:
And, therefore, was it rightly said   30
That Ossian, last of all his race!
Lies buried in this lonely place.

VIII.

STEPPING WESTWARD.

[Composed June 3, 1805.—Published 1807.]

While my Fellow-traveller and I were walking
by the side of Loch Ketterine, one fine evening
after sunset, in our road to a Hut where, in the
course of our Tour, we had been hospitably
entertained some weeks before, we met, in one
of the loneliest parts of that solitary region,
two well-dressed Women, one of whom said to
us, by way of greeting, "What, you are step-
ping westward?"

"*WHAT, you are stepping westward?*"—
    "*Yea.*"
—'Twould be a *wildish* destiny,
If we, who thus together roam
In a strange Land, and far from home,
Were in this place the guests of Chance: 5
Yet who would stop, or fear to advance,
Though home or shelter he had none,
With such a sky to lead him on?

The dewy ground was dark and cold;
Behind, all gloomy to behold;   10
And stepping westward seemed to be
A kind of *heavenly* destiny:
I liked the greeting; 'twas a sound
Of something without place or bound;
And seemed to give me spiritual right   15
To travel through that region bright.

The voice was soft, and she who spake
Was walking by her native lake:
The salutation had to me
The very sound of courtesy: 20
Its power was felt; and while my eye
Was fixed upon the glowing Sky,
The echo of the voice enwrought
A human sweetness with the thought
Of travelling through the world that lay
Before me in my endless way.   26

IX.

THE SOLITARY REAPER.

[Composed Nov. 1805.—Published 1807.]

BEHOLD her, single in the field,
Yon solitary Highland Lass!
Reaping and singing by herself;
Stop here, or gently pass!
Alone she cuts and binds the grain,   5
And sings a melancholy strain;
O listen! for the Vale profound
Is overflowing with the sound.

No Nightingale did ever chaunt
More welcome notes to weary bands   10
Of travellers in some shady haunt,
Among Arabian sands:
A voice so thrilling ne'er was heard
In spring-time from the Cuckoo-bird,
Breaking the silence of the seas   15
Among the farthest Hebrides.

Will no one tell me what she sings?—
Perhaps the plaintive numbers flow
For old, unhappy, far-off things,
And battles long ago: 20
Or is it some more humble lay,
Familiar matter of to-day?
Some natural sorrow, loss, or pain,
That has been, and may be again?

Whate'er the theme, the Maiden sang   25
As if her song could have no ending;
I saw her singing at her work,
And o'er the sickle bending;—
I listened, motionless and still;
And, as I mounted up the hill,   30
The music in my heart I bore,
Long after it was heard no more.

X.

ADDRESS TO KILCHURN CASTLE, UPON LOCH AWE.

[Composed ll. 1–3, 1803; finished "long after."—
Published 1827.]

"From the top of the hill a most impressive
scene opened upon our view,—a ruined Castle
on an Island (for an Island the flood had made
it) at some distance from the shore, backed by
a Cove of the Mountain Cruachan, down which
came a foaming stream. The Castle occupied
every foot of the Island that was visible to us,
appearing to rise out of the water,—mists rest-
ed upon the mountain side, with spots of sun-
shine; there was a mild desolation in the low
grounds, a solemn grandeur in the mountains,
and the Castle was wild, yet stately—not dis-
mantled of turrets—nor the walls broken down,
though obviously a ruin."—*Extract from the
Journal of my Companion.*

CHILD of loud-throated War! the moun-
    tain Stream
Roars in thy hearing; but thy hour of rest
Is come, and thou art silent in thy age;
Save when the wind sweeps by and
    sounds are caught
Ambiguous, neither wholly thine nor
    theirs.   5
Oh! there is life that breathes not;
    Powers there are
That touch each other to the quick in
    modes
Which the gross world no sense hath to
    perceive,
No soul to dream of. What art Thou,
    from care
Cast off—abandoned by thy rugged Sire,
Nor by soft Peace adopted; though, in
    place   11
And in dimension, such that thou might'st
    seem
But a mere footstool to yon sovereign
    Lord,
Huge Cruachan, (a thing that meaner hills
Might crush, nor know that it had suffered
    harm;)   15
Yet he, not loth, in favour of thy claims
To reverence, suspends his own; submit-
    ting
All that the God of Nature hath con-
    ferred,

All that he holds in common with the stars,
To the memorial majesty of Time   20
Impersonated in thy calm decay!
Take, then, thy seat, Vicegerent unre-
    proved!
Now, while a farewell gleam of evening
    light
Is fondly lingering on thy shattered front,
Do thou, in turn, be paramount; and rule
Over the pomp and beauty of a scene   26
Whose mountains, torrents, lake, and
    woods, unite
To pay thee homage; and with these are
    joined,
In willing admiration and respect,
Two Hearts, which in thy presence might
    be called   30
Youthful as Spring.—Shade of departed
    Power,
Skeleton of unfleshed humanity,
The chronicle were welcome that should
    call
Into the compass of distinct regard
The toils and struggles of thy infant
    years!   35
Yon foaming flood seems motionless as ice;
Its dizzy turbulence eludes the eye,
Frozen by distance; so, majestic Pile,
To the perception of this Age, appear
Thy fierce beginnings, softened and sub-
    dued   40
And quieted in character—the strife,
The pride, the fury uncontrollable,
Lost on the aerial heights of the Cru-
    sades![1]

XI.

ROB ROY'S GRAVE.

[Composed between June 1805 and Feb. 1806.—
Published 1807.]

The history of Rob Roy is sufficiently known;
his grave is near the head of Loch Ketterine,
in one of those small pinfold-like Burial-
grounds, of neglected and desolate appearance,
which the traveller meets with in the High-
lands of Scotland.

A FAMOUS man is Robin Hood,
The English ballad-singer's joy!

---

[1] The tradition is, that the Castle was built by
a Lady during the absence of her Lord in Pales-
tine.

And Scotland has a thief as good,
An outlaw of as daring mood;
She has her brave ROB ROY!　5
Then clear the weeds from off his
　　Grave,
And let us chant a passing stave,
In honour of that Hero brave!

Heaven gave Rob Roy a dauntless heart
And wondrous length and strength of
　　arm:　10
Nor craved he more to quell his foes,
　Or keep his friends from harm.

Yet was Rob Roy as *wise* as brave;
Forgive me if the phrase be strong;—
A Poet worthy of Rob Roy　15
　　Must scorn a timid song.

Say, then, that he was wise as brave;
As wise in thought as bold in deed:
For in the principles of things
　　He sought his moral creed.　20

Said generous Rob, "What need of books?
Burn all the statutes and their shelves:
They stir us up against our kind;
　And worse, against ourselves.

"We have a passion—make a law,　25
Too false to guide us or control!
And for the law itself we fight
　In bitterness of soul.

"And, puzzled, blinded thus, we lose
Distinctions that are plain and few:　30
These find I graven on my heart:
　　That tells me what to do.

"The creatures see of flood and field,
And those that travel on the wind!
With them no strife can last; they
　live　35
　In peace, and peace of mind.

"For why?—because the good old rule
Sufficeth them, the simple plan,
That they should take, who have the
　power,
And they should keep who can.　40

"A lesson that is quickly learned,
A signal this which all can see!
Thus nothing here provokes the strong
　To wanton cruelty.

"All freakishness of mind is checked;　45
He tamed, who foolishly aspires;
While to the measure of his might
　Each fashions his desires.

"All kinds, and creatures, stand and fall
By strength of prowess or of wit:　50
'Tis God's appointment who must sway,
　And who is to submit.

"Since, then, the rule of right is plain,
And longest life is but a day;
To have my ends, maintain my rights,　55
　I'll take the shortest way."

And thus among these rocks he lived,
Through summer heat and winter snow:
The Eagle, he was lord above,
　And Rob was lord below.　60

So was it—*would*, at least, have been
But through untowardness of fate;
For Polity was then too strong—
　He came an age too late;

Or shall we say an age too soon?　65
For, were the bold Man living *now*,
How might he flourish in his pride,
　With buds on every bough!

Then rents and factors, rights of chase,
Sheriffs, and lairds and their domains,　70
Would all have seemed but paltry things,
　Not worth a moment's pains.

Rob Roy had never lingered here,
To these few meagre Vales confined;
But thought how wide the world, the
　times　75
　How fairly to his mind!

And to his Sword he would have said,
"Do Thou my sovereign will enact
From land to land through half the earth!
　Judge thou of law and fact!　80

"'Tis fit that we should do our part,
Becoming that mankind should learn
That we are not to be surpassed
　In fatherly concern.

"Of old things all are over old,　85
Of good things none are good enough:—
We'll show that we can help to frame
　A world of other stuff.

"I, too, will have my kings that take
From me the sign of life and death :   90
Kingdoms shall shift about, like clouds,
  Obedient to my breath."

And, if the word had been fulfilled,
As *might* have been, then, thought of joy !
France would have had her present Boast,
  And we our own Rob Roy !   96

Oh ! say not so; compare them not;
I would not wrong thee, Champion brave !
Would wrong thee nowhere ; least of all
  Here standing by thy grave.   100

For Thou, although with some wild
  thoughts,
Wild Chieftain of a savage Clan !
Hadst this to boast of; thou didst love
  The *liberty* of man.

And, had it been thy lot to live   105
With us who now behold the light,
Thou wouldst have nobly stirred thyself,
  And battled for the Right.

For thou wert still the poor man's stay,
The poor man's heart, the poor man's
  hand;   110
And all the oppressed, who wanted
  strength,
  Had thine at their command.

Bear witness many a pensive sigh
Of thoughtful Herdsman when he strays
Alone upon Loch Veol's heights,   115
  And by Loch Lomond's braes.

And, far and near, through vale and hill,
Are faces that attest the same ;
The proud heart flashing through the eyes,
  At sound of Rob Roy's name.   120

XII.

SONNET.

COMPOSED AT —— CASTLE.

[Composed September 18, 1803.—Published 1807.]

DEGENERATE Douglas ! oh, the unworthy
  Lord !
Whom mere despite of heart could so
  far please,
And love of havoc, (for with such disease

Fame taxes him,) that he could send
  forth word
To level with the dust a noble horde,   5
A brotherhood of venerable Trees,
Leaving an ancient dome, and towers
  like these,
Beggared and outraged !—Many hearts
  deplored
The fate of those old Trees; and oft
  with pain
The traveller, at this day, will stop and
  gaze   10
On wrongs, which Nature scarcely seems
  to heed :
For sheltered places, bosoms, nooks, and
  bays,
And the pure mountains, and the gentle
  Tweed,
And the green silent pastures, yet remain.

XIII.

YARROW UNVISITED.

[Composed 1803.—Published 1807.]

See the various Poems the scene of which is laid
  upon the banks of the Yarrow; in particular,
  the exquisite Ballad of Hamilton beginning—
  " Busk ye, busk ye, my bonny, bonny Bride,
  Busk ye, busk ye, my winsome Marrow !"

FROM Stirling castle we had seen
The mazy Forth unravelled ;
Had trod the banks of Clyde, and Tay,
And with the Tweed had travelled ;
And when we came to Clovenford,   5
Then said my "*winsome Marrow*,"
"Whate'er betide, we'll turn aside,
  And see the Braes of Yarrow."

"Let Yarrow folk, *frae* Selkirk town,
Who have been buying, selling,   10
Go back to Yarrow, 'tis their own ;
Each maiden to her dwelling !
On Yarrow's banks let herons feed,
Hares couch, and rabbits burrow !
But we will downward with the Tweed, 15
  Nor turn aside to Yarrow.

"There's Galla Water, Leader Haughs,
Both lying right before us ;
And Dryborough, where with chiming
  Tweed
The lintwhites sing in chorus ;   20

There's pleasant Tiviot-dale, a land
Made blithe with plough and harrow:
Why throw away a needful day
To go in search of Yarrow?

"What's Yarrow but a river bare,   25
That glides the dark hills under?
There are a thousand such elsewhere
As worthy of your wonder."
—Strange words they seemed of slight
    and scorn;
My True-love sighed for sorrow;   30
And looked me in the face, to think
I thus could speak of Yarrow!

"Oh! green," said I, "are Yarrow's
    holms,
And sweet is Yarrow flowing!
Fair hangs the apple frae the rock,[1]   35
But we will leave it growing.
O'er hilly path, and open Strath,
We'll wander Scotland thorough;
But, though so near, we will not turn
Into the dale of Yarrow.   40

"Let beeves and home-bred kine partake
The sweets of Burn-mill meadow;
The swan on still St. Mary's Lake
Float double, swan and shadow!
We will not see them; will not go,   45
To-day, nor yet to-morrow;
Enough if in our hearts we know
There's such a place as Yarrow.

"Be Yarrow stream unseen, unknown!
It must, or we shall rue it: 50
We have a vision of our own;
Ah! why should we undo it?
The treasured dreams of times long past,
We'll keep them, winsome Marrow!
For when we're there, although 'tis fair,
'Twill be another Yarrow!   56

"If Care with freezing years should come,
And wandering seem but folly,—
Should we be loth to stir from home,
And yet be melancholy;   60
Should life be dull, and spirits low,
'Twill soothe us in our sorrow,
That earth hath something yet to show,
The bonny holms of Yarrow!"

---

[1] See Hamilton's Ballad as above.

XIV.
SONNET.

IN THE PASS OF KILLICRANKY.

An invasion being expected, October, 1803.

[Composed October, 1803.—Published 1807.]

Six thousand veterans practised in war's
    game,
Tried men, at Killicranky were arrayed
Against an equal host that wore the plaid,
Shepherds and herdsmen.—Like a whirl-
    wind came
The Highlanders, the slaughter spread
    like flame;   5
And Garry, thundering down his moun-
    tain-road,
Was stopped, and could not breathe
    beneath the load
Of the dead bodies.—'Twas a day of shame
For them whom precept and the pedantry
Of cold mechanic battle do enslave.   10
O for a single hour of that Dundee,
Who on that day the word of onset gave!
Like conquest would the Men of Eng-
    land see;
And her Foes find a like inglorious grave.

XV.
THE MATRON OF JEDBOROUGH
AND HER HUSBAND.

[Composed between 1803–1805.—Published 1807.]

At Jedborough, my companion and I went into
    private lodgings for a few days; and the fol-
    lowing Verses were called forth by the charac-
    ter and domestic situation of our Hostess.

Age! twine thy brows with fresh spring
    flowers,
And call a train of laughing Hours;
And bid them dance, and bid them sing;
And thou, too, mingle in the ring!
Take to thy heart a new delight;   5
If not, make merry in despite
That there is One who scorns thy power:—
But dance! for under Jedborough Tower
A Matron dwells who, though she bears
The weight of more than seventy years,   10
Lives in the light of youthful glee,
And she will dance and sing with thee.

Nay! start not at that Figure—there!
Him who is rooted to his chair!
Look at him—look again! for he   15
Hath long been of thy family.
With legs that move not, if they can,
And useless arms, a trunk of man,
He sits, and with a vacant eye;
A sight to make a stranger sigh!   20
Deaf, drooping, that is now his doom:
His world is in this single room:
Is this a place for mirthful cheer?
Can merry-making enter here?

The joyous Woman is the Mate   25
Of him in that forlorn estate!
He breathes a subterraneous damp;
But bright as Vesper shines her lamp:
He is as mute as Jedborough Tower:
She jocund as it was of yore,   30
With all its bravery on; in times
When, all alive with merry chimes,
Upon a sun-bright morn of May,
It roused the Vale to holiday.

I praise thee, Matron! and thy due   35
Is praise, heroic praise, and true!
With admiration I behold
Thy gladness unsubdued and bold:
Thy looks, thy gestures, all present
The picture of a life well spent: 40
This do I see; and something more;
A strength unthought of heretofore!
Delighted am I for thy sake;
And yet a higher joy partake:
Our Human-nature throws away   45
Its second twilight, and looks gay;
A land of promise and of pride
Unfolding, wide as life is wide.

Ah! see her helpless Charge! enclosed
Within himself as seems, composed;   50
To fear of loss, and hope of gain,
The strife of happiness and pain,
Utterly dead! yet in the guise
Of little infants, when their eyes
Begin to follow to and fro   55
The persons that before them go,
He tracks her motions, quick or slow.
Her buoyant spirit can prevail
Where common cheerfulness would fail;
She strikes upon him with the heat   60
Of July suns; he feels it sweet;

An animal delight though dim!
'Tis all that now remains for him!

The more I looked, I wondered more—
And, while I scanned them o'er and o'er,
Some inward trouble suddenly   66
Broke from the Matron's strong black
    eye—
A remnant of uneasy light,
A flash of something over-bright!
Nor long this mystery did detain   70
My thoughts;—she told in pensive strain
That she had borne a heavy yoke,
Been stricken by a twofold stroke;
Ill health of body; and had pined
Beneath worse ailments of the mind.   75

So be it!—but let praise ascend
To Him who is our lord and friend!
Who from disease and suffering
Hath called for thee a second spring;
Repaid thee for that sore distress   80
By no untimely joyousness;
Which makes of thine a blissful state;
And cheers thy melancholy Mate!

XVI.

[Composed September 25, 1803.—Published 1815.]

FLY, some kind Harbinger, to Grasmere-
    dale!
Say that we come, and come by this day's
    light;
Fly upon swiftest wing round field and
    height,
But chiefly let one Cottage hear the tale;
There let a mystery of joy prevail,   5
The kitten frolic, like a gamesome sprite,
And Rover whine, as at a second sight
Of near-approaching good that shall not
    fail:
And from that Infant's face let joy
    appear;   9
Yea, let our Mary's one companion child—
That hath her six weeks' solitude beguiled
With intimations manifold and dear,
While we have wandered over wood and
    wild—
Smile on his Mother now with bolder
    cheer.   14

XVII.

THE BLIND HIGHLAND BOY.

A TALE TOLD BY THE FIRE-SIDE, AFTER
RETURNING TO THE VALE OF GRASMERE.

[Composed probably December, 1806.—Published
1807.]

Now we are tired of boisterous joy,
Have romped enough, my little Boy !
Jane hangs her head upon my breast,
And you shall bring your stool and rest;
  This corner is your own.   5

There ! take your seat, and let me see
That you can listen quietly :
And, as I promised, I will tell
That strange adventure which befell
  A poor blind Highland Boy.   10

A *Highland* Boy !—why call him so ?
Because, my Darlings, ye must know
That, under hills which rise like towers,
Far higher hills than these of ours !
  He from his birth had lived.   15

He ne'er had seen one earthly sight ;
The sun, the day ; the stars, the night ;
Or tree, or butterfly, or flower,
Or fish in stream, or bird in bower,
  Or woman, man, or child.   20

And yet he neither drooped nor pined,
Nor had a melancholy mind ;
For God took pity on the Boy,
And was his friend ; and gave him joy
  Of which we nothing know.   25

His Mother, too, no doubt, above
Her other children him did love :
For was she here, or was she there,
She thought of him with constant care,
  And more than mother's love.   30

And proud she was of heart, when clad
In crimson stockings, tartan plaid,
And bonnet with a feather gay,
To Kirk he on the sabbath day
  Went hand in hand with her.   35

A dog, too, had he ; not for need,
But one to play with and to feed ;
Which would have led him, if bereft
Of company or friends, and left
  Without a better guide.   40

And then the bagpipes he could blow—
And thus from house to house would go;
And all were pleased to hear and see,
For none made sweeter melody
  Than did the poor blind Boy.   45

Yet he had many a restless dream ;
Both when he heard the eagles scream,
And when he heard the torrents roar,
And heard the water beat the shore
  Near which their cottage stood.   50

Beside a lake their cottage stood,
Not small like ours, a peaceful flood ;
But one of mighty size, and strange ;
That, rough or smooth, is full of change,
  And stirring in its bed.   55

For to this lake, by night and day,
The great Sea-water finds its way
Through long, long windings of the hills,
And drinks up all the pretty rills
  And rivers large and strong :   60

Then hurries back the road it came—
Returns, on errand still the same ;
This did it when the earth was new ;
And this for evermore will do,
  As long as earth shall last.   65

And, with the coming of the tide,
Come boats and ships that safely ride
Between the woods and lofty rocks ;
And to the shepherds with their flocks
  Bring tales of distant lands.   70

And of those tales, whate'er they were,
The blind Boy always had his share ;
Whether of mighty towns, or vales
With warmer suns and softer gales,
  Or wonders of the Deep.   75

Yet more it pleased him, more it stirred,
When from the water-side he heard
The shouting, and the jolly cheers ;
The bustle of the mariners
  In stillness or in storm.   80

But what do his desires avail ?
For He must never handle sail ;
Nor mount the mast, nor row, nor float
In sailor's ship, or fisher's boat,
  Upon the rocking waves.   85

His Mother often thought, and said,
What sin would be upon her head
If she should suffer this: "My Son,
Whate'er you do, leave this undone;
    The danger is so great."   90

Thus lived he by Loch Leven's side
Still sounding with the sounding tide,
And heard the billows leap and dance,
Without a shadow of mischance,
    Till he was ten years old.   95

When one day (and now mark me well,
Ye soon shall know how this befell)
He in a vessel of his own
On the swift flood is hurrying down,
    Down to the mighty Sea.   100

In such a vessel never more
May human creature leave the shore!
If this or that way he should stir,
Woe to the poor blind Mariner!
    For death will be his doom.   105

But say what bears him?—Ye have seen
The Indian's bow, his arrows keen,
Rare beasts, and birds with plumage
    bright;
Gifts which, for wonder or delight,
    Are brought in ships from far.   110

Such gifts had those seafaring men
Spread round that haven in the glen;
Each hut, perchance, might have its own;
And to the Boy they all were known—
    He knew and prized them all.   115

The rarest was a Turtle-shell
Which he, poor Child, had studied well;
A shell of ample size, and light
As the pearly car of Amphitrite,
    That sportive dolphins drew.   120

And, as a Coracle that braves
On Vaga's breast the fretful waves,
This shell upon the deep would swim,
And gaily lift its fearless brim
    Above the tossing surge.   125

And this the little blind Boy knew;
And he a story strange yet true
Had heard, how in a shell like this
An English Boy, O thought of bliss!
    Had stoutly launched from shore;   130

Launched from the margin of a bay
Among the Indian isles, where lay
His father's ship, and had sailed far—
To join that gallant ship of war,
    In his delightful shell.   135

Our Highland Boy oft visited
The house that held this prize; and, led
By choice or chance, did thither come
One day when no one was at home,
    And found the door unbarred.   140

While there he sate, alone and blind,
That story flashed upon his mind;—
A bold thought roused him, and he took
The shell from out its secret nook,
    And bore it on his head.   145

He launched his vessel,—and in pride
Of spirit, from Loch Leven's side,
Stepped into it—his thoughts all free
As the light breezes that with glee
    Sang through the adventurer's hair.

A while he stood upon his feet;   151
He felt the motion—took his seat;
Still better pleased as more and more
The tide retreated from the shore,
    And sucked, and sucked him in.   155

And there he is in face of Heaven.
How rapidly the Child is driven!
The fourth part of a mile, I ween,
He thus had gone, ere he was seen
    By any human eye.   160

But when he was first seen, oh me
What shrieking and what misery!
For many saw; among the rest
His Mother, she who loved him best,
    She saw her poor blind Boy.   165

But for the child, the sightless Boy,
It is the triumph of his joy!
The bravest traveller in balloon,
Mounting as if to reach the moon,
    Was never half so blessed.   170

And let him, let him go his way,
Alone, and innocent, and gay!
For, if good Angels love to wait
On the forlorn unfortunate,
    This Child will take no harm.   175

But now the passionate lament,
Which from the crowd on shore was sent,
The cries which broke from old and young
In Gaelic, or the English tongue,
    Are stifled—all is still.   180

And quickly with a silent crew
A boat is ready to pursue;
And from the shore their course they take,
And swiftly down the running lake
    They follow the blind Boy.   185

But soon they move with softer pace;
So have ye seen the fowler chase
On Grasmere's clear unruffled breast
A youngling of the wild-duck's nest
    With deftly-lifted oar;   190

Or as the wily sailors crept
To seize (while on the Deep it slept)
The hapless creature which did dwell
Erewhile within the dancing shell,
    They steal upon their prey.   195

With sound the least that can be made,
They follow, more and more afraid,
More cautious as they draw more near;
But in his darkness he can hear,
    And guesses their intent.   200

"*Lei-gha—Lei-gha*"—he then cried out,
"*Lei-gha—Lei-gha*"—with eager shout;
Thus did he cry, and thus did pray,
And what he meant was "Keep away,
    And leave me to myself!"   205

Alas! and when he felt their hands——
You've often heard of magic wands,
That with a motion overthrow
A palace of the proudest show,
    Or melt it into air: 210

So all his dreams—that inward light
With which his soul had shone so bright—
All vanished;—'twas a heartfelt cross
To him, a heavy, bitter loss,
    As he had ever known.   215

But hark! a gratulating voice,
With which the very hills rejoice:
'Tis from the crowd, who tremblingly
Have watched the event, and now can see
    That he is safe at last.   220

And then, when he was brought to land,
Full sure they were a happy band,
Which, gathering round, did on the banks
Of that great Water give God thanks,
    And welcomed the poor Child.   225

And in the general joy of heart
The blind Boy's little dog took part;
He leapt about, and oft did kiss
His master's hands in sign of bliss,
    With sound like lamentation.   230

But most of all, his Mother dear,
She who had fainted with her fear,
Rejoiced when waking she espies
The Child; when she can trust her eyes,
    And touches the blind Boy.   235

She led him home, and wept amain,
When he was in the house again:
Tears flowed in torrents from her eyes;
She kissed him—how could she chastise?
    She was too happy far.   240

Thus, after he had fondly braved
The perilous Deep, the Boy was saved;
And, though his fancies had been wild,
Yet he was pleased and reconciled
    To live in peace on shore.   245

And in the lonely Highland dell
Still do they keep the Turtle-shell;
And long the story will repeat
Of the blind Boy's adventurous feat,
    And how he was preserved.   250

Note.—It is recorded in "Dampier's Voyages,"
that a boy, son of the captain of a Man-of-War,
seated himself in a Turtle-shell, and floated in
it from the shore to his father's ship, which lay
at anchor at the distance of half a mile. In
deference to the opinion of a Friend, I have
substituted such a shell for the less elegant ves-
sel in which my blind Voyager did actually en-
trust himself to the dangerous current of Loch
Leven, as was related to me by an eye-witness.

MEMORIALS OF A TOUR IN SCOTLAND,

1814.

————◆◆————

I.

SUGGESTED BY A BEAUTIFUL RUIN UPON
ONE OF THE ISLANDS OF LOCH LOMOND,
A PLACE CHOSEN FOR THE RETREAT OF
A SOLITARY INDIVIDUAL, FROM WHOM
THIS HABITATION ACQUIRED THE NAME
OF

THE BROWNIE'S CELL.

[Composed perhaps 1814.—Published 1820.]

I.

To barren heath, bleak moor, and quaking
 fen,
Or depth of labyrinthine glen;
Or into trackless forest set
With trees, whose lofty umbrage met;
World-wearied Men withdrew of yore; 5
(Penance their trust, and prayer their
 store;)
And in the wilderness were bound
To such apartments as they found;
Or with a new ambition raised;
That God might suitably be praised. 10

II.

High lodged the *Warrior*, like a bird of
 prey;
Or where broad waters round him lay:
But this wild Ruin is no ghost
Of his devices—buried, lost!
Within this little lonely isle 15
There stood a consecrated Pile;
Where tapers burned, and mass was sung,
For them whose timid Spirits clung
To mortal succour, though the tomb
Had fixed, for ever fixed, their doom! 20

III.

Upon those servants of another world
When madding Power her bolts had
 hurled,
Their habitation shook;—it fell,
And perished, save one narrow cell;
Whither, at length, a Wretch retired 25
Who neither grovelled nor aspired:
He, struggling in the net of pride,
The future scorned, the past defied;
Still tempering, from the unguilty forge
Of vain conceit, an iron scourge! 30

IV

Proud Remnant was he of a fearless Race,
Who stood and flourished face to face
With their perennial hills;—but Crime,
Hastening the stern decrees of Time,
Brought low a Power, which from its
 home 35
Burst, when repose grew wearisome;
And, taking impulse from the sword,
And, mocking its own plighted word,
Had found, in ravage widely dealt,
Its warfare's bourn, its travel's belt! 40

V.

All, all were dispossessed, save him whose
 smile
Shot lightning through this lonely Isle!
No right had he but what he made
To this small spot, his leafy shade;
But the ground lay within that ring 45
To which he only dared to cling;
Renouncing here, as worse than dead,
The craven few who bowed the head

Beneath the change; who heard a claim
How loud! yet lived in peace with
    shame.   50

VI.

From year to year this shaggy Mortal
    went
(So seemed it) down a strange descent:
Till they, who saw his outward frame,
Fixed on him an unhallowed name;
Him, free from all malicious taint,   55
And guiding, like the Patmos Saint,
A pen unwearied—to indite,
In his lone Isle, the dreams of night;
Impassioned dreams, that strove to span
The faded glories of his Clan!   60

VII.

Suns that through blood their western
    harbour sought,
And stars that in their courses fought;
Towers rent, winds combating with
    woods,
Lands deluged by unbridled floods;
And beast and bird that from the spell 65
Of sleep took import terrible;—
These types mysterious (if the show
Of battle and the routed foe
Had failed) would furnish an array
Of matter for the dawning day!   70

VIII.

How disappeared He?—ask the newt and
    toad,
Inheritors of his abode;
The otter crouching undisturbed,
In her dank cleft;—but be thou curbed,
O froward Fancy! 'mid a scene   75
Of aspect winning and serene;
For those offensive creatures shun
The inquisition of the sun!
And in this region flowers delight,
And all is lovely to the sight.   80

IX.

Spring finds not here a melancholy breast,
When she applies her annual test
To dead and living; when her breath
Quickens, as now, the withered heath;—
Nor flaunting Summer—when he throws
His soul into the briar-rose;   86

Or calls the lily from her sleep
Prolonged beneath the bordering deep;
Nor Autumn, when the viewless wren
Is warbling near the BROWNIE'S Den.   90

X.

Wild Relique! beauteous as the chosen
    spot
In Nysa's isle, the embellished grot;
Whither, by care of Libyan Jove,
(High Servant of paternal Love)
Young Bacchus was conveyed—to lie 95
Safe from his step-dame Rhea's eye;
Where bud, and bloom, and fruitage,
    glowed,
Close-crowding round the infant-god;
All colours,—and the liveliest streak
A foil to his celestial cheek!   100

II.

COMPOSED AT CORA LINN,

IN SIGHT OF WALLACE'S TOWER.

[Composed perhaps 1814.—Published 1820.]

"— How Wallace fought for Scotland, left the
    name
Of Wallace to be found, like a wild flower,
All over his dear Country; left the deeds
Of Wallace, like a family of ghosts,
To people the steep rocks and river banks,
Her natural sanctuaries, with a local soul
Of independence and stern liberty."—*MS.*

LORD of the vale! astounding Flood;
The dullest leaf in this thick wood
Quakes—conscious of thy power;
The caves reply with hollow moan;
And vibrates, to its central stone,   5
Yon time-cemented Tower!

And yet how fair the rural scene!
For thou, O Clyde, hast ever been
Beneficent as strong;
Pleased in refreshing dews to steep 10
The little trembling flowers that peep
Thy shelving rocks among.

Hence all who love their country, love
To look on thee—delight to rove
Where they thy voice can hear;   15
And, to the patriot-warrior's Shade,
Lord of the vale! to Heroes laid
In dust, that voice is dear!

Along thy banks, at dead of night
Sweeps visibly the Wallace Wight ;　20
Or stands, in warlike vest,
Aloft, beneath the moon's pale beam,
A Champion worthy of the stream,
Yon grey tower's living crest !

But clouds and envious darkness hide　25
A Form not doubtfully descried :—
Their transient mission o'er,
O say to what blind region flee
These Shapes of awful phantasy ?
To what untrodden shore ?　30

Less than divine command they spurn ;
But this we from the mountains learn,
And this the valleys show ;
That never will they deign to hold
Communion where the heart is cold　35
To human weal and woe.

The man of abject soul in vain
Shall walk the Marathonian plain ;
Or thrid the shadowy gloom,
That still invests the guardian Pass,　40
Where stood, sublime, Leonidas
Devoted to the tomb.

And let no Slave his head incline,
Or kneel, before the votive shrine
By Uri's lake, where Tell　45
Leapt, from his storm-vext boat, to land,
Heaven's Instrument, for by his hand
That day the Tyrant fell.

III.

EFFUSION

IN THE PLEASURE-GROUND ON THE BANKS
OF THE BRAN, NEAR DUNKELD.

[Composed 1814 (?).—Published 1827.]

"The waterfall, by a loud roaring, warned us
when we must expect it. We were first, how-
ever, conducted into a small apartment, where
the Gardener desired us to look at a picture
of Ossian, which, while he was telling us the his-
tory of the young Artist who executed the
work, disappeared, parting in the middle—
flying asunder as by the touch of magic—and
lo! we are at the entrance of a splendid apart-
ment, which was almost dizzy and alive with
waterfalls, that tumbled in all directions; the
great cascade, opposite the window, which
faced us, being reflected in innumerable mir-
rors upon the ceiling and against the walls."—
*Extract from the Journal of my Fellow-Tra-
veller.*

WHAT He—who, mid the kindred throng
Of Heroes that inspired his song,
Doth yet frequent the hill of storms,
The stars dim-twinkling through their
　　forms !
What ! Ossian here—a painted Thrall,　5
Mute fixture on a stuccoed wall ;
To serve—an unsuspected screen
For show that must not yet be seen ;
And, when the moment comes, to part
And vanish by mysterious art ;　10
Head, harp, and body, split asunder,
For ingress to a world of wonder :
A gay saloon, with waters dancing
Upon the sight wherever glancing ;
One loud cascade in front, and lo !　15
A thousand like it, white as snow—
Streams on the walls, and torrent-foam
As active round the hollow dome,
Illusive cataracts ! of their terrors
Not stripped, nor voiceless in the mirrors,
That catch the pageant from the flood　21
Thundering adown a rocky wood.
What pains to dazzle and confound !
What strife of colour, shape and sound
In this quaint medley, that might seem 25
Devised out of a sick man's dream !
Strange scene, fantastic and uneasy
As ever made a maniac dizzy,
When disenchanted from the mood
That loves on sullen thoughts to brood ! 30

O Nature—in thy changeful visions,
Through all thy most abrupt transitions
Smooth, graceful, tender, or sublime—
Ever averse to pantomime,
Thee neither do they know nor us　35
Thy servants, who can trifle thus ;
Else verily the sober powers
Of rock that frowns, and stream that
　　roars,
Exalted by congenial sway
Of Spirits, and the undying Lay,　40
And Names that moulder not away,
Had wakened some redeeming thought
More worthy of this favoured Spot ;
Recalled some feeling—to set free
The Bard from such indignity !　45

The Effigies[1] of a valiant Wight
I once beheld, a Templar Knight;
Not prostrate, not like those that rest
On tombs, with palms together prest,
But sculptured out of living stone,   50
And standing upright and alone,
Both hands with rival energy
Employed in setting his sword free
From its dull sheath—stern sentinel
Intent to guard St. Robert's cell;   55
As if with memory of the affray
Far distant, when, as legends say,
The Monks of Fountain's thronged to force
From its dear home the Hermit's corse,
That in their keeping it might lie,   60
To crown their abbey's sanctity.
So had they rushed into the grot
Of sense despised, a world forgot,
And torn him from his loved retreat,
Where altar-stone and rock-hewn seat   65
Still hint that quiet best is found,
Even by the *Living*, under ground;
But a bold Knight, the selfish aim
Defeating, put the Monks to shame,
There where you see his Image stand   70
Bare to the sky, with threatening brand
Which lingering NID is proud to show
Reflected in the pool below.

Thus, like the men of earliest days,
Our sires set forth their grateful praise:
Uncouth the workmanship, and rude !   76
But, nursed in mountain solitude,
Might some aspiring artist dare
To seize whate'er, through misty air,
A ghost, by glimpses, may present   80
Of imitable lineament,
And give the phantom an array
That less should scorn the abandoned clay;
Then let him hew with patient stroke
An Ossian out of mural rock,   85
And leave the figurative Man—
Upon thy margin, roaring Bran !—
Fixed, like the Templar of the steep,
An everlasting watch to keep;
With local sanctities in trust,   90
More precious than a hermit's dust;

---

[1] On the banks of the river Nld, near Knares-borough.

And virtues through the mass infused,
Which old idolatry abused.

What though the Granite would deny
All fervour to the sightless eye;   95
And touch from rising suns in vain
Solicit a Memnonian strain;
Yet, in some fit of anger sharp,
The wind might force the deep-grooved harp
To utter melancholy moans   100
Not unconnected with the tones
Of soul-sick flesh and weary bones ;
While grove and river notes would lend,
Less deeply sad, with these to blend !

Vain pleasures of luxurious life,   105
For ever with yourselves at strife ;
Through town and country both deranged
By affectations interchanged,
And all the perishable gauds
That heaven-deserted man applauds;   110
When will your hapless patrons learn
To watch and ponder—to discern
The freshness, the everlasting youth,
Of admiration sprung from truth;
From beauty infinitely growing   115
Upon a mind with love o'erflowing—
To sound the depths of every Art
That seeks its wisdom through the heart?

Thus (where the intrusive Pile, ill-graced
With baubles of theatric taste,   120
O'erlooks the torrent breathing showers
On motley bands of alien flowers
In stiff confusion set or sown,
Till Nature cannot find her own,
Or keep a remnant of the sod   125
Which Caledonian Heroes trod)
I mused ; and, thirsting for redress,
Recoiled into the wilderness.

IV.

YARROW VISITED.

SEPTEMBER, 1814.

[Composed 1814.—Published 1815.]

(See page 292.)

AND is this—Yarrow?—*This* the Stream
Of which my fancy cherished,
So faithfully, a waking dream?
An image that hath perished !

O that some Minstrel's harp were near, 5
To utter notes of gladness,
And chase this silence from the air,
That fills my heart with sadness!

Yet why?—a silvery current flows
With uncontrolled meanderings; 10
Nor have these eyes by greener hills
Been soothed, in all my wanderings.
And, through her depths, Saint Mary's Lake
Is visibly delighted;
For not a feature of those hills 15
Is in the mirror slighted.

A blue sky bends o'er Yarrow vale,
Save where that pearly whiteness
Is round the rising sun diffused,
A tender hazy brightness; 20
Mild dawn of promise! that excludes
All profitless dejection;
Though not unwilling here to admit
A pensive recollection.

Where was it that the famous Flower 25
Of Yarrow Vale lay bleeding?
His bed perchance was yon smooth mound
On which the herd is feeding:
And haply from this crystal pool,
Now peaceful as the morning, 30
The Water-wraith ascended thrice—
And gave his doleful warning.

Delicious is the Lay that sings
The haunts of happy Lovers,
The path that leads them to the grove, 35
The leafy grove that covers:
And Pity sanctifies the Verse
That paints, by strength of sorrow,
The unconquerable strength of love;
Bear witness, rueful Yarrow! 40

But thou, that didst appear so fair
To fond imagination,
Dost rival in the light of day
Her delicate creation:

Meek loveliness is round thee spread, 45
A softness still and holy;
The grace of forest charms decayed,
And pastoral melancholy.

That region left, the vale unfolds
Rich groves of lofty stature, 50
With Yarrow winding through the pomp
Of cultivated nature;
And, rising from those lofty groves,
Behold a Ruin hoary!
The shattered front of Newark's Towers,
Renowned in Border story. 56

Fair scenes for childhood's opening bloom,
For sportive youth to stray in;
For manhood to enjoy his strength;
And age to wear away in! 60
Yon cottage seems a bower of bliss,
A covert for protection
Of tender thoughts, that nestle there—
The brood of chaste affection.

How sweet, on this autumnal day, 65
The wild-wood fruits to gather,
And on my True-love's forehead plant
A crest of blooming heather!
And what if I enwreathed my own! 70
'Twere no offence to reason;
The sober Hills thus deck their brows
To meet the wintry season.

I see—but not by sight alone,
Loved Yarrow, have I won thee;
A ray of fancy still survives— 75
Her sunshine plays upon thee!
Thy ever-youthful waters keep
A course of lively pleasure;
And gladsome notes my lips can breathe,
Accordant to the measure. 80

The vapours linger round the Heights,
They melt, and soon must vanish;
One hour is theirs, nor more is mine—
Sad thought, which I would banish,
But that I know, where'er I go, 85
Thy genuine image, Yarrow!
Will dwell with me—to heighten joy,
And cheer my mind in sorrow.

POEMS

DEDICATED TO NATIONAL

INDEPENDENCE AND LIBERTY.

PART I.

I.

COMPOSED BY THE SEA-SIDE, NEAR CALAIS,
AUGUST, 1802.

[Composed August, 1802.—Published 1807.]

FAIR Star of evening, Splendour of the
  west,
Star of my Country!—on the horizon's
  brink
Thou hangest, stooping, as might seem,
  to sink
On England's bosom; yet well pleased to
  rest,
Meanwhile, and be to her a glorious
  crest   5
Conspicuous to the Nations. Thou, I
  think,
Shouldst be my Country's emblem; and
  shouldst wink,
Bright Star! with laughter on her ban-
  ners, drest
In thy fresh beauty. There! that dusky
  spot
Beneath thee, that is England; there she
  lies.   10
Blessings be on you both! one hope, one
  lot,
One life, one glory!—I, with many a fear
For my dear Country, many heartfelt
  sighs,
Among men who do not love her, linger
  here.

II.

CALAIS, AUGUST, 1802.

[Composed August, 1802.—Published January 29,
1803 (*Morning Post* [1]); 1807.]

Is it a reed that's shaken by the wind,
Or what is it that ye go forth to see?
Lords, lawyers, statesmen, squires of low
  degree,
Men known, and men unknown, sick,
  lame, and blind,
Post forward all, like creatures of one
  kind,   5
With first-fruit offerings crowd to bend
  the knee
In France, before the new-born Majesty.
'Tis ever thus. Ye men of prostrate mind,
A seemly reverence may be paid to
  power;
But that's a loyal virtue, never sown   10
In haste, nor springing with a transient
  shower:
When truth, when sense, when liberty
  were flown,
What hardship had it been to wait an
  hour?
Shame on you, feeble Heads, to slavery
  prone!

---

[1] This Sonnet (II.), as well as Nos. IV., V., VIII., IX.,
XVI. and XVII., appear in the *Morning Post* with
the signature W. L. D.,—initials which probably
stand for *Wordsworthius Libertati dedicavit.*—
ED.

III.

COMPOSED NEAR CALAIS, ON THE ROAD
LEADING TO ARDRES, AUGUST 7, 1802.

[Composed August, 1802.—Published 1807.]

JONES! as from Calais southward you
and I
Went pacing side by side, this public
Way
Streamed with the pomp of a too-credu-
lous day,[1]
When faith was pledged to new-born
Liberty:
A homeless sound of joy was in the sky: 5
From hour to hour the antiquated Earth
Beat like the heart of Man: songs, gar-
lands, mirth,
Banners, and happy faces, far and nigh!
And now, sole register that these things
were,
Two solitary greetings have I heard,   10
"*Good morrow, Citizen!*" a hollow word,
As if a dead man spake it! Yet despair
Touches me not, though pensive as a bird
Whose vernal coverts winter hath laid
bare[2].

IV.

1801.

[Composed May 21, 1802.—Published September 6,
1802 (*Morning Post*); January 29, 1803 (*Ibid.*);
1807.]

I GRIEVED for Buonaparté, with a vain
And an unthinking grief! The tenderest
mood
Of that Man's mind—what can it be?
what food
Fed his first hopes? what knowledge
could *he* gain?
'Tis not in battles that from youth we
train   5
The Governor who must be wise and
good,
And temper with the sternness of the
brain
Thoughts motherly, and meek as woman-
hood.
Wisdom doth live with children round
her knees:

Books, leisure, perfect freedom, and the
talk   10
Man holds with week-day man in the
hourly walk
Of the mind's business: these are the
degrees
By which true Sway doth mount; this is
the stalk
True Power doth grow on; and her
rights are these.

V.

CALAIS, AUGUST 15, 1802.

[Composed August 15, 1802.—Published February
26, 1803 (*Morning Post*); 1807.]

FESTIVALS have I seen that were not
names:
This is young Buonaparté's natal day,
And his is henceforth an established
sway—
Consul for life. With worship France
proclaims
Her approbation, and with pomps and
games.   5
Heaven grant that other Cities may be gay!
Calais is not: and I have bent my way
To the sea-coast, noting that each man
frames
His business as he likes. Far other show
My youth here witnessed, in a prouder
time;   10
The senselessness of joy was then sub-
lime!
Happy is he, who, caring not for Pope,
Consul, or King, can sound himself to
know
The destiny of Man, and live in hope.

VI.

ON THE EXTINCTION OF THE VENETIAN
REPUBLIC[3].

[Composed probably August, 1802.—Published
1807.]

ONCE did She hold the gorgeous east in
fee;
And was the safeguard of the west: the
worth
Of Venice did not fall below her birth,

---

[1] July 14, 1790   [2] See Note, p. 903   [3] By the treaty of Campo Formio, 1797.—ED.

Venice, the eldest Child of Liberty. 4
She was a maiden City, bright and free;
No guile seduced, no force could violate;
And, when she took unto herself a Mate,
She must espouse the everlasting Sea.
And what if she had seen those glories
   fade,
Those titles vanish, and that strength
   decay; 10
Yet shall some tribute of regret be paid
When her long life hath reached its final
   day:
Men are we, and must grieve when even
   the Shade
Of that which once was great is passed
   away.

VII.

THE KING OF SWEDEN.

[Composed probably August, 1802.—Published
1807.]

THE Voice of song from distant lands
   shall call
To that great King: shall hail the crownèd
   Youth
Who, taking counsel of unbending Truth,
By one example hath set forth to all
How they with dignity may stand; or
   fall, 5
If fall they must. Now, whither doth it
   tend?
And what to him and his shall be the
   end?
That thought is one which neither can
   appal
Nor cheer him; for the illustrious Swede
   hath done
The thing which ought to be; is raised
   above 10
All consequences: work he hath begun
Of fortitude, and piety, and love,
Which all his glorious ancestors approve:
The heroes bless him, him their rightful
   son[1].

---

[1] See note.—W. (The "crownèd Youth" was
Gustavus IV. of Sweden: born 1778; crowned
1792; abdicated 1809. See Part II., Sonnets xx.,
xxi.—Ed.)

VIII.

TO TOUSSAINT L'OUVERTURE [2].

[Composed probably August, 1802.—Published
February 2, 1803 (*Morning Post*); 1807.]

TOUSSAINT, the most unhappy man of
   men!
Whether the whistling Rustic tend his
   plough
Within thy hearing, or thy head be now
Pillowed in some deep dungeon's earless
   den;—
O miserable Chieftain! where and when
Wilt thou find patience! Yet die not;
   do thou 6
Wear rather in thy bonds a cheerful
   brow:
Though fallen thyself, never to rise again,
Live, and take comfort. Thou hast left
   behind
Powers that will work for thee; air,
   earth, and skies; 10
There's not a breathing of the common
   wind
That will forget thee; thou hast great
   allies;
Thy friends are exultations, agonies,
And love, and man's unconquerable mind.

IX.

SEPTEMBER 1, 1802.

[Composed September 1, 1802.—Published Feb-
ruary 11, 1803 (*Morning Post*); 1807.]

Among the capricious acts of tyranny that dis-
graced those times, was the chasing of all
Negroes from France by decree of the govern-
ment: we had a Fellow-passenger who was one
of the expelled.

WE had a female Passenger who came
From Calais with us, spotless in array,—
A white-robed Negro, like a lady gay,
Yet downcast as a woman fearing blame;
Meek, destitute, as seemed, of hope or
   aim 5

---

[2] François Dominique Toussaint, surnamed
L'Ouverture, was governor of St. Domingo, and
chief of the African slaves enfranchised by the
decree of the French Convention (1794). He re-
sisted Napoleon's edict re-establishing slavery in
St. Domingo, was arrested and sent to Paris in
June, 1802, and there died after ten months' im-
prisonment in April, 1803.—Ed.

She sate, from notice turning not away,
But on all proffered intercourse did lay
A weight of languid speech, or to the same
No sign of answer made by word or face:
Yet still her eyes retained their tropic fire,
That, burning independent of the mind,
Joined with the lustre of her rich attire 12
To mock the Outcast—O ye Heavens, be
    kind !
And feel, thou Earth, for this afflicted Race !

X.

COMPOSED IN THE VALLEY NEAR DOVER, ON THE DAY OF LANDING.

[Composed August 30, 1802.—Published 1807.]

HERE, on our native soil, we breathe once
    more.
The cock that crows, the smoke that curls,
    that sound
Of bells;—those boys who in yon meadow-
    ground
In white-sleeved shirts are playing; and
    the roar
Of the waves breaking on the chalky
    shore;—   5
All, all are English. Oft have I looked
    round
With joy in Kent's green vales; but never
    found
Myself so satisfied in heart before.
Europe is yet in bonds; but let that pass,
Thought for another moment. Thou art
    free,   10
My Country ! and 'tis joy enough and
    pride
For one hour's perfect bliss, to tread the
    grass
Of England once again, and hear and see,
With such a dear Companion at my side.

XI.

SEPTEMBER, 1802. NEAR DOVER.

[Composed September, 1802.—Published 1807.]

INLAND, within a hollow vale, I stood ;
And saw, while sea was calm and air was
    clear,
The coast of France—the coast of France
    how near !
Drawn almost into frightful neighbour-
    hood.
I shrunk; for verily the barrier flood   5

Was like a lake, or river bright and fair,
A span of waters; yet what power is
    there !
What mightiness for evil and for good !
Even so doth God protect us if we be
Virtuous and wise. Winds blow, and
    waters roll,   10
Strength to the brave, and Power, and
    Deity ;
Yet in themselves are nothing ! One de-
    cree
Spake laws to *them*, and said that by the
    soul
Only, the Nations shall be great and free.

XII.

THOUGHT OF A BRITON ON THE SUBJUGA-TION OF SWITZERLAND.

[Composed probably early in 1807.—Published
    1807.]

Two Voices are there ; one is of the sea,
One of the mountains; each a mighty
    Voice :
In both from age to age thou didst rejoice,
They were thy chosen music, Liberty !
There came a Tyrant, and with holy glee 5
Thou fought'st against him; but hast
    vainly striven;
Thou from thy Alpine holds at length art
    driven,
Where not a torrent murmurs heard by
    thee.
Of one deep bliss thine ear hath been
    bereft:
Then cleave, O cleave to that which still
    is left ;   10
For, high-souled Maid, what sorrow would
    it be
That Mountain floods should thunder as
    before,
And Ocean bellow from his rocky shore,
And neither awful Voice be heard by
    thee !

XIII.

WRITTEN IN LONDON, SEPTEMBER, 1802.

[Composed September, 1802.—Published 1807.]

O FRIEND ! I know not which way I must
    look
For comfort, being, as I am, opprest,
To think that now our life is only drest

For show; mean handy-work of crafts-
man, cook,
Or groom!—We must run glittering like
a brook 5
In the open sunshine, or we are unblest:
The wealthiest man among us is the best:
No grandeur now in nature or in book
Delights us. Rapine, avarice, expense,
This is idolatry; and these we adore: 10
Plain living and high thinking are no
more:
The homely beauty of the good old cause
Is gone; our peace, our fearful innocence,
And pure religion breathing household
laws.

XIV.

LONDON, 1802.

[Composed September, 1802.—Published 1807.]

MILTON! thou shouldst be living at this
hour:
England hath need of thee: she is a fen
Of stagnant waters: altar, sword, and
pen,
Fireside, the heroic wealth of hall and
bower,
Have forfeited their ancient English
dower 5
Of inward happiness. We are selfish men;
Oh! raise us up, return to us again;
And give us manners, virtue, freedom,
power.
Thy soul was like a Star, and dwelt apart;
Thou hadst a voice whose sound was like
the sea: 10
Pure as the naked heavens, majestic, free,
So didst thou travel on life's common way,
In cheerful godliness; and yet thy heart
The lowliest duties on herself did lay.

XV.

[Composed probably 1802.—Published 1807.

GREAT men have been among us; hands
that penned
And tongues that uttered wisdom—better
none:
The later Sidney, Marvel, Harrington,

Young Vane, and others who called Mil-
ton friend.
These moralists could act and compre-
hend: 5
They knew how genuine glory was put on;
Taught us how rightfully a nation shone
In splendour: what strength was, that
would not bend
But in magnanimous meekness. France,
'tis strange,
Hath brought forth no such souls as we
had then. 10
Perpetual emptiness! unceasing change!
No single volume paramount, no code,
No master spirit, no determined road;
But equally a want of books and men!

XVI.

[Composed 1802 or 1803.—Published April 16.
1803 (*Morning Post*); 1807.]

IT is not to be thought of that the Flood
Of British freedom, which, to the open sea
Of the world's praise, from dark antiquity
Hath flowed, "with pomp of waters, un-
withstood," 4
Roused though it be full often to a mood
Which spurns the check of salutary bands,
That this most famous Stream in bogs
and sands
Should perish; and to evil and to good
Be lost for ever. In our halls is hung
Armoury of the invincible Knights of old:
We must be free or die, who speak the
tongue 11
That Shakspeare spake; the faith and
morals hold
Which Milton held.—In every thing we
are sprung
Of Earth's first blood, have titles mani-
fold.

XVII.

[Composed 1802 or 1803.—Published September
17, 1803 (*Morning Post*); 1807.]

WHEN I have borne in memory what has
tamed
Great Nations, how ennobling thoughts
depart
When men change swords for ledgers,
and desert

The student's bower for gold, some fears
  unnamed
I had, my Country—am I to be blamed?
Now, when I think of thee, and what
  thou art,   6
Verily, in the bottom of my heart,
Of those unfilial fears I am ashamed.
For dearly must we prize thee; we who
  find
In thee a bulwark for the cause of
  men;   10
And I by my affection was beguiled:
What wonder if a Poet now and then,
Among the many movements of his mind,
Felt for thee as a lover or a child!

XVIII.

OCTOBER, 1803.

[Composed October, 1803.—Published 1807.]

ONE might believe that natural miseries
Had blasted France, and made of it a land
Unfit for men; and that in one great
  band
Her sons were bursting forth, to dwell at
  ease.
But 'tis a chosen soil, where sun and
  breeze
Shed gentle favours: rural works are
  there,
And ordinary business without care;
Spot rich in all things that can soothe
  and please!
How piteous then that there should be
  such dearth
Of knowledge; that whole myriads should
  unite   10
To work against themselves such fell
  despite:
Should come in frenzy and in drunken
  mirth,
Impatient to put out the only light
Of Liberty that yet remains on earth!

XIX.

[Composed 1803 (?).—Published 1807.]

THERE is a bondage worse, far worse, to
  bear
Than his who breathes, by roof, and floor,
  and wall,
Pent in, a Tyrant's solitary Thrall:

'Tis his who walks about in the open
  air,
One of a Nation who, henceforth, must
  wear   5
Their fetters in their souls. For who
  could be,
Who, even the best, in such condition,
  free
From self-reproach, reproach that he must
  share
With Human-nature? Never be it ours
To see the sun how brightly it will
  shine,   10
And know that noble feelings, manly
  powers,
Instead of gathering strength, must droop
  and pine;
And earth with all her pleasant fruits
  and flowers
Fade, and participate in man's decline.

XX.

OCTOBER, 1803.

[Composed October, 1803.—Published 1807.]

THESE times strike monied worldlings
  with dismay:
Even rich men, brave by nature, taint
  the air
With words of apprehension and de-
  spair:
While tens of thousands, thinking on the
  affray,
Men unto whom sufficient for the day   5
And minds not stinted or untilled are
  given,
Sound, healthy, children of the God of
  heaven,
Are cheerful as the rising sun in
  May.
What do we gather hence but firmer
  faith
That every gift of noble origin   10
Is breathed upon by Hope's perpetual
  breath;
That virtue and the faculties within
Are vital,—and that riches are akin
To fear, to change, to cowardice, and
  death?

XXI.

[Composed probably 1803.—Published 1807.]

ENGLAND! the time is come when thou
    shouldst wean
Thy heart from its emasculating food;
The truth should now be better under-
    stood;
Old things have been unsettled; we have
    seen
Fair seed-time, better harvest might have
    been   5
But for thy trespasses; and, at this day,
If for Greece, Egypt, India, Africa,
Aught good were destined, thou wouldst
    step between.
England! all nations in this charge agree:
But worse, more ignorant in love and
    hate,   10
Far—far more abject, is thine Enemy:
Therefore the wise pray for thee, though
    the freight
Of thy offences be a heavy weight:
Oh grief that Earth's best hopes rest all
    with Thee!

XXII.

OCTOBER, 1803.

[Composed October, 1803.—Published 1807.]

WHEN, looking on the present face of
    things,
I see one man, of men the meanest too!
Raised up to sway the world, to do, undo,
With mighty Nations for his underlings,
The great events with which old story
    rings   5
Seem vain and hollow; I find nothing
    great:
Nothing is left which I can venerate;
So that a doubt almost within me springs
Of Providence, such emptiness at length
Seems at the heart of all things. But,
    great God!   10
I measure back the steps which I have
    trod;
And tremble, seeing whence proceeds the
    strength
Of such poor Instruments, with thoughts
    sublime
I tremble at the sorrow of the time.

XXIII.

TO THE MEN OF KENT. OCTOBER, 1803.

[Composed Oct. 1803.—Published 1807.]

VANGUARD of Liberty, ye men of Kent,
Ye children of a Soil that doth advance
Her haughty brow against the coast of
    France,
Now is the time to prove your hardiment!
To France be words of invitation sent! 5
They from their fields can see the coun-
    tenance
Of your fierce war, may ken the glittering
    lance,
And hear you shouting forth your brave
    intent.
Left single, in bold parley, ye, of yore,
Did from the Norman win a gallant
    wreath;   10
Confirmed the charters that were yours
    before;—
No parleying now. In Britain is one
    breath;
We all are with you now from shore to
    shore;—
Ye men of Kent, 'tis victory or death!

XXIV.

[Composed ?.—Published 1837.]

WHAT if our numbers barely could defy
The arithmetic of babes, must foreign
    hordes,
Slaves, vile as ever were befooled by
    words,
Striking through English breasts the
    anarchy
Of Terror, bear us to the ground, and tie
Our hands behind our backs with felon
    cords?   6
Yields every thing to discipline of swords?
Is man as good as man, none low, none
    high?—
Nor discipline nor valour can withstand
The shock, nor quell the inevitable rout,
When in some great extremity breaks
    out   11
A people, on their own beloved Land
Risen, like one man, to combat in the
    sight
Of a just God for liberty and right.

XXV.

LINES ON THE EXPECTED INVASION.
1803.

[Composed 1803.—Published: vol. of 1842.]

COME ye—who, if (which Heaven avert!)
  the Land
Were with herself at strife, would take
  your stand,
Like gallant Falkland, by the Monarch's
  side,
And, like Montrose, make Loyalty your
  pride—
Come ye—who, not less zealous, might
  display   5
Banners at enmity with regal sway,
And, like the Pyms and Miltons of that
  day,
Think that a State would live in sounder
  health
If Kingship bowed its head to Common-
  wealth—
Ye too—whom no discreditable fear   10
Would keep, perhaps with many a fruit-
  less tear,
Uncertain what to choose and how to
  steer—
And ye—who might mistake for sober
  sense
And wise reserve the plea of indolence—
Come ye—whate'er your creed—O waken
  all,   15
Whate'er your temper, at your Country's
  call;
Resolving (this a free-born Nation can)
To have one Soul, and perish to a man,
Or save this honoured Land from every
  Lord   19
But British reason and the British sword.

XXVI.

ANTICIPATION.   OCTOBER, 1803.

[Composed October, 1803.—Published 1803 (*The
Poetical Register*, iii. 340); 1804 (*The Anti-
Gallican*); 1807.]

SHOUT, for a mighty Victory is won!
On British ground the Invaders are laid
  low;
The breath of Heaven has drifted them
  like snow,

And left them lying in the silent sun,
Never to rise again!—the work is done. 5
Come forth, ye old men, now in peaceful
  show
And greet your sons! drums beat and
  trumpets blow!
Make merry, wives! ye little children,
  stun
Your grandame's ears with pleasure of
  your noise!
Clap, infants, clap your hands! Divine
  must be   10
That triumph, when the very worst, the
  pain,
And even the prospect of our brethren
  slain,
Hath something in it which the heart
  enjoys:—
In glory will they sleep and endless
  sanctity.

XXVII.

NOVEMBER, 1806.

[Composed 1806.—Published 1807.]

ANOTHER year!—another deadly blow!
Another mighty Empire[1] overthrown!
And We are left, or shall be left, alone;
The last that dare to struggle with the
  Foe.
'Tis well! from this day forward we shall
  know   5
That in ourselves our safety must be
  sought;
That by our own right hands it must be
  wrought;
That we must stand unpropped, or be
  laid low.
O dastard whom such foretaste doth not
  cheer!
We shall exult, if they who rule the land
Be men who hold its many blessings
  dear,   11
Wise, upright, valiant; not a servile band,
Who are to judge of danger which they
  fear,
And honour which they do not under-
  stand.

---

[1] Written after the overthrow of Prussia in the
battle of Jena, October 14, 1806.—ED.

XXVIII.

ODE.

I.

[Composed probably January, 1816.—Published:
vol. of 1816.]

WHO rises on the banks of Seine,
And binds her temples with the civic
wreath?
What joy to read the promise of her mien!
How sweet to rest her wide-spread wings
beneath!
  But they are ever playing, 5
  And twinkling in the light,
  And, if a breeze be straying,
  That breeze she will invite;
And stands on tiptoe, conscious she is
fair,
And calls a look of love into her face, 10
And spreads her arms, as if the general air
Alone could satisfy her wide embrace.
—Melt, Principalities, before her melt!
Her love ye hailed—her wrath have felt!
But She through many a change of form
hath gone, 15
And stands amidst you now an armèd
creature,
Whose panoply is not a thing put on,
But the live scales of a portentous nature;
That, having forced its way from birth to
birth,
Stalks round—abhorred by Heaven, a
terror to the Earth! 20

II.

I marked the breathings of her dragon
crest:
My Soul, a sorrowful interpreter,
In many a midnight vision bowed
Before the ominous aspect of her spear;
Whether the mighty beam, in scorn up-
held, 25
Threatened her foes,—or, pompously at
rest,
Seemed to bisect her orbèd shield,
As stretches a blue bar of solid cloud
Across the setting sun and all the fiery
west.

III.

So did she daunt the Earth, and God
defy! 30
And, wheresoe'er she spread her sove-
reignty,
Pollution tainted all that was most pure.
—Have we not known—and live we not
to tell—
That Justice seemed to hear her final
knell?
Faith buried deeper in her own deep
breast 35
Her stores, and sighed to find them
insecure!
And Hope was maddened by the drops
that fell
From shades, her chosen place of short-
lived rest.
Shame followed shame, and woe sup-
planted woe—
Is this the only change that time can
show? 40
How long shall vengeance sleep? Ye
patient Heavens, how long?
—Infirm ejaculation! from the tongue
Of Nations wanting virtue to be strong
Up to the measure of accorded might,
And daring not to feel the majesty of
right! 45

IV.

Weak Spirits are there—who would ask,
Upon the pressure of a painful thing,
The lion's sinews, or the eagle's wing;
Or let their wishes loose, in forest-glade,
  Among the lurking powers 50
  Of herbs and lowly flowers,
Or seek, from saints above, miraculous
aid—
That Man may be accomplished for a
task
Which his own nature hath enjoined;—
and why?
If, when that interference hath relieved
him, 55
  He must sink down to languish
In worse than former helplessness—and lie
  Till the caves roar,—and imbecility
  Again engendering anguish,
The same weak wish returns, that had
before deceived him. 60

V.

But Thou, supreme Disposer! may'st
    not speed
The course of things, and change the
    creed
Which hath been held aloft before men's
    sight
Since the first framing of societies,
Whether, as bards have told in ancient
    song,   65
Built up by soft seducing harmonies;
Or prest together by the appetite,
    And by the power, of wrong.

PART II.

I.

ON A CELEBRATED EVENT IN ANCIENT
HISTORY [1].

[Composed ?.—Published 1815.]

A ROMAN Master stands on Grecian
    ground,
And to the people at the Isthmian
    Games
Assembled, He, by a herald's voice, pro-
    claims
THE LIBERTY OF GREECE:—the words
    rebound   4
Until all voices in one voice are drowned;
Glad acclamation by which air was
    rent!
And birds, high flying in the element,
Dropped to the earth, astonished at the
    sound!
Yet were the thoughtful grieved; and
    still that voice
Haunts, with sad echoes, musing Fancy's
    ear: 10
Ah! that a *Conqueror's* words should be
    so dear:
Ah! that a *boon* could shed such rap-
    turous joys!
A gift of that which is not to be given
By all the blended powers of Earth and
    Heaven.

[1] i.e. the proclamation of the Liberty of Greece
by T. Quintius Flamininus, the conqueror of Phi-
lip of Macedon (B.C. 196).—ED.

II.

UPON THE SAME EVENT.

[Composed ?.—Published 1815.]

WHEN, far and wide, swift as the beams
    of morn
The tidings passed of servitude repealed,
And of that joy which shook the Isth-
    mian Field,
The rough Ætolians smiled with bitter
    scorn.
"'Tis known," cried they, "that he, who
    would adorn   5
His envied temples with the Isthmian
    crown,
Must either win, through effort of his own,
The prize, or be content to see it worn
By more deserving brows.—Yet so ye prop,
Sons of the brave who fought at Ma-
    rathon,   10
Your feeble spirits! Greece her head hath
    bowed,
As if the wreath of liberty thereon
Would fix itself as smoothly as a cloud,
Which, at Jove's will, descends on Pe-
    lion's top."

III.

TO THOMAS CLARKSON, ON THE FINAL PASS-
ING OF THE BILL FOR THE ABOLITION OF
THE SLAVE TRADE. MARCH, 1807.

[Composed March, 1807.—Published 1807.]

CLARKSON! it was an obstinate hill to
    climb:
How toilsome—nay, how dire—it was, by
    thee
Is known; by none, perhaps, so feelingly:
But thou, who, starting in thy fervent
    prime,
Didst first lead forth that enterprise sub-
    lime,   5
Hast heard the constant Voice its charge
    repeat,
Which, out of thy young heart's oracular
    seat,
First roused thee.—O true yoke-fellow
    of Time,
Duty's intrepid liegeman, see, the palm 9
Is won, and by all Nations shall be worn!
The blood-stained Writing is for ever torn;

And thou henceforth wilt have a good
man's calm,
A great man's happiness; thy zeal shall find
Repose at length, firm friend of human
kind!

IV.

A PROPHECY.

FEBRUARY, 1807.

[Composed 1807.—Published 1807.]

HIGH deeds, O Germans, are to come
from you!
Thus in your books the record shall be
found,
"A watchword was pronounced, a potent
sound—
ARMINIUS!—all the people quaked like dew
Stirred by the breeze; they rose, a Nation,
true, 5
True to herself—the mighty Germany,
She of the Danube and the Northern Sea,
She rose, and off at once the yoke she
threw.
All power was given her in the dreadful
trance;
Those new-born Kings [1] she withered like
a flame." 10
—Woe to them all! but heaviest woe and
shame
To that Bavarian who could first advance
His banner in accursed league with
France,
First open traitor to the German name!

V.

COMPOSED BY THE SIDE OF GRASMERE
LAKE.

[Composed 1807.—Published 1819.]

CLOUDS, lingering yet, extend in solid bars
Through the grey west; and lo! these
waters, steeled
By breezeless air to smoothest polish, yield

[1] i.e. The heads of twelve sovereign houses of
the Empire who, by treaty signed at Paris (July
12, 1806) declared themselves finally severed from
Germany, and united into the Confederation of
the Rhine under the Protectorate of Napoleon.
The *Bavarian* (line 12) was Frederick Augustus,
Elector of Saxony, with whom Napoleon (Dec.
11, 1806) concluded a treaty admitting him into
the Confederation of the Rhine.—ED.

A vivid repetition of the stars;
Jove, Venus, and the ruddy crest of Mars
Amid his fellows beauteously revealed 6
At happy distance from earth's groaning
field,
Where ruthless mortals wage incessant
wars.
Is it a mirror?—or the nether Sphere
Opening to view the abyss in which she
feeds 10
Her own calm fires?—But list! a voice
is near;
Great Pan himself low-whispering through
the reeds,
"Be thankful, thou; for, if unholy deeds
Ravage the world, tranquillity is here!"

VI.

[Composed ?.—Published 1827.]

Go back to antique ages, if thine eyes
The genuine mien and character would
trace
Of the rash Spirit that still holds her
place, 3
Prompting the world's audacious vanities!
Go back, and see the Tower of Babel rise;
The pyramid extend its monstrous base,
For some Aspirant of our short-lived race,
Anxious an aery name to immortalize.
There, too, ere wiles and politic dispute
Gave specious colouring to aim and act,
See the first mighty Hunter leave the
brute— 11
To chase mankind, with men in armies
packed
For his field-pastime high and absolute,
While, to dislodge his game, cities are
sacked!

VII.

COMPOSED WHILE THE AUTHOR WAS EN-
GAGED IN WRITING A TRACT OCCASIONED
BY THE CONVENTION OF CINTRA.

[Composed November or December, 1808.—
Published 1815.]

NOT 'mid the World's vain objects that
enslave
The free-born Soul—that World whose
vaunted skill
In selfish interest perverts the will,

Whose factions lead astray the wise and
brave—
Not there; but in dark wood and rocky
cave,   5
And hollow vale which foaming torrents
fill
With omnipresent murmur as they rave
Down their steep beds, that never shall
be still:
Here, mighty Nature! in this school
sublime
I weigh the hopes and fears of suffering
Spain;   10
For her consult the auguries of time,
And through the human heart explore
my way;
And look and listen—gathering, whence
I may,
Triumph, and thoughts no bondage can
restrain.

VIII.

COMPOSED AT THE SAME TIME AND ON THE
SAME OCCASION.

[Composed November or December, 1808.—
Published 1815.]

I DROPPED my pen; and listened to the
Wind
That sang of trees up-torn and vessels
tost—
A midnight harmony; and wholly lost
To the general sense of men by chains
confined
Of business, care, or pleasure; or re-
signed   5
To timely sleep. Thought I, the impas-
sioned strain,
Which, without aid of numbers, I sus-
tain,
Like acceptation from the World will
find.
Yet some with apprehensive ear shall
drink
A dirge devoutly breathed o'er sorrows
past;   10
And to the attendant promise will give
heed—
The prophecy,—like that of this wild
blast,

Which, while it makes the heart with
sadness shrink,
Tells also of bright calms that shall
succeed.

IX.

HOFER[1].

[Composed 1809.—Published Oct. 26, 1809 (*The
Friend*); 1815].

OF mortal parents is the Hero born
By whom the undaunted Tyrolese are led?
Or is it Tell's great Spirit, from the dead
Returned to animate an age forlorn?
He comes like Phœbus through the gates
of morn   5
When dreary darkness is discomfited,
Yet mark his modest state! upon his head,
That simple crest, a heron's plume, is worn.
O Liberty! they stagger at the shock
From van to rear—and with one mind
would flee,   10
But half their host is buried:—rock on
rock
Descends:—beneath this godlike War-
rior, see!
Hills, torrents, woods, embodied to be-
moan
The Tyrant, and confound his cruelty.

X.

[Composed 1809.—Published October 26, 1809
(*The Friend*); 1815.]

ADVANCE—come forth from thy Tyrolean
ground,
Dear Liberty! stern Nymph of soul un-
tamed;
Sweet Nymph, O rightly of the moun-
tains named!
Through the long chain of Alps from
mound to mound
And o'er the eternal snows, like Echo,
bound;   5
Like Echo, when the hunter train at dawn
Have roused her from her sleep: and
forest-lawn,

---

[1] Andreas Hofer, an innkeeper, led the Tyro-
lese for a time successfully, but was defeated by
the Bavarians in October 1809, and tried by court-
martial and shot in 1810.—ED.

Cliffs, woods and caves, her viewless steps
   resound
And babble of her pastime!—On, dread
   Power!
With such invisible motion speed thy
   flight,   10
Through hanging clouds, from craggy
   height to height,
Through the green vales and through the
   herdsman's bower—
That all the Alps may gladden in thy
   might,
Here, there, and in all places at one hour.

XI.

FEELINGS OF THE TYROLESE.

[Composed 1809.—Published December 21, 1809
    (*The Friend*); 1815.]

THE Land we from our fathers had in
   trust,
And to our children will transmit, or die;
This is our maxim, this our piety;
And God and Nature say that it is just.
That which we *would* perform in arms—
   we must!   5
We read the dictate in the infant's eye;
In the wife's smile; and in the placid sky;
And, at our feet, amid the silent dust
Of them that were before us.—Sing aloud
Old songs, the precious music of the
   heart!   10
Give, herds and flocks, your voices to the
   wind!
While we go forth, a self-devoted crowd,
With weapons grasped in fearless hands,
   to assert
Our virtue, and to vindicate mankind.

XII.

[Composed 1809.—Published November 16, 1809
    (*The Friend*); 1815.]

ALAS! what boots the long laborious quest
Of moral prudence, sought through good
   and ill;
Or pains abstruse—to elevate the will,
And lead us on to that transcendent rest
Where every passion shall the sway
   attest   5

Of Reason, seated on her sovereign hill;
What is it but a vain and curious skill,
If sapient Germany must lie deprest,
Beneath the brutal sword?—Her haughty
   Schools
Shall blush; and may not we with sorrow
   say,   10
A few strong instincts and a few plain
   rules,
Among the herdsmen of the Alps, have
   wrought
More for mankind at this unhappy day
Than all the pride of intellect and
   thought?

XIII.

[Composed 1809.—Published December 21, 1809
    (*The Friend*); 1815.]

AND is it among rude untutored Dales,
There, and there only, that the heart is
   true?
And, rising to repel or to subdue,
Is it by rocks and woods that man pre-
   vails?
Ah no! though Nature's dread protection
   fails,   5
There is a bulwark in the soul. This
   knew
Iberian Burghers when the sword they
   drew
In Zaragoza, naked to the gales
Of fiercely-breathing war. The truth
   was felt
By Palafox, and many a brave compeer,
Like him of noble birth and noble mind;
By ladies, meek-eyed women without
   fear;   12
And wanderers of the street, to whom is
   dealt
The bread which without industry they
   find.

XIV.

[Composed 1809.—Published December 21, 1809
    The Friend); 1815.]

O'ER the wide earth, on mountain and on
   plain,
Dwells in the affections and the soul of
   man
A Godhead, like the universal PAN;

But more exalted, with a brighter train:
And shall his bounty be dispensed in
    vain,   5
Showered equally on city and on field,
And neither hope nor steadfast promise
    yield
In these usurping times of fear and
    pain?
Such doom awaits us. Nay, forbid it
    Heaven!
We know the arduous strife, the eternal
    laws   10
To which the triumph of all good is
    given,
High sacrifice, and labour without pause,
Even to the death:—else wherefore should
    the eye
Of man converse with immortality?

XV.

ON THE FINAL SUBMISSION OF THE TYROLESE.

[Composed 1809.—Published December 21, 1809
(*The Friend*); 1815.]

IT was a *moral* end for which they
    fought;
Else how, when mighty Thrones were put
    to shame,
Could they, poor Shepherds, have pre-
    served an aim,
A resolution, or enlivening thought?
Nor hath that moral good been *vainly*
    sought;   5
For in their magnanimity and fame
Powers have they left, an impulse, and a
    claim
Which neither can be overturned nor
    bought.
Sleep, Warriors, sleep! among your hills
    repose!
We know that ye, beneath the stern
    control   10
Of awful prudence, keep the unvan-
    quished soul:
And when, impatient of her guilt and
    woes,
Europe breaks forth; then, Shepherds!
    shall ye rise
For perfect triumph o'er your Enemies.

XVI.

[Composed 1809.—Published 1815.]

HAIL, Zaragoza! If with unwet eye
We can approach, thy sorrow to behold,
Yet is the heart not pitiless nor cold;
Such spectacle demands not tear or sigh.
These desolate remains are trophies high
Of more than martial courage in the breast
Of peaceful civic virtue: they attest
Thy matchless worth to all posterity.
Blood flowed before thy sight without
    remorse;
Disease consumed thy vitals; War up-
    heaved   10
The ground beneath thee with volcanic
    force:
Dread trials! yet encountered and sus-
    tained
Till not a wreck of help or hope remained,
And law was from necessity received[1].

XVII.

[Composed 1809 (?)—Published 1815.]

SAY, what is Honour?—'Tis the finest sense
Of *justice* which the human mind can frame,
Intent each lurking frailty to disclaim,   3
And guard the way of life from all offence
Suffered or done. When lawless violence
Invades a Realm, so pressed that in the
    scale   6
Of perilous war her weightiest armies fail,
Honour is hopeful elevation,—whence
Glory, and triumph. Yet with politic skill
Endangered States may yield to terms
    unjust;   10
Stoop their proud heads, but not unto
    the dust—
A Foe's most favourite purpose to fulfil:
Happy occasions oft by self-mistrust
Are forfeited; but infamy doth kill.

XVIII[2].

[Composed October or November, 1809.]—Pub-
lished 1815.]

THE martial courage of a day is vain,
An empty noise of death the battle's roar,
If vital hope be wanting to restore,

---

[1] Saragossa surrendered February 20, 1809.—ED.
[2] Written apparently on the occasion of the
Peace of Vienna, signed Oct. 10, 1809.—ED.

Or fortitude be wanting to sustain,
Armies or kingdoms. We have heard a
    strain 5
Of triumph, how the ·labouring Danube
    bore
A weight of hostile corses: drenched
    with gore
Were the wide fields, the hamlets heaped
    with slain.
Yet see (the mighty tumult overpast)
Austria a Daughter of her Throne hath
    sold ! 10
And her Tyrolean Champion we be-
    hold
Murdered, like one ashore by shipwreck
    cast,
Murdered without relief. Oh ! blind as
    bold,
To think that such assurance can stand
    fast !

XIX.

[Composed after May, 1809.—Published 1815.]

BRAVE Schill[1] ! by death delivered, take
    thy flight
From Prussia's timid region. Go, and
    rest
With heroes, 'mid the islands of the
    Blest,
Or in the fields of empyrean light.
A meteor wert thou crossing a dark
    night : 5
Yet shall thy name, conspicuous and
    sublime,
Stand in the spacious firmament of time,
Fixed as a star : such glory is thy right.
Alas ! it may not be : for earthly fame
Is Fortune's frail dependant; yet there
    lives 10
A Judge, who, as man claims by merit,
    gives ;
To whose all-pondering mind a noble
    aim,
Faithfully kept, is as a noble deed ;
In whose pure sight all virtue doth suc-
    ceed.

[1] Killed at Stralsund, May 31, 1809.—ED.

XX.

[Composed 1809.—Published 1815.]

CALL not the royal Swede[2] unfortunate,
Who never did to Fortune bend the knee;
Who slighted fear ; rejected steadfastly
Temptation ; and whose kingly name and
    state
Have "perished by his choice, and not
    his fate !" 5
Hence lives He, to his inner self en-
    deared ;
And hence, wherever virtue is revered,
He sits a more exalted Potentate,
Throned in the hearts of men. Should
    Heaven ordain
That this great Servant of a righteous
    cause 10
Must still have sad or vexing thoughts to
    endure,
Yet may a sympathising spirit pause,
Admonished by these truths, and quench
    all pain
In thankful joy and gratulation pure.

XXI.

[Composed 1809.—Published 1815.]

LOOK now on that Adventurer who hath
    paid
His vows to Fortune ; who, in cruel-slight
Of virtuous hope, of liberty, and right,
Hath followed wheresoe'er a way was
    made
By the blind Goddess,—ruthless, undis-
    mayed ; 5
And so hath gained at length a prosper-
    ous height,
Round which the elements of worldly
    might
Beneath his haughty feet, like clouds, are
    laid.
O joyless power that stands by lawless
    force !
Curses are *his* dire portion, scorn, and
    hate, 10

[2] Gustavus IV. (see Part I., Sonnet VII.) abdi-
cated early in 1809. In this and the following
Sonnet he is contrasted with Napoleon. See
Wordsworth's note to Sonnet VII., Part I. of this
series.—ED.

Internal darkness and unquiet breath;
And, if old judgments keep their sacred
  course,
Him from that height shall Heaven pre-
  cipitate
By violent and ignominious death.

XXII.

[Composed probably 1809.—Published 1815.]

Is there a power that can sustain and
  cheer
The captive chieftain, by a tyrant's doom,
Forced to descend into his destined tomb—
A dungeon dark! where he must waste
  the year,
And lie cut off from all his heart holds
  dear;   5
What time his injured country is a stage
Whereon deliberate Valour and the rage
Of righteous Vengeance side by side ap-
  pear,
Filling from morn to night the heroic
  scene
With deeds of hope and everlasting
  praise:—   10
Say can he think of this with mind serene
And silent fetters? Yes, if visions bright
Shine on his soul, reflected from the days
When he himself was tried in open light.

XXIII.

1810.

[Composed 1810.—Published 1815.]

Ah! where is Palafox[1]? Nor tongue nor
  pen
Reports of him, his dwelling or his grave!
Does yet the unheard-of vessel ride the
  wave?
Or is she swallowed up, remote from ken
Of pitying human nature? Once again   5

[1] Don Joseph Palafox-y-Melzi (1780–1847), fam-
ed for his stubborn defence of Saragossa, on the
surrender of that fortress by the general to whom,
owing to illness, he had been compelled to resign
the command, was taken prisoner (February, 1809)
and sent to Vincennes, where he was detained for
nearly five years. On the restoration of Ferdi-
nand VII. he was sent back to Madrid, and in
1814 was appointed Captain-General of Arragon;
but soon after retired into private life, from which
he never again emerged.—ED.

Methinks that we shall hail thee, Cham-
  pion brave,
Redeemed to baffle that imperial Slave,
And through all Europe cheer desponding
  men
With new-born hope. Unbounded is the
  might
Of martyrdom, and fortitude, and right.
Hark, how thy Country triumphs!—
  Smilingly   11
The Eternal looks upon her sword that
  gleams,
Like his own lightning, over mountains
  high,
On rampart, and the banks of all her
  streams.

XXIV.

[Composed 1810.—Published 1815.]

In due observance of an ancient rite,
The rude Biscayans, when their children lie
Dead in the sinless time of infancy,
Attire the peaceful corse in vestments
  white;
And, in like sign of cloudless triumph
  bright,   5
They bind the unoffending creature's brows
With happy garlands of the pure white
  rose:
Then do a festal company unite
In choral song; and, while the uplifted
  cross
Of Jesus goes before, the child is borne 10
Uncovered to his grave: 'tis closed,—her
  loss
The Mother *then* mourns, as she needs
  must mourn;
But soon, through Christian faith, is grief
  subdued:
And joy returns, to brighten fortitude.

XXV.

FEELINGS OF A NOBLE BISCAYAN AT ONE OF
THOSE FUNERALS.

1810.

[Composed 1810.—Published 1815.]

Yet, yet, Biscayans! we must meet our
  Foes
With firmer soul, yet labour to regain
Our ancient freedom: else 'twere worse
  than vain

To gather round the bier these festal
  shows.
A garland fashioned of the pure white
  rose   5
Becomes not one whose father is a
  slave:
Oh, bear the infant covered to his grave!
These venerable mountains now enclose
A people sunk in apathy and fear.
If this endure, farewell, for us, all good!
The awful light of heavenly innocence
Will fail to illuminate the infant's bier;
And guilt and shame, from which is no
  defence,
Descend on all that issues from our blood.

XXVI.

THE OAK OF GUERNICA.

[Composed 1810.—Published 1815.]

The ancient oak of Guernica, says Laborde in
his account of Biscay, is a most venerable
natural monument. Ferdinand and Isabella,
in the year 1476, after hearing Mass in the
church of Santa Maria de la Antigua, repaired
to this tree, under which they swore to the
Biscayans to maintain their *fueros* (privileges).
What other interest belongs to it in the minds
of this people will appear from the following

SUPPOSED ADDRESS TO THE SAME. 1810.

OAK of Guernica! Tree of holier power
Than that which in Dodona did enshrine
(So faith too fondly deemed) a voice di-
  vine
Heard from the depths of its aerial bower—
How canst thou flourish at this blighting
  hour?   5
What hope, what joy can sunshine bring
  to thee,
Or the soft breezes from the Atlantic sea,
The dews of morn, or April's tender
  shower?
Stroke merciful and welcome would that
  be
Which should extend thy branches on the
  ground,   10
If never more within their shady round
Those lofty-minded Lawgivers shall meet,
Peasant and lord, in their appointed seat,
Guardians of Biscay's ancient liberty.

XXVII.

INDIGNATION OF A HIGH-MINDED
SPANIARD.

1810.

[Composed 1810.—Published 1815.]

WE can endure that He should waste our
  lands,
Despoil our temples, and by sword and
  flame
Return us to the dust from which we
  came;
Such food a Tyrant's appetite demands;
And we can brook the thought that by
  his hands   5
Spain may be overpowered, and he possess,
For his delight, a solemn wilderness
Where all the brave lie dead. But, when
  of bands
Which he will break for us he dares to
  speak,
Of benefits, and of a future day   10
When our enlightened minds shall bless
  his sway;
Then, the strained heart of fortitude proves
  weak;
Our groans, our blushes, our pale cheeks
  declare
That he has power to inflict what we lack
  strength to bear.

XXVIII.

[Composed probably 1810.—Published 1815.]

AVAUNT all specious pliancy of mind
In men of low degree, all smooth pre-
  tence!
I better like a blunt indifference,
And self-respecting slowness, disinclined
To win me at first sight: and be there
  joined   5
Patience and temperance with this high
  reserve,
Honour that knows the path and will not
  swerve;
Affections which, if put to proof, are kind;
And piety towards God. Such men of old
Were England's native growth; and
  throughout Spain   10
(Thanks to high God) forests of such re-
  main:

Then for that Country let our hopes be
    bold ;
For matched with these shall policy prove
    vain,
Her arts, her strength, her iron, and her
    gold.

XXIX.

1810.

[Composed 1810.—Published 1815.]

O'ERWEENING Statesmen have full long
    relied
On fleets and armies, and external wealth :
But from *within* proceeds a Nation's
    health ;
Which shall not fail, though poor men
    cleave with pride
To the paternal floor ; or turn aside,   5
In the thronged city, from the walks of
    gain,
As being all unworthy to detain
A Soul by contemplation sanctified.
There are who cannot languish in this
    strife,
Spaniards of every rank, by whom the
    good   10
Of such high course was felt and under-
    stood ;
Who to their Country's cause have bound
    a life
Erewhile, by solemn consecration, given
To labour, and to prayer, to nature, and
    to heaven[1].

XXX.

THE FRENCH AND THE SPANISH GUERILLAS.

[Composed 1810 or 1811.—Published 1815.]

HUNGER, and sultry heat, and nipping blast
From bleak hill-top, and length of march
    by night
Through heavy swamp, or over snow-clad
    height—
These hardships ill-sustained, these dan-
    gers past,
The roving Spanish Bands are reached at
    last,   5

[1] See Laborde's character of the Spanish peo-
ple; from him the sentiment of these last two
lines is taken.

Charged, and dispersed like foam : but as
    a flight
Of scattered quails by signs do reunite,
So these,—and, heard of once again, are
    chased
With combinations of long-practised art
And newly-kindled hope; but they are
    fled—   10
Gone are they, viewless as the buried
    dead :
Where now ?—Their sword is at the Foe-
    man's heart !
And thus from year to year his walk they
    thwart,
And hang like dreams around his guilty
    bed.

XXXI.

SPANISH GUERILLAS.

1811.

[Composed 1811.—Published 1815.]

THEY seek, are sought ; to daily battle led,
Shrink not, though far outnumbered by
    their Foes,
For they have learnt to open and to close
The ridges of grim war ; and at their head
Are captains such as erst their country
    bred   5
Or fostered, self-supported chiefs,—like
    those
Whom hardy Rome was fearful to oppose ;
Whose desperate shock the Carthaginian
    fled.
In One who lived unknown a shepherd's
    life
Redoubted Viriathus breathes again ;   10
And Mina[2], nourished in the studious
    shade,
With that great Leader vies, who, sick of
    strife
And bloodshed, longed in quiet to be laid
In some green island of the western main.

[2] Don Esprez y Mina, leader of the Guerillas of
Navarre, had been educated for the priesthood.
The "great Leader" (l. 12) is the Roman general
Sertorius, whose romantic story profoundly stir-
red Wordsworth's imagination (See Prelude I.,
ll. 190–202). Viriathus (l. 10), the renowned shep-
herd-leader of the Lusitanians against the arms
of Rome.—ED.

XXXII.

1811.

[Composed 1811.—Published 1815.]

THE power of Armies is a visible thing,
Formal, and circumscribed in time and
    space ;
But who the limits of that power shall
    trace
Which a brave People into light can bring
Or hide, at will,—for freedom combating
By just revenge inflamed? No foot may
    chase,   6
No eye can follow, to a fatal place
That power, that spirit, whether on the
    wing
Like the strong wind, or sleeping like the
    wind
Within its awful caves.—From year to year
Springs this indigenous produce far and
    near ;   11
No craft this subtle element can bind,
Rising like water from the soil, to find
In every nook a lip that it may cheer.

XXXIII.

1811.

[Composed 1811.—Published 1815.]

HERE pause : the poet claims at least this
    praise,
That virtuous Liberty hath been the scope
Of his pure song, which did not shrink
    from hope
In the worst moment of these evil days ;
From hope, the paramount *duty* that
    Heaven lays,   5
For its own honour, on man's suffering
    heart.
Never may from our souls one truth de-
    part—
That an accursed thing it is to gaze
On prosperous tyrants with a dazzled eye ;
Nor—touched with due abhorrence of
    their guilt   10
For whose dire ends tears flow, and blood
    is spilt,
And justice labours in extremity—
Forget thy weakness, upon which is built,
O wretched man, the throne of tyranny !

XXXIV.

THE FRENCH ARMY IN RUSSIA.

1812–13.

[Composed Feb., 1816.—Published : vol. of 1816.]

HUMANITY, delighting to behold
A fond reflection of her own decay,
Hath painted Winter like a traveller old,
Propped on a staff, and, through the
    sullen day,
In hooded mantle, limping o'er the plain,
As though his weakness were disturbed
    by pain :   6
Or, if a juster fancy should allow
An undisputed symbol of command,
The chosen sceptre is a withered bough,
Infirmly grasped within a palsied hand.
These emblems suit the helpless and for-
    lorn,   11
But mighty Winter the device shall scorn.

For he it was—dread Winter ! who beset,
Flinging round van and rear his ghastly net,
That host, when from the regions of the
    Pole   15
They shrunk, insane ambition's barren
    goal—
That host, as huge and strong as e'er defied
Their God, and placed their trust in
    human pride !
As fathers persecute rebellious sons,
He smote the blossoms of their warrior
    youth ;   20
He called on Frost's inexorable tooth
Life to consume in Manhood's firmest
    hold ;
Nor spared the reverend blood that feebly
    runs ;
For why—unless for liberty enrolled
And sacred home—ah ! why should hoary
    Age be bold ?   25
Fleet the Tartar's reinless steed,
But fleeter far the pinions of the Wind,
Which from Siberian caves the Monarch
    freed,
And sent him forth, with squadrons of his
    kind,
And bade the Snow their ample backs
    bestride,   30
      And to the battle ride.

No pitying voice commands a halt,
No courage can repel the dire assault ;
Distracted, spiritless, benumbed, and
   blind,
Whole legions sink—and, in one instant,
   find   35
Burial and death : look for them—and
   descry,
When morn returns, beneath the clear
   blue sky,
A soundless waste, a trackless vacancy !

XXXV.

ON THE SAME OCCASION.

[Composed 1816.—Published 1816.]

YE Storms, resound the praises of your
   King !
And ye mild Seasons—in a sunny clime,
Midway on some high hill, while father
   Time
Looks on delighted—meet in festal ring,
And loud and long of Winter's triumph
   sing !   5
Sing ye, with blossoms crowned, and
   fruits, and flowers,
Of Winter's breath surcharged with sleety
   showers,
And the dire flapping of his hoary
   wing !
Knit the blithe dance upon the soft green
   grass ;
With feet, hands, eyes, looks, lips, report
   your gain ;   10
Whisper it to the billows of the main,
And to the aerial zephyrs as they pass,
That old decrepit Winter—*He* hath
   slain
That Host, which rendered all your boun-
   ties vain !

XXXVI.

[Composed November or December, 1822.—
Published 1827.]

BY Moscow self-devoted to a blaze
Of dreadful sacrifice ; by Russian blood
Lavished in fight with desperate hardi-
   hood ;

The unfeeling Elements no claim shall
   raise
To 'rob our Human-nature of just
   praise   5
For what she did and suffered. Pledges
   sure
Of a deliverance absolute and pure
She gave, if Faith might tread the beaten
   ways
Of Providence. But now did the Most
   High
Exalt his still small voice ;—to quell that
   Host   10
Gathered his power, a manifest ally ;
He, whose heaped waves confounded the
   proud boast
Of Pharaoh, said to Famine, Snow, and
   Frost,
" Finish the strife by deadliest victory !"

XXXVII.

THE GERMANS ON THE HEIGHTS OF
HOCHHEIM.

[Composed 1820.—Published 1822 (*Memorials of
a Tour,* &c.).]

ABRUPTLY paused the strife ;—the field
   throughout
Resting upon his arms each warrior stood,
Checked in the very act and deed of blood,
With breath suspended, like a listening
   scout.
O Silence ! thou wert mother of a shout 5
That through the texture of yon azure
   dome
Cleaves its glad way, a cry of harvest
   home
Uttered to Heaven in ecstasy devout !
The barrier Rhine hath flashed, through
   battle-smoke,
On men who gaze heart-smitten by the
   view,   10
As if all Germany had felt the shock !
—Fly, wretched Gauls ! ere they the
   charge renew
Who have seen—themselves now casting
   off the yoke—
The unconquerable Stream his course
   pursue.

XXXVIII.

NOVEMBER, 1813.

[Composed November, 1813.—Published 1815.]

Now that all hearts are glad, all faces
bright,
Our aged Sovereign sits, to the ebb and
flow
Of states and kingdoms, to their joy or
woe,
Insensible. He sits deprived of sight,
And lamentably wrapped in twofold night,
Whom no weak hopes deceived ; whose
mind ensued,   6
Through perilous war, with regal fortitude,
Peace that should claim respect from law-
less Might.
Dread King of Kings, vouchsafe a ray
divine
To his forlorn condition ! let thy grace 10
Upon his inner soul in mercy shine ;
Permit his heart to kindle, and to embrace
(Though it were only for a moment's
space)
The triumphs of this hour[1] ; for they are
THINE !

XXXIX.

ODE.

1814.

[Composed Jan., 1816.—Published : vol. of 1816.]

——————————Carmina possumus
Donare, et pretium dicere muneri.
Non incisa notis marmora publicis,
Per quae spiritus et vita redit bonis
Post mortem ducibus
——————————clarius indicant
Laudes, quam ——————Pierides ; neque,
Si chartae sileant quod bene feceris,
Mercedem tuleris.——HOR. Car. 8. Lib. 4. 11 *sq.*

I.

WHEN the soft hand of sleep had closed
the latch
On the tired household of corporeal sense,
And Fancy, keeping unreluctant watch,
Was free her choicest favours to dispense ;

I saw, in wondrous pérspective displayed,
A landscape more august than happiest
skill   6
Of pencil ever clothed with light and
shade ;
An intermingled pomp of vale and hill,
City, and naval stream, suburban grove,
And stately forest where the wild deer
rove ;   10
Nor wanted lurking hamlet, dusky towns,
And scattered rural farms of aspect
bright ;
And, here and there, between the pas-
toral downs,
The azure sea upswelled upon the sight.
Fair prospect, such as Britain only
shows !   15
But not a living creature could be seen
Through its wide circuit, that, in deep
repose,
And, even to sadness, lonely and serene,
Lay hushed ; till—through a portal in
the sky
Brighter than brightest loop-hole, in a
storm,   20
Opening before the sun's triumphant
eye—
Issued, to sudden view, a glorious Form !
Earthward it glided with a swift descent :
Saint George himself this Visitant must
be ;
And, ere a thought could ask on what
intent   25
He sought the regions of humanity,
A thrilling voice was heard, that vivified
City and field and flood ;—aloud it cried—

"Though from my celestial home,
Like a Champion, armed I come ;   30
On my helm the dragon crest,
And the red cross on my breast ;
I, the Guardian of this Land,
Speak not now of toilsome duty ;
Well obeyed was that command—   35
Whence bright days of festive beauty ;
Haste, Virgins, haste !—the flowers which
summer gave
Have perished in the field ;
But the green thickets plenteously shall
yield
Fit garlands for the brave,   40

[1] i.e. the final overthrow of Napoleon at Leip-
zig, Oct. 16–19, 1813.—ED.

That will be welcome, if by you entwined;
Haste, Virgins, haste; and you, ye Ma-
　　trons grave,
Go forth with rival youthfulness of mind,
　　And gather what ye find
Of hardy laurel and wild holly boughs—
To deck your stern Defenders' modest
　　brows!　　　　　　　　　　　　46
　　Such simple gifts prepare,
Though they have gained a worthier meed,
　　And in due time shall share
Those palms and amaranthine wreaths
Unto their martyred Countrymen de-
　　creed,　　　　　　　　　　　　51
In realms where everlasting freshness
　　breathes!"

II.

And lo! with crimson banners proudly
　　streaming,
And upright weapons innocently gleaming,
Along the surface of a spacious plain　55
Advance in order the redoubted Bands,
And there receive green chaplets from
　　the hands
　　Of a fair female train—
　　Maids and Matrons, dight
　　In robes of dazzling white;　　　60
While from the crowd bursts forth a
　　rapturous noise
By the cloud-capt hills retorted;
　　And a throng of rosy boys
　　In loose fashion tell their joys;
And grey-haired sires, on staffs sup-
　　ported,　　　　　　　　　　　65
Look round, and by their smiling seem
　　to say,
"Thus strives a grateful Country to
　　display
The mighty debt which nothing can
　　repay!"

III.

Anon before my sight a palace rose　69
Built of all precious substances,—so pure
And exquisite, that sleep alone bestows
Ability like splendour to endure:
Entered, with streaming thousands,
　　through the gate,
I saw the banquet spread beneath a Dome
　　of state,

A lofty Dome, that dared to emulate　75
The heaven of sable night
With starry lustre; yet had power to
　　throw
Solemn effulgence, clear as solar light,
Upon a princely company below,
While the vault rang with choral har-
　　mony,　　　　　　　　　　　　80
Like some Nymph-haunted grot beneath
　　the roaring sea.
—No sooner ceased that peal, than on the
　　verge
Of exultation hung a dirge
Breathed from a soft and lonely instru-
　　ment,
　　That kindled recollections　　85
　　Of agonised affections;
And, though some tears the strain at-
　　tended,
　　The mournful passion ended
In peace of spirit, and sublime content!

IV.

But garlands wither; festal shows de-
　　part,　　　　　　　　　　　　90
Like dreams themselves; and sweetest
　　sound—
　　(Albeit of effect profound)
　　It was and it is gone!
Victorious England! bid the silent Art
Reflect, in glowing hues that shall not
　　fade,　　　　　　　　　　　　95
Those high achievements; even as she
　　arrayed
With second life the deed of Marathon
　　Upon Athenian walls;
So may she labour for thy civic halls:
　　And be the guardian spaces　100
　　Of consecrated places,
As nobly graced by Sculpture's patient
　　toil;
And let imperishable Columns rise
Fixed in the depths of this courageous
　　soil;
Expressive signals of a glorious strife, 105
And competent to shed a spark divine
Into the torpid breast of daily life;—
Records on which, for pleasure of all
　　eyes,
　　The morning sun may shine
With gratulation thoroughly benign! 110

V.

And ye, Pierian Sisters, sprung from
    Jove
And sage Mnemosyne,—full long de-
    barred
From your first mansions, exiled all too
    long
From many a hallowed stream and grove,
Dear native regions where ye wont to
    rove,   115
Chanting for patriot heroes the reward
    Of never-dying song!
Now (for, though Truth descending from
    above
The Olympian summit hath destroyed for
    aye   119
Your kindred Deities, *Ye* live and move,
Spared for obeisance from perpetual love,
For privilege redeemed of godlike sway)
Now, on the margin of some spotless
    fountain,
Or top serene of unmolested mountain,
Strike audibly the noblest of your lyres,
And for a moment meet the soul's de-
    sires!   126
That I, or some more favoured Bard, may
    hear
What ye, celestial Maids! have often
    sung
Of Britain's acts,—may catch it with rapt
    ear,
And give the treasure to our British
    tongue!   130
So shall the characters of that proud page
Support their mighty theme from age
    to age;
And, in the desert places of the earth,
When they to future empires have given
    birth,
So shall the people gather and believe 135
The bold report, transferred to every
    clime;
And the whole world, not envious but
    admiring,
    And to the like aspiring,
Own—that the progeny of this fair Isle
Had power as lofty actions to achieve 140
As were performed in man's heroic prime;
Nor wanted, when their fortitude had held
Its even tenor, and the foe was quelled,

A corresponding virtue to beguile
The hostile purpose of wide-wasting
    Time—   145
That not in vain they laboured to secure,
For their great deeds, perpetual memory,
And fame as largely spread as land and
    sea,
By Works of spirit high and passion pure!

XL.

FEELINGS OF A FRENCH ROYALIST, ON THE
DISINTERMENT OF THE REMAINS OF THE
DUKE D'ENGHIEN.

[Composed 1816.—Published: vol. of 1816.]

DEAR Reliques! from a pit of vilest
    mould
Uprisen—to lodge among ancestral kings;
And to inflict shame's salutary stings
On the remorseless hearts of men grown
    old
In a blind worship; men perversely bold
Even to this hour,—yet, some shall now
    forsake   6
Their monstrous Idol if the dead e'er
    spake,
To warn the living; if truth were ever
    told
By aught redeemed out of the hollow
    grave:
O murdered Prince! meek, loyal, pious,
    brave!   10
The power of retribution once was given:
But 'tis a rueful thought that willow
    bands
So often tie the thunder-wielding hands
Of Justice sent to earth from highest
    Heaven!

XLI.

OCCASIONED BY THE BATTLE OF WATERLOO.

(The last six lines intended for an Inscription.)

FEBRUARY, 1816.

[Composed 1816.—Published Feb. 4, 1816 (*The Champion*); vol. of 1816.]

INTREPID sons of Albion! not by you
Is life despised; ah no, the spacious earth
Ne'er saw a race who held, by right of
    birth,

So many objects to which love is due:
Ye slight not life—to God and Nature
    true;   5
But death, becoming death, is dearer far,
When duty bids you bleed in open war:
Hence hath your prowess quelled that
    impious crew.
Heroes!—for instant sacrifice prepared;
Yet filled with ardour and on triumph
    bent   10
'Mid direst shocks of mortal accident—
To you who fell, and you whom slaughter
    spared
To guard the fallen, and consummate the
    event,
Your Country rears this sacred Monu-
    ment!

XLII.

SIEGE OF VIENNA RAISED BY JOHN SOBIESKI.

FEBRUARY, 1816.

[Composed Jan., 1816.—Published Feb. 4, 1816
(*The Champion*); vol. of 1816.]

OH, for a kindling touch from that pure
    flame
Which ministered, erewhile, to a sacrifice
Of gratitude, beneath Italian skies,
In words like these: "Up, Voice of song!
    proclaim
Thy saintly rapture with celestial aim: 5
For lo! the Imperial City stands released
From bondage threatened by the em-
    battled East,
And Christendom respires; from guilt
    and shame
Redeemed, from miserable fear set free
By one day's feat, one mighty victory. 10
—Chant the Deliverer's praise in every
    tongue!
The Cross shall spread, the Crescent hath
    waxed dim;
He conquering, as in joyful Heaven is
    sung,
HE CONQUERING THROUGH GOD, AND GOD
    BY HIM [1]."

---

[1] See Filicaia's Ode.

XLIII.

OCCASIONED BY THE BATTLE OF WATERLOO. FEBRUARY, 1816.

[Composed February, 1816.—Published: vol.
of 1816.]

THE Bard—whose soul is meek as dawn-
    ing day,
Yet trained to judgments righteously
    severe,
Fervid, yet conversànt with holy fear,
As recognising one Almighty sway:
He—whose experienced eye can pierce the
    array   5
Of past events; to whom, in vision clear,
The aspiring heads of future things
    appear,
Like mountain-tops whose mists have
    rolled away—
Assoiled from all encumbrance of our
    time [2],
He only, if such breathe, in strains
    devout   10
Shall comprehend this victory sublime;
Shall worthily rehearse the hideous rout,
The triumph hail, which from their peace-
    ful clime
Angels might welcome with a choral
    shout!

XLIV.

[Composed ? (perhaps 1816).—Published 1827.]

EMPERORS and Kings, how oft have
    temples rung
With impious thanksgiving, the Al-
    mighty's scorn!
How oft above their altars have been
    hung
Trophies that led the good and wise to
    mourn   4
Triumphant wrong, battle of battle born,
And sorrow that to fruitless sorrow clung!
Now, from Heaven-sanctioned victory,
    Peace is sprung;
In this firm hour Salvation lifts her horn.
Glory to arms! But, conscious that the
    nerve

---

[2] "From all this world's encumbrance did him-
self assoil."—SPENSER.

Of popular reason, long mistrusted, freed
Your thrones, ye Powers, from duty fear
   to swerve!   11
Be just, be grateful; nor, the oppressor's
   creed
Reviving, heavier chastisement deserve
Than ever forced unpitied hearts to bleed.

XLV.

ODE.

1815.

[Composed 1816.—Published: volume of 1816.]

I.

IMAGINATION—ne'er before content,
But aye ascending, restless in her pride
From all that martial feats could yield
To her desires, or to her hopes present—
Stooped to the Victory on that Belgic
   field   5
Achieved, this closing deed magnificent,
   And with the embrace was satisfied.
   —Fly, ministers of Fame,
With every help that ye from earth and
   heaven may claim!
Bear through the world these tidings of
   delight!   10
—Hours, Days, and Months, *have* borne
   them in the sight
Of mortals, hurrying like a sudden shower
   That landward stretches from the sea,
   The morning's splendours to devour;
But this swift travel scorns the company
Of irksome change, or threats from sad-
   dening power.   16
   —*The shock is given—the Adversaries*
   bleed—
   Lo, Justice triumphs! Earth is freed!
Joyful annunciation!—it went forth—
It pierced the caverns of the sluggish
   North—   20
   It found no barrier on the ridge
Of Andes—frozen gulfs became its
   bridge—
The vast Pacific gladdens with the
   freight—
Upon the Lakes of Asia 'tis bestowed—
The Arabian desert shapes a willing
   road   25
   Across her burning breast,

For this refreshing incense from the
   West!—
   —Where snakes and lions breed,
Where towns and cities thick as stars
   appear,
Wherever fruits are gathered, and
   where'er   30
The upturned soil receives the hopeful
   seed—
While the Sun rules, and cross the shades
   of night—
The unwearied arrow hath pursued its
   flight!
The eyes of good men thankfully give
   heed,
   And in its sparkling progress read 35
Of virtue crowned with glory's deathless
   meed:
Tyrants exult to hear of kingdoms won,
And slaves are pleased to learn that
   mighty feats are done;
Even the proud Realm, from whose dis-
   tracted borders
This messenger of good was launched
   in air,   40
France, humbled France, amid her wild
   disorders,
Feels, and hereafter shall the truth
   declare,
That she too lacks not reason to rejoice,
And utter England's name with sadly-
   plausive voice.

II.

O genuine glory, pure renown!   45
And well might it beseem that mighty
   Town
Into whose bosom earth's best treasures
   flow,
To whom all persecuted men retreat;
If a new Temple lift her votive brow
High on the shore of silver Thames—to
   greet   50
The peaceful guest advancing from afar.
Bright be the Fabric, as a star
Fresh risen, and beautiful within!—there
   meet
Dependence infinite, proportion just;
A Pile that Grace approves, and Time
   can trust   55
With his most sacred wealth, heroic dust.

III.

But if the valiant of this land
In reverential modesty demand,
That all observance, due to them, be paid
Where their serene progenitors are laid ;
Kings, warriors, high-souled poets, saint-
    like sages,   61
England's illustrious sons of long, long
    ages ;
Be it not unordained that solemn rites,
Within the circuit of those Gothic walls,
Shall be performed at pregnant intervals ;
Commemoration holy that unites   66
The living generations with the dead ;
    By the deep soul-moving sense
    Of religious eloquence,—
    By visual pomp, and by the tie   70
    Of sweet and threatening harmony ;
    Soft notes, awful as the omen
    Of destructive tempests coming,
    And escaping from that sadness
    Into elevated gladness ;   75
    While the white-robed choir attendant,
    Under mouldering banners pendant,
Provoke all potent symphonies to raise
    Songs of victory and praise,
For them who bravely stand unhurt, or
    bled   80
With medicable wounds, or found their
    graves
Upon the battle field, or under ocean's
    waves ;
Or were conducted home in single state,
And long procession—there to lie,
Where their sons' sons, and all posterity,
Unheard by them, their deeds shall
    celebrate !   86

IV.

Nor will the God of peace and love
Such martial service disapprove.
He guides the Pestilence—the cloud
Of locusts travels on his breath ;   90
The region that in hope was ploughed
His drought consumes, his mildew taints
    with death ;
He springs the hushed Volcano's mine,
He puts the Earthquake on her still
    design,

Darkens the sun, hath bade the forest sink,
And, drinking towns and cities, still can
    drink   96
Cities and towns—'tis Thou—the work is
    Thine !—
The fierce Tornado sleeps within Thy
    courts—
    He hears the word—he flies—
    And navies perish in their ports ;   100
For Thou art angry with Thine enemies !
    For these, and mourning for our
    errors,
    And sins, that point their terrors,
We bow our heads before Thee, and we
    laud
And magnify Thy name, Almighty God !
    But Man is Thy most awful instru-
    ment,   106
    In working out a pure intent [1] ;
Thou cloth'st the wicked in their dazzling
    mail,
And for Thy righteous purpose they
    prevail ;
    Thine arm from peril guards the
    coasts   110
    Of them who in Thy laws delight :
Thy presence turns the scale of doubtful
    fight,
Tremendous God of Battles, Lord of
    Hosts !

V.

Forbear :—to Thee—
Father and Judge of all, with fervent
    tongue,   115
    But in a gentler strain
Of contemplation, by no sense of wrong
(Too quick and keen) incited to disdain
Of pity pleading from the heart in vain—
    To Thee—To Thee,   120
Just God of christianised Humanity,
Shall praises be poured forth, and thanks
    ascend,
That Thou hast brought our warfare to
    an end,

---

[1] Lines 106, 107 were, in 1845, substituted for
the four following lines at which many had stum-
bled :—

    "But Thy most dreaded instrument,
    In working out a pure intent,
    Is Man—arrayed for mutual slaughter,
    —Yea, Carnage is thy daughter !"—Ed.

And that we need no second victory !
Blest, above measure blest,   125
If on Thy love our Land her hopes shall
    rest,
And all the Nations labour to fulfil
Thy law, and live henceforth in peace, in
    pure good will.

XLVI.

ODE.

THE MORNING OF THE DAY APPOINTED FOR
A GENERAL THANKSGIVING.   JANUARY 18,
1816.

Composed January, 1816.—Published: vol. of 1816.]

I.

HAIL, orient Conqueror of gloomy Night !
Thou that canst shed the bliss of gratitude
On hearts howe'er insensible or rude ;
Whether thy punctual visitations smite
The haughty towers where monarchs
    dwell ;   5
Or thou, impartial Sun, with presence
    bright
Cheer'st the low threshold of the pea-
    sant's cell !
Not unrejoiced I see thee climb the sky
In naked splendour, clear from mist or
    haze,
Or cloud approaching to divert the rays,
Which even in deepest winter testify 11
    Thy power and majesty,
Dazzling the vision that presumes to gaze.
—Well does thine aspect usher in this
    Day ;
As aptly suits therewith that modest pace
    Submitted to the chains   16
That bind thee to the path which God
    ordains
    That thou shalt trace,
Till, with the heavens and earth, thou
    pass away !
Nor less, the stillness of these frosty
    plains,   20
Their utter stillness, and the silent grace
Of yon ethereal summits white with snow,
(Whose tranquil pomp and spotless purity
    Report of storms gone by
    To us who tread below),   25
Do with the service of this Day accord.
—Divinest Object which the uplifted eye

Of mortal man is suffered to behold ;
Thou, who upon those snow-clad Heights
    hast poured
Meek lustre, nor forget'st the humble Vale ;
Thou who dost warm Earth's universal
    mould,   31
And for thy bounty wert not unadored
    By pious men of old ;
Once more, heart-cheering Sun, I bid thee
    hail !
Bright be thy course to-day, let not this
    promise fail !   35

II.

'Mid the deep quiet of this morning
    hour,
All nature seems to hear me while I speak,
By feelings urged that do not vainly seek
Apt language, ready as the tuneful notes
That stream in blithe succession from the
    throats   40
    Of birds, in leafy bower,
Warbling a farewell to a vernal shower.
—There is a radiant though a short-lived
    flame,
That burns for Poets in the dawning east ;
And oft my soul hath kindled at the same,
When the captivity of sleep had ceased ; 46
But He who fixed immoveably the frame
Of the round world, and built, by laws as
    strong,
    A solid refuge for distress—
    The towers of righteousness ;   50
He knows that from a holier altar came
The quickening spark of this day's sacri-
    fice ;
Knows that the source is nobler whence
    doth rise
    The current of this matin song ;
    That deeper far it lies   55
Than aught dependent on the fickle skies.

III.

    Have we not conquered ?—by the venge-
        ful sword ?
Ah no, by dint of Magnanimity ;
That curbed the baser passions, and left
    free
A loyal band to follow their liege Lord
Clear-sighted Honour, and his staid Com-
    peers,   61
Along a track of most unnatural years ;

In execution of heroic deeds
Whose memory, spotless as the crystal
    beads
Of morning dew upon the untrodden
    meads,   65
Shall live enrolled above the starry
    spheres.
He, who in concert with an earthly string
Of Britain's acts would sing,
He with enraptured voice will tell
Of One whose spirit no reverse could
    quell;   70
Of One that 'mid the failing never failed—
Who paints how Britain struggled and
    prevailed
Shall represent her labouring with an eye
Of circumspect humanity;
Shall show her clothed with strength and
    skill   75
All martial duties to fulfil;
Firm as a rock in stationary fight;
In motion rapid as the lightning's gleam;
Fierce as a flood-gate bursting at mid-
    night
To rouse the wicked from their giddy
    dream—   80
Woe, woe to all that face her in the
    field !
Appalled she may not be, and cannot
    yield.

IV.

And thus is *missed* the sole true glory
That can belong to human story !
At which they only shall arrive   85
Who through the abyss of weakness
    dive.
The very humblest are too proud of heart;
And one brief day is rightly set apart
For Him who lifteth up and layeth low;
For that Almighty God to whom we owe,
Say not that we have vanquished—but
    that we survive.   91

V.

How dreadful the dominion of the impure !
Why should the Song be tardy to proclaim
That less than power unbounded could
    not tame

That soul of Evil—which, from Hell let
    loose,   95
Had filled the astonished world with such
    abuse
As boundless patience only could endure?
—Wide-wasted regions—cities wrapt in
    flame—
Who sees, may lift a streaming eye
To Heaven;—who never saw, may heave
    a sigh;   100
But the foundation of our nature shakes,
And with an infinite pain the spirit aches,
When desolated countries, towns on fire,
    Are but the avowed attire
Of warfare waged with desperate mind 105
Against the life of virtue in mankind;
    Assaulting without ruth
    The citadels of truth;
While the fair gardens of civility,
    By ignorance defaced,   110
    By violence laid waste,
Perish without reprieve for flower or tree !

VI.

A crouching purpose—a distracted will—
Opposed to hopes that battened upon
    scorn,
And to desires whose ever waning horn
Not all the light of earthly power could
    fill;   116
Opposed to dark, deep plots of patient
    skill,
And to celerities of lawless force;
Which, spurning God, had flung away
    remorse—
What could they gain but shadows of re-
    dress?   120
—So bad proceeded propagating worse;
And discipline was passion's dire excess.
Widens the fatal web, its lines extend,
And deadlier poisons in the chalice blend.
When will your trials teach you to be
    wise?   125
—O prostrate Lands, consult your agonies !

VII.

No more—the guilt is banished,
And, with the guilt, the shame is fled;
And, with the guilt and shame, the Woe
    hath vanished,

Shaking the dust and ashes from her
    head!   130
—No more—these lingerings of distress
Sully the limpid stream of thankfulness.
What robe can Gratitude employ
So seemly as the radiant vest of Joy?
What steps so suitable as those that move
In prompt obedience to spontaneous
    measures   136
Of glory, and felicity, and love,
Surrendering the whole heart to sacred
    pleasures?

VIII.

O Britain! dearer far than life is dear,
    If one there be   140
    Of all thy progeny
Who can forget thy prowess, never more
Be that ungrateful Son allowed to hear
Thy green leaves rustle or thy torrents
    roar.
As springs the lion from his den,   145
    As from a forest-brake
    Upstarts a glistering snake,
The bold Arch-despot re-appeared;—
    again
Wide Europe heaves, impatient to be cast,
    With all her armèd Powers,   150
    On that offensive soil, like waves upon
    a thousand shores.
The trumpet blew a universal blast!
But Thou art foremost in the field:—
    there stand:
Receive the triumph destined to thy hand!
All States have glorified themselves;—
    their claims   155
Are weighed by Providence, in balance
    even;
And now, in preference to the mightiest
    names,
To Thee the exterminating sword is given.
Dread mark of approbation, justly gained!
Exalted office, worthily sustained!   160

IX.

Preserve, O Lord! within our hearts
The memory of Thy favour,
That else insensibly departs,
And loses its sweet savour!

Lodge it within us!—as the power of
    light   165
Lives inexhaustibly in precious gems,
Fixed on the front of Eastern diadems,
So shine our thankfulness for ever bright!
What offering, what transcendent monu-
    ment
Shall our sincerity to Thee present?   170
—Not work of hands; but trophies that
    may reach
To highest Heaven—the labour of the
    Soul;
That builds, as thy unerring precepts
    teach,
Upon the internal conquests made by
    each,
Her hope of lasting glory for the whole.
Yet will not heaven disown nor earth
    ·   gainsay   176
The outward service of this day;
Whether the worshippers entreat
Forgiveness from God's mercy-seat;
Or thanks and praises to His throne
    ascend   180
That He has brought our warfare to an
    end,
And that we need no second victory!——
Ha! what a ghastly sight for man to see;
And to the heavenly saints in peace who
    dwell,
    For a brief moment, terrible;   185
But, to Thy sovereign penetration, fair,
Before whom all things are, that were,
All judgments that have been, or e'er
    shall be;
Links in the chain of Thy tranquillity!
Along the bosom of this favoured Nation,
Breathe Thou, this day, a vital undula-
    tion!   191
    Let all who do this land inherit
    Be conscious of Thy moving spirit!
Oh, 'tis a goodly Ordinance,—the sight,
Though sprung from bleeding war, is one
    of pure delight;   195
Bless Thou the hour, or ere the hour
    arrive,
When a whole people shall kneel down in
    prayer,
And, at one moment, in one rapture, strive
With lip and heart to tell their gratitude
    For Thy protecting care,   200

Their solemn joy—praising the Eternal
  Lord
    For tyranny subdued,
And for the sway of equity renewed,
For liberty confirmed, and peace restored!

X.

  But hark—the summons!—down the
    placid lake   205
Floats the soft cadence of the church-
    tower bells;
Bright shines the Sun, as if his beams
    would wake
The tender insects sleeping in their cells;
Bright shines the Sun—and not a breeze
    to shake
The drops that tip the melting icicles. 210
    O, enter now his Temple gate!
Inviting words—perchance already flung
(As the crowd press devoutly down the
    aisle
Of some old Minster's venerable pile)
From voices into zealous passion stung,
While the tubed engine feels the inspiring
    blast,   216
And has begun—its clouds of sound to
    cast
    Forth towards empyreal Heaven,
      As if the fretted roof were riven.
Us humbler ceremonies now await;   220

But in the bosom, with devout respect
The banner of our joy we will erect,
And strength of love our souls shall
    elevate:
For to a few collected in His name,   224
Their heavenly Father will incline an ear
Gracious to service hallowed by its aim;—
Awake! the majesty of God revere!
  Go—and with foreheads meekly bowed
Present your prayers—go—and rejoice
    aloud—
    The Holy One will hear!   230
And what, 'mid silence deep, with faith
    sincere,
Ye, in your low and undisturbed estate,
Shall simply feel and purely meditate—
Of warnings—from the unprecedented
    might,
Which, in our time, the impious have
    disclosed;   235
And of more arduous duties thence imposed
Upon the future advocates of right;
    Of mysteries revealed,
      And judgments unrepealed,
    Of earthly revolution,   240
      And final retribution,—
  To his omniscience will appear
An offering not unworthy to find place,
On this high Day of Thanks, before the
    Throne of Grace!

MEMORIALS OF A TOUR ON THE CONTINENT[1].

1820.

—··—

DEDICATION.

(SENT WITH THESE POEMS, IN MS., TO ——.)

DEAR Fellow-travellers! think not that the Muse,
To You presenting these memorial Lays,
Can hope the general eye thereon would gaze,
As on a mirror that gives back the hues
Of living Nature; no—though free to choose
The greenest bowers, the most inviting ways,
The fairest landscapes and the brightest days—
Her skill she tried with less ambitious views.
For You she wrought: Ye only can supply
The life, the truth, the beauty: she confides
In that enjoyment which with You abides.
Trusts to your love and vivid memory;
Thus far contented, that for You her verse
Shall lack not power the "meeting soul to pierce!"

W. WORDSWORTH.

RYDAL MOUNT, *Nov.*, 1821.

I.

FISH-WOMEN.—ON LANDING AT CALAIS.

'TIS said, fantastic ocean doth enfold
The likeness of whate'er on land is seen;
But if the Nereid Sisters and their Queen,
Above whose heads the tide so long hath
    rolled,
The Dames resemble whom we here behold,
How fearful were it down through open-
    ing waves   6

To sink, and meet them in their fretted
    caves,
Withered, grotesque, immeasurably old,
And shrill and fierce in accent!—Fear it
    not:
For they Earth's fairest daughters do
    excel;   10
Pure undecaying beauty is their lot;
Their voices into liquid music swell,
Thrilling each pearly cleft and sparry
    grot,
The undisturbed abodes where Sea-
    nymphs dwell!

II.

BRUGÈS.

BRUGÈS I saw attired with golden light
(Streamed from the west) as with a robe
    of power:
The splendour fled; and now the sunless
    hour,
That, slowly making way for peaceful
    night,
Best suits with fallen grandeur, to my
    sight   5
Offers the beauty, the magnificence,
And sober graces, left her for defence
Against the injuries of time, the spite
Of fortune, and the desolating storms

---

[1] These *Memorials* were published as a separate volume early in 1822. The poems were mostly written between January and November, 1821, the latest written of all, the *Dedication*, being dated November. To save needless repetition, none of the following poems will be furnished with the usual chronological note, except those to which the preceding observation does not apply. Where the usual note is wanting, the following general note may be taken as appropriate:—Composed 1821.—Published 1822.—Exceptions will be duly noted.—ED.

Of future war. Advance not—spare to
hide,   10
O gentle Power of darkness! these mild
hues;
Obscure not yet these silent avenues
Of stateliest architecture, where the Forms
Of nun-like females, with soft motion,
glide!

III.

BRUGÈS.

THE Spirit of Antiquity—enshrined
In sumptuous buildings, vocal in sweet song,
In picture, speaking with heroic tongue,
And with devout solemnities entwined—
Mounts to the seat of grace within the
mind: 5
Hence Forms that glide with swan-like
ease along,
Hence motions, even amid the vulgar
throng,
To an harmonious decency confined:
As if the streets were consecrated ground,
The city one vast temple, dedicate   10
To mutual respect in thought and deed;
To leisure, to forbearances sedate;
To social cares from jarring passions freed;
A deeper peace than that in deserts found!

IV.

INCIDENT AT BRUGÈS.

[Composed after July, 1828.—Published: vol.
of 1835.]

IN Brugès town is many a street
Whence busy life hath fled;
Where, without hurry, noiseless feet
The grass-grown pavement tread.
There heard we, halting in the shade   5
Flung from a Convent-tower,
A harp that tuneful prelude made
To a voice of thrilling power.

The measure, simple truth to tell,
Was fit for some gay throng;   10
Though from the same grim turret fell
The shadow and the song.
When silent were both voice and chords,
The strain seemed doubly dear,
Yet sad as sweet,—for *English* words   15
Had fallen upon the ear.

It was a breezy hour of eve;
And pinnacle and spire
Quivered and seemed almost to heave,
Clothed with innocuous fire;   20
But, where we stood, the setting sun
Showed little of his state;
And, if the glory reached the Nun,
'Twas through an iron grate.

Not always is the heart unwise,   25
Nor pity idly born,
If even a passing Stranger sighs
For them who do not mourn.
Sad is thy doom, self-solaced dove,
Captive, whoe'er thou be!   30
Oh! what is beauty, what is love,
And opening life to thee?

Such feeling pressed upon my soul,
A feeling sanctified
By one soft trickling tear that stole   35
From the Maiden at my side;
Less tribute could she pay than this,
Borne gaily o'er the sea,
Fresh from the beauty and the bliss
Of English liberty?   40

V.

AFTER VISITING THE FIELD OF WATERLOO.

A WINGÈD Goddess—clothed in vesture
wrought
Of rainbow colours; One whose port was
bold,
Whose overburthened hand could scarcely
hold
The glittering crowns and garlands which
it brought—
Hovered in air above the far-famed Spot.
She vanished; leaving prospect blank and
cold   6
Of wind-swept corn that wide around us
rolled
In dreary billows, wood, and meagre cot,
And monuments that soon must disap-
pear:
Yet a dread local recompense we found;
While glory seemed betrayed, while
patriot-zeal   11
Sank in our hearts, we felt as men *should*
feel

With such vast hoards of hidden carnage
near,
And horror breathing from the silent
ground !

VI.

BETWEEN NAMUR AND LIEGE.

WHAT lovelier home could gentle Fancy
choose?
Is this the stream, whose cities, heights,
and plains,
War's favourite playground, are with
crimson stains
Familiar, as the Morn with pearly dews ?
The Morn, that now, along the silver
MEUSE,   5
Spreading her peaceful ensigns, calls the
swains
To tend their silent boats and ringing
wains,
Or strip the bough whose mellow fruit
bestrews
The ripening corn beneath it. As mine
eyes
Turn from the fortified and threatening
hill,   10
How sweet the prospect of yon watery
glade,
With its grey rocks clustering in pensive
shade—
That, shaped like old monastic turrets,
rise
From the smooth meadow-ground, serene
and still !

VII.

AIX-LA-CHAPELLE.

WAS it to disenchant, and to undo.
That we approached the Seat of Charle-
maine?
To sweep from many an old romantic
strain
That faith which no devotion may renew !
Why does this puny Church present to
view   5
Her feeble columns? and that scanty
chair !
This sword that one of our weak times
might wear !
Objects of false pretence, or meanly true !

If from a traveller's fortune I might claim
A palpable memorial of that day,   10
Then would I seek the Pyrenean Breach
That ROLAND clove with huge two-handed
sway,
And to the enormous labour left his name,
Where unremitting frosts the rocky cres-
cent bleach.

VIII.

IN THE CATHEDRAL AT COLOGNE.

O FOR the help of Angels to complete
This Temple—Angels governed by a plan
Thus far pursued (how gloriously !) by
Man,
Studious that *He* might not disdain the seat
Who dwells in heaven ! But that aspir-
ing heat   5
Hath failed ; and now, ye Powers ! whose
gorgeous wings
And splendid aspect yon emblazonings
But faintly picture, 'twere an office meet
For you, on these unfinished shafts to try
The midnight virtues of your harmony :—
This vast design might tempt you to
repeat   11
Strains that call forth upon empyreal
ground
Immortal Fabrics, rising to the sound
Of penetrating harps and voices sweet !

IX.

IN A CARRIAGE, UPON THE BANKS OF THE RHINE.

AMID this dance of objects sadness steals
O'er the defrauded heart—while sweep-
ing by,
As in a fit of Thespian jollity,
Beneath her vine-leaf crown the green
Earth reels :
Backward, in rapid evanescence, wheels 5
The venerable pageantry of Time,
Each beetling rampart, and each tower
sublime,
And what the Dell unwillingly reveals
Of lurking cloistral arch, through trees
espied
Near the bright River's edge. Yet why
repine ?   10
To muse, to creep, to halt at will, to gaze—

Such sweet wayfaring—of life's spring
the pride,
Her summer's faithful joy—*that* still is
mine,
And in fit measure cheers autumnal days.

X.

HYMN,

FOR THE BOATMEN, AS THEY APPROACH
THE RAPIDS UNDER THE CASTLE OF
HEIDELBERG.

JESU! bless our slender Boat,
  By the current swept along;
Loud its threatenings—let them not
  Drown the music of a song
Breathed thy mercy to implore,   5
Where these troubled waters roar!

Saviour, for our warning, seen
  Bleeding on that precious Rood;
If, while through the meadows green
  Gently wound the peaceful flood,   10
We forgot Thee, do not Thou
Disregard Thy Suppliants now!

Hither, like yon ancient Tower
  Watching o'er the River's bed,
Fling the shadow of thy power,   15
  Else we sleep among the dead;
Thou who trod'st the billowy sea,
Shield us in our jeopardy!

Guide our Bark among the waves;
  Through the rocks our passage smooth;
Where the whirlpool frets and raves   21
  Let Thy love its anger soothe:
All our hope is placed in Thee;
Miserere Domine[1]!

XI.

THE SOURCE OF THE DANUBE.

NOT, like his great Compeers, indignantly
Doth DANUBE spring to life[2]! The wan-
  dering Stream
(Who loves the Cross, yet to the Cres-
  cent's gleam
Unfolds a willing breast) with infant glee
Slips from his prison walls: and Fancy,
  free   5

To follow in his track of silver light,
Mounts on rapt wing, and with a mo-
  ment's flight
Hath reached the encincture of that
  gloomy sea
Whose waves the Orphean lyre forbad to
  meet
In conflict; whose rough winds forgot
  their jars   10
To waft the heroic progeny of Greece;
When the first Ship sailed for the Golden
  Fleece—
ARGO—exalted for that daring feat
To fix in heaven her shape distinct with
  stars.

XII.

ON APPROACHING THE STAUB-BACH,
LAUTERBRUNNEN.

UTTERED by whom, or how inspired—
  designed
For what strange service, does this con-
  cert reach
Our ears, and near the dwellings of man-
  kind!
'Mid fields familiarised to human
  speech?—
No Mermaids warble—to allay the wind   5
Driving some vessel toward a dangerous
  beach—
More thrilling melodies; Witch answer-
  ing Witch,
To chant a love-spell, never intertwined
Notes shrill and wild with art more
  musical:
Alas! that from the lips of abject Want
Or Idleness in tatters mendicant   11
The strain should flow—free Fancy to
  enthral,
And with regret and useless pity haunt
This bold, this bright, this sky-born,
  WATERFALL[3]!

XIII.

THE FALL OF THE AAR—HANDEC.

FROM the fierce aspect of this River,
  throwing
His giant body o'er the steep rock's brink,
Back in astonishment and fear we shrink:

---

[1] See Note, p. 905.   [2] See Note, ibid.   [3] See Note, p. 905

But, gradually a calmer look bestowing,
Flowers we espy beside the torrent grow-
        ing;   5
Flowers that peep forth from many a
        cleft and chink,
And, from the whirlwind of his anger,
        drink
Hues ever fresh, in rocky fortress blowing:
They suck—from breath that, threaten-
        ing to destroy,   9
Is more benignant than the dewy eve—
Beauty, and life, and motions as of joy:
Nor doubt but HE to whom yon Pine-
        trees nod
Their heads in sign of worship, Nature's
        God,
These humbler adorations will receive.

XIV.

MEMORIAL

NEAR THE OUTLET OF THE LAKE OF THUN.

"DEM
ANDENKEN
MEINES FREUNDES
ALOYS REDING
MDCCCXVIII."

Aloys Reding, it will be remembered, was Cap-
tain-General of the Swiss forces, which, with a
courage and perseverance worthy of the cause,
opposed the flagitious and too successful at-
tempt of Buonaparte to subjugate their coun-
try.

AROUND a wild and woody hill
A gravelled pathway treading,
We reached a votive Stone that bears
The name of Aloys Reding.

Well judged the Friend who placed it
        there   5
For silence and protection;
And haply with a finer care
Of dutiful affection.

The Sun regards it from the West;
And, while in summer glory   10
He sets, his sinking yields a type
Of that pathetic story:

And oft he tempts the patriot Swiss
Amid the grove to linger;
Till all is dim, save this bright Stone   15
Touched by his golden finger.

XV.

COMPOSED IN ONE OF THE CATHOLIC CANTONS[1].

DOOMED as we are our native dust
To wet with many a bitter shower,
It ill befits us to disdain
The altar, to deride the fane,
Where simple Sufferers bend, in trust   5
To win a happier hour.

I love, where spreads the village lawn,
Upon some knee-worn cell to gaze:
Hail to the firm unmoving cross,
Aloft, where pines their branches toss ! 10
And to the chapel far withdrawn,
That lurks by lonely ways !

Where'er we roam—along the brink
Of Rhine—or by the sweeping Po,
Through Alpine vale, or champaign wide,
Whate'er we look on, at our side   16
Be Charity !—to bid us think,
And feel, if we would know.

XVI.

AFTER-THOUGHT[2].

[Composed 1832.—Published 1832.]

OH Life ! without thy chequered scene
Of right and wrong, of weal and woe,
Success and failure, could a ground
For magnanimity be found;
For faith, 'mid ruined hopes, serene?   5
Or whence could virtue flow?

[Composed 1837.—Published 1837.]

Pain entered through a ghastly breach—
Nor while sin lasts must effort cease;
Heaven upon earth's an empty boast;
But, for the bowers of Eden lost,   10
Mercy has placed within our reach
A portion of God's peace.

---

[1] The three stanzas comprised under this title
originally (1822) formed part of the poem No.
XXIV. of this series, being the 5th, 4th, and 9th
stanzas of that piece. In 1827 they were detach-
ed and arranged as now to form a separate poem.
In 1832 a stanza (now stanza i. of *After-thought*,
No. XVI.) was added to them. This again was taken
from them in 1837, and formed, along with a
second added stanza, into the independent poem
entitled *After-thought.*—ED.

[2] See Editor's note to No. XV.

XVII.

SCENE ON THE LAKE OF BRIENTZ.

"WHAT know we of the Blest above
But that they sing and that they love?"
Yet, if they ever did inspire
A mortal hymn, or shaped the choir,
Now, where those harvest-Damsels float
Homeward in their rugged Boat,   6
(While all the ruffling winds are fled—
Each slumbering on some mountain's
    head),
Now, surely, hath that gracious aid
Been felt, that influence is displayed.   10
Pupils of Heaven, in order stand
The rustic Maidens, every hand
Upon a Sister's shoulder laid,—
To chant, as glides the boat along,
A simple, but a touching, song;   15
To chant, as Angels do above,
The melodies of Peace in love!

XVIII.

ENGELBERG, THE HILL OF ANGELS[1].

FOR gentlest uses, oft-times Nature takes
The work of Fancy from her willing
    hands;
And such a beautiful creation makes
As renders needless spells and magic
    wands,
And for the boldest tale belief commands.
When first mine eyes beheld that famous
    Hill   6
The sacred ENGELBERG, celestial Bands,
With intermingling motions soft and still,
Hung round its top, on wings that
    changed their hues at will.

Clouds do not name those Visitants;
    they were   10
The very Angels whose authentic lays,
Sung from that heavenly ground in mid-
    dle air,
Made known the spot where piety should
    raise
A holy Structure to the Almighty's praise.
Resplendent Apparition! if in vain   15
My ears did listen, 'twas enough to gaze;

And watch the slow departure of the
    train,
Whose skirts the glowing Mountain
    thirsted to detain.

XIX.

OUR LADY OF THE SNOW.

MEEK Virgin Mother, more benign
Than fairest Star, upon the height
Of thy own mountain[2], set to keep
Lone vigils through the hours of sleep,
What eye can look upon thy shrine   5
Untroubled at the sight?

These crowded offerings as they hang
In sign of misery relieved,
Even these, without intent of theirs,
Report of comfortless despairs,   10
Of many a deep and cureless pang
And confidence deceived.

To Thee, in this aerial cleft,
As to a common centre, tend
All sufferers that no more rely   15
On mortal succour—all who sigh
And pine, of human hope bereft,
Nor wish for earthly friend.

And hence, O Virgin Mother mild!
Though plenteous flowers around thee
    blow,   20
Not only from the dreary strife
Of Winter, but the storms of life,
Thee have thy Votaries aptly styled,
OUR LADY OF THE SNOW.

Even for the Man who stops not here,   25
But down the irriguous valley hies,
Thy very name, O Lady! flings,
O'er blooming fields and gushing springs
A tender sense of shadowy fear,
And chastening sympathies!   30

Nor falls that intermingling shade
To summer-gladsomeness unkind:
It chastens only to requite
With gleams of fresher, purer, light;
While, o'er the flower-enamelled glade,   35
More sweetly breathes the wind.

---

[1] See Note, p. 905.   [2] Mount Righi.

But on!—a tempting downward way,
A verdant path before us lies;
Clear shines the glorious sun above;
Then give free course to joy and love,   40
Deeming "the evil of the day
Sufficient for the wise."

XX.

EFFUSION,

IN PRESENCE OF THE PAINTED TOWER OF TELL, AT ALTORF.

This Tower stands upon the spot where grew the
Linden Tree against which his Son is said to
have been placed, when the Father's archery
was put to proof under circumstances so famous
in Swiss Story.

WHAT though the Italian pencil wrought
    not here,
Nor such fine skill as did the meed bestow
On Marathonian valour, yet the tear
Springs forth in presence of this gaudy
    show,
While narrow cares their limits overflow.
Thrice happy, burghers, peasants, war-
    riors old,   6
Infants in arms, and ye, that as ye go
Homeward or schoolward, ape what ye
    behold;
Heroes before your time, in frolic fancy
    bold!

And when that calm Spectatress from
    on high   10
Looks down—the bright and solitary
    Moon,
Who never gazes but to beautify;
And snow-fed torrents, which the blaze
    of noon
Roused into fury, murmur a soft tune
That fosters peace, and gentleness recalls;
Then might the passing Monk receive a
    boon   16
Of saintly pleasure from these pictured
    walls,
While on the warlike groups the mellow-
    ing lustre falls.

How blest the souls who when their
    trials come
Yield not to terror or despondency,   20

But face like that sweet Boy their mortal
    doom,
Whose head the ruddy apple tops,
    while he
Expectant stands beneath the linden
    tree:
He quakes not like the timid forest game,
But smiles—the hesitating shaft to free;
Assured that Heaven its justice will pro-
    claim,   26
And to his Father give its own unerring
    aim.

XXI.

THE TOWN OF SCHWYTZ.

BY antique Fancy trimmed—though
    lowly, bred
To dignity—in thee, O SCHWYTZ! are seen
The genuine features of the golden mean;
Equality by Prudence governèd,
Or jealous Nature ruling in her stead;   5
And, therefore, art thou blest with peace,
    serene
As that of the sweet fields and meadows
    green
In unambitious compass round thee
    spread.
Majestic BERNE, high on her guardian
    steep,
Holding a central station of command,   10
Might well be styled this noble body's
    HEAD;
Thou, lodged 'mid mountainous entrench-
    ments deep,
Its HEART; and ever may the heroic Land
Thy name, O SCHWYTZ, in happy freedom
    keep[1]!

XXII.

ON HEARING THE "RANZ DES VACHES" ON
THE TOP OF THE PASS OF ST. GOTHARD.

I LISTEN—but no faculty of mine
Avails those modulations to detect,
Which, heard in foreign lands, the Swiss
    affect

[1] Nearly 500 years (says Ebel, speaking of the
French Invasion) had elapsed, when, for the first
time, foreign soldiers were seen upon the fron-
tiers of this small Canton, to impose upon it the
laws of their governors.

With tenderest passion; leaving him to
   pine
(So fame reports) and die,—his sweet-
   breathed kine   5
Remembering, and green Alpine pastures
   decked
With vernal flowers. Yet may we not
   reject
The tale as fabulous.—Here while I re-
   cline,
Mindful how others by this simple Strain
Are moved, for me—upon this Mountain
   named   10
Of God himself from dread pre-eminence—
Aspiring thoughts, by memory reclaimed,
Yield to the Music's touching influence;
And joys of distant home my heart en-
   chain.

XXIII.

FORT FUENTES.

The Ruins of Fort Fuentes form the crest of a
rocky eminence that rises from the plain at
the head of the lake of Como, commanding
views up the Valteline, and toward the town
of Chiavenna. The prospect in the latter
direction is characterised by melancholy sub-
limity. We rejoiced at being favoured with a
distinct view of those Alpine heights; not, as
we had expected from the breaking up of the
storm, steeped in celestial glory, yet in com-
munion with clouds floating or stationary—
scatterings from heaven. The Ruin is interest-
ing both in mass and in detail. An Inscription,
upon elaborately-sculptured marble lying on
the ground, records that the Fort had been
erected by Count Fuentes in the year 1600,
during the reign of Philip the Third; and the
Chapel, about twenty years after, by one of his
Descendants. Marble pillars of gateways are
yet standing, and a considerable part of the
Chapel walls: a smooth green turf has taken
place of the pavement, and we could see no
trace of altar or image; but everywhere some-
thing to remind one of former splendour, and
of devastation and tumult. In our ascent we
had passed abundance of wild vines intermin-
gled with bushes: near the ruins were some
ill tended, but growing willingly; and rock,
turf, and fragments of the pile, are alike co-
vered or adorned with a variety of flowers,
among which the rose-coloured pink was grow-

ing in great beauty. While descending, we
discovered on the ground, apart from the
path, and at a considerable distance from the
ruined Chapel, a statue of a Child in pure
white marble, uninjured by the explosion that
had driven it so far down the hill. "How lit-
tle," we exclaimed, "are these things valued
here! Could we but transport this pretty Image
to our own garden!"—Yet it seemed it would
have been a pity any one should remove it from
its couch in the wilderness, which may be its
own for hundreds of years.—*Extract from
Journal.*

DREAD hour! when, upheaved by war's
   sulphurous blast,
This sweet-visaged Cherub of Parian
   stone
So far from the holy enclosure was cast,
   To couch in this thicket of brambles
     alone,
To rest where the lizard may bask in the
   palm   5
   Of his half-open hand pure from blemish
     or speck;
And the green, gilded snake, without
   troubling the calm
   Of the beautiful countenance, twine
     round his neck;
Where haply (kind service to Piety due!)
   When winter the grove of its mantle
     bereaves,   10
Some bird (like our own honoured red-
   breast) may strew
   The desolate Slumberer with moss and
     with leaves.

FUENTES once harboured the good and the
   brave,
   Nor to her was the dance of soft
     pleasure unknown:
Her banners for festal enjoyment did wave
   While the thrill of her fifes thro' the
     mountains was blown: 16

Now gads the wild vine o'er the pathless
   ascent:—
   O silence of Nature, how deep is thy
     sway,
When the whirlwind of human destruc-
   tion is spent,
   Our tumults appeased, and our strifes
     passed away!   20

XXIV.

THE CHURCH OF SAN SALVADOR.

SEEN FROM THE LAKE OF LUGANO.

This Church was almost destroyed by lightning a few years ago, but the altar and the image of the Patron Saint were untouched. The Mount, upon the summit of which the Church is built, stands amid the intricacies of the Lake of Lugano; and is, from a hundred points of view, its principal ornament, rising to the height of 2,000 feet, and, on one side, nearly perpendicular. The ascent is toilsome; but the traveller who performs it will be amply rewarded. Splendid fertility, rich woods and dazzling waters, seclusion and confinement of view contrasted with sea-like extent of plain fading into the sky; and this again, in an opposite quarter, with an horizon of the loftiest and boldest Alps—unite in composing a prospect more diversified by magnificence, beauty, and sublimity, than perhaps any other point in Europe, of so inconsiderable an elevation, commands.

THOU sacred Pile! whose turrets rise
From yon steep mountain's loftiest stage,
Guarded by lone San Salvador;
Sink (if thou must) as heretofore,
To sulphurous bolts a sacrifice, 5
But ne'er to human rage!

On Horeb's top, on Sinai, deigned
To rest the universal Lord:
Why leap the fountains from their cells
Where everlasting Bounty dwells?— 10
That, while the Creature is sustained,
His God may be adored.

Cliffs, fountains, rivers, seasons, times—
Let all remind the soul of heaven;
Our slack devotion needs them all; 15
And Faith—so oft of sense the thrall,
While she, by aid of Nature, climbs—
May hope to be forgiven.

Glory, and patriotic Love,
And all the Pomps of this frail "spot 20
Which men call Earth," have yearned to seek,
Associate with the simply meek,
Religion in the sainted grove,
And in the hallowed grot.

Thither, in time of adverse shocks, 25
Of fainting hopes and backward wills,
Did mighty Tell repair of old—
A Hero cast in Nature's mould,
Deliverer of the steadfast rocks
And of the ancient hills! 30

He, too, of battle-martyrs chief!
Who, to recall his daunted peers,
For victory shaped an open space,
By gathering with a wide embrace,
Into his single breast, a sheaf 35
Of fatal Austrian spears[1].

XXV.

THE ITALIAN ITINERANT, AND THE SWISS GOATHERD.

PART I.

I.

Now that the farewell tear is dried,
Heaven prosper thee, be hope thy guide!
Hope be thy guide, adventurous Boy;
The wages of thy travel, joy!
Whether for London bound—to trill 5
Thy mountain notes with simple skill;
Or on thy head to poise a show
Of Images in seemly row;
The graceful form of milk-white Steed,
Or Bird that soared with Ganymede; 10
Or through our hamlets thou wilt bear
The sightless Milton, with his hair
Around his placid temples curled;
And Shakspeare at his side—a freight,
If clay could think and mind were weight,
For him who bore the world! 16
Hope be thy guide, adventurous Boy;
The wages of thy travel, joy!

II.

But thou, perhaps, (alert as free
Though serving sage philosophy), 20
Wilt ramble over hill and dale,
A Vender of the well-wrought Scale,

---

[1] Arnold Winkelried, at the battle of Sempach, broke an Austrian phalanx in this manner. The event is one of the most famous in the annals of Swiss heroism; and pictures and prints of it are frequent throughout the country.

Whose sentient tube instructs to time
A purpose to a fickle clime:
Whether thou choose this useful part,   25
Or minister to finer art,
Though robbed of many a cherished dream,
And crossed by many a shattered scheme,
What stirring wonders wilt thou see
In the proud Isle of liberty!   30
Yet will the Wanderer sometimes pine
With thoughts which no delights can chase,
Recall a Sister's last embrace,
His Mother's neck entwine;
Nor shall forget the Maiden coy   35
That *would* have loved the bright-haired Boy!

III.

My Song, encouraged by the grace
That beams from his ingenuous face,
For this Adventurer scruples not
To prophesy a golden lot;   40
Due recompense, and safe return
To Como's steeps—his happy bourne!
Where he, aloft in garden-glade,
Shall tend, with his own dark-eyed Maid,
The towering maize, and prop the twig   45
That ill supports the luscious fig;
Or feed his eye in paths sun-proof
With purple of the trellis-roof,
That through the jealous leaves escapes
From Cadenabbia's pendent grapes.   50
—Oh might he tempt that Goatherd-child
To share his wanderings! him whose look
Even yet my heart can scarcely brook,
So touchingly he smiled—
As with a rapture caught from heaven—
For unasked alms in pity given.   56

PART II.

I.

With nodding plumes, and lightly drest
Like foresters in leaf-green vest,
The Helvetian Mountaineers, on ground
For Tell's dread archery renowned,   60
Before the target stood—to claim
The guerdon of the steadiest aim.
Loud was the rifle-gun's report—
A startling thunder quick and short!
But, flying through the heights around,   65

Echo prolonged a tell-tale sound
Of hearts and hands alike "prepared
The treasures they enjoy to guard!"
And, if there be a favoured hour
When Heroes are allowed to quit   70
The tomb, and on the clouds to sit
With tutelary power,
On their Descendants shedding grace—
This was the hour, and that the place.

II.

But Truth inspired the Bards of old   75
When of an iron age they told,
Which to unequal laws gave birth,
And drove Astræa from the earth.
—A gentle Boy (perchance with blood
As noble as the best endued,   80
But seemingly a Thing despised;
Even by the sun and air unprized;
For not a tinge or flowery streak
Appeared upon his tender cheek)
Heart-deaf to those rebounding notes,   85
Apart, beside his silent goats,
Sate watching in a forest shed,
Pale, ragged, with bare feet and head;
Mute as the snow upon the hill,
And, as the saint he prays to, still.   90
Ah, what avails heroic deed?
What liberty? if no defence
Be won for feeble Innocence.
Father of all! though wilful Manhood read
His punishment in soul-distress,   95
Grant to the morn of life its natural blessedness!

XXVI.

THE LAST SUPPER, BY LEONARDO DA VINCI,
IN THE REFECTORY OF THE CONVENT OF
MARIA DELLA GRAZIA—MILAN[1].

Tho' searching damps and many an envious flaw
Have marred this Work; the calm ethereal grace,
The love deep-seated in the Saviour's face,
The mercy, goodness, have not failed to awe
The Elements; as they do melt and thaw

---

[1] See Note p. 906.

The heart of the Beholder—and erase 6
(At least for one rapt moment) every trace
Of disobedience to the primal law.
The annunciation of the dreadful truth
Made to the Twelve,—till survives: lip, fore-
head, cheek, 10
And hand reposing on the board in ruth
Of what it utters, while the unguilty seek
Unquestionable meanings—still bespeak
A labour worthy of eternal youth !

XXVII.

THE ECLIPSE OF THE SUN, 1820.

HIGH on her speculative tower
Stood Science waiting for the hour
When Sol was destined to endure
That darkening of his radiant face
Which Superstition strove to chase, 5
Erewhile, with rites impure.

Afloat beneath Italian skies,
Through regions fair as Paradise
We gaily passed,—till Nature wrought
A silent and unlooked-for change, 10
That checked the desultory range
Of joy and sprightly thought.

Where'er was dipped the toiling oar,
The waves danced round us as before,
As lightly, though of altered hue, 15
'Mid recent coolness, such as falls
At noontide from umbrageous walls
That screen the morning dew.

No vapour stretched its wings; no cloud
Cast far or near a murky shroud; 20
The sky an azure field displayed;
'Twas sunlight sheathed and gently
charmed,
Of all its sparkling rays disarmed,
And as in slumber laid,—

Or something night and day between, 25
Like moonshine—but the hue was green;
Still moonshine, without shadow, spread
On jutting rock, and curvèd shore,
Where gazed the peasant from his door,
And on the mountain's head. 30

It tinged the Julian steeps—it lay,
Lugano! on thy ample bay;
The solemnising veil was drawn

O'er villas, terraces, and towers;
To Albogasio's olive bowers, 35
Porlezza's verdant lawn.

But Fancy with the speed of fire
Hath past to Milan's loftiest spire,
And there alights 'mid that aerial host
Of Figures human and divine[1], 40
White as the snows of Apennine
Indúrated by frost.

Awe-stricken she beholds the array
That guards the Temple night and day;
Angels she sees—that might from heaven
have flown, 45
And Virgin-saints, who not in vain
Have striven by purity to gain
The beatific crown—

Sees long-drawn files, concentric rings
Each narrowing above each;—the wings,
The uplifted palms, the silent marble
lips 51
The starry zone of sovereign height[2]—
All steeped in this portentous light !
All suffering dim eclipse !

Thus after Man had fallen (if aught 55
These perishable spheres have wrought
May with that issue be compared)
Throngs of celestial visages,
Darkening like water in the breeze,
A holy sadness shared. 60

Lo ! while I speak, the labouring Sun
His glad deliverance has begun:
The cypress waves her sombre plume
More cheerily; and town and tower,
The vineyard and the olive-bower, 65
Their lustre re-assume !

O Ye, who guard and grace my home
While in far-distant lands we roam,
What countenance hath this Day put on
for you?
While we look round with favoured eyes,
Did sullen mists hide lake and skies 71
And mountains from your view?

Or was it given you to behold
Like vision, pensive though not cold,

---

[1] See Note, p. 906.
[2] Above the highest circle of figures is a zone
of metallic stars.

From the smooth breast of gay Winander-
　　mere?　　　　　　　　　　　　　　75
Saw ye the soft yet awful veil
Spread over Grasmere's lovely dale,
Helvellyn's brow severe?

I ask in vain—and know far less
If sickness, sorrow, or distress　　　80
Have spared my Dwelling to this hour;
Sad blindness! but ordained to prove
Our faith in Heaven's unfailing love
And all-controlling power.

XXVIII.

THE THREE COTTAGE GIRLS.

I.

How blest the Maid whose heart—yet
　　free
From Love's uneasy sovereignty—
Beats with a fancy running high,
Her simple cares to magnify;
Whom Labour, never urged to toil,　　5
Hath cherished on a healthful soil;
Who knows not pomp, who heeds not
　　pelf;
Whose heaviest sin it is to look
Askance upon her pretty Self
Reflected in some crystal brook;　　10
Whom grief hath spared—who sheds no
　　tear
But in sweet pity; and can hear
Another's praise from envy clear.

II.

Such (but O lavish Nature! why
That dark unfathomable eye,　　　15
Where lurks a Spirit that replies
To stillest mood of softest skies,
Yet hints at peace to be o'erthrown,
Another's first, and then her own?)
Such, haply, yon ITALIAN Maid,　　20
Our Lady's laggard Votaress,
Halting beneath the chestnut shade
To accomplish there her loveliness:
Nice aid maternal fingers lend;
A Sister serves with slacker hand;　　25
Then, glittering like a star, she joins the
　　festal band.

III.

How blest (if truth may entertain
Coy fancy with a bolder strain)
The HELVETIAN Girl—who daily braves,
In her light skiff, the tossing waves,　　30
And quits the bosom of the deep
Only to climb the rugged steep!
—Say whence that modulated shout!
From Wood-nymph of Diana's throng?
Or does the greeting to a rout　　35
Of giddy Bacchanals belong?
Jubilant outcry! rock and glade
Resounded—but the voice obeyed
The breath of an Helvetian Maid.

IV.

Her beauty dazzles the thick wood;　　40
Her courage animates the flood;
Her steps the elastic green-sward meets
Returning unreluctant sweets;
The mountains (as ye heard) rejoice
Aloud, saluted by her voice!　　　45
Blithe Paragon of Alpine grace,
Be as thou art—for through thy veins
The blood of Heroes runs its race!
And nobly wilt thou brook the chains
That, for the virtuous, Life prepares;　　50
The fetters which the Matron wears,
The patriot Mother's weight of anxious
　　cares!

V.

"Sweet HIGHLAND Girl[1]! a very shower
Of beauty was thy earthly dower,"
When thou didst flit before mine eyes,　　55
Gay vision under sullen skies,
While Hope and Love around thee played,
Near the rough Falls of Inversneyd!
Have they, who nursed the blossom, seen
No breach of promise in the fruit?　　60
Was joy, in following joy, as keen
As grief can be in grief's pursuit?
When youth had flown did hope still bless
Thy goings—or the cheerfulness　　64
Of innocence survive to mitigate distress?

VI.

But from our course why turn—to tread
A way with shadows overspread;

---

[1] See address to a Highland Girl, p. 287.

Where what we gladliest would believe
Is feared as what may most deceive?   69
Bright Spirit, not with amaranth crowned
But heath-bells from thy native ground,
Time cannot thin thy flowing hair,
Nor take one ray of light from Thee;
For in my Fancy thou dost share
The gift of immortality;   75
And there shall bloom, with Thee allied,
The Votaress by Lugano's side;
And that intrepid Nymph, on Uri's steep
  descried!

XXIX.

THE COLUMN INTENDED BY BUONAPARTE
FOR A TRIUMPHAL EDIFICE IN MILAN,
NOW LYING BY THE WAY-SIDE IN THE
SIMPLON PASS.

AMBITION—following down this far-famed
  slope
Her Pioneer, the snow-dissolving Sun,
While clarions prate of kingdoms to be
  won—
Perchance, in future ages, here may stop;
Taught to mistrust her flattering horoscope
By admonition from this prostrate Stone!
Memento uninscribed of Pride o'erthrown,
Vanity's hieroglyphic; a choice trope
In Fortune's rhetoric. Daughter of the
  Rock,
Rest where thy course was stayed by
  Power divine!   10
The Soul transported sees, from hint of
  thine,
Crimes which the great Avenger's hand
  provoke,
Hears combats whistling o'er the ensan-
  guined heath:
What groans! what shrieks! what quiet-
  ness in death!

XXX.

STANZAS,

COMPOSED IN THE SIMPLON PASS.

VALLOMBROSA! I longed in thy shadiest
  wood
To slumber, reclined on the moss-covered
  floor,
To listen to ANIO's precipitous flood,

When the stillness of evening hath
  deepened its roar;
To range through the Temples of PAESTUM,
  to muse   5
In POMPEII preserved by her burial in
  earth;
On pictures to gaze where they drank in
  their hues;
And murmur sweet songs on the ground
  of their birth!

The beauty of Florence, the grandeur of
  Rome,
Could I leave them unseen, and not yield
  to regret?   10
With a hope (and no more) for a season to
  come,
Which ne'er may discharge the magnificent
  debt?
Thou fortunate Region! whose Greatness
  inurned
Awoke to new life from its ashes and dust;
Twice-glorified fields! if in sadness I
  turned   15
From your infinite marvels, the sadness
  was just.

Now, risen ere the light-footed Chamois
  retires
From dew-sprinkled grass to heights
  guarded with snow,
Toward the mists that hang over the land
  of my Sires,
From the climate of myrtles contented I
  go.   20
My thoughts become bright like yon
  edging of Pines
On the steep's lofty verge: how it black-
  ened the air!
But, touched from behind by the Sun, it
  now shines
With threads that seem part of his own
  silver hair.

Though the toil of the way with dear
  Friends we divide,   25
Though by the same zephyr our temples
  be fanned
As we rest in the cool orange-bower side
  by side,
A yearning survives which few hearts
  shall withstand:

Each step hath its value while homeward
    we move ;—
O joy when the girdle of England appears !
What moment in life is so conscious of
    love,   31
Of love in the heart made more happy by
    tears ?

XXXI.

ECHO, UPON THE GEMMI.

WHAT beast of chase hath broken from
    the cover ?
Stern GEMMI listens to as full a cry,
As multitudinous a harmony
Of sounds as rang the heights of Latmos
    over,
When, from the soft couch of her sleeping
    Lover,   5
Up-starting, Cynthia skimmed the moun-
    tain-dew
In keen pursuit—and gave, where'er she
    flew,
Impetuous motion to the Stars above her.
A solitary Wolf-dog, ranging on
Through the bleak concave, wakes this
    wondrous chime   10
Of aery voices looked in unison—
Faint — far-off — near — deep — solemn
    and sublime !—
So, from the body of one guilty deed,
A thousand ghostly fears, and haunting
    thoughts, proceed !

XXXII.

PROCESSIONS.

SUGGESTED ON A SABBATH MORNING IN
THE VALE OF CHAMOUNY.

To appease the Gods ; or public thanks to
    yield ;
Or to solicit knowledge of events,
Which in her breast Futurity concealed ;
And that the past might have its true
    intents
Feelingly told by living monuments—   5
Mankind of yore were prompted to devise
Rites such as yet Persepolis presents
Graven on her cankered walls, solemnities
That moved in long array before admiring
    eyes.

The Hebrews thus, carrying in joyful
    state   10
Thick boughs of palm, and willows from
    the brook,
Marched round the altar—to commemo-
    rate
How, when their course they through the
    desert took,
Guided by signs which ne'er the sky for-
    sook,
They lodged in leafy tents and cabins
    low ;   15
Green boughs were borne, while, for the
    blast that shook
Down to the earth the walls of Jericho,
Shouts rise, and storms of sound from
    lifted trumpets blow !

And thus, in order, 'mid the sacred grove
Fed in the Libyan waste by gushing
    wells,   20
The priests and damsels of Ammonian
    Jove
Provoked responses with shrill canticles ;
While, in a ship begirt with silver bells,
They round his altar bore the hornèd
    God,
Old Cham, the solar Deity, who dwells 25
Aloft, yet in a tilting vessel rode,
When universal sea the mountains over-
    flowed.

Why speak of Roman Pomps ? the
    haughty claims
Of Chiefs triumphant after ruthless wars ;
The feast of Neptune—and the Cereal
    Games,   30
With images, and crowns, and empty
    cars ;
The dancing Salii—on the shields of Mars
Smiting with fury ; and a deeper dread
Scattered on all sides by the hideous
    jars
Of Corybantian cymbals, while the head 35
Of Cybelè was seen, sublimely turreted !

At length a Spirit more subdued and
    soft
Appeared—to govern Christian pageant-
    ries :
The Cross, in calm procession, borne aloft
Moved to the chant of sober litanies. 40

Even such, this day, came wafted on the
    breeze
From a long train—in hooded vestments
    fair
Enwrapt—and winding, between Alpine
    trees
Spiry and dark, around their House of
    prayer,
Below the icy bed of bright ARGENTIERE. 45

Still in the vivid freshness of a dream,
The pageant haunts me as it met our
    eyes !
Still, with those white-robed Shapes—a
    living Stream,
The glacier Pillars join in solemn guise [1]
For the same service, by mysterious ties ;
Numbers exceeding credible account   51
Of number, pure and silent Votaries
Issuing or issued from a wintry fount ;
The impenetrable heart of that exalted
    Mount !

They, too, who send so far a holy gleam
While they the Church engird with
    motion slow,   56
A product of that awful Mountain seem,
Poured from his vaults of everlasting
    snow ;
Not virgin lilies marshalled in bright row,
Not swans descending with the stealthy
    tide,   60
A livelier sisterly resemblance show
Than the fair Forms, that in long order
    glide,
Bear to the glacier band—those Shapes
    aloft descried.

Trembling, I look upon the secret springs
Of that licentious craving in the mind 65
To act the God among external things,
To bind, on apt suggestion, or unbind ;
And marvel not that antique Faith in-
    clined
To crowd the world with metamorphosis,
Vouchsafed in pity or in wrath assigned ;
Such insolent temptations wouldst thou
    miss,   71
Avoid these sights ; nor brood o'er Fable's
    dark abyss !

[1] See Note. p. 906.

XXXIII.

ELEGIAC STANZAS.

The lamented Youth, whose untimely death gave
occasion to these elegiac verses, was Frederick
William Goddard, from Boston in North Ame-
rica. He was in his twentieth year, and had
resided for some time with a clergyman in the
neighbourhood of Geneva for the completion
of his education. Accompanied by a fellow-
pupil, a native of Scotland, he had just set out
on a Swiss tour when it was his misfortune to
fall in with a friend of mine who was hastening
to join our party. The travellers, after spend-
ing a day together on the road from Berne and
at Soleure, took leave of each other at night,
the young men having intended to proceed
directly to Zurich. But early in the morning
my friend found his new acquaintance, who
were informed of the object of his journey,
and the friends he was in pursuit of, equipped
to accompany him. We met at Lucerne the
succeeding evening, and Mr. G. and his fellow-
student became in consequence our travelling
companions for a couple of days. We ascend-
ed the Righi together ; and, after contemplat-
ing the sunrise from that noble mountain, we
separated at an hour and on a spot well suited
to the parting of those who were to meet no
more. Our party descended through the val-
ley of Our Lady of the Snow, and our late com-
panions, to Art. We had hoped to meet in a
few weeks at Geneva ; but on the third suc-
ceeding day (on the 21st of August) Mr. God-
dard perished, being overset in a boat while
crossing the Lake of Zurich. His companion
saved himself by swimming, and was hospitably
received in the mansion of a Swiss gentleman
(M. Keller) situated on the eastern coast of
the lake. The corpse of poor Goddard was
cast ashore on the estate of the same gentle-
man, who generously performed all the rites
of hospitality which could be rendered to the
dead as well as to the living. He caused a
handsome mural monument to be erected in
the church of Küsnacht, which records the
premature fate of the young American, and
on the shores too of the lake the traveller may
read an inscription pointing out the spot where
the body was deposited by the waves.

LULLED by the sound of pastoral bells,
Rude Nature's Pilgrims did we go,
From the dread summit of the Queen [2]
Of mountains, through a deep ravine,

[2] Mount Righi—Regina Montium.

Where, in her holy chapel, dwells 5
"Our Lady of the Snow."

The sky was blue, the air was mild;
Free were the streams and green the
    bowers;
As if, to rough assaults unknown,
The genial spot had *ever* shown 10
A countenance that as sweetly smiled—
The face of summer-hours.

And we were gay, our hearts at ease;
With pleasure dancing through the frame
We journeyed; all we knew of care— 15
Our path that straggled here and there;
Of trouble—but the fluttering breeze;
Of Winter—but a name.

If foresight could have rent the veil
Of three short days—but hush—no more !
Calm is the grave, and calmer none 21
Than that to which thy cares are gone,
Thou Victim of the stormy gale;
Asleep on ZURICH's shore !

Oh GODDARD!—what art thou?—a name—
A sunbeam followed by a shade ! 26
Nor more, for aught that time supplies,
The great, the experienced, and the wise !
Too much from this frail earth we claim,
And therefore are betrayed. 30

We met, while festive mirth ran wild,
Where, from a deep lake's mighty urn,
Forth slips, like an enfranchised slave,
A sea-green river, proud to lave,
With current swift and undefiled, 35
The towers of old LUCERNE.

We parted upon solemn ground
Far-lifted towards the unfading sky;
But all our thoughts were *then* of Earth,
That gives to common pleasures birth; 40
And nothing in our hearts we found
That prompted even a sigh.

Fetch, sympathising Powers of air,
Fetch, ye that post o'er seas and lands,
Herbs moistened by Virginian dew, 45
A most untimely grave to strew,
Whose turf may never know the care
Of *kindred* human hands !

Beloved by every gentle Muse
He left his Transatlantic home: 50
Europe, a realised romance,
Had opened on his eager glance;
What present bliss !—what golden views !
What stores for years to come !

Though lodged within no vigorous frame,
His soul her daily tasks renewed, 56
Blithe as the lark on sun-gilt wings
High poised—or as the wren that sings
In shady places, to proclaim
Her modest gratitude. 60

Not vain is sadly-uttered praise;
The words of truth's memorial vow
Are sweet as morning fragrance shed
From flowers 'mid GOLDAU's ruins bred;
As evening's fondly-lingering rays, 65
On RIGHI's silent brow.

Lamented youth ! to thy cold clay
Fit obsequies the Stranger paid;
And piety shall guard the Stone
Which hath not left the spot unknown 70
Where the wild waves resigned their
    prey—
And *that* which marks thy bed.

And, when thy Mother weeps for Thee,
Lost Youth ! a solitary Mother;
This tribute from a casual Friend 75
A not unwelcome aid may lend,
To feed the tender luxury,
The rising pang to smother[1].

XXXIV.

SKY-PROSPECT—FROM THE PLAIN OF
FRANCE.

Lo ! in the burning west, the craggy nape
Of a proud Ararat ! and, thereupon,
The Ark, her melancholy voyage done !
Yon rampant cloud mimics a lion's shape;
There, combats a huge crocodile—agape 5

[1] The persuasion here expressed was not
groundless. The first human consolation that
the afflicted Mother felt was derived from this
tribute to her son's memory, a fact which the
author learned, at his own residence, from her
Daughter, who visited Europe some years after-
wards.—Goldau is one of the villages desolated
by the fall of part of the Mountain Rossberg.

A golden spear to swallow! and that
  brown
And massy grove, so near yon blazing
  town,
Stirs and recedes—destruction to escape!
Yet all is harmless—as the Elysian shades
Where Spirits dwell in undisturbed re-
  pose—   10
Silently disappears, or quickly fades:
Meek Nature's evening comment on the
  shows
That for oblivion take their daily birth
From all the fuming vanities of Earth!

XXXV.

ON BEING STRANDED NEAR THE HARBOUR OF BOULOGNE[1].

WHY cast ye back upon the Gallic shore,
Ye furious waves! a patriotic Son
Of England—who in hope her coast had
  won,
His project crowned, his pleasant travel
  o'er?
Well—let him pace this noted beach once
  more,   5
That gave the Roman his triumphal
  shells;
That saw the Corsican his cap and bells
Haughtily shake, a dreaming Con-
  queror!—
Enough: my Country's cliffs I can behold,
And proudly think, beside the chafing
  sea,   10
Of checked ambition, tyranny controlled,
And folly cursed with endless memory:
These local recollections ne'er can cloy;
Such ground I from my very heart enjoy!

XXXVI.

AFTER LANDING—THE VALLEY OF DOVER. NOVEMBER, 1820.

WHERE be the noisy followers of the
  game
Which faction breeds? the turmoil where,
  that passed
Through Europe, echoing from the news-
  man's blast,

And filled our hearts with grief for
  England's shame?
Peace greets us;—rambling on without
  an aim   5
We mark majestic herds of cattle, free
To ruminate, couched on the grassy lea;
And hear far-off the mellow horn proclaim
The Season's harmless pastime. Ruder
  sound
Stirs not; enrapt I gaze with strange
  delight,   10
While consciousnesses, not to be disowned,
Here only serve a feeling to invite
That lifts the spirit to a calmer height,
And makes this rural stillness more pro-
  found.

XXXVII.

AT DOVER.

[Composed 1837.—Published: Sonnet-vol. of 1838;
  ed. 1845.]

FROM the Pier's head, musing, and with
  increase
Of wonder, I have watched this sea-side
  Town,
Under the white cliff's battlemented
  crown,
Hushed to a depth of more than Sabbath
  peace:
The streets and quays are thronged, but
  why disown   5
Their natural utterance? whence this
  strange release
From social noise—silence elsewhere un-
  known?—
A Spirit whispered, "Let all wonder
  cease;
Ocean's o'erpowering murmurs have set
  free
Thy sense from pressure of life's common
  din;   10
As the dread Voice that speaks from out
  the sea
Of God's eternal Word, the Voice of
  Time
Doth deaden, shocks of tumult, shrieks of
  crime,
The shouts of folly, and the groans of
  sin."

---

[1] See Note, p. 906.

XXXVIII.

DESULTORY STANZAS,

UPON RECEIVING THE PRECEDING SHEETS
FROM THE PRESS.

[Composed 1822.—Published 1822.]

Is then the final page before me spread,
Nor further outlet left to mind or heart?
Presumptuous Book! too forward to be
  read,
How can I give thee license to depart?
One tribute more: unbidden feelings
  start   5
Forth from their coverts; slighted objects
  rise;
My spirit is the scene of such wild art
As on Parnassus rules, when lightning
  flies,
Visibly leading on the thunder's har-
  monies.

All that I saw returns upon my view,   10
All that I heard comes back upon my
  ear,
All that I felt this moment doth renew;
And where the feet with no unmanly fear
Recoiled—and wings alone could travel—
  there
I move at ease; and meet contending
  themes   15
That press upon me, crossing the career
Of recollections vivid as the dreams
Of midnight,—cities, plains, forests, and
  mighty streams.

Where Mortal never breathed I dare to
  sit
Among the interior Alps, gigantic crew, 20
Who triumphed o'er diluvian power!—
  and yet
What are they but a wreck and residue,
Whose only business is to perish!—true
To which sad course, these wrinkled Sons
  of Time
Labour their proper greatness to sub-
  due;   25
Speaking of death alone, beneath a clime
Where life and rapture flow in plenitude
  sublime.

Fancy hath flung for me an airy bridge
Across thy long deep Valley, furious
  Rhone!
Arch that *here* rests upon the granite
  ridge   30
Of Monte Rosa—*there* on frailer stone
Of secondary birth, the Jung-frau's cone;
And, from that arch, down-looking on the
  Vale
The aspect I behold of every zone;
A sea of foliage, tossing with the gale, 35
Blithe Autumn's purple crown, and
  Winter's icy mail!

Far as St. Maurice, from yon eastern
  Forks[1],
Down the main avenue my sight can
  range:
And all its branchy vales, and all that
  lurks
Within them, church, and town, and hut,
  and grange,   40
For my enjoyment meet in vision strange;
Snows, torrents;—to the region's utmost
  bound,
Life, Death, in amicable interchange;—
But list! the avalanche—the hush pro-
  found
That follows—yet more awful than that
  awful sound!   45

Is not the chamois suited to his place?
The eagle worthy of her ancestry?
—Let Empires fall; but ne'er shall Ye
  disgrace
Your noble birthright, ye that occupy
Your council-seats beneath the open
  sky,   50
On Sarnen's Mount[2], there judge of fit
  and right,
In simple democratic majesty;
Soft breezes fanning your rough brows—
  the might
And purity of nature spread before your
  sight!

From this appropriate Court renowned
  Lucerne   55

---

[1] At the head of the Valais. See Note, p. 906.
[2] See Note, p. 906.

Calls me to pace her honoured Bridge[1]
    that cheers
The Patriot's heart with pictures rude and
    stern,
An uncouth Chronicle of glorious years.
Like portraiture, from loftier source,
    endears
That work of kindred frame, which spans
    the lake   60
Just at the point of issue, where it fears
The form and motion of a stream to
    take;
Where it begins to stir, *yet* voiceless as a
    snake.

Volumes of sound, from the Cathedral
    rolled,
This long-roofed Vista penetrate—but
    see,   65
One after one, its tablets, that unfold
The whole design of Scripture history;
From the first tasting of the fatal Tree,
Till the bright Star appeared in eastern
    skies,
Announcing, ONE was born mankind to
    free;   70
His acts, his wrongs, his final sacrifice;
Lessons for every heart, a Bible for all
    eyes.

[1] See Note, p. 906.

Our pride misleads, our timid likings
    kill.
—Long may these homely Works devised
    of old,
These simple efforts of Helvetian skill, 75
Aid, with congenial influence, to uphold
The State,—the Country's destiny to
    mould;
Turning, for them who pass, the common
    dust
Of servile opportunity to gold;
Filling the soul with sentiments au-
    gust—   80
The beautiful, the brave, the holy, and
    the just!

No more; Time halts not in his noiseless
    march—
Nor turns, nor winds, as doth the liquid
    flood;
Life slips from underneath us, like that
    arch
Of airy workmanship whereon we stood, 85
Earth stretched below, heaven in our
    neighbourhood.
Go forth, my little Book! pursue thy way;
Go forth, and please the gentle and the
    good;
Nor be a whisper stifled, if it say
That treasures, yet untouched, may grace
    some future Lay.   90

MEMORIALS OF A TOUR IN ITALY[1],

1837.

—••—

TO HENRY CRABB ROBINSON.

COMPANION! by whose buoyant Spirit cheered,
In whose experience trusting, day by day
Treasures I gained with zeal that neither feared
The toils nor felt the crosses of the way,
These records take, and happy should I be
Were but the Gift a meet Return to thee
For kindnesses that never ceased to flow,
And prompt self-sacrifice to which I owe
Far more than any heart but mine can know.

W. WORDSWORTH.

RYDAL MOUNT,
   Feb. 14th, 1842.

The Tour of which the following Poems are very
inadequate remembrances was shortened by
report, too well founded, of the prevalence of
Cholera at Naples. To make some amends
for what was reluctantly left unseen in the
South of Italy, we visited the Tuscan Sanc-
tuaries among the Apennines, and the princi-
pal Italian Lakes among the Alps. Neither of
those lakes, nor of Venice, is there any notice
in these Poems, chiefly because I have touched
upon them elsewhere. See, in particular, "De-
scriptive Sketches," "Memorials of a Tour on
the Continent in 1820," and a Sonnet upon
the extinction of the Venetian Republic.

I.

MUSINGS NEAR AQUAPENDENTE.

APRIL, 1837.

[Composed 1837.—Published: vol. of 1842.]

YE Apennines! with all your fertile vales
Deeply embosomed, and your winding
   shores
Of either sea, an Islander by birth,
A Mountaineer by habit, would resound
Your praise, in meet accordance with
   your claims   5
Bestowed by Nature, or from man's great
   deeds
Inherited:—presumptuous thought!—it
   fled
Like vapour, like a towering cloud, dis-
   solved.
Not, therefore, shall my mind give way to
   sadness;—
Yon snow-white torrent-fall, plumb down
   it drops   10
Yet ever hangs or seems to hang in air,
Lulling the leisure of that high-perched
   town,
AQUAPENDENTE, in her lofty site
Its neighbour and its namesake—town,
   and flood
Forth flashing out of its own gloomy
   chasm   15
Bright sunbeams—the fresh verdure of
   this lawn
Strewn with grey rocks, and on the
   horizon's verge,
O'er intervenient waste, through glimmer-
   ing haze,
Unquestionably kenned, that cone-shaped
   hill
With fractured summit, no indifferent
   sight   20
To travellers, from such comforts as are
   thine,
Bleak Radicofani! escaped with joy—
These are before me; and the varied scene
May well suffice, till noon-tide's sultry
   heat

---

[1] This group of Poems first appeared in the volume entitled *Poems, Chiefly of Early and Late Years,* published in 1842. The Sonnets all, or almost all, belong to the year, December, 1840—December, 1841. Where no note recording dates of composition and of publication is given, it is to be assumed that the poem was written in 1840–41, and published (as described above) in 1842.—ED.

Relax, to fix and satisfy the mind   25
Passive yet pleased. What! with this
    Broom in flower
Close at my side! She bids me fly to greet
Her sisters, soon like her to be attired
With golden blossoms opening at the feet
Of my own Fairfield. The glad greeting
    given,   30
Given with a voice and by a look re-
    turned
Of old companionship, Time counts not
    minutes
Ere, from accustomed paths, familiar
    fields,
The local Genius hurries me aloft,   34
Transported over that cloud-wooing hill,
Seat Sandal, a fond suitor of the clouds,
With dream-like smoothness, to Hel-
    vellyn's top,
There to alight upon crisp moss and range,
Obtaining ampler boon, at every step,
Of visual sovereignty — hills multitu-
    dinous,   40
(Not Apennine can boast of fairer), hills
Pride of two nations, wood and lake and
    plains,
And prospect right below of deep coves
    shaped
By skeleton arms, that, from the moun-
    tain's trunk
Extended, clasp the winds, with mutual
    moan   45
Struggling for liberty, while undis-
    mayed
The shepherd struggles with them. On-
    ward thence
And downward by the skirt of Greenside
    fell,
And by Glenridding-screes, and low Glen-
    coign,
Places forsaken now, though loving still   50
The Muses, as they loved them in the
    days
Of the old minstrels and the border
    bards.—
But here am I fast bound; and let it pass,
The simple rapture;—who that travels far
To feed his mind with watchful eyes could
    share   55
Or wish to share it?—One there surely
    was,

"The Wizard of the North," with anxious
    hope
Brought to this genial climate, when
    disease
Preyed upon body and mind—yet not the
    less
Had his sunk eye kindled at those dear
    words   60
That spake of bards and minstrels; and
    his spirit
Had flown with mine to old Helvellyn's
    brow,
Where once together, in his day of
    strength,
We stood rejoicing, as if earth were free
From sorrow, like the sky above our
    heads.   65

Years followed years, and when, upon
    the eve
Of his last going from Tweed-side, thought
    turned,
Or by another's sympathy was led,
To this bright land, Hope was for him no
    friend,
Knowledge no help; Imagination shaped
No promise. Still, in more than ear-deep
    seats,   71
Survives for me, and cannot but survive
The tone of voice which wedded borrowed
    words
To sadness not their own, when, with
    faint smile
Forced by intent to take from speech its
    edge,   75
He said, "When I am there, although 'tis
    fair,
'Twill be another Yarrow." Prophecy
More than fulfilled, as gay Campania's
    shores
Soon witnessed, and the city of seven hills,
Her sparkling fountains, and her moulder-
    ing tombs;   80
And more than all, that Eminence which
    showed
Her splendours, seen, not felt, the while
    he stood
A few short steps (painful they were)
    apart
From Tasso's Convent-haven, and retired
    grave.

Peace to their Spirits! why should
Poesy　　　　　　　　　　　85
Yield to the lure of vain regret, and hover
In gloom on wings with confidence out-
　spread
To move in sunshine?—Utter thanks, my
　Soul!
Tempered with awe, and sweetened by
　compassion
For them who in the shades of sorrow
　dwell,　　　　　　　　　　　90
That I—so near the term to human life
Appointed by man's common heritage,
Frail as the frailest, one withal (if that
Deserve a thought) but little known to
　fame—
Am free to rove where Nature's loveliest
　looks,　　　　　　　　　　　95
Art's noblest relics, history's rich be-
　quests,
Failed to reanimate and but feebly cheered
The whole world's Darling—free to rove
　at will
O'er high and low, and if requiring rest,
Rest from enjoyment only.
　　　　　　Thanks poured forth 100
For what thus far hath blessed my wander-
　ings, thanks
Fervent but humble as the lips can breathe
Where gladness seems a duty—let me
　guard
Those seeds of expectation which the fruit
Already gathered in this favoured Land
Enfolds within its core. The faith be
　mine,　　　　　　　　　　　106
That He who guides and governs all,
　approves
When gratitude, though disciplined to
　look
Beyond these transient spheres, doth wear
　a crown
Of earthly hope put on with trembling
　hand;　　　　　　　　　　　110
Nor is least pleased, we trust, when golden
　beams,
Reflected through the mists of age, from
　hours
Of innocent delight, remote or recent,
Shoot but a little way—'tis all they can—
Into the doubtful future. Who would
　keep　　　　　　　　　　　115

Power must resolve to cleave to it through
　life,
Else it deserts him, surely as he lives.
Saints would not grieve nor guardian
　angels frown
If one—while tossed, as was my lot to be,
In a frail bark urged by two slender
　oars　　　　　　　　　　　120
Over waves rough and deep, that, when
　they broke,
Dashed their white foam against the
　palace walls
Of Genoa the superb—should there be led
To meditate upon his own appointed tasks,
However humble in themselves, with
　thoughts　　　　　　　　　125
Raised and sustained by memory of Him
Who oftentimes within those narrow
　bounds
Rocked on the surge, there tried his
　spirit's strength
And grasp of purpose, long ere sailed his
　ship
To lay a new world open.
　　　　　　Nor less prized 130
Be those impressions which incline the
　heart
To mild, to lowly, and to seeming weak,
Bend that way her desires. The dew, the
　storm—
The dew whose moisture fell in gentle
　drops
On the small hyssop destined to be-
　come,　　　　　　　　　　　135
By Hebrew ordinance devoutly kept,
A purifying instrument—the storm
That shook on Lebanon the cedar's top,
And as it shook, enabling the blind roots
Further to force their way, endowed its
　trunk　　　　　　　　　　　140
With magnitude and strength fit to up-
　hold
The glorious temple—did alike proceed
From the same gracious will, were both an
　offspring
Of bounty infinite.
　　　　　Between Powers that aim
Higher to lift their lofty heads, im-
　pelled　　　　　　　　　　　145
By no profane ambition, Powers that
　thrive

By conflict, and their opposites, that trust
In lowliness—a mid-way tract there lies
Of thoughtful sentiment for every mind
Pregnant with good. Young, Middle-
    aged, and Old,   150
From century on to century, must have
    known
The emotion—nay, more fitly were it
    said—
The blest tranquillity that sunk so deep
Into my spirit, when I paced, enclosed
In Pisa's Campo Santo, the smooth
    floor   155
Of its Arcades paved with sepulchral
    slabs,
And through each window's open fret-
    work looked
O'er the blank Area of sacred earth
Fetched from Mount Calvary, or haply
    delved
In precincts nearer to the Saviour's
    tomb,   160
By hands of men, humble as brave, who
    fought
For its deliverance—a capacious field
That to descendants of the dead it holds
And to all living mute memento breathes,
More touching far than aught which on
    the walls   165
Is pictured, or their epitaphs can speak,
Of the changed City's long-departed
    power,
Glory, and wealth, which, perilous as
    they are,
Here did not kill, but nourished, Piety.
And, high above that length of cloistral
    roof,   170
Peering in air and backed by azure sky,
To kindred contemplations ministers
The Baptistery's dome, and that which
    swells
From the Cathedral pile; and with the
    twain
Conjoined in prospect mutable or fixed 175
(As hurry on in eagerness the feet,
Or pause) the summit of the Leaning-
    tower.
Nor less remuneration waits on him
Who having left the Cemetery stands
In the Tower's shadow, of decline and
    fall   180

Admonished not without some sense of
    fear,
Fear that soon vanishes before the sight
Of splendour unextinguished, pomp un-
    scathed,
And beauty unimpaired. Grand in itself,
And for itself, the assemblage, grand and
    fair   185
To view, and for the mind's consenting
    eye
A type of age in man, upon its front
Bearing the world-acknowledged evidence
Of past exploits, nor fondly after more
Struggling against the stream of destiny,
But with its peaceful majesty content. 191
—Oh what a spectacle at every turn
The Place unfolds, from pavement skin-
    ned with moss,
Or grass-grown spaces, where the heavi-
    est foot
Provokes no echoes, but must softly
    tread ;   195
Where Solitude with Silence paired stops
    short
Of Desolation, and to Ruin's scythe
Decay submits not.
                    But where'er my steps
Shall wander, chiefly let me cull with
    care
Those images of genial beauty, oft   200
Too lovely to be pensive in themselves
But by reflexion made so, which do best
And fitliest serve to crown with fragrant
    wreaths
Life's cup when almost filled with years,
    like mine.
—How lovely robed in forenoon light
    and shade,   205
Each ministering to each, didst thou
    appear
Savona, Queen of territory fair
As aught that marvellous coast thro' all
    its length
Yields to the Stranger's eye. Remem-
    brance holds
As a selected treasure thy one cliff, 210
That, while it wore for melancholy crest
A shattered Convent, yet rose proud to
    have
Clinging to its steep sides a thousand
    herbs

And shrubs, whose pleasant looks gave
    proof how kind
The breath of air can be where earth
    had else   215
Seemed churlish. And behold, both far
    and near,
Garden and field all decked with orange
    bloom,
And peach and citron, in Spring's mild-
    est breeze
Expanding; and, along the smooth shore
    curved
Into a natural port, a tideless sea,   220
To that mild breeze with motion and
    with voice
Softly responsive; and, attuned to all
Those vernal charms of sight and sound,
    appeared
Smooth space of turf which from the
    guardian fort
Sloped seaward, turf whose tender April
    green,   225
In coolest climes too fugitive, might even
    here
Plead with the sovereign Sun for longer
    stay
Than his unmitigated beams allow,
Nor plead in vain, if beauty could pre-
    serve,
From mortal change, aught that is born
    on earth   230
Or doth on time depend.
                While on the brink
Of that high Convent-crested cliff I
    stood,
Modest Savona! over all did brood
A pure poetic Spirit—as the breeze,
Mild—as the verdure, fresh—the sun-
    shine, bright—   235
Thy gentle Chiabrera!—not a stone,
Mural or level with the trodden floor,
In Church or Chapel, if my curious quest
Missed not the truth, retains a single
    name
Of young or old, warrior, or saint, or sage,
To whose dear memories his sepulchral
    verse   241
Paid simple tribute, such as might have
    flowed
From the clear spring of a plain English
    heart,

Say rather, one in native fellowship
With all who want not skill to couple
    grief   245
With praise, as genuine admiration
    prompts.
The grief, the praise, are severed from
    their dust,
Yet in his page the records of that worth
Survive, uninjured;—glory then to words,
Honour to word-preserving Arts, and
    hail   250
Ye kindred local influences that still,
If Hope's familiar whispers merit faith,
Await my steps when they the breezy
    height
Shall range of philosophic Tusculum;
Or Sabine vales explored inspire a wish
To meet the shade of Horace by the
    side   256
Of his Bandusian fount; or I invoke
His presence to point out the spot where
    once
He sate, and eulogised with earnest pen
Peace, leisure, freedom, moderate de-
    sires;   260
And all the immunities of rural life
Extolled, behind Vacuna's crumbling fane.
Or let me loiter, soothed with what is
    given,
Nor asking more, on that delicious Bay,
Parthenope's Domain—Virgilian haunt,
Illustrated with never-dying verse,   266
And, by the Poet's laurel-shaded tomb,
Age after age to Pilgrims from all lands
Endeared.
              And who—if not a man as cold
In heart as dull in brain—while pacing
    ground   270
Chosen by Rome's legendary Bards, high
    minds
Out of her early struggles well inspired
To localise heroic acts—could look
Upon the spots with undelighted eye,
Though even to their last syllable the
    Lays   275
And very names of those who gave them
    birth
Have perished?—Verily, to her utmost
    depth,
Imagination feels what Reason fears not
To recognise, the lasting virtue lodged

In those bold fictions that, by deeds
assigned 280
To the Valerian, Fabian, Curian Race,
And others like in fame, created Powers
With attributes from History derived,
By Poesy irradiate, and yet graced,
Through marvellous felicity of skill, 285
With something more propitious to high
aims
Than either, pent within her separate
sphere,
Can oft with justice claim.
                    And not disdaining
Union with those primeval energies
To virtue consecrate, stoop ye from your
height 290
Christian Traditions! at my Spirit's call
Descend, and, on the brow of ancient
Rome
As she survives in ruin, manifest
Your glories mingled with the brightest
hues
Of her memorial halo, fading, fading, 295
But never to be extinct while Earth
endures.
O come, if undishonoured by the prayer,
From all her Sanctuaries!—Open for my
feet
Ye Catacombs, give to mine eyes a
glimpse
Of the Devout, as, 'mid your glooms
convened 300
For safety, they of yore enclasped the
Cross
On knees that ceased from trembling, or
intoned
Their orisons with voices half-suppressed,
But sometimes heard. or fancied to be
heard,
Even at this hour.
                    And thou Mamertine prison, 305
Into that vault receive me from whose
depth
Issues, revealed in no presumptuous vi-
sion,
Albeit lifting human to divine,
A Saint, the Church's Rock, the mystic
Keys
Grasped in his hand; and lo! with up-
right sword 310
Prefiguring his own impendent doom,

The Apostle of the Gentiles; both pre-
pared
To suffer pains with heathen scorn and
hate
Inflicted;—blessèd Men, for so to Heaven
They follow their dear Lord!
                    Time flows—nor winds, 315
Nor stagnates, nor precipitates his course,
But many a benefit borne upon his breast
For human-kind sinks out of sight, is
gone,
No one knows how; nor seldom is put
forth 319
An angry arm that snatches good away,
Never perhaps to reappear. The Stream
Has to our generation brought and brings
Innumerable gains; yet we, who now
Walk in the light of day, pertain full
surely
To a chilled age, most pitiably shut out
From that which *is* and actuates, by
forms, 326
Abstractions, and by lifeless fact to fact
Minutely linked with diligence unin-
spired,
Unrectified, unguided, unsustained,
By godlike insight. To this fate is
doomed 330
Science, wide-spread and spreading still
as be
Her conquests, in the world of sense made
known.
So with the internal mind it fares; and so
With morals, trusting, in contempt or
fear
Of vital principle's controlling law, 335
To her purblind guide Expediency;
and so
Suffers religious faith. Elate with view
Of what is won, we overlook or scorn
The best that should keep pace with it,
and must,
Else more and more the general mind
will droop, 340
Even as if bent on perishing. There
lives
No faculty within us which the Soul
Can spare, and humblest earthly Weal
demands,
For dignity not placed beyond her reach,
Zealous co-operation of all means 345

Given or acquired, to raise us from the
 mire,
And liberate our hearts from low pur-
 suits.
By gross Utilities enslaved we need   348
More of ennobling impulse from the past,
If to the future aught of good must come
Sounder and therefore holier than the ends
Which, in the giddiness of self-applause,
We covet as supreme. O grant the crown
That Wisdom wears, or take his treacher-
 ous staff
From Knowledge!—If the Muse, whom
 I have served   355
This day, be mistress of a single pearl
Fit to be placed in that pure diadem;
Then, not in vain, under these chestnut
 boughs
Reclined, shall I have yielded up my soul
To transports from the secondary founts
Flowing of time and place, and paid to
 both   361
Due homage; nor shall fruitlessly have
 striven,
By love of beauty moved, to enshrine in
 verse
Accordant meditations, which in times
Vexed and disordered, as our own, may
 shed   365
Influence, at least among a scattered few,
To soberness of mind and peace of heart
Friendly; as here to my repose hath been
This flowering broom's dear neighbour-
 hood, the light
And murmur issuing from yon pendent
 flood,   370
And all the varied landscape. Let us now
Rise, and to-morrow greet magnificent
 Rome[1].

II.

THE PINE OF MONTE MARIO AT ROME.

I saw far off the dark top of a Pine
Look like a cloud—a slender stem the
 tie
That bound it to its native earth—poised
 high
'Mid evening hues, along the horizon line,
Striving in peace each other to out-
 shine.   5
But when I learned the Tree was living
 there,
Saved from the sordid axe by Beaumont's
 care,
Oh, what a gush of tenderness was
 mine!
The rescued Pine-tree, with its sky so
 bright
And cloud-like beauty, rich in thoughts
 of home,   10
Death-parted friends, and days too swift
 in flight,
Supplanted the whole majesty of Rome
(Then first apparent from the Pincian
 Height)
Crowned with St. Peter's everlasting
 Dome[2].

III.

AT ROME.

Is this, ye Gods, the Capitolian Hill?
Yon petty Steep in truth the fearful
 Rock,
Tarpeian named of yore, and keeping
 still
That name, a local Phantom proud to
 mock
The Traveller's expectation?—Could our
 Will   5
Destroy the ideal Power within, 'twere
 done
Thro' what men see and touch,—slaves
 wandering on,
Impelled by thirst of all but Heaven-
 taught skill.
Full oft, our wish obtained, deeply we
 sigh;
Yet not unrecompensed are they who
 learn,   10
From that depression raised, to mount on
 high
With stronger wing, more clearly to dis-
 cern
Eternal things; and, if need be, defy
Change, with a brow not insolent, though
 stern.

---

[1] See Note, p. 907.

[2] See Note, p. 907.

IV.

AT ROME. — REGRETS. — IN ALLUSION TO
NIEBUHR, AND OTHER MODERN HISTO-
RIANS.

THOSE old credulities, to nature dear,
Shall they no longer bloom upon the stock
Of History, stript naked as a rock
'Mid a dry desert? What is it we hear?
The glory of Infant Rome must dis-
 appear,   5
Her morning splendours vanish, and their
 place
Know them no more. If Truth, who
 veiled her face
With those bright beams yet hid it not,
 must steer
Henceforth a humbler course perplexed
 and slow;   9
One solace yet remains for us who came
Into this world in days when story lacked
Severe research, that in our hearts we
 know
How, for exciting youth's heroic flame,
Assent is power, belief the soul of fact.

V.

CONTINUED.

COMPLACENT Fictions were they, yet the
 same
Involved a history of no doubtful sense,
History that proves by inward evidence
From what a precious source of truth it
 came.
Ne'er could the boldest Eulogist have
 dared   5
Such deeds to paint, such characters to
 frame,
But for coeval sympathy prepared
To greet with instant faith their loftiest
 claim.
None but a noble people could have loved
Flattery in Ancient Rome's pure-minded
 style: 10
Not in like sort the Runic Scald was
 moved;
He, nursed 'mid savage passions that
 defile
Humanity, sang feats that well might call
For the blood-thirsty mead of Odin's
 riotous Hall.

VI.

PLEA FOR THE HISTORIAN.

FORBEAR to deem the Chronicler unwise,
Ungentle, or untouched by seemly ruth,
Who, gathering up all that Time's en-
 vious tooth
Has spared of sound and grave realities,
Firmly rejects those dazzling flatteries, 5
Dear as they are to unsuspecting Youth,
That might have drawn down Clio from
 the skies
To vindicate the majesty of truth.
Such was her office while she walked with
 men,
A Muse, who, not unmindful of her Sire
All-ruling Jove, whate'er the theme
 might be   11
Revered her Mother, sage Mnemosyne,
And taught her faithful servants how the
 lyre
Should animate, but not mislead, the pen[1].

VII.

AT ROME.

THEY—who have seen the noble Roman's
 scorn
Break forth at thought of laying down
 his head,
When the blank day is over, garreted
In his ancestral palace, where, from morn
To night, the desecrated floors are worn 5
By feet of purse-proud strangers; they—
 who have read
In one meek smile, beneath a peasant's shed,
How patiently the weight of wrong is
 borne;
They—who have heard some learned
 Patriot treat
Of freedom, with mind grasping the
 whole theme   10
From ancient Rome, downwards through
 that bright dream
Of Commonwealths, each city a starlike
 seat
Of rival glory; they—fallen Italy—
Nor must, nor will, nor can, despair of
 Thee!

---

[1] Quem virum——lyra——
——sumes celebrare Clio?

VIII.

NEAR ROME, IN SIGHT OF ST. PETER'S.

LONG has the dew been dried on tree and
lawn;
O'er man and beast a not unwelcome boon
Is shed, the languor of approaching noon;
To shady rest withdrawing or withdrawn
Mute are all creatures, as this couchant
fawn,   5
Save insect-swarms that hum in air
afloat,
Save that the Cock is crowing, a shrill
note,
Startling and shrill as that which roused
the dawn.
—Heard in that hour, or when, as now,
the nerve
Shrinks from the note as from a mis-
timed thing,   10
Oft for a holy warning may it serve,
Charged with remembrance of *his* sudden
sting,
His bitter tears, whose name the Papal
Chair
And yon resplendent Church are proud
to bear.

IX.

AT ALBANO.

DAYS passed—and Monte Calvo would
not clear
His head from mist; and, as the wind
sobbed through
Albano's dripping Ilex avenue,
My dull forebodings in a Peasant's ear
Found casual vent. She said, "Be of
good cheer;   5
Our yesterday's procession did not sue
In vain; the sky will change to sunny
blue,
Thanks to our Lady's grace." I smiled
to hear,
But not in scorn:—the Matron's Faith
may lack
The heavenly sanction needed to ensure
Fulfilment; but, we trust, her upward
track   11
Stops not at this low point, nor wants
the lure

Of flowers the Virgin without fear may
own,
For by her Son's blest hand the seed was
sown.

X.

NEAR Anio's stream I spied a gentle Dove
Perched on an olive branch, and heard
her cooing
'Mid new-born blossoms that soft airs
were wooing,
While all things present told of joy and
love.
But restless Fancy left that olive grove 5
To hail the exploratory Bird renewing
Hope for the few, who, at the world's
undoing,
On the great flood were spared to live and
move.
O bounteous Heaven! signs true as dove
and bough
Brought to the ark are coming evermore,
Given though we seek them not, but,
while we plough   11
This sea of life without a visible shore,
Do neither promise ask nor grace implore
In what alone is ours, the living Now.

XI.

FROM THE ALBAN HILLS, LOOKING TOWARDS ROME.

FORGIVE, illustrious Country! these deep
sighs,
Heaved less for thy bright plains and
hills bestrown
With monuments decayed or overthrown,
For all that tottering stands or prostrate
lies,
Than for like scenes in moral vision
shown,   5
Ruin perceived for keener sympathies;
Faith crushed, yet proud of weeds, her
gaudy crown;
Virtues laid low, and mouldering ener-
gies.
Yet why prolong this mournful strain?—
Fallen Power,
Thy fortunes, twice exalted, might pro-
voke   10

Verse to glad notes prophetic of the
  hour
When thou, uprisen, shalt break thy
  double yoke,
And enter, with prompt aid from the
  Most High,
On the third stage of thy great destiny.

XII.

NEAR THE LAKE OF THRASYMENE.

WHEN here with Carthage Rome to con-
  flict came,
An earthquake, mingling with the bat-
  tle's shock,
Checked not its rage; unfelt the ground
  did rock,
Sword dropped not, javelin kept its
  deadly aim.—
Now all is sun-bright peace. Of that
  day's shame,   5
Or glory, not a vestige seems to endure,
Save in this Rill that took from blood the
  name [1]
Which yet it bears, sweet Stream! as
  crystal pure.
So may all trace and sign of deeds aloof
From the true guidance of humanity,   10
Thro' Time and Nature's influence, purify
Their spirit; or, unless they for reproof
Or warning serve, thus let them all, on
  ground
That gave them being, vanish to a sound.

XIII.

NEAR THE SAME LAKE.

FOR action born, existing to be tried,
Powers manifold we have that intervene
To stir the heart that would too closely
  screen
Her peace from images to pain allied.
What wonder if at midnight, by the side
Of Sanguinetto or broad Thrasymene,   6
The clang of arms is heard, and phantoms
  glide,
Unhappy ghosts in troops by moonlight
  seen;
And singly thine, O vanquished Chief!
  whose corse,

---

[1] Sanguinetto.

Unburied, lay hid under heaps of
  slain: 10
But who is He—the Conqueror? Would
  he force
His way to Rome? Ah, no,—round hill
  and plain
Wandering, he haunts, at fancy's strong
  command,
This spot—his shadowy death-cup in his
  hand.

XIV.

THE CUCKOO AT LAVERNA.

MAY 25, 1837.

[Composed June, July, 1837.—Published: vol. of
  1842.]

LIST—'twas the Cuckoo.—O with what
  delight
Heard I that voice! and catch it now,
  though faint,
Far off and faint, and melting into air,
Yet not to be mistaken. Hark again!
Those louder cries give notice that the
  Bird,   5
Although invisible as Echo's self,
Is wheeling hitherward. Thanks, happy
  Creature,
For this unthought-of greeting!
                          While allured
From vale to hill, from hill to vale led on,
We have pursued, through various lands,
  a long   10
And pleasant course; flower after flower
  has blown,
Embellishing the ground that gave them
  birth
With aspects novel to my sight; but still
Most fair, most welcome, when they
  drank the dew
In a sweet fellowship with kinds beloved,
For old remembrance sake. And oft—
  where Spring   16
Displayed her richest blossoms among files
Of orange-trees bedecked with glowing
  fruit
Ripe for the hand, or under a thick shade
Of Ilex, or, if better suited to the hour, 20
The lightsome Olive's twinkling canopy—
Oft have I heard the Nightingale and
  Thrush

Blending as in a common English grove
Their love-songs; but, where'er my feet
    might roam,
Whate'er assemblages of new and old, 25
Strange and familiar, might beguile the
    way,
A gratulation from that vagrant Voice
Was wanting;—and most happily till
    now.

For see, Laverna! mark the far-famed
    Pile,
High on the brink of that precipitous
    rock, 30
Implanted like a Fortress, as in truth
It is, a Christian Fortress, garrisoned
In faith and hope, and dutiful obedience,
By a few Monks, a stern society,
Dead to the world and scorning earth-
    born joys. 35
Nay—though the hopes that drew, the
    fears that drove,
St. Francis, far from Man's resort, to
    abide
Among these sterile heights of Apennine,
Bound him, nor, since he raised yon
    House, have ceased
To bind his spiritual Progeny, with rules
Stringent as flesh can tolerate and live; 41
His milder Genius (thanks to the good
    God
That made us) over those severe restraints
Of mind, that dread heart-freezing disci-
    pline,
Doth sometimes here predominate, and
    works 45
By unsought means for gracious purposes;
For earth through heaven, for heaven, by
    changeful earth,
Illustrated, and mutually endeared.

Rapt though He were above the power
    of sense,
Familiarly, yet out of the cleansed heart
Of that once sinful Being overflowed 51
On sun, moon, stars, the nether elements,
And every shape of creature they sustain,
Divine affections; and with beast and
    bird
(Stilled from afar—such marvel story
    tells— 55

By casual outbreak of his passionate
    words,
And from their own pursuits in field or
    grove
Drawn to his side by look or act of love
Humane, and virtue of his innocent life)
He wont to hold companionship so free,
So pure, so fraught with knowledge and
    delight, 61
As to be likened in his Followers' minds
To that which our first Parents, ere the
    fall
From their high state darkened the Earth
    with fear,
Held with all Kinds in Eden's blissful
    bowers. 65

Then question not that, 'mid the austere
    Band,
Who breathe the air he breathed, tread
    where he trod,
Some true Partakers of his loving spirit
Do still survive, and, with those gentle
    hearts
Consorted, Others, in the power, the
    faith, 70
Of a baptized imagination, prompt
To catch from Nature's humblest monitors
Whate'er they bring of Impulses sublime.

Thus sensitive must be the Monk,
    though pale
With fasts, with vigils worn, depressed by
    years, 75
Whom in a sunny glade I chanced to see,
Upon a pine-tree's storm-uprooted trunk,
Seated alone, with forehead sky-ward
    raised,
Hands clasped above the crucifix he wore
Appended to his bosom, and lips closed 80
By the joint pressure of his musing mood
And habit of his vow. That ancient
    Man—
Nor haply less the Brother whom I
    marked,
As we approached the Convent gate,
    aloft
Looking far forth from his aerial cell, 85
A young Ascetic—Poet, Hero, Sage,
He might have been, Lover belike he
    was—

If they received into a conscious ear
The notes whose first faint greeting
startled me,
Whose sedulous iteration thrilled with
joy   90
My heart—may have been moved like me
to think,
Ah ! not like me who walk in the world's
ways,
On the great Prophet, styled *the Voice
of One
Crying amid the wilderness,* and given,
Now that their snows must melt, their
herbs and flowers   95
Revive, their obstinate winter pass away,
That awful name to Thee, thee, simple
Cuckoo,
Wandering in solitude, and evermore
Foretelling and proclaiming, ere thou
leave
This thy last haunt beneath Italian skies   99
To carry thy glad tidings over heights
Still loftier, and to climes more near the
Pole.

Voice of the Desert, fare-thee-well ;
sweet Bird !
If that substantial title please thee more,
Farewell !—but go thy way, no need hast
thou   105
Of a good wish sent after thee ; from
bower
To bower as green, from sky to sky as
clear,
Thee gentle breezes waft—or airs that meet
Thy course and sport around thee softly
fan—
Till Night, descending upon hill and vale,
Grants to thy mission a brief term of
silence,   111
And folds thy pinions up in blest repose.

XV.

AT THE CONVENT OF CAMALDOLI.

GRIEVE for the Man who hither came
bereft,
And seeking consolation from above ;
Nor grieve the less that skill to him was
left
To paint this picture of his lady-love :

Can she, a blessèd saint, the work ap-
prove ?   5
And O, good Brethren of the cowl, a
thing
So fair, to which with peril he must cling,
Destroy in pity, or with care remove.
That bloom—those eyes—can they assist
to bind
Thoughts that would stray from Heaven?
The dream must cease   10
To be ; by Faith, not sight, his soul must
live ;
Else will the enamoured Monk too
surely find
How wide a space can part from inward
peace
The most profound repose his cell can
give.

XVI.

CONTINUED.

THE world forsaken, all its busy cares
And stirring interests shunned with de-
sperate flight,
All trust abandoned in the healing might
Of virtuous action ; all that courage dares,
Labour accomplishes, or patience bears—
Those helps rejected, they, whose minds
perceive   6
How subtly works man's weakness, sighs
may heave
For such a One beset with cloistral snares.
Father of Mercy ! rectify his view,
If with his vows this object ill agree ;   10
Shed over it Thy grace, and thus subdue
Imperious passion in a heart set free :—
That earthly love may to herself be true,
Give him a soul that cleaveth unto Thee[1].

XVII.

AT THE EREMITE OR UPPER CONVENT
OF CAMALDOLI.

WHAT aim had they, the Pair of Monks,
in size
Enormous, dragged, while side by side
they sate,
By panting steers up to this convent
gate?

---

[1] See Note, p. 907.

How, with empurpled cheeks and pam-
    pered eyes,
Dare they confront the lean austerities 5
Of Brethren who, here fixed, on Jesu
    wait
In sackcloth, and God's anger deprecate
Through all that humbles flesh and mor-
    tifies?
Strange contrast!—verily the world of
    dreams,
Where mingle, as for mockery combined,
Things in their very essences at strife, 11
Shows not a sight incongruous as the
    extremes
That everywhere, before the thoughtful
    mind,
Meet on the solid ground of waking life[1].

XVIII.
AT VALLOMBROSA.

Thick as autumnal leaves that strew the brooks
In Vallombrosa, where Etrurian shades
High over-arch'd embower[2].
                PARADISE LOST.

"VALLOMBROSA—I longed in thy shadiest
    wood
To slumber, reclined on the moss-covered
    floor!"
Fond wish that was granted at last, and
    the Flood,
That lulled me asleep, bids me listen once
    more.
Its murmur how soft! as it falls down the
    steep, 5
Near that Cell—yon sequestered Retreat
    high in air—
Where our Milton was wont lonely vigils
    to keep
For converse with God, sought through
    study and prayer.

The Monks still repeat the tradition with
    pride,
And its truth who shall doubt? for his
    Spirit is here; 10
In the cloud-piercing rocks doth her
    grandeur abide,

In the pines pointing heavenward her
    beauty austere;
In the flower-besprent meadows his genius
    we trace
Turned to humbler delights, in which
    youth might confide,
That would yield him fit help while pre-
    figuring that Place 15
Where, if Sin had not entered, Love never
    had died.

When with life lengthened out came a
    desolate time,
And darkness and danger had compassed
    him round,
With a thought he would flee to these
    haunts of his prime,
And here once again a kind shelter be
    found. 20
And let me believe that when nightly the
    Muse
Did waft him to Sion, the glorified hill,
Here also, on some favoured height, he
    would choose
To wander, and drink inspiration at
    will.

Vallombrosa! of thee I first heard in the
    page 25
Of that holiest of Bards, and the name for
    my mind
Had a musical charm, which the winter
    of age
And the changes it brings had no power
    to unbind.
And now, ye Miltonian shades! under
    you
I repose, nor am forced from sweet fancy
    to part, 30
While your leaves I behold and the brooks
    they will strew,
And the realised vision is clasped to my
    heart.

Even so, and unblamed, we rejoice as we
    may
In Forms that must perish, frail objects
    of sense;
Unblamed—if the Soul be intent on the
    day 35
When the Being of Beings shall summon
    her hence.

---

[1] See Note, p. 907.
[2] See for the two *first lines*, "Stanzas composed in the Simplon Pass," p. 345.

For he and he only with wisdom is blest
Who, gathering true pleasures wherever
  they grow,
Looks up in all places, for joy or for
  rest,
To the Fountain whence Time and
  Eternity flow.   40

XIX.

AT FLORENCE.

UNDER the shadow of a stately Pile,
The dome of Florence, pensive and alone,
Nor giving heed to aught that passed the
  while,
I stood, and gazed upon a marble stone,
The laurelled Dante's favourite seat. A
  throne,   5
In just esteem, it rivals; though no
  style
Be there of decoration to beguile
The mind, depressed by thought of great-
  ness flown.
As a true man, who long had served the
  lyre,
I gazed with earnestness, and dared no
  more.   10
But in his breast the mighty Poet bore
A Patriot's heart, warm with undying
  fire.
Bold with the thought, in reverence I sate
  down,
And, for a moment, filled that empty
  Throne.

XX.

BEFORE THE PICTURE OF THE BAPTIST, BY RAPHAEL, IN THE GALLERY AT FLORENCE.

THE Baptist might have been ordained to
  cry
Forth from the towers of that huge Pile,
  wherein
His Father served Jehovah; but how
  win
Due audience, how for aught but scorn
  defy
The obstinate pride and wanton revelry 5
Of the Jerusalem below, her sin
And folly, if they with united din

Drown not at once mandate and pro-
  phecy?
Therefore the Voice spake from the De-
  sert, thence
To Her, as to her opposite in peace,   10
Silence, and holiness, and innocence,
To Her and to all Lands its warning
  sent,
Crying with earnestness that might not
  cease,
"Make straight a highway for the Lord—
  repent!"

XXI.

AT FLORENCE.—FROM MICHAEL ANGELO[1].

RAPT above earth by power of one fair
  face,
Hers in whose sway alone my heart de-
  lights,
I mingle with the blest on those pure
  heights
Where Man, yet mortal, rarely finds a
  place.
With Him who made the Work that Work
  accords   5
So well, that by its help and through His
  grace
I raise my thoughts, inform my deeds and
  words,
Clasping her beauty in my soul's em-
  brace.
Thus, if from two fair eyes mine cannot
  turn,
I feel how in their presence doth abide 10
Light which to God is both the way and
  guide;
And, kindling at their lustre, if I burn,
My noble fire emits the joyful ray
That through the realms of glory shines
  for aye.

---

[1] This and the following Sonnet may possibly
have been two of the fifteen Sonnets which in
1805 Wordsworth essayed to translate from the
Italian of Michael Angelo. A rough draft of No.
XXII. is given by Mr. Dykes Campbell from a note-
book belonging to S. T. Coleridge. See *Coleridge's
Poetical Works*, p. 474. Mr. Campbell, unfortu-
nately, does not give the date of the entry, or of
the note-book.—ED.

XXII.

AT FLORENCE.—FROM MICHAEL ANGELO.

ETERNAL Lord! eased of a cumbrous load,
And loosened from the world, I turn to
　　Thee;
Shun, like a shattered bark, the storm,
　　and flee
To Thy protection for a safe abode.
The crown of thorns, hands pierced upon
　　the tree,　　　　　　　　　　5
The meek, benign, and lacerated face,
To a sincere repentance promise grace,
To the sad soul give hope of pardon free.
With justice mark not Thou, O Light
　　divine,
My fault, nor hear it with Thy sacred
　　ear;　　　　　　　　　　　　10
Neither put forth that way Thy arm
　　severe;
Wash with Thy blood my sins; thereto
　　incline
More readily the more my years require
Help, and forgiveness speedy and entire.

XXIII.

AMONG THE RUINS OF A CONVENT IN THE APENNINES.

YE Trees! whose slender roots entwine
　　Altars that piety neglects;
Whose infant arms enclasp the shrine
　　Which no devotion now respects;
If not a straggler from the herd　　　5
Here ruminate, nor shrouded bird,
Chanting her low-voiced hymn, take pride
In aught that ye would grace or hide—
How sadly is your love misplaced,
Fair Trees, your bounty run to waste!　10

Ye, too, wild Flowers! that no one heeds,
And ye—full often spurned as weeds—
In beauty clothed, or breathing sweetness
From fractured arch and mouldering
　　wall—
Do but more touchingly recall　　　15
Man's headstrong violence and Time's
　　fleetness,
Making the precincts ye adorn
Appear to sight still more forlorn.

XXIV.

IN LOMBARDY.

SEE, where his difficult way that Old Man
　　wins
Bent by a load of Mulberry leaves!—most
　　hard
Appears *his* lot, to the small Worm's
　　compared,
For whom his toil with early day begins.
Acknowledging no task-master, at will　5
(As if her labour and her ease were twins)
She seems to work, at pleasure to lie
　　still;—
And softly sleeps within the thread she
　　spins.
So fare they—the Man serving as her
　　Slave.
Ere long their fates do each to each
　　conform:　　　　　　　　　　10
Both pass into new being,—but the Worm,
Transfigured, sinks into a hopeless grave;
His volant Spirit will, he trusts, ascend
To bliss unbounded, glory without end.

XXV.

AFTER LEAVING ITALY.

FAIR Land! Thee all men greet with joy;
　　how few,
Whose souls take pride in freedom, virtue,
　　fame,
Part from thee without pity dyed in
　　shame:
I could not—while from Venice we with-
　　drew,
Led on till an Alpine strait confined our
　　view　　　　　　　　　　　　5
Within its depths, and to the shore we came
Of Lago Morto, dreary sight and name,
Which o'er sad thoughts a sadder colour
　　ing threw.
Italia! on the surface of thy spirit,
(Too aptly emblemed by that torpid lake)
Shall a few partial breezes only creep?—11
Be its depths quickened; what thou dost
　　inherit
Of the world's hopes, dare to fulfil; awake,
Mother of Heroes, from thy death-like
　　sleep!

XXVI.

CONTINUED.

As indignation mastered grief, my tongue
Spake bitter words; words that did ill
    agree
With those rich stores of Nature's imagery,
And divine Art, that fast to memory
    clung—
Thy gifts, magnificent Region, ever young
In the sun's eye, and in his sister's
    sight   6
How beautiful! how worthy to be sung
In strains of rapture, or subdued delight!
I feign not; witness that unwelcome shock
That followed the first sound of German
    speech,   10
Caught the far-winding barrier Alps
    among.
In that announcement, greeting seemed
    to mock
Parting; the casual word had power to
    reach
My heart, and filled that heart with con-
    flict strong.

XXVII.

COMPOSED AT RYDAL ON MAY MORNING, 1838.

[Composed May 1, 1838.—Published: Sonnet-vol.
of 1838; vol. of 1842.]

IF with old love of you, dear Hills! I
    share
New love of many a rival image brought
From far, forgive the wanderings of my
    thought:
Nor art thou wronged, sweet May! when
    I compare
Thy present birth-morn with thy last, so
    fair,   5
So rich to me in favours. For my lot
Then was, within the famed Egerian Grot
To sit and muse, fanned by its dewy air
Mingling with thy soft breath! That
    morning too,
Warblers I heard their joy unbosoming 10
Amid the sunny, shadowy, Colosseum;
Heard them, unchecked by aught of sad-
    dening hue,

For victories there won by flower-crowned
    Spring,
Chant in full choir their innocent Te
    Deum.

XXVIII.

THE PILLAR OF TRAJAN.

[Composed 1825.—Published 1827 [1].]

WHERE towers are crushed, and unfor-
    bidden weeds
O'er mutilated arches shed their seeds;
And temples, doomed to milder change,
    unfold
A new magnificence that vies with old;
Firm in its pristine majesty hath stood 5
A votive Column, spared by fire and
    flood:—
And, though the passions of man's fretful
    race
Have never ceased to eddy round its base,
Not injured more by touch of meddling
    hands
Than a lone obelisk, 'mid Nubian sands, 10
Or aught in Syrian deserts left to save
From death the memory of the good and
    brave.
Historic figures round the shaft embost
Ascend, with lineaments in air not lost:
Still as he turns, the charmed spectator
    sees   15
Group winding after group with dream-
    like ease;
Triumphs in sun-bright gratitude dis-
    played,
Or softly stealing into modest shade.
—So, pleased with purple clusters to en-
    twine
Some lofty elm-tree, mounts the daring
    vine;   20
The woodbine so, with spiral grace, and
    breathes
Wide-spreading odours from her flowery
    wreaths.

[1] Included among *Poems of Sentiment and
Reflection* in edd. 1827–43. First placed in this
Series in ed. 1845. The preceding Sonnet (XXVII.)
was included amongst the *Miscellaneous Sonnets*
in the volume of 1842, and first found its present
place in ed. 1845.—ED.

Borne by the Muse from rills in shep-
    herds' ears
Murmuring but one smooth story for all
    years,
I gladly commune with the mind and
    heart   25
Of him who thus survives by classic art,
His actions witness, venerate his mien,
And study Trajan as by Pliny seen;
Behold how fought the Chief whose con-
    quering sword
Stretched far as earth might own a single
    lord;   30
In the delight of moral prudence schooled,
How feelingly at home the Sovereign
    ruled;
Best of the good—in pagan faith allied
To more than Man, by virtue deified.

Memorial Pillar! 'mid the wrecks of
    Time   35
Preserve thy charge with confidence
    sublime—
The exultations, pomps, and cares of
    Rome,
Whence half the breathing world received
    its doom;
Things that recoil from language; that,
    if shown   39
By apter pencil, from the light had flown.
A Pontiff, Trajan *here* the Gods implores,
There greets an Embassy from Indian
    shores;
Lo! he harangues his cohorts—*there* the
    storm
Of battle meets him in authentic form!
Unharnessed, naked, troops of Moorish
    horse   45
Sweep to the charge; more high, the
    Dacian force,
To hoof and finger mailed;—yet, high or
    low,

None bleed, and none lie prostrate but
    the foe;
In every Roman, through all turns of
    fate,
Is Roman dignity inviolate;   50
Spirit in him pre-eminent, who guides,
Supports, adorns, and over all presides;
Distinguished only by inherent state
From honoured Instruments that round
    him wait;
Rise as he may, his grandeur scorns the
    test   55
Of outward symbol, nor will deign to rest
On aught by which another is deprest.
—Alas! that One thus disciplined could
    toil
To enslave whole nations on their native
    soil;
So emulous of Macedonian fame,   60
That, when his age was measured with his
    aim,
He drooped, 'mid else unclouded victories,
And turned his eagles back with deep-
    drawn sighs:
O weakness of the Great! O folly of the
    Wise!

Where now the haughty Empire that
    was spread   65
With such fond hope? her very speech is
    dead;
Yet glorious Art the power of Time defies,
And Trajan still, through various enter-
    prise,
Mounts, in this fine illusion, toward the
    skies:
Still are we present with the imperial
    Chief,   70
Nor cease to gaze upon the bold Relief
Till Rome, to silent marble unconfined,
Becomes with all her years a vision of the
    Mind.

The Egyptian Maid;

OR,

The Romance of the Water Lily.

[Composed 1830.—Published 1835.]

For the names and persons in the following poem see the "History of the renowned Prince Arthur and his Knights of the Round Table;" for the rest the Author is answerable; only it may be proper to add that the Lotus, with the bust of the Goddess appearing to rise out of the full-blown flower, was suggested by the beautiful work of ancient art, once included among the Townley Marbles, and now in the British Museum.

WHILE Merlin paced the Cornish sands,
Forth-looking toward the rocks of Scilly,
The pleased Enchanter was aware
Of a bright Ship that seemed to hang in air,
Yet was she work of mòrtal hands,   5
And took from men her name—THE WATER LILY.

Soft was the wind, that landward blew;
And, as the Moon, o'er some dark hill ascendant,
Grows from a little edge of light
To a full orb, this Pinnace bright   10
Became, as nearer to the coast she drew,
More glorious, with spread sail and streaming pendant.

Upon this wingèd Shape so fair
Sage Merlin gazed with admiration:
Her lineaments, thought he, surpass   15
Aught that was ever shown in magic glass;
Was ever built with patient care;
Or, at a touch, produced by happiest transformation.

Now, though a Mechanist, whose skill
Shames the degenerate grasp of modern science,   20
Grave Merlin (and belike the more
For practising occult and perilous lore)
Was subject to a freakish will
That sapped good thoughts, or scared them with defiance.

Provoked to envious spleen, he cast   25
An altered look upon the advancing Stranger
Whom he had hailed with joy, and cried,
"My Art shall help to tame her pride—"
Anon the breeze became a blast,
And the waves rose, and sky portended danger.   30

With thrilling word, and potent sign
Traced on the beach, his work the Sorcerer urges;
The clouds in blacker clouds are lost,
Like spiteful Fiends that vanish, crossed
By Fiends of aspect more malign;   35
And the winds roused the Deep with fiercer scourges.

But worthy of the name she bore
Was this Sea-flower, this buoyant Galley;
Supreme in loveliness and grace
Of motion, whether in the embrace   40
Of trusty anchorage, or scudding o'er
The main flood roughened into hill and valley.

Behold, how wantonly she laves
Her sides, the Wizard's craft confound-
   ing;
Like something out of Ocean sprung 45
To be for ever fresh and young,
Breasts the sea-flashes, and huge waves
Top-gallant high, rebounding and re-
   bounding!

But Ocean under magic heaves,
And cannot spare the Thing he
   cherished: 50
Ah! what avails that she was fair,
Luminous, blithe, and debonair?
The storm has stripped her of her leaves;
The Lily floats no longer!—She hath
   perished.

Grieve for her, she deserves no less; 55
So like, yet so unlike, a living Creature!
No heart had she, no busy brain;
Though loved, she could not love again;
Though pitied, *feel* her own distress;
Nor aught that troubles us, the fools of
   Nature.   60

Yet is there cause for gushing tears;
So richly was this Galley laden,
A fairer than herself she bore,
And, in her struggles, cast ashore;
A lovely One, who nothing hears 65
Of wind or wave—a meek and guileless
   Maiden.

Into a cave had Merlin fled
From mischief, caused by spells himself
   had muttered;
And while, repentant all too late,
In moody posture there he sate, 70
He heard a voice, and saw, with half-
   raised head,
A Visitant by whom these words were
   uttered:—

"On Christian service this frail Bark
Sailed" (hear me, Merlin!) "under high
   protection,
Though on her prow a sign of heathen
   power   75
Was carved—a Goddess with a Lily
   flower,
The old Egyptian's emblematic mark
Of joy immortal and of pure affection.

"Her course was for the British strand;
Her freight, it was a Damsel peer-
   less;
God reigns above, and Spirits strong 81
May gather to avenge this wrong
Done to the Princess, and her Land
Which she in duty left, sad but not cheer-
   less.

"And to Caerleon's loftiest tower 85
Soon will the Knights of Arthur's
   Table
A cry of lamentation send;
And all will weep who there attend,
To grace that Stranger's bridal hour, 89
For whom the sea was made unnavi-
   gable.

"Shame! should a Child of royal line
Die through the blindness of thy
   malice?"
Thus to the Necromancer spake
Nina, the Lady of the Lake,
A gentle Sorceress, and benign, 95
Who ne'er embittered any good man's
   chalice.

"What boots," continued she, "to
   mourn?
To expiate thy sin endeavour:
From the bleak isle where she is laid, 99
Fetched by our art, the Egyptian Maid
May yet to Arthur's court be borne
Cold as she is, ere life be fled for ever.

"My pearly Boat, a shining Light,
That brought me down that sunless
   river,
Will bear me on from wave to wave, 105
And back with her to this sea-cave;—
Then Merlin! for a rapid flight
Through air, to thee my Charge will I
   deliver.

"The very swiftest of thy cars   109
Must, when my part is done, be ready;
Meanwhile, for further guidance, look
Into thy own prophetic book;
And, if that fail, consult the Stars
To learn thy course; farewell! be prompt
   and steady."

This scarcely spoken, she again   115
Was seated in her gleaming shallop,
That, o'er the yet-distempered Deep,
Pursued its way with bird-like sweep,
Or like a steed, without a rein,
Urged o'er the wilderness in sportive
    gallop.   120

Soon did the gentle Nina reach
That Isle without a house or haven;
Landing, she found not what she sought,
Nor saw of wreck or ruin aught   124
But a carved Lotus cast upon the beach
By the fierce waves, a flower in marble
    graven.

Sad relique, but how fair the while !
For gently each from each retreating
With backward curve, the leaves re-
    vealed
The bosom half, and half concealed,   130
Of a Divinity, that seemed to smile
On Nina, as she passed, with hopeful
    greeting.

No quest was hers of vague desire,
Of tortured hope and purpose shaken !
Following the margin of a bay,   135
She spied the lonely Cast-away,
Unmarred, unstripped of her attire,
But with closed eyes,—of breath and
    bloom forsaken.

Then Nina, stooping down, embraced,
With tenderness and mild emotion,   140
The Damsel, in that trance embound;
And, while she raised her from the
    ground,
And in the pearly shallop placed,
Sleep fell upon the air, and stilled the
    ocean.

The turmoil hushed, celestial springs   145
Of music opened, and there came a
    blending
Of fragrance, underived from earth,
With gleams that owed not to the sun
    their birth,
And that soft rustling of invisible wings
Which Angels make, on works of love
    descending.   150

And Nina heard a sweeter voice
Than if the Goddess of the flower had
    spoken :
"Thou hast achieved, fair Dame ! what
    none
Less pure in spirit could have done;
Go, in thy enterprise rejoice !   155
Air, earth, sea, sky, and heaven, success
    betoken."

So cheered, she left that Island bleak,
A bare rock of the Scilly cluster;
And, as they traversed the smooth brine,
The self-illumined Brigantine   160
Shed, on the Slumberer's cold wan cheek
And pallid brow, a melancholy lustre.

Fleet was their course, and when they
    came
To the dim cavern, whence the river
Issued into the salt-sea flood,   165
Merlin, as fixed in thought he stood,
Was thus accosted by the Dame :
"Behold to thee my Charge I now deliver!

"But where attends thy chariot —
    where?"—   169
Quoth Merlin, "Even as I was bidden,
So have I done; as trusty as thy barge
My vehicle shall prove—O precious
    Charge !
If this be sleep, how soft ! if death, how
    fair !
Much have my books disclosed, but the
    end is hidden."

He spake; and gliding into view   175
Forth from the grotto's dimmest
    chamber
Came two mute Swans, whose plumes
    of dusky white
Changed, as the pair approached the light,
Drawing an ebon car, their hue
(Like clouds of sunset) into lucid amber.

Once more did gentle Nina lift   181
The Princess, passive to all changes :
The car received her:—then up-went
Into the ethereal element
The Birds with progress smooth and
    swift   185
As thought, when through bright regions
    memory ranges.

Sage Merlin, at the Slumberer's side,
Instructs the Swans their way to mea-
  sure;
And soon Caerleon's towers appeared,
And notes of minstrelsy were heard 190
From rich pavilions spreading wide,
For some high day of long-expected plea-
  sure.

Awe-stricken stood both Knights and
  Dames
Ere on firm ground the car alighted;
Eftsoons astonishment was past,   195
For in that face they saw the last
Last lingering look of clay, that tames
All pride; by which all happiness is
  blighted.

Said Merlin: "Mighty King, fair Lords,
Away with feast and tilt and tourney! 200
Ye saw, throughout this royal House,
Ye heard, a rocking marvellous
Of turrets, and a clash of swords
Self-shaken, as I closed my airy journey.

Lo! by a destiny well known   205
To mortals, joy is turned to sorrow;
This is the wished for Bride, the Maid
Of Egypt, from a rock conveyed
Where she by shipwreck had been
  thrown;
Ill sight! but grief may vanish ere the
  morrow."   210

"Though vast thy power, thy words are
  weak,"
Exclaimed the King, "a mockery hate-
  ful;
Dutiful Child, her lot how hard!
Is this her piety's reward?
Those watery locks, that bloodless cheek!
O winds without remorse! O shore un-
  grateful!   216

"Rich robes are fretted by the moth;
Towers, temples, fall by stroke of
  thunder;
Will that, or deeper thoughts, abate
A Father's sorrow for her fate?   220
He will repent him of his troth;
His brain will burn, his stout heart split
  asunder.

"Alas! and I have caused this woe;
For, when my prowess from invading
  Neighbours   224
Had freed his Realm, he plighted word
That he would turn to Christ our Lord,
And his dear Daughter on a Knight
  bestow
Whom I should choose for love and match-
  less labours.

"Her birth was heathen; but a fence
Of holy Angels round her hovered: 230
A Lady added to my court
So fair, of such divine report
And worship, seemed a recompense
For fifty kingdoms by my sword re-
  covered.

"Ask not for whom, O Champions true!
She was reserved by me her life's be-
  trayer;   236
She who was meant to be a bride
Is now a corse: then put aside
Vain thoughts, and speed ye, with
  observance due
Of Christian rites, in Christian ground to
  lay her."   240

"The tomb," said Merlin, "may not close
Upon her yet, earth hide her beauty;
Not froward to thy sovereign will
Esteem me, Liege! if I, whose skill
Wafted her hither, interpose   245
To check this pious haste of erring duty.

"My books command me to lay bare
The secret thou art bent on keeping:
Here must a high attest be given,
What Bridegroom was for her ordained
  by Heaven: 250
And in my glass significants there are
Of things that may to gladness turn this
  weeping.

"For this, approaching, One by One,
Thy Knights must touch the cold hand
  of the Virgin;
So, for the favoured One, the Flower
  may bloom   255
Once more: but, if unchangeable her
  doom,
If life departed be for ever gone,
Some blest assurance, from this cloud
  emerging,

"May teach him to bewail his loss;
Not with a grief that, like a vapour,
rises   260
And melts; but grief devout that shall
endure,
And a perpetual growth secure
Of purposes which no false thought
shall cross,
A harvest of high hopes and noble enter-
prises."

"So be it," said the King;—"anon, 265
Here, where the Princess lies, begin the
trial;
Knights each in order as ye stand
Step forth."—To touch the pallid hand
Sir Agravaine advanced; no sign he
won
From Heaven or earth;—Sir Kaye had
like denial.   270

Abashed, Sir Dinas turned away;
Even for Sir Percival was no disclo-
sure;
Though he, devoutest of all Champions,
ere
He reached that ebon car, the bier
Whereon diffused like snow the Damsel
lay,   275
Full thrice had crossed himself in meek
composure.

Imagine (but ye Saints! who can?)
How in still air the balance trembled—
The wishes, peradventure the despites
That overcame some not ungenerous
Knights;   280
And all the thoughts that lengthened
out a span
Of time to Lords and Ladies thus as-
sembled.

What patient confidence was here!
And there how many bosoms panted!
While drawing toward the car Sir
Gawaine, mailed   285
For tournament, his beaver vailed,
And softly touched; but, to his princely
cheer
And high expectancy, no sign was
granted.

Next, disencumbered of his harp,
Sir Tristram, dear to thousands as a
brother,   290
Came to the proof, nor grieved that
there ensued
No change;—the fair Izonda he had
wooed
With love too true, a love with pangs
too sharp,
From hope too distant, not to dread
another.

Not so Sir Launcelot;—from Heaven's
grace   295
A sign he craved, tired slave of vain
contrition;
The royal Guinever looked passing glad
When his touch failed.—Next came
Sir Galahad;
He paused, and stood entranced by that
still face
Whose features he had seen in noontide
vision.   300

For late, as near a murmuring stream
He rested 'mid an arbour green and
shady,
Nina, the good Enchantress, shed
A light around his mossy bed;
And, at her call, a waking dream   305
Prefigured to his sense the Egyptian Lady.

Now, while his bright-haired front he
bowed,
And stood, far-kenned by mantle furred
with ermine,
As o'er the insensate Body hung
The enrapt, the beautiful, the young,
Belief sank deep into the crowd   311
That he the solemn issue would deter-
mine.

Nor deem it strange; the Youth had
worn
That very mantle on a day of glory,
The day when he achieved that match-
less feat,   315
The marvel of the PERILOUS SEAT,
Which whosoe'er approached of strength
was shorn,
Though King or Knight the most re-
nowned in story.

He touched with hesitating hand—
And lo! those Birds, far-famed through
    Love's dominions,   320
The Swans, in triumph clap their
    wings;
And their necks play, involved in rings,
Like sinless snakes in Eden's happy
    land;—
"Mine is she," cried the Knight;—again
    they clapped their pinions.

"Mine was she—mine she is, though dead,
And to her name my soul shall cleave
    in sorrow;"   326
Whereat a tender twilight streak
Of colour dawned upon the Damsel's
    cheek;
And her lips, quickening with uncertain
    red,
Seemed from each other a faint warmth
    to borrow.   330

Deep was the awe, the rapture high,
Of love emboldened, hope with dread
    entwining,
When, to the mouth, relenting Death
Allowed a soft and flower-like breath,
Precursor to a timid sigh,   335
To lifted eyelids, and a doubtful shining.

In silence did King Arthur gaze
Upon the signs that pass away or tarry;
In silence watched the gentle strife
Of Nature leading back to life;   340
Then eased his soul at length by praise
Of God, and Heaven's pure Queen—the
    blissful Mary.

Then said he, "Take her to thy heart,
Sir Galahad! a treasure, that God
    giveth,
Bound by indissoluble ties to thee   345
Through mortal change and immor-
    tality;
Be happy and unenvied, thou who art
A goodly Knight that hath no peer that
    liveth!"

Not long the Nuptials were delayed;
And sage tradition still rehearses   350
The pomp, the glory of that hour
When toward the altar from her bower
King Arthur led the Egyptian Maid,
And Angels carolled these far-echoed
    verses;—

Who shrinks not from alliance   355
Of evil with good Powers
To God proclaims defiance,
And mocks whom he adores.

A Ship to Christ devoted
From the Land of Nile did go;   360
Alas! the bright Ship floated,
An Idol at her prow.

By magic domination,
The Heaven-permitted vent
Of purblind mortal passion,   365
Was wrought her punishment.

The Flower, the Form within it,
What served they in her need?
Her port she could not win it,
Nor from mishap be freed.   370

The tempest overcame her,
And she was seen no more;
But gently, gently blame her—
She cast a Pearl ashore.

The Maid to Jesu hearkened,   375
And kept to Him her faith,
Till sense in death was darkened,
Or sleep akin to death.

But Angels round her pillow
Kept watch, a viewless band;   380
And, billow favouring billow,
She reached the destined strand.

Blest Pair! whate'er befall you,
Your faith in Him approve
Who from frail earth can call you   385
To bowers of endless love!

THE RIVER DUDDON.

A SERIES OF SONNETS [1].

[Composed between 1806-1820.—Published 1820.]

The River Duddon rises upon Wrynose Fell, on the confines of Westmoreland, Cumberland, and Lancashire; and, having served as a boundary to the two last Counties for the space of about twenty-five miles, enters the Irish Sea, between the Isle of Walney and the Lordship of Millum.

TO THE REV. DR. WORDSWORTH

(WITH THE SONNETS TO THE RIVER DUDDON, AND OTHER POEMS IN THIS COLLECTION, 1820).

[Composed Christmastide, 1819.—Published 1820.]

The Minstrels played their Christmas tune
To-night beneath my cottage-eaves;
While, smitten by a lofty moon,
The encircling laurels, thick with leaves,
Gave back a rich and dazzling sheen,   5
That overpowered their natural green.

Through hill and valley every breeze
Had sunk to rest with folded wings:
Keen was the air, but could not freeze,
Nor check, the music of the strings;   10
So stout and hardy were the band
That scraped the chords with strenuous hand!

And who but listened?—till was paid
Respect to every Inmate's claim:
The greeting given, the music played,   15
In honour of each household name,
Duly pronounced with lusty call,
And "Merry Christmas" wished to all!

O Brother! I revere the choice
That took thee from thy native hills;   20
And it is given thee to rejoice:
Though public care full often tills
(Heaven only witness of the toil)
A barren and ungrateful soil.

Yet, would that Thou, with me and mine,   25
Hadst heard this never-failing rite;
And seen on other faces shine
A true revival of the light
Which Nature and these rustic Powers,
In simple childhood, spread through ours!   30

For pleasure hath not ceased to wait
On these expected annual rounds;
Whether the rich man's sumptuous gate
Call forth the unelaborate sounds,
Or they are offered at the door   35
That guards the lowliest of the poor.

How touching, when, at midnight, sweep
Snow-muffled winds, and all is dark,
To hear—and sink again to sleep!
Or, at an earlier call, to mark,   40
By blazing fire, the still suspense
Of self-complacent innocence;

The mutual nod,—the grave disguise
Of hearts with gladness brimming o'er;
And some unbidden tears that rise   45
For names once heard, and heard no more;
Tears brightened by the serenade
For infant in the cradle laid.

Ah! not for emerald fields alone,
With ambient streams more pure and bright 50
Than fabled Cytherea's zone
Glittering before the Thunderer's sight,
Is to my heart of hearts endeared
The ground where we were born and reared!

---

[1] These Sonnets (No. XXVII. excepted) appeared early in 1820, in a volume entitled *The River Duddon, A Series of Sonnets: Vaudracour and Julia: and other Poems. To which is annexed A Topographical Description of the Country of the Lakes, in the North of England.* They were written at various intervals between 1806 and 1820. Sonnet No. XIV. (*O Mountain Stream!*) was written before April, 1807, when it first appeared amongst the *Miscellaneous Sonnets* of *Poems in Two Volumes;* and Sonnet No. XXVII. (*Fallen, and diffused*) was published in 1819, along with *The Waggoner;* included, in the collective (4 vol.) ed. of 1820, amongst the *Miscellaneous Sonnets;* and, in ed. 1827, transferred to its present place in this Series.—ED.

Hail, ancient Manners! sure defence, 55
Where they survive, of wholesome laws;
Remnants of love whose modest sense
Thus into narrow room withdraws;
Hail, Usages of pristine mould,
And ye that guard them, Mountains old! 60

Bear with me, Brother! quench the thought
That slights this passion, or condemns;
If thee fond Fancy ever brought
From the proud margin of the Thames,
And Lambeth's venerable towers, 65
To humbler streams, and greener bowers.

Yes, they can make, who fail to find,
Short leisure even in busiest days;
Moments, to cast a look behind,
And profit by those kindly rays 70
That through the clouds do sometimes steal,
And all the far-off past reveal.

Hence, while the imperial City's din
Beats frequent on thy satiate ear,
A pleased attention I may win 75
To agitations less severe,
That neither overwhelm nor cloy,
But fill the hollow vale with joy!

I.

NOT envying Latian shades—if yet they
throw
A grateful coolness round that crystal
Spring,
Bandusia, prattling as when long ago
The Sabine Bard was moved her praise to
sing;
Careless of flowers that in perennial blow
Round the moist marge of Persian foun-
tains cling; 6
Heedless of Alpine torrents thundering
Through ice-built arches radiant as hea-
ven's bow;
I seek the birthplace of a native Stream.—
All hail, ye mountains! hail, thou morn-
ing light! 10
Better to breathe at large on this clear
height
Than toil in needless sleep from dream to
dream:
Pure flow the verse, pure, vigorous, free,
and bright,
For Duddon, long-loved Duddon, is my
theme!

II.

CHILD of the clouds! remote from every
taint
Of sordid industry thy lot is cast;
Thine are the honours of the lofty waste;
Not seldom, when with heat the valleys
faint,
Thy handmaid Frost with spangled tissue
quaint 5
Thy cradle decks;—to chant thy birth,
thou hast
No meaner Poet than the whistling Blast,
And Desolation is thy Patron-saint!
She guards thee, ruthless Power! who
would not spare
Those mighty forests, once the bison's
screen, 10
Where stalked the huge deer to his shaggy
lair[1]
Through paths and alleys roofed with
darkest green;
Thousands of years before the silent air
Was pierced by whizzing shaft of hunter
keen!

III.

HOW shall I paint thee?—Be this naked
stone
My seat, while I give way to such intent;
Pleased could my verse, a speaking monu-
ment,
Make to the eyes of men thy features
known. 4
But as of all those tripping lambs not one
Outruns his fellows, so hath Nature lent
To thy beginning nought that doth pre-
sent
Peculiar ground for hope to build upon.
To dignify the spot that gives thee birth
No sign of hoar Antiquity's esteem 10
Appears, and none of modern Fortune's
care;
Yet thou thyself hast round thee shed
a gleam
Of brilliant moss, instinct with freshness
rare;
Prompt offering to thy Foster-mother,
Earth!

---

[1] The deer alluded to is the Leigh, a gigantic
species long since extinct.

IV.

TAKE, cradled Nursling of the mountain, take
This parting glance, no negligent adieu !
A Protean change seems wrought while I pursue
The curves, a loosely-scattered chain doth make ;
Or rather thou appear'st a glistering snake,
Silent, and to the gazer's eye untrue,   6
Thridding with sinuous lapse the rushes, through
Dwarf willows gliding, and by ferny brake.
Starts from a dizzy steep the undaunted Rill
Robed instantly in garb of snow-white foam ;   10
And laughing dares the Adventurer, who hath clomb
So high, a rival purpose to fulfil ;
Else let the dastard backward wend, and roam,
Seeking less bold achievement, where he will !

V.

SOLE listener, Duddon ! to the breeze that played
With thy clear voice, I caught the fitful sound
Wafted o'er sullen moss and craggy mound—
Unfruitful solitudes, that seemed to upbraid
The sun in heaven !—but now, to form a shade   5
For Thee, green alders have together wound
Their foliage ; ashes flung their arms around ;
And birch-trees risen in silver colonnade.
And thou hast also tempted here to rise,
'Mid sheltering pines, this Cottage rude and grey ;   10
Whose ruddy children, by the mother's eyes
Carelessly watched, sport through the summer day,
Thy pleased associates :—light as endless May
On infant bosoms lonely Nature lies.

VI.

FLOWERS.

ERE yet our course was graced with social trees
It lacked not old remains of hawthorn bowers,
Where small birds warbled to their paramours ;
And, earlier still, was heard the hum of bees ;
I saw them ply their harmless robberies,
And caught the fragrance which the sundry flowers,   6
Fed by the stream with soft perpetual showers,
Plenteously yielded to the vagrant breeze.
There bloomed the strawberry of the wilderness ;
The trembling eyebright showed her sapphire blue,   10
The thyme her purple, like the blush of Even ;
And if the breath of some to no caress
Invited, forth they peeped so fair to view,
All kinds alike seemed favourites of Heaven.

VII.

"CHANGE me, some God, into that breathing rose !"
The love-sick Stripling fancifully sighs,
The envied flower beholding, as it lies
On Laura's breast, in exquisite repose ;
Or he would pass into her bird, that throws   5
The darts of song from out its wiry cage ;
Enraptured,—could he for himself engage
The thousandth part of what the Nymph bestows ;
And what the little careless innocent
Ungraciously receives. Too daring choice !
There are whose calmer mind it would content   11
To be an unculled floweret of the glen,
Fearless of plough and scythe ; or darkling wren
That tunes on Duddon's banks her slender voice.

VIII.

WHAT aspect bore the Man who roved or
    fled,
First of his tribe, to this dark dell—who
    first
In this pellucid Current slaked his thirst?
What hopes came with him? what designs
    were spread
Along his path? His unprotected bed 5
What dreams encompassed? Was the in-
    truder nursed
In hideous usages, and rights accursed,
That thinned the living and disturbed the
    dead?
No voice replies;—both air and earth are
    mute;
And Thou, blue Streamlet, murmuring
    yield'st no more   10
Than a soft record, that, whatever fruit
Of ignorance thou might'st witness hereto-
    fore,
Thy function was to heal and to restore,
To soothe and cleanse, not madden and
    pollute!

IX

THE STEPPING-STONES.

THE struggling Rill insensibly is grown
Into a Brook of loud and stately march,
Crossed ever and anon by plank or arch;
And, for like use, lo! what might seem
    a zone
Chosen for ornament—stone matched with
    stone   5
In studied symmetry, with interspace
For the clear waters to pursue their race
Without restraint. How swiftly have
    they flown,
Succeeding—still succeeding! Here the
    Child
Puts, when the high-swoln Flood runs
    fierce and wild,   10
His budding courage to the proof; and
    here
Declining Manhood learns to note the sly
And sure encroachments of infirmity,
Thinking how fast time runs, life's end
    how near!

X.

THE SAME SUBJECT.

NOT so that Pair whose youthful spirits
    dance
With prompt emotion, urging them to
    pass;
A sweet confusion checks the Shepherd-
    lass;
Blushing she eyes the dizzy flood askance;
To stop ashamed—too timid to advance; 5
She ventures once again—another pause!
His outstretched hand He tauntingly
    withdraws—
She sues for help with piteous utterance!
Chidden she chides again; the thrilling
    touch
Both feel, when he renews the wished-for
    aid: 10
Ah! if their fluttering hearts should stir
    too much,
Should beat too strongly, both may be
    betrayed.
The frolic Loves, who, from yon high
    rock, see
The struggle, clap their wings for vic-
    tory!

XI.

THE FAERY CHASM.

No fiction was it of the antique age:
A sky-blue stone, within this sunless cleft,
Is of the very footmarks unbereft
Which tiny Elves impressed;—on that
    smooth stage
Dancing with all their brilliant equipage 5
In secret revels—haply after theft
Of some sweet Babe—Flower stolen, and
    coarse Weed left
For the distracted Mother to assuage
Her grief with, as she might!—But, where,
    oh! where
Is traceable a vestige of the notes   10
That ruled those dances wild in charac-
    ter?—
Deep underground? Or in the upper air,
On the shrill wind of midnight? or where
    floats
O'er twilight fields the autumnal gossa-
    mer?

XII.

HINTS FOR THE FANCY.

On, loitering Muse—the swift Stream
    chides us—on !
Albeit his deep-worn channel doth im-
    mure
Objects immense portrayed in miniature,
Wild shapes for many a strange compari-
    son !
Niagaras, Alpine passes, and anon   5
Abodes of Naiads, calm abysses pure,
Bright liquid mansions, fashioned to en-
    dure
When the broad oak drops, a leafless
    skeleton,
And the solidities of mortal pride,
Palace and tower, are crumbled into
    dust !—   10
The Bard who walks with Duddon for his
    guide,
Shall find such toys of fancy thickly set :
Turn from the sight, enamoured Muse—
    we must ;
And, if thou canst, leave them without
    regret !

XIII.

OPEN PROSPECT.

Hail to the fields—with Dwellings
    sprinkled o'er,
And one small hamlet, under a green hill
Clustering, with barn and byre, and
    spouting mill !
A glance suffices ;—should we wish for
    more,
Gay June would scorn us. But when
    bleak winds roar   5
Through the stiff lance-like shoots of
    pollard ash,
Dread swell of sound ! loud as the gusts
    that lash
The matted forests of Ontario's shore
By wasteful steel unsmitten—then would I
Turn into port ; and, reckless of the
    gale,   10
Reckless of angry Duddon sweeping by,
While the warm hearth exalts the mantling
    ale,

Laugh with the generous household
    heartily
At all the merry pranks of Donnerdale !

XIV.

[Comp. before April, 1807 (1806 ?).—Pub. 1807 [1].]

O mountain Stream ! the Shepherd and
    his Cot
Are privileged Inmates of deep solitude ;
Nor would the nicest Anchorite exclude
A field or two of brighter green, or plot
Of tillage-ground, that seemeth like a
    spot   5
Of stationary sunshine :—thou hast viewed
These only, Duddon ! with their paths
    renewed
By fits and starts, yet this contents thee
    not.
Thee hath some awful Spirit impelled to
    leave,
Utterly to desert, the haunts of men,   10
Though simple thy companions were and
    few ;
And through this wilderness a passage
    cleave
Attended but by thy own voice, save
    when
The clouds and fowls of the air thy way
    pursue !

XV.

From this deep chasm, where quivering
    sunbeams play
Upon its loftiest crags, mine eyes behold
A gloomy niche, capacious, blank, and
    cold ;
A concave free from shrubs and mosses
    grey ;
In semblance fresh, as if, with dire
    affray,   5
Some Statue, placed amid these regions
    old
For tutelary service, thence had rolled,
Startling the flight of timid Yesterday !
Was it by mortals sculptured ?—weary
    slaves
Of slow endeavour ! or abruptly cast   10
Into rude shape by fire, with roaring blast

[1] See Editor's note, p. 375.

Tempestuously let loose from central
    caves?
Or fashioned by the turbulence of waves,
Then, when o'er highest hills the Deluge
    passed?

XVI.

AMERICAN TRADITION.

SUCH fruitless questions may not long
    beguile
Or plague the fancy 'mid the sculptured
    shows
Conspicuous yet where Oroonoko flows;
There would the Indian answer with a
    smile
Aimed at the White Man's ignorance the
    while,   5
Of the GREAT WATERS telling how they
    rose,
Covered the plains, and, wandering where
    they chose,
Mounted through every intricate defile,
Triumphant.—Inundation wide and deep,
O'er which his Fathers urged, to ridge
    and steep   10
Else unapproachable, their buoyant way;
And carved, on mural cliff's undreaded
    side,
Sun, moon, and stars, and beast of chase
    or prey;
Whate'er they sought, shunned, loved, or
    deified [1]!

XVII.

RETURN.

A DARK plume fetch me from yon blasted
    yew,
Perched on whose top the Danish Raven
    croaks;
Aloft, the imperial Bird of Rome invokes
Departed ages, shedding where he flew
Loose fragments of wild wailing, that
    bestrew   5
The clouds and thrill the chambers of the
    rocks;
And into silence hush the timorous flocks,
That, calmly couching while the nightly
    dew

Moistened each fleece, beneath the twink-
    ling stars
Slept amid that lone Camp on Hardknot's
    height [2],   10
Whose Guardians bent the knee to Jove
    and Mars:
Or near that mystic Round of Druid
    frame
Tardily sinking by its proper weight
Deep into patient Earth, from whose
    smooth breast it came!

XVIII.

SEATHWAITE CHAPEL.

SACRED Religion! "mother of form and
    fear,"
Dread arbitress of mutable respect,
New rites ordaining when the old are
    wrecked,
Or cease to please the fickle worshipper;
Mother of Love! (that name best suits
    thee here)   5
Mother of Love! for this deep vale, protect
Truth's holy lamp, pure source of bright
    effect,
Gifted to purge the vapoury atmosphere
That seeks to stifle it;—as in those days
When this low Pile [3] a Gospel Teacher
    knew,   10
Whose good works formed an endless
    retinue:
A Pastor such as Chaucer's verse por-
    trays;
Such as the heaven-taught skill of Herbert
    drew;
And tender Goldsmith crowned with
    deathless praise!

XIX.

TRIBUTARY STREAM.

MY frame hath often trembled with de-
    light
When hope presented some far-distant
    good,
That seemed from heaven descending,
    like the flood
Of yon pure waters, from their aery height
Hurrying, with lordly Duddon to unite; 5

---

[1] See Humboldt's Personal Narrative.

[2] See Note, p. 908.   [3] See Note p. 908.

Who, 'mid a world of images imprest
On the calm depth of his transparent
    breast,
Appears to cherish most that Torrent
    white,
The fairest, softest, liveliest of them all !
And seldom hath ear listened to a tune 10
More lulling than the busy hum of Noon,
Swoln by that voice—whose murmur
    musical
Announces to the thirsty fields a boon
Dewy and fresh, till showers again shall
    fall.

XX.

THE PLAIN OF DONNERDALE.

THE old inventive Poets, had they seen,
Or rather felt, the entrancement that
    detains
Thy waters, Duddon ! 'mid these flowery
    plains ;
The still repose, the liquid lapse serene,
Transferred to bowers imperishably
    green,   5
Had beautified Elysium ! But these
    chains
Will soon be broken ;—a rough course
    remains,
Rough as the past ; where Thou, of placid
    mien,
Innocuous as a firstling of the flock,
And countenanced like a soft cerulean
    sky,   10
Shalt change thy temper ; and, with many
    a shock
Given and received in mutual jeopardy,
Dance, like a Bacchanal, from rock to
    rock,
Tossing her frantic thyrsus wide and
    high !

XXI.

WHENCE that low voice?—A whisper from
    the heart,
That told of days long past, when here
    I roved
With friends and kindred tenderly be-
    loved ;
Some who had early mandates to depart,

Yet are allowed to steal my path athwart
By Duddon's side ; once more do we
    unite,   6
Once more beneath the kind Earth's
    tranquil light ;
And smothered joys into new being start.
From her unworthy seat, the cloudy stall
Of Time, breaks forth triumphant Me-
    mory ;   10
Her glistening tresses bound, yet light
    and free
As golden locks of birch, that rise and fall
On gales that breathe too gently to recall
Aught of the fading year's inclemency !

XXII.

TRADITION.

A LOVE-LORN Maid, at some far-distant
    time,
Came to this hidden pool, whose depths
    surpass
In crystal clearness Dian's looking-glass ;
And, gazing, saw that Rose, which from
    the prime
Derives its name, reflected as the chime 5
Of echo doth reverberate some sweet
    sound :
The starry treasure from the blue pro-
    found
She longed to ravish ;—shall she plunge,
    or climb
The humid precipice, and seize the guest
Of April, smiling high in upper air?   10
Desperate alternative ! what fiend could
    dare
To prompt the thought?—Upon the steep
    rock's breast
The lonely Primrose yet renews its bloom,
Untouched memento of her hapless doom !

XXIII.

SHEEP-WASHING.

SAD thoughts, avaunt !—partake we their
    blithe cheer
Who gathered in betimes the unshorn
    flock
To wash the fleece, where haply bands of
    rock,

Checking the stream, make a pool smooth
and clear
As this we look on. Distant Mountains
hear,　　　　　5
Hear and repeat, the turmoil that unites
Clamour of boys with innocent despites
Of barking dogs, and bleatings from
strange fear.
And what if Duddon's spotless flood
receive
Unwelcome mixtures as the uncouth
noise　　　　　10
Thickens, the pastoral River will forgive
Such wrong; nor need *we* blame the
licensed joys,
Though false to Nature's quiet equipoise:
Frank are the sports, the stains are fugitive.

XXIV.

THE RESTING-PLACE.

MID-NOON is past;—upon the sultry mead
No zephyr breathes, no cloud its shadow
throws:
If we advance unstrengthened by repose,
Farewell the solace of the vagrant reed!
This Nook—with woodbine hung and
straggling weed,　　　　　5
Tempting recess as ever pilgrim chose,
Half grot, half arbour—proffers to enclose
Body and mind, from molestation freed,
In narrow compass—narrow as itself:
Or if the Fancy, too industrious Elf,　　10
Be loth that we should breathe awhile
exempt
From new incitements friendly to our task,
Here wants not stealthy prospect, that
may tempt
Loose Idless to forego her wily mask.

XXV.

METHINKS 'twere no unprecedented feat
Should some benignant Minister of air
Lift, and encircle with a cloudy chair,
The One for whom my heart shall ever beat
With tenderest love;—or, if a safer seat 5
Atween his downy wings be furnished,
there
Would lodge her, and the cherished bur-
den bear
O'er hill and valley to this dim retreat!

Rough ways my steps have trod;—too
rough and long
For her companionship; here dwells soft
ease:　　　　　10
With sweets that she partakes not some
distaste
Mingles, and lurking consciousness of
wrong;
Languish the flowers; the waters seem to
waste
Their vocal charm; their sparklings cease
to please.

XXVI.

RETURN, Content! for fondly I pursued,
Even when a child, the Streams—unheard,
unseen;
Through tangled woods, impending rocks
between;
Or, free as air, with flying inquest viewed
The sullen reservoirs whence their bold
brood—　　　　　5
Pure as the morning, fretful, boisterous,
keen,
Green as the salt-sea billows, white and
green—
Poured down the hills, a choral multi-
tude!
Nor have I tracked their course for scanty
gains;
They taught me random cares and truant
joys,　　　　　10
That shield from mischief and preserve
from stains
Vague minds, while men are growing out
of boys;
Maturer Fancy owes to their rough noise
Impetuous thoughts that brook not servile
reins.

XXVII.

[Composed probably between 1815-1819.—Pub-
lished 1819[1].]

FALLEN, and diffused into a shapeless
heap,
Or quietly self-buried in earth's mould,
Is that embattled House, whose massy
Keep

---

[1] See Editor's Note, p. 375.

Flung from yon cliff a shadow large and
   cold.
There dwelt the gay, the bountiful, the
   bold ;   5
Till nightly lamentations, like the sweep
Of winds—though winds were silent—
   struck a deep
And lasting terror through that ancient
   Hold.
Its line of Warriors fled;—they shrunk
   when tried
By ghostly power:—but Time's unsparing
   hand   10
Hath plucked such foes, like weeds, from
   out the land ;
And now, if men with men in peace abide,
All other strength the weakest may with-
   stand,
All worse assaults may safely be defied.

XXVIII.
JOURNEY RENEWED.

I ROSE while yet the cattle, heat-opprest,
Crowded together under rustling trees
Brushed by the current of the water-
   breeze ;
And for *their* sakes, and love of all that
   rest,
On Duddon's margin, in the sheltering
   nest ;   5
For all the startled scaly tribes that slink
Into his coverts, and each fearless link
Of dancing insects forged upon his breast;
For these, and hopes and recollections
   worn
Close to the vital seat of human clay ; 10
Glad meetings, tender partings, that up-
   stay
The drooping mind of absence, by vows
   sworn
In his pure presence near the trysting
   thorn—
I thanked the Leader of my onward way.

XXIX.

No record tells of lance opposed to lance,
Horse charging horse, 'mid these retired
   domains ;
Tells that their turf drank purple from
   the veins

Of heroes, fallen, or struggling to advance,
Till doubtful combat issued in a trance 5
Of victory, that struck through heart and
   reins
Even to the inmost seat of mortal pains,
And lightened o'er the pallid countenance.
Yet, to the loyal and the brave, who lie
In the blank earth, neglected and for-
•   lorn,   10
The passing Winds memorial tribute pay ;
The Torrents chant their praise, inspiring
   scorn
Of power usurped ; with proclamation
   high,
And glad acknowledgment, of lawful sway.

XXX.

WHO swerves from innocence, who makes
   divorce
Of that serene companion—a good name,
Recovers not his loss ; but walks with
   shame,
With doubt, with fear, and haply with
   remorse :
And oft-times he—who, yielding to the
   force   5
Of chance-temptation, ere his journey end,
From chosen comrade turns, or faithful
   friend—
In vain shall rue the broken intercourse.
Not so with such as loosely wear the chain
That binds them, pleasant River ! to thy
   side :—   10
Through the rough copse wheel thou with
   hasty stride ;
I choose to saunter o'er the grassy plain,
Sure, when the separation has been tried,
That we, who part in love, shall meet
   again.

XXXI.

THE KIRK OF ULPHA to the pilgrim's eye
Is welcome as a star, that doth present
Its shining forehead through the peaceful
   rent
Of a black cloud diffused o'er half the sky :
Or as a fruitful palm-tree towering high 5
O'er the parched waste beside an Arab's
   tent ;
Or the Indian tree whose branches, down-
   ward bent,

Take root again, a boundless canopy.
How sweet were leisure! could it yield no
    more
Than 'mid that wave-washed Churchyard
    to recline,   10
From pastoral graves extracting thoughts
    divine;
Or there to pace, and mark the summits hoar
Of distant moon-lit mountains faintly
    shine,
Soothed by the unseen River's gentle roar.

XXXII.

NOT hurled precipitous from steep to
    steep;
Lingering no more 'mid flower-enamelled
    lands
And blooming thickets; nor by rocky
    bands
Held; but in radiant progress toward the
    Deep
Where mightiest rivers into powerless
    sleep   5
Sink, and forget their nature—now ex-
    pands
Majestic Duddon, over smooth flat sands
Gliding in silence with unfettered sweep!
Beneath an ampler sky a region wide
Is opened round him:—hamlets, towers,
    and towns,   10
And blue-topped hills, behold him from
    afar;
In stately mien to sovereign Thames allied
Spreading his bosom under Kentish
    downs,
With commerce freighted, or triumphant
    war.

XXXIII.

CONCLUSION.

BUT here no cannon thunders to the gale;
Upon the wave no haughty pendants cast
A crimson splendour: lowly is the mast

That rises here, and humbly spread, the
    sail;
While, less disturbed than in the narrow
    Vale   5
Through which with strange vicissitudes
    he passed,
The Wanderer seeks that receptacle vast
Where all his unambitious functions fail.
And may thy Poet, cloud-born Stream!
    be free—
The sweets of earth contentedly resigned,
And each tumultuous working left be-
    hind   11
At seemly distance—to advance like Thee;
Prepared, in peace of heart, in calm of
    mind
And soul, to mingle with Eternity!

XXXIV.

AFTER-THOUGHT.

I THOUGHT of Thee, my partner and my
    guide,
As being past away.—Vain sympathies!
For, backward, Duddon! as I cast my
    eyes,
I see what was, and is, and will abide;
Still glides the Stream, and shall for ever
    glide;   5
The Form remains, the Function never
    dies;
While we, the brave, the mighty, and the
    wise,
We Men, who in our morn of youth de-
    fied
The elements, must vanish;—be it so!
Enough, if something from our hands have
    power   10
To live, and act, and serve the future hour;
And if, as toward the silent tomb we go,
Through love, through hope, and faith's
    transcendent dower,
We feel that we are greater than we know.

YARROW REVISITED, AND OTHER POEMS.

COMPOSED (TWO EXCEPTED) DURING A TOUR IN SCOTLAND, AND ON THE
ENGLISH BORDER, IN THE AUTUMN OF 1831[1].

————◆————

TO

SAMUEL ROGERS, ESQ.,

AS A TESTIMONY OF FRIENDSHIP AND ACKNOWLEDGMENT OF INTELLECTUAL
OBLIGATIONS, THESE MEMORIALS ARE AFFECTIONATELY INSCRIBED.

RYDAL MOUNT, *Dec.* 11, 1834.

————◆————

The following Stanzas are a memorial of a day
passed with Sir Walter Scott and other Friends
visiting the Banks of the Yarrow under his
guidance, immediately before his departure
from Abbotsford, for Naples.

The title "Yarrow Revisited" will stand in no
need of explanation for Readers acquainted
with the Author's previous poems suggested
by that celebrated Stream.

I.

THE gallant Youth, who may have gained,
  Or seeks, a "winsome Marrow,"
Was but an Infant in the lap
  When first I looked on Yarrow;
Once more, by Newark's Castle-gate   5
  Long left without a warder,
I stood, looked, listened, and with Thee,
  Great Minstrel of the Border!

Grave thoughts ruled wide on that sweet
    day,
  Their dignity installing   10
In gentle bosoms, while sere leaves
  Were on the bough, or falling;

But breezes played, and sunshine gleam-
    ed—
  The forest to embolden;
Reddened the fiery hues, and shot   15
  Transparence through the golden.

For busy thoughts the Stream flowed on
  In foamy agitation;
And slept in many a crystal pool
  For quiet contemplation: 20
No public and no private care
  The freeborn mind enthralling,
We made a day of happy hours,
  Our happy days recalling.

Brisk Youth appeared, the Morn of
    Youth,   25
  With freaks of graceful folly,—
Life's temperate Noon, her sober Eve,
  Her Night not melancholy;
Past, present, future, all appeared
  In harmony united,   30
Like guests that meet, and some from far,
  By cordial love invited.

---

[1] The poems of this series, with two exceptions (conjectured by Prof. Knight to be Nos. XV. and
XVII.), were written during the autumn of 1831, and first published in the vol. of 1835 entitled, *Yarrow
Revisited, and Other Poems.* In order to avoid needless repetition, separate chronological notes
will not be added to the individual poems of the series, save where the particulars of composition or
publication differ in some respect from those now given.—ED.

And if, as Yarrow, through the woods
 And down the meadow ranging,
Did meet us with unaltered face, 35
 Though we were changed and changing;
If, *then*, some natural shadows spread
 Our inward prospect over,
The soul's deep valley was not slow
 Its brightness to recover. 40

Eternal blessings on the Muse,
 And her divine employment!
The blameless Muse, who trains her Sons
 For hope and calm enjoyment;
Albeit sickness, lingering yet, 45
 Has o'er their pillow brooded;
And Care waylays their steps—a Sprite
 Not easily eluded.

For thee, O SCOTT! compelled to change
 Green Eildon-hill and Cheviot 50
For warm Vesuvio's vine-clad slopes;
 And leave thy Tweed and Tiviot
For mild Sorento's breezy waves;
 May classic Fancy, linking
With native Fancy her fresh aid, 55
 Preserve thy heart from sinking!

Oh! while they minister to thee,
 Each vying with the other,
May Health return to mellow Age,
 With Strength, her venturous brother;
And Tiber, and each brook and rill 61
 Renowned in song and story,
With unimagined beauty shine,
 Nor lose one ray of glory!

For Thou, upon a hundred streams, 65
 By tales of love and sorrow,
Of faithful love, undaunted truth,
 Hast shed the power of Yarrow;
And streams unknown, hills yet unseen,
 Wherever they invite Thee, 70
At parent Nature's grateful call,
 With gladness must requite Thee.

A gracious welcome shall be thine,
 Such looks of love and honour
As thy own Yarrow gave to me 75
 When first I gazed upon her;
Beheld what I had feared to see,
 Unwilling to surrender
Dreams treasured up from early days,
 The holy and the tender. 80

And what, for this frail world, were all
 That mortals do or suffer,
Did no responsive harp, no pen,
 Memorial tribute offer?
Yea, what were mighty Nature's self? 85
 Her features, could they win us,
Unhelped by the poetic voice
 That hourly speaks within us?

Nor deem that localised Romance
 Plays false with our affections; 90
Unsanctifies our tears—made sport
 For fanciful dejections:
Ah, no! the visions of the past
 Sustain the heart in feeling
Life as she is—our changeful Life, 95
 With friends and kindred dealing.

Bear witness, Ye, whose thoughts that day
 In Yarrow's groves were centred;
Who through the silent portal arch
 Of mouldering Newark entered; 100
And clomb the winding stair that once
 Too timidly was mounted
By the "last Minstrel," (not the last!)
 Ere he his Tale recounted.

Flow on for ever, Yarrow Stream! 105
 Fulfil thy pensive duty,
Well pleased that future Bards should
 chant
For simple hearts thy beauty;
To dream-light dear while yet unseen,
 Dear to the common sunshine, 110
And dearer still, as now I feel,
 To memory's shadowy moonshine!

II.

ON THE DEPARTURE OF SIR WALTER SCOTT FROM ABBOTSFORD, FOR NAPLES.

[Composed September, 1831.—Published 1833 (*Literary Souvenir* of Alaric Watts); vol. of 1835.]

A TROUBLE, not of clouds, or weeping rain,
Nor of the setting sun's pathetic light
Engendered, hangs o'er Eildon's triple
 height:
Spirits of Power, assembled there, com-
 plain
For kindred Power departing from their
 sight; 5

While Tweed, best pleased in chanting a
    blithe strain,
Saddens his voice again, and yet again.
Lift up your hearts, ye Mourners! for the
    might
Of the whole world's good wishes with
    him goes;
Blessings and prayers in nobler retinue
Than sceptred king or laurelled conqueror
    knows,   11
Follow this wondrous Potentate. Be true,
Ye winds of ocean, and the midland sea,
Wafting your Charge to soft Parthenope!

III.

A PLACE OF BURIAL IN THE SOUTH OF SCOTLAND.

PART fenced by man, part by a rugged
    steep
That curbs a foaming brook, a Grave-
    yard lies;
The hare's best couching-place for fear-
    less sleep;
Which moonlit elves, far seen by credulous
    eyes,
Enter in dance. Of church, or sabbath ties,
No vestige now remains; yet thither creep
Bereft Ones, and in lowly anguish weep
Their prayers out to the wind and naked
    skies.
Proud tomb is none; but rudely-sculp-
    tured knights,
By humble choice of plain old times, are
    seen   10
Level with earth, among the hillocks
    green:
Union not sad, when sunny daybreak
    smites
The spangled turf, and neighbouring
    thickets ring
With *jubilate* from the choirs of spring!

IV.

ON THE SIGHT OF A MANSE IN THE SOUTH OF SCOTLAND.

SAY, ye far-travelled clouds, far-seeing
    hills—
Among the happiest-looking homes of men
Scattered all Britain over, through deep
    glen,

On airy upland, and by forest rills,
And o'er wide plains cheered by the lark
    that trills   5
His sky-born warblings—does aught meet
    your ken
More fit to animate the Poet's pen,
Aught that more surely by its aspect
    fills
Pure minds with sinless envy, than the
    Abode
Of the good Priest: who, faithful through
    all hours   10
To his high charge, and truly serving
    God,
Has yet a heart and hand for trees and
    flowers,
Enjoys the walks his predecessors trod,
Nor covets lineal rights in lands and
    towers.

V.

COMPOSED IN ROSLIN CHAPEL DURING A STORM.

THE wind is now thy organist;—a clank
(We know not whence) ministers for a
    bell
To mark some change of service. As the
    swell
Of music reached its height, and even
    when sank
The notes, in prelude, ROSLIN! to a
    blank   5
Of silence, how it thrilled thy sumptuous
    roof,
Pillars, and arches,—not in vain time-
    proof,
Though Christian rites be wanting! From
    what bank
Came those live herbs? by what hand
    were they sown
Where dew falls not, where rain-drops
    seem unknown?   10
Yet in the Temple they a friendly niche
Share with their sculptured fellows, that,
    green-grown,
Copy their beauty more and more, and
    preach,
Though mute, of all things blending into
    one.

VI.

THE TROSACHS.

THERE's not a nook within this solemn
    Pass
But were an apt confessional for One
Taught by his summer spent, his autumn
    gone,
That Life is but a tale of morning grass
Withered at eve. From scenes of art
    which chase   5
That thought away, turn, and with watch-
    ful eyes
Feed it 'mid Nature's old felicities,
Rocks, rivers, and smooth lakes more
    clear than glass
Untouched, unbreathed upon. Thrice
    happy quest,
If from a golden perch of aspen spray 10
(October's workmanship to rival May)
The pensive warbler of the ruddy breast
That moral sweeten by a heaven-taught
    lay,
Lulling the year, with all its cares, to
    rest !

VII.

THE pibroch's note, discountenanced or
    mute ;
The Roman kilt, degraded to a toy
Of quaint apparel for a half-spoilt boy ;
The target mouldering like ungathered
    fruit ;   4
The smoking steam-boat eager in pur-
    suit,
As eagerly pursued ; the umbrella spread
To weather-fend the Celtic herdsman's
    head—
All speak of manners withering to the
    root,
And of old honours, too, and passions
    high :
Then may we ask, though pleased that
    thought should range   10
Among the conquests of civility,
Survives imagination—to the change
Superior? Help to virtue does she give?
If not, O Mortals, better cease to live !

VIII.

COMPOSED IN THE GLEN OF LOCH ETIVE.

"THIS Land of Rainbows spanning glens
    whose walls,
Rock-built, are hung with rainbow-
    coloured mists—
Of far-stretched Meres whose salt flood
    never rests—
Of tuneful Caves and playful Waterfalls—
Of Mountains varying momently their
    crests—   5
Proud be this Land ! whose poorest huts
    are halls
Where Fancy entertains becoming guests ;
While native song the heroic Past recalls."
Thus, in the net of her own wishes caught,
The Muse exclaimed ; but Story now must
    hide   10
Her trophies, Fancy crouch ; the course
    of pride
Has been diverted, other lessons taught,
That make the Patriot-spirit bow her
    head
Where the all-conquering Roman feared
    to tread.

IX.

EAGLES.

Composed at Dunollie Castle in the bay of Oban

DISHONOURED Rock and Ruin ! that, by
    law
Tyrannic, keep the Bird of Jove em-
    barred
Like a lone criminal whose life is spared.
Vexed is he, and screams loud. The last
    I saw
Was on the wing ; stooping, he struck
    with awe   5
Man, bird, and beast ; then, with a consort
    paired,
From a bold headland, their loved aery's
    guard,
Flew high above Atlantic waves, to draw
Light from the fountain of the setting
    sun.
Such was this Prisoner once ; and when
    his plumes   10
The sea-blast ruffles as the storm comes on,

Then, for a moment, he, in spirit, resumes
His rank 'mong freeborn creatures that
    live free,
His power, his beauty, and his majesty.

X.

IN THE SOUND OF MULL.

TRADITION, be thou mute! Oblivion,
    throw
Thy veil in mercy o'er the records, hung
Round strath and mountain, stamped by
    the ancient tongue
On rock and ruin darkening as we go,—
Spots where a word, ghost-like, survives
    to show   5
What crimes from hate, or desperate love,
    have sprung;
From honour misconceived, or fancied
    wrong,
What feuds, not quenched but fed by
    mutual woe.
Yet, though a wild vindictive Race, un-
    tamed
By civil arts and labours of the pen,   10
Could gentleness be scorned by those
    fierce Men,
Who, to spread wide the reverence they
    claimed
For patriarchal occupations, named
Yon towering Peaks, "Shepherds of Etive
    Glen[1]?"

XI.

SUGGESTED AT TYNDRUM IN A STORM.

ENOUGH of garlands, of the Arcadian
    crook,
And all that Greece and Italy have sung
Of Swains reposing myrtle groves among!
Ours couch on naked rocks,—will cross a
    brook
Swoln with chill rains, nor ever cast a
    look   5
This way or that, or give it even a thought
More than by smoothest pathway may be
    brought
Into a vacant mind. Can written book
Teach what *they* learn? Up, hardy Moun-
    taineer!

---

[1] In Gaelic, *Buachaill Eite.*

And guide the Bard, ambitious to be One
Of Nature's privy council, as thou art,   11
On cloud-sequestered heights, that see
    and hear
To what dread Powers He delegates his
    part
On Earth, who works in the heaven of
    heavens, alone.

XII.

THE EARL OF BREADALBANE'S RUINED MAN-SION, AND FAMILY BURIAL-PLACE, NEAR KILLIN.

WELL sang the Bard who called the grave,
    in strains
Thoughtful and sad, the "narrow house."
    No style
Of fond sepulchral flattery can beguile
Grief of her sting; nor cheat, where he
    detains
The sleeping dust, stern Death. How
    reconcile   5
With truth, or with each other, decked
    remains
Of a once warm Abode, and that *new* Pile,
For the departed, built with curious pains
And mausolean pomp? Yet here they
    stand
Together,—'mid trim walks and artful
    bowers,   10
To be looked down upon by ancient hills,
That, for the living and the dead, demand
And prompt a harmony of genuine
    powers;
Concord that elevates the mind, and
    stills.

XIII.

"REST AND BE THANKFUL."

At the Head of Glencroe.

DOUBLING and doubling with laborious
    walk,
Who, that has gained at length the
    wished-for Height,
This brief this simple wayside Call can
    slight,
And rests not thankful? Whether cheered
    by talk
With some loved friend, or by the unseen
    hawk   5

Whistling to clouds and sky-born streams,
    that shine
At the sun's outbreak, as with light divine,
Ere they descend to nourish root and
    stalk
Of valley flowers. Nor, while the limbs
    repose,
Will we forget that, as the fowl can keep
Absolute stillness, poised aloft in air, 11
And fishes front, unmoved, the torrent's
    sweep,—
So may the Soul, through powers that
    Faith bestows,
Win rest, and ease, and peace, with bliss
    that Angels share.

XIV.

HIGHLAND HUT.

SEE what gay wild flowers deck this
    earth-built Cot,
Whose smoke, forth-issuing whence and
    how it may,
Shines in the greeting of the sun's first ray
Like wreaths of vapour without stain or
    blot.
The limpid mountain-rill avoids it not; 5
And why shouldst thou?—If rightly
    trained and bred,
Humanity is humble, finds no spot
Which her Heaven-guided feet refuse to
    tread.
The walls are cracked, sunk is the flowery
    roof,
Undressed the pathway leading to the
    door; 10
But love, as Nature loves, the lonely
    Poor;
Search, for their worth, some gentle heart
    wrong-proof,
Meek, patient, kind, and, were its trials
    fewer,
Belike less happy.—Stand no more aloof[1]!

XV.

THE HIGHLAND BROACH.

The exact resemblance which the old Broach
(still in use, though rarely met with, among
the Highlanders) bears to the Roman Fibula

[1] See Note p. 915.

must strike every one, and concurs with the
plaid and kilt to recall to mind the commu-
nication which the ancient Romans had with
this remote country.

IF to Tradition faith be due,
And echoes from old verse speak true,
Ere the meek Saint, Columba, bore
Glad tidings to Iona's shore,
No common light of nature blessed 5
The mountain region of the west,
A land where gentle manners ruled
O'er men in dauntless virtues schooled,
That raised, for centuries, a bar
Impervious to the tide of war: 10
Yet peaceful Arts did entrance gain
Where haughty Force had striven in vain;
And, 'mid the works of skilful hands,
By wanderers brought from foreign lands
And various climes, was not unknown 15
The clasp that fixed the Roman Gown;
The Fibula, whose shape, I ween,
Still in the Highland Broach is seen,
The silver Broach of massy frame,
Worn at the breast of some grave Dame
On road or path, or at the door 21
Of fern-thatched hut on heathy moor:
But delicate of yore its mould,
And the material finest gold;
As might beseem the fairest Fair, 25
Whether she graced a royal chair,
Or shed, within a vaulted hall,
No fancied lustre on the wall
Where shields of mighty heroes hung,
While Fingal heard what Ossian sung. 30

The heroic Age expired—it slept
Deep in its tomb:—the bramble crept
O'er Fingal's hearth; the grassy sod
Grew on the floors his sons had trod:
Malvina! where art thou? Their state 35
The noblest-born must abdicate;
The fairest, while with fire and sword
Come Spoilers—horde impelling horde,
Must walk the sorrowing mountains, drest
By ruder hands in homelier vest. 40
Yet still the female bosom lent,
And loved to borrow, ornament;
Still was its inner world a place
Reached by the dews of heavenly grace;
Still pity to this last retreat 45
Clove fondly; to his favourite seat

Love wound his way by soft approach,
Beneath a massier Highland Broach.

When alternations came of rage
Yet fiercer, in a darker age;   50
And feuds, where, clan encountering clan,
The weaker perished to a man;
For maid and mother, when despair
Might else have triumphed, baffling
    prayer,
One small possession lacked not power,
Provided in a calmer hour,   56
To meet such need as might befall—
Roof, raiment, bread, or burial:
For woman, even of tears bereft,
The hidden silver Broach was left.   60

As generations come and go,
Their arts, their customs, ebb and flow;
Fate, fortune, sweep strong powers away,
And feeble, of themselves, decay;
What poor abodes the heirloom hide,   65
In which the castle once took pride !
Tokens, once kept as boasted wealth,
If saved at all, are saved by stealth.
Lo ! ships, from seas by nature barred,
Mount along ways by man prepared;   70
And in far-stretching vales, whose streams
Seek other seas, their canvas gleams.
Lo ! busy towns spring up, on coasts
Thronged yesterday by airy ghosts;
Soon, like a lingering star forlorn   75
Among the novelties of morn,
While young delights on old encroach,
Will vanish the last Highland Broach.

But when, from out their viewless bed,
Like vapours, years have rolled and
    spread;   80
And this poor verse, and worthier lays,
Shall yield no light of love or praise;
Then, by the spade, or cleaving plough,
Or torrent from the mountain's brow,
Or whirlwind, reckless what his might 85
Entombs, or forces into light;
Blind Chance, a volunteer ally,
That oft befriends Antiquity,
And clears Oblivion from reproach,   89
May render back the Highland Broach[1].

---

[1] How much the Broach is sometimes prized
by persons in humble stations may be gathered
from an occurrence mentioned to me by a female

XVI.

THE BROWNIE.

Upon a small island, not far from the head of
Loch Lomond, are some remains of an ancient
building, which was for several years the abode
of a solitary Individual, one of the last surviv-
ors of the clan of Macfarlane, once powerful in
that neighbourhood. Passing along the shore
opposite this island in the year 1814, the Au-
thor learned these particulars, and that this
person then living there had acquired the ap-
pellation of "The Brownie." See "The Brownie's
Cell," to which the following is a sequel.

"How disappeared he?" Ask the newt
    and toad;
Ask of his fellow-men, and they will tell
How he was found, cold as an icicle,
Under an arch of that forlorn abode;
Where he, unpropped, and by the gather-
    ing flood   5
Of years hemmed round, had dwelt, pre-
    pared to try
Privation's worst extremities, and die
With no one near save the omnipresent
    God.
Verily so to live was an awful choice—
A choice that wears the aspect of a doom;
But in the mould of mercy all is cast   11
For Souls familiar with the eternal Voice;
And this forgotten Taper to the last
Drove from itself, we trust, all frightful
    gloom.

XVII.

TO THE PLANET VENUS, AN EVENING STAR.

Composed at Loch Lomond.

THOUGH joy attend Thee orient at the
    birth
Of dawn, it cheers the lofty spirit most
To watch thy course when Daylight, fled
    from earth,

---

friend. She had had an opportunity of benefit-
ing a poor old woman in her own hut, who, wish-
ing to make a return, said to her daughter in
Erse, in a tone of plaintive earnestness, "I would
give anything I have, but I *hope* she does not
wish for my Broach !" and, uttering these words,
she put her hand upon the Broach which fasten-
ed her kerchief, and which, she imagined, had
attracted the eye of her benefactress.

In the grey sky hath left his lingering
    Ghost,
Perplexed as if between a splendour lost
And splendour slowly mustering. Since
    the Sun,   6
The absolute, the world-absorbing One,
Relinquished half his empire to the host
Emboldened by thy guidance, holy Star,
Holy as princely, who that looks on thee
Touching, as now, in thy humility   11
The mountain-borders of this seat of care,
Can question that thy countenance is
    bright,
Celestial Power, as much with love as light?

XVIII.

BOTHWELL CASTLE.

(Passed unseen, on account of stormy weather.)

IMMURED in Bothwell's towers, at times
    the Brave
(So beautiful is Clyde) forgot to mourn
The liberty they lost at Bannockburn.
Once on those steeps *I* roamed at large,
    and have   4
In mind the landscape, as if still in sight;
The river glides, the woods before me wave;
Then why repine that now In vain I crave
Needless renewal of an old delight?
Better to thank a dear and long-past day
For joy its sunny hours were free to give
Than blame the present, that our wish
    hath crost.   11
Memory, like sleep, hath powers which
    dreams obey,
Dreams, vivid dreams, that are not fugitive;
How little that she cherishes is lost!

XIX.

PICTURE OF DANIEL IN THE LIONS' DEN,
AT HAMILTON PALACE.

AMID a fertile region green with wood
And fresh with rivers, well did it become
The ducal Owner, in his palace-home
To naturalise this tawny Lion brood;
Children of Art, that claim strange bro-
    therhood   5
(Couched in their den) with those that
    roam at large
Over the burning wilderness, and charge

The wind with terror while they roar for
    food.
Satiate are *these;* and stilled to eye and
    ear;
Hence, while we gaze, a more enduring
    fear!   10
Yet is the Prophet calm, nor would the
    cave
Daunt him—if his Companions, now be-
    drowsed
Outstretched and listless, were by hunger
    roused:
Man placed him here, and God, he knows,
    can save.

XX.

THE AVON.

(A feeder of the Annan.)

AVON—a precious, an immortal name!
Yet is it one that other rivulets bear
Like this unheard-of, and their channels
    wear
Like this contented, though unknown to
    Fame:
For great and sacred is the modest claim
Of Streams to Nature's love, where'er
    they flow;   6
And ne'er did Genius alight them, as they
    go,
Tree, flower, and green herb, feeding
    without blame.
But Praise can waste her voice on work
    of tears,
Anguish, and death: full oft where inno-
    cent blood   10
Has mixed its current with the limpid
    flood,
Her heaven - offending trophies Glory
    rears:
Never for like distinction may the good
Shrink from *thy* name, pure Rill, with
    unpleased ears.

XXI.

SUGGESTED BY A VIEW FROM AN EMINENCE
IN INGLEWOOD FOREST.

THE forest huge of ancient Caledon
Is but a name, no more is Inglewood,
That swept from hill to hill, from flood to
    flood:

On her last thorn the nightly moon has
   shone;
Yet still, though unappropriate Wild be
   none,   5
Fair parks spread wide where Adam Bell
   might deign
With Clym o' the Clough, were they alive
   again,
To kill for merry feast their venison.
Nor wants the holy Abbot's gliding Shade
His church with monumental wreck be-
   strown;   10
The feudal Warrior-chief, a Ghost un-
   laid,
Hath still his castle, though a skele-
   ton,
That he may watch by night, and lessons
   con
Of power that perishes, and rights that
   fade.

XXII.

HART'S-HORN TREE, NEAR PENRITH.

HERE stood an Oak, that long had borne
   affixed
To his huge trunk, or, with more subtle
   art,
Among its withering topmost branches
   mixed,
The palmy antlers of a hunted Hart,
Whom the Dog Hercules pursued—his
   part   5
Each desperately sustaining, till at last
Both sank and died, the life-veins of the
   chased
And chaser bursting here with one dire
   smart.
Mutual the victory, mutual the defeat!
High was the trophy hung with pitiless
   pride;   10
Say, rather, with that generous sym-
   pathy
That wants not, even in rudest breasts, a
   seat;
And, for this feeling's sake, let no one
   chide
Verse that would guard thy memory,
   HART'S-HORN TREE[1]!

---

[1] See Note, p. 917.

XXIII.

FANCY AND TRADITION.

[Composed 1833.—Published 1835.]

THE Lovers took within this ancient
   grove
Their last embrace; beside those crystal
   springs
The Hermit saw the Angel spread his
   wings
For instant flight; the Sage in yon alcove
Sate musing; on that hill the Bard would
   rove,   5
Not mute, where now the linnet only
   sings:
Thus everywhere to truth Tradition
   clings,
Or Fancy localises Powers we love.
Were only History licensed to take note
Of things gone by, her meagre monu-
   ments   10
Would ill suffice for persons and events:
There is an ampler page for man to quote,
A readier book of manifold contents,
Studied alike in palace and in cot.

XXIV.

COUNTESS' PILLAR.

On the roadside between Penrith and Appleby,
   there stands a pillar with the following inscrip-
   tion:—

"This pillar was erected, in the year 1656, by
   Anne Countess Dowager of Pembroke, &c. for
   a memorial of her last parting with her pious
   mother, Margaret Countess Dowager of Cum-
   berland, on the 2d of April, 1616; in memory
   whereof she hath left an annuity of £4 to be dis-
   tributed to the poor of the parish of Brougham,
   every 2d day of April for ever, upon the stone
   table placed hard by. Laus Deo!"

WHILE the Poor gather round, till the
   end of time
May this bright flower of Charity display
Its bloom, unfolding at the appointed day;
Flower than the loveliest of the vernal
   prime
Lovelier—transplanted from heaven's
   purest clime!   5
"Charity never faileth:" on that creed,
More than on written testament or deed,
The pious Lady built with hope sublime.

Alms on this stone to be dealt out, *for
        ever!*
"LAUS DEO." Many a Stranger passing
        by   10
Has with that Parting mixed a filial sigh,
Blest its humane Memorial's fond en-
        deavour;
And, fastening on those lines an eye tear-
        glazed,
Has ended, though no Clerk, with "God
        be praised!"

XXV.

ROMAN ANTIQUITIES.

(From the Roman Station at Old Penrith.)

How profitless the relics that we cull,
Troubling the last holds of ambitious
        Rome,
Unless they chasten fancies that presume
Too high, or idle agitations lull!
Of the world's flatteries if the brain be
        full,   5
To have no seat for thought were better
        doom,
Like this old helmet, or the eyeless skull
Of him who gloried in its nodding plume.
Heaven out of view, our wishes what are
        they?
Our fond regrets tenacious in their grasp?
The Sage's theory? the Poet's lay?—   11
Mere Fibulæ without a robe to clasp;
Obsolete lamps, whose light no time re-
        calls;
Urns without ashes, tearless lacrymals!

XXVI.

APOLOGY,

FOR THE FOREGOING POEMS.

No more: the end is sudden and abrupt,
Abrupt—as without preconceived design
Was the beginning; yet the several Lays
Have moved in order, to each other bound
By a continuous and acknowledged tie 5
Though unapparent—like those Shapes
        distinct

That yet survive ensculptured on the
        walls
Of palaces, or temples, 'mid the wreck
Of famed Persepolis; each following each,
As might beseem a stately embassy,   10
In set array; these bearing in their hands
Ensign of civil power, weapon of war,
Or gift to be presented at the throne
Of the Great King; and others, as they
        go
In priestly vest, with holy offerings
        charged,   15
Or leading victims drest for sacrifice.
Nor will the Power we serve, that sacred
        Power,
The Spirit of humanity, disdain
A ministration humble but sincere,
That from a threshold loved by every
        Muse   20
Its impulse took—that sorrow-stricken
        door,
Whence, as a current from its fountain-
        head,
Our thoughts have issued, and our feelings
        flowed,
Receiving, willingly or not, fresh strength
From kindred sources; while around us
        sighed   25
(Life's three first seasons having passed
        away)
Leaf-scattering winds; and hoar-frost
        sprinklings fell
(Foretaste of winter) on the moorland
        heights;
And every day brought with it tidings
        new
Of rash change, ominous for the public
        weal.   30
Hence, if dejection has too oft encroached
Upon that sweet and tender melancholy
Which may itself be cherished and ca-
        ressed
More than enough; a fault so natural
(Even with the young, the hopeful, or the
        gay)   35
For prompt forgiveness will not sue in
        vain.

The White Doe of Rylstone;

OR,

The Fate of the Nortons.

[Composed 1807-1808.—Published 1815 (4to); collective ed. 1820.]

ADVERTISEMENT.

During the Summer of 1807 I visited, for the first time, the beautiful country that surrounds Bolton Priory in Yorkshire; and the Poem of "The White Doe," founded upon a Tradition connected with that place, was composed at the close of the same year.

DEDICATION.

In trellised shed with clustering roses gay,
And, MARY! oft beside our blazing fire,
When years of wedded life were as a day
Whose current answers to the heart's desire,
Did we together read in Spenser's Lay   5
How Una, sad of soul—in sad attire,
The gentle Una, of celestial birth,
To seek her Knight went wandering o'er the earth.

Ah, then, Belovèd! pleasing was the smart,
And the tear precious in compassion shed   10
For Her, who, pierced by sorrow's thrilling dart,
Did meekly bear the pang unmerited;
Meek as that emblem of her lowly heart
The milk-white Lamb which in a line she led,—
And faithful, loyal in her innocence,   15
Like the brave Lion slain in her defence.

Notes could we hear as of a faery shell
Attuned to words with sacred wisdom fraught;
Free Fancy prized each specious miracle,
And all its finer inspiration caught;   20
Till in the bosom of our rustic Cell
We by a lamentable change were taught
That "bliss with mortal Man may not abide:"
How nearly joy and sorrow are allied!

For us the stream of fiction ceased to flow,   25
For us the voice of melody was mute.
—But, as soft gales dissolve the dreary snow,
And give the timid herbage leave to shoot,
Heaven's breathing influence failed not to bestow
A timely promise of unlooked-for fruit,   30
Fair fruit of pleasure and serene content
From blossoms wild of fancies innocent.

It soothed us—it beguiled us—then, to hear
Once more of troubles wrought by magic spell;
And griefs whose aery motion comes not near   35
The pangs that tempt the Spirit to rebel:
Then, with mild Una in her sober cheer,
High over hill and low adown the dell
Again we wandered, willing to partake
All that she suffered for her dear Lord's sake.   40

Then, too, this Song of mine once more could please,
Where anguish, strange as dreams of restless sleep,
Is tempered and allayed by sympathies
Aloft ascending, and descending deep,
Even to the inferior Kinds; whom forest-trees   45
Protect from beating sunbeams, and the sweep
Of the sharp winds;—fair Creatures!—to whom Heaven
A calm and sinless life, with love, hath given.

This tragic Story cheered us; for it speaks
Of female patience winning firm repose;   50
And, of the recompense that conscience seeks,
A bright, encouraging, example shows;
Needful when o'er wide realms the tempest breaks,
Needful amid life's ordinary woes;—
Hence not for them unfitted who would bless   55
A happy hour with holier happiness.

He serves the Muses erringly and ill,
Whose aim is pleasure light and fugitive:
O, that my mind were equal to fulfil
The comprehensive mandate which they give—   60
Vain aspiration of an earnest will!
Yet in this moral Strain a power may live,
Belovèd Wife! such solace to impart
As it hath yielded to thy tender heart.

RYDAL MOUNT, WESTMORELAND,
April 20, 1815.

"Action is transitory—a step, a blow,
The motion of a muscle—this way or that—
'Tis done; and in the after-vacancy
We wonder at ourselves like men betrayed:
Suffering is permanent, obscure and dark,
And has the nature of infinity[1].
Yet through that darkness (infinite though it seem
And irremoveable) gracious openings lie,
By which the soul—with patient steps of thought
Now toiling, wafted now on wings of prayer—
May pass in hope, and, though from mortal bonds
Yet undelivered, rise with sure ascent
Even to the fountain-head of peace divine."

"They that deny a God destroy Man's nobility:
for certainly Man is of kin to the Beast by his
Body, and if he be not of kin to God by his Spirit,
he is a base ignoble Creature. It destroys like-
wise Magnanimity, and the raising of humane Na-
ture: for take an example of a Dog, and mark
what a generosity and courage he will put on,
when he finds himself maintained by a Man, who
to him is instead of a God, or Melior Natura.
Which courage is manifestly such as that Crea-
ture without that confidence of a better Nature
than his own could never attain. So Man, when
he resteth and assureth himself upon Divine pro-
tection and favour, gathereth a force and faith
which human Nature in itself could not obtain."

LORD BACON.

Canto First.

FROM Bolton's old monastic tower
The bells ring loud with gladsome power;
The sun shines bright; the fields are gay
With people in their best array
Of stole and doublet, hood and scarf,   5
Along the banks of crystal Wharf,
Through the Vale retired and lowly,
Trooping to that summons holy.
And, up among the moorlands, see
What sprinklings of blithe company!   10
Of lasses and of shepherd grooms,
That down the steep hills force their way,
Like cattle through the budded brooms;
Path, or no path, what care they?
And thus in joyous mood they hie   15
To Bolton's mouldering Priory.

[1] These six lines ("Action is transitory . . . .
infinity") are quoted from the Tragedy of *The
Borderers*, Act III., Scene v. (ll. 1539-1544). The
entire passage ("Action . . . divine") was added
in 1837.—ED.

What would they there?—full fifty
     years
That sumptuous Pile, with all its peers,
Too harshly hath been doomed to taste
The bitterness of wrong and waste: 20
Its courts are ravaged; but the tower
Is standing with a voice of power,
That ancient voice which wont to call
To mass or some high festival;
And in the shattered fabric's heart   25
Remaineth one protected part;
A Chapel, like a wild-bird's nest,
Closely embowered and trimly drest;
And thither young and old repair,
This Sabbath-day, for praise and prayer.

Fast the churchyard fills;—anon   31
Look again, and they all are gone;
The cluster round the porch, and the
     folk
Who sate in the shade of the Prior's
     Oak!
And scarcely have they disappeared   35
Ere the prelusive hymn is heard:—
With one consent the people rejoice,
Filling the church with a lofty voice!
They sing a service which they feel:
For 'tis the sunrise now of zeal;   40
Of a pure faith the vernal prime—
In great Eliza's golden time.

A moment ends the fervent din,
And all is hushed, without and within;
For though the priest, more tranquilly,
Recites the holy liturgy,   46
The only voice which you can hear
Is the river murmuring near.
—When soft!—the dusky trees between,
And down the path through the open
     green,   50
Where is no living thing to be seen;
And through yon gateway, where is
     found,
Beneath the arch with ivy bound,
Free entrance to the churchyard ground—
Comes gliding in with lovely gleam,   55
Comes gliding in serene and slow,
Soft and silent as a dream,
A solitary Doe!
White she is as lily of June,
And beauteous as the silver moon   60

When out of sight the clouds are driven
And she is left alone in heaven;
Or like a ship some gentle day
In sunshine sailing far away,
A glittering ship, that hath the plain 65
Of ocean for her own domain.

Lie silent in your graves, ye dead!
Lie quiet in your churchyard bed!
Ye living, tend your holy cares;
Ye multitude, pursue your prayers; 70
And blame not me if my heart and sight
Are occupied with one delight!
'Tis a work for sabbath hours
If I with this bright Creature go:
Whether she be of forest bowers, 75
From the bowers of earth below;
Or a Spirit for one day given,
A pledge of grace from purest heaven.

What harmonious pensive changes
Wait upon her as she ranges 80
Round and through this Pile of state
Overthrown and desolate!
Now a step or two her way
Leads through space of open day,
Where the enamoured sunny light 85
Brightens her that was so bright;
Now doth a delicate shadow fall,
Falls upon her like a breath,
From some lofty arch or wall,
As she passes underneath: 90
Now some gloomy nook partakes
Of the glory that she makes,—
High-ribbed vault of stone, or cell,
With perfect cunning framed as well
Of stone, and ivy, and the spread 95
Of the elder's bushy head;
Some jealous and forbidding cell,
That doth the living stars repel,
And where no flower hath leave to dwell.

The presence of this wandering Doe 100
Fills many a damp obscure recess
With lustre of a saintly show;
And, reappearing, she no less
Sheds on the flowers that round her blow
A more than sunny liveliness, 105
But say, among these holy places,
Which thus assiduously she paces,
Comes she with a votary's task,
Rite to perform, or boon to ask?

Fair Pilgrim! harbours she a sense 110
Of sorrow, or of reverence?
Can she be grieved for quire or shrine,
Crushed as if by wrath divine?
For what survives of house where God
Was worshipped, or where Man abode;
For old magnificence undone; 116
Or for the gentler work begun
By Nature, softening and concealing,
And busy with a hand of healing?
Mourns she for lordly chamber's hearth
That to the sapling ash gives birth; 121
For dormitory's length laid bare
Where the wild rose blossoms fair;
Or altar, whence the cross was rent,
Now rich with mossy ornament? 125
—She sees a warrior carved in stone,
Among the thick weeds, stretched alone;
A warrior, with his shield of pride
Cleaving humbly to his side,
And hands in resignation prest, • 130
Palm to palm, on his tranquil breast;
As little she regards the sight
As a common creature might:
If she be doomed to inward care,
Or service, it must lie elsewhere. 135
—But hers are eyes serenely bright,
And on she moves—with pace how light!
Nor spares to stoop her head, and taste
The dewy turf with flowers bestrown;
And thus she fares, until at last 140
Beside the ridge of a grassy grave
In quietness she lays her down;
Gentle as a weary wave
Sinks, when the summer breeze hath died,
Against an anchored vessel's side; 145
Even so, without distress, doth she
Lie down in peace, and lovingly.

The day is placid in its going,
To a lingering motion bound,
Like the crystal stream now flowing 150
With its softest summer sound:
So the balmy minutes pass,
While this radiant Creature lies
Couched upon the dewy grass,
Pensively with downcast eyes. 155
—But now again the people raise
With awful cheer a voice of praise;
It is the last, the parting song;
And from the temple forth they throng,.

And quickly spread themselves abroad,
While each pursues his several road. 161
But some—a variegated band
Of middle-aged, and old, and young,
And little children by the hand
Upon their leading mothers hung— 165
With mute obeisance gladly paid
Turn towards the spot where, full in view,
The white Doe, to her service true,
Her sabbath couch has made.

It was a solitary mound; 170
Which two spears' length of level ground
Did from all other graves divide:
As if in some respect of pride;
Or melancholy's sickly mood,
Still shy of human neighbourhood; 175
Or guilt, that humbly would express
A penitential loneliness.

"Look, there she is, my Child! draw
    near;
She fears not, wherefore should we fear?
She means no harm;"—but still the Boy,
To whom the words were softly said, 181
Hung back, and smiled, and blushed for
    joy,
A shame faced blush of glowing red!
Again the Mother whispered low,
"Now you have seen the famous Doe; 185
From Rylstone she hath found her way
Over the hills this sabbath day;
Her work, whate'er it be, is done,
And she will depart when we are gone;
Thus doth she keep, from year to year,
Her sabbath morning, foul or fair." 191

Bright was the Creature, as in dreams
The Boy had seen her, yea, more bright;
But is she truly what she seems?
He asks with insecure delight, 195
Asks of himself, and doubts,—and still
The doubt returns against his will:
Though he, and all the standers-by,
Could tell a tragic history
Of facts divulged, wherein appear 200
Substantial motive, reason clear,
Why thus the milk-white Doe is found
Couchant beside that lonely mound;
And why she duly loves to pace
The circuit of this hallowed place. 205

Nor to the Child's enquiring mind
Is such perplexity confined:
For, spite of sober Truth that sees
A world of fixed remembrances
Which to this mystery belong, 210
If, undeceived, my skill can trace
The characters of every face,
There lack not strange delusion here,
Conjecture vague, and idle fear,
And superstitious fancies strong, 215
Which do the gentle Creature wrong.

That bearded, staff-supported Sire—
Who in his boyhood often fed
Full cheerily on convent-bread
And heard old tales by the convent-fire,
And to his grave will go with scars, 221
Relics of long and distant wars—
That Old Man, studious to expound
The spectacle, is mounting high
To days of dim antiquity; 225
When Lady Aäliza mourned
Her Son, and felt in her despair
The pang of unavailing prayer;
Her Son in Wharf's abysses drowned,
The noble Boy of Egremound. 230
From which affliction—when the grace
Of God had in her heart found place—
A pious structure, fair to see,
Rose up, this stately Priory!
The Lady's work;—but now laid low;
To the grief of her soul that doth come
    and go, 236
In the beautiful form of this innocent
    Doe:
Which, though seemingly doomed in its
    breast to sustain
A softened remembrance of sorrow and
    pain,
Is spotless, and holy, and gentle, and
    bright; 240
And glides o'er the earth like an angel of
    light.

Pass, pass who will, yon chantry
    door;
And through the chink in the fractured
    floor
Look down, and see a griesly sight;
A vault where the bodies are buried
    upright! 245

There, face by face, and hand by hand,
The Claphams and Mauleverers stand;
And, in his place, among son and sire,
Is John de Clapham, that fierce Esquire,
A valiant man, and a name of dread   250
In the ruthless wars of the White and
    Red;
Who dragged Earl Pembroke from Ban-
    bury church
And smote off his head on the stones of
    the porch!
Look down among them, if you dare;
Oft does the White Doe loiter there,   255
Prying into the darksome rent;
Nor can it be with good intent:
So thinks that Dame of haughty air,
Who hath a Page her book to hold,
And wears a frontlet edged with gold. 260
Harsh thoughts with her high mood
    agree—
Who counts among her ancestry
Earl Pembroke, slain so impiously!

That slender Youth, a scholar pale,
From Oxford come to his native vale,   265
He also hath his own conceit:
It is, thinks he, the gracious Fairy,
Who loved the Shepherd-lord to meet
In his wanderings solitary:
Wild notes she in his hearing sang,   270
A song of Nature's hidden powers;
That whistled like the wind, and rang
Among the rocks and holly bowers.
'Twas said that She all shapes could
    wear;
And oftentimes before him stood,   275
Amid the trees of some thick wood,
In semblance of a lady fair;
And taught him signs, and showed him
    sights,
In Craven's dens, on Cumbrian heights;
When under cloud of fear he lay,   280
A shepherd clad in homely grey;
Nor left him at his later day.
And hence when he, with spear and
    shield,
Rode full of years to Flodden-field,
His eye could see the hidden spring,   285
And how the current was to flow;
The fatal end of Scotland's King,
And all that hopeless overthrow.

But not in wars did he delight,
This Clifford wished for worthier might;
Nor in broad pomp, or courtly state;   291
Him his own thoughts did elevate,—
Most happy in the shy recess
Of Barden's lowly quietness.
And choice of studious friends had he   295
Of Bolton's dear fraternity;
Who, standing on this old church tower,
In many a calm propitious hour,
Perused, with him, the starry sky;
Or, in their cells, with him did pry   300
For other lore,—by keen desire
Urged to close toil with chemic fire;
In quest belike of transmutations
Rich as the mine's most bright creations.
But they and their good works are fled,
And all is now disquieted—   306
And peace is none, for living or dead!

Ah, pensive Scholar, think not so,
But look again at the radiant Doe!
What quiet watch she seems to keep,   310
Alone, beside that grassy heap!
Why mention other thoughts unmeet
For vision so composed and sweet?
While stand the people in a ring,
Gazing, doubting, questioning;   315
Yea, many overcome in spite
Of recollections clear and bright;
Which yet do unto some impart
An undisturbed repose of heart.
And all the assembly own a law   320
Of orderly respect and awe;
But see—they vanish one by one,
And last, the Doe herself is gone.

Harp! we have been full long beguiled
By vague thoughts, lured by fancies
    wild;   325
To which, with no reluctant strings,
Thou hast attuned thy murmurings;
And now before this Pile we stand
In solitude, and utter peace:
But, Harp! thy murmurs may not cease—
A Spirit, with his angelic wings,   331
In soft and breeze-like visitings,
Has touched thee—and a Spirit's hand:
A voice is with us—a command
To chant, in strains of heavenly glory, 335
A tale of tears, a mortal story!

Canto Second.

THE Harp in lowliness obeyed;
And first we sang of the greenwood shade
And a solitary Maid;
Beginning, where the song must end,　340
With her, and with her sylvan Friend;
The Friend, who stood before her sight,
Her only unextinguished light;
Her last companion in a dearth
Of love, upon a hopeless earth.　345

For She it was—this Maid, who wrought
Meekly, with foreboding thought,
In vermeil colours and in gold
An unblest work; which, standing by,
Her Father did with joy behold,—　350
Exulting in its imagery;
A Banner, fashioned to fulfil
Too perfectly his headstrong will:
For on this Banner had her hand　354
Embroidered (such her Sire's command)
The sacred Cross; and figured there
The five dear wounds our Lord did bear;
Full soon to be uplifted high,
And float in rueful company!

It was the time when England's Queen
Twelve years had reigned, a Sovereign
　　dread;　361
Nor yet the restless crown had been
Disturbed upon her virgin head;
But now the inly-working North
Was ripe to send its thousands forth,　365
A potent vassalage, to fight
In Percy's and in Neville's right,
Two Earls fast leagued in discontent,
Who gave their wishes open vent;
And boldly urged a general plea,　370
The rites of ancient piety
To be triumphantly restored,
By the stern justice of the sword!
And that same Banner, on whose breast
The blameless Lady had exprest　375
Memorials chosen to give life
And sunshine to a dangerous strife;
That Banner, waiting for the Call,
Stood quietly in Rylstone-hall.

It came; and Francis Norton said,　380
"O Father! rise not in this fray—
The hairs are white upon your head;

Dear Father, hear me when I say
It is for you too late a day!
Bethink you of your own good name:　385
A just and gracious Queen have we,
A pure religion, and the claim
Of peace on our humanity.—
'Tis meet that I endure your scorn;
I am your son, your eldest born;　390
But not for lordship or for land,
My Father, do I clasp your knees;
The Banner touch not, stay your hand,
This multitude of men disband,
And live at home in blameless ease;　395
For these my brethren's sake, for me;
And, most of all, for Emily!"

Tumultuous noises filled the hall;
And scarcely could the Father hear
That name—pronounced with a dying
　　fall—　400
The name of his only Daughter dear,
As on the banner which stood near
He glanced a look of holy pride,
And his moist eyes were glorified;
Then did he seize the staff, and say:　405
"Thou, Richard, bear'st thy father's name,
Keep thou this ensign till the day
When I of thee require the same:
Thy place be on my better hand;
And seven as true as thou, I see,　410
Will cleave to this good cause and me."
He spake, and eight brave sons straight-
　　way
All followed him, a gallant band!

Thus, with his sons, when forth he came
The sight was hailed with loud acclaim
And din of arms and minstrelsy,　416
From all his warlike tenantry,
All horsed and harnessed with him to
　　ride,—
A voice to which the hills replied!

But Francis, in the vacant hall,　420
Stood silent under dreary weight,—
A phantasm, in which roof and wall
Shook, tottered, swam before his sight;
A phantasm like a dream of night!
Thus overwhelmed, and desolate,　425
He found his way to a postern-gate;
And, when he waked, his languid eye
Was on the calm and silent sky;

With air about him breathing sweet, 429
And earth's green grass beneath his feet;
Nor did he fail ere long to hear
A sound of military cheer,
Faint—but it reached that sheltered spot;
He heard, and it disturbed him not.

There stood he, leaning on a lance 435
Which he had grasped unknowingly,
Had blindly grasped in that strong trance,
That dimness of heart-agony;
There stood he, cleansed from the despair
And sorrow of his fruitless prayer. 440
The past he calmly hath reviewed:
But where will be the fortitude
Of this brave man, when he shall see
That Form beneath the spreading tree,
And know that it is Emily? 445

He saw her where in open view
She sate beneath the spreading yew—
Her head upon her lap, concealing
In solitude her bitter feeling:
"Might ever son *command* a sire, 450
The act were justified to-day."
This to himself—and to the Maid,
Whom now he had approached, he said—
"Gone are they,—they have their desire;
And I with thee one hour will stay, 455
To give thee comfort if I may."

She heard, but looked not up, nor spake;
And sorrow moved him to partake
Her silence; then his thoughts turned
round,
And fervent words a passage found. 460

"Gone are they, bravely, though misled;
With a dear Father at their head!
The Sons obey a natural lord;
The Father had given solemn word
To noble Percy; and a force 465
Still stronger, bends him to his course.
This said, our tears to-day may fall
As at an innocent funeral.
In deep and awful channel runs
This sympathy of Sire and Sons; 470
Untried our Brothers have been loved
With heart by simple nature moved;
And now their faithfulness is proved:
For faithful we must call them, bearing
That soul of conscientious daring. 475

—There were they all in circle—there
Stood Richard, Ambrose, Christopher,
John with a sword that will not fail,
And Marmaduke in fearless mail,
And those bright Twins were side by side;
And there, by fresh hopes beautified, 481
Stood He, whose arm yet lacks the power
Of man, our youngest, fairest flower!
I, by the right of eldest born,
And in a second father's place, 485
Presumed to grapple with their scorn,
And meet their pity face to face;
Yea, trusting in God's holy aid,
I to my Father knelt and prayed;
And one, the pensive Marmaduke, 490
Methought, was yielding inwardly,
And would have laid his purpose by,
But for a glance of his Father's eye,
Which I myself could scarcely brook.

"Then be we, each and all, forgiven! 495
Thou, chiefly thou, my Sister dear,
Whose pangs are registered in heaven—
The stifled sigh, the hidden tear,
And smiles, that dared to take their place,
Meek filial smiles, upon thy face, 500
As that unhallowed Banner grew
Beneath a loving old Man's view.
Thy part is done—thy painful part;
Be thou then satisfied in heart!
A further, though far easier, task 505
Than thine hath been, my duties ask;
With theirs my efforts cannot blend,
I cannot for such cause contend;
Their aims I utterly forswear;
But I in body will be there. 510
Unarmed and naked will I go,
Be at their side, come weal or woe:
On kind occasions I may wait,
See, hear, obstruct, or mitigate.
Bare breast I take and an empty
hand [1]."— 515
Therewith he threw away the lance,
Which he had grasped in that strong
trance;
Spurned it, like something that would
stand
Between him and the pure intent
Of love on which his soul was bent. 520

[1] See the Old Ballad,—"The Rising of the North."

"For thee, for thee, is left the sense
Of trial past without offence
To God or man; such innocence,
Such consolation, and the excess
Of an unmerited distress;   525
In that thy very strength must lie.
—O Sister, I could prophesy!
The time is come that rings the knell
Of all we loved, and loved so well:
Hope nothing, if I thus may speak   530
To thee, a woman, and thence weak:
Hope nothing, I repeat; for we
Are doomed to perish utterly:
'Tis meet that thou with me divide
The thought while I am by thy side, 535
Acknowledging a grace in this,
A comfort in the dark abyss.
But look not for me when I am gone,
And be no farther wrought upon:
Farewell all wishes, all debate,   540
All prayers for this cause, or for that!
Weep, if that aid thee; but depend
Upon no help of outward friend;
Espouse thy doom at once, and cleave
To fortitude without reprieve.   545
For we must fall, both we and ours—
This Mansion and these pleasant bowers,
Walks, pools, and arbours, homestead,
     hall—
Our fate is theirs, will reach them all;
The young horse must forsake his manger,
And learn to glory in a Stranger;   551
The hawk forget his perch; the hound
Be parted from his ancient ground:
The blast will sweep us all away—
One desolation, one decay!   555
And even this Creature!" which words
     saying,
He pointed to a lovely Doe,
A few steps distant, feeding, straying;
Fair creature, and more white than snow!
"Even she will to her peaceful woods 560
Return, and to her murmuring floods,
And be in heart and soul the same
She was before she hither came;
Ere she had learned to love us all,
Herself beloved in Rylstone-hall.   565
—But thou, my Sister, doomed to be
The last leaf on a blasted tree;
If not in vain we breathed the breath
Together of a purer faith;

If hand in hand we have been led,   570
And thou, (O happy thought this day!)
Not seldom foremost in the way;
If on one thought our minds have fed,
And we have in one meaning read;
If, when at home our private weal   575
Hath suffered from the shock of zeal,
Together we have learned to prize
Forbearance and self-sacrifice;
If we like combatants have fared,
And for this issue been prepared;   580
If thou art beautiful, and youth
And thought endue thee with all truth—
Be strong;—be worthy of the grace
Of God, and fill thy destined place:
A Soul, by force of sorrows high,   585
Uplifted to the purest sky
Of undisturbed humanity!"

He ended,—or she heard no more;
He led her from the yew-tree shade,
And at the mansion's silent door,   590
He kissed the consecrated Maid;
And down the valley then pursued,
Alone, the armèd Multitude.

Canto Third.

Now joy for you who from the towers
Of Brancepeth look in doubt and fear, 595
Telling melancholy hours!
Proclaim it, let your Masters hear
That Norton with his band is near!
The watchmen from their station high
Pronounced the word,—and the Earls
     descry,   600
Well-pleased, the armèd Company
Marching down the banks of Were.

Said fearless Norton to the pair
Gone forth to greet him on the plain—
"This meeting, noble Lords! looks fair,
I bring with me a goodly train;   606
Their hearts are with you: hill and dale
Have helped us: Ure we crossed, and
     Swale,
And horse and harness followed—see
The best part of their Yeomanry!   610
—Stand forth, my Sons!—these eight are
     mine,
Whom to this service I commend;

Which way soe'er our fate incline,
These will be faithful to the end ;   614
They are my all"—voice failed him here—
"My all save one, a Daughter dear !
Whom I have left, Love's mildest birth,
The meekest Child on this blessed earth.
I had—but these are by my side,
These Eight, and this is a day of pride !
The time is ripe. With festive din   621
Lo ! how the people are flocking in,—
Like hungry fowl to the feeder's hand
When snow lies heavy upon the land."

He spake bare truth ; for far and near
From every side came noisy swarms   626
Of Peasants in their homely gear ;
And, mixed with these, to Brancepeth
    came
Grave Gentry of estate and name,
And Captains known for worth in arms ;
And prayed the Earls in self-defence 631
To rise, and prove their innocence.—
"Rise, noble Earls, put forth your might
For holy Church, and the People's right !"

The Norton fixed, at this demand,   635
His eye upon Northumberland,
And said ; "The Minds of Men will own
No loyal rest while England's Crown
Remains without an Heir, the bait
Of strife and factions desperate ;   640
Who, paying deadly hate in kind
Through all things else, in this can find
A mutual hope, a common mind ;
And plot, and pant to overwhelm
All ancient honour in the realm.   645
—Brave Earls ! to whose heroic veins
Our noblest blood is given in trust,
To you a suffering State complains,
And ye must raise her from the dust.
With wishes of still bolder scope   650
On you we look, with dearest hope ;
Even for our Altars—for the prize
In Heaven, of life that never dies ;
For the old and holy Church we mourn,
And must in joy to her return.   655
Behold !"—and from his Son whose stand
Was on his right, from that guardian
    hand
He took the Banner, and unfurled
The precious folds—"behold," said he,
"The ransom of a sinful world ;   660

Let this your preservation be ;
The wounds of hands and feet and side,
And the sacred Cross on which Jesus died.
—This bring I from an ancient hearth,
These Records wrought in pledge of love
By hands of no ignoble birth,   666
A Maid o'er whom the blessed Dove
Vouchsafed in gentleness to brood
While she the holy work pursued."
"Uplift the Standard !" was the cry 670
From all the listeners that stood round,
"Plant it,—by this we live or die."
The Norton ceased not for that sound,
But said ; "The prayer which ye have
    heard,
Much injured Earls ! by these preferred,
Is offered to the Saints, the sigh   676
Of tens of thousands, secretly."
"Uplift it !" cried once more the Band,
And then a thoughtful pause ensued :
"Uplift it !" said Northumberland— 680
Whereat from all the multitude
Who saw the Banner reared on high
In all its dread emblazonry
A voice of uttermost joy brake out :
The transport was rolled down the river
    of Were,   685
And Durham, the time-honoured Durham,
    did hear,
And the towers of Saint Cuthbert were
    stirred by the shout !

Now was the North in arms:—they
    shine
In warlike trim from Tweed to Tyne,
At Percy's voice : and Neville sees   690
His Followers gathering in from Tees,
From Were, and all the little rills
Concealed among the forkèd hills—
Seven hundred Knights, Retainers all
Of Neville, at their Master's call   695
Had sate together in Raby Hall !
Such strength that Earldom held of yore;
Nor wanted at this time rich store
Of well-appointed chivalry.
—Not loth the sleepy lance to wield, 700
And greet the old paternal shield,
They heard the summons ;—and, further-
    more,
Horsemen and Foot of each degree,
Unbound by pledge of fealty,

Appeared, with free and open hate   705
Of novelties in Church and State;
Knight, burgher, yeoman, and esquire,
And Romish priest, in priest's attire.
And thus, in arms, a zealous Band
Proceeding under joint command,   710
To Durham first their course they bear;
And in Saint Cuthbert's ancient seat
Sang mass,—and tore the book of prayer,—
And trod the bible beneath their feet.

Thence marching southward smooth
      and free   715
"They mustered their host at Wetherby,
Full sixteen thousand fair to see[1];"
The Choicest Warriors of the North!
But none for beauty and for worth
Like those eight Sons—who, in a ring, 720
(Ripe men, or blooming in life's spring)
Each with a lance, erect and tall,
A falchion, and a buckler small,
Stood by their Sire, on Clifford-moor,
To guard the Standard which he bore. 725
On foot they girt their Father round;
And so will keep the appointed ground
Where'er their march: no steed will he
Henceforth bestride;—triumphantly
He stands upon this grassy sod,   730
Trusting himself to the earth, and God.
Rare sight to embolden and inspire!
Proud was the field of Sons and Sire;
Of him the most; and, sooth to say,
No shape of man in all the array   735
So graced the sunshine of that day.
The monumental pomp of age
Was with this goodly Personage;
A stature undepressed in size,
Unbent, which rather seemed to rise,   740
In open victory o'er the weight
Of seventy years, to loftier height;
Magnific limbs of withered state;
A face to fear and venerate;   744
Eyes dark and strong; and on his head
Bright locks of silver hair, thick spread,
Which a brown morion half-concealed,
Light as a hunter's of the field;
And thus, with girdle round his waist,
Whereon the Banner-staff might rest   750
At need, he stood, advancing high
The glittering, floating Pageantry.

Who sees him?—thousands see, and One
With unparticipated gaze;
Who, 'mong those thousands, friend hath
      none,   755
And treads in solitary ways.
He, following wheresoe'er he might,
Hath watched the Banner from afar,
As shepherds watch a lonely star,
Or mariners the distant light   760
That guides them through a stormy
      night.
And now, upon a chosen plot
Of rising ground, yon heathy spot!
He takes alone his far-off stand,
With breast unmailed, unweaponed hand.
Bold is his aspect; but his eye
Is pregnant with anxiety,
While, like a tutelary Power,
He there stands fixed from hour to
      hour:
Yet sometimes in more humble guise 770
Upon the turf-clad height he lies
Stretched, herdsman-like, as if to bask
In sunshine were his only task,
Or by his mantle's help to find
A shelter from the nipping wind: 775
And thus, with short oblivion blest,
His weary spirits gather rest.
Again he lifts his eyes; and lo!
The pageant glancing to and fro;
And hope is wakened by the sight,   780
He thence may learn, ere fall of night,
Which way the tide is doomed to flow.

To London were the Chieftains bent;
But what avails the bold intent?
A Royal army is gone forth   785
To quell the RISING OF THE NORTH;
They march with Dudley at their head,
And, in seven days' space, will to York
      be led!—
Can such a mighty host be raised
Thus suddenly, and brought so near?   790
The Earls upon each other gazed,
And Neville's cheek grew pale with fear;
For, with a high and valiant name,
He bore a heart of timid frame;
And bold if both had been, yet they   795
"Against so many may not stay[2]."

[1] From the Old Ballad.

[2] From the Old Ballad.

Back therefore will they hie to seize
A strong Hold on the banks of Tees;
There wait a favourable hour,
Until Lord Dacre with his power   800
From Naworth come; and Howard's aid
Be with them openly displayed.

While through the Host, from man to
    man,
A rumour of this purpose ran,
The Standard trusting to the care   805
Of him who heretofore did bear
That charge, impatient Norton sought
The Chieftains to unfold his thought,
And thus abruptly spake;—"We yield
(And can it be?) an unfought field!—   810
How oft has strength, the strength of
    heaven,
To few triumphantly been given!
Still do our very children boast
Of mitred Thurston—what a Host
He conquered!—Saw we not the Plain
(And flying shall behold again)   816
Where faith was proved?—while to battle
    moved
The Standard, on the Sacred Wain
That bore it, compassed round by a bold
Fraternity of Barons old;   820
And with those grey-haired champions
    stood,
Under the saintly ensigns three,
The infant Heir of Mowbray's blood—
All confident of victory!—
Shall Percy blush, then, for his name? 825
Must Westmoreland be asked with shame
Whose were the numbers, where the loss,
In that other day of Neville's Cross?
When the Prior of Durham with holy
    hand
Raised, as the Vision gave command, 830
Saint Cuthbert's Relic—far and near
Kenned on the point of a lofty spear;
While the Monks prayed in Maiden's
    Bower
To God descending in his power.
Less would not at our need be due   835
To us, who war against the Untrue;—
The delegates of Heaven we rise,
Convoked the impious to chastise:
We, we, the sanctities of old
Would re-establish and uphold: 840

Be warned"—His zeal the Chiefs con-
    founded,
But word was given, and the trumpet
    sounded:
Back through the melancholy Host
Went Norton, and resumed his post.
Alas! thought he, and have I borne   845
This Banner raised with joyful pride,
This hope of all posterity,
By those dread symbols sanctified;
Thus to become at once the scorn
Of babbling winds as they go by,   850
A spot of shame to the sun's bright eye,
To the light clouds a mockery!
—"Even these poor eight of mine would
    stem—"
Half to himself, and half to them   854
He spake—"would stem, or quell, a force
Ten times their number, man and horse;
This by their own unaided might,
Without their father in their sight,
Without the Cause for which they fight;
A Cause, which on a needful day   860
Would breed us thousands brave as
    they."
—So speaking, he his reverend head
Raised toward that Imagery once more:
But the familiar prospect shed
Despondency unfelt before: 865
A shock of intimations vain,
Dismay, and superstitious pain,
Fell on him, with the sudden thought
Of her by whom the work was wrought:—
Oh! wherefore was her countenance
    bright   870
With love divine and gentle light?
She would not, could not, disobey,
But her Faith leaned another way.
Ill tears she wept; I saw them fall,
I overheard her as she spake   875
Sad words to that mute Animal,
The White Doe, in the hawthorn brake;
She steeped, but not for Jesu's sake,
This Cross in tears: by her, and One
Unworthier far we are undone—   880
Her recreant Brother—he prevailed
Over that tender Spirit—assailed
Too oft, alas! by her whose head
In the cold grave hath long been laid:
She first in reason's dawn beguiled   885
Her docile, unsuspecting Child:

Far back—far back my mind must go
To reach the well-spring of this woe!

While thus he brooded, music sweet
Of border tunes was played to cheer 890
The footsteps of a quick retreat;
But Norton lingered in the rear,
Stung with sharp thoughts; and, ere the last
From his distracted brain was cast,
Before his Father, Francis stood, 895
And spake in firm and earnest mood.

"Though here I bend a suppliant knee
In reverence, and unarmed, I bear
In your indignant thoughts my share;
Am grieved this backward march to see
So careless and disorderly. 901
I scorn your Chiefs—men who would lead,
And yet want courage at their need:
Then look at them with open eyes!
Deserve they further sacrifice?— 905
If—when they shrink, nor dare oppose
In open field their gathering foes,
(And fast, from this decisive day,
Yon multitude must melt away;)
If now I ask a grace not claimed 910
While ground was left for hope; unblamed
Be an endeavour that can do
No injury to them or you.
My Father! I would help to find
A place of shelter, till the rage 915
Of cruel men do like the wind
Exhaust itself and sink to rest;
Be Brother now to Brother joined!
Admit me in the equipage
Of your misfortunes, that at least, 920
Whatever fate remain behind,
I may bear witness in my breast
To your nobility of mind!"

"Thou Enemy, my bane and blight!
Oh! bold to fight the Coward's fight 925
Against all good"—but why declare,
At length, the issue of a prayer
Which love had prompted, yielding scope
Too free to one bright moment's hope?
Suffice it that the Son, who strove 930
With fruitless effort to allay
That passion, prudently gave way;
Nor did he turn aside to prove
His Brothers' wisdom or their love—

But calmly from the spot withdrew; 935
His best endeavours to renew,
Should e'er a kindlier time ensue.

Canto Fourth.

'Tis night: in silence looking down,
The Moon from cloudless ether sees
A Camp, and a beleaguered Town, 940
And Castle like a stately crown
On the steep rocks of winding Tees;—
And southward far, with moor between,
Hill-top, and flood, and forest green, 944
The bright Moon sees that valley small
Where Rylstone's old sequestered Hall
A venerable image yields
Of quiet to the neighbouring fields;
While from one pillared chimney breathes
The smoke, and mounts in silver wreaths.
—The courts are hushed;—for timely sleep 951
The greyhounds to their kennel creep;
The peacock in the broad ash-tree
Aloft is roosted for the night,
He who in proud prosperity 955
Of colours manifold and bright
Walked round, affronting the daylight;
And higher still, above the bower
Where he is perched, from yon lone Tower
The hall-clock in the clear moonshine 960
With glittering finger points at nine.

Ah! who could think that sadness here
Hath any sway? or pain, or fear?
A soft and lulling sound is heard
Of streams inaudible by day; 965
The garden pool's dark surface, stirred
By the night insects in their play,
Breaks into dimples small and bright;
A thousand, thousand rings of light
That shape themselves and disappear 970
Almost as soon as seen:—and lo!
Not distant far, the milk-white Doe—
The same who quietly was feeding
On the green herb, and nothing heeding,
When Francis, uttering to the Maid 975
His last words in the yew-tree shade,
Involved whate'er by love was brought
Out of his heart, or crossed his thought,
Or chance presented to his eye,
In one sad sweep of destiny— 980

The same fair Creature, who hath found
Her way into forbidden ground ;
Where now—within this spacious plot
For pleasure made, a goodly spot,
With lawns and beds of flowers, and
    shades   985
Of trellis-work in long arcades,
And cirque and crescent framed by wall
Of close-clipt foliage green and tall,
Converging walks, and fountains gay,
And terraces in trim array—   990
Beneath yon cypress spiring high,
With pine and cedar spreading wide
Their darksome boughs on either side,
In open moonlight doth she lie ;
Happy as others of her kind,   995
That, far from human neighbourhood,
Range unrestricted as the wind,
Through park, or chase, or savage wood.

But see the consecrated Maid
Emerging from a cedar shade   1000
To open moonshine, where the Doe
Beneath the cypress-spire is laid ;
Like a patch of April snow—
Upon a bed of herbage green,
Lingering in a woody glade   1005
Or behind a rocky screen—
Lonely relic ! which, if seen
By the shepherd, is passed by
With an inattentive eye.
Nor more regard doth She bestow   1010
Upon the uncomplaining Doe
Now couched at ease, though oft this day
Not unperplexed nor free from pain,
When she had tried, and tried in vain,
Approaching in her gentle way,   1015
To win some look of love, or gain
Encouragement to sport or play ;
Attempts which still the heart-sick Maid
Rejected, or with slight repaid.

Yet Emily is soothed ;—the breeze   1020
Came fraught with kindly sympathies.
As she approached yon rustic Shed
Hung with late-flowering woodbine,
    spread
Along the walls and overhead,
The fragrance of the breathing flowers
Revived a memory of those hours   1026
When here, in this remote alcove,

(While from the pendent woodbine came
Like odours, sweet as if the same)
A fondly-anxious Mother strove   1030
To teach her salutary fears
And mysteries above her years.
Yes, she is soothed : an Image faint,
And yet not faint—a presence bright
Returns to her—that blessèd Saint   1035
Who with mild looks and language mild
Instructed here her darling Child,
While yet a prattler on the knee,
To worship in simplicity
The invisible God, and take for guide
The faith reformed and purified.   1041

'Tis flown—the Vision, and the sense
Of that beguiling influence ;
"But oh ! thou Angel from above,
Mute Spirit of maternal love,   1045
That stood'st before my eyes, more clear
Than ghosts are fabled to appear
Sent upon embassies of fear ;
As thou thy presence hast to me
Vouchsafed, in radiant ministry   1050
Descend on Francis ; nor forbear
To greet him with a voice, and say ;—
'If hope be a rejected stay,
Do thou, my christian Son, beware
Of that most lamentable snare,   1055
The self-reliance of despair !'"

Then from within the embowered retreat
Where she had found a grateful seat
Perturbed she issues. She will go !
Herself will follow to the war,   1060
And clasp her Father's knees ;—ah, no !
She meets the insuperable bar,
The injunction by her Brother laid ;
His parting charge—but ill obeyed—
That interdicted all debate,   1065
All prayer for this cause or for that ;
All efforts that would turn aside
The headstrong current of their fate :
Her duty is to stand and wait ;
In resignation to abide   1070
The shock, AND FINALLY SECURE
O'ER PAIN AND GRIEF A TRIUMPH PURE.
—She feels it, and her pangs are checked.
But now, as silently she paced
The turf, and thought by thought was
    chased,   1075

Came One who, with sedate respect,
Approached, and, greeting her, thus
    spake;
"An old man's privilege I take:
Dark is the time—a woeful day!
Dear daughter of affliction, say   1080
How can I serve you? point the way."

"Rights have you, and may well be
    bold:
You with my Father have grown old
In friendship—strive—for his sake go—
Turn from us all the coming woe: 1085
This would I beg; but on my mind
A passive stillness is enjoined.
On you, if room for mortal aid
Be left, is no restriction laid;
You not forbidden to recline   1090
With hope upon the Will divine."

"Hope," said the old Man, "must
    abide
With all of us, whate'er betide.
In Craven's Wilds is many a den,
To shelter persecuted men: 1095
Far under ground is many a cave,
Where they might lie as in the grave,
Until this storm hath ceased to rave:
Or let them cross the River Tweed,
And be at once from peril freed!"   1100

"Ah tempt me not!" she faintly
    sighed;
"I will not counsel nor exhort,
With my condition satisfied;
But you, at least, may make report
Of what befalls;—be this your task—1105
This may be done;—'tis all I ask!"

She spake—and from the Lady's sight
The Sire, unconscious of his age,
Departed promptly as a Page
Bound on some errand of delight.   1110
—The noble Francis—wise as brave,
Thought he, may want not skill to save.
With hopes in tenderness concealed,
Unarmed he followed to the field;   1114
Him will I seek: the insurgent Powers
Are now besieging Barnard's Towers,—
"Grant that the Moon which shines this
    night
May guide them in a prudent flight!"

But quick the turns of chance and
    change,
And knowledge has a narrow range; 1120
Whence idle fears, and needless pain,
And wishes blind, and efforts vain.—
The Moon may shine, but cannot be
Their guide in flight—already she
Hath witnessed their captivity.   1125
She saw the desperate assault
Upon that hostile castle made;—
But dark and dismal is the vault
Where Norton and his sons are laid!
Disastrous issue!—he had said   1130
"This night yon faithless Towers must
    yield,
Or we for ever quit the field.
—Neville is utterly dismayed,
For promise fails of Howard's aid;
And Dacre to our call replies   1135
That *he* is unprepared to rise.
My heart is sick;—this weary pause
Must needs be fatal to our cause.
The breach is open—on the wall,
This night,—the Banner shall be plant-
    ed!"   1140
—'Twas done: his Sons were with him—
    all;
They belt him round with hearts un-
    daunted
And others follow;—Sire and Son
Leap down into the court;—"'Tis won"—
They shout aloud—but Heaven decreed
That with their joyful shout should close
The triumph of a desperate deed
Which struck with terror friends and
    foes!
The friend shrinks back—the foe recoils
From Norton and his filial band;   1150
But they, now caught within the toils,
Against a thousand cannot stand;—
The foe from numbers courage drew,
And overpowered that gallant few.
"A rescue for the Standard!" cried 1155
The Father from within the walls;
But, see, the sacred Standard falls!—
Confusion through the Camp spread
    wide:
Some fled; and some their fears detained:
But ere the Moon had sunk to rest   1160
In her pale chambers of the west,
Of that rash levy nought remained.

Canto Fifth.

High on a point of rugged ground
Among the wastes of Rylstone Fell,
Above the loftiest ridge or mound   1165
Where foresters or shepherds dwell,
An edifice of warlike frame
Stands single—Norton Tower its name—
It fronts all quarters, and looks round
O'er path and road, and plain and dell,
Dark moor, and gleam of pool and stream,
Upon a prospect without bound.

The summit of this bold ascent—
Though bleak and bare, and seldom free
As Pendle-hill or Pennygent   1175
From wind, or frost, or vapours wet—
Had often heard the sound of glee
When there the youthful Nortons met,
To practise games and archery :   1179
How proud and happy they ! the crowd
Of Lookers-on how pleased and proud !
And from the scorching noon-tide sun,
From showers, or when the prize was
        won,
They to the Tower withdrew, and there
Would mirth run round, with generous
        fare ;   1185
And the stern old Lord of Rylstone-hall
Was happiest, proudest, of them all !

But now, his Child, with anguish pale,
Upon the height walks to and fro ;
'Tis well that she hath heard the tale,   1190
Received the bitterness of woe :
For she *had* hoped, had hoped and feared,
Such rights did feeble nature claim ;
And oft her steps had hither steered,
Though not unconscious of self-blame ;
For she her brother's charge revered,   1196
His farewell words ; and by the same,
Yea, by her brother's very name,
Had, in her solitude, been cheered.   1199

Beside the lonely watch-tower stood
That grey-haired Man of gentle blood,
Who with her Father had grown old
In friendship ; rival hunters they,
And fellow warriors in their day ;
To Rylstone he the tidings brought ;   1205
Then on this height the Maid had sought,
And, gently as he could, had told

The end of that dire Tragedy,
Which it had been his lot to see.

To him the Lady turned ; "You said
That Francis lives, *he* is not dead ?"   1211

"Your noble brother hath been spared ;
To take his life they have not dared ;
On him and on his high endeavour   1214
The light of praise shall shine for ever !
Nor did he (such Heaven's will) in vain
His solitary course maintain ;
Not vainly struggled in the might
Of duty, seeing with clear sight ;
He was their comfort to the last,   1220
Their joy till every pang was past.

"I witnessed when to York they
        came—
What, Lady, if their feet were tied ;
They might deserve a good Man's blame ;
But marks of infamy and shame—   1225
These were their triumph, these their
        pride ;
Nor wanted 'mid the pressing crowd
Deep feeling, that found utterance loud,
'Lo, Francis comes,' there were who cried,
'A Prisoner once, but now set free !   1230
'Tis well, for he the worst defied
Through force of natural piety ;
He rose not in this quarrel, he,
For concord's sake and England's good,
Suit to his Brothers often made   1235
With tears, and of his Father prayed—
And when he had in vain withstood
Their purpose—then did he divide,
He parted from them ; but at their side
Now walks in unanimity.   1240
Then peace to cruelty and scorn,
While to the prison they are borne,
Peace, peace to all indignity !'

"And so in Prison were they laid—
Oh hear me, hear me, gentle Maid,   1245
For I am come with power to bless,
By scattering gleams, through your dis-
        tress,
Of a redeeming happiness.
Me did a reverent pity move
And privilege of ancient love   1250
And, in your service making bold,
Entrance I gained to that strong-hold."

"Your Father gave me cordial greet-
   ing;
But to his purposes, that burned
Within him, instantly returned: 1255
He was commanding and entreating,
And said—'We need not stop, my Son!
Thoughts press, and time is hurrying
   on'—
And so to Francis he renewed   1259
His words, more calmly thus pursued.

  "'Might this our enterprise have sped,
Change wide and deep the Land had seen,
A renovation from the dead,
A spring-tide of immortal green: 1264
The darksome altars would have blazed
Like stars when clouds are rolled away;
Salvation to all eyes that gazed,
Once more the Rood had been upraised
To spread its arms, and stand for aye.
Then, then—had I survived to see   1270
New life in Bolton Priory;
The voice restored, the eye of Truth
Re-opened that inspired my youth;
To see her in her pomp arrayed—
This Banner (for such vow I made)   1275
Should on the consecrated breast
Of that same Temple have found rest,
I would myself have hung it high,
Fit offering of glad victory!   1279

  "'A shadow of such thought remains
To cheer this sad and pensive time;
A solemn fancy yet sustains
One feeble Being—bids me climb
Even to the last—one effort more
To attest my Faith, if not restore.   1285

  "'Hear then,' said he, 'while I im-
   part,
My Son, the last wish of my heart.
The Banner strive thou to regain;
And, if the endeavour prove not vain,
Bear it—to whom if not to thee   1290
Shall I this lonely thought consign?—
Bear it to Bolton Priory,
And lay it on Saint Mary's shrine;
To wither in the sun and breeze
'Mid those decaying sanctities.   1295
There let at least the gift be laid,
The testimony there displayed;

Bold proof that with no selfish aim,
But for lost Faith and Christ's dear
   name,
I helmeted a brow though white,   1300
And took a place in all men's sight;
Yea, offered up this noble Brood,
This fair unrivalled Brotherhood,
And turned away from thee, my Son!
And left—but be the rest unsaid,   1305
The name untouched, the tear unshed;—
My wish is known, and I have done:
Now promise, grant this one request,
This dying prayer, and be thou blest!'

  "Then Francis answered—'Trust thy
   Son,   1310
For, with God's will, it shall be done!'—

  "The pledge obtained, the solemn word
Thus scarcely given, a noise was heard,
And Officers appeared in state
To lead the prisoners to their fate.   1315
They rose, oh! wherefore should I fear
To tell, or, Lady, you to hear?
They rose—embraces none were given—
They stood like trees when earth and
   heaven   1319
Are calm; they knew each other's worth,
And reverently the Band went forth.
They met, when they had reached the door,
One with profane and harsh intent
Placed there—that he might go before
And, with that rueful Banner borne   1325
Aloft in sign of taunting scorn,
Conduct them to their punishment:
So cruel Sussex, unrestrained
By human feeling, had ordained.
The unhappy Banner Francis saw,   1330
And, with a look of calm command
Inspiring universal awe,
He took it from the soldier's hand;
And all the people that stood round   1334
Confirmed the deed in peace profound.
—High transport did the Father shed
Upon his Son—and they were led,
Led on, and yielded up their breath;
Together died, a happy death!—
But Francis, soon as he had braved   1340
That insult, and the Banner saved,
Athwart the unresisting tide
Of the spectators occupied

In admiration or dismay,
Bore instantly his Charge away."   1345

These things, which thus had in the
    sight
And hearing passed of Him who stood
With Emily, on the Watch-tower height,
In Rylstone's woeful neighbourhood,
He told; and oftentimes with voice   1350
Of power to comfort or rejoice;
For deepest sorrows that aspire
Go high, no transport ever higher.
"Yes—God is rich in mercy," said
The old Man to the silent Maid,   1355
"Yet, Lady! shines, through this black
    night,
One star of aspect heavenly bright;
Your brother lives—he lives—is come
Perhaps already to his home;
Then let us leave this dreary place."   1360
She yielded, and with gentle pace,
Though without one uplifted look,
To Rylstone-hall her way she took.

Canto Sixth.

WHY comes not Francis?—From the
    doleful City
He fled,—and, in his flight, could hear   1365
The death-sounds of the Minster-bell:
That sullen stroke pronounced farewell
To Marmaduke, cut off from pity!
To Ambrose that! and then a knell
For him, the sweet half-opened Flower!
For all—all dying in one hour!   1371
—Why comes not Francis? Thoughts of
    love
Should bear him to his Sister dear
With the fleet motion of a dove;
Yea, like a heavenly messenger   1375
Of speediest wing, should he appear.
Why comes he not?—for westward fast
Along the plain of York he past;
Reckless of what impels or leads,
Unchecked he hurries on;—nor heeds 1380
The sorrow, through the Villages,
Spread by triumphant cruelties
Of vengeful military force,
And punishment without remorse.
He marked not, heard not, as he fled; 1385
All but the suffering heart was dead
For him abandoned to blank awe,

To vacancy, and horror strong:
And the first object which he saw,
With conscious sight, as he swept along—
It was the Banner in his hand!   1391
He felt—and made a sudden stand.

He looked about like one betrayed:
What hath he done? what promise made?
Oh weak, weak moment! to what end 1395
Can such a vain oblation tend,
And he the Bearer?—Can he go
Carrying this instrument of woe,
And find, find anywhere, a right
To excuse him in his Country's sight? 1400
No; will not all men deem the change
A downward course, perverse and strange?
Here is it;—but how? when? must she,
The unoffending Emily,
Again this piteous object see?   1405

Such conflict long did he maintain,
Nor liberty nor rest could gain:
His own life into danger brought
By this sad burden—even that thought,
Exciting self-suspicion strong,   1410
Swayed the brave man to his wrong.
And how—unless it were the sense
Of all-disposing Providence,
Its will unquestionably shown—
How has the Banner clung so fast   1415
To a palsied, and unconscious hand;
Clung to the hand to which it passed
Without impediment? And why
But that Heaven's purpose might be
    known
Doth now no hindrance meet his eye, 1420
No intervention, to withstand
Fulfilment of a Father's prayer
Breathed to a Son forgiven, and blest
When all resentments were at rest,
And life in death laid the heart bare?—
Then, like a spectre sweeping by,   1426
Rushed through his mind the prophecy
Of utter desolation made
To Emily in the yew-tree shade:
He sighed, submitting will and power 1430
To the stern embrace of that grasping
    hour.
"No choice is left, the deed is mine—
Dead are they, dead!—and I will go,
And, for their sakes, come weal or woe,
Will lay the Relic on the shrine."   1435

So forward with a steady will
He went, and traversed plain and hill;
And up the vale of Wharf his way
Pursued;—and, at the dawn of day,
Attained a summit whence his eyes 1440
Could see the Tower of Bolton rise.
There Francis for a moment's space
Made halt—but hark! a noise behind
Of horsemen at an eager pace!
He heard, and with misgiving mind. 1445
—'Tis Sir George Bowes who leads the
    Band:
They come, by cruel Sussex sent;
Who, when the Nortons from the hand
Of death had drunk their punishment,
Bethought him, angry and ashamed, 1450
How Francis, with the Banner claimed
As his own charge, had disappeared,
By all the standers-by revered.
His whole bold carriage (which had
    quelled
Thus far the Opposer, and repelled 1455
All censure, enterprise so bright
That even bad men had vainly striven
Against that overcoming light)
Was then reviewed, and prompt word
    given,
That to what place soever fled 1460
He should be seized, alive or dead.

The troop of horse have gained the
    height
Where Francis stood in open sight.
They hem him round—"Behold the
    proof,"
They cried, "the Ensign in his hand! 1465
He did not arm, he walked aloof!
For why?—to save his Father's land;
Worst Traitor of them all is he,
A Traitor dark and cowardly!"

"I am no Traitor," Francis said, 1470
"Though this unhappy freight I bear;
And must not part with. But beware;—
Err not, by hasty zeal misled,
Nor do a suffering Spirit wrong,
Whose self-reproaches are too strong!"
At this he from the beaten road 1476
Retreated towards a brake of thorn,
That like a place of vantage showed;
And there stood bravely, though forlorn.

In self-defence with warlike brow 1480
He stood,—nor weaponless was now;
He from a Soldier's hand had snatched
A spear,—and, so protected, watched
The Assailants, turning round and round;
But from behind with treacherous wound
A Spearman brought him to the ground.
The guardian lance, as Francis fell,
Dropped from him; but his other hand
The Banner clenched; till, from out the
    Band,
One, the most eager for the prize, 1490
Rushed in; and—while, O grief to tell!
A glimmering sense still left, with eyes
Unclosed the noble Francis lay—
Seized it, as hunters seize their prey;
But not before the warm life-blood 1495
Had tinged more deeply, as it flowed,
The wounds the broidered Banner
    showed,
Thy fatal work, O Maiden, innocent as
    good!

Proudly the Horsemen bore away
The Standard; and where Francis lay 1500
There was he left alone, unwept,
And for two days unnoticed slept.
For at that time bewildering fear
Possessed the country, far and near;
But, on the third day, passing by 1505
One of the Norton Tenantry
Espied the uncovered Corse; the Man
Shrunk as he recognised the face,
And to the nearest homesteads ran
And called the people to the place. 1510
—How desolate is Rylstone-hall!
This was the instant thought of all;
And if the lonely Lady there
Should be; to her they cannot bear
This weight of anguish and despair. 1515
So, when upon sad thoughts had prest
Thoughts sadder still, they deemed it
    best
That, if the Priest should yield assent
And no one hinder their intent,
Then, they, for Christian pity's sake, 1520
In holy ground a grave would make;
And straightway buried he should be
In the Churchyard of the Priory.

Apart, some little space, was made
The grave where Francis must be laid.

In no confusion or neglect   1526
This did they,—but in pure respect
That he was born of gentle blood;
And that there was no neighbourhood
Of kindred for him in that ground: 1530
So to the Churchyard they are bound,
Bearing the body on a bier;
And psalms they sing—a holy sound
That hill and vale with sadness hear.

But Emily hath raised her head,   1535
And is again disquieted;
She must behold!—so many gone,
Where is the solitary One?
And forth from Rylstone-hall stepped
she,—
To seek her Brother forth she went, 1540
And tremblingly her course she bent
Toward Bolton's ruined Priory.
She comes, and in the vale hath heard
The funeral dirge;—she sees the knot
Of people, sees them in one spot—   1545
And darting like a wounded bird
She reached the grave, and with her
breast
Upon the ground received the rest,—
The consummation, the whole ruth
And sorrow of this final truth!   1550

Canto Seventh.

"Powers there are
That touch each other to the quick—in modes
Which the gross world no sense hath to perceive,
No soul to dream of[1]."

THOU Spirit, whose angelic hand
Was to the harp a strong command,
Called the submissive strings to wake
In glory for this Maiden's sake,
Say, Spirit! whither hath she fled   1555
To hide her poor afflicted head?
What mighty forest in its gloom
Enfolds her?—is a rifted tomb
Within the wilderness her seat?
Some island which the wild waves
beat—   1560
Is that the Sufferer's last retreat?
Or some aspiring rock, that shrouds
Its perilous front in mists and clouds?

High-climbing rock, low sunless dale,
Sea, desert, what do these avail?   1565
Oh take her anguish and her fears
Into a deep recess of years!

'Tis done;—despoil and desolation
O'er Rylstone's fair domain have blown;
Pools, terraces, and walks are sown   1570
With weeds; the bowers are overthrown,
Or have given way to slow mutation,
While, in their ancient habitation
The Norton name hath been unknown.
The lordly Mansion of its pride   1575
Is stripped; the ravage hath spread wide
Through park and field, a perishing
That mocks the gladness of the Spring!
And, with this silent gloom agreeing,
Appears a joyless human Being,   1580
Of aspect such as if the waste
Were under her dominion placed.
Upon a primrose bank, her throne
Of quietness, she sits alone;
Among the ruins of a wood,   1585
Erewhile a covert bright and green,
And where full many a brave tree stood,
That used to spread its boughs, and ring
With the sweet bird's carolling.
Behold her, like a virgin Queen,   1590
Neglecting in imperial state
These outward images of fate,
And carrying inward a serene
And perfect sway, through many a thought
Of chance and change, that hath been
brought   1595
To the subjection of a holy,
Though stern and rigorous, melancholy!
The like authority, with grace
Of awfulness, is in her face,—
There hath she fixed it; yet it seems 1600
To o'ershadow by no native right
That face, which cannot lose the gleams,
Lose utterly the tender gleams,
Of gentleness and meek delight,
And loving-kindness ever bright: 1605
Such is her sovereign mien:—her dress
(A vest with woollen cincture tied,
A hood of mountain-wool undyed)
Is homely,—fashioned to express
A wandering Pilgrim's humbleness.   1610

And she *hath* wandered, long and far,
Beneath the light of sun and star;

[1] See *Address to Kilchurn Castle* (*Memorials of a Tour in Scotland*, 1803), ll. 6–9.—ED

Hath roamed in trouble and in grief,
Driven forward like a withered leaf,
Yea, like a ship at random blown   1615
To distant places and unknown.
But now she dares to seek a haven
Among her native wilds of Craven;
Hath seen again her Father's roof,
And put her fortitude to proof;   1620
The mighty sorrow hath been borne,
And she is thoroughly forlorn:
Her soul doth in itself stand fast,
Sustained by memory of the past
And strength of Reason; held above 1625
The infirmities of mortal love;
Undaunted, lofty, calm, and stable,
And awfully impenetrable.

And so—beneath a mouldered tree,
A self-surviving leafless oak   1630
By unregarded age from stroke
Of ravage saved—sate Emily.
There did she rest, with head reclined,
Herself most like a stately flower,
(Such have I seen) whom chance of
      birth   1635
Hath separated from its kind,
To live and die in a shady bower,
Single on the gladsome earth.

When, with a noise like distant thunder,
A troop of deer came sweeping by; 1640
And, suddenly, behold a wonder!
For One, among those rushing deer,
A single One, in mid career
Hath stopped, and fixed her large full eye
Upon the Lady Emily;   1645
A Doe most beautiful, clear-white,
A radiant creature, silver-bright!

Thus checked, a little while it stayed;
A little thoughtful pause it made;
And then advanced with stealth-like
      pace,   1650
Drew softly near her, and more near—
Looked round—but saw no cause for fear;
So to her feet the Creature came,
And laid its head upon her knee,
And looked into the Lady's face,   1655
A look of pure benignity,
And fond unclouded memory.
It is, thought Emily, the same,
The very Doe of other years!—

The pleading look the Lady viewed, 1660
And, by her gushing thoughts subdued,
She melted into tears—
A flood of tears that flowed apace
Upon the happy Creature's face.

Oh, moment ever blest! O Pair   1665
Beloved of Heaven, Heaven's chosen care,
This was for you a precious greeting;
And may it prove a fruitful meeting!
Joined are they, and the sylvan Doe
Can she depart? can she forego   1670
The Lady, once her playful peer,
And now her sainted Mistress dear?
And will not Emily receive
This lovely chronicler of things
Long past, delights and sorrowings? 1675
Lone Sufferer! will not she believe
The promise in that speaking face;
And welcome, as a gift of grace,
The saddest thought the Creature brings?

That day, the first of a re-union   1680
Which was to teem with high communion,
That day of balmy April weather,
They tarried in the wood together.
And when, ere fall of evening dew,
She from her sylvan haunt withdrew, 1685
The White Doe tracked with faithful pace
The Lady to her dwelling-place;
That nook where, on paternal ground,
A habitation she had found,
The Master of whose humble board 1690
Once owned her Father for his Lord;
A hut, by tufted trees defended,
Where Rylstone brook with Wharf is
      blended.

When Emily by morning light
Went forth, the Doe stood there in
      sight.   1695
She shrunk:—with one frail shock of pain
Received and followed by a prayer,
She saw the Creature once again;
Shun will she not, she feels, will bear;—
But, wheresoever she looked round, 1700
All now was trouble-haunted ground;
And therefore now she deems it good
Once more this restless neighbourhood
To leave.—Unwooed, yet unforbidden,
The White Doe followed up the vale, 1705
Up to another cottage, hidden

In the deep fork of Amerdale;
And there may Emily restore
Herself, in spots unseen before.
—Why tell of mossy rock, or tree,   1710
By lurking Dernbrook's pathless side,
Haunts of a strengthening amity
That calmed her, cheered, and fortified?
For she hath ventured now to read
Of time, and place, and thought, and
       deed—   1715
Endless history that lies
In her silent Follower's eyes;
Who with a power like human reason
Discerns the favourable season,
Skilled to approach or to retire,—   1720
From looks conceiving her desire;
From look, deportment, voice, or mien,
That vary to the heart within.
If she too passionately wreathed
Her arms, or over-deeply breathed,   1725
Walked quick or slowly, every mood
In its degree was understood;
Then well may their accord be true,
And kindliest intercourse ensue.
—Oh! surely 'twas a gentle rousing   1730
When she by sudden glimpse espied
The White Doe on the Mountain browsing,
Or in the meadow wandered wide!
How pleased, when down the Straggler sank
Beside her, on some sunny bank!   1735
How soothed, when in thick bower en-
       closed,
They, like a nested pair, reposed!
Fair Vision! when it crossed the Maid
Within some rocky cavern laid,
The dark cave's portal gliding by,   1740
White as whitest cloud on high
Floating through the azure sky.
—What now is left for pain or fear?
That Presence, dearer and more dear,
While they, side by side, were straying,
And the shepherd's pipe was playing,
Did now a very gladness yield
At morning to the dewy field,
And with a deeper peace endued
The hour of moonlight solitude.   1750

With her Companion, in such frame
Of mind, to Rylstone back she came;
And, ranging through the wasted groves,
Received the memory of old loves,

Undisturbed and undistrest,   1755
Into a soul which now was blest
With a soft spring-day of holy,
Mild, and grateful, melancholy:
Not sunless gloom or unenlightened,
But by tender fancies brightened.   1760

When the bells of Rylstone played
Their sabbath music—"God us aÿde!"
That was the sound they seemed to speak;
Inscriptive legend which I ween
May on these holy bells be seen,   1765
That legend and her Grandsire's name;
And oftentimes the Lady meek
Had in her childhood read the same;
Words which she slighted at that day;
But now, when such sad change was
       wrought,   1770
And of that lonely name she thought,
The bells of Rylstone seemed to say,
While she sate listening in the shade,
With vocal music, "God us aÿde;"
And all the hills were glad to bear   1775
Their part in this effectual prayer.

Nor lacked she Reason's firmest power;
But with the White Doe at her side
Up would she climb to Norton Tower,
And thence look round her far and
       wide,   1780
Her fate there measuring;—all is stilled,—
The weak One hath subdued her heart;
Behold the prophecy fulfilled,
Fulfilled, and she sustains her part!
But here her Brother's words have
       failed;   1785
Here hath a milder doom prevailed;
That she, of him and all bereft,
Hath yet this faithful Partner left;
This one Associate that disproves
His words remains for her, and loves. 1790
If tears are shed, they do not fall
For loss of him—for one, or all;
Yet sometimes, sometimes doth she weep
Moved gently in her soul's soft sleep;
A few tears down her cheek descend   1795
For this her last and living Friend.

Bless, tender Hearts, their mutual lot,
And bless for both this savage spot;
Which Emily doth sacred hold
For reasons dear and manifold—   1800

Here hath she, here before her sight,
Close to the summit of this height,
The grassy rock-encircled Pound
In which the Creature first was found.
So beautiful the timid Thrall   1805
(A spotless Youngling white as foam)
Her youngest Brother brought it home;
The youngest, then a lusty boy,
Bore it, or led, to Rylstone-hall
With heart brimful of pride and joy!   1810

But most to Bolton's sacred Pile,
On favouring nights, she loved to go;
There ranged through cloister, court, and aisle,
Attended by the soft-paced Doe;
Nor feared she in the still moonshine   1815
To look upon Saint Mary's shrine;
Nor on the lonely turf that showed
Where Francis slept in his last abode.
For that she came; there oft she sate
Forlorn, but not disconsolate: 1820
And when she from the abyss returned
Of thought, she neither shrunk nor mourned;
Was happy that she lived to greet
Her mute Companion as it lay
In love and pity at her feet;   1825
How happy in its turn to meet
The recognition! the mild glance
Beamed from that gracious countenance;
Communication, like the ray
Of a new morning, to the nature   1830
And prospects of the inferior Creature!

A mortal Song we sing, by dower
Encouraged of celestial power;
Power which the viewless Spirit shed
By whom we were first visited;   1835
Whose voice we heard, whose hand and wings
Swept like a breeze the conscious strings,
When, left in solitude, erewhile
We stood before this ruined Pile,
And, quitting unsubstantial dreams,   1840
Sang in this Presence kindred themes;
Distress and desolation spread
Through human hearts, and pleasure dead,—
Dead—but to live again on earth,
A second and yet nobler birth;   1845

Dire overthrow, and yet how high
The re-ascent in sanctity!
From fair to fairer; day by day
A more divine and loftier way!
Even such this blessèd Pilgrim trod,   1850
By sorrow lifted towards her God;
Uplifted to the purest sky
Of undisturbed mortality.
Her own thoughts loved she; and could bend
A dear look to her lowly Friend;   1855
There stopped; her thirst was satisfied
With what this innocent spring supplied:
Her sanction inwardly she bore,
And stood apart from human cares:
But to the world returned no more,   1860
Although with no unwilling mind
Help did she give at need, and joined
The Wharfdale peasants in their prayers.
At length, thus faintly, faintly tied
To earth, she was set free, and died.   1865
Thy soul, exalted Emily,
Maid of the blasted family,
Rose to the God from whom it came!
—In Rylstone Church her mortal frame
Was buried by her Mother's side.   1870

Most glorious sunset! and a ray
Survives—the twilight of this day—
In that fair Creature whom the fields
Support, and whom the forest shields;
Who, having filled a holy place,   1875
Partakes, in her degree, Heaven's grace;
And bears a memory and a mind
Raised far above the law of kind;
Haunting the spots with lonely cheer
Which her dear Mistress once held dear: 1880
Loves most what Emily loved most—
The enclosure of this churchyard ground;
Here wanders like a gliding ghost,
And every sabbath here is found;
Comes with the people when the bells   1885
Are heard among the moorland dells,
Finds entrance through yon arch, where way
Lies open on the sabbath day;
Here walks amid the mournful waste
Of prostrate altars, shrines defaced,   1890
And floors encumbered with rich show
Of fret-work imagery laid low;

Paces softly, or makes halt,
By fractured cell, or tomb, or vault;
By plate of monumental brass   1895
Dim-gleaming among weeds and grass,
And sculptured Forms of Warriors brave:
But chiefly by that single grave,
That one sequestered hillock green,
The pensive visitant is seen.   1900
There doth the gentle Creature lie

With those adversities unmoved;
Calm spectacle, by earth and sky
In their benignity approved!
And aye, methinks, this hoary Pile,   1905
Subdued by outrage and decay,
Looks down upon her with a smile,
A gracious smile, that seems to say—
"Thou, thou art not a Child of Time,
But Daughter of the Eternal Prime!"   1910

ECCLESIASTICAL SONNETS.

IN SERIES[1].

[Composed mostly in 1821.—Published 1822.]

—◆—

PART I.

FROM THE INTRODUCTION OF CHRISTIANITY INTO BRITAIN TO THE CONSUMMATION OF THE PAPAL DOMINION.

"A verse may catch a wandering Soul, that flies
Profounder Tracts, and by a blest surprise
Convert delight into a Sacrifice[2]."

I.

INTRODUCTION.

I, who accompanied with faithful pace
Cerulean Duddon from its cloud-fed
    spring,
And loved with spirit ruled by his to
    sing
Of mountain-quiet and boon nature's
    grace;
I, who essayed the nobler Stream to
    trace   5
Of Liberty, and smote the plausive
    string
Till the checked torrent, proudly triumph-
    ing,
Won for herself a lasting resting-place;
Now seek upon the heights of Time the
    source
Of a HOLY RIVER, on whose banks are
    found   10
Sweet pastoral flowers, and laurels that
    have crowned

Full oft the unworthy brow of lawless
    force;
And, for delight of him who tracks its
    course,
Immortal amaranth and palms abound.

II.

CONJECTURES.

IF there be prophets on whose spirits
    rest
Past things, revealed like future, they
    can tell
What Powers, presiding o'er the sacred
    well
Of Christian Faith, this savage Island
    blessed
With its first bounty. Wandering through
    the west,   5
Did holy Paul[3] a while in Britain dwell,
And call the Fountain forth by miracle,
And with dread signs the nascent Stream
    invest?

---

[1] The *Ecclesiastical Sonnets* (first so called in 1837; previously *Ecclesiastical Sketches*) were writ-
ten for the most part in 1821, and published in 1822. Chronological notes are attached only to those
sonnets to which this observation does not apply.—ED.

[2] This motto, from George Herbert, was added in 1827.—ED.   [3] See Note, p. 920.

Or He, whose bonds dropped off, whose
    prison doors
Flew open, by an Angel's voice un-
    barred ?   10
Or some of humbler name, to these wild
    shores
Storm-driven; who, having seen the cup
    of woe
Pass from their Master, sojourned here to
    guard
The precious Current they had taught to
    flow ?

III.

TREPIDATION OF THE DRUIDS.

SCREAMS round the Arch-druid's brow the
    sea-mew [1]—white
As Menai's foam; and toward the mystic
    ring
Where Augurs stand, the Future ques-
    tioning,
Slowly the cormorant aims her heavy
    flight,
Portending ruin to each baleful rite   5
That, in the lapse of ages, hath crept o'er
Diluvian truths, and patriarchal lore.
Haughty the Bard : can these meek doc-
    trines blight
His transports? wither his heroic strains?
But all shall be fulfilled;—the Julian
    spear   10
A way first opened; and, with Roman
    chains,
The tidings come of Jesus crucified;
They come—they spread—the weak, the
    suffering, hear;
Receive the faith, and in the hope abide.

IV.

DRUIDICAL EXCOMMUNICATION.

MERCY and Love have met thee on thy
    road,
Thou wretched Outcast, from the gift of
    fire
And food cut off by sacerdotal ire,

---

[1] This water-fowl was, among the Druids, an
emblem of those traditions connected with the
Deluge that made an important part of their
mysteries. The Cormorant was a bird of bad
omen.

From every sympathy that Man be-
    stowed !
Yet shall it claim our reverence, that to
    God,   5
Ancient of days ! that to the eternal Sire,
These jealous Ministers of law aspire,
As to the one sole fount whence wisdom
    flowed,
Justice, and order. Tremblingly escaped,
As if with prescience of the coming
    storm,   10
That intimation when the stars were
    shaped;
And still, 'mid yon thick woods, the
    primal truth
Glimmers through many a superstitious
    form
That fills the Soul with unavailing ruth.

V.

UNCERTAINTY.

DARKNESS surrounds us; seeking, we are
    lost
On Snowdon's wilds, amid Brigantian
    coves,
Or where the solitary shepherd roves
Along the plain of Sarum, by the ghost
Of Time and shadows of Tradition crost;
And where the boatman of the Western
    Isles   6
Slackens his course—to mark those holy
    piles
Which yet survive on bleak Iona's coast.
Nor these, nor monuments of eldest
    name,
Nor Taliesin's unforgotten lays,   10
Nor characters of Greek or Roman fame,
To an unquestionable Source have led;
Enough—if eyes, that sought the foun-
    tain-head
In vain, upon the growing Rill may gaze.

VI.

PERSECUTION.

LAMENT ! for Dioclet1an's fiery sword
Works busy as the lightning; but instinct
With malice ne'er to deadliest weapon
    linked,
Which God's ethereal storehouses afford:

Against the Followers of the incarnate
   Lord   5
It rages;—some are smitten in the field—
Some pierced to the heart through the
   ineffectual shield
Of sacred home;—with pomp are others
   gored
And dreadful respite. Thus was Alban
   tried,
England's first Martyr, whom no threats
   could shake;   10
Self-offered victim, for his friend he died,
And for the faith; nor shall his name
   forsake
That Hill, whose flowery platform seems
   to rise
By Nature decked for holiest sacrifice[1].

VII.

RECOVERY.

As, when a storm hath ceased, the birds
   regain
Their cheerfulness, and busily retrim
Their nests, or chant a gratulating hymn
To the blue ether and bespangled plain;
Even so, in many a re-constructed fane, 5
Have the survivors of this Storm renewed
Their holy rites with vocal gratitude:
And solemn ceremonials they ordain
To celebrate their great deliverance;
Most feelingly instructed 'mid their
   fear—   10
That persecution, blind with rage ex-
   treme,
May not the less, through Heaven's mild
   countenance,
Even in her own despite, both feed and
   cheer;
For all things are less dreadful than they
   seem.

VIII.

TEMPTATIONS FROM ROMAN REFINE-
MENTS.

WATCH, and be firm! for soul-subduing
   vice,
Heart-killing luxury, on your steps await.

---

[1] See Note, p. 920.

Fair houses, baths, and banquets delicate,
And temples flashing, bright as polar
   ice,
Their radiance through the woods—may
   yet suffice   5
To sap your hardy virtue, and abate
Your love of Him upon whose forehead
   sate
The crown of thorns; whose life-blood
   flowed, the price
Of your redemption. Shun the insidious
   arts
That Rome provides, less dreading from
   her frown   10
Than from her wily praise, her peaceful
   gown,
Language, and letters;—these, though
   fondly viewed
As humanising graces, are but parts
And instruments of deadliest servitude!

IX.

DISSENSIONS.

THAT heresies should strike (if truth be
   scanned
Presumptuously) their roots both wide
   and deep,
Is natural as dreams to feverish sleep.
Lo! Discord at the altar dares to stand
Uplifting toward high Heaven her fiery
   brand,   5
A cherished Priestess of the new-bap-
   tized!
But chastisement shall follow peace de-
   spised.
The Pictish cloud darkens the enervate
   land
By Rome abandoned; vain are suppliant
   cries,
And prayers that would undo her forced
   farewell;   10
For she returns not.—Awed by her own
   knell,
She casts the Britons upon strange
   Allies,
Soon to become more dreaded enemies
Than heartless misery called them to
   repel.

X.

STRUGGLE OF THE BRITONS AGAINST THE BARBARIANS.

RISE !—they *have* risen : of brave Aneurin
    ask
How they have scourged old foes, per-
    fidious friends :
The Spirit of Caractacus descends
Upon the Patriots, animates their task ;—
Amazement runs before the towering
    casque   5
Of Arthur, bearing through the stormy
    field
The virgin sculptured on his Christian
    shield :—
Stretched in the sunny light of victory
    bask
The Host that followed Urien as he strode
O'er heaps of slain ;—from Cambrian
    wood and moss   10
Druids descend, auxiliars of the Cross ;
Bards, nursed on blue Plinlimmon's still
    abode,
Rush on the fight, to harps preferring
    swords,
And everlasting deeds to burning words !

XI.

SAXON CONQUEST.

NOR wants the cause the panic-striking
    aid
Of hallelujahs [1] tost from hill to hill—
For instant victory. But Heaven's high
    will
Permits a second and a darker shade
Of Pagan night. Afflicted and dismayed,
The Relics of the sword flee to the moun-
    tains :   6
O wretched Land ! whose tears have
    flowed like fountains ;
Whose arts and honours in the dust are
    laid
By men yet scarcely conscious of a care
For other monuments than those of
    Earth ;   10
Who, as the fields and woods have given
    them birth,

Will build their savage fortunes only
    there ;
Content, if foss, and barrow, and the
    girth
Of long-drawn rampart, witness what
    they were.

XII.

MONASTERY OF OLD BANGOR [2].

THE oppression of the tumult—wrath and
    scorn—
The tribulation—and the gleaming blades—
Such is the impetuous spirit that per-
    vades
The song of Taliesin ;—Ours shall mourn
The *unarmed* Host who by their prayers
    would turn   5
The sword from Bangor's walls, and guard
    the store
Of Aboriginal and Roman lore,
And Christian monuments, that now
    must burn
To senseless ashes. Mark ! how all things
    swerve
From their known course, or vanish like
    a dream ;   10
Another language spreads from coast to
    coast ;
Only perchance some melancholy Stream
And some indignant Hills old names pre-
    serve,
When laws, and creeds, and people all are
    lost !

XIII.

CASUAL INCITEMENT.

A BRIGHT-HAIRED company of youthful
    slaves,
Beautiful strangers, stand within the
    pale
Of a sad market, ranged for public sale,
Where Tiber's stream the immortal City
    laves :
ANGLI by name ; and not an ANGEL
    waves   5
His wing who could seem lovelier to
    man's eye
Than they appear to holy Gregory ;

---

[1] See Note, p. 921.

[2] See Note, p. 921.

Who, having learnt that name, salvation craves
For Them, and for their Land. The earnest Sire,
His questions urging, feels, in slender ties   10
Of chiming sound, commanding sympathies;
DE-IRIANS—he would save them from God's IRE;
Subjects of Saxon ÆLLA—they shall sing
Glad HALLE-lujahs to the eternal King!

XIV.

GLAD TIDINGS.

FOR ever hallowed be this morning fair,
Blest be the unconscious shore on which ye tread,
And blest the silver Cross, which ye, instead
Of martial banner, in procession bear;
The Cross preceding Him who floats in air,   5
The pictured Saviour!—By Augustin led,
They come—and onward travel without dread,
Chanting in barbarous ears a tuneful prayer—
Sung for themselves, and those whom they would free!
Rich conquest waits them:—the tempestuous sea   10
Of Ignorance, that ran so rough and high
And heeded not the voice of clashing swords,
These good men humble by a few bare words,
And calm with fear of God's divinity.

XV.

PAULINUS[1].

BUT to remote Northumbria's royal Hall,
Where thoughtful Edwin, tutored in the school
Of sorrow, still maintains a heathen rule,
Who comes with functions apostolical?
Mark him, of shoulders curved, and stature tall,   5

Black hair, and vivid eye, and meagre cheek,
His prominent feature like an eagle's beak;
A Man whose aspect doth at once appal
And strike with reverence. The Monarch leans
Toward the pure truths this Delegate propounds,   10
Repeatedly his own deep mind he sounds
With careful hesitation,—then convenes
A synod of his Councillors:—give ear,
And what a pensive Sage doth utter, hear!

XVI.

PERSUASION.

"MAN'S life is like a Sparrow, mighty King!
That—while at banquet with your Chiefs you sit
Housed near a blazing fire—is seen to flit
Safe from the wintry tempest. Fluttering,
Here did it enter; there, on hasty wing,   5
Flies out, and passes on from cold to cold;
But whence it came we know not, nor behold
Whither it goes. Even such, that transient Thing,
The human Soul; not utterly unknown
While in the Body lodged, her warm abode;   10
But from what world She came, what woe or weal
On her departure waits, no tongue hath shown;
This mystery if the Stranger can reveal,
His be a welcome cordially bestowed[2]!"

XVII.

CONVERSION.

PROMPT transformation works the novel Lore;
The Council closed, the Priest in full career
Rides forth, an armèd man, and hurls a spear

To desecrate the Fane which heretofore
He served in folly. Woden falls, and
    Thor   5
Is overturned ; the mace, in battle heaved
(So might they dream) till victory was
    achieved,
Drops, and the God himself is seen no
    more.
Temple and Altar sink, to hide their
    shame
Amid oblivious weeds. *"O come to me,* 10
Ye heavy laden!" such the inviting voice
Heard near fresh streams[1] ; and thou-
    sands, who rejoice
In the new Rite—the pledge of sanctity,
Shall, by regenerate life, the promise
    claim.

XVIII.

APOLOGY.

NOR scorn the aid which Fancy oft doth
    lend
The Soul's eternal interests to promote :
Death, darkness, danger, are our natural
    lot ;
And evil Spirits *may* our walk attend
For aught the wisest know or compre-
    hend ;   5
Then be *good* Spirits free to breathe a note
Of elevation ; let their odours float
Around these Converts ; and their glories
    blend,
The midnight stars outshining, or the blaze
Of the noon-day. Nor doubt that golden
    cords   10
Of good works, mingling with the visions,
    raise
The Soul to purer worlds : and *who* the line
Shall draw, the limits of the power define,
That even imperfect faith to man affords ?

XIX.

PRIMITIVE SAXON CLERGY[2].

How beautiful your presence, how benign,
Servants of God ! who not a thought will
    share
With the vain world ; who, outwardly as
    bare

---

[1] See Note, p. 921.   [2] See Note· ibid

As winter trees, yield no fallacious sign
That the firm soul is clothed with fruit
    divine !   5
Such Priest, when service worthy of his
    care
Has called him forth to breathe the
    common air,
Might seem a saintly Image from its
    shrine
Descended :—happy are the eyes that meet
The Apparition ; evil thoughts are stayed
At his approach, and low-bowed necks
    entreat   11
A benediction from his voice or hand ;
Whence grace, through which the heart
    can understand,
And vows, that bind the will, in silence
    made.

XX.

OTHER INFLUENCES.

AH, when the Body, round which in love
    we clung,
Is chilled by death, does mutual service
    fail ?
Is tender pity then of no avail ?
Are intercessions of the fervent tongue
A waste of hope ?—From this sad source
    have sprung   5
Rites that console the Spirit, under grief
Which ill can brook more rational relief :
Hence, prayers are shaped amiss, and
    dirges sung
For Souls whose doom is fixed ! The way
    is smooth
For Power that travels with the human
    heart :   10
Confession ministers the pang to soothe
In him who at the ghost of guilt doth
    start.
Ye holy Men, so earnest in your care,
Of your own mighty instruments beware !

XXI.

SECLUSION.

LANCE, shield, and sword relinquished—
    at his side
A bead-roll, in his hand a claspèd book,
Or staff more harmless than a shepherd's
    crook,

The war-worn Chieftain quits the world—
  to hide
His thin autumnal locks where Monks
  abide   5
In cloistered privacy. But not to dwell
In soft repose he comes. Within his cell,
Round the decaying trunk of human pride,
At morn, and eve, and midnight's silent
  hour,
Do penitential cogitations cling;   10
Like ivy, round some ancient elm, they
  twine
In grisly folds and strictures serpentine;
Yet, while they strangle, a fair growth
  they bring,
For recompense—their own perennial
  bower.

XXII.

CONTINUED.

METHINKS that to some vacant hermitage
My feet would rather turn—to some dry
  nook
Scooped out of living rock, and near a
  brook
Hurled down a mountain-cove from stage
  to stage,
Yet tempering, for my sight, its bustling
  rage   5
In the soft heaven of a translucent pool;
Thence creeping under sylvan arches cool,
Fit haunt of shapes whose glorious equi-
  page
Would elevate my dreams. A beechen bowl,
A maple dish, my furniture should be; 10
Crisp, yellow leaves my bed; the hooting
  owl
My night-watch: nor should e'er the
  crested fowl
From thorp or vill his matins sound
  for me,
Tired of the world and all its industry.

XXIII.

REPROOF.

BUT what if One, through grove or flowery
  mead,
Indulging thus at will the creeping feet
Of a voluptuous indolence, should meet

Thy hovering Shade, O venerable Bede!
The saint, the scholar, from a circle freed
Of toil stupendous, in a hallowed seat   6
Of learning, where thou heard'st the bil-
  lows beat
On a wild coast, rough monitors to feed
Perpetual industry. Sublime Recluse!
The recreant soul, that dares to shun the
  debt   10
Imposed on human kind, must first forget
Thy diligence, thy unrelaxing use
Of a long life; and, in the hour of death,
The last dear service of thy passing
  breath[1]!

XXIV.

SAXON MONASTERIES, AND LIGHTS AND SHADES OF THE RELIGION.

BY such examples moved to unbought
  pains,
The people work like congregated bees;
Eager to build the quiet Fortresses
Where Piety, as they believe, obtains
From Heaven a *general* blessing; timely
  rains   5
Or needful sunshine; prosperous enter-
  prise,
Justice and peace:—bold faith! yet also
  rise
The sacred Structures for less doubtful
  gains.
The Sensual think with reverence of the
  palms
Which the chaste Votaries seek, beyond
  the grave;   10
If penance be redeemable, thence alms
Flow to the poor, and freedom to the slave;
And if full oft the Sanctuary save
Lives black with guilt, ferocity it calms.

XXV.

MISSIONS AND TRAVELS.

NOT sedentary all: there are who roam
To scatter seeds of life on barbarous
  shores;
Or quit with zealous step their knee-worn
  floors

---

[1] He expired dictating the last words of a
translation of St. John's Gospel.

To seek the general mart of Christendom;
Whence they, like richly-laden merchants,
 come   5
To their belovèd cells:—or shall we say
That, like the Red-cross Knight, they
 urge their way,
To lead in memorable triumph home
Truth, their immortal Una? Babylon,
Learnèd and wise, hath perished utterly,
Nor leaves her Speech one word to aid
 the sigh   11
That would lament her;—Memphis, Tyre,
 are gone
With all their Arts,—but classic lore
 glides on
By these Religious saved for all posterity.

XXVI.

ALFRED.

BEHOLD a pupil of the monkish gown,
The pious ALFRED, King to Justice dear!
Lord of the harp and liberating spear;
Mirror of Princes! Indigent Renown
Might range the starry ether for a crown
Equal to *his* deserts, who, like the year, 6
Pours forth his bounty, like the day doth
 cheer,
And awes like night with mercy-tempered
 frown.
Ease from this noble miser of his time
No moment steals; pain narrows not his
 cares [1].   10
Though small his kingdom as a spark or
 gem,
Of Alfred boasts remote Jerusalem,
And Christian India, through her wide-
 spread clime,
In sacred converse gifts with Alfred shares.

XXVII.

HIS DESCENDANTS.

WHEN thy great soul was freed from
 mortal chains,
Darling of England! many a bitter
 shower
Fell on thy tomb; but emulative power

Flowed in thy line through undegenerate
 veins.
The Race of Alfred covet glorious pains 5
When dangers threaten, dangers ever new!
Black tempests bursting, blacker still in
 view!
But manly sovereignty its hold retains;
The root sincere, the branches bold to strive
With the fierce tempest, while, within
 the round   10
Of their protection, gentle virtues thrive;
As oft, 'mid some green plot of open
 ground,
Wide as the oak extends its dewy gloom,
The fostered hyacinths spread their pur-
 ple bloom.

XXVIII.

INFLUENCE ABUSED.

URGED by Ambition, who with subtlest
 skill
Changes her means, the Enthusiast as a
 dupe
Shall soar, and as a hypocrite can stoop,
And turn the instruments of good to ill,
Moulding the credulous people to his will.
Such DUNSTAN:—from its Benedictine
 coop   6
Issues the master Mind, at whose fell
 swoop
The chaste affections tremble to fulfil
Their purposes. Behold, pre-signified,
The Might of spiritual sway! his
 thoughts, his dreams,   10
Do in the supernatural world abide:
So vaunt a throng of Followers, filled
 with pride
In what they see of virtues pushed to
 extremes,
And sorceries of talent misapplied.

XXIX.

DANISH CONQUESTS.

WOE to the Crown that doth the Cowl
 obey [2]!
Dissension, checking arms that would
 restrain
The incessant Rovers of the northern main,

[1] See Note, p. 921.

[2] See Note, p. 921.

Helps to restore and spread a Pagan
    sway:
But Gospel-truth is potent to allay   5
Fierceness and rage; and soon the cruel
    Dane
Feels, through the influence of her gentle
    reign,
His native superstitions melt away.
Thus often, when thick gloom the east
    o'ershrouds,
The full-orbed Moon, slow-climbing, doth
    appear   10
Silently to consume the heavy clouds;
How no one can resolve; but every eye
Around her sees, while air is hushed,
    a clear
And widening circuit of ethereal sky.

XXX.
CANUTE.

A PLEASANT music floats along the Mere,
From Monks in Ely chanting service high,
While-as Canùte the King is rowing by:
"My Oarsmen," quoth the mighty King,
    "draw near,
That we the sweet song of the Monks
    may hear!"   5
He listens (all past conquests and all
    schemes
Of future vanishing like empty dreams)
Heart-touched, and haply not without a
    tear.
The Royal Minstrel, ere the choir is still,
While his free Barge skims the smooth
    flood along,   10
Gives to that rapture an accordant
    Rhyme [1].
O suffering Earth! be thankful; sternest
    clime
And rudest age are subject to the thrill
Of heaven-descended Piety and Song.

XXXI.
THE NORMAN CONQUEST.

THE woman-hearted Confessor prepares
The evanescence of the Saxon line.
Hark! 'tis the tolling Curfew!—the stars
    shine;

---

[1] Which is still extant.

But of the lights that cherish household
    cares
And festive gladness, burns not one that
    dares   5
To twinkle after that dull stroke of thine,
Emblem and instrument, from Thames to
    Tyne,
Of force that daunts, and cunning that
    ensnares!
Yet as the terrors of the lordly bell,
That quench, from hut to palace, lamps
    and fires,   10
Touch not the tapers of the sacred quires;
Even so a thraldom, studious to expel
Old laws, and ancient customs to derange,
To Creed or Ritual brings no fatal change.

XXXII.
[Composed ?.—Published 1837.]

COLDLY we spake. The Saxons, over-
    powered
By wrong triumphant through its own
    excess,
From fields laid waste, from house and
    home devoured
By flames, look up to heaven and crave
    redress
From God's eternal justice. Pitiless   5
Though men be, there are angels that can
    feel
For wounds that death alone has power
    to heal,
For penitent guilt, and innocent distress.
And has a Champion risen in arms to try
His Country's virtue, fought, and breathes
    no more;   10
Him in their hearts the people canonize;
And far above the mine's most precious ore
The least small pittance of bare mould
    they prize
Scooped from the sacred earth where his
    dear relics lie.

XXXIII.
THE COUNCIL OF CLERMONT.

"AND shall," the Pontiff asks, "profane-
    ness flow
From Nazareth—source of Christian piety,
From Bethlehem, from the Mounts of
    Agony

And glorified Ascension? Warriors, go,
With prayers and blessings we your path
    will sow; 5
Like Moses hold our hands erect, till ye
Have chased far off by righteous victory
These sons of Amalek, or laid them
    low!"—
"God willeth it," the whole assembly
    cry;
Shout which the enraptured multitude
    astounds! 10
The Council-roof and Clermont's towers
    reply;—
"God willeth it," from hill to hill re-
    bounds,
And, in awe-stricken Countries far and
    nigh,
Through "Nature's hollow arch" that
    voice resounds [1].

XXXIV.

CRUSADES.

The turbaned Race are poured in thicken-
    ing swarms
Along the west; though driven from
    Aquitaine,
The Crescent glitters on the towers of
    Spain;
And soft Italia feels renewed alarms;
The scimitar, that yields not to the
    charms 5
Of ease, the narrow Bosphorus will dis-
    dain;
Nor long (that crossed) would Grecian
    hills detain
Their tents, and check the current of
    their arms.
Then blame not those who, by the
    mightiest lever
Known to the moral world, Imagination,
Upheave, so seems it, from her natural
    station 11
All Christendom:—they sweep along (was
    never
So huge a host!)—to tear from the Un-
    believer
The precious Tomb, their haven of sal-
    vation.

---

[1] The decision of this council was believed to be instantly known in remote parts of Europe.

XXXV.

RICHARD I.

Redoubted King, of courage leonine,
I mark thee, Richard! urgent to equip
Thy warlike person with the staff and
    scrip;
I watch thee sailing o'er the midland
    brine;
In conquered Cyprus see thy Bride
    decline 5
Her blushing cheek, love-vows upon her
    lip,
And see love-emblems streaming from thy
    ship,
As thence she holds her way to Palestine.
My Song, a fearless homager, would
    attend
Thy thundering battle-axe as it cleaves
    the press 10
Of war, but duty summons her away
To tell—how, finding in the rash distress
Of those Enthusiasts a subservient friend,
To giddier heights hath clomb the Papal
    sway.

XXXVI.

AN INTERDICT.

Realms quake by turns: proud Arbitress
    of grace,
The Church, by mandate shadowing forth
    the power
She arrogates o'er heaven's eternal door,
Closes the gates of every sacred place.
Straight from the sun and tainted air's
    embrace 5
All sacred things are covered: cheerful
    morn
Grows sad as night—no seemly garb is
    worn,
Nor is a face allowed to meet a face
With natural smiles of greeting. Bells
    are dumb;
Ditches are graves—funereal rites denied;
And in the churchyard he must take his
    bride 11
Who dares be wedded! Fancies thickly
    come
Into the pensive heart ill fortified,
And comfortless despairs the soul benumb.

XXXVII.

PAPAL ABUSES.

As with the Stream our voyage we
pursue,
The gross materials of this world pre-
sent
A marvellous study of wild accident;
Uncouth proximities of old and new;
And bold transfigurations, more untrue 5
(As might be deemed) to disciplined
intent
Than aught the sky's fantastic element,
When most fantastic, offers to the view.
Saw we not Henry scourged at Becket's
Shrine?
Lo! John self-stripped of his insignia:—
crown,   10
Sceptre and mantle, sword and ring, laid
down
At a proud Legate's feet! The spears that
line
Baronial halls the opprobrious insult
feel;
And angry Ocean roars a vain appeal.

XXXVIII.

SCENE IN VENICE.

BLACK Demons hovering o'er his mitred
head,
To Cæsar's Successor the Pontiff spake;
"Ere I absolve thee, stoop! that on thy
neck
Levelled with earth this foot of mine may
tread."
Then he, who to the altar had been led, 5
He, whose strong arm the Orient could
not check,
He, who had held the Soldan at his
beck,
Stooped, of all glory disinherited,
And even the common dignity of man!—
Amazement strikes the crowd: while
many turn   10
Their eyes away in sorrow, others burn
With scorn, invoking a vindictive ban
From outraged Nature; but the sense of
most
In abject sympathy with power is lost.

XXXIX.

PAPAL DOMINION.

UNLESS to Peter's Chair the viewless wind
Must come and ask permission when to
blow,
What further empire would it have? for now
A ghostly Domination, unconfined
As that by dreaming Bards to Love
assigned,   5
Sits there in sober truth—to raise the low,
Perplex the wise, the strong to over-
throw;
Through earth and heaven to bind and to
unbind!—
Resist—the thunder quails thee!—crouch
—rebuff
Shall be thy recompense! from land to
land   10
The ancient thrones of Christendom are
stuff
For occupation of a magic wand,
And 'tis the Pope that wields it:—
whether rough
Or smooth his front, our world is in his
hand!

PART II.

TO THE CLOSE OF THE TROUBLES IN
THE REIGN OF CHARLES I.

I.

[Composed ?.—Published 1845.]

How soon—alas! did Man, created pure—
By Angels guarded, deviate from the line
Prescribed to duty:—woeful forfeiture
He made by wilful breach of law divine.
With like perverseness did the Church
abjure   5
Obedience to her Lord, and haste to
twine,
'Mid Heaven-born flowers that shall for
aye endure,
Weeds on whose front the world had
fixed her sign.
O Man,—if with thy trials thus it fares,
If good can smooth the way to evil choice,

From all rash censure be the mind kept
free;   11
He only judges right who weighs, com-
pares,
And, in the sternest sentence which his
voice
Pronounces, ne'er abandons Charity.

II.

[Composed ?.—Published 1845.]

FROM false assumption rose, and fondly
hailed
By superstition, spread the Papal power;
Yet do not deem the Autocracy prevailed
Thus only, even in error's darkest hour.
She daunts, forth-thundering from her
spiritual tower   5
Brute rapine, or with gentle lure she tames.
Justice and Peace through Her uphold
their claims;
And Chastity finds many a sheltering
bower.
Realm there is none that if controlled or
sway'd
By her commands partakes not, in degree,
Of good, o'er manners arts and arms,
diffused: 11
Yes, to thy domination, Roman See,
Tho' miserably, oft monstrously, abused
By blind ambition, be this tribute paid.

III.

CISTERTIAN MONASTERY.

"*HERE Man more purely lives, less oft
doth fall,*
*More promptly rises, walks with stricter
heed,*
More safely rests, dies happier, is freed
*Earlier from cleansing fires, and gains
withal*
A brighter crown[1]."—On yon Cistertian wall
That confident assurance may be read; 6
And, to like shelter, from the world have
fled
Increasing multitudes. The potent call
Doubtless shall cheat full oft the heart's
desires;
Yet, while the rugged Age on pliant knee
Vows to rapt Fancy humble fealty,   11

[1] See Note, p. 921.

A gentler life spreads round the holy
spires;
Where'er they rise, the sylvan waste
retires,
And aery harvests crown the fertile lea.

IV.

[Composed ?.—Published 1835.]

DEPLORABLE his lot who tills the ground,
His whole life long tills it, with heartless
toil
Of villain-service, passing with the soil
To each new Master, like a steer or hound,
Or like a rooted tree, or stone earth-
bound;   5
But mark how gladly, through their own
domains,
The Monks relax or break these iron
chains;
While Mercy, uttering, through their
voice, a sound
Echoed in Heaven, cries out, "Ye Chiefs,
abate
These legalized oppressions! Man—whose
name   10
And nature God disdained not; Man—
whose soul
Christ died for—cannot forfeit his high
claim
To live and move exempt from all control
Which fellow-feeling doth not mitigate!'

V.

MONKS AND SCHOOLMEN.

RECORD we too, with just and faithful pen,
That many hooded Cenobites there are,
Who in their private cells have yet a care
Of public quiet; unambitious Men,
Counsellors for the world, of piercing ken;
Whose fervent exhortations from afar   6
Move Princes to their duty, peace or war;
And oft-times in the most forbidding den
Of solitude, with love of science strong,
How patiently the yoke of thought they
bear!   10
How subtly glide its finest threads along!
Spirits that crowd the intellectual sphere
With mazy boundaries, as the astronomer
With orb and cycle girds the starry
throng.

VI.

OTHER BENEFITS.

AND, not in vain embodied to the sight,
Religion finds even in the stern retreat
Of feudal sway her own appropriate seat;
From the collegiate pomps on Windsor's
    height
Down to the humbler altar, which the
    Knight   5
And his Retainers of the embattled hall
Seek in domestic oratory small,
For prayer in stillness, or the chanted
    rite;
Then chiefly dear, when foes are planted
    round,
Who teach the intrepid guardians of the
    place—   10
Hourly exposed to death, with famine
    worn,
And suffering under many a perilous
    wound—
How sad would be their durance, if for-
    lorn
Of offices dispensing heavenly grace!

VII.

CONTINUED.

AND what melodious sounds at times
    prevail!
And, ever and anon, how bright a gleam
Pours on the surface of the turbid Stream!
What heartfelt fragrance mingles with
    the gale
That swells the bosom of our passing sail!
For where, but on *this* River's margin,
    blow   6
Those flowers of chivalry, to bind the
    brow
Of hardihood with wreaths that shall not
    fail?—
Fair Court of Edward! wonder of the
    world!
I see a matchless blazonry unfurled   10
Of wisdom, magnanimity, and love;
And meekness tempering honourable
    pride;
The lamb is couching by the lion's side,
And near the flame-eyed eagle sits the
    dove.

VIII.

CRUSADERS.

FURL we the sails, and pass with tardy
    oars
Through these bright regions, casting
    many a glance
Upon the dream-like issues—the romance
Of many-coloured life that Fortune pours
Round the Crusaders, till on distant
    shores   5
Their labours end; or they return to lie,
The vow performed, in cross-legged effigy,
Devoutly stretched upon their chancel
    floors.
Am I deceived? Or is their requiem
    chanted
By voices never mute when Heaven un-
    ties   10
Her inmost, softest, tenderest harmonies;
Requiem which Earth takes up with voice
    undaunted,
When she would tell how Brave, and
    Good, and Wise,
For their high guerdon not in vain have
    panted!

IX.

[Composed 1842.—Published 1845.]

As faith thus sanctified the warrior's crest
While from the Papal Unity there came,
What feebler means had failed to give,
    one aim
Diffused thro' all the regions of the
    West;
So does her Unity its power attest   5
By works of Art, that shed, on the out-
    ward frame
Of worship, glory and grace, which who
    shall blame.
That ever looked to heaven for final rest?
Hail countless Temples! that so well
    befit
Your ministry; that, as ye rise and take
Form spirit and character from holy
    writ,   11
Give to devotion, wheresoe'er awake,
Pinions of high and higher sweep, and
    make
The unconverted soul with awe submit.

X.

[Composed 1842.—Published 1845.]

WHERE long and deeply hath been fixed
    the root
In the blest soil of gospel truth, the Tree,
(Blighted or scathed tho' many branches
    be,
Put forth to wither, many a hopeful
    shoot)
Can never cease to bear celestial fruit.   5
Witness the Church that oft-times, with
    effect
Dear to the saints, strives earnestly to
    eject
Her bane, her vital energies recruit.
Lamenting, do not hopelessly repine
When such good work is doomed to be
    undone,   10
The conquests lost that were so hardly
    won:—
All promises vouchsafed by Heaven will
    shine
In light confirmed while years their course
    shall run,
Confirmed alike in progress and decline.

XI.

TRANSUBSTANTIATION.

ENOUGH! for see, with dim association
The tapers burn; the odorous incense feeds
A greedy flame; the pompous mass pro-
    ceeds;
The Priest bestows the appointed conse-
    cration;   4
And, while the HOST is raised, its elevation
An awe and supernatural horror breeds;
And all the people bow their heads, like
    reeds
To a soft breeze, in lowly adoration.
This Valdo brooks not. On the banks of
    Rhone
He taught, till persecution chased him
    thence,   10
To adore the Invisible, and Him alone.
Nor are his Followers loth to seek defence,
'Mid woods and wilds, on Nature's craggy
    throne,
From rites that trample upon soul and
    sense.

XII.

THE VAUDOIS.

[Composed ?.—Published 1835.]

BUT whence came they who for the Saviour
    Lord
Have long borne witness as the Scriptures
    teach?—
Ages ere Valdo raised his voice to preach
In Gallic ears the unadulterate Word,
Their fugitive Progenitors explored   5
Subalpine vales, in quest of safe retreats
Where that pure Church survives, though
    summer heats
Open a passage to the Romish sword,
Far as it dares to follow. Herbs self-
    sown,
And fruitage gathered from the chestnut-
    wood,   10
Nourish the sufferers then; and mists,
    that brood
O'er chasms with new-fallen obstacles
    bestrown,
Protect them; and the eternal snow that
    daunts
Aliens, is God's good winter for their
    haunts.

XIII.

[Composed ?.—Published 1835.]

PRAISED be the Rivers, from their moun-
    tain springs
Shouting to Freedom, "Plant thy banners
    here!"
To harassed Piety, "Dismiss thy fear,
And in our caverns smooth thy ruffled
    wings!"
Nor be unthanked their final lingerings—
Silent, but not to high-souled Passion's
    ear—   6
'Mid reedy fens wide-spread and marshes
    drear,
Their own creation. Such glad wel-
    comings
As Po was heard to give where Venice
    rose
Hailed from aloft those Heirs of truth
    divine   10
Who near his fountains sought obscure
    repose,

Yet came prepared as glorious lights to
    shine,
Should that be needed for their sacred
    Charge;
Blest Prisoners They, whose spirits were
    at large!

XIV.

WALDENSES.

THOSE had given earliest notice, as the
    lark
Springs from the ground the morn to
    gratulate;
Or rather rose the day to antedate,
By striking out a solitary spark,
When all the world with midnight gloom
    was dark.—   5
Then followed the Waldensian bands,
    whom Hate
In vain endeavours to exterminate,
Whom Obloquy pursues with hideous
    bark[1]:
But they desist not;—and the sacred fire,
Rekindled thus, from dens and savage
    woods   10
Moves, handed on with never-ceasing care,
Through courts, through camps, o'er
    limitary floods;
Nor lacks this sea-girt Isle a timely share
Of the new Flame, not suffered to expire.

XV.

ARCHBISHOP CHICHELEY TO HENRY V.

"WHAT beast in wilderness or cultured
    field
The lively beauty of the leopard shows?
What flower in meadow-ground or garden
    grows
That to the towering lily doth not yield?
Let both meet only on thy royal shield!   5
Go forth, great King! claim what thy
    birth bestows;
Conquer the Gallic lily which thy foes
Dare to usurp;—thou hast a sword to
    wield,
And Heaven will crown the right."—The
    mitred Sire

[1] See Note, p. 922.

Thus spake—and lo! a Fleet, for Gaul
    addrest,   10
Ploughs her bold course across the won-
    dering seas;
For, sooth to say, ambition, in the breast
Of youthful heroes, is no sullen fire,
But one that leaps to meet the fanning
    breeze.

XVI.

WARS OF YORK AND LANCASTER.

THUS is the storm abated by the craft
Of a shrewd Counsellor, eager to protect
The Church, whose power hath recently
    been checked,
Whose monstrous riches threatened. So
    the shaft
Of victory mounts high, and blood is
    quaffed   5
In fields that rival Cressy and Poictiers—
Pride to be washed away by bitter tears!
For deep as hell itself, the avenging
    draught
Of civil slaughter. Yet, while temporal
    power
Is by these shocks exhausted, spiritual
    truth   10
Maintains the else endangered gift of life;
Proceeds from infancy to lusty youth;
And, under cover of this woeful strife,
Gathers unblighted strength from hour
    to hour.

XVII.

WICLIFFE.

ONCE more the Church is seized with
    sudden fear,
And at her call is Wicliffe disinhumed:
Yea, his dry bones to ashes are consumed
And flung into the brook that travels
    near;
Forthwith that ancient Voice which
    Streams can hear   5
Thus speaks (that Voice which walks upon
    the wind,
Though seldom heard by busy human
    kind)—
"As thou these ashes, little Brook! wilt
    bear
Into the Avon, Avon to the tide
Of Severn, Severn to the narrow seas,   10

Into main Ocean they, this deed accurst
An emblem yields to friends and enemies
How the bold Teacher's Doctrine, sancti-
    fied
By truth, shall spread, throughout the
    world dispersed."

XVIII.

CORRUPTIONS OF THE HIGHER CLERGY.

"WOE to you, Prelates! rioting in ease
And cumbrous wealth—the shame of your
    estate;
You, on whose progress dazzling trains
    await
Of pompous horses; whom vain titles
    please;
Who will be served by others on their
    knees,   5
Yet will yourselves to God no service
    pay;
Pastors who neither take nor point the
    way
To Heaven; for, either lost in vanities
Ye have no skill to teach, or if ye know
And speak the word ——" Alas! of
    fearful things   10
'Tis the most fearful when the people's
    eye
Abuse hath cleared from vain imaginings;
And taught the general voice to prophesy
Of Justice armed, and Pride to be laid
    low.

XIX.

ABUSE OF MONASTIC POWER.

AND what is Penance with her knotted
    thong;
Mortification with the shirt of hair,
Wan cheek, and knees indúrated with
    prayer,
Vigils, and fastings rigorous as long;
If cloistered Avarice scruple not to wrong
The pious, humble, useful Secular,   6
And rob the people of his daily care,
Scorning that world whose blindness
    makes her strong?
Inversion strange! that, unto One who
    lives
For self, and struggles with himself alone,

The amplest share of heavenly favour
    gives;   11
That to a Monk allots, both in the esteem
Of God and man, place higher than to him
Who on the good of others builds his
    own!

XX.

MONASTIC VOLUPTUOUSNESS.

YET more,—round many a Convent's
    blazing fire
Unhallowed threads of revelry are spun;
There Venus sits disguisèd like a Nun,—
While Bacchus, clothed in semblance of
    a Friar,
Pours out his choicest beverage high and
    higher   5
Sparkling, until it cannot choose but run
Over the bowl, whose silver lip hath won
An instant kiss of masterful desire—
To stay the precious waste. Through
    every brain
The domination of the sprightly juice   10
Spreads high conceits to madding Fancy
    dear,
Till the arched roof, with resolute abuse
Of its grave echoes, swells a choral strain
Whose votive burthen is—"OUR KING-
    DOM'S HERE!"

XXI.

DISSOLUTION OF THE MONASTERIES.

THREATS come which no submission may
    assuage,
No sacrifice avert, no power dispute;
The tapers shall be quenched, the belfries
    mute,
And, 'mid their choirs unroofed by selfish
    rage,
The warbling wren shall find a leafy cage;
The gadding bramble hang her purple
    fruit;   6
And the green lizard and the gilded newt
Lead unmolested lives, and die of age.
The owl of evening and the woodland fox
For their abode the shrines of Waltham
    choose: 10
Proud Glastonbury can no more refuse
To stoop her head before these desperate
    shocks—

She whose high pomp displaced, as story
tells,
Arimathean Joseph's wattled cells.

XXII.

THE SAME SUBJECT.

THE lovely Nun (submissive, but more
meek
Through saintly habit than from effort
due
To unrelenting mandates that pursue
With equal wrath the steps of strong and
weak)
Goes forth—unveiling timidly a cheek   5
Suffused with blushes of celestial hue,
While through the Convent's gate to open
view
Softly she glides, another home to seek.
Not Iris, issuing from her cloudy shrine,
An Apparition more divinely bright!   10
Not more attractive to the dazzled sight
Those watery glories, on the stormy brine
Poured forth, while summer suns at dis-
tance shine,
And the green vales lie hushed in sober
light!

XXIII.

CONTINUED.

YET many a Novice of the cloistral shade,
And many chained by vows, with eager
glee
The warrant hail, exulting to be free;
Like ships before whose keels, full long
embayed
In polar ice, propitious winds have made
Unlooked-for outlet to an open sea,   6
Their liquid world, for bold discovery,
In all her quarters temptingly displayed!
Hope guides the young; but when the old
must pass
The threshold, whither shall they turn to
find   10
The hospitality—the alms (alas!
Alms may be needed) which that House
bestowed?
Can they, in faith and worship, train the
mind
To keep this new and questionable road?

XXIV.

SAINTS.

YE, too, must fly before a chasing hand,
Angels and Saints, in every hamlet
mourned!
Ah! if the old idolatry be spurned,
Let not your radiant Shapes desert the
Land:
Her adoration was not your demand,   5
The fond heart proffered it—the servile
heart;
And therefore are ye summoned to de-
part,
Michael, and thou, St. George, whose
flaming brand
The Dragon quelled; and valiant Mar-
garet   9
Whose rival sword a like Opponent slew:
And rapt Cecilia, seraph-haunted Queen
Of harmony; and weeping Magdalene,
Who in the penitential desert met
Gales sweet as those that over Eden
blew!

XXV

THE VIRGIN.

MOTHER! whose virgin bosom was un-
crost
With the least shade of thought to sin
allied;
Woman! above all women glorified,
Our tainted nature's solitary boast;
Purer than foam on central ocean tost;   5
Brighter than eastern skies at daybreak
strewn
With fancied roses, than the unblemished
moon
Before her wane begins on heaven's blue
coast;
Thy Image falls to earth. Yet some, I
ween,
Not unforgiven the suppliant knee might
bend,   10
As to a visible Power, in which did
blend
All that was mixed and reconciled in
Thee
Of mother's love with maiden purity,
Of high with low, celestial with terrene!

XXVI.

APOLOGY.

NOT utterly unworthy to endure
Was the supremacy of crafty Rome;
Age after age to the arch of Christendom
Aerial keystone haughtily secure;
Supremacy from Heaven transmitted
    pure,   5
As many hold; and, therefore, to the
    tomb
Pass, some through fire—and by the scaf-
    fold some—
Like saintly Fisher, and unbending More.
"Lightly for both the bosom's lord did
    sit
Upon his throne;" unsoftened, undis-
    mayed   10
By aught that mingled with the tragic
    scene
Of pity or fear; and More's gay genius
    played
With the inoffensive sword of native wit,
Than the bare axe more luminous and
    keen.

XXVII.

IMAGINATIVE REGRETS.

DEEP is the lamentation! Not alone
From Sages justly honoured by mankind;
But from the ghostly tenants of the wind,
Demons and Spirits, many a dolorous
    groan
Issues for that dominion overthrown: 5
Proud Tiber grieves, and far-off Ganges,
    blind
As his own worshippers: and Nile, re-
    clined
Upon his monstrous urn, the farewell
    moan
Renews. Through every forest, cave, and
    den,
Where frauds were hatched of old, hath
    sorrow past—   10
Hangs o'er the Arabian Prophet's native
    Waste,
Where once his airy helpers schemed and
    planned
'Mid spectral lakes bemocking thirsty
    men,
And stalking pillars built of fiery sand.

XXVIII.

REFLECTIONS.

GRANT that by this unsparing hurricane
Green leaves with yellow mixed are torn
    away,
And goodly fruitage with the mother-
    spray;
'Twere madness—wished we, therefore, to
    detain,
With hands stretched forth in mollified
    disdain,   5
The "trumpery" that ascends in bare
    display—
Bulls, pardons, relics, cowls black, white,
    and grey—
Upwhirled, and flying o'er the ethereal
    plain
Fast bound for Limbo Lake. And yet
    not choice
But habit rules the unreflecting herd,   10
And airy bonds are hardest to disown;
Hence, with the spiritual sovereignty
    transferred
Unto itself, the Crown assumes a voice
Of reckless mastery, hitherto unknown.

XXIX.

TRANSLATION OF THE BIBLE.

BUT, to outweigh all harm, the sacred
    Book,
In dusty sequestration wrapt too long,
Assumes the accents of our native tongue;
And he who guides the plough, or wields
    the crook,
With understanding spirit now may look
Upon her records, listen to her song,   6
And sift her laws—much wondering that
    the wrong,
Which Faith has suffered, Heaven could
    calmly brook.
Transcendent Boon! noblest that earthly
    King
Ever bestowed to equalize and bless   10
Under the weight of mortal wretched-
    ness!
But passions spread like plagues, and
    thousands wild
With bigotry shall tread the Offering
Beneath their feet, detested and defiled.

XXX.

THE POINT AT ISSUE.

[Composed ?.—Published 1827.]

FOR what contend the wise?—for no-
　　thing less
Than that the Soul, freed from the bonds
　　of Sense,
And to her God restored by evidence
Of things not seen, drawn forth from
　　their recess,
Root there, and not in forms, her holi-
　　ness;—　　　　　　　　　　　　　5
For Faith, which to the Patriarchs did
　　dispense
Sure guidance, ere a ceremonial fence
Was needful round men thirsting to
　　transgress;—
For Faith, more perfect still, with which
　　the Lord
Of all, himself a Spirit, in the youth　10
Of Christian aspiration, deigned to fill
The temples of their hearts who, with his
　　word
Informed, were resolute to do his will,
And worship him in spirit and in truth.

XXXI.

EDWARD VI.

"SWEET is the holiness of Youth"—so
　　felt
Time-honoured Chaucer speaking through
　　that Lay
By which the Prioress beguiled the way,
And many a Pilgrim's rugged heart did
　　melt.
Hadst thou, loved Bard! whose spirit
　　often dwelt　　　　　　　　　　　5
In the clear land of vision, but foreseen
King, child, and seraph, blended in the
　　mien
Of pious Edward kneeling as he knelt
In meek and simple infancy, what joy
For universal Christendom had thrilled
Thy heart! what hopes inspired thy
　　genius, skilled,　　　　　　　　11
(O great Precursor, genuine morning Star)
The lucid shafts of reason to employ,
Piercing the Papal darkness from afar!

XXXII.

EDWARD SIGNING THE WARRANT FOR
THE EXECUTION OF JOAN OF KENT.

THE tears of man in various measure
　　gush
From various sources; gently overflow
From blissful transport some—from clefts
　　of woe
Some with ungovernable impulse rush;
And some, coeval with the earliest blush
Of infant passion, scarcely dare to show　6
Their pearly lustre—coming but to go;
And some break forth when others' sor-
　　rows crush
The sympathising heart. Nor these, nor
　　yet
The noblest drops to admiration known,
To gratitude, to injuries forgiven—　11
Claim Heaven's regard like waters that
　　have wet
The innocent eyes of youthful Monarchs
　　driven
To pen the mandates nature doth disown.

XXXIII.

REVIVAL OF POPERY.

[Composed ?.—Published 1827.]

THE saintly Youth has ceased to rule,
　　discrowned
By unrelenting Death. O People keen
For change, to whom the new looks al-
　　ways green!
Rejoicing did they cast upon the ground
Their Gods of wood and stone; and, at
　　the sound　　　　　　　　　　　5
Of counter-proclamation, now are seen,
(Proud triumph is it for a sullen Queen!)
Lifting them up, the worship to confound
Of the Most High. Again do they in-
　　voke
The Creature, to the Creature glory
　　give;　　　　　　　　　　　　10
Again with frankincense the altars smoke
Like those the Heathen served; and mass
　　is sung;
And prayer, man's rational prerogative,
Runs through blind channels of an un-
　　known tongue.

XXXIV.

LATIMER AND RIDLEY.

[Composed ?.—Published 1827.]

How fast the Marian death-list is un-
  rolled !
See Latimer and Ridley in the might
Of Faith stand coupled for a common
  flight !
One (like those prophets whom God sent
  of old)
Transfigured[1], from this kindling hath
  foretold   5
A torch of inextinguishable light;
The Other gains a confidence as bold ;
And thus they foil their enemy's despite.
The penal instruments, the shows of
  crime,
Are glorified while this once-mitred pair
Of saintly Friends the "murtherer's chain
  partake,   11
Corded, and burning at the social stake :"
Earth never witnessed object more sub-
  lime
In constancy, in fellowship more fair !

XXXV.

CRANMER.

OUTSTRETCHING flameward his upbraided
  hand
(O God of mercy, may no earthly Seat
Of judgment such presumptuous doom
  repeat !)
Amid the shuddering throng doth Cran-
  mer stand ;
Firm as the stake to which with iron
  band   5
His frame is tied ; firm from the naked
  feet
To the bare head. The victory is com-
  plete ;
The shrouded Body to the Soul's com-
  mand
Answers with more than Indian forti-
  tude,
Through all her nerves with finer sense
  endued,   10
Till breath departs in blissful aspiration :

[1] See Note, p. 922

Then, 'mid the ghastly ruins of the fire,
Behold the unalterable heart entire,
Emblem of faith untouched, miraculous
  attestation[2] !

XXXVI.

GENERAL VIEW OF THE TROUBLES OF THE REFORMATION.

AID, glorious Martyrs, from your fields
  of light,
Our mortal ken ! Inspire a perfect trust
(While we look round) that Heaven's de-
  crees are just :
Which few can hold committed to a fight
That shows, ev'n on its better side, the
  might   5
Of proud Self-will, Rapacity, and Lust,
'Mid clouds enveloped of polemic dust,
Which showers of blood seem rather to
  incite
Than to allay. Anathemas are hurled
From both sides ; veteran thunders (the
  brute test   10
Of truth) are met by fulminations new—
Tartarean flags are caught at, and un-
  furled—
Friends strike at friends—the flying shall
  pursue—
And Victory sickens, ignorant where to
  rest !

XXXVII.

ENGLISH REFORMERS IN EXILE.

SCATTERING, like birds escaped the fowl-
  er's net,
Some seek with timely flight a foreign
  strand ;
Most happy, re-assembled in a land
By dauntless Luther freed, could they
  forget
Their Country's woes. But scarcely have
  they met,   5
Partners in faith, and brothers in distress,
Free to pour forth their common thank-
  fulness,
Ere hope declines :—their union is beset
With speculative notions rashly sown,

[2] For the belief in this fact, see the contem-
porary Historians.

Whence thickly-sprouting growth of poi-
sonous weeds ;   10
Their forms are broken staves ; their
passions, steeds
That master them. How enviably blest
Is he who can, by help of grace, enthrone
The peace of God within his single
breast !

XXXVIII.

ELIZABETH.

HAIL, Virgin Queen! o'er many an en-
vious bar
Triumphant, snatched from many a trea-
cherous wile !
All hail, sage Lady, whom a grateful Isle
Hath blest, respiring from that dismal
war
Stilled by thy voice! But quickly from
afar   5
Defiance breathes with more malignant
aim ;
And alien storms with home-bred fer-
ments claim
Portentous fellowship. Her silver car,
By sleepless prudence ruled, glides slow-
ly on ;
Unhurt by violence, from menaced taint
Emerging pure, and seemingly more
bright :   11
Ah! wherefore yields it to a foul con-
straint
Black as the clouds its beams dispersed,
while shone,
By men and angels blest, the glorious
light?

XXXIX.

EMINENT REFORMERS.

METHINKS that I could trip o'er heaviest
soil,
Light as a buoyant bark from wave to
wave,
Were mine the trusty staff that JEWEL
gave
To youthful HOOKER, in familiar style
The gift exalting, and with playful
smile[1]:   5

---

[1] See Note, p. 922.

For thus equipped, and bearing on his
head
The Donor's farewell blessing, can he
dread
Tempest, or length of way, or weight of
toil?—
More sweet than odours caught by him
who sails
Near spicy shores of Araby the blest,   10
A thousand times more exquisitely sweet,
The freight of holy feeling which we meet,
In thoughtful moments, wafted by the
gales
From fields where good men walk, or
bowers wherein they rest.

XL.

THE SAME.

HOLY and heavenly Spirits as they are,
Spotless in life, and eloquent as wise,
With what entire affection do they prize
Their Church reformed ! labouring with
earnest care
To baffle all that may her strength im-
pair ;   5
That Church, the unperverted Gospel's
seat ;
In their afflictions a divine retreat ;
Source of their liveliest hope, and tender-
est prayer !—
The truth exploring with an equal mind,
In doctrine and communion they have
sought   10
Firmly between the two extremes to
steer ;
But theirs the wise man's ordinary lot,
To trace right courses for the stubborn
blind,
And prophesy to ears that will not hear.

XLI.

DISTRACTIONS.

MEN, who have ceased to reverence, soon
defy
Their forefathers ; lo! sects are formed,
and split
With morbid restlessness :—the ecstatic fit
Spreads wide ; though special mysteries
multiply,

The Saints must govern is their common
   cry;   5
And so they labour, deeming Holy Writ
Disgraced by aught that seems content to
   sit
Beneath the roof of settled Modesty.
The Romanist exults; fresh hope he
   draws
From the confusion, craftily incites   10
The overweening, personates the mad—
To heap disgust upon the worthier Cause:
Totters the Throne; the new-born Church
   is sad,
For every wave against her peace unites.

XLII.

GUNPOWDER PLOT.

FEAR hath a hundred eyes that all agree
To plague her beating heart; and there is
   one
(Nor idlest that!) which holds com-
   munion
With things that were not, yet were
   meant to be.
Aghast within its gloomy cavity   5
That eye (which sees as if fulfilled and done
Crimes that might stop the motion of the
   sun)
Beholds the horrible catastrophe
Of an assembled Senate unredeemed
From subterranean Treason's darkling
   power: 10
Merciless act of sorrow infinite!
Worse than the product of that dismal
   night,
When gushing, copious as a thunder-
   shower,
The blood of Huguenots through Paris
   streamed.

XLIII.

ILLUSTRATION.

THE JUNG-FRAU AND THE FALL OF THE
RHINE NEAR SCHAFFHAUSEN.

THE Virgin-Mountain[1], wearing like a
   Queen
A brilliant crown of everlasting snow,

---

[1] The Jung-frau.

Sheds ruin from her sides; and men
   below
Wonder that aught of aspect so serene
Can link with desolation. Smooth and
   green,   5
And seeming, at a little distance, slow,
The waters of the Rhine; but on they
   go
Fretting and whitening, keener and more
   keen;
Till madness seizes on the whole wide
   Flood,
Turned to a fearful Thing whose nostrils
   breathe   10
Blasts of tempestuous smoke—wherewith
   he tries
To hide himself, but only magnifies;
And doth in more conspicuous torment
   writhe,
Deafening the region in his ireful mood.

XLIV.

TROUBLES OF CHARLES THE FIRST

EVEN such the contrast that, where'er we
   move,
To the mind's eye Religion doth pre-
   sent;
Now with her own deep quietness con-
   tent;
Then, like the mountain, thundering from
   above
Against the ancient pine-trees of the
   grove   5
And the Land's humblest comforts. Now
   her mood
Recalls the transformation of the flood,
Whose rage the gentle skies in vain re-
   prove,
Earth cannot check. O terrible excess
Of headstrong will! Can this be Piety?
No—some fierce Maniac hath usurped her
   name;   11
And scourges England struggling to be
   free:
Her peace destroyed! her hopes a wilder-
   ness!
Her blessings cursed—her glory turned to
   shame!

XLV.

LAUD [1].

PREJUDGED by foes determined not to spare,
An old weak Man for vengeance thrown
 aside,
Laud, "in the painful art of dying" tried,
(Like a poor bird entangled in a snare
Whose heart still flutters, though his
 wings forbear   5
To stir in useless struggle) hath relied
On hope that conscious innocence sup-
 plied,
And in his prison breathes celestial air.
Why tarries then thy chariot? Wherefore
 stay,
O Death! the ensanguined yet triumphant
 wheels,   10
Which thou prepar'st, full often, to convey
(What time a State with madding faction
 reels)
The Saint or Patriot to the world that heals
All wounds, all perturbations doth allay?

XLVI.

AFFLICTIONS OF ENGLAND.

HARP! couldst thou venture, on thy
 boldest string,
The faintest note to echo which the blast
Caught from the hand of Moses as it
 passed
O'er Sinai's top, or from the Shepherd-
 king,
Early awake, by Siloa's brook, to sing 5
Of dread Jehovah; then should wood and
 waste
Hear also of that name, and mercy cast
Off to the mountains, like a covering
Of which the Lord was weary. Weep,
 oh! weep,
Weep with the good, beholding King and
 Priest   10
Despised by that stern God to whom they
 raise
Their suppliant hands; but holy is the
 feast
He keepeth; like the firmament his ways:
His statutes like the chambers of the deep.

PART III.

FROM THE RESTORATION TO THE PRE-
SENT TIMES.

I.

I SAW the figure of a lovely Maid
Seated alone beneath a darksome tree,
Whose fondly-overhanging canopy
Set off her brightness with a pleasing shade.
No Spirit was she; *that* my heart be-
 trayed,   5
For she was one I loved exceedingly;
But while I gazed in tender reverie
(Or was it sleep that with my Fancy
 played?)
The bright corporeal presence—form and
 face—
Remaining still distinct grew thin and
 rare,   10
Like sunny mist;—at length the golden
 hair,
Shape, limbs, and heavenly features, keep-
 ing pace
Each with the other in a lingering race
Of dissolution, melted into air.

II.

PATRIOTIC SYMPATHIES.

LAST night, without a voice, that Vision
 spake
Fear to my Soul, and sadness which
 might seem
Wholly dissevered from our present
 theme;
Yet, my belovèd Country! I partake
Of kindred agitations for thy sake; 5
Thou, too, dost visit oft my midnight
 dream;
Thy glory meets me with the earliest
 beam
Of light, which tells that Morning is
 awake.
If aught impair thy beauty or destroy,
Or but forbode destruction, I deplore 10
With filial love the sad vicissitude;
If thou hast fallen, and righteous Hea-
 ven restore
The prostrate, then my spring-time is
 renewed,
And sorrow bartered for exceeding joy.

III.

CHARLES THE SECOND.

WHO comes—with rapture greeted, and
   caressed
With frantic love—his kingdom to regain?
Him Virtue's Nurse, Adversity, in vain
Received, and fostered in her iron breast:
For all she taught of hardiest and of best,
Or would have taught, by discipline of pain
And long privation, now dissolves amain,
Or is remembered only to give zest
To wantonness.—Away, Circean revels!
But for what gain? if England soon
   must sink   10
Into a gulf which all distinction levels—
That bigotry may swallow the good name,
And, with that draught, the life-blood:
   misery, shame,
By Poets loathed; from which Historians
   shrink!

IV.

LATITUDINARIANISM.

YET Truth is keenly sought for, and the
   wind
Charged with rich words poured out in
   thought's defence;
Whether the Church inspire that elo-
   quence,
Or a Platonic Piety confined
To the sole temple of the inward mind; 5
And One there is who builds immortal lays,
Though doomed to tread in solitary ways,
Darkness before and danger's voice behind;
Yet not alone, nor helpless to repel
Sad thoughts; for from above the starry
   sphere   10
Come secrets, whispered nightly to his ear;
And the pure spirit of celestial light
Shines through his soul—"that he may
   see and tell
Of things invisible to mortal sight."

V.

WALTON'S BOOK OF LIVES.

THERE are no colours in the fairest sky
So fair as these. The feather, whence the
   pen
Was shaped that traced the lives of these
   good men,
Dropped from an Angel's wing. With
   moistened eye
We read of faith and purest charity   5
In Statesman, Priest, and humble Citizen:
Oh could we copy their mild virtues, then
What joy to live, what blessedness to
   die!
Methinks their very names shine still and
   bright;
Apart—like glow-worms on a summer
   night;   10
Or lonely tapers when from far they fling
A guiding ray; or seen—like stars on high,
Satellites burning in a lucid ring
Around meek Walton's heavenly memory.

VI.

CLERICAL INTEGRITY.

NOR shall the eternal roll of praise reject
Those Unconforming; whom one rigorous
   day
Drives from their Cures, a voluntary prey
To poverty, and grief, and disrespect,
And some to want—as if by tempests
   wrecked   5
On a wild coast; how destitute! did They
Feel not that Conscience never can be-
   tray,
That peace of mind is Virtue's sure effect.
Their altars they forego, their homes they
   quit,
Fields which they love, and paths they
   daily trod,   10
And cast the future upon Providence;
As men the dictate of whose inward sense
Outweighs the world; whom self-deceiving
   wit
Lures not from what they deem the cause
   of God.

VII.

PERSECUTION OF THE SCOTTISH COVE-
NANTERS.

[Composed ?.—Published 1827.]

WHEN Alpine Vales threw forth a sup-
   pliant cry,
The majesty of England interposed
And the sword stopped; the bleeding
   wounds were closed;
And Faith preserved her ancient purity.

How little boots that precedent of good, 5
Scorned or forgotten, Thou canst testify,
For England's shame, O Sister Realm !
    from wood,
Mountain, and moor, and crowded street,
    where lie
The headless martyrs of the Covenant,
Slain by Compatriot-protestants that
    draw   10
From councils senseless as intolerant
Their warrant. Bodies fall by wild sword-
    law ;
But who would force the Soul tilts with a
    straw
Against a Champion cased in adamant.

VIII.

ACQUITTAL OF THE BISHOPS.

A VOICE, from long-expecting thousands
    sent,
Shatters the air, and troubles tower and
    spire ;
For Justice hath absolved the innocent,
And Tyranny is balked of her desire :
Up, down, the busy Thames—rapid as
    fire   5
Coursing a train of gunpowder—it went,
And transport finds in every street a vent,
Till the whole City rings like one vast
    quire.
The Fathers urge the People to be still,
With outstretched hands and earnest
    speech—in vain !   10
Yea, many, haply wont to entertain
Small reverence for the mitre's offices,
And to Religion's self no friendly will,
A Prelate's blessing ask on bended knees.

IX.

WILLIAM THE THIRD.

CALM as an under-current, strong to draw
Millions of waves into itself, and run,
From sea to sea, impervious to the sun
And ploughing storm, the spirit of Nassau
Swerves not, (how blest if by religious
    awe   5
Swayed, and thereby enabled to contend
With the wide world's commotions) from
    its end

Swerves not—diverted by a casual law.
Had mortal action e'er a nobler scope?
The Hero comes to liberate, not defy ;   10
And while he marches on with steadfast
    hope,
Conqueror beloved ! expected anxiously !
The vacillating Bondman of the Pope
Shrinks from the verdict of his steadfast
    eye.

X.

OBLIGATIONS OF CIVIL TO RELIGIOUS
LIBERTY.

UNGRATEFUL Country, if thou e'er forget
The sons who for thy civil rights have
    bled !
How, like a Roman, Sidney bowed his
    head,
And Russell's milder blood the scaffold
    wet ;
But these had fallen for profitless regret 5
Had not thy holy Church her champions
    bred,
And claims from other worlds inspirited
The star of Liberty to rise. Nor yet
(Grave this within thy heart !) if spiritual
    things
Be lost, through apathy, or scorn, or fear,
Shalt thou thy humbler franchises sup-
    port,   11
However hardly won or justly dear:
What came from heaven to heaven by
    nature clings,
And, if dissevered thence, its course is
    short.

XI.

SACHEVEREL.

[Composed ?.—Published 1827.]

A SUDDEN conflict rises from the swell
Of a proud slavery met by tenets strained
In Liberty's behalf. Fears, true or
    feigned,
Spread through all ranks; and lo ! the
    Sentinel
Who loudest rang his pulpit 'larum bell,
Stands at the Bar, absolved by female
    eyes   6
Mingling their glances with grave flat-
    teries

Lavished on *Him*—that England may
    rebel
Against her ancient virtue. HIGH and
    Low,
Watchwords of Party, on all tongues are
    rife;   10
As if a Church, though sprung from
    heaven, must owe
To opposites and fierce extremes her
    life,—
Not to the golden mean, and quiet flow
Of truths that soften hatred, temper
    strife.

XII.

[Composed ?.—Published 1827.]

DOWN a swift Stream, thus far, a bold
    design
Have we pursued, with livelier stir of
    heart
Than his who sees, borne forward by the
    Rhine,
The living landscapes greet him, and
    depart;
Sees spires fast sinking—up again to start!
And strives the towers to number, that
    recline   6
O'er the dark steeps, or on the horizon line
Striding with shattered crests his eye
    athwart.
So have we hurried on with troubled
    pleasure:
Henceforth, as on the bosom of a stream
That slackens, and spreads wide a watery
    gleam,   11
We, nothing loth a lingering course to
    measure,
May gather up our thoughts, and mark at
    leisure
How widely spread the interests of our
    theme.

XIII.

ASPECTS OF CHRISTIANITY IN AMERICA.

I.—THE PILGRIM FATHERS.

[Composed 1842.—Published: vol. of 1842.]

WELL worthy to be magnified are they
Who, with sad hearts, of friends and
    country took
A last farewell, their loved abodes forsook,

And hallowed ground in which their
    fathers lay;
Then to the new-found World explored
    their way,   5
That so a Church, unforced, uncalled to
    brook
Ritual restraints, within some sheltering
    nook
Her Lord might worship and his word
    obey
In freedom. Men they were who could
    not bend;
Blest Pilgrims, surely, as they took for
    guide   10
A will by sovereign Conscience sancti-
    fied;
Blest while their Spirits from the woods
    ascend
Along a Galaxy that knows no end,
But in His glory who for Sinners died.

XIV.

II. CONTINUED.

[Composed 1842.—Published: vol. of 1842.]

FROM Rite and Ordinance abused they
    fled
To Wilds where both were utterly un-
    known;
But not to them had Providence fore-
    shown
What benefits are missed, what evils
    bred,
In worship neither raised nor limited   5
Save by Self-will. Lo! from that distant
    shore,
For Rite and Ordinance, Piety is led
Back to the Land those Pilgrims left of
    yore,
Led by her own free choice. So Truth
    and Love
By Conscience governed do their steps
    retrace.—   10
Fathers! your Virtues, such the power
    of grace,
Their spirit, in your Children, thus ap-
    prove.
Transcendent over time, unbound by
    place,
Concord and Charity in circles move.

XV.

III. CONCLUDED.—AMERICAN EPISCOPACY.

[Composed 1842.—Published: vol. of 1842.].

PATRIOTS informed with Apostolic light
Were they who, when their Country had
  been freed,
Bowing with reverence to the ancient
  creed,
Fixed on the frame of England's Church
  their sight,
And strove in filial love to reunite   5
What force had severed. Thence they
  fetched the seed
Of Christian unity, and won a meed
Of praise from Heaven. To Thee, O
  saintly WHITE,
Patriarch of a wide-spreading family,
Remotest lands and unborn times shall
  turn,   10
Whether they would restore or build—to
  Thee,
As one who rightly taught how zeal should
  burn,
As one who drew from out Faith's holiest
  urn
The purest stream of patient Energy.

XVI.

[Composed ?.—Published 1845.]

BISHOPS and Priests, blessèd are ye, if
  deep
(As yours above all offices is high)
Deep in your hearts the sense of duty lie;
Charged as ye are by Christ to feed and
  keep
From wolves your portion of His chosen
  sheep: 5
Labouring as ever in your Master's sight,
Making your hardest task your best
  delight,
What perfect glory ye in Heaven shall
  reap!—
But in the solemn Office which ye sought
And undertook premonished, if unsound
Your practice prove, faithless though but
  in thought,   11
Bishops and Priests, think what a gulf
  profound

Awaits you then, if they were rightly
  taught
Who framed the Ordinance by your lives
  disowned!

XVII.

PLACES OF WORSHIP.

As star that shines dependent upon star
Is to the sky while we look up in love;
As to the deep fair ships which though
  they move
Seem fixed, to eyes that watch them from
  afar;
As to the sandy desert fountains are,   5
With palm-groves shaded at wide inter-
  vals,
Whose fruit around the sun-burnt Native
  falls
Of roving tired or desultory war—
Such to this British Isle her christian
  Fanes,
Each linked to each for kindred services;
Her Spires, her Steeple-towers with
  glittering vanes   11
Far-kenned, her Chapels lurking among
  trees,
Where a few villagers on bended knees
Find solace which a busy world disdains.

XVIII.

PASTORAL CHARACTER.

A GENIAL hearth, a hospitable board,
And a refined rusticity, belong
To the neat mansion, where, his flock
  among,
The learned Pastor dwells, their watchful
  Lord.
Though meek and patient as a sheathèd
  sword;   5
Though pride's least lurking thought
  appear a wrong
To human kind; though peace be on his
  tongue,
Gentleness in his heart—can earth afford
Such genuine state, pre-eminence so free,
As when, arrayed in Christ's authority, 10
He from the pulpit lifts his awful hand;
Conjures, implores, and labours all he can
For re-subjecting to divine command
The stubborn spirit of rebellious man?

XIX.

THE LITURGY.

YES, if the intensities of hope and fear
Attract us still, and passionate exercise
Of lofty thoughts, the way before us lies
Distinct with signs, through which in set
    career,
As through a zodiac, moves the ritual
    year   5
Of England's Church; stupendous mys-
    teries!
Which whoso travels in her bosom eyes,
As he approaches them, with solemn
    cheer.
Upon that circle traced from sacred story
We only dare to cast a transient glance,
Trusting in hope that Others may ad-
    vance   11
With mind intent upon the King of
    Glory,
From his mild advent till his countenance
Shall dissipate the seas and mountains
    hoary.

XX.

BAPTISM.

[Composed ?.—Published 1827.]

DEAR be the Church that, watching o'er
    the needs
Of Infancy, provides a timely shower
Whose virtue changes to a christian
    Flower
A Growth from sinful Nature's bed of
    weeds!—
Fitliest beneath the sacred roof proceeds 5
The ministration; while parental Love
Looks on, and Grace descendeth from
    above
As the high service pledges now, now
    pleads.
There, should vain thoughts outspread
    their wings and fly
To meet the coming hours of festal mirth,
The tombs—which hear and answer that
    brief cry,   11
The Infant's notice of his second birth—
Recall the wandering Soul to sympathy
With what man hopes from Heaven, yet
    fears from Earth.

XXI.

SPONSORS.

[Composed ?.—Published 1832.]

FATHER! to God himself we cannot give
A holier name! then lightly do not bear
Both names conjoined, but of thy spiritual
    care
Be duly mindful: still more sensitive
Do Thou, in truth a second Mother, strive
Against disheartening custom, that by
    Thee   6
Watched, and with love and pious in-
    dustry
Tended at need, the adopted Plant may
    thrive
For everlasting bloom. Benign and pure
This Ordinance, whether loss it would
    supply,   10
Prevent omission, help deficiency,
Or seek to make assurance doubly sure.
Shame if the consecrated Vow be found
An idle form, the Word an empty sound!

XXII.

CATECHISING.

FROM Little down to Least, in due degree,
Around the Pastor, each in new-wrought
    vest,
Each with a vernal posy at his breast,
We stood, a trembling, earnest Company!
With low soft murmur, like a distant bee,
Some spake, by thought-perplexing fears
    betrayed;   6
And some a bold unerring answer made:
How fluttered then thy anxious heart for
    me,
Belovèd Mother! Thou whose happy
    hand
Had bound the flowers I wore, with faith-
    ful tie: 10
Sweet flowers! at whose inaudible com-
    mand
Her countenance, phantom-like, doth re-
    appear:
O lost too early for the frequent tear,
And ill requited by this heartfelt sigh[1]!

[1] See Bishop Wordsworth's *Memoirs of Wil-
liam Wordsworth,* I., 8; and *The Prelude,*
Bk. V., ll. 256–293.—ED.

XXIII.

CONFIRMATION.

[Composed ?.—Published 1827.]

THE Young-ones gathered in from hill
		and dale,
With holiday delight on every brow:
'Tis past away; far other thoughts pre-
		vail;
For they are taking the baptismal Vow
Upon their conscious selves; their own
		lips speak					5
The solemn promise. Strongest sinews
		fail,
And many a blooming, many a lovely,
		cheek
Under the holy fear of God turns pale;
While on each head his lawn-robed
		servant lays
An apostolic hand, and with prayer seals
The Covenant. The Omnipotent will
		raise					11
Their feeble Souls; and bear with *his*
		regrets,
Who, looking round the fair assemblage,
		feels
That ere the Sun goes down their child-
		hood sets.

XXIV.

CONFIRMATION CONTINUED.

[Composed ?.—Published 1827.]

I SAW a Mother's eye intensely bent
Upon a Maiden trembling as she knelt;
In and for whom the pious Mother felt
Things that we judge of by a light too
		faint:
Tell, if ye may, some star-crowned Muse,
		or Saint!					5
Tell what rushed in, from what she was
		relieved—
Then, when her Child the hallowing touch
		received,
And such vibration through the Mother
		went
That tears burst forth amain. Did gleams
		appear?
Opened a vision of that blissful place		10

Where dwells a Sister-child? And was
		power given
Part of her lost One's glory back to trace
Even to this Rite? For thus *She* knelt,
		and, ere
The summer-leaf had faded, passed to
		Heaven.

XXV.

SACRAMENT.

[Composed ?.—Published 1827.]

BY chain yet stronger must the Soul be
		tied:
One duty more, last stage of this ascent,
Brings to thy food, mysterious Sacra-
		ment!
The Offspring, haply at the Parent's side;
But not till They, with all that do abide	5
In Heaven, have lifted up their hearts to
		laud
And magnify the glorious name of God,
Fountain of Grace, whose Son for sinners
		died.
Ye, who have duly weighed the summons,
		pause
No longer: ye, whom to the saving rite	10
The Altar calls; come early under laws
That can secure for you a path of light
Through gloomiest shade; put on (nor
		dread its weight)
Armour divine, and conquer in your
		cause!

XXVI.

THE MARRIAGE CEREMONY.

[Composed 1842.—Published 1845.]

THE Vested Priest before the Altar
		stands;
Approach, come gladly, ye prepared, in
		sight
Of God and chosen friends, your troth to
		plight
With the symbolic ring, and willing
		hands
Solemnly joined. Now sanctify the bands
O Father!—to the Espoused thy blessing
		give,					6
That mutually assisted they may live

Obedient, as here taught, to thy commands.

So prays the Church, to consecrate a Vow
"The which would endless matrimony
make;" 10

Union that shadows forth and doth partake

A mystery potent human love to endow

With heavenly, each more prized for the other's sake;

Weep not, meek Bride! uplift thy timid brow.

XXVII.

THANKSGIVING AFTER CHILDBIRTH.

[Composed 1842 (?).—Published 1845.]

WOMAN! the Power who left His throne on high,

And deigned to wear the robe of flesh we wear,

The Power that thro' the straits of Infancy

Did pass dependent on maternal care,

His own humanity with Thee will share, 5

Pleased with the thanks that in His People's eye

Thou offerest up for safe Delivery

From Childbirth's perilous throes. And should the Heir

Of thy fond hopes hereafter walk inclined

To courses fit to make a mother rue 10

That ever he was born, a glance of mind

Cast upon this observance may renew

A better will; and, in the imagined view

Of thee thus kneeling, safety he may find.

XXVIII.

VISITATION OF THE SICK.

[Composed 1842 (?).—Published 1845.]

THE Sabbath bells renew the inviting peal;

Glad music! yet there be that, worn with pain

And sickness, listen where they long have lain,

In sadness listen. With maternal zeal

Inspired, the Church sends ministers to kneel 5

Beside the afflicted; to sustain with prayer,

And soothe the heart confession hath laid bare—

That pardon, from God's throne, may set its seal

On a true Penitent. When breath departs

From one disburthened so, so comforted,

His Spirit Angels greet; and ours be hope 11

That, if the Sufferer rise from his sick-bed,

Hence he will gain a firmer mind, to cope

With a bad world, and foil the Tempter's arts.

XXIX.

THE COMMINATION SERVICE.

[Composed 1842 (?).—Published 1845.]

SHUN not this Rite, neglected, yea abhorred,

By some of unreflecting mind, as calling

Man to curse man, (thought monstrous and appalling).

Go thou and hear the threatenings of the *Lord;*

Listening within his Temple see his sword

Unsheathed in wrath to strike the offender's head, 6

Thy own, if sorrow for thy sin be dead,

Guilt unrepented, pardon unimplored.

Two aspects bears Truth needful for salvation;

Who knows not *that?*—yet would this delicate age 10

Look only on the Gospel's brighter page:

Let light and dark duly our thoughts employ;

So shall the fearful words of Commination

Yield timely fruit of peace and love and joy.

XXX.

FORMS OF PRAYER AT SEA.

[Composed 1842 (?).—Published 1845.]

To kneeling Worshippers no earthly floor
Gives holier invitation than the deck
Of a storm-shattered Vessel saved from Wreck

(When all that Man could do availed no
    more)
By Him who raised the Tempest and
    restrains: 5
Happy the crew who this have felt, and
    pour
Forth for His mercy, as the Church
    ordains,
Solemn thanksgiving. Nor will *they* im-
    plore
In vain who, for a rightful cause, give
    breath
To words the Church prescribes aiding
    the lip   10
For the heart's sake, ere ship with hostile
    ship
Encounters, armed for work of pain and
    death.
Suppliants! the God to whom your cause
    ye trust
Will listen, and ye know that He is just.

XXXI.
FUNERAL SERVICE.

[Composed 1842.—Published 1845.]

FROM the Baptismal hour, thro' weal and
    woe,
The Church extends her care to thought
    and deed;
Nor quits the Body when the Soul is
    freed,
The mortal weight cast off to be laid low.
Blest Rite for him who hears in faith,
    "I know   5
That my Redeemer liveth,"—hears each
    word
That follows—striking on some kindred
    chord
Deep in the thankful heart;—yet tears
    will flow.
Man is as grass that springeth up at morn,
Grows green, and is cut down and wither-
    eth   10
Ere nightfall—truth that well may claim
    a sigh,
Its natural echo; but hope comes reborn
At Jesu's bidding. We rejoice, "O
    Death,
Where is thy Sting?—O Grave, where is
    thy Victory?".

XXXII.
RURAL CEREMONY [1].

CLOSING the sacred Book which long has
    fed
Our meditations, give we to a day
Of annual joy one tributary lay;
This day, when, forth by rustic music
    led,
The village Children, while the sky is red
With evening lights, advance in long
    array   6
Through the still churchyard, each with
    garland gay,
That, carried sceptre-like, o'ertops the
    head
Of the proud Bearer. To the wide church-
    door,
Charged with these offerings which their
    fathers bore   10
For decoration in the Papal time,
The innocent Procession softly moves:—
The spirit of Laud is pleased in heaven's
    pure clime,
And Hooker's voice the spectacle ap-
    proves!

XXXIII.
REGRETS.

WOULD that our scrupulous Sires had
    dared to leave
Less scanty measure of those graceful
    rites
And usages, whose due return invites
A stir of mind too natural to deceive;
Giving to Memory help when she would
    weave   5
A crown for Hope!—I dread the boasted
    lights
That all too often are but fiery blights,
Killing the bud o'er which in vain we
    grieve.
Go, seek, when Christmas snows discom-
    fort bring,
The counter Spirit found in some gay
    church   10
Green with fresh holly, every pew a
    perch

[1] See Note, p. 923.

In which the linnet or the thrush might
sing,
Merry and loud and safe from prying
search,
Strains offered only to the genial Spring.

XXXIV.
MUTABILITY.

FROM low to high doth dissolution climb,
And sink from high to low, along a
scale
Of awful notes, whose concord shall not
fail;
A musical but melancholy chime,
Which they can hear who meddle not
with crime,   5
Nor avarice, nor over-anxious care.
Truth fails not; but her outward forms
that bear
The longest date do melt like frosty rime,
That in the morning whitened hill and
plain
And is no more; drop like the tower
sublime   10
Of yesterday, which royally did wear
His crown of weeds, but could not even
sustain
Some casual shout that broke the silent
air,
Or the unimaginable touch of Time.

XXXV.
OLD ABBEYS.

MONASTIC Domes! following my down-
ward way,
Untouched by due regret I marked your
fall!
Now, ruin, beauty, ancient stillness, all
Dispose to judgments temperate as we lay
On our past selves in life's declining day:
For as, by discipline of Time made wise,
We learn to tolerate the infirmities
And faults of others—gently as he may,
So with our own the mild Instructor deals,
Teaching us to forget them or forgive. 10
Perversely curious, then, for hidden ill
Why should we break Time's charitable
seals?
Once ye were holy, ye are holy still;
Your spirit freely let me drink, and live.

XXXVI.
EMIGRANT FRENCH CLERGY.
[Composed ?.—Published 1827.]

EVEN while I speak, the sacred roofs of
France
Are shattered into dust; and self-exiled
From altars threatened, levelled, or de-
filed,
Wander the Ministers of God, as chance
Opens a way for life, or consonance   5
Of faith invites. More welcome to no land
The fugitives than to the British strand,
Where priest and layman with the vigil-
ance
Of true compassion greet them. Creed
and test
Vanish before the unreserved embrace 10
Of catholic humanity:—distrest
They came,—and, while the moral tem-
pest roars
Throughout the Country they have left,
our shores
Give to their Faith a fearless resting-
place.

XXXVII.
CONGRATULATION.

THUS all things lead to Charity, secured
By THEM who blessed the soft and happy
gale
That landward urged the great Deliverer's
sail,
Till in the sunny bay his fleet was
moored!
Propitious hour! had we, like them,
endured   5
Sore stress of apprehension[1], with a mind
Sickened by injuries, dreading worse de-
signed,
From month to month trembling and un-
assured,
How had we then rejoiced! But we have
felt,
As a loved substance, their futurity: 10
Good, which they dared not hope for, we
have seen;

---

[1] See Note, p. 923.

A State whose generous will through
    earth is dealt;
A State—which, balancing herself be-
    tween
Licence and slavish order, dares be free.

XXXVIII.

NEW CHURCHES.

BUT liberty, and triumphs on the Main,
And laurelled armies, not to be with-
    stood—
What serve they? if, on transitory good
Intent, and sedulous of abject gain,
The State (ah, surely not preserved in
    vain!)   5
Forbear to shape due channels which the
    Flood
Of sacred truth may enter—till it brood
O'er the wide realm, as o'er the Egyptian
    plain
The all-sustaining Nile. No more—the
    time
Is conscious of her want; through
    England's bounds,   10
In rival haste, the wished-for Temples
    rise!
I hear their sabbath bells' harmonious
    chime
Float on the breeze—the heavenliest of
    all sounds
That vale or hill prolongs or multiplies!

XXXIX.

CHURCH TO BE ERECTED.

BE this the chosen site; the virgin sod,
Moistened from age to age by dewy eve,
Shall disappear, and grateful earth receive
The corner-stone from hands that build
    to God.
Yon reverend hawthorns, hardened to
    the rod   5
Of winter storms, yet budding cheerfully;
Those forest oaks of Druid memory,
Shall long survive, to shelter the Abode
Of genuine Faith. Where, haply, 'mid
    this band
Of daisies, shepherds sate of yore and
    wove   10
May-garlands, there let the holy altar
    stand

For kneeling adoration;—while—above,
Broods, visibly portrayed, the mystic
    Dove,
That shall protect from blasphemy the
    Land.

XL.

CONTINUED.

MINE ear has rung, my spirit sunk sub-
    dued,
Sharing the strong emotion of the crowd,
When each pale brow to dread hosannas
    bowed
While clouds of incense mounting veiled
    the rood,
That glimmered like a pine-tree dimly
    viewed   5
Through Alpine vapours. Such appal-
    ling rite
Our Church prepares not, trusting to the
    might
Of simple truth with grace divine imbued;
Yet will we not conceal the precious
    Cross,
Like men ashamed: the Sun with his
    first smile   10
Shall greet that symbol crowning the low
    Pile;
And the fresh air of incense-breathing morn
Shall wooingly embrace it; and green
    moss
Creep round its arms through centuries
    unborn.

XLI.

NEW CHURCHYARD.

THE encircling ground, in native turf
    arrayed,
Is now by solemn consecration given
To social interests, and to favouring
    Heaven;
And where the rugged colts their gambols
    played,
And wild deer bounded through the
    forest glade,   5
Unchecked as when by merry Outlaw
    driven,
Shall hymns of praise resound at morn
    and even;
And soon, full soon, the lonely Sexton's
    spade

Shall wound the tender sod. Encincture
    small,
But infinite its grasp of weal and woe! 10
Hopes, fears, in never-ending ebb and
    flow;—
The spousal trembling, and the "dust to
    dust,"
The prayers, the contrite struggle, and
    the trust
That to the Almighty Father looks
    through all.

XLII.

CATHEDRALS, ETC.

OPEN your gates, ye everlasting Piles!
Types of the spiritual Church which God
    hath reared;
Not loth we quit the newly-hallowed
    sward
And humble altar, 'mid your sumptuous
    aisles
To kneel, or thrid your intricate defiles, 5
Or down the nave to pace in motion slow;
Watching, with upward eye, the tall
    tower grow
And mount, at every step, with living
    wiles
Instinct—to rouse the heart and lead the
    will
By a bright ladder to the world above. 10
Open your gates, ye Monuments of love
Divine! thou Lincoln, on thy sovereign
    hill!
Thou, stately York! and Ye, whose
    splendours cheer
Isis and Cam, to patient Science dear!

XLIII.

INSIDE OF KING'S COLLEGE CHAPEL, CAMBRIDGE[1].

TAX not the royal Saint with vain ex-
    pense,
With ill-matched aims the Architect who
    planned—
Albeit labouring for a scanty band

[1] Wordsworth appears to have written one at
least of these sonnets (XLIII.-XLV.), and perhaps
wrote all three, during a visit to his brother
Christopher (Master of Trinity) at Cambridge,
Nov.-Dec., 1820.—ED.

Of white-robed Scholars only—this im-
    mense
And glorious Work of fine intelligence! 5
Give all thou canst; high Heaven rejects
    the lore
Of nicely-calculated less or more;
So deemed the man who fashioned for the
    sense
These lofty pillars, spread that branching
    roof
Self-poised, and scooped into ten thou-
    sand cells, 10
Where light and shade repose, where
    music dwells
Lingering—and wandering on as loth to
    die;
Like thoughts whose very sweetness yield-
    eth proof
That they were born for immortality.

XLIV.

THE SAME.

WHAT awful pérspective! while from our
    sight
With gradual stealth the lateral windows
    hide
Their Portraitures, their stone-work glim-
    mers, dyed
In the soft chequerings of a sleepy light.
Martyr, or King, or sainted Eremite, 5
Whoe'er ye be, that thus, yourselves un-
    seen,
Imbue your prison-bars with solemn sheen,
Shine on, until ye fade with coming
    Night!—
But, from the arms of silence—list! O list!
The music bursteth into second life; 10
The notes luxuriate, every stone is kissed
By sound, or ghost of sound, in mazy
    strife;
Heart-thrilling strains, that cast, before
    the eye
Of the devout, a veil of ecstasy!

XLV.

CONTINUED.

THEY dreamt not of a perishable home
Who thus could build. Be mine, in
    hours of fear
Or grovelling thought, to seek a refuge
    here;

Or through the aisles of Westminster to
　　roam;
Where bubbles burst, and folly's dancing
　　foam　　　　　　　　　　　　　　5
Melts, if it cross the threshold; where the
　　wreath
Of awe-struck wisdom droops: or let my
　　path
Lead to that younger Pile, whose sky-
　　like dome
Hath typified by reach of daring art
Infinity's embrace; whose guardian crest,
The silent Cross, among the stars shall
　　spread　　　　　　　　　　　　　11
As now, when She hath also seen her
　　breast
Filled with mementos, satiate with its part
Of grateful England's overflowing Dead.

XLVI.

EJACULATION.

GLORY to God! and to the Power who came
In filial duty, clothed with love divine,
That made His human tabernacle shine
Like Ocean burning with purpureal flame;
Or like the Alpine Mount, that takes its
　　name　　　　　　　　　　　　　5
From roseate hues, far kenned at morn
　　and even,
In hours of peace, or when the storm is
　　driven
Along the nether region's rugged frame!
Earth prompts—Heaven urges; let us
　　seek the light,

Studious of that pure intercourse begun　10
When first our infant brows their lustre
　　won;
So, like the Mountain, may we grow
　　more bright
From unimpeded commerce with the Sun,
At the approach of all-involving night.

XLVII.

CONCLUSION.

WHY sleeps the future, as a snake en-
　　rolled,
Coil within coil, at noon-tide? For the
　　WORD
Yields, if with unpresumptuous faith
　　explored,
Power at whose touch the sluggard shall
　　unfold
His drowsy rings. Look forth!—that
　　Stream behold,　　　　　　　　5
THAT STREAM upon whose bosom we
　　have passed
Floating at ease while nations have
　　effaced
Nations, and Death has gathered to his
　　fold
Long lines of mighty Kings—look forth,
　　my Soul!　　　　　　　　　　　,
(Nor in this vision be thou slow to trust)
The living Waters, less and less by guilt
Stained and polluted, brighten as they
　　roll,
Till they have reached the eternal City—
　　built
For the perfected Spirits of the just!

EVENING VOLUNTARIES.

I.

[Composed 1832.—Published 1835.]

CALM is the fragrant air, and loth to lose
Day's grateful warmth, tho' moist with
    falling dews.
Look for the stars, you'll say that there
    are none;
Look up a second time, and, one by one,
You mark them twinkling out with silvery
    light,   5
And wonder how they could elude the
    sight!
The birds, of late so noisy in their bowers,
Warbled a while with faint and fainter
    powers,
But now are silent as the dim-seen flowers:
Nor does the village Church-clock's iron
    tone   10
The time's and season's influence disown;
Nine beats distinctly to each other bound
In drowsy sequence—how unlike the
    sound
That, in rough winter, oft inflicts a fear
On fireside listeners, doubting what they
    hear!   15
The shepherd, bent on rising with the sun,
Had closed his door before the day was
    done,
And now with thankful heart to bed doth
    creep,
And joins his little children in their sleep.
The bat, lured forth where trees the lane
    o'ershade,   20
Flits and reflits along the close arcade;
The busy dor-hawk chases the white moth
With burring note, which Industry and
    Sloth
Might both be pleased with, for it suits
    them both.
A stream is heard—I see it not, but
    know   25
By its soft music whence the waters flow:

Wheels and the tread of hoofs are heard
    no more;
One boat there was, but it will touch the
    shore
With the next dipping of its slackened
    oar;
Faint sound, that, for the gayest of the
    gay,   30
Might give to serious thought a moment's
    sway,
As a last token of man's toilsome day!

II.

ON A HIGH PART OF THE COAST OF CUMBERLAND.

Easter Sunday, April 7.

THE AUTHOR'S SIXTY-THIRD BIRTH-DAY.

[Composed April 7, 1833.—Published 1835.]

THE Sun, that seemed so mildly to retire,
Flung back from distant climes a stream-
    ing fire,
Whose blaze is now subdued to tender
    gleams,
Prelude of night's approach with soothing
    dreams.
Look round;—of all the clouds not one is
    moving;   5
'Tis the still hour of thinking, feeling,
    loving.
Silent, and steadfast as the vaulted sky,
The boundless plain of waters seems to
    lie:—
Comes that low sound from breezes rust-
    ling o'er
The grass-crowned headland that conceals
    the shore?   10
No; 'tis the earth-voice of the mighty sea,
Whispering how meek and gentle he
    can be!

Thou Power supreme! who, arming to
    rebuke
Offenders, dost put off the gracious look,
And clothe thyself with terrors like the
    flood   15
Of Ocean roused into his fiercest mood,
Whatever discipline thy Will ordain
For the brief course that must for me
    remain;
Teach me with quick-eared spirit to rejoice
In admonitions of thy softest voice!   20
Whate'er the path these mortal feet may
    trace,
Breathe through my soul the blessing of
    thy grace,
Glad, through a perfect love, a faith
    sincere
Drawn from the wisdom that begins with
    fear,
Glad to expand; and, for a season, free   25
From finite cares, to rest absorbed in
    Thee!

III.

(BY THE SEA-SIDE.)

[Composed 1833.—Published 1835.]

The sun is couched, the sea fowl gone to
    rest,
And the wild storm hath somewhere found
    a nest;.
Air slumbers—wave with wave no longer
    strives,
Only a heaving of the deep survives,
A tell-tale motion! soon will it be laid,   5
And by the tide alone the water swayed.
Stealthy withdrawings, interminglings
    mild
Of light with shade in beauty reconciled—
Such is the prospect far as sight can
    range,
The soothing recompense, the welcome
    change.   10
Where now the ships that drove before
    the blast,
Threatened by angry breakers as they
    passed;
And by a train of flying clouds bemocked;
Or, in the hollow surge, at anchor rocked
As on a bed of death? Some lodge in
    peace,   15

Saved by His care who bade the tempest
    cease;
And some, too heedless of past danger,
    court
Fresh gales to waft them to the far-off
    port;
But near, or hanging sea and sky between,
Not one of all those wingèd powers is
    seen,   20
Seen in her course, nor 'mid this quiet
    heard;
Yet oh! how gladly would the air be
    stirred
By some acknowledgment of thanks and
    praise,
Soft in its temper as those vesper lays
Sung to the Virgin while accordant
    oars   25
Urge the slow bark along Calabrian
    shores;
A sea-born service through the mountains
    felt
Till into one loved vision all things melt:
Or like those hymns that soothe with
    graver sound
The gulfy coast of Norway iron-bound;   30
And, from the wide and open Baltic, rise
With punctual care, Lutherian harmonies,
Hush, not a voice is here! but why repine,
Now when the star of eve comes forth to
    shine
On British waters with that look be-
    nign?   35
Ye mariners, that plough your onward
    way,
Or in the haven rest, or sheltering bay,
May silent thanks at least to God be given
With a full heart; "our thoughts are *heard*
    in heaven!"

IV.

[Composed 1834.—Published 1835.]

Not in the lucid intervals of life
That come but as a curse to party-strife;
Not in some hour when Pleasure with a
    sigh
Of languor puts his rosy garland by;
Not in the breathing-times of that poor
    slave   5
Who daily piles up wealth in Mammon's
    cave—

Is Nature felt, or can be; nor do words,
Which practised talent readily affords,
Prove that her hand has touched re-
sponsive chords;
Nor has her gentle beauty power to
move   10
With genuine rapture and with fervent
love
The soul of Genius, if he dare to take
Life's rule from passion craved for passion's
sake;
Untaught that meekness is the cherished
bent
Of all the truly great and all the
innocent.   15

But who *is* innocent? By grace divine,
Not otherwise, O Nature! we are thine,
Through good and evil thine, in just degree
Of rational and manly sympathy.
To all that Earth from pensive hearts is
stealing,   20
And Heaven is now to gladdened eyes
revealing,
Add every charm the Universe can show
Through every change its aspects under-
go—
Care may be respited, but not repealed;
No perfect cure grows on that bounded
field.   25
Vain is the pleasure, a false calm the
peace,
If He, through whom alone our conflicts
cease,
Our virtuous hopes without relapse ad-
vance,
Come not to speed the Soul's deliverance;
To the distempered Intellect refuse   30
His gracious help, or give what we abuse.

V.

(BY THE SIDE OF RYDAL MERE.)

[Composed 1834.—Published 1835.]

THE linnet's warble, sinking towards a
close,
Hints to the thrush 'tis time for their
repose;
The shrill-voiced thrush is heedless, and
again
The monitor revives his own sweet strain;

But both will soon be mastered, and the
copse   5
Be left as silent as the mountain-tops,
Ere some commanding star dismiss to rest
The throng of rooks, that now, from twig
or nest,
(After a steady flight on home-bound
wings,
And a last game of mazy hoverings   10
Around their ancient grove) with cawing
noise
Disturb the liquid music's equipoise.

O Nightingale! Who ever heard thy
song
Might here be moved, till Fancy grows
so strong
That listening sense is pardonably cheated
Where wood or stream by thee was never
greeted.   16
Surely, from fairest spots of favoured
lands,
Were not some gifts withheld by jealous
hands,
This hour of deepening darkness here
would be
As a fresh morning for new harmony; 20
And lays as prompt would hail the dawn
of Night:
A *dawn* she has both beautiful and bright,
When the East kindles with the full
moon's light;
Not like the rising sun's impatient glow
Dazzling the mountains, but an overflow
Of solemn splendour, in mutation slow.

Wanderer by spring with gradual pro-
gress led,
For sway profoundly felt as widely spread;
To king, to peasant, to rough sailor, dear,
And to the soldier's trumpet-wearied ear;
How welcome wouldst thou be to this
green Vale   31
Fairer than Tempe! Yet, sweet Night-
ingale!
From the warm breeze that bears thee on,
alight
At will, and stay thy migratory flight;
Build, at thy choice, or sing, by pool or
fount,   35
Who shall complain, or call thee to
account?

The wisest, happiest, of our kind are they
That ever walk content with Nature's
way,
God's goodness—measuring bounty as it
may;
For whom the gravest thought of what
they miss,   40
Chastening the fulness of a present bliss,
Is with that wholesome office satisfied,
While unrepining sadness is allied
In thankful bosoms to a modest pride.

VI.

[Composed 1834.—Published 1835.]

SOFT as a cloud is yon blue Ridge—the
Mere
Seems firm as solid crystal, breathless,
clear,
And motionless; and, to the gazer's eye,
Deeper than ocean, in the immensity
Of its vague mountains and unreal sky!   5
But, from the process in that still retreat,
Turn to minuter changes at our feet;
Observe how dewy Twilight has with-
drawn
The crowd of daisies from the shaven lawn,
And has restored to view its tender
green,   10
That, while the sun rode high, was lost
beneath their dazzling sheen.
—An emblem this of what the sober Hour
Can do for minds disposed to feel its
power!
Thus oft, when we in vain have wished
away
The petty pleasures of the garish day,   15
Meek eve shuts up the whole usurping
host
(Unbashful dwarfs each glittering at his
post)
And leaves the disencumbered spirit free
To reassume a staid simplicity.

'Tis well—but what are helps of time
and place,   20
When wisdom stands in need of nature's
grace;
Why do good thoughts, invoked or not,
descend,
Like Angels from their bowers, our virtues
to befriend;

If yet To-morrow, unbelied, may say,
"I come to open out, for fresh display,
The elastic vanities of yesterday?"   26

VII.

[Composed 1834.—Published 1835.]

THE leaves that rustled on this oak-
crowned hill,
And sky that danced among those leaves,
are still;
Rest smooths the way for sleep; in field
and bower
Soft shades and dews have shed their
blended power
On drooping eyelid and the closing
flower;   5
Sound is there none at which the faintest
heart
Might leap, the weakest nerve of super-
stition start;
Save when the Owlet's unexpected scream
Pierces the ethereal vault; and ('mid the
gleam
Of unsubstantial imagery, the dream,   10
From the hushed vale's realities, trans-
ferred
To the still lake) the imaginative Bird
Seems, 'mid inverted mountains, not un-
heard.

Grave Creature!—whether, while the
moon shines bright
On thy wings opened wide for smoothest
flight,   15
Thou art discovered in a roofless tower,
Rising from what may once have been a
lady's bower;
Or spied where thou sitt'st moping in
thy mew
At the dim centre of a churchyard yew;
Or from a rifted crag or ivy tod   20
Deep in a forest, thy secure abode,
Thou giv'st, for pastime's sake, by shriek
or shout,
A puzzling notice of thy whereabout—
May the night never come, nor day be
seen,
When I shall scorn thy voice or mock thy
mien!   25

In classic ages men perceived a soul
Of sapience in thy aspect, headless Owl!

Thee Athens reverenced in the studious
  grove ;
And near the golden sceptre grasped by
  Jove,
His Eagle's favourite perch, while round
  him sate   30
The Gods revolving the decrees of Fate,
Thou, too, wert present at Minerva's side:—
Hark to that second larum !—far and
  wide
The elements have heard, and rock and
  cave replied.

VIII.

[Composed June 8, 1802.—Published 1807 ; omit-
ted from edd. 1815-1832 ; republished 1835.]

This *Impromptu* appeared, many years ago,
among the Author's poems, from which, in
subsequent editions, it was excluded. It is
reprinted at the request of the Friend in
whose presence the lines were thrown off.

THE sun has long been set,
  The stars are out by twos and threes,
The little birds are piping yet
  Among the bushes and trees ;
There's a cuckoo, and one or two thrushes,
And a far-off wind that rushes,   6
And a sound of water that gushes,
And the cuckoo's sovereign cry
Fills all the hollow of the sky.
  Who would go "parading"   10
In London, " and masquerading,"
On such a night of June
With that beautiful soft half-moon,
And all these innocent blisses ?
On such a night as this is !   15

IX.

COMPOSED UPON AN EVENING OF EXTRAORDINARY SPLENDOUR AND BEAUTY.

[Composed 1818.—Published 1820.]

I.

HAD this effulgence disappeared
With flying haste, I might have sent,
Among the speechless clouds, a look
Of blank astonishment ;
But 'tis endued with power to stay,   5
And sanctify one closing day,

That frail Mortality may see—
What is ?—ah no, but what *can* be !
Time was when field and watery cove
With modulated echoes rang,   10
While choirs of fervent Angels sang
Their vespers in the grove ;
Or, crowning, star-like, each some sove-
  reign height,
Warbled, for heaven above and earth
  below,
Strains suitable to both.—Such holy rite,
Methinks, if audibly repeated now   16
From hill or valley, could not move
Sublimer transport, purer love,
Than doth this silent spectacle—the
  gleam—
The shadow—and the peace supreme !   20

II.

No sound is uttered,—but a deep
And solemn harmony pervades
The hollow vale from steep to steep,
And penetrates the glades.
Far-distant images draw nigh,   25
Called forth by wondrous potency
Of beamy radiance, that imbues
Whate'er it strikes with gem-like hues !
In vision exquisitely clear,
Herds range along the mountain side ;   30
And glistening antlers are descried ;
And gilded flocks appear.
Thine is the tranquil hour, purpureal
  Eve !
But long as god-like wish, or hope di-
  vine,
Informs my spirit, ne'er can I believe   35
That this magnificence is wholly thine !
—From worlds not quickened by the sun
A portion of the gift is won ;
An intermingling of Heaven's pomp is
  spread
On ground which British shepherds
  tread !   40

III.

And if there be whom broken ties
Afflict, or injuries assail,
Yon hazy ridges to their eyes
Present a glorious scale,
Climbing suffused with sunny air,   45
To stop—no record hath told where !

And tempting Fancy to ascend,
And with immortal Spirits blend!
—Wings at my shoulders seem to play;
But, rooted here, I stand and gaze   50
On those bright steps that heavenward
    raise
Their practicable way.
Come forth, ye drooping old men, look
    abroad,
And see to what fair countries ye are
    bound!
And if some traveller, weary of his road,
Hath slept since noon-tide on the grassy
    ground,   56
Ye Genii! to his covert speed;
And wake him with such gentle heed
As may attune his soul to meet the
    dower
Bestowed on this transcendent hour!   60

IV.

Such hues from their celestial Urn
Were wont to stream before mine eye,
Where'er it wandered in the morn
Of blissful infancy.
This glimpse of glory, why renewed?   65
Nay, rather speak with gratitude:
For, if a vestige of those gleams
Survived, 'twas only in my dreams.
Dread Power! whom peace and calmness
    serve
No less than Nature's threatening voice,
If aught unworthy be my choice,   71
From THEE if I would swerve;
Oh, let Thy grace remind me of the light
Full early lost, and fruitlessly deplored;
Which, at this moment, on my waking
    sight   75
Appears to shine, by miracle restored;
My soul, though yet confined to earth,
Rejoices in a second birth!
—'Tis past, the visionary splendour fades;
And night approaches with her shades.   80

Note—The multiplication of mountain-ridges,
described at the commencement of the third
Stanza of this Ode as a kind of Jacob's Ladder,
leading to Heaven, is produced either by watery
vapours, or sunny haze;—in the present instance
by the latter cause. Allusions to the Ode en-
titled "Intimations of Immortality" pervade the
last Stanza of the foregoing Poem.

X.

COMPOSED BY THE SEA-SHORE.

[Composed 1833.—Published 1845.]

WHAT mischief cleaves to unsubdued re-
    gret,
How fancy sickens by vague hopes beset;
How baffled projects on the spirit prey,
And fruitless wishes eat the heart away,
The Sailor knows; he best, whose lot is
    cast   5
On the relentless sea that holds him fast
On chance dependent, and the fickle star
Of power, through long and melancholy
    war.
O sad it is, in sight of foreign shores,
Daily to think on old familiar doors,   10
Hearths loved in childhood, and ancestral
    floors;
Or, tossed about along a waste of foam,
To ruminate on that delightful home
Which with the dear Betrothèd *was* to
    come;
Or came and was and is, yet meets the eye
Never but in the world of memory;   16
Or in a dream recalled, whose smoothest
    range
Is crossed by knowledge, or by dread, of
    change,
And if not so, whose perfect joy makes
    sleep
A thing too bright for breathing man to
    keep.   20
Hail to the virtues which that perilous life
Extracts from Nature's elemental strife;
And welcome glory won in battles fought
As bravely as the foe was keenly sought.
But to each gallant Captain and his crew
A less imperious sympathy is due,   26
Such as my verse now yields, while moon-
    beams play
On the mute sea in this unruffled bay;
Such as will promptly flow from every
    breast,
Where good men, disappointed in the
    quest   30
Of wealth and power and honours, long
    for rest;
Or, having known the splendours of
    success,
Sigh for the obscurities of happiness.

XI.

[Composed ?.—Published : vol. of 1842.]

THE Crescent-moon, the Star of Love,
Glories of evening, as ye there are seen
With but a span of sky between—
Speak one of you, my doubts remove,
Which is the attendant Page and which
 the Queen?   5

XII.

TO THE MOON.

COMPOSED BY THE SEASIDE,—ON THE
COAST OF CUMBERLAND.

[Composed 1835.—Published 1837.]

WANDERER ! that stoop'st so low, and
 com'st so near
To human life's unsettled atmosphere ;
Who lov'st with Night and Silence to
 partake,
So might it seem, the cares of them that
 wake ;
And, through the cottage-lattice softly
 peeping,   5
Dost shield from harm the humblest of
 the sleeping ;
What pleasure once encompassed those
 sweet names
Which yet in thy behalf the Poet claims,
An idolizing dreamer as of yore !—
I slight them all ; and, on this sea-beat
 shore   10
Sole-sitting, only can to thoughts attend
That bid me hail thee as the SAILOR's
 FRIEND ;
So call thee for heaven's grace through
 thee made known
By confidence supplied and mercy shown,
When not a twinkling star or beacon's
 light   15
Abates the perils of a stormy night ;
And for less obvious benefits, that find
Their way, with thy pure help, to heart
 and mind ;
Both for the adventurer starting in life's
 prime ;
And veteran ranging round from clime to
 clime,   20

Long-baffled hope's slow fever in his
 veins,
And wounds and weakness oft his labour's
 sole remains.

The aspiring Mountains and the wind-
 ing Streams,
Empress of Night ! are gladdened by thy
 beams ;
A look of thine the wilderness pervades, 25
And penetrates the forest's inmost shades ;
Thou, chequering peaceably the minster's
 gloom,
Guid'st the pale Mourner to the lost one's
 tomb ;
Canst reach the Prisoner—to his grated
 cell
Welcome, though silent and intangible !—
And lives there one, of all that come and
 go   31
On the great waters toiling to and fro,
One, who has watched thee at some quiet
 hour
Enthroned aloft in undisputed power,
Or crossed by vapoury streaks and clouds
 that move   35
Catching the lustre they in part reprove—
Nor sometimes felt a fitness in thy sway
To call up thoughts that shun the glare
 of day,
And make the serious happier than the
 gay ?

Yes, lovely Moon ! if thou so mildly
 bright   40
Dost rouse, yet surely in thy own despite,
To fiercer mood the frenzy-stricken
 brain,
Let me a compensating faith maintain ;
That there's a sensitive, a tender, part
Which thou canst touch in every human
 heart,   45
For healing and composure.—But as least
And mightiest billows ever have confessed
Thy domination ; as the whole vast Sea
Feels through her lowest depths thy sove-
 reignty ;
So shines that countenance with especial
 grace   50
On them who urge the keel her *plains* to
 trace

Furrowing its way right onward. The
  most rude,
Cut off from home and country, may have
  stood—
Even till long gazing hath bedimmed his
  eye,
Or the mute rapture ended in a sigh— 55
Touched by accordance of thy placid
  cheer,
With some internal lights to memory dear,
Or fancies stealing forth to soothe the
  breast
Tired with its daily share of earth's un-
  rest,—
Gentle awakenings, visitations meek ; 60
A kindly influence whereof few will speak,
Though it can wet with tears the hardiest
  cheek.

And when thy beauty in the shadowy
  cave
Is hidden, buried in its monthly grave ;
Then, while the Sailor, 'mid an open sea
Swept by a favouring wind that leaves
.   thought free, 66
Paces the deck—no star perhaps in sight,
And nothing save the moving ship's own
  light
To cheer the long dark hours of vacant
  night—
Oft with his musings does thy image blend,
In his mind's eye thy crescent horns ascend,
And thou art still, O Moon, that SAILOR'S
  FRIEND !

XIII.
TO THE MOON.
(RYDAL.)

[Composed 1835.—Published 1837.]

QUEEN of the stars !—so gentle, so benign,
That ancient Fable did to thee assign,
When darkness creeping o'er thy silver
  brow
Warned thee these upper regions to
  forego,
Alternate empire in the shades below— 5
A Bard, who, lately near the wide-spread
  sea
Traversed by gleaming ships, looked up
  to thee

With grateful thoughts, doth now thy
  rising hail
From the close confines of a shadowy vale.
Glory of night, conspicuous yet serene, 10
Nor less attractive when by glimpses
  seen
Through cloudy umbrage, well might that
  fair face,
And all those attributes of modest grace,
In days when Fancy wrought unchecked
  by fear,
Down to the green earth fetch thee from
  thy sphere,   15
To sit in leafy woods by fountains clear !

O still beloved (for thine, meek Power,
  are charms
That fascinate the very Babe in arms,
While he, uplifted towards thee, laughs
  outright,
Spreading his little palms in his glad
  Mother's sight)   20
O still beloved, once worshipped ! Time,
  that frowns
In his destructive flight on earthly crowns,
Spares thy mild splendour ; still those
  far-shot beams
Tremble on dancing waves and rippling
  streams
With stainless touch, as chaste as when
  thy praise   25
Was sung by Virgin-choirs in festal lays ;
And through dark trials still dost thou
  explore
Thy way for increase punctual as of yore,
When teeming Matrons—yielding to rude
  faith
In mysteries of birth and life and death 30
And painful struggle and deliverance—
  prayed
Of thee to visit them with lenient aid.
What though the rites be swept away, the
  fanes
Extinct that echoed to the votive strains ;
Yet thy mild aspect does not, cannot,
  cease
Love to promote and purity and peace ;
And Fancy, unreproved, even yet may
  trace   37
Faint types of suffering in thy beamless
  face.

Then, silent Monitress! let us—not
blind
To worlds unthought of till the searching
mind   40
Of Science laid them open to mankind—
Told, also, how the voiceless heavens de-
clare
God's glory; and acknowledging thy
share
In that blest charge; let us—without
offence
To aught of highest, holiest, influence—
Receive whatever good 'tis given thee to
dispense.   46
May sage and simple, catching with one
eye
The moral intimations of the sky,
Learn from thy course, where'er their
own be taken,
"To look on tempests, and be never
shaken;"   50
To keep with faithful step the appointed
way
Eclipsing or eclipsed, by night or day,
And from example of thy monthly range
Gently to brook decline and fatal change;
Meek, patient, steadfast, and with loftier
scope,   55
Than thy revival yields, for gladsome
hope!

XIV.

TO LUCCA GIORDANO.

[Composed 1846.—Published 1850.]

GIORDANO, verily thy Pencil's skill
Hath here portrayed with Nature's hap-
piest grace
The fair Endymion couched on Latmos-
hill;
And Dian gazing on the Shepherd's
face
In rapture,—yet suspending her embrace,
As not unconscious with what power the
thrill   6
Of her most timid touch his sleep would
chase,
And, with his sleep, that beauty calm and
still.

Oh may this work have found its last re-
treat
Here in a Mountain-bard's secure abode,
One to whom, yet a School-boy, Cynthia
showed   11
A face of love which he in love would
greet,
Fixed, by her smile, upon some rocky
seat;
Or lured along where green-wood paths
he trod.

RYDAL MOUNT, 1846.

XV.

[Composed 1846.—Published 1850.]

WHO but is pleased to watch the moon on
high
Travelling where she from time to time
enshrouds
Her head, and nothing loth her Majesty
Renounces, till among the scattered clouds
One with its kindling edge declares that
soon   5
Will reappear before the uplifted eye
A Form as bright, as beautiful a moon,
To glide in open prospect through clear
sky.
Pity that such a promise e'er should
prove
False in the issue, that yon seeming space
Of sky should be in truth the steadfast
face   11
Of a cloud flat and dense, through which
must move
(By transit not unlike man's frequent
doom)
The Wanderer lost in more determined
gloom.

XVI.

[Composed 1846.—Published 1850.]

WHERE lies the truth? has Man, in wis-
dom's creed,
A pitiable doom; for respite brief
A care more anxious, or a heavier grief?
Is he ungrateful, and doth little heed

God's bounty, soon forgotten ; or indeed,
Must Man, with labour born, awake to
    sorrow   6
When Flowers rejoice and Larks with
    rival speed
Spring from their nests to bid the Sun
    good morrow?
They mount for rapture as their songs
    proclaim

Warbled in hearing both of earth and
    sky ;   10
But o'er the contrast wherefore heave
    a sigh?
Like those aspirants let us soar—our aim,
Through life's worst trials, whether shocks
    or snares,
A happier, brighter, purer Heaven than
    theirs.

POEMS

Having been prevented by the lateness of the season, in 1831, from visiting Staffa and Iona, the author made these the principal objects of a short tour in the summer of 1833, of which the following Series of Poems is a Memorial. The course pursued was down the Cumberland river Derwent, and to Whitehaven; thence (by the Isle of Man, where a few days were passed) up the Frith of Clyde to Greenock, then to Oban, Staffa, Iona; and back towards England, by Loch Awe, Inverary, Loch Goil-head, Greenock, and through parts of Renfrewshire, Ayrshire, and Dumfries-shire, to Carlisle, and thence up the river Eden, and homewards by Ullswater.

I.

ADIEU, Rydalian Laurels! that have
grown
And spread as if ye knew that days
might come
When ye would shelter in a happy home,
On this fair Mount, a Poet of your own,
One who ne'er ventured for a Delphic
crown 5
To sue the God; but, haunting your green
shade
All seasons through, is humbly pleased to
braid
Ground-flowers, beneath your guardian-
ship, self-sown.
Farewell! no Minstrels now with harp
new-strung
For summer wandering quit their house-
hold bowers; 10
Yet not for this wants Poesy a tongue
To cheer the Itinerant on whom she
pours
Her spirit, while he crosses lonely moors,
Or musing sits forsaken halls among.

II.

WHY should the Enthusiast, journeying
through this Isle,
Repine as if his hour were come too late?
Not unprotected in her mouldering state,
Antiquity salutes him with a smile,
'Mid fruitful fields that ring with jocund
toil, 5
And pleasure-grounds where Taste, re-
fined Co-mate
Of Truth and Beauty, strives to imitate,
Far as she may, primeval Nature's style.
Fair Land! by Time's parental love made
free,
By Social Order's watchful arms em-
braced; 10
With unexampled union meet in thee,
For eye and mind, the present and the
past;
With golden prospect for futurity,
If that be reverenced which ought to
last.

III.

THEY called Thee MERRY ENGLAND, in
old time;
A happy people won for thee that name
With envy heard in many a distant
clime;
And, spite of change, for me thou keep'st
the same
Endearing title, a responsive chime 5
To the heart's fond belief; though some
there are
Whose sterner judgments deem that word
a snare
For inattentive Fancy, like the lime
Which foolish birds are caught with. Can, I ask,
This face of rural beauty be a mask 10
For discontent, and poverty, and crime;

---

[1] The Poems of this Series were for the most part composed in 1833, and published for the first time in the volume of 1835 entitled *Yarrow Revisited, and Other Poems*. Chronological notes are attached only to those pieces to which this observation does not apply. See Nos. XXVII, XLIII, and XLVI.—ED.

These spreading towns a cloak for lawless
will?
Forbid it, Heaven!—and MERRY ENG-
LAND still
Shall be thy rightful name, in prose and
rhyme!

IV.

TO THE RIVER GRETA, NEAR KESWICK.

GRETA, what fearful listening! when huge
stones
Rumble along thy bed, block after block:
Or, whirling with reiterated shock,
Combat, while darkness aggravates the
groans:
But if thou (like Cocytus from the moans
Heard on his rueful margin) thence wert
named   6
The Mourner, thy true nature was de-
famed,
And the habitual murmur that atones
For thy worst rage, forgotten. Oft as
Spring
Decks, on thy sinuous banks, her thou-
sand thrones,   10
Seats of glad instinct and love's carol-
ling,
The concert, for the happy, then may vie
With liveliest peals of birth-day har-
mony:
To a grieved heart the notes are benisons.

V.

TO THE RIVER DERWENT.

AMONG the mountains were we nursed,
loved Stream!
Thou near the eagle's nest—within brief
sail,
I, of his bold wing floating on the gale,
Where thy deep voice could lull me!
Faint the beam
Of human life when first allowed to
gleam   5
On mortal notice.—Glory of the vale,
Such thy meek outset, with a crown,
though frail,
Kept in perpetual verdure by the steam
Of thy soft breath!—Less vivid wreath
entwined

Nemean victor's brow; less bright was
worn,   10
Meed of some Roman chief—in triumph
borne
With captives chained; and shedding
from his car
The sunset splendours of a finished war
Upon the proud enslavers of mankind!

VI.

IN SIGHT OF THE TOWN OF COCKER-
MOUTH.

(Where the Author was born, and his Father's
remains are laid.)

A POINT of life between my Parent's dust,
And yours, my buried Little-ones! am I;
And to those graves looking habitually
In kindred quiet I repose my trust.
Death to the innocent is more than just, 5
And, to the sinner, mercifully bent;
So may I hope, if truly I repent
And meekly bear the ills which bear I
must:
And You, my Offspring! that do still
remain,
Yet may outstrip me in the appointed
race,   10
If e'er, through fault of mine, in mutual
pain
We breathed together for a moment's
space,
The wrong, by love provoked, let love
arraign,
And only love keep in your hearts a
place.

VII.

ADDRESS FROM THE SPIRIT OF COCKER-
MOUTH CASTLE.

"THOU look'st upon me, and dost fondly
think,
Poet! that, stricken as both are by years,
We, differing once so much, are now
Compeers,
Prepared, when each has stood his time,
to sink
Into the dust. Erewhile a sterner link 5
United us; when thou, in boyish play,
Entering my dungeon, didst become a prey

To soul-appalling darkness. Not a blink
Of light was there;—and thus did I, thy
    Tutor,
Make thy young thoughts acquainted
    with the grave;   10
While thou wert chasing the winged
    butterfly
Through my green courts; or climbing, a
    bold suitor,
Up to the flowers whose golden progeny
Still round my shattered brow in beauty
    wave."

VIII.

NUN'S WELL, BRIGHAM.

THE cattle crowding round this beverage
    clear
To slake their thirst, with reckless hoofs
    have trod
The encircling turf into a barren clod;
Through which the waters creep, then
    disappear,
Born to be lost in Derwent flowing near;
Yet o'er the brink, and round the lime-
    stone cell   6
Of the pure spring (they call it the "Nun's
    Well,"
Name that first struck by chance my
    startled ear)
A tender Spirit broods—the pensive
    Shade   9
Of ritual honours to this Fountain paid
By hooded Votaresses with saintly cheer;
Albeit oft the Virgin-mother mild
Looked down with pity upon eyes be-
    guiled
Into the shedding of "too soft a tear."

IX.

TO A FRIEND.

On the banks of the Derwent.

PASTOR and Patriot!—at whose bidding
    rise
These modest walls, amid a flock that need,
For one who comes to watch them and
    to feed,
A fixed Abode—keep down presageful
    sighs.
Threats, which the unthinking only can
    despise,   5

Perplex the Church; but be thou firm,—
    be true
To thy first hope, and this good work
    pursue,
Poor as thou art. A welcome sacrifice
Dost Thou prepare, whose sign will be
    the smoke
Of thy new hearth; and sooner shall its
    wreaths,   10
Mounting while earth her morning in-
    cense breathes,
From wandering fiends of air receive a yoke,
And straightway cease to aspire, than
    God disdain
This humble tribute as ill-timed or vain.

X.

MARY QUEEN OF SCOTS.

Landing at the mouth of the Derwent, Work-
    ington.

DEAR to the Loves, and to the Graces
    vowed,
The Queen drew back the wimple that
    she wore;   3
And to the throng, that on the Cumbrian
    shore
Her landing hailed, how touchingly she
    bowed!
And like a Star (that, from a heavy cloud
Of pine-tree foliage poised in air, forth
    darts,   6
When a soft summer gale at evening parts
The gloom that did its loveliness enshroud)
She smiled; but Time, the old Saturnian
    seer,
Sighed on the wing as her foot pressed
    the strand,   10
With step prelusive to a long array
Of woes and degradations hand in hand—
Weeping captivity, and shuddering fear
Stilled by the ensanguined block of
    Fotheringay!

XI.

STANZAS

SUGGESTED IN A STEAMBOAT OFF SAINT
BEES' HEADS, ON THE COAST OF CUM-
BERLAND.

IF Life were slumber on a bed of down,
Toil unimposed, vicissitude unknown,

Sad were our lot : no hunter of the hare
Exults like him whose javelin from the lair
Has roused the lion ; no one plucks the
   rose,   5
Whose proffered beauty in safe shelter
   blows
'Mid a trim garden's summer luxuries,
With joy like his who climbs, on hands
   and knees,
For some rare plant, yon Headland of
   St. Bees.

This independence upon oar and sail,   10
This new indifference to breeze or gale,
This straight-lined progress, furrowing
   a flat lea,
And regular as if locked in certainty—
Depress the hours. Up, Spirit of the
   storm !
That Courage may find something to
   perform ;   15
That Fortitude, whose blood disdains to
   freeze
At Danger's bidding, may confront the
   seas,
Firm as the towering Headlands of
   St. Bees.

Dread cliff of Baruth ! *that* wild wish
   may sleep,
Bold as if men and creatures of the Deep
Breathed the same element ; too many
   wrecks   21
Have struck thy sides, too many ghastly
   decks
Hast thou looked down upon, that such
   a thought
Should here be welcome, and in verse
   enwrought :
With thy stern aspect better far agrees 25
Utterance of thanks that we have past
   with ease,
As millions thus shall do, the Headlands
   of St. Bees.

Yet, while each useful Art augments her
   store,
What boots the gain if Nature should
   lose more?
And Wisdom, as she holds a Christian
   place   30
In man's intelligence sublimed by grace?

When Bega sought of yore the Cumbrian
   coast,
Tempestuous winds her holy errand
   crossed :
She knelt in prayer—the waves their
   wrath appease ;
And, from her vow well weighed in Hea-
   ven's decrees,   35
Rose, where she touched the strand, the
   Chantry of St. Bees.

"Cruel of heart were they, bloody of
   hand,"
Who in these Wilds then struggled for
   command ;
The strong were merciless, without hope
   the weak ;
Till this bright Stranger came, fair as
   day-break,   40
And as a cresset true that darts its length
Of beamy lustre from a tower of strength ;
Guiding the mariner through troubled seas,
And cheering oft his peaceful reveries,
Like the fixed Light that crowns yon
   Headland of St. Bees.   45

To aid the Votaress, miracles believed
Wrought in men's minds, like miracles
   achieved ;
So piety took root ; and Song might tell
What humanizing virtues near her cell
Sprang up, and spread their fragrance
   wide around ;   50
How savage bosoms melted at the sound
Of gospel-truth enchained in harmonies
Wafted o'er waves, or creeping through
   close trees,
From her religious Mansion of St. Bees.

When her sweet Voice, that instrument
   of love,   55
Was glorified, and took its place, above
The silent stars, among the angelic quire,
Her chantry blazed with sacrilegious fire,
And perished utterly ; but her good deeds
Had sown the spot, that witnessed them,
   with seeds   60
Which lay in earth expectant, till a breeze
With quickening impulse answered their
   mute pleas,
And lo ! a *statelier* pile, the Abbey of
   St. Bees.

There are the naked clothed, the hungry
 fed;
And Charity extendeth to the dead 65
Her intercessions made for the soul's rest
Of tardy penitents; or for the best
Among the good (when love might else
 have slept,
Sickened, or died) in pious memory kept:
Thanks to the austere and simple De-
 votees, 70
Who, to that service bound by venial
 fees,
Keep watch before the altars of St. Bees.

Are not, in sooth, their Requiem's sacred
 ties
Woven out of passion's sharpest agonies,
Subdued, composed, and formalized by
 art, 75
To fix a wiser sorrow in the heart?
The prayer for them whose hour is past
 away
Says to the Living, profit while ye may!
A little part, and that the worst, he sees
Who thinks that priestly cunning holds
 the keys 80
That best unlock the secrets of St. Bees.

Conscience, the timid being's inmost light,
Hope of the dawn and solace of the night,
Cheers these Recluses with a steady ray
In many an hour when judgment goes
 astray. 85
Ah! scorn not hastily their rule who try
Earth to despise, and flesh to mortify;
Consume with zeal, in wingèd ecstasies
Of prayer and praise forget their rosaries,
Nor hear the loudest surges of St. Bees. 90

Yet none so prompt to succour and pro-
 tect
The forlorn traveller, or sailor wrecked
On the bare coast; nor do they grudge
 the boon
Which staff and cockle hat and sandal
 shoon
Claim for the pilgrim: and, though chid-
 ings sharp 95
May sometimes greet the strolling min-
 strel's harp,
It is not then when, swept with sportive
 ease,

It charms a feast-day throng of all de-
 grees,
Brightening the archway of revered St.
 Bees.

How did the cliffs and echoing hills re-
 joice 100
What time the Benedictine Brethren's
 voice,
Imploring, or commanding with meet
 pride,
Summoned the Chiefs to lay their feuds
 aside,
And under one blest ensign serve the
 Lord
In Palestine. Advance, indignant Sword!
Flaming till thou from Paynim hands
 release 106
That Tomb, dread centre of all sanctities
Nursed in the quiet Abbey of St. Bees.

But look we now to them whose minds
 from far
Follow the fortunes which they may not
 share. 110
While in Judea Fancy loves to roam,
She helps to make a Holy-land at home:
The Star of Bethlehem from its sphere
 invites
To sound the crystal depth of maiden
 rights;
And wedded Life, through scriptural
 mysteries, 115
Heavenward ascends with all her charities,
Taught by the hooded Celibates of St.
 Bees.

Nor be it e'er forgotten how by skill
Of cloistered Architects, free their souls
 to fill
With love of God, throughout the Land
 were raised 120
Churches, on whose symbolic beauty
 gazed
Peasant and mail-clad Chief with pious
 awe;
As at this day men seeing what they
 saw,
Or the bare wreck of faith's solemnities,
Aspire to more than earthly destinies; 125
Witness yon Pile that greets us from
 St. Bees.

Yet more; around those Churches,
    gathered Towns
Safe from the feudal Castle's haughty
    frowns;
Peaceful abodes, where Justice might
    uphold
Her scales with even hand, and culture
    mould   130
The heart to pity, train the mind in care
For rules of life, sound as the Time could
    bear.
Nor dost thou fail, thro' abject love of ease,
Or hindrance raised by sordid purposes,
To bear thy part in this good work,
    St. Bees.   135

Who with the ploughshare clove the
    barren moors,
And to green meadows changed the
    swampy shores?
Thinned the rank woods; and for the
    cheerful grange
Made room where wolf and boar were
    used to range?
Who taught, and showed by deeds, that
    gentler chains   140
Should bind the vassal to his lord's
    domains?
The thoughtful Monks, intent their God
    to please,
For Christ's dear sake, by human
    sympathies
Poured from the bosom of thy Church,
    St. Bees!

But all availed not; by a mandate given
Through lawless will the Brotherhood
    was driven   146
Forth from their cells; their ancient
    House laid low
In Reformation's sweeping overthrow.
But now once more the local Heart
    revives,
The inextinguishable Spirit strives.   150
Oh may that Power who hushed the
    stormy seas,
And cleared a way for the first Votaries,
Prosper the new-born College of St. Bees!

Alas! the Genius of our age, from Schools
Less humble, draws her lessons, aims, and
    rules.   155

To Prowess guided by her insight keen
Matter and Spirit are as one Machine;
Boastful Idolatress of formal skill
She in her own would merge the eternal
    will:
Better, if Reason's triumphs match with
    these,   160
Her flight before the bold credulities
That furthered the first teaching of St.
    Bees[1].

XII.

**IN THE CHANNEL, BETWEEN THE COAST
    OF CUMBERLAND AND THE ISLE OF
    MAN.**

RANGING the heights of Scawfell or Black-
    comb,
In his lone course the Shepherd oft will
    pause,
And strive to fathom the mysterious laws
By which the clouds, arrayed in light or
    gloom,
On Mona settle, and the shapes assume   5
Of all her peaks and ridges. What he
    draws
From sense, faith, reason, fancy, of the
    cause,
He will take with him to the silent tomb.
Or by his fire, a child upon his knee,
Haply the untaught Philosopher may
    speak   10
Of the strange sight, nor hide his theory
That satisfies the simple and the meek,
Blest in their pious ignorance, though weak
To cope with Sages undevoutly free.

XIII.

AT SEA OFF THE ISLE OF MAN.

BOLD words affirmed, in days when faith
    was strong
And doubts and scruples seldom teased
    the brain,
That no adventurer's bark had power to
    gain
These shores if he approached them bent
    on wrong;

[1] See "Excursion," seventh part; and "Eccle-
siastical Sketches," second part, near the be-
ginning.

For, suddenly up-conjured from the
Main,   5
Mists rose to hide the Land—that search,
though long
And eager, might be still pursued in vain.
O Fancy, what an age was *that* for song !
That age, when not by *laws* inanimate,
As men believed, the waters were im-
pelled,   10
The air controlled, the stars their courses
held ;
But element and orb on *acts* did wait
Of *Powers* endued with visible form, in-
stinct
With will, and to their work by passion
linked.

XIV.

DESIRE we past illusions to recall ?
To reinstate wild Fancy, would we hide
Truths whose thick veil Science has
drawn aside ?
No,—let this Age, high as she may, instal
In her esteem the thirst that wrought
man's fall,   5
The universe is infinitely wide ;
And conquering Reason, if self-glorified,
Can nowhere move uncrossed by some
new wall
Or gulf of mystery, which thou alone,
Imaginative Faith ! canst overleap,   10
In progress toward the fount of Love,—
the throne
Of Power whose ministers the records
keep
Of periods fixed, and laws established,
less
Flesh to exalt than prove its nothingness.

XV.

ON ENTERING DOUGLAS BAY, ISLE OF
MAN.

" Dignum laude virum Musa vetat mori."

THE feudal Keep, the bastions of Cohorn,
Even when they rose to check or to repel
Tides of aggressive war, oft served as
well
Greedy ambition, armed to treat with
scorn

Just limits ; but yon Tower, whose smiles
adorn   5
This perilous bay, stands clear of all
offence ;
Blest work it is of love and innocence,
A Tower of refuge built for the else
forlorn.
Spare it, ye waves, and lift the mariner,
Struggling for life, into its saving arms !
Spare, too, the human helpers ! Do they
stir   11
'Mid your fierce shock like men afraid to
die ?
No ; their dread service nerves the heart
it warms,
And they are led by noble HILLARY.[1]

XVI.

BY THE SEA-SHORE, ISLE OF MAN.

WHY stand we gazing on the sparkling
Brine,
With wonder smit by its transparency,
And all-enraptured with its purity ?—
Because the unstained, the clear, the
crystalline,
Have ever in them something of benign ;
Whether in gem, in water, or in sky,   6
A sleeping infant's brow, or wakeful eye
Of a young maiden, only not divine.
Scarcely the hand forbears to dip its palm
For beverage drawn as from a mountain-
well.   10
Temptation centres in the liquid Calm ;
Our daily raiment seems no obstacle
To instantaneous plunging in, deep Sea !
And revelling in long embrace with thee[2].

XVII.

ISLE OF MAN.

A YOUTH too certain of his power to
wade
On the smooth bottom of this clear bright
sea,
To sight so shallow, with a bather's glee,
Leapt from this rock, and but for timely
aid

---

[1] See Note, p. 924.
[2] The sea-water on the coast of the Isle of Man
is singularly pure and beautiful.

He, by the alluring element betrayed,   5
Had perished. Then might Sea-nymphs
      (and with sighs
Of self-reproach) have chanted elegies
Bewailing his sad fate, when he was laid
In peaceful earth: for, doubtless, he was
      frank,
Utterly in himself devoid of guile;   10
Knew not the double-dealing of a smile;
Nor aught that makes men's promises
      a blank,
Or deadly snare: and He survives to bless
The Power that saved him in his strange
      distress.

XVIII.

ISLE OF MAN.

DID pangs of grief for lenient time too
      keen,
Grief that devouring waves had caused—
      or guilt
Which they had witnessed, sway the man
      who built
This Homestead, placed where nothing
      could be seen,
Nought heard, of ocean troubled or serene?
A tired Ship-soldier on paternal land,   6
That o'er the channel holds august com-
      mand,
The dwelling raised,—a veteran Marine.
He, in disgust, turned from the neigh-
      bouring sea
To shun the memory of a listless life   10
That hung between two callings. May
      no strife
More hurtful here beset him, doomed
      though free,
Self-doomed, to worse inaction, till his eye
Shrink from the daily sight of earth and
      sky!

XIX.

BY A RETIRED MARINER.

A Friend of the Author.

FROM early youth I ploughed the restless
      Main,
My mind as restless and as apt to change;
Through every clime and ocean did I range,
In hope at length a competence to gain;

For poor to Sea I went, and poor I still
      remain.   5
Year after year I strove, but strove in vain,
And hardships manifold did I endure,
For Fortune on me never deigned to
      smile;
Yet I at last a resting-place have found,
With just enough life's comforts to procure,
In a snug Cove on this our favoured Isle,
A peaceful spot where Nature's gifts
      abound;
Then sure I have no reason to complain,
Though poor to Sea I went, and poor
      I still remain.

XX.

AT BALA-SALA, ISLE OF MAN.

Supposed to be written by a Friend.

BROKEN in fortune, but in mind entire
And sound in principle, I seek repose
Where ancient trees this convent-pile
      enclose[1],
In ruin beautiful. When vain desire
Intrudes on peace, I pray the eternal Sire
To cast a soul-subduing shade on me,   6
A grey-haired, pensive, thankful Refugee;
A shade—but with some sparks of hea-
      venly fire
Once to these cells vouchsafed. And
      when I note
The old Tower's brow yellowed as with
      the beams   10
Of sunset ever there, albeit streams
Of stormy weather-stains that semblance
      wrought,
I thank the silent Monitor, and say
"Shine so, my aged brow, at all hours of
      the day!"

XXI.

TYNWALD HILL.

ONCE on the top of Tynwald's formal
      mound
(Still marked with green turf circles
      narrowing
Stage above stage) would sit this Island's
      King,

------

[1] Rushen Abbey.

The laws to promulgate, enrobed and
    crowned;
While, compassing the little mound
    around,   5
Degrees and Orders stood, each under
    each:
Now, like to things within fate's easiest
    reach,
The power is merged, the pomp a grave
    has found.
Off with yon cloud, old Snafell! that
    thine eye
Over three Realms may take its widest
    range;   10
And let, for them, thy fountains utter
    strange
Voices, thy winds break forth in pro-
    phecy,
If the whole State must suffer mortal
    change,
Like Mona's miniature of sovereignty.

XXII.

DESPOND who will—*I* heard a voice ex-
    claim,
"Though fierce the assault, and shattered
    the defence,
It cannot be that Britain's social frame,
The glorious work of time and provi-
    dence,
Before a flying season's rash pretence   5
Should fall; that She, whose virtue put
    to shame,
When Europe prostrate lay, the Con-
    queror's aim,
Should perish, self-subverted. Black and
    dense
The cloud is; but brings *that* a day of
    doom
To Liberty? Her sun is up the while, 10
That orb whose beams round Saxon
    Alfred shone:
Then laugh, ye innocent Vales! ye
    Streams, sweep on,
Nor let one billow of our heaven-blest
    Isle
Toss in the fanning wind a humbler
    plume."

XXIII.

IN THE FRITH OF CLYDE, AILSA CRAG.

During an Eclipse of the Sun, July 17.

SINCE risen from ocean, ocean to defy,
Appeared the Crag of Ailsa, ne'er did
    morn
With gleaming lights more gracefully
    adorn
His sides, or wreathe with mist his fore-
    head high:
Now, faintly darkening with the sun's
    eclipse,   5
Still is he seen, in lone sublimity,
Towering above the sea and little ships;
For dwarfs the tallest seem while sailing
    by,
Each for her haven; with her freight of
    Care,
Pleasure, or Grief, and Toil that seldom
    looks   10
Into the secret of to-morrow's fare;
Though poor, yet rich, without the wealth
    of books,
Or aught that watchful Love to Nature
    owes
For her mute Powers, fixed Forms, or
    transient Shows.

XXIV.

ON THE FRITH OF CLYDE.

In a Steamboat.

ARRAN! a single-crested Teneriffe,
A St. Helena next—in shape and hue,
Varying her crowded peaks and ridges
    blue;
Who but must covet a cloud-seat, or skiff
Built for the air, or wingèd Hippogriff? 5
That he might fly, where no one could
    pursue,
From this dull Monster and her sooty
    crew;
And, as a God, light on thy topmost cliff.
Impotent wish! which reason would
    despise
If the mind knew no union of extremes,
No natural bond between the boldest
    schemes   11

Ambition frames and heart-humilities.
Beneath stern mountains many a soft
    vale lies,
And lofty springs give birth to lowly
    streams.

XXV.

ON REVISITING DUNOLLY CASTLE.

See former Series, p. 388.

THE captive Bird was gone;—to cliff or
    moor
Perchance had flown, delivered by the
    storm;
Or he had pined, and sunk to feed the
    worm:
Him found we not: but, climbing a tall
    tower,
There saw, impaved with rude fidelity   5
Of art mosaic, in a roofless floor,
An Eagle with stretched wings, but beam-
    less eye—
An Eagle that could neither wail nor soar.
Effigy of the Vanished—(shall I dare
To call thee so?) or symbol of fierce deeds
And of the towering courage which past
    times   11
Rejoiced in—take whate'er thou be, a share,
Not undeserved, of the memorial rhymes
That animate my way where'er it leads!

XXVI.

THE DUNOLLY EAGLE.

NOT to the clouds, not to the cliff, he flew;
But when a storm, on sea or mountain
    bred,
Came and delivered him, alone he sped
Into the castle-dungeon's darkest mew.
Now near his master's house in open view
He dwells, and hears indignant tempests
    howl,   6
Kennelled and chained. Ye tame domestic
    fowl,
Beware of him! Thou, saucy cockatoo,
Look to thy plumage and thy life!—The
    roe,
Fleet as the west wind, is for *him* no
    quarry;   10
Balanced in ether he will never tarry,
Eyeing the sea's blue depths. Poor Bird!
    even so

Doth man of brother man a creature make
That clings to slavery for its own sad sake.

XXVII.

WRITTEN IN A BLANK LEAF OF MACPHERSON'S OSSIAN.

[Composed 1824.—Published 1827.]

OFT have I caught, upon a fitful breeze,
Fragments of far-off melodies,
With ear not coveting the whole,
A part so charmed the pensive soul:
While a dark storm before my sight   5
Was yielding, on a mountain height
Loose vapours have I watched, that won
Prismatic colours from the sun;
Nor felt a wish that heaven would show
The image of its perfect bow.   10
What need, then, of these finished Strains?
Away with counterfeit Remains!
An abbey in its lone recess,
A temple of the wilderness,
Wrecks though they be, announce with
    feeling   15
The majesty of honest dealing.
Spirit of Ossian! if imbound
In language thou may'st yet be found,
If aught (intrusted to the pen
Or floating on the tongues of men,   20
Albeit shattered and impaired)
Subsist thy dignity to guard,
In concert with memorial claim
Of old grey stone, and high-born name
That cleaves to rock or pillared cave   25
Where moans the blast, or beats the wave,
Let Truth, stern arbitress of all,
Interpret that Original,
And for presumptuous wrongs atone;—
Authentic words be given, or none!   30

Time is not blind;—yet He, who spares
Pyramid pointing to the stars,
Hath preyed with ruthless appetite
On all that marked the primal flight
Of the poetic ecstasy   35
Into the land of mystery.
No tongue is able to rehearse
One measure, Orpheus! of thy verse;
Musæus, stationed with his lyre
Supreme among the Elysian quire,   40
Is, for the dwellers upon earth,
Mute as a lark ere morning's birth.

Why grieve for these, though past away
The music, and extinct the lay?
When thousands, by severer doom,   45
Full early to the silent tomb
Have sunk, at Nature's call; or strayed
From hope and promise, self-betrayed;
The garland withering on their brows;
Stung with remorse for broken vows; 50
Frantic—else how might they rejoice?
And friendless, by their own sad choice!

Hail, Bards of mightier grasp! on you
I chiefly call, the chosen Few,
Who cast not off the acknowledged guide,
Who faltered not, nor turned aside; 56
Whose lofty genius could survive
Privation, under sorrow thrive;
In whom the fiery Muse revered
The symbol of a snow-white beard, 60
Bedewed with meditative tears
Dropped from the lenient cloud of years.

Brothers in soul! though distant times
Produced you nursed in various climes,
Ye, when the orb of life had waned, 65
A plenitude of love retained:
Hence, while in you each sad regret
By corresponding hope was met,
Ye lingered among human kind,
Sweet voices for the passing wind; 70
Departing sunbeams, loth to stop,
Though smiling on the last hill-top!
Such to the tender-hearted maid
Even ere her joys begin to fade;
Such, haply, to the rugged chief 75
By fortune crushed, or tamed by grief,
Appears, on Morven's lonely shore,
Dim-gleaming through imperfect lore,
The Son of Fingal; such was blind
Maeonides of ampler mind; 80
Such Milton, to the fountain-head
Of glory by Urania led!

XXVIII.

CAVE OF STAFFA.

WE saw, but surely, in the motley crowd,
Not One of us has felt the far-famed sight;
How *could* we feel it? each the other's
    blight,
Hurried and hurrying, volatile and loud.
O for those motions only that invite 5

The Ghost of Fingal to his tuneful Cave
By the breeze entered, and wave after
    wave
Softly embosoming the timid light!
And by *one* Votary who at will might
    stand 9
Gazing and take into his mind and heart,
With undistracted reverence, the effect
Of those proportions where the almighty
    hand
That made the worlds, the sovereign
    Architect,
Has deigned to work as if with human
    Art!

XXIX.

CAVE OF STAFFA.

After the Crowd had departed.

THANKS for the lessons of this Spot—fit
    school
For the presumptuous thoughts that would
    assign
Mechanic laws to agency divine;
And, measuring heaven by earth, would
    overrule
Infinite Power. The pillared vestibule, 5
Expanding yet precise, the roof embowed,
Might seem designed to humble man,
    when proud
Of his best workmanship by plan and tool.
Down-bearing with his whole Atlantic
    weight
Of tide and tempest on the Structure's
    base,   10
And flashing to that Structure's topmost
    height,
Ocean has proved its strength, and of its
    grace
In calms is conscious, finding for his
    freight
Of softest music some responsive place.

XXX.

CAVE OF STAFFA.

YE shadowy Beings, that have rights and
    claims
In every cell of Fingal's mystic Grot,
Where are ye? Driven or venturing to
    the spot,

Our fathers glimpses caught of your thin
Frames,
And, by your mien and bearing, knew
your names;   5
And they could hear *his* ghostly song
who trod
Earth, till the flesh lay on him like a load,
While he struck his desolate harp without
hopes or aims.
Vanished ye are, but subject to recall;
Why keep *we* else the instincts whose
dread law   10
Ruled here of yore, till what men felt
they saw,
Not by black arts but magic natural!
If eyes be still sworn vassals of belief,
Yon light shapes forth a Bard, that shade
a Chief.

XXXI.

FLOWERS ON THE TOP OF THE PILLARS AT THE ENTRANCE OF THE CAVE.

HOPE smiled when your nativity was cast,
Children of Summer! Ye fresh Flowers
that brave
What Summer here escapes not, the fierce
wave,
And whole artillery of the western blast,
Battering the Temple's front, its long-
drawn nave   5
Smiting, as if each moment were their last.
But ye, bright Flowers, on frieze and
architrave
Survive, and once again the Pile stands
fast:
Calm as the Universe, from specular towers
Of heaven contemplated by Spirits pure
With mute astonishment, it stands sus-
tained   11
Through every part in symmetry, to
endure,
Unhurt, the assault of Time with all his
hours,
As the supreme Artificer ordained.

XXXII.

IONA.

ON to Iona!—What can she afford
To *us* save matter for a thoughtful sigh,
Heaved over ruin with stability

In urgent contrast? To diffuse the WORD
(Thy Paramount, mighty Nature! and
Time's Lord)   5
Her Temples rose, 'mid pagan gloom; but
why,
Even for a moment, has our verse de-
plored
Their wrongs, since they fulfilled their
destiny?
And when, subjected to a common doom
Of mutability, those far-famed Piles   10
Shall disappear from both the sister Isles,
Iona's Saints, forgetting not past days,
Garlands shall wear of amaranthine bloom,
While heaven's vast sea of voices chants
their praise.

XXXIII.

IONA.

Upon Landing.

How sad a welcome! To each voyager
Some ragged child holds up for sale a store
Of wave-worn pebbles, pleading on the
shore
Where once came monk and nun with
gentle stir,
Blessings to give, news ask, or suit prefer.
Yet is yon neat trim church a grateful
speck   6
Of novelty amid the sacred wreck
Strewn far and wide. Think, proud
Philosopher!
Fallen though she be, this Glory of the
west,
Still on her sons the beams of mercy
shine;   10
And "hopes, perhaps more heavenly
bright than thine,
A grace by thee unsought and unpossest,
A faith more fixed, a rapture more divine
Shall gild their passage to eternal rest."

XXXIV.

THE BLACK STONES OF IONA.

[See Martin's *Voyage among the Western Isles.*]

HERE on their knees men swore: the
stones were black,
Black in the people's minds and words,
yet they
Were at that time, as now, in colour grey.

But what is colour, if upon the rack
Of conscience souls are placed by deeds
    that lack   5
Concord with oaths? What differ night
    and day
Then, when before the Perjured on his way
Hell opens, and the heavens in vengeance
    crack
Above his head uplifted in vain prayer
To Saint, or Fiend, or to the Godhead
    whom   10
He had insulted — Peasant, King, or
    Thane?
Fly where the culprit may, guilt meets a
    doom;
And, from invisible worlds at need laid
    bare,
Come links for social order's awful chain.

XXXV.

HOMEWARD we turn. Isle of Columba's Cell,
Where Christian piety's soul-cheering
    spark
(Kindled from Heaven between the light
    and dark
Of time) shone like the morning-star,
    farewell!—
And fare thee well, to Fancy visible,   5
Remote St. Kilda, lone and loved sea-
    mark
For many a voyage made in her swift
    bark,
When with more hues than in the rainbow
    dwell
Thou a mysterious intercourse dost hold, 9
Extracting from clear skies and air serene,
And out of sun-bright waves, a lucid veil,
That thickens, spreads, and, mingling
    fold with fold,
Makes known, when thou no longer canst
    be seen,
Thy whereabout, to warn the approaching
    sail.

XXXVI.

GREENOCK.

Per me si va nella Città dolente.

WE have not passed into a doleful City,
We who were led to-day down a grim dell,
By some too boldly named "the Jaws of
    Hell:"

Where be the wretched ones, the sights
    for pity?
These crowded streets resound no plain-
    tive ditty:—   5
As from the hive where bees in summer
    dwell,
Sorrow seems here excluded; and that
    knell,
It neither damps the gay, nor checks the
    witty.
Alas! too busy Rival of old Tyre,
Whose merchants Princes were, whose
    decks were thrones;   10
Soon may the punctual sea in vain re-
    spire
To serve thy need, in union with that
    Clyde
Whose nursling current brawls o'er mossy
    stones,
The poor, the lonely, herdsman's joy and
    pride.

XXXVII.

"THERE!" said a Stripling, pointing with
    meet pride
Towards a low roof with green trees half
    concealed,
"Is Mosgiel Farm; and that's the very
    field
Where Burns ploughed up the Daisy."
    Far and wide
A plain below stretched seaward, while,
    descried   5
Above sea-clouds, the Peaks of Arran
    rose;
And, by that simple notice, the repose
Of earth, sky, sea, and air, was vivi-
    fied.
Beneath "the random *bield* of clod or
    stone"
Myriads of daisies have shone forth in
    flower   10
Near the lark's nest, and in their natural
    hour
Have passed away; less happy than the
    One
That, by the unwilling ploughshare, died
    to prove
The tender charm of poetry and love.

XXXVIII.

THE RIVER EDEN, CUMBERLAND.

EDEN! till now thy beauty had I viewed
By glimpses only, and confess with shame
That verse of mine, whate'er its varying
    mood,
Repeats but once the sound of thy sweet
    name:
Yet fetched from Paradise that honour
    came,   5
Rightfully borne; for Nature gives thee
    flowers
That have no rivals among British bowers;
And thy bold rocks are worthy of their
    fame.
Measuring thy course, fair Stream! at
    length I pay
To my life's neighbour dues of neighbour-
    hood;   10
But I have traced thee on thy winding
    way
With pleasure sometimes by this thought
    restrained—
For things far off we toil, while many a
    good
Not sought, because too near, is never
    gained.

XXXIX.

MONUMENT OF MRS. HOWARD

(by Nollekens),

In Wetheral Church, near Corby, on the banks
of the Eden.

STRETCHED on the dying Mother's lap,
    lies dead
Her new-born Babe; dire ending of bright
    hope!
But Sculpture here, with the divinest
    scope
Of luminous faith, heavenward hath raised
    that head
So patiently; and through one hand has
    spread   5
A touch so tender for the insensate Child—
(Earth's lingering love to parting re-
    conciled,
Brief parting, for the spirit is all but
    fled)—

That we, who contemplate the turns of
    life
Through this still medium, are consoled
    and cheered;   10
Feel with the Mother, think the severed
    Wife
Is less to be lamented than revered;
And own that Art, triumphant over strife
And pain, hath powers to Eternity en-
    deared.

XL.

SUGGESTED BY THE FOREGOING.

TRANQUILLITY! the sovereign aim wert
    thou
In heathen schools of philosophic lore;
Heart-stricken by stern destiny of yore
The Tragic Muse thee served with thought-
    ful vow;
And what of hope Elysium could allow 5
Was fondly seized by Sculpture, to restore
Peace to the Mourner. But when He
    who wore
The crown of thorns around his bleeding
    brow
Warmed our sad being with celestial
    light,
Then Arts, which still had drawn a soften-
    ing grace   10
From shadowy fountains of the Infinite,
Communed with that Idea face to face:
And move around it now as planets run,
Each in its orbit round the central Sun.

XLI.

NUNNERY.

THE floods are roused, and will not soon
    be weary;
Down from the Pennine Alps[1] how fiercely
    sweeps
CROGLIN, the stately Eden's tributary!
He raves, or through some moody passage
    creeps
Plotting new mischief—out again he leaps
Into broad light, and sends, through
    regions airy,   6
That voice which soothed the Nuns while
    on the steeps

---

[1] The chain of Crossfell.

They knelt in prayer, or sang to blissful
  Mary.
That union ceased: then, cleaving easy
  walks
Through crags, and smoothing paths beset
  with danger,   10
Came studious Taste; and many a pensive
  stranger
Dreams on the banks, and to the river talks.
What change shall happen next to Nun-
  nery Dell?
Canal, and Viaduct, and Railway, tell!

XLII.

STEAMBOATS, VIADUCTS, AND RAIL-
WAYS.

MOTIONS and Means, on land and sea at
  war
With old poetic feeling, not for this,
Shall ye, by Poets even, be judged amiss!
Nor shall your presence, howsoe'er it mar
The loveliness of Nature, prove a bar   5
To the Mind's gaining that prophetic sense
Of future change, that point of vision,
  whence
May be discovered what in soul ye are.
In spite of all that beauty may disown
In your harsh features, Nature doth em-
  brace   10
Her lawful offspring in Man's art; and
  Time,
Pleased with your triumphs o'er his
  brother Space,
Accepts from your bold hands the prof-
  fered crown
Of hope, and smiles on you with cheer
  sublime.

XLIII.

THE MONUMENT COMMONLY CALLED
LONG MEG AND HER DAUGHTERS,
NEAR THE RIVER EDEN.

[Composed 1821.—Published 1822 [1]; ed. 1827.]

A WEIGHT of awe, not easy to be borne,
Fell suddenly upon my Spirit—cast
From the dread bosom of the unknown
  past,

---

[1] In the little book entitled, *A Description of
the Scenery of the Lakes*, etc.—ED.

When first I saw that family forlorn.
Speak Thou, whose massy strength and
  stature scorn   5
The power of years—pre-eminent, and
  placed
Apart, to overlook the circle vast—
Speak, Giant-mother! tell it to the Morn
While she dispels the cumbrous shades of
  Night;
Let the Moon hear, emerging from a
  cloud;   10
At whose behest uprose on British ground
That Sisterhood, in hieroglyphic round
Forth-shadowing, some have deemed, the
  infinite
The inviolable God, that tames the
  proud [2]!

XLIV.

LOWTHER.

LOWTHER! in thy majestic Pile are seen
Cathedral pomp and grace, in apt accord
With the baronial castle's sterner mien;
Union significant of God adored,
And charters won and guarded by the
  sword   5
Of ancient honour; whence that goodly
  state
Of polity which wise men venerate,
And will maintain, if God his help afford.
Hourly the democratic torrent swells;
For airy promises and hopes suborned   10
The strength of backward - looking
  thoughts is scorned.
Fall if ye must, ye Towers and Pinnacles,
With what ye symbolise; authentic Story
Will say, Ye disappeared with England's
  Glory!

XLV.

TO THE EARL OF LONSDALE.

"Magistratus indicat virum."

LONSDALE! it were unworthy of a Guest,
Whose heart with gratitude to thee in-
  clines,
If he should speak, by fancy touched, of
  signs

---

[2] See Note, p. 925.

On thy Abode harmoniously imprest,
Yet be unmoved with wishes to attest   5
How in thy mind and moral frame agree
Fortitude, and that Christian Charity
Which, filling, consecrates the human
    breast.
And if the Motto on thy 'scutcheon teach
With truth, "THE MAGISTRACY SHOWS
    THE MAN;"   10
That searching test thy public course has
    stood;
As will be owned alike by bad and good,
Soon as the measuring of life's little span
Shall place thy virtues out of Envy's
    reach[1].

XLVI.

THE SOMNAMBULIST.

[Composed before 1827 (1807–8?).—Published
1835.]

LIST, ye who pass by Lyulph's Tower[2]
    At eve; how softly then
Doth Aira-force, that torrent hoarse,
    Speak from the woody glen!
Fit music for a solemn vale!   5
    And holier seems the ground
To him who catches on the gale
    The spirit of a mournful tale,
Embodied in the sound.

Not far from that fair site whereon   10
    The Pleasure-house is reared,
As story says, in antique days
    A stern-browed house appeared;
Foil to a Jewel rich in light
    There set, and guarded well;   15
Cage for a Bird of plumage bright,
Sweet-voiced, nor wishing for a flight
    Beyond her native dell.

To win this bright Bird from her cage,
    To make this Gem their own,   20
Came Barons bold, with store of gold,
    And Knights of high renown;

---

[1] See Note, p. 925.
[2] A pleasure-house built by the late Duke of
Norfolk upon the banks of Ullswater. FORCE is
the word used in the Lake District for Water-
fall.

But one She prized, and only one;
    Sir Eglamore was he;
Full happy season, when was known,   25
Ye Dales and Hills! to you alone
    Their mutual loyalty—

Known chiefly, Aira! to thy glen,
    Thy brook, and bowers of holly;
Where Passion caught what Nature
    taught,   30
    That all but love is folly;
Where Fact with Fancy stooped to play;
    Doubt came not, nor regret—
To trouble hours that winged their way,
As if through an immortal day   35
    Whose sun could never set.

But in old times Love dwelt not long
    Sequestered with repose;
Best throve the fire of chaste desire,
    Fanned by the breath of foes.   40
"A conquering lance is beauty's test,
    And proves the Lover true;"
So spake Sir Eglamore, and pressed
    The drooping Emma to his breast,
    And looked a blind adieu.   45

They parted.—Well with him it fared
    Through wide-spread regions errant;
A knight of proof in love's behoof,
    The thirst of fame his warrant:
And She her happiness can build   50
    On woman's quiet hours;
Though faint, compared with spear and
    shield,
The solace beads and masses yield,
    And needlework and flowers.

Yet blest was Emma when she heard   55
    Her Champion's praise recounted;
Though brain would swim, and eyes grow
    dim,
    And high her blushes mounted;
Or when a bold heroic lay
    She warbled from full heart;   60
Delightful blossoms for the *May*
Of absence! but they will not stay,
    Born only to depart.

Hope wanes with her, while lustre fills
    Whatever path he chooses;   65
As if his orb, that owns no curb,
    Received the light hers loses.

He comes not back; an ampler space
　Requires for nobler deeds;
He ranges on from place to place,　70
Till of his doings is no trace,
　But what her fancy breeds.

His fame may spread, but in the past
　Her spirit finds its centre;
Clear sight She has of what he was,　75
　And that would now content her.
"Still is he my devoted Knight?"
　The tear in answer flows;
Month falls on month with heavier
　weight;
Day sickens round her, and the night　80
　Is empty of repose.

In sleep She sometimes walked abroad,
　Deep sighs with quick words blending,
Like that pale Queen whose hands are
　seen
With fancied spots contending;　85
But *she* is innocent of blood,—
　The moon is not more pure
That shines aloft, while through the wood
She thrids her way, the sounding Flood
　Her melancholy lure!　90

While 'mid the fern-brake sleeps the doe,
　And owls alone are waking,
In white arrayed, glides on the Maid
　The downward pathway taking,
That leads her to the torrent's side　95
　And to a holly bower;
By whom on this still night descried?
By whom in that lone place espied?
　By thee, Sir Eglamore!

A wandering Ghost, so thinks the Knight,
　His coming step has thwarted,　101
Beneath the boughs that heard their
　vows,
　Within whose shade they parted.
Hush, hush, the busy Sleeper see!
　Perplexed her fingers seem,　105
As if they from the holly tree
Green twigs would pluck, as rapidly
　Flung from her to the stream.

What means the Spectre? Why intent
　To violate the Tree,　110
Thought Eglamore, by which I swore
　Unfading constancy?

Here am I, and to-morrow's sun,
　To her I left, shall prove
That bliss is ne'er so surely won　115
As when a circuit has been run
　Of valour, truth, and love.

So from the spot whereon he stood,
　He moved with stealthy pace;
And, drawing nigh, with his living eye,
　He recognised the face;　121
And whispers caught, and speeches small,
　Some to the green-leaved tree,
Some muttered to the torrent-fall;—
"Roar on, and bring him with thy call;
　I heard, and so may He!"　126

Soul-shattered was the Knight, nor knew
　If Emma's Ghost it were,
Or boding Shade, or if the Maid
　Her very self stood there.　130
He touched; what followed who shall
　tell?
The soft touch snapped the thread
Of slumber—shrieking back she fell,
And the Stream whirled her down the
　dell
　Along its foaming bed.　135

In plunged the Knight!—when on firm
　ground
　The rescued Maiden lay,
Her eyes grew bright with blissful light,
　Confusion passed away;
She heard, ere to the throne of grace　140
　Her faithful Spirit flew,
His voice—beheld his speaking face;
And, dying, from his own embrace,
　She felt that he was true.

So was he reconciled to life:　145
　Brief words may speak the rest;
Within the dell he built a cell,
　And there was Sorrow's guest;
In hermits' weeds repose he found,
　From vain temptations free;　150
Beside the torrent dwelling—bound
By one deep heart-controlling sound,
　And awed to piety.

Wild stream of Aira, hold thy course,
　Nor fear memorial lays,　155
Where clouds that spread in solemn
　shade,
　Are edged with golden rays!

Dear art thou to the light of heaven,
　Though minister of sorrow ;
Sweet is thy voice at pensive even ;　160
And thou, in lovers' hearts forgiven,
　Shalt take thy place with Yarrow !

XLVII.

TO CORDELIA M———.

Hallsteads, Ullswater.

NOT in the mines beyond the western main,
You say, Cordelia, was the metal sought,
Which a fine skill, of Indian growth, has
　wrought
Into this flexible yet faithful Chain ;
Nor is it silver of romantic Spain ;　5
But from our loved Helvellyn's depths
　was brought,
Our own domestic mountain.　Thing and
　thought
Mix strangely ; trifles light, and partly
　vain,
Can prop, as you have learnt, our nobler
　being :
Yes, Lady, while about your neck is
　wound　10
(Your casual glance oft meeting) this
　bright cord,

What witchery, for pure gifts of inward
　seeing,
Lurks in it, Memory's Helper, Fancy's
　Lord,
For precious tremblings in your bosom
　found !

XLVIII.

MOST sweet it is with unuplifted eyes
To pace the ground, if path be there or
　none,
While a fair region round the traveller
　lies
Which he forbears again to look upon ;　4
Pleased rather with some soft ideal scene,
The work of Fancy, or some happy tone
Of meditation, slipping in between
The beauty coming and the beauty gone.
If Thought and Love desert us, from that
　day
Let us break off all commerce with the
　Muse :　10
With Thought and Love companions of
　our way,
Whate'er the senses take or may refuse,
The Mind's internal heaven shall shed
　her dews
Of inspiration on the humblest lay

POEMS OF
SENTIMENT AND REFLECTION.

————•◦•————

I.

EXPOSTULATION AND REPLY.

[Composed 1798.—Published 1798.]

"WHY, William, on that old grey stone,
Thus for the length of half a day,
Why, William, sit you thus alone,
And dream your time away?

"Where are your books?—that light be-
    queathed   5
To Beings else forlorn and blind!
Up! up! and drink the spirit breathed
From dead men to their kind.

"You look round on your Mother Earth,
As if she for no purpose bore you;   10
As if you were her first-born birth,
And none had lived before you!"

One morning thus, by Esthwaite lake,
When life was sweet, I knew not why,
To me my good friend Matthew spake, 15
And thus I made reply:

"The eye—it cannot choose but see;
We cannot bid the ear be still;
Our bodies feel, where'er they be,
Against or with our will.   20

"Nor less I deem that there are Powers
Which of themselves our minds impress;
That we can feed this mind of ours
In a wise passiveness.

"Think you, 'mid all this mighty sum 25
Of things for ever speaking,
That nothing of itself will come,
But we must still be seeking?

"—Then ask not wherefore, here, alone,
Conversing as I may,   30
I sit upon this old grey stone,
And dream my time away."

II.

THE TABLES TURNED.

AN EVENING SCENE ON THE SAME SUBJECT.

[Composed 1798.—Published 1798.]

UP! up! my Friend, and quit your
    books;
Or surely you'll grow double:
Up! up! my Friend, and clear your
    looks;
Why all this toil and trouble?

The sun, above the mountain's head, 5
A freshening lustre mellow
Through all the long green fields has
    spread,
His first sweet evening yellow.

Books! 'tis a dull and endless strife:
Come, hear the woodland linnet, 10
How sweet his music! on my life,
There's more of wisdom in it.

And hark! how blithe the throstle sings!
He, too, is no mean preacher:
Come forth into the light of things, 15
Let Nature be your Teacher.

She has a world of ready wealth,
Our minds and hearts to bless—
Spontaneous wisdom breathed by health,
Truth breathed by cheerfulness. 20

One impulse from a vernal wood
May teach you more of man,
Of moral evil and of good,
Than all the sages can.

Sweet is the lore which Nature brings; 25
Our meddling intellect
Mis-shapes the beauteous forms of
    things:—
We murder to dissect.

Enough of Science and of Art;
Close up those barren leaves;   30
Come forth, and bring with you a heart
That watches and receives.

III.

LINES WRITTEN IN EARLY SPRING.

[Composed 1798.—Published 1798.]

I HEARD a thousand blended notes,
While in a grove I sate reclined,
In that sweet mood when pleasant
    thoughts
Bring sad thoughts to the mind.

To her fair works did Nature link   5
The human soul that through me ran;
And much it grieved my heart to think
What man has made of man.

Through primrose tufts, in that green
    bower,
The periwinkle trailed its wreaths;   10
And 'tis my faith that every flower
Enjoys the air it breathes.

The birds around me hopped and played,
Their thoughts I cannot measure:—
But the least motion which they made, 15
It seemed a thrill of pleasure.

The budding twigs spread out their fan,
To catch the breezy air;
And I must think, do all I can,
That there was pleasure there.   20

If this belief from heaven be sent,
If such be Nature's holy plan,
Have I not reason to lament
What man has made of man?

IV.

A CHARACTER.

[Composed probably September or October, 1800.
—Published 1800.]

I MARVEL how Nature could ever find
    space
For so many strange contrasts in one
    human face:
There's thought and no thought, and
    there's paleness and bloom
And bustle and sluggishness, pleasure
    and gloom.

There's weakness, and strength both re-
    dundant and vain;   5
Such strength as, if ever affliction and
    pain
Could pierce through a temper that's soft
    to disease,
Would be rational peace—a philosopher's
    ease.

There's indifference, alike when he fails
    or succeeds,
And attention full ten times as much as
    there needs;   10
Pride where there's no envy, there's so
    much of joy;
And mildness, and spirit both forward
    and coy.

There's freedom, and sometimes a diffi-
    dent stare
Of shame scarcely seeming to know that
    she's there,
There's virtue, the title it surely may
    claim,   15
Yet wants heaven knows what to be
    worthy the name.

This picture from nature may seem to
    depart,
Yet the Man would at once run away
    with your heart;
And I for five centuries right gladly
    would be
Such an odd such a kind happy creature
    as he.   20

V.

TO MY SISTER.

[Composed 1798.—Published 1798.]

IT is the first mild day of March:
Each minute sweeter than before,
The redbreast sings from the tall larch
That stands beside our door.

There is a blessing in the air,   5
Which seems a sense of joy to yield
To the bare trees, and mountains bare,
And grass in the green field.

My sister! ('tis a wish of mine)
Now that our morning meal is done,   10
Make haste, your morning task resign;
Come forth and feel the sun.

Edward will come with you;—and, pray,
Put on with speed your woodland dress;
And bring no book: for this one day   15
We'll give to idleness.

No joyless forms shall regulate
Our living calendar:
We from to-day, my Friend, will date
The opening of the year.   20

Love, now a universal birth,
From heart to heart is stealing,
From earth to man, from man to earth:
—It is the hour of feeling.

One moment now may give us more   25
Than years of toiling reason:
Our minds shall drink at every pore
The spirit of the season.

Some silent laws our hearts will make,
Which they shall long obey: 30
We for the year to come may take
Our temper from to-day.

And from the blessed power that rolls
About, below, above,
We'll frame the measure of our souls: 35
They shall be tuned to love.

Then come, my Sister! come, I pray,
With speed put on your woodland dress;
And bring no book: for this one day
We'll give to idleness.   40

VI.

SIMON LEE,

THE OLD HUNTSMAN;

With an incident in which he was concerned.

[Composed 1798.—Published 1798.]

In the sweet shire of Cardigan,
Not far from pleasant Ivor-hall,
An old Man dwells, a little man,—
'Tis said he once was tall.
Full five-and-thirty years he lived   5
A running huntsman merry;
And still the centre of his cheek
Is red as a ripe cherry.

No man like him the horn could sound,
And hill and valley rang with glee   10
When Echo bandied, round and round,
The halloo of Simon Lee.

In those proud days, he little cared
For husbandry or tillage;
To blither tasks did Simon rouse   15
The sleepers of the village.

He all the country could outrun,
Could leave both man and horse behind;
And often, ere the chase was done,
He reeled, and was stone-blind.   20
And still there's something in the world
At which his heart rejoices;
For when the chiming hounds are out,
He dearly loves their voices!

But, oh the heavy change!—bereft   25
Of health, strength, friends, and kindred,
    see!
Old Simon to the world is left
In liveried poverty.
His Master's dead,—and no one now
Dwells in the Hall of Ivor;   30
Men, dogs, and horses, all are dead;
He is the sole survivor.

And he is lean and he is sick;
His body, dwindled and awry,
Rests upon ankles swoln and thick;   35
His legs are thin and dry.
One prop he has, and only one,
His wife, an aged woman,
Lives with him, near the waterfall,
Upon the village Common.   40

Beside their moss-grown hut of clay,
Not twenty paces from the door,
A scrap of land they have, but they
Are poorest of the poor.
This scrap of land he from the heath   45
Enclosed when he was stronger;
But what to them avails the land
Which he can till no longer?

Oft, working by her Husband's side,
Ruth does what Simon cannot do;   50
For she, with scanty cause for pride,
Is stouter of the two.
And, though you with your utmost skill
From labour could not wean them,
'Tis little, very little—all   55
That they can do between them.

Few months of life has he in store
As he to you will tell,
For still, the more he works, the more
Do his weak ankles swell.   60

My gentle Reader, I perceive
How patiently you've waited,
And now I fear that you expect
Some tale will be related.

O Reader! had you in your mind   65
Such stores as silent thought can bring,
O gentle Reader! you would find
A tale in every thing.
What more I have to say is short,
And you must kindly take it: 70
It is no tale; but, should you think,
Perhaps a tale you'll make it.

One summer-day I chanced to see
This old Man doing all he could
To unearth the root of an old tree,   75
A stump of rotten wood.
The mattock tottered in his hand;
So vain was his endeavour,
That at the root of the old tree
He might have worked for ever.   80

"You're overtasked, good Simon Lee,
Give me your tool," to him I said;
And at the word right gladly he
Received my proffered aid.
I struck, and with a single blow   85
The tangled root I severed,
At which the poor old Man so long
And vainly had endeavoured.

The tears into his eyes were brought,
And thanks and praises seemed to run   90
So fast out of his heart, I thought
They never would have done.
—I've heard of hearts unkind, kind deeds
With coldness still returning;
Alas! the gratitude of men   95
Hath oftener left me mourning.

VII.

WRITTEN IN GERMANY,

ON ONE OF THE COLDEST DAYS OF THE CENTURY.

[Composed 1799.—Published 1800.]

The Reader must be apprised that the Stoves in North Germany generally have the impression of a galloping horse upon them, this being part of the Brunswick Arms.

A PLAGUE on your languages, German and Norse!
Let me have the song of the kettle;

And the tongs and the poker, instead of that horse
That gallops away with such fury and force
On this dreary dull plate of black metal. 5

See that Fly,—a disconsolate creature! perhaps
A child of the field or the grove;
And, sorrow for him! the dull treacherous heat
Has seduced the poor fool from his winter retreat,
And he creeps to the edge of my stove. 10

Alas! how he fumbles about the domains
Which this comfortless oven environ!
He cannot find out in what track he must crawl,
Now back to the tiles, then in search of the wall,
And now on the brink of the iron. 15

Stock-still there he stands like a traveller bemazed:
The best of his skill he has tried;
His feelers, methinks, I can see him put forth
To the east and the west, to the south and the north,
But he finds neither guide-post nor guide.

His spindles sink under him, foot, leg, and thigh!   21
His eyesight and hearing are lost;
Between life and death his blood freezes and thaws;
And his two pretty pinions of blue dusky gauze
Are glued to his sides by the frost. 25

No brother, no mate has he near him—while I
Can draw warmth from the cheek of my Love;
As blest and as glad, in this desolate gloom,
As if green summer grass were the floor of my room,
And woodbines were hanging above. 30

Yet, God is my witness, thou small helpless Thing!
Thy life I would gladly sustain

Till summer come up from the south, and
    with crowds
Of thy brethren a march thou shouldst
    sound through the clouds,
And back to the forests again!   35

VIII.

A POET'S EPITAPH.

[Composed 1799.—Published 1800.]

ART thou a Statist in the van
Of public conflicts trained and bred?
—First learn to love one living man;
Then may'st thou think upon the dead.

A Lawyer art thou?—draw not nigh!   5
Go, carry to some fitter place
The keenness of that practised eye,
The hardness of that sallow face.

Art thou a Man of purple cheer?
A rosy Man, right plump to see?   10
Approach; yet, Doctor, not too near,
This grave no cushion is for thee.

Or art thou one of gallant pride,
A Soldier and no man of chaff?
Welcome!—but lay thy sword aside,   15
And lean upon a peasant's staff.

Physician art thou?—one, all eyes,
Philosopher!—a fingering slave,
One that would peep and botanize
Upon his mother's grave?   20

Wrapt closely in thy sensual fleece,
O turn aside,—and take, I pray,
That he below may rest in peace,
Thy ever-dwindling soul, away!

A Moralist perchance appears;   25
Led, Heaven knows how! to this poor
    sod:
And he has neither eyes nor ears;
Himself his world, and his own God;

One to whose smooth-rubbed soul can cling
Nor form, nor feeling, great or small;   30
A reasoning, self-sufficing thing,
An intellectual All-in-all!

Shut close the door; press down the latch;
Sleep in thy intellectual crust;
Nor lose ten tickings of thy watch   35
Near this unprofitable dust

But who is He, with modest looks,
And clad in homely russet brown?
He murmurs near the running brooks
A music sweeter than their own.   40

He is retired as noontide dew,
Or fountain in a noon-day grove;
And you must love him, ere to you
He will seem worthy of your love.

The outward shows of sky and earth,   45
Of hill and valley, he has viewed;
And impulses of deeper birth
Have come to him in solitude.

In common things that round us lie
Some random truths he can impart,—   50
The harvest of a quiet eye
That broods and sleeps on his own heart.

But he is weak; both Man and Boy,
Hath been an idler in the land;
Contented if he might enjoy   55
The things which others understand.

—Come hither in thy hour of strength;
Come, weak as is a breaking wave!
Here stretch thy body at full length;
Or build thy house upon this grave.   60

IX.

TO THE DAISY.

[Composed 1802.—Published 1807.]

BRIGHT Flower! whose home is every-
    where,
Bold in maternal Nature's care,
And all the long year through the heir
    Of joy and sorrow;
Methinks that there abides in thee   5
Some concord with humanity,
Given to no other flower I see
    The forest thorough!

Is it that Man is soon deprest?
A thoughtless Thing! who, once unblest,
Does little on his memory rest,   11
    Or on his reason,
And Thou wouldst teach him how to
    find
A shelter under every wind,
A hope for times that are unkind   15
    And every season?

Thou wander'st the wide world about,
Unchecked by pride or scrupulous doubt,
With friends to greet thee, or without,
    Yet pleased and willing;   20
Meek, yielding to the occasion's call,
And all things suffering from all,
Thy function apostolical
    In peace fulfilling.

X.

MATTHEW.

[Composed 1799.—Published 1800.]

In the School of ———— is a tablet, on which
are inscribed, in gilt letters, the Names of the
several persons who have been Schoolmasters
there since the foundation of the School, with
the time at which they entered upon and quitted
their office. Opposite to one of those Names
the Author wrote the following lines.

If Nature, for a favourite child,
In thee hath tempered so her clay,
That every hour thy heart runs wild,
Yet never once doth go astray,

Read o'er these lines; and then review   5
This tablet, that thus humbly rears
In such diversity of hue
Its history of two hundred years.

—When through this little wreck of fame,
Cipher and syllable! thine eye   10
Has travelled down to Matthew's name,
Pause with no common sympathy.

And if a sleeping tear should wake,
Then be it neither checked nor stayed:
For Matthew a request I make   15
Which for himself he had not made.

Poor Matthew, all his frolics o'er,
Is silent as a standing pool;
Far from the chimney's merry roar,
And murmur of the village school.   20

The sighs which Matthew heaved were
    sighs
Of one tired out with fun and madness;
The tears which came to Matthew's eyes
Were tears of light, the dew of gladness.

Yet sometimes, when the secret cup   25
Of still and serious thought went round,
It seemed as if he drank it up—
He felt with spirit so profound.

—Thou soul of God's best earthly mould!
Thou happy Soul! and can it be   30
That these two words of glittering gold
Are all that must remain of thee?

XI.

THE TWO APRIL MORNINGS.

[Composed 1799.—Published 1800.]

We walked along, while bright and red
Uprose the morning sun;
And Matthew stopped, he looked, and
    said,
"The will of God be done!"

A village schoolmaster was he,   5
With hair of glittering grey;
As blithe a man as you could see
On a spring holiday.

And on that morning, through the grass,
And by the steaming rills,   10
We travelled merrily, to pass
A day among the hills.

"Our work," said I, "was well begun,
Then from thy breast what thought,
Beneath so beautiful a sun,   15
So sad a sigh has brought?"

A second time did Matthew stop;
And fixing still his eye
Upon the eastern mountain-top,
To me he made reply: 20

"Yon cloud with that long purple cleft
Brings fresh into my mind
A day like this which I have left
Full thirty years behind.

"And just above yon slope of corn   25
Such colours, and no other,
Were in the sky, that April morn,
Of this the very brother.

"With rod and line I sued the sport
Which that sweet season gave,   30
And, to the churchyard come, stopped
    short
Beside my daughter's grave.

"Nine summers had she scarcely seen,
The pride of all the vale;
And then she sang;—she would have
    been   35
A very nightingale.

"Six feet in earth my Emma lay ;
And yet I loved her more,
For so it seemed, than till that day
I e'er had loved before.   40

"And, turning from her grave, I met,
Beside the churchyard yew,
A blooming Girl, whose hair was wet
With points of morning dew.

"A basket on her head she bare ;   45
Her brow was smooth and white :
To see a child so very fair,
It was a pure delight !

"No fountain from its rocky cave
E'er tripped with foot so free ;   50
She seemed as happy as a wave
That dances on the sea.

"There came from me a sigh of pain
Which I could ill confine ;
I looked at her, and looked again :   55
And did not wish her mine !"

Matthew is in his grave, yet now,
Methinks, I see him stand,
As at that moment, with a bough
Of wilding in his hand.   60

XII.

THE FOUNTAIN.

A CONVERSATION.

[Composed 1799.—Published 1800.]

WE talked with open heart, and tongue
Affectionate and true,
A pair of friends, though I was young,
And Matthew seventy-two.

We lay beneath a spreading oak,   5
Beside a mossy seat ;
And from the turf a fountain broke,
And gurgled at our feet.

"Now, Matthew !" said I, "let us match
This water's pleasant tune   10
With some old border-song, or catch
That suits a summer's noon ;

"Or of the church-clock and the chimes
Sing here beneath the shade,
That half-mad thing of witty rhymes   15
Which you last April made !"

In silence Matthew lay, and eyed
The spring beneath the tree ;
And thus the dear old Man replied,
The grey-haired man of glee :   20

"No check, no stay, this Streamlet fears ;
How merrily it goes !
'Twill murmur on a thousand years,
And flow as now it flows.

"And here, on this delightful day,   25
I cannot choose but think
How oft, a vigorous man, I lay
Beside this fountain's brink.

"My eyes are dim with childish tears,
My heart is idly stirred,   30
For the same sound is in my ears
Which in those days I heard.

"Thus fares it still in our decay :
And yet the wiser mind
Mourns less for what age takes away   35
Than what it leaves behind.

"The blackbird amid leafy trees,
The lark above the hill,
Let loose their carols when they please,
Are quiet when they will.   40

"With Nature never do *they* wage
A foolish strife ; they see
A happy youth, and their old age
Is beautiful and free :

"But we are pressed by heavy laws ;   45
And often, glad no more,
We wear a face of joy, because
We have been glad of yore.

"If there be one who need bemoan
His kindred laid in earth,   50
The household hearts that were his own ;
It is the man of mirth.

"My days, my Friend, are almost gone,
My life has been approved,
And many love me ! but by none   55
Am I enough beloved."

"Now both himself and me he wrongs,
The man who thus complains !
I live and sing my idle songs
Upon these happy plains ;   60

"And, Matthew, for thy children dead
I'll be a son to thee!"
At this he grasped my hand, and said,
"Alas! that cannot be."

We rose up from the fountain-side; 65
And down the smooth descent
Of the green sheep-track did we glide;
And through the wood we went;

And, ere we came to Leonard's rock,
He sang those witty rhymes 70
About the crazy old church-clock,
And the bewildered chimes.

XIII.

PERSONAL TALK.

[Composed ?.—Published 1807.]

I.

I AM not One who much or oft delight
To season my fireside with personal
talk,—
Of friends, who live within an easy walk,
Or neighbours, daily, weekly, in my
sight:
And, for my chance-acquaintance, ladies
bright, 5
Sons, mothers, maidens withering on the
stalk,
These all wear out of me, like Forms with
chalk
Painted on rich men's floors, for one feast-
night.
Better than such discourse doth silence
long,
Long, barren silence, square with my
desire; 10
To sit without emotion, hope, or aim,
In the loved presence of my cottage-fire,
And listen to the flapping of the flame,
Or kettle whispering its faint under-
song.

II.

"Yet life," you say, "is life; we have
seen and see, 15
And with a living pleasure we describe;
And fits of sprightly malice do but
bribe
The languid mind into activity.

Sound sense, and love itself, and mirth
and glee
Are fostered by the comment and the
gibe." 20
Even be it so: yet still among your
tribe,
Our daily world's true Worldlings, rank
not me!
Children are blest, and powerful; their
world lies
More justly balanced; partly at their feet,
And part far from them:—sweetest
melodies 25
Are those that are by distance made
more sweet;
Whose mind is but the mind of his own
eyes,
He is a Slave; the meanest we can meet!

III.

Wings have we,—and as far as we can
go
We may find pleasure: wilderness and
wood, 30
Blank ocean and mere sky, support that
mood
Which with the lofty sanctifies the low.
Dreams, books, are each a world; and
books, we know,
Are a substantial world, both pure and
good:
Round these, with tendrils strong as flesh
and blood, 35
Our pastime and our happiness will
grow.
There find I personal themes, a plenteous
store,
Matter wherein right voluble I am,
To which I listen with a ready ear;
Two shall be named, pre-eminently dear,—
The gentle Lady married to the Moor; 41
And heavenly Una with her milk-white
Lamb.

IV.

Nor can I not believe but that hereby
Great gains are mine; for thus I live
remote
From evil-speaking; rancour, never
sought, 45

Comes to me not; malignant truth, or
   lie.
Hence have I genial seasons, hence have I
Smooth passions, smooth discourse, and
   joyous thought:
And thus from day to day my little
   boat
Rocks in its harbour, lodging peaceably.
Blessings be with them — and eternal
   praise,   51
Who gave us nobler loves, and nobler
   cares—
The Poets, who on earth have made us
   heirs
Of truth and pure delight by heavenly
   lays!
Oh! might my name be numbered among
   theirs,   55
Then gladly would I end my mortal
   days.

XIV.

ILLUSTRATED BOOKS AND NEWSPAPERS.

[Composed 1846.—Published 1850.]

DISCOURSE was deemed Man's noblest
   attribute,
And written words the glory of his
   hand;
Then followed. Printing with enlarged
   command
For thought—dominion vast and absolute
For spreading truth, and making love
   expand.   5
Now prose and verse sunk into disrepute
Must lacquey a dumb Art that best can
   suit
The taste of this once-intellectual Land.
A backward movement surely have we
   here,
From manhood—back to childhood; for
   the age—   10
Back towards caverned life's first rude
   career.
Avaunt this vile abuse of pictured page!
Must eyes be all in all, the tongue and
   ear
Nothing? Heaven keep us from a lower
   stage!

XV.

TO THE SPADE OF A FRIEND.

(AN AGRICULTURIST.)

Composed while we were labouring together in
his pleasure-ground.

[Composed (probably) 1806.—Published 1807.]

SPADE! with which Wilkinson hath tilled
   his lands,
And shaped these pleasant walks by
   Emont's side,
Thou art a tool of honour in my hands;
I press thee, through the yielding soil,
   with pride.   4

Rare master has it been thy lot to know;
Long hast Thou served a man to reason true;
Whose life combines the best of high and
   low,
The labouring many and the resting few;

Health, meekness, ardour, quietness secure,
And industry of body and of mind;   10
And elegant enjoyments, that are pure
As nature is;—too pure to be refined.

Here often hast Thou heard the Poet sing
In concord with his river murmuring by;
Or in some silent field, while timid spring
Is yet uncheered by other minstrelsy. 16

Who shall inherit Thee when death has
   laid
Low in the darksome cell thine own dear
   lord?
That man will have a trophy, humble
   Spade!   19
A trophy nobler than a conqueror's sword.

If he be one that feels, with skill to part
False praise from true, or, greater from
   the less,
Thee will he welcome to his hand and
   heart,
Thou monument of peaceful happiness!

He will not dread with Thee a toilsome
   day—   25
Thee his loved servant, his inspiring
   mate!
And, when Thou art past service, worn
   away,
No dull oblivious nook shall hide thy fate.

His thrift thy uselessness will never scorn;
An *heir-loom* in his cottage wilt Thou
be:—   30
High will he hang thee up, well pleased
to adorn
His rustic chimney with the last of
Thee !

XVI.
A NIGHT THOUGHT.

[Composed ?.—Published 1837 (*The Tribute:
edited by Lord Northampton*); vol. of 1842.]

Lo ! where the Moon along the sky
Sails with her happy destiny;
Oft is she hid from mortal eye
    Or dimly seen,
But when the clouds asunder fly   5
    How bright her mien !

Far different we—a froward race,
Thousands though rich in Fortune's grace
With cherished sullenness of pace
    Their way pursue,   10
Ingrates who wear a smileless face
    The whole year through.

If kindred humours e'er would make
My spirit droop for drooping's sake,
From Fancy following in thy wake,   15
    Bright ship of heaven !
A counter impulse let me take
    And be forgiven.

XVII.
INCIDENT

CHARACTERISTIC OF A FAVOURITE DOG.

[Composed 1805.—Published 1807.]

On his morning rounds the Master
Goes to learn how all things fare;
Searches pasture after pasture,
Sheep and cattle eyes with care;
And, for silence or for talk,   5
He hath comrades in his walk;
Four dogs, each pair of different breed,
Distinguished two for scent, and two for
    speed.

See a hare before him started !
—Off they fly in earnest chase;   10
Every dog is eager-hearted,
All the four are in the race:

And the hare whom they pursue,
Knows from instinct what to do;
Her hope is near: no turn she makes;   15
But, like an arrow, to the river takes.

Deep the river was, and crusted
Thinly by a one night's frost;
But the nimble Hare hath trusted
To the ice, and safely crost;   20
She hath crost, and without heed
All are following at full speed,
When, lo ! the ice, so thinly spread,
Breaks—and the, greyhound, DART, is
    overhead !

Better fate have PRINCE and SWALLOW—
See them cleaving to the sport !   26
MUSIC has no heart to follow,
Little MUSIC, she stops short.
She hath neither wish nor heart,
Hers is now another part: 30
A loving creature she, and brave !
And fondly strives her struggling friend
    to save.

From the brink her paws she stretches,
Very hands as you would say !
And afflicting moans she fetches,   35
As he breaks the ice away.
For herself she hath no fears,—
Him alone she sees and hears,—
Makes efforts with complainings; nor
    gives o'er
Until her fellow sinks to re-appear no
    more.   40

XVIII.
TRIBUTE

TO THE MEMORY OF THE SAME DOG.

[Composed 1805.—Published 1807.]

Lie here, without a record of thy worth,
Beneath a covering of the common earth !
It is not from unwillingness to praise,
Or want of love, that here no Stone we
    raise;
More thou deserv'st; but *this* man gives
    to man,   5
Brother to brother, *this* is all we can.
Yet they to whom thy virtues made thee
    dear
Shall find thee through all changes of the
    year:

This Oak points out thy grave; the silent
      tree
Will gladly stand a monument of thee. 10

We grieved for thee, and wished thy
      end were past;
And willingly have laid thee here at last:
For thou hadst lived till every thing that
      cheers
In thee had yielded to the weight of years;
Extreme old age had wasted thee away, 15
And left thee but a glimmering of the day;
Thy ears were deaf, and feeble were thy
      knees,—
I saw thee stagger in the summer breeze,
Too weak to stand against its sportive
      breath,
And ready for the gentlest stroke of
      death.   20
It came, and we were glad; yet tears were
      shed;
Both man and woman wept when thou
      wert dead;
Not only for a thousand thoughts that
      were,
Old household thoughts, in which thou
      hadst thy share;
But for some precious boons vouchsafed
      to thee,   25
Found scarcely anywhere in like degree!
For love, that comes wherever life and
      sense
Are given by God, in thee was most
      intense;
A chain of heart, a feeling of the mind,
A tender sympathy, which did thee bind
Not only to us Men, but to thy Kind: 31
Yea, for thy fellow-brutes in thee we saw
A soul of love, love's intellectual law:—
Hence, if we wept, it was not done in
      shame;
Our tears from passion and from reason
      came,   35
And, therefore, shalt thou be an honoured
      name!

XIX.

FIDELITY.

[Composed 1805.—Published 1807.]

A BARKING sound the Shepherd hears,
A cry as of a dog or fox;

He halts—and searches with his eyes
Among the scattered rocks:
And now at distance can discern   5
A stirring in a brake of fern;
And instantly a dog is seen,
Glancing through that covert green.

The Dog is not of mountain breed;
Its motions, too, are wild and shy;   10
With something, as the Shepherd thinks,
Unusual in its cry:
Nor is there any one in sight
All round, in hollow or on height;
Nor shout, nor whistle strikes his ear; 15
What is the creature doing here?

It was a cove, a huge recess,
That keeps, till June, December's snow;
A lofty precipice in front,
A silent tarn [1] below!   20
Far in the bosom of Helvellyn,
Remote from public road or dwelling,
Pathway, or cultivated land;
From trace of human foot or hand.

There sometimes doth a leaping fish   25
Send through the tarn a lonely cheer;
The crags repeat the raven's croak,
In symphony austere;
Thither the rainbow comes—the cloud—
And mists that spread the flying shroud;
And sunbeams; and the sounding blast,
That, if it could, would hurry past; 32
But that enormous barrier holds it fast.

Not free from boding thoughts, a while
The Shepherd stood; then makes his way
O'er rocks and stones, following the Dog
As quickly as he may;
Nor far had gone before he found
A human skeleton on the ground;
The appalled Discoverer with a sigh   40
Looks round, to learn the history.

From those abrupt and perilous rocks
The Man had fallen, that place of fear!
At length upon the Shepherd's mind
It breaks, and all is clear: 45
He instantly recalled the name,
And who he was, and whence he came;
Remembered, too, the very day
On which the Traveller passed this way.

[1] Tarn is a *small* Mere or Lake, mostly high
up in the mountains.

But hear a wonder, for whose sake 50
This lamentable tale I tell!
A lasting monument of words
This wonder merits well.
The Dog, which still was hovering nigh,
Repeating the same timid cry, 55
This Dog, had been through three months'
  , space
A dweller in that savage place.

Yes, proof was plain that, since the day
When this ill-fated Traveller died,
The Dog had watched about the spot, 60
Or by his master's side:
How nourished here through such long
  time
He knows, who gave that love sublime;
And gave that strength of feeling, great
Above all human estimate! 65

XX.

ODE TO DUTY.

[Composed 1805.—Published 1807.]

"Jam non consilio bonus, sed more eò perductus,
  ut non tantum rectè facere possim, sed nisi
  rectè facere non possim."

STERN Daughter of the Voice of God!
O Duty! if that name thou love
Who art a light to guide, a rod
To check the erring, and reprove;
Thou, who art victory and law 5
When empty terrors overawe;
From vain temptations dost set free;
And calm'st the weary strife of frail
  humanity!

There are who ask not if thine eye
Be on them; who, in love and truth, 10
Where no misgiving is, rely
Upon the genial sense of youth:
Glad Hearts! without reproach or blot;
Who do thy work, and know it not:
Oh! if through confidence misplaced 15
They fail, thy saving arms, dread Power!
  around them cast.

Serene will be our days and bright,
And happy will our nature be,
When love is an unerring light,
And joy its own security. 20

And they a blissful course may hold
Even now, who, not unwisely bold,
Live in the spirit of this creed;
Yet seek thy firm support, according to
  their need.

I, loving freedom, and untried; 25
No sport of every random gust,
Yet being to myself a guide,
Too blindly have reposed my trust:
And oft, when in my heart was heard
Thy timely mandate, I deferred 30
The task, in smoother walks to stray;
But thee I now would serve more strictly,
  if I may.

Through no disturbance of my soul,
Or strong compunction in me wrought,
I supplicate for thy control; 35
But in the quietness of thought:
Me this unchartered freedom tires;
I feel the weight of chance-desires:
My hopes no more must change their
  name,
I long for a repose that ever is the
  same. 40

[Yet not the less would I throughout
Still act according to the voice
Of my own wish; and feel past doubt
That my submissiveness was choice:
Not seeking in the school of pride
For "precepts over dignified,"
Denial and restraint I prize
No farther than they breed a second Will
  more wise[1].]

Stern Lawgiver! yet thou dost wear
The Godhead's most benignant grace;
Nor know we anything so fair
As is the smile upon thy face:
Flowers laugh before thee on their beds 45
And fragrance in thy footing treads;
Thou dost preserve the stars from wrong;
And the most ancient heavens, through
  Thee, are fresh and strong.

To humbler functions, awful Power!
I call thee: I myself commend 50
Unto thy guidance from this hour;
Oh, let my weakness have an end!

---

[1] In ed. 1807 only—ED.

Give unto me, made lowly wise,
The spirit of self-sacrifice;
The confidence of reason give;   55
And in the light of truth thy Bondman
    let me live!

XXI.

CHARACTER OF THE HAPPY
WARRIOR.

[Composed December 1805 or January 1806.—
Published 1807.]

WHO is the happy Warrior? Who is he
That every man in arms should wish
    to be?
—It is the generous Spirit, who, when
    brought
Among the tasks of real life, hath
    wrought
Upon the plan that pleased his boyish
    thought: 5
Whose high endeavours are an inward
    light
That makes the path before him always
    bright:
Who, with a natural instinct to discern
What knowledge can perform, is diligent
    to learn;
Abides by this resolve, and stops not
    there,   10
But makes his moral being his prime
    care;
Who, doomed to go in company with
    Pain,
And Fear, and Bloodshed, miserable
    train!
Turns his necessity to glorious gain;
In face of these doth exercise a power 15
Which is our human nature's highest
    dower;
Controls them and subdues, transmutes,
    bereaves
Of their bad influence, and their good
    receives:
By objects, which might force the soul to
    abate
Her feeling, rendered more compas-
    sionate;   20
Is placable—because occasions rise
So often that demand such sacrifice;
More skilful in self-knowledge, even
    more pure,

As tempted more; more able to endure,
As more exposed to suffering and dis-
    tress;   25
Thence, also, more alive to tenderness.
—'Tis he whose law is reason; who
    depends
Upon that law as on the best of friends;
Whence, in a state where men are tempted
    still
To evil for a guard against worse ill, 30
And what in quality or act is best
Doth seldom on a right foundation rest,
He labours good on good to fix, and owes
To virtue every triumph that he knows:
—Who, if he rise to station of command,
Rises by open means; and there will
    stand   36
On honourable terms, or else retire,
And in himself possess his own desire;
Who comprehends his trust, and to the
    same
Keeps faithful with a singleness of aim;
And therefore does not stoop, nor lie in
    wait   41
For wealth, or honours, or for worldly
    state;
Whom they must follow; on whose head
    must fall,
Like showers of manna, if they come
    at all:
Whose powers shed round him in the
    common strife,   45
Or mild concerns of ordinary life,
A constant influence, a peculiar grace;
But who, if he be called upon to face
Some awful moment to which Heaven
    has joined
Great issues, good or bad for human
    kind,   50
Is happy as a Lover; and attired
With sudden brightness, like a Man
    inspired;
And, through the heat of conflict, keeps
    the law
In calmness made, and sees what he
    foresaw;
Or if an unexpected call succeed,   55
Come when it will, is equal to the need:
—He who, though thus endued as with a
    sense
And faculty for storm and turbulence,

Is yet a Soul whose master-bias leans
To homefelt pleasures and to gentle
    scenes;   60
Sweet images! which, wheresoe'er he be,
Are at his heart; and such fidelity
It is his darling passion to approve;
More brave for this, that he hath much to
    love:——
'Tis, finally, the Man, who, lifted high, 65
Conspicuous object in a Nation's eye,
Or left unthought-of in obscurity,—
Who, with a toward or untoward lot,
Prosperous or adverse, to his wish or not—
Plays, in the many games of life, that one
Where what he most doth value must be
    won: 71
Whom neither shape of danger can
    dismay,
Nor thought of tender happiness betray;
Who, not content that former worth
    stand fast,
Looks forward, persevering to the last, 75
From well to better, daily self-surpast:
Who, whether praise of him must walk
    the earth
For ever, and to noble deeds give birth,
Or he must fall, to sleep without his fame,
And leave a dead unprofitable name— 80
Finds comfort in himself and in his cause;
And, while the mortal mist is gathering,
    draws
His breath in confidence of Heaven's
    applause:
This is the happy Warrior; this is He 84
That every Man in arms should wish to be.

XXII.
THE FORCE OF PRAYER[1];
OR,
THE FOUNDING OF BOLTON PRIORY.

A TRADITION.

[Composed 1807.—Published 1815 (4to, along with
The White Doe of Rylstone); ed. 1815.]

"𝔚𝔥𝔞𝔱 𝔦𝔰 𝔤𝔬𝔬𝔡 𝔣𝔬𝔯 𝔞 𝔟𝔬𝔬𝔱𝔩𝔢𝔰𝔰 𝔟𝔢𝔫𝔢?"
With these dark words begins my Tale;
And their meaning is, whence can comfort
    spring
When Prayer is of no avail?

[1] See "The White Doe of Rylstone."

"𝔚𝔥𝔞𝔱 𝔦𝔰 𝔤𝔬𝔬𝔡 𝔣𝔬𝔯 𝔞 𝔟𝔬𝔬𝔱𝔩𝔢𝔰𝔰 𝔟𝔢𝔫𝔢?" 5
The Falconer to the Lady said;
And she made answer "ENDLESS SORROW!"
For she knew that her Son was dead.

She knew it by the Falconer's words, 9
And from the look of the Falconer's eye;
And from the love which was in her soul
For her youthful Romilly.

—Young Romilly through Barden woods
Is ranging high and low;
And holds a greyhound in a leash, 15
To let slip upon buck or doe.

The pair have reached that fearful chasm,
How tempting to bestride!
For lordly Wharf is there pent in
With rocks on either side. 20

The striding-place is called THE STRID,
A name which it took of yore:
A thousand years hath it borne that
    name,
And shall a thousand more.

And hither is young Romilly come, 25
And what may now forbid
That he, perhaps for the hundredth time,
Shall bound across THE STRID?

He sprang in glee,—for what cared he
That the river was strong, and the rocks
    were steep?— 30
But the greyhound in the leash hung
    back,
And checked him in his leap.

The Boy is in the arms of Wharf,
And strangled by a merciless force;
For never more was young Romilly seen
Till he rose a lifeless corse. 36

Now there is stillness in the vale,
And long, unspeaking, sorrow:
Wharf shall be to pitying hearts
A name more sad than Yarrow. 40

If for a Lover the Lady wept,
A solace she might borrow
From death, and from the passion of
    death:—
Old Wharf might heal her sorrow.

She weeps not for the wedding-day 45
Which was to be to-morrow:
Her hope was a further-looking hope,
And hers is a mother's sorrow.

He was a tree that stood alone,
And proudly did its branches wave; 50
And the root of this delightful tree
Was in her husband's grave !

Long, long in darkness did she sit,
And her first words were, "Let there be
In Bolton, on the field of Wharf, 55
A stately Priory !"

The stately Priory was reared;
And Wharf, as he moved along,
To matins joined a mournful voice,
Nor failed at even-song. 60

And the Lady prayed in heaviness
That looked not for relief !
But slowly did her succour come,
And a patience to her grief.

Oh ! there is never sorrow of heart 65
That shall lack a timely end,
If but to God we turn, and ask
Of Him to be our friend !

XXIII.

A FACT, AND AN IMAGINATION;

OR,

CANUTE AND ALFRED, ON THE SEA-SHORE.

[Composed 1816.—Published 1820.]

THE Danish Conqueror, on his royal
chair,
Mustering a face of haughty sovereignty,
To aid a covert purpose, cried—"O ye
Approaching Waters of the deep, that
share
With this green isle my fortunes, come
not where 5
Your Master's throne is set."—Deaf was
the Sea;
Her waves rolled on, respecting his decree
Less than they heed a breath of wanton
air.
—Then Canute, rising from the invaded
throne,

Said to his servile Courtiers,—"Poor the
reach, 10
The undisguised extent, of mortal sway !
He only is a King, and he alone
Deserves the name (this truth the billows
preach)
Whose everlasting laws, sea, earth, and
heaven obey."

This just reproof the prosperous Dane
Drew from the influx of the main, 16
For some whose rugged northern mouths
would strain
At oriental flattery;
And Canute (fact more worthy to be
known)
From that time forth did for his brows
disown 20
The ostentatious symbol of a crown;
Esteeming earthly royalty
Contemptible as vain.

Now hear what one of elder days,
Rich theme of England's fondest praise, 25
Her darling Alfred, *might* have spoken;
To cheer the remnant of his host
When he was driven from coast to coast,
Distressed and harassed, but with mind
unbroken:

"My faithful followers, lo ! the tide is
spent 30
That rose, and steadily advanced to fill
The shores and channels, working Na-
ture's will
Among the mazy streams that backward
went,
And in the sluggish pools where ships are
pent:
And now, his task performed, the flood
stands still, 35
At the green base of many an inland
hill,
In placid beauty and sublime content !
Such the repose that sage and hero find;
Such measured rest the sedulous and good
Of humbler name; whose souls do, like
the flood 40
Of Ocean, press right on; or gently wind,
Neither to be diverted nor withstood
Until they reach the bounds by Heaven
assigned."

XXIV.

[Composed 1816.—Published 1820.]

" *A LITTLE onward lend thy guiding hand*
To these dark steps, a little further on! "
—What trick of memory to *my* voice hath
    brought
This mournful iteration? For though
    Time,
The Conqueror, crowns the Conquered,
    on this brow   5
Planting his favourite silver diadem,
Nor he, nor minister of his—intent
To run before him, hath enrolled me yet,
Though not unmenaced, among those who
    lean
Upon a living staff, with borrowed sight.
—O my own Dora, my belovèd child!   11
Should that day come—but hark! the
    birds salute
The cheerful dawn, brightening for me
    the east;
For me, thy natural leader, once again
Impatient to conduct thee, not as erst   15
A tottering infant, with compliant stoop
From flower to flower supported; but to
    curb
Thy nymph-like step swift bounding o'er
    the lawn,
Along the loose rocks, or the slippery
    verge
Of foaming torrents.—From thy orisons
Come forth; and, while the morning air
    is yet   21
Transparent as the soul of innocent youth,
Let me, thy happy guide, now point thy way,
And now precede thee, winding to and fro,
Till we by perseverance gain the top   25
Of some smooth ridge, whose brink pre-
    cipitous
Kindles intense desire for powers withheld
From this corporeal frame; whereon who
    stands
Is seized with strong incitement to push
    forth
His arms, as swimmers use, and plunge—
    dread thought,   30
For pastime plunge—into the "abrupt
    abyss,"
Where ravens spread their plumy vans,
    at ease!

And yet more gladly thee would I
    conduct
Through woods and spacious forests,—to
    behold
There how the Original of human art,   35
Heaven-prompted Nature, measures and
    erects
Her temples, fearless for the stately work,
Though waves, to every breeze, its high-
    arched roof,
And storms the pillars rock. But we
    such schools
Of reverential awe will chiefly seek   40
In the still summer noon, while beams of
    light,
Reposing here, and in the aisles beyond
Traceably gliding through the dusk, recall
To mind the living presences of nuns;
A gentle, pensive, white-robed sisterhood,
Whose saintly radiance mitigates the
    gloom   46
Of those terrestrial fabrics, where they
    serve,
To Christ, the Sun of righteousness,
    espoused.

Now also shall the page of classic lore,
To these glad eyes from bondage freed,
    again   50
Lie open; and the book of Holy Writ,
Again unfolded, passage clear shall yield
To heights more glorious still, and into
    shades
More awful, where, advancing hand in
    hand,
We may be taught, O Darling of my care!
To calm the affections, elevate the soul,
And consecrate our lives to truth and
    love.

XXV.

ODE TO LYCORIS.

MAY, 1817.

[Composed May, 1817.—Published 1820.]

I.

An age hath been when Earth was proud
Of lustre too intense
To be sustained; and Mortals bowed
The front in self-defence.

Who *then,* if Dian's crescent gleamed, 5
Or Cupid's sparkling arrow streamed
While on the wing the Urchin played,
Could fearlessly approach the shade?
—Enough for one soft vernal day,
If I, a bard of ebbing time, 10
And nurtured in a fickle clime,
May haunt this hornèd bay ;
Whose amorous water multiplies
The flitting halcyon's vivid dyes ; 14
And smooths her liquid breast—to show
These swan-like specks of mountain snow,
White as the pair that slid along the
plains
Of heaven, when Venus held the reins !

II.

In youth we love the darksome lawn
Brushed by the owlet's wing ; 20
Then, Twilight is preferred to Dawn,
And Autumn to the Spring.
Sad fancies do we then affect,
In luxury of disrespect
To our own prodigal excess 25
Of too familiar happiness.
Lycoris (if such name befit
Thee, thee my life's celestial sign !)
When Nature marks the year's decline,
Be ours to welcome it ; 30
Pleased with the harvest hope that runs
Before the path of milder suns ;
Pleased while the sylvan world displays
Its ripeness to the feeding gaze ;
Pleased when the sullen winds resound
the knell 35
Of the resplendent miracle.

III.

But something whispers to my heart
That, as we downward tend,
Lycoris ! life requires an *art*
To which our souls must bend ; 40
A skill—to balance and supply ;
And, ere the flowing fount be dry,
As soon it must, a sense to sip,
Or drink, with no fastidious lip.
Then welcome, above all, the Guest 45
Whose smiles, diffused o'er land and sea,
Seem to recall the Deity
Of youth into the breast :

May pensive Autumn ne'er present
A claim to her disparagement ! 50
While blossoms and the budding spray
Inspire us in our own decay ;
Still, as we nearer draw to life's dark
goal,
Be hopeful Spring the favourite of the
Soul !

XXVI.

TO THE SAME.

[Composed 1817.—Published 1820.]

ENOUGH of climbing toil !—Ambition
treads
Here, as 'mid busier scenes, ground steep
and rough,
Or slippery even to peril ! and each step,
As we for most uncertain recompense
Mount toward the empire of the fickle
clouds, 5
Each weary step, dwarfing the world
below,
Induces, for its old familiar sights,
Unacceptable feelings of contempt,
With wonder mixed—that Man could
e'er be tied,
In anxious bondage, to such nice array 10
And formal fellowship of petty things !
—Oh ! 'tis the *heart* that magnifies this
life,
Making a truth and beauty of her own ;
And moss-grown alleys, circumscribing
shades, 14
And gurgling rills, assist her in the work
More efficaciously than realms outspread,
As in a map, before the adventurer's
gaze—
Ocean and Earth contending for regard.

The umbrageous woods are left—how
far beneath !
But lo ! where darkness seems to guard
the mouth 20
Of yon wild cave, whose jaggèd brows are
fringed
With flaccid threads of ivy, in the still
And sultry air, depending motionless.
Yet cool the space within, and not un-
cheered
(As whoso enters shall ere long perceive)
By stealthy influx of the timid day 26

Mingling with night, such twilight to
compose
As Numa loved; when, in the Egerian
grot,
From the sage Nymph appearing at his
wish
He gained whate'er a regal mind might
ask,   30
Or need, of counsel breathed through lips
divine.

   Long as the heat shall rage, let that
dim cave
Protect us, there deciphering as we may
Diluvian records; or the sighs of Earth
Interpreting; or counting for old Time 35
His minutes, by reiterated drops,
Audible tears, from some invisible source
That deepens upon fancy—more and more
Drawn toward the centre whence those
sighs creep forth
To awe the lightness of humanity.   40
Or, shutting up thyself within thyself,
There let me see thee sink into a mood
Of gentler thought, protracted till thine eye
Be calm as water when the winds are gone,
And no one can tell whither. Dearest
Friend!   45
We two[1] have known such happy hours
together
That, were power granted to replace
them (fetched
From out the pensive shadows where they
lie)
In the first warmth of their original sun-
shine,
Loth should I be to use it: passing sweet
Are the domains of tender memory!   51

XXVII.

SEPTEMBER, 1819.

[Composed September, 1819.—Published 1820.]

THE sylvan slopes with corn-clad fields
Are hung, as if with golden shields,
Bright trophies of the sun!
Like a fair sister of the sky,
Unruffled doth the blue lake lie,   5
The mountains looking on.

---

1 "We two": edd. 1820-1843; "we too": edd.
1845, 1849-50.—ED.

And, sooth to say, yon vocal grove,
Albeit uninspired by love,
By love untaught to ring,
May well afford to mortal ear   10
An impulse more profoundly dear
Than music of the Spring.

For *that* from turbulence and heat
Proceeds, from some uneasy seat
In nature's struggling frame,   15
Some region of impatient life:
And jealousy, and quivering strife,
Therein a portion claim.

This, this is holy;—while I hear
These vespers of another year,   20
This hymn of thanks and praise,
My spirit seems to mount above
The anxieties of human love,
And earth's precarious days.

But list!—though winter storms be nigh,
Unchecked is that soft harmony: 26
There lives Who can provide
For all His creatures; and in Him,
Even like the radiant Seraphim,
These choristers confide.

XXVIII.

UPON THE SAME OCCASION

[Composed September, 1819.—Published 1820].

DEPARTING summer hath assumed
An aspect tenderly illumed,
The gentlest look of spring;
That calls from yonder leafy shade
Unfaded, yet prepared to fade,   5
A timely carolling.

No faint and hesitating trill,
Such tribute as to winter chill
The lonely redbreast pays!
Clear, loud, and lively is the din,   10
From social warblers gathering in
Their harvest of sweet lays.

Nor doth the example fail to cheer
Me, conscious that my leaf is sere,
And yellow on the bough:—   15
Fall, rosy garlands, from my head!
Ye myrtle wreaths, your fragrance shed
Around a younger brow!

Yet will I temperately rejoice;
Wide is the range, and free the choice   20
Of undiscordant themes;
Which, haply, kindred souls may prize
Not less than vernal ecstasies,
And passion's feverish dreams.

For deathless powers to verse belong,   25
And they like Demi-gods are strong
On whom the Muses smile;
But some their function have disclaimed,
Best pleased with what is aptliest framed
To enervate and defile.   30

Not such the initiatory strains
Committed to the silent plains
In Britain's earliest dawn:
Trembled the groves, the stars grew pale,
While all-too-daringly the veil   35
Of nature was withdrawn!

Nor such the spirit-stirring note
When the live chords Alcæus smote,
Inflamed by sense of wrong;
Woe! woe to Tyrants! from the lyre   40
Broke threateningly, in sparkles dire
Of fierce vindictive song.

And not unhallowed was the page
By wingèd Love inscribed, to assuage
The pangs of vain pursuit;   45
Love listening while the Lesbian Maid
With finest touch of passion swayed
Her own Æolian lute.

O ye, who patiently explore
The wreck of Herculanean lore,   50
What rapture! could ye seize
Some Theban fragment, or unroll
One precious, tender-hearted, scroll
Of pure Simonides.

That were, indeed, a genuine birth   55
Of poesy; a bursting forth
Of genius from the dust:
What Horace gloried to behold,
What Maro loved, shall we enfold?
Can haughty Time be just!   60

XXIX.

MEMORY.

[Composed 1823.—Published 1827.]

A PEN—to register; a key—
That winds through secret wards;

Are well assigned to Memory
By allegoric Bards.

As aptly, also, might be given   5
A Pencil to her hand;
That, softening objects, sometimes even
Outstrips the heart's demand;

That smoothes foregone distress, the lines
Of lingering care subdues,   10
Long-vanished happiness refines,
And clothes in brighter hues;

Yet, like a tool of Fancy, works
Those Spectres to dilate
That startle Conscience, as she lurks   15
Within her lonely seat.

O! that our lives, which flee so fast,
In purity were such,
That not an image of the past
Should fear that pencil's touch!   20

Retirement then might hourly look
Upon a soothing scene,
Age steal to his allotted nook
Contented and serene;

With heart as calm as lakes that sleep,   25
In frosty moonlight glistening;
Or mountain rivers, where they creep
Along a channel smooth and deep,
To their own far-off murmurs listening.

XXX.

[Composed 1829.—Published 1835.]

THIS Lawn, a carpet all alive
With shadows flung from leaves—to strive
  In dance, amid a press
Of sunshine, an apt emblem yields
Of Worldlings revelling in the fields   5
  Of strenuous idleness;

Less quick the stir when tide and breeze
Encounter, and to narrow seas
  Forbid a moment's rest;
The medley less when boreal Lights   10
Glance to and fro, like aery Sprites
  To feats of arms addrest!

Yet, spite of all this eager strife,
This ceaseless play, the genuine life
  That serves the steadfast hours,   15
Is in the grass beneath, that grows
Unheeded, and the mute repose
  Of sweetly-breathing flowers.

XXXI.

HUMANITY.

[Composed 1829.—Published 1835.]

The Rocking-stones, alluded to in the beginning
of the following verses, are supposed to have
been used, by our British ancestors, both for
judicial and religious purposes. Such stones
are not uncommonly found, at this day, both
in Great Britain and in Ireland.

WHAT though the Accused, upon his own
　　appeal
To righteous Gods when man has ceased
　　to feel,
Or at a doubting Judge's stern command,
Before the STONE OF POWER no longer
　　stand—
To take his sentence from the balanced
　　Block,　　　　　　　　　　　5
As, at his touch, it rocks, or seems to
　　rock;
Though, in the depths of sunless groves,
　　no more
The Druid-priest the hallowed Oak adore;
Yet, for the Initiate, rocks and whisper-
　　ing trees
Do still perform mysterious offices!　10
And functions dwell in beast and bird
　　that sway
The reasoning mind, or with the fancy
　　play,
Inviting, at all seasons, ears and eyes
To watch for undelusive auguries:—
Not uninspired appear their simplest
　　ways;　　　　　　　　　　　15
Their voices mount symbolical of praise—
To mix with hymns that Spirits make
　　and hear;
And to fallen man their innocence is
　　dear.
Enraptured Art draws from those sacred
　　springs
Streams that reflect the poetry of things!
Where Christian Martyrs stand in hues
　　portrayed,　　　　　　　　　　21
That, might a wish avail, would never
　　fade,
Borne in their hands the lily and the
　　palm
Shed round the altar a celestial calm;

There, too, behold the lamb and guileless
　　dove　　　　　　　　　　　25
Prest in the tenderness of virgin love
To saintly bosoms!—Glorious is the blend-
　　ing
Of right affections climbing or descending
Along a scale of light and life, with cares
Alternate; carrying holy thoughts and
　　prayers　　　　　　　　　　30
Up to the sovereign seat of the Most
　　High;
Descending to the worm in charity;
Like those good Angels whom a dream of
　　night
Gave, in the field of Luz, to Jacob's sight
All, while *he* slept, treading the pendent
　　stairs　　　　　　　　　　35
Earthward or heavenward, radiant mes-
　　sengers,
That, with a perfect will in one accord
Of strict obedience, serve the Almighty
　　Lord;
And with untired humility forbore
To speed their errand by the wings they
　　wore.　　　　　　　　　　40

What a fair world were ours for verse
　　to paint,
If Power could live at ease with self-
　　restraint!
Opinion bow before the naked sense
Of the great Vision,—faith in Providence;
Merciful over all his creatures, just　45
To the least particle of sentient dust;
But fixing by immutable decrees
Seedtime and harvest for his purposes!
Then would be closed the restless oblique
　　eye
That looks for evil like a treacherous spy;
Disputes would then relax, like stormy
　　winds　　　　　　　　　　51
That into breezes sink; impetuous minds
By discipline endeavour to grow meek
As Truth herself, whom they profess to
　　seek.
Then Genius, shunning fellowship with
　　Pride,　　　　　　　　　　55
Would braid his golden locks at Wis-
　　dom's side;
Love ebb and flow untroubled by caprice;
And not alone *harsh* tyranny would cease,

But unoffending creatures find release
From qualified oppression, whose de-
   fence   60
Rests on a hollow plea of recompense;
Thought-tempered wrongs, for each hu-
   mane respect
Oft worse to bear, or deadlier in effect.
Witness those glances of indignant scorn
From some high-minded Slave, impelled
   to spurn   65
The kindness that would make him less
   forlorn ;
Or, if the soul to bondage be subdued,
His look of pitiable gratitude !

   Alas for thee, bright Galaxy of Isles,
Whose day departs in pomp, returns
   with smiles—   70
To greet the flowers and fruitage of a
   land,
As the sun mounts, by sea-born breezes
   fanned ;
A land whose azure mountain-tops are
   seats
For Gods in council, whose green vales,
   retreats
Fit for the shades of heroes, mingling
   there   75
To breathe Elysian peace in upper air.

   Though cold as winter, gloomy as the
   grave,
Stone-walls a prisoner make, but not
   a slave.
Shall man assume a property in man ?
Lay on the moral will a withering ban ?
Shame that our laws at distance still
   protect   81
Enormities, which they at home reject !
"Slaves cannot breathe in England"—
   yet that boast
Is but a mockery ! when from coast to
   coast,
Though *fettered* slave be none, her floors
   and soil   85
Groan underneath a weight of slavish
   toil,
For the poor Many, measured out by
   rules
Fetched with cupidity from heartless
   schools,

That to an Idol, falsely called "the
   Wealth
Of Nations," sacrifice a People's health,
Body and mind and soul; a thirst so
   keen   91
Is ever urging on the vast machine
Of sleepless Labour, 'mid whose dizzy
   wheels
The Power least prized is that which
   thinks and feels.

   Then, for the pastimes of this delicate age,
And all the heavy or light vassalage 96
Which for their sakes we fasten, as may
   suit
Our varying moods, on human kind or
   brute,
'Twere well in little, as in great, to pause,
Lest Fancy trifle with eternal laws. 100
Not from his fellows only man may learn
Rights to compare and duties to discern !
All creatures and all objects, in degree,
Are friends and patrons of humanity.
There are to whom the garden, grove,
   and field,   105
Perpetual lessons of forbearance yield ;
Who would not lightly violate the grace
The lowliest flower possesses in its place;
Nor shorten the sweet life, too fugitive,
Which nothing less than Infinite Power
   could give.   110

XXXII.

[Composed 1846.—Published 1850.]

THE unremitting voice of nightly streams
That wastes so oft, we think, its tuneful
   powers,
If neither soothing to the worm that
   gleams
Through dewy grass, nor small birds
   hushed in bowers,
Nor unto silent leaves and drowsy
   flowers,—   5
That voice of unpretending harmony
(For who what is shall measure by what
   seems
To be, or not to be,
Or tax high Heaven with prodigality?)
Wants not a healing influence that can
   creep   10
Into the human breast, and mix with sleep

To regulate the motion of our dreams
For kindly issues—as through every clime
Was felt near murmuring brooks in
    earliest time;
As, at this day, the rudest swains who
    dwell   15
Where torrents roar, or hear the tinkling
    knell
Of water-breaks, with grateful heart
    could tell.

XXXIII.

THOUGHTS ON THE SEASONS.

[Composed 1829.—Published 1835.]

FLATTERED with promise of escape
    From every hurtful blast,
Spring takes, O sprightly May! thy
    shape,
    Her loveliest and her last.

Less fair is summer riding high   5
    In fierce solstitial power,
Less fair than when a lenient sky
    Brings on her parting hour.

When earth repays with golden sheaves
    The labours of the plough,   10
And ripening fruits and forest leaves
    All brighten on the bough;

What pensive beauty autumn shows,
    Before she hears the sound
Of winter rushing in, to close   15
    The emblematic round!

Such be our Spring, our Summer such;
    So may our Autumn blend
With hoary Winter, and Life touch,
    Through heaven-born hope, her end! 20

XXXIV.

TO —.

UPON THE BIRTH OF HER FIRST-BORN
CHILD, MARCH, 1833.

[Composed March, 1833.—Published 1835.]

"Tum porro puer, ut saevis projectus ab undis
Navita, nudus humi jacet," &c.—LUCRETIUS.

LIKE a shipwrecked Sailor tost
By rough waves on a perilous coast,
Lies the Babe, in helplessness

And in tenderest nakedness,
Flung by labouring Nature forth   5
Upon the mercies of the earth.
Can its eyes beseech?—no more
Than the hands are free to implore:
Voice but serves for one brief cry;
Plaint was it? or prophecy   10
Of sorrow that will surely come?
Omen of man's grievous doom!

But, O Mother! by the close
Duly granted to thy throes;
By the silent thanks, now tending   15
Incense-like to Heaven, descending
Now to mingle and to move
With the gush of earthly love,
As a debt to that frail Creature,
Instrument of struggling Nature   20
For the blissful calm, the peace
Known but to this *one* release—
Can the pitying spirit doubt
That for human-kind springs out
From the penalty a sense   25
Of more than mortal recompense?

As a floating summer cloud,
Though of gorgeous drapery proud,
To the sun-burnt traveller,
Or the stooping labourer,   30
Oft-times makes its bounty known
By its shadow round him thrown;
So, by chequerings of sad cheer,
Heavenly Guardians, brooding near,
Of their presence tell—too bright   35
Haply for corporeal sight!
Ministers of grace divine
Feelingly their brows incline
O'er this seeming Castaway
Breathing, in the light of day,   40
Something like the faintest breath
That has power to baffle death—
Beautiful, while very weakness
Captivates like passive meekness.

And, sweet Mother! under warrant   45
Of the universal Parent,
Who repays in season due
Them who have, like thee, been true
To the filial chain let down
From his everlasting throne,   50
Angels hovering round thy couch,
With their softest whispers vouch,

That—whatever griefs may fret,
Cares entangle, sins beset,
This thy First-born, and with tears   55
Stain her cheek in future years—
Heavenly succour, not denied
To the babe, whate'er betide,
Will to the woman be supplied!

Mother! blest be thy calm ease;   60
Blest the starry promises,—
And the firmament benign
Hallowed be it, where they shine!
Yes, for them whose souls have scope
Ample for a wingèd hope,   65
And can earthward bend an ear
For needful listening, pledge is here,
That, if thy new-born Charge shall tread
In thy footsteps, and be led
By that other Guide, whose light   70
Of manly virtues, mildly bright,
Gave him first the wished-for part
In thy gentle virgin heart;
Then, amid the storms of life
Presignified by that dread strife   75
Whence ye have escaped together,
She may look for serene weather;
In all trials sure to find
Comfort for a faithful mind;
Kindlier issues, holier rest,   80
Than even now await her prest,
Conscious Nursling, to thy breast!

XXXV.

THE WARNING.

A SEQUEL TO THE FOREGOING.

[Composed 1833.—Published 1835.]

LIST, the winds of March are blowing;
Her ground-flowers shrink, afraid of
      showing
Their meek heads to the nipping air,
Which ye feel not, happy pair!
Sunk into a kindly sleep.   5
We, meanwhile, our hope will keep;
And if Time leagued with adverse Change
(Too busy fear!) shall cross its range,
Whatsoever check they bring,
Anxious duty hindering,   10
To like hope our prayers will cling.

Thus, while the ruminating spirit feeds
Upon the events of home as life proceeds,
Affections pure and holy in their source
Gain a fresh impulse, run a livelier course;
Hopes that within the Father's heart
      prevail,   16
Are in the experienced Grandsire's slow
      to fail;
And if the harp pleased his gay youth, it
      rings
To his grave touch with no unready
      strings,
While thoughts press on, and feelings
      overflow,   20
And quick words round him fall like
      flakes of snow.

Thanks to the Powers that yet main-
      tain their sway,
And have renewed the tributary Lay.
Truths of the heart flock in with eager
      pace,
And FANCY greets them with a fond
      embrace;   25
Swift as the rising sun his beams extends
She shoots the tidings forth to distant
      friends;
Their gifts she hails (deemed precious, as
      they prove
For the unconscious Babe so prompt a
      love!)—
But from this peaceful centre of delight
Vague sympathies have urged her to take
      flight: 31
Rapt into upper regions, like the bee
That sucks from mountain-heath her
      honey fee,
Or, like the warbling lark intent to shroud
His head in sunbeams or a bowery cloud,
She soars—and here and there her pinions
      rest   36
On proud towers, like this humble cot-
      tage, blest
With a new visitant, an infant guest—
Towers where red streamers flout the
      breezy sky
In pomp foreseen by her creative eye, 40
When feasts shall crowd the hall, and
      steeple bells
Glad proclamation make, and heights
      and dells

Catch the blithe music as it sinks and
swells,
And harboured ships, whose pride is on
the sea,
Shall hoist their topmost flags in sign of
glee,   45
Honouring the hope of noble ancestry.

But who (though neither reckoning ills
assigned
By Nature, nor reviewing in the mind
The track that was, and is, and must be,
worn   49
With weary feet by all of woman born)—
Shall *now* by such a gift with joy be moved,
Nor feel the fulness of that joy reproved?
Not He, whose last faint memory will
command
The truth that Britain was his native
land;
Whose infant soul was tutored to confide
In the cleansed faith for which her mar-
tyrs died;   56
Whose boyish ear the voice of her renown
With rapture thrilled; whose Youth re-
vered the crown
Of Saxon liberty that Alfred wore,
Alfred, dear Babe, thy great Progenitor!
—Not He, who from her mellowed prac-
tice drew   61
His social sense of just, and fair, and
true;
And saw, thereafter, on the soil of France
Rash Polity begin her maniac dance,
Foundations broken up, the deeps run
wild,   65
Nor grieved to see (himself not unbe-
guiled)—
Woke from the dream, the dreamer to
upbraid,
And learn how sanguine expectations fade
When novel trusts by folly are betrayed,—
To see Presumption, turning pale, refrain
From further havoc, but repent in vain,—
Good aims lie down, and perish in the
road   72
Where guilt had urged them on with
ceaseless goad,
Proofs thickening round her that on
public ends
Domestic virtue vitally depends,   75

That civic strife can turn the happiest
hearth
Into a grievous sore of self-tormenting
earth.

Can such a One, dear Babe! though
glad and proud
To welcome thee, repel the fears that
crowd
Into his English breast, and spare to quake
Less for his own than for thy innocent
sake?   81
Too late—or, should the providence of
God
Lead, through dark ways by sin and sor-
row trod,
Justice and peace to a secure abode,
Too soon—thou com'st into this breathing
world;   85
Ensigns of mimic outrage are unfurled.
Who shall preserve or prop the tottering
Realm?
What hand suffice to govern the state-
helm?
If in the aims of men the surest test
Of good or bad (whate'er be sought for or
profest)   90
Lie in the means required, or ways
ordained,
For compassing the end, else never gained;
Yet governors and governed both are
blind
To this plain truth, or fling it to the wind;
If to expedience principle must bow;   95
Past, future, shrinking up beneath the
incumbent Now;
If cowardly concession still must feed
The thirst for power in men who ne'er
concede;
Nor turn aside, unless to shape a way
For domination at some riper day;   100
If generous Loyalty must stand in awe
Of subtle Treason, in his mask of law,
Or with bravado insolent and hard,
Provoking punishment, to win reward;
If office help the factious to conspire, 105
And they who *should* extinguish, fan the
fire—
Then, will the sceptre be a straw, the
crown
Sit loosely, like the thistle's crest of down;

To be blown off at will, by Power that
    spares it
In cunning patience, from the head that
    wears it. 110

Lost people, trained to theoretic feud!
Lost above all, ye labouring multitude!
Bewildered whether ye, by slanderous
    tongues
Deceived, mistake calamities for wrongs;
And over fancied usurpations brood, 115
Oft snapping at revenge in sullen mood;
Or, from long stress of real injuries fly
To desperation for a remedy;
In bursts of outrage spread your judg-
    ments wide,
And to your wrath cry out, "Be thou our
    guide;" 120
Or, bound by oaths, come forth to tread
    earth's floor
In marshalled thousands, darkening street
    and moor
With the worst shape mock-patience ever
    wore;
Or, to the giddy top of self-esteem
By Flatterers carried, mount into a
    dream 125
Of boundless suffrage, at whose sage
    behest
Justice shall rule, disorder be supprest,
And every man sit down as Plenty's
    Guest!
—O for a bridle bitted with remorse
To stop your Leaders in their headstrong
    course! 130
Oh may the Almighty scatter with His
    grace
These mists, and lead you to a safer place,
By paths no human wisdom can fore-
    trace!
May He pour round you, from worlds far
    above
Man's feverish passions, His pure light of
    love, 135
That quietly restores the natural mien
To hope, and makes truth willing to be
    seen!
Else shall your blood-stained hands in
    frenzy reap
Fields gaily sown when promises were
    cheap.— 139

Why is the Past belied with wicked art,
The Future made to play so false a part,
Among a people famed for strength of
    mind,
Foremost in freedom, noblest of man-
    kind?
We act as if we joyed in the sad tune
Storms make in rising, valued in the
    moon 145
Nought but her changes. Thus, ungrate-
    ful Nation!
If thou persist, and, scorning modera-
    tion,
Spread for thyself the snares of tribu-
    lation,
Whom, then, shall meekness guard? What
    saving skill
Lie in forbearance, strength in standing
    still? 150
—Soon shall the widow (for the speed of
    Time
Nought equals when the hours are winged
    with crime)
Widow, or wife, implore on tremulous
    knee,
From him who judged her lord, a like
    decree;
The skies will weep o'er old men deso-
    late: 155
Ye little-ones! Earth shudders at your
    fate,
Outcasts and homeless orphans——

But turn, my Soul, and from the sleep-
    ing pair
Learn thou the beauty of omniscient care!
Be strong in faith, bid anxious thoughts
    lie still; 160
Seek for the good and cherish it—the ill
Oppose, or bear with a submissive will.

XXXVI.

[Composed 1833.—Published 1835.]

IF this great world of joy and pain
    Revolve in one sure track;
If freedom, set, will rise again,
    And virtue, flown, come back;
Woe to the purblind crew who fill 5
    The heart with each day's care;
Nor gain, from past or future, skill
    To bear, and to forbear!

XXXVII.

THE LABOURER'S NOON-DAY HYMN.

[Composed 1834.—Published 1835.]

UP to the throne of God is borne
The voice of praise at early morn,
And he accepts the punctual hymn
Sung as the light of day grows dim:

Nor will he turn his ear aside   5
From holy offerings at noontide.
Then here reposing let us raise
A song of gratitude and praise.

What though our burthen be not light
We need not toil from morn to night;   10
The respite of the mid-day hour
Is in the thankful Creature's power.

Blest are the moments, doubly blest,
That, drawn from this one hour of rest,
Are with a ready heart bestowed   15
Upon the service of our God!

Each field is then a hallowed spot,
An altar is in each man's cot,
A church in every grove that spreads
Its living roof above our heads.   20

Look up to Heaven! the industrious Sun
Already half his race hath run,
He cannot halt nor go astray,
But our immortal Spirits may.

Lord! since his rising in the East,   25
If we have faltered or transgressed,
Guide, from thy love's abundant source,
What yet remains of this day's course:

Help with thy grace, through life's short
        day,
Our upward and our downward way;   30
And glorify for us the west,
When we shall sink to final rest.

XXXVIII.

ODE.

COMPOSED ON MAY MORNING.

[Composed 1826.—Published 1835.]

WHILE from the purpling east departs
The star that led the dawn,
Blithe Flora from her couch upstarts,
For May is on the lawn.

A quickening hope, a freshening glee,   5
Foreran the expected Power,
Whose first-drawn breath from bush and
        tree
Shakes off that pearly shower.

All Nature welcomes Her whose sway
Tempers the year's extremes;   10
Who scattereth lustres o'er noon-day,
Like morning's dewy gleams;
While mellow warble, sprightly trill,
The tremulous heart excite;
And hums the balmy air to still   15
The balance of delight.

Time was, blest Power! when youths and
        maids
At peep of dawn would rise,
And wander forth, in forest glades
Thy birth to solemnize.   20
Though mute the song—to grace the rite
Untouched the hawthorn bough,
Thy Spirit triumphs o'er the slight;
Man changes, but not Thou!

Thy feathered Lieges bill and wings   25
In love's disport employ;
Warmed by thy influence, creeping things
Awake to silent joy:
Queen art thou still for each gay plant
Where the slim wild deer roves;   30
And served in depths where fishes haunt
Their own mysterious groves.

Cloud-piercing peak, and trackless heath,
Instinctive homage pay;
Nor wants the dim-lit cave a wreath   35
To honour thee, sweet May!
Where cities fanned by thy brisk airs
Behold a smokeless sky,
Their puniest flower-pot-nursling dares
To open a bright eye.   40

And if, on this thy natal morn,
The pole, from which thy name
Hath not departed, stands forlorn
Of song and dance and game;
Still from the village-green a vow   45
Aspires to thee addrest,
Wherever peace is on the brow,
Or love within the breast.

Yes! where Love nestles thou canst
        teach
The soul to love the more;   50

Hearts also shall thy lessons reach
  That never loved before.
Stript is the haughty one of pride,
  The bashful freed from fear,
While rising, like the ocean-tide,   55
  In flows the joyous year.

Hush, feeble lyre! weak words refuse
  The service to prolong!
To yon exulting thrush the Muse
  Entrusts the imperfect song;   60
His voice shall chant, in accents clear,
  Throughout the live-long day,
Till the first silver star appear,
  The sovereignty of May.

XXXIX.

TO MAY.

[Composed 1826-34.—Published 1835.]

THOUGH many suns have risen and set
  Since thou, blithe May, wert born,
And Bards, who hailed thee, may forget
  Thy gifts, thy beauty scorn;
There are who to a birthday strain   5
  Confine not harp and voice,
But evermore throughout thy reign
  Are grateful and rejoice!

Delicious odours! music sweet,
  Too sweet to pass away!   10
Oh for a deathless song to meet
  The soul's desire—a lay
That, when a thousand years are told,
  Should praise thee, genial Power!
Through summer heat, autumnal cold,   15
  And winter's dreariest hour.

Earth, sea, thy presence feel—nor less,
  If yon ethereal blue
With its soft smile the truth express,
  The heavens have felt it too.   20
The inmost heart of man if glad
  Partakes a livelier cheer;
And eyes that cannot but be sad
  Let fall a brightened tear.

Since thy return, through days and weeks
  Of hope that grew by stealth,   25
How many wan and faded cheeks
  Have kindled into health!

The Old, by thee revived, have said,
  "Another year is ours;"   30
And wayworn Wanderers, poorly fed,
  Have smiled upon thy flowers.

Who tripping lisps a merry song
  Amid his playful peers?
The tender Infant who was long   35
  A prisoner of fond fears;
But now, when every sharp-edged blast
  Is quiet in its sheath,
His Mother leaves him free to taste
  Earth's sweetness in thy breath.   40

Thy help is with the weed that creeps
  Along the humblest ground;
No cliff so bare but on its steeps
  Thy favours may be found;
But most on some peculiar nook   45
  That our own hands have drest,
Thou and thy train are proud to look,
  And seem to love it best.

And yet how pleased we wander forth
  When May is whispering, "Come!   50
Choose from the bowers of virgin earth
  The happiest for your home;
Heaven's bounteous love through me is spread
  From sunshine, clouds, winds, waves,
Drops on the mouldering turret's head,   55
  And on your turf-clad graves!"

Such greeting heard, away with sighs
  For lilies that must fade,
Or "the rathe primrose as it dies
  Forsaken" in the shade!   60
Vernal fruitions and desires
  Are linked in endless chase;
While, as one kindly growth retires,
  Another takes its place.

And what if thou, sweet May, hast known   65
  Mishap by worm and blight;
If expectations newly blown
  Have perished in thy sight;
If loves and joys, while up they sprung,
  Were caught as in a snare;   70
Such is the lot of all the young,
  However bright and fair.

Lo! Streams that April could not check
  Are patient of thy rule;

Gurgling in foamy water-break, 75
Loitering in glassy pool :
By thee, thee only, could be sent
Such gentle mists as glide,
Curling with unconfirmed intent,
On that green mountain's side. 80

How delicate the leafy veil
Through which yon house of God
Gleams 'mid the peace of this deep dale
By few but shepherds trod !
And lowly huts, near beaten ways, 85
No sooner stand attired
In thy fresh wreaths, than they for
praise
Peep forth, and are admired.

Season of fancy and of hope,
Permit not for one hour 90
A blossom from thy crown to drop,
Nor add to it a flower !
Keep, lovely May, as if by touch
Of self-restraining art,
This modest charm of not too much, 95
Part seen, imagined part !

XL.

LINES

SUGGESTED BY A PORTRAIT FROM THE
PENCIL OF F. STONE.

[Composed 1834.—Published 1835.]

BEGUILED into forgetfulness of care
Due to the day's unfinished task ; of pen
Or book regardless, and of that fair
scene
In Nature's prodigality displayed
Before my window, oftentimes and long 5
I gaze upon a Portrait whose mild gleam
Of beauty never ceases to enrich
The common light; whose stillness charms
the air,
Or seems to charm it, into like repose ;
Whose silence, for the pleasure of the
ear, 10
Surpasses sweetest music. There she sits
With emblematic purity attired
In a white vest, white as her marble neck
Is, and the pillar of the throat would be
But for the shadow by the drooping chin
Cast into that recess—the tender shade,

The shade and light, both there and every-
where,
And through the very atmosphere she
breathes,
Broad, clear, and toned harmoniously,
with skill
That might from nature have been learnt
in the hour 20
When the lone shepherd sees the morning
spread
Upon the mountains. Look at her,
whoe'er
Thou be that, kindling with a poet's soul,
Hast loved the painter's true Promethean
craft
Intensely—from Imagination take 25
The treasure,—what mine eyes behold see
thou,
Even though the Atlantic ocean roll
between.

A silver line, that runs from brow to
crown
And in the middle parts the braided hair,
Just serves to show how delicate a soil 30
The golden harvest grows in; and those
eyes,
Soft and capacious as a cloudless sky
Whose azure depth their colour emulates,
Must needs be conversant with upward
looks,
Prayer's voiceless service ; but now, seek-
ing nought 35
And shunning nought, their own peculiar
life
Of motion they renounce, and with the
head
Partake its inclination towards earth
In humble grace, and quiet pensiveness
Caught at the point where it stops short
of sadness. 40

Offspring of soul-bewitching Art, make
me
Thy confidant ! say, whence derived that
air
Of calm abstraction ? Can the ruling
thought
Be with some lover far away, or one
Crossed by misfortune, or of doubted
faith ? 45

Inapt conjecture! Childhood here, a
 moon
Crescent in simple loveliness serene,
Has but approached the gates of woman-
 hood,
Not entered them; her heart is yet
 unpierced
By the blind Archer-god; her fancy
 free: 50
The fount of feeling, if unsought else-
 where,
Will not be found.
    Her right hand, as it lies
Across the slender wrist of the left arm
Upon her lap reposing, holds—but mark
How slackly, for the absent mind per-
 mits   55
No firmer grasp—a little wild-flower,
 joined
As in a posy, with a few pale ears
Of yellowing corn, the same that over-
 topped
And in their common birthplace sheltered
 it
Till they were plucked together; a blue
 flower   60
Called by the thrifty husbandman a weed;
But Ceres, in her garland, might have
 worn
That ornament, unblamed. The floweret,
 held
In scarcely conscious fingers, was, she
 knows,
(Her Father told her so) in youth's gay
 dawn   65
Her Mother's favourite; and the orphan
 Girl,
In her own dawn—a dawn less gay and
 bright,
Loves it, while there in solitary peace
She sits, for that departed Mother's sake.
—Not from a source less sacred is derived
(Surely I do not err) that pensive air 71
Of calm abstraction through the face
 diffused
And the whole person.
    Words have something told
More than the pencil can, and verily
More than is needed, but the precious
 Art   75
Forgives their interference—Art divine,

That both creates and fixes, in despite
Of Death and Time, the marvels it hath
 wrought.

Strange contrasts have we in this world
 of ours!
That posture, and the look of filial love 80
Thinking of past and gone, with what is
 left
Dearly united, might be swept away
From this fair Portrait's fleshly Archetype,
Even by an innocent fancy's slightest
 freak
Banished, nor ever, haply, be restored 85
To their lost place, or meet in harmony
So exquisite; but *here* do they abide,
Enshrined for ages. Is not then the Art
Godlike, a humble branch of the divine,
In visible quest of immortality, 90
Stretched forth with trembling hope?—In
 every realm,
From high Gibraltar to Siberian plains,
Thousands, in each variety of tongue
That Europe knows, would echo this
 appeal;
One above all, a Monk who waits on God
In the magnific Convent built of yore 96
To sanctify the Escurial palace. He—
Guiding, from cell to cell and room to
 room,
A British Painter (eminent for truth
In character, and depth of feeling, shown
By labours that have touched the hearts
 of kings,   101
And are endeared to simple cottagers)—
Came, in that service, to a glorious work,
Our Lord's Last Supper, beautiful as
 when first
The appropriate Picture, fresh from
 Titian's hand,   105
Graced the Refectory: and there, while
 both
Stood with eyes fixed upon that master-
 piece,
The hoary Father in the Stranger's ear
Breathed out these words:—"Here daily
 do we sit,   109
Thanks given to God for daily bread, and
 here
Pondering the mischiefs of these restless
 times,

And thinking of my Brethren, dead, dispersed,
Or changed and changing, I not seldom gaze
Upon this solemn Company unmoved
By shock of circumstance, or lapse of years,   115
Until I cannot but believe that they—
They are in truth the Substance, we the Shadows."

So spake the mild Jeronymite, his griefs
Melting away within him like a dream
Ere he had ceased to gaze, perhaps to speak: 120
And I, grown old, but in a happier land,
Domestic Portrait! have to verse consigned
In thy calm presence those heart-moving words:
Words that can soothe, more than they agitate;
Whose spirit, like the angel that went down   125
Into Bethesda's pool, with healing virtue
Informs the fountain in the human breast
Which by the visitation was disturbed.
——But why this stealing tear? Companion mute,
On thee I look, not sorrowing; fare thee well,   130
My Song's Inspirer, once again farewell[1]!

XLI.

THE FOREGOING SUBJECT RESUMED.

[Composed 1834.—Published 1835.]

AMONG a grave fraternity of Monks,
For One, but surely not for One alone,
Triumphs, in that great work, the Painter's skill,
Humbling the body, to exalt the soul;
Yet representing, amid wreck and wrong

And dissolution and decay, the warm   6
And breathing life of flesh, as if already
Clothed with impassive majesty, and graced
With no mean earnest of a heritage
Assigned to it in future worlds. Thou, too,   10
With thy memorial flower, meek Portraiture!
From whose serene companionship I passed
Pursued by thoughts that haunt me still; thou also—
Though but a simple object, into light
Called forth by those affections that endear   15
The private hearth; though keeping thy sole seat
In singleness, and little tried by time,
Creation, as it were, of yesterday—
With a congenial function art endued
For each and all of us, together joined 20
In course of nature under a low roof
By charities and duties that proceed
Out of the bosom of a wiser vow.
To a like salutary sense of awe
Or sacred wonder, growing with the power   25
Of meditation that attempts to weigh,
In faithful scales, things and their opposites,
Can thy enduring quiet gently raise
A household small and sensitive,—whose love,
Dependent as in part its blessings are 30
Upon frail ties dissolving or dissolved
On earth, will be revived, we trust, in heaven[2].

---

[1] The pile of buildings composing the palace and convent of San Lorenzo, has, in common usage, lost its proper name in that of the *Escurial*, a village at the foot of the hill upon which the splendid edifice, built by Philip the Second, stands. It need scarcely be added that Wilkie is the painter alluded to.

[2] In the class entitled "Musings," in Mr. Southey's Minor Poems, is one upon his own miniature Picture, taken in childhood, and another upon a landscape painted by Gaspar Poussin. It is possible that every word of the above verses, though similar in subject, might have been written had the author been unacquainted with those beautiful effusions of poetic sentiment. But, for his own satisfaction, he must be allowed thus publicly to acknowledge the pleasure those two Poems of his Friend have given him, and the grateful influence they have upon his mind as often as he reads them, or thinks of them.

XLII.

[Composed 1844.—Published 1845.]

So fair, so sweet, withal so sensitive,
Would that the little Flowers were born
  to live,
Conscious of half the pleasure which they
  give;

That to this mountain-daisy's self were
  known
The beauty of its star-shaped shadow,
  thrown   5
On the smooth surface of this naked
  stone!

And what if hence a bold desire should
  mount
High as the Sun, that he could take
  account
Of all that issues from his glorious
  fount!

So might he ken how by his sovereign
  aid   10
These delicate companionships are
  made;
And how he rules the pomp of light and
  shade;

And were the Sister-power that shines by
  night
So privileged, what a countenance of de-
  light
Would through the clouds break forth on
  human sight!   15

Fond fancies! wheresoe'er shall turn thine
  eye
On earth, air, ocean, or the starry
  sky,
Converse with Nature in pure sym-
  pathy;

All vain desires, all lawless wishes
  quelled,
Be Thou to love and praise alike im-
  pelled,   20
Whatever boon is granted or withheld.

XLIII.

**UPON SEEING A COLOURED DRAW-
ING OF THE BIRD OF PARADISE
IN AN ALBUM.**

[Composed 1835-6.—Published 1837.]

Who rashly strove thy Image to portray?
Thou buoyant minion of the tropic air;
How could he think of the live creature—
  gay
With a divinity of colours, drest
In all her brightness, from the dancing
  crest   5
Far as the last gleam of the filmy train
Extended and extending to sustain
The motions that it graces — and for-
  bear
To drop his pencil! Flowers of every
  clime
Depicted on these pages smile at time; 10
And gorgeous insects copied with nice
  care
Are here, and likenesses of many a shell
Tossed ashore by restless waves,
Or in the diver's grasp fetched up from
  caves
Where sea-nymphs might be proud to
  dwell: 15
But whose rash hand (again I ask) could
  dare,
'Mid casual tokens and promiscuous
  shows,
To circumscribe this Shape in fixed re-
  pose;
Could imitate for indolent survey,
Perhaps for touch profane,   20
Plumes that might catch, but cannot
  keep, a stain;
And, with cloud-streaks lightest and lofti-
  est, share
The sun's first greeting, his last farewell
  ray!

Resplendent Wanderer! followed with
  glad eyes
Where'er her course; mysterious Bird! 25
To whom, by wondering Fancy stirred,
Eastern Islanders have given
A holy name—the Bird of Heaven!

And even a title higher still,
The Bird of God! whose blessed will   30
She seems performing as she flies
Over the earth and through the skies
In never-wearied search of Paradise—
Region that crowns her beauty with the
    name
She bears for *us*—for us how blest,   35
How happy at all seasons, could like aim
Uphold our Spirits urged to kindred flight
On wings that fear no glance of God's
    pure sight,
No tempest from his breath, their pro-
    mised rest
Seeking with indefatigable quest   40
Above a world that deems itself most
    wise
When most enslaved by gross realities!

SONNETS

DEDICATED TO LIBERTY AND ORDER.

I.

COMPOSED AFTER READING A NEWSPAPER OF THE DAY.

[Composed 1831.—Published 1835.]

"PEOPLE! your chains are severing link
    by link;
Soon shall the Rich be levelled down—the
    Poor
Meet them half way." Vain boast! for
    These, the more
They thus would rise, must low and lower
    sink
Till, by repentance stung, they fear to
    think;   5
While all lie prostrate, save the tyrant
    few
Bent in quick turns each other to undo,
And mix the poison, they themselves
    must drink.
Mistrust thyself, vain Country! cease to
    cry,
"Knowledge will save me from the
    threatened woe."   10
For if than other rash ones more thou
    know,
Yet on presumptuous wing as far would
    fly
Above thy knowledge as they dared to go,
Thou wilt provoke a heavier penalty.

II.

UPON THE LATE GENERAL FAST.
MARCH, 1832.

[Composed 1832.—Published 1838.]

RELUCTANT call it was; the rite delayed;
And in the Senate some there were who
    doffed
The last of their humanity, and scoffed
At providential judgments, undismayed
By their own daring. But the People
    prayed   5
As with one voice; their flinty heart grew
    soft
With penitential sorrow, and aloft
Their spirit mounted, crying, "God us
    aid!"
Oh that with aspirations more intense,
Chastised by self-abasement more pro-
    found,   10
This People, once so happy, so renowned
For liberty, would seek from God defence
Against far heavier ill, the pestilence
Of revolution, impiously unbound!

III.

[Composed probably 1833.—Published 1838.]

SAID Secrecy to Cowardice and Fraud,
Falsehood and Treachery, in close council
    met,
Deep under ground, in Pluto's cabinet,
"The frost of England's pride will soon
    be thawed;
Hooded the open brow that overawed   5
Our schemes; the faith and honour, never
    yet
By us with hope encountered, be upset;—
For once I burst my bands, and cry, ap-
    plaud!"
Then whispered she, "The Bill is carrying
    out!"
They heard, and, starting up, the Brood
    of Night   10
Clapped hands, and shook with glee their
    matted locks;
All Powers and Places that abhor the
    light
Joined in the transport, echoed back their
    shout,
Hurrah for————[1], hugging his Ballot-
    box!

---

[1] i.e. Grote.—ED.

IV.

[Composed 1838.—Published 1838.]

BLEST Statesman He, whose Mind's un-
selfish will
Leaves him at ease among grand thoughts:
whose eye
Sees that, apart from magnanimity,
Wisdom exists not; nor the humbler skill
Of Prudence, disentangling good and ill 5
With patient care. What tho' assaults
run high,
They daunt not him who holds his mi-
nistry,
Resolute, at all hazards, to fulfil
Its duties;—prompt to move, but firm to
wait,—
Knowing, things rashly sought are rarely
found; 10
That, for the functions of an ancient
State—
Strong by her charters, free because im-
bound,
Servant of Providence, not slave of Fate—
Perilous is sweeping change, all chance
unsound.

V.

IN ALLUSION TO VARIOUS RECENT HIS-
TORIES AND NOTICES OF THE FRENCH
REVOLUTION.

[Composed ?.—Published 1842.]

PORTENTOUS change when History can
appear
As the cool Advocate of foul device;
Reckless audacity extol, and jeer
At consciences perplexed with scruples
nice!
They who bewail not, must abhor, the
sneer 5
Born of Conceit, Power's blind Idolater;
Or haply sprung from vaunting Coward-
ice
Betrayed by mockery of holy fear.
Hath it not long been said the wrath of
Man
Works not the righteousness of God? Oh
bend, 10
Bend, ye Perverse! to judgments from
on High,

Laws that lay under Heaven's perpetual
ban
All principles of action that transcend
The sacred limits of humanity.

VI.

CONTINUED.

[Composed ?.—Published 1842.]

WHO ponders National events shall find
An awful balancing of loss and gain,
Joy based on sorrow, good with ill com-
bined,
And proud deliverance issuing out of
pain
And direful throes; as if the All-ruling
Mind, 5
With whose perfection it consists to
ordain
Volcanic burst, earthquake, and hurri-
cane,
Dealt in like sort with feeble human kind
By laws immutable. But woe for him
Who thus deceived shall lend an eager
hand 10
To social havoc. Is not Conscience ours,
And Truth, whose eye guilt only can
make dim;
And Will, whose office, by divine com-
mand,
Is to control and check disordered Powers?

VII.

CONCLUDED.

[Composed ?.—Published 1842.]

LONG-FAVOURED England! be not thou
misled
By monstrous theories of alien growth,
Lest alien frenzy seize thee, waxing
wroth,
Self-smitten till thy garments reek dyed
red
With thy own blood, which tears in tor-
rents shed 5
Fail to wash out, tears flowing ere thy
troth
Be plighted, not to ease but sullen sloth,
Or wan despair—the ghost of false hope
fled
Into a shameful grave. Among thy youth,

My Country! if such warning be held
    dear,   10
Then shall a Veteran's heart be thrilled
    with joy,
One who would gather from eternal truth,
For time and season, rules that work to
    cheer—
Not scourge, to save the People—not
    destroy.

VIII.

[Composed 1839.—Published 1842.]

MEN of the Western World! in Fate's
    dark book
Whence these opprobrious leaves of dire
    portent?
Think ye your British Ancestors forsook
Their native Land, for outrage provi-
    dent;
From unsubmissive necks the bridle
    shook   5
To give, in their Descendants, freer vent
And wider range to passions turbulent,
To mutual tyranny a deadlier look?
Nay, said a voice, soft as the south wind's
    breath,
Dive through the stormy surface of the
    flood   10
To the great current flowing underneath;
Explore the countless springs of silent
    good;
So shall the truth be better understood,
And thy grieved Spirit brighten strong
    in faith.

IX.

TO THE PENNSYLVANIANS.

[Composed probably January or February, 1845.
    —Published 1845.]

DAYS undefiled by luxury or sloth,
Firm self-denial, manners grave and staid,
Rights equal, laws with cheerfulness
    obeyed,
Words that require no sanction from an
    oath,
And simple honesty a common growth— 5
This high repute, with bounteous Nature's
    aid,
Won confidence, now ruthlessly betrayed

At will, your power the measure of your
    troth!—
All who revere the memory of Penn
Grieve for the land on whose wild woods
    his name   10
Was fondly grafted with a virtuous aim,
Renounced, abandoned by degenerate Men
For state-dishonour black as ever came
To upper air from Mammon's loathsome
    den.

X.

AT BOLOGNA, IN REMEMBRANCE OF THE LATE INSURRECTIONS, 1837.

I.

[Composed probably 1837.—Published: vol. of 1842.]

AH why deceive ourselves! by no mere fit
Of sudden passion roused shall men attain
True freedom where for ages they have
    lain
Bound in a dark abominable pit,
With life's best sinews more and more
    unknit.   5
Here, there, a banded few who loathe the
    chain
May rise to break it: effort worse than
    vain
For thee, O great Italian nation, split
Into those jarring fractions.—Let thy
    scope
Be one fixed mind for all; thy rights
    approve   10
To thy own conscience gradually re-
    newed;
Learn to make Time the father of wise
    Hope;
Then trust thy cause to the arm of Forti-
    tude,
The light of Knowledge, and the warmth
    of Love.

XI.

CONTINUED.

II.

[Composed probably 1837.—Published: vol. of 1842.]

HARD task! exclaim the undisciplined,
    to lean
On Patience coupled with such slow en-
    deavour,
That long-lived servitude must last for
    ever.

Perish the grovelling few, who, prest
  between
Wrongs and the terror of redress, would
  wean   5
Millions from glorious aims. Our chains
  · to sever
Let us break forth in tempest now or
  never !—
What, is there then no space for golden
  mean
And gradual progress?—Twilight leads
  to day,
And, even within the burning zones of
  earth,   10
The hastiest sunrise yields a temperate
  ray ;
The softest breeze to fairest flowers gives
  birth :
Think not that Prudence dwells in dark
  abodes,
She scans the future with the eye of
  gods.

XII.

CONCLUDED.

III.

[Composed probably 1837.—Published: vol. of
1842.]

As leaves are to the tree whereon they
  grow
And wither, every human generation
Is to the Being of a mighty nation,
Locked in our world's embrace through
  weal and woe ;
Thought that should teach the zealot to
  forego   5
Rash schemes, to abjure all selfish agita-
  tion,
And seek through noiseless pains and
  moderation
The unblemished good they only can
  bestow.
Alas ! with most, who weigh futurity
Against time present, passion holds the
  scales :   10
Hence equal ignorance of both prevails,
And nations sink ; or, struggling to be
  free,

Are doomed to flounder on, like wounded
  whales
Tossed on the bosom of a stormy sea.

XIII.

[Composed January or February, 1845.—Pub-
lished 1845.]

YOUNG ENGLAND—what is then become
  of Old,
Of dear Old England? Think they she is
  dead,
Dead to the very name? Presumption fed
On empty air ! That name will keep its
  hold
In the true filial bosom's inmost fold   5
For ever.—The Spirit of Alfred, at the
  head
Of all who for her rights watched, toiled
  and bled,
Knows that this prophecy is not too bold.
What—how ! shall she submit in will and
  deed
To Beardless Boys—an imitative race,   10
The *servum pecus* of a Gallic breed?
Dear Mother ! if thou *must* thy steps re-
  trace,
Go where at least meek Innocency dwells ;
Let Babes and Sucklings be thy oracles.

XIV.

[Composed ?.—Published 1842.]

FEEL for the wrongs to universal ken
Daily exposed, woe that unshrouded lies ;
And seek the Sufferer in his darkest den,
Whether conducted to the spot by sighs
And moanings, or he dwells (as if the
  wren   5
Taught him concealment) hidden from all
  eyes
In silence and the awful modesties
Of sorrow ;—feel for all, as brother Men !
Rest not in hope want's icy chain to thaw
By casual boons and formal charities ;   10
Learn to be just, just through impartial
  law ;
Far as ye may, erect and equalize ;
And, what ye cannot reach by statute,
  draw
Each from his fountain of self-sacrifice !

SONNETS UPON THE PUNISHMENT
OF DEATH.

IN SERIES.

[Composed 1839-40.—Published December, 1841 (*Quarterly Review*); vol. of 1842.]

I.

SUGGESTED BY THE VIEW OF LANCAS-
TER CASTLE (ON THE ROAD FROM
THE SOUTH).

THIS Spot—at once unfolding sight so
    fair
Of sea and land, with yon grey towers
    that still
Rise up as if to lord it over air—
Might soothe in human breasts the sense
    of ill,
Or charm it out of memory; yea, might
    fill   5
The heart with joy and gratitude to God
For all his bounties upon man bestowed:
Why bears it then the name of "Weeping
    Hill"?
Thousands, as toward yon old Lancastrian
    Towers,
A prison's crown, along this way they
    past   10
For lingering durance or quick death
    with shame,
From this bare eminence thereon have
    cast
Their first look—blinded as tears fell in
    showers
Shed on their chains; and hence that
    doleful name.

II.

TENDERLY do we feel by Nature's law
For worst offenders: though the heart
    will heave
With indignation, deeply moved we
    grieve,

In after-thought, for Him who stood in
    awe
Neither of God nor man, and only saw, 5
Lost wretch, a horrible device enthroned
On proud temptations, till the victim
    groaned
Under the steel his hand had dared to
    draw.
But O, restrain compassion, if its course,
As oft befalls, prevent or turn aside   10
Judgments and aims and acts whose
    higher source
Is sympathy with the unforewarned, who
    died
Blameless—with them that shuddered
    o'er his grave,
And all who from the law firm safety
    crave.

III.

THE Roman Consul doomed his sons to
    die
Who had betrayed their country. The
    stern word
Afforded (may it through all time afford)
A theme for praise and admiration high.
Upon the surface of humanity   5
He rested not; its depths his mind
    explored;
He felt; but his parental bosom's lord
Was Duty,—Duty calmed his agony.
And some, we know, when they by wilful
    act
A single human life have wrongly taken,
Pass sentence on themselves, confess the
    fact,   11
And, to atone for it, with soul unshaken

Kneel at the feet of Justice, and, for
　　faith
Broken with all mankind, solicit death.

IV.

Is *Death*, when evil against good has
　　fought
With such fell mastery that a man may
　　dare
By deeds the blackest purpose to lay
　　bare—
Is Death, for one to that condition
　　brought,—
For him, or any one,—the thing that
　　ought　　　　　　　　　　　　　5
To be *most* dreaded? Lawgivers, beware,
Lest, capital pains remitting till ye spare
The murderer, ye, by sanction to that
　　thought,
Seemingly given, debase the general mind;
Tempt the vague will tried standards to
　　disown;　　　　　　　　　　　10
Nor only palpable restraints unbind,
But upon Honour's head disturb the
　　crown,
Whose absolute rule permits not to with-
　　stand
In the weak love of life his least com-
　　mand.

V.

Not to the object specially designed,
Howe'er momentous in itself it be,
Good to promote or curb depravity,
Is the wise Legislator's view confined.
His Spirit, when most severe, is oft most
　　kind;　　　　　　　　　　　　5
As all Authority in earth depends
On Love and Fear, their several powers
　　he blends,
Copying with awe the one Paternal
　　mind.
Uncaught by processes in show humane,
He feels how far the act would derogate
From even the humblest functions of the
　　State;　　　　　　　　　　　11
If she, self-shorn of Majesty, ordain
That never more shall hang upon her
　　breath
The last alternative of Life or Death.

VI.

Ye brood of Conscience—Spectres! that
　　frequent
The bad man's restless walk, and haunt
　　his bed—
Fiends in your aspect, yet beneficent
In act, as hovering Angels when they
　　spread
Their wings to guard the unconscious
　　Innocent—　　　　　　　　　5
Slow be the Statutes of the land to share
A laxity that could not but impair
Your power to punish crime, and so
　　prevent.
And ye, Beliefs! coiled serpent-like
　　about
The adage on all tongues, "Murder will
　　out,"　　　　　　　　　　　10
How shall your ancient warnings work
　　for good
In the full might they hitherto have
　　shown,
If for deliberate shedder of man's blood
Survive not Judgment that requires his
　　own?

VII.

Before the world had past her time of
　　youth
While polity and discipline were weak,
The precept eye for eye, and tooth for
　　tooth,
Came forth—a light, though but as of
　　daybreak,
Strong as could then be borne. A Master
　　meek　　　　　　　　　　　5
Proscribed the spirit fostered by that
　　rule,
Patience *his* law, long-suffering *his* school,
And love the end, which all through
　　peace must seek.
But lamentably do they err who strain
His mandates, given rash impulse to
　　control　　　　　　　　　　10
And keep vindictive thirstings from the
　　soul,
So far that, if consistent in their scheme,
They must forbid the State to inflict a
　　pain,
Making of social order a mere dream.

VIII.

FIT retribution, by the moral code
Determined, lies beyond the State's embrace,
Yet, as she may, for each peculiar case
She plants well-measured terrors in the road
Of wrongful acts. Downward it is and broad,   5
And, the main fear once doomed to banishment,
Far oftener then, bad ushering worse event,
Blood would be spilt that in his dark abode
Crime might lie better hid. And, should the change
Take from the horror due to a foul deed,
Pursuit and evidence so far must fail,   11
And, guilt escaping, passion then might plead
In angry spirits for her old free range,
And the "wild justice of revenge" prevail.

IX.

THOUGH to give timely warning and deter
Is one great aim of penalty, extend
Thy mental vision further and ascend
Far higher, else full surely shalt thou err.
What is a State? The wise behold in her   5
A creature born of time, that keeps one eye
Fixed on the statutes of Eternity,
To which her judgments reverently defer.
Speaking through Law's dispassionate voice the State   9
Endues her conscience with external life
And being, to preclude or quell the strife
Of individual will, to elevate
The grovelling mind, the erring to recall,
And fortify the moral sense of all.

X.

OUR bodily life, some plead, that life the shrine
Of an immortal spirit, is a gift
So sacred, so informed with light divine,
That no tribunal, though most wise to sift
Deed and intent, should turn the Being adrift   5

Into that world where penitential tear
May not avail, nor prayer have for God's ear
A voice—that world whose veil no hand can lift
For earthly sight. "Eternity and Time,"
They urge, "have interwoven claims and rights   10
Not to be jeopardised through foulest crime:
The sentence rule by mercy's heaven-born lights."
Even so; but measuring not by finite sense
Infinite Power, perfect Intelligence.

XI.

AH, think how one compelled for life to abide
Locked in a dungeon needs must eat the heart
Out of his own humanity, and part
With every hope that mutual cares provide;
And, should a less unnatural doom confide   5
In life-long exile on a savage coast,
Soon the relapsing penitent may boast
Of yet more heinous guilt, with fiercer pride.
Hence thoughtful Mercy, Mercy sage and pure,
Sanctions the forfeiture that Law demands,   10
Leaving the final issue in His hands
Whose goodness knows no change, whose love is sure,
Who sees, foresees; who cannot judge amiss,
And wafts at will the contrite soul to bliss.

XII.

SEE the Condemned alone within his cell
And prostrate at some moment when remorse
Stings to the quick, and, with resistless force,
Assaults the pride she strove in vain to quell.
Then mark him, him who could so long rebel,   5

The crime confessed, a kneeling Penitent
Before the Altar, where the Sacrament
Softens his heart, till from his eyes
    outwell
Tears of salvation. Welcome death! while
    Heaven
Does in this change exceedingly rejoice;
While yet the solemn heed the State hath
    given　　　　　　　　　　　　　11
Helps him to meet the last Tribunal's
    voice
In faith, which fresh offences, were he
    cast
On old temptations, might for ever blast.

XIII.

CONCLUSION.

YES, though He well may tremble at the
    sound
Of his own voice, who from the judgment-
    seat
Sends the pale Convict to his last retreat
In death; though Listeners shudder all
    around,
They know the dread requital's source
    profound;　　　　　　　　　　　　5
Nor is, they feel, its wisdom obsolete—
(Would that it were!) the sacrifice un-
    meet
For Christian Faith. But hopeful signs
    abound;
The social rights of man breathe purer
    air;
Religion deepens her preventive care;　10

Then, moved by needless fear of past
    abuse,
Strike not from Law's firm hand that
    awful rod,
But leave it thence to drop for lack of
    use:
Oh, speed the blessed hour, Almighty
    God!

XIV.

APOLOGY.

THE formal World relaxes her cold chain
For One who speaks in numbers; ampler
    scope
His utterance finds; and, conscious of the
    gain,
Imagination works with bolder hope
The cause of grateful reason to sustain;　5
And, serving Truth, the heart more
    strongly beats
Against all barriers which his labour
    meets
In lofty place, or humble Life's domain.
Enough;—before us lay a painful road,
And guidance have I sought in duteous
    love　　　　　　　　　　　　　　10
From Wisdom's heavenly Father. Hence
    hath flowed
Patience, with trust that, whatsoe'er the
    way
Each takes in this high matter, all may
    move
Cheered with the prospect of a brighter
    day.

MISCELLANEOUS POEMS.

I.

EPISTLE

TO SIR GEORGE HOWLAND BEAUMONT, BART.

From the South-west Coast of Cumberland.—1811.

[Composed 1811.—Published: vol. of 1842.]

FAR from our home by Grasmere's quiet
    Lake,
From the Vale's peace which all her
    fields partake,
Here on the bleakest point of Cumbria's
    shore
We sojourn stunned by Ocean's ceaseless
    roar;
While, day by day, grim neighbour! huge
    Black Comb   5
Frowns deepening visibly his native
    gloom,
Unless, perchance rejecting in despite
What on the Plain *we* have of warmth
    and light,
In his own storms he hides himself from
    sight.
Rough is the time; and thoughts, that
    would be free   10
From heaviness, oft fly, dear Friend, to
    thee;
Turn from a spot where neither sheltered
    road
Nor hedge-row screen invites my steps
    abroad;
Where one poor Plane-tree, having as it
    might
Attained a stature twice a tall man's
    height,   15
Hopeless of further growth, and brown
    and sere
Through half the summer, stands with
    top cut sheer,

Like an unshifting weathercock which
    proves
How cold the quarter that the wind best
    loves,
Or like a Centinel that, evermore   20
Darkening the window, ill defends the
    door
Of this unfinished house—a Fortress bare,
Where strength has been the Builder's
    only care;
Whose rugged walls may still for years
    demand
The final polish of the Plasterer's hand. 25
—This Dwelling's Inmate more than three
    weeks' space
And oft a Prisoner in the cheerless place,
I—of whose touch the fiddle would com-
    plain,
Whose breath would labour at the flute in
    vain,
In music all unversed, nor blessed with
    skill   30
A bridge to copy, or to paint a mill,
Tired of my books, a scanty company!
And tired of listening to the boisterous
    sea—
Pace between door and window mutter-
    ing rhyme,
An old resource to cheat a froward time!
Though these dull hours (mine is it, or
    their shame?)   36
Would tempt me to renounce that humble
    aim.
—But if there be a Muse who, free to
    take
Her seat upon Olympus, doth forsake
Those heights (like Phœbus when his
    golden locks   40
He veiled, attendant on Thessalian flocks)
And, in disguise, a Milkmaid with her
    pail
Trips down the pathways of some winding
    dale;

Or, like a Mermaid, warbles on the
shores
To fishers mending nets beside their
doors ;   45
Or, Pilgrim-like, on forest moss reclined,
Gives plaintive ditties to the heedless
wind,
Or listens to its play among the boughs
Above her head and so forgets her vows—
If such a Visitant of Earth there be   50
And she would deign this day to smile
on me
And aid my verse, content with local
bounds
Of natural beauty and life's daily rounds,
Thoughts, chances, sights, or doings,
which we tell
Without reserve to those whom we love
well—   55
Then haply, Beaumont ! words in current
clear
Will flow, and on a welcome page ap-
pear
Duly before thy sight, unless they perish
here.

What shall I treat of? News from
Mona's Isle?
Such have we, but unvaried in its style ;
No tales of Runagates fresh landed,
whence   61
And wherefore fugitive or on what pre-
tence ;
Of feasts, or scandal, eddying like the
wind
Most restlessly alive when most confined.
Ask not of me, whose tongue can best
appease   65
The mighty tumults of the HOUSE OF
KEYS ;
The last year's cup whose Ram or Heifer
gained,
What slopes are planted, or what mosses
drained :
An eye of fancy only can I cast
On that proud pageant now at hand or
past,   70
When full five hundred boats in trim
array,
With nets and sails outspread and stream-
ers gay,

And chanted hymns and stiller voice of
prayer,
For the old Manx-harvest to the Deep
repair,
Soon as the herring-shoals at distance
shine   75
Like beds of moonlight shifting on the
brine.

Mona from our Abode is daily seen,
But with a wilderness of waves between ;
And by conjecture only can we speak
Of aught transacted there in bay or creek ;
No tidings reach us thence from town or
field,   81
Only faint news her mountain-sunbeams
yield,
And some we gather from the misty air,
And some the hovering clouds, our tele-
graph, declare.
But these poetic mysteries I withhold ; 85
For Fancy hath her fits both hot and cold,
And should the colder fit with You be on
When You might read, my credit would
be gone.

Let more substantial themes the pen
engage,
And nearer interests culled from the
opening stage   90
Of our migration.—Ere the welcome dawn
Had from the east her silver star with-
drawn,
The Wain stood ready, at our Cottage-
door,
Thoughtfully freighted with a various
store ;
And long or ere the uprising of the Sun
O'er dew-damped dust our journey was
begun,   96
A needful journey, under favouring skies,
Through peopled Vales ; yet something
in the guise
Of those old Patriarchs when from well
to well
They roamed through Wastes where now
the tented Arabs dwell.   100

Say first, to whom did we the charge
confide,
Who promptly undertook the Wain to
guide

Up many a sharply-twining road and
 down,
And over many a wide hill's craggy
 crown,
Through the quick turns of many a hollow
 nook, 105
And the rough bed of many an unbridged
 brook?
A blooming Lass—who in her better hand
Bore a light switch, her sceptre of com-
 mand
When, yet a slender Girl, she often led,
Skilful and bold, the horse and burthen-
 ed *sled*[1] 110
From the peat-yielding Moss on Gowdar's
 head.
What could go wrong with such a Cha-
 rioteer
For goods and chattels, or those Infants
 dear,
A Pair who smilingly sat side by side,
Our hope confirming that the salt-sea
 tide, 115
Whose free embraces we were bound to
 seek,
Would their lost strength restore and
 freshen the pale cheek?
Such hope did either Parent entertain
Pacing behind along the silent lane.

 Blithe hopes and happy musings soon
 took flight, 120
For lo! an uncouth melancholy sight—
On a green bank a creature stood forlorn
Just half protruded to the light of morn,
Its hinder part concealed by hedge-row
 thorn.
The Figure called to mind a beast of prey
Stript of its frightful powers by slow
 decay, 126
And, though no longer upon rapine bent,
Dim memory keeping of its old intent.
We started, looked again with anxious
 eyes,
And in that griesly object recognise 130
The Curate's Dog—his long-tried friend,
 for they,
As well we knew, together had grown
 grey.

---

[1] A local word for sledge.

The Master died, his drooping servant's
 grief
Found at the Widow's feet some sad
 relief;
Yet still he lived in pining discontent,
Sadness which no indulgence could pre-
 vent; 136
Hence whole day wanderings, broken
 nightly sleeps
And lonesome watch that out of doors he
 keeps;
Not oftentimes, I trust, as we, poor brute!
Espied him on his legs sustained, blank,
 mute, 140
And of all visible motion destitute,
So that the very heaving of his breath
Seemed stopt, though by some other
 power than death.
Long as we gazed upon the form and face,
A mild domestic pity kept its place, 145
Unscared by thronging fancies of strange
 hue
That haunted us in spite of what we
 knew.
Even now I sometimes think of him as lost
In second-sight appearances, or crost
By spectral shapes of guilt, or to the
 ground, 150
On which he stood, by spells unnatural
 bound,
Like a gaunt shaggy Porter forced to wait
In days of old romance at Archimago's
 gate.

 Advancing Summer, Nature's law ful-
 filled, 154
The choristers in every grove had stilled;
But we, we lacked not music of our own,
For lightsome Fanny had thus early
 thrown,
Mid the gay prattle of those infant
 tongues,
Some notes prelusive, from the round of
 songs
With which, more zealous than the live-
 liest bird 160
That in wild Arden's brakes was ever heard,
Her work and her work's partners she
 can cheer,
The whole day long, and all days of the
 year.

Thus gladdened from our own dear
  Vale we pass
And soon approach Diana's Looking-glass!
To Loughrigg-tarn, round clear and bright
  as heaven,   166
Such name Italian fancy would have
  given,
Ere on its banks the few grey cabins rose
That yet disturb not its concealed repose
More than the feeblest wind that idly
  blows.   170

Ah, Beaumont! when an opening in
  the road
Stopped me at once by charm of what it
  showed,
The encircling region vividly exprest
Within the mirror's depth, a world at
  rest—
Sky streaked with purple, grove and
  craggy bield[1],   175
And the smooth green of many a pen-
  dent field,
And, quieted and soothed, a torrent
  small,
A little daring would-be waterfall,
One chimney smoking and its azure
  wreath,
Associate all in the calm Pool beneath,
With here and there a faint imperfect
  gleam   181
Of water-lilies veiled in misty steam—
What wonder at this hour of stillness
  deep,
A shadowy link 'tween wakefulness and
  sleep,
When Nature's self, amid such blending,
  seems   185
To render visible her own soft dreams,
If, mixed with what appeared of rock,
  lawn, wood,
Fondly embosomed in the tranquil flood,
A glimpse I caught of that Abode, by
  Thee
Designed to rise in humble privacy,   190
A lowly Dwelling, here to be outspread,
Like a small Hamlet, with its bashful
  head

Half hid in native trees. Alas 'tis not,
Nor ever was; I sighed, and left the spot
Unconscious of its own untoward lot, 195
And thought in silence, with regret too
  keen,
Of unexperienced joys that might have
  been;
Of neighbourhood and intermingling arts,
And golden summer days uniting cheer-
  ful hearts.
But time, irrevocable time, is flown, 200
And let us utter thanks for blessings
  sown
And reaped—what hath been, and what
  is, our own.

Not far we travelled ere a shout of glee,
Startling us all, dispersed my reverie;
Such shout as many a sportive echo meet-
  ing   205
Oft-times from Alpine *chalets* sends a
  greeting.
Whence the blithe hail? behold a Peasant
  stand
On high, a kerchief waving in her hand!
Not unexpectant that by early day
Our little Band would thrid this moun-
  tain way,   210
Before her cottage on the bright hill-side
She hath advanced with hope to be de-
  scried.
Right gladly answering signals we dis-
  played,
Moving along a tract of morning shade,
And vocal wishes sent of like good will
To our kind Friend high on the sunny
  hill—   216
Luminous region, fair as if the prime
Were tempting all astir to look aloft or
  climb;
Only the centre of the shining cot
With door left open makes a gloomy spot,
Emblem of those dark corners sometimes
  found   221
Within the happiest breast on earthly
  ground.

Rich prospect left behind of stream
  and vale,
And mountain-tops, a barren ridge we
  scale;

---

[1] A word common in the country, signifying
shelter, as in Scotland.

Descend and reach, in Yewdale's depths,
a plain   225
With haycocks studded, striped with
yellowing grain—
An area level as a Lake and spread
Under a rock too steep for man to tread,
Where sheltered from the north and bleak
north-west
Aloft the Raven hangs a visible nest, 230
Fearless of all assaults that would her
brood molest.

Hot sunbeams fill the steaming vale; but
hark,
At our approach, a jealous watch-dog's
bark,
Noise that brings forth no liveried Page
of state,
But the whole household, that our coming
wait.   235
With Young and Old warm greetings we
exchange,
And jocund smiles, and toward the lowly
Grange
Press forward by the teasing dogs un-
scared.
Entering, we find the morning meal pre-
pared:
So down we sit, though not till each had
cast   240
Pleased looks around the delicate repast—
Rich cream, and snow-white eggs fresh
from the nest,
With amber honey from the mountain's
breast;
Strawberries from lane or woodland, offer-
ing wild   244
Of children's industry, in hillocks piled;
Cakes for the nonce, and butter fit to lie
Upon a lordly dish; frank hospitality
Where simple art with bounteous nature
vied,
And cottage comfort shunned not seemly
pride.

Kind Hostess! Handmaid also of the
feast,   250
If thou be lovelier than the kindling East,
Words by thy presence unrestrained may
speak
Of a perpetual dawn from brow and
cheek

Instinct with light whose sweetest pro-
mise lies,
Never retiring, in thy large dark eyes, 255
Dark but to every gentle feeling true,
As if their lustre flowed from ether's
purest blue.

Let me not ask what tears may have
been wept
By those bright eyes, what weary vigils
kept,
Beside that hearth what sighs may have
been heaved   260
For wounds inflicted, nor what toil relieved
By fortitude and patience, and the grace
Of heaven in pity visiting the place.
Not unadvisedly those secret springs
I leave unsearched: enough that memory
clings,   265
Here as elsewhere, to notices that make
Their own significance for hearts awake,
To rural incidents, whose genial powers
Filled with delight three summer morn-
ing hours.

More could my pen report of grave or gay
That through our gipsy travel cheered the
way;   271
But, bursting forth above the waves, the
Sun
Laughs at my pains, and seems to say,
"Be done."
Yet, Beaumont, thou wilt not, I trust,
reprove
This humble offering made by Truth to
Love,   275
Nor chide the Muse that stooped to break
a spell
Which might have else been on me yet:—
                                    FAREWELL.

UPON PERUSING THE FOREGOING EPISTLE THIRTY YEARS AFTER ITS COMPOSITION.

[Composed 1841.—Published: vol. of 1842.]

Soon did the Almighty Giver of all rest
Take those dear young Ones to a fearless
nest;
And in Death's arms has long reposed the
Friend
For whom this simple Register was
penned.

Thanks to the moth that spared it for
 our eyes;   5
And Strangers even the slighted Scroll
 may prize,
Moved by the touch of kindred sym-
 pathies.
For—save the calm repentance sheds o'er
 strife
Raised by remembrances of misused life,
The light from past endeavours purely
 willed   10
And by Heaven's favour happily fulfilled;
Save hope that we, yet bound to Earth,
 may share
The joys of the Departed—what so fair
As blameless pleasure, not without some
 tears,
Reviewed through Love's transparent veil
 of years?   15

Note.—LOUGHRIGG TARN, alluded to in the fore-
going Epistle, resembles, though much smaller in
compass, the Lake Nemi, or *Speculum Dianæ*
as it is often called, not only in its clear waters
and circular form, and the beauty immediately
surrounding it, but also as being overlooked by
the eminence of Langdale Pikes as Lake Nemi is
by that of Monte Calvo. Since this Epistle was
written Loughrigg Tarn has lost much of its
beauty by the felling of many natural clumps of
wood, relics of the old forest, particularly upon
the farm called "The Oaks," from the abundance
of that tree which grew there.

It is to be regretted, upon public grounds, that
Sir George Beaumont did not carry into effect
his intention of constructing here a Summer
Retreat in the style I have described; as his taste
would have set an example how buildings, with
all the accommodations modern society requires,
might be introduced even into the most secluded
parts of this country without injuring their native
character. The design was not abandoned from
failure of inclination on his part, but in conse-
quence of local untowardness which need not be
particularised.

II.

GOLD AND SILVER FISHES IN A VASE.

[Composed 1829.—Published 1835.]

THE soaring lark is blest as proud
 When at heaven's gate she sings;
The roving bee proclaims aloud
 Her flight by vocal wings;

While Ye, in lasting durance pent, 5
 Your silent lives employ
For something more than dull content,
 Though haply less than joy.

Yet might your glassy prison seem
 A place where joy is known, 10
Where golden flash and silver gleam
 Have meanings of their own;
While, high and low, and all about,
 Your motions, glittering Elves!
Ye weave—no danger from without, 15
 And peace among yourselves.

Type of a sunny human breast
 Is your transparent cell;
Where Fear is but a transient guest,
 No sullen Humours dwell; 20
Where, sensitive of every ray
 That smites this tiny sea,
Your scaly panoplies repay
 The loan with usury.

How beautiful!—Yet none knows why 25
 This ever-graceful change,
Renewed—renewed incessantly—
 Within your quiet range.
Is it that ye with conscious skill
 For mutual pleasure glide; 30
And sometimes, not without your will,
 Are dwarfed, or magnified?

Fays, Genii of gigantic size!
 And now, in twilight dim,
Clustering like constellated eyes 35
 In wings of Cherubim,
When the fierce orbs abate their glare;—
 Whate'er your forms express,
Whate'er ye seem, whate'er ye are—
 All leads to gentleness. 40

Cold though your nature be, 'tis pure;
 Your birthright is a fence
From all that haughtier kinds endure
 Through tyranny of sense.
Ah! not alone by colours bright 45
 Are Ye to heaven allied,
When, like essential Forms of light,
 Ye mingle, or divide.

For day-dreams soft as e'er beguiled
 Day-thoughts while limbs repose; 50
For moonlight fascinations mild,
 Your gift, ere shutters close—

Accept, mute Captives! thanks and
praise;
And may this tribute prove
That gentle admirations raise   55
Delight resembling love.

III.

LIBERTY.

SEQUEL TO THE PRECEDING.

Addressed to a friend; the gold and silver fishes
having been removed to a pool in the pleasure-
ground of Rydal Mount.

"The liberty of a people consists in being govern-
ed by laws which they have made for them-
selves, under whatever form it be of govern-
ment. The liberty of a private man, in being
master of his own time and actions, as far
as may consist with the laws of God and of his
country. Of this latter we are here to dis-
course."—COWLEY.

[Composed 1829.—Published 1835.]

THOSE breathing Tokens of your kind
regard,
(Suspect not, Anna, that their fate is
hard;
Not soon does aught to which mild fancies
cling
In lonely spots, become a slighted thing;)
Those silent Inmates now no longer share,
Nor do they need, our hospitable care,   6
Removed in kindness from their glassy
Cell
To the fresh waters of a living Well—
An elfin pool so sheltered that its rest
No winds disturb; the mirror of whose
breast   10
Is smooth as clear, save where with dim-
ples small
A fly may settle, or a blossom fall.
—There swims, of blazing sun and beating
shower
Fearless (but how obscured!) the golden
Power,
That from his bauble prison used to cast
Gleams by the richest jewel unsurpast; 16
And near him, darkling like a sullen
Gnome,
The silver Tenant of the crystal dome;

Dissevered both from all the mysteries
Of hue and altering shape that charmed
all eyes.   20
Alas! they pined, they languished while
they shone;
And, if not so, what matters beauty gone
And admiration lost, by change of place
That brings to the inward creature no
disgrace?
But if the change restore his birthright,
then,   25
Whate'er the difference, boundless is the
gain.
Who can divine what impulses from God
Reach the caged lark, within a town-
abode,
From his poor inch or two of daisied sod?
O yield him back his privilege!—No sea 30
Swells like the bosom of a man set free;
A wilderness is rich with liberty.
Roll on, ye spouting whales, who die or
keep
Your independence in the fathomless
Deep!
Spread, tiny nautilus, the living sail; 35
Dive, at thy choice, or brave the freshening
gale!
If unreproved the ambitious eagle mount
Sunward to seek the daylight in its fount,
Bays, gulfs, and ocean's Indian width,
shall be,
Till the world perishes, a field for thee! 40

While musing here I sit in shadow cool,
And watch these mute Companions, in
the pool,
(Among reflected boughs of leafy trees)
By glimpses caught—disporting at their
ease,
Enlivened, braced, by hardy luxuries, 45
I ask what warrant fixed them (like a
spell
Of witchcraft fixed them) in the crystal
cell;
To wheel with languid motion round and
round,
Beautiful, yet in mournful durance bound.
Their peace, perhaps, our lightest footfall
marred;   50
On their quick sense our sweetest music
jarred;

And whither could they dart, if seized
　　with fear?
No sheltering stone, no tangled root was
　　near.
When fire or taper ceased to cheer the
　　room,
They wore away the night in starless
　　gloom;　　　　　　　　　　　　55
And when the sun first dawned upon the
　　streams,
How faint their portion of his vital beams!
Thus, and unable to complain, they fared,
While not one joy of ours by them was
　　shared.

Is there a cherished bird (I venture
　　now　　　　　　　　　　　　60
To snatch a sprig from Chaucer's reverend
　　brow)—
Is there a brilliant fondling of the cage,
Though sure of plaudits on his costly
　　stage,
Though fed with dainties from the snow-
　　white hand
Of a kind mistress, fairest of the land, 65
But gladly would escape; and, if need
　　were,
Scatter the colours from the plumes that
　　bear
The emancipated captive through blithe
　　air
Into strange woods, where he at large
　　may live
On best or worst which they and Nature
　　give?　　　　　　　　　　　　70
The beetle loves his unpretending track,
The snail the house he carries on his
　　back;
The far-fetched worm with pleasure would
　　disown
The bed we give him, though of softest
　　down;
A noble instinct; in all kinds the same, 75
All ranks! What Sovereign, worthy of
　　the name,
If doomed to breathe against his lawful
　　will
An element that flatters him—to kill,
But would rejoice to barter outward show
For the least boon that freedom can be-
　　stow?　　　　　　　　　　　　80

But most the Bard is true to inborn
　　right,
Lark of the dawn, and Philomel of night,
Exults in freedom, can with rapture vouch
For the dear blessings of a lowly couch,
A natural meal—days, months, from
　　Nature's hand;　　　　　　　　85
Time, place, and business, all at his com-
　　mand!—
Who bends to happier duties, who more
　　wise
Than the industrious Poet, taught to
　　prize,
Above all grandeur, a pure life uncrossed
By cares in which simplicity is lost? 90
That life—the flowery path that winds by
　　stealth—
Which Horace needed for his spirit's
　　health;
Sighed for, in heart and genius, overcome
By noise and strife, and questions weari-
　　some,
And the vain splendours of Imperial
　　Rome?—　　　　　　　　　　95
Let easy mirth his social hours inspire,
And fiction animate his sportive lyre,
Attuned to verse that, crowning light
　　Distress
With garlands, cheats her into happiness;
Give me the humblest note of those sad
　　strains　　　　　　　　　　　100
Drawn forth by pressure of his gilded
　　chains,
As a chance-sunbeam from his memory
　　fell
Upon the Sabine farm he loved so well;
Or when the prattle of Bandusia's spring
Haunted his ear—he only listening— 105
He proud to please, above all rivals, fit
To win the palm of gaiety and wit;
He, doubt not, with involuntary dread,
Shrinking from each new favour to be
　　shed,
By the world's Ruler, on his honoured
　　head!　　　　　　　　　　　110

In a deep vision's intellectual scene,
Such earnest longings and regrets as keen
Depressed the melancholy Cowley, laid
Under a fancied yew-tree's luckless
　　shade;

A doleful bower for penitential song, 115
Where Man and Muse complained of
    mutual wrong;
While Cam's ideal current glided by,
And antique towers nodded their fore-
    heads high,
Citadels dear to studious privacy.
But Fortune, who had long been used to
    sport 120
With this tried Servant of a thankless
    Court,
Relenting met his wishes; and to you
The remnant of his days at least was true;
You, whom, though long deserted, he
    loved best;
You, Muses, books, fields, liberty, and rest!

Far happier they who, fixing hope and
    aim 126
On the humanities of peaceful fame,
Enter betimes with more than martial fire
The generous course, aspire, and still
    aspire;
Upheld by warnings heeded not too late
Stifle the contradictions of their fate, 131
And to one purpose cleave, their Being's
    godlike mate!

Thus, gifted Friend, but with the placid
    brow
That woman ne'er should forfeit, keep *thy*
    vow;
With modest scorn reject whate'er would
    blind 135
The ethereal eyesight, cramp the wingèd
    mind!
Then, with a blessing granted from above
To every act, word, thought, and look of love,
Life's book for Thee may lie unclosed, till
    age
Shall with a thankful tear bedrop its latest
    page[1]. 140

IV.

POOR ROBIN[2].

[Composed March, 1840.—Published: vol. of 1842.]

Now when the primrose makes a splendid
    show,
And lilies face the March-winds in full
    blow,
And humbler growths as moved with one
    desire
Put on, to welcome spring, their best
    attire,
Poor Robin is yet flowerless; but how
    gay 5
With his red stalks upon this sunny day!
And, as his tufts of leaves he spreads,
    content
With a hard bed and scanty nourishment,
Mixed with the green, some shine not
    lacking power
To rival summer's brightest scarlet flower;
And flowers they well might seem to
    passers-by 11
If looked at only with a careless eye;
Flowers—or a richer produce (did it suit
The season) sprinklings of ripe strawberry
    fruit.

But while a thousand pleasures come
    unsought, 15
Why fix upon his wealth or want a
    thought?
Is the string touched in prelude to a lay
Of pretty fancies that would round him
    play
When all the world acknowledged elfin
    sway?

[1] There is now, alas! no possibility of the anticipation, with which the above Epistle concludes, being realised: nor were the verses ever seen by the Individual for whom they were intended. She accompanied her husband, the Rev. Wm. Fletcher, to India, and died of cholera, at the age of thirty-two or thirty-three years, on her way from Shalapore to Bombay, deeply lamented by all who knew her.

Her enthusiasm was ardent, her piety stead-fast; and her great talents would have enabled her to be eminently useful in the difficult path of life to which she had been called. The opinion she entertained of her own performances, given to the world under her maiden name, Jewsbury, was modest and humble, and, indeed, far below their merits; as is often the case with those who are making trial of their powers, with a hope to discover what they are best fitted for. In one quality, viz. quickness in the motions of her mind, she had, within the range of the Author's acquaintance, no equal.

[2] The small wild Geranium known by that term.

Or does it suit our humour to commend 20
Poor Robin as a sure and crafty friend,
Whose practice teaches, spite of names to
 show
Bright colours whether they deceive or
 no?—
Nay, we would simply praise the free
 good-will
With which, though slighted, he, on naked
 hill 25
Or in warm valley, seeks his part to fill;
Cheerful alike if bare of flowers as now,
Or when his tiny gems shall deck his
 brow:
Yet more, we wish that men by men
 despised,
And such as lift their foreheads over-
 prized, 30
Should sometimes think, where'er they
 chance to spy
This child of Nature's own humility,
What recompense is kept in store or left
For all that seem neglected or bereft;
With what nice care equivalents are
 given, 35
How just, how bountiful, the hand of
 Heaven.

V.

THE GLEANER.

SUGGESTED BY A PICTURE.

[Composed 1828.—Published, as "The Country
Girl," 1829 (*The Keepsake*); ed. 1832.]

THAT happy gleam of vernal eyes,
Those locks from summer's golden skies,
 That o'er thy brow are shed;
That cheek—a kindling of the morn,
That lip—a rose-bud from the thorn, 5
 I saw; and Fancy sped
To scenes Arcadian, whispering, through
 soft air,
Of bliss that grows without a care,
And happiness that never flies—
(How can it where love never dies?) 10
Whispering of promise, where no blight
Can reach the innocent delight;
Where pity, to the mind conveyed
In pleasure, is the darkest shade
That Time, unwrinkled grandsire, flings
From his smoothly gliding wings. 16

What mortal form, what earthly face
Inspired the pencil, lines to trace,
And mingle colours, that should breed
Such rapture, nor want power to feed; 2c
For had thy charge been idle flowers,
Fair Damsel! o'er my captive mind,
To truth and sober reason blind,
'Mid that soft air, those long-lost bowers,
The sweet illusion might have hung, for
 hours. 25

Thanks to this tell-tale sheaf of corn,
That touchingly bespeaks thee born
Life's daily tasks with them to share
Who, whether from their lowly bed
They rise, or rest the weary head, 30
Ponder the blessing they entreat
From Heaven, and *feel* what they repeat,
While they give utterance to the prayer
That asks for daily bread.

VI.

TO A REDBREAST

(IN SICKNESS).

[Composed ?.—Published: vol. of 1842.]

STAY, little cheerful Robin! stay,
 And at my casement sing,
Though it should prove a farewell lay
 And this our parting spring.

Though I, alas! may ne'er enjoy 5
 The promise in thy song;
A charm, *that* thought can not destroy,
 Doth to thy strain belong.

Methinks that in my dying hour
 Thy song would still be dear, 10
And with a more than earthly power
 My passing Spirit cheer.

Then, little Bird, this boon confer,
 Come, and my requiem sing,
Nor fail to be the harbinger 15
 Of everlasting Spring.

S. H.

VII.

[Composed 1846.—Published 1850.]

I KNOW an aged Man constrained to dwell
In a large house of public charity,
Where he abides, as in a Prisoner's cell,
With numbers near, alas! no company.

When he could creep about, at will,
   though poor   5
And forced to live on alms, this old Man
   fed
A Redbreast, one that to his cottage door
Came not, but in a lane partook his bread.

There, at the root of one particular tree,
An easy seat this worn-out Labourer
   found   10
While Robin pecked the crumbs upon his
   knee
Laid one by one, or scattered on the
   ground.

Dear intercourse was theirs, day after
   day;
What signs of mutual gladness when they
   met!
Think of their common peace, their sim-
   ple play,   15
The parting moment and its fond regret.

Months passed in love that failed not to
   fulfil,
In spite of season's change, its own
   demand,
By fluttering pinions here and busy bill;
There by caresses from a tremulous hand.

Thus in the chosen spot a tie so strong   21
Was formed between the solitary pair,
That when his fate had housed him 'mid
   a throng
The Captive shunned all converse prof-
   fered there.

Wife, children, kindred, they were dead
   and gone;   25
But, if no evil hap his wishes crossed,
One living Stay was left, and on that
   one
Some recompense for all that he had lost.

O that the good old Man had power to
   prove,
By message sent through air or visible
   token,   30
That still he loves the Bird, and still
   must love;
That friendship lasts though fellowship
   is broken!

VIII.

SONNET.

TO AN OCTOGENARIAN.

[Composed 1846.—Published 1850.]

AFFECTIONS lose their object; Time brings
   forth
No successors; and, lodged in memory,
If love exist no longer, it must die,—
Wanting accustomed food, must pass
   from earth,
Or never hope to reach a second birth.   5
This sad belief, the happiest that is left
To thousands, share not Thou; howe'er
   bereft,
Scorned, or neglected, fear not such a
   dearth.
Though poor and destitute of friends thou
   art,
Perhaps the sole survivor of thy race,   10
One to whom Heaven assigns that mourn-
   ful part
The utmost solitude of age to face,
Still shall be left some corner of the heart
Where Love for living Thing can find a
   place.

IX.

FLOATING ISLAND.

These lines are by the Author of the Address to
the Wind, &c., published heretofore along with
my poems. Those to a Redbreast are by a de-
ceased female Relative.

[Composed ?.—Published: vol. of 1842.]

HARMONIOUS Powers with Nature work
On sky, earth, river, lake and sea;
Sunshine and cloud, whirlwind and breeze,
All in one duteous task agree.

Once did I see a slip of earth   5
(By throbbing waves long undermined)
Loosed from its hold; how, no one knew,
But all might see it float, obedient to the
   wind;

Might see it, from the mossy shore
Dissevered, float upon the Lake,   10
Float with its crest of trees adorned
On which the warbling birds their pas-
   time take.

Food, shelter, safety, there they find;
There berries ripen, flowerets bloom;
There insects live their lives, and die; 15
A peopled world it is; in size a tiny
    room.

And thus through many seasons' space
This little Island may survive;
But Nature, though we mark her not,
Will take away, may cease to give. 20

Perchance when you are wandering forth
Upon some vacant sunny day,
Without an object, hope, or fear,
Thither your eyes may turn—the Isle is
    passed away;

Buried beneath the glittering Lake, 25
Its place no longer to be found;
Yet the lost fragments shall remain
To fertilise some other ground.
                                D. W.

X.

[Composed ?.—Published 1850.]

How beautiful the Queen of Night, on
    high
Her way pursuing among scattered clouds,
Where, ever and anon, her head she
    shrouds
Hidden from view in dense obscurity.
But look, and to the watchful eye   5
A brightening edge will indicate that
    soon
We shall behold the struggling Moon
Break forth,—again to walk the clear blue
    sky.

XI.

"Late, late yestreen I saw the new moone
Wi' the auld moone in hir arme."
            Ballad of Sir Patrick Spence,
                        Percy's Reliques.

[Composed 1826.—Published 1827.]

ONCE I could hail (howe'er serene the
    sky)
The Moon re-entering her monthly round,
No faculty yet given me to espy
The dusky Shape within her arms im-
    bound,

That thin memento of effulgence lost   5
Which some have named her Prede-
    cessor's ghost.

Young, like the Crescent that above me
    shone,
Nought I perceived within it dull or dim;
All that appeared was suitable to One
Whose fancy had a thousand fields to
    skim;   10
To expectations spreading with wild
    growth,
And hope that kept with me her plighted
    troth.

I saw (ambition quickening at the view)
A silver boat launched on a boundless
    flood;
A pearly crest, like Dian's when it threw
Its brightest splendour round a leafy
    wood;   16
But not a hint from under-ground, no
    sign
Fit for the glimmering brow of Proser-
    pine.

Or was it Dian's self that seemed to
    move
Before me?—nothing blemished the fair
    sight;   20
On her I looked whom jocund Fairies
    love,
Cynthia, who puts the *little* stars to
    flight,
And by that thinning magnifies the great,
For exaltation of her sovereign state.

And when I learned to mark the spectral
    Shape   25
As each new Moon obeyed the call of
    Time,
If gloom fell on me, swift was my es-
    cape;
Such happy privilege hath life's gay
    Prime,
To see or not to see, as best may please
A buoyant Spirit, and a heart at ease. 30

Now, dazzling Stranger! when thou
    meet'st my glance,
Thy dark Associate ever I discern;
Emblem of thoughts too eager to advance

While I salute my joys, thoughts sad or
   stern;
Shades of past bliss, or phantoms that, to
   gain   35
Their fill of promised lustre, wait in vain.

So changes mortal Life with fleeting
   years;
A mournful change, should Reason fail
   to bring
The timely insight that can temper fears,
And from vicissitude remove its sting; 40
While Faith aspires to seats in that
   domain
Where joys are perfect—neither wax nor
   wane.

XII.

TO THE LADY FLEMING,

ON SEEING THE FOUNDATION PREPAR-
ING FOR THE ERECTION OF RYDAL
CHAPEL, WESTMORELAND.

[Composed 1823.—Published 1827.]

I.

BLEST is this Isle—our native Land;
Where battlement and moated gate
Are objects only for the hand
Of hoary Time to decorate;
Where shady hamlet, town that breathes
Its busy smoke in social wreaths,   6
No rampart's stern defence require,
Nought but the heaven-directed spire,
And steeple tower (with pealing bells
Far-heard)—our only citadels.   10

II.

O Lady! from a noble line
Of chieftains sprung, who stoutly bore
The spear, yet gave to works divine
A bounteous help in days of yore,
(As records mouldering in the Dell   15
Of Nightshade[1] haply yet may tell;)
Thee kindred aspirations moved
To build, within a vale beloved,
For Him upon whose high behests
All peace depends, all safety rests.   20

[1] Bekangs Ghyll—or the dell of Nightshade—
in which stands St. Mary's Abbey in Low Fur-
ness.

III.

How fondly will the woods embrace
This daughter of thy pious care,
Lifting her front with modest grace
To make a fair recess more fair;
And to exalt the passing hour;   25
Or soothe it with a healing power
Drawn from the Sacrifice fulfilled,
Before this rugged soil was tilled,
Or human habitation rose
To interrupt the deep repose!   30

IV.

Well may the villagers rejoice!
Nor heat, nor cold, nor weary ways,
Will be a hindrance to the voice
That would unite in prayer and praise;
More duly shall wild wandering Youth
Receive the curb of sacred truth,   36
Shall tottering Age, bent earthward, hear
The Promise, with uplifted ear;
And all shall welcome the new ray
Imparted to their sabbath-day.   40

V.

Nor deem the Poet's hope misplaced,
His fancy cheated—that can see
A shade upon the future cast,
Of time's pathetic sanctity;
Can hear the monitory clock   45
Sound o'er the lake with gentle shock
At evening, when the ground beneath
Is ruffled o'er with cells of death;
Where happy generations lie,
Here tutored for eternity.   50

VI.

Lives there a man whose sole delights
Are trivial pomp and city noise,
Hardening a heart that loathes or slights
What every natural heart enjoys?
Who never caught a noon-tide dream   55
From murmur of a running stream;
Could strip, for aught the prospect yields
To him, their verdure from the fields;
And take the radiance from the clouds
In which the sun his setting shrouds.   60

VII.

A soul so pitiably forlorn,
If such do on this earth abide,
May season apathy with scorn,
May turn indifference to pride;
And still be not unblest—compared   65
With him who grovels, self-debarred
From all that lies within the scope
Of holy faith and Christian hope;
Or, shipwrecked, kindles on the coast
False fires, that others may be lost.   70

VIII.

Alas! that such perverted zeal
Should spread on Britain's favoured
      ground!
That public order, private weal,
Should e'er have felt or feared a wound
From champions of the desperate law   75
Which from their own blind hearts they
      draw;
Who tempt their reason to deny
God, whom their passions dare defy,
And boast that they alone are free
Who reach this dire extremity!   80

IX.

But turn we from these bold bad
      men;
The way, mild Lady! that hath led
Down to their "dark opprobrious den,"
Is all too rough for Thee to tread.
Softly as morning vapours glide   85
Down Rydal-cove from Fairfield's side,
Should move the tenor of *his* song
Who means to charity no wrong;
Whose offering gladly would accord
With this day's work, in thought and
      word.   90

X.

Heaven prosper it! may peace, and love,
And hope, and consolation, fall,
Through its meek influence, from above,
And penetrate the hearts of all;
All who, around the hallowed Fane,   95
Shall sojourn in this fair domain;
Grateful to Thee, while service pure,
And ancient ordinance, shall endure,
For opportunity bestowed   99
To kneel together, and adore their God!

XIII.

ON THE SAME OCCASION.

Oh! gather whencesoe'er ye safely may
The help which slackening Piety requires;
Nor deem that he perforce must go astray
Who treads upon the footmarks of his sires.

Our churches, invariably perhaps, stand east and
west, but *why* is by few persons *exactly* known;
nor, that the degree of deviation from *due* east
often noticeable in the ancient ones was deter-
mined, in each particular case, by the point in
the horizon, at which the sun rose upon the
day of the saint to whom the church was dedi-
cated. These observances of our ancestors, and
the causes of them, are the subject of the fol-
lowing stanzas.

[Composed 1823.—Published 1827.]

WHEN in the antique age of bow and spear
And feudal rapine clothed with iron mail,
Came ministers of peace, intent to rear
The Mother Church in yon sequestered
      vale;

Then, to her Patron Saint a previous rite 5
Resounded with deep swell and solemn
      close,
Through unremitting vigils of the night,
Till from his couch the wished-for day-
      uprose.

He rose, and straight—as by divine com-
      mand,
They, who had waited for that sign to trace
Their work's foundation, gave with care-
      ful hand   11
To the high altar its determined place;

Mindful of Him Who in the Orient born
There lived, and on the cross His life re-
      signed,
And Who, from out the regions of the
      morn,   15
Issuing in pomp, shall come to judge
      mankind.

So taught *their* creed;—nor failed the
      eastern sky,
'Mid these more awful feelings, to infuse
The sweet and natural hopes that shall
      not die,
Long as the sun his gladsome course
      renews.   20

For us hath such prelusive vigil ceased;
Yet still we plant, like men of elder days
Our Christian altar faithful to the east,
Whence the tall window drinks the morn-
    ing rays;

That obvious emblem giving to the eye 25
Of meek devotion, which erewhile it gave,
That symbol of the day-spring from on high,
Triumphant o'er the darkness of the grave.

XIV.

THE HORN OF EGREMONT CASTLE.

[Composed 1806.—Published 1807.]

Ere the Brothers through the gateway
Issued forth with old and young,
To the Horn Sir Eustace pointed
Which for ages there had hung.
Horn it was which none could sound,   5
No one upon living ground,
Save He who came as rightful Heir
To Egremont's Domains and Castle fair.

Heirs from times of earliest record
Had the House of Lucie born,   10
Who of right had held the Lordship
Claimed by proof upon the Horn:
Each at the appointed hour
Tried the Horn,—it owned his power;
He was acknowledged: and the blast,   15
Which good Sir Eustace sounded, was
    the last.

With his lance Sir Eustace pointed,
And to Hubert thus said he,
"What I speak this Horn shall witness
For thy better memory.   20
Hear, then, and neglect me not!
At this time, and on this spot,
The words are uttered from my heart,
As my last earnest prayer ere we depart.

"On good service we are going   25
Life to risk by sea and land,
In which course if Christ our Saviour
Do my sinful soul demand,
Hither come thou back straightway,
Hubert, if alive that day;   30
Return, and sound the Horn, that we
May have a living House still left in thee!"

"Fear not," quickly answered Hubert;
"As I am thy Father's son,

What thou askest, noble Brother,   35
With God's favour shall be done."
So were both right well content:
Forth they from the Castle went,
And at the head of their Array
To Palestine the Brothers took their way.

Side by side they fought (the Lucies   41
Were a line for valour famed)
And where'er their strokes alighted,
There the Saracens were tamed.
Whence, then, could it come — the
    thought—   45
By what evil spirit brought?
Oh! can a brave Man wish to take
His Brother's life, for Lands' and Castle's
    sake?

"Sir!" the Ruffians said to Hubert,
"Deep he lies in Jordan flood."   50
Stricken by this ill assurance,
Pale and trembling Hubert stood.
"Take your earnings."—Oh! that I
Could have *seen* my Brother die!
It was a pang that vexed him then;   55
And oft returned, again, and yet again.

Months passed on, and no Sir Eustace!
Nor of him were tidings heard;
Wherefore, bold as day, the Murderer
Back again to England steered.   60
To his Castle Hubert sped;
Nothing has he now to dread.
But silent and by stealth he came,
And at an hour which nobody could name.

None could tell if it were night-time,   65
Night or day, at even or morn;
No one's eye had seen him enter,
No one's ear had heard the Horn.
But bold Hubert lives in glee:
Months and years went smilingly;   70
With plenty was his table spread;
And bright the Lady is who shares his bed.

Likewise he had sons and daughters;
And, as good men do, he sate
At his board by these surrounded,   75
Flourishing in fair estate.
And while thus in open day
Once he sate, as old books say,
A blast was uttered from the Horn,
Where by the Castle-gate it hung forlorn.

'Tis the breath of good Sir Eustace! 81
He is come to claim his right:
Ancient castle, woods, and mountains
Hear the challenge with delight.
Hubert! though the blast be blown 85
He is helpless and alone:
Thou hast a dungeon, speak the word!
And there he may be lodged, and thou
    be Lord.

Speak!—astounded Hubert cannot;
And, if power to speak he had, 90
All are daunted, all the household
Smitten to the heart, and sad.
'Tis Sir Eustace; if it be
Living man, it must be he!
Thus Hubert thought in his dismay, 95
And by a postern-gate he slunk away.

Long, and long was he unheard of:
To his Brother then he came,
Made confession, asked forgiveness,
Asked it by a brother's name, 100
And by all the saints in heaven;
And of Eustace was forgiven:
Then in a convent went to hide
His melancholy head, and there he died.

But Sir Eustace, whom good angels 105
Had preserved from murderers' hands,
And from Pagan chains had rescued,
Lived with honour on his lands.
Sons he had, saw sons of theirs:
And through ages, heirs of heirs, 110
A long posterity renowned,
Sounded the Horn which they alone could
    sound.

XV.

GOODY BLAKE AND HARRY GILL.

A TRUE STORY.

[Composed 1798.—Published 1798.]

OH! what's the matter? what's the
    matter?
What is't that ails young Harry Gill?
That evermore his teeth they chatter,
Chatter, chatter, chatter still!
Of waistcoats Harry has no lack, 5
Good duffle grey, and flannel fine;
He has a blanket on his back,
And coats enough to smother nine.

In March, December, and in July,
'Tis all the same with Harry Gill; 10
The neighbours tell, and tell you truly,
His teeth they chatter, chatter still.
At night, at morning, and at noon,
'Tis all the same with Harry Gill;
Beneath the sun, beneath the moon, 15
His teeth they chatter, chatter still!

Young Harry was a lusty drover,
And who so stout of limb as he?
His cheeks were red as ruddy clover;
His voice was like the voice of three. 20
Old Goody Blake was old and poor;
Ill fed she was, and thinly clad;
And any man who passed her door
Might see how poor a hut she had.

All day she spun in her poor dwelling: 25
And then her three hours' work at night,
Alas! 'twas hardly worth the telling,
It would not pay for candle-light.
Remote from sheltered village-green,
On a hill's northern side she dwelt, 30
Where from sea-blasts the hawthorns
    lean,
And hoary dews are slow to melt.

By the same fire to boil their pottage,
Two poor old Dames, as I have known,
Will often live in one small cottage; 35
But she, poor Woman! housed alone.
'Twas well enough, when summer came,
The long, warm, lightsome summer-day,
Then at her door the *canty* Dame
Would sit, as any linnet, gay. 40

But when the ice our streams did fetter,
Oh then how her old bones would shake!
You would have said, if you had met her,
'Twas a hard time for Goody Blake.
Her evenings then were dull and dead: 45
Sad case it was, as you may think,
For very cold to go to bed;
And then for cold not sleep a wink.

O joy for her! whene'er in winter
The winds at night had made a rout; 50
And scattered many a lusty splinter
And many a rotten bough about.
Yet never had she, well or sick,
As every man who knew her says,
A pile beforehand, turf or stick, 55
Enough to warm her for three days.

Now, when the frost was past enduring,
And made her poor old bones to ache,
Could any thing be more alluring
Than an old hedge to Goody Blake?   60
And, now and then, it must be said,
When her old bones were cold and chill,
She left her fire, or left her bed,
To seek the hedge of Harry Gill.

Now Harry he had long suspected   65
This trespass of old Goody Blake;
And vowed that she should be detected—
That he on her would vengeance take.
And oft from his warm fire he'd go,
And to the fields his road would take;   70
And there, at night, in frost and snow,
He watched to seize old Goody Blake.

And once, behind a rick of barley,
Thus looking out did Harry stand:
The moon was full and shining clearly,   75
And crisp with frost the stubble land.
—He hears a noise—he's all awake—
Again?—on tip-toe down the hill
He softly creeps—'tis Goody Blake;
She's at the hedge of Harry Gill!   80

Right glad was he when he beheld her:
Stick after stick did Goody pull:
He stood behind a bush of elder,
Till she had filled her apron full.
When with her load she turned about,   85
The by-way back again to take;
He started forward, with a shout,
And sprang upon poor Goody Blake.

And fiercely by the arm he took her,
And by the arm he held her fast,   90
And fiercely by the arm he shook her,
And cried, "I've caught you then at
   last!"
Then Goody, who had nothing said,
Her bundle from her lap let fall;
And, kneeling on the sticks, she prayed 95
To God that is the judge of all.

She prayed, her withered hand uprearing,
While Harry held her by the arm—
"God! who art never out of hearing,
O may he never more be warm!"   100
The cold, cold moon above her head,
Thus on her knees did Goody pray;
Young Harry heard what she had said:
And icy cold he turned away.

He went complaining all the morrow   105
That he was cold and very chill:
His face was gloom, his heart was sorrow,
Alas! that day for Harry Gill!
That day he wore a riding-coat,
But not a whit the warmer he: 110
Another was on Thursday brought,
And ere the Sabbath he had three.

'Twas all in vain, a useless matter,
And blankets were about him pinned;
Yet still his jaws and teeth they clatter,
Like a loose casement in the wind.   116
And Harry's flesh it fell away;
And all who see him say, 'tis plain,
That, live as long as live he may,
He never will be warm again.   120

No word to any man he utters,
A-bed or up, to young or old;
But ever to himself he mutters,
"Poor Harry Gill is very cold."
A-bed or up, by night or day;   125
His teeth they chatter, chatter still.
Now think, ye farmers all, I pray,
Of Goody Blake and Harry Gill!

XVI.

PRELUDE.

PREFIXED TO THE VOLUME ENTITLED
   "POEMS CHIEFLY OF EARLY AND
   LATE YEARS."

[Composed March, 1842.—Published: vol. of 1842.]

IN desultory walk through orchard
   grounds,
Or some deep chestnut grove, oft have
   I paused
The while a Thrush, urged rather than
   restrained
By gusts of vernal storm, attuned his
   song
To his own genial instincts; and was
   heard   5
(Though not without some plaintive tones
   between)
To utter, above showers of blossom swept
From tossing boughs, the promise of a
   calm,
Which the unsheltered traveller might
   receive

With thankful spirit. The descant, and
   the wind   10
That seemed to play with it in love or
   scorn,
Encouraged and endeared the strain of
   words
That haply flowed from me, by fits of
   silence
Impelled to livelier pace. But now, my
   Book!
Charged with those lays, and others of
   like mood,   15
Or loftier pitch if higher rose the theme,
Go, single—yet aspiring to be joined
With thy Forerunners that through many
   a year
Have faithfully prepared each other's
   way—
Go forth upon a mission best fulfilled 20
When and wherever, in this changeful
   world,
Power hath been given to please for
   higher ends
Than pleasure only; gladdening to pre-
   pare
For wholesome sadness, troubling to re-
   fine,
Calming to raise; and, by a sapient Art
Diffused through all the mysteries of our
   Being,   26
Softening the toils and pains that have
   not ceased
To cast their shadows on our mother Earth
Since the primeval doom. Such is the
   grace
Which, though unsued for, fails not to
   descend   30
With heavenly inspiration; such the aim
That Reason dictates; and, as even the
   wish
Has virtue in it, why should hope to me
Be wanting that sometimes, where fancied
   ills
Harass the mind and strip from off the
   bowers   35
Of private life their natural pleasantness,
A Voice—devoted to the love whose seeds
Are sown in every human breast, to
   beauty
Lodged within compass of the humblest
   sight,

To cheerful intercourse with wood and
   field,   40
And sympathy with man's substantial
   griefs—
Will not be heard in vain? And in those
   days
When unforeseen distress spreads far and
   wide
Among a People mournfully cast down,
Or into anger roused by venal words 45
In recklessness flung out to overturn
The judgment, and divert the general
   heart
From mutual good—some strain of thine,
   my Book!
Caught at propitious intervals, may win
Listeners who not unwillingly admit 50
Kindly emotion tending to console
And reconcile; and both with young and
   old
Exalt the sense of thoughtful gratitude
For benefits that still survive, by faith
In progress, under laws divine, main-
   tained.   55
    RYDAL MOUNT, *March* 26, 1842.

XVII.

TO A CHILD.

WRITTEN IN HER ALBUM.

[Composed 1834.—Published 1835.]

SMALL service is true service while it
   lasts:
Of humblest Friends, bright Creature!
   scorn not one:
The Daisy, by the shadow that it casts,
Protects the lingering dew-drop from the
   Sun.

XVIII.

LINES

WRITTEN IN THE ALBUM OF THE
COUNTESS OF LONSDALE.

[Composed November 5, 1834.—Published 1835.]

LADY! a Pen (perhaps with thy regard,
Among the Favoured, favoured not the
   least)
Left, 'mid the Records of this Book
   inscribed,

Deliberate traces, registers of thought
And feeling, suited to the place and time
That gave them birth:—months passed,
   and still this hand,   6
That had not been too timid to imprint
Words which the virtues of thy Lord
   inspired,
Was yet not bold enough to write of
   Thee.
And why that scrupulous reserve? In
   sooth   10
The blameless cause lay in the Theme
   itself.

Flowers are there many that delight to
   strive
With the sharp wind, and seem to court
   the shower,
Yet are by nature careless of the sun
Whether he shine on them or not; and
   some,   15
Where'er he moves along the unclouded
   sky,
Turn a broad front full on his flattering
   beams:
Others do rather from their notice shrink,
Loving the dewy shade,—a humble band,
Modest and sweet, a progeny of earth, 20
Congenial with thy mind and character,
High-born Augusta!
        Witness, Towers and Groves!
And Thou, wild Stream, that giv'st the
   honoured name
Of Lowther to this ancient Line, bear
   witness
From thy most secret haunts; and ye
   Parterres,   25
Which She is pleased and proud to call
   her own,
Witness how oft upon my noble Friend
Mute offerings, tribute from an inward
   sense
Of admiration and respectful love,
Have waited—till the affections could no
   more   30
Endure that silence, and broke out in
   song,
Snatches of music taken up and dropt
Like those self-solacing, those under,
   notes
Trilled by the redbreast, when autumnal
   leaves

Are thin upon the bough. Mine, only
   mine,   35
The pleasure was, and no one heard the
   praise,
Checked, in the moment of its issue,
   checked
And reprehended, by a fancied blush
From the pure qualities that called it
   forth.

Thus Virtue lives debarred from Vir-
   tue's meed;   40
Thus, Lady, is retiredness a veil
That, while it only spreads a softening
   charm
O'er features looked at by discerning
   eyes,
Hides half their beauty from the common
   gaze;
And thus, even on the exposed and
   breezy hill   45
Of lofty station, female goodness walks,
When side by side with lunar gentleness,
As in a cloister. Yet the grateful Poor
(Such the immunities of low estate,
Plain Nature's enviable privilege,   50
Her sacred recompense for many wants)
Open their hearts before Thee, pouring
   out
All that they think and feel, with tears
   of joy;
And benedictions not unheard in hea-
   ven:
And friend in the ear of friend, where
   speech is free   55
To follow truth, is eloquent as they.

Then let the Book receive in these
   prompt lines
A just memorial; and thine eyes consent
To read that they, who mark thy course,
   behold
A life declining with the golden light   60
Of summer, in the season of sere leaves;
See cheerfulness undamped by stealing
   Time;
See studied kindness flow with easy
   stream,
Illustrated with inborn courtesy;
And an habitual disregard of self   65
Balanced by vigilance for others' weal.

And shall the Verse not tell of lighter
   gifts
With these ennobling attributes con-
   joined
And blended, in peculiar harmony,
By Youth's surviving spirit? What agile
   grace!   70
A nymph-like liberty, in nymph-like
   form,
Beheld with wonder; whether floor or
   path
Thou tread; or sweep—borne on the
   managed steed—
Fleet as the shadows, over down or field,
Driven by strong winds at play among
   the clouds.   75

Yet one word more—one farewell word—
   a wish
Which came, but it has passed into a
   prayer—
That, as thy sun in brightness is de-
   clining,
So—at an hour yet distant for *their* sakes
Whose tender love, here faltering on the
   way   80
Of a diviner love, will be forgiven—
So may it set in peace, to rise again
For everlasting glory won by faith.

XIX.

GRACE DARLING.

[Composed 1843.—Published 1845.]

AMONG the dwellers in the silent fields
The natural heart is touched, and public
   way
And crowded street resound with ballad
   strains,
Inspired by ONE whose very name be-
   speaks
Favour divine, exalting human love;   5
Whom, since her birth on bleak North-
   umbria's coast,
Known unto few but prized as far as
   known,
A single Act endears to high and low
Through the whole land—to Manhood,
   moved in spite
Of the world's freezing cares—to generous
   Youth—   10

To Infancy, that lisps her praise—to Age
Whose eye reflects it, glistening through
   a tear
Of tremulous admiration. Such true fame
Awaits her *now;* but, verily, good deeds
Do no imperishable record find   15
Save in the rolls of heaven, where hers
   may live
A theme for angels, when they celebrate
The high-souled virtues which forgetful
   earth
Has witnessed. Oh! that winds and
   waves could speak
Of things which their united power called
   forth   20
From the pure depths of her humanity!
A Maiden gentle, yet, at duty's call,
Firm and unflinching, as the Lighthouse
   reared
On the Island-rock, her lonely dwelling-
   place;
Or like the invincible Rock itself that
   braves,   25
Age after age, the hostile elements,
As when it guarded holy Cuthbert's cell.

All night the storm had raged, nor
   ceased, nor paused,
When, as day broke, the Maid, through
   misty air,
Espies far off a Wreck, amid the surf,   30
Beating on one of those disastrous isles—
Half of a Vessel, half—no more; the rest
Had vanished, swallowed up with all
   that there
Had for the common safety striven in vain,
Or thither thronged for refuge. With
   quick glance   35
Daughter and Sire through optic-glass
   discern,
Clinging about the remnant of this Ship,
Creatures—how precious in the Maiden's
   sight!
For whom, belike, the old Man grieves
   still more
Than for their fellow-sufferers engulfed
Where every parting agony is hushed,   41
And hope and fear mix not in further strife.
"But courage, Father! let us out to sea—
A few may yet be saved." The Daughter's
   words,

Her earnest tone, and look beaming with
   faith, 45
Dispel the Father's doubts: nor do they
   lack
The noble-minded Mother's helping hand
To launch the boat; and with her blessing
   cheered,
And inwardly sustained by silent prayer,
Together they put forth, Father and Child!
Each grasps an oar, and struggling on
   they go— 51
Rivals in effort; and, alike intent
Here to elude and there surmount, they
   watch
The billows lengthening, mutually crossed
And shattered, and re-gathering their
   might; 55
As if the tumult, by the Almighty's will
Were, in the conscious sea, roused and
   prolonged
That woman's fortitude—so tried, so
   proved—
May brighten more and more !

              True to the mark,
They stem the current of that perilous
   gorge, 60
Their arms still strengthening with the
   strengthening heart,
Though danger, as the Wreck is neared,
   becomes
More imminent. Not unseen do they
   approach ;
And rapture, with varieties of fear
Incessantly conflicting, thrills the frames
Of those who, in that dauntless energy, 66
Foretaste deliverance; but the least
   perturbed
Can scarcely trust his eyes, when he
   perceives
That of the pair—tossed on the waves to
   bring
Hope to the hopeless, to the dying, life—
One is a Woman, a poor earthly sister, 71
Or, be the Visitant other than she seems,
A guardian Spirit sent from pitying
   Heaven,
In woman's shape. But why prolong the
   tale,
Casting weak words amid a host of
   thoughts 75

Armed to repel them? Every hazard
   faced
And difficulty mastered, with resolve
That no one breathing should be left to
   perish,
This last remainder of the crew are all
Placed in the little boat, then o'er the
   deep 80
Are safely borne, landed upon the beach,
And, in fulfilment of God's mercy, lodged
Within the sheltering Lighthouse.—
   Shout, ye Waves !
Send forth a song of triumph. Waves
   and Winds,
Exult in this deliverance wrought through
   faith 85
In Him whose Providence your rage hath
   served !
Ye screaming Sea-mews, in the concert
   join !
And would that some immortal Voice—a
   Voice
Fitly attuned to all that gratitude
Breathes out from floor or couch, through
   pallid lips 90
Of the survivors—to the clouds might
   bear—
Blended with praise of that parental love,
Beneath whose watchful eye the Maiden
   grew
Pious and pure, modest and yet so brave,
Though young so wise, though meek so
   resolute— 95
Might carry to the clouds and to the
   stars,
Yea, to celestial Choirs, GRACE DARLING's
   name !

XX.

THE RUSSIAN FUGITIVE.

PART I.

[Composed 1830.—Published 1835.]

ENOUGH of rose-bud lips, and eyes
   Like harebells bathed in dew,
Of cheek that with carnation vies,
   And veins of violet hue;
Earth wants not beauty that may scorn 5
   A likening to frail flowers;
Yea, to the stars, if they were born
   For seasons and for hours.

Through Moscow's gates, with gold un-
  barred,
  Stepped One at dead of night,   10
Whom such high beauty could not guard
  From meditated blight;
By stealth she passed, and fled as fast
  As doth the hunted fawn,
Nor stopped, till in the dappling east 15
  Appeared unwelcome dawn.

Seven days she lurked in brake and field,
Seven nights her course renewed,
Sustained by what her scrip might yield,
  Or berries of the wood;   20
At length, in darkness travelling on,
  When lowly doors were shut,
The haven of her hope she won,
  Her Foster-mother's hut.

"To put your love to dangerous proof 25
  I come," said she, "from far;
For I have left my Father's roof,
  In terror of the Czar."
No answer did the Matron give,
  No second look she cast,   30
But hung upon the Fugitive,
  Embracing and embraced.

She led the Lady to a seat
  Beside the glimmering fire,
Bathed duteously her wayworn feet, 35
  Prevented each desire:—
The cricket chirped, the house-dog dozed,
  And on that simple bed,
Where she in childhood had reposed,
  Now rests her weary head.   40

When she, whose couch had been the sod,
  Whose curtain pine or thorn,
Had breathed a sigh of thanks to God,
  Who comforts the forlorn;
While over her the Matron bent 45
  Sleep sealed her eyes, and stole
Feeling from limbs with travel spent,
  And trouble from the soul.

Refreshed, the Wanderer rose at morn,
  And soon again was dight 50
In those unworthy vestments worn
  Through long and perilous flight;
And "O beloved Nurse," she said,
  "My thanks with silent tears
Have unto Heaven and You been paid: 55
  Now listen to my fears!

"Have you forgot"—and here she smiled—
  "The babbling flatteries
You lavished on me when a child
  Disporting round your knees? 60
I was your lambkin, and your bird,
  Your star, your gem, your flower;
Light words, that were more lightly
    heard
  In many a cloudless hour!

"The blossom you so fondly praised 65
  Is come to bitter fruit;
A mighty One upon me gazed;
  I spurned his lawless suit,
And must be hidden from his wrath:
  You, Foster-father dear, 70
Will guide me in my forward path;
  I may not tarry here!

"I cannot bring to utter woe
  Your proved fidelity."—
"Dear child, sweet Mistress, say not so!
  For you we both would die." 76
"Nay, nay, I come with semblance
    feigned
  And cheek embrowned by art;
Yet, being inwardly unstained,
  With courage will depart." 80

"But whither would you, could you, flee?
  A poor Man's counsel take;
The Holy Virgin gives to me
  A thought for your dear sake;
Rest, shielded by our Lady's grace, 85
  And soon shall you be led
Forth to a safe abiding-place,
  Where never foot doth tread."

PART II.

The dwelling of this faithful pair
  In a straggling village stood, 90
For One who breathed unquiet air
  A dangerous neighbourhood;
But wide around lay forest ground
  With thickets rough and blind;
And pine-trees made a heavy shade 95
  Impervious to the wind.

And there, sequestered from the sight,
  Was spread a treacherous swamp,
On which the noonday sun shed light
  As from a lonely lamp; 100

And midway in the unsafe morass,
  A single Island rose
Of firm dry ground, with healthful grass
  Adorned, and shady boughs.

The Woodman knew, for such the craft
  This Russian vassal plied, 106
That never fowler's gun, nor shaft
  Of archer, there was tried;
A sanctuary seemed the spot
  From all intrusion free; 110
And there he planned an artful Cot
  For perfect secrecy.

With earnest pains unchecked by dread
  Of Power's far-stretching hand,
The bold good Man his labour sped 115
  At nature's pure command;
Heart-soothed, and busy as a wren,
  While, in a hollow nook,
She moulds her sight-eluding den
  Above a murmuring brook. 120

His task accomplished to his mind,
  The twain ere break of day
Creep forth, and through the forest wind
  Their solitary way;
Few words they speak, nor dare to slack
  Their pace from mile to mile, 126
Till they have crossed the quaking marsh,
  And reached the lonely Isle.

The sun above the pine-trees showed
  A bright and cheerful face; 130
And Ina looked for her abode,
  The promised hiding-place;
She sought in vain, the Woodman smiled;
  No threshold could be seen,
Nor roof, nor window;—all seemed wild
  As it had ever been. 136

Advancing, you might guess an hour,
  The front with such nice care
Is masked, "if house it be or bower,"
  But in they entered are; 140
As shaggy as were wall and roof
  With branches intertwined,
So smooth was all within, air-proof,
  And delicately lined:

And hearth was there, and maple dish,
  And cups in seemly rows, 146
And couch—all ready to a wish
  For nurture or repose;

And Heaven doth to her virtue grant
  That there she may abide 150
In solitude, with every want
  By cautious love supplied.

No queen before a shouting crowd
  Led on in bridal state,
E'er struggled with a heart so proud, 155
  Entering her palace gate;
Rejoiced to bid the world farewell,
  No saintly anchoress
E'er took possession of her cell
  With deeper thankfulness. 160

"Father of all, upon thy care
  And mercy am I thrown;
Be thou my safeguard!"—such her prayer
  When she was left alone,
Kneeling amid the wilderness 165
  When joy had passed away,
And smiles, fond efforts of distress
  To hide what they betray!

The prayer is heard, the Saints have seen,
  Diffused through form and face, 170
Resolves devotedly serene;
  That monumental grace
Of Faith, which doth all passions tame
  That Reason *should* control;
And shows in the untrembling frame 175
  A statue of the soul.

PART III.

'Tis sung in ancient minstrelsy
  That Phœbus wont to wear
The leaves of any pleasant tree
  Around his golden hair; 180
Till Daphne, desperate with pursuit
  Of his imperious love,
At her own prayer transformed, took root,
  A laurel in the grove.

Then did the Penitent adorn 185
  His brow with laurel green;
And 'mid his bright locks never shorn
  No meaner leaf was seen;
And poets sage, through every age,
  About their temples wound 190
The bay; and conquerors thanked the Gods,
  With laurel chaplets crowned.

Into the mists of fabling Time
  So far runs back the praise
Of Beauty, that disdains to climb   195
  Along forbidden ways;
That scorns temptation; power defies
  Where mutual love is not;
And to the tomb for rescue flies
  When life would be a blot.   200

To this fair Votaress a fate
  More mild doth Heaven ordain
Upon her Island desolate;
  And words, not breathed in vain,
Might tell what intercourse she found,
  Her silence to endear;   206
What birds she tamed, what flowers the
    ground
  Sent forth her peace to cheer.

To one mute Presence, above all,
  Her soothed affections clung,   210
A picture on the cabin wall
  By Russian usage hung—
The Mother-maid, whose countenance
    bright
  With love abridged the day;
And, communed with by taper-light, 215
  Chased spectral fears away.

And oft, as either Guardian came,
  The joy in that retreat
Might any common friendship shame,
  So high their hearts would beat;   220
And to the lone Recluse, whate'er
  They brought, each visiting
Was like the crowding of the year
  With a new burst of spring.

But when she of her Parents thought, 225
  The pang was hard to bear;
And, if with all things not enwrought,
  That trouble still is near.
Before her flight she had not dared
  Their constancy to prove,   230
Too much the heroic Daughter feared
  The weakness of their love.

Dark is the past to them, and dark
  The future still must be,
Till pitying Saints conduct her bark 235
  Into a safer sea—
Or gentle Nature close her eyes,
  And set her Spirit free

From the altar of this sacrifice,
  In vestal purity.   240

Yet, when above the forest-glooms
  The white swans southward passed,
High as the pitch of their swift plumes
  Her fancy rode the blast;
And bore her toward the fields of France,
  Her Father's native land,   246
To mingle in the rustic dance,
  The happiest of the band!

Of those belovèd fields she oft
  Had heard her Father tell   250
In phrase that now with echoes soft
  Haunted her lonely cell;
She saw the hereditary bowers,
  She heard the ancestral stream;
The Kremlin and its haughty towers 255
  Forgotten like a dream!

PART IV.

THE ever-changing Moon had traced
  Twelve times her monthly round,
When through the unfrequented Waste
  Was heard a startling sound;   260
A shout thrice sent from one who chased
  At speed a wounded deer,
Bounding through branches interlaced,
  And where the wood was clear.

The fainting creature took the marsh, 265
  And toward the Island fled,
While plovers screamed with tumult
    harsh
  Above his antlered head;
This, Ina saw; and, pale with fear,
  Shrunk to her citadel;   270
The desperate deer rushed on, and near
  The tangled covert fell.

Across the marsh, the game in view,
  The Hunter followed fast,
Nor paused, till o'er the stag he blew 275
  A death-proclaiming blast;
Then, resting on her upright mind,
  Came forth the Maid—"In me
Behold," she said, "a stricken Hind
  Pursued by destiny!   280

"From your deportment, Sir! I deem
  That you have worn a sword,
And will not hold in light esteem
  A suffering woman's word;

There is my covert, there perchance 285
  I might have lain concealed,
My fortunes hid, my countenance
  Not even to you revealed.

"Tears might be shed, and I might pray,
  Crouching and terrified, 290
That what has been unveiled to-day,
  You would in mystery hide;
But I will not defile with dust
  The knee that bends to adore
The God in heaven;—attend, be just; 295
  This ask I, and no more!

"I speak not of the winter's cold
  For summer's heat exchanged,
While I have lodged in this rough hold,
  From social life estranged; 300
Nor yet of trouble and alarms:
  High Heaven is my defence;
And every season has soft arms
  For injured Innocence.

"From Moscow to the Wilderness 305
  It was my choice to come,
Lest virtue should be harbourless,
  And honour want a home;
And happy were I, if the Czar
  Retain his lawless will, 310
To end life here like this poor deer,
  Or a lamb on a green hill."

"Are you the Maid," the Stranger cried,
  "From Gallic parents sprung,
Whose vanishing was rumoured wide, 315
  Sad theme for every tongue;
Who foiled an Emperor's eager quest?
  You, Lady, forced to wear
These rude habiliments, and rest
  Your head in this dark lair!" 320

But wonder, pity, soon were quelled;
  And in her face and mien
The soul's pure brightness he beheld
  Without a veil between:
He loved, he hoped,—a holy flame 325
  Kindled 'mid rapturous tears;
The passion of a moment came
  As on the wings of years.

"Such bounty is no gift of chance,"
  Exclaimed he: "righteous Heaven, 330

Preparing your deliverance,
  To me the charge hath given.
The Czar full oft in words and deeds
  Is stormy and self-willed;
But, when the Lady Catherine pleads, 335
  His violence is stilled.

"Leave open to my wish the course,
  And I to her will go;
From that humane and heavenly source
  Good, only good, can flow." 340
Faint sanction given, the Cavalier
  Was eager to depart,
Though question followed question, dear
  To the Maiden's filial heart.

Light was his step,—his hopes, more light, 345
  Kept pace with his desires;
And the fifth morning gave him sight
  Of Moscow's glittering spires.
He sued:—heart-smitten by the wrong,
  To the lorn Fugitive 350
The Emperor sent a pledge as strong
  As sovereign power could give.

O more than mighty change! If e'er
  Amazement rose to pain,
And joy's excess produced a fear 355
  Of something void and vain;
'Twas when the Parents, who had mourned
  So long the lost as dead,
Beheld their only Child returned
  The household floor to tread. 360

Soon gratitude gave way to love
  Within the Maiden's breast;
Delivered and Deliverer move
  In bridal garments drest;
Meek Catherine had her own reward; 365
  The Czar bestowed a dower;
And universal Moscow shared
  The triumph of that hour.

Flowers strewed the ground; the nuptial feast
  Was held with costly state; 370
And there, 'mid many a noble guest,
  The Foster-parents sate;
Encouraged by the imperial eye,
  They shrank not into shade;
Great was their bliss, the honour high 375
  To them and nature paid!

INSCRIPTIONS.

I.

IN THE GROUNDS OF COLEORTON, THE
SEAT OF SIR GEORGE BEAUMONT,
BART., LEICESTERSHIRE.

[Composed 1808.—Published 1815.]

THE embowering rose, the acacia, and the
   pine,
Will not unwillingly their place resign ;
If but the Cedar thrive that near them
   stands,
Planted by Beaumont's and by Words-
   worth's hands.
One wooed the silent Art with studious
   pains :   5
These groves have heard the Other's pen-
   sive strains ;
Devoted thus, their spirits did unite
By interchange of knowledge and delight.
May Nature's kindliest powers sustain
   the Tree,
And Love protect it from all injury !   10
And when its potent branches, wide out-
   thrown,
Darken the brow of this memorial Stone,
Here may some Painter sit in future days,
Some future Poet meditate his lays ;   14
Not mindless of that distant age renowned
When Inspiration hovered o'er this ground,
The haunt of him who sang how spear and
   shield
In civil conflict met on Bosworth-field ;
And of that famous Youth, full soon
   removed
From earth, perhaps by Shakespeare's
   self approved,   20
Fletcher's Associate, Jonson's Friend be-
   loved.

II.

IN A GARDEN OF THE SAME.

[Composed 1811 (?).—Published 1815.]

OFT is the medal faithful to its trust
When temples, columns, towers, are laid
   in dust ;
And 'tis a common ordinance of fate
That things obscure and small outlive the
   great :
Hence, when yon mansion and the flowery
   trim   5
Of this fair garden, and its alleys dim,
And all its stately trees, are passed away,
This little Niche, unconscious of decay,
Perchance may still survive. And be it
   known
That it was scooped within the living
   stone,—   10
Not by the sluggish and ungrateful pains
Of labourer plodding for his daily gains,
But by an industry that wrought in love ;
With help from female hands, that proudly
   strove
To aid the work, what time these walks
   and bowers   15
Were shaped to cheer dark winter's lonely
   hours.

III.

WRITTEN AT THE REQUEST OF SIR
GEORGE BEAUMONT, BART., AND IN
HIS NAME, FOR AN URN, PLACED BY
HIM AT THE TERMINATION OF A
NEWLY-PLANTED AVENUE, IN THE
SAME GROUNDS.

[Composed November, 1811.—Published 1815.]

YE Lime-trees, ranged before this hal-
   lowed Urn,
Shoot forth with lively power at Spring's
   return ;
And be not slow a stately growth to rear
Of pillars, branching off from year to year,
Till they have learned to frame a dark-
   some aisle ;—   5
That may recall to mind that awful Pile
Where Reynolds, 'mid our country's
   noblest dead,
In the last sanctity of fame is laid.

—There, though by right the excelling
    Painter sleep
Where Death and Glory a joint sabbath
    keep,   10
Yet not the less his Spirit would hold dear
Self - hidden praise, and Friendship's
    private tear:
Hence, on my patrimonial grounds, have I
Raised this frail tribute to his memory;
From youth a zealous follower of the Art
That he professed; attached to him in
    heart;   16
Admiring, loving, and with grief and pride
Feeling what England lost when Reynolds
    died.

IV.

FOR A SEAT IN THE GROVES OF COLEORTON.

[Composed November 19, 1811.—Published 1815.]

BENEATH yon eastern ridge, the craggy
    bound,
Rugged and high, of Charnwood's forest
    ground,
Stand yet, but, Stranger! hidden from
    thy view,
The ivied Ruins of forlorn GRACE DIEU;
Erst a religious House, which day and night
With hymns resounded, and the chanted
    rite: 6
And when those rites had ceased, the Spot
    gave birth
To honourable Men of various worth:
There, on the margin of a streamlet wild,
Did Francis Beaumont sport, an eager
    child;   10
There, under shadow of the neighbouring
    rocks,
Sang youthful tales of shepherds and
    their flocks;
Unconscious prelude to heroic themes,
Heart-breaking tears, and melancholy
    dreams
Of slighted love, and scorn, and jealous rage,
With which his genius shook the buskined
    stage.   16
Communities are lost, and Empires die,
And things of holy use unhallowed lie;
They perish;—but the Intellect can raise,
From airy words alone, a Pile that ne'er
    decays.   20

V.

WRITTEN WITH A PENCIL UPON A STONE IN THE WALL OF THE HOUSE (AN OUT-HOUSE), ON THE ISLAND AT GRASMERE.

[Composed 1800.—Published 1800.]

RUDE is this Edifice, and Thou hast seen
Buildings, albeit rude, that have main-
    tained
Proportions more harmonious, and ap-
    proached
To closer fellowship with ideal grace.
But take it in good part:—alas! the poor
Vitruvius of our village had no help   6
From the great City; never, upon leaves
Of red Morocco folio saw displayed,
In long succession, pre-existing ghosts
Of Beauties yet unborn—the rustic Lodge
Antique, and Cottage with verandah
    graced,   11
Nor lacking, for fit company, alcove,
Green-house, shell-grot, and moss-lined
    hermitage.
Thou see'st a homely Pile, yet to these
    walls
The heifer comes in the snow-storm, and
    here   15
The new-dropped lamb finds shelter from
    the wind.
And hither does one Poet sometimes row
His pinnace, a small vagrant barge, up-
    piled
With plenteous store of heath and withered
    fern,
(A lading which he with his sickle cuts, 20
Among the mountains) and beneath this
    roof
He makes his summer couch, and here at
    noon
Spreads out his limbs, while, yet unshorn,
    the Sheep,
Panting beneath the burthen of their wool,
Lie round him, even as if they were a part
Of his own Household: nor, while from
    his bed   26
He looks, through the open door-place,
    toward the lake
And to the stirring breezes, does he want
Creations lovely as the work of sleep—
Fair sights, and visions of romantic joy!

VI.

WRITTEN WITH A SLATE PENCIL ON A STONE, ON THE SIDE OF THE MOUNTAIN OF BLACK COMB.

[Composed 1813.—Published 1815.]

STAY, bold Adventurer; rest awhile thy limbs
On this commodious Seat! for much remains
Of hard ascent before thou reach the top
Of this huge Eminence,—from blackness named,
And, to far-travelled storms of sea and land,   5
A favourite spot of tournament and war!
But thee may no such boisterous visitants
Molest; may gentle breezes fan thy brow;
And neither cloud conceal, nor misty air
Bedim, the grand terraqueous spectacle,   10
From centre to circumference, unveiled!
Know, if thou grudge not to prolong thy rest,
That on the summit whither thou art bound,
A geographic Labourer pitched his tent,
With books supplied and instruments of art,   15
To measure height and distance; lonely task,
Week after week pursued!—To him was given
Full many a glimpse (but sparingly bestowed
On timid man) of Nature's processes
Upon the exalted hills. He made report
That once, while there he plied his studious work   21
Within that canvass Dwelling, colours, lines,
And the whole surface of the out-spread map,
Became invisible: for all around
Had darkness fallen—unthreatened, unproclaimed—   25
As if the golden day itself had been
Extinguished in a moment; total gloom,
In which he sate alone, with unclosed eyes,
Upon the blinded mountain's silent top!

VII.

WRITTEN WITH A SLATE PENCIL UPON A STONE, THE LARGEST OF A HEAP LYING NEAR A DESERTED QUARRY, UPON ONE OF THE ISLANDS AT RYDAL.

[Composed 1800.—Published 1800.]

STRANGER! this hillock of mis-shapen stones
Is not a Ruin spared or made by time,
Nor, as perchance thou rashly deem'st, the Cairn
Of some old British Chief: 'tis nothing more
Than the rude embryo of a little Dome   5
Or Pleasure-house, once destined to be built
Among the birch-trees of this rocky isle.
But, as it chanced, Sir William having learned
That from the shore a full-grown man might wade,   9
And make himself a freeman of this spot
At any hour he chose, the prudent Knight
Desisted, and the quarry and the mound
Are monuments of his unfinished task.
The block on which these lines are traced, perhaps,
Was once selected as the corner-stone   15
Of that intended Pile, which would have been
Some quaint odd plaything of elaborate skill,
So that, I guess, the linnet and the thrush,
And other little builders who dwell here,
Had wondered at the work. But blame him not,   20
For old Sir William was a gentle Knight,
Bred in this vale, to which he appertained
With all his ancestry. Then peace to him,
And for the outrage which he had devised
Entire forgiveness!—But if thou art one   25
On fire with thy impatience to become
An inmate of these mountains,—if, disturbed
By beautiful conceptions, thou hast hewn
Out of the quiet rock the elements
Of thy trim Mansion destined soon to blaze   30

In snow-white splendour,—think again;
  and, taught
By old Sir William and his quarry, leave
Thy fragments to the bramble and the
  rose;
There let the vernal slow-worm sun him-
  self,
And let the redbreast hop from stone to
  stone. 35

VIII.

[Composed 1830 (? 1831).—Published 1835.]

IN these fair vales hath many a Tree
  At Wordsworth's suit been spared;
And from the builder's hand this Stone,
For some rude beauty of its own,
  Was rescued by the Bard: 5
So let it rest; and time will come
  When here the tender-hearted
May heave a gentle sigh for him,
  As one of the departed.

IX.

[Composed 1826.—Published 1835.]

THE massy Ways, carried across these
  heights
By Roman perseverance, are destroyed,
Or hidden under ground, like sleeping
  worms.
How venture then to hope that Time will
  spare
This humble Walk? Yet on the moun-
  tain's side 5
A POET's hand first shaped it; and the
  steps
Of that same Bard—repeated to and fro
At morn, at noon, and under moonlight
  skies
Through the vicissitudes of many a year—
Forbade the weeds to creep o'er its grey
  line. 10
No longer, scattering to the heedless winds
The vocal raptures of fresh poesy,
Shall he frequent these precincts; locked
  no more
In earnest converse with belovèd Friends,
Here will he gather stores of ready bliss, 15
As from the beds and borders of a garden
Choice flowers are gathered! But, if
  Power may spring

Out of a farewell yearning—favoured more
Than kindred wishes mated suitably
With vain regrets—the Exile would con-
  sign 20
This Walk, his loved possession, to the
  care
Of those pure Minds that reverence the
  Muse.

X.

INSCRIPTIONS SUPPOSED TO BE FOUND
IN AND NEAR A HERMIT'S CELL.

[This group (X.—XIV.) was composed 1818.—Pub-
lished 1820.]

I.

HOPES what are they?—Beads of morning
Strung on slender blades of grass;
Or a spider's web adorning
In a strait and treacherous pass.

What are fears but voices airy? 5
Whispering harm where harm is not;
And deluding the unwary
Till the fatal bolt is shot!

What is glory?—in the socket
See how dying tapers fare! 10
What is pride?—a whizzing rocket
That would emulate a star.

What is friendship?—do not trust her,
Nor the vows which she has made;
Diamonds dart their brightest lustre 15
From a palsy-shaken head.

What is truth?—a staff rejected;
Duty?—an unwelcome clog;
Joy?—a moon by fits reflected
In a swamp or watery bog; 20

Bright, as if through ether steering,
To the Traveller's eye it shone:
He hath hailed it re-appearing—
And as quickly it is gone;

Such is Joy—as quickly hidden, 25
Or mis-shapen to the sight,
And by sullen weeds forbidden
To resume its native light.

What is youth?—a dancing billow,
(Winds behind, and rocks before!) 30
Age?—a drooping, tottering willow
On a flat and lazy shore.

What is peace?—when pain is over,
And love ceases to rebel,
Let the last faint sigh discover   35
That precedes the passing-knell!

XI.
INSCRIBED UPON A ROCK.
II.

PAUSE, Traveller! whosoe'er thou be
Whom chance may lead to this retreat,
Where silence yields reluctantly
Even to the fleecy straggler's bleat;

Give voice to what my hand shall trace, 5
And fear not lest an idle sound
Of words unsuited to the place
Disturb its solitude profound.

I saw this Rock, while vernal air
Blew softly o'er the russet heath,   10
Uphold a Monument as fair
As church or abbey furnisheth.

Unsullied did it meet the day,
Like marble, white, like ether, pure;
As if, beneath, some hero lay,   15
Honoured with costliest sepulture.

My fancy kindled as I gazed;
And, even as the sun shone forth,
The flattered structure glistened, blazed,
And seemed the proudest thing on earth.

But frost had reared the gorgeous Pile 21
Unsound as those which Fortune builds—
To undermine with secret guile,
Sapped by the very beam that gilds.

And, while I gazed, with sudden shock 25
Fell the whole Fabric to the ground;
And naked left this dripping Rock,
With shapeless ruin spread around!

XII.
III.

HAST thou seen, with flash incessant,
Bubbles gliding under ice,
Bodied forth and evanescent,
No one knows by what device?

Such are thoughts!—A wind-swept
          meadow   5
Mimicking a troubled sea,
Such is life; and death a shadow
From the rock eternity!

XIII.
NEAR THE SPRING OF THE HERMITAGE.
IV.

TROUBLED long with warring notions
Long impatient of Thy rod,
I resign my soul's emotions
Unto Thee, mysterious God!

What avails the kindly shelter   5
Yielded by this craggy rent,
If my spirit toss and welter
On the waves of discontent?

Parching Summer hath no warrant
To consume this crystal Well;   10
Rains, that make each rill a torrent,
Neither sully it nor swell.

Thus, dishonouring not her station,
Would my Life present to Thee,
Gracious God, the pure oblation   15
Of divine tranquillity!

XIV.
V.

NOT seldom, clad in radiant vest,
Deceitfully goes forth the Morn;
Not seldom Evening in the west
Sinks smilingly forsworn.

The smoothest seas will sometimes prove,
To the confiding Bark, untrue;   6
And, if she trust the stars above
They can be treacherous too.

The umbrageous Oak, in pomp outspread,
Full oft, when storms the welkin rend, 10
Draws lightning down upon the head
It promised to defend.

But Thou art true, incarnate Lord,
Who didst vouchsafe for man to die;
Thy smile is sure, Thy plighted word   15
No change can falsify!

I bent before Thy gracious throne,
And asked for peace on suppliant knee;
And peace was given,—nor peace alone,
But faith sublimed to ecstasy!   20

XV.

FOR THE SPOT WHERE THE HERMITAGE
STOOD ON ST. HERBERT'S ISLAND,
DERWENT-WATER.

[Composed 1800.—Published 1800.]

IF thou in the dear love of some one
    Friend
Hast been so happy that thou know'st
    what thoughts
Will sometimes in the happiness of love
Make the heart sink, then wilt thou
    reverence
This quiet spot; and, Stranger! not un-
    moved   5
Wilt thou behold this shapeless heap of
    stones,
The desolate ruins of St. Herbert's Cell.
Here stood his threshold; here was spread
    the roof
That sheltered him, a self-secluded Man,
After long exercise in social cares   10
And offices humane, intent to adore
The Deity, with undistracted mind,
And meditate on everlasting things,
In utter solitude.—But he had left
A Fellow-labourer, whom the good Man
    loved   15
As his own soul. And, when with eye
    upraised
To heaven he knelt before the crucifix,
While o'er the lake the cataract of Lo-
    dore
Pealed to his orisons, and when he paced
Along the beach of this small isle and
    thought   20
Of his Companion, he would pray that
    both
(Now that their earthly duties were ful-
    filled)
Might die in the same moment. Nor in
    vain
So prayed he:—as our chronicles report,
Though here the Hermit numbered his
    last day   25
Far from St. Cuthbert his belovèd Friend,
Those holy Men both died in the same
    hour.

XVI.

ON THE BANKS OF A ROCKY STREAM.

[Composed ?.—Published 1850.]

BEHOLD an emblem of our human mind
Crowded with thoughts that need a settled
    home,
Yet, like to eddying balls of foam
Within this whirlpool, they each other
    chase
Round and round, and neither find   5
An outlet nor a resting-place!
Stranger, if such disquietude be thine,
Fall on thy knees and sue for help divine.

SELECTIONS FROM CHAUCER.

MODERNISED.

———◆◆———

I.

THE PRIORESS' TALE.

"Call up him who left half told
The story of Cambuscan bold."

In the following Poem no further deviation from the original has been made than was necessary for the fluent reading and instant understanding of the Author: so much, however, is the language altered since Chaucer's time, especially in pronunciation, that much was to be removed, and its place supplied with as little incongruity as possible. The ancient accent has been retained in a few conjunctions, as *alsò* and *alwày*, from a conviction that such sprinklings of antiquity would be admitted, by persons of taste, to have a graceful accordance with the subject. The fierce bigotry of the Prioress forms a fine background for her tender-hearted sympathies with the Mother and Child; and the mode in which the story is told amply atones for the extravagance of the miracle.

[Written 1801.—Published 1820.]

I.

"O LORD, our Lord! how wondrously,"
    (quoth she)
"Thy name in this large world is spread
    abroad!
For not alone by men of dignity
Thy worship is performed and precious
    laud;
But by the mouths of children, gracious
    God!   5
Thy goodness is set forth; they when they
    lie
Upon the breast Thy name do glorify.

II.

"Wherefore in praise, the worthiest that
    I may,
Jesu! of Thee, and the white Lily-flower
Which did Thee bear, and is a Maid for
    aye,   10
To tell a story I will use my power;
Not that I may increase her honour's
    dower,

For she herself is honour, and the root
Of goodness, next her Son, our soul's best
    boot.

III.

"O Mother Maid! O Maid and Mother
    free!   15
O bush unburnt! burning in Moses'
    sight!
That down didst ravish from the Deity,
Through humbleness, the Spirit that did
    alight
Upon thy heart, whence, through that
    glory's might,
Conceivèd was the Father's sapience,   20
Help me to tell it in thy reverence!

IV.

"Lady! thy goodness, thy magnificence,
Thy virtue, and thy great humility,
Surpass all science and all utterance;
For sometimes, Lady! ere men pray to
    thee   25
Thou goest before in thy benignity,

The light to us vouchsafing of thy prayer,
To be our guide unto thy Son so dear.

V.

"My knowledge is so weak, O blissful
        Queen!
To tell abroad thy mighty worthiness, 30
That I the weight of it may not sustain;
But as a child of twelvemonths old or less,
That laboureth his language to express,
Even so fare I; and therefore, I thee pray,
Guide thou my song which I of thee shall
        say.   35

VI.

"There was in Asia, in a mighty town,
'Mong Christian folk, a street where Jews
        might be,
Assigned to them and given them for
        their own
By a great Lord, for gain and usury,
Hateful to Christ and to His company; 40
And through this street who list might
        ride and wend;
Free was it, and unbarred at either end.

VII.

"A little school of Christian people stood
Down at the farther end, in which there
        were
A nest of children come of Christian
        blood,   45
That learnèd in that school from year to
        year
Such sort of doctrine as men usèd there,
That is to say, to sing and read alsò,
As little children in their childhood do.

VIII.

"Among these children was a Widow's
        son,   50
A little scholar[1], scarcely seven years old,
Who day by day unto this school hath
        gone,
And eke, when he the image did behold
Of Jesu's Mother, as he had been told,
This Child was wont to kneel adown and
        say   55
Ave Marie, as he goeth by the way.

IX.

"This Widow thus her little Son hath
        taught
Our blissful Lady, Jesu's Mother dear,
To worship aye, and he forgat it not;
For simple[2] infant hath a ready ear.   60
Sweet is the holiness of youth: and hence,
Calling to mind this matter when I may,
Saint Nicholas in my presence standeth
        aye,
For he so young to Christ did reverence.

X.

"This little Child, while in the school he
        sate   65
His Primer conning with an earnest
        cheer,
The whilst the rest their anthem-book
        repeat
The *Alma Redemptoris* did he hear;
And as he durst he drew him near and
        near,
And hearkened to the words and to the
        note,   70
Till the first verse he learned it all by rote.

XI.

"This Latin knew he nothing what it
        said,
For he too tender was of age to know;
But to his comrade he repaired, and
        prayed
That he the meaning of this song would
        show,   75
And unto him declare why men sing so;
This oftentimes, that he might be at ease,
This child did him beseech on his bare
        knees.

XII.

"His Schoolfellow, who elder was than he,
Answered him thus:—'This song, I have
        heard say,   80
Was fashioned for our blissful Lady free;
Her to salute, and also her to pray
To be our help upon our dying day:
If there is more in this, I know it not;
Song do I learn,—small grammar I have
        got.'   85

---

[1] *Clergeon* (Chaucer); i.e. chorister.—Ed.

[2] *Sely* (Chaucer); i.e. happy. Line 61 was in-
terpolated by Wordsworth.—Ed.

XIII.

"'And is this song fashioned in rever-
ence
Of Jesu's Mother?' said this Innocent;
'Now, certès, I will use my diligence
To con it all ere Christmas-tide be spent;
Although I for my Primer shall be shent,
And shall be beaten three times in an
hour,   91
Our Lady I will praise with all my power.'

XIV.

"His Schoolfellow, whom he had so be-
sought,
As they went homeward taught him
privily
And then he sang it well and fearlessly,
From word to word according to the
note: 96
Twice in a day it passèd through his
throat;
Homeward and schoolward whensoe'er he
went,
On Jesu's Mother fixed was his intent.

XV.

"Through all the Jewry (this before
said I)   100
This little Child, as he came to and fro,
Full merrily then would he sing and cry,
O *Alma Redemptoris!* high and low:
The sweetness of Christ's Mother piercèd
so
His heart, that her to praise, to her to
pray,   105
He cannot stop his singing by the way.

XVI.

"The Serpent, Satan, our first foe, that
hath
His wasp's nest in Jew's heart, upswelled
—'O woe,
O Hebrew people!' said he in his wrath,
'Is it an honest thing? Shall this be so?
That such a Boy where'er he lists shall go
In your despite, and sing his hymns and
saws,
Which is against the reverence of our
laws!'

XVII.

"From that day forward have the Jews
conspired   114
Out of the world this Innocent to chase;
And to this end a Homicide they hired,
That in an alley had a privy place,
And, as the Child 'gan to the school to
pace,
This cruel Jew him seized, and held him
fast
And cut his throat, and in a pit him
cast.   120

XVIII.

"I say that him into a pit they threw,
A loathsome pit, whence noisome scents
exhale;
O cursèd folk! away, ye Herods new!
What may your ill intentions you avail?
Murder will out; certès it will not fail;
Know, that the honour of high God may
spread,   126
The blood cries out on your accursèd deed.

XIX.

"O Martyr 'stablished in virginity!
Now may'st thou sing for aye before the
throne,
Following the Lamb celestial," quoth
she,   130
"Of which the great Evangelist, Saint
John,
In Patmos wrote, who saith of them that
go
Before the Lamb singing continually,
That never fleshly woman they did know.

XX.

"Now this poor Widow waiteth all that
night   135
After her little Child, and he came not;
For which, by earliest glimpse of morning
light,
With face all pale with dread and busy
thought,
She at the School and elsewhere him hath
sought,
Until thus far she learned, that he had
been   140
In the Jews' street, and there he last was
seen.

XXI.

"With Mother's pity in her breast en-
    closed
She goeth, as she were half out of her
    mind,
To every place wherein she hath supposed
By likelihood her little Son to find;   145
And ever on Christ's Mother meek and
    kind
She cried, till to the Jewry she was
    brought,
And him among the accursèd Jews she
    sought.

XXII.

"She asketh, and she piteously doth pray
To every Jew that dwelleth in that place
To tell her if her child had passed that
    way;   151
They all said—Nay; but Jesu of His grace
Gave to her thought, that in a little
    space
She for her Son in that same spot did
    cry
Where he was cast into a pit hard by. 155

XXIII.

"O Thou great God that dost perform
    Thy laud
By mouths of Innocents, lo! here Thy
    might;
This gem of chastity, this emerald,
And eke of martyrdom this ruby bright,
There, where with mangled throat he lay
    upright,   160
The *Alma Redemptoris* 'gan to sing
So loud, that with his voice the place did
    ring.

XXIV.

"The Christian folk that through the
    Jewry went
Come to the spot in wonder at the thing;
And hastily they for the Provost sent; 165
Immediately he came, not tarrying,
And praiseth Christ that is our heavenly
    King,
And eke His Mother, honour of Mankind:
Which done, he bade that they the Jews
    should bind.

XXV.

"This Child with piteous lamentation
    then   170
Was taken up, singing his song alwày;
And with procession great and pomp of
    men
To the next Abbey him they bare away;
His Mother swooning by the body lay:
And scarcely could the people that were
    near   175
Remove this second Rachel from the
    bier.

XXVI.

"Torment and shameful death to every
    one
This Provost doth for those bad Jews
    prepare
That of this murder wist, and that anon:
Such wickedness his judgments cannot
    spare;   180
Who will do evil, evil shall he bear;
Them therefore with wild horses did he
    draw,
And after that he hung them by the law.

XXVII.

"Upon his bier this Innocent doth lie
Before the altar while the Mass doth
    last: 185
The Abbot with his convent's company
Then sped themselves to bury him full
    fast;
And, when they holy water on him cast,
Yet spake this Child when sprinkled was
    the water;
And sang, O *Alma Redemptoris Mater!* 190

XXVIII.

"This Abbot, for he was a holy man,
As all Monks are, or surely ought to be,
In supplication to the Child began
Thus saying, 'O dear Child! I summon
    thee
In virtue of the holy Trinity   195
Tell me the cause why thou dost sing this
    hymn,
Since that thy throat is cut, as it doth
    seem.'

XXIX.

"'My throat is cut unto the bone, I
trow,'
Said this young Child, 'and by the law of
kind
I should have died, yea many hours ago;
But Jesus Christ, as in the books ye
find,   201
Will that His glory last, and be in mind;
And, for the worship of His Mother dear,
Yet may I sing, O *Alma!* loud and clear.

XXX.

"'This well of mercy, Jesu's Mother
sweet,   205
After my knowledge I have loved alwây;
And in the hour when I my death did
meet
To me she came, and thus to me did say,
'Thou in thy dying sing this holy lay,'
As ye have heard; and soon as I had
sung   210
Methought she laid a grain upon my
tongue.

XXXI.

"'Wherefore I sing, nor can from song
refrain,
In honour of that blissful Maiden free,
Till from my tongue off-taken is the grain;
And after that thus said she unto me; 215
'My little Child, then will I come for
thee
Soon as the grain from off thy tongue they
take:
Be not dismayed, I will not thee forsake!'

XXXII.

"This holy Monk, this Abbot—him
mean I,
Touched then his tongue, and took away
the grain;   220
And he gave up the ghost full peacefully;
And, when the Abbot had this wonder
seen,
His salt tears trickled down like showers
of rain;
And on his face he dropped upon the
ground,
And still he lay as if he had been bound.

XXXIII.

"Eke the whole Convent on the pave-
ment lay,   226
Weeping and praising Jesu's Mother
dear;
And after that they rose, and took their
way,
And lifted up this Martyr from the bier,
And in a tomb of precious marble clear 230
Enclosed his uncorrupted body sweet[1].—
Where'er he be, God grant us him to
meet!

XXXIV.

"Young Hew of Lincoln! in like sort laid
low
By cursèd Jews—thing well and widely
known,
For it was done a little while ago—   235
Pray also thou for us, while here we tarry
Weak sinful folk, that God, with pitying
eye,
In mercy would His mercy multiply
On us, for reverence of His Mother Mary!"

II.

THE CUCKOO AND THE NIGHTIN-
GALE.

[Written 1801.—Published 1841 (R. H. Horne's
*The Poems of Geoffrey Chaucer, Modern-
ised*); vol. of 1842.]

I.

THE God of Love—*ah, benedicite!*
How mighty and how great a Lord is he!
For he of low hearts can make high, of high
He can make low, and unto death bring
nigh;
And hard hearts he can make them kind
and free.   5

II.

Within a little time, as hath been found,
He can make sick folk whole and fresh
and sound;
Them who are whole in body and in
mind,
He can make sick,—bind can he and un-
bind
All that he will have bound, or have un-
bound.   10

---

[1] *Enclosèd they his little body sweet* (Chaucer)
—ED.

III.

To tell his might my wit may not suffice;
Foolish men he can make them out of
    wise;—
For he may do all that he will devise;
Loose livers he can make abate their
    vice,
And proud hearts can make tremble in
    a trice.   15

IV.

In brief, the whole of what he will, he
    may;
Against him dare not any wight say
    nay;
To humble or afflict whome'er he will,
To gladden or to grieve, he hath like
    skill;
But most his might he sheds on the eve
    of May.   20

V.

For every true heart, gentle heart and
    free,
That with him is, or thinketh so to be,
Now against May shall have some stir-
    ring—whether
To joy, or be it to some mourning; never
At other time, methinks, in like degree. 25

VI.

For now when they may hear the small
    birds' song,
And see the budding leaves the branches
    throng,
This unto their rememberance doth bring
All kinds of pleasure mix'd with sorrow-
    ing;
And longing of sweet thoughts that ever
    long.   30

VII.

And of that longing heaviness doth come,
Whence oft great sickness grows of heart
    and home;
Sick are they all for lack of their desire;
And thus in May their hearts are set on
    fire,
So that they burn forth in great martyr-
    dom.   35

VIII.

In sooth, I speak from feeling, what
    though now
Old am I, and to genial pleasure slow;
Yet have I felt of sickness through the
    May,
Both hot and cold, and heart-aches every
    day,—
How hard, alas! to bear, I only know. 40

IX.

Such shaking doth the fever in me keep
Through all this May that I have little
    sleep;
And also 'tis not likely unto me,
That any living heart should sleepy be
In which Love's dart its fiery point doth
    steep.   45

X.

But tossing lately on a sleepless bed,
I of a token thought which Lovers heed;
How among them it was a common tale,
That it was good to hear the Nightingale,
Ere the vile Cuckoo's note be utterèd. 50

XI.

And then I thought anon as it was day,
I gladly would go somewhere to essay
If I perchance a Nightingale might hear,
For yet had I heard none, of all that year,
And it was then the third night of the May.

XII.

And soon as I a glimpse of day espied, 56
No longer would I in my bed abide,
But straightway to a wood that was hard by,
Forth did I go, alone and fearlessly,
And held the pathway down by a brook-
    side;   60

XIII.

Till to a lawn I came all white and green,
I in so fair a one had never been.
The ground was green, with daisy powder-
    ed over;
Tall were the flowers, the grove a lofty
    cover [1],
All green and white; and nothing else was
    seen.   65

---

[1] *The flowers and the grass alike all high*
(Chaucer); i.e. grass and daisies being of equal
height.—Ed.

XIV.

There sate I down among the fair fresh
  flowers,
And saw the birds come tripping from
  their bowers,
Where they had rested them all night;
  and they,
Who were so joyful at the light of day,
Began to honour May with all their
  powers.   70

XV.

Well did they know that service all by
  rote,
And there was many and many a lovely
  note,
Some, singing loud, as if they had com-
  plained;
Some with their notes another manner
  feigned;
And some did sing all out with the full
  throat.   75

XVI.

They pruned themselves, and made them-
  selves right gay,
Dancing and leaping light upon the spray;
And ever two and two together were,
The same as they had chosen for the year,
Upon Saint Valentine's returning day. 80

XVII.

Meanwhile the stream, whose bank I sate
  upon,
Was making such a noise as it ran on
Accordant to the sweet Birds' harmony;
Methought that it was the best melody
Which ever to man's ear a passage won. 85

XVIII.

And for delight, but how I never wot,
I in a slumber and a swoon was caught,
Not all asleep and yet not waking wholly;
And as I lay, the Cuckoo, bird unholy, 89
Broke silence, or I heard him in my
  thought.

XIX.

And that was right upon a tree fast by,
And who was then ill satisfied but I?

Now, God, quoth I, that died upon the
  rood,
From thee and thy base throat, keep all
  that's good,
Full little joy have I now of thy cry.   95

XX.

And, as I with the Cuckoo thus 'gan
  chide,
In the next bush that was me fast beside,
I heard the lusty Nightingale so sing,
That her clear voice made a loud rioting,
Echoing thorough all the green wood
  wide.   100

XXI.

Ah! good sweet Nightingale! for my
  heart's cheer,
Hence hast thou stayed a little while too
  long;
For we have had the sorry Cuckoo here,
And she hath been before thee with her
  song;
Evil light on her! she hath done me
  wrong.   105

XXII.

But hear you now a wondrous thing, I
  pray;
As long as in that swooning-fit I lay,
Methought I wist right well what these
  birds meant,
And had good knowing both of their
  intent,
And of their speech, and all that they
  would say.   110

XXIII.

The Nightingale thus in my hearing
  spake:—
Good Cuckoo, seek some other bush or
  brake,
And, prithee, let us that can sing dwell
  here;
For every wight eschews thy song to hear,
Such uncouth singing verily dost thou
  make.   115

XXIV.

What! quoth she then, what is't that ails
  thee now?
It seems to me I sing as well as thou;

For mine's a song that is both true and
    plain,—
Although I cannot quaver so in vain
As thou dost in thy throat, I wot not
    how.   120

XXV.

All men may understanding have of me,
But, Nightingale, so may they not of
    thee;
For thou hast many a foolish and quaint
    cry:—
Thou say'st OSEE, OSEE, then how may I
Have knowledge, I thee pray, what this
    may be?   125

XXVI.

Ah, fool! quoth she, wist thou not what
    it is?
Oft as I say OSEE, OSEE, I wis,
Then mean I, that I should be wonderous
    fain
That shamefully they one and all were
    slain,
Whoever against Love mean aught amiss.

XXVII.

And also would I that they all were dead,
Who do not think in love their life to
    lead;
For who is loth the God of Love to obey,
Is only fit to die, I dare well say,
And for that cause OSEE I cry; take
    heed!   135

XXVIII.

Ay, quoth the Cuckoo, that is a quaint
    law,
That all must love or die; but I withdraw,
And take my leave of all such company,
For mine intent it neither is to die,
Nor ever while I live Love's yoke to
    draw.   140

XXIX.

For lovers, of all folk that be alive,
The most disquiet have and least do
    thrive;
Most feeling have of sorrow, woe and care,
And the least welfare cometh to their
    share;
What need is there against the truth to
    strive?   145

XXX.

What! quoth she, thou art all out of thy
    mind,
That in thy churlishness a cause canst
    find
To speak of Love's true Servants in this
    mood;
For in this world no service is so good
To every wight that gentle is of kind.   150

XXXI.

For thereof comes all goodness and all
    worth;
All gentiless and honour thence come
    forth;
Thence worship comes, content and true
    heart's pleasure,
And full-assurèd trust, joy without mea-
    sure,   154
And jollity, fresh cheerfulness, and mirth;

XXXII.

And bounty, lowliness, and courtesy,
And seemliness, and faithful company,
And dread of shame that will not do
    amiss;
For he that faithfully Love's servant is,
Rather than be disgraced, would chuse
    to die.   160

XXXIII.

And that the very truth it is which I
Now say—in such belief I'll live and
    die;
And Cuckoo, do thou so, by my advice.
Then, quoth she, let me never hope for
    bliss,
If with that counsel I do e'er comply.   165

XXXIV.

Good Nightingale! thou speakest won-
    drous fair,
Yet for all that, the truth is found else-
    where;
For Love in young folk is but rage, I
    wis;
And Love in old folk a great dotage is;
Who most it useth, him 'twill most
    impair.   170

XXXV.

For thereof come all contraries to gladness;
Thence sickness comes, and overwhelming sadness,
Mistrust and jealousy, despite, debate,
Dishonour, shame, envy importunate,
Pride, anger, mischief, poverty, and madness.   175

XXXVI.

Loving is aye an office of despair,
And one thing is therein which is not fair;
For whoso gets of love a little bliss,
Unless it alway stay with him, I wis
He may full soon go with an old man's hair.   180

XXXVII.

And, therefore, Nightingale! do thou keep nigh,
For trust me well, in spite of thy quaint cry,
If long time from thy mate thou be, or far,
Thou 'it be as others that forsaken are;
Then shalt thou raise a clamour as do I.

XXXVIII.

Fie, quoth she, on thy name, Bird ill beseen!   186
The God of Love afflict thee with all teen,
For thou art worse than mad a thousand fold;
For many a one hath virtues manifold,
Who had been nought, if Love had never been.   190

XXXIX.

For evermore his servants Love amendeth,
And he from every blemish them defendeth;
And maketh them to burn, as in a fire,
In loyalty, and worshipful desire,
And, when it likes him, joy enough them sendeth.   195

XL.

Thou Nightingale! the Cuckoo said, be still,
For Love no reason hath but his own will;—
For to th' untrue he oft gives ease and joy;
True lovers doth so bitterly annoy,
He lets them perish through that grievous ill.   200

XLI.

With such a master would I never be [1];
For he, in sooth, is blind, and may not see,
And knows not when he hurts and when he heals;
Within this court full seldom Truth avails,
So diverse in his wilfulness is he.   205

XLII.

Then of the Nightingale did I take note,
How from her inmost heart a sigh she brought,
And said, Alas! that ever I was born,
Not one word have I now, I am so forlorn,—
And with that word, she into tears burst out.   210

XLIII.

Alas, alas! my very heart will break,
Quoth she, to hear this churlish bird thus speak
Of Love, and of his holy services;
Now, God of Love! thou help me in some wise,
That vengeance on this Cuckoo I may wreak.   215

XLIV.

And so methought I started up anon,
And to the brook I ran and got a stone,
Which at the Cuckoo hardily I cast,
And he for dread did fly away full fast;
And glad, in sooth, was I when he was gone.   220

---

[1] From a manuscript in the Bodleian, as are also stanzas 44 and 45, which are necessary to complete the sense.

XLV.

And as he flew, the Cuckoo, ever and aye,
Kept crying, "Farewell!—farewell, Pop-
injay!"
As if in scornful mockery of me;
And on I hunted him from tree to tree,
Till he was far, all out of sight, away. 225

XLVI.

Then straightway came the Nightingale
to me,
And said,. Forsooth, my friend, do I
thank thee,
That thou wert near to rescue me; and
now,
Unto the God of Love I make a vow,
That all this May I will thy songstress
be. 230

XLVII.

Well satisfied, I thanked her, and she
said,
By this mishap no longer be dismayed,
Though thou the Cuckoo heard, ere thou
heard'st me;
Yet if I live it shall amended be,
When next May comes, if I am not
afraid. 235

XLVIII.

And one thing will I counsel thee also,
The Cuckoo trust not thou, nor his Love's
saw;
All that she said is an outrageous lie.
Nay, nothing shall me bring thereto,
quoth I,
For Love, and it hath done me mighty
woe. 240

XLIX.

Yea, hath it? use, quoth she, this
medicine;
This May-time, every day before thou
dine,
Go look on the fresh daisy; then say I,
Although for pain thou may'st be like to
die,
Thou wilt be eased, and less wilt droop
and pine. 245

L.

And mind always that thou be good and
true,
And I will sing one song, of many new,
For love of thee, as loud as I may cry; 248
And then did she begin this song full
high,
"Beshrew all them that are in love
untrue."

LI.

And soon as she had sung it to the end,
Now farewell, quoth she, for I hence
must wend;
And, God of Love, that can right well
and may,
Send unto thee as mickle joy this day,
As ever he to Lover yet did send. 255

LII.

Thus takes the Nightingale her leave of
me;
I pray to God with her always to be,
And joy of love to send her evermore;
And shield us from the Cuckoo and her
lore,
For there is not so false a bird as she. 260

LIII.

Forth then she flew, the gentle Nightin-
gale,
To all the Birds that lodged within that
dale,
And gathered each and all into one
place;
And them besought to hear her doleful
case,
And thus it was that she began her tale.

LIV.

The Cuckoo—'tis not well that I should
hide 266
How she and I did each the other chide,
And without ceasing, since it was day-
light;
And now I pray you all to do me right
Of that false Bird whom Love can not
abide. 270

LV.

Then spake one Bird, and full assent all
gave;
This matter asketh counsel good as grave,
For birds we are—all here together
brought;
And, in good sooth, the Cuckoo here is
not;　　　　　　　　　　　　274
And therefore we a Parliament will have.

LVI.

And thereat shall the Eagle be our Lord,
And other Peers whose names are on
record;
A summons to the Cuckoo shall be sent,
And judgment there be given; or that
intent
Failing, we finally shall make accord.　280

LVII.

And all this shall be done, without a nay,
The morrow after Saint Valentine's day,
Under a maple that is well beseen,
Before the chamber-window of the Queen,
At Woodstock, on the meadow green and
gay.　　　　　　　　　　　　285

LVIII.

She thankèd them; and then her leave
she took,
And flew into a hawthorn by that brook;
And there she sate and sung—upon that
tree—
"For term of life Love shall have hold
of me"—
So loudly, that I with that song awoke.

Unlearned Book and rude, as well I
know,　　　　　　　　　　　291
For beauty thou hast none, nor elo-
quence,
Who did on thee the hardiness bestow
To appear before my Lady? but a sense
Thou surely hast of her benevolence,　295
Whereof her hourly bearing proof doth
give;
For of all good she is the best alive.

Alas, poor Book! for thy unworthiness,
To show to her some pleasant meanings
writ
In winning words, since through her
gentiless,　　　　　　　　　300

Thee she accepts as for her service fit!
Oh! it repents me I have neither wit
Nor leisure unto thee more worth to give;
For of all good she is the best alive.

Beseech her meekly with all lowliness, 305
Though I be far from her I reverence,
To think upon my truth and steadfastness,
And to abridge my sorrow's violence,
Caused by the wish, as knows your
sapience,
She of her liking proof to me would give;
For of all good she is the best alive.　311

L'ENVOY.

Pleasure's Aurora, Day of gladsomeness!
Luna by night, with heavenly influence
Illumined! root of beauty and goodnesse,
Write, and allay by your beneficence　315
My sighs breathed forth in silence,—
comfort give!
Since of all good you are the best alive.

EXPLICIT.

III.

TROILUS AND CRESIDA.

[Written 1801.—Same dates of publication as II.]

Next morning Troilus began to clear
His eyes from sleep, at the first break of
day,
And unto Pandarus, his own Brother dear,
For love of God, full piteously did say,
We must the Palace see of Cresida;　5
For since we yet may have no other feast,
Let us behold her Palace at the least!

And therewithal to cover his intent[1]
A cause he found into the Town to go,
And they right forth to Cresid's Palace
went;　　　　　　　　　　　10
But, Lord, this simple Troilus was woe,
Him thought his sorrowful heart would
break in two;
For when he saw her doors fast bolted all,
Well nigh for sorrow down he 'gan to fall.

Therewith when this true Lover 'gan
behold,　　　　　　　　　　　15
How shut was every window of the place,

---

[1] His meiny for to blend (Chaucer); i.e. to hoodwink his followers.—Ed.

Like frost he thought his heart was icy cold;
For which, with changèd, pale, and
    deadly face,
Without word uttered, forth he 'gan to
    pace;
And on his purpose bent so fast to ride,
That no wight his continuance[1] espied. 21

Then said he thus,—O Palace desolate!
O house of houses, once so richly dight!
O Palace empty and disconsolate!
Thou lamp of which extinguished is the
    light; 25
O Palace whilom day that now art night,
Thou ought'st to fall and I to die; since she
Is gone who held us both in sovereignty.

O, of all houses once the crownèd boast!
Palace illumined with the sun of bliss; 30
O ring of which the ruby now is lost,
O cause of woe, that cause has been of
    bliss:
Yet, since I may no better, would I kiss
Thy cold doors; but I dare not for this
    rout;
Farewell, thou shrine of which the Saint
    is out! 35

Therewith he cast on Pandarus an eye,
With changèd face, and piteous to be-
    hold;
And when he might his time aright espy,
Aye as he rode, to Pandarus he told
Both his new sorrow and his joys of old,
So piteously, and with so dead a hue, 41
That every wight might on his sorrow rue.

Forth from the spot he rideth up and
    down,
And everything to his rememberànce
Came as he rode by places of the town 45
Where he had felt such perfect pleasure
    once.
Lo, yonder saw I mine own Lady dance,
And in that Temple she with her bright
    eyes,
My Lady dear, first bound me captive-
    wise.

And yonder with joy-smitten heart have I
Heard my own Cresid's laugh; and once
    at play 51

---

[1] *Countenance* (Chaucer).—Ed.

I yonder saw her eke full blissfully;
And yonder once she unto me 'gan say—
Now, my sweet Troilus, love me well, I
    pray!
And there so graciously did me behold,
That hers unto the death my heart I
    hold. 56

And at the corner of that self-same house
Heard I my most beloved Lady dear,
So womanly, with voice melodious 59
Singing so well, so goodly, and so clear,
That in my soul methinks I yet do hear
The blissful sound; and in that very
    place
My Lady first me took unto her grace.

O blissful God of Love! then thus he
    cried,
When I the process have in memory, 65
How thou hast wearied me on every side,
Men thence a book might make, a history;
What need to seek a conquest over me,
Since I am wholly at thy will? what joy
Hast thou thy own liege subjects to de-
    stroy? 70

Dread Lord! so fearful when provoked,
    thine ire
Well hast thou wreaked on me by pain
    and grief;
Now mercy, Lord! thou know'st well I
    desire
Thy grace above all pleasures first and
    chief;
And live and die I will in thy belief; 75
For which I ask for guerdon but one
    boon,
That Cresida again thou send me soon.

Constrain her heart as quickly to return,
As thou dost mine with longing her to see,
Then know I well that she would not
    sojourn. 80
Now, blissful Lord, so cruel do not be
Unto the blood of Troy, I pray of thee,
As Juno was unto the Theban blood,
From whence to Thebes came griefs in
    multitude.

And after this he to the gate did go 85
Whence Cresid rode, as if in haste she
    was;

And up and down there went, and to
and fro,
And to himself full oft he said, alas!
From hence my hope and solace forth
did pass.
O would the blissful God now for his joy,
I might her see again coming to Troy! 91

And up to yonder hill was I her guide;
Alas, and there I took of her my leave;
Yonder I saw her to her Father ride,
For very grief of which my heart shall
cleave;—   95
And hither home I came when it was eve;
And here I dwell an outcast from all joy,
And shall, unless I see her soon in Troy.

And of himself did he imagine oft,
That he was blighted, pale, and waxen less
Than he was wont; and that in whispers
soft   101
Men said, what may it be, can no one
guess
Why Troilus hath all this heaviness?
All which he of himself conceited wholly
Out of his weakness and his melancholy.

Another time he took into his head,   106
That every wight, who in the way passed
by,
Had of him ruth, and fancied that they
said,
I am right sorry Troilus will die:
And thus a day or two drove wearily; 110
As ye have heard; such life 'gan he to
lead
As one that standeth betwixt hope and
dread.

For which it pleased him in his songs to
show
The occasion of his woe, as best he might;
And made a fitting song, of words but
few,   115
Somewhat his woeful heart to make more
light;
And when he was removed from all men's
sight,
With a soft voice, he of his Lady dear,
That absent was, 'gan sing as ye may hear.

O star, of which I lost have all the light, 120
With a sore heart well ought I to bewail,

That ever dark in torment, night by night,
Toward my death with wind I steer and
sail [1];
For which upon the tenth night if thou fail
With thy bright beams to guide me but
one hour,   125
My ship and me Charybdis will devour.

As soon as he this song had thus sung
through,
He fell again into his sorrows old;
And every night, as was his wont to do,
Troilus stood the bright moon to behold;
And all his trouble to the moon he told, 131
And said: I wis, when thou art horn'd
anew,
I shall be glad if all the world be true.

Thy horns were old as now upon that
morrow,
When hence did journey my bright Lady
dear,   135
That cause is of my torment and my
sorrow;
For which, oh, gentle Luna, bright and
clear,
For love of God, run fast above thy sphere;
For when thy horns begin once more to
spring,
Then shall she come, that with her bliss
may bring.   140

The day is more, and longer every night
Than they were wont to be—for he
thought so;
And that the sun did take his course not
right,
By longer way than he was wont to go;
And said, I am in constant dread I trow,
That Phäeton his son is yet alive,   146
His too fond father's car amiss to drive.

Upon the walls fast also would he walk,
To the end that he the Grecian host might
see;   149
And ever thus he to himself would talk:—
Lo! yonder is my own bright Lady free;
Or yonder is it that the tents must be;
And thence does come this air which is so
sweet,
That in my soul I feel the joy of it.

---

[1] *With wind in stern I sail* (Chaucer).—ED.

And certainly this wind, that more and
more   155
By moments thus increaseth in my
face,
Is of my Lady's sighs heavy and sore;
I prove it thus; for in no other space
Of all this town, save only in this place,
Feel I a wind, that soundeth so like
pain;   160
It saith, Alas, why severed are we
twain?

A weary while in pain he tosseth thus,
Till fully passed and gone was the ninth
night;
And ever at his side stood Pandarus,
Who busily made use of all his might   165
To comfort him, and make his heart more
light;
Giving him always hope, that she the
morrow
Of the tenth day will come, and end his
sorrow.

POEMS REFERRING TO THE PERIOD
OF OLD AGE.

I.

THE OLD CUMBERLAND BEGGAR.

The class of Beggars, to which the Old Man here described belongs, will probably soon be extinct. It consisted of poor, and, mostly, old and infirm persons, who confined themselves to a stated round in their neighbourhood, and had certain fixed days, on which, at different houses, they regularly received alms, sometimes in money, but mostly in provisions.

[Composed 1797.—Published 1800.]

I saw an aged Beggar in my walk;
And he was seated, by the highway side,
On a low structure of rude masonry
Built at the foot of a huge hill, that they
Who lead their horses down the steep
    rough road   5
May thence remount at ease. The aged
    Man
Had placed his staff across the broad
    smooth stone
That overlays the pile; and, from a bag
All white with flour, the dole of village
    dames,
He drew his scraps and fragments, one
    by one;   10
And scanned them with a fixed and
    serious look
Of idle computation. In the sun,
Upon the second step of that small pile,
Surrounded by those wild unpeopled hills,
He sat, and ate his food in solitude: 15
And ever, scattered from his palsied hand,
That, still attempting to prevent the
    waste,
Was baffled still, the crumbs in little
    showers
Fell on the ground; and the small moun-
    tain birds,
Not venturing yet to peck their destined
    meal,   20
Approached within the length of half his
    staff.

  Him from my childhood have I known;
    and then
He was so old, he seems not older now;
He travels on, a solitary Man,
So helpless in appearance, that for him 25
The sauntering Horseman throws not
    with a slack
And careless hand his alms upon the
    ground,
But stops,—that he may safely lodge the
    coin
Within the old Man's hat; nor quits
    him so,
But still, when he has given his horse the
    rein,   30
Watches the aged Beggar with a look
Sidelong, and half-reverted. She who
    tends
The toll-gate, when in summer at her
    door
She turns her wheel, if on the road she
    sees
The aged Beggar coming, quits her work,
And lifts the latch for him that he may
    pass.   36
The post-boy, when his rattling wheels
    o'ertake
The aged Beggar in the woody lane,
Shouts to him from behind; and, if thus
    warned
The old man does not change his course,
    the boy   40
Turns with less noisy wheels to the road-
    side,
And passes gently by, without a curse
Upon his lips or anger at his heart.

He travels on, a solitary Man ;
His age has no companion. On the
 ground   45
His eyes are turned, and, as he moves
 along,
They move along the ground ; and, ever-
 more,
Instead of common and habitual sight
Of fields with rural works, of hill and
 dale,
And the blue sky, one little span of earth
Is all his prospect. Thus, from day to
 day,   51
Bow-bent, his eyes for ever on the ground,
He plies his weary journey ; seeing still,
And seldom knowing that he sees, some
 straw,
Some scattered leaf, or marks which, in
 one track,   55
The nails of cart or chariot-wheel have
 left
Impressed on the white road,—in the
 same line,
At distance still the same. Poor Tra-
 veller !
His staff trails with him ; scarcely do his
 feet
Disturb the summer dust ; he is so still 60
In look and motion, that the cottage curs,
Ere he has passed the door, will turn
 away,
Weary of barking at him. Boys and girls,
The vacant and the busy, maids and
 youths,
And urchins newly breeched—all pass
 him by :   65
Him even the slow-paced waggon leaves
 behind.

But deem not this Man useless.—States-
 men ! ye
Who are so restless in your wisdom, ye
Who have a broom still ready in your
 hands
To rid the world of nuisances ; ye proud,
Heart-swoln, while in your pride ye con-
 template   71
Your talents, power, or wisdom, deem
 him not
A burthen of the earth ! 'Tis Nature's law
That none, the meanest of created things,

Of forms created the most vile and
 brute,   75
The dullest or most noxious, should exist
Divorced from good—a spirit and pulse
 of good,
A life and soul, to every mode of being
Inseparably linked. Then be assured
That least of all can aught—that ever
 owned   80
The heaven-regarding eye and front sub-
 lime
Which man is born to—sink, howe'er de-
 pressed,
So low as to be scorned without a sin ;
Without offence to God cast out of view ;
Like the dry remnant of a garden-flower 85
Whose seeds are shed, or as an implement
Worn out and worthless. While from
 door to door,
This old Man creeps, the villagers in him
Behold a record which together binds
Past deeds and offices of charity,   90
Else unremembered, and so keeps alive
The kindly mood in hearts which lapse of
 years,
And that half-wisdom half-experience
 gives,
Make slow to feel, and by sure steps
 resign
To selfishness and cold oblivious cares. 95
Among the farms and solitary huts,
Hamlets and thinly-scattered villages,
Where'er the aged Beggar takes his
 rounds,
The mild necessity of use compels
To acts of love ; and habit does the work
Of reason ; yet prepares that after-joy
Which reason cherishes. And thus the
 soul,   102
By that sweet taste of pleasure unpursued,
Doth find herself insensibly disposed
To virtue and true goodness.
                              Some there are,
By their good works exalted, lofty minds,
And meditative, authors of delight
And happiness, which to the end of time
Will live, and spread, and kindle : even
 such minds
In childhood, from this solitary Being, 110
Or from like wanderer, haply have re-
 ceived

(A thing more precious far than all that
    books
Or the solicitudes of love can do !)
That first mild touch of sympathy and
    thought,
In which they found their kindred with
    a world   115
Where want and sorrow were. The easy
    man
Who sits at his own door,—and, like the
    pear
That overhangs his head from the green
    wall,
Feeds in the sunshine; the robust and
    young,
The prosperous and unthinking, they who
    live   120
Sheltered, and flourish in a little grove
Of their own kindred ;—all behold in him
A silent monitor, which on their minds
Must needs impress a transitory thought
Of self-congratulation, to the heart   125
Of each recalling his peculiar boons,
His charters and exemptions; and, per-
    chance,
Though he to no one give the fortitude
And circumspection needful to preserve
His present blessings, and to husband up
The respite of the season, he, at least, 131
And 'tis no vulgar service, makes them
    felt.

Yet further.———Many, I believe, there
    are
Who live a life of virtuous decency,
Men who can hear the Decalogue and
    feel   135
No self-reproach ; who of the moral law
Established in the land where they abide
Are strict observers ; and not negligent
In acts of love to those with whom they
    dwell,
Their kindred, and the children of their
    blood.   140
Praise be to such, and to their slumbers
    peace !
—But of the poor man ask, the abject
    poor ;
Go, and demand of him, if there be here
In this cold abstinence from evil deeds,
And these inevitable charities,   145

Wherewith to satisfy the human soul?
No—man is dear to man ; the poorest poor
Long for some moments in a weary life
When they can know and feel that they
    have been,
Themselves, the fathers and the dealers-
    out   150
Of some small blessings ; have been kind
    to such
As needed kindness, for this single cause,
That we have all of us one human heart.
—Such pleasure is to one kind Being
    known,
My neighbour, when with punctual care,
    each week,   155
Duly as Friday comes, though pressed
    herself
By her own wants, she from her store of
    meal
Takes one unsparing handful for the scrip
Of this old Mendicant, and, from her door
Returning with exhilarated heart,   160
Sits by her fire, and builds her hope in
    heaven.

Then let him pass, a blessing on his
    head !
And while in that vast solitude to which
The tide of things has borne him, he
    appears   164
To breathe and live but for himself alone,
Unblamed, uninjured, let him bear about
The good which the benignant law of
    Heaven
Has hung around him : and, while life is
    his,
Still let him prompt the unlettered vil-
    lagers
To tender offices and pensive thoughts.
—Then let him pass, a blessing on his
    head !   171
And, long as he can wander, let him
    breathe
The freshness of the valleys ; let his blood
Struggle with frosty air and winter snows;
And let the chartered wind that sweeps
    the heath   175
Beat his grey locks against his withered
    face.
Reverence the hope whose vital anxious-
    ness

Gives the last human interest to his heart.
May never HOUSE, misnamed of IN-
   DUSTRY,
Make him a captive!—for that pent-up
   din,   180
Those life-consuming sounds that clog the
   air,
Be his the natural silence of old age!
Let him be free of mountain solitudes;
And have around him, whether heard or
   not,
The pleasant melody of woodland birds.
Few are his pleasures: if his eyes have
   now   186
Been doomed so long to settle upon earth
That not without some effort they behold
The countenance of the horizontal sun,
Rising or setting, let the light at least
Find a free entrance to their languid
   orbs,   191
And let him, *where* and *when* he will, sit
   down
Beneath the trees, or on a grassy bank
Of highway side, and with the little birds
Share his chance-gathered meal; and,
   finally,   195
As in the eye of Nature he has lived,
So in the eye of Nature let him die!

II.

THE FARMER OF TILSBURY VALE.

[Composed 1800.—Published July 21, 1800 (*Morn-
ing Post*); ed. 1815.]

'TIS not for the unfeeling, the falsely
   refined,
The squeamish in taste, and the narrow
   of mind,
And the small critic wielding his delicate
   pen,
That I sing of old Adam, the pride of old
   men.

He dwells in the centre of London's wide
   Town;   5
His staff is a sceptre—his grey hairs a
   crown;
And his bright eyes look brighter, set off
   by the streak
Of the unfaded rose that still blooms on
   his cheek.

'Mid the dews, in the sunshine of morn,—
   'mid the joy
Of the fields, he collected that bloom,
   when a boy;   10
That countenance there fashioned, which,
   spite of a stain
That his life hath received, to the last
   will remain.

A Farmer he was; and his house far and
   near
Was the boast of the country for excellent
   cheer;
How oft have I heard in sweet Tilsbury
   Vale   15
Of the silver-rimmed horn whence he
   dealt his mild ale!

Yet Adam was far as the farthest from
   ruin,
His fields seemed to know what their
   Master was doing;
And turnips, and corn-land, and meadow,
   and lea,
All caught the infection—as generous as
   he.   20

Yet Adam prized little the feast and the
   bowl,—
The fields better suited the ease of his
   soul:
He strayed through the fields like an
   indolent wight,
The quiet of nature was Adam's delight.

For Adam was simple in thought; and
   the poor,   25
Familiar with him, made an inn of his
   door:
He gave them the best that he had; or,
   to say
What less may mislead you, they took it
   away.

Thus thirty smooth years did he thrive
   on his farm:
The Genius of plenty preserved him from
   harm: 30
At length, what to most is a season of
   sorrow,
His means are run out,—he must beg, or
   must borrow.

To the neighbours he went,—all were free
    with their money;
For his hive had so long been replenished
    with honey,
That they dreamt not of dearth;—He
    continued his rounds,   35
Knocked here—and knocked there, pounds
    still adding to pounds.

He paid what he could with his ill-gotten
    pelf,
And something, it might be, reserved for
    himself:
Then (what is too true) without hinting a
    word,
Turned his back on the country—and off
    like a bird.   40

You lift up your eyes!—but I guess that
    you frame
A judgment too harsh of the sin and the
    shame;
In him it was scarcely a business of art,
For this he did all in the *ease* of his
    heart.

To London—a sad emigration I ween—
With his grey hairs he went from the
    brook and the green,   46
And there, with small wealth but his legs
    and his hands,
As lonely he stood as a crow on the sands.

All trades, as need was, did old Adam
    assume,—
Served as stable-boy, errand-boy, porter,
    and groom;   50
But nature is gracious, necessity kind,
And, in spite of the shame that may lurk
    in his mind,

He seems ten birthdays younger, is green
    and is stout;
Twice as fast as before does his blood run
    about;
You would say that each hair of his beard
    was alive,   55
And his fingers as busy as bees in a hive.

For he's not like an Old Man that leisure-
    ly goes
About work that he knows, in a track
    that he knows;

But often his mind is compelled to demur,
And you guess that the more then his
    body must stir.   60

In the throng of the town like a stranger
    is he,
Like one whose own country's far over
    the sea;
And Nature, while through the great city
    he hies,
Full ten times a day takes his heart by
    surprise.

This gives him the fancy of one that is
    young,   65
More of soul in his face than of words on
    his tongue;
Like a maiden of twenty he trembles and
    sighs,
And tears of fifteen will come into his
    eyes.

What's a tempest to him, or the dry
    parching heats?
Yet he watches the clouds that pass over
    the streets;   70
With a look of such earnestness often will
    stand,
You might think he'd twelve reapers at
    work in the Strand.

Where proud Covent-garden, in desolate
    hours
Of snow and hoar-frost, spreads her fruits
    and her flowers,
Old Adam will smile at the pains that
    have made   75
Poor winter look fine in such strange
    masquerade.

'Mid coaches and chariots, a waggon of
    straw,
Like a magnet, the heart of old Adam
    can draw;
With a thousand soft pictures his memory
    will teem,
And his hearing is touched with the
    sounds of a dream.   80

Up the Haymarket hill he oft whistles his
    way,
Thrusts his hands in a waggon, and smells
    at the hay;

He thinks of the fields he so often hath
    mown,
And is happy as if the rich freight were
    his own.

But chiefly to Smithfield he loves to re-
    pair,—   85
If you pass by at morning, you'll meet
    with him there.
The breath of the cows you may see him
    inhale,
And his heart all the while is in Tilsbury
    Vale.

Now farewell, old Adam! when low thou
    art laid,
May one blade of grass spring up over
    thy head;   90
And I hope that thy grave, wheresoever
    it be,
Will hear the wind sigh through the leaves
    of a tree.

III.

THE SMALL CELANDINE.

[Composed 1804.—Published 1807.]

THERE is a Flower, the lesser Celandine,
That shrinks, like many more, from cold
    and rain ;
And, the first moment that the sun may
    shine,
Bright as the sun himself, 'tis out again !

When hailstones have been falling, swarm
    on swarm,   5
Or blasts the green field and the trees dis-
    trest,
Oft have I seen it muffled up from harm,
In close self-shelter, like a Thing at rest.

But lately, one rough day, this Flower I
    passed
And recognised it, though an altered
    form,   10
Now standing forth an offering to the
    blast,
And buffeted at will by rain and storm.

I stopped, and said with inly-muttered
    voice,
"It doth not love the shower, nor seek
    the cold :

This neither is its courage nor its choice,
But its necessity in being old.   16

"The sunshine may not cheer it, nor the
    dew ;
It cannot help itself in its decay ;
Stiff in its members, withered, changed
    of hue."
And, in my spleen, I smiled that it was
    grey.   20

To be a Prodigal's Favourite—then, worse
    truth,
A Miser's Pensioner—behold our lot !
O Man, that from thy fair and shining
    youth
Age might but take the things Youth
    needed not !

IV.

THE TWO THIEVES;

OR,

THE LAST STAGE OF AVARICE.

[Composed 1800.—Published 1800.]

O NOW that the genius of Bewick were
    mine,
And the skill which he learned on the
    banks of the Tyne,
Then the Muses might deal with me just
    as they chose,
For I'd take my last leave both of verse
    and of prose.

What feats would I work with my magical
    hand !   5
Book-learning and books should be
    banished the land :
And, for hunger and thirst and such
    troublesome calls,
Every ale-house should then have a feast
    on its walls.

The traveller would hang his wet clothes
    on a chair ;
Let them smoke, let them burn, not a
    straw would he care !   10
For the Prodigal Son, Joseph's Dream
    and his sheaves,
Oh, what would they be to my tale of two
    Thieves ?

The One, yet unbreeched, is not three
    birthdays old,
His Grandsire that age more than thirty
    times told;
There are ninety good seasons of fair and
    foul weather   15
Between them, and both go a-pilfering
    together.

With chips is the carpenter strewing his
    floor?
Is a cart-load of turf at an old woman's
    door?
Old Daniel his hand to the treasure will
    slide!
And his Grandson's as busy at work by
    his side.   20

Old Daniel begins; he stops short—and
    his eye,
Through the lost look of dotage, is cunning
    and sly:
'Tis a look which at this time is hardly
    his own,
But tells a plain tale of the days that are
    flown.

He once had a heart which was moved by
    the wiles   25
Of manifold pleasures and many desires:
And what if he cherished his purse?
    'Twas no more
Than treading a path trod by thousands
    before.

'Twas a path trod by thousands; but
    Daniel is one
Who went something farther than others
    have gone,   30
And now with old Daniel you see how it
    fares;
You see to what end he has brought his
    grey hairs.

The pair sally forth hand in hand: ere
    the sun
Has peered o'er the beeches, their work is
    begun:
And yet, into whatever sin they may
    fall,   35
This child but half knows it, and that not
    at all.

They hunt through the streets with de-
    liberate tread,
And each, in his turn, becomes leader or
    led;
And, wherever they carry their plots and
    their wiles,
Every face in the village is dimpled with
    smiles.   40

Neither checked by the rich nor the needy
    they roam;
For the grey-headed Sire has a daughter
    at home,
Who will gladly repair all the damage
    that's done;
And three, were it asked, would be ren-
    dered for one.

Old Man! whom so oft I with pity have
    eyed,   45
I love thee, and love the sweet Boy at thy
    side:
Long yet may'st thou live! for a teacher
    we see
That lifts up the veil of our nature in thee.

V.

ANIMAL TRANQUILLITY AND DECAY.

[Composed 1798 (? 1797).—Published 1798.]

THE little hedgerow birds,
That peck along the road, regard him
    not.
He travels on, and in his face, his step,
His gait, is one expression: every limb,
His look and bending figure, all bespeak
A man who does not move with pain, but
    moves   6
With thought.—He is insensibly subdued
To settled quiet: he is one by whom
All effort seems forgotten; one to whom
Long patience hath such mild composure
    given,   10
That patience now doth seem a thing of
    which
He hath no need. He is by nature led
To peace so perfect that the young behold
With envy, what the Old Man hardly
    feels.

EPITAPHS AND ELEGIAC PIECES.

EPITAPHS

TRANSLATED FROM CHIABRERA.

I.

[Composed ?.—Published 1837.]

WEEP not, belovèd Friends! nor let the
    air
For me with sighs be troubled. Not from
    life
Have I been taken; this is genuine life
And this alone—the life which now I live
In peace eternal; where desire and joy 5
Together move in fellowship without
    end.—
Francesco Ceni willed that, after death,
His tombstone thus should speak for him.
    And surely
Small cause there is for that fond wish of
    ours
Long to continue in this world; a world
That keeps not faith, nor yet can point a
    hope   11
To good, whereof itself is destitute.

II.

[Composed 1809 or 1810.—Published February 22,
1810 (*The Friend*); ed. 1815.]

PERHAPS some needful service of the State
Drew TITUS from the depth of studious
    bowers,
And doomed him to contend in faithless
    courts,
Where gold determines between right and
    wrong.
Yet did at length his loyalty of heart   5
And his pure native genius, lead him
    back
To wait upon the bright and gracious
    Muses,
Whom he had early loved. And not in
    vain
Such course he held! Bologna's learned
    schools

Were gladdened by the Sage's voice, and
    hung   10
With fondness on those sweet Nestorian
    strains.
There pleasure crowned his days; and all
    his thoughts
A roseate fragrance breathed[1].—O human
    life,
That never art secure from dolorous
    change!
Behold a high injunction suddenly   15
To Arno's side hath brought him, and he
    charmed
A Tuscan audience: but full soon was
    called
To the perpetual silence of the grave.
Mourn, Italy, the loss of him who stood
A Champion steadfast and invincible, 20
To quell the rage of literary War!

III.

[Composed 1809 or 1810.—Published February 22,
1810 (*The Friend*); ed. 1815.]

O THOU who movest onward with a mind
Intent upon thy way, pause, though in
    haste!
'Twill be no fruitless moment. I was
    born
Within Savona's walls, of gentle blood.
On Tiber's banks my youth was dedicate
To sacred studies; and the Roman Shep-
    herd   6
Gave to my charge Urbino's numerous
    flock.
Well did I watch, much laboured, nor
    had power
To escape from many and strange indig-
    nities;

---

[1] Ivi vivea giocondo e i suoi pensieri
Erano tutti rose.

The Translator had not skill to come nearer
to his original.

Was smitten by the great ones of the
    world,   10
But did not fall; for Virtue braves all
    shocks,
Upon herself resting immovably.
Me did a kindlier fortune then invite
To serve the glorious Henry, King of
    France,
And in his hands I saw a high reward 15
Stretched out for my acceptance,—but
    Death came.
Now, Reader, learn from this my fate,
    how false,
How treacherous to her promise, is the
    world;
And trust in God—to whose eternal doom
Must bend the sceptred Potentates of
    earth.   20

IV.

[Composed 1809.—Published December 28, 1809
    (*The Friend*); ed. 1815.]

THERE never breathed a man who, when
    his life
Was closing, might not of that life relate
Toils long and hard.—The warrior will
    report
Of wounds, and bright swords flashing in
    the field,
And blast of trumpets. He who hath
    been doomed   5
To bow his forehead in the courts of kings,
Will tell of fraud and never-ceasing hate,
Envy and heart-inquietude, derived
From intricate cabals of treacherous
    friends.
I, who on shipboard lived from earliest
    youth,   10
Could represent the countenance horrible
Of the vexed waters, and the indignant
    rage
Of Auster and Boötes. Fifty years
Over the well-steered galleys did I rule:—
From huge Pelorus to the Atlantic
    pillars,   15
Rises no mountain to mine eyes unknown;
And the broad gulfs I traversed oft and
    oft.
Of every cloud which in the heavens
    might stir

I knew the force; and hence the rough
    sea's pride
Availed not to my Vessel's overthrow. 20
What noble pomp and frequent have
    not I
On regal decks beheld! yet in the end
I learned that one poor moment can
    suffice
To equalize the lofty and the low.
We sail the sea of life—a *Calm* One
    finds,   25
And One a *Tempest*—and, the voyage o'er,
Death is the quiet haven of us all.
If more of my condition ye would know,
Savona was my birthplace, and I sprang
Of noble parents: seventy years and three
Lived I—then yielded to a slow disease.

V.

[Composed ?.—Published 1837.]

TRUE is it that Ambrosio Salinero
With an untoward fate was long involved
In odious litigation; and full long,
Fate harder still! had he to endure as-
    saults
Of racking malady. And true it is   5
That not the less a frank courageous heart
And buoyant spirit triumphed over pain;
And he was strong to follow in the steps
Of the fair Muses. Not a covert path
Leads to the dear Parnassian forest's shade,
That might from him be hidden; not a
    track   11
Mounts to pellucid Hippocrene, but he
Had traced its windings.—This Savona
    knows,
Yet no sepulchral honours to her Son
She paid, for in our age the heart is ruled
Only by gold. And now a simple stone
Inscribed with this memorial here is
    raised   17
By his bereft, his lonely, Chiabrera.
Think not, O Passenger! who read'st the
    lines
That an exceeding love hath dazzled me;
No—he was One whose memory ought to
    spread   21
Where'er Permessus bears an honoured
    name,
And live as long as its pure stream shall
    flow.

VI.

[Composed 1809.—Published December 28, 1809
(*The Friend*); ed. 1815.]

DESTINED to war from very infancy
Was I, Roberto Dati, and I took
In Malta the white symbol of the Cross:
Nor in life's vigorous season did I shun
Hazard or toil; among the sands was seen
Of Lybia; and not seldom, on the banks 6
Of wide Hungarian Danube, 'twas my lot
To hear the sanguinary trumpet sounded.
So lived I, and repined not at such fate:
This only grieves me, for it seems a
    wrong,   10
That stripped of arms I to my end am
    brought
On the soft down of my paternal home.
Yet haply Arno shall be spared all cause
To blush for me. Thou, loiter not nor halt
In thy appointed way, and bear in mind
How fleeting and how frail is human life!

VII.

[Composed ?.—Published 1837.]

O FLOWER of all that springs from gentle
    blood,
And all that generous nurture breeds to
    make
Youth amiable; O friend so true of soul
To fair Aglaia; by what envy moved,
Lelius! has death cut short thy brilliant
    day   5
In its sweet opening? and what dire
    mishap
Has from Savona torn her best delight?
For thee she mourns, nor e'er will cease
    to mourn;
And, should the out-pourings of her eyes
    suffice not
For her heart's grief, she will entreat
    Sebeto   10
Not to withhold his bounteous aid, Sebeto
Who saw thee, on his margin, yield to
    death,
In the chaste arms of thy belovèd Love!
What profit riches? what does youth
    avail?
Dust are our hopes;—I, weeping bitterly,
Penned these sad lines, nor can forbear
    to pray   16

That every gentle Spirit hither led
May read them not without some bitter
    tears.

VIII.

[Composed 1809.—Published January 4, 1810
(*The Friend*); ed. 1815.]

NOT without heavy grief of heart did He
On whom the duty fell (for at that time
The father sojourned in a distant land)
Deposit in the hollow of this tomb
A brother's Child, most tenderly beloved!
FRANCESCO was the name the Youth had
    borne,   6
POZZOBONNELLI his illustrious house;
And, when beneath this stone the Corse
    was laid,
The eyes of all Savona streamed with tears.
Alas! the twentieth April of his life   10
Had scarcely flowered: and at this early
    time,
By genuine virtue he inspired a hope
That greatly cheered his country: to his
    kin
He promised comfort; and the flattering
    thoughts
His friends had in their fondness enter-
    tained[1],   15
He suffered not to languish or decay.
Now is there not good reason to break forth
Into a passionate lament?—O Soul!
Short while a Pilgrim in our nether world,
Do thou enjoy the calm empyreal air; 20
And round this earthly tomb let roses rise,
An everlasting spring! in memory
Of that delightful fragrance which was
    once
From thy mild manners quietly exhaled.

IX.

[Composed 1809.—Published January 4, 1810
(*The Friend*); ed. 1815.]

PAUSE, courteous Spirit!—Baldi suppli-
    cates
That Thou, with no reluctant voice, for
    him

---

[1] In justice to the Author, I subjoin the ori-
ginal:

————— e degli amici
Non lasciava languire i bei pensieri.

Here laid in mortal darkness, wouldst
    prefer
A prayer to the Redeemer of the world.
This to the dead by sacred right belongs;
All else is nothing.—Did occasion suit   6
To tell his worth, the marble of this tomb
Would ill suffice: for Plato's lore sublime,
And all the wisdom of the Stagyrite,
Enriched and beautified his studious
    mind: 10
With Archimedes also he conversed
As with a chosen friend; nor did he leave
Those laureat wreaths ungathered which
    the Nymphs
Twine near their loved Permessus.—
    Finally,
Himself above each lower thought up-
    lifting,   15
His ears he closed to listen to the songs
Which Sion's Kings did consecrate of
    old;
And his Permessus found on Lebanon.
A blessèd Man! who of protracted days
Made not, as thousands do, a vulgar
    sleep;   20
But truly did *He* live his life. Urbino,
Take pride in him!—O Passenger, fare-
    well!

I.

[Composed ?.—Published 1835.]

By a blest Husband guided, Mary came
From nearest kindred, Vernon her new
    name;
She came, though meek of soul, in seemly
    pride
Of happiness and hope, a youthful Bride.
O dread reverse! if aught *be* so, which
    proves   5
That God will chasten whom he dearly
    loves.
Faith bore her up through pains in mercy
    given,
And troubles that were each a step to
    Heaven:
Two Babes were laid in earth before she
    died;
A third now slumbers at the Mother's
    side;   10

Its Sister-twin survives, whose smiles
    afford
A trembling solace to her widowed Lord.

Reader! if to thy bosom cling the pain
Of recent sorrow combated in vain;
Or if thy cherished grief have failed to
    thwart   15
Time still intent on his insidious part,
Lulling the mourner's best good thoughts
    asleep,
Pilfering regrets we would, but cannot,
    keep;
Bear with Him—judge *Him* gently who
    makes known
His bitter loss by this memorial Stone; 20
And pray that in his faithful breast the
    grace
Of resignation find a hallowed place.

II.

[Composed 1812 (?).—Published 1837.]

Six months to six years added he re-
    mained
Upon this sinful earth, by sin unstained:
O blessèd Lord! whose mercy then re-
    moved
A Child whom every eye that looked on
    loved;
Support us, teach us calmly to resign
What we possessed, and now is wholly
    thine!

III.

CENOTAPH.

In affectionate remembrance of Frances Fermor,
  whose remains are deposited in the church of
  Claines, near Worcester, this stone is erected
  by her sister, Dame Margaret, wife of Sir George
  Beaumont, Bart., who, feeling not less than the
  love of a brother for the deceased, commends
  this memorial to the care of his heirs and suc-
  cessors in the possession of this place.

[Composed 1824.—Published 1842.]

By vain affections unenthralled,
Though resolute when duty called
To meet the world's broad eye,
Pure as the holiest cloistered nun
That ever feared the tempting sun,   5
Did Fermor live and die.

This Tablet, hallowed by her name,
One heart-relieving tear may claim;
But if the pensive gloom
Of fond regret be still thy choice,   10
Exalt thy spirit, hear the voice
Of Jesus from her tomb!
"I AM THE WAY, THE TRUTH, AND THE
        LIFE."

IV.

EPITAPH

IN THE CHAPEL-YARD OF LANGDALE,
        WESTMORELAND.

[Composed 1841.—Published: vol. of 1842.]

By playful smiles, (alas! too oft
A sad heart's sunshine) by a soft
And gentle nature, and a free
Yet modest hand of charity,
Through life was OWEN LLOYD endeared 5
To young and old; and how revered
Had been that pious spirit, a tide
Of humble mourners testified,
When, after pains dispensed to prove
The measure of God's chastening love, 10
Here, brought from far, his corse found
        rest,—
Fulfilment of his own request;—
Urged less for this Yew's shade, though he
Planted with such fond hope the tree;
Less for the love of stream and rock, 15
Dear as they were, than that his Flock,
When they no more their Pastor's voice
Could hear to guide them in their choice
Through good and evil, help might have,
Admonished, from his silent grave,   20
Of righteousness, of sins forgiven,
For peace on earth and bliss in heaven.

V.

ADDRESS TO THE SCHOLARS OF
THE VILLAGE SCHOOL OF ——.

[Composed 1798.—Published: vol. of 1842.]

I COME, ye little noisy Crew,
Not long your pastime to prevent;
I heard the blessing which to you
Our common Friend and Father sent.
I kissed his cheek before he died;   5
And when his breath was fled,

I raised, while kneeling by his side,
His hand:—it dropped like lead.
Your hands, dear Little-ones, do all
That can be done, will never fall   10
Like his till they are dead.
By night or day, blow foul or fair,
Ne'er will the best of all your train
Play with the locks of his white hair,
Or stand between his knees again.   15

Here did he sit confined for hours;
But he could see the woods and plains,
Could hear the wind and mark the showers
Come streaming down the streaming
        panes.
Now stretched beneath his grass-green
        mound   20
He rests a prisoner of the ground.
He loved the breathing air,
He loved the sun, but if it rise
Or set, to him where now he lies,
Brings not a moment's care.   25
Alas! what idle words; but take
The Dirge which for our Master's sake
And yours, love prompted me to make.
The rhymes so homely in attire
With learnèd ears may ill agree,   30
But chanted by your Orphan Quire
Will make a touching melody.

DIRGE.

Mourn, Shepherd, near thy old grey stone;
Thou Angler, by the silent flood;
And mourn when thou art all alone,   35
Thou Woodman, in the distant wood!

Thou one blind Sailor, rich in joy
Though blind, thy tunes in sadness hum;
And mourn, thou poor half-witted Boy!
Born deaf, and living deaf and dumb. 40

Thou drooping sick Man, bless the Guide
Who checked or turned thy headstrong
        youth,
As he before had sanctified
Thy infancy with heavenly truth.

Ye Striplings, light of heart and gay, 45
Bold settlers on some foreign shore,
Give, when your thoughts are turned this
        way,
A sigh to him whom we deplore.

For us who here in funeral strain
With one accord our voices raise,　50
Let sorrow overcharged with pain
Be lost in thankfulness and praise.

And when our hearts shall feel a sting
From ill we meet or good we miss,
May touches of his memory bring　55
Fond healing, like a mother's kiss.

BY THE SIDE OF THE GRAVE SOME YEARS AFTER.

Long time his pulse hath ceased to beat;
But benefits, his gift, we trace—
Expressed in every eye we meet
Round this dear Vale, his native place.　60

To stately Hall and Cottage rude
Flowed from his life what still they hold,
Light pleasures, every day renewed;
And blessings half a century old.

Oh true of heart, of spirit gay,　65
Thy faults, where not already gone
From memory, prolong their stay
For charity's sweet sake alone.

Such solace find we for our loss;
And what beyond this thought we crave
Comes in the promise from the Cross,　71
Shining upon thy happy grave[1].

VI.

ELEGIAC STANZAS,

SUGGESTED BY A PICTURE OF PEELE
CASTLE, IN A STORM, PAINTED BY
SIR GEORGE BEAUMONT.

[Composed 1805.—Published 1807.]

I was thy neighbour once, thou rugged
Pile!
Four summer weeks I dwelt in sight of
thee:
I saw thee every day; and all the while
Thy Form was sleeping on a glassy sea.

So pure the sky, so quiet was the air!　5
So like, so very like, was day to day!
Whene'er I looked, thy Image still was
there;
It trembled, but it never passed away.

How perfect was the calm! it seemed no
sleep;
No mood, which season takes away, or
brings:　10
I could have fancied that the mighty
Deep
Was even the gentlest of all gentle
Things.

Ah! then, if mine had been the Painter's
hand,
To express what then I saw; and add
the gleam,　14
The light that never was, on sea or land,
The consecration, and the Poet's dream;

I would have planted thee, thou hoary
Pile
Amid a world how different from this!
Beside a sea that could not cease to smile;
On tranquil land, beneath a sky of bliss.

Thou shouldst have seemed a treasure-
house divine　21
Of peaceful years; a chronicle of heaven;—
Of all the sunbeams that did ever shine
The very sweetest had to thee been given.

A Picture had it been of lasting ease,　25
Elysian quiet, without toil or strife;
No motion but the moving tide, a breeze,
Or merely silent Nature's breathing life.

Such, in the fond illusion of my heart,
Such Picture would I at that time have
made:　30
And seen the soul of truth in every part,
A steadfast peace that might not be be-
trayed.

So once it would have been,—'tis so no
more;
I have submitted to a new control:
A power is gone, which nothing can re-
store;　35
A deep distress hath humanised my Soul.

Not for a moment could I now behold
A smiling sea, and be what I have been:
The feeling of my loss will ne'er be old;
This, which I know, I speak with mind
serene.　40

---

[1] See upon the subject of the three foregoing
pieces "Matthew," &c., &c., pp. 486–489.

Then, Beaumont, Friend! who would
   have been the Friend,
If he had lived, of Him whom I deplore,
This work of thine I blame not, but com-
   mend;
This sea in anger, and that dismal shore.

O 'tis a passionate Work!—yet wise and
   well,   45
Well chosen is the spirit that is here;
That Hulk which labours in the deadly
   swell,
This rueful sky, this pageantry of fear!

And this huge Castle, standing here
   sublime,
I love to see the look with which it
   braves,   50
Cased in the unfeeling armour of old
   time,
The lightning, the fierce wind, and tramp-
   ling waves.

Farewell, farewell the heart that lives
   alone,
Housed in a dream, at distance from the
   Kind!
Such happiness, wherever it be known,
Is to be pitied; for 'tis surely blind.   56

But welcome fortitude, and patient cheer,
And frequent sights of what is to be
   borne!
Such sights, or worse, as are before me
   here.—
Not without hope we suffer and we
   mourn.   60

VII.

TO THE DAISY.

[Composed 1805.—Published 1815.]

SWEET Flower! belike one day to have
A place upon thy Poet's grave,
I welcome thee once more:
But He, who was on land, at sea,
My Brother, too, in loving thee,   5
Although he loved more silently,
Sleeps by his native shore.

Ah! hopeful, hopeful was the day
When to that Ship he bent his way,
To govern and to guide: 10
His wish was gained: a little time

Would bring him back in manhood's prime
And free for life, these hills to climb,
With all his wants supplied.

And full of hope day followed day   15
While that stout Ship at anchor lay
Beside the shores of Wight;
The May had then made all things green;
And, floating there, in pomp serene,
That Ship was goodly to be seen,   20
His pride and his delight!

Yet then, when called ashore, he sought
The tender peace of rural thought:
In more than happy mood
To your abodes, bright daisy Flowers! 25
He then would steal at leisure hours,
And loved you glittering in your bowers,
A starry multitude.

But hark the word!—the ship is gone;—
Returns from her long course:—anon   30
Sets sail:—in season due,
Once more on English earth they stand:
But, when a third time from the land
They parted, sorrow was at hand
For Him and for his crew.   35

Ill-fated Vessel!—ghastly shock!
—At length delivered from the rock,
The deep she hath regained;
And through the stormy night they steer;
Labouring for life, in hope and fear,   40
To reach a safer shore—how near,
Yet not to be attained!

"Silence!" the brave Commander cried;
To that calm word a shriek replied,
It was the last death-shriek.   45
—A few (my soul oft sees that sight)
Survive upon the tall mast's height;
But one dear remnant of the night—
For Him in vain I seek.

Six weeks beneath the moving sea   50
He lay in slumber quietly;
Unforced by wind or wave
To quit the Ship for which he died,
(All claims of duty satisfied;)
And there they found him at her side; 55
And bore him to the grave.

Vain service! yet not vainly done
For this, if other end were none,

That He, who had been cast
Upon a way of life unmeet   60
For such a gentle Soul and sweet,
Should find an undisturbed retreat
Near what he loved, at last—

That neighbourhood of grove and field
To Him a resting-place should yield,   65
A meek man and a brave !
The birds shall sing and ocean make
A mournful murmur for *his* sake ;
And Thou, sweet Flower, shalt sleep and wake
Upon his senseless grave.   70

VIII.

ELEGIAC VERSES,

IN MEMORY OF MY BROTHER, JOHN WORDSWORTH,

Commander of the E. I. Company's ship, the Earl of Abergavenny, in which he perished by calamitous shipwreck, Feb. 6th, 1805. Composed near the Mountain track, that leads from Grasmere through Grisdale Hawes, where it descends towards Patterdale.

[Composed 1805.—Published : vol. of 1842.]

I.

THE Sheep-boy whistled loud, and lo !
That instant, startled by the shock,
The Buzzard mounted from the rock
Deliberate and slow :
Lord of the air, he took his flight ;   5
Oh ! could he on that woeful night
Have lent his wing, my Brother dear,
For one poor moment's space to Thee,
And all who struggled with the Sea,
When safety was so near.   10

II.

Thus in the weakness of my heart
I spoke (but let that pang be still)
When rising from the rock at will,
I saw the Bird depart.
And let me calmly bless the Power   15
That meets me in this unknown Flower,
Affecting type of him I mourn !
With calmness suffer and believe,
And grieve, and know that I must grieve,
Not cheerless, though forlorn.   20

III.

Here did we stop ; and here looked round
While each into himself descends,
For that last thought of parting Friends
That is not to be found.   24
Hidden was Grasmere Vale from sight,
Our home and his, his heart's delight,
His quiet heart's selected home.
But time before him melts away,
And he hath feeling of a day
Of blessedness to come.   30

IV.

Full soon in sorrow did I weep,
Taught that the mutual hope was dust,
In sorrow, but for higher trust,
How miserably deep !
All vanished in a single word,   35
A breath, a sound, and scarcely heard.
Sea—Ship—drowned—Shipwreck—so it came,
The meek, the brave, the good, was gone ;
He who had been our living John
Was nothing but a name.   40

V.

That was indeed a parting ! oh,
Glad am I, glad that it is past ;
For there were some on whom it cast
Unutterable woe.
But they as well as I have gains ;—   45
From many a humble source, to pains
Like these, there comes a mild release ;
Even here I feel it, even this Plant
Is in its beauty ministrant
To comfort and to peace.   50

VI.

He would have loved thy modest grace,
Meek Flower ! To Him I would have said,
"It grows upon its native bed
Beside our Parting-place ;
There, cleaving to the ground, it lies   55
With multitude of purple eyes,
Spangling a cushion green like moss ;
But we will see it, joyful tide !
Some day, to see it in its pride,
The mountain will we cross."   60

VII.

—Brother and friend, if verse of mine
Have power to make thy virtues known,
Here let a monumental Stone
Stand—sacred as a Shrine;
And to the few who pass this way,   65
Traveller or Shepherd, let it say,
Long as these mighty rocks endure,—
Oh do not Thou too fondly brood,
Although deserving of all good,
On any earthly hope, however pure[1]!   70

IX.

SONNET.

[Composed 1846.—Published 1850.]

WHY should we weep or mourn, Angelic
    boy,
For such thou wert ere from our sight
    removed,
Holy, and ever dutiful—beloved
From day to day with never-ceasing joy,
And hopes as dear as could the heart
    employ   5
In aught to earth pertaining? Death has
    proved
His might, nor less his mercy, as behoved—
Death conscious that he only could destroy
The bodily frame. That beauty is laid low
To moulder in a far-off field of Rome; 10
But Heaven is now, blest Child, thy
    Spirit's home:
When such divine communion, which we
    know,
Is felt, thy Roman burial-place will be
Surely a sweet remembrancer of Thee.

X.

LINES

Composed at Grasmere, during a walk one Even-
ing, after a stormy day, the Author having
just read in a Newspaper that the dissolution
of Mr. Fox was hourly expected.

[Composed September (?), 1806.—Published 1807.]

LOUD is the Vale! the Voice is up
With which she speaks when storms are
    gone,

A mighty unison of streams!
Of all her Voices, One!

Loud is the Vale;—this inland Depth   5
In peace is roaring like the Sea;
Yon star upon the mountain-top
Is listening quietly.

Sad was I, even to pain deprest,
Importunate and heavy load[2]!   10
The Comforter hath found me here,
Upon this lonely road;

And many thousands now are sad—
Wait the fulfilment of their fear;
For he must die who is their stay,   15
Their glory disappear.

A Power is passing from the earth
To breathless Nature's dark abyss;
But when the great and good depart
What is it more than this—   20

That Man, who is from God sent forth,
Doth yet again to God return?—
Such ebb and flow must ever be,
Then wherefore should we mourn?

XI.

INVOCATION TO THE EARTH.

FEBRUARY, 1816.

[Composed February, 1816.—Published 1816.]

I.

"REST, rest, perturbèd Earth!
O rest, thou doleful Mother of Man-
    kind!"
A Spirit sang in tones more plaintive than
    the wind:
"From regions where no evil thing has
    birth
I come—thy stains to wash away,   5
Thy cherished fetters to unbind,
And open thy sad eyes upon a milder
    day.
The Heavens are thronged with martyrs
    that have risen
    From out thy noisome prison;
    The penal caverns groan   10

---

[1] The plant alluded to is the Moss Campion
(Silene acaulis, of Linnæus). See Note, p. 925
See among the Poems on the "Naming of
Places," No. VI.

[2] Importuna e grave salma.
              MICHAEL ANGELO.

With tens of thousands rent from off the
　　tree
Of hopeful life,—by battle's whirlwind
　　blown
Into the deserts of Eternity.
Unpitied havoc! Victims unlamented!
But not on high, where madness is re-
　　sented,　　　　　　　　　　15
And murder causes some sad tears to flow,
Though, from the widely-sweeping blow,
The choirs of Angels spread, triumphant-
　　ly augmented.

II.

"False Parent of Mankind!
　　Obdurate, proud, and blind,　　20
I sprinkle thee with soft celestial dews,
Thy lost, maternal heart to re-infuse!
Scattering this far-fetched moisture from
　　my wings,
Upon the act a blessing I implore,　　24
Of which the rivers in their secret springs,
The rivers stained so oft with human gore,
Are conscious;—may the like return no
　　more!
May Discord—for a Seraph's care
Shall be attended with a bolder prayer—
May she, who once disturbed the seats of
　　bliss　　　　　　　　　　30
　　These mortal spheres above,
Be chained for ever to the black abyss!
And thou, O rescued Earth, by peace and
　　love,
And merciful desires, thy sanctity ap-
　　prove!"　　　　　　　　　34

The Spirit ended his mysterious rite,
And the pure vision closed in darkness
　　infinite.

XII.

LINES

WRITTEN ON A BLANK LEAF IN A COPY
OF THE AUTHOR'S POEM "THE EX-
CURSION," UPON HEARING OF THE
DEATH OF THE LATE VICAR OF
KENDAL.

[Composed November 13, 1814.—Published 1815.]

To public notice, with reluctance strong,
Did I deliver this unfinished Song;

Yet for one happy issue;—and I look
With self-congratulation on the Book
Which pious, learned, MURFITT saw and
　　read;—　　　　　　　　　5
Upon my thoughts his saintly Spirit fed;
He conned the new-born Lay with grate-
　　ful heart—
Foreboding not how soon he must de-
　　part;
Unweeting that to him the joy was given
Which good men take with them from
　　earth to heaven.　　　　　10

XIII.

ELEGIAC STANZAS.

(ADDRESSED TO SIR G. H. B. UPON THE
DEATH OF HIS SISTER-IN-LAW.)

[Composed probably Dec. 1824.—Published 1827.]

O FOR a dirge! But why complain?
Ask rather a triumphal strain
When FERMOR'S race is run;
A garland of immortal boughs
To twine around the Christian's brows, 5
Whose glorious work is done.

We pay a high and holy debt;
No tears of passionate regret
Shall stain this votive lay;
Ill-worthy, Beaumont! were the grief 10
That flings itself on wild relief
When Saints have passed away.

Sad doom, at Sorrow's shrine to kneel,
For ever covetous to feel,
And impotent to bear!　　　　15
Such once was hers—to think and think
On severed love, and only sink
From anguish to despair!

But nature to its inmost part
Faith had refined; and to her heart 20
A peaceful cradle given:
Calm as the dew-drop's, free to rest
Within a breeze-fanned rose's breast
Till it exhales to Heaven.

Was ever Spirit that could bend 25
So graciously?—that could descend,
Another's need to suit,
So promptly from her lofty throne?—
In works of love, in these alone,
How restless, how minute!　　　30

Pale was her hue; yet mortal cheek
Ne'er kindled with a livelier streak
When aught had suffered wrong,—
When aught that breathes had felt a
    wound;
Such look the Oppressor might confound,
However proud and strong. 36

But hushed be every thought that springs
From out the bitterness of things;
Her quiet is secure;
No thorns can pierce her tender feet, 40
Whose life was, like the violet, sweet,
As climbing jasmine, pure—

As snowdrop on an infant's grave,
Or lily heaving with the wave
That feeds it and defends; 45
As Vesper, ere the star hath kissed
The mountain top, or breathed the mist
That from the vale ascends.

Thou takest not away, O Death!
Thou strikest—absence perisheth, 50
Indifference is no more;
The future brightens on our sight;
For on the past hath fallen a light
That tempts us to adore.

XIV.

ELEGIAC MUSINGS.

IN THE GROUNDS OF COLEORTON HALL,
THE SEAT OF THE LATE SIR G. H.
BEAUMONT, BART.

In these grounds stands the Parish Church,
wherein is a mural monument bearing an
Inscription which, in deference to the earnest
request of the deceased, is confined to name,
dates, and these words:—"Enter not into judg-
ment with thy servant, O Lord!"

[Composed November, 1830.—Published 1835.]

WITH copious eulogy in prose or rhyme
Graven on the tomb we struggle against
    Time,
Alas, how feebly! but our feelings rise
And still we struggle when a good man
    dies.
Such offering BEAUMONT dreaded and for-
    bade, 5
A spirit meek in self-abasement clad.

Yet *here* at least, though few have num-
    bered days
That shunned so modestly the light of
    praise,
His graceful manners, and the temperate
    ray
Of that arch fancy which would round
    him play, 10
Brightening a converse never known to
    swerve
From courtesy and delicate reserve;
That sense, the bland philosophy of life,
Which checked discussion ere it warmed
    to strife;
Those rare accomplishments, and varied
    powers, 15
Might have their record among sylvan
    bowers.
Oh, fled for ever! vanished like a blast
That shook the leaves in myriads as it
    passed;—
Gone from this world of earth, air, sea,
    and sky,
From all its spirit-moving imagery, 20
Intensely studied with a painter's eye,
A poet's heart; and, for congenial view,
Portrayed with happiest pencil, not un-
    true
To common recognitions while the line 24
Flowed in a course of sympathy divine;—
Oh! severed, too abruptly, from delights
That all the seasons shared with equal
    rights;—
Rapt in the grace of undismantled age,
From soul-felt music, and the treasured
    page
Lit by that evening lamp which loved to
    shed 30
Its mellow lustre round thy honoured
    head;
While Friends beheld thee give with eye,
    voice, mien,
More than theatric force to Shakspeare's
    scene;—
If thou hast heard me—if thy Spirit know
Aught of these bowers and whence their
    pleasures flow; 35
If things in our remembrance held so
    dear,
And thoughts and projects fondly che-
    rished here,

To thy exalted nature only seem
Time's vanities, light fragments of earth's
    dream—
Rebuke us not!—The mandate is obeyed
That said, "Let praise be mute where
    I am laid;"   41
The holier deprecation, given in trust
To the cold marble, waits upon thy dust;
Yet have we found how slowly genuine
    grief
From *silent* admiration wins relief.   45
Too long abashed thy Name is like a rose
That doth "within itself its sweetness
    close;"
A drooping daisy changed into a cup
In which her bright-eyed beauty is shut up.
Within these groves, where still are flit-
    ting by   50
Shades of the Past, oft noticed with a sigh,
Shall stand a votive Tablet, haply free,
When towers and temples fall, to speak
    of Thee!
If sculptured emblems of our mortal doom
Recall not there the wisdom of the Tomb,
Green ivy risen from out the cheerful earth
Will fringe the lettered stone; and herbs
    spring forth,
Whose fragrance, by soft dews and rain
    unbound,
Shall penetrate the heart without a wound;
While truth and love their purposes fulfil,
Commemorating genius, talent, skill,   61
That could not lie concealed where Thou
    wert known;
Thy virtues *He* must judge, and He alone,
The God upon whose mercy they are
    thrown.

XV.

WRITTEN AFTER THE DEATH OF CHARLES LAMB.

[Composed November, 1835.—Published 1837.]

To a good Man of most dear memory
This Stone is sacred. Here he lies apart
From the great city where he first drew
    breath,
Was reared and taught; and humbly
    earned his bread,
To the strict labours of the merchant's
    desk   5

By duty chained. Not seldom did those
    tasks
Tease, and the thought of time so spent
    depress,
His spirit, but the recompense was high;
Firm Independence, Bounty's rightful
    sire;
Affections, warm as sunshine, free as air;
And when the precious hours of leisure
    came,   11
Knowledge and wisdom, gained from con-
    verse sweet
With books, or while he ranged the
    crowded streets
With a keen eye, and overflowing heart:
So genius triumphed over seeming wrong,
And poured out truth in works by thought-
    ful love   16
Inspired—works potent over smiles and
    tears.
And as round mountain-tops the lightning
    plays,
Thus innocently sported, breaking forth
As from a cloud of some grave sympathy,
Humour and wild instinctive wit, and all
The vivid flashes of his spoken words. 22
From the most gentle creature nursed in
    fields
Had been derived the name he bore—
    a name,
Wherever Christian altars have been
    raised,   25
Hallowed to meekness and to innocence;
And if in him meekness at times gave way,
Provoked out of herself by troubles
    strange,
Many and strange, that hung about his
    life;
Still, at the centre of his being, lodged 30
A soul by resignation sanctified:
And if too often, self-reproached, he felt
That innocence belongs not to our kind,
A power that never ceased to abide in him,
Charity, 'mid the multitude of sins   35
That she can cover, left not his exposed
To an unforgiving judgment from just
    Heaven.
O, he was good, if e'er a good Man lived!
.   .   .   .
From a reflecting mind and sorrowing
    heart

Those simple lines flowed with an earnest
wish,   40
Though but a doubting hope, that they
might serve
Fitly to guard the precious dust of him
Whose virtues called them forth. That
aim is missed;
For much that truth most urgently re-
quired
Had from a faltering pen been asked in
: vain: 45
Yet, haply, on the printed page received,
The imperfect record, there, may stand
unblamed
As long as verse of mine shall breathe the
air
Of memory, or see the light of love.

Thou wert a scorner of the fields, my
Friend,   50
But more in show than truth; and from
the fields,
And from the mountains, to thy rural
grave
Transported, my soothed spirit hovers o'er
Its green untrodden turf, and blowing
flowers;
And taking up a voice shall speak (tho'
still   55
Awed by the theme's peculiar sanctity
Which words less free presumed not even
to touch)
Of that fraternal love, whose heaven-lit
lamp
From infancy, through manhood, to the
last
Of threescore years, and to thy latest
hour,   60
Burnt on with ever-strengthening light,
enshrined
Within thy bosom.
                    "Wonderful" hath been
The love established between man and
man,
"Passing the love of women;" and be-
tween
Man and his help-mate in fast wedlock
joined   65
Through God, is raised a spirit and soul
of love
Without whose blissful influence Paradise

Had been no Paradise; and earth were
now
A waste where creatures bearing human
form,
Direst of savage beasts, would roam in
fear,   70
Joyless and comfortless. Our days glide
on;
And let him grieve who cannot choose
but grieve
That he hath been an Elm without his Vine,
And her bright dower of clustering chari-
ties,
That, round his trunk and branches,
might have clung   75
Enriching and adorning. Unto thee,
Not so enriched, not so adorned, to thee
Was given (say rather thou of later birth
Wert given to her) a Sister—'tis a word
Timidly uttered, for she *lives*, the meek,
The self-restraining, and the ever-kind; 81
In whom thy reason and intelligent heart
Found—for all interests, hopes, and tender
cares,
All softening, humanising, hallowing
powers,
Whether withheld, or for her sake un-
sought—   85
More than sufficient recompense!
                              Her love
(What weakness prompts the voice to tell
it here?)
Was as the love of mothers; and when
years,
Lifting the boy to man's estate, had called
The long-protected to assume the part 90
Of a protector, the first filial tie
Was undissolved; and, in or out of sight,
Remained imperishably interwoven
With life itself. Thus, 'mid a shifting
world,
Did they together testify of time   95
And season's difference—a double tree
With two collateral stems sprung from
one root;
Such were they—such thro' life they *might*
have been
In union, in partition only such;
Otherwise wrought the will of the Most
High;   100
Yet, thro' all visitations and all trials,

Still they were faithful; like two vessels
    launched
From the same beach one ocean to explore
With mutual help, and sailing—to their
    league
True, as inexorable winds, or bars   105
Floating or fixed of polar ice, allow.

But turn we rather, let my spirit turn
With thine, O silent and invisible Friend!
To those dear intervals, nor rare nor brief,
When reunited, and by choice withdrawn
From miscellaneous converse, ye were
    taught   111
That the remembrance of foregone distress,
And the worse fear of future ill (which oft
Doth hang around it, as a sickly child
Upon its mother) may be both alike   115
Disarmed of power to unsettle present
    good
So prized, and things inward and outward
    held
In such an even balance, that the heart
Acknowledges God's grace, his mercy
    feels,
And in its depth of gratitude is still.   120

O gift divine of quiet sequestration!
The hermit, exercised in prayer and
    praise,
And feeding daily on the hope of heaven,
Is happy in his vow, and fondly cleaves
To life-long singleness; but happier far
Was to your souls, and, to the thoughts
    of others,   126
A thousand times more beautiful ap-
    peared,
Your *dual* loneliness. The sacred tie
Is broken; yet why grieve? for Time but
    holds
His moiety in trust, till Joy shall lead   130
To the blest world where parting is un-
    known.

XVI.

EXTEMPORE EFFUSION UPON THE DEATH OF JAMES HOGG.

[Composed November, 1835.—Published December 12, 1835 (*The Athenæum*); ed. 1837.]

WHEN first, descending from the moor-
    lands,
I saw the Stream of Yarrow glide

Along a bare and open valley,
  The Ettrick Shepherd was my guide.

When last along its banks I wandered,   5
Through groves that had begun to shed
Their golden leaves upon the pathways,
  My steps the Border-minstrel led.

The mighty Minstrel breathes no longer,
'Mid mouldering ruins low he lies;   10
And death upon the braes of Yarrow,
  Has closed the Shepherd-poet's eyes:

Nor has the rolling year twice measured,
From sign to sign, its steadfast course,
Since every mortal power of Coleridge   15
  Was frozen at its marvellous source;

The rapt One, of the godlike forehead,
The heaven-eyed creature sleeps in earth:
And Lamb, the frolic and the gentle,
  Has vanished from his lonely hearth.   20

Like clouds that rake the mountain-sum-
    mits,
Or waves that own no curbing hand,
How fast has brother followed brother,
  From sunshine to the sunless land!

Yet I, whose lids from infant slumber   25
Were earlier raised, remain to hear
A timid voice, that asks in whispers,
  "Who next will drop and disappear?"

Our haughty life is crowned with dark-
    ness,
Like London with its own black wreath,
On which with thee, O Crabbe! forth-
    looking,   31
I gazed from Hampstead's breezy heath.

As if but yesterday departed,
Thou too art gone before; but why,
O'er ripe fruit, seasonably gathered,   35
  Should frail survivors heave a sigh?

Mourn rather for that holy Spirit,
Sweet as the spring, as ocean deep;
For Her who, ere her summer faded,
  Has sunk into a breathless sleep.   40

No more of old romantic sorrows,
For slaughtered Youth or love-lorn Maid!
With sharper grief is Yarrow smitten,
And Ettrick mourns with her their Poet
    dead [1].

----

[1] See Note, p. 926.

XVII.

INSCRIPTION

FOR A MONUMENT IN CROSTHWAITE
CHURCH, IN THE VALE OF KESWICK.

[Composed 1843.—Published 1845.]

YE vales and hills whose beauty hither
    drew
The poet's steps, and fixed him here, on you
His eyes have closed! And ye, lov'd
    books, no more
Shall Southey feed upon your precious lore,
To works that ne'er shall forfeit their
    renown,   5
Adding immortal labours of his own—
Whether he traced historic truth, with zeal
For the State's guidance, or the Church's
    weal,

Or Fancy, disciplined by studious art,
Inform'd his pen, or wisdom of the
    heart,
Or judgments sanctioned in the Patriot's
    mind   11
By reverence for the rights of all man-
    kind.
Wide were his aims, yet in no human
    breast
Could private feelings meet for holier
    rest.
His joys, his griefs, have vanished like
    a cloud   15
From Skiddaw's top; but he to heaven
    was vowed
Through his industrious life, and Christian
    faith
Calmed in his soul the fear of change and
    death.

ODE.

—*⋅*—

INTIMATIONS OF IMMORTALITY FROM RECOLLECTIONS OF EARLY CHILDHOOD.

The Child is father of the Man;
And I could wish my days to be
Bound each to each by natural piety.

[Composed 1803 (? 1802)–1806.—Published 1807.]

I.

THERE was a time when meadow, grove,
    and stream,
The earth, and every common sight,
    To me did seem
    Apparelled in celestial light,
The glory and the freshness of a dream.
It is not now as it hath been of yore;—
    Turn wheresoe'er I may,
    By night or day,
The things which I have seen I now can
    see no more.

II.

    The Rainbow comes and goes, 10
    And lovely is the Rose,
    The Moon doth with delight
Look round her when the heavens are
    bare,
    Waters on a starry night
    Are beautiful and fair;   15
The sunshine is a glorious birth;
But yet I know, where'er I go,
That there hath past away a glory from
    the earth.

III.

Now, while the birds thus sing a joyous
    song,
  And while the young lambs bound   20
    As to the tabor's sound,
To me alone there came a thought of
    grief:
A timely utterance gave that thought
    relief,
    And I again am strong:
The cataracts blow their trumpets from
    the steep;   25
No more shall grief of mine the season
    wrong;
I hear the Echoes through the mountains
    throng,
The Winds come to me from the fields of
    sleep,
    And all the earth is gay;
        Land and sea   30
    Give themselves up to jollity,
    And with the heart of May
  Doth every Beast keep holiday;—
    Thou Child of Joy,
Shout round me, let me hear thy shouts,
    thou happy Shepherd-boy!   35

IV.

Ye blessèd Creatures, I have heard the
    call
  Ye to each other make; I see
The heavens laugh with you in your
    jubilee;
My heart is at your festival,
    My head hath its coronal,   40
The fulness of your bliss, I feel—I feel it
    all.
    Oh evil day! if I were sullen
  While Earth herself is adorning,
    This sweet May-morning,
  And the Children are culling   45
    On every side,
In a thousand valleys far and wide,
Fresh flowers; while the sun shines
    warm,
And the Babe leaps up on his Mother's
    arm:—
    I hear, I hear, with joy I hear!   50
  —But there's a Tree, of many, one,

A single Field which I have looked upon,
Both of them speak of something that is
    gone:
    The Pansy at my feet
    Doth the same tale repeat: 55
Whither is fled the visionary gleam?
Where is it now, the glory and the dream?

V.

Our birth is but a sleep and a forgetting:
The Soul that rises with us, our life's Star,
    Hath had elsewhere its setting,   60
    And cometh from afar:
    Not in entire forgetfulness,
    And not in utter nakedness,
But trailing clouds of glory do we come
    From God, who is our home: 65
Heaven lies about us in our infancy!
Shades of the prison-house begin to close
    Upon the growing Boy,
But He beholds the light, and whence it
    flows,
    He sees it in his joy;   70
The Youth, who daily farther from the east
    Must travel, still is Nature's Priest,
    And by the vision splendid
    Is on his way attended;
At length the Man perceives it die away,
And fade into the light of common day. 76

VI.

Earth fills her lap with pleasures of her
    own;
Yearnings she hath in her own natural
    kind,
And, even with something of a Mother's
    mind,
    And no unworthy aim,   80
    The homely Nurse doth all she can
To make her Foster-child, her Inmate
    Man,
    Forget the glories he hath known,
And that imperial palace whence he came.

VII.

Behold the Child among his new-born
    blisses,   85
A six years' Darling of a pigmy size!
See, where 'mid work of his own hand he
    lies,
Fretted by sallies of his mother's kisses,

With light upon him from his father's
eyes!
See, at his feet, some little plan or chart,
Some fragment from his dream of human
life, 91
Shaped by himself with newly-learned art;
    A wedding or a festival,
    A mourning or a funeral;
      And this hath now his heart, 95
    And unto this he frames his song:
    Then will he fit his tongue
To dialogues of business, love, or strife;
    But it will not be long
    Ere this be thrown aside, 100
    And with new joy and pride
The little Actor cons another part;
Filling from time to time his "humorous
stage"
With all the Persons, down to palsied
Age,
That Life brings with her in her equipage;
    As if his whole vocation 106
    Were endless imitation.

VIII.

Thou, whose exterior semblance doth belie
    Thy Soul's immensity;
Thou best Philosopher, who yet dost
keep 110
Thy heritage, thou Eye among the blind,
That, deaf and silent, read'st the eternal
deep,
Haunted for ever by the eternal mind,—
    Mighty Prophet! Seer blest!
    On whom those truths do rest, 115
Which we are toiling all our lives to find,
In darkness lost, the darkness of the
grave;
Thou, over whom thy Immortality
Broods like the Day, a Master o'er a Slave,
A Presence which is not to be put by; 120
    [To whom the grave
Is but a lonely bed without the sense or
sight
    Of day or the warm light,
A place of thought where we in waiting
lie;[1]]

[1] Found in edd. 1807 and 1815; omitted from
ed. 1820 and all subsequent issues in consequence
of Coleridge's adverse criticism. See *Biographia
Literaria*, chap. xxii.—Ed.

Thou little Child, yet glorious in the
might 125
Of heaven-born freedom on thy being's
height,
Why with such earnest pains dost thou
provoke
The years to bring the inevitable yoke,
Thus blindly with thy blessedness at
strife?
Full soon thy Soul shall have her earthly
freight, 130
And custom lie upon thee with a weight,
Heavy as frost, and deep almost as life!

IX.

    O joy! that in our embers
    Is something that doth live,
    That nature yet remembers 135
    What was so fugitive!
The thought of our past years in me doth
breed
Perpetual benediction: not indeed
For that which is most worthy to be
blest;
Delight and liberty, the simple creed 140
Of Childhood, whether busy or at rest,
With new-fledged hope still fluttering in
his breast:—
    Not for these I raise
    The song of thanks and praise;
    But for those obstinate questionings
    Of sense and outward things, 146
    Fallings from us, vanishings;
    Blank misgivings of a Creature
Moving about in worlds not realised,
High instincts before which our mortal
Nature 150
Did tremble like a guilty Thing surprised:
    But for those first affections,
    Those shadowy recollections,
    Which, be they what they may, 154
Are yet the fountain-light of all our day,
Are yet a master-light of all our seeing;
    Uphold us, cherish, and have power
to make
Our noisy years seem moments in the
being
Of the eternal Silence: truths that wake,
    To perish never: 160
Which neither listlessness, nor mad en-
deavour,

Nor Man nor Boy,
Nor all that is at enmity with joy,
Can utterly abolish or destroy !
    Hence in a season of calm weather
      Though inland far we be,   166
Our Souls have sight of that immortal
      sea
    Which brought us hither,
    Can in a moment travel thither,
And see the Children sport upon the
      shore,   170
And hear the mighty waters rolling ever-
      more.

X.

Then sing, ye Birds, sing, sing a joyous
      song !
    And let the young Lambs bound
    As to the tabor's sound !
We in thought will join your throng,   175
    Ye that pipe and ye that play,
    Ye that through your hearts to-
      day
    Feel the gladness of the May !
What though the radiance which was
      once so bright
Do now for ever taken from my sight,   180
    Though nothing can bring back the
      hour
Of splendour in the grass, of glory in the
      flower ;
    We will grieve not, rather find
    Strength in what remains behind ;
    In the primal sympathy   185
    Which having been must ever be ;

In the soothing thoughts that spring
Out of human suffering ;
In the faith that looks through
    death,
In years that bring the philosophic mind.

XI.

And O, ye Fountains, Meadows, Hills,
      and Groves,   191
Forebode not any severing of our loves !
Yet in my heart of hearts I feel your
      might ;
I only have relinquished one delight
To live beneath your more habitual sway.
I love the Brooks which down their
      channels fret,   196
Even more than when I tripped lightly
      as they ;
The innocent brightness of a new-born Day
      Is lovely yet ;
The Clouds that gather round the setting
      sun   200
Do take a sober colouring from an eye
That hath kept watch o'er man's mor-
      tality ;
Another race hath been, and other palms
      are won.
Thanks to the human heart by which we
      live,
Thanks to its tenderness, its joys, and
      fears,   205
To me the meanest flower that blows can
      give
Thoughts that do often lie too deep for
      tears.

APPENDIX: POEMS OF 1793[1].

An Evening Walk.

REPRINTED FROM THE QUARTO OF 1793.

AN EVENING WALK. AN EPISTLE; IN VERSE. ADDRESSED TO A YOUNG LADY, FROM THE LAKES OF THE NORTH OF ENGLAND. BY W. WORDSWORTH, B.A., OF ST. JOHN'S, CAMBRIDGE. LONDON: PRINTED FOR J. JOHNSON, ST. PAUL'S CHURCHYARD. 1793.

ARGUMENT.

General Sketch of the Lakes.—Author's Regret of his Youth passed amongst them.—Short description of Noon.—Cascade Scene.—Noontide Retreat.—Precipice and Sloping Lights.—Face of Nature as the Sun declines.—Mountain Farm, and the Cock.—Slate Quarry.—Sunset.—Superstition of the Country, connected with that Moment.—Swans.—Female Beggar.—Twilight Objects.—Twilight Sounds.—Western Lights.—Spirits.—Night.—Moonlight.—Hope.—Night Sounds.—Conclusion.

FAR from my dearest friend, 'tis mine to rove
Thro' bare grey dell, high wood, and pastoral cove;
His wizard course where hoary Derwent takes
Thro' craggs, and forest glooms, and opening lakes,
Staying his silent waves, to hear the roar   5
That stuns the tremulous cliffs of high Lodore:
Where silver rocks the savage prospect chear
Of giant yews that frown on Rydale's mere;
Where peace to Grasmere's lonely island leads,
To willowy hedgerows, and to emerald meads;   10
Leads to her bridge, rude church, and cottag'd grounds,
Her rocky sheepwalks, and her woodland bounds;
Where, bosom'd deep, the shy Winander[2] peeps
'Mid clust'ring isles, and holly-sprinkl'd steeps;
Where twilight glens endear my Esthwaite's shore,   15
And memory of departed pleasures, more.

Fair scenes! with other eyes, than once, I gaze,
The ever-varying charm your round displays,
Than when, erewhile, I taught, "a happy child,"
The echoes of your rocks my carols wild: 20

---

[1] The *Errata* of these Poems are here rectified in the text.—ED.
[2] These lines are only applicable to the middle part of that lake.

Then did no ebb of chearfulness demand
Sad tides of joy from Melancholy's hand;
In youth's wild eye the livelong day was
    bright,
The sun at morning, and the stars of
    night,
Alike, when first the vales the bittern
    fills,   25
Or the first woodcocks[1] roam'd the moon-
    light hills.

Return Delights! with whom my road
    begun,
When Life rear'd laughing up her morn-
    ing sun;
When Transport kiss'd away my april tear,
"Rocking as in a dream the tedious
    year;"   30
When link'd with thoughtless Mirth I
    cours'd the plain,
And hope itself was all I knew of pain.
For then, ev'n then, the little heart would
    beat
At times, while young Content forsook
    her seat,
And wild Impatience, panting upward,
    show'd   35
Where tipp'd with gold the mountain
    summits glow'd.
Alas! the idle tale of man is found
Depicted in the dial's moral round;
With Hope Reflexion blends her social
    rays
To gild the total tablet of his days;   40
Yet still, the sport of some malignant
    Pow'r,
He knows but from its shade the present
    hour.

While, Memory at my side, I wander here,
Starts at the simplest sight th' unbidden
    tear,   44
A form discover'd at the well-known seat,
A spot, that angles at the riv'let's feet,
The ray the cot of morning trav'ling nigh,
And sail that glides the well-known alders
    by.

But why, ungrateful, dwell on idle pain?
To shew her yet some joys to me remain,
Say, will my friend, with soft affection's ear,
The history of a poet's ev'ning hear?

When, in the south, the wan noon brood-
    ing still,
Breath'd a pale steam around the glaring
    hill,
And shades of deep embattl'd clouds were
    seen   55
Spotting the northern cliffs with lights
    between;
Gazing the tempting shades to them
    deny'd,
When stood the shorten'd herds amid the
    tide,
Where, from the barren wall's unshelter'd
    end,
Long rails into the shallow lake extend;
When schoolboys stretch'd their length
    upon the green   61
And round the humming elm, a glimmer-
    ing scene!
In the brown park, in flocks, the troubl'd
    deer
Shook the still twinkling tail and glanc-
    ing ear;
When horses in the wall-girt intake[2]
    stood,   65
Unshaded, eying far below, the flood,
Crouded behind the swain, in mute dis-
    tress,
With forward neck the closing gate to
    press;
And long, with wistful gaze, his walk
    survey'd,
Till dipp'd his pathway in the river
    shade;   70

—Then Quiet led me up the huddling rill,
Bright'ning with water-breaks the som-
    brous gill[3];
To where, while thick above the branches
    close,
In dark-brown bason its wild waves re-
    pose,

---

[1] In the beginning of winter, these mountains, in the moonlight nights, are covered with immense quantities of woodcocks; which, in the dark nights, retire into the woods.

[2] The word *intake* is local, and signifies a mountain-inclosure.

[3] Gill is also, I believe, a term confined to this country. Glen, gill, and dingle, have the same meaning.

Inverted shrubs, and moss of darkest
green,   75
Cling from the rocks, with pale wood-
weeds between ;
Save that, atop, the subtle sunbeams
shine,
On wither'd briars that o'er the craggs
recline ;
Sole light admitted here, a small cascade,
Illumes with sparkling foam the twilight
shade.   80
Beyond, along the visto of the brook,
Where antique roots its bustling path
o'erlook,
The eye reposes on a secret bridge[1]
Half grey, half shagg'd with ivy to its
ridge.

—Sweet rill, farewel ! To-morrow's noon
again,   85
Shall hide me wooing long thy wildwood
strain ;
But now the sun has gain'd his western
road,
And eve's mild hour invites my steps
abroad.

While, near the midway cliff, the silver'd
kite
In many a whistling circle wheels her
flight ;   90
Slant wat'ry lights, from parting clouds
a-pace,
Travel along the precipice's base ;
Chearing its naked waste of scatter'd
stone
By lychens grey, and scanty moss o'er-
grown,
Where scarce the foxglove peeps, and
thistle's beard,   95
And desert stone-chat, all day long, is
heard.

How pleasant, as the yellowing sun de-
clines,
And with long rays and shades the land-
scape shines ;

To mark the birches' stems all golden
light,
That lit the dark slant woods with silvery
white !   100
The willows weeping trees, that twink-
ling hoar,
Glanc'd oft upturn'd along the breezy
shore,
Low bending o'er the colour'd water, fold
Their moveless boughs and leaves like
threads of gold ;
The skiffs with naked masts at anchor
laid,   105
Before the boat-house peeping thro' the
shade ;
Th' unwearied glance of woodman's echo'd
stroke ;
And curling from the trees the cottage
smoke.

Their pannier'd train a groupe of potters
goad,
Winding from side to side up the steep
road ;   110
The peasant from yon cliff of fearful edge
Shot, down the headlong pathway darts
his sledge ;
Bright beams the lonely mountain horse
illume,
Feeding 'mid purple heath, "green rings[2],"
and broom ;
While the sharp slope the slacken'd team
confounds,   115
Downward[3] the pond'rous timber-wain
resounds ;
Beside their sheltering cross[4] of wall, the
flock
Feeds on in light, nor thinks of winter's
shock ;
In foamy breaks the rill, with merry
song,
Dash'd down the rough rock, lightly leaps
along ;   120

[2] " Vivid rings of green." GREENWOOD'S Poem
on Shooting.

[3] "Down the rough slope the pond'rous waggon
rings."   BEATTIE.

[4] These rude structures, to protect the flocks,
are frequent in this country : the traveller may
recollect one in Withburne, another upon Whin-
latter.

[1] The reader, who has made the tour of this
country, will recognize, in this description, the
features which characterize the lower waterfall
in the gardens of Rydale.

From lonesome chapel at the mountain's feet,
Three humble bells their rustic chime repeat;
Sounds from the water-side the hammer'd boat;
And blasted quarry thunders heard remote.

Ev'n here, amid the sweep of endless woods, 125
Blue pomp of lakes, high cliffs, and falling floods,
Not undelightful are the simplest charms
Found by the verdant door of mountain farms.

Sweetly[1] ferocious round his native walks,
Gaz'd by his sister-wives, the monarch stalks; 130
Spur clad his nervous feet, and firm his tread,
A crest of purple tops his warrior head.
Bright sparks his black and haggard eye-ball hurls
Afar, his tail he closes and unfurls;
Whose state, like pine-trees, waving to and fro, 135
Droops, and o'er canopies his regal brow,
On tiptoe rear'd he blows his clarion throat,
Threaten'd by faintly answering farms remote.

Bright'ning the cliffs between where sombrous pine,
And yew-trees o'er the silver rocks recline, 140
I love to mark the quarry's moving trains,
Dwarf pannier'd steeds, and men, and numerous wains:
How busy the enormous hive within,
While Echo dallies with the various din!
Some hardly heard their chissel's clinking sound, 145
Toil, small as pigmies, in the gulph profound;

Some, dim between th' aereal cliffs descry'd,
O'erwalk the viewless plank from side to side;
These by the pale-blue rocks that ceaseless ring
Glad from their airy baskets hang and sing. 150

Hung o'er a cloud, above the steep that rears
It's edge all flame, the broad'ning sun appears;
A long blue bar it's ægis orb divides,
And breaks the spreading of it's golden tides;
And now it touches on the purple steep
That flings his shadow on the pictur'd deep. 156
Cross the calm lake's blue shades the cliffs aspire,
With tow'rs and woods a "prospect all on fire;"
The coves and secret hollows thro' a ray
Of fainter gold a purple gleam betray;
The gilded turf arrays in richer green 161
Each speck of lawn the broken rocks between;
Deep yellow beams the scatter'd boles illume,
Far in the level forest's central gloom;
Waving his hat, the shepherd in the vale
Directs his winding dog the cliffs to scale,
That, barking busy 'mid the glittering rocks,
Hunts, where he points, the intercepted flocks;
Where oaks o'erhang the road the radiance shoots
On tawny earth, wild weeds, and twisted roots; 170
The Druid[2] stones their lighted fane unfold,
And all the babbling brooks are liquid gold;

[1] "Dolcemente feroce."—TASSO.
In this description of the cock, I remembered a spirited one of the same animal in the l'Agriculture, ou Les Georgiques Françoises of M. Rossuet.

[2] Not far from Broughton is a Druid monument, of which I do not recollect that any tour descriptive of this country makes mention. Perhaps this poem may fall into the hands of some curious traveller, who may thank me for informing him, that up the Duddon, the river which forms the æstuary at Broughton, may be found some of the most romantic scenery of these mountains.

Sunk[1] to a curve the day-star lessens
   still,
Gives one bright glance, and sinks behind
   the hill.

In these lone vales, if aught of faith may
   claim,   175
Thin silver hairs, and ancient hamlet
   fame;
When up the hills, as now, retreats the
   light,
Strange apparitions mock the village
   sight.

A desperate form appears, that spurs his
   steed,
Along the midway cliffs with violent
   speed;   180
Unhurt pursues his lengthen'd flight,
   while all
Attend, at every stretch, his headlong
   fall.
Anon, in order mounts a gorgeous show
Of horsemen shadows winding to and
   fro;
And now the van is gilt with evening's
   beam,   185
The rear thro' iron brown betrays a sullen
   gleam;
Lost[2] gradual o'er the heights in pomp
   they go,
While silent stands th' admiring vale
   below;
Till, but the lonely beacon all is fled,
That tips with eve's last gleam his spiry
   head.   190
Now while the solemn evening Shadows
   sail,
On red slow-waving pinions down the
   vale,
And, fronting the bright west in stronger
   lines,
The oak its dark'ning boughs and foliage
   twines,
I love beside the glowing lake to stray,
Where winds the road along the secret
   bay;   196

By rills that tumble down the woody
   steeps,
And run in transport to the dimpling
   deeps;
Along the "wild meand'ring" shore to
   view,
Obsequious Grace the winding swan pur-
   sue.   200
He swells his lifted chest, and backward
   flings
His bridling neck between his tow'ring
   wings;
Stately, and burning in his pride, di-
   vides
And glorying looks around, the silent
   tides:
On as he floats, the silver'd waters glow,
Proud of the varying arch and moveless
   form of snow.   206
While tender Cares and mild domestic
   Loves,
With furtive watch pursue her as she
   moves;
The female with a meeker charm suc-
   ceeds,
And her brown little ones around her
   leads,   210
Nibbling the water lilies as they pass,
Or playing wanton with the floating
   grass:
She in a mother's care, her beauty's
   pride
Forgets, unweary'd watching every side,
She calls them near, and with affection
   sweet   215
Alternately relieves their weary feet;
Alternately[3] they mount her back, and
   rest
Close by her mantling wings' embraces
   prest.

Long may ye roam these hermit waves
   that sleep,
In birch besprinkl'd cliffs embosom'd
   deep;   220
These fairy holms untrodden, still, and
   green,
Whose shades protect the hidden wave
   serene;

---

[1] From Thomson: see Scott's Critical Essays.
[2] See a description of an appearance of this
kind in Clark's "Survey of the Lakes," accompa-
nied with vouchers of its veracity that may amuse
the reader.

[3] This is a fact of which I have been an eye-
witness.

Whence fragrance scents the water's
desart gale,
The violet, and the lily [1] of the vale;
Where, tho' her far-off twilight ditty
steal,   225
They not the trip of harmless milkmaid
feel.

Yon tuft conceals your home, your cottage
bow'r,
Fresh water rushes strew the verdant
floor;
Long grass and willows form the woven
wall,
And swings above the roof the poplar
tall.   230
Thence issuing oft, unwieldly as ye
stalk,
Ye crush with broad black feet your
flow'ry walk;
Safe from your door ye hear at breezy
morn,
The hound, the horse's tread, and mellow
horn;
At peace inverted your lithe necks ye
lave,   235
With the green bottom strewing o'er the
wave;
No ruder sound your desart haunts in-
vades,
Than waters dashing wild, or rocking
shades.
Ye ne'er, like hapless human wanderers,
throw
Your young on winter's winding sheet of
snow.   240

Fair swan! by all a mother's joys caress'd,
Haply some wretch has ey'd, and call'd
thee bless'd;
Who faint, and beat by summer's breath-
less ray,
Hath dragg'd her babes along this weary
way;
While arrowy fire extorting feverish
groans,   245
Shot stinging through her stark o'er-
labour'd bones.

—With backward gaze, lock'd joints, and
step of pain,
Her seat scarce left, she strives, alas! in
vain,
To teach their limbs along the burning
road
A few short steps to totter with their
load,   250
Shakes her numb arm that slumbers with
its weight,
And eyes through tears the mountain's
shadeless height;
And bids her soldier come her woes to
share,
Asleep on Bunker's charnel hill [2] afar;
For hope's deserted well why wistful
look?   255
Chok'd is the pathway, and the pitcher
broke.

I see her now, deny'd to lay her head,
On cold blue nights, in hut or straw-built
shed;
Turn to a silent smile their sleepy cry,
By pointing to a shooting star on high:
I hear, while in the forest depth he sees,
The Moon's fix'd gaze between the open-
ing trees,
In broken sounds her elder grief demand,
And skyward lift, like one that prays, his
hand,
If, in that country, where he dwells
afar,   265
His father views that good, that kindly
star;
—Ah me! all light is mute amid the
gloom,
The interlunar cavern of the tomb.
—When low-hung clouds each star of
summer hide,
And fireless are the valleys far and
wide,   270
Where the brook brawls along the painful
road,
Dark with bat haunted ashes stretching
broad,
The distant clock forgot, and chilling dew,
Pleas'd thro' the dusk their breaking
smiles to view,

---

[1] The lily of the valley is found in great abun-
dance in the smaller islands of Winandermere.

[2] Substituted in *Errata* for the words of the
text:—"Minden's charnel plain."—Ed.

Oft has she taught them on her lap to play
Delighted, with the glow-worm's harm-
less ray   276
Toss'd light from hand to hand; while
on the ground
Small circles of green radiance gleam
around.

Oh! when the bitter showers her path
assail,
And roars between the hills the torrent
gale,   280
—No more her breath can thaw their
fingers cold,
Their frozen arms her neck no more can
fold;
Scarce heard, their chattering lips her
shoulder chill,
And her cold back their colder bosoms
thrill;
All blind she wilders o'er the lightless
heath,   285
Led by Fear's cold wet hand, and dogg'd
by Death;
Death, as she turns her neck the kiss to
seek,
Breaks off the dreadful kiss with angry
shriek.
Snatch'd from her shoulder with despair-
ing moan,
She clasps them at that dim-seen roofless
stone.—   290
"Now ruthless Tempest launch thy dead-
liest dart!
Fall fires—but let us perish heart to
heart."
Weak roof a cow'ring form two babes to
shield,
And faint the fire a dying heart can yield;
Press the sad kiss, fond mother! vainly
fears   295
Thy flooded cheek to wet them with its
tears;
Soon shall the Light'ning hold before thy
head
His torch, and shew them slumbering in
their bed,
No tears can chill them, and no bosom
warms,
Thy breast their death-bed, coffin'd in
thine arms.   300

Sweet are the sounds that mingle from
afar,
Heard by calm lakes, as peeps the folding
star,
Where the duck dabbles 'mid the rustling
sedge,
And feeding pike starts from the water's
edge,
Or the swan stirs the reeds, his neck and
bill   305
Wetting, that drip upon the water still;
And heron, as resounds the trodden shore,
Shoots upward, darting his long neck
before.
While, by the scene compos'd, the breast
subsides,
Nought wakens or disturbs it's tranquil
tides;   310
Nought but the char that for the may-fly
leaps,
And breaks the mirror of the circling
deeps;
Or clock, that blind against the wanderer
born,
Drops at his feet, and stills his droning
horn.
—The whistling swain that plods his ring-
ing way   315
Where the slow waggon winds along the
bay;
The sugh[1] of swallow flocks that twitter-
ing sweep,
The solemn curfew swinging long and
deep;
The talking boat that moves with pensive
sound,
Or drops his anchor down with plunge
profound;   320
Of boys that bathe remote the faint
uproar,
And restless piper wearying out the shore;
These all to swell the village murmurs
blend,
That soften'd from the water-head
descend.

---

[1] "Sugh," a Scotch word, expressive, as Mr.
Gilpin explains it, of the sound of the motion
of a stick through the air, or of the wind passing
through the trees. See Burns' Cotter's Saturday
Night.

While in sweet cadence rising small and
　　still　　　　　　　　　　　　　325
The far-off minstrels of the haunted hill,
As the last bleating of the fold expires,
Tune in the mountain dells their water
　　lyres.

Now with religious awe the farewell light
Blends with the solemn colouring of the
　　night;　　　　　　　　　　　　330
'Mid groves of clouds that crest the moun-
　　tain's brow,
And round the West's proud lodge their
　　shadows throw,
Like Una[1] shining on her gloomy way,
The half seen form of Twilight roams
　　astray;
Thence, from three paly loopholes mild
　　and small,　　　　　　　　　　335
Slow lights upon the lake's still bosom
　　fall,
Beyond the mountain's giant reach that
　　hides
In deep determin'd gloom his subject
　　tides.
—'Mid the dark steeps repose the shadowy
　　streams,
As touch'd with dawning moonlight's
　　hoary gleams,　　　　　　　　340
Long streaks of fairy light the wave
　　illume
With bordering lines of intervening gloom,
Soft o'er the surface creep the lustres pale
Tracking with silvering path the change-
　　ful gale.
—'Tis restless magic all; at once the
　　bright　　　　　　　　　　　　345
Breaks on the shade, the shade upon the
　　light,
Fair Spirits are abroad; in sportive chase
Brushing with lucid wands the water's
　　face,
While music stealing round the glimmer-
　　ing deeps
Charms the tall circle of th' enchanted
　　steeps.　　　　　　　　　　　　350

—As thro' th' astonish'd woods the notes
　　ascend,
The mountain streams their rising song
　　suspend;
Below Eve's listening Star the sheep walk
　　stills
It's drowsy tinklings on th' attentive
　　hills;
The milkmaid stops her ballad, and her
　　pail　　　　　　　　　　　　　355
Stays it's low murmur in th' unbreathing
　　vale;
No night-duck clamours for his wilder'd
　　mate,
Aw'd, while below the Genii hold their
　　state.—
—The pomp is fled, and mute the won-
　　drous strains,
No wrack of all the pageant scene re-
　　mains,　　　　　　　　　　　　360
So[2] vanish those fair Shadows, human joys,
But Death alone their vain regret de-
　　stroys.

Unheeded Night has overcome the vales,
On the dark earth the baffl'd vision fails,
If peep between the clouds a star on
　　high,　　　　　　　　　　　　365
There turns for glad repose the weary
　　eye;
The latest lingerer of the forest train,
The lone black fir, forsakes the faded
　　plain;
Last evening sight, the cottage smoke no
　　more,
Lost in the deepen'd darkness, glimmers
　　hoar;　　　　　　　　　　　　370
High towering from the sullen dark-brown
　　mere,
Like a black wall, the mountain steeps
　　appear,
Thence red from different heights with
　　restless gleam
Small cottage lights across the water
　　stream,
Nought else of man or life remains be-
　　hind　　　　　　　　　　　　375
To call from other worlds the wilder'd
　　mind,

---

[1] Alluding to this passage of Spenser—
　　　　"Her angel face
　　As the great eye of Heaven shined bright,
　　And made a sunshine in that shady place."

[2] "So break those glittering shadows, human joys."
　　　　　　　　　　　　　　YOUNG.

Till pours the wakeful bird her solemn
  strains
Heard[1] by the night-calm of the wat'ry
  plains.
—No purple prospects now the mind
  employ
Glowing in golden sunset tints of joy, 380
But o'er the sooth'd accordant heart we
  feel
A sympathetic twilight slowly steal,
And ever, as we fondly muse, we find
The soft gloom deep'ning on the tranquil
  mind.
Stay! pensive, sadly-pleasing visions,
  stay! 385
Ah no! as fades the vale, they fade away.
Yet still the tender, vacant gloom re-
  mains,
Still the cold cheek its shuddering tear
  retains.

The bird, with fading light who ceas'd to
  thread
Silent the hedge or steaming rivulet's
  bed, 390
From his grey re-appearing tower shall
  soon
Salute with boding note the rising moon,
Frosting with hoary light the pearly
  ground,
And pouring deeper blue to Æther's
  bound;
Rejoic'd her solemn pomp of clouds to
  fold 395
In robes of azure, fleecy white, and gold,
While rose and poppy, as the glow-worm
  fades,
Checquer with paler red the thicket shades.
  Now o'er the eastern hill, where Dark-
  ness broods
O'er all its vanish'd dells, and lawns, and
  woods 400
Where but a mass of shade the sight can
  trace,
She lifts in silence up her lovely face;
Above the gloomy valley flings her light,
Far to the western slopes with hamlets
  white;

And gives, where woods the checquer'd
  upland strew, 405
To the green corn of summer autumn's hue.
  Thus Hope, first pouring from her
  blessed horn
Her dawn, far lovelier than the Moon's
  own morn;
'Till higher mounted, strives in vain to
  chear
The weary hills, impervious, black'ning
  near; 410
—Yet does she still, undaunted, throw the
  while
On darling spots remote her tempting
  smile.
—Ev'n now she decks for me a distant
  scene,
(For dark and broad the gulph of time
  between)
Gilding that cottage with her fondest ray,
(Sole bourn, sole wish, sole object of my
  way; 416
How fair it's lawn and silvery woods
  appear!
How sweet it's streamlet murmurs in mine
  ear!)
Where we, my friend, to golden days
  shall rise,
'Till our small share of hardly-paining sighs
(For sighs will ever trouble human breath)
Creep hush'd into the tranquil breast of
  Death.
  But now the clear-bright Moon her
  zenith gains,
And rimy without speck extend the
  plains;
The deepest dell the mountain's breast
  displays, 425
Scarce hides a shadow from her searching
  rays;
From the dark-blue "faint silvery threads"
  divide
The hills, while gleams below the azure
  tide;
The scene is waken'd, yet its peace un-
  broke,
By silver'd wreaths of quiet charcoal
  smoke, 430
That, o'er the ruins of the fallen wood,
Steal down the hills, and spread along
  the flood.

---

[1] "Charming the night-calm with her powerful
song." A line of one of our older poets.

The song of mountain streams unheard by
   day,
Now hardly heard, beguiles my home-
   ward way.
All air is, as the sleeping water, still, 435
List'ning th' aëreal music of the hill,
Broke only by the slow clock tolling deep,
Or shout that wakes the ferry-man from
   sleep,
Soon follow'd by his hollow-parting oar,
And echo'd hoof approaching the far
   shore;   440

Sound of clos'd gate, across the water
   born,
Hurrying the feeding hare thro' rustling
   corn;
The tremulous sob of the complaining
   owl;
And at long intervals the mill-dog's
   howl;
The distant forge's swinging thump pro-
   found;   445
Or yell in the deep woods of lonely
   hound.

𝔇escriptive 𝔖ketches.

REPRINTED FROM THE QUARTO OF 1793.

DESCRIPTIVE SKETCHES. IN VERSE. TAKEN DURING A PEDESTRIAN TOUR IN THE ITALIAN, GRISON, SWISS, AND SAVOYARD ALPS. BY W. WORDSWORTH, B.A., OF ST. JOHN'S, CAMBRIDGE. "LOCA PASTORUM DESERTA ATQUE OTIA DIA."—*Lucret.* "CASTELLA IN TUMULIS—ET LONGE SALTUS LATEQUE VACANTES."—*Virgil.* LONDON: PRINTED FOR J. JOHNSON, ST. PAUL'S CHURCHYARD. 1793.

TO THE REV. ROBERT JONES, FELLOW OF ST. JOHN'S COLLEGE, CAMBRIDGE.

DEAR SIR,—However desirous I might have been of giving you proofs of the high place you hold in my esteem, I should have been cautious of wounding your delicacy by thus publicly addressing you, had not the circumstance of my having accompanied you amongst the Alps, seemed to give this dedication a propriety sufficient to do away any scruples which your modesty might otherwise have suggested.

In inscribing this little work to you I consult my heart. You know well how great is the difference between two companions lolling in a post chaise, and two travellers plodding slowly along the road, side by side, each with his little knapsack of necessaries upon his shoulders. How much more of heart between the two latter!

I am happy in being conscious I shall have one reader who will approach the conclusion of these few pages with regret. You they must certainly interest, in reminding you of moments to which you can hardly look back without a pleasure not the less dear from a shade of melancholy. You will meet with few images without recollecting the spot where we observed them together, consequently, whatever is feeble in my design, or spiritless in my colouring, will be amply supplied by your own memory.

With still greater propriety I might have inscribed to you a description of some of the features of your native mountains, through which we have wandered together, in the same manner, with so much pleasure. But the sea-sunsets which give such splendour to the vale of Clwyd, Snowdon, the chair of Idris, the quiet village of Bethkelert, Menai and her druids, the Alpine steeps of the Conway, and the still more interesting windings of the wizard stream of the Dee remain yet untouched. Apprehensive that my pencil may never be exercised on these subjects, I cannot let slip this opportunity of thus publicly assuring you with how much affection and esteem, I am, Dear Sir, Your most obedient very humble servant. W. WORDSWORTH.

ARGUMENT.

Happiness (if she had been to be found on Earth) amongst the Charms of Nature.—Pleasures of the pedestrian Traveller.—Author crosses France to the Alps.—Present state of the Grande Chartreuse.—Lake of Como.—Time, Sunset.—Same Scene, Twilight.—Same Scene, Morning, it's Voluptuous Character; Old Man and Forest Cottage Music.—River Tusa.—Via Mala and Grison Gypsey.—Valley of Sckellenenthal.—Lake of Uri.—Stormy Sunset.—Chapel of William Tell.—Force of Local Emotion. Chamois Chaser.—View of the higher Alps.—Manner of Life of a Swiss Mountaineer interspersed with Views of the higher Alps.—Golden Age of the Alps.—Life and Views continued.—Ranz des Vaches, famous Swiss Air.—Abbey of Einsiedlen and it's Pilgrims.—Valley of Chamouny.—Mont Blanc.—Slavery of Savoy.—Influence of Liberty on Cottage Happiness.—France.—Wish for the Extirpation of Slavery.—Conclusion.

WERE there, below, a spot of holy ground,
By Pain and her sad family unfound,
Sure, Nature's GOD that spot to man had giv'n,
Where murmuring rivers join the song of ev'n ;
Where falls the purple morning far and wide   5
In flakes of light upon the mountainside ;
Where summer Suns in ocean sink to rest,
Or moonlight Upland lifts her hoary breast ;
Where Silence, on her night of wing, o'erbroods
Unfathom'd dells and undiscover'd woods ;
Where rocks and groves the power of waters shakes   11
In cataracts, or sleeps in quiet lakes.
But doubly pitying Nature loves to show'r
Soft on his wounded heart her healing pow'r,
Who plods o'er hills and vales his road forlorn,   15
Wooing her varying charms from eve to morn.
No sad vacuities his heart annoy,
Blows not a Zephyr but it whispers joy ;

For him lost flowers their idle sweets exhale ;
He tastes the meanest note that swells the gale ;   20
For him sod-seats the cottage-door adorn,
And peeps the far-off spire, his evening bourn !
Dear is the forest frowning o'er his head,
And dear the green-sward to his velvet tread ;
Moves there a cloud o'er mid-day's flaming eye?   25
Upward he looks—and calls it luxury ;
Kind Nature's charities his steps attend,
In every babbling brook he finds a friend,
While chast'ning thoughts of sweetest use, bestow'd
By Wisdom, moralize his pensive road.
Host of his welcome inn, the noon-tide bow'r,   31
To his spare meal he calls the passing poor ;
He views the Sun uprear his golden fire,
Or sink, with heart alive like Memnon's [1] lyre ;
Blesses the Moon that comes with kindest ray   35
To light him shaken by his viewless way.
With bashful fear no cottage children steal
From him, a brother at the cottage meal,
His humble looks no shy restraint impart,
Around him plays at will the virgin heart.
While unsuspended wheels the village dance,   41
The maidens eye him with inquiring glance,
Much wondering what sad stroke of crazing Care
Or desperate Love could lead a wanderer there.
Me, lur'd by hope her sorrows to remove,   45
A heart, that could not much itself approve,
O'er Gallia's wastes of corn dejected led,
Her [2] road elms rustling thin above my head,

---

[1] The lyre of Memnon is reported to have emitted melancholy or cheerful tones, as it was touched by the sun's evening or morning rays.

[2] There are few people whom it may be neces-

Or through her truant pathway's native
charms,
By secret villages and lonely farms,　50
To where the Alps, ascending white in
air,
Toy with the Sun, and glitter from afar.
　Ev'n now I sigh at hoary Chartreuse'
doom
Weeping beneath his chill of mountain
gloom
Where now is fled that Power whose frown
severe　55
Tam'd "sober Reason" till she crouch'd
in fear?
That breath'd a death-like peace these
woods around,
Broke only by th' unvaried torrent's
sound,
Or prayer-bell by the dull cicada
drown'd.
The cloister startles at the gleam of arms,
And Blasphemy the shuddering fane
alarms;　61
Nod the cloud-piercing pines their troubl'd
heads,
Spires, rocks, and lawns, a browner night
o'erspreads.
Strong terror checks the female peasant's
sighs,
And start th' astonish'd shades at female
eyes.　65
The thundering tube the aged angler hears,
And swells the groaning torrent with his
tears.
From Bruno's forest screams the frighted
jay,
And slow th' insulted eagle wheels away.
The cross with hideous laughter Demons
mock,　70
By angels[1] planted on the aereal rock.
The "parting Genius" sighs with hollow
breath
Along the mystic streams of Life and
Death[2],

Swelling the outcry dull, that long re-
sounds
Portentous, thro' her old woods' trackless
bounds,　75
Deepening her echoing torrents' awful
peal
And bidding paler shades her form con-
ceal,
Vallombre[3], 'mid her falling fanes, de-
plores,
For ever broke, the sabbath of her bow'rs.
　More pleas'd, my foot the hidden
margin roves　80
Of Como bosom'd deep in chestnut groves.
No meadows thrown between, the giddy
steeps
Tower, bare or silvan, from the narrow
deeps.
To towns, whose shades of no rude sound
complain,
To ringing team unknown and grating
wain,　85
To flat-roof'd towns, that touch the water's
bound,
Or lurk in woody sunless glens profound,
Or from the bending rocks obtrusive cling,
And o'er the whiten'd wave their shadows
fling;
Wild round the steeps the little[4] path-
way twines,　90
And Silence loves it's purple roof of vines.
The viewless lingerer hence, at evening,
sees
From rock-hewn steps the sail between
the trees;
Or marks, mid opening cliffs, fair dark-
ey'd maids
Tend the small harvest of their garden
glades,　95
Or, led by distant warbling notes, sur-
veys,
With hollow ringing ears and darkening
gaze,

---

sary to inform, that the sides of many of the
post-roads in France are planted with a row of
trees.
　[1] Alluding to crosses seen on the tops of the
spiry rocks of the Chartreuse, which have every
appearance of being inaccessible.
　[2] Names of rivers at the Chartreuse.

　[3] Name of one of the vallies of the Chartreuse.
　[4] If any of my readers should ever visit the
Lake of Como, I recommend it to him to take
a stroll along this charming little pathway; he
must chuse the evening, as it is on the western
side of the Lake. We pursued it from the foot
of the water to its head: it is once interrupted
by a ferry.

Binding the charmed soul in powerless
  trance,
Lip-dewing Song and ringlet-tossing
  Dance,
Where sparkling eyes and breaking smiles
  illume   100
The bosom'd cabin's lyre-enliven'd gloom;
Or stops the solemn mountain-shades to
  view
Stretch, o'er their pictur'd mirror, broad
  and blue,
Tracking the yellow sun from steep to
  steep,
As up th' opposing hills, with tortoise
  foot, they creep.   105
Here half a village shines, in gold ar-
  ray'd,
Bright as the moon, half hides itself in
  shade.
From the dark sylvan roofs the restless
  spire,
Inconstant glancing, mounts like spring-
  ing fire,   109
There, all unshaded, blazing forests throw
Rich golden verdure on the waves below.
Slow glides the sail along th' illumined
  shore,
And steals into the shade his lazy oar.
Soft bosoms breathe around contagious
  sighs,
And amourous music on the water dies.
Heedless how Pliny, musing here, sur-
  vey'd
Old Roman boats and figures thro' the
  shade,
Pale Passion, overpower'd, retires and
  woos
The thicket, where th' unlisten'd stock-
  dove coos.
  How bless'd, delicious Scene! the eye
  that greets   120
Thy open beauties, or thy lone retreats;
Th' unwearied sweep of wood thy cliffs
  that scales,
The never-ending waters of thy vales;
The cots, those dim religious groves em-
  bow'r,
Or, under rocks that from the water tow'r
Insinuated, sprinkling all the shore,   126
Each with his household boat beside the
  door,

Whose flaccid sails in forms fantastic
  droop,
Bright'ning the gloom where thick the
  forests stoop;
—Thy torrents shooting from the clear-
  blue sky,   130
Thy towns, like swallows' nests that cleave
  on high;
That glimmer hoar in eve's last light,
  descry'd
Dim from the twilight water's shaggy
  side,
Whence lutes and voices down th' en-
  chanted woods
Steal, and compose the oar-forgotten
  floods,   135
While Evening's solemn bird melodious
  weeps,
Heard, by star-spotted bays, beneath the
  steeps;
—Thy lake, mid smoking woods, that
  blue and grey
Gleams, streak'd or dappled, hid from
  morning's ray
Slow-travelling down the western hills, to
  fold   140
It's green-ting'd margin in a blaze of gold;
From thickly-glittering spires the matin-
  bell
Calling the woodman from his desert cell,
A summons to the sound of oars, that pass,
Spotting the steaming deeps, to early
  mass;   145
Slow swells the service o'er the water
  born,
While fill each pause the ringing woods of
  morn.
  Farewel! those forms that, in thy
  noon-tide shade,
Rest, near their little plots of wheaten
  glade;
Those steadfast eyes, that beating breasts
  inspire   150
To throw the "sultry ray" of young De-
  sire;
Those lips, whose tides of fragrance come,
  and go,
Accordant to the cheek's unquiet glow;
Those shadowy breasts in love's soft light
  array'd,
And rising, by the moon of passion sway'd.

—Thy fragrant gales and lute-resounding
   streams,   156
Breathe o'er the failing soul voluptuous
   dreams;
While Slavery, forcing the sunk mind to
   dwell
On joys that might disgrace the captive's
   cell,
Her shameless timbrel shakes along thy
   marge,   160
And winds between thine isles the vocal
   barge.
   Yet, arts are thine that rock th' un-
   sleeping heart,
And smiles to Solitude and Want im-
   part.
I lov'd, mid thy most desert woods
   astray,
With pensive step to measure my slow
   way[1],   165
By lonely, silent cottage-doors to roam,
The far-off peasant's day-deserted home;
Once did I pierce to where a cabin
   stood,
The redbreast peace had bury'd it in
   wood,
There, by the door a hoary-headed sire
Touch'd with his wither'd hand an aged
   lyre,   171
Beneath an old-grey oak as violets lie,
Stretch'd at his feet with steadfast, up-
   ward eye,
His children's children join'd the holy
   sound,
A hermit—with his family around.   175
Hence shall we seek where fair Locarno
   smiles
Embower'd in walnut slopes and citron
   isles,
Or charms that smile on Tusa's evening
   stream,
While mid dim towers and woods her[2]
   waters gleam:

---

[1]   "Solo, e pensoso i più deserti campi
      Vò misurando à passi tardi, e lenti."—
                                    PETRARCH.
[2] The river along whose banks you descend in
crossing the Alps by the Semplon pass. From
the striking contrast of it's features, this pass I
should imagine to be the most interesting among
the Alps.

From the bright wave, in solemn gloom,
   retire   180
The dull-red steeps, and darkening still,
   aspire,
To where afar rich orange lustres glow
Round undistinguish'd clouds, and rocks,
   and snow;
Or, led where Viamala's chasms con-
   fine
Th' indignant waters of the infant Rhine,
Bend o'er th' abyss?—the else impervious
   gloom   186
His burning eyes with fearful light
   illume.
The Grison gypsey here her tent has
   plac'd,
Sole human tenant of the piny waste;
Her tawny skin, dark eyes, and glossy
   locks,   190
Bend o'er the smoke that curls beneath
   the rocks.

—The mind condemn'd, without reprieve,
   to go
O'er life's long deserts with it's charge of
   woe,
With sad congratulation joins the ⎫
   train,   ⎬195
Where beasts and men together o'er ⎥
   the plain   ⎭
Move on,—a mighty caravan of pain; ⎠
Hope, strength, and courage, social suffer-
   ing brings,
Freshening the waste of sand with shades
   and springs,
—She solitary through the desert drear
Spontaneous wanders, hand in hand with
   Fear.   200
A giant moan along the forest swells
Protracted, and the twilight storm fore-
   tells,
And, ruining from the cliffs their deafen-
   ing load
Tumbles, the wildering Thunder slips
   abroad;
On the high summits Darkness comes
   and goes,   205
Hiding their fiery clouds, their rocks, and
   snows;
The torrent, travers'd by the lustre broad,
Starts like a horse beside the flashing road;

In the roof'd[1] bridge, at that despairing
hour,
She seeks a shelter from the battering
show'r.   210
—Fierce comes the river down; the crash-
ing wood
Gives way, and half it's pines torment
the flood;
Fearful[2], beneath, the Water-spirits call,
And the bridge vibrates, tottering to its
fall.
—Heavy, and dull, and cloudy is the
night,   215
No star supplies the comfort of it's light,
Glimmer the dim-lit Alps, dilated, round,
And one sole light shifts in the vale
profound;
While, opposite, the waning moon hangs
still,
And red, above her melancholy hill. 220
By the deep quiet gloom appall'd, she sighs,
Stoops her sick head, and shuts her weary
eyes.
—Breaking th' ascending roar of desert
floods,
And insect buzz, that stuns the sultry
woods,
She hears, upon the mountain forest's brow,
The death-dog, howling loud and long,
below;   226
On viewless fingers counts the valley-
clock,
Followed by drowsy crow of midnight cock.
—Bursts from the troubl'd Larch's giant
boughs
The pie, and chattering breaks the night's
repose.   230
Low barks the fox: by Havoc rouz'd the
bear,
Quits, growling, the white bones that
strew his lair;
The dry leaves stir as with the serpent's
walk,
And, far beneath, Banditti voices talk;

Behind her hill the Moon, all crimson,
rides,   235
And his red eyes the slinking water
hides;
Then all is hushed; the bushes rustle near,
And with strange tinglings sings her
fainting ear.
—Vex'd by the darkness, from the piny
gulf
Ascending, nearer howls the famish'd
wolf,   240
While thro' the stillness scatters wild
dismay,
Her babe's small cry, that leads him to
his prey.
  Now, passing Urseren's open vale
serene,
Her quiet streams, and hills of downy
green,
Plunge with the Russ embrown'd by
Terror's breath,   245
Where danger roofs the narrow walks of
death;
By floods, that, thundering from their
dizzy height,
Swell more gigantic on the steadfast sight;
Black drizzling craggs, that beaten by
the din,
Vibrate, as if a voice complain'd within;
Bare steeps, where Desolation stalks,
afraid,   251
Unsteadfast, by a blasted yew upstay'd;
By cells[3] whose image, trembling as he
prays,
Awe struck, the kneeling peasant scarce
surveys;
Loose-hanging rocks the Day's bless'd eye
that hide,   255
And crosses[4] rear'd to Death on every
side,
Which with cold kiss Devotion planted
near,
And, bending, water'd with the human
tear,

---

[1] Most of the bridges among the Alps are of
wood and covered: these bridges have a heavy
appearance, and rather injure the effect of the
scenery in some places.

[2] "Red came the river down, and loud, and oft
The angry Spirit of the water shriek'd."
                            HOME'S *Douglas.*

[3] The Catholic religion prevails here. These
cells are, as is well known, very common in the
Catholic countries, planted, like Roman tombs,
along the road side.

[4] Crosses commemorative of the deaths of tra-
vellers by the fall of snow, and other accidents
very common along this dreadful road.

Soon fading "silent" from her upward
    eye,
Unmov'd with each rude form of Danger
    nigh,   260
Fix'd on the anchor left by him who saves
Alike in whelming snows and roaring
    waves.
  On as we move, a softer prospect opes,
Calm huts, and lawns between, and sylvan
    slopes.
While mists, suspended on th' expiring
    gale,   265
Moveless o'er-hang the deep secluded vale,
The beams of evening, slipping soft be-
    tween,
Light up of tranquil joy a sober scene;
Winding it's dark-green wood and eme-
    rald glade,
The still vale lengthens underneath the
    shade;   270
While in soft gloom the scattering bowers
    recede,
Green dewy lights adorn the freshen'd
    mead,
Where solitary forms illumin'd stray
Turning with quiet touch the valley's
    hay,
On the low [1] brown wood-huts delighted
    sleep   275
Along the brighten'd gloom reposing
    deep.
While pastoral pipes and streams the
    landscape lull,
And bells of passing mules that tinkle
    dull,
In solemn shapes before th' admiring eye
Dilated hang the misty pines on high,
Huge convent domes with pinnacles and
    tow'rs,   281
And antique castles seen thro' drizzling
    show'rs.
  From such romantic dreams my soul
    awake,
Lo! Fear looks silent down on Uri's lake,
By whose unpathway'd margin still and
    dread   285
Was never heard the plodding peasant's
    tread.

---

[1] The houses in the more retired Swiss valleys
are all built of wood.

Tower like a wall the naked rocks, or
    reach
Far o'er the secret water dark with beach,
More high, to where creation seems to
    end,
Shade above shade the desert pines as-
    cend,   290
And still, below, where mid the savage
    scene
Peeps out a little speck of smiling green,
There with his infants man undaunted
    creeps
And hangs his small wood-hut upon the
    steeps.
A garden-plot the desert air perfumes,
'Mid the dark pines a little orchard
    blooms,   296
A zig-zag path from the domestic skiff
Threading the painful cragg surmounts
    the cliff.
—Before those hermit doors, that never
    know   299
The face of traveller passing to and fro,
No peasant leans upon his pole, to tell
For whom at morning toll'd the funeral
    bell,
Their watch-dog ne'er his angry bark for-
    goes,
Touch'd by the beggar's moan of human
    woes,
The grassy seat beneath their casement
    shade   305
The pilgrim's wistful eye hath never
    stay'd.
—There, did the iron Genius not dis-
    dain
The gentle Power that haunts the myrtle
    plain,
There might the love-sick maiden sit, and
    chide
Th' insuperable rocks and severing tide,
There watch at eve her lover's sun-gilt
    sail   311
Approaching, and upbraid the tardy gale,
There list at midnight till is heard no
    more,
Below, the echo of his parting oar,
There hang in fear, when growls the
    frozen stream,   315
To guide his dangerous tread the taper's
    gleam.

'Mid stormy vapours ever driving by,
Where ospreys, cormorants, and herons
   cry,
Where hardly giv'n the hopeless waste to
   chear
Deny'd the bread of life the foodful ear,
Dwindles the pear on autumn's latest
   spray,   321
And apple sickens pale in summer's ray,
Ev'n here Content has fix'd her smiling
   reign
With Independence child of high Dis-
  . dain.
Exulting mid the winter of the skies,
Shy as the jealous chamois, Freedom
   flies,   326
And often grasps her sword, and often
   eyes,
Her crest a bough of Winter's bleakest
   pine,
Strange "weeds" and alpine plants her
   helm entwine,
And wildly-pausing oft she hangs aghast,
While thrills the "Spartan fife" between
   the blast.   331
'Tis storm; and hid in mist from hour
   to hour
All day the floods a deeper murmur
   pour,
And mournful sounds, as of a Spirit
   lost,
Pipe wild along the hollow-blustering
   coast,   335
'Till the Sun walking on his western
   field
Shakes from behind the clouds his flash-
   ing shield.
Triumphant on the bosom of the storm,
Glances the fire-clad eagle's wheeling
   form ;
Eastward, in long perspective glittering,
   shine   340
The wood-crown'd cliffs that o'er the lake
   recline ;
Wide o'er the Alps a hundred streams
   unfold,
At once to pillars turn'd that flame with
   gold ;
Behind his sail the peasant strives to
   shun
The west that burns like one dilated sun.

Where in a mighty crucible expire   346
The mountains, glowing hot, like coals of
   fire [1].
But lo ! the boatman, over-aw'd, before
The pictur'd fane of Tell suspends his oar:
Confused the Marathonian tale appears,
While burn in his full eyes the glorious
   tears.   351
And who but feels a power of strong con-
   troul,
Felt only there, oppress his labouring
   soul,
Who walks, where honour'd men of an'
   cient days
Have wrought with god-like arm the
   deeds of praise?   355
Say, who, by thinking on Canadian hills,
Or wild Aosta lull'd by Alpine rills,
On Zutphen's plain ; or where with
   soften'd gaze
The old grey stones the plaided chief
   surveys,
Can guess the high resolve, the cherish'd
   pain   360
Of him whom passion rivets to the plain,
Where breath'd the gale that caught
   Wolfe's happiest sigh,
And the last sun-beam fell on Bayard's eye,
Where bleeding Sydney from the cup
   retir'd,
And glad Dundee in "faint huzza's" ex-
   pir'd.   365

---

[1] I had once given to these sketches the title
of Picturesque ; but the Alps are insulted in ap-
plying to them that term. Whoever, in attempt-
ing to describe their sublime features, should
confine himself to the cold rules of painting
would give his reader but a very imperfect idea
of those emotions which they have the irresisti-
ble power of communicating to the most impas-
sive imaginations. The fact is, that controuling
influence, which distinguishes the Alps from all
other scenery, is derived from images which dis-
dain the pencil. Had I wished to make a picture
of this scene I had thrown much less light into
it. But I consulted nature and my feelings. The
ideas excited by the stormy sunset I am here
describing owed their sublimity to that deluge of
light, or rather of fire, in which nature had wrap-
ped the immense forms around me ; any intru-
sion of shade, by destroying the unity of the
impression, had necessarily diminished it's gran-
deur.

But now with other soul I stand alone
Sublime upon this far-surveying cone,
And watch from pike[1] to pike amid the
   sky
Small as a bird the chamois-chaser fly.
'Tis his with fearless step at large to roam
Thro' wastes, of Spirits wing'd the solemn
   home,   371
Thro'[2] vacant worlds where Nature never
   gave
A brook to murmur or a bough to wave,
Which unsubstantial Phantoms sacred
   keep;
Thro' worlds where Life and Sound, and
   Motion sleep,   375
Where Silence still her death-like reign
   extends,
Save when the startling cliff unfrequent
   rends:
In the deep snow the mighty ruin drown'd,
Mocks the dull ear of Time with deaf
   abortive sound;
—To mark a planet's pomp and steady
   light   380
In the least star of scarce-appearing night,
And neighbouring moon, that coasts the
   vast profound,
Wheel pale and silent her diminish'd
   round,
While far and wide the icy summits blaze
Rejoicing in the glory of her rays;   385
The star of noon that glitters small and
   bright,
Shorn of his beams, insufferably white,
And flying fleet behind his orb to view
Th' interminable sea of sable blue.
—Of cloudless suns no more ye frost-built
   spires   390
Refract in rainbow hues the restless fires!
Ye dewy mists the arid rocks o'er-spread
Whose slippery face derides his deathful
   tread!
—To wet the peak's impracticable sides
He opens of his feet the sanguine tides,

Weak and more weak the issuing current
   eyes   396
Lapp'd by the panting tongue of thirsty
   skies[3].
—At once bewildering mists around him
   close,
And cold and hunger are his least of
   woes;   399
The Demon of the snow with angry roar
Descending, shuts for aye his prison door.
Craz'd by the strength of hope at morn
   he eyes
As sent from heav'n the raven of the skies,
Then with despair's whole weight his
   spirits sink,
No bread to feed him, and the snow his
   drink,   405
While ere his eyes can close upon the
   day,
The eagle of the Alps o'ershades his prey.
—Meanwhile his wife and child with
   cruel hope
All night the door at every moment ope;
Haply that child in fearful doubt may
   gaze,   410
Passing his father's bones in future days,
Start at the reliques of that very thigh,
On which so oft he prattled when a boy.
   Hence shall we turn where, heard with
   fear afar,
Thunders thro' echoing pines the head-
   long Aar?   415
Or rather stay to taste the mild delights
Of pensive Underwalden's[4] pastoral
   heights?
—Is there who mid these awful wilds
   has seen
The native Genii walk the mountain
   green?
Or heard, while other worlds their charms
   reveal,   420
Soft music from th' aereal summit steal?

---

[1] Pike is a word very commonly used in the north of England, to signify a high mountain of the conic form, as Langdale pike, &c.

[2] For most of the images in the next sixteen verses I am indebted to M. Raymond's interesting observations annexed to his translation of Coxe's Tour in Switzerland.

[3] The rays of the sun drying the rocks frequently produce on their surface a dust so subtile and slippery, that the wretched chamois-chasers are obliged to bleed themselves in the legs and feet in order to secure a footing.

[4] The people of this Canton are supposed to be of a more melancholy disposition than the other inhabitants of the Alps: this, if true, may proceed from their living more secluded.

While o'er the desert, answering every
close,
Rich steam of sweetest perfume comes
and goes.
—And sure there is a secret Power that
reigns
Here, where no trace of man the spot
profanes, 425
Nought but the herds that pasturing up-
ward creep,
Hung dim-discover'd from the dangerous
steep,
Or summer hamlet [1], flat and bare, on high
Suspended, mid the quiet of the sky. 429
How still! no irreligious sound or sight
Rouzes the soul from her severe delight.
An idle voice the sabbath region fills
Of Deep that calls to Deep across the hills,
Broke only by the melancholy sound
Of drowsy bells for ever tinkling round;
Faint wail of eagle melting into blue 436
Beneath the cliffs, and pine-woods steady
sugh [2];
The solitary heifer's deepen'd low;
Or rumbling heard remote of falling snow.
Save that, the stranger seen below, the
boy 440
Shouts from the echoing hills with savage
joy.

When warm from myrtle bays and
tranquil seas,
Comes on, to whisper hope, the vernal
breeze [3],
When hums the mountain bee in May's
glad ear,
And emerald isles to spot the heights
appear, 445
When shouts and lowing herds the valley
fill,
And louder torrents stun the noon-tide
hill,

When fragrant scents beneath th' en-
chanted tread
Spring up, his little all around him spread,
The pastoral Swiss begins the cliffs to
scale, 450
To silence leaving the deserted vale,
Up the green mountain tracking Sum-
mer's feet,
Each twilight earlier call'd the Sun to
meet,
With earlier smile the ray of morn to view
Fall on his shifting hut that gleams mid
smoking dew; 455
Bless'd with his herds, as in the patri-
arch's age,
The summer long to feed from stage to
stage;
O'er azure pikes serene and still, they go,
And hear the rattling thunder far below;
Or lost at eve in sudden mist the day 460
Attend, or dare with minute-steps their
way;
Hang from the rocks that tremble o'er
the steep,
And tempt the icy valley yawning deep,
O'er-walk the chasmy torrent's foam-lit
bed,
Rock'd on the dizzy larch's narrow tread,
Whence Danger leans and pointing ghast-
ly, joys 466
To mock the mind with "desperation's
toys";
Or steal beneath loose mountains, half-
deterr'd,
That sigh and shudder to the lowing herd.
—I see him, up the midway cliff he creeps
To where a scanty knot of verdure peeps,
Thence down the steep a pile of grass he
throws
The fodder of his herds in winter snows.
Far different life to what tradition hoar
Transmits of days more bless'd in times
of yore [4]. 475

---

[1] These summer hamlets are most probably (as
I have seen observed by a critic in the *Gentle-
man's Magazine*) what Virgil alludes to in the
expression "Castella in tumulis."

[2] Sugh, a Scotch word expressive of the sound
of the wind through the trees.

[3] This wind, which announces the spring to the
Swiss, is called in their language Foen; and is
according to M. Raymond the Syroco of the
Italians.

[4] This tradition of the golden age of the Alps,
as M. Raymond observes, is highly interesting,
interesting not less to the philosopher than to
the poet. Here I cannot help remarking, that
the superstitions of the Alps appear to be far
from possessing that poetical character which so
eminently distinguishes those of Scotland and
the other mountainous northern countries. The

Then Summer lengthen'd out his season
  bland,
And with rock-honey flow'd the happy
  land.
Continual fountains welling chear'd the
  waste,
And plants were wholesome, now of dead-
  ly taste.
Nor Winter yet his frozen stores had
  pil'd   480
Usurping where the fairest herbage
  smil'd ;
Nor Hunger forc'd the herds from pas-
  tures bare
For scanty food the treacherous cliffs to
  dare.
Then the milk-thistle bad those herds
  demand
Three times a day the pail and welcome
  hand.   485
But human vices have provok'd the rod
Of angry Nature to avenge her God.
Thus does the father to his sons relate,
On the lone mountain top, their chang'd
  estate.   489
Still, Nature, ever just, to him imparts
Joys only given to uncorrupted hearts.
—'Tis morn : with gold the verdant moun-
  tain glows,
More high, the snowy peaks with hues of
  rose.
Far stretch'd beneath the many-tinted
  hills,
A mighty waste of mist the valley fills,
A solemn sea ! whose vales and moun-
  tains round   496
Stand motionless, to awful silence bound.
A gulf of gloomy blue, that opens wide
And bottomless, divides the midway tide.
Like leaning masts of stranded ships
  appear   500
The pines that near the coast their sum-
  mits rear
Of cabins, woods, and lawns a pleasant
  shore
Bounds calm and clear the chaos still
  and hoar ;

Devil with his horns, &c., seems to be, in their
idea, the principal agent that brings about the
sublime natural revolutions that take place daily
before the'r eyes.

Loud thro' that midway gulf ascending,
  sound
Unnumber'd streams with hollow roar
  profound.   505
Mounts thro' the nearer mist the chaunt
  of birds,
And talking voices, and the low of herds,
The bark of dogs, the drowsy tinkling bell,
And wild-wood mountain lutes of saddest
  swell.
Think not, suspended from the cliff on
  high   510
He looks below with undelighted eye.
—No vulgar joy is his, at even tide
Stretch'd on the scented mountain's pur-
  ple side.
For as the pleasures of his simple day
Beyond his native valley hardly stray, 515
Nought round it's darling precincts can
  he find
But brings some past enjoyment to his
  mind,
While Hope that ceaseless leans on Plea-
  sure's urn
Binds her wild wreathes, and whispers
  his return.
  Once Man entirely free, alone and
  wild,   520
Was bless'd as free—for he was Nature's
  child.
He, all superior but his God disdain'd,
Walk'd none restraining, and by none
  restrain'd,
Confess'd no law but what his reason
  taught,
Did all he wish'd, and wish'd but what he
  ought.   525
As Man in his primæval dower ar-
  ray'd
The image of his glorious sire display'd,
Ev'n so, by vestal Nature guarded, here
The traces of primæval Man appear.
The native dignity no forms debase, 530
The eye sublime, and surly lion-grace.
The slave of none, of beasts alone the lord,
He marches with his flute, his book, and
  sword,
Well taught by that to feel his rights,
  prepar'd
With this "the blessings he enjoys to
  guard."   535

And as on glorious ground he draws his
breath,
Where Freedom oft, with Victory and
Death,
Hath seen in grim array amid their
Storms
Mixed with auxiliar Rocks, three hundred
Forms [1];
While twice ten thousand corselets at the
view   540
Dropp'd loud at once, Oppression shriek'd,
and flew.
Oft as those sainted Rocks before him
spread,
An unknown power connects him with
the dead.
For images of other worlds are there,
Awful the light, and holy is the air.   545
Uncertain thro' his fierce uncultur'd soul
Like lighted tempests troubled transports
roll ;
To viewless realms his Spirit towers
amain,
Beyond the senses and their little reign.
And oft, when pass'd that solemn vision
by,   550
He holds with God himself communion
high,
When the dread peal of swelling torrents
fills
The sky-roof'd temple of the eternal
hills,
And savage Nature humbly joins the
rite,
While flash her upward eyes severe de-
light.   555
Or gazing from the mountain's silent brow,
Bright stars of ice and azure worlds of
snow,

Where needle peaks of granite shooting
bare
Tremble in ever-varying tints of air,
Great joy by horror tam'd dilates his
heart,   560
And the near heav'ns their own delights
impart.
—When the Sun bids the gorgeous scene
farewell,
Alps overlooking Alps their state up-
swell ;
Huge Pikes of Darkness named, of Fear [2]
and Storms,
Lift, all serene, their still, illumin'd
forms,   565
In sea-like reach of prospect round him
spread,
Ting'd like an angel's smile all rosy red.
When downward to his winter hut he
goes,
Dear and more dear the lessening circle
grows,
The hut which from the hills his eyes
employs   570
So oft, the central point of all his joys.
And as a swift by tender cares oppress'd
Peeps often ere she dart into her nest,
So to th' untrodden floor, where round
him looks
His father helpless as the babe he
rocks,   575
Oft he descends to nurse the brother
pair,
Till storm and driving ice blockade him
there ;
There hears, protected by the woods
behind.
Secure, the chiding of the baffled wind,
Hears Winter, calling all his Terrors
round,   580
Rush down the living rocks with whirl-
wind sound.
Thro' Nature's vale his homely pleasures
glide
Unstain'd by envy, discontent, and pride,
The bound of all his vanity to deck
With one bright bell a favourite heifer's
neck ;   585

[1] Alluding to several battles which the Swiss
in very small numbers have gained over their
oppressors, the house of Austria ; and in par-
ticular, to one fought at Naeffels near Glarus,
where three hundred and thirty men defeated
an army of between fifteen and twenty thousand
Austrians. Scattered over the valley are to be
found eleven stones, with this inscription 1388,
the year the battle was fought, marking out as
I was told upon the spot, the several places where
the Austrians attempting to make a stand were
repulsed anew.

[2] As Schreck-Horn, the pike of terror. Wetter-
Horn the pike of storms, &c., &c.

Content upon some simple annual feast,
Remember'd half the year, and hop'd the
   rest,
If dairy produce, from his inner hoard,
Of thrice ten summers consecrate the
   board.
—Alas! in every clime a flying ray   590
Is all we have to chear our wintry way,
Condemn'd, in mists and tempests ever
   rife,
To pant slow up the endless Alp of life.
"Here," cried a swain, whose venerable
   head
Bloom'd with the snow-drops of Man's
   narrow bed,   595
Last night, while by his dying fire, as
   clos'd
The day, in luxury my limbs repos'd,
"Here Penury oft from misery's mount
   will guide
Ev'n to the summer door his icy tide,
And here the avalanche of Death destroy
The little cottage of domestic Joy.   601
But, ah! th' unwilling mind may more
   than trace
The general sorrows of the human race:
The churlish gales, that unremitting blow
Cold from necessity's continual snow, 605
To us the gentle groups of bliss deny
That on the noon-day bank of leisure lie.
Yet more; the tyrant Genius, still at strife
With all the tender Charities of life,
When close and closer they begin to
   strain,   610
No fond hand left to staunch th' unclosing
   vein,
Tearing their bleeding ties leaves Age to
   groan
On his wet bed, abandon'd and alone.
For ever, fast as they of strength become
To pay the filial debt, for food to roam,
The father forc'd by Powers that only
   deign   616
That solitary Man disturb their reign,
From his bare nest amid the storms of
   heaven
Drives, eagle-like, his sons as he was
   driven,
His last dread pleasure! watches to the
   plain—   620
And never, eagle-like, beholds again."

When the poor heart has all its joys
   resign'd,
Why does their sad remembrance cleave
   behind?
Lo! by the lazy Seine the exile roves,
Or where thick sails illume Batavia's
   groves;   625
Soft o'er the waters mournful measures
   swell,
Unlocking bleeding Thought's "memorial
   cell;"
At once upon his heart Despair has set
Her seal, the mortal tear his cheek has wet;
Strong poison not a form of steel can brave
Bows his young hairs with sorrow to the
   grave[1].   631
   Gay lark of hope thy silent song
   resume!
Fair smiling lights the purpled hills
   illume!
Soft gales and dews of life's delicious
   morn,
And thou! lost fragrance of the heart
   return!   635
Soon[2] flies the little joy to man allow'd,
And tears before him travel like a cloud.
For come Diseases on, and Penury's rage,
Labour, and Pain, and Grief, and joyless
   Age,
And Conscience dogging close his bleeding
   way   640
Cries out, and leads her Spectres to their
   prey,
'Till Hope-deserted, long in vain his
   breath
Implores the dreadful untried sleep of
   Death.
—Mid savage rocks and seas of snow that
   shine
Between interminable tracts of pine, 645
Round a lone fane the human Genii
   mourn,
Where fierce the rays of woe collected
   burn.

---

[1] The effect of the famous air, called in French
Ranz des Vaches, upon the Swiss troops removed
from their native country is well known, as also
the injunction of not playing it on pain of death,
before the regiments of that nation, in the service
of France and Holland.

[2] Optima quaeque dies, &c.

—From viewless lamps a ghastly dimness
   falls,
And ebbs uncertain on the troubled walls,
Dim dreadful faces thro' the gloom
   appear,   650
Abortive Joy, and Hope that works in
   fear,
While strives a secret Power to hush the
   croud,
Pain's wild rebellious burst proclaims her
   rights aloud.
  Oh give not me that eye of hard
   disdain
That views undimm'd Einsiedlen's wretch-
   ed fane[1].   655
Mid muttering prayers all sounds of tor-
   ment meet,
Dire clap of hands, distracted chase of
   feet,
While loud and dull ascends the weeping
   cry,
Surely in other thoughts contempt may
   die.
If the sad grave of human ignorance
   bear   660
One flower of hope—Oh pass and leave it
   there.
—The tall Sun, tip toe on an Alpine
   spire,
Flings o'er the desert blood-red streams
   of fire.
At such an hour there are who love to
   stray,
And meet the gladdening pilgrims on
   their way.   665
—Now with joy's tearful kiss each other
   greet,
Nor longer naked be your way-worn feet,
For ye have reach'd at last the happy
   shore,
Where the charm'd worm of pain shall
   gnaw no more.
How gayly murmur and how sweetly
   taste   670
The fountains[2] rear'd for you amid the
   waste!

Yes I will see you when ye first behold
Those turrets tipp'd by hope with morn-
   ing gold,
And watch, while on your brows the cross
   ye make,
Round your pale eyes a wintry lustre
   wake.   675
—Without one hope her written griefs to
   blot,
Save in the land where all things are
   forgot,
My heart, alive to transports long un-
   known,
Half wishes your delusion were it's
   own.
Last let us turn to where Chamouny[3]
   shields,   680
Bosom'd in gloomy woods, her golden
   fields,
Five streams of ice amid her cots de-
   scend,
And with wild flowers and blooming
   orchards blend,
A scene more fair than what the Grecian
   feigns
Of purple lights and ever vernal
   plains.   685
Here lawns and shades by breezy rivulets
   fann'd,
Here all the Seasons revel hand in
   hand.
—Red stream the cottage lights; the
   landscape fades,
Erroneous wavering mid the twilight
   shades.
Alone ascends that mountain nam'd of
   white[4]   690
That dallies with the Sun the summer
   night.
Six thousand years amid his lonely bounds
The voice of Ruin, day and night, re-
   sounds.

---

[1] This shrine is resorted to, from a hope of relief, by multitudes, from every corner of the Catholick world, labouring under mental or bodily afflictions.

[2] Rude fountains built and covered with sheds for the accommodation of the pilgrims, in their ascent of the mountain. Under those sheds the sentimental traveller and the philosopher may find interesting sources of meditation.

[3] This word is pronounced upon the spot Chàmouny, I have taken the liberty of reading it long thinking it more musical.

[4] It is only from the higher part of the valley of Chàmouny that Mont Blanc is visible.

Where Horror-led his sea of ice assails,
Havoc and Chaos blast a thousand vales,
In waves, like two enormous serpents,
wind 696
And drag their length of deluge train
behind.
Between the pine's enormous boughs
descry'd
Serene he towers, in deepest purple dy'd;
Glad Day-light laughs upon his top of
snow, 700
Glitter the stars above, and all is black
below.
  At such an hour I heav'd the human
sigh,
When roar'd the sullen Arve in anger by,
That not for thee, delicious vale! unfold
Thy reddening orchards, and thy fields of
gold; 705
That thou, the slave of slaves[1], art
doom'd to pine,
While no Italian arts their charms combine
To teach the skirt of thy dark cloud to
shine;
For thy poor babes that, hurrying from
the door,
With pale-blue hands, and eyes that fix'd
implore, 710
Dead muttering lips, and hair of hungry
white,
Besiege the traveller whom they half
affright.
—Yes, were it mine, the cottage meal to
share
Forc'd from my native mountains bleak
and bare;
O'er Anet's[2] hopeless seas of marsh to
stray, 715
Her shrill winds roaring round my lonely
way;
To scent the sweets of Piedmont's breath-
ing rose,
And orange gale that o'er Lugano blows;
In the wide range of many a weary round,
Still have my pilgrim feet unfailing
found, 720

As despot courts their blaze of gems
display,
Ev'n by the secret cottage far away
The lily of domestic joy decay;
While Freedom's farthest hamlets bless-
ings share,
Found still beneath her smile, and only
there. 725
The casement shade more luscious wood-
bine binds,
And to the door a neater pathway winds,
At early morn the careful housewife, led
To cull her dinner from it's garden bed,
Of weedless herbs a healthier prospect
sees, 730
While hum with busier joy her happy
bees;
In brighter rows her table wealth aspires,
And laugh with merrier blaze her even-
ing fires;
Her infant's cheeks with fresher roses
glow,
And wilder graces sport around their
brow; 735
By clearer taper lit a cleanlier board
Receives at supper hour her tempting
hoard;
The chamber hearth with fresher boughs
is spread,
And whiter is the hospitable bed.
—And thou! fair favoured region! which
my soul 740
Shall love, 'till Life has broke her golden
bowl,
Till Death's cold touch her cistern-wheel
assail,
And vain regret and vain desire shall fail;
Tho' now, where erst the grey-clad peasant
stray'd,
To break the quiet of the village shade
Gleam war's[3] discordant habits thro' the
trees, 746
And the red banner mock the sullen
breeze;
'Tho' now no more thy maids their voices
suit
To the low-warbled breath of twilight
lute,

[1] It is scarce necessary to observe that these lines were written before the emancipation of Savoy.

[2] A vast extent of marsh so called near the lake of Neufchatel.

[3] This, as may be supposed, was written before France became the seat of war.

And heard, the pausing village hum be-
tween,　　　　　　　　　　　　750
No solemn songstress lull the fading green,
Scared by the fife, and rumbling drum's
alarms,
And the short thunder, and the flash of
arms;
While, as Night bids the startling uproar
die,
Sole sound, the sourd[1] renews his mourn-
ful cry:　　　　　　　　　　　　755
—Yet, hast thou found that Freedom
spreads her pow'r
Beyond the cottage hearth, the cottage
door:
All nature smiles; and owns beneath her
eyes
Her fields peculiar, and peculiar skies.
Yes, as I roam'd where Loiret's[2] waters
glide　　　　　　　　　　　　　760
Thro' rustling aspins heard from side to
side,

[1] An insect so called, which emits a short,
melancholy cry, heard, at the close of the summer
evenings, on the banks of the Loire.

[2] The river Loiret, which has the honour of
giving name to a department, rises out of the
earth at a place, called La Source, a league and
a half south-east of Orleans, and taking at once
the character of a considerable stream, winds
under a most delicious bank on its left, with a
flat country of meadows, woods, and vineyards
on its right, till it falls into the Loire about three
or four leagues below Orleans. The hand of false
taste has committed on its banks those outrages
which the Abbé de Lille so pathetically deprecates
in those charming verses descriptive of the Seine,
visiting in secret the retreat of his friend Watelet.
Much as the Loiret, in its short course, suffers
from injudicious ornament, yet are there spots
to be wished upon its banks as soothing as medi-
tation could wish for: the curious traveller may
meet with some of them where it loses itself
among the mills in the neighbourhood of the
villa called La Fontaine. The walks of La Source,
where it takes its rise, may, in the eyes of some
people, derive an additional interest from the
recollection that they were the retreat of Boling-
broke during his exile, and that here it was that
his philosophical works were chiefly composed.
The inscriptions of which he speaks in one of his
letters to Swift descriptive of this spot, are not,
I believe, now extant. The gardens have been
modelled within these twenty years according to
a plan evidently not dictated by the taste of the
friend of Pope.

When from october clouds a milder
light
Fell, where the blue flood rippled into
white,
Methought from every cot the watchful
bird
Crowed with ear-piercing power 'till then
unheard;　　　　　　　　　　765
Each clacking mill, that broke the mur-
muring streams,
Rock'd the charm'd thought in more de-
lightful dreams,
Chasing those long long dreams the fall-
ing leaf
Awoke a fainter pang of moral grief;
The measured echo of the distant flail　770
Winded in sweeter cadence down the
vale;
A more majestic tide the water[3] roll'd
And glowed the sun-gilt groves in richer
gold:
—Tho' Liberty shall soon, indignant, raise
Red on his hills his beacon's comet
blaze;
Bid from on high his lonely cannon
sound,
And on ten thousand hearths his shout
rebound;
His larum-bell from village-tow'r to tow'r
Swing on th' astounded ear it's dull un-
dying roar:
Yet, yet rejoice, tho' Pride's perverted
ire　　　　　　　　　　　　　780
Rouze Hell's own aid, and wrap thy hills
in fire.
Lo! from th' innocuous flames, a lovely
birth!
With it's own Virtues springs another
earth:
Nature, as in her prime, her virgin reign
Begins, and Love and Truth compose her
train;　　　　　　　　　　　　785
With pulseless hand, and fix'd unwearied
gaze,
Unbreathing Justice her still beam sur-
veys:

[3] The duties upon many of the French rivers
were so exorbitant that the poorer people, de-
prived of the benefit of water carriage, were
obliged to transport their goods by land.

No more, along thy vales and viny groves,
Whole hamlets disappearing as he moves,
With cheeks o'erspread by smiles of bale-
ful glow,   790
On his pale horse shall fell Consumption
go.

  Oh give, great God, to Freedom's waves
to ride
Sublime o'er Conquest, Avarice, and
Pride,
To break, the vales where Death with
Famine scow'rs,
And dark Oppression builds her thick-
ribb'd tow'rs;   795
Where Machination her fell soul re-
signs,
Fled panting to the centre of her
mines;
Where Persecution decks with ghastly
smiles
Her bed, his mountains mad Ambition
piles;
Where Discord stalks dilating, every
hour,   800
And crouching fearful at the feet of
Pow'r,
Like Lightnings eager for th' almighty
word,
Look up for sign of havoc, Fire and
Sword[1],
—Give them, beneath their breast while
Gladness springs,
To brood the nations o'er with Nile-like
wings;   805
And grant that every sceptred child of
clay,
Who cries, presumptuous, "here their
tides shall stay,"
Swept in their anger from th' affrighted
shore,
With all his creatures sink—to rise no
more.

  To-night, my friend, within this humble
cot   810
Be the dead load of mortal ills forgot,
Renewing, when the rosy summits glow
At morn, our various journey, sad and
slow.

---

[1] ————————— And, at his heels,
Leash'd in like hounds, should Famine,
Sword, and Fire,
Crouch for employment.

SUPPLEMENT OF PIECES NOT APPEARING IN THE EDITION OF 1849-50;

ARRANGED IN CHRONOLOGICAL ORDER.

I.

LINES

WRITTEN AS A SCHOOL EXERCISE AT HAWKSHEAD, ANNO ÆTATIS 14.

[Composed 1784-5.—Published 1851 (*Memoirs of W.*].

"I was called upon, among other scholars," Wordsworth says, "to write verses upon the completion of the second centenary from the foundation of the school in 1585, by Archbishop Sandys. The verses were much admired, far more than they deserved, for they were but a tame imitation of Pope's versification, and a little in his style. This exercise, however, put it into my head to compose verses from the impulse of my own mind, and I wrote, while yet a schoolboy, a long poem running upon my own adventures, and the scenery of the country in which I was brought up. The only part of that poem which has been preserved is the conclusion of it, which stands at the beginning of my collected Poems." (See *Extract from the Conclusion of a Poem*, &c., page 1.)—ED.

"And has the Sun his flaming chariot driven
Two hundred times around the ring of heaven,
Since Science first, with all her sacred train,
Beneath yon roof began her heavenly reign?
While thus I mused, methought, before mine eyes,   5
The Power of EDUCATION seemed to rise;
Not she whose rigid precepts trained the boy
Dead to the sense of every finer joy,
Nor that vile wretch who bade the tender age
Spurn Reason's law and humour Passion's rage;   10
But she who trains the generous British youth
In the bright paths of fair majestic Truth:
Emerging slow from Academus' grove
In heavenly majesty she seem'd to move.

Stern was her forehead, but a smile serene
'Soften'd the terrors of her awful mien.'   16
Close at her side were all the powers, design'd
To curb, exalt, reform the tender mind :
With panting breast, now pale as winter snows,
Now flush'd as Hebe, Emulation rose;   20
And hue far deeper than the Tyrian dye;
Shame follow'd after with reverted eye,
Last Industry appear'd with steady pace,
A smile sat beaming on her pensive face.
I gazed upon the visionary train,   25
Threw back my eyes, return'd, and gazed again.
When lo ! the heavenly goddess thus began,
Through all my frame the pleasing accents ran.

" 'When Superstition left the golden light
And fled indignant to the shades of night ;
When pure Religion rear'd the peaceful breast   31
And lull'd the warring passions into rest,
Drove far away the savage thoughts that roll
In the dark mansions of the bigot's soul,
Enlivening Hope display'd her cheerful ray,
And beam'd on Britain's sons a brighter day;   36
So when on Ocean's face the storm subsides,
Hush'd are the winds and silent are the tides;
The God of day, in all the pomp of light,
Moves through the vault of heaven, and dissipates the night ;   40
Wide o'er the main a trembling lustre plays,
The glittering waves reflect the dazzling blaze;
Science with joy saw Superstition fly
Before the lustre of Religion's eye;
With rapture she beheld Britannia smile,
Clapp'd her strong wings, and sought the cheerful isle,   46
The shades of night no more the soul involve,
She sheds her beam, and, lo ! the shades dissolve;

No jarring monks, to gloomy cell confined,
With mazy rules perplex the weary mind;
No shadowy forms entice the soul aside, 51
Secure she walks, Philosophy her guide.
Britain, who long her warriors had adored,
And deem'd all merit centred in the sword;
Britain, who thought to stain the field was
    fame, 55
Now honour'd Edward's less than Bacon's
    name.

Her sons no more in listed fields advance
To ride the ring, or toss the beamy lance;
No longer steel their indurated hearts
To the mild influence of the finer arts; 60
Quick to the secret grotto they retire
To court majestic truth, or wake the golden
    lyre;
By generous Emulation taught to rise,
The seats of learning brave the distant
    skies.
Then noble Sandys, inspir'd with great
    design, 65
Reared Hawkshead's happy roof, and call'd
    it mine.
There have I loved to show the tender age
The golden precepts of the classic page;
To lead the mind to those Elysian plains
Where, throned in gold, immortal Science
    reigns; 70
Fair to the view is sacred Truth display'd,
In all the majesty of light array'd,
To teach, on rapid wings, the curious soul
To roam from heaven to heaven, from pole
    to pole,
From thence to search the mystic cause of
    things 75
And follow Nature to her secret springs;
Nor less to guide the fluctuating youth
Firm in the sacred paths of moral truth,
To regulate the mind's disordered frame,
And quench the passions kindling into
    flame; 80
The glimmering fires of Virtue to enlarge,
And purge from Vice's dross my tender
    charge.
Oft have I said, the paths of Fame pursue,
And all that Virtue dictates, dare to do;
Go to the world, peruse the book of man,
And learn from thence thy own defects to
    scan; 86
Severely honest, break no plighted trust,
But coldly rest not here—be more than
    just;
Join to the rigours of the sires of Rome
The gentler manners of the private dome;
When Virtue weeps in agony of woe, 91
Teach from the heart the tender tear to
    flow;
If Pleasure's soothing song thy soul en-
    tice,
Or all the gaudy pomp of splendid Vice,

Arise superior to the Siren's power, 95
The wretch, the short-lived vision of an
    hour;
Soon fades her cheek, her blushing beauties
    fly,
As fades the chequer'd bow that paints the
    sky.

"'So shall thy sire, whilst hope his
    breast inspires,
And wakes anew life's glimmering trem-
    bling fires, 100
Hear Britain's sons rehearse thy praise
    with joy,
Look up to heaven, and bless his darling
    boy.
If e'er these precepts quell'd the passions'
    strife,
If e'er they smooth'd the rugged walks of
    life,
If e'er they pointed forth the blissful way
That guides the spirit to eternal day, 106
Do thou, if gratitude inspire thy breast,
Spurn the soft fetters of lethargic rest.
Awake, awake! and snatch the slumbering
    lyre,
Let this bright morn and Sandys the song
    inspire.' 110

"I look'd obedience: the celestial Fair
    Smiled like the morn, and vanish'd into
    air."

II.

SONNET, ON SEEING MISS HELEN MARIA WILLIAMS WEEP AT A TALE OF DISTRESS.

[Composed 1787.—Published March, 1787 (*The European Magazine*, Vol. XI., p. 202); never reprinted by W.

She wept.—Life's purple tide began to
    flow
In languid streams through every thrilling
    vein;
Dim were my swimming eyes—my pulse
    beat slow,
And my full heart was swell'd to dear
    delicious pain. 4
Life left my loaded heart, and closing eye;
A sigh recall'd the wanderer to my breast;
Dear was the pause of life, and dear the
    sigh
That call'd the wanderer home, and home
    to rest.
That tear proclaims—in thee each virtue
    dwells,
And bright will shine in misery's midnight
    hour; 10
As the soft star of dewy evening tells

What radiant fires were drown'd by day's
    malignant pow'r,
That only wait the darkness of the night
To cheer the wand'ring wretch with hospi-
    table light.

AXIOLOGUS.

III.

THE BIRTH OF LOVE.

[Composed 1795 (?).—Published 1795.]

Reprinted from a vol. entitled *Poems by Francis
Wrangham, M.A.* A translation (signed
Wordsworth) of some French stanzas signed
Anon.; never reprinted by Wordsworth—ED.

WHEN Love was born of heavenly line,
    What dire intrigues disturbed *Cythera's*
      joy!
Till VENUS cried, "A mother's heart is
    mine;
None but myself shall nurse my boy."

But, infant as he was, the child   5
    In that divine embrace enchanted lay;
And, by the beauty of the vase beguil'd,
    Forgot the beverage—and pin'd away.

"And must my offspring languish in my
    sight?"
    (Alive to all a mother's pain,   10
The Queen of Beauty thus her court ad-
    dress'd)
"No: Let the most discreet of all my
    train
Receive him to her breast:
    Think all, he is the God of young
      delight."   14

Then TENDERNESS with CANDOUR join'd,
    And GAIETY the charming office sought;
Nor even DELICACY stayed behind:
    But none of those fair Graces brought
Wherewith to nurse the child—and still he
    pin'd.
Some fond hearts to COMPLIANCE seem'd
    inclin'd;   20
    But she had surely spoil'd the boy:
    And sad experience forbade a thought
On the wild Goddess of VOLUPTUOUS
    JOY.

Long undecided lay th' important choice,
Till of the beauteous court, at length, a
    voice   25
Pronounced the name of HOPE:—The
    conscious child
Stretched forth his little arms and smil'd.

'Tis said ENJOYMENT (who averr'd
    The charge belong'd to her alone)
Jealous that HOPE had been preferr'd   30
    Laid snares to make the babe her own.

Of INNOCENCE the garb she took,
    The blushing mien and downcast look;
      And came her services to proffer:
And HOPE (what has not HOPE believ'd!)
By that seducing air deceiv'd,   36
    Accepted of the offer.

It happen'd that, to sleep inclin'd,
    Deluded HOPE for one short hour
      To that false INNOCENCE'S power   40
Her little charge consign'd.

The Goddess then her lap with sweetmeats
    fill'd
    And gave, in handfuls gave, the treach-
      erous store:
A wild delirium first the infant thrill'd;
    But soon upon her breast he sunk—to
      wake no more.   45

IV.

THE CONVICT.

[Composed ?.—Published 1798; never reprinted
by W.]

THE glory of evening was spread through
    the west;
    —On the slope of a mountain I stood,
While the joy that precedes the calm season
    of rest
    Rang loud through the meadow and
      wood.

"And must we then part from a dwelling
    so fair?"   5
    In the pain of my spirit I said,
And with a deep sadness I turned, to
    repair
    To the cell where the convict is laid.

The thick-ribbèd walls that o'ershadow the
    gate
    Resound; and the dungeons unfold: 10
I pause; and at length, through the glim-
    mering grate,
    That outcast of pity behold.

His black matted hair on his shoulder is
    bent,
    And deep is the sigh of his breath,
And with steadfast dejection his eyes are
    intent   15
    On the fetters that link him to death.

'Tis sorrow enough on that visage to gaze,
    That body dismiss'd from his care;
Yet my fancy has pierced to his heart, and
    pourtrays
    More terrible images there.   20

His bones are consumed, and his life-blood
    is dried,
  With wishes the past to undo ;
And his crime, through the pains that o'er-
    whelm him, descried,
  Still blackens and grows on his view.

When from the dark synod, or blood-
    reeking field,   25
  To his chamber the monarch is led,
All soothers of sense their soft virtue shall
    yield,
  And quietness pillow his head.

But if grief, self-consumed, in oblivion
    would doze,
  And conscience her tortures appease, 30
'Mid tumult and uproar this man must
    repose ;
  In the comfortless vault of disease.

When his fetters at night have so press'd
    on his limbs,
  That the weight can no longer be borne,
If, while a half-slumber his memory be-
    dims,   35
  The wretch on his pallet should turn,

While the jail-mastiff howls at the dull
    clanking chain,
  From the roots of his hair there shall
    start
A thousand sharp punctures of cold-
    sweating pain,
  And terror shall leap at his heart.   40

But now he half-raises his deep-sunken
    eye,
  And the motion unsettles a tear ;
The silence of sorrow it seems to supply,
  And asks of me why I am here.

" Poor victim ! no idle intruder has stood
  With o'erweening complacence our state
    to compare,   46
But one, whose first wish is the wish to be
    good,
  Is come as a brother thy sorrows to
    share.

" At thy name though compassion her
    nature resign,
  Though in virtue's proud mouth thy
    report be a stain,   50
My care, if the arm of the mighty were
    mine,
  Would plant thee where yet thou
    might'st blossom again."

V.

ANDREW JONES.

[Composed probably 1800.—Published 1800, 1802,
  1805 (*Lyrical Ballads*) ; ed. 1815 ; omitted from
  edd. 1820—1849-50.]

I HATE that Andrew Jones : he'll breed
His children up to waste and pillage.
I wish the press-gang or the drum
Would, with its rattling music, come,
And sweep him from the village !   5

I said not this, because he loves
Through the long day to swear and tipple ;
But for the poor dear sake of one
To whom a foul deed he had done,
A friendless Man, a travelling Cripple ! 10

For this poor crawling helpless wretch
Some Horseman who was passing by,
A penny on the ground had thrown ;
But the poor Cripple was alone
And could not stoop—no help was nigh.

Inch-thick the dust lay on the ground   16
For it had long been droughty weather ;
So with his staff the Cripple wrought
Among the dust till he had brought
The halfpennies together.   20

It chanc'd that Andrew pass'd that way
Just at the time ; and there he found
The Cripple in the mid-day heat
Standing alone, and at his feet
He saw the penny on the ground.   25

He stooped and took the penny up :
And when the Cripple nearer drew,
Quoth Andrew, " Under half-a-crown,
What a man finds is all his own,
And so, my Friend, good-day to you."   30

And *hence* I say, that Andrew's boys
Will all be train'd to waste and pillage ;
And wish'd the press-gang, or the drum
Would, with its rattling music, come,
And sweep him from the village !   35

VI.

"ON NATURE'S INVITATION DO
I COME."

[Composed probably in 1800.—Published 1851.]

ON Nature's invitation do I come,
By Reason sanctioned. Can the choice
    mislead,
That made the calmest, fairest spot on
    earth,
With all its unappropriated good,
My own ; and not mine only, for with me

Entrenched—say rather peacefully em-
bowered—   6
Under yon orchard, in yon humble cot,
A younger orphan of a Home extinct,
The only daughter of my parents dwells :
Aye, think on that, my heart, and cease to
stir ;   10
Pause upon that, and let the breathing
frame
No longer breathe, but all be satisfied.
Oh, if such silence be not thanks to God
For what hath been bestowed, then where,
where then
Shall gratitude find rest? Mine eyes did
ne'er   15
Fix on a lovely object, nor my mind
Take pleasure in the midst of happy
thoughts,
But either she, whom now I have, who now
Divides with me this loved abode, was
there,
Or not far off. Where'er my footsteps
turned,   20
Her voice was like a hidden Bird that sang ;
The thought of her was like a flash of light
Or an unseen companionship, a breath
Or fragrance independent of the wind.
In all my goings, in the new and old   25
Of all my meditations, and in this
Favourite of all, in this the most of all. . . .
Embrace me then, ye hills, and close me in.
Now in the clear and open day I feel   29
Your guardianship : I take it to my heart ;
'Tis like the solemn shelter of the night.
But I would call thee beautiful ; for mild,
And soft, and gay, and beautiful thou art,
Dear valley, having in thy face a smile,
Though peaceful, full of gladness. Thou
art pleased,   35
Pleased with thy crags, and woody steeps,
thy Lake,
Its one green Island, and its winding shores,
The multitude of little rocky hills,
Thy Church, and cottages of mountain-
stone
Clustered like stars some few, but single
most,   40
And lurking dimly in their shy retreats,
Or glancing at each other cheerful looks,
Like separated stars with clouds between.

VII.[1]

"BLEAK SEASON WAS IT, TURBU-
LENT AND WILD."

[Composed (possibly) in 1800.—Published 1851.]

BLEAK season was it, turbulent and wild,
When hitherward we journeyed, side by
side,

---

[1] Nos. VI. and VII. are extracts, given by Bishop

Through bursts of sunshine and through
flying showers,
Paced the long Vales, how long they were,
and yet
How fast that length of way was left
behind,   5
Wensley's rich Vale and Sedbergh's naked
heights.
The frosty wind, as if to make amends
For its keen breath, was aiding to our
steps,
And drove us onward as two ships at sea ;
Or, like two birds, companions in mid-air,
Parted and reunited by the blast.   11
Stern was the face of nature ; we rejoiced
In that stern countenance ; for our souls
thence drew
A feeling of their strength. The naked
trees,
The icy brooks, as on we passed, appeared
To question us, "Whence come ye? To
what end?"   16

VIII.

AMONG ALL LOVELY THINGS MY
LOVE HAD BEEN.

[Composed April 12, 1802.—Published 1807 ;
never reprinted by W.]

AMONG all lovely things my Love had
been ;
Had noted well the stars, all flowers that
grew
About her home ; but she had never seen
A Glow-worm, never one, and this I knew.

While riding near her home one stormy
night   5
A single Glow-worm did I chance to espy ;
I gave a fervent welcome to the sight,
And from my Horse I leapt ; great joy
had I.

Upon a leaf the Glow-worm did I lay,
To bear it with me through the stormy
night :   10
And, as before, it shone without dismay ;
Albeit putting forth a fainter light.

When to the Dwelling of my Love I came,
I went into the Orchard quietly ;
And left the Glow-worm, blessing it by
name,   15
Laid safely by itself, beneath a Tree.

Wordsworth in his *Memoirs* of the poet (1851),
from *The Recluse, Book I., Part I., Home at
Grasmere* ;—a poem which, being copyright, is
not included in this volume. For two other
extracts from the same poem see *Water-Fowl,*
page 218, and the *Preface to The Excursion.*—
ED.

The whole next day, I hoped, and hoped
  with fear;
At night the Glow-worm shone beneath
  the Tree:
I led my Lucy to the spot, "Look here!"
Oh! joy it was for her, and joy for me[1]!

IX.

SONNET[2].

[Composed ?.—Published October 10, 1803 (*Morning Post*); never reprinted by W.]

I FIND it written of Simonides
  That travelling in strange countries
    once he found
A corpse that lay expos'd upon the
    ground,
For which, with pains, he caused due
    obsequies
To be performed, and paid all holy fees. 5
  Soon after, this man's Ghost unto him
    came
And told him not to sail as was his aim,
On board a ship then ready for the seas.
  Simonides, admonished by the ghost,
Remained behind; the ship the following
    day   10
Set sail, was wrecked, and all on board
    were lost.
Thus was the tenderest Poet that could be,
  Who sang in ancient Greece his moving
    lay,
Saved out of many by his piety.

X.

GEORGE AND SARAH GREEN[3].

[Composed 1808.—Published September, 1839 (*Tait's Edinburgh Magazine*); never printed by W.]

WHO weeps for strangers? Many wept
  For George and Sarah Green;
Wept for that pair's unhappy fate,
  Whose grave may here be seen.

---

[1] The incident described in this poem took place in 1795—probably at Racedown—between the poet and his sister Dorothy.—ED.

[2] This sonnet bears no signature in the *Morning Post*, but Coleridge, in an unpublished letter, assigns it to Wordsworth. Cf. line 12 with line 53 of the Poem, No. II., on *September*, 1819 (*Poems of Sentiment*, XXVIII; p. 498), and with a passage in the *Essay on Epitaphs* (page 929) in which the story of this sonnet is related in prose.—ED.

[3] See De Quincey's *Early Memorials of Grasmere*.—ED.

By night, upon these stormy fells,   5
  Did wife and husband roam;
Six little ones at home had left,
  And could not find that home.

For *any* dwelling-place of man
  As vainly did they seek.   10
He perish'd; and a voice was heard—
  The widow's lonely shriek.

Not many steps, and she was left
  A body without life—
A few short steps were the chain that
    bound   15
  The husband to the wife.

Now do those sternly-featured hills
  Look gently on this grave;
And quiet *now* are the depths of air,
  As a sea without a wave.   20

But deeper lies the heart of peace
  In quiet more profound;
The heart of quietness is here
  Within this churchyard bound.

And from all agony of mind   25
  It keeps them safe, and far
From fear and grief, and from all need
  Of sun or guiding star.

O darkness of the grave! how deep,
  After that living night—   30
That last and dreary living one
  Of sorrow and affright?

O sacred marriage-bed of death,
  That keeps them side by side
In bond of peace, in bond of love,   35
  That may not be untied!

XI.

TRANSLATION OF PART OF THE FIRST BOOK OF THE ÆNEID.

[Written c. 1816.—Published 1832 (*The Philological Museum*); not reprinted by W.]

TO THE EDITORS OF THE "PHILOLOGICAL MUSEUM."

YOUR letter, reminding me of an expectation I some time since held out to you of allowing some specimens of my translation from the Æneid to be printed in the "Philological Museum," was not very acceptable; for I had abandoned the thought of ever sending into the world any part of that experiment—for it was nothing more—an experiment begun for amusement, and I now think a less fortunate one than when I first named it to you. Having been displeased in modern translations with the additions of incongruous matter, I began to translate with a resolve to keep clear of that fault, by adding nothing; but I became convinced that a spirited translation can scarcely be accomplished in the English language without admitting a principle of compensation. On this point, however, I do not wish to insist, and merely send the following passage, taken at random, from a wish to comply with your request.—W. W.

But Cytherea, studious to invent
Arts yet untried, upon new counsels bent,
Resolves that Cupid, chang'd in form and
    face
To young Ascanius, should assume his
    place;
Present the maddening gifts, and kindle
    heat   5
Of passion at the bosom's inmost seat.
She dreads the treacherous house, the
    double tongue;
She burns, she frets—by Juno's rancour
    stung;
The calm of night is powerless to remove
These cares, and thus she speaks to winged
    Love: 10

"O son, my strength, my power! who
    dost despise
(What, save thyself, none dares through
    earth and skies)
The giant-quelling bolts of Jove, I flee,
O son, a suppliant to thy deity!
What perils meet Æneas in his course,   15
How Juno's hate with unrelenting force
Pursues thy brother—this to thee is
    known;
And oft-times hast thou made my griefs
    thine own.
Him now the generous Dido by soft chains
Of bland entreaty at her court detains;   20
Junonian hospitalities prepare
Such apt occasion that I dread a snare.
Hence, ere some hostile God can intervene,
Would I, by previous wiles, inflame the
    queen
With passion for Æneas, such strong love
That at my beck, mine only, she shall
    move.   26
Hear, and assist;—the father's mandate
    calls
His young Ascanius to the Tyrian walls;
He comes, my dear delight,—and costliest
    things
Preserv'd from fire and flood for presents
    brings.   30
Him will I take, and in close covert keep,
'Mid groves Idalian, lull'd to gentle sleep,
Or on Cythera's far-sequestered steep,
That he may neither know what hope is
    mine,
Nor by his presence traverse the design.   35
Do thou, but for a single night's brief
    space,
Dissemble; be that boy in form and face.

And when enraptured Dido shall receive
Thee to her arms, and kisses interweave
With many a fond embrace, while joy runs
    high,   40
And goblets crown the proud festivity,
Instil thy subtle poison, and inspire,
At every touch, an unsuspected fire."

Love, at the word, before his mother's
    sight
Puts off his wings, and walks, with proud
    delight,   45
Like young Iulus; but the gentlest dews
Of slumber Venus sheds, to circumfuse
The true Ascanius steep'd in placid rest;
Then wafts him, cherish'd on her careful
    breast,
Through upper air to an Idalian glade,   50
Where he on soft *amaracus* is laid,
With breathing flowers embraced, and
    fragrant shade.
But Cupid, following cheerily his guide
Achates, with the gifts to Carthage hied;
And, as the hall he entered, there, between
The sharers of her golden couch, was seen
Reclin'd in festal pomp the Tyrian queen.
The Trojans too (Æneas at their head),
On couches lie, with purple overspread:
Meantime in canisters is heap'd the bread,
Pellucid water for the hands is borne,   61
And napkins of smooth texture, finely
    shorn.
Within are fifty handmaids, who prepare,
As they in order stand, the dainty fare;
And fume the household deities with store
Of odorous incense; while a hundred more
Match'd with an equal number of like age,
But each of manly sex, a docile page,
Marshal the banquet, giving with due grace
To cup or viand its appointed place.   70
The Tyrians rushing in, an eager band,
Their painted couches seek, obedient to
    command.
They look with wonder on the gifts—they
    gaze
Upon Iulus, dazzled with the rays
That from his ardent countenance are
    flung,   75
And charm'd to hear his simulating tongue;
Nor pass unprais'd the robe and veil divine,
Round which the yellow flowers and wan-
    dering foliage twine.

But chiefly Dido, to the coming ill
Devoted, strives in vain her vast desires to
    fill;   80
She views the gifts; upon the child then
    turns
Insatiable looks, and gazing burns.
To ease a father's cheated love he hung
Upon Æneas, and around him clung;

Then seeks the queen; with her his arts he
    tries; 85
She fastens on the boy enamour'd eyes,
Clasps in her arms, nor weens (O lot
    unblest!)
How great a God, incumbent o'er her breast,
Would fill it with his spirit. He, to please
His Acidalian mother, by degrees 90
Blots out Sichæus, studious to remove
The dead, by influx of a living love,
By stealthy entrance of a perilous guest,
Troubling a heart that had been long at rest.

Now when the viands were withdrawn,
    and ceas'd 95
The first division of the splendid feast,
While round a vacant board the chiefs
    recline,
Huge goblets are brought forth; they
    crown the wine;
Voices of gladness roll the walls around;
Those gladsome voices from the courts
    rebound; 100
From gilded rafters many a blazing light
Depends, and torches overcome the night.
The minutes fly—till, at the queen's com-
    mand,
A bowl of state is offered to her hand;
Then she, as Belus wont, and all the line
From Belus, filled it to the brim with
    wine; 106
Silence ensued. "O Jupiter, whose care
Is hospitable dealing, grant my prayer!
Productive day be this of lasting joy
To Tyrians, and these exiles driven from
    Troy; 110
A day to future generations dear!
Let Bacchus, donor of soul-quick'ning
    cheer,
Be present; kindly Juno, be thou near!
And, Tyrians, may your choicest favours
    wait
Upon this hour, the bond to celebrate!"
She spake and shed an offering on the
    board; 116
Then sipp'd the bowl whence she the wine
    had pour'd
And gave to Bitias, urging the prompt lord;
He rais'd the bowl, and took a long deep
    draught;
Then every chief in turn the beverage
    quaff'd. 120

Graced with redundant hair, Iopas sings
The lore of Atlas, to resounding strings,
The labours of the Sun, the lunar wander-
    ings;
Whence human kind, and brute; what
    natural powers
Engender lightning, whence are falling
    showers. 125

He chaunts Arcturus,—that fraternal
    twain
The glittering Bears,—the Pleiads fraught
    with rain;
—Why suns in winter, shunning heaven's
    steep heights
Post seaward,—what impedes the tardy
    nights.
The learned song from Tyrian hearers
    draws 130
Loud shouts,—the Trojans echo the ap-
    plause.
—But, lengthening out the night with
    converse new,
Large draughts of love unhappy Dido
    drew;
Of Priam ask'd, of Hector,—o'er and
    o'er—
What arms the son of bright Aurora
    wore;— 135
What steeds the car of Diomed could
    boast;
Among the leaders of the Grecian host
How looked Achilles—their dread para-
    mount—
"But nay—the fatal wiles, O guest,
    recount,
Retrace the Grecian cunning from its
    source, 140
Your own grief and your friends'—your
    wandering course;
For now, till this seventh summer have
    ye rang'd
The sea, or trod the earth, to peace
    estrang'd."

XII.

SONNET.

AUTHOR'S VOYAGE DOWN THE RHINE
(THIRTY YEARS AGO).

[Composed probably 1821.—Published 1822 (*Me-
morials of a Tour on the Continent*, 1820);
never reprinted by W.]

THE confidence of Youth our only Art,
And Hope gay Pilot of the bold design,
We saw the living Landscapes of the
    Rhine,
Reach after reach, salute us and depart;
Slow sink the Spires,—and up again they
    start! 5
But who shall count the Towers as they
    recline
O'er the dark steeps, or on the horizon
    line
Striding, with shattered crests, the eye
    athwart?

More touching still, more perfect was the
  pleasure,
When hurrying forward till the slack'ning
  stream   10
Spread like a spacious Mere, we there
  could measure
A smooth free course along the watery
  gleam,
Think calmly on the past, and mark at
  leisure
Features which else had vanished like
  a dream.

XIII.

A CENTO MADE BY WORDSWORTH.

[Published 1835 (*Yarrow Revisited and other
  Poems*); never reprinted by W.]

For printing [the following piece] some reason
should be given, as not a word of it is original:
it is simply a fine stanza of Akenside, connected
with a still finer from Beattie, by a couplet
from Thomson. This practice, in which the
author sometimes indulges, of linking together,
in his own mind, favourite passages from dif-
ferent authors, seems in itself unobjectionable:
but, as the *publishing* such compilations might
lead to confusion in literature, he should deem
himself inexcusable in giving this specimen,
were it not from a hope that it might open to
others a harmless source of *private* gratifica-
tion.—W. W.

THRONED in the Sun's descending car
What Power unseen diffuses far
This tenderness of mind?
What Genius smiles on yonder flood?
What God in whispers from the wood   5
Bids every thought be kind?

O ever pleasing Solitude,
Companion of the wise and good,
Thy shades, thy silence, now be mine,
Thy charms my only theme;   10
My haunt the hollow cliff whose Pine
  Waves o'er the gloomy stream;
Whence the scared Owl on pinions grey
  Breaks from the rustling boughs,
And down the lone vale sails away   15
  To more profound repose!

XIV.

INSCRIPTION ON A ROCK AT RYDAL
MOUNT. (1838.)

WOULDST thou be gathered to Christ's
  chosen flock,
Shun the broad way too easily explored,
And let thy path be hewn out of the Rock,
The living Rock of God's eternal Word.

XV.

PROTEST AGAINST THE BALLOT.
(1838.)

[Composed 1838.—Published 1838 (collected vol.
  of *Sonnets*); 1839 (Supplement to ed. 1842);
  afterwards omitted by W.]

FORTH rushed from Envy sprung and
  Self-conceit,
A Power misnamed the SPIRIT of RE-
  FORM,
And through the astonished Island swept
  in storm,
Threatening to lay all Orders at her feet
That crossed her way. Now stoops she to
  entreat   5
Licence to hide at intervals her head
Where she may work, safe, undisquieted,
In a close Box, covert for Justice meet.
St. George of England! keep a watchful
  eye
Fixed on the Suitor; frustrate her re-
  quest—   10
Stifle her hope; for, if the State comply,
From such Pandorian gift may come a
  Pest
Worse than the Dragon that bowed low
  his crest,
Pierced by thy spear in glorious victory.

XVI.

A POET TO HIS GRANDCHILD.

SEQUEL TO "A PLEA FOR AUTHORS[1]."

[Composed 1838.—Same dates and mode of pub-
  lication as XV.; omitted from edd. 1843—1849-
  50.]

"SON of my buried Son, while thus thy
  hand
Is clasping mine, it saddens me to think
How Want may press thee down, and with
  thee sink
Thy Children left unfit, through vain de-
  mand
Of culture, even to feel or understand   5
My simplest Lay that to their memory
May cling;—hard fate! which haply need
  not be
Did Justice mould the Statutes of the
  Land.
A Book time-cherished and an honoured
  name
Are high rewards; but bound they Nature's
  claim   10
Or Reason's? No—hopes spun in timid
  line

---

[1] See page 280.—ED.

From out the bosom of a modest home
Extend through unambitious years to come,
My careless Little-one, for thee and thine!"

May 23, 1838.

XVII.

ON A PORTRAIT OF I. F. [ISABELLA FENWICK], PAINTED BY MARGARET GILLIES[1].

WE gaze—nor grieve to think that we
    must die,
But that the precious love this friend hath
    sown
Within our hearts, the love whose flower
    hath blown
Bright as if heaven were ever in its eye,
Will pass so soon from human memory; 5
And not by strangers to our blood alone,
But by our best descendants be unknown,
Unthought of—this may surely claim a
    sigh.
Yet, blessed Art, we yield not to dejection;
Thou against Time so feelingly dost strive.
Where'er, preserved in this most true
    reflection, 11
An image of her soul is kept alive,
Some lingering fragrance of the pure
    affection,
Whose flower with us will vanish, must
    survive.

RYDAL MOUNT, *New Year's Day,* 1840.

XVIII.

TO I. F.

THE star which comes at close of day to
    shine
More heavenly bright than when it leads
    the morn,
Is Friendship's emblem, whether the for-
    lorn
She visiteth, or, shedding light benign
Through shades that solemnize Life's calm
    decline, 5
Doth make the happy happier. This have
    we
Learnt, Isabel, from thy society,
Which now we too unwillingly resign
Though for brief absence. But farewell!
    the page
Glimmers before my sight through thank-
    ful tears, 10
Such as start forth, not seldom, to approve
Our truth, when we, old yet unchilled by age,

---

[1] XVII. and XVIII. were first published (1851) in the *Memoirs of William Wordsworth,* by his nephew, the late Bishop of Lincoln.—ED.

Call thee, though known but for a few
    fleet years,
The heart-affianced sister of our love!

RYDAL MOUNT, *Feb.* 1840.

XIX.

"WHEN SEVERN'S SWEEPING FLOOD HAD OVERTHROWN."

In 1842 a bazaar was held in Cardiff Castle to raise funds for the building of a Church. Wordsworth assisted by contributing this Sonnet, which was printed and sold along with verses by James Montgomery and others (cf. Prof. Knight's note, in his edition of the *Poems,* Vol. VIII.).—ED.

WHEN Severn's sweeping flood had over-
    thrown
St. Mary's Church, the preacher then
    would cry:—
"Thus, Christian people, God his might
    hath shown
That ye to him your love may testify;
Haste, and rebuild the pile."—But not
    a stone 5
Resumed its place. Age after age went by,
And Heaven still lacked its due, though
    piety
In secret did, we trust, her loss bemoan.
But now her Spirit hath put forth its
    claim 9
In Power, and Poesy would lend her voice;
Let the new Church be worthy of its aim,
That in its beauty Cardiff may rejoice!
Oh! in the past if cause there was for
    shame,
Let not our times halt in their better
    choice.

RYDAL MOUNT, *Jan.* 23, 1842.

XX.

THE EAGLE AND THE DOVE.

[Composed 1842 (?).—Published 1842 (*La Petite Chouannerie ou Histoire d'un Collège Breton sous l'Empire.* By A. F. Rio).]

SHADE of Caractacus, if spirits love
The cause they fought for in their earthly
    home,
To see the Eagle ruffled by the Dove
May soothe thy memory of the chains of
    Rome.

These children claim thee for their sire;
    the breath 5
Of thy renown, from Cambrian mountains,
    fans
A flame within them that despises death
And glorifies the truant youth of Vannes.

With thy own scorn of tyrants they
  advance,
But truth divine has sanctified their rage,
A silver cross enchased with Flowers of
  France   11
Their badge, attests the holy fight they
  wage.

The shrill defiance of the young crusade
Their veteran foes mock as an idle noise;
But unto Faith and Loyalty comes aid   15
From Heaven, gigantic force to beardless
  boys.

XXI.

LINES

INSCRIBED IN A COPY OF HIS POEMS
SENT TO THE QUEEN FOR THE ROYAL
LIBRARY AT WINDSOR.

DEIGN, Sovereign Mistress! to accept a
  lay,
  No Laureate offering of elaborate art;
But salutation taking its glad way
  From deep recesses of a loyal heart.

Queen, Wife and Mother! may All-judging
  Heaven   5
  Shower with a bounteous hand on Thee
    and Thine
Felicity that only can be given
  On earth to goodness blest by grace
    divine.

Lady! devoutly honoured and beloved
  Through every realm confided to thy
    sway;   10
May'st thou pursue thy course by God
  approved,
  And He will teach thy people to obey.

As thou art wont, thy sovereignty adorn
  With woman's gentleness, yet firm and
    staid;
So shall that earthly crown thy brows have
  worn   15
  Be changed for one whose glory cannot
    fade.

And now by duty urged, I lay this Book
  Before thy Majesty, in humble trust
That on its simplest pages thou wilt look
  With a benign indulgence more than
    just.   20

Nor wilt thou blame an aged Poet's prayer,
  That issuing hence may steal into thy
    mind
Some solace under weight of royal care,
  Or grief—the inheritance of humankind.

For know we not that from celestial
  spheres,   25
When Time was young, an inspiration
  came
(Oh were it mine!) to hallow saddest tears,
  And help life onward in its noblest aim.
                        W. W.

January 9th, 1846.

XXII.

ODE ON THE INSTALLATION OF HIS ROYAL HIGHNESS PRINCE ALBERT AS CHANCELLOR OF THE UNIVERSITY OF CAMBRIDGE, JULY, 1847[1].

[Composed 1847.—Published 1847.]

FOR thirst of power that Heaven dis-
  owns,
  For temples, towers, and thrones
Too long insulted by the Spoiler's shock,
  Indignant Europe cast
  Her stormy foe at last   5
To reap the whirlwind on a Libyan rock.
  War is passion's basest game
  Madly played to win a name:
Up starts some tyrant, Earth and Heaven
  to dare,
  The servile million bow;   10
But will the Lightning glance aside to
  spare
  The Despot's laurelled brow?

War is mercy, glory, fame,
  Waged in Freedom's holy cause,
  Freedom, such as man may claim   15
  Under God's restraining laws.
  Such is Albion's fame and glory,
  Let rescued Europe tell the story.
But lo! what sudden cloud has darkened
  all
  The land as with a funeral pall?   20
The Rose of England suffers blight,
The Flower has drooped, the Isle's delight:
  Flower and bud together fall;
A Nation's hopes lie crushed in Claremont's
  desolate Hall.

Time a chequered mantle wears—   25
  Earth awakes from wintry sleep:
Again the Tree a blossom bears;
  Cease, Britannia, cease to weep!
Hark to the peals on this bright May-
  morn!
They tell that your future Queen is born.
  A Guardian Angel fluttered   31
  Above the babe, unseen;

---

[1] The poet's nephew Christopher (late Bishop of Lincoln) aided in the composition of this "commanded" Ode.—ED.

One word he softly uttered,
It named the future Queen;   34
And a joyful cry through the Island rang,
As clear and bold as the trumpet's clang,
As bland as the reed of peace:
"VICTORIA be her name!"
For righteous triumphs are the base
Whereon Britannia rests her peaceful
fame.   40

Time, in his mantle's sunniest fold
Uplifted in his arms the child,
And while the fearless infant smiled,
Her happier destiny foretold:—
"Infancy, by Wisdom mild,   45
Trained to health and artless beauty;
Youth, by pleasure unbeguiled
From the lore of lofty duty;
Womanhood in pure renown,
Seated on her lineal throne;   50
Leaves of myrtle in her Crown,
Fresh with lustre all their own.
Love, the treasure worth possessing
More than all the world beside,
This shall be her choicest blessing,   55
Oft to royal hearts denied."

That eve, the Star of Brunswick shone
With steadfast ray benign
On Gotha's ducal roof, and on
The softly flowing Leine,   60
Nor failed to gild the spires of Bonn,
And glittered on the Rhine.
Old Camus, too, on that prophetic night
Was conscious of the ray;
And his willows whispered in its light,   65
Not to the Zephyr's sway,
But with a Delphic life, in sight
Of this auspicious day—
This day, when Granta hails her chosen
Lord,
And, proud of her award,   70
Confiding in that Star serene,
Welcomes the Consort of a happy Queen.

Prince, in these collegiate bowers,
Where science, leagued with holier truth,
Guards the sacred heart of youth,   75
Solemn monitors are ours.
These reverend aisles, these hallowed
towers,
Raised by many a hand august,
Are haunted by majestic Powers,
The Memories of the Wise and Just,   80
Who, faithful to a pious trust,
Here, in the Founder's Spirit sought
To mould and stamp the ore of thought
In that bold form and impress high
That best betoken patriot loyalty.   85
Not in vain those Sages taught,—
True disciples, good as great,

Have pondered here their country's weal,
Weighed the Future by the Past,
Learned how social frames may last,   90
And how a Land may rule its fate
By constancy inviolate,
Though worlds to their foundations reel
The sport of factious Hate or godless Zeal.

Albert, in thy race we cherish   95
A Nation's strength that will not perish
While England's sceptred Line
True to the King of Kings is found;
Like that Wise ancestor of thine
Who threw the Saxon shield o'er Luther's
life   100
When first, above the yells of bigot strife,
The trumpet of the Living Word
Assumed a voice of deep portentous sound,
From gladdened Elbe to startled Tiber
heard.
What shield more sublime   105
E'er was blazoned or sung?
And the PRINCE whom we greet
From its Hero is sprung.
Resound, resound the strain
That hails him for our own!   110
Again, again, and yet again,
For the Church, the State, the Throne!
And that Presence fair and bright,
Ever blest wherever seen,
Who deigns to grace our festal rite,   115
The Pride of the Islands, VICTORIA
THE QUEEN!

XXIII.

QUINZAIN

CONJECTURALLY ASSIGNED TO WORDS-
WORTH.

[Composed ?.—Published 1802 (*Morning Post*);
never reprinted by W.]

A writer (E. H. C.) in the *Athenæum* of
November 4, 1893, suggests that the following
lines, which appeared in the *Morning Post* on
February 9, 1802, were probably composed by
Wordsworth. "It may be remembered," writes
E. H. C., "that the phrase 'monthly grave' is to be
found in *Lines to the Moon* (1835); and in one of
Wordsworth's latest sonnets, that *To Lucca
Giordano*, the aged poet turns with pleasure
to the delightful vision of 'young Endymion,
couched on Latmos Hill.'" The suggestion is
undoubtedly a happy one. The rhyme-arrange-
ment of these lines resembles that of the piece
beginning, *With how sad steps, O Moon, thou
climb'st the Sky*, which first appeared in *Poems
in Two Volumes* (1807), but may have been
written in or about 1802. Both pieces appear to
be experiments in metre. They are neither
sonnets nor quatorzains, but *quinzains*, or
stanzas consisting of fifteen lines each; though
that published in 1807 was subsequently curtailed

by one line and placed amongst the *Miscellane-ous Sonnets* (1815 onwards). Moreover, the turn of the sentence in lines 8 and 9—the repetition of the substantive (*Nymphs*) in apposition, quali-fied by an adjective or adjectival phrase—is of frequent occurrence in Wordsworth's poetry. Cf. *Misc. Son.*, Part II., xx., ll. 7, 8:—

> "As if to vindicate her beauty's right,
> Her beauty thoughtlessly disparaged."—ED.[1]

WRITTEN IN A GROTTO.

O Moon! if e'er I joyed when thy soft light
  Danc'd to the murmuring rill on Lo-
    mond's wave,
Or sighed for thy sweet presence some dark
  night,
  When thou wert hidden in thy monthly
    grave;

If e'er, on wings which active fancy gave,
  I sought thy golden vale with dancing
    flight,   6
Then, stretcht at ease in some sequestered
  cave,
  Gaz'd on thy lovely Nymphs with fond
    delight,
Thy Nymphs with more than earthly
  beauty bright;
If e'er thy beam, as Smyrna's shepherds
  tell,   10
  Soft as the gentle kiss of amorous maid
On the closed eyes of young Endymion fell,
  That he might wake to clasp thee in the
    shade:
Each night, while I recline within this cell,
Guide hither, O sweet Moon, the maid I love
  so well.   15

---

[1] [Mr. T. E. Casson points out (1926) that there is no very close resemblance between the rhyme-arrangement of the above and that of the piece beginning *With how sad steps* in its original form of fifteen lines, now subjoined for comparison (for the 14 line form see p. 266):

> 'With how sad steps, O Moon, thou climb'st the sky,
> How silently, and with how wan a face!"
> Where art thou? Thou whom I have seen on high
> Running among the clouds a Wood-nymph's race?
> Unhappy Nuns, whose common breath's a sigh
> Which they would stifle, move at such a pace!
> The Northern Wind, to call thee to the chace,
> Must blow tonight his bugle horn. Had I
> The power of Merlin, Goddess! this should be:
> And all the Stars now shrouded up in heaven,
> Should sally forth to keep thee company.
> What strife would then be yours, fair Creatures, driv'n
> Now up, now down, and sparkling in your glee!
> But, Cynthia, should to Thee the palm be giv'n,
> Queen both for beauty and for majesty.]

The Prelude;

OR,

Growth of a Poet's Mind;

AN AUTOBIOGRAPHICAL POEM.

ADVERTISEMENT.

[BY THE EDITOR OF 1850.]

THE following Poem was commenced in the beginning of the year 1799, and completed in the summer of 1805 [1].

The design and occasion of the work are described by the Author in his Preface to the "Excursion," first published in 1814, where he thus speaks:—

"Several years ago, when the Author retired to his native mountains with the hope of being enabled to construct a literary work that might live, it was a reasonable thing that he should take a review of his own mind, and examine how far Nature and Education had qualified him for such an employment.

"As subsidiary to this preparation, he undertook to record, in verse, the origin and progress of his own powers, as far as he was acquainted with them.

"That work, addressed to a dear friend, most distinguished for his knowledge and genius, and to whom the Author's intellect is deeply indebted, has been long finished; and the result of the investigation which gave rise to it, was a determination to compose a philosophical Poem, containing views of Man, Nature, and Society, and to be entitled the "Recluse;" as having for its principal subject the sensations and opinions of a poet living in retirement.

"The preparatory poem is biographical, and conducts the history of the Author's mind to the point when he was emboldened to hope that his faculties were sufficiently matured for entering upon the arduous labour which he had proposed to himself; and the two works have the same kind of relation to each other, if he may so express himself, as the Ante-chapel has to the body of a Gothic Church. Continuing this allusion, he may be permitted to add, that his minor pieces, which have been long before the public, when they shall be properly arranged, will be found by the attentive reader to have such connection with the main work as may give them claim to be likened to the little cells, oratories, and sepulchral recesses, ordinarily included in those edifices."

Such was the Author's language in the year 1814.

It will thence be seen, that the present Poem was intended to be introductory to the "Recluse," and that the "Recluse," if completed, would have consisted of Three Parts. Of these, the Second Part alone, viz. the "Excursion," was finished, and given to the world by the Author.

The First Book of the First Part of the "Recluse" still [1850] remains in manuscript; but the Third Part was only planned. The materials of which it would have been formed have, however, been incorporated, for the most part, in the Author's other Publications, written subsequently to the "Excursion."

The Friend, to whom the present Poem is addressed, was the late SAMUEL TAYLOR COLERIDGE, who was resident in Malta, for the restoration of his health, when the greater part of it was composed.

Mr. Coleridge read a considerable portion of the Poem while he was abroad; and his feelings, on hearing it recited by the Author (after his return to his own country) are recorded in his Verses, addressed to Mr. Wordsworth, which will be found in the "Sibylline Leaves," p. 197, ed. 1817, or "Poetical Works, by S. T. Coleridge," vol. i., p. 206.

RYDAL MOUNT,
    July 13th, 1850.

---

[1] For further information regarding the dates of composition of the several Books of *The Prelude* see *The Prelude*, ed. by E. de Selincourt, 2nd ed., 1928.

The Prelude.

BOOK FIRST.

INTRODUCTION—CHILDHOOD AND SCHOOL-TIME.

OH THERE is blessing in this gentle breeze,
A visitant that while it fans my cheek
Doth seem half-conscious of the joy it
   brings
From the green fields, and from yon
   azure sky.
Whate'er its mission, the soft breeze can
   come   5
To none more grateful than to me; es-
   caped
From the vast city, where I long had
   pined
A discontented sojourner: now free,
Free as a bird to settle where I will.
What dwelling shall receive me? in what
   vale   10
Shall be my harbour? underneath what
   grove
Shall I take up my home? and what
   clear stream
Shall with its murmur lull me into rest?
The earth is all before me. With a heart
Joyous, nor scared at its own liberty, 15
I look about; and should the chosen
   guide
Be nothing better than a wandering
   cloud,
I cannot miss my way. I breathe again!
Trances of thought and mountings of the
   mind
Come fast upon me: it is shaken off, 20
That burthen of my own unnatural self,
The heavy weight of many a weary day
Not mine, and such as were not made
   for me.
Long months of peace (if such bold word
   accord
With any promises of human life), 25
Long months of ease and undisturbed
   delight

Are mine in prospect; whither shall I
   turn,
By road or pathway, or through trackless
   field,
Up hill or down, or shall some floating
   thing   29
Upon the river point me out my course?

Dear Liberty! Yet what would it avail
But for a gift that consecrates the joy?
For I, methought, while the sweet breath
   of heaven
Was blowing on my body, felt within
A correspondent breeze, that gently
   moved   35
With quickening virtue, but is now be-
   come
A tempest, a redundant energy,
Vexing its own creation. Thanks to both,
And their congenial powers, that, while
   they join
In breaking up a long-continued frost, 40
Bring with them vernal promises, the
   hope
Of active days urged on by flying hours,—
Days of sweet leisure, taxed with patient
   thought
Abstruse, nor wanting punctual service
   high,   44
Matins and vespers of harmonious verse!

Thus far, O Friend! did I, not used to
   make
A present joy the matter of a song,
Pour forth that day my soul in measured
   strains
That would not be forgotten, and are
   here
Recorded: to the open fields I told 50
A prophecy: poetic numbers came

Spontaneously to clothe in priestly robe
A renovated spirit singled out,
Such hope was mine, for holy services.
My own voice cheered me, and, far more,
    the mind's   55
Internal echo of the imperfect sound;
To both I listened, drawing from them
    both
A cheerful confidence in things to come.

  Content and not unwilling now to give
A respite to this passion, I paced on   60
With brisk and eager steps; and came,
    at length,
To a green shady place, where down I
    sate
Beneath a tree, slackening my thoughts
    by choice,
And settling into gentler happiness.
'Twas autumn, and a clear and placid day,
With warmth, as much as needed, from a
    sun   66
Two hours declined towards the west;
    a day
With silver clouds, and sunshine on the
    grass,
And in the sheltered and the sheltering
    grove
A perfect stillness. Many were the
    thoughts   70
Encouraged and dismissed, till choice
    was made
Of a known Vale, whither my feet should
    turn,
Nor rest till they had reached the very
    door
Of the one cottage which methought I
    saw.   74
No picture of mere memory ever looked
So fair; and while upon the fancied scene
I gazed with growing love, a higher
    power
Than Fancy gave assurance of some work
Of glory there forthwith to be begun,
Perhaps too there performed. Thus long
    I mused,   80
Nor e'er lost sight of what I mused upon,
Save when, amid the stately grove of
    oaks,
Now here, now there, an acorn, from its
    cup

Dislodged, through sere leaves rustled, or
    at once
To the bare earth dropped with a start-
    ling sound.   85
From that soft couch I rose not, till the
    sun
Had almost touched the horizon; casting
    then
A backward glance upon the curling
    cloud
Of city smoke, by distance ruralised;
Keen as a Truant or a Fugitive,   90
But as a Pilgrim resolute, I took,
Even with the chance equipment of that
    hour,
The road that pointed toward the chosen
    Vale.
It was a splendid evening, and my soul
Once more made trial of her strength,
    nor lacked   95
Æolian visitations; but the harp
Was soon defrauded, and the banded
    host
Of harmony dispersed in straggling
    sounds,
And lastly utter silence! "Be it so;
Why think of anything but present
    good?"   100
So, like a home-bound labourer, I pursued
My way beneath the mellowing sun, that
    shed
Mild influence; nor left in me one wish
Again to bend the Sabbath of that time
To a servile yoke. What need of many
    words?   105
A pleasant loitering journey, through
    three days
Continued, brought me to my hermitage.
I spare to tell of what ensued, the life
In common things—the endless store of
    things,
Rare, or at least so seeming, every day
Found all about me in one neighbour-
    hood—   111
The self-congratulation, and, from morn
To night, unbroken cheerfulness serene.
But speedily an earnest longing rose
To brace myself to some determined aim,
Reading or thinking; either to lay up
New stores, or rescue from decay the old
By timely interference: and therewith

Came hopes still higher, that with out-
 ward life
I might endue some airy phantasies 120
That had been floating loose about for
 years,
And to such beings temperately deal
 forth
The many feelings that oppressed my
 heart.
That hope hath been discouraged; wel-
 come light
Dawns from the east, but dawns to dis-
 appear 125
And mock me with a sky that ripens not
Into a steady morning: if my mind,
Remembering the bold promise of the
 past,
Would gladly grapple with some noble
 theme,
Vain is her wish; where'er she turns she
 finds 130
Impediments from day to day renewed.

And now it would content me to yield
 up
Those lofty hopes awhile, for present
 gifts
Of humbler industry. But, oh, dear
 Friend!
The Poet, gentle creature as he is, 135
Hath, like the Lover, his unruly times;
His fits when he is neither sick nor well,
Though no distress be near him but his
 own
Unmanageable thoughts: his mind, best
 pleased
While she as duteous as the mother dove
Sits brooding, lives not always to that
 end, 141
But like the innocent bird, hath goadings
 on
That drive her as in trouble through the
 groves;
With me is now such passion, to be
 blamed
No otherwise than as it lasts too long. 145

When, as becomes a man who would
 prepare
For such an arduous work, I through
 myself

Make rigorous inquisition, the report
Is often cheering; for I neither seem
To lack that first great gift, the vital
 soul, 150
Nor general Truths, which are them-
 selves a sort
Of Elements and Agents, Under-powers,
Subordinate helpers of the living mind:
Nor am I naked of external things,
Forms, images, nor numerous other aids
Of less regard, though won perhaps with
 toil 156
And needful to build up a Poet's praise.
Time, place, and manners do I seek, and
 these
Are found in plenteous store, but no-
 where such 159
As may be singled out with steady choice;
No little band of yet remembered names
Whom I, in perfect confidence, might
 hope
To summon back from lonesome banish-
 ment,
And make them dwellers in the hearts of
 men
Now living, or to live in future years. 165
Sometimes the ambitious Power of choice,
 mistaking
Proud spring tide swellings for a regular
 sea,
Will settle on some British theme, some
 old
Romantic tale by Milton left unsung;
More often turning to some gentle place
Within the groves of Chivalry, I pipe 171
To shepherd swains, or seated harp in
 hand,
Amid reposing knights by a river side
Or fountain, listen to the grave reports
Of dire enchantments faced and over-
 come 175
By the strong mind, and tales of warlike
 feats,
Where spear encountered spear, and
 sword with sword
Fought, as if conscious of the blazonry
That the shield bore, so glorious was the
 strife;
Whence inspiration for a song that winds
Through ever-changing scenes of votive
 quest 181

Wrongs to redress, harmonious tribute paid
To patient courage and unblemished
 truth,
To firm devotion, zeal unquenchable,
And Christian meekness hallowing faith-
 ful loves.   185
Sometimes, more sternly moved, I would
 relate
How vanquished Mithridates northward
 passed,
And, hidden in the cloud of years, became
Odin, the Father of a race by whom
Perished the Roman Empire: how the
 friends   190
And followers of Sertorius, out of Spain
Flying, found shelter in the Fortunate
 Isles,
And left their usages, their arts and laws,
To disappear by a slow gradual death,
To dwindle and to perish one by one, 195
Starved in those narrow bounds: but
 not the soul
Of Liberty, which fifteen hundred years
Survived, and, when the European came
With skill and power that might not be
 withstood,
Did, like a pestilence, maintain its hold
And wasted down by glorious death that
 race   201
Of natural heroes: or I would record
How, in tyrannic times, some high-souled
 man,
Unnamed among the chronicles of kings,
Suffered in silence for Truth's sake; or
 tell,   205
How that one Frenchman[1], through con-
 tinued force
Of meditation on the inhuman deeds
Of those who conquered first the Indian
 Isles,
Went single in his ministry across
The Ocean; not to comfort the op-
 pressed,   210
But, like a thirsty wind, to roam about
Withering the Oppressor: how Gustavus
 sought
Help at his need in Dalecarlia's mines:

---

[1] Dominique de Gourgues, who in 1567 sailed
to Florida to avenge the massacre of the French
by the Spaniards.—Ed. of 1850.

How Wallace fought for Scotland; left
 the name
Of Wallace to be found, like a wild
 flower,   215
All over his dear Country; left the
 deeds
Of Wallace, like a family of Ghosts,
To people the steep rocks and river
 banks,
Her natural sanctuaries, with a local soul
Of independence and stern liberty.   220
Sometimes it suits me better to invent
A tale from my own heart, more near akin
To my own passions and habitual thoughts;
Some variegated story, in the main
Lofty, but the unsubstantial structure
 melts   225
Before the very sun that brightens it,
Mist into air dissolving! Then a wish,
My last and favourite aspiration, mounts
With yearning toward some philosophic
 song
Of Truth that cherishes our daily life; 230
With meditations passionate from deep
Recesses in man's heart, immortal verse
Thoughtfully fitted to the Orphean lyre;
But from this awful burthen I full soon
Take refuge and beguile myself with
 trust   235
That mellower years will bring a riper
 mind
And clearer insight. Thus my days are
 past
In contradiction; with no skill to part
Vague longing, haply bred by want of
 power,
From paramount impulse not to be with-
 stood,   240
A timorous capacity from prudence,
From circumspection, infinite delay.
Humility and modest awe themselves
Betray me, serving often for a cloak 244
To a more subtle selfishness; that now
Locks every function up in blank reserve,
Now dupes me, trusting to an anxious eye
That with intrusive restlessness beats off
Simplicity and self-presented truth.
Ah! better far than this, to stray about
Voluptuously through fields and rural
 walks,   251
And ask no record of the hours, resigned

To vacant musing, unreproved neglect
Of all things, and deliberate holiday. 254
Far better never to have heard the name
Of zeal and just ambition, than to live
Baffled and plagued by a mind that every
    hour
Turns recreant to her task; takes heart
    again,
Then feels immediately some hollow
    thought
Hang like an interdict upon her hopes.
This is my lot; for either still I find 261
Some imperfection in the chosen theme,
Or see of absolute accomplishment
Much wanting, so much wanting, in my-
    self,
That I recoil and droop, and seek repose
In listlessness from vain perplexity, 266
Unprofitably travelling toward the grave,
Like a false steward who hath much
    received
And renders nothing back.
            Was it for this
That one, the fairest of all rivers, loved
To blend his murmurs with my nurse's
    song, 271
And, from his alder shades and rocky falls,
And from his fords and shallows, sent a
    voice
That flowed along my dreams? For this,
    didst thou, 274
O Derwent! winding among grassy holms
Where I was looking on, a babe in arms,
Make ceaseless music that composed my
    thoughts
To more than infant softness, giving me
Amid the fretful dwellings of mankind
A foretaste, a dim earnest, of the calm
That Nature breathes among the hills
    and groves. 281

When he had left the mountains and
    received
On his smooth breast the shadow of those
    towers
That yet survive, a shattered monument
Of feudal sway, the bright blue river
    passed 285
Along the margin of our terrace walk;
A tempting playmate whom we dearly
    loved.

Oh, many a time have I, a five years'
    child,
In a small mill-race severed from his
    stream,
Made one long bathing of a summer's
    day; 290
Basked in the sun, and plunged and
    basked again
Alternate, all a summer's day, or scoured
The sandy fields, leaping through flowery
    groves
Of yellow ragwort; or when rock and
    hill,
The woods, and distant Skiddaw's lofty
    height, 295
Were bronzed with deepest radiance,
    stood alone
Beneath the sky, as if I had been born
On Indian plains, and from my mother's
    hut
Had run abroad in wantonness, to sport,
A naked savage, in the thunder shower.

Fair seed-time had my soul, and I grew
    up 301
Fostered alike by beauty and by fear:
Much favoured in my birthplace, and no
    less
In that beloved Vale to which erelong
We were transplanted—there were we let
    loose 305
For sports of wider range. Ere I had
    told
Ten birth-days, when among the mountain-
    slopes
Frost, and the breath of frosty wind, had
    snapped
The last autumnal crocus, 'twas my joy
With store of springes o'er my shoulder
    hung 310
To range the open heights where wood-
    cocks run
Among the smooth green turf. Through
    half the night,
Scudding away from snare to snare, I
    plied
That anxious visitation;—moon and stars
Were shining o'er my head. I was alone,
And seemed to be a trouble to the peace
That dwelt among them. Sometimes it
    befell 317

In these night wanderings, that a strong
  desire
O'erpowered my better reason, and the
  bird
Which was the captive of another's toil
Became my prey; and when the deed
  was done   321
I heard among the solitary hills
Low breathings coming after me, and
  sounds
Of undistinguishable motion, steps
Almost as silent as the turf they trod. 325

Nor less when spring had warmed the
  cultured Vale,
Roved we as plunderers where the mother-
  bird
Had in high places built her lodge;
  though mean
Our object and inglorious, yet the end
Was not ignoble. Oh! when I have
  hung   330
Above the raven's nest, by knots of grass
And half-inch fissures in the slippery
  rock
But ill sustained, and almost (so it
  seemed)
Suspended by the blast that blew amain,
Shouldering the naked crag, oh, at that
  time   335
While on the perilous ridge I hung alone,
With what strange utterance did the loud
  dry wind
Blow through my ear! the sky seemed
  not a sky
Of earth—and with what motion moved
  the clouds!

Dust as we are, the immortal spirit
  grows   340
Like harmony in music; there is a dark
Inscrutable workmanship that reconciles
Discordant elements, makes them cling
  together
In one society. How strange that all
The terrors, pains, and early miseries, 345
Regrets, vexations, lassitudes interfused
Within my mind, should e'er have borne
  a part,
And that a needful part, in making up
The calm existence that is mine when I

Am worthy of myself! Praise to the
  end!   350
Thanks to the means which Nature
  deigned to employ;
Whether her fearless visitings, or those
That came with soft alarm, like hurtless
  light
Opening the peaceful clouds; or she may
  use
Severer interventions, ministry   355
More palpable, as best might suit her
  aim.

One summer evening (led by her) I
  found
A little boat tied to a willow tree
Within a rocky cave, its usual home.
Straight I unloosed her chain, and stepping
  in   360
Pushed from the shore. It was an act of
  stealth
And troubled pleasure, nor without the
  voice
Of mountain-echoes did my boat move on;
Leaving behind her still, on either side,
Small circles glittering idly in the moon,
Until they melted all into one track   366
Of sparkling light. But now, like one
  who rows,
Proud of his skill, to reach a chosen point
With an unswerving line, I fixed my view
Upon the summit of a craggy ridge,   370
The horizon's utmost boundary; for above
Was nothing but the stars and the grey
  sky.
She was an elfin pinnace; lustily
I dipped my oars into the silent lake,
And, as I rose upon the stroke, my boat
Went heaving through the water like
  a swan;   376
When, from behind that craggy steep till
  then
The horizon's bound, a huge peak, black
  and huge,
As if with voluntary power instinct
Upreared its head. I struck and struck
  again,   380
And growing still in stature the grim
  shape
Towered up between me and the stars,
  and still,

For so it seemed, with purpose of its own
And measured motion like a living thing,
Strode after me. With trembling oars
    I turned,   385
And through the silent water stole my
    way
Back to the covert of the willow tree;
There in her mooring-place I left my
    bark,—
And through the meadows homeward
    went, in grave   389
And serious mood; but after I had seen
That spectacle, for many days, my brain
Worked with a dim and undetermined
    sense
Of unknown modes of being; o'er my
    thoughts
There hung a darkness, call it solitude
Or blank desertion. No familiar shapes 395
Remained, no pleasant images of trees,
Of sea or sky, no colours of green fields;
But huge and mighty forms, that do not
    live
Like living men, moved slowly through
    the mind
By day, and were a trouble to my dreams.

Wisdom and Spirit of the universe! 401
Thou Soul that art the eternity of thought,
That givest to forms and images a breath
And everlasting motion, not in vain
By day or star-light thus from my first
    dawn   405
Of childhood didst thou intertwine for
    me
The passions that build up our human
    soul;
Not with the mean and vulgar works of
    man,
But with high objects, with enduring
    things—
With life and nature—purifying thus 410
The elements of feeling and of thought,
And sanctifying, by such discipline,
Both pain and fear, until we recognise
A grandeur in the beatings of the heart.
Nor was this fellowship vouchsafed to me
With stinted kindness. In November
    days,   416
When vapours rolling down the valley
    made

A lonely scene more lonesome, among
    woods,
At noon and 'mid the calm of summer
    nights,
When, by the margin of the trembling
    lake,   420
Beneath the gloomy hills homeward I
    went
In solitude, such intercourse was mine;
Mine was it in the fields both day and
    night,
And by the waters, all the summer long.

And in the frosty season, when the sun
Was set, and visible for many a mile 426
The cottage windows blazed through
    twilight gloom,
I heeded not their summons: happy time
It was indeed for all of us—for me
It was a time of rapture! Clear and loud
The village clock tolled six,—I wheeled
    about,   431
Proud and exulting like an untired horse
That cares not for his home. All shod
    with steel,
We hissed along the polished ice in
    games
Confederate, imitative of the chase   435
And woodland pleasures,—the resounding
    horn,
The pack loud chiming, and the hunted
    hare.
So through the darkness and the cold we
    flew,
And not a voice was idle; with the din
Smitten, the precipices rang aloud;   440
The leafless trees and every icy crag
Tinkled like iron; while far distant hills
Into the tumult sent an alien sound
Of melancholy not unnoticed, while the
    stars
Eastward were sparkling clear, and in the
    west   445
The orange sky of evening died away.
Not seldom from the uproar I retired
Into a silent bay, or sportively
Glanced sideway, leaving the tumultuous
    throng,
To cut across the reflex of a star   450
That fled, and, flying still before me,
    gleamed

Upon the glassy plain; and oftentimes,
When we had given our bodies to the
　　wind,
And all the shadowy banks on either side
Came sweeping through the darkness,
　　spinning still　　　　　　　　455
The rapid line of motion, then at once
Have I, reclining back upon my heels,
Stopped short; yet still the solitary cliffs
Wheeled by me—even as if the earth had
　　rolled
With visible motion her diurnal round!
Behind me did they stretch in solemn
　　train,　　　　　　　　　　　461
Feebler and feebler, and I stood and
　　watched
Till all was tranquil as a dreamless sleep.

Ye Presences of Nature in the sky
And on the earth! Ye Visions of the
　　hills!　　　　　　　　　　　465
And Souls of lonely places! can I think
A vulgar hope was yours when ye em-
　　ployed
Such ministry, when ye through many
　　a year
Haunting me thus among my boyish
　　sports,
On caves and trees, upon the woods and
　　hills,　　　　　　　　　　　470
Impressed upon all forms the characters
Of danger or desire; and thus did make
The surface of the universal earth
With triumph and delight, with hope
　　and fear,
Work like a sea?
　　　　　　Not uselessly employed,
Might I pursue this theme through every
　　change　　　　　　　　　　476
Of exercise and play, to which the year
Did summon us in his delightful round.

We were a noisy crew; the sun in
　　heaven
Beheld not vales more beautiful than
　　ours;　　　　　　　　　　　480
Nor saw a band in happiness and joy
Richer, or worthier of the ground they
　　trod.
I could record with no reluctant voice
The woods of autumn, and their hazel
　　bowers

With milk-white clusters hung; the rod
　　and line,　　　　　　　　　485
True symbol of hope's foolishness, whose
　　strong
And unreproved enchantment led us on
By rocks and pools shut out from every
　　star,
All the green summer, to forlorn cascades
Among the windings hid of mountain
　　brooks.　　　　　　　　　490
—Unfading recollections! at this hour
The heart is almost mine with which
　　I felt,
From some hill-top on sunny afternoons,
The paper kite high among fleecy clouds
Pull at her rein like an impetuous
　　courser;　　　　　　　　　495
Or, from the meadows sent on gusty
　　days,
Beheld her breast the wind, then suddenly
Dashed headlong, and rejected by the
　　storm.

Ye lowly cottages wherein we dwelt,
A ministration of your own was yours; 500
Can I forget you, being as you were
So beautiful among the pleasant fields
In which ye stood? or can I here forget
The plain and seemly countenance with
　　which
Ye dealt out your plain comforts? Yet
　　had ye　　　　　　　　　505
Delights and exultations of your own.
Eager and never weary we pursued
Our home-amusements by the warm peat-
　　fire
At evening, when with pencil, and smooth
　　slate
In square divisions parcelled out and all
With crosses and with cyphers scribbled
　　o'er,　　　　　　　　　　511
We schemed and puzzled, head opposed
　　to head
In strife too humble to be named in
　　verse:
Or round the naked table, snow-white
　　deal,
Cherry or maple, sate in close array, 515
And to the combat, Loo or Whist, led on
A thick-ribbed army; not, as in the
　　world,

Neglected and ungratefully thrown by
Even for the very service they had
   wrought,
But husbanded through many a long
   campaign.   520
Uncouth assemblage was it, where no few
Had changed their functions; some,
   plebeian cards
Which Fate, beyond the promise of their
   birth,
Had dignified, and called to represent
The persons of departed potentates.   525
Oh, with what echoes on the board they
   fell!
Ironic diamonds,—clubs, hearts, diamonds,
   spades,
A congregation piteously akin!
Cheap matter offered they to boyish wit,
Those sooty knaves, precipitated down
With scoffs and taunts, like Vulcan out
   of heaven: 531
The paramount ace, a moon in her eclipse,
Queens gleaming through their splen-
   dour's last decay,
And monarchs surly at the wrongs sus-
   tained
By royal visages. Meanwhile abroad 535
Incessant rain was falling, or the frost
Raged bitterly, with keen and silent
   tooth;
And, interrupting oft that eager game,
From under Esthwaite's splitting fields
   of ice
The pent-up air, struggling to free itself,
Gave out to meadow-grounds and hills
   a loud   541
Protracted yelling, like the noise of
   wolves
Howling in troops along the Bothnic
   Main.

Nor, sedulous as I have been to trace
How Nature by extrinsic passion first 545
Peopled the mind with forms sublime or
   fair,
And made me love them, may I here
   omit
How other pleasures have been mine, and
   joys
Of subtler origin; how I have felt,
Not seldom even in that tempestuous time,

Those hallowed and pure motions of the
   sense   551
Which seem, in their simplicity, to own
An intellectual charm; that calm delight
Which, if I err not, surely must belong
To those first-born affinities that fit   555
Our new existence to existing things,
And, in our dawn of being, constitute
The bond of union between life and joy.

Yes, I remember when the changeful
   earth,
And twice five summers on my mind had
   stamped   560
The faces of the moving year, even then
I held unconscious intercourse with beauty
Old as creation, drinking in a pure
Organic pleasure from the silver wreaths
Of curling mist, or from the level plain 565
Of waters coloured by impending clouds.

The sands of Westmoreland, the creeks
   and bays
Of Cumbria's rocky limits, they can tell
How, when the Sea threw off his evening
   shade
And to the shepherd's hut on distant hills
Sent welcome notice of the rising moon,
How I have stood, to fancies such as
   these
A stranger, linking with the spectacle 573
No conscious memory of a kindred sight,
And bringing with me no peculiar sense
Of quietness or peace; yet have I stood,
Even while mine eye hath moved o'er
   many a league
Of shining water, gathering as it seemed,
Through every hair-breadth in that field
   of light,
New pleasure like a bee among the
   flowers.   580

Thus oft amid those fits of vulgar joy
Which, through all seasons, on a child's
   pursuits
Are prompt attendants, 'mid that giddy
   bliss
Which, like a tempest, works along the
   blood
And is forgotten; even then I felt   585
Gleams like the flashing of a shield;—the
   earth

And common face of Nature spake to me
Remembered things; sometimes, 'tis
    true,
By chance collisions and quaint accidents
(Like those ill-sorted unions, work sup-
    posed   590
Of evil-minded fairies), yet not vain
Nor profitless, if haply they impressed
Collateral objects and appearances,
Albeit lifeless then, and doomed to sleep
Until maturer seasons called them forth
To impregnate and to elevate the mind.
—And if the vulgar joy by its own
    weight
Wearied itself out of the memory,
The scenes which were a witness of that
    joy
Remained in their substantial lineaments
Depicted on the brain, and to the eye   601
Were visible, a daily sight; and thus
By the impressive discipline of fear,
By pleasure and repeated happiness,
So frequently repeated, and by force   605
Of obscure feelings representative
Of things forgotten, these same scenes so
    bright,
So beautiful, so majestic in themselves,
Though yet the day was distant, did
    become
Habitually dear, and all their forms   610
And changeful colours by invisible links
Were fastened to the affections.
                        I began
My story early—not misled, I trust,
By an infirmity of love for days
Disowned by memory—ere the breath of
    spring   615
Planting my snowdrops among winter
    snows:
Nor will it seem to thee, O Friend! so
    prompt
In sympathy, that I have lengthened out
With fond and feeble tongue a tedious tale.
Meanwhile, my hope has been, that I
    might fetch   620

Invigorating thoughts from former years;
Might fix the wavering balance of my
    mind,
And haply meet reproaches too, whose
    power
May spur me on, in manhood now
    mature,
To honourable toil. Yet should these
    hopes   625
Prove vain, and thus should neither I be
    taught
To understand myself, nor thou to know
With better knowledge how the heart
    was framed
Of him thou lovest; need I dread from
    thee
Harsh judgments, if the song be loth to
    quit   630
Those recollected hours that have the
    charm
Of visionary things, those lovely forms
And sweet sensations that throw back
    our life,
And almost make remotest infancy
A visible scene, on which the sun is
    shining?   635

One end at least hath been attained;
    my mind
Hath been revived, and if this genial
    mood
Desert me not, forthwith shall be brought
    down
Through later years the story of my life.
The road lies plain before me;—'tis a
    theme   640
Single and of determined bounds; and
    hence
I choose it rather at this time, than work
Of ampler or more varied argument,
Where I might be discomfited and lost:
And certain hopes are with me, that to
    thee   645
This labour will be welcome, honoured
    Friend!

BOOK SECOND.

SCHOOL-TIME—(Continued).

Thus far, O Friend! have we, though leaving much
Unvisited, endeavoured to retrace
The simple ways in which my childhood walked;
Those chiefly that first led me to the love
Of rivers, woods, and fields. The passion yet 5
Was in its birth, sustained as might befall
By nourishment that came unsought; for still
From week to week, from month to month, we lived
A round of tumult. Duly were our games
Prolonged in summer till the day-light failed: 10
No chair remained before the doors; the bench
And threshold steps were empty; fast asleep
The labourer, and the old man who had sate
A later lingerer; yet the revelry
Continued and the loud uproar: at last,
When all the ground was dark, and twinkling stars 16
Edged the black clouds, home and to bed we went,
Feverish with weary joints and beating minds.
Ah! is there one who ever has been young,
Nor needs a warning voice to tame the pride 20
Of intellect and virtue's self-esteem?
One is there, though the wisest and the best
Of all mankind, who covets not at times
Union that cannot be;—who would not give,
If so he might, to duty and to truth 25
The eagerness of infantine desire?
A tranquillising spirit presses now
On my corporeal frame, so wide appears
The vacancy between me and those days
Which yet have such self-presence in my mind, 30
That, musing on them, often do I seem
Two consciousnesses, conscious of myself
And of some other Being. A rude mass
Of native rock, left midway in the square
Of our small market village, was the goal
Or centre of these sports; and when, returned 36
After long absence, thither I repaired,
Gone was the old grey stone, and in its place
A smart Assembly-room usurped the ground
That had been ours. There let the fiddle scream, 40
And be ye happy! Yet, my Friends! I know
That more than one of you will think with me
Of those soft starry nights, and that old Dame
From whom the stone was named, who there had sate,
And watched her table with its huckster's wares 45
Assiduous, through the length of sixty years.

We ran a boisterous course; the year span round
With giddy motion. But the time approached
That brought with it a regular desire
For calmer pleasures, when the winning forms 50
Of Nature were collaterally attached
To every scheme of holiday delight
And every boyish sport, less grateful else
And languidly pursued.
                                When summer came,

Our pastime was, on bright half-holi-
   days,   55
To sweep along the plain of Windermere
With rival oars; and the selected bourne
Was now an Island musical with birds
That sang and ceased not; now a Sister
   Isle
Beneath the oaks' umbrageous covert,
   sown   60
With lilies of the valley like a field;
And now a third small Island, where sur-
   vived
In solitude the ruins of a shrine
Once to Our Lady dedicate, and served
Daily with chaunted rites. In such a
   race   65
So ended, disappointment could be none,
Uneasiness, or pain, or jealousy:
We rested in the shade, all pleased alike,
Conquered and conqueror. Thus the
   pride of strength,
And the vain-glory of superior skill,   70
Were tempered; thus was gradually pro-
   duced
A quiet independence of the heart;
And to my Friend who knows me I may
   add,
Fearless of blame, that hence for future
   days
Ensued a diffidence and modesty,   75
And I was taught to feel, perhaps too
   much,
The self-sufficing power of Solitude.

Our daily meals were frugal, Sabine
   fare!
More than we wished we knew the bless-
   ing then
Of vigorous hunger — hence corporeal
   strength   80
Unsapped by delicate viands; for, ex-
   clude
A little weekly stipend, and we lived
Through three divisions of the quartered
   year
In penniless poverty. But now to school
From the half-yearly holidays returned,
We came with weightier purses, that
   sufficed   86
To furnish treats more costly than the
   Dame

Of the old grey stone, from her scant
   board, supplied.
Hence rustic dinners on the cool green
   ground,
Or in the woods, or by a river side   90
Or shady fountain, while among the
   leaves
Soft airs were stirring, and the mid-day
   sun
Unfelt shone brightly round us in our joy.
Nor is my aim neglected if I tell
How sometimes, in the length of those
   half-years,   95
We from our funds drew largely;—proud
   to curb,
And eager to spur on, the galloping steed;
And with the cautious inn-keeper, whose
   stud
Supplied our want, we haply might
   employ
Sly subterfuge, if the adventure's bound
Were distant: some famed temple where
   of yore   101
The Druids worshipped, or the antique
   walls
Of that large abbey, where within the
   Vale
Of Nightshade, to St. Mary's honour
   built,
Stands yet a mouldering pile with frac-
   tured arch,   105
Belfry, and images, and living trees;
A holy scene!—Along the smooth green
   turf
Our horses grazed. To more than inland
   peace,
Left by the west wind sweeping overhead
From a tumultuous ocean, trees and
   towers   110
In that sequestered valley may be seen,
Both silent and both motionless alike;
Such the deep shelter that is there, and
   such
The safeguard for repose and quietness.

Our steeds remounted and the summons
   given,   115
With whip and spur we through the
   chauntry flew
In uncouth race, and left the cross-legged
   knight,

And the stone-abbot, and that single
    wren
Which one day sang so sweetly in the
    nave
Of the old church, that—though from
    recent showers   120
The earth was comfortless, and, touched
    by faint
Internal breezes, sobbings of the place
And respirations, from the roofless walls
The shuddering ivy dripped large drops—
    yet still
So sweetly 'mid the gloom the invisible
    bird   125
Sang to herself, that there I could have
    made
My dwelling-place, and lived for ever
    there
To hear such music. Through the walls
    we flew
And down the valley, and, a circuit made
In wantonness of heart, through rough
    and smooth   130
We scampered homewards. Oh, ye rocks
    and streams,
And that still spirit shed from evening
    air!
Even in this joyous time I sometimes
    felt
Your presence, when with slackened step
    we breathed
Along the sides of the steep hills, or when
Lighted by gleams of moonlight from the
    sea   136
We beat with thundering hoofs the level
    sand.

Midway on long Winander's eastern
    shore,
Within the crescent of a pleasant bay,
A tavern stood; no homely - featured
    house,   140
Primeval like its neighbouring cottages,
But 'twas a splendid place, the door be-
    set
With chaises, grooms, and liveries, and
    within
Decanters, glasses, and the blood-red wine.
In ancient times, or ere the Hall was
    built   145
On the large island, had this dwelling been

More worthy of a poet's love, a hut,
Proud of its one bright fire and sycamore
    shade.
But—though the rhymes were gone that
    once inscribed
The threshold, and large golden cha-
    racters,   150
Spread o'er the spangled sign-board, had
    dislodged
The old Lion and usurped his place, in
    slight
And mockery of the rustic painter's
    hand—
Yet, to this hour, the spot to me is dear
With all its foolish pomp. The garden
    lay   155
Upon a slope surmounted by a plain
Of a small bowling-green; beneath us
    stood
A grove, with gleams of water through
    the trees
And over the tree-tops; nor did we want
Refreshment, strawberries and mellow
    cream.   160
There, while through half an afternoon
    we played
On the smooth platform, whether skill
    prevailed
Or happy blunder triumphed, bursts of
    glee
Made all the mountains ring. But, ere
    nightfall,
When in our pinnace we returned at
    leisure   165
Over the shadowy lake, and to the beach
Of some small island steered our course
    with one,
The Minstrel of the Troop, and left him
    there,
And rowed off gently, while he blew his
    flute
'Alone upon the rock—oh, then, the calm
And dead still water lay upon my mind
Even with a weight of pleasure, and the
    sky,
Never before so beautiful, sank down
Into my heart, and held me like a dream!
Thus were my sympathies enlarged, and
    thus   175
Daily the common range of visible things
Grew dear to me: already I began

To love the sun; a boy I loved the sun,
Not as I since have loved him, as a pledge
And surety of our earthly life, a light 180
Which we behold and feel we are alive;
Nor for his bounty to so many worlds—
But for this cause, that I had seen him
 lay
His beauty on the morning hills, had
 seen
The western mountain touch his setting
 orb,   185
In many a thoughtless hour, when, from
 excess
Of happiness, my blood appeared to flow
For its own pleasure, and I breathed with
 joy.
And, from like feelings, humble though
 intense,
To patriotic and domestic love   190
Analogous, the moon to me was dear;
For I could dream away my purposes,
Standing to gaze upon her while she
 hung
Midway between the hills, as if she knew
No other region, but belonged to thee, 195
Yea, appertained by a peculiar right
To thee and thy grey huts, thou one dear
 Vale!

 Those incidental charms which first
  attached
My heart to rural objects, day by day
Grew weaker, and I hasten on to tell 200
How Nature, intervenient till this time
And secondary, now at length was sought
For her own sake. But who shall parcel
 out
His intellect by geometric rules,
Split like a province into round and
 square?   205
Who knows the individual hour in which
His habits were first sown, even as a
 seed?
Who that shall point as with a wand and
 say
"This portion of the river of my mind
Came from yon fountain?" Thou, my
 Friend! art one   210
More deeply read in thy own thoughts;
 to thee
Science appears but what in truth she is,

Not as our glory and our absolute boast,
But as a succedaneum, and a prop
To our infirmity. No officious slave 215
Art thou of that false secondary power
By which we multiply distinctions, then
Deem that our puny boundaries are
 things
That we perceive, and not that we have
 made.
To thee, unblinded by these formal arts,
The unity of all hath been revealed, 221
And thou wilt doubt, with me less aptly
 skilled
Than many are to range the faculties
In scale and order, class the cabinet
Of their sensations, and in voluble phrase
Run through the history and birth of
 each   226
As of a single independent thing.
Hard task, vain hope, to analyse the
 mind,
If each most obvious and particular
 thought,
Not in a mystical and idle sense,   230
But in the words of Reason deeply
 weighed,
Hath no beginning.
    Blest the infant Babe,
(For with my best conjecture I would
 trace
Our Being's earthly progress,) blest the
 Babe,
Nursed in his Mother's arms, who sinks
 to sleep,   235
Rocked on his Mother's breast; who with
 his soul
Drinks in the feelings of his Mother's
 eye!
For him, in one dear Presence, there
 exists
A virtue which irradiates and exalts
Objects through widest intercourse of
 sense.   240
No outcast he, bewildered and depressed:
Along his infant veins are interfused
The gravitation and the filial bond
Of nature that connect him with the
 world.
Is there a flower, to which he points with
 hand   245
Too weak to gather it, already love

Drawn from love's purest earthly fount
   for him
Hath beautified that flower; already
   shades
Of pity cast from inward tenderness
Do fall around him upon aught that bears
Unsightly marks of violence or harm. 251
Emphatically such a Being lives,
Frail creature as he is, helpless and frail,
An inmate of this active universe:
For feeling has to him imparted power
That through the growing faculties of
   sense   256
Doth like an agent of the one great Mind
Create, creator and receiver both,
Working but in alliance with the works
Which it beholds.—Such, verily, is the
   first   260
Poetic spirit of our human life,
By uniform control of after years,
In most, abated or suppressed; in some,
Through every change of growth and of
   decay,
Pre-eminent till death.

         From early days, 265
Beginning not long after that first time
In which, a Babe, by intercourse of touch
I held mute dialogues with my Mother's
   heart,
I have endeavoured to display the means
Whereby this infant sensibility,   270
Great birthright of our being, was in me
Augmented and sustained. Yet is a path
More difficult before me; and I fear
That in its broken windings we shall need
The chamois' sinews, and the eagle's
   wing: 275
For now a trouble came into my mind
From unknown causes. I was left alone
Seeking the visible world, nor knowing
   why.
The props of my affections were removed,
And yet the building stood, as if sus-
   tained   280
By its own spirit! All that I beheld
Was dear, and hence to finer influxes
The mind lay open, to a more exact
And close communion. Many are our
   joys   284
In youth, but oh! what happiness to live
When every hour brings palpable access

Of knowledge, when all knowledge is
   delight,
And sorrow is not there! The seasons
   came,
And every season wheresoe'er I moved
Unfolded transitory qualities,   290
Which, but for this most watchful power
   of love,
Had been neglected; left a register
Of permanent relations, else unknown.
Hence life, and change, and beauty, soli-
   tude
More active even than "best society"—
Society made sweet as solitude   296
By silent inobtrusive sympathies,
And gentle agitations of the mind
From manifold distinctions, difference
Perceived in things, where, to the un-
   watchful eye,   300
No difference is, and hence, from the
   same source,
Sublimer joy; for I would walk alone,
Under the quiet stars, and at that time
Have felt whate'er there is of power in
   sound   304
To breathe an elevated mood, by form
Or image unprofaned; and I would stand,
If the night blackened with a coming
   storm,
Beneath some rock, listening to notes
   that are
The ghostly language of the ancient earth,
Or make their dim abode in distant
   winds.   310
Thence did I drink the visionary power;
And deem not profitless those fleeting
   moods
Of shadowy exultation: not for this,
That they are kindred to our purer mind
And intellectual life; but that the soul,
Remembering how she felt, but what she
   felt   316
Remembering not, retains an obscure
   sense
Of possible sublimity, whereto
With growing faculties she doth aspire,
With faculties still growing, feeling still
That whatsoever point they gain, they
   yet   321
Have something to pursue.

         And not alone,

'Mid gloom and tumult, but no less 'mid
　　fair
And tranquil scenes, that universal power
And fitness in the latent qualities　　325
And essences of things, by which the mind
Is moved with feelings of delight, to me
Came strengthened with a superadded soul,
A virtue not its own.　My morning walks
Were early;—oft before the hours of
　　school　　330
I travelled round our little lake, five
　　miles
Of pleasant wandering.　Happy time!
　　more dear
For this, that one was by my side, a
　　Friend[1],
Then passionately loved; with heart how
　　full
Would he peruse these lines!　For many
　　years　　335
Have since flowed in between us, and,
　　our minds
Both silent to each other, at this time
We live as if those hours had never been.
Nor seldom did I lift our cottage latch
Far earlier, ere one smoke-wreath had
　　risen　　340
From human dwelling, or the vernal
　　thrush
Was audible; and sate among the woods
Alone upon some jutting eminence,
At the first gleam of dawn-light, when the
　　Vale,
Yet slumbering, lay in utter solitude.　345
How shall I seek the origin? where find
Faith in the marvellous things which then
　　I felt?
Oft in these moments such a holy-calm
Would overspread my soul, that bodily
　　eyes
Were utterly forgotten, and what I saw
Appeared like something in myself, a
　　dream,　　351
A prospect in the mind.
　　　　　　　'Twere long to tell
What spring and autumn, what the winter
　　snows,
And what the summer shade, what day
　　and night,

[1] Rev. John Fleming, of Rayrigg, Windermere.
—Ed. of 1850.

Evening and morning, sleep and waking
　　thought,　　355
From sources inexhaustible, poured forth
To feed the spirit of religious love
In which I walked with Nature.　But let
　　this
Be not forgotten, that I still retained
My first creative sensibility;　　360
That by the regular action of the world
My soul was unsubdued.　A plastic power
Abode with me; a forming hand, at times
Rebellious, acting in a devious mood;
A local spirit of his own, at war　　365
With general tendency, but, for the most,
Subservient strictly to external things
With which it communed.　An auxiliar
　　light
Came from my mind, which on the setting
　　sun
Bestowed new splendour; the melodious
　　birds,　　370
The fluttering breezes, fountains that run
　　on
Murmuring so sweetly in themselves,
　　obeyed
A like dominion, and the midnight storm
Grew darker in the presence of my eye:
Hence my obeisance, my devotion hence
And hence my transport.
　　　　　　Nor should this, perchance,
Pass unrecorded, that I still had loved
The exercise and produce of a toil,
Than analytic industry to me
More pleasing, and whose character I
　　deem　　380
Is more poetic as resembling more
Creative agency.　The song would speak
Of that interminable building reared
By observation of affinities
In objects where no brotherhood exists
To passive minds.　My seventeenth year
　　was come;　　386
And, whether from this habit rooted now
So deeply in my mind, or from excess
In the great social principle of life
Coercing all things into sympathy,　　390
To unorganic natures were transferred
My own enjoyments; or the power of truth
Coming in revelation, did converse
With things that really are; I, at this
　　time,

Saw blessings spread around me like a sea.
Thus while the days flew by, and years
  passed on,   396
From Nature and her overflowing soul
I had received so much, that all my
  thoughts
Were steeped in feeling; I was only then
Contented, when with bliss ineffable   400
I felt the sentiment of Being spread
O'er all that moves and all that seemeth
  still;
O'er all that, lost beyond the reach of
  thought
And human knowledge, to the human eye
Invisible, yet liveth to the heart;   405
O'er all that leaps and runs, and shouts
  and sings,
Or beats the gladsome air; o'er all that
  glides
Beneath the wave, yea, in the wave itself,
And mighty depth of waters. Wonder not
If high the transport, great the joy I felt
Communing in this sort through earth
  and heaven   411
With every form of creature, as it looked
Towards the Uncreated with a counte-
  nance
Of adoration, with an eye of love.   414
One song they sang, and it was audible,
Most audible, then, when the fleshly ear,
O'ercome by humblest prelude of that
  strain,
Forgot her functions, and slept undis-
  turbed.

If this be error, and another faith
Find easier access to the pious mind,   420
Yet were I grossly destitute of all
Those human sentiments that make this
  earth
So dear, if I should fail with grateful voice
To speak of you, ye mountains, and ye
  lakes
And sounding cataracts, ye mists and
  winds   425
That dwell among the hills where I was
  born.
If in my youth I have been pure in heart,
If, mingling with the world, I am content
With my own modest pleasures, and have
  lived

With God and Nature communing, re-
  moved   430
From little enmities and low desires,
The gift is yours; if in these times of fear
This melancholy waste of hopes o'er-
  thrown,
If, 'mid indifference and apathy,   434
And wicked exultation when good men
On every side fall off, we know not how,
To selfishness, disguised in gentle names
Of peace and quiet and domestic love,
Yet mingled not unwillingly with sneers
On visionary minds; if, in this time   440
Of dereliction and dismay, I yet
Despair not of our nature, but retain
A more than Roman confidence, a faith
That fails not, in all sorrow my support,
The blessing of my life; the gift is yours,
Ye winds and sounding cataracts! 'tis
  yours,
Ye mountains! thine, O Nature! Thou
  hast fed
My lofty speculations; and in thee,
For this uneasy heart of ours, I find
A never-failing principle of joy   450
And purest passion.
             Thou, my Friend! wert reared
In the great city, 'mid far other scenes;
But we, by different roads, at length have
  gained
The self-same bourne. And for this cause
  to thee
I speak, unapprehensive of contempt, 455
The insinuated scoff of coward tongues,
And all that silent language which so oft
In conversation between man and man
Blots from the human countenance all trace
Of beauty and of love. For thou hast
  sought   460
The truth in solitude, and, since the days
That gave thee liberty, full long desired,
To serve in Nature's temple, thou hast been
The most assiduous of her ministers;   464
In many things my brother, chiefly here
In this our deep devotion.
             Fare thee well!
Health and the quiet of a healthful mind
Attend thee! seeking oft the haunts of men,
And yet more often living with thyself,
And for thyself, so haply shall thy days
Be many, and a blessing to mankind. 471

BOOK THIRD.

RESIDENCE AT CAMBRIDGE.

It was a dreary morning when the wheels
Rolled over a wide plain o'erhung with
   clouds,
And nothing cheered our way till first
   we saw
The long-roofed chapel of King's College
   lift
Turrets and pinnacles in answering files,
Extended high above a dusky grove.   6

  Advancing, we espied upon the road
A student clothed in gown and tasselled
   cap,
Striding along as if o'ertasked by Time,
Or covetous of exercise and air;   10
He passed—nor was I master of my eyes
Till he was left an arrow's flight behind.
As near and nearer to the spot we drew,
It seemed to suck us in with an eddy's
   force.
Onward we drove beneath the Castle;
   caught,   15
While crossing Magdalene Bridge, a
   glimpse of Cam;
And at the *Hoop* alighted, famous Inn.

  My spirit was up, my thoughts were
   full of hope;
Some friends I had, acquaintances who
   there
Seemed friends, poor simple schoolboys,
   now hung round   20
With honour and importance: in a world
Of welcome faces up and down I roved;
Questions, directions, warnings and ad-
   vice,
Flowed in upon me, from all sides; fresh
   day   24
Of pride and pleasure! to myself I seemed
A man of business and expense, and went

From shop to shop about my own affairs,
To Tutor or to Tailor, as befell,
From street to street with loose and care-
   less mind.

  I was the Dreamer, they the Dream;
   I roamed   30
Delighted through the motley spectacle;
Gowns grave, or gaudy, doctors, students,
   streets,
Courts, cloisters, flocks of churches, gate-
   ways, towers:
Migration strange for a stripling of the
   hills,
A northern villager.

          As if the change   35
Had waited on some Fairy's wand, at once
Behold me rich in monies, and attired
In splendid garb, with hose of silk, and
   hair
Powdered like rimy trees, when frost is
   keen.
My lordly dressing-gown, I pass it by, 40
With other signs of manhood that sup-
   plied
The lack of beard.—The weeks went
   roundly on,
With invitations, suppers, wine and fruit,
Smooth housekeeping within, and all
   without
Liberal, and suiting gentleman's array. 45

  The Evangelist St. John my patron was:
Three Gothic courts are his, and in the
   first
Was my abiding-place, a nook obscure;
Right underneath, the College kitchens
   made
A humming sound, less tuneable than
   bees,   50

But hardly less industrious; with shrill
notes
Of sharp command and scolding inter-
mixed.
Near me hung Trinity's loquacious clock,
Who never let the quarters, night or day,
Slip by him unproclaimed, and told the
hours   55
Twice over with a male and female voice.
Her pealing organ was my neighbour too;
And from my pillow, looking forth by
light
Of moon or favouring stars, I could be-
hold
The antechapel where the statue stood 60
Of Newton with his prism and silent face,
The marble index of a mind for ever
Voyaging through strange seas of Thought,
alone.

Of College labours, of the Lecturer's
room
All studded round, as thick as chairs
could stand,   65
With loyal students faithful to their
books,
Half-and-half idlers, hardy recusants,
And honest dunces—of happier days,
Examinations, when the man was weighed
As in a balance! of excessive hopes,   70
Tremblings withal and commendable
fears,
Small jealousies, and triumphs good or
bad—
Let others that know more speak as they
know.
Such glory was but little sought by me,
And little won. Yet from the first crude
days   75
Of settling time in this untried abode,
I was disturbed at times by prudent
thoughts,
Wishing to hope without a hope, some
fears
About my future worldly maintenance,
And, more than all, a strangeness in the
mind,   80
A feeling that I was not for that hour,
Nor for that place. But wherefore be
cast down?
For (not to speak of Reason and her pure

Reflective acts to fix the moral law
Deep in the conscience, nor of Christian
Hope,   85
Bowing her head before her sister Faith
As one far mightier), hither I had come,
Bear witness Truth, endowed with holy
powers
And faculties, whether to work or feel.
Oft when the dazzling show no longer new
Had ceased to dazzle, ofttimes did I quit
My comrades, leave the crowd, buildings
and groves,
And as I paced alone the level fields
Far from those lovely sights and sounds
sublime
With which I had been conversant, the
mind   95
Drooped not; but there into herself re-
turning,
With prompt rebound seemed fresh as
heretofore.
At least I more distinctly recognised
Her native instincts: let me dare to speak
A higher language, say that now I felt
What independent solaces were mine, 101
To mitigate the injurious sway of place
Or circumstance, how far soever changed
In youth, or to be changed in after years
As if awakened, summoned, roused, con-
strained,   105
I looked for universal things; perused
The common countenance of earth and
sky:
Earth, nowhere unembellished by some
trace
Of that first Paradise whence man was
driven;
And sky, whose beauty and bounty are
expressed   110
By the proud name she bears—the name
of Heaven.
I called on both to teach me what they
might;
Or turning the mind in upon herself,
Pored, watched, expected, listened, spread
my thoughts
And spread them with a wider creeping;
felt   115
Incumbencies more awful, visitings
Of the Upholder of the tranquil soul,
That tolerates the indignities of Time,

And, from the centre of Eternity
All finite motions overruling, lives   120
In glory immutable. But peace ! enough
Here to record that I was mounting now
To such community with highest truth—
A track pursuing, not untrod before,
From strict analogies by thought sup-
    plied   125
Or consciousnesses not to be subdued.
To every natural form, rock, fruit, or
    flower,
Even the loose stones that cover the high-
    way,
I gave a moral life: I saw them feel,
Or linked them to some feeling: the great
    mass   130
Lay bedded in a quickening soul, and all
That I beheld respired with inward
    meaning.
Add that whate'er of Terror or of Love
Or Beauty, Nature's daily face put on
From transitory passion, unto this   135
I was as sensitive as waters are
To the sky's influence; in a kindred mood
Of passion was obedient as a lute
That waits upon the touches of the wind.
Unknown, unthought of, yet I was most
    rich—   140
I had a world about me—'twas my own;
I made it, for it only lived to me,
And to the God who sees into the heart.
Such sympathies, though rarely, were be-
    trayed   144
By outward gestures and by visible looks:
Some called it madness—so indeed it was,
If child-like fruitfulness in passing joy,
If steady moods of thoughtfulness ma-
    tured
To inspiration, sort with such a name;
If prophecy be madness; if things viewed
By poets in old time, and higher up   151
By the first men, earth's first inhabitants,
May in these tutored days no more be
    seen
With undisordered sight. But leaving
    this,
It was no madness, for the bodily eye 155
Amid my strongest workings evermore
Was searching out the lines of difference
As they lie hid in all external forms,
Near or remote, minute or vast; an eye

Which, from a tree, a stone, a withered
    leaf,   160
To the broad ocean and the azure heavens
Spangled with kindred multitudes of
    stars,
Could find no surface where its power
    might sleep;
Which spake perpetual logic to my soul,
And by an unrelenting agency   165
Did bind my feelings even as in a chain.

    And here, O Friend ! have I retraced
    my life
Up to an eminence, and told a tale
Of matters which not falsely may be
    called
The glory of my youth. Of genius,
    power,   170
Creation and divinity itself
I have been speaking, for my theme has
    been
What passed within me. Not of outward
    things
Done visibly for other minds, words, signs,
Symbols or actions, but of my own heart
Have I been speaking, and my youthful
    mind.   176
O Heavens ! how awful is the might of
    souls,
And what they do within themselves
    while yet
The yoke of earth is new to them, the
    world
Nothing but a wild field where they were
    sown.   180
This is, in truth, heroic argument,
This genuine prowess, which I wished to
    touch
With hand however weak, but in the
    main
It lies far hidden from the reach of words.
Points have we all of us within our souls
Where all stand single; this I feel, and
    make   186
Breathings for incommunicable powers;
But is not each a memory to himself ?—
And, therefore, now that we must quit
    this theme,
I am not heartless, for there's not a man
That lives who hath not known his god-
    like hours,   191

And feels not what an empire we inherit
As natural beings in the strength of
    Nature.

No more: for now into a populous plain
We must descend. A Traveller I am, 195
Whose tale is only of himself; even so,
So be it, if the pure of heart be prompt
To follow, and if thou, my honoured
    Friend!
Who in these thoughts art ever at my
    side,
Support, as heretofore, my fainting steps.

It hath been told, that when the first
    delight   201
That flashed upon me from this novel
    show
Had failed, the mind returned into her-
    self;
Yet true it is, that I had made a change
In climate, and my nature's outward coat
Changed also slowly and insensibly. 206
Full oft the quiet and exalted thoughts
Of loneliness gave way to empty noise
And superficial pastimes; now and then
Forced labour, and more frequently forced
    hopes;   210
And, worst of all, a treasonable growth
Of indecisive judgments, that impaired
And shook the mind's simplicity.—And
    yet
This was a gladsome time. Could I be-
    hold—
Who, less insensible than sodden clay 215
In a sea-river's bed at ebb of tide,
Could have beheld,—with undelighted
    heart,
So many happy youths, so wide and fair
A congregation in its budding-time
Of health, and hope, and beauty, all at
    once   220
So many divers samples from the growth
Of life's sweet season—could have seen
    unmoved
That miscellaneous garland of wild flowers
Decking the matron temples of a place
So famous through the world? To me, at
    least,   225
It was a goodly prospect: for, in sooth,
Though I had learnt betimes to stand
    unpropped,

And independent musings pleased me so
That spells seemed on me when I was
    alone,
Yet could I only cleave to solitude   230
In lonely places; if a throng was near
That way I leaned by nature; for my
    heart
Was social, and loved idleness and joy.

Not seeking those who might participate
My deeper pleasures (nay, I had not once,
Though not unused to mutter lonesome
    songs,   236
Even with myself divided such delight,
Or looked that way for aught that might
    be clothed
In human language), easily I passed
From the remembrances of better things,
And slipped into the ordinary works 241
Of careless youth, unburdened, unalarmed.
Caverns there were within my mind which
    sun
Could never penetrate, yet did there not
Want store of leafy *arbours* where the
    light   245
Might enter in at will. Companionships,
Friendships, acquaintances, were welcome
    all.
We sauntered, played, or rioted; we
    talked
Unprofitable talk at morning hours;
Drifted about along the streets and
    walks,   250
Read lazily in trivial books, went forth
To gallop through the country in blind
    zeal
Of senseless horsemanship, or on the breast
Of Cam sailed boisterously, and let the
    stars
Come forth, perhaps without one quiet
    thought.   255

Such was the tenour of the second act
In this new life. Imagination slept,
And yet not utterly. I could not print
Ground where the grass had yielded to
    the steps
Of generations of illustrious men,   260
Unmoved. I could not always lightly
    pass
Through the same gateways, sleep where
    they had slept,

Wake where they waked, range that in-
    closure old,
That garden of great intellects, undis-
    turbed.
Place also by the side of this dark sense
Of nobler feeling, that those spiritual
    men,   266
Even the great Newton's own ethereal
    self,
Seemed humbled in these precincts thence
    to be
The more endeared. Their several me-
    mories here
(Even like their persons in their portraits
    clothed   270
With the accustomed garb of daily life)
Put on a lowly and a touching grace
Of more distinct humanity, that left
All genuine admiration unimpaired.

Beside the pleasant Mill of Trompington
I laughed with Chaucer; in the hawthorn
    shade   276
Heard him, while birds were warbling,
    tell his tales
Of amorous passion. And that gentle
    Bard,
Chosen by the Muses for their Page of
    State—
Sweet Spenser, moving through his clouded
    heaven   280
With the moon's beauty and the moon's
    soft pace,
I called him Brother, Englishman, and
    Friend!
Yea, our blind Poet, who, in his later day,
Stood almost single; uttering odious
    truth—
Darkness before, and danger's voice be-
    hind,   285
Soul awful—if the earth has ever lodged
An awful soul—I seemed to see him here
Familiarly, and in his scholar's dress
Bounding before me, yet a stripling
    youth—
A boy, no better, with his rosy cheeks 290
Angelical, keen eye, courageous look,
And conscious step of purity and pride.
Among the band of my compeers was one
Whom chance had stationed in the very
    room

Honoured by Milton's name. O tempe-
    rate Bard!   295
Be it confest that, for the first time,
    seated
Within thy innocent lodge and oratory,
One of a festive circle, I poured out
Libations, to thy memory drank, till
    pride
And gratitude grew dizzy in a brain 300
Never excited by the fumes of wine
Before that hour, or since. Then, forth
    I ran
From the assembly; through a length of
    streets,
Ran, ostrich-like, to reach our chapel door
In not a desperate or opprobrious time,
Albeit long after the importunate bell 306
Had stopped, with wearisome Cassandra
    voice
No longer haunting the dark winter night.
Call back, O Friend! a moment to thy
    mind,
The place itself and fashion of the rites. 310
With careless ostentation shouldering up
My surplice, through the inferior throng
    I clove
Of the plain Burghers, who in audience
    stood
On the last skirts of their permitted
    ground,
Under the pealing organ. Empty
    thoughts!   315
I am ashamed of them: and that great
    Bard,
And thou, O Friend! who in thy ample
    mind
Hast placed me high above my best
    deserts,
Ye will forgive the weakness of that hour,
In some of its unworthy vanities, 320
Brother to many more.

                In this mixed sort
The months passed on, remissly, not given
    up
To wilful alienation from the right, 323
Or walks of open scandal, but in vague
And loose indifference, easy likings, aims
Of a low pitch—duty and zeal dismissed,
Yet Nature, or a happy course of things
Not doing in their stead the needful work.
The memory languidly revolved, the heart

Reposed in noontide rest, the inner pulse
Of contemplation almost failed to beat. 331
Such life might not inaptly be compared
To a floating island, an amphibious spot
Unsound, of spongy texture, yet withal
Not wanting a fair face of water-weeds
And pleasant flowers. The thirst of living
    praise, 336
Fit reverence for the glorious Dead, the
    sight
Of those long vistas, sacred catacombs,
Where mighty *minds* lie visibly entombed,
Have often stirred the heart of youth,
    and bred 340
A fervent love of rigorous discipline.—
Alas! such high emotion touched not me.
Look was there none within these walls
    to shame
My easy spirits, and discountenance 344
Their light composure, far less to instil
A calm resolve of mind, firmly addressed
To puissant efforts. Nor was this the
    blame
Of others but my own; I should, in truth,
As far as doth concern my single self,
Misdeem most widely, lodging it else-
    where: 350
For I, bred up 'mid Nature's luxuries,
Was a spoiled child, and, rambling like
    the wind,
As I had done in daily intercourse
With those crystalline rivers, solemn
    heights,
And mountains, ranging like a fowl of
    the air, 355
I was ill-tutored for captivity;
To quit my pleasure, and, from month to
    month,
Take up a station calmly on the perch
Of sedentary peace. Those lovely forms
Had also left less space within my mind,
Which, wrought upon instinctively, had
    found 361
A freshness in those objects of her love,
A winning power, beyond all other power.
Not that I slighted books,—that were to
    lack
All sense,—but other passions in me
    ruled, 365
Passions more fervent, making me less
    prompt

To in-door study than was wise or well,
Or suited to those years. Yet I, though
    used
In magisterial liberty to rove,
Culling such flowers of learning as might
    tempt 370
A random choice, could shadow forth a
    place
(If now I yield not to a flattering dream)
Whose studious aspect should have bent
    me down
To instantaneous service; should at once
Have made me pay to science and to arts
And written lore, acknowledged my liege
    lord, 376
A homage frankly offered up, like that
Which I had paid to Nature. Toil and
    pains
In this recess, by thoughtful Fancy built,
Should spread from heart to heart; and
    stately groves, 380
Majestic edifices, should not want
A corresponding dignity within.
The congregating temper that pervades
Our unripe years, not wasted, should be
    taught
To minister to works of high attempt—
Works which the enthusiast would per-
    form with love. 386
Youth should be awed, religiously pos-
    sessed
With a conviction of the power that waits
On knowledge, when sincerely sought and
    prized 389
For its own sake, on glory and on praise
If but by labour won, and fit to endure.
The passing day should learn to put
    aside
Her trappings here, should strip them off
    abashed
Before antiquity and steadfast truth
And strong book-mindedness; and over
    all 395
A healthy sound simplicity should reign,
A seemly plainness, name it what you
    will,
Republican or pious.
                If these thoughts
Are a gratuitous emblazonry
That mocks the recreant age *we* live in,
    then 400

Be Folly and False-seeming free to affect
Whatever formal gait of discipline
Shall raise them highest in their own
    esteem—
Let them parade among the Schools at
    will,
But spare the House of God. Was ever
    known   405
The witless shepherd who persists to
    drive
A flock that thirsts not to a pool disliked?
A weight must surely hang on days begun
And ended with such mockery. Be wise,
Ye Presidents and Deans, and, till the
    spirit   410
Of ancient times revive, and youth be
    trained
At home in pious service, to your bells
Give seasonable rest, for 'tis a sound
Hollow as ever vexed the tranquil air;
And your officious doings bring disgrace
On the plain steeples of our English
    Church,   416
Whose worship, 'mid remotest village
    trees,
Suffers for this. Even Science, too, at
    hand
In daily sight of this irreverence,
Is smitten thence with an unnatural taint,
Loses her just authority, falls beneath
Collateral suspicion, else unknown.   422
This truth escaped me not, and I confess,
That having 'mid my native hills given
    loose
To a schoolboy's vision, I had raised a
    pile   425
Upon the basis of the coming time,
That fell in ruins round me. Oh, what
    joy
To see a sanctuary for our country's youth
Informed with such a spirit as might be
Its own protection; a primeval grove,   430
Where, though the shades with cheerful-
    ness were filled,
Nor indigent of songs warbled from crowds
In under-coverts, yet the countenance
Of the whole place should bear a stamp
    of awe;
A habitation sober and demure   435
For ruminating creatures; a domain
For quiet things to wander in; a haunt

In which the heron should delight to feed
By the sby rivers, and the pelican   439
Upon the cypress spire in lonely thought
Might sit and sun himself.—Alas! alas!
In vain for such solemnity I looked;
Mine eyes were crossed by butterflies,
    ears vexed
By chattering popinjays; the inner heart
Seemed trivial, and the impresses without
Of a too gaudy region.
                        Different sight 446
Those venerable Doctors saw of old,
When all who dwelt within these famous
    walls
Led in abstemiousness a studious life;
When, in forlorn and naked chambers
    cooped   450
And crowded, o'er the ponderous books
    they hung
Like caterpillars eating out their way
In silence, or with keen devouring noise
Not to be tracked or fathered. Princes
    then
At matins froze, and couched at curfew-
    time,   455
Trained up through piety and zeal to
    prize
Spare diet, patient labour, and plain
    weeds.
O seat of Arts! renowned throughout the
    world!
Far different service in those homely days
The Muses' modest nurslings underwent
From their first childhood: in that glo-
    rious time   461
When Learning, like a stranger come
    from far,
Sounding through Christian lands her
    trumpet, roused
Peasant and king; when boys and youths,
    the growth
Of ragged villages and crazy huts,   465
Forsook their homes, and, errant in the
    quest
Of Patron, famous school or friendly nook,
Where, pensioned, they in shelter might
    sit down,
From town to town and through wide
    scattered realms
Journeyed with ponderous folios in their
    hands;   470

And often, starting from some covert place,
Saluted the chance comer on the road,
Crying, "An obolus, a penny give
To a poor scholar!"—when illustrious
 men,
Lovers of truth, by penury constrained,
Bucer, Erasmus, or Melancthon, read 476
Before the doors or windows of their cells
By moonshine through mere lack of taper
 light.

 But peace to vain regrets! We see but
  darkly
Even when we look behind us, and best
  things   480
Are not so pure by nature that they needs
Must keep to all, as fondly all believe,
Their highest promise. If the mariner,
When at reluctant distance he hath
 passed
Some tempting island, could but know
  the ills   485
That must have fallen upon him had he
 brought
His bark to land upon the wished-for
 shore,
Good cause would oft be his to thank the
 surf
Whose white belt scared him thence, or
 wind that blew
Inexorably adverse: for myself 490
I grieve not; happy is the gownèd youth,
Who only misses what I missed, who falls
No lower than I fell.
     I did not love,
Judging not ill perhaps, the timid
 course
Of our scholastic studies; could have
 wished   495
To see the river flow with ampler range
And freer pace; but more, far more, I
 grieved
To see displayed among an eager few,
Who in the field of contest persevered,
Passions unworthy of youth's generous
 heart   500
And mounting spirit, pitiably repaid,
When so disturbed, whatever palms are
 won.
From these I turned to travel with the
 shoal

Of more unthinking natures, easy minds
And pillowy; yet not wanting love that
 makes   505
The day pass lightly on, when foresight
 sleeps,
And wisdom and the pledges inter-
 changed
With our own inner being are forgot.

Yet was this deep vacation not given up
To utter waste. Hitherto I had stood 510
In my own mind remote from social life,
(At least from what we commonly so
 name,)
Like a lone shepherd on a promontory
Who lacking occupation looks far forth
Into the boundless sea, and rather makes
Than finds what he beholds. And sure
 it is,   516
That this first transit from the smooth
 delights
And wild outlandish walks of simple
 youth
To something that resembles an approach
Towards human business, to a privileged
 world   520
Within a world, a midway residence
With all its intervenient imagery,
Did better suit my visionary mind,
Far better, than to have been bolted
 forth,   524
Thrust out abruptly into Fortune's way
Among the conflicts of substantial life;
By a more just gradation did lead on
To higher things; more naturally ma-
 tured,
For permanent possession, better fruits,
Whether of truth or virtue, to ensue. 530
In serious mood, but oftener, I confess,
With playful zest of fancy, did we note
(How could we less?) the manners and the
 ways
Of those who lived distinguished by the
 badge
Of good or ill report; or those with whom
By frame of Academic discipline 536
We were perforce connected, men whose
 sway
And known authority of office served
To set our minds on edge, and did no
 more.

Nor wanted we rich pastime of this
  kind,   540
Found everywhere, but chiefly in the
  ring
Of the grave Elders, men unscoured,
  grotesque
In character, tricked out like aged trees
Which through the lapse of their in-
  firmity
Give ready place to any random seed 545
That chooses to be reared upon their
  trunks.

 Here on my view, confronting vividly
Those shepherd swains whom I had lately
  left,
Appeared a different aspect of old age;
How different! yet both distinctly
  marked,   550
Objects embossed to catch the general
  eye,
Or portraitures for special use designed,
As some might seem, so aptly do they
  serve
To illustrate Nature's book of rudiments—
That book upheld as with maternal care
When she would enter on her tender
  scheme   556
Of teaching comprehension with delight,
And mingling playful with pathetic
  thoughts.

 The surfaces of artificial life
And manners finely wrought, the delicate
  race   560
Of colours, lurking, gleaming up and
  down
Through that state arras woven with silk
  and gold;
This wily interchange of snaky hues,
Willingly or unwillingly revealed,
I neither knew nor cared for; and as
  such   565
Were wanting here, I took what might be
  found
Of less elaborate fabric. At this day
I smile, in many a mountain solitude
Conjuring up scenes as obsolete in freaks
Of character, in points of wit as broad, 570
As aught by wooden images performed
For entertainment of the gaping crowd
At wake or fair. And oftentimes do flit

Remembrances before me of old men—
Old humourists, who have been long in
  their graves,   575
And having almost in my mind put off
Their human names, have into phantoms
  passed
Of texture midway between life and
  books.

 I play the loiterer: 'tis enough to note
That here in dwarf proportions were
  expressed   580
The limbs of the great world; its eager
  strifes
Collaterally pourtrayed, as in mock fight,
A tournament of blows, some hardly dealt
Though short of mortal combat; and
  whate'er   584
Might in this pageant be supposed to hit
An artless rustic's notice, this way less,
More that way, was not wasted upon
  me—
And yet the spectacle may well demand
A more substantial name, no mimic
  show,
Itself a living part of a live whole, 590
A creek in the vast sea; for, all degrees
And shapes of spurious fame and short-
  lived praise
Here sate in state, and fed with daily
  alms
Retainers won away from solid good;
And here was Labour, his own bond-
  slave; Hope,   595
That never set the pains against the
  prize;
Idleness halting with his weary clog,
And poor misguided Shame, and witless
  Fear,
And simple Pleasure foraging for Death;
Honour misplaced, and Dignity astray;
Feuds, factions, flatteries, enmity, and
  guile,   601
Murmuring submission, and bald govern-
  ment,
(The idol weak as the idolater),
And Decency and Custom starving Truth,
And blind Authority beating with his
  staff   605
The child that might have led him;
  Emptiness

Followed as of good omen, and meek Worth
Left to herself unheard of and unknown.

Of these and other kindred notices
I cannot say what portion is in truth   610
The naked recollection of that time,
And what may rather have been called to life
By after-meditation. But delight
That, in an easy temper lulled asleep,
Is still with Innocence its own reward, 615
This was not wanting. Carelessly I roamed
As through a wide museum from whose stores
A casual rarity is singled out
And has its brief perusal, then gives way
To others, all supplanted in their turn;

Till 'mid this crowded neighbourhood of things   621
That are by nature most unneighbourly,
The head turns round and cannot right itself;
And though an aching and a barren sense
Of gay confusion still be uppermost,   625
With few wise longings and but little love,
Yet to the memory something cleaves at last,
Whence profit may be drawn in times to come.

Thus in submissive idleness, my Friend!
The labouring time of autumn, winter, spring,   630
Eight months! rolled pleasingly away;
the ninth
Came and returned me to my native hills.

BOOK FOURTH.

SUMMER VACATION.

BRIGHT was the summer's noon when quickening steps
Followed each other till a dreary moor
Was crossed, a bare ridge clomb, upon whose top
Standing alone, as from a rampart's edge,
I overlooked the bed of Windermere,   5
Like a vast river, stretching in the sun.
With exultation, at my feet I saw
Lake, islands, promontories, gleaming bays,
A universe of Nature's fairest forms
Proudly revealed with instantaneous burst,   10
Magnificent, and beautiful, and gay.
I bounded down the hill shouting amain
For the old Ferryman; to the shout the rocks
Replied, and when the Charon of the flood
Had staid his oars, and touched the jutting pier,   15
I did not step into the well-known boat

Without a cordial greeting. Thence with speed
Up the familiar hill I took my way
Towards that sweet Valley[1] where I had been reared;
'Twas but a short hour's walk, ere veering round   20
I saw the snow-white church upon her hill
Sit like a thronèd Lady, sending out
A gracious look all over her domain.
Yon azure smoke betrays the lurking town;
With eager footsteps I advance and reach
The cottage threshold where my journey closed.   26
Glad welcome had I, with some tears, perhaps,
From my old Dame, so kind and motherly,
While she perused me with a parent's pride.
The thoughts of gratitude shall fall like dew

---

[1] Hawkshead.

Upon thy grave, good creature! While
   my heart   31
Can beat never will I forget thy name.
Heaven's blessing be upon thee where
   thou liest
After thy innocent and busy stir
In narrow cares, thy little daily growth 35
Of calm enjoyments, after eighty years,
And more than eighty, of untroubled life,
Childless, yet by the strangers to thy
   blood
Honoured with little less than filial love.
What joy was mine to see thee once
   again,   40
Thee and thy dwelling, and a crowd of
   things
About its narrow precincts all beloved,
And many of them seeming yet my own!
Why should I speak of what a thousand
   hearts
Have felt, and every man alive can
   guess?   45
The rooms, the court, the garden were not
   left
Long unsaluted, nor the sunny seat
Round the stone table under the dark
   pine,
Friendly to studious or to festive hours;
Nor that unruly child of mountain birth,
The froward brook, who, soon as he was
   boxed   51
Within our garden, found himself at once,
As if by trick insidious and unkind,
Stripped of his voice and left to dimple
   down
(Without an effort and without a will) 55
A channel paved by man's officious care.
I looked at him and smiled, and smiled
   again,
And in the press of twenty thousand
   thoughts,
"Ha," quoth I, "pretty prisoner, are you
   there!"
Well might sarcastic Fancy then have
   whispered,   60
"An emblem here behold of thy own life;
In its late course of even days with all
Their smooth enthralment;" but the
   heart was full,
Too full for that reproach. My aged
   Dame

Walked proudly at my side: she guided
   me;   65
I willing, nay—nay, wishing to be led.
—The face of every neighbour whom
   I met
Was like a volume to me; some were
   hailed
Upon the road, some busy at their work,
Unceremonious greetings interchanged
With half the length of a long field
   between.   71
Among my schoolfellows I scattered
   round
Like recognitions, but with some con-
   straint
Attended, doubtless, with a little pride,
But with more shame, for my habili-
   ments,   75
The transformation wrought by gay
   attire.
Not less delighted did I take my place
At our domestic table: and, dear Friend!
In this endeavour simply to relate
A Poet's history, may I leave untold 80
The thankfulness with which I laid me
   down
In my accustomed bed, more welcome
   now
Perhaps than if it had been more desired
Or been more often thought of with
   regret;
That lowly bed whence I had heard the
   wind   85
Roar, and the rain beat hard; where I so
   oft
Had lain awake on summer nights to
   watch
The moon in splendour couched among
   the leaves
Of a tall ash, that near our cottage stood;
Had watched her with fixed eyes while to
   and fro   90
In the dark summit of the waving tree
She rocked with every impulse of the
   breeze.

Among the favourites whom it pleased
   me well
To see again, was one by ancient right
Our inmate, a rough terrier of the hills; 95
By birth and call of nature pre-ordained

To hunt the badger and unearth the fox
Among the impervious crags, but having
　　been
From youth our own adopted, he had
　　passed　　　　　　　　　　　　99
Into a gentler service. And when first
The boyish spirit flagged, and day by day
Along my veins I kindled with the stir,
The fermentation, and the vernal heat
Of poesy, affecting private shades
Like a sick Lover, then this dog was
　　used　　　　　　　　　　　　　105
To watch me, an attendant and a friend,
Obsequious to my steps early and late,
Though often of such dilatory walk
Tired, and uneasy at the halts I made.
A hundred times when, roving high and
　　low,　　　　　　　　　　　　110
I have been harassed with the toil of
　　verse,
Much pains and little progress, and at
　　once
Some lovely Image in the song rose up
Full-formed, like Venus rising from the
　　sea ;　　　　　　　　　　　　114
Then have I darted forwards to let loose
My hand upon his back with stormy joy,
Caressing him again and yet again,
And when at evening on the public way
I sauntered, like a river murmuring
And talking to itself when all things
　　else　　　　　　　　　　　　120
Are still, the creature trotted on before ;
Such was his custom ; but whene'er he
　　met
A passenger approaching, he would turn
To give me timely notice, and straight-
　　way,
Grateful for that admonishment, I hushed
My voice, composed my gait, and, with
　　the air　　　　　　　　　　　126
And mien of one whose thoughts are free,
　　advanced
To give and take a greeting that might
　　save
My name from piteous rumours, such as
　　wait
On men suspected to be crazed in brain.

Those walks well worthy to be prized
　　and loved—　　　　　　　　131

Regretted !—that word, too, was on my
　　tongue,
But they were richly laden with all good,
And cannot be remembered but with
　　thanks
And gratitude, and perfect joy of heart—
Those walks in all their freshness now
　　came back　　　　　　　　136
Like a returning Spring. When first I
　　made
Once more the circuit of our little lake,
If ever happiness hath lodged with man,
That day consummate happiness was
　　mine,　　　　　　　　　　　140
Wide-spreading, steady, calm, contem-
　　plative.
The sun was set, or setting, when I left
Our cottage door, and evening soon
　　brought on
A sober hour, not winning or serene,
For cold and raw the air was, and un-
　　tuned ;　　　　　　　　　　145
But as a face we love is sweetest then
When sorrow damps it, or, whatever look
It chance to wear, is sweetest if the heart
Have fulness in herself ; even so with me
It fared that evening. Gently did my
　　soul　　　　　　　　　　　　150
Put off her veil, and self-transmuted,
　　stood
Naked, as in the presence of her God.
While on I walked, a comfort seemed to
　　touch
A heart that had not been disconsolate :
Strength came where weakness was not
　　known to be,　　　　　　　155
At least not felt ; and restoration came
Like an intruder knocking at the door
Of unacknowledged weariness. I took
The balance, and with firm hand weighed
　　myself.
—Of that external scene which round me
　　lay,　　　　　　　　　　　　160
Little, in this abstraction, did I see ;
Remembered less ; but I had inward
　　hopes
And swellings of the spirit, was rapt and
　　soothed,
Conversed with promises, had glimmer-
　　ing views　　　　　　　　164
How life pervades the undecaying mind ;

How the immortal soul with God-like
power
Informs, creates, and thaws the deepest
sleep
That time can lay upon her; how on
earth
Man, if he do but live within the light
Of high endeavours, daily spreads abroad
His being armed with strength that can-
not fail.   171
Nor was there want of milder thoughts,
of love,
Of innocence, and holiday repose;
And more than pastoral quiet, 'mid the
stir   174
Of boldest projects, and a peaceful end
At last, or glorious, by endurance won.
Thus musing, in a wood I sate me down
Alone, continuing there to muse: the
slopes
And heights meanwhile were slowly over-
spread
With darkness, and before a rippling
breeze   180
The long lake lengthened out its hoary
line,
And in the sheltered coppice where I
sate,
Around me from among the hazel leaves,
Now here, now there, moved by the
straggling wind,   184
Came ever and anon a breath-like sound,
Quick as the pantings of the faithful dog,
The off and on companion of my walk;
And such, at times, believing them to be,
I turned my head to look if he were
there;
Then into solemn thought I passed once
more.   190

A freshness also found I at this time
In human Life, the daily life of those
Whose occupations really I loved;
The peaceful scene oft filled me with
surprise
Changed like a garden in the heat of
spring,   195
After an eight-days' absence. For (to
omit
The things which were the same and yet
appeared

Far otherwise) amid this rural solitude,
A narrow Vale where each was known to
all,
'Twas not indifferent to a youthful mind
To mark some sheltering bower or sunny
nook,   201
Where an old man had used to sit alone,
Now vacant; pale-faced babes whom I
had left ·
In arms, now rosy prattlers at the feet
Of a pleased grandame tottering up and
down;   205
And growing girls whose beauty, filched
away
With all its pleasant promises, was gone
To deck some slighted playmate's homely
cheek.

Yes, I had something of a subtler sense,
And often looking round was moved to
smiles   210
Such as a delicate work of humour breeds;
I read, without design, the opinions,
thoughts,
Of those plain-living people now observed
With clearer knowledge; with another
eye
I saw the quiet woodman in the woods,
The shepherd roam the hills. With new
delight,   216
This chiefly, did I note my grey-haired
Dame;
Saw her go forth to church or other work
Of state, equipped in monumental trim;
Short velvet cloak, (her bonnet of the
like),   220
A mantle such as Spanish Cavaliers
Wore in old time. Her smooth domestic
life,
Affectionate without disquietude,
Her talk, her business, pleased me; and
no less
Her clear though shallow stream of piety
That ran on Sabbath days a fresher
course;   226
With thoughts unfelt till now I saw her
read
Her Bible on hot Sunday afternoons,
And loved the book, when she had
dropped asleep
And made of it a pillow for her head. 230

Nor less do I remember to have felt,
Distinctly manifested at this time,
A human-heartedness about my love
For objects hitherto the absolute wealth
Of my own private being and no more;
Which I had loved, even as a blessed
     spirit   236
Or Angel, if he were to dwell on earth,
Might love in individual happiness.
But now there opened on me other
     thoughts
Of change, congratulation or regret,   240
A pensive feeling! It spread far and
     wide;
The trees, the mountains shared it, and
     the brooks,
The stars of Heaven, now seen in their
     old haunts—
White Sirius glittering o'er the southern
     crags,
Orion with his belt, and those fair Seven,
Acquaintances of every little child,   246
And Jupiter, my own beloved star!
Whatever shadings of mortality,
Whatever imports from the world of
     death
Had come among these objects here-
     before,   250
Were, in the main, of mood less tender:
     strong,
Deep, gloomy were they, and severe;
     the scatterings
Of awe or tremulous dread, that had
     given way
In later youth to yearnings of a love
Enthusiastic, to delight and hope.   255

As one who hangs down-bending from
     the side
Of a slow-moving boat, upon the breast
Of a still water, solacing himself
With such discoveries as his eye can
     make
Beneath him in the bottom of the deep,
Sees many beauteous sights—weeds, fishes,
     flowers,   261
Grots, pebbles, roots of trees, and fancies
     more,
Yet often is perplexed and cannot part
The shadow from the substance, rocks
     and sky,

Mountains and clouds, reflected in the
     depth   265
Of the clear flood, from things which
     there abide
In their true dwelling; now is crossed by
     gleam
Of his own image, by a sunbeam now,
And wavering motions sent he knows not
     whence,
Impediments that make his task more
     sweet;   270
Such pleasant office have we long pursued
Incumbent o'er the surface of past time
With like success, nor often have ap-
     peared
Shapes fairer or less doubtfully discerned
Than these to which the Tale, indulgent
     Friend!   275
Would now direct thy notice. Yet in
     spite
Of pleasure won, and knowledge not
     withheld,
There was an inner falling off—I loved,
Loved deeply all that had been loved
     before,
More deeply even than ever: but a
     swarm.   280
Of heady schemes jostling each other,
     gawds,
And feast and dance, and public revelry,
And sports and games (too grateful in
     themselves,
Yet in themselves less grateful, I believe,
Than as they were a badge glossy and
     fresh   285
Of manliness and freedom) all conspired
To lure my mind from firm habitual
     quest
Of feeding pleasures, to depress the zeal
And damp those yearnings which had
     once been mine—
A wild, unworldly-minded youth, given
     up   290
To his own eager thoughts. It would
     demand
Some skill, and longer time than may be
     spared,
To paint these vanities, and how they
     wrought
In haunts where they, till now, had been
     unknown.

It seemed the very garments that I wore
Preyed on my strength, and stopped the
quiet stream   296
Of self-forgetfulness.
        Yes, that heartless chase
Of trivial pleasures was a poor exchange
For books and nature at that early age.
'Tis true, some casual knowledge might
be gained   300
Of character or life; but at that time,
Of manners put to school I took small
note,
And all my deeper passions lay else-
where.
Far better had it been to exalt the mind
By solitary study, to uphold   305
Intense desire through meditative peace;
And yet, for chastisement of these re-
grets,
The memory of one particular hour
Doth here rise up against me. 'Mid a
throng
Of maids and youths, old men, and
matrons staid,   310
A medley of all tempers, I had passed
The night in dancing, gaiety, and mirth,
With din of instruments and shuffling
feet,
And glancing forms, and tapers glittering,
And unaimed prattle flying up and down;
Spirits upon the stretch, and here and
there   316
Slight shocks of young love-liking inter-
spersed,
Whose transient pleasure mounted to the
head,
And tingled through the veins. Ere we
retired,
The cock had crowed, and now the
eastern sky   320
Was kindling, not unseen, from humble
copse
And open field, through which the path-
way wound,
And homeward led my steps. Magni-
ficent
The morning rose, in memorable pomp,
Glorious as e'er I had beheld—in front,
The sea lay laughing at a distance; near,
The solid mountains shone, bright as the
clouds,   327

Grain-tinctured, drenched in empyrean
light;
And in the meadows and the lower
grounds
Was all the sweetness of a common
dawn—   330
Dews, vapours, and the melody of birds,
And labourers going forth to till the
fields.
Ah! need I say, dear Friend! that to
the brim
My heart was full; I made no vows, but
vows
Were then made for me; bond unknown
to me   335
Was given, that I should be, else sinning
greatly,
A dedicated Spirit. On I walked
In thankful blessedness, which yet sur-
vives.

Strange rendez-vous my mind was at
that time,
A parti-coloured show of grave and gay,
Solid and light, short-sighted and pro-
found;   341
Of inconsiderate habits and sedate,
Consorting in one mansion unreproved.
The worth I knew of powers that I
possessed,
Though slighted and too oft misused.
Besides,   345
That summer, swarming as it did with
thoughts
Transient and idle, lacked not intervals
When Folly from the frown of fleeting Time
Shrunk, and the mind experienced in
herself
Conformity as just as that of old   350
To the end and written spirit of God's
works,
Whether held forth in Nature or in Man,
Through pregnant vision, separate or
conjoined.

When from our better selves we have
too long
Been parted by the hurrying world, and
droop,   355
Sick of its business, of its pleasures tired,
How gracious, how benign, is Solitude;

How potent a mere image of her sway;
Most potent when impressed upon the
   mind
With an appropriate human centre—
   hermit,   360
Deep in the bosom of the wilderness;
Votary (in vast cathedral, where no foot
Is treading, where no other face is seen)
Kneeling at prayers; or watchman on
   the top   364
Of lighthouse, beaten by Atlantic waves;
Or as the soul of that great Power is met
Sometimes embodied on a public road,
When, for the night deserted, it assumes
A character of quiet more profound
Than pathless wastes.

          Once, when those summer
   months   370
Were flown, and autumn brought its
   annual show
Of oars with oars contending, sails with
   sails,
Upon Winander's spacious breast, it
   chanced
That—after I had left a flower-decked
   room
(Whose in-door pastime, lighted up, sur-
   vived   375
To a late hour), and spirits overwrought
Were making night do penance for a day
Spent in a round of strenuous idleness—
My homeward course led up a long
   ascent,
Where the road's watery surface, to the
   top   380
Of that sharp rising, glittered to the moon
And bore the semblance of another stream
Stealing with silent lapse to join the
   brook
That murmured in the vale. All else
   was still;
No living thing appeared in earth or air,
And, save the flowing water's peaceful
   voice,   386
Sound there was none—but, lo! an un-
   couth shape,
Shown by a sudden turning of the road,
So near that, slipping back into the shade
Of a thick hawthorn, I could mark him
   well,   390
Myself unseen. He was of stature tall,

A span above man's common measure,
   tall,
Stiff, lank, and upright; a more meagre
   man
Was never seen before by night or day.
Long were his arms, pallid his hands;
   his mouth   395
Looked ghastly in the moonlight: from
   behind,
A mile-stone propped him; I could also
   ken
That he was clothed in military garb,
Though faded, yet entire. Companion-
   less,   399
No dog attending, by no staff sustained,
He stood, and in his very dress appeared
A desolation, a simplicity,
To which the trappings of a gaudy world
Make a strange back-ground. From his
   lips, ere long,
Issued low muttered sounds, as if of pain
Or some uneasy thought; yet still his
   form   406
Kept the same awful steadiness—at his
   feet
His shadow lay, and moved not. From
   self-blame
Not wholly free, I watched him thus; at
   length   409
Subduing my heart's specious cowardice,
I left the shady nook where I had stood
And hailed him. Slowly from his resting-
   place
He rose, and with a lean and wasted arm
In measured gesture lifted to his head
Returned my salutation; then resumed
His station as before; and when I asked
His history, the veteran, in reply,   417
Was neither slow nor eager; but, un-
   moved,
And with a quiet uncomplaining voice,
A stately air of mild indifference,   420
He told in few plain words a soldier's
   tale—
That in the Tropic Islands he had served,
Whence he had landed scarcely three
   weeks past;
That on his landing he had been dis-
   missed,
And now was travelling towards his
   native home.   425

This heard, I said, in pity, "Come with
   me."
He stooped, and straightway from the
   ground took up
An oaken staff by me yet unobserved—
A staff which must have dropt from his
   slack hand
And lay till now neglected in the grass.
Though weak his step and cautious, he
   appeared   431
To travel without pain, and I beheld,
With an astonishment but ill suppressed,
His ghostly figure moving at my side;
Nor could I, while we journeyed thus,
   forbear   435
To turn from present hardships to the
   past,
And speak of war, battle, and pestilence,
Sprinkling this talk with questions, better
   spared,
On what he might himself have seen or
   felt.   439
He all the while was in demeanour calm,
Concise in answer; solemn and sublime
He might have seemed, but that in all he
   said
There was a strange half-absence, as of
   one
Knowing too well the importance of his
   theme,   444
But feeling it no longer.   Our discourse
Soon ended, and together on we passed
In silence through a wood gloomy and
   still.

Up-turning, then, along an open field,
We reached a cottage.   At the door I
   knocked,
And earnestly to charitable care   450
Commended him as a poor friendless
   man,
Belated and by sickness overcome.
Assured that now the traveller would
   repose
In comfort, I entreated that henceforth
He would not linger in the public ways,
But ask for timely furtherance and help
Such as his state required.   At this re-
   proof,   457
With the same ghastly mildness in his
   look,
He said, "My trust is in the God of
   Heaven,
And in the eye of him who passes me!"

The cottage door was speedily unbar-
   red,   461
And now the soldier touched his hat once
   more
With his lean hand, and in a faltering
   voice,
Whose tone bespake reviving interests
Till then unfelt, he thanked me; I re-
   turned   465
The farewell blessing of the patient man,
And so we parted.   Back I cast a look,
And lingered near the door a little space,
Then sought with quiet heart my distant
   home.

BOOK FIFTH.

BOOKS.

WHEN Contemplation, like the night-
   calm felt
Through earth and sky, spreads widely,
   and sends deep
Into the soul its tranquillising power,
Even then I sometimes grieve for thee,
   O Man,
Earth's paramount Creature! not so much
   for woes   5

That thou endurest; heavy though that
   weight be,
Cloud-like it mounts, or touched with
   light divine
Doth melt away; but for those palms
   achieved,
Through length of time, by patient exercise
Of study and hard thought; there, there,
   it is   10

That sadness finds its fuel. Hitherto,
In progress through this Verse, my mind
   hath looked
Upon the speaking face of earth and
   heaven
As her prime teacher, intercourse with
   man
Established by the sovereign Intellect, 15
Who through that bodily image hath
   diffused,
As might appear to the eye of fleeting
   time,
A deathless spirit. Thou also, man! hast
   wrought,
For commerce of thy nature with herself,
Things that aspire to unconquerable life;
And yet we feel—we cannot choose but
   feel—   21
That they must perish. Tremblings of
   the heart
It gives, to think that our immortal
   being
No more shall need such garments; and
   yet man,
As long as he shall be the child of earth,
Might almost "weep to have" what he
   may lose,   26
Nor be himself extinguished, but survive,
Abject, depressed, forlorn, disconsolate.
A thought is with me sometimes, and I
   say,—
Should the whole frame of earth by in-
   ward throes   30
Be wrenched, or fire come down from far
   to scorch
Her pleasant habitations, and dry up
Old Ocean, in his bed left singed and bare,
Yet would the living Presence still sub-
   sist
Victorious, and composure would ensue,
And kindlings like the morning—presage
   sure   36
Of day returning and of life revived.
But all the meditations of mankind,
Yea, all the adamantine holds of truth
By reason built, or passion, which itself 40
Is highest reason in a soul sublime;
The consecrated works of Bard and Sage,
Sensuous or intellectual, wrought by men,
Twin labourers and heirs of the same
   hopes;

Where would they be? Oh! why hath
   not the Mind   45
Some element to stamp her image on
In nature somewhat nearer to her own?
Why, gifted with such powers to send
   abroad
Her spirit, must it lodge in shrines so
   frail?

One day, when from my lips a like
   complaint   50
Had fallen in presence of a studious
   friend,
He with a smile made answer, that in truth
'Twas going far to seek disquietude;
But on the front of his reproof confessed
That he himself had oftentimes given
   way   55
To kindred hauntings. Whereupon I
   told,
That once in the stillness of a summer's
   noon,
While I was seated in a rocky cave
By the sea-side, perusing, so it chanced,
The famous history of the errant knight
Recorded by Cervantes, these same
   thoughts   61
Beset me, and to height unusual rose,
While listlessly I sate, and, having closed
The book, had turned my eyes toward
   the wide sea.
On poetry and geometric truth,   65
And their high privilege of lasting life,
From all internal injury exempt,
I mused; upon these chiefly: and at
   length,
My senses yielding to the sultry air,
Sleep seized me, and I passed into a
   dream.   70
I saw before me stretched a boundless
   plain
Of sandy wilderness, all black and void,
And as I looked around, distress and fear
Came creeping over me, when at my side,
Close at my side, an uncouth shape
   appeared   75
Upon a dromedary, mounted high,
He seemed an Arab of the Bedouin
   tribes:
A lance he bore, and underneath one arm
A stone, and in the opposite hand a shell

Of a surpassing brightness. At the sight
Much I rejoiced, not doubting but a
    guide   81
Was present, one who with unerring skill
Would through the desert lead me; and
    while yet
I looked and looked, self-questioned what
    this freight
Which the new-comer carried through
    the waste   85
Could mean, the Arab told me that the
    stone
(To give it in the language of the dream)
Was "Euclid's Elements;" and "This,"
    said he,
"Is something of more worth;" and at
    the word
Stretched forth the shell, so beautiful in
    shape,   90
In colour so resplendent, with command
That I should hold it to my ear. I did so,
And heard that instant in an unknown
    tongue,
Which yet I understood, articulate sounds,
A loud prophetic blast of harmony;   95
An Ode, in passion uttered, which fore-
    told
Destruction to the children of the earth
By deluge, now at hand. No sooner
    ceased
The song, than the Arab with calm look
    declared
That all would come to pass of which the
    voice   100
Had given forewarning, and that he
    himself
Was going then to bury those two books:
The one that held acquaintance with the
    stars,
And wedded soul to soul in purest bond
Of reason, undisturbed by space or time;
The other that was a god, yea many
    gods,   106
Had voices more than all the winds, with
    power
To exhilarate the spirit, and to soothe,
Through every clime, the heart of human
    kind.
While this was uttering, strange as it
    may seem,   110
I wondered not, although I plainly saw

The one to be a stone, the other a shell;
Nor doubted once but that they both
    were books,
Having a perfect faith in all that passed.
Far stronger, now, grew the desire I felt
To cleave unto this man; but when I
    prayed   116
To share his enterprise, he hurried on
Reckless of me: I followed, not unseen,
For oftentimes he cast a backward look,
Grasping his twofold treasure.—Lance in
    rest,   120
He rode, I keeping pace with him; and
    now
He, to my fancy, had become the knight
Whose tale Cervantes tells; yet not the
    knight,
But was an Arab of the desert too;
Of these was neither, and was both at
    once.   125
His countenance, meanwhile, grew more
    disturbed;
And, looking backwards when he looked,
    mine eyes
Saw, over half the wilderness diffused,
A bed of glittering light: I asked the
    cause:
"It is," said he, "the waters of the deep
Gathering upon us;" quickening then
    the pace   131
Of the unwieldy creature he bestrode,
He left me: I called after him aloud;
He heeded not; but, with his twofold
    charge   134
Still in his grasp, before me, full in view,
Went hurrying o'er the illimitable waste,
With the fleet waters of a drowning
    world
In chase of him; whereat I waked in
    terror,
And saw the sea before me, and the book,
In which I had been reading, at my side.

Full often, taking from the world of
    sleep   141
This Arab phantom, which I thus beheld,
This semi-Quixote, I to him have given
A substance, fancied him a living man,
A gentle dweller in the desert, crazed 145
By love and feeling, and internal thought
Protracted among endless solitudes;

Have shaped him wandering upon this
quest!
Nor have I pitied him; but rather felt
Reverence was due to a being thus em-
ployed;   150
And thought that, in the blind and awful
lair
Of such a madness, reason did lie couched.
Enow there are on earth to take in charge
Their wives, their children, and their
virgin loves,
Or whatsoever else the heart holds dear;
Enow to stir for these; yea, will I say, 156
Contemplating in soberness the approach
Of an event so dire, by signs in earth
Or heaven made manifest, that I could
share
That maniac's fond anxiety, and go   160
Upon like errand. Oftentimes at least
Me hath such strong entrancement over-
come,
When I have held a volume in my hand,
Poor earthly casket of immortal verse,
Shakespeare, or Milton, labourers divine!

Great and benign, indeed, must be the
power   166
Of living nature, which could thus so
long
Detain me from the best of other guides
And dearest helpers, left unthanked, un-
praised.
Even in the time of lisping infancy,   170
And later down, in prattling childhood,
even
While I was travelling back among those
days,
How could I ever play an ingrate's part?
Once more should I have made those
bowers resound,
By intermingling strains of thankfulness
With their own thoughtless melodies; at
least   176
It might have well beseemed me to repeat
Some simply fashioned tale, to tell again,
In slender accents of sweet verse, some tale
That did bewitch me then, and soothes
me now.   180
O Friend! O Poet! brother of my soul,
Think not that I could pass along un-
touched

By these remembrances. Yet wherefore
speak?
Why call upon a few weak words to say
What is already written in the hearts 185
Of all that breathe?—what in the path of
all
Drops daily from the tongue of every
child,
Wherever man is found? The trickling
tear
Upon the cheek of listening Infancy
Proclaims it, and the insuperable look 190
That drinks as if it never could be full.

That portion of my story I shall leave
There registered: whatever else of power
Or pleasure sown, or fostered thus, may be
Peculiar to myself, let that remain   195
Where still it works, though hidden from
all search
Among the depths of time. Yet is it just
That here, in memory of all books which
lay
Their sure foundations in the heart of
man,
Whether by native prose, or numerous
verse,   200
That in the name of all inspirèd souls—
From Homer the great Thunderer, from
the voice
That roars along the bed of Jewish song,
And that more varied and elaborate,
Those trumpet-tones of harmony that
shake   205
Our shores in England,—from those
loftiest notes
Down to the low and wren-like warblings,
made
For cottagers and spinners at the wheel,
And sun-burnt travellers resting their
tired limbs,
Stretched under wayside hedge-rows,
ballad tunes,   210
Food for the hungry ears of little ones,
And of old men who have survived their
joys—
'Tis just that in behalf of these, the works,
And of the men that framed them,
whether known,
Or sleeping nameless in their scattered
graves,   215

That I should here assert their rights, attest

Their honours, and should, once for all, pronounce

Their benediction; speak of them as Powers

For ever to be hallowed; only less,

For what we are and what we may become,   220

Than Nature's self, which is the breath of God,

Or His pure Word by miracle revealed.

Rarely and with reluctance would I stoop

To transitory themes; yet I rejoice,

And, by these thoughts admonished, will pour out   225

Thanks with uplifted heart, that I was reared

Safe from an evil which these days have laid

Upon the children of the land, a pest

That might have dried me up, body and soul.

This verse is dedicate to Nature's self, 230

And things that teach as Nature teaches: then,

Oh! where had been the Man, the Poet where,

Where had we been, we two, belovèd Friend!

If in the season of unperilous choice,

In lieu of wandering, as we did, through vales   235

Rich with indigenous produce, open ground

Of Fancy, happy pastures ranged at will,

We had been followed, hourly watched, and noosed,

Each in his several melancholy walk

Stringed like a poor man's heifer at its feed,   240

Led through the lanes in forlorn servitude;

Or rather like a stallèd ox debarred

From touch of growing grass, that may not taste

A flower till it have yielded up its sweets

A prelibation to the mower's scythe. 245

Behold the parent hen amid her brood,

Though fledged and feathered, and well pleased to part

And straggle from her presence, still a brood,

And she herself from the maternal bond

Still undischarged; yet doth she little more   250

Than move with them in tenderness and love,

A centre to the circle which they make;

And now and then, alike from need of theirs

And call of her own natural appetites,

She scratches, ransacks up the earth for food,   255

Which they partake at pleasure. Early died

My honoured Mother, she who was the heart

And hinge of all our learnings and our loves:

She left us destitute, and, as we might,

Trooping together. Little suits it me 260

To break upon the sabbath of her rest

With any thought that looks at others' blame;

Nor would I praise her but in perfect love.

Hence am I checked: but let me boldly say,

In gratitude, and for the sake of truth,

Unheard by her, that she, not falsely taught,   266

Fetching her goodness rather from times past,

Than shaping novelties for times to come,

Had no presumption, no such jealousy,

Nor did by habit of her thoughts mistrust   270

Our nature, but had virtual faith that He

Who fills the mother's breast with innocent milk,

Doth also for our nobler part provide,

Under His great correction and control,

As innocent instincts, and as innocent food;   275

Or draws for minds that are left free to trust

In the simplicities of opening life

Sweet honey out of spurned or dreaded weeds.

This was her creed, and therefore she was
   pure
From anxious fear of error or mishap, 280
And evil, overweeningly so called ;
Was not puffed up by false unnatural
   hopes,
Nor selfish with unnecessary cares,
Nor with impatience from the season
   asked
More than its timely produce ; rather
   loved   285
The hours for what they are, than from
   regard
Glanced on their promises in restless
   pride.
Such was she—not from faculties more
   strong
Than others have, but from the times,
   perhaps,
And spot in which she lived, and through
   a grace   290
Of modest meekness, simple-mindedness,
A heart that found benignity and hope,
Being itself benign.
            My drift I fear
Is scarcely obvious ; but, that common
   sense
May try this modern system by its fruits,
Leave let me take to place before her
   sight   296
A specimen pourtrayed with faithful
   hand.
Full early trained to worship seemliness,
This model of a child is never known
To mix in quarrels ; that were far be-
   neath   300
Its dignity ; with gifts he bubbles o'er
As generous as a fountain ; selfishness
May not come near him, nor the little
   throng
Of flitting pleasures tempt him from his
   path ;
The wandering beggars propagate his
   name,   305
Dumb creatures find him tender as a nun,
And natural or supernatural fear,
Unless it leap upon him in a dream,
Touches him not. To enhance the wonder,
   see
How arch his notices, how nice his sense
Of the ridiculous ; not blind is he   311

To the broad follies of the licensed world,
Yet innocent himself withal, though
   shrewd,
And can read lectures upon innocence ;
A miracle of scientific lore,   315
Ships he can guide across the pathless
   sea,
And tell you all their cunning ; he can
   read
The inside of the earth, and spell the
   stars ;
He knows the policies of foreign lands ;
Can string you names of districts, cities,
   towns,   320
The whole world over, tight as beads of
   dew
Upon a gossamer thread ; he sifts, he
   weighs ;
All things are put to question ; he must
   live
Knowing that he grows wiser every day
Or else not live at all, and seeing too   325
Each little drop of wisdom as it falls
Into the dimpling cistern of his heart :
For this unnatural growth the trainer
   blame,
Pity the tree.—Poor human vanity,
Wert thou extinguished, little would be
   left   330
Which he could truly love ; but how es-
   cape ?
For, ever as a thought of purer birth
Rises to lead him toward a better clime,
Some intermeddler still is on the watch
To drive him back, and pound him, like
   a stray,   335
Within the pinfold of his own conceit.
Meanwhile old grandame earth is grieved
   to find
The playthings, which her love designed
   for him,
Unthought of : in their woodland beds
   the flowers   339
Weep, and the river sides are all forlorn.
Oh ! give us once again the wishing-cap
Of Fortunatus, and the invisible coat
Of Jack the Giant-killer, Robin Hood,
And Sabra in the forest with St. George !
The child, whose love is here, at least,
   doth reap   345
One precious gain, that he forgets himself.

These mighty workmen of our later age,
Who, with a broad highway, have over-
      bridged
The froward chaos of futurity,
Tamed to their bidding; they who have
      the skill   350
To manage books, and things, and make
      them act
On infant minds as surely as the sun
Deals with a flower; the keepers of our
      time,
The guides and wardens of our faculties,
Sages who in their prescience would control
All accidents, and to the very road   356
Which they have fashioned would confine
      us down,
Like engines; when will their presump-
      tion learn,
That in the unreasoning progress of the
      world
A wiser spirit is at work for us,   360
A better eye than theirs, most prodigal
Of blessings, and most studious of our
      good,
Even in what seem our most unfruitful
      hours?

There was a Boy[1]: ye knew him well,
      ye cliffs   364
And islands of Winander!—many a time
At evening, when the earliest stars began
To move along the edges of the hills,
Rising or setting, would he stand alone
Beneath the trees or by the glimmering
      lake,
And there, with fingers interwoven, both
      hands   370
Pressed closely palm to palm, and to his
      mouth
Uplifted, he, as through an instrument,
Blew mimic hootings to the silent owls,
That they might answer him; and they
      would shout
Across the watery vale, and shout again,
Responsive to his call, with quivering
      peals,   376
And long halloos and screams, and echoes
      loud,
Redoubled and redoubled, concourse wild

Of jocund din; and, when a lengthened
      pause
Of silence came and baffled his best skill,
Then sometimes, in that silence while he
      hung   381
Listening, a gentle shock of mild surprise
Has carried far into his heart the voice
Of mountain torrents; or the visible scene
Would enter unawares into his mind,   385
With all its solemn imagery, its rocks,
Its woods, and that uncertain heaven,
      received
Into the bosom of the steady lake.

This Boy was taken from his mates,
      and died
In childhood, ere he was full twelve years
      old.   390
Fair is the spot, most beautiful the vale
Where he was born; the grassy church-
      yard hangs
Upon a slope above the village school,
And through that churchyard when my
      way has led   394
On summer evenings, I believe that there
A long half hour together I have stood
Mute, looking at the grave in which he
      lies!
Even now appears before the mind's clear
      eye
That self-same village church; I see her
      sit
(The thronèd Lady whom erewhile we
      hailed)   400
On her green hill, forgetful of this Boy
Who slumbers at her feet,—forgetful, too,
Of all her silent neighbourhood of graves,
And listening only to the gladsome sounds
That, from the rural school ascending,
      play   405
Beneath her and about her. May she long
Behold a race of young ones like to those
With whom I herded!—(easily, indeed,
We might have fed upon a fatter soil
Of arts and letters—but be that for-
      given)—   410
A race of real children; not too wise,
Too learned, or too good; but wanton,
      fresh,
And bandied up and down by love and
      hate;

Not unresentful where self-justified;
Fierce, moody, patient, venturous, modest,
　　shy;　　　　　　　　　　　　415
Mad at their sports like withered leaves
　　in winds;
Though doing wrong and suffering, and
　　full oft
Bending beneath our life's mysterious
　　weight
Of pain, and doubt, and fear, yet yielding
　　not
In happiness to the happiest upon earth.
Simplicity in habit, truth in speech,　421
Be these the daily strengtheners of their
　　minds;
May books and Nature be their early joy!
And knowledge, rightly honoured with
　　that name—
Knowledge not purchased by the loss of
　　power!　　　　　　　　　　　425

　Well do I call to mind the very week
When I was first intrusted to the care
Of that sweet Valley; when its paths, its
　　shores,
And brooks were like a dream of novelty
To my half-infant thoughts; that very
　　week,　　　　　　　　　　　　430
While I was roving up and down alone,
Seeking I knew not what, I chanced to
　　cross
One of those open fields, which, shaped
　　like ears,
Make green peninsulas on Esthwaite's
　　Lake:
Twilight was coming on, yet through the
　　gloom　　　　　　　　　　　　435
Appeared distinctly on the opposite shore
A heap of garments, as if left by one
Who might have there been bathing.
　　Long I watched,
But no one owned them; meanwhile the
　　calm lake
Grew dark with all the shadows on its
　　breast,　　　　　　　　　　　440
And, now and then, a fish up-leaping
　　snapped
The breathless stillness. The succeeding
　　day,
Those unclaimed garments telling a plain
　　tale

Drew to the spot an anxious crowd; some
　　looked
In passive expectation from the shore,
While from a boat others hung o'er the
　　deep,　　　　　　　　　　　　446
Sounding with grappling irons and long
　　poles.
At last, the dead man, 'mid that beauteous
　　scene
Of trees and hills and water, bolt upright
Rose, with his ghastly face, a spectre
　　shape　　　　　　　　　　　　450
Of terror; yet no soul-debasing fear,
Young as I was, a child not nine years old,
Possessed me, for my inner eye had seen
Such sights before, among the shining
　　streams
Of faery land, the forest of romance.　455
Their spirit hallowed the sad spectacle
With decoration of ideal grace;
A dignity, a smoothness, like the works
Of Grecian art, and purest poesy.

　A precious treasure had I long pos-
　　sessed,　　　　　　　　　　　460
A little yellow, canvas-covered book,
A slender abstract of the Arabian tales;
And, from companions in a new abode,
When first I learnt, that this dear prize
　　of mine
Was but a block hewn from a mighty
　　quarry—　　　　　　　　　　465
That there were four large volumes, laden
　　all
With kindred matter, 'twas to me, in
　　truth,
A promise scarcely earthly. Instantly,
With one not richer than myself, I made
A covenant that each should lay aside
The moneys he possessed, and hoard up
　　more,　　　　　　　　　　　471
Till our joint savings had amassed enough
To make this book our own. Through
　　several months,
In spite of all temptation, we preserved
Religiously that vow; but firmness failed,
Nor were we ever masters of our wish.

　And when thereafter to my father's
　　house　　　　　　　　　　　477
The holidays returned me, there to find

That golden store of books which I had
   left,
What joy was mine! How often in the
   course   480
Of those glad respites, though a soft west
   wind
Ruffled the waters to the angler's wish,
For a whole day together, have I lain
Down by thy side, O Derwent! murmur-
   ing stream,
On the hot stones, and in the glaring
   sun,   485
And there have read, devouring as I read,
Defrauding the day's glory, desperate!
Till with a sudden bound of smart re-
   proach,
Such as an idler deals with in his shame,
I to the sport betook myself again.   490

A gracious spirit o'er this earth pre-
   sides,
And o'er the heart of man : invisibly
It comes, to works of unreproved delight,
And tendency benign, directing those
Who care not, know not, think not what
   they do.   495
The tales that charm away the wakeful
   night
In Araby, romances; legends penned
For solace by dim light of monkish lamps;
Fictions, for ladies of their love, devised
By youthful squires; adventures endless,
   spun   500
By the dismantled warrior in old age,
Out of the bowels of those very schemes
In which his youth did first extravagate;
These spread like day, and something in
   the shape
Of these will live till man shall be no
   more.   505
Dumb yearnings, hidden appetites, are
   ours,
And *they must* have their food. Our
   childhood sits,
Our simple childhood, sits upon a throne
That hath more power than all the ele-
   ments.   509
I guess not what this tells of Being past,
Nor what it augurs of the life to come;
But so it is, and, in that dubious hour,
That twilight when we first begin to see

This dawning earth, to recognise, ex-
   pect,   514
And, in the long probation that ensues,
The time of trial, ere we learn to live
In reconcilement with our stinted powers;
To endure this state of meagre vassalage,
Unwilling to forego, confess, submit,
Uneasy and unsettled, yoke-fellows   520
To custom, mettlesome, and not yet tamed
And humbled down;—oh! then we feel,
   we feel,
We know where we have friends. Ye
   dreamers, then,   523
Forgers of daring tales! we bless you then,
Impostors, drivellers, dotards, as the ape
Philosophy will call you: *then* we feel
With what, and how great might ye are
   in league,
Who make our wish our power, our
   thought a deed,
An empire, a possession,—ye whom time
And seasons serve; all Faculties;—to
   whom
Earth crouches, the elements are potter's
   clay,   531
Space like a heaven filled up with northern
   lights,
Here, nowhere, there, and everywhere at
   once.

Relinquishing this lofty eminence
For ground, though humbler, not the less
   a tract   535
Of the same isthmus, which our spirits
   cross
In progress from their native continent
To earth and human life, the Song might
   dwell
On that delightful time of growing youth
When craving for the marvellous gives
   way   540
To strengthening love for things that we
   have seen;
When sober truth and steady sympathies,
Offered to notice by less daring pens,
Take firmer hold of us, and words them-
   selves
Move us with conscious pleasure.
                              I am sad
At thought of raptures now for ever
   flown;   546

Almost to tears I sometimes could be sad
To think of, to read over, many a page,
Poems withal of name, which at that time
Did never fail to entrance me, and are
now   550
Dead in my eyes, dead as a theatre
Fresh emptied of spectators. Twice five
years
Or less I might have seen, when first my
mind
With conscious pleasure opened to the
charm
Of words in tuneful order, found them
sweet   555
For their own *sakes*, a passion, and a
power;
And phrases pleased me chosen for de-
light,
For pomp, or love. Oft, in the public
roads
Yet unfrequented, while the morning
light
Was yellowing the hill tops, I went
abroad   560
With a dear friend, and for the better
part
Of two delightful hours we strolled along
By the still borders of the misty lake,
Repeating favourite verses with one voice,
Or conning more, as happy as the birds
That round us chaunted. Well might we
be glad,   566
Lifted above the ground by airy fancies,
More bright than madness or the dreams
of wine;
And, though full oft the objects of our
love
Were false, and in their splendour over-
wrought,   570
Yet was there surely then no vulgar
power
Working within us,—nothing less, in
truth,
Than that most noble attribute of man,

Though yet untutored and inordinate,
That wish for something loftier, more
adorned,   575
Than is the common aspect, daily garb,
Of human life. What wonder, then, if
sounds
Of exultation echoed through the groves!
For, images, and sentiments, and words,
And everything encountered or pursued
In that delicious world of poesy,   581
Kept holiday, a never-ending show,
With music, incense, festival, and flowers!

Here must we pause: this only let me
add,
From heart-experience, and in humblest
sense   585
Of modesty, that he, who in his youth
A daily wanderer among woods and fields
With living Nature hath been intimate,
Not only in that raw unpractised time
Is stirred to ecstasy, as others are,   590
By glittering verse; but further, doth
receive,
In measure only dealt out to himself,
Knowledge and increase of enduring joy
From the great Nature that exists in
works
Of mighty Poets. Visionary power   595
Attends the motions of the viewless winds,
Embodied in the mystery of words:
There, darkness makes abode, and all the
host
Of shadowy things work endless changes,
—there,   599
As in a mansion like their proper home,
Even forms and substances are circum-
fused
By that transparent veil with light divine,
And, through the turnings intricate of
verse,
Present themselves as objects recognised,
In flashes, and with glory not their
own.   605

BOOK SIXTH.

CAMBRIDGE AND THE ALPS.

THE leaves were fading when to Esth-
    waite's banks
And the simplicities of cottage life
I bade farewell; and, one among the
    youth
Who, summoned by that season, reunite
As scattered birds troop to the fowler's
    lure,   5
Went back to Granta's cloisters, not so
    prompt
Or eager, though as gay and undepressed
In mind, as when I thence had taken flight
A few short months before. I turned my
    face
Without repining from the coves and
    heights   10
Clothed in the sunshine of the withering
    fern;
Quitted, not loth, the mild magnificence
Of calmer lakes and louder streams; and
    you,
Frank-hearted maids of rocky Cumber-
    land,
You and your not unwelcome days of
    mirth   15
Relinquished, and your nights of revelry,
And in my own unlovely cell sate down
In lightsome mood—such privilege has
    youth
That cannot take long leave of pleasant
    thoughts.

  The bonds of indolent society   20
Relaxing in their hold, henceforth I lived
More to myself. Two winters may be
    passed
Without a separate notice: many books
Were skimmed, devoured, or studiously
    perused,
But with no settled plan. I was detached
Internally from academic cares;   26

Yet independent study seemed a course
Of hardy disobedience towards friends
And kindred, proud rebellion and un-
    kind.
This spurious virtue, rather let it bear 30
A name it more deserves, this cowardice,
Gave treacherous sanction to that over-
    love
Of freedom which encouraged me to turn
From regulations even of my own
As from restraints and bonds. Yet who
    can tell—   35
Who knows what thus may have been
    gained, both then
And at a later season, or preserved;
What love of nature, what original
    strength
Of contemplation, what intuitive truths,
The deepest and the best, what keen
    research,   40
Unbiassed, unbewildered, and unawed?

  The Poet's soul was with me at that
    time;
Sweet meditations, the still overflow
Of present happiness, while future years
Lacked not anticipations, tender dreams,
No few of which have since been realised;
And some remain, hopes for my future
    life.   47
Four years and thirty, told this very
    week,
Have I been now a sojourner on earth,
By sorrow not unsmitten; yet for me 50
Life's morning radiance hath not left the
    hills,
Her dew is on the flowers. Those were
    the days
Which also first emboldened me to trust
With firmness, hitherto but lightly
    touched

By such a daring thought, that I might
    leave   55
Some monument behind me which pure
    hearts
Should reverence. The instinctive hum-
    bleness,
Maintained even by the very name and
    thought
Of printed books and authorship, began
To melt away; and further, the dread
    awe   60
Of mighty names was softened down and
    seemed
Approachable, admitting fellowship
Of modest sympathy. Such aspect now,
Though not familiarly, my mind put on,
Content to observe, to achieve, and to
    enjoy.   65

    All winter long, whenever free to
    choose,
Did I by night frequent the College
    groves
And tributary walks; the last, and oft
The only one, who had been lingering
    there
Through hours of silence, till the porter's
    bell,   70
A punctual follower on the stroke of nine,
Rang with its blunt unceremonious voice,
Inexorable summons! Lofty elms,
Inviting shades of opportune recess,
Bestowed composure on a neighbourhood
Unpeaceful in itself. A single tree   76
With sinuous trunk, boughs exquisitely
    wreathed,
Grew there; an ash which Winter for
    himself
Decked as in pride, and with outlandish
    grace:
Up from the ground, and almost to the
    top,   80
The trunk and every master branch were
    green
With clustering ivy, and the lightsome
    twigs
And outer spray profusely tipped with
    seeds
That hung in yellow tassels, while the air
Stirred them, not voiceless. Often have
    I stood   85

Foot-bound uplooking at this lovely tree
Beneath a frosty moon. The hemisphere
Of magic fiction, verse of mine perchance
May never tread; but scarcely Spenser's
    self
Could have more tranquil visions in his
    youth,   90
Or could more bright appearances create
Of human forms with superhuman powers,
Than I beheld loitering on calm clear
    nights
Alone, beneath this fairy work of earth.

On the vague reading of a truant youth
'Twere idle to descant. My inner judg-
    ment   96
Not seldom differed from my taste in
    books,
As if it appertained to another mind,
And yet the books which then I valued
    most
Are dearest to me *now;* for, having
    scanned,   100
Not heedlessly, the laws, and watched
    the forms
Of Nature, in that knowledge I possessed
A standard, often usefully applied,
Even when unconsciously, to things re-
    moved
From a familiar sympathy.—In fine,   105
I was a better judge of thoughts than
    words,
Misled in estimating words, not only
By common inexperience of youth,
But by the trade in classic niceties,
The dangerous craft of culling term and
    phrase   110
From languages that want the living
    voice
To carry meaning to the natural heart;
To tell us what is passion, what is truth,
What reason, what simplicity and sense.

    Yet may we not entirely overlook   115
The pleasure gathered from the rudi-
    ments
Of geometric science. Though advanced
In these enquiries, with regret I speak,
No farther than the threshold, there I
    found
Both elevation and composed delight:

With Indian awe and wonder, ignorance
    pleased	121
With its own struggles, did I meditate
On the relation those abstractions bear
To Nature's laws, and by what process led,
Those immaterial agents bowed their
    heads	125
Duly to serve the mind of earth-born man;
From star to star, from kindred sphere to
    sphere,
From system on to system without end.

    More frequently from the same source
      I drew
A pleasure quiet and profound, a sense
Of permanent and universal sway,	131
And paramount belief; there, recognised
A type, for finite natures, of the one
Supreme Existence, the surpassing life
Which—to the boundaries of space and
    time,	135
Of melancholy space and doleful time,
Superior, and incapable of change,
Nor touched by welterings of passion—is,
And hath the name of, God. Transcen-
    dent peace
And silence did await upon these thoughts
That were a frequent comfort to my
    youth.	141

    'Tis told by one whom stormy waters
      threw,
With fellow-sufferers by the shipwreck
    spared,
Upon a desert coast, that having brought
To land a single volume, saved by chance,
A treatise of Geometry, he wont,	146
Although of food and clothing destitute,
And beyond common wretchedness de-
    pressed,
To part from company and take this book
(Then first a self-taught pupil in its
    truths)	150
To spots remote, and draw his diagrams
With a long staff upon the sand, and thus
Did oft beguile his sorrow, and almost
Forget his feeling: so (if like effect
From the same cause produced, 'mid
    outward things	155
So different, may rightly be compared),
So was it then with me, and so will be

With Poets ever. Mighty is the charm
Of those abstractions to a mind beset
With images, and haunted by herself,
And specially delightful unto me	161
Was that clear synthesis built up aloft
So gracefully; even then when it ap-
    peared
Not more than a mere plaything, or a toy
To sense embodied: not the thing it is
In verity, an independent world,	166
Created out of pure intelligence.

    Such dispositions then were mine un-
      earned
By aught, I fear, of genuine desert—
Mine, through heaven's grace and inborn
    aptitudes.	170
And not to leave the story of that time
Imperfect, with these habits must be
    joined
Moods melancholy, fits of spleen, that
    loved
A pensive sky, sad days, and piping
    winds,
The twilight more than dawn, autumn
    than spring;	175
A treasured and luxurious gloom of choice
And inclination mainly, and the mere
Redundancy of youth's contentedness.
—To time thus spent, add multitudes of
    hours
Pilfered away, by what the Bard who
    sang	180
Of the Enchanter Indolence hath called
"Good-natured lounging," and behold a
    map
Of my collegiate life—far less intense
Than duty called for, or, without regard
To duty, *might* have sprung up of itself
By change of accidents, or even, to
    speak	186
Without unkindness, in another place.
Yet why take refuge in that plea?—the
    fault,
This I repeat, was mine; mine be the
    blame.

    In summer, making quest for works of
      art,	190
Or scenes renowned for beauty, I ex-
    plored

That streamlet whose blue current works
  its way
Between romantic Dovedale's spiry rocks;
Pried into Yorkshire dales, or hidden
  tracts
Of my own native region, and was blest
Between these sundry wanderings with
  a joy   196
Above all joys, that seemed another morn
Risen on mid noon; blest with the
  presence, Friend!
Of that sole Sister, her who hath been
  long
Dear to thee also, thy true friend and
  mine,   200
Now, after separation desolate,
Restored to me—such absence that she
  seemed
A gift then first bestowed. The varied
  banks
Of Emont, hitherto unnamed in song,
And that monastic castle, 'mid tall trees,
Low-standing by the margin of the
  stream,   206
A mansion visited (as fame reports)
By Sidney, where, in sight of our Hel-
  vellyn,
Or stormy Cross fell, snatches he might
  pen
Of his Arcadia, by fraternal love   210
Inspired;—that river and those moulder-
  ing towers
Have seen us side by side, when, having
  clomb
The darksome windings of a broken stair,
And crept along a ridge of fractured wall,
Not without trembling, we in safety
  looked   215
Forth, through some Gothic window's
  open space,
And gathered with one mind a rich
  reward
From the far-stretching landscape, by
  the light
Of morning beautified, or purple eve;
Or, not less pleased, lay on some turret's
  head,   220
Catching from tufts of grass and hare-
  bell flowers
Their faintest whisper to the passing
  breeze,

Given out while mid-day heat oppressed
  the plains.

Another maid there was, who also shed
A gladness o'er that season, then to me,
By her exulting outside look of youth 226
And placid under-countenance, first en-
  deared;
That other spirit, Coleridge! who is now
So near to us, that meek confiding heart,
So reverenced by us both. O'er paths
  and fields   230
In all that neighbourhood, through nar-
  row lanes
Of eglantine, and through the shady
  woods,
And o'er the Border Beacon, and the
  waste
Of naked pools, and common crags that
  lay
Exposed on the bare fell, were scattered
  love,   235
The spirit of pleasure, and youth's golden
  gleam.
O Friend! we had not seen thee at that
  time,
And yet a power is on me, and a strong
Confusion, and I seem to plant thee there,
Far art thou wandered now in search of
  health   240
And milder breezes,—melancholy lot!
But thou art with us, with us in the past,
The present, with us in the times to come.
There is no grief, no sorrow, no despair,
No languor, no dejection, no dismay, 245
No absence scarcely can there be, for
  those
Who love as we do. Speed thee well!
  divide
With us thy pleasure; thy returning
  strength,
Receive it daily as a joy of ours;
Share with us thy fresh spirits, whether
  gift   250
Of gales Etesian or of tender thoughts.

I, too, have been a wanderer; but, alas!
How different the fate of different men.
Though mutually unknown, yea, nursed
  and reared   254
As if in several elements, we were framed

To bend at last to the same discipline,
Predestined, if two beings ever were,
To seek the same delights, and have one
    health,
One happiness. Throughout this narra-
    tive,
Else sooner ended, I have borne in
    mind   260
For whom it registers the birth, and
    marks the growth,
Of gentleness, simplicity, and truth,
And joyous loves, that hallow innocent
    days
Of peace and self-command. Of rivers,
    fields,
And groves I speak to thee, my Friend !
    to thee,   265
Who, yet a liveried schoolboy, in the
    depths
Of the huge city, on the leaded roof
Of that wide edifice, thy school and home,
Wert used to lie and gaze upon the clouds
Moving in heaven; or, of that pleasure
    tired,   270
To shut thine eyes, and by internal light
See trees, and meadows, and thy native
    stream,
Far distant, thus beheld from year to year
Of a long exile. Nor could I forget,
In this late portion of my argument, 275
That scarcely, as my term of pupilage
Ceased, had I left those academic bowers
When thou wert thither guided. From
    the heart
Of London, and from cloisters there, thou
    camest,
And didst sit down in temperance and
    peace,   280
A rigorous student. What a stormy
    course
Then followed. Oh ! it is a pang that
    calls
For utterance, to think what easy change
Of circumstances might to thee have
    spared
A world of pain, ripened a thousand
    hopes,   285
For ever withered. Through this retro-
    spect
Of my collegiate life I still have had
Thy after-sojourn in the self-same place

Present before my eyes, have played with
    times
And accidents as children do with cards,
Or as a man, who, when his house is
    built,   291
A frame locked up in wood and stone,
    doth still,
As impotent fancy prompts, by his fire-
    side,
Rebuild it to his liking. I have thought
Of thee, thy learning, gorgeous eloquence,
And all the strength and plumage of thy
    youth,   296
Thy subtle speculations, toils abstruse
Among the schoolmen, and Platonic forms
Of wild ideal pageantry, shaped out
From things well-matched or ill, and
    words for things,   300
The self-created sustenance of a mind
Debarred from Nature's living images,
Compelled to be a life unto herself,
And unrelentingly possessed by thirst
Of greatness, love, and beauty. Not
    alone,   305
Ah ! surely not in singleness of heart
Should I have seen the light of evening
    fade
From smooth Cam's silent waters: had
    we met,
Even at that early time, needs must I
    trust
In the belief, that my maturer age, 310
My calmer habits, and more steady voice,
Would with an influence benign have
    soothed,
Or chased away, the airy wretchedness
That battened on thy youth. But thou
    hast trod
A march of glory, which doth put to
    shame   315
These vain regrets; health suffers in thee,
    else
Such grief for thee would be the weakest
    thought
That ever harboured in the breast of man.

A passing word erewhile did lightly
    touch
On wanderings of my own, that now
    embraced   320
With livelier hope a region wider far.

When the third summer freed us from
restraint,
A youthful friend, he too a mountaineer,
Not slow to share my wishes, took his
staff,
And sallying forth, we journeyed side by
side,   325
Bound to the distant Alps. A hardy
slight
Did this unprecedented course imply
Of college studies and their set rewards;
Nor had, in truth, the scheme been
formed by me   329
Without uneasy forethought of the pain,
The censures, and ill-omening of those
To whom my worldly interests were
dear.
But Nature then was sovereign in my
mind,
And mighty forms, seizing a youthful
fancy,   334
Had given a charter to irregular hopes.
In any age of uneventful calm
Among the nations, surely would my
heart
Have been possessed by similar desire;
But Europe at that time was thrilled
with joy,
France standing on the top of golden
hours,   340
And human nature seeming born again.

Lightly equipped, and but a few brief
looks
Cast on the white cliffs of our native shore
From the receding vessel's deck, we
chanced
To land at Calais on the very eve   345
Of that great federal day; and there we
saw,
In a mean city, and among a few,
How bright a face is worn when joy of
one
Is joy for tens of millions. Southward
thence
We held our way, direct through hamlets,
towns,   350
Gaudy with reliques of that festival,
Flowers left to wither on triumphal arcs,
And window-garlands. On the public
roads,

And, once, three days successively,
through paths
By which our toilsome journey was
abridged,   355
Among sequestered villages we walked
And found benevolence and blessedness
Spread like a fragrance everywhere, when
spring
Hath left no corner of the land un-
touched:
Where elms for many and many a league
in files   360
With their thin umbrage, on the stately
roads
Of that great kingdom, rustled o'er our
heads,
For ever near us as we paced along:
How sweet at such a time, with such
delight
On every side, in prime of youthful
strength,   365
To feed a Poet's tender mélancholy
And fond conceit of sadness, with the
sound
Of undulations varying as might please
The wind that swayed them; once, and
more than once,
Unhoused beneath the evening star we
saw   370
Dances of liberty, and, in late hours
Of darkness, dances in the open air
Deftly prolonged, though grey-haired
lookers on
Might waste their breath in chiding.
                          Under hills—
The vine-clad hills and slopes of Bur-
gundy,   375
Upon the bosom of the gentle Saone
We glided forward with the flowing
stream.
Swift Rhone! thou wert the *wings* on
which we cut
A winding passage with majestic ease
Between thy lofty rocks. Enchanting
show   380
Those woods and farms and orchards
did present,
And single cottages and lurking towns,
Reach after reach, succession without end
Of deep and stately vales! A lonely
pair

Of strangers, till day closed, we sailed
    along,   385
Clustered together with a merry crowd
Of those emancipated, a blithe host
Of travellers, chiefly delegates returning
From the great spousals newly solemnized
At their chief city, in the sight of Heaven.
Like bees they swarmed, gaudy and gay
    as bees;   391
Some vapoured in the unruliness of joy,
And with their swords flourished as if to
    fight
The saucy air. In this proud company
We landed—took with them our evening
    meal,   395
Guests welcome almost as the angels were
To Abraham of old. The supper done,
With flowing cups elate and happy
    thoughts
We rose at signal given, and formed a
    ring
And, hand in hand, danced round and
    round the board;   400
All hearts were open, every tongue was
    loud
With amity and glee; we bore a name
Honoured in France, the name of English-
    men,
And hospitably did they give us hail,
As their forerunners in a glorious course;
And round and round the board we
    danced again.   406
With these blithe friends our voyage we
    renewed
At early dawn. The monastery bells
Made a sweet jingling in our youthful
    ears;
The rapid river flowing without noise,   410
And each uprising or receding spire
Spake with a sense of peace, at intervals
Touching the heart amid the boisterous
    crew
By whom we were encompassed. Taking
    leave
Of this glad throng, foot-travellers side
    by side,   415
Measuring our steps in quiet, we pursued
Our journey, and ere twice the sun had
    set
Beheld the Convent of Chartreuse, and
    there

Rested within an awful *solitude*:
Yes; for even then no other than a place
Of soul-affecting *solitude* appeared   421
That far-famed region, though our eyes
    had seen,
As toward the sacred mansion we ad-
    vanced,
Arms flashing, and a military glare
Of riotous men commissioned to expel 425
The blameless inmates, and belike subvert
That frame of social being, which so long
Had bodied forth the ghostliness of
    things
In silence visible and perpetual calm.
—"Stay, stay your sacrilegious hands!"—
    The voice   430
Was Nature's, uttered from her Alpine
    throne;
I heard it then, and seem to hear it now—
"Your impious work forbear: perish
    what may,
Let this one temple last, be this one spot
Of earth devoted to eternity!"   435
She ceased to speak, but while St. Bruno's
    pines
Waved their dark tops, not silent as they
    waved,
And while below, along their several beds,
Murmured the sister streams of Life and
    Death,
Thus by conflicting passions pressed, my
    heart   440
Responded; "Honour to the patriot's
    zeal!
Glory and hope to new-born Liberty!
Hail to the mighty projects of the time!
Discerning sword that Justice wields, do
    thou
Go forth and prosper; and, ye purging
    fires,   445
Up to the loftiest towers of Pride ascend,
Fanned by the breath of angry Provi-
    dence.
But oh! if Past and Future be the wings
On whose support harmoniously con-
    joined
Moves the great spirit of human know-
    ledge, spare   450
These courts of mystery, where a step
    advanced
Between the portals of the shadowy rocks

Leaves far behind life's treacherous vani-
    ties,
For penitential tears and trembling hopes
Exchanged—to equalise in God's pure
    sight   455
Monarch and peasant: be the house
    redeemed
With its unworldly votaries, for the sake
Of conquest over sense, hourly achieved
Through faith and meditative reason,
    resting
Upon the word of heaven-imparted truth,
Calmly triumphant; and for humbler
    claim   461
Of that imaginative impulse sent
From these majestic floods, yon shining
    cliffs,
The untransmuted shapes of many worlds,
Cerulean ether's pure inhabitants,   465
These forests unapproachable by death,
That shall endure as long as man endures,
To think, to hope, to worship, and to
    feel,
To struggle, to be lost within himself
In trepidation, from the blank abyss   470
To look with bodily eyes, and be con-
    soled."
Not seldom since that moment have I
    wished
That thou, O Friend! the trouble or the
    calm
Hadst shared, when, from profane regards
    apart,
In sympathetic reverence we trod   475
The floors of those dim cloisters, till that
    hour,
From their foundation, strangers to the
    presence
Of unrestricted and unthinking man.
Abroad, how cheeringly the sunshine lay
Upon the open lawns! Vallombre's
    groves   480
Entering, we fed the soul with darkness;
    thence
Issued, and with uplifted eyes beheld,
In different quarters of the bending sky,
The cross of Jesus stand erect, as if
Hands of angelic powers had fixed it
    there,   485
Memorial reverenced by a thousand
    storms;

Yet then, from the undiscriminating
    sweep
And rage of one State-whirlwind, in-
    secure.

'Tis not my present purpose to retrace
That variegated journey step by step. 490
A march it was of military speed,
And Earth did change her images and
    forms
Before us, fast as clouds are changed in
    heaven.
Day after day, up early and down late,
From hill to vale we dropped, from vale
    to hill   495
Mounted—from province on to province
    swept,
Keen hunters in a chase of fourteen
    weeks,
Eager as birds of prey, or as a ship
Upon the stretch, when winds are blow-
    ing fair:
Sweet coverts did we cross of pastoral
    life,   500
Enticing valleys, greeted them and left
Too soon, while yet the very flash and
    gleam
Of salutation were not passed away.
Oh! sorrow for the youth who could have
    seen
Unchastened, unsubdued, unawed, un-
    raised   505
To patriarchal dignity of mind,
And pure simplicity of wish and will,
Those sanctified abodes of peaceful man,
Pleased (though to hardship born, and
    compassed round
With danger, varying as the seasons
    change),   510
Pleased with his daily task, or, if not
    pleased,
Contented, from the moment that the
    dawn
(Ah! surely not without attendant gleams
Of soul-illumination) calls him forth
To industry, by glistenings flung on rocks,
Whose evening shadows lead him to re-
    pose.   516

Well might a stranger look with bound-
    ing heart
Down on a green recess, the first I saw

Of those deep haunts, an aboriginal vale,
Quiet and lorded over and possessed   520
By naked huts, wood-built, and sown like
    tents
Or Indian cabins over the fresh lawns
And by the river side.

           That very day,
From a bare ridge we also first beheld
Unveiled the summit of Mont Blanc, and
    grieved   525
To have a soulless image on the eye
That had usurped upon a living thought
That never more could be. The wondrous
    Vale
Of Chamouny stretched far below, and
    soon
With its dumb cataracts and streams of
    ice,   530
A motionless array of mighty waves,
Five rivers broad and vast, made rich
    amends,
And reconciled us to realities;
There small birds warble from the leafy
    trees,
The eagle soars high in the element,   535
There doth the reaper bind the yellow
    sheaf,
The maiden spread the haycock in the sun,
While Winter like a well-tamed lion
    walks,
Descending from the mountain to make
    sport   539
Among the cottages by beds of flowers.

    Whate'er in this wide circuit we beheld,
Or heard, was fitted to our unripe state
Of intellect and heart. With such a book
Before our eyes, we could not choose but
    read
Lessons of genuine brotherhood, the plain
And universal reason of mankind,   546
The truths of young and old. Nor, side
    by side
Pacing, two social pilgrims, or alone
Each with his humour, could we fail to
    abound
In dreams and fictions, pensively com-
    posed: 550
Dejection taken up for pleasure's sake,
And gilded sympathies, the willow
    wreath,

And sober posies of funereal flowers,
Gathered among those solitudes sublime
From formal gardens of the lady Sorrow,
Did sweeten many a meditative hour.   556

    Yet still in me with those soft luxuries
Mixed something of stern mood, an
    under-thirst
Of vigour seldom utterly allayed:
And from that source how different a sad-
    ness   560
Would issue, let one incident make
    known.
When from the Vallais we had turned,
    and clomb
Along the Simplon's steep and rugged
    road,
Following a band of muleteers, we reached
A halting-place, where all together took
Their noon-tide meal. Hastily rose our
    guide,   566
Leaving us at the board; awhile we
    lingered,
Then paced the beaten downward way
    that led
Right to a rough stream's edge, and there
    broke off;
The only track now visible was one   570
That from the torrent's further brink
    held forth
Conspicuous invitation to ascend
A lofty mountain. After brief delay
Crossing the unbridged stream, that road
    we took,
And clomb with eagerness, till anxious
    fears   575
Intruded, for we failed to overtake
Our comrades gone before. By fortunate
    chance,
While every moment added doubt to
    doubt,
A peasant met us, from whose mouth we
    learned
That to the spot which had perplexed us
    first   580
We must descend, and there should find
    the road,
Which in the stony channel of the stream
Lay a few steps, and then along its banks;
And, that our future course, all plain to
    sight,

Was downwards, with the current of that
     stream.   585
Loth to believe what we so grieved to hear,
For still we had hopes that pointed to
     the clouds,
We questioned him again, and yet again;
But every word that from the peasant's
     lips
Came in reply, translated by our feelings,
Ended in this,—*that we had crossed the
     Alps.*   591

    Imagination—here the Power so called
Through sad incompetence of human
     speech,
That awful Power rose from the mind's
     abyss
Like an unfathered vapour that enwraps,
At once, some lonely traveller. I was
     lost;   596
Halted without an effort to break through;
But to my conscious soul I now can say—
" I recognise thy glory :" in such strength
Of usurpation, when the light of sense
Goes out, but with a flash that has re-
     vealed   601
The invisible world, doth greatness make
     abode,
There harbours ; whether we be young or
     old,
Our destiny, our being's heart and home,
Is with infinitude, and only there ;   605
With hope it is, hope that can never die,
Effort, and expectation, and desire,
And something evermore about to be.
Under such banners militant, the soul
Seeks for no trophies, struggles for no
     spoils   610
That may attest her prowess, blest in
     thoughts
That are their own perfection and reward,
Strong in herself and in beatitude
That hides her, like the mighty flood of
     Nile
Poured from his fount of Abyssinian
     clouds   615
To fertilise the whole Egyptian plain.

    The melancholy slackening that ensued
Upon those tidings by the peasant given
Was soon dislodged. Downwards we
     hurried fast,

And, with the half-shaped road which we
     had missed,   620
Entered a narrow chasm. [1] The brook and
     road
Were fellow-travellers in this gloomy
     strait,
And with them did we journey several
     hours
At a slow pace. The immeasurable height
Of woods decaying, never to be decayed,
The stationary blasts of waterfalls,   626
And in the narrow rent at every turn
Winds thwarting winds, bewildered and
     forlorn,
The torrents shooting from the clear blue
     sky,
The rocks that muttered close upon our
     ears,   630
Black drizzling crags that spake by the
     way-side
As if a voice were in them, the sick sight
And giddy prospect of the raving stream,
The unfettered clouds and region of the
     Heavens,
Tumult and peace, the darkness and the
     light—   635
Were all like workings of one mind, the
     features
Of the same face, blossoms upon one tree ;
Characters of the great Apocalypse,
The types and symbols of Eternity,
Of first, and last, and midst, and without
     end.   640

    That night our lodging was a house
     that stood
Alone, within the valley, at a point
Where, tumbling from aloft, a torrent
     swelled
The rapid stream whose margin we had
     trod ;
A dreary mansion, large beyond all need,
With high and spacious rooms, deafened
     and stunned   646
By noise of waters, making innocent sleep
Lie melancholy among weary bones.

    Uprisen betimes, our journey we re-
     newed,

---

[1] See page 186.

Led by the stream, ere noon-day magni-
fied   650
Into a lordly river, broad and deep,
Dimpling along in silent majesty,
With mountains for its neighbours, and
in view
Of distant mountains and their snowy
tops,
And thus proceeding to Locarno's Lake,
Fit resting-place for such a visitant. 656
Locarno! spreading out in width like
Heaven,
How dost thou cleave to the poetic heart,
Bask in the sunshine of the memory;
And Como! thou, a treasure whom the
earth   660
Keeps to herself, confined as in a depth
Of Abyssinian privacy. I spake
Of thee, thy chestnut woods, and garden
plots
Of Indian corn tended by dark-eyed
maids;
Thy lofty steeps, and pathways roofed
with vines,   665
Winding from house to house, from town
to town,
Sole link that binds them to each other;
walks,
League after league, and cloistral avenues,
Where silence dwells if music be not
there:
While yet a youth undisciplined in verse,
Through fond ambition of that hour, I
strove   671
To chant your praise; nor can approach
you now
Ungreeted by a more melodious Song,
Where tones of Nature smoothed by
learned Art
May flow in lasting current. Like a
breeze   675
Or sunbeam over your domain I passed
In motion without pause; but ye have
left
Your beauty with me, a serene accord
Of forms and colours, passive, yet en-
dowed
In their submissiveness with power as
sweet   680
And gracious, almost might I dare to say,
As virtue is, or goodness; sweet as love,

Or the remembrance of a generous deed,
Or mildest visitations of pure thought,
When God, the giver of all joy, is thanked
Religiously, in silent blessedness;   685
Sweet as this last herself, for such it is.

With those delightful pathways we ad-
vanced,
For two days' space, in presence of the
Lake,
That, stretching far among the Alps,
assumed   690
A character more stern. The second
night,
From sleep awakened, and misled by
sound
Of the church clock telling the hours with
strokes
Whose import then we had not learned,
we rose
By moonlight, doubting not that day was
nigh,   695
And that meanwhile, by no uncertain
path,
Along the winding margin of the lake,
Led, as before, we should behold the
scene,
Hushed in profound repose. We left the
town
Of Gravedona with this hope; but soon
Were lost, bewildered among woods im-
mense,   701
And on a rock sate down, to wait for day.
An open place it was, and overlooked,
From high, the sullen water far beneath,
On which a dull red image of the moon
Lay bedded, changing oftentimes its form
Like an uneasy snake. From hour to
hour
We sate and sate, wondering as if the
night
Had been ensnared by witchcraft. On
the rock
At last we stretched our weary limbs for
sleep,   710
But *could not* sleep, tormented by the
stings
Of insects, which with noise like that of
noon
Filled all the woods: the cry of unknown
birds;

The mountains more by blackness visible
And their own size, than any outward
    light;   715
The breathless wilderness of clouds; the
    clock
That told, with unintelligible voice,
The widely parted hours; the noise of
    streams,
And sometimes rustling motions nigh at
    hand,
That did not leave us free from personal
    fear;   720
And, lastly, the withdrawing moon, that
    set
Before us, while she still was high in
    heaven;—
These were our food; and such a summer's
    night
Followed that pair of golden days that
    shed
On Como's Lake, and all that round it
    lay,   725
Their fairest, softest, happiest influence.

But here I must break off, and bid
    farewell
To days, each offering some new sight, or
    fraught
With some untried adventure, in a course
Prolonged till sprinklings of autumnal
    snow   730
Checked our unwearied steps. Let this
    alone
Be mentioned as a parting word, that not
In hollow exultation, dealing out
Hyperboles of praise comparative;   734
Not rich one moment to be poor for ever;
Not prostrate, overborne, as if the mind
Herself were nothing, a mere pensioner
On outward forms—did we in presence
    stand
Of that magnificent region. On the front
Of this whole Song is written that my
    heart   740
Must, in such Temple, needs have offered
    up
A different worship. Finally, whate'er
I saw, or heard, or felt, was but a stream
That flowed into a kindred stream; a gale,
Confederate with the current of the soul,

To speed my voyage; every sound or
    sight,   746
In its degree of power, administered
To grandeur or to tenderness,—to the one
Directly, but to tender thoughts by means
Less often instantaneous in effect;   750
Led me to these by paths that, in the
    main,
Were more circuitous, but not less sure
Duly to reach the point marked out by
    Heaven.

Oh, most belovèd Friend! a glorious
    time,
A happy time that was; triumphant looks
Were then the common language of all
    eyes;   756
As if awaked from sleep, the Nations
    hailed
Their great expectancy: the fife of war
Was then a spirit-stirring sound indeed,
A blackbird's whistle in a budding grove.
We left the Swiss exulting in the fate 761
Of their near neighbours; and, when
    shortening fast
Our pilgrimage, nor distant far from
    home,
We crossed the Brabant armies on the
    fret
For battle in the cause of Liberty.   765
A stripling, scarcely of the household
    then
Of social life, I looked upon these things
As from a distance; heard, and saw, and
    felt,
Was touched, but with no intimate con-
    cern;
I seemed to move along them, as a bird 770
Moves through the air, or as a fish
    pursues
Its sport, or feeds in its proper element;
I wanted not that joy, I did not need
Such help; the ever-living universe,
Turn where I might, was opening out its
    glories,   775
And the independent spirit of pure youth
Called forth, at every season, new de-
    lights
Spread round my steps like sunshine o'er
    green fields.

BOOK SEVENTH.

RESIDENCE IN LONDON.

SIX changeful years have vanished since
 I first
Poured out (saluted by that quickening
 breeze
Which met me issuing from the City's
 walls)
A glad preamble to this Verse: I sang
Aloud, with fervour irresistible   5
Of short-lived transport, like a torrent
 bursting,
From a black thunder-cloud, down Scafell's
 side
To rush and disappear. But soon broke
 forth
(So willed the Muse) a less impetuous
 stream,
That flowed awhile with unabating
 strength,   10
Then stopped for years; not audible
 again
Before last primrose-time. Belovèd
 Friend!
The assurance which then cheered some
 heavy thoughts
On thy departure to a foreign land
Has failed; too slowly moves the promised
 work.   15
Through the whole summer have I been
 at rest,
Partly from voluntary holiday,
And part through outward hindrance.
 But I heard,
After the hour of sunset yester-even,
Sitting within doors between light and
 dark,   20
A choir of redbreasts gathered somewhere
 near
My threshold,—minstrels from the distant
 woods
Sent in on Winter's service, to announce,
With preparation artful and benign,
That the rough lord had left the surly
 North   25
On his accustomed journey. The delight,
Due to this timely notice, unawares
Smote me, and, listening, I in whispers
 said,
"Ye heartsome Choristers, ye and I will
 be
Associates, and, unscared by blustering
 winds,   30
Will chant together." Thereafter, as the
 shades
Of twilight deepened, going forth, I spied
A glow-worm underneath a dusky plume
Or canopy of yet unwithered fern,
Clear-shining, like a hermit's taper seen
Through a thick forest. Silence touched
 me here   36
No less than sound had done before; the
 child
Of Summer, lingering, shining, by her-
 self,
The voiceless worm on the unfrequented
 hills,
Seemed sent on the same errand with the
 choir   40
Of Winter that had warbled at my door,
And the whole year breathed tenderness
 and love.

The last night's genial feeling over-
 flowed
Upon this morning, and my favourite
 grove,
Tossing in sunshine its dark boughs
 aloft,   45
As if to make the strong wind visible,
Wakes in me agitations like its own,
A spirit friendly to the Poet's task,
Which we will now resume with lively
 hope,

Nor checked by aught of tamer argument,
That lies before us, needful to be told. 51

    Returned from that excursion [1]. soon I
      bade
Farewell for ever to the sheltered seats
Of gownèd students, quitted hall and
    bower,
And every comfort of that privileged
    ground,   55
Well pleased to pitch a vagrant tent
    among
The unfenced regions of society.

    Yet, undetermined to what course of
      life
I should adhere, and seeming to possess
A little space of intermediate time   60
At full command, to London first I turned,
In no disturbance of excessive hope,
By personal ambition unenslaved,
Frugal as there was need, and, though
    self-willed,
From dangerous passions free. Three
    years had flown   65
Since I had felt in heart and soul the shock
Of the huge town's first presence, and had
    passed
Her endless streets, a transient visitant:
Now, fixed amid that concourse of man-
    kind   69
Where Pleasure whirls about incessantly,
And life and labour seem but one, I filled
An idler's place; an idler well content
To have a house (what matter for a home?)
That owned him; living cheerfully abroad
With unchecked fancy ever on the stir, 75
And all my young affections out of doors.

    There was a time when whatsoe'er is
      feigned
Of airy palaces, and gardens built
By Genii of romance; or hath in grave
Authentic history been set forth of Rome,
Alcairo, Babylon, or Persepolis;   81
Or given upon report by pilgrim friars,
Of golden cities ten months' journey deep
Among Tartarian wilds—fell short, far
    short,
Of what my fond simplicity believed   85

[1] See page 680.

And thought of London—held me by a
    chain
Less strong of wonder and obscure de-
    light.
Whether the bolt of childhood's Fancy
    shot
For me beyond its ordinary mark,
'Twere vain to ask; but in our flock of
    boys   /   90
Was One, a cripple from his birth, whom
    chance
Summoned from school to London; for-
    tunate
And envied traveller! When the Boy
    returned,
After short absence, curiously I scanned
His mien and person, nor was free, in
    sooth,   95
From disappointment, not to find some
    change
In look and air, from that new region
    brought,
As if from Fairy-land. Much I questioned
    him;
And every word he uttered, on my ears
Fell flatter than a cagèd parrot's note, 100
That answers unexpectedly awry,
And mocks the prompter's listening.
    Marvellous things
Had vanity (quick Spirit that appears
Almost as deeply seated and as strong
In a Child's heart as fear itself) con-
    ceived   105
For my enjoyment. Would that I could
    now
Recall what then I pictured to myself,
Of mitred Prelates, Lords in ermine clad,
The King, and the King's Palace, and,
    not last,
Nor least, Heaven bless him! the re-
    nowned Lord Mayor: 110
Dreams not unlike to those which once
    begat
A change of purpose in young Whitting-
    ton,
When he, a friendless and a drooping
    boy,
Sate on a stone, and heard the bells speak
    out   114
Articulate music. Above all, one thought
Baffled my understanding: how men lived

Even next-door neighbours, as we say, yet
   still
Strangers, not knowing each the other's
   name.

O, wond'rous power of words, by simple
   faith
Licensed to take the meaning that we love !
Vauxhall and Ranelagh ! I then had
   heard   121
Of your green groves, and wilderness of
   lamps
Dimming the stars, and fireworks magical,
And gorgeous ladies, under splendid
   domes,   124
Floating in dance, or warbling high in air
The songs of spirits ! Nor had Fancy fed
With less delight upon that other class
Of marvels, broad-day wonders perma-
   nent :
The River proudly bridged ; the dizzy top
And Whispering Gallery of St. Paul's ;
   the tombs   130
Of Westminster ; the Giants of Guild-
   hall ;
Bedlam, and those carved maniacs at the
   gates,
Perpetually recumbent ; Statues—man,
And the horse under him—in gilded pomp
Adorning flowery gardens, 'mid vast
   squares ;   135
The Monument, and that Chamber of the
   Tower
Where England's sovereigns sit in long
   array,
Their steeds bestriding,—every mimic
   shape
Cased in the gleaming mail the monarch
   wore,
Whether for gorgeous tournament ad-
   dressed,   140
Or life or death upon the battle-field.
Those bold imaginations in due time
Had vanished, leaving others in their
   stead :
And now I looked upon the living scene ;
Familiarly perused it ; oftentimes,   145
In spite of strongest disappointment,
   pleased
Through courteous self-submission, as a tax
Paid to the object by prescriptive right.

Rise up, thou monstrous ant-hill on the
   plain
Of a too busy world ! Before me flow,
Thou endless stream of men and moving
   things !   151
Thy every-day appearance, as it strikes—
With wonder heightened, or sublimed by
   awe—
On strangers, of all ages ; the quick dance
Of colours, lights, and forms ; the deafen-
   ing din ;   155
The comers and the goers face to face,
Face after face ; the string of dazzling
   wares,
Shop after shop, with symbols, blazoned
   names,
And all the tradesman's honours over-
   head :
Here, fronts of houses, like a title-page,
With letters huge inscribed from top to
   toe ;   161
Stationed above the door, like guardian
   saints,
There, allegoric shapes, female or male,
Or physiognomies of real men.
Land-warriors, kings, or admirals of the
   sea,   165
Boyle, Shakspeare, Newton, or the attrac-
   tive head
Of some quack-doctor, famous in his
   day.

Meanwhile the roar continues, till at
   length,
Escaped as from an enemy, we turn
Abruptly into some sequestered nook,
Still as a sheltered place when winds blow
   loud !   171
At leisure, thence, through tracts of thin
   resort,
And sights and sounds that come at
   intervals,
We take our way. A raree-show is here,
With children gathered round ; another
   street   175
Presents a company of dancing dogs,
Or dromedary, with an antic pair
Of monkeys on his back ; a minstrel band
Of Savoyards ; or, single and alone,   179
An English ballad-singer. Private courts,
Gloomy as coffins, and unsightly lanes

Thrilled by some female vendor's scream,
belike
The very shrillest of all London cries,
May then entangle our impatient steps;
Conducted through those labyrinths, un-
awares,   185
To privileged regions and inviolate,
Where from their airy lodges studious
lawyers
Look out on waters, walks, and gardens
green.

Thence back into the throng, until we
reach,
Following the tide that slackens by
degrees,   190
Some half-frequented scene, where wider
streets
Bring straggling breezes of suburban air.
Here files of ballads dangle from dead
walls;
Advertisements, of giant-size, from high
Press forward, in all colours, on the sight;
These, bold in conscious merit, lower
down;   196
That, fronted with a most imposing word,
Is, peradventure, one in masquerade.
As on the broadening causeway we ad-
vance,
Behold, turned upwards, a face hard and
strong   200
In lineaments, and red with over-toil.
'Tis one encountered here and every-
where;
A travelling cripple, by the trunk cut short,
And stumping on his arms. In sailor's
garb
Another lies at length, beside a range
Of well-formed characters, with chalk in-
scribed   206
Upon the smooth flat stones: the Nurse
is here,
The Bachelor, that loves to sun himself,
The military Idler, and the Dame,
That field-ward takes her walk with decent
steps.   210

Now homeward through the thickening
hubbub, where
See, among less distinguishable shapes,
The begging scavenger, with hat in hand;

The Italian, as he thrids his way with care,
Steadying, far-seen, a frame of images
Upon his head; with basket at his breast
The Jew; the stately and slow-moving
Turk,
With freight of slippers piled beneath his
arm!

Enough;—the mighty concourse I sur-
veyed
With no unthinking mind, well pleased
to note   220
Among the crowd all specimens of man,
Through all the colours which the sun
bestows,
And every character of form and face:
The Swede, the Russian; from the genial
south,
The Frenchman and the Spaniard; from
remote   225
America, the Hunter-Indian; Moors,
Malays, Lascars, the Tartar, the Chinese,
And Negro Ladies in white muslin gowns.

At leisure, then, I viewed, from day to
day,
The spectacles within doors,—birds and
beasts   230
Of every nature, and strange plants con
vened
From every clime; and, next, those sights
that ape
The absolute presence of reality,
Expressing, as in mirror, sea and land,
And what earth is, and what she has to
show.   235
I do not here allude to subtlest craft,
By means refined attaining purest ends,
But imitations, fondly made in plain
Confession of man's weakness and his
loves.
Whether the Painter, whose ambitious
skill   240
Submits to nothing less than taking in
A whole horizon's circuit, do with power,
Like that of angels or commissioned
spirits,
Fix us upon some lofty pinnacle,
Or in a ship on waters, with a world   245
Of life, and life-like mockery beneath,
Above, behind, far stretching and before;

Or more mechanic artist represent
By scale exact, in model, wood or clay,
From blended colours also borrowing
    help,   250
Some miniature of famous spots or
    things,—
St. Peter's Church ; or, more aspiring aim,
In microscopic vision, Rome herself ;
Or, haply, some choice rural haunt,—the
    Falls
Of Tivoli ; and, high upon that steep, 255
The Sibyl's mouldering Temple ! every
    tree,
Villa, or cottage, lurking among rocks
Throughout the landscape; tuft, stone,
    scratch minute—
All that the traveller sees when he is
    there.   259

  Add to these exhibitions, mute and still,
Others of wider scope, where living men,
Music, and shifting pantomimic scenes,
Diversified the allurement. Need I fear
To mention by its name, as in degree,
Lowest of these and humblest in attempt,
Yet richly graced with honours of her own,
Half-rural Sadler's Wells ? Though at that
    time   .   267
Intolerant, as is the way of youth
Unless itself be pleased, here more than
    once
Taking my seat, I saw (nor blush to add,
With ample recompense) giants and
    dwarfs,   271
Clowns, conjurors, posture-masters, har-
    lequins,
Amid the uproar of the rabblement,
Perform their feats. Nor was it mean
    delight
To watch crude Nature work in untaught
    minds ;   275
To note the laws and progress of belief ;
Though obstinate on this way, yet on that
How willingly we travel, and how far !
To have, for instance, brought upon the
    scene
The champion, Jack the Giant-killer : Lo !
He dons his coat of darkness: on the
    stage   281
Walks, and achieves his wonders, from
    the eye

Of living Mortal covert, "as the moon
Hid in her vacant interlunar cave."
Delusion bold ! and how can it be wrought?
The garb he wears is black as death, the
    word   286
"Invisible" flames forth upon his chest.

  Here, too, were "forms and pressures
    of the time,"
Rough, bold, as Grecian comedy displayed
When Art was young; dramas of living
    men,   290
And recent things yet warm with life ;
    a sea-fight,
Shipwreck, or some domestic incident
Divulged by Truth and magnified by
    Fame ;
Such as the daring brotherhood of late
Set forth, too serious theme for that light
    place—   295
I mean, O distant Friend ! a story drawn
From our own ground,—the Maid of
    Buttermere,—
And how, unfaithful to a virtuous wife
Deserted and deceived, the Spoiler came
And wooed the artless daughter of the
    hills,   300
And wedded her, in cruel mockery
Of love and marriage bonds. These words
    to thee
Must needs bring back the moment when
    we first,
Ere the broad world rang with the maiden's
    name,   304
Beheld her serving at the cottage inn ;
Both stricken, as she entered or withdrew,
With admiration of her modest mien
And carriage, marked by unexampled
    grace.
We since that time not unfamiliarly
Have seen her,—her discretion have
    observed,   310
Her just opinions, delicate reserve,
Her patience, and humility of mind
Unspoiled by commendation and the
    excess
Of public notice—an offensive light
To a meek spirit suffering inwardly. 315

  From this memorial tribute to my theme
I was returning, when, with sundry forms

Commingled—shapes which met me in the
    way
That we must tread—thy image rose
    again,
Maiden of Buttermere! She lives in
    peace   320
Upon the spot where she was born and
    reared;
Without contamination doth she live
In quietness, without anxiety:
Beside the mountain-chapel, sleeps in
    earth
Her new-born infant, fearless as a lamb
That, thither driven from some unshel-
    tered place,   326
Rests underneath the little rock-like pile
When storms are raging. Happy are they
    both—
Mother and child!—These feelings, in
    themselves
Trite, do yet scarcely seem so when I
    think   330
On those ingenuous moments of our youth
Ere we have learnt by use to slight the
    crimes
And sorrows of the world. Those simple
    days
Are now my theme; and, foremost of the
    scenes,   334
Which yet survive in memory, appears
One, at whose centre sate a lovely Boy,
A sportive infant, who, for six months'
    space,
Not more, had been of age to deal about
Articulate prattle—Child as beautiful
As ever clung around a mother's neck, 340
Or father fondly gazed upon with pride.
There, too, conspicuous for stature tall
And large dark eyes, beside her infant
    stood
The mother; but, upon her cheeks dif-
    fused,
False tints too well accorded with the
    glare   345
From play-house lustres thrown without
    reserve
On every object near. The Boy had been
The pride and pleasure of all lookers-on
In whatsoever place, but seemed in this
A sort of alien scattered from the clouds.
Of lusty vigour, more than infantine 351

He was in limb, in cheek a summer rose
Just three parts blown—a cottage-child—
    if e'er,
By cottage-door on breezy mountain-side,
Or in some sheltering vale, was seen a
    babe   355
By Nature's gift so favoured. Upon
    a board
Decked with refreshments had this child
    been placed,
His little stage in the vast theatre,
And there he sate surrounded with a
    throng
Of chance spectators, chiefly dissolute
    men   360
And shameless women, treated and
    caressed;
Ate, drank, and with the fruit and glasses
    played,
While oaths and laughter and indecent
    speech
Were rife about him as the songs of birds
Contending after showers. The mother
    now   365
Is fading out of memory, but I see
The lovely Boy as I beheld him then
Among the wretched and the falsely
    gay,
Like one of those who walked with hair
    unsinged
Amid the fiery furnace. Charms and
    spells   370
Muttered on black and spiteful instiga
    tion
Have stopped, as some believe, the kind-
    liest growths.
Ah, with how different spirit might a
    prayer
Have been preferred, that this fair crea-
    ture, checked
By special privilege of Nature's love, 375
Should in his childhood be detained for
    ever!
But with its universal freight the tide
Hath rolled along, and this bright in-
    nocent,
Mary! may now have lived till he could
    look
With envy on thy nameless babe that
    sleeps,   380
Beside the mountain-chapel, undisturbed.

Four rapid years had scarcely then
    been told
Since, travelling southward from our
    pastoral hills,
I heard, and for the first time in my life,
The voice of woman utter blasphemy—
Saw woman as she is, to open shame 386
Abandoned, and the pride of public vice;
I shuddered, for a barrier seemed at once
Thrown in, that from humanity divorced
Humanity, splitting the race of man 390
In twain, yet leaving the same outward
    form.
Distress of mind ensued upon the sight,
And ardent meditation. Later years
Brought to such spectacle a milder sad-
    ness,
Feelings of pure commiseration, grief 395
For the individual and the overthrow
Of her soul's beauty ; farther I was then
But seldom led, or wished to go ; in truth
The sorrow of the passion stopped me
    there.

But let me now, less moved, in order
    take 400
Our argument. Enough is said to show
How casual incidents of real life,
Observed where pastime only had been
    sought,
Outweighed, or put to flight, the set
    events
And measured passions of the stage,
    albeit 405
By Siddons trod in the fulness of her
    power.
Yet was the theatre my dear delight ;
The very gilding, lamps and painted
    scrolls,
And all the mean upholstery of the place,
Wanted not animation, when the tide 410
Of pleasure ebbed but to return as fast
With the ever-shifting figures of the
    scene,
Solemn or gay : whether some beauteous
    dame
Advanced in radiance through a deep
    recess
Of thick entangled forest, like the moon
Opening the clouds ; or sovereign king,
    announced 416

With flourishing trumpet, came in full-
    blown state
Of the world's greatness, winding round
    with train
Of courtiers, banners, and a length of
    guards ;
Or captive led in abject weeds, and
    jingling 420
His slender manacles ; or romping girl
Bounced, leapt, and pawed the air ; or
    mumbling sire,
A scare-crow pattern of old age dressed up
In all the tatters of infirmity
All loosely put together, hobbled in, 425
Stumping upon a cane with which he
    smites,
From time to time, the solid boards, and
    makes them
Prate somewhat loudly of the whereabout
Of one so overloaded with his years.
But what of this ! the laugh, the grin,
    grimace, 430
The antics striving to outstrip each other,
Were all received, the least of them not
    lost,
With an unmeasured welcome. Through
    the night,
Between the show, and many-headed
    mass 434
Of the spectators, and each several nook
Filled with its fray or brawl, how eagerly
And with what flashes, as it were, the
    mind
Turned this way—that way ! sportive and
    alert
And watchful, as a kitten when at play,
While winds are eddying round her,
    among straws 440
And rustling leaves. Enchanting age and
    sweet !
Romantic almost, looked at through a
    space,
How small, of intervening years ! For
    then,
Though surely no mean progress had been
    made
In meditations holy and sublime, 445
Yet something of a girlish child-like gloss
Of novelty survived for scenes like these ;
Enjoyment haply handed down from
    times

When at a country-playhouse, some rude
    barn
Tricked out for that proud use, if I per-
    chance   450
Caught, on a summer evening through
    a chink
In the old wall, an unexpected glimpse
Of daylight, the bare thought of where
    I was
Gladdened me more than if I had been
    led
Into a dazzling cavern of romance,   455
Crowded with Genii busy among works
Not to be looked at by the common sun.

   The matter that detains us now may
    seem,
To many, neither dignified enough
Nor arduous, yet will not be scorned by
    them,   460
Who, looking inward, have observed the
    ties.
That bind the perishable hours of life
Each to the other, and the curious props
By which the world of memory and
    thought
Exists and is sustained. More lofty
    themes,   465
Such as at least do wear a prouder face,
Solicit our regard; but when I think
Of these, I feel the imaginative power
Languish within me; even then it slept,
When, pressed by tragic sufferings, the
    heart   470
Was more than full; amid my sobs and
    tears
It slept, even in the pregnant season of
    youth.
For though I was most passionately moved
And yielded to all changes of the scene
With an obsequious promptness, yet the
    storm   475
Passed not beyond the suburbs of the
    mind;
Save when realities of act and mien,
The incarnation of the spirits that move
In harmony amid the Poet's world,
Rose to ideal grandeur, or, called forth 480
By power of contrast, made me recognise,
As at a glance, the things which I had
    shaped,

And yet not shaped, had seen and scarcely
    seen,
When, having closed the mighty Shak-
    speare's page,
I mused, and thought, and felt, in soli-
    tude.   485

   Pass we from entertainments, that are
    such
Professedly, to others titled higher,
Yet, in the estimate of youth at least,
More near akin to those than names
    imply,—
I mean the brawls of lawyers in their
    courts   490
Before the ermined judge, or that great
    stage
Where senators, tongue-favoured men,
    perform,
Admired and envied. Oh! the beating
    heart,
When one among the prime of these rose
    up,—
One, of whose name from childhood we
    had heard   495
Familiarly, a household term, like those,
The Bedfords, Glosters, Salisburys, of old
Whom the fifth Harry talks of. Silence!
    hush!
This is no trifler, no short-flighted wit,
No stammerer of a minute, painfully   500
Delivered. No! the Orator hath yoked
The Hours, like young Aurora, to his car:
Thrice welcome Presence! how can pa-
    tience e'er
Grow weary of attending on a track
That kindles with such glory! All are
    charmed,   505
Astonished; like a hero in romance,
He winds away his never-ending horn;
Words follow words, sense seems to follow
    sense:
What memory and what logic! till the
    strain   509
Transcendent, superhuman as it seemed,
Grows tedious even in a young man's ear.

   Genius of Burke! forgive the pen
    seduced
By specious wonders, and too slow to tell
Of what the ingenuous, what bewildered
    men,

Beginning to mistrust their boastful
  guides,   515
And wise men, willing to grow wiser,
  caught,
Rapt auditors! from thy most eloquent
  tongue—
Now mute, for ever mute in the cold
  grave.
I see him,—old, but vigorous in age,—
Stand like an oak whose stag-horn
  branches start   520
Out of its leafy brow, the more to awe
The younger brethren of the grove. But
  some—
While he forewarns, denounces, launches
  forth,
Against all systems built on abstract
  rights,
Keen ridicule; the majesty proclaims 525
Of Institutes and Laws, hallowed by time;
Declares the vital power of social ties
Endeared by Custom; and with high
  disdain,
Exploding upstart Theory, insists
Upon the allegiance to which men are
  born—   530
Some—say at once a froward multitude—
Murmur (for truth is hated, where not
  loved)
As the winds fret within the Æolian cave,
Galled by their monarch's chain. The
  times were big
With ominous change, which, night by
  night, provoked   535
Keen struggles, and black clouds of
  passion raised;
But memorable moments intervened,
When Wisdom, like the Goddess from
  Jove's brain,
Broke forth in armour of resplendent
  words,
Startling the Synod. Could a youth, and
  one   540
In ancient story versed, whose breast had
  heaved
Under the weight of classic eloquence,
Sit, see, and hear, unthankful, uninspired?

Nor did the Pulpit's oratory fail
To achieve its higher triumph. Not un-
  felt   545

Were its admonishments, nor lightly
  heard
The awful truths delivered thence by
  tongues
Endowed with various power to search
  the soul;
Yet ostentation, domineering, oft
Poured forth harangues, how sadly out of
  place!—   550
There have I seen a comely bachelor,
Fresh from a toilette of two hours, ascend
His rostrum, with seraphic glance look up,
And, in a tone elaborately low
Beginning, lead his voice through many
  a maze   555
A minuet course; and, winding up his
  mouth,
From time to time, into an orifice
Most delicate, a lurking eyelet, small,
And only not invisible, again
Open it out, diffusing thence a smile   560
Of rapt irradiation, exquisite.
Meanwhile the Evangelists, Isaiah, Job,
Moses, and he who penned, the other day,
The Death of Abel, Shakspeare, and the
  Bard
Whose genius spangled o'er a gloomy
  theme   565
With fancies thick as his inspiring stars,
And Ossian (doubt not—'tis the naked
  truth)
Summoned from streamy Morven—each
  and all
Would, in their turns, lend ornaments
  and flowers
To entwine the crook of eloquence that
  helped   570
This pretty Shepherd, pride of all the
  plains,
To rule and guide his captivated flock.

I glance but at a few conspicuous
  marks,
Leaving a thousand others, that, in hall,
Court, theatre, conventicle, or shop, 575
In public room or private, park or street,
Each fondly reared on his own pedestal,
Looked out for admiration. Folly, vice,
Extravagance in gesture, mien, and dress,
And all the strife of singularity,   580
Lies to the ear, and lies to every sense—

Of these, and of the living shapes they
   wear,
There is no end. Such candidates for
   regard,
Although well pleased to be where they
   were found,
I did not hunt after, nor greatly prize, 585
Nor made unto myself a secret boast
Of reading them with quick and curious
   eye;
But, as a common produce, things that
   are
To-day, to-morrow will be, took of them
Such willing note, as, on some errand
   bound   590
That asks not speed, a traveller might
   bestow
On sea-shells that bestrew the sandy
   beach,
Or daisies swarming through the fields of
   June.

But foolishness and madness in parade,
Though most at home in this their dear
   domain,   595
Are scattered everywhere, no rarities,
Even to the rudest novice of the Schools.
Me, rather, it employed, to note, and
   keep
In memory, those individual sights
Of courage, or integrity, or truth,   600
Or tenderness, which there, set off by foil,
Appeared more touching. One will I
   select;
A Father—for he bore that sacred name—
Him saw I, sitting in an open square,
Upon a corner-stone of that low wall, 605
Wherein were fixed the iron pales that
   fenced
A spacious grass-plot; there, in silence,
   sate
This One Man, with a sickly babe out-
   stretched
Upon his knee, whom he had thither
   brought
For sunshine, and to breathe the fresher
   air.   610
Of those who passed, and me who looked
   at him,
He took no heed; but in his brawny
   arms

(The Artificer was to the elbow bare,
And from his work this moment had been
   stolen)
He held the child, and, bending over it,
As if he were afraid both of the sun   616
And of the air, which he had come to
   seek,
Eyed the poor babe with love un-
   utterable.

As the black storm upon the mountain-
   top
Sets off the sunbeam in the valley, so 620
That huge fermenting mass of human-
   kind
Serves as a solemn background, or relief,
To single forms and objects, whence they
   draw,
For feeling and contemplative regard, 624
More than inherent liveliness and power.
How oft, amid those overflowing streets,
Have I gone forward with the crowd, and
   said
Unto myself, "The face of every one
That passes by me is a mystery!"
Thus have I looked, nor ceased to look,
   oppressed   630
By thoughts of what and whither, when
   and how,
Until the shapes before my eyes became
A second-sight procession, such as glides
Over still mountains, or appears in
   dreams;
And once, far-travelled in such mood,
   beyond   635
The reach of common indication, lost
Amid the moving pageant, I was smitten
Abruptly, with the view (a sight not rare)
Of a blind Beggar, who, with upright
   face,
Stood, propped against a wall, upon his
   chest   640
Wearing a written paper, to explain
His story, whence he came, and who he
   was.
Caught by the spectacle my mind turned
   round
As with the might of waters; an apt type
This label seemed of the utmost we can
   know,   645
Both of ourselves and of the universe;

And, on the shape of that unmoving man,
His steadfast face and sightless eyes,
        I gazed,
As if admonished from another world.

Though reared upon the base of out-
        ward things,   650
Structures like these the excited spirit
        mainly
Builds for herself; scenes different there
        are,
Full-formed, that take, with small internal
        help,
Possession of the faculties,—the peace
That comes with night; the deep solem-
        nity   655
Of nature's intermediate hours of rest,
When the great tide of human life stands
        still;
The business of the day to come, unborn,
Of that gone by, locked up, as in the
        grave;
The blended calmness of the heavens and
        earth,   660
Moonlight and stars, and empty streets,
        and sounds
Unfrequent as in deserts; at late hours
Of winter evenings, when unwholesome
        rains
Are falling hard, with people yet astir,
The feeble salutation from the voice 665
Of some unhappy woman, now and then
Heard as we pass, when no one looks
        about,
Nothing is listened to. But these, I fear,
Are falsely catalogued; things that are,
        are not,
As the mind answers to them, or the
        heart   670
Is prompt, or slow, to feel. What say
        you, then,
To times, when half the city shall break
        out
Full of one passion, vengeance, rage, or
        fear?
To executions, to a street on fire,
Mobs, riots, or rejoicings? From these
        sights   675
Take one,—that ancient festival, the Fair,
Holden where martyrs suffered in past
        time,

And named of St. Bartholomew; there,
        see
A work completed to our hands, that
        lays,
If any spectacle on earth can do,   680
The whole creative powers of man asleep!—
For once, the Muse's help will we implore,
And she shall lodge us, wafted on her
        wings,
Above the press and danger of the crowd,
Upon some showman's platform. What
        a shock   685
For eyes and ears! what anarchy and
        din,
Barbarian and infernal,—a phantasma,
Monstrous in colour, motion, shape, sight,
        sound!
Below, the open space, through every
        nook
Of the wide area, twinkles, is alive 690
With heads; the midway region, and
        above,
Is thronged with staring pictures and
        huge scrolls,
Dumb proclamations of the Prodigies;
With chattering monkeys dangling from
        their poles,
And children whirling in their round-
        abouts;   695
With those that stretch the neck and
        strain the eyes,
And crack the voice in rivalship, the
        crowd
Inviting; with buffoons against buffoons
Grimacing, writhing, screaming,—him
        who grinds
The hurdy-gurdy, at the fiddle weaves,
Rattles the salt-box, thumps the kettle-
        drum,   701
And him who at the trumpet puffs his
        cheeks,
The silver-collared Negro with his timbrel,
Equestrians, tumblers, women, girls, and
        boys,
Blue-breeched, pink-vested, with high-
        towering plumes.—   705
All moveables of wonder, from all parts,
Are here—Albinos, painted Indians,
        Dwarfs,
The Horse of knowledge, and the learned
        Pig,

The Stone-eater, the man that swallows
fire,
Giants, Ventriloquists, the Invisible Girl,
The Bust that speaks and moves its
goggling eyes,   711
The Wax-work, Clock-work, all the mar-
vellous craft
Of modern Merlins, Wild Beasts, Puppet-
shows,
All out-o'-the-way, far-fetched, perverted
things,
All freaks of nature, all Promethean
thoughts   715
Of man, his dulness, madness, and their
feats
All jumbled up together, to compose
A Parliament of Monsters. Tents and
Booths
Meanwhile, as if the whole were one vast
mill,
Are vomiting, receiving on all sides,   720
Men, Women, three-years' Children, Babes
in arms.

Oh, blank confusion! true epitome
Of what the mighty City is herself,
To thousands upon thousands of her sons,
Living amid the same perpetual whirl   725
Of trivial objects, melted and reduced
To one identity, by differences
That have no law, no meaning, and no
end—
Oppression, under which even highest
minds
Must labour, whence the strongest are
not free.   730
But though the picture weary out the eye,
By nature an unmanageable sight,
It is not wholly so to him who looks
In steadiness, who hath among least
things   734
An under-sense of greatest; sees the parts
As parts, but with a feeling of the whole.
This, of all acquisitions, first awaits
On sundry and most widely different
modes

Of education, nor with least delight
On that through which I passed. At-
tention springs,   740
And comprehensiveness and memory flow,
From early converse with the works of
God
Among all regions; chiefly where appear
Most obviously simplicity and power.
Think, how the everlasting streams and
woods,   745
Stretched and still stretching far and
wide, exalt
The roving Indian, on his desert sands:
What grandeur not unfelt, what pregnant
show
Of beauty, meets the sun-burnt Arab's
eye:
And, as the sea propels, from zone to
zone,   750
Its currents; magnifies its shoals of life
Beyond all compass; spreads, and sends
aloft
Armies of clouds,—even so, its powers
and aspects
Shape for mankind, by principles as fixed,
The views and aspirations of the soul   755
To majesty. Like virtue have the forms
Perennial of the ancient hills; nor less
The changeful language of their coun-
tenances
Quickens the slumbering mind, and aids
the thoughts,
However multitudinous, to move   760
With order and relation. This, if still,
As hitherto, in freedom I may speak,
Not violating any just restraint,
As may be hoped, of real modesty,—
This did I feel, in London's vast do-
main.   765
The Spirit of Nature was upon me there;
The soul of Beauty and enduring Life
Vouchsafed her inspiration, and diffused,
Through meagre lines and colours, and
the press
Of self-destroying, transitory things,   770
Composure, and ennobling Harmony.

BOOK EIGHTH.

RETROSPECT.—LOVE OF NATURE LEADING TO LOVE OF MAN.

WHAT sounds are those, Helvellyn, that are heard
Up to thy summit, through the depth of air
Ascending, as if distance had the power
To make the sounds more audible? What crowd
Covers, or sprinkles o'er, yon village green?   5
Crowd seems it, solitary hill! to thee,
Though but a little family of men,
Shepherds and tillers of the ground—betimes
Assembled with their children and their wives,
And here and there a stranger interspersed.   10
They hold a rustic fair—a festival,
Such as, on this side now, and now on that,
Repeated through his tributary vales,
Helvellyn, in the silence of his rest,
Sees annually, if clouds towards either ocean   15
Blown from their favourite resting-place, or mists
Dissolved, have left him an unshrouded head.
Delightful day it is for all who dwell
In this secluded glen, and eagerly
They give it welcome. Long ere heat of noon,   20
From byre or field the kine were brought; the sheep
Are penned in cotes; the chaffering is begun.
The heifer lows, uneasy at the voice
Of a new master; bleat the flocks aloud.
Booths are there none; a stall or two is here;   25

A lame man or a blind, the one to beg,
The other to make music; hither, too,
From far, with basket, slung upon her arm,
Of hawker's wares—books, pictures, combs, and pins—
Some aged woman finds her way again,   30
Year after year, a punctual visitant!
There also stands a speech-maker by rote,
Pulling the strings of his boxed rareeshow;
And in the lapse of many years may come
Prouder itinerant, mountebank, or he   35
Whose wonders in a covered wain lie hid.
But one there is, the loveliest of them all,
Some sweet lass of the valley, looking out
For gains, and who that sees her would not buy?
Fruits of her father's orchard are her wares,   40
And with the ruddy produce she walks round
Among the crowd, half pleased with, half ashamed
Of her new office, blushing restlessly.
The children now are rich, for the old to-day
Are generous as the young; and, if content   45
With looking on, some ancient wedded pair
Sit in the shade together, while they gaze,
"A cheerful smile unbends the wrinkled brow,
The days departed start again to life,
And all the scenes of childhood reappear,
Faint, but more tranquil, like the changing sun   51

To him who slept at noon and wakes at
    eve [1]."
Thus gaiety and cheerfulness prevail,
Spreading from young to old, from old to
    young,
And no one seems to want his share.—
    Immense   55
Is the recess, the circumambient world
Magnificent, by which they are embraced:
They move about upon the soft green
    turf:
How little they, they and their doings,
    seem,
And all that they can further or obstruct!
Through utter weakness pitiably dear, 61
As tender infants are: and yet how
    great !
For all things serve them; them the
    morning light
Loves, as it glistens on the silent rocks;
And them the silent rocks, which now
    from high   65
Look down upon them; the reposing
    clouds;
The wild brooks prattling from invisible
    haunts;
And old Helvellyn, conscious of the stir
Which animates this day their calm
    abode.

With deep devotion, Nature, did I feel,
In that enormous City's turbulent world
Of men and things, what benefit I owed
To thee, and those domains of rural peace,
Where to the sense of beauty first my
    heart
Was opened; tract more exquisitely fair
Than that famed paradise of ten thousand
    trees,   76
Or Gehol's matchless gardens, for delight
Of the Tartarian dynasty composed
(Beyond that mighty wall, not fabulous,
China's stupendous mound) by patient
    toil   80
Of myriads and boon nature's lavish help;
There, in a clime from widest empire
    chosen,
Fulfilling (could enchantment have done
    more?)

A sumptuous dream of flowery lawns, with
    domes
Of pleasure sprinkled over, shady dells 85
For eastern monasteries, sunny mounts
With temples crested, bridges, gondolas,
Rocks, dens, and groves of foliage taught
    to melt
Into each other their obsequious hues,
Vanished and vanishing in subtle chase, 90
Too fine to be pursued; or standing forth
In no discordant opposition, strong .
And gorgeous as the colours side by side
Bedded among rich plumes of tropic
    birds;
And mountains over all, embracing all; 95
And all the landscape, endlessly enriched
With waters running, falling, or asleep.

But lovelier far than this, the paradise
Where I was reared; in Nature's primi-
    tive gifts
Favoured no less, and more to every
    sense   100
Delicious, seeing that the sun and sky,
The elements, and seasons as they change,
Do find a worthy fellow-labourer there—
Man free, man working for himself, with
    choice
Of time, and place, and object; by his
    wants,   105
His comforts, native occupations, cares,
Cheerfully led to individual ends
Or social, and still followed by a train
Unwooed, unthought-of even—simplicity,
And beauty, and inevitable grace.   110

Yea, when a glimpse of those imperial
    bowers
Would to a child be transport over-great,
When but a half-hour's roam through such
    a place
Would leave behind a dance of images,
That shall break in upon his sleep for
    weeks;   115
Even then the common haunts of the
    green earth,
And ordinary interests of man,
Which they embosom, all without regard
As both may seem, are fastening on the
    heart
Insensibly, each with the other's help. 120

---

[1] From the *Malvern Hills* of Joseph Cottle.

For me, when my affections first were led
From kindred, friends, and playmates, to
    partake
Love for the human creature's absolute
    self,
That noticeable kindliness of heart
Sprang out of fountains, there abounding
    most,   125
Where sovereign Nature dictated the
    tasks
And occupations which her beauty
    adorned,
And Shepherds were the men that pleased
    me first ;
Not such as Saturn ruled 'mid Latian
    wilds,
With arts and laws so tempered, that
    their lives   130
Left, even to us toiling in this late day,
A bright tradition of the golden age ;
Not such as, 'mid Arcadian fastnesses
Sequestered, handed down among them-
    selves
Felicity, in Grecian song renowned ; 135
Nor such as—when an adverse fate had
    driven,
From house and home, the courtly band
    whose fortunes
Entered, with Shakspeare's genius, the
    wild woods
Of Arden—amid sunshine or in shade
Culled the best fruits of Time's uncounted
    hours,   140
Ere Phœbe sighed for the false Gany-
    mede ;
Or there where Perdita and Florizel
Together danced, Queen of the feast, and
    King ;
Nor such as Spenser fabled. True it is,
That I had heard (what he perhaps had
    seen)   145
Of maids at sunrise bringing in from far
Their May-bush, and along the street in
    flocks
Parading with a song of taunting rhymes,
Aimed at the laggards slumbering within
    doors ;
Had also heard, from those who yet re-
    membered,   150
Tales of the May-pole dance, and wreaths
    that decked

Porch, door-way, or kirk-pillar ; and of
    youths,
Each with his maid, before the sun was
    up,
By annual custom, issuing forth in troops,
To drink the waters of some sainted well,
And hang it round with garlands. Love
    survives ;   156
But, for such purpose, flowers no longer
    grow :
The times, too sage, perhaps too proud,
    have dropped
These lighter graces ; and the rural ways
And manners which my childhood looked
    upon   160
Were the unluxuriant produce of a life
Intent on little but substantial needs,
Yet rich in beauty, beauty that was felt.
But images of danger and distress,
Man suffering among awful Powers and
    Forms ;   165
Of this I heard, and saw enough to make
Imagination restless ; nor was free
Myself from frequent perils ; nor were
    tales
Wanting,—the tragedies of former times,
Hazards and strange escapes, of which
    the rocks   170
Immutable, and everflowing streams,
Where'er I roamed, were speaking monu-
    ments.

Smooth life had flock and shepherd in
    old time,
Long springs and tepid winters, on the
    banks
Of delicate Galesus ; and no less   175
Those scattered along Adria's myrtle
    shores :
Smooth life had herdsman, and his snow-
    white herd
To triumphs and to sacrificial rites
Devoted, on the inviolable stream
Of rich Clitumnus ; and the goat-herd
    lived   180
As calmly, underneath the pleasant brows
Of cool Lucretilis, where the pipe was
    heard
Of Pan, Invisible God, thrilling the rocks
With tutelary music, from all harm
The fold protecting. I myself, mature

In manhood then, have seen a pastoral
    tract   186
Like one of these, where Fancy might
    run wild,
Though under skies less generous, less
    serene:
There, for her own delight had Nature
    framed
A pleasure-ground, diffused a fair ex-
    panse   190
Of level pasture, islanded with groves
And banked with woody risings; but the
    Plain
Endless, here opening widely out, and
    there
Shut up in lesser lakes or beds of lawn
And intricate recesses, creek or bay   195
Sheltered within a shelter, where at large
The shepherd strays, a rolling hut his
    home.
Thither he comes with spring-time, there
    abides
All summer, and at sunrise ye may hear
His flageolet to liquid notes of love   200
Attuned, or sprightly fife resounding far.
Nook is there none, nor tract of that
    vast space
Where passage opens, but the same shall
    have
In turn its visitant, telling there his hours
In unlaborious pleasure, with no task
More toilsome than to carve a beechen
    bowl   206
For spring or fountain, which the traveller
    finds,
When through the region he pursues at
    will
His devious course. A glimpse of such
    sweet life
I saw when, from the melancholy walls
Of Goslar, once imperial, I renewed   211
My daily walk along that wide cham-
    paign,
That, reaching to her gates, spreads east
    and west,
And northwards, from beneath the moun-
    tainous verge
Of the Hercynian forest. Yet, hail to
    you   215
Moors, mountains, headlands, and ye
    hollow vales,

Ye long deep channels for the Atlantic's
    voice,
Powers of my native region! Ye that
    seize
The heart with firmer grasp! Your snows
    and streams
Ungovernable, and your terrifying winds,
That howl so dismally for him who
    treads   221
Companionless your awful solitudes!
There, 'tis the shepherd's task the winter
    long
To wait upon the storms: of their
    approach
Sagacious, into sheltering coves he drives
His flock, and thither from the homestead
    bears   226
A toilsome burden up the craggy ways,
And deals it out, their regular nourish-
    ment
Strewn on the frozen snow. And when
    the spring
Looks out, and all the pastures dance
    with lambs,   230
And when the flock, with warmer weather,
    climbs
Higher and higher, him his office leads
To watch their goings, whatsoever track
The wanderers choose. For this he quits
    his home
At day-spring, and no sooner doth the
    sun   235
Begin to strike him with a fire-like heat,
Than he lies down upon some shining
    rock,
And breakfasts with his dog. When they
    have stolen,
As is their wont, a pittance from strict
    time,
For rest not needed or exchange of love,
Then from his couch he starts; and now
    his feet   241
Crush out a livelier fragrance from the
    flowers
Of lowly thyme, by Nature's skill en-
    wrought
In the wild turf: the lingering dews of
    morn
Smoke round him, as from hill to hill he
    hies,   245
His staff protending like a hunter's spear,

Or by its aid leaping from crag to crag,
And o'er the brawling beds of unbridged
streams.
Philosophy, methinks, at Fancy's call,
Might deign to follow him through what
he does   250
Or sees in his day's march; himself he
feels,
In those vast regions where his service
lies,
A freeman, wedded to his life of hope
And hazard, and hard labour inter-
changed
With that majestic indolence so dear 255
To native man. A rambling schoolboy,
thus
I felt his presence in his own domain,
As of a lord and master, or a power,
Or genius, under Nature, under God,
Presiding; and severest solitude   260
Had more commanding looks when he
was there.
When up the lonely brooks on rainy days
Angling I went, or trod the trackless hills
By mists bewildered, suddenly mine eyes
Have glanced upon him distant a few
steps,   265
In size a giant, stalking through thick
fog,
His sheep like Greenland bears; or, as he
stepped
Beyond the boundary line of some hill-
shadow,
His form hath flashed upon me, glorified
By the deep radiance of the setting sun:
Or him have I descried in distant sky, 271
A solitary object and sublime,
Above all height! like an aerial cross
Stationed alone upon a spiry rock
Of the Chartreuse, for worship. Thus
was man   275
Ennobled outwardly before my sight,
And thus my heart was early introduced
To an unconscious love and reverence
Of human nature; hence the human form
To me became an index of delight,   280
Of grace and honour, power and worthi-
ness.
Meanwhile this creature—spiritual almost
As those of books, but more exalted far;
Far more of an imaginative form

Than the gay Corin of the groves, who
lives   285
For his own fancies, or to dance by the
hour,
In coronal, with Phyllis in the midst—
Was, for the purposes of kind, a man
With the most common; husband, father;
learned,
Could teach, admonish; suffered with the
rest   290
From vice and folly, wretchedness and
fear;
Of this I little saw, cared less for it,
But something must have felt.
                    Call ye these appearances—
Which I beheld of shepherds in my
youth,
This sanctity of Nature given to man—
A shadow, a delusion, ye who pore   296
On the dead letter, miss the spirit of
things;
Whose truth is not a motion or a shape
Instinct with vital functions, but a block
Or waxen image which yourselves have
made,   300
And ye adore! But blessèd be the God
Of Nature and of Man that this was so;
That men before my inexperienced eyes
Did first present themselves thus purified,
Removed, and to a distance that was fit:
And so we all of us in some degree   306
Are led to knowledge, wheresoever led,
And howsoever; were it otherwise,
And we found evil fast as we find good
In our first years, or think that it is found,
How could the innocent heart bear up
and live!   311
But doubly fortunate my lot; not here
Alone, that something of a better life
Perhaps was round me than it is the
privilege
Of most to move in, but that first I
looked   315
At man through objects that were great
or fair;
First communed with him by their help.
And thus
Was founded a sure safeguard and de-
fence
Against the weight of meanness, selfish
cares,

Coarse manners, vulgar passions, that
    beat in   320
On all sides from the ordinary world
In which we traffic. Starting from this
    point
I had my face turned toward the truth,
    began
With an advantage furnished by that
    kind
Of prepossession, without which the soul
Receives no knowledge that can bring
    forth good,   326
No genuine insight ever comes to her.
From the restraint of over-watchful eyes
Preserved, I moved about, year after year,
Happy, and now most thankful that my
    walk   330
Was guarded from too early intercourse
With the deformities of crowded life,
And those ensuing laughters and con-
    tempts,
Self-pleasing, which, if we would wish to
    think
With a due reverence on earth's rightful
    lord,   335
Here placed to be the inheritor of
    heaven,
Will not permit us, but pursue the mind,
That to devotion willingly would rise,
Into the temple and the temple's heart.

Yet deem not, Friend! that human
    kind with me   340
Thus early took a place pre-eminent;
Nature herself was, at this unripe time,
But secondary to my own pursuits
And animal activities, and all
Their trivial pleasures; and when these
    had drooped   345
And gradually expired, and Nature,
    prized
For her own sake, became my joy, even
    then—
And upwards through late youth, until
    not less
Than two-and-twenty summers had been
    told—
Was Man in my affections and regards
Subordinate to her, her visible forms 351
And viewless agencies: a passion, she,
A rapture often, and immediate love

Ever at hand; he, only a delight
Occasional, an accidental grace,   355
His hour being not yet come. Far less
    had then
The inferior creatures, beast or bird,
    attuned
My spirit to that gentleness of love
(Though they had long been carefully
    observed),   359
Won from me those minute obeisances
Of tenderness, which I may number now
With my first blessings. Nevertheless,
    on these
The light of beauty did not fall in vain,
Or grandeur circumfuse them to no end.

But when that first poetic faculty 365
Of plain Imagination and severe,
No longer a mute influence of the soul,
Ventured, at some rash Muse's earnest
    call,
To try her strength among harmonious
    words;
And to book-notions and the rules of art
Did knowingly conform itself; there
    came   371
Among the simple shapes of human life
A wilfulness of fancy and conceit:
And Nature and her objects beautified
These fictions, as in some sort, in their
    turn,   375
They burnished her. From touch of this
    new power
Nothing was safe: the elder-tree that
    grew
Beside the well-known charnel-house had
    then
A dismal look; the yew-tree had its
    ghost,   379
That took his station there for ornament:
The dignities of plain occurrence then
Were tasteless, and truth's golden mean,
    a point
Where no sufficient pleasure could be
    found.
Then, if a widow, staggering with the
    blow
Of her distress, was known to have turned
    her steps   385
To the cold grave in which her husband
    slept,

One night, or haply more than one,
    through pain
Or half-insensate impotence of mind,
The fact was caught at greedily, and
    there
She must be visitant the whole year
    through,   390
Wetting the turf with never-ending tears.

Through quaint obliquities I might
    pursue
These cravings; when the foxglove, one
    by one,
Upwards through every stage of the tall
    stem,   394
Had shed beside the public way its bells,
And stood of all dismantled, save the last
Left at the tapering ladder's top, that
    seemed
To bend as doth a slender blade of grass
Tipped with a rain-drop, Fancy loved to
    seat,
Beneath the plant despoiled, but crested
    still   400
With this last relic, soon itself to fall,
Some vagrant mother, whose arch little
    ones,
All unconcerned by her dejected plight,
Laughed as with rival eagerness their
    hands
Gathered the purple cups that round
    them lay,   405
Strewing the turf's green slope.
                        A diamond light
(Whene'er the summer sun, declining,
    smote
A smooth rock wet with constant springs)
    was seen
Sparkling from out a copse-clad bank
    that rose
Fronting our cottage. Oft beside the
    hearth   410
Seated, with open door, often and long
Upon this restless lustre have I gazed,
That made my fancy restless as itself.
'Twas now for me a burnished silver
    shield   414
Suspended over a knight's tomb, who lay
Inglorious, buried in the dusky wood:
An entrance now into some magic cave
Or palace built by fairies of the rock;

Nor could I have been bribed to disen-
    chant
The spectacle, by visiting the spot.   420
Thus wilful Fancy, in no hurtful mood,
Engrafted far-fetched shapes on feelings
    bred
By pure Imagination: busy Power
She was, and with her ready pupil
    turned
Instinctively to human passions, then
Least understood. Yet, 'mid the fervent
    swarm   426
·Of these vagaries, with an eye so rich
As mine was through the bounty of a
    grand
And lovely region, I had forms distinct
To steady me: each airy thought re-
    volved   430
Round a substantial centre, which at
    once
Incited it to motion, and controlled.
I did not pine like one in cities bred,
As was thy melancholy lot, dear Friend!
Great Spirit as thou art, in endless
    dreams   435
Of sickliness, disjoining, joining, things
Without the light of knowledge. Where
    the harm,
If, when the woodman languished with
    disease
Induced by sleeping nightly on the
    ground   439
Within his sod-built cabin, Indian-wise,
I called the pangs of disappointed love,
And all the sad etcetera of the wrong,
To help him to his grave? Meanwhile the
    man,
If not already from the woods retired
To die at home, was haply as I knew,
Withering by slow degrees, 'mid gentle
    airs,   446
Birds, running streams, and hills so
    beautiful
On golden evenings, while the charcoal
    pile
Breathed up its smoke, an image of his
    ghost
Or spirit that full soon must take her
    flight.   450
Nor shall we not be tending towards that
    point

Of sound humanity to which our Tale
Leads, though by sinuous ways, if here
    I show
How Fancy, in a season when she wove
Those slender cords, to guide the uncon-
    scious Boy   455
For the Man's sake, could feed at Na-
    ture's call
Some pensive musings which might well
    beseem
Maturer years.
        A grove there is whose boughs
Stretch from the western marge of Thur-
    ston-mere,
With length of shade so thick, that whoso
    glides   460
Along the line of low-roofed water, moves
As in a cloister. Once—while, in that
    shade
Loitering, I watched the golden beams of
    light
Flung from the setting sun, as they
    reposed
In silent beauty on the naked ridge   465
Of a high eastern hill—thus flowed my
    thoughts
In a pure stream of words fresh from the
    heart:
Dear native Regions, wheresoe'er shall
    close
My mortal course, there will I think on
    you;   469
Dying, will cast on you a backward look;
Even as this setting sun (albeit the Vale
Is no where touched by one memorial
    gleam)
Doth with the fond remains of his last
    power
Still linger, and a farewell lustre sheds
On the dear mountain-tops where first he
    rose.   475

    Enough of humble arguments; recall,
My Song! those high emotions which thy
    voice
Has heretofore made known; that burst-
    ing forth
Of sympathy, inspiring and inspired,
When everywhere a vital pulse was felt,
And all the several frames of things, like
    stars,   481

Through every magnitude distinguish-
    able,
Shone mutually indebted, or half lost
Each in the other's blaze, a galaxy
Of life and glory. In the midst stood
    Man,   485
Outwardly, inwardly contemplated,
As, of all visible natures, crown, though
    born
Of dust, and kindred to the worm; a
    Being,
Both in perception and discernment, first
In every capability of rapture,   490
Through the divine effect of power and
    love;
As, more than anything we know, in-
    stinct
With godhead, and, by reason and by
    will,
Acknowledging dependency sublime.

    Ere long, the lonely mountains left,
    I moved,   495
Begirt, from day to day, with temporal
    shapes
Of vice and folly thrust upon my view,
Objects of sport, and ridicule, and scorn,
Manners and characters discriminate,
And little bustling passions that eclipse,
As well they might, the impersonated
    thought,   501
The idea, or abstraction of the kind.

    An Idler among academic bowers,
Such was my new condition, as at large
Has been set forth; yet here the vulgar
    light   505
Of present, actual, superficial life,
Gleaming through colouring of other
    times,
Old usages and local privilege,
Was welcome, softened, if not solemnised.
This notwithstanding, being brought
    more near   510
To vice and guilt, forerunning wretched-
    ness,
I trembled,—thought, at times, of human
    life
With an indefinite terror and dismay,
Such as the storms and angry elements
Had bred in me; but gloomier far, a dim

Analogy to uproar and misrule,   516
Disquiet, danger, and obscurity.

It might be told (but wherefore speak
of things
Common to all?) that, seeing, I was led
Gravely to ponder—judging between good
And evil, not as for the mind's delight
But for her guidance—one who was to *act*,
As sometimes to the best of feeble means
I did, by human sympathy impelled;
And, through dislike and most offensive
pain,   525
Was to the truth conducted; of this
faith
Never forsaken, that, by acting well,
And understanding, I should learn to love
The end of life, and everything we know.

Grave Teacher, stern Preceptress! for
at times   530
Thou canst put on an aspect most severe;
London, to thee I willingly return.
Erewhile my verse played idly with the
flowers
Enwrought upon thy mantle; satisfied
With that amusement, and a simple look
Of child-like inquisition now and then
Cast upwards on thy countenance, to
detect
Some inner meanings which might har-
bour there.
But how could I in mood so light indulge,
Keeping such fresh remembrance of the
day,   540
When, having thridded the long labyrinth
Of the suburban villages, I first
Entered thy vast dominion? On the roof
Of an itinerant vehicle I sate,
With vulgar men about me, trivial forms
Of houses, pavement, streets, of men and
things,—   546
Mean shapes on every side: but, at the
instant,
When to myself it fairly might be said,
The threshold now is overpast, (how
strange
That aught external to the living mind
Should have such mighty sway! yet so it
was),   551
A weight of ages did at once descend

Upon my heart; no thought embodied,
no
Distinct remembrances, but weight and
power,—
Power growing under weight: alas! I
feel   555
That I am trifling: 'twas a moment's
pause,—
All that took place within me came and
went
As in a moment; yet with Time it dwells,
And grateful memory, as a thing divine.

The curious traveller, who, from open
day,   560
Hath passed with torches into some huge
cave,
The Grotto of Antiparos, or the Den
In old time haunted by that Danish
Witch,
Yordas; he looks around and sees the
vault
Widening on all sides; sees, or thinks he
sees,   565
Erelong, the massy roof above his head,
That instantly unsettles and recedes,—
Substance and shadow, light and dark-
ness, all
Commingled, making up a canopy
Of shapes and forms and tendencies to
shape   570
That shift and vanish, change and inter-
change
Like spectres,—ferment silent and sub-
lime!
That after a short space works less and
less,
Till, every effort, every motion gone,
The scene before him stands in perfect
view   575
Exposed, and lifeless as a written book!—
But let him pause awhile, and look again,
And a new quickening shall succeed, at
first
Beginning timidly, then creeping fast,
Till the whole cave, so late a senseless
mass,   580
Busies the eye with images and forms
Boldly assembled,—here is shadowed
forth
From the projections, wrinkles, cavities,

A variegated landscape,—there the shape
Of some gigantic warrior clad in mail, 585
The ghostly semblance of a hooded monk,
Veiled nun, or pilgrim resting on his
    staff:
Strange congregation! yet not slow to
    meet
Eyes that perceive through minds that
    can inspire.

Even in such sort had I at first been
    moved,   590
Nor otherwise continued to be moved,
As I explored the vast metropolis,
Fount of my country's destiny and the
    world's;
That great emporium, chronicle at once
And burial-place of passions, and their
    home   595
Imperial, their chief living residence.

With strong sensations teeming as it
    did
Of past and present, such a place must
    needs
Have pleased me, seeking knowledge at
    that time
Far less than craving power; yet know-
    ledge came,   600
Sought or unsought, and influxes of
    power
Came, of themselves, or at her call de-
    rived
In fits of kindliest apprehensiveness,
From all sides, when whate'er was in
    itself
Capacious found, or seemed to find, in
    me   605
A correspondent amplitude of mind;
Such is the strength and glory of our
    youth!
The human nature unto which I felt
That I belonged, and reverenced with
    love,
Was not a punctual presence, but a spirit
Diffused through time and space, with
    aid derived   611
Of evidence from monuments, erect,
Prostrate, or leaning towards their com-
    mon rest
In earth, the widely scattered wreck
    sublime

Of vanished nations, or more clearly
    drawn   615
From books and what they picture and
    record.

'Tis true, the history of our native land,
With those of Greece compared and
    popular Rome,
And in our high-wrought modern narra-
    tives
Stript of their harmonising soul, the life
Of manners and familiar incidents, 621
Had never much delighted me. And
    less
Than other intellects had mine been used
To lean upon extrinsic circumstance
Of record or tradition; but a sense 625
Of what in the Great City had been done
And suffered, and was doing, suffering,
    still,
Weighed with me, could support the test
    of thought;
And, in despite of all that had gone by,
Or was departing never to return, 630
There I conversed with majesty and
    power
Like independent natures. Hence the
    place
Was thronged with impregnations like
    the Wilds
In which my early feelings had been
    nursed—
Bare hills and valleys, full of caverns,
    rocks,   635
And audible seclusions, dashing lakes,
Echoes and waterfalls, and pointed crags
That into music touch the passing wind.
Here then my young imagination found
No uncongenial element; could here 640
Among new objects serve or give com-
    mand,
Even as the heart's occasions might re-
    quire,
To forward reason's else too scrupulous
    march.
The effect was, still more elevated views
Of human nature. Neither vice nor guilt,
Debasement undergone by body or mind,
Nor all the misery forced upon my sight,
Misery not lightly passed, but sometimes
    scanned   648

Most feelingly, could overthrow my trust
In what we *may* become; induce belief
That I was ignorant, had been falsely
　　　taught,　　　　651
A solitary, who with vain conceits
Had been inspired, and walked about in
　　dreams.
From those sad scenes when meditation
　　turned,
Lo! everything that was indeed divine
Retained its purity inviolate,　　　656
Nay brighter shone, by this portentous
　　gloom
Set off; such opposition as aroused
The mind of Adam, yet in Paradise
Though fallen from bliss, when in the
　　East he saw　　　660
Darkness ere day's mid course, and morn-
　　ing light
More orient in the western cloud, that
　　drew
O'er the blue firmament a radiant white,
Descending slow with something heavenly
　　fraught.　　　664

Add also, that among the multitudes
Of that huge city, oftentimes was seen
Affectingly set forth, more than else-
　　where

Is possible, the unity of man,
One spirit over ignorance and vice
Predominant in good and evil hearts;
One sense for moral judgments, as one
　　eye　　　671
For the sun's light. The soul when
　　smitten thus
By a sublime *idea*, whencesoe'er
Vouchsafed for union or communion,
　　feeds
On the pure bliss, and takes her rest with
　　God.　　　675

Thus from a very early age, O Friend!
My thoughts by slow gradations had
　　been drawn
To human-kind, and to the good and ill
Of human life: Nature had led me on;
And oft amid the "busy hum" I seemed
To travel independent of her help,　681
As if I had forgotten her; but no,
The world of human-kind outweighed not
　　hers
In my habitual thoughts; the scale of
　　love,
Though filling daily, still was light, com-
　　pared　　　685
With that in which *her* mighty objects
　　lay.

BOOK NINTH.

RESIDENCE IN FRANCE.

EVEN as a river,—partly (it might seem)
Yielding to old remembrances, and
　　swayed
In part by fear to shape a way direct,
That would engulph him soon in the
　　ravenous sea—
Turns, and will measure back his course,
　　far back,　　　5
Seeking the very regions which he crossed
In his first outset; so have we, my
　　Friend!
Turned and returned with intricate de-
　　lay.

Or as a traveller, who has gained the brow
Of some aerial Down, while there he halts
For breathing-time, is tempted to review
The region left behind him; and, if
　　aught　　　12
Deserving notice have escaped regard,
Or been regarded with too careless eye,
Strives, from that height, with one and
　　yet one more　　　15
Last look, to make the best amends he
　　may:
So have we lingered. Now we start
　　afresh

With courage, and new hope risen on our
　　toil.
Fair greetings to this shapeless eagerness,
Whene'er it comes ! needful in work so
　　long,　　　　　　　　　　　　　　20
Thrice needful to the argument which
　　now
Awaits us ! Oh, how much unlike the
　　past !

Free as a colt at pasture on the hill,
I ranged at large, through London's wide
　　· domain,
Month after month. Obscurely did I
　　live,　　　　　　　　　　　　　　25
Not seeking frequent intercourse with
　　men,
By literature, or elegance, or rank,
Distinguished. Scarcely was a year thus
　　spent
Ere I forsook the crowded solitude,　　9
With less regret for its luxurious pomp,
And all the nicely-guarded shows of art,
Than for the humble book-stalls in the
　　streets,
Exposed to eye and hand where'er I
　　turned.

France lured me forth, the realm that
　　I had crossed
So lately, journeying toward the snow-
　　clad Alps.　　　　　　　　　　35
But now, relinquishing the scrip and
　　staff,
And all enjoyment which the summer sun
Sheds round the steps of those who meet
　　the day
With motion constant as his own, I went
Prepared to sojourn in a pleasant town,
Washed by the current of the stately
　　Loire. ·　　　　　　　　　　41

Through Paris lay my readiest course,
　　and there
Sojourning a few days, I visited
In haste, each spot of old or recent fame,
The latter chiefly ; from the field of Mars
Down to the suburbs of St. Antony,　46
And from Mont Martre southward to
　　the Dome
Of Geneviève. In both her clamorous
　　Halls,

The National Synod and the Jacobins,
I saw the Revolutionary Power　　50
Toss like a ship at anchor, rocked by
　　storms ;
The Arcades I traversed, in the Palace
　　huge
Of Orleans ; coasted round and round the
　　line
Of Tavern, Brothel, Gaming-house, and
　　Shop,
Great rendezvous of worst and best, the
　　walk　　　　　　　　　　　　55
Of all who had a purpose, or had not ;
I stared and listened, with a stranger's
　　ears,
To Hawkers and Haranguers, hubbub
　　wild !
And hissing Factionists with ardent eyes,
In knots, or pairs, or single. Not a look
Hope takes, or Doubt or Fear is forced
　　to wear,　　　　　　　　　　61
But seemed there present ; and I scanned
　　them all,
Watched every gesture uncontrollable,
Of anger, and vexation, and despite,
All side by side, and struggling face to
　　face,　　　　　　　　　　　　65
With gaiety and dissolute idleness.

Where silent zephyrs sported with the
　　dust
Of the Bastille, I sate in the open sun,
And from the rubbish gathered up a stone,
And pocketed the relic, in the guise　70
Of an enthusiast ; yet, in honest truth,
I looked for something that I could not
　　find,
Affecting more emotion than I felt ;
For 'tis most certain, that these various
　　sights,
However potent their first shock, with
　　me　　　　　　　　　　　　　75
Appeared to recompense the traveller's
　　pains
Less than the painted Magdalene of Le
　　Brun,
A beauty exquisitely wrought, with hair
Dishevelled, gleaming eyes, and rueful
　　cheek
Pale and bedropped with everflowing
　　tears.　　　　　　　　　　　　80

But hence to my more permanent abode
I hasten; there, by novelties in speech,
Domestic manners, customs, gestures,
looks,
And all the attire of ordinary life,
Attention was engrossed; and, thus
amused,   85
I stood, 'mid those concussions, uncon-
cerned,
Tranquil almost, and careless as a flower
Glassed in a greenhouse, or a parlour
shrub
That spreads its leaves in unmolested
peace,
While every bush and tree, the country
through,   90
Is shaking to the roots: indifference this
Which may seem strange: but I was un-
prepared
With needful knowledge, had abruptly
passed
Into a theatre, whose stage was filled
And busy with an action far advanced.
Like others, I had skimmed, and some-
times read   96
With care, the master-pamphlets of the
day;
Nor wanted such half-insight as grew
wild
Upon that meagre soil, helped out by
talk   99
And public news; but having never seen
A chronicle that might suffice to show
Whence the main organs of the public
power
Had sprung, their transmigrations, when
and how
Accomplished, giving thus unto events
A form and body; all things were to me
Loose and disjointed, and the affections
left   106
Without a vital interest. At that time,
Moreover, the first storm was overblown,
And the strong hand of outward violence
Locked up in quiet. For myself, I fear
Now in connection with so great a theme
To speak (as I must be compelled to do)
Of one so unimportant; night by night
Did I frequent the formal haunts of men,
Whom, in the city, privilege of birth 115
Sequestered from the rest, societies

Polished in arts, and in punctilio versed;
Whence, and from deeper causes, all dis-
course
Of good and evil of the time was shunned
With scrupulous care; but these restric-
tions soon   120
Proved tedious, and I gradually with-
drew
Into a noisier world, and thus ere long
Became a patriot; and my heart was all
Given to the people, and my love was
theirs.

A band of military Officers,   125
Then stationed in the city, were the chief
Of my associates: some of these wore
swords
That had been seasoned in the wars, and
all
Were men well-born; the chivalry of
France.
In age and temper differing, they had yet
One spirit ruling in each heart; alike 131
(Save only one, hereafter to be named)
Were bent upon undoing what was done:
This was their rest and only hope; there-
with
No fear had they of bad becoming worse,
For worst to them was come; nor would
have stirred,   136
Or deemed it worth a moment's thought
to stir,
In anything, save only as the act
Looked thitherward. One, reckoning by
years,
Was in the prime of manhood, and ere-
while   140
He had sate lord in many tender hearts;
Though heedless of such honours now,
and changed:
His temper was quite mastered by the
times,
And they had blighted him, had eaten
away
The beauty of his person, doing wrong
Alike to body and to mind: his port, 146
Which once had been erect and open, now
Was stooping and contracted, and a face,
Endowed by Nature with her fairest gifts
Of symmetry and light and bloom, ex-
pressed,   150

As much as any that was ever seen,
A ravage out of season, made by thoughts
Unhealthy and vexatious. With the hour,
That from the press of Paris duly brought
Its freight of public news, the fever came,   155
A punctual visitant, to shake this man,
Disarmed his voice and fanned his yellow cheek
Into a thousand colours; while he read,
Or mused, his sword was haunted by his touch
Continually, like an uneasy place   160
In his own body. 'Twas in truth an hour
Of universal ferment; mildest men
Were agitated; and commotions, strife
Of passions and opinions, filled the walls
Of peaceful houses with unquiet sounds.
The soil of common life, was, at that time,   166
Too hot to tread upon. Oft said I then,
And not then only, "What a mockery this
Of history, the past and that to come!
Now do I feel how all men are deceived,
Reading of nations and their works, in faith,   171
Faith given to vanity and emptiness;
Oh! laughter for the page that would reflect
To future times the face of what now is!"
The land all swarmed with passion, like a plain   175
Devoured by locusts,—Carra, Gorsas,—add
A hundred other names, forgotten now,
Nor to be heard of more; yet, they were powers,
Like earthquakes, shocks repeated day by day,
And felt through every nook of town and field.   180

Such was the state of things. Meanwhile the chief
Of my associates stood prepared for flight
To augment the band of emigrants in arms
Upon the borders of the Rhine, and leagued
With foreign foes mustered for instant war.   185
This was their undisguised intent, and they
Were waiting with the whole of their desires
The moment to depart.
                              An Englishman,
Born in a land whose very name appeared
To license some unruliness of mind;   190
A stranger, with youth's further privilege,
And the indulgence that a half-learnt speech
Wins from the courteous; I, who had been else
Shunned and not tolerated, freely lived
With these defenders of the Crown, and talked,   195
And heard their notions; nor did they disdain
The wish to bring me over to their cause.

But though untaught by thinking or by books
To reason well of polity or law,
And nice distinctions, then on every tongue,   200
Of natural rights and civil; and to acts
Of nations and their passing interests,
(If with unworldly ends and aims compared)
Almost indifferent, even the historian's tale   204
Prizing but little otherwise than I prized
Tales of the poets, as it made the heart
Beat high, and filled the fancy with fair forms,
Old heroes and their sufferings and their deeds;
Yet in the regal sceptre, and the pomp
Of orders and degrees, I nothing found
Then, or had ever, even in crudest youth,
That dazzled me, but rather what I mourned
And ill could brook, beholding that the best
Ruled not, and feeling that they ought to rule.

For, born in a poor district, and which yet   215
Retaineth more of ancient homeliness,

Than any other nook of English ground,
It was my fortune scarcely to have seen,
Through the whole tenour of my school-
day time,
The face of one, who, whether boy or
man,   220
Was vested with attention or respect
Through claims of wealth or blood; nor
was it least
Of many benefits, in later years
Derived from academic institutes
And rules, that they held something up
to view   225
Of a Republic, where all stood thus far
Upon equal ground; that we were bro-
thers all
In honour, as in one community,
Scholars and gentlemen; where, further-
more,
Distinction open lay to all that came, 230
And wealth and titles were in less esteem
Than talents, worth, and prosperous in-
dustry.
Add unto this, subservience from the
first
To presences of God's mysterious power
Made manifest in Nature's sovereignty,
And fellowship with venerable books, 236
To sanction the proud workings of the
soul,
And mountain liberty. It could not be
But that one tutored thus should look
with awe
Upon the faculties of man, receive   240
Gladly the highest promises, and hail,
As best, the government of equal rights
And individual worth. And hence, O
Friend!
If at the first great outbreak I rejoiced
Less than might well befit my youth, the
cause   245
In part lay here, that unto me the events
Seemed nothing out of nature's certain
course,
A gift that was come rather late than
soon.
No wonder, then, if advocates like these,
Inflamed by passion, blind with pre-
judice,   250
And stung with injury, at this riper day,
Were impotent to make my hopes put on

The shape of theirs, my understanding
bend
In honour to their honour: zeal, which
yet   254
Had slumbered, now in opposition burst
Forth like a Polar summer: every word
They uttered was a dart, by counter-
winds
Blown back upon themselves; their reason
seemed
Confusion-stricken by a higher power
Than human understanding, their dis-
course   260
Maimed, spiritless: and, in their weak-
ness strong,
I triumphed.
            Meantime, day by day, the roads
Were crowded with the bravest youth of
France,
And all the promptest of her spirits,
linked
In gallant soldiership, and posting on
To meet the war upon her frontier
bounds.   266
Yet at this very moment do tears start
Into mine eyes: I do not say I weep—
I wept not then,—but tears have dimmed
my sight,
In memory of the farewells of that time,
Domestic severings, female fortitude 271
At dearest separation, patriot love
And self-devotion, and terrestrial hope,
Encouraged with a martyr's confidence;
Even files of strangers merely seen but
once,   275
And for a moment, men from far with
sound
Of music, martial tunes, and banners
spread,
Entering the city, here and there a face,
Or person singled out among the rest,
Yet still a stranger and beloved as such;
Even by these passing spectacles my
heart   281
Was oftentimes uplifted, and they seemed
Arguments sent from Heaven to prove
the cause
Good, pure, which no one could stand up
against,
Who was not lost, abandoned, selfish,
proud,   285

Mean, miserable, wilfully depraved,
Hater perverse of equity and truth.

Among that band of Officers was one,
Already hinted at [1], of other mould—
A patriot, thence rejected by the rest, 290
And with an oriental loathing spurned,
As of a different caste. A meeker man
Than this lived never, nor a more benign,
Meek though enthusiastic. Injuries
Made *him* more gracious, and his nature
then   295
Did breathe its sweetness out most sen-
sibly,
As aromatic flowers on Alpine turf,
When foot hath crushed them. He
through the events
Of that great change wandered in perfect
faith,
As through a book, an old romance, or
tale   300
Of Fairy, or some dream of actions
wrought
Behind the summer clouds. By birth he
ranked
With the most noble, but unto the poor
Among mankind he was in service bound,
As by some tie invisible, oaths professed
To a religious order. Man he loved 306
As man; and, to the mean and the
obscure,
And all the homely in their homely works,
Transferred a courtesy which had no air
Of condescension; but did rather seem
A passion and a gallantry, like that 311
Which he, a soldier, in his idler day
Had paid to woman: somewhat vain he
was,
Or seemed so, yet it was not vanity,
But fondness, and a kind of radiant joy
Diffused around him, while he was in-
tent   316
On works of love or freedom, or revolved
Complacently the progress of a cause,
Whereof he was a part: yet this was
meek
And placid, and took nothing from the
man   320
That was delightful. Oft in solitude

---

[1] See line 132, p. 711.—Ed.

With him did I discourse about the end
Of civil government, and its wisest forms;
Of ancient loyalty, and chartered rights,
Custom and habit, novelty and change;
Of self-respect, and virtue in the few 326
For patrimonial honour set apart,
And ignorance in the labouring multitude.
For he, to all intolerance indisposed,
Balanced these contemplations in his
mind;   330
And I, who at that time was scarcely
dipped
Into the turmoil, bore a sounder judgment
Than later days allowed; carried about me,
With less alloy to its integrity,
The experience of past ages, as, through
help   335
Of books and common life, it makes sure
way
To youthful minds, by objects over near
Not pressed upon, nor dazzled or misled
By struggling with the crowd for present
ends.

But though not deaf, nor obstinate to
find   340
Error without excuse upon the side
Of them who strove against us, more
delight
We took, and let this freely be confessed,
In painting to ourselves the miseries 344
Of royal courts, and that voluptuous life
Unfeeling, where the man who is of soul
The meanest thrives the most; where
dignity,
True personal dignity, abideth not;
A light, a cruel, and vain world cut off
From the natural inlets of just sentiment,
From lowly sympathy and chastening
truth: 351
Where good and evil interchange their
names,
And thirst for bloody spoils abroad is
paired
With vice at home. We added dearest
themes—
Man and his noble nature, as it is 355
The gift which God has placed within his
power,
His blind desires and steady faculties
Capable of clear truth, the one to break

Bondage, the other to build liberty
On firm foundations, making social life,
Through knowledge spreading and im-
    perishable,   361
As just in regulation, and as pure
As individual in the wise and good.

We summoned up the honourable deeds
Of ancient Story, thought of each bright
    spot,   365
That would be found in all recorded time,
Of truth preserved and error passed
    away;
Of single spirits that catch the flame
    from Heaven,
And how the multitudes of men will feed
And fan each other; thought of sects,
    how keen   370
They are to put the appropriate nature on,
Triumphant over every obstacle
Of custom, language, country, love, or
    hate,
And what they do and suffer for their
    creed;
How far they travel, and how long en-
    dure;   375
How quickly mighty Nations have been
    formed,
From least beginnings; how, together
    locked
By new opinions, scattered tribes have
    made
One body, spreading wide as clouds in
    heaven.
To aspirations then of our own minds 380
Did we appeal; and, finally, beheld
A living confirmation of the whole
Before us, in a people from the depth
Of shameful imbecility uprisen,
Fresh as the morning star. Elate we
    looked   385
Upon their virtues; saw, in rudest men,
Self-sacrifice the firmest; generous love,
And continence of mind, and sense of
    right,
Uppermost in the midst of fiercest strife.

Oh, sweet it is, in academic groves, 390
Or such retirement, Friend! as we have
    known
In the green dales beside our Rotha's
    stream,

Greta, or Derwent, or some nameless rill,
To ruminate, with interchange of talk,
On rational liberty, and hope in man, 395
Justice and peace. But far more sweet
    such toil—
Toil, say I, for it leads to thoughts ab-
    struse—
If nature then be standing on the brink
Of some great trial, and we hear the voice
Of one devoted,—one whom circumstance
Hath called upon to embody his deep
    sense
In action, give it outwardly a shape,
And that of benediction, to the world.
Then doubt is not, and truth is more
    than truth,—
A hope it is, and a desire; a creed 405
Of zeal, by an authority Divine
Sanctioned, of danger, difficulty, or death.
Such conversation, under Attic shades,
Did Dion hold with Plato; ripened thus
For a deliverer's glorious task,—and such
He, on that ministry already bound, 411
Held with Eudemus and Timonides,
Surrounded by adventurers in arms,
When those two vessels with their daring
    freight,
For the Sicilian Tyrant's overthrow, 415
Sailed from Zacynthus,—philosophic war,
Led by Philosophers. With harder fate,
Though like ambition, such was he, O
    Friend!
Of whom I speak. So BEAUPUY (let the
    name
Stand near the worthiest of Antiquity)
Fashioned his life; and many a long dis-
    course,   421
With like persuasion honoured, we main-
    tained:
He, on his part, accoutred for the worst,
He perished fighting, in supreme com-
    mand,
Upon the borders of the unhappy Loire[1],
For liberty, against deluded men, 426
His fellow country-men; and yet most
    blessed
In this, that he the fate of later times

---

[1] An error. Beaupuy died at Emmendingen,
shot while in command of a division of the Army
of the Rhine and the Moselle.—ED.

Lived not to see, nor what we now behold,
Who have as ardent hearts as he had
    then [1].   430

Along that very Loire, with festal mirth
Resounding at all hours, and innocent yet
Of civil slaughter, was our frequent walk;
Or in wide forests of continuous shade,
Lofty and over-arched, with open space
Beneath the trees, clear footing many
    a mile—   436
A solemn region. Oft amid those haunts,
From earnest dialogues I slipped in
    thought,
And let remembrance steal to other times,
When o'er those interwoven roots, moss-
    clad,   440
And smooth as marble or a waveless sea,
Some Hermit, from his cell forth-strayed,
    might pace
In sylvan meditation undisturbed;
As on the pavement of a Gothic church
Walks a lone Monk, when service hath
    expired,   445
In peace and silence. But if e'er was
    heard,—
Heard, though unseen,—a devious tra-
    veller,
Retiring or approaching from afar
With speed and echoes loud of trampling
    hoofs
From the hard floor reverberated, then 450
It was Angelica thundering through the
    woods
Upon her palfrey, or that gentle maid
Erminia, fugitive as fair as she.
Sometimes methought I saw a pair of
    knights
Joust underneath the trees, that as in storm
Rocked high above their heads; anon,
    the din   456
Of boisterous merriment, and music's roar,
In sudden proclamation, burst from haunt
Of Satyrs in some viewless glade, with
    dance
Rejoicing o'er a female in the midst,   460
A mortal beauty, their unhappy thrall.

[1] For the story of W's. relations with Beaupuy,
see *Le Général Michel Beaupuy*, by MM. Georges
Bussière and Emile Legouis: Chap. II.—Ed.

The width of those huge forests, unto me
A novel scene, did often in this way
Master my fancy while I wandered on
With that revered companion. And some-
    times—   465
When to a convent in a meadow green,
By a brook-side, we came, a roofless pile,
And not by reverential touch of Time
Dismantled, but by violence abrupt—
In spite of those heart-bracing colloquies,
In spite of real fervour, and of that   471
Less genuine and wrought up within
    myself—
I could not but bewail a wrong so harsh,
And for the Matin-bell to sound no more
Grieved, and the twilight taper, and the
    cross   475
High on the topmost pinnacle, a sign
(How welcome to the weary traveller's
    eyes!)
Of hospitality and peaceful rest.
And when the partner of those varied walks
Pointed upon occasion to the site   480
Of Romorentin, home of ancient kings,
To the imperial edifice of Blois,
Or to that rural castle, name now slipped
From my remembrance, where a lady
    lodged,
By the first Francis wooed, and bound to
    him   485
In chains of mutual passion, from the
    tower,
As a tradition of the country tells,
Practised to commune with her royal
    knight
By cressets and love-beacons, intercourse
'Twixt her high-seated residence and his
Far off at Chambord on the plain beneath;
Even here, though less than with the
    peaceful house
Religious, 'mid those frequent monuments
Of Kings, their vices and their better
    deeds,
Imagination, potent to inflame   495
At times with virtuous wrath and noble
    scorn,
Did also often mitigate the force
Of civic prejudice, the bigotry,
So call it, of a youthful patriot's mind;
And on these spots with many gleams
    I looked   500

Of chivalrous delight. Yet not the less,
Hatred of absolute rule, where will of one
Is law for all, and of that barren pride
In them who, by immunities unjust,
Between the sovereign and the people
     stand,   505
His helper and not theirs, laid stronger
     hold
Daily upon me, mixed with pity too
And love; for where hope is, there love
     will be
For the abject multitude. And when we
     chanced
One day to meet a hunger-bitten girl, 510
Who crept along fitting her languid gait
Unto a heifer's motion, by a cord
Tied to her arm, and picking thus from
     the lane
Its sustenance, while the girl with pallid
     hands   514
Was busy knitting in a heartless mood
Of solitude, and at the sight my friend
In agitation said, "'Tis against *that*
That we are fighting," I with him be-
     lieved
That a benignant spirit was abroad
Which might not be withstood, that
     poverty   520
Abject as this would in a little time
Be found no more, that we should see the
     earth
Unthwarted in her wish to recompense
The meek, the lowly, patient child of toil,
All institutes for ever blotted out   525
That legalised exclusion, empty pomp
Abolished, sensual state and cruel power,
Whether by edict of the one or few ;
And finally, as sum and crown of all,
Should see the people having a strong
     hand   530
In framing their own laws ; whence better
     days
To all mankind. But, these things set
     apart,
Was not this single confidence enough
To animate the mind that ever turned
A thought to human welfare,—that,
     henceforth   535
Captivity by mandate without law
Should cease ; and open accusation lead
To sentence in the hearing of the world,

And open punishment, if not the air
Be free to breathe in, and the heart of
     man   540
Dread nothing ? From this height I shall
     not stoop
To humbler matter that detained us oft
In thought or conversation, public acts,
And public persons, and emotions wrought
Within the breast, as ever-varying winds
Of record or report swept over us ;   546
But I might here, instead, repeat a tale[1],
Told by my Patriot friend, of sad events,
That prove to what low depth had struck
     the roots,
How widely spread the boughs, of that
     old tree   550
Which, as a deadly mischief, and a foul
And black dishonour, France was weary of.

O, happy time of youthful lovers, (thus
The story might begin,) oh, balmy time,
In which a love-knot on a lady's brow,
Is fairer than the fairest star in Heaven !
So might—and with that prelude *did*
     begin   557
The record ; and, in faithful verse, was
     given
The doleful sequel.
                    But our little bark
On a strong river boldly hath been
     launched ;   560
And from the driving current should we
     turn
To loiter wilfully within a creek,
Howe'er attractive, Fellow voyager !
Wouldst thou not chide? Yet deem not
     my pains lost :
For Vaudracour and Julia (so were
     named   565
The ill-fated pair) in that plain tale will
     draw
Tears from the hearts of others, when
     their own
Shall beat no more. Thou, also, there
     may'st read,
At leisure, how the enamoured youth was
     driven,   569
By public power abased, to fatal crime,
Nature's rebellion against monstrous law ;

[1] *Vaudracour and Julia*, p. 121.—ED.

How, between heart and heart, oppres-
  sion thrust
Her mandates, severing whom true love
  had joined,
Harassing both; until he sank and
  pressed
The couch his fate had made for him;
  supine,   575
Save when the stings of viperous remorse,
Trying their strength, enforced him to
  start up,
Aghast and prayerless. Into a deep wood

He fled, to shun the haunts of human
  kind;
There dwelt, weakened in spirit more
  and more;   580
Nor could the voice of Freedom, which
  through France
Full speedily resounded, public hope,
Or personal memory of his own worst
  wrongs,
Rouse him; but, hidden in those gloomy
  shades,   584
His days he wasted,—an imbecile mind.

BOOK TENTH.

RESIDENCE IN FRANCE.—(CONTINUED).

IT was a beautiful and silent day
That overspread the countenance of earth,
Then fading with unusual quietness,—
A day as beautiful as e'er was given
To soothe regret, though deepening what
  it soothed,   5
When by the gliding Loire I paused, and
  cast
Upon his rich domains, vineyard and
  tilth,
Green meadow-ground, and many-coloured
  woods,
Again, and yet again, a farewell look;
Then from the quiet of that scene passed
  on,   10
Bound to the fierce Metropolis. From
  his throne
The King had fallen, and that invading
  host—
Presumptuous cloud, on whose black
  front was written
The tender mercies of the dismal wind
That bore it—on the plains of Liberty   15
Had burst innocuous. Say in bolder
  words,
They—who had come elate as eastern
  hunters
Banded beneath the Great Mogul, when
  he
Erewhile went forth from Agra or Lahore,
Rajahs and Omrahs in his train, intent   20
To drive their prey enclosed within a ring

Wide as a province, but, the signal given,
Before the point of the life-threatening
  spear
Narrowing itself by moments—they, rash
  men,
Had seen the anticipated quarry turned
Into avengers, from whose wrath they
  fled   26
In terror. Disappointment and dismay
Remained for all whose fancies had run
  wild
With evil expectations; confidence   29
And perfect triumph for the better cause.

The State, as if to stamp the final seal
On her security, and to the world
Show what she was, a high and fearless
  soul,
Exulting in defiance, or heart-stung
By sharp resentment, or belike to taunt
With spiteful gratitude the baffled
  League,   36
That had stirred up her slackening facul-
  ties
To a new transition, when the King was
  crushed,
Spared not the empty throne, and in
  proud haste
Assumed the body and venerable name
Of a Republic. Lamentable crimes,   41
'Tis true, had gone before this hour, dire
  work

Of massacre, in which the senseless sword
Was prayed to as a judge; but these were
　　past,
Earth free from them for ever, as was
　　thought,—　　　　　　　　　　45
Ephemeral monsters, to be seen but once!
Things that could only show themselves
　　and die.

Cheered with this hope, to Paris I
　　returned,
And ranged, with ardour heretofore un-
　　felt,
The spacious city, and in progress passed
The prison where the unhappy Monarch
　　lay,　　　　　　　　　　　　51
Associate with his children and his wife
In bondage; and the palace, lately
　　stormed
With roar of cannon by a furious host. 54
I crossed the square (an empty area then !)
Of the Carrousel, where so late had lain
The dead, upon the dying heaped, and
　　gazed
On this and other spots, as doth a man 58
Upon a volume whose contents he knows
Are memorable, but from him locked up,
Being written in a tongue he cannot read,
So that he questions the mute leaves with
　　pain,
And half upbraids their silence. But
　　that night
I felt most deeply in what world I was,
What ground I trod on, and what air I
　　breathed.　　　　　　　　　　65
High was my room and lonely, near the
　　roof
Of a large mansion or hotel, a lodge
That would have pleased me in more
　　quiet times;
Nor was it wholly without pleasure then.
With unextinguished taper I kept
　　watch,　　　　　　　　　　　70
Reading at intervals; the fear gone by
Pressed on me almost like a fear to come.
I thought of those September massacres,
Divided from me by one little month,
Saw them and touched: the rest was con-
　　jured up　　　　　　　　　　75
From tragic fictions or true history,
Remembrances and dim admonishments.

The horse is taught his manage, and no
　　star
Of wildest course but treads back his own
　　steps;
For the spent hurricane the air pro-
　　vides　　　　　　　　　　　80
As fierce a successor; the tide retreats
But to return out of its hiding-place
In the great deep; all things have second
　　birth;
The earthquake is not satisfied at once;
And in this way I wrought upon my-
　　self,　　　　　　　　　　　85
Until I seemed to hear a voice that cried,
To the whole city, "sleep no more." The
　　trance
Fled with the voice to which it had given
　　birth;
But vainly comments of a calmer mind
Promised soft peace and sweet forgetful-
　　ness.　　　　　　　　　　　90
The place, all hushed and silent as it was,
Appeared unfit for the repose of night,
Defenceless as a wood where tigers roam.

With early morning towards the Palace
　　walk
Of Orleans eagerly I turned; as yet　95
The streets were still; not so those long
　　Arcades;
There, 'mid a peal of ill-matched sounds
　　and cries,
That greeted me on entering, I could
　　hear
Shrill voices from the hawkers in the
　　throng,
Bawling, "Denunciation of the Crimes 100
Of Maximilian Robespierre;" the hand,
Prompt as the voice, held forth a printed
　　speech,
The same that had been recently pro-
　　nounced,
When Robespierre, not ignorant for what
　　mark
Some words of indirect reproof had
　　been　　　　　　　　　　　105
Intended, rose in hardihood, and dared
The man who had an ill surmise of him
To bring his charge in openness; whereat,
When a dead pause ensued, and no one
　　stirred,

In silence of all present, from his seat   110
Louvet walked single through the avenue,
And took his station in the Tribune, say-
    ing,
"I, Robespierre, accuse thee!" Well is
    known
The inglorious issue of that charge, and
    how
He, who had launched the startling thun-
    derbolt,   115
The one bold man, whose voice the attack
    had sounded,
Was left without a follower to discharge
His perilous duty, and retire lamenting
That Heaven's best aid is wasted upon
    men
Who to themselves are false.
           But these are things   120
Of which I speak, only as they were storm
Or sunshine to my individual mind,
No further. Let me then relate that
    now—
In some sort seeing with my proper eyes
That Liberty, and Life, and Death would
    soon   125
To the remotest corners of the land
Lie in the arbitrement of those who ruled
The capital City; what was struggled for,
And by what combatants victory must be
    won;
The indecision on their part whose aim
Seemed best, and the straightforward
    path of those   131
Who in attack or in defence were strong
Through their impiety—my inmost soul
Was agitated; yea, I could almost
Have prayed that throughout earth upon
    all men,   135
By patient exercise of reason made
Worthy of liberty, all spirits filled
With zeal expanding in Truth's holy light,
The gift of tongues might fall, and power
    arrive
From the four quarters of the winds to
    do   140
For France, what without help she could
    not do,
A work of honour; think not that to this
I added, work of safety: from all doubt
Or trepidation for the end of things
Far was I, far as angels are from guilt.   145

Yet did I grieve, nor only grieved, but
    thought
Of opposition and of remedies:
An insignificant stranger and obscure,
And one, moreover, little graced with
    power
Of eloquence even in my native speech,
And all unfit for tumult or intrigue,   151
Yet would I at this time with willing
    heart
Have undertaken for a cause so great
Service however dangerous. I revolved,
How much the destiny of Man had
    still   155
Hung upon single persons; that there
    was,
Transcendent to all local patrimony,
One nature, as there is one sun in heaven;
That objects, even as they are great,
    thereby
Do come within the reach of humblest
    eyes;   160
That Man is only weak through his mis-
    trust
And want of hope where evidence divine
Proclaims to him that hope should be
    most sure;
Nor did the inexperience of my youth
Preclude conviction, that a spirit strong
In hope, and trained to noble aspira-
    tions,   166
A spirit thoroughly faithful to itself,
Is for Society's unreasoning herd
A domineering instinct, serves at once
For way and guide, a fluent receptacle   170
That gathers up each petty straggling rill
And vein of water, glad to be rolled on
In safe obedience; that a mind, whose
    rest
Is where it ought to be, in self-restraint,
In circumspection and simplicity,   175
Falls rarely in entire discomfiture
Below its aim, or meets with, from with-
    out,
A treachery that foils it or defeats;
And, lastly, if the means on human will,
Frail human will, dependent should be-
    tray   180
Him who too boldly trusted them, I felt
That 'mid the loud distractions of the
    world

A sovereign voice subsists within the soul,
Arbiter undisturbed of right and wrong,
Of life and death, in majesty severe   185
Enjoining, as may best promote the aims
Of truth and justice, utter sacrifice,
From whatsoever region of our cares
Or our infirm affections Nature pleads,
Earnest and blind, against the stern
    decree.   190

  On the other side, I called to mind
    those truths
That are the commonplaces of the
    schools—
(A theme for boys, too hackneyed for
    their sires,)
Yet, with a revelation's liveliness,
In all their comprehensive bearings known
And visible to philosophers of old,   196
Men who, to business of the world un-
    trained,
Lived in the shade; and to Harmodius
    known
And his compeer Aristogiton, known
To Brutus—that tyrannic power is weak,
Hath neither gratitude, nor faith, nor
    love,   201
Nor the support of good or evil men
To trust in; that the godhead which is
    ours
Can never utterly be charmed or stilled;
That nothing hath a natural right to last
But equity and reason; that all else   206
Meets foes irreconcilable, and at best
Lives only by variety of disease.

  Well might my wishes be intense, my
    thoughts
Strong and perturbed, not doubting at
    that time   210
But that the virtue of one paramount
    mind
Would have abashed those impious
    crests—have quelled
Outrage and bloody power, and—in de-
    spite
Of what the People long had been and
    were
Through ignorance and false teaching,
    sadder proof   215
Of immaturity, and—in the teeth
Of desperate opposition from without—

Have cleared a passage for just govern-
    ment,
And left a solid birthright to the State,
Redeemed, according to example given
By ancient lawgivers.
                    In this frame of mind,
Dragged by a chain of harsh necessity,
So seemed it,—now I thankfully acknow-
    ledge,
Forced by the gracious providence of
    Heaven,—
To England I returned, else (though
    assured   225
That I both was and must be of small
    weight,
No better than a landsman on the deck
Of a ship struggling with a hideous storm)
Doubtless, I should have then made
    common cause
With some who perished; haply perished
    too,   230
A poor mistaken and bewildered offer-
    ing,—
Should to the breast of Nature have gone
    back,
With all my resolutions, all my hopes,
A Poet only to myself, to men
Useless, and even, beloved Friend! a
    soul   235
To thee unknown!
                    Twice had the trees let fall
Their leaves, as often Winter had put on
His hoary crown, since I had seen the
    surge
Beat against Albion's shore, since ear of
    mine
Had caught the accents of my native
    speech   240
Upon our native country's sacred ground.
A patriot of the world, how could I glide
Into communion with her sylvan shades,
Erewhile my tuneful haunt? It pleased
    me more
To abide in the great City, where I
    found   245
The general air still busy with the stir
Of that first memorable onset made
By a strong levy of humanity
Upon the traffickers in Negro blood;
Effort which, though defeated, had re-
    called   250

To notice old forgotten principles,
And through the nation spread a novel
    heat
Of virtuous feeling. For myself, I own
That this particular strife had wanted
    power
To rivet my affections; nor did now   255
Its unsuccessful issue much excite
My sorrow; for I brought with me the
    faith
That, if France prospered, good men
    would not long
Pay fruitless worship to humanity,
And this most rotten branch of human
    shame,   260
Object, so seemed it, of superfluous pains,
Would fall together with its parent tree.
What, then, were my emotions, when in
    arms
Britain put forth her freeborn strength
    in league,
Oh, pity and shame! with those confede-
    rate Powers!   265
Not in my single self alone I found,
But in the minds of all ingenuous youth,
Change and subversion from that hour.
    No shook
Given to my moral nature had I known
Down to that very moment; neither lapse
Nor turn of sentiment that might be
    named   271
A revolution, save at this one time;
All else was progress on the self-same
    path
On which, with a diversity of pace,
I had been travelling: this a stride at
    once   275
Into another region. As a light
And pliant harebell, swinging in the
    breeze
On some grey rock—its birthplace—so
    had I
Wantoned, fast rooted on the ancient
    tower
Of my belovèd country, wishing not   280
A happier fortune than to wither there:
Now was I from that pleasant station torn
And tossed about in whirlwind. I re-
    joiced,
Yea, afterwards—truth most painful to
    record!—

Exulted, in the triumph of my soul,   285
When Englishmen by thousands were
    o'erthrown,
Left without glory on the field, or driven,
Brave hearts! to shameful flight. It was
    a grief,—
Grief call it not, 'twas anything but
    that,—   289
A conflict of sensations without name,
Of which he only, who may love the sight
Of a village steeple, as I do, can judge,
When, in the congregation bending all
To their great Father, prayers were offer-
    ed up,
Or praises for our country's victories;
And, 'mid the simple worshippers, per-
    chance   296
I only, like an uninvited guest
Whom no one owned, sate silent, shall
    I add,
Fed on the day of vengeance yet to come.

Oh! much have they to account for, who
    could tear,   300
By violence, at one decisive rent,
From the best youth in England their
    dear pride,
Their joy, in England; this, too, at a
    time
In which worst losses easily might wear
The best of names, when patriotic love
Did of itself in modesty give way,   306
Like the Precursor when the Deity
Is come Whose harbinger he was; a time
In which apostasy from ancient faith
Seemed but conversion to a higher creed;
Withal a season dangerous and wild,   311
A time when sage Experience would have
    snatched
Flowers out of any hedge-row to compose
A chaplet in contempt of his grey locks.

When the proud fleet that bears the
    red-cross flag   315
In that unworthy service was prepared
To mingle, I beheld the vessels lie,
A brood of gallant creatures, on the deep;
I saw them in their rest, a sojourner
Through a whole month of calm and glassy
•   days   320
In that delightful island which protects

Their place of convocation—there I heard,
Each evening, pacing by the still sea-
    shore,
A monitory sound that never failed,—
The sunset cannon. While the orb went
    down   325
In the tranquillity of nature, came
That voice, ill requiem! seldom heard by
    me
Without a spirit overcast by dark
Imaginations, sense of woes to come,
Sorrow for human kind, and pain of
    heart.   330

  In France, the men, who, for their
    desperate ends,
Had plucked up mercy by the roots, were
    glad
Of this new enemy. Tyrants, strong
    before
In wicked pleas, were strong as demons
    now;
And thus, on every side beset with foes,
The goaded land waxed mad; the crimes
    of few   336
Spread into madness of the many; blasts
From hell came sanctified like airs from
    heaven.
The sternness of the just, the faith of
    those
Who doubted not that Providence had
    times   340
Of vengeful retribution, theirs who
    throned
The human Understanding paramount
And made of that their God, the hopes
    of men
Who were content to barter short-lived
    pangs
For a paradise of ages, the blind rage 345
Of insolent tempers, the light vanity
Of intermeddlers, steady purposes
Of the suspicious, slips of the indiscreet,
And all the accidents of life were pressed
Into one service, busy with one work. 350
The Senate stood aghast, her prudence
    quenched,
Her wisdom stifled, and her justice scared,
Her frenzy only active to extol
Past outrages, and shape the way for new,
Which no one dared to oppose or mitigate.

Domestic carnage now filled the whole
    year   356
With feast-days; old men from the
    chimney-nook,
The maiden from the bosom of her love,
The mother from the cradle of her babe,
The warrior from the field—all perished,
    all—   360
Friends, enemies, of all parties, ages,
    ranks,
Head after head, and never heads enough
For those that bade them fall. They
    found their joy,
They made it proudly, eager as a child,
(If like desires of innocent little ones 365
May with such heinous appetites be com-
    pared),
Pleased in some open field to exercise
A toy that mimics with revolving wings
The motion of a wind-mill; though the air
Do of itself blow fresh, and make the
    vanes   370
Spin in his eyesight, *that* contents him
    not,
But, with the plaything at arm's length,
    he sets
His front against the blast, and runs
    amain,
That it may whirl the faster.

                Amid the depth
Of those enormities, even thinking minds
Forgot, at seasons, whence they had their
    being;   376
Forgot that such a sound was ever heard
As Liberty upon earth: yet all beneath
Her innocent authority was wrought,
Nor could have been, without her blessèd
    name.   380
The illustrious wife of Roland, in the
    hour
Of her composure, felt that agony,
And gave it vent in her last words. O
    Friend!
It was a lamentable time for man,
Whether a hope had e'er been his or not;
A woeful time for them whose hopes
    survived   386
The shock; most woeful for those few
    who still
Were flattered, and had trust in human
    kind:

They had the deepest feeling of the grief.
Meanwhile the Invaders fared as they
　　deserved :　　　　　　　　　　　390
The Herculean Commonwealth had put
　　forth her arms,
And throttled with an infant godhead's
　　might
The snakes about her cradle ; that was
　　well,
And as it should be ; yet no cure for them
Whose souls were sick with pain of what
　　would be　　　　　　　　　　　395
Hereafter brought in charge against man-
　　kind.
Most melancholy at that time, O Friend !
Were my day-thoughts,—my nights were
　　miserable ;
Through months, through years, long after
　　the last beat
Of those atrocities, the hour of sleep　400
To me came rarely charged with natural
　　gifts,
Such ghastly visions had I of despair
And tyranny, and implements of death ;
And innocent victims sinking under fear,
And momentary hope, and worn-out
　　prayer,　　　　　　　　　　　405
Each in his separate cell, or penned in
　　crowds
For sacrifice, and struggling with forced
　　mirth
And levity in dungeons, where the dust
Was laid with tears.　Then suddenly the
　　scene
Changed, and the unbroken dream en-
　　tangled me　　　　　　　　　　410
In long orations, which I strove to plead
Before unjust tribunals,—with a voice
Labouring, a brain confounded, and a sense,
Death-like, of treacherous desertion, felt
In the last place of refuge—my own soul.

When I began in youth's delightful
　　prime　　　　　　　　　　　　416
To yield myself to Nature, when that
　　strong
And holy passion overcame me first,
Nor day nor night, evening or morn, was
　　free
From its oppression.　But, O Power
　　Supreme !　　　　　　　　　　420

Without Whose care this world would
　　cease to breathe,
Who from the Fountain of Thy grace dost
　　fill
The veins that branch through every
　　frame of life,
Making man what he is, creature divine,
In single or in social eminence,　　425
Above the rest raised infinite ascents
When reason that enables him to be
Is not sequestered—what a change is
　　here !
How different ritual for this after-worship,
What countenance to promote this second
　　love !　　　　　　　　　　　430
The first was service paid to things which
　　lie
Guarded within the bosom of Thy will.
Therefore to serve was high beatitude ;
Tumult was therefore gladness, and the
　　fear
Ennobling, venerable ; sleep secure,　435
And waking thoughts more rich than
　　happiest dreams.

But as the ancient Prophets, borne
　　aloft
In vision, yet constrained by natural laws
With them to take a troubled human
　　heart,
Wanted not consolations, nor a creed　440
Of reconcilement, then when they de-
　　nounced,
On towns and cities, wallowing in the
　　abyss
Of their offences, punishment to come ;
Or saw, like other men, with bodily eyes,
Before them, in some desolated place, 445
The wrath consummate and the threat
　　fulfilled ;
So, with devout humility be it said,
So, did a portion of that spirit fall
On me uplifted from the vantage-ground
Of pity and sorrow to a state of being
That through the time's exceeding fierce-
　　ness saw　　　　　　　　　　451
Glimpses of retribution, terrible,
And in the order of sublime behests :
But, even if that were not, amid the awe
Of unintelligible chastisement,　　455
Not only acquiescences of faith

Survived, but daring sympathies with
    power,
Motions not treacherous or profane, else
    why
Within the folds of no ungentle breast
Their dread vibration to this hour pro-
    longed?   460
Wild blasts of music thus could find their
    way
Into the midst of turbulent events;
So that worst tempests might be listened
    to.
Then was the truth received into my
    heart,
That, under heaviest sorrow earth can
    bring,   465
If from the affliction somewhere do not
    grow
Honour which could not else have been,
    a faith,
An elevation, and a sanctity,
If new strength be not given nor old
    restored,
The blame is ours, not Nature's.   When
    a taunt   470
Was taken up by scoffers in their pride,
Saying, "Behold the harvest that we reap
From popular government and equality,"
I clearly saw that neither these nor aught
Of wild belief engrafted on their names
By false philosophy had caused the woe,
But a terrific reservoir of guilt
And ignorance filled up from age to age,
That could no longer hold its loathsome
    charge,
But burst and spread in deluge through
    the land.   480

    And as the desert hath green spots, the
        sea
Small islands scattered amid stormy
    waves,
So that disastrous period did not want
Bright sprinklings of all human excellence,
To which the silver wands of saints in
    Heaven   485
Might point with rapturous joy.   Yet not
    the less,
For those examples, in no age surpassed,
Of fortitude and energy and love,
And human nature faithful to herself

Under worst trials, was I driven to think
Of the glad times when first I traversed
    France   491
A youthful pilgrim; above all reviewed
That eventide, when under windows bright
With happy faces and with garlands hung,
And through a rainbow-arch that spanned
    the street,   495
Triumphal pomp for liberty confirmed,
I paced, a dear companion at my side,
The town of Arras, whence with promise
    high
Issued, on delegation to sustain
Humanity and right, that Robespierre, 500
He who thereafter, and in how short time!
Wielded the sceptre of the Atheist crew.
When the calamity spread far and wide—
And this same city, that did then appear
To outrun the rest in exultation, groaned
Under the vengeance of her cruel son, 506
As Lear reproached the winds—I could
    almost
Have quarrelled with that blameless
    spectacle
For lingering yet an image in my mind
To mock me under such a strange re-
    verse.   510

    O Friend! few happier moments have
        been mine
Than that which told the downfall of this
    Tribe
So dreaded, so abhorred.   The day de-
    serves
A separate record.   Over the smooth sands
Of Leven's ample estuary lay   515
My journey, and beneath a genial sun,
With distant prospect among gleams of
    sky
And clouds, and intermingling mountain-
    tops,
In one inseparable glory clad,
Creatures of one ethereal substance met
In consistory, like a diadem   521
Or crown of burning seraphs as they sit
In the empyrean.   Underneath that pomp
Celestial, lay unseen the pastoral vales
Among whose happy fields I had grown
    up   525
From childhood.   On the fulgent spec-
    tacle,

That neither passed away nor changed,
I gazed
Enrapt; but brightest things are wont to
draw
Sad opposites out of the inner heart,
As even their pensive influence drew from
mine.   530
How could it otherwise? for not in vain
That very morning had I turned aside
To seek the ground where, 'mid a throng
of graves,
An honoured teacher of my youth was
laid,
And on the stone were graven by his
desire   535
Lines from the churchyard elegy of Gray.
This faithful guide, speaking from his
death-bed,
Added no farewell to his parting counsel,
But said to me, "My head will soon lie
low;"
And when I saw the turf that covered
him,   540
After the lapse of full eight years, those
words,
With sound of voice and countenance of
the Man,
Came back upon me, so that some few
tears
Fell from me in my own despite. But
now
I thought, still traversing that widespread
plain,   545
With tender pleasure of the verses graven
Upon his tombstone, whispering to my-
self:
He loved the Poets, and, if now alive,
Would have loved me, as one not desti-
tute
Of promise, nor belying the kind hope
That he had formed, when I, at his com-
mand,   551
Began to spin, with toil, my earliest
songs.

As I advanced, all that I saw or felt
Was gentleness and peace. Upon a small
And rocky island near, a fragment stood
(Itself like a sea rock) the low remains 556
(With shells encrusted, dark with briny
weeds)

Of a dilapidated structure, once
A Romish chapel, where the vested priest
Said matins at the hour that suited those
Who crossed the sands with ebb of
morning tide.   561
Not far from that still ruin all the
plain
Lay spotted with a variegated crowd
Of vehicles and travellers, horse and foot,
Wading beneath the conduct of their
guide   565
In loose procession through the shallow
stream
Of inland waters; the great sea mean-
while
Heaved at safe distance, far retired. I
paused,
Longing for skill to paint a scene so
bright
And cheerful, but the foremost of the
band   570
As he approached, no salutation given
In the familiar language of the day,
Cried, "Robespierre is dead!"—nor was
a doubt,
After strict question, left within my
mind
That he and his supporters all were
fallen.   575

Great was my transport, deep my
gratitude
To everlasting Justice, by this fiat
Made manifest. "Come now, ye golden
times,"
Said I forth-pouring on those open sands
A hymn of triumph: "as the morning
comes   580
From out the bosom of the night, come
ye:
Thus far our trust is verified; behold!
They who with clumsy desperation
brought
A river of Blood, and preached that
nothing else
Could cleanse the Augean stable, by the
might   585
Of their own helper have been swept
away;
Their madness stands declared and
visible;

Elsewhere will safety now be sought, and
    earth
March firmly towards righteousness and
    peace."—
Then schemes I framed more calmly,
    when and how   590
The madding factions might be tran-
    quillised,
And how through hardships manifold and
    long
The glorious renovation would proceed.
Thus interrupted by uneasy bursts
Of exultation, I pursued my way   595

Along that very shore which I had
    skimmed
In former days, when—spurring from the
    Vale
Of Nightshade, and St. Mary's mouldering
    fane,
And the stone abbot, after circuit made
In wantonness of heart, a joyous band
Of schoolboys hastening to their distant
    home   601
Along the margin of the moonlight sea—
We beat with thundering hoofs the level
    sand.

BOOK ELEVENTH.

FRANCE.—(Concluded).

From that time forth, Authority in
    France
Put on a milder face; Terror had ceased,
Yet everything was wanting that might
    give
Courage to them who looked for good by
    light
Of rational Experience, for the shoots   5
And hopeful blossoms of a second spring:
Yet, in me, confidence was unimpaired;
The Senate's language, and the public acts
And measures of the Government, though
    both
Weak, and of heartless omen, had not
    power   10
To daunt me; in the People was my
    trust,
And in the virtues which mine eyes had
    seen.
I knew that wound external could not
    take
Life from the young Republic; that new
    foes
Would only follow, in the path of shame,
Their brethren, and her triumphs be in
    the end   16
Great, universal, irresistible.
This intuition led me to confound
One victory with another, higher far,—
Triumphs of unambitious peace at home,

And noiseless fortitude. Beholding still
Resistance strong as heretofore, I thought
That what was in degree the same was
    likewise
The same in quality,—that, as the worse
Of the two spirits then at strife remained
Untired, the better, surely, would pre-
    serve   26
The heart that first had roused him.
    Youth maintains,
In all conditions of society,
Communion more direct and intimate
With Nature,—hence, ofttimes, with
    reason too—   30
Than age or manhood, even. To Nature,
    then,
Power had reverted: habit, custom, law,
Had left an interregnum's open space
For *her* to move about in, uncontrolled.
Hence could I see how Babel-like their
    task,   35
Who, by the recent deluge stupefied,
With their whole souls went culling from
    the day
Its petty promises, to build a tower
For their own safety; laughed with my
    compeers
At gravest heads, by enmity to France
Distempered, till they found, in every
    blast   41

Forced from the street-disturbing news-
man's horn,
For her great cause record or prophecy
Of utter ruin.   How might we believe
That wisdom could, in any shape, come
     near   45
Men clinging to delusions so insane?
And thus, experience proving that no few
Of our opinions had been just, we took
Like credit to ourselves where less was due,
And thought that other notions were as
     sound,   50
Yea, could not but be right, because we
     saw
That foolish men opposed them.
                To a strain
More animated I might here give way,
And tell, since juvenile errors are my theme,
What in those days through Britain was
     performed   55
To turn *all* judgments out of their right
     course ;
But this is passion over-near ourselves,
Reality too close and too intense,
And intermixed with something, in my
     mind,
Of scorn and condemnation personal,   60
That would profane the sanctity of verse.
Our Shepherds, this say merely, at that
     time
Acted, or seemed at least to act, like men
Thirsting to make the guardian crook of
     law
A tool of murder; they who ruled the
     State,—   65
Though with such awful proof before
     their eyes
That he, who would sow death, reaps
     death, or worse,
And can reap nothing better,—child-like
     longed
To imitate, not wise enough to avoid ;
Or left (by mere timidity betrayed)   70
The plain straight road, for one no better
     chosen
Than if their wish had been to undermine
Justice, and make an end of Liberty.

   But from these bitter truths I must
     return
To my own history. It hath been told

That I was led to take an eager part   76
In arguments of civil polity,
Abruptly, and indeed before my time :
I had approached, like other youths, the
     shield
Of human nature from the golden side,
And would have fought, even to the
     death, to attest   81
The quality of the metal which I saw.
What there is best in individual man,
Of wise in passion, and sublime in power,
Benevolent in small societies,   85
And great in large ones, I had oft re-
     volved,
Felt deeply, but not thoroughly under-
     stood
By reason : nay, far from it ; they were yet,
As cause was given me afterwards to learn,
Not proof against the injuries of the
     day ;   90
Lodged only at the sanctuary's door,
Not safe within its bosom. Thus pre-
     pared,
And with such general insight into evil,
And of the bounds which sever it from
     good,
As books and common intercourse with
     life   95
Must needs have given to the inex-
     perienced mind,
When the world travels in a beaten road,
Guide faithful as is needed—I began
To meditate with ardour on the rule
And management of nations ; what it is
And ought to be ; and strove to learn
     how far   101
Their power or weakness, wealth or
     poverty,
Their happiness or misery, depends
Upon their laws, and fashion of the State.

O pleasant exercise of hope and joy [1] !
For mighty were the auxiliars which then
     stood   106
Upon our side, us who were strong in
     love !
Bliss was it in that dawn to be alive,
But to be young was very Heaven ! O
     times,

---

[1] See page 208.—ED.

In which the meagre, stale, forbidding
     ways   110
Of custom, law, and statute, took at once
The attraction of a country in romance!
When Reason seemed the most to assert
     her rights
When most intent on making of herself
A prime enchantress—to assist the work,
Which then was going forward in her
     name!   116
Not favoured spots alone, but the whole
     Earth,
The beauty wore of promise—that which
     sets
(As at some moments might not be un-
     felt
Among the bowers of Paradise itself) 120
The budding rose above the rose full
     blown.
What temper at the prospect did not
     wake
To happiness unthought of? The inert
Were roused, and lively natures rapt
     away!
They who had fed their childhood upon
     dreams,   125
The play-fellows of fancy, who had made
All powers of swiftness, subtilty, and
     strength
Their ministers,—who in lordly wise had
     stirred
Among the grandest objects of the sense,
And dealt with whatsoever they found
     there   130
As if they had within some lurking right
To wield it;—they, too, who of gentle
     mood
Had watched all gentle motions, and to
     these
Had fitted their own thoughts, schemers
     more mild,
And in the region of their peaceful
     selves;—   135
Now was it that *both* found, the meek
     and lofty
Did both find, helpers to their hearts'
     desire,
And stuff at hand, plastic as they could
     wish,—
Were called upon to exercise their skill,
Not in Utopia,—subterranean fields,—

Or some secreted island, Heaven knows
     where!   141
But in the very world, which is the world
Of all of us,—the place where, in the end,
We find our happiness, or not at all!

Why should I not confess that Earth
     was then   145
To me, what an inheritance, new-fallen,
Seems, when the first time visited, to one
Who thither comes to find in it his home?
He walks about and looks upon the spot
With cordial transport, moulds it and
     remoulds,   150
And is half pleased with things that are
     amiss,
'Twill be such joy to see them disappear.

An active partisan, I thus convoked
From every object pleasant circumstance
To suit my ends; I moved among man-
     kind   155
With genial feelings still predominant;
When erring, erring on the better part,
And in the kinder spirit; placable,
Indulgent, as not uninformed that men
See as they have been taught—Antiquity
Gives rights to error; and aware, no less,
That throwing off oppression must be
     work
As well of License as of Liberty;
And above all—for this was more than
     all—   164
Not caring if the wind did now and then
Blow keen upon an eminence that gave
Prospect so large into futurity;
In brief, a child of Nature, as at first,
Diffusing only those affections wider
That from the cradle had grown up with
     me,   170
And losing, in no other way than light
Is lost in light, the weak in the more
     strong.

In the main outline, such it might be
     said
Was my condition, till with open war
Britain opposed the liberties of France.
This threw me first out of the pale of
     love;   176
Soured and corrupted, upwards to the
     source,

My sentiments; was not, as hitherto,
A swallowing up of lesser things in great,
But change of them into their contraries;
And thus a way was opened for mis-
   takes   181
And false conclusions, in degree as gross,
In kind more dangerous. What had been
   a pride,
Was now a shame; my likings and my
   loves
Ran in new channels, leaving old ones
   dry;   185
And hence a blow that, in maturer age,
Would but have touched the judgment,
   struck more deep
Into sensations near the heart: mean-
   time,
As from the first, wild theories were
   afloat,
To whose pretensions, sedulously urged,
I had but lent a careless ear, assured   191
That time was ready to set all things
   right,
And that the multitude, so long op-
   pressed,
Would be oppressed no more.
              But when events
Brought less encouragement, and unto
   these   195
The immediate proof of principles no
   more
Could be entrusted, while the events
   themselves,
Worn out in greatness, stripped of
   novelty,
Less occupied the mind, and sentiments
Could through my understanding's natural
   growth   200
No longer keep their ground, by faith
   maintained
Of inward consciousness, and hope that
   laid
Her hand upon her object—evidence
Safer, of universal application, such
As could not be impeached, was sought
   elsewhere.   205

But now, become oppressors in their
   turn,
Frenchmen had changed a war of self-
   defence

For one of conquest, losing sight of all
Which they had struggled for: up mounted
   now,   209
Openly in the eye of earth and heaven,
The scale of liberty. I read her doom,
With anger vexed, with disappointment
   sore,
But not dismayed, nor taking to the
   shame
Of a false prophet. While resentment
   rose
Striving to hide, what nought could heal,
   the wounds   215
Of mortified presumption, I adhered
More firmly to old tenets, and, to prove
Their temper, strained them more; and
   thus, in heat
Of contest, did opinions every day
Grow into consequence, till round my
   mind   220
They clung, as if they were its life, nay
   more,
The very being of the immortal soul.

This was the time, when, all things
   tending fast
To depravation, speculative schemes—
That promised to abstract the hopes of
   Man   225
Out of his feelings, to be fixed thence-
   forth
For ever in a purer element—
Found ready welcome. Tempting region
   that
For Zeal to enter and refresh herself,
Where passions had the privilege to work,
And never hear the sound of their own
   names.   231
But, speaking more in charity, the dream
Flattered the young, pleased with ex-
   tremes, nor least
With that which makes our Reason's
   naked self
The object of its fervour. What delight!
How glorious! in self-knowledge and self-
   rule,   236
To look through all the frailties of the
   world,
And, with a resolute mastery shaking off
Infirmities of nature, time, and place,
Build social upon personal Liberty,   240

Which, to the blind restraints of general
    laws
Superior, magisterially adopts
One guide, the light of circumstances,
    flashed
Upon an independent intellect.
Thus expectation rose again; thus hope,
From her first ground expelled, grew
    proud once more.   246
Oft, as my thoughts were turned to hu-
    man kind,
I scorned indifference; but, inflamed with
    thirst
Of a secure intelligence, and sick   249
Of other longing, I pursued what seemed
A more exalted nature; wished that Man
Should start out of his earthy, worm-like
    state,
And spread abroad the wings of Liberty,
Lord of himself, in undisturbed delight—
A noble aspiration! *yet* I feel   255
(Sustained by worthier as by wiser
    thoughts)
The aspiration, nor shall ever cease
To feel it;—but return we to our course.

Enough, 'tis true—could such a plea
    excuse
Those aberrations—had the clamorous
    friends   260
Of ancient Institutions said and done
To bring disgrace upon their very names;
Disgrace, of which, custom and written
    law,
And sundry moral sentiments as props
Or emanations of those institutes,   265
Too justly bore a part. A veil had been
Uplifted; why deceive ourselves? in sooth,
'Twas even so; and sorrow for the man
Who either had not eyes wherewith to
    see,
Or, seeing, had forgotten! A strong shock
Was given to old opinions; all men's
    minds   271
Had felt its power, and mine was both let
    loose,
Let loose and goaded. After what hath
    been
Already said of patriotic love,
Suffice it here to add, that, somewhat
    stern   275

In temperament, withal a happy man,
And therefore bold to look on painful
    things,
Free likewise of the world, and thence
    more bold,
I summoned my best skill, and toiled,
    intent
To anatomise the frame of social life;
Yea, the whole body of society   281
Searched to its heart. Share with me,
    Friend! the wish
That some dramatic tale, endued with
    shapes
Livelier, and flinging out less guarded
    words
Than suit the work we fashion, might set
    forth   285
What then I learned, or think I learned,
    of truth,
And the errors into which I fell, betrayed
By present objects, and by reasonings
    false
From their beginnings, inasmuch as drawn
Out of a heart that had been turned aside
From Nature's way by outward accidents,
And which was thus confounded, more
    and more
Misguided, and misguiding. So I fared,
Dragging all precepts, judgments, maxims,
    creeds,   294
Like culprits to the bar; calling the mind,
Suspiciously, to establish in plain day
Her titles and her honours; now believ-
    ing,
Now disbelieving; endlessly perplexed
With impulse, motive, right and wrong,
    the ground
Of obligation, what the rule and whence
The sanction; till, demanding formal
    proof,   301
And seeking it in everything, I lost
All feeling of conviction, and, in fine,
Sick, wearied out with contrarieties,   304
Yielded up moral questions in despair.

This was the crisis of that strong disease,
This the soul's last and lowest ebb; I
    drooped,
Deeming our blessèd reason of least use
Where wanted most: "The lordly at-
    tributes   309

Of will and choice," I bitterly exclaimed,
"What are they but a mockery of a Being
Who hath in no concerns of his a test
Of good and evil; knows not what to fear
Or hope for, what to covet or to shun;
And who, if those could be discerned,
     would yet   315
Be little profited, would see, and ask
Where is the obligation to enforce?
And, to acknowledged law rebellious, still,
As selfish passion urged, would act amiss;
The dupe of folly, or the slave of crime."

Depressed, bewildered thus, I did not
     walk   321
With scoffers, seeking light and gay re-
     venge
From indiscriminate laughter, nor sate
     down
In reconcilement with an utter waste
Of intellect; such sloth I could not brook,
(Too well I loved, in that my spring of
     life,   326
Pains-taking thoughts, and truth, their
     dear reward)
But turned to abstract science, and there
     sought
Work for the reasoning faculty enthroned
Where the disturbances of space and
     time—   330
Whether in matter's various properties
Inherent, or from human will and power
Derived—find no admission. Then it was—
Thanks to the bounteous Giver of all
     good !—
That the belovèd Sister in whose sight
Those days were passed, now speaking in
     a voice   336
Of sudden admonition—like a brook
That did but *cross* a lonely road, and
     now
Is seen, heard, felt, and caught at every
     turn,
Companion never lost through many a
     league—   340
Maintained for me a saving intercourse
With my true self; for, though bedimmed
     and changed
Much, as it seemed, I was no further
     changed
Than as a clouded and a waning moon:

She whispered still that brightness would
     return,   345
She, in the midst of all, preserved me still
A Poet, made me seek beneath that name,
And that alone, my office upon earth;
And, lastly, as hereafter will be shown,
If willing audience fail not, Nature's self,
By all varieties of human love   351
Assisted, led me back through opening
     day
To those sweet counsels between head
     and heart
Whence grew that genuine knowledge,
     fraught with peace,
Which, through the later sinkings of this
     cause,   355
Hath still upheld me, and upholds me now
In the catastrophe (for so they dream,
And nothing less), when, finally to close
And seal up all the gains of France, a
     Pope
Is summoned in to crown an Emperor—
This last opprobrium, when we see a
     people,   361
That once looked up in faith, as if to
     Heaven
For manna, take a lesson from the dog
Returning to his vomit; when the sun
That rose in splendour, was alive, and
     moved   365
In exultation with a living pomp
Of clouds—his glory's natural retinue—
Hath dropped all functions by the gods
     bestowed,
And, turned into a gewgaw, a machine,
Sets like an Opera phantom.
           Thus, O Friend !
Through times of honour and through
     times of shame   371
Descending, have I faithfully retraced
The perturbations of a youthful mind
Under a long-lived storm of great events—
A story destined for thy ear, who now,
Among the fallen of nations, dost abide
Where Etna, over hill and valley, casts
His shadow stretching towards Syracuse,
The city of Timoleon ! Righteous Heaven !
How are the mighty prostrated ! They
     first,   380
They first of all that breathe should have
     awaked

When the great voice was heard from out
   the tombs
Of ancient heroes. If I suffered grief
For ill-requited France, by many deemed
A trifler only in her proudest day;   385
Have been distressed to think of what
   she once
Promised, now is; a far more sober cause
Thine eyes must see of sorrow in a land,
To the reanimating influence lost
Of memory, to virtue lost and hope,   390
Though with the wreck of loftier years
   bestrewn.

But indignation works where hope is
   not,
And thou, O Friend! wilt be refreshed.
   There is
One great society alone on earth:
The noble Living and the noble Dead.   395

Thine be such converse strong and sa-
   native,
A ladder for thy spirit to reascend
To health and joy and pure contented-
   ness;
To me the grief confined, that thou art
   gone
From this last spot of earth, where Free-
   dom now   400
Stands single in her only sanctuary;
A lonely wanderer art gone, by pain
Compelled and sickness, at this latter day,
This sorrowful reverse for all mankind.
I feel for thee, must utter what I feel: 405
The sympathies erewhile in part dis-
   charged,
Gather afresh, and will have vent again:
My own delights do scarcely seem to me
My own delights; the lordly Alps them-
   selves,
Those rosy peaks, from which the Morn-
   ing looks   410
Abroad on many nations, are no more
For me that image of pure gladsomeness
Which they were wont to be. Through
   kindred scenes,
For purpose, at a time, how different!
Thou tak'st thy way, carrying the heart
   and soul   415
That Nature gives to Poets, now by
   thought

Matured, and in the summer of their
   strength.
Oh! wrap him in your shades, ye giant
   woods,
On Etna's side; and thou, O flowery field
Of Enna! is there not some nook of thine,
From the first playtime of the infant
   world   421
Kept sacred to restorative delight,
When from afar invoked by anxious love?

Child of the mountains, among shep-
   herds reared,
Ere yet familiar with the classic page, 425
I learnt to dream of Sicily; and lo,
The gloom, that, but a moment past, was
   deepened
At thy command, at her command gives
   way;
A pleasant promise, wafted from her
   shores,
Comes o'er my heart: in fancy I behold
Her seas yet smiling, her once happy
   vales;   431
Nor can my tongue give utterance to a name
Of note belonging to that honoured isle,
Philosopher or Bard, Empedocles,
Or Archimedes, pure abstracted soul! 435
That doth not yield a solace to my grief:
And, O Theocritus[1], so far have some
Prevailed among the powers of heaven
   and earth,
By their endowments, good or great, that
   they
Have had, as thou reportest, miracles
Wrought for them in old time: yea, not
   unmoved,   441
When thinking on my own beloved friend,
I hear thee tell how bees with honey fed
Divine Comates, by his impious lord
Within a chest imprisoned; how they
   came   445
Laden from blooming grove or flowery field,
And fed him there, alive, month after
   month,
Because the goatherd, blessed man! had
   lips
Wet with the Muses' nectar.

                  Thus I soothe

---

[1] *Theocrit. Idyll.* vii. 78.—ED.

The pensive moments by this calm fire-
side,   450
And find a thousand bounteous images
To cheer the thoughts of those I love, and
mine.
Our prayers have been accepted; thou
wilt stand
On Etna's summit, above earth and sea,
Triumphant, winning from the invaded
heavens   455
Thoughts without bound, magnificent de-
signs,
Worthy of poets who attuned their harps
In wood or echoing cave, for discipline
Of heroes; or, in reverence to the gods,
'Mid temples, served by sapient priests,
and choirs   460
Of virgins crowned with roses. Not in
vain
Those temples, where they in their ruins
yet
Survive for inspiration, shall attract
Thy solitary steps: and on the brink 464
Thou wilt recline of pastoral Arethuse;
Or, if that fountain be in truth no more,
Then, near some other spring—which by
the name
Thou gratulatest, willingly deceived—
I see thee linger a glad votary,   469
And not a captive pining for his home.

BOOK TWELFTH.

IMAGINATION AND TASTE, HOW IMPAIRED AND RESTORED.

LONG time have human ignorance and
guilt
Detained us, on what spectacles of woe
Compelled to look, and inwardly op-
pressed
With sorrow, disappointment, vexing
thoughts,
Confusion of the judgment, zeal decayed,
And, lastly, utter loss of hope itself   6
And things to hope for! Not with these
began
Our song, and not with these our song
must end.—
Ye motions of delight, that haunt the
sides
Of the green hills; ye breezes and soft
airs,   10
Whose subtle intercourse with breathing
flowers,
Feelingly watched, might teach Man's
haughty race
How without injury to take, to give
Without offence; ye who, as if to show
The wondrous influence of power gently
used,   15
Bend the complying heads of lordly pines,
And, with a touch, shift the stupendous
clouds
Through the whole compass of the sky;
ye brooks,
Muttering along the stones, a busy noise
By day, a quiet sound in silent night; 20
Ye waves, that out of the great deep steal
forth
In a calm hour to kiss the pebbly shore,
Not mute, and then retire, fearing no
storm;
And you, ye groves, whose ministry it is
To interpose the covert of your shades, 25
Even as a sleep, between the heart of man
And outward troubles, between man him-
self,
Not seldom, and his own uneasy heart:
Oh! that I had a music and a voice
Harmonious as your own, that I might
tell   30
What ye have done for me. The morning
shines,
Nor heedeth Man's perverseness; Spring
returns,—

I saw the Spring return, and could rejoice,
In common with the children of her love,
Piping on boughs, or sporting on fresh
    fields,   35
Or boldly seeking pleasure nearer heaven
On wings that navigate cerulean skies.
So neither were complacency, nor peace,
Nor tender yearnings, wanting for my
    good
Through these distracted times; in Na-
    ture still   40
Glorying, I found a counterpoise in her,
Which, when the spirit of evil reached
    its height,
Maintained for me a secret happiness.

This narrative, my Friend! hath chiefly
    told
Of intellectual power, fostering love,   45
Dispensing truth, and, over men and
    things,
Where reason yet might hesitate, diffusing
Prophetic sympathies of genial faith :
So was I favoured—such my happy lot—
Until that natural graciousness of mind
Gave way to overpressure from the times
And their disastrous issues. What availed,
When spells forbade the voyager to land,
That fragrant notice of a pleasant shore
Wafted, at intervals, from many a bower
Of blissful gratitude and fearless love? 56
Dare I avow that wish was mine to see,
And hope that future times *would* surely
    see,
The man to come, parted, as by a gulph,
From him who had been ; that I could no
    more   60
Trust the elevation which had made me
    one
With the great family that still survives
To illuminate the abyss of ages past,
Sage, warrior, patriot, hero; for it seemed
That their best virtues were not free from
    taint   65
Of something false and weak, that could
    not stand
The open eye of Reason. Then I said,
"Go to the Poets, they will speak to thee
More perfectly of purer creatures ;—yet
If reason be nobility in man,   70
Can aught be more ignoble than the man

Whom they delight in, blinded as he is
By prejudice, the miserable slave
Of low ambition or distempered love?"

In such strange passion, if I may once
    more   75
Review the past, I warred against my-
    self—
A bigot to a new idolatry—
Like a cowled monk who hath forsworn
    the world,
Zealously laboured to cut off my heart
From all the sources of her former
    strength ;   80
And as, by simple waving of a wand,
The wizard instantaneously dissolves
Palace or grove, even so could I unsoul
As readily by syllogistic words
Those mysteries of being which have
    made,   85
And shall continue evermore to make,
Of the whole human race one brother-
    hood.

What wonder, then, if, to a mind so far
Perverted, even the visible Universe
Fell under the dominion of a taste   90
Less spiritual, with microscopic view
Was scanned, as I had scanned the moral
    world?

O Soul of Nature! excellent and fair!
That didst rejoice with me, with whom I,
    too,
Rejoiced through early youth, before the
    winds   95
And roaring waters, and in lights and
    shades
That marched and countermarched about
    the hills
In glorious apparition, Powers on whom
I daily waited, now all eye and now   99
All ear ; but never long without the heart
Employed, and man's unfolding intellect:
O Soul of Nature ! that, by laws divine
Sustained and governed, still dost over-
    flow
With an impassioned life, what feeble
    ones
Walk on this earth ! how feeble have I
    been   105

When thou wert in thy strength ! Nor
  this through stroke
Of human suffering, such as justifies
Remissness and inaptitude of mind,
But through presumption; even in plea-
  sure pleased   109
Unworthily, disliking here, and there
Liking; by rules of mimic art transferred
To things above all art; but more,—for
  this,
Although a strong infection of the age,
Was never much my habit—giving way
To a comparison of scene with scene, 115
Bent overmuch on superficial things,
Pampering myself with meagre novelties
Of colour and proportion; to the moods
Of time and season, to the moral power,
The affections and the spirit of the place,
Insensible. Nor only did the love   121
Of sitting thus in judgment interrupt
My deeper feelings, but another cause,
More subtle and less easily explained,
That almost seems inherent in the crea-
  ture,   125
A twofold frame of body and of mind.
I speak in recollection of a time
When the bodily eye, in every stage of life
The most despotic of our senses, gained
Such strength in me as often hold my
  mind   130
In absolute dominion. Gladly here,
Entering upon abstruser argument,
Could I endeavour to unfold the means
Which Nature studiously employs to
  thwart
This tyranny, summons all the senses
  each   135
To counteract the other, and themselves,
And makes them all, and the objects with
  which all
Are conversant, subservient in their turn
To the great ends of Liberty and Power.
But leave we this: enough that my
  delights   140
(Such as they were) were sought insati-
  ably.
Vivid the transport, vivid though not
  profound;
I roamed from hill to hill, from rock to
  rock,
Still craving combinations of new forms,

New pleasure, wider empire for the sight,
Proud of her own endowments, and re-
  joiced   146
To lay the inner faculties asleep.
Amid the turns and counterturns, the
  strife
And various trials of our complex being,
As we grow up, such thraldom of that
  sense   150
Seems hard to shun. And yet I knew a
  maid,
A young enthusiast, who escaped these
  bonds;
Her eye was not the mistress of her
  heart;
Far less did rules prescribed by passive
  taste,
Or barren intermeddling subtleties, 155
Perplex her mind; but, wise as women
  are
When genial circumstance hath favoured
  them,
She welcomed what was given, and craved
  no more;
Whate'er the scene presented to her view
That was the best, to that she was attuned
By her benign simplicity of life,   161
And through a perfect happiness of soul,
Whose variegated feelings were in this
Sisters, that they were each some new
  delight.
Birds in the bower, and lambs in the
  green field,   165
Could they have known her, would have
  loved; methought
Her very presence such a sweetness
  breathed,
That flowers, and trees, and even the
  silent hills,
And everything she looked on, should
  have had
An intimation how she bore herself   170
Towards them and to all creatures. God
  delights
In such a being; for, her common
  thoughts
Are piety, her life is gratitude.

  Even like this maid, before I was called
    forth   174
From the retirement of my native hills,

I loved whate'er I saw: nor lightly loved,
But most intensely; never dreamt of
  aught
More grand, more fair, more exquisitely
  framed
Than those few nooks to which my happy
  feet
Were limited. I had not at that time
Lived long enough, nor in the least sur-
  vived   181
The first diviner influence of this world,
As it appears to unaccustomed eyes.
Worshipping then among the depth of
  things,
As piety ordained; could I submit   185
To measured admiration, or to aught
That should preclude humility and love?
I felt, observed, and pondered; did not
  judge,
Yea, never thought of judging; with the
  gift
Of all this glory filled and satisfied. 190
And afterwards, when through the gor-
  geous Alps
Roaming, I carried with me the same
  heart:
In truth, the degradation—howsoe'er
Induced, effect, in whatsoe'er degree,
Of custom that prepares a partial scale
In which the little oft outweighs the
  great;   196
Or any other cause that hath been
  named;
Or lastly, aggravated by the times
And their impassioned sounds, which
  well might make   199
The milder minstrelsies of rural scenes
Inaudible—was transient; I had known
Too forcibly, too early in my life,
Visitings of imaginative power
For this to last: I shook the habit off
Entirely and for ever, and again   205
In Nature's presence stood, as now I
  stand,
A sensitive being, a *creative* soul.

There are in our existence spots of
  time,
That with distinct pre-eminence retain
A renovating virtue, whence, depressed
By false opinion and contentious thought,

Or aught of heavier or more deadly
  weight,
In trivial occupations, and the round
Of ordinary intercourse, our minds   214
Are nourished and invisibly repaired;
A virtue, by which pleasure is enhanced,
That penetrates, enables us to mount,
When high, more high, and lifts us up
  when fallen.
This efficacious spirit chiefly lurks
Among those passages of life that give
Profoundest knowledge to what point,
  and how,   221
The mind is lord and master—outward
  sense
The obedient servant of her will. Such
  moments
Are scattered everywhere, taking their
  date
From our first childhood. I remember
  well,   225
That once, while yet my inexperienced
  hand
Could scarcely hold a bridle, with proud
  hopes
I mounted, and we journeyed towards
  the hills:
An ancient servant of my father's house
Was with me, my encourager and guide:
We had not travelled long, ere some
  mischance   231
Disjoined me from my comrade; and,
  through fear
Dismounting, down the rough and stony
  moor
I led my horse, and, stumbling on, at
  length
Came to a bottom, where in former times
A murderer had been hung in iron chains.
The gibbet-mast had mouldered down,
  the bones   237
And iron case were gone; but on the
  turf,
Hard by, soon after that fell deed was
  wrought,
Some unknown hand had carved the
  murderer's name.   240
The monumental letters were inscribed
In times long past; but still, from year
  to year,
By superstition of the neighbourhood,

The grass is cleared away, and to this
   hour
The characters are fresh and visible: 245
A casual glance had shown them, and I
   fled,
Faltering and faint, and ignorant of the
   road:
Then, reascending the bare common, saw
A naked pool that lay beneath the hills,
The beacon on the summit, and, more
   near,   250
A girl, who bore a pitcher on her head,
And seemed with difficult steps to force
   her way
Against the blowing wind. It was, in
   truth,
An ordinary sight; but I should need
Colours and words that are unknown to
   man,   255
To paint the visionary dreariness
Which, while I looked all round for my
   lost guide,
Invested moorland waste, and naked pool,
The beacon crowning the lone eminence,
The female and her garments vexed and
   tossed   260
By the strong wind. When, in the blessèd
   hours
Of early love, the loved one at my side,
I roamed, in daily presence of this scene,
Upon the naked pool and dreary crags,
And on the melancholy beacon, fell   265
A spirit of pleasure and youth's golden
   gleam;
And think ye not with radiance more
   sublime
For these remembrances, and for the
   power
They had left behind? So feeling comes
   in aid
Of feeling, and diversity of strength   270
Attends us, if but once we have been
   strong.
Oh! mystery of man, from what a depth
Proceed thy honours. I am lost, but see
In simple childhood something of the
   base
On which thy greatness stands; but this
   I feel,   275
That from thyself it comes, that thou
   must give,

Else never canst receive. The days gone
   by
Return upon me almost from the dawn
Of life: the hiding-places of man's power
Open; I would approach them, but they
   close.   280
I see by glimpses now; when age comes
   on,
May scarcely see at all; and I would
   give,
While yet we may, as far as words can
   give,
Substance and life to what I feel, enshrin-
   ing,
Such is my hope, the spirit of the Past
For future restoration.—Yet another 286
Of these memorials:—
               One Christmas-time,
On the glad eve of its dear holidays,
Feverish, and tired, and restless, I went
   forth
Into the fields, impatient for the sight
Of those led palfreys that should bear us
   home;   291
My brothers and myself. There rose a
   crag,
That, from the meeting-point of two
   highways
Ascending, overlooked them both, far
   stretched;
Thither, uncertain on which road to fix
My expectation, thither I repaired,   296
Scout-like, and gained the summit; 'twas
   a day
Tempestuous, dark, and wild, and on the
   grass
I sate half-sheltered by a naked wall;
Upon my right hand couched a single
   sheep,   300
Upon my left a blasted hawthorn stood;
With those companions at my side, I
   watched,
Straining my eyes intensely, as the mist
Gave intermitting prospect of the copse
And plain beneath. Ere we to school
   returned,—   305
That dreary time,—ere we had been ten
   days
Sojourners in my father's house, he died,
And I and my three brothers, orphans
   then,

Followed his body to the grave. The event,
With all the sorrow that it brought, appeared   310
A chastisement; and when I called to mind
That day so lately past, when from the crag
I looked in such anxiety of hope;
With trite reflections of morality,   314
Yet in the deepest passion, I bowed low
To God, Who thus corrected my desires;
And, afterwards, the wind and sleety rain,
And all the business of the elements,
The single sheep, and the one blasted tree,
And the bleak music from that old stone wall,   320
The noise of wood and water, and the mist
That on the line of each of those two roads

Advanced in such indisputable shapes;
All these were kindred spectacles and sounds
To which I oft repaired, and thence would drink,   325
As at a fountain; and on winter nights,
Down to this very time, when storm and rain
Beat on my roof, or, haply, at noon-day,
While in a grove I walk, whose lofty trees,
Laden with summer's thickest foliage, rock   330
In a strong wind, some working of the spirit,
Some inward agitations thence are brought,
Whate'er their office, whether to beguile
Thoughts over busy in the course they took,
Or animate an hour of vacant ease.   335

BOOK THIRTEENTH.

IMAGINATION AND TASTE, HOW IMPAIRED AND RESTORED.—(Concluded).

From Nature doth emotion come, and
    moods
Of calmness equally are Nature's gift:
This is her glory; these two attributes
Are sister horns that constitute her
    strength.
Hence Genius, born to thrive by inter-
    change   5
Of peace and excitation, finds in her
His best and purest friend; from her
    receives
That energy by which he seeks the truth,
From her that happy stillness of the
    mind
Which fits him to receive it when un-
    sought.   10

Such benefit the humblest intellects
Partake of, each in their degree; 'tis mine
To speak, what I myself have known and
    felt;
Smooth task! for words find easy way,
    inspired
By gratitude, and confidence in truth. 15
Long time in search of knowledge did I
    range
The field of human life, in heart and
    mind
Benighted; but, the dawn beginning
    now
To re-appear, 'twas proved that not in
    vain
I had been taught to reverence a Power
That is the visible quality and shape 21
And image of right reason; that matures
Her processes by steadfast laws; gives
    birth
To no impatient or fallacious hopes,
No heat of passion or excessive zeal, 25
No vain conceits; provokes to no quick
    turns

Of self-applauding intellect; but trains
To meekness, and exalts by humble faith;
Holds up before the mind intoxicate 29
With present objects, and the busy dance
Of things that pass away, a temperate show
Of objects that endure; and by this course
Disposes her, when over-fondly set
On throwing off incumbrances, to seek
In man, and in the frame of social life, 35
Whate'er there is desirable and good
Of kindred permanence, unchanged in
    form
And function, or, through strict vicissi-
    tude
Of life and death, revolving. Above all
Were re-established now those watchful
    thoughts   40
Which, seeing little worthy or sublime
In what the Historian's pen so much de-
    lights
To blazon—power and energy detached
From moral purpose—early tutored me
To look with feelings of fraternal love 45
Upon the unassuming things that hold
A silent station in this beauteous world.

Thus moderated, thus composed, I found
Once more in Man an object of delight,
Of pure imagination, and of love;   50
And, as the horizon of my mind enlarged,
Again I took the intellectual eye
For my instructor, studious more to see
Great truths, than touch and handle
    little ones.
Knowledge was given accordingly; my
    trust   55
Became more firm in feelings that had
    stood
The test of such a trial; clearer far
My sense of excellence—of right and
    wrong:
The promise of the present time retired

Into its true proportion; sanguine schemes,
Ambitious projects, pleased me less; I
 sought   61
For present good in life's familiar face,
And built thereon my hopes of good to
 come.

With settling judgments now of what
 would last
And what would disappear; prepared to
 find   65
Presumption, folly, madness, in the men
Who thrust themselves upon the passive
 world
As Rulers of the world; to see in these,
Even when the public welfare is their aim,
Plans without thought, or built on theo-
 ries   70
Vague and unsound; and having brought
 the books
Of modern statists to their proper test,
Life, human life, with all its sacred claims
Of sex and age, and heaven-descended
 rights,
Mortal, or those beyond the reach of
 death;   75
And having thus discerned how dire a
 thing
Is worshipped in that idol proudly named
"The Wealth of Nations," *where* alone
 that wealth
Is lodged, and how increased; and having
 gained
A more judicious knowledge of the worth
And dignity of individual man, 81
No composition of the brain, but man
Of whom we read, the man whom we be-
 hold
With our own eyes—I could not but
 enquire—
Not with less interest than heretofore, 85
But greater, though in spirit more sub-
 dued—
Why is this glorious creature to be found
One only in ten thousand? What one is,
Why may not millions be? What bars
 are thrown
By Nature in the way of such a hope? 90
Our animal appetites and daily wants,
Are these obstructions insurmountable?
If not, then others vanish into air.

"Inspect the basis of the social pile:
Enquire," said I, "how much of mental
 power   95
And genuine virtue they possess who live
By bodily toil, labour exceeding far
Their due proportion, under all the weight
Of that injustice which upon ourselves
Ourselves entail." Such estimate to frame
I chiefly looked (what need to look
 beyond?)   101
Among the natural abodes of men,
Fields with their rural works; recalled
 to mind
My earliest notices; with these compared
The observations made in later youth,
And to that day continued.—For, the
 time   106
Had never been when throes of mighty
 Nations
And the world's tumult unto me could
 yield,
How far soe'er transported and possessed,
Full measure of content; but still I
 craved   110
An intermingling of distinct regards
And truths of individual sympathy
Nearer ourselves. Such often might be
 gleaned
From the great City, else it must have
 proved
To me a heart-depressing wilderness; 115
But much was wanting: therefore did I
 turn
To you, ye pathways, and ye lonely roads;
Sought you enriched with everything I
 prized,
With human kindnesses and simple joys.

Oh! next to one dear state of bliss,
 vouchsafed   120
Alas! to few in this untoward world,
The bliss of walking daily in life's prime
Through field or forest with the maid we
 love,
While yet our hearts are young, while yet
 we breathe   124
Nothing but happiness, in some lone nook,
Deep vale, or anywhere, the home of both,
From which it would be misery to stir:
Oh! next to such enjoyment of our youth,
In my esteem, next to such dear delight,

Was that of wandering on from day to
day   130
Where I could meditate in peace, and cull
Knowledge that step by step might lead
me on
To wisdom; or, as lightsome as a bird
Wafted upon the wind from distant lands,
Sing notes of greeting to strange fields or
groves,   135
Which lacked not voice to welcome me in
turn:
And, when that pleasant toil had ceased
to please,
Converse with men, where if we meet a
face
We almost meet a friend, on naked
heaths
With long long ways before, by cottage
bench,   140
Or well-spring where the weary traveller
rests.

Who doth not love to follow with his eye
The windings of a public way? the sight,
Familiar object as it is, hath wrought
On my imagination since the morn   145
Of childhood, when a disappearing line,
One daily present to my eyes, that crossed
The naked summit of a far-off hill
Beyond the limits that my feet had trod,
Was like an invitation into space   150
Boundless, or guide into eternity.
Yes, something of the grandeur which
invests
The mariner who sails the roaring sea
Through storm and darkness, early in my
mind
Surrounded, too, the wanderers of the
earth;   155
Grandeur as much, and loveliness far
more.
Awed have I been by strolling Bedlam-
ites;
From many other uncouth vagrants
(passed
In fear) have walked with quicker step;
but why
Take note of this? When I began to
enquire,   160
To watch and question those I met, and
speak

Without reserve to them, the lonely roads
Were open schools in which I daily read
With most delight the passions of man-
kind,
Whether by words, looks, sighs, or tears,
revealed;   165
There saw into the depth of human souls,
Souls that appear to have no depth at all
To careless eyes. And—now convinced
at heart
How little those formalities, to which
With overweening trust alone we give
The name of Education, have to do   171
With real feeling and just sense; how vain
A correspondence with the talking world
Proves to the most; and called to make
good search
If man's estate, by doom of Nature yoked
With toil, be therefore yoked with igno-
rance;   176
If virtue be indeed so hard to rear,
And intellectual strength so rare a boon—
I prized such walks still more, for there
I found
Hope to my hope, and to my pleasure
peace   180
And steadiness, and healing and repose
To every angry passion. There I heard,
From mouths of men obscure and lowly,
truths
Replete with honour; sounds in unison
With loftiest promises of good and fair.

There are who think that strong af-
fection, love   186
Known by whatever name, is falsely
deemed
A gift, to use a term which they would use,
Of vulgar nature; that its growth requires
Retirement, leisure, language purified
By manners studied and elaborate;   191
That whoso feels such passion in its
strength
Must live within the very light and air
Of courteous usages refined by art.
True is it, where oppression worse than
death   195
Salutes the being at his birth, where grace
Of culture hath been utterly unknown,
And poverty and labour in excess
From day to day pre-occupy the ground

Of the affections, and to Nature's self 200
Oppose a deeper nature; there, indeed,
Love cannot be; nor does it thrive with
    ease
Among the close and overcrowded haunts
Of cities, where the human heart is sick,
And the eye feeds it not, and cannot
    feed. 205
—Yes, in those wanderings deeply did
    I feel
How we mislead each other; above all,
How books mislead us, seeking their re-
    ward
From judgments of the wealthy Few,
    who see
By artificial lights; how they debase 210
The Many for the pleasure of those Few;
Effeminately level down the truth
To certain general notions, for the sake
Of being understood at once, or else
Through want of better knowledge in the
    heads 215
That framed them; flattering self-conceit
    with words,
That, while they most ambitiously set
    forth
Extrinsic differences, the outward marks
Whereby society has parted man
From man, neglect the universal heart. 220

Here, calling up to mind what then
    I saw,
A youthful traveller, and see daily now
In the familiar circuit of my home,
Here might I pause, and bend in reve-
    rence
To Nature, and the power of human
    minds, 225
To men as they are men within them-
    selves.
How oft high service is performed within,
When all the external man is rude in
    show, —
Not like a temple rich with pomp and
    gold,
But a mere mountain-chapel, that protects
Its simple worshippers from sun and
    shower. 231
Of these, said I, shall be my song; of
    these,
If future years mature me for the task,

Will I record the praises, making verse
Deal boldly with substantial things; in
    truth 235
And sanctity of passion, speak of these,
That justice may be done, obeisance paid
Where it is due: thus haply shall I teach,
Inspire; through unadulterated ears
Pour rapture, tenderness, and hope, —my
    theme 240
No other than the very heart of man,
As found among the best of those who
    live—
Not unexalted by religious faith,
Nor uninformed by books, good books,
    though few—
In Nature's presence: thence may I
    select 245
Sorrow, that is not sorrow, but delight;
And miserable love, that is not pain
To hear of, for the glory that redounds
Therefrom to human kind, and what we
    are.
Be mine to follow with no timid step 250
Where knowledge leads me: it shall be
    my pride
That I have dared to tread this holy
    ground,
Speaking no dream, but things oracular;
Matter not lightly to be heard by those
Who to the letter of the outward pro-
    mise 255
Do read the invisible soul; by men adroit
In speech, and for communion with the
    world
Accomplished; minds whose faculties are
    then
Most active when they are most eloquent,
And elevated most when most admired.
Men may be found of other mould than
    these, 261
Who are their own upholders, to them-
    selves
Encouragement, and energy, and will,
Expressing liveliest thoughts in lively
    words 264
As native passion dictates. Others, too,
There are among the walks of homely life
Still higher, men for contemplation
    framed,
Shy, and unpractised in the strife of
    phrase:

Meek men, whose very souls perhaps
would sink
Beneath them, summoned to such inter-
course :   270
Theirs is the language of the heavens, the
power,
The thought, the image, and the silent joy:
Words are but under-agents in their
souls ;
When they are grasping with their great-
est strength,
They do not breathe among them: this
I speak   275
In gratitude to God, Who feeds our
hearts
For His own service; knoweth, loveth us,
When we are unregarded by the world.

Also, about this time did I receive
Convictions still more strong than hereto-
fore,   280
Not only that the inner frame is good,
And graciously composed, but that, no
less,
Nature for all conditions wants not
power
To consecrate, if we have eyes to see,
The outside of her creatures, and to
breathe   285
Grandeur upon the very humblest face
Of human life. I felt that the array
Of act and circumstance, and visible form,
Is mainly to the pleasure of the mind
What passion makes them; that mean-
while the forms   290
Of Nature have a passion in themselves,
That intermingles with those works of
man
To which she summons him; although
the works
Be mean, have nothing lofty of their own;
And that the Genius of the Poet hence 295
May boldly take his way among mankind
Wherever Nature leads; that he hath
stood
By Nature's side among the men of old,
And so shall stand for ever. Dearest
Friend !
If thou partake the animating faith   300
That Poets, even as Prophets, each with
each

Connected in a mighty scheme of truth,
Have each his own peculiar faculty,
Heaven's gift, a sense that fits him to
perceive
Objects unseen before, thou wilt not
blame   305
The humblest of this band who dares to
hope
That unto him hath also been vouchsafed
An insight that in some sort he possesses,
A privilege whereby a work of his,
Proceeding from a source of untaught
things,   310
Creative and enduring, may become
A power like one of Nature's. To a hope
Not less ambitious once among the wilds
Of Sarum's Plain, my youthful spirit was
raised ;
There, as I ranged at will the pastoral
downs   315
Trackless and smooth, or paced the bare
white roads
Lengthening in solitude their dreary line,
Time with his retinue of ages fled
Backwards, nor checked his flight until I
saw
Our dim ancestral Past in vision clear;
Saw multitudes of men, and, here and
there,   321
A single Briton clothed in wolf-skin vest,
With shield and stone-axe, stride across
the wold ;
The voice of spears was heard, the rattling
spear
Shaken by arms of mighty bone, in
strength,   325
Long mouldered, of barbaric majesty.
I called on Darkness—but before the word
Was uttered, midnight darkness seemed
to take
All objects from my sight; and lo ! again
The Desert visible by dismal flames ; 330
It is the sacrificial altar, fed
With living men—how deep the groans !
the voice
Of those that crowd the giant wicker
thrills
The monumental hillocks, and the pomp
Is for both worlds, the living and the dead.
At other moments—(for through that
wide waste   336

Three summer days I roamed) where'er
 the Plain
Was figured o'er with circles, lines, or
 mounds,
That yet survive, a work, as some divine,
Shaped by the Druids, so to represent
Their knowledge of the heavens, and
 image forth   341
The constellations—gently was I charmed
Into a waking dream, a reverie
That, with believing eyes, where'er I
 turned,
Beheld long-bearded teachers, with white
 wands   345
Uplifted, pointing to the starry sky,
Alternately, and plain below, while breath
Of music swayed their motions, and the
 waste
Rejoiced with them and me in those
 sweet sounds.

 This for the past, and things that may
  be viewed   350
Or fancied in the obscurity of years
From monumental hints: and thou, O
 Friend!
Pleased with some unpremeditated strains
That served those wanderings to beguile,
 hast said

That then and there my mind had exer-
 cised   355
Upon the vulgar forms of present things,
The actual world of our familiar days,
Yet higher power; had caught from them
 a tone,
An image, and a character, by books
Not hitherto reflected. Call we this 360
A partial judgment—and yet why? for
 then
We were as strangers; and I may not
 speak
Thus wrongfully of verse, however rude,
Which on thy young imagination, trained
In the great City, broke like light from far.
Moreover, each man's Mind is to herself
Witness and judge; and I remember well
That in life's every-day appearances
I seemed about this time to gain clear sight
Of a new world—a world, too, that was fit
To be transmitted, and to other eyes 371
Made visible; as ruled by those fixed laws
Whence spiritual dignity originates,
Which do both give it being and maintain
A balance, an ennobling interchange 375
Of action from without and from within;
The excellence, pure function, and best
 power
Both of the object seen, and eye that sees.

BOOK FOURTEENTH.

CONCLUSION.

In one of those excursions (may they ne'er
Fade from remembrance!) through the
    Northern tracts
Of Cambria ranging with a youthful
    friend,
I left Bethgelert's huts at couching-time,
And westward took my way, to see the
    sun   5
Rise, from the top of Snowdon. To the
    door
Of a rude cottage at the mountain's base
We came, and roused the shepherd who
    attends
The adventurous stranger's steps, a trusty
    guide;
Then, cheered by short refreshment, sal-
    lied forth.   10

It was a close, warm, breezeless summer
    night,
Wan, dull, and glaring, with a dripping
    fog
Low-hung and thick that covered all the
    sky;
But, undiscouraged, we began to climb
The mountain-side. The mist soon girt
    us round,   15
And, after ordinary travellers' talk
With our conductor, pensively we sank
Each into commerce with his private
    thoughts:
Thus did we breast the ascent, and by
    myself
Was nothing either seen or heard that
    checked   20
Those musings or diverted, save that once
The shepherd's lurcher, who, among the
    crags,
Had to his joy unearthed a hedgehog,
    teased

His coiled-up prey with barkings turbu-
    lent.
This small adventure, for even such it
    seemed   25
In that wild place and at the dead of
    night,
Being over and forgotten, on we wound
In silence as before. With forehead bent
Earthward, as if in opposition set
Against an enemy, I panted up   30
With eager pace, and no less eager
    thoughts.
Thus might we wear a midnight hour
    away,
Ascending at loose distance each from
    each,
And I, as chanced, the foremost of the
    band;
When at my feet the ground appeared to
    brighten,   35
And with a step or two seemed brighter
    still;
Nor was time given to ask or learn the
    cause,
For instantly a light upon the turf
Fell like a flash, and lo! as I looked up,
The Moon hung naked in a firmament 40
Of azure without cloud, and at my feet
Rested a silent sea of hoary mist.
A hundred hills their dusky backs up-
    heaved
All over this still ocean; and beyond,
Far, far beyond, the solid vapours stretched,
In headlands, tongues, and promontory
    shapes,   46
Into the main Atlantic, that appeared
To dwindle, and give up his majesty,
Usurped upon far as the sight could reach.
Not so the ethereal vault; encroachment
    none   50

Was there, nor loss; only the inferior stars
Had disappeared, or shed a fainter light
In the clear presence of the full-orbed
    Moon,
Who, from her sovereign elevation, gazed
Upon the billowy ocean, as it lay   55
All meek and silent, save that through a
    rift—
Not distant from the shore whereon we
    stood,
A fixed, abysmal, gloomy, breathing-
    place—
Mounted the roar of waters, torrents,
    streams
Innumerable, roaring with one voice!   60
Heard over earth and sea, and, in that
    hour,
For so it seemed, felt by the starry
    heavens.

When into air had partially dissolved
That vision, given to spirits of the night
And three chance human wanderers, in
    calm thought   65
Reflected, it appeared to me the type
Of a majestic intellect, its acts
And its possessions, what it has and
    craves,
What in itself it is, and would become.
There I beheld the emblem of a mind   70
That feeds upon infinity, that broods
Over the dark abyss, intent to hear
Its voices issuing forth to silent light
In one continuous stream; a mind sus-
    tained
By recognitions of transcendent power,
In sense conducting to ideal form,   76
In soul of more than mortal privilege.
One function, above all, of such a mind
Had Nature shadowed there, by putting
    forth,
'Mid circumstances awful and sublime, 80
That mutual domination which she loves
To exert upon the face of outward things,
So moulded, joined, abstracted, so en-
    dowed
With interchangeable supremacy,
That men, least sensitive, see, hear, per-
    ceive,   85
And cannot choose but feel. The power,
    which all

Acknowledge when thus moved, which
    Nature thus
To bodily sense exhibits, is the express
Resemblance of that glorious faculty
That higher minds bear with them as
    their own.   90
This is the very spirit in which they deal
With the whole compass of the universe:
They from their native selves can send
    abroad
Kindred mutations; for themselves create
A like existence; and, whene'er it dawns
Created for them, catch it, or are caught
By its inevitable mastery,
Like angels stopped upon the wing by
    sound
Of harmony from Heaven's remotest
    spheres.
Them the enduring and the transient
    both   100
Serve to exalt; they build up greatest
    things
From least suggestions; ever on the
    watch,
Willing to work and to be wrought upon,
They need not extraordinary calls
To rouse them; in a world of life they
    live,   105
By sensible impressions not enthralled,
But by their quickening impulse made
    more prompt
To hold fit converse with the spiritual
    world,
And with the generations of mankind
Spread over time, past, present, and to
    come,   110
Age after age, till Time shall be no more.
Such minds are truly from the Deity,
For they are Powers; and hence the
    highest bliss
That flesh can know is theirs—the con-
    sciousness
Of Whom they are, habitually infused
Through every image and through every
    thought,   116
And all affections by communion raised
From earth to heaven, from human to
    divine;
Hence endless occupation for the Soul,
Whether discursive or intuitive;   120
Hence cheerfulness for acts of daily life,

Emotions which best foresight need not
    fear,
Most worthy then of trust when most
    intense.
Hence, amid ills that vex and wrongs
    that crush
Our hearts—if here the words of Holy
    Writ   125
May with fit reverence be applied—that
    peace
Which passeth understanding, that repose
In moral judgments which from this pure
    source
Must come, or will by man be sought in
    vain.

Oh! who is he that hath his whole life
    long   130
Preserved, enlarged, this freedom in him-
    self?
For this alone is genuine liberty:
Where is the favoured being who hath
    held
That course unchecked, unerring, and un-
    tired,
In one perpetual progress smooth and
    bright?—   135
A humbler destiny have we retraced,
And told of lapse and hesitating choice,
And backward wanderings along thorny
    ways:
Yet—compassed round by mountain soli-
    tudes,
Within whose solemn temple I received
My earliest visitations, careless then   141
Of what was given me; and which now I
    range,
A meditative, oft a suffering, man—
Do I declare—in accents which, from
    truth
Deriving cheerful confidence, shall blend
Their modulation with these vocal
    streams—   146
That, whatsoever falls my better mind,
Revolving with the accidents of life,
May have sustained, that, howsoe'er mis-
    led,
Never did I, in quest of right and wrong,
Tamper with conscience from a private
    aim;   151
Nor was in any public hope the dupe

Of selfish passions; nor did ever yield
Wilfully to mean cares or low pursuits,
But shrunk with apprehensive jealousy
From every combination which might aid
The tendency, too potent in itself,
Of use and custom to bow down the soul
Under a growing weight of vulgar sense,
And substitute a universe of death   160
For that which moves with light and life
    informed,
Actual, divine, and true. To fear and love,
To love as prime and chief, for there fear
    ends,
Be this ascribed; to early intercourse,
In presence of sublime or beautiful forms,
With the adverse principles of pain and
    joy—   166
Evil as one is rashly named by men
Who know not what they speak. By love
    subsists
All lasting grandeur, by pervading love;
That gone, we are as dust.—Behold the
    fields   170
In balmy spring-time full of rising flowers
And joyous creatures; see that pair, the
    lamb
And the lamb's mother, and their tender
    ways
Shall touch thee to the heart; thou call-
    est this love,
And not inaptly so, for love it is,   175
Far as it carries thee. In some green
    bower
Rest, and be not alone, but have thou there
The One who is thy choice of all the
    world:
There linger, listening, gazing, with de-
    light
Impassioned, but delight how pitiable!
Unless this love by a still higher love   181
Be hallowed, love that breathes not with-
    out awe;
Love that adores, but on the knees of
    prayer,
By heaven inspired; that frees from
    chains the soul,
Lifted, in union with the purest, best,   185
Of earth-born passions, on the wings of
    praise
Bearing a tribute to the Almighty's
    Throne.

This spiritual Love acts not nor can
   exist
Without Imagination, which, in truth,
Is but another name for absolute power
And clearest insight, amplitude of mind,
And Reason in her most exalted mood.
This faculty hath been the feeding source
Of our long labour: we have traced the
   stream
From the blind cavern whence is faintly
   heard   195
Its natal murmur; followed it to light
And open day; accompanied its course
Among the ways of Nature, for a time
Lost sight of it bewildered and engulphed;
Then given it greeting as it rose once
   more   200
In strength, reflecting from its placid
   breast
The works of man and face of human life;
And lastly, from its progress have we
   drawn
Faith in life endless, the sustaining
   thought
Of human Being, Eternity, and God. 205

   Imagination having been our theme,
So also hath that intellectual Love,
For they are each in each, and cannot
   stand
Dividually.—Here must thou be, O Man!
Power to thyself; no Helper hast thou
   here;   210
Here keepest thou in singleness thy state:
No other can divide with thee this work:
No secondary hand can intervene
To fashion this ability; 'tis thine,
The prime and vital principle is thine 215
In the recesses of thy nature, far
From any reach of outward fellowship,
Else is not thine at all. But joy to him,
Oh, joy to him who here hath sown, hath
   laid
Here, the foundation of his future years!
For all that friendship, all that love can
   do,   221
All that a darling countenance can look
Or dear voice utter, to complete the man,
Perfect him, made imperfect in himself,
All shall be his: and he whose soul hath
   risen   225

Up to the height of feeling intellect
Shall want no humbler tenderness; his
   heart
Be tender as a nursing mother's heart;
Of female softness shall his life be full,
Of humble cares and delicate desires, 230
Mild interests and gentlest sympathies.

   Child of my parents! Sister of my soul!
Thanks in sincerest verse have been else-
   where
Poured out for all the early tenderness
Which I from thee imbibed: and 'tis
   most true   235
That later seasons owed to thee no less;
For, spite of thy sweet influence and the
   touch
Of kindred hands that opened out the
   springs
Of genial thought in childhood, and in spite
Of all that unassisted I had marked 240
In life or nature of those charms minute
That win their way into the heart by
   stealth,
Still, to the very going-out of youth,
I too exclusively esteemed *that* love,
And sought *that* beauty, which, as Milton
   sings,   245
Hath terror in it. Thou didst soften down
This over-sternness; but for thee, dear
   Friend!
My soul, too reckless of mild grace, had
   stood
In her original self too confident,
Retained too long a countenance severe;
A rock with torrents roaring, with the
   clouds   251
Familiar, and a favourite of the stars:
But thou didst plant its crevices with
   flowers,
Hang it with shrubs that twinkle in the
   breeze,
And teach the little birds to build their
   nests   255
And warble in its chambers. At a time
When Nature, destined to remain so long
Foremost in my affections, had fallen back
Into a second place, pleased to become
A handmaid to a nobler than herself, 260
When every day brought with it some
   new sense

Of exquisite regard for common things,
And all the earth was budding with these
   gifts
Of more refined humanity, thy breath,
Dear Sister! was a kind of gentler spring
That went before my steps. Thereafter
   came   266
One whom with thee friendship had early
   paired;
She came, no more a phantom to adorn
A moment, but an inmate of the heart,
And yet a spirit, there for me enshrined
To penetrate the lofty and the low;   271
Even as one essence of pervading light
Shines in the brightest of ten thousand
   stars,
And the meek worm that feeds her lonely
   lamp
Couched in the dewy grass.
              With such a theme,
Coleridge! with this my argument, of
   thee   276
Shall I be silent? O capacious Soul!
Placed on this earth to love and under-
   stand,
And from thy presence shed the light of
   love,
Shall I be mute, ore thou be spoken of?
Thy kindred influence to my heart of
   hearts   281
Did also find its way. Thus fear relaxed
Her overweening grasp; thus thoughts
   and things
In the self-haunting spirit learned to take
More rational proportions; mystery,   285
The incumbent mystery of sense and soul,
Of life and death, time and eternity,
Admitted more habitually a mild
Interposition—a serene delight
In closelier gathering cares, such as be-
   come   290
A human creature, howsoe'er endowed,
Poet, or destined for a humbler name;
And so the deep enthusiastic joy,
The rapture of the hallelujah sent
From all that breathes and is, was chas-
   tened, stemmed   295
And balanced by pathetic truth, by trust
In hopeful reason, leaning on the stay
Of Providence; and in reverence for
   duty,

Here, if need be, struggling with storms,
   and there
Strewing in peace life's humblest ground
   with herbs,   300
At every season green, sweet at all hours.

And now, O Friend! this history is
   brought
To its appointed close: the discipline
And consummation of a Poet's mind,
In everything that stood most prominent,
Have faithfully been pictured; we have
   reached   306
The time (our guiding object from the
   first)
When we may, not presumptuously, I
   hope,
Suppose my powers so far confirmed, and
   such   309
My knowledge, as to make me capable
Of building up a Work that shall endure.
Yet much hath been omitted, as need
   was;
Of books how much! and even of the
   other wealth
That is collected among woods and fields,
Far more: for Nature's secondary grace
Hath hitherto been barely touched upon,
The charm more superficial that attends
Her works, as they present to Fancy's
   choice
Apt illustrations of the moral world,
Caught at a glance, or traced with curi-
   ous pains.   320

Finally, and above all, O Friend! (I
   speak
With due regret) how much is overlooked
In human nature and her subtle ways,
As studied first in our own hearts, and
   then   324
In life among the passions of mankind,
Varying their composition and their hue,
Where'er we move, under the diverse
   shapes
That individual character presents
To an attentive eye. For progress meet,
Along this intricate and difficult path,
Whate'er was wanting, something had I
   gained,   331
As one of many schoolfellows compelled,

In hardy independence, to stand up
Amid conflicting interests, and the shock
Of various tempers; to endure and note
What was not understood, though known
    to be;   336
Among the mysteries of love and hate,
Honour and shame, looking to right and
    left,
Unchecked by innocence too delicate,
And moral notions too intolerant,   340
Sympathies too contracted. Hence, when
    called
To take a station among men, the step
Was easier, the transition more secure,
More profitable also; for the mind   344
Learns from such timely exercise to keep
In wholesome separation the two natures,
The one that feels, the other that observes.

    Yet one word more of personal con-
    cern;—
Since I withdrew unwillingly from France,
I led an undomestic wanderer's life,   350
In London chiefly harboured, whence I
    roamed,
Tarrying at will in many a pleasant spot
Of rural England's cultivated vales
Or Cambrian solitudes. A youth—(he
    bore
The name of Calvert—it shall live, if
    words   355
Of mine can give it life,) in firm belief
That by endowments not from me with-
    held
Good might be furthered—in his last
    decay
By a bequest sufficient for my needs
Enabled me to pause for choice, and
    walk   360
At large and unrestrained, nor damped
    too soon
By mortal cares. Himself no Poet, yet
Far less a common follower of the world,
He deemed that my pursuits and labours
    lay
Apart from all that leads to wealth, or
    even   365
A necessary maintenance insures,
Without some hazard to the finer sense;
He cleared a passage for me, and the
    stream

Flowed in the bent of Nature.
                      Having now
Told what best merits mention, further
    pains   370
Our present purpose seems not to require,
And I have other tasks. Recall to mind
The mood in which this labour was be-
    gun,
O Friend! The termination of my course
Is nearer now, much nearer; yet even
    then,   375
In that distraction and intense desire,
I said unto the life which I had lived,
Where art thou? Hear I not a voice from
    thee
Which 'tis reproach to hear? Anon I
    rose
As if on wings, and saw beneath me
    stretched   380
Vast prospect of the world which I had
    been
And was; and hence this Song, which
    like a lark
I have protracted, in the unwearied
    heavens
Singing, and often with more plaintive
    voice
To earth attempered and her deep-drawn
    sighs,   385
Yet centring all in love, and in the end
All gratulant, if rightly understood.

    Whether to me shall be allotted life,
And, with life, power to accomplish aught
    of worth,
That will be deemed no insufficient plea
For having given the story of myself,   391
Is all uncertain: but, beloved Friend!
When, looking back, thou seest, in clearer
    view
Than any liveliest sight of yesterday,
That summer, under whose indulgent
    skies,   395
Upon smooth Quantock's airy ridge we
    roved
Unchecked, or loitered 'mid her sylvan
    combs,
Thou in bewitching words, with happy
    heart,
Didst chaunt the vision of that Ancient
    Man,

The bright-eyed Mariner, and rueful
woes   400
Didst utter of the Lady Christabel;
And I, associate with such labour, steeped
In soft forgetfulness the livelong hours,
Murmuring of him who, joyous hap, was
found,
After the perils of his moonlight ride, 405
Near the loud waterfall; or her who sate
In misery near the miserable Thorn;—
When thou dost to that summer turn thy
thoughts,
And hast before thee all which then we
were,
To thee, in memory of that happiness,
It will be known, by thee at least, my
Friend!   411
Felt, that the history of a Poet's mind
Is labour not unworthy of regard:
To thee the work shall justify itself.

The last and later portions of this gift
Have been prepared, not with the buoy-
ant spirits   416
That were our daily portion when we
first
Together wantoned in wild Poesy,
But, under pressure of a private grief,
Keen and enduring, which the mind and
heart,   420
That in this meditative history
Have been laid open, needs must make
me feel
More deeply, yet enable me to bear
More firmly; and a comfort now hath
risen
From hope that thou art near, and wilt
be soon   425
Restored to us in renovated health;
When, after the first mingling of our
tears

'Mong other consolations, we may draw
Some pleasure from this offering of my
love.

Oh! yet a few short years of useful life,
And all will be complete, thy race be
run,   431
Thy monument of glory will be raised;
Then, though (too weak to tread the ways
of truth)
This age fall back to old idolatry,   434
Though men return to servitude as fast
As the tide ebbs, to ignominy and shame
By nations sink together, we shall still
Find solace—knowing what we have
learnt to know,
Rich in true happiness if allowed to be
Faithful alike in forwarding a day   440
Of firmer trust, joint labourers in the
work
(Should Providence such grace to us
vouchsafe)
Of their deliverance, surely yet to come.
Prophets of Nature, we to them will
speak
A lasting inspiration, sanctified   445
By reason, blest by faith: what we have
loved,
Others will love, and we will teach them
how;
Instruct them how the mind of man
becomes
A thousand times more beautiful than
the earth
On which he dwells, above this frame of
things   450
(Which, 'mid all revolution in the hopes
And fears of men, doth still remain un-
changed)
In beauty exalted, as it is itself
Of quality and fabric more divine.

The Excursion

—◆—

TO THE RIGHT HONOURABLE

WILLIAM, EARL OF LONSDALE, K.G.,

ETC., ETC.

OFT, through thy fair domains, illustrious Peer!
In youth I roamed, on youthful pleasures bent;
And mused in rocky cell or sylvan tent,
Beside swift-flowing Lowther's current clear.
—Now, by thy care befriended, I appear
Before thee, LONSDALE, and this Work present,
A token (may it prove a monument!)
Of high respect and gratitude sincere.
Gladly would I have waited till my task
Had reached its close; but Life is insecure,
And Hope full oft fallacious as a dream:
Therefore, for what is here produced, I ask
Thy favour; trusting that thou wilt not deem
The offering, though imperfect, premature.

                                    WILLIAM WORDSWORTH

RYDAL MOUNT, WESTMORELAND,
    July 29. 1814.

PREFACE TO THE EDITION OF 1814.

THE Title-page announces that this is only a portion of a poem; and the Reader must be here apprised that it belongs to the second part of a long and laborious Work, which is to consist of three parts.— The Author will candidly acknowledge that, if the first of these had been completed, and in such a manner as to satisfy his own mind, he should have preferred the natural order of publication, and have given that to the world first; but, as the second division of the Work was designed to refer more to passing events, and to an existing state of things, than the others were meant to do, more continuous exertion was naturally bestowed upon it, and greater progress made here than in the rest of the poem; and as this part does not depend upon the preceding, to a degree which will materially injure its own peculiar interest, the Author, complying with the earnest entreaties of some valued Friends, presents the following pages to the Public.

It may be proper to state whence the poem, of which "The Excursion" is a part, derives its Title of THE RECLUSE.— Several years ago, when the Author retired to his native mountains, with the hope of being enabled to construct a literary Work that might live, it was a reasonable thing that he should take a review of his own mind, and examine how far Nature and Education had qualified him for such employment. As subsidiary to this preparation, he undertook to record, in verse, the origin and progress of his own powers, as far as he was acquainted with them. That Work, addressed to a dear Friend, most distinguished for his knowledge and genius, and to whom the Author's Intellect is deeply indebted, has been long finished; and the result of the investigation which gave rise to it was a determination to compose a philosophical poem, containing views of Man, Nature, and Society; and to be entitled, "The Recluse;" as having for its principal subject the sensations and opinions of a poet living in retirement.— The preparatory poem is biographical, and conducts the history of the Author's mind to the point when he was emboldened to hope that his faculties were sufficiently matured for entering upon the arduous labour which he had proposed to himself; and the two Works have the same kind of relation to each other, if he may so express himself, as the ante-chapel has to the body of a gothic church. Continuing this allusion, he may be permitted to add, that his minor Pieces, which have been long before the Public, when they shall be properly arranged, will be found by the attentive Reader to have such connection with the main Work as may give them claim to be likened to the little cells, oratories, and sepulchral recesses, ordinarily included in those edifices.

The Author would not have deemed himself justified in saying, upon this occasion, so much of performances either unfinished, or unpublished, if he had not thought that the labour bestowed by him upon what he has heretofore and now laid before the Public, entitled him to candid attention for such a statement as he thinks necessary to throw light upon his endeavours to please and, he would hope, to benefit his countrymen.—Nothing further need be added, than that the first and third parts of "The Recluse" will consist chiefly of meditations in the Author's own person; and that in the intermediate part ("The Excursion") the intervention of characters speaking is employed, and something of a dramatic form adopted.

It is not the Author's intention formally to announce a system: it was more animating to him to proceed in a different course; and if he shall succeed in conveying to the mind clear thoughts, lively images, and strong feelings, the Reader will have no difficulty in extracting the

system for himself. And in the mean-
time the following passage, taken from
the conclusion of the first book of "The
Recluse," may be acceptable as a kind of
Prospectus of the design and scope of the
whole Poem.

"On Man, on Nature, and on Human Life,
Musing in solitude, I oft perceive
Fair trains of imagery before me rise,
Accompanied by feelings of delight
Pure, or with no unpleasing sadness mixed ;   5
And I am conscious of affecting thoughts
And dear remembrances, whose presence soothes
Or elevates the Mind, intent to weigh
The good and evil of our mortal state.
—To these emotions, whencesoe'er they come,   10
Whether from breath of outward circumstance,
Or from the Soul—an impulse to herself—
I would give utterance in numerous verse.
Of Truth, of Grandeur, Beauty, Love, and Hope,
And melancholy Fear subdued by Faith ;   15
Of blessèd consolations in distress ;
Of moral strength, and intellectual Power ;
Of joy in widest commonalty spread ;
Of the individual Mind that keeps her own
Inviolate retirement, subject there   20
To Conscience only, and the law supreme
Of that Intelligence which governs all—
I sing :—'fit audience let me find though few!'

"So prayed, more gaining than he asked, the
Bard—
In holiest mood. Urania, I shall need   25
Thy guidance, or a greater Muse, if such
Descend to earth or dwell in highest heaven!
For I must tread on shadowy ground, must sink
Deep—and, aloft ascending, breathe in worlds
To which the heaven of heavens is but a veil.   30
All strength—all terror, single or in bands,
That ever was put forth in personal form—
Jehovah—with his thunder, and the choir
Of shouting Angels, and the empyreal thrones—
I pass them unalarmed. Not Chaos, not   35
The darkest pit of lowest Erebus,
Nor aught of blinder vacancy, scooped out
By help of dreams—can breed such fear and awe
As fall upon us often when we look
Into our Minds, into the Mind of Man—   40
My haunt, and the main region of my song.
—Beauty—a living Presence of the earth,
Surpassing the most fair ideal Forms
Which craft of delicate Spirits hath composed
From earth's materials—waits upon my steps ;
Pitches her tents before me as I move,   46
An hourly neighbour. Paradise, and groves
Elysian, Fortunate Fields—like those of old
Sought in the Atlantic Main—why should they be
A history only of departed things,   50

Or a mere fiction of what never was?
For the discerning intellect of Man,
When wedded to this goodly universe
In love and holy passion, shall find these
A simple produce of the common day.   55
—I, long before the blissful hour arrives,
Would chant, in lonely peace, the spousal verse
Of this great consummation :—and, by words
Which speak of nothing more than what we are,
Would I arouse the sensual from their sleep   60
Of Death, and win the vacant and the vain
To noble raptures ; while my voice proclaims
How exquisitely the individual Mind
(And the progressive powers perhaps no less
Of the whole species) to the external World   65
Is fitted :—and how exquisitely, too—
Theme this but little heard of among men—
The external World is fitted to the Mind ;
And the creation (by no lower name
Can it be called) which they with blended might
Accomplish :—this is our high argument.   71
—Such grateful haunts foregoing, if I oft
Must turn elsewhere—to travel near the tribes
And fellowships of men, and see ill sights
Of madding passions mutually inflamed ;   75
Must hear Humanity in fields and groves
Pipe solitary anguish ; or must hang
Brooding above the fierce confederate storm
Of sorrow, barricadoed evermore
Within the walls of cities—may these sounds   80
Have their authentic comment ; that even these
Hearing, I be not downcast or forlorn !—
Descend, prophetic Spirit ! that inspir'st
The human Soul of universal earth,
Dreaming on things to come ; and dost possess
A metropolitan temple in the hearts   86
Of mighty Poets : upon me bestow
A gift of genuine insight ; that my Song
With star-like virtue in its place may shine,
Shedding benignant influence, and secure,   90
Itself, from all malevolent effect
Of those mutations that extend their sway
Throughout the nether sphere !—And if with
this
I mix more lowly matter ; with the thing
Contemplated, describe the Mind and Man   95
Contemplating ; and who, and what he was—
The transitory Being that beheld
This Vision ; when and where, and how he
lived ;—
Be not this labour useless. If such theme
May sort with highest objects, then—dread
Power !   100
Whose gracious favour is the primal source
Of all illumination,—may my Life
Express the image of a better time,
More wise desires, and simpler manners ;—nurse
My Heart in genuine freedom :—all pure thoughts
Be with me ;—so shall thy unfailing love   106
Guide, and support, and cheer me to the end !"

The Excursion

—•—

BOOK FIRST.

THE WANDERER.

ARGUMENT.

A summer forenoon.—The Author reaches a ruined Cottage upon a Common, and there meets with a revered Friend, the Wanderer, of whose education and course of life he gives an account.—The Wanderer, while resting under the shade of the Trees that surround the Cottage, relates the History of its last Inhabitant.

'TWAS summer, and the sun had mounted
   high :
Southward the landscape indistinctly
   glared
Through a pale steam; but all the north-
   ern downs,
In clearest air ascending, showed far off
A surface dappled o'er with shadows
   flung   5
From brooding clouds; shadows that lay
   in spots
Determined and unmoved, with steady
   beams
Of bright and pleasant sunshine inter-
   posed ;
To him most pleasant who on soft cool
   moss
Extends his careless limbs along the
   front   10
Of some huge cave, whose rocky ceiling
   casts
A twilight of its own, an ample shade,
Where the wren warbles, while the dream-
   ing man,
Half conscious of the soothing melody,
With side-long eye looks out upon the
   scene,   15
By power of that impending covert,
   thrown
To finer distance. Mine was at that hour
Far other lot, yet with good hope that
   soon
Under a shade as grateful I should find
Rest, and be welcomed there to livelier
   joy.   20

Across a bare wide Common I was toiling
With languid steps that by the slippery
   turf
Were baffled; nor could my weak arm
   disperse
The host of insects gathering round my
   face,
And ever with me as I paced along.   25

Upon that open moorland stood a grove,
The wished-for port to which my course
   was bound.
Thither I came, and there, amid the
   gloom
Spread by a brotherhood of lofty elms,
Appeared a roofless Hut; four naked
   walls   30
That stared upon each other !—I looked
   round,
And to my wish and to my hope espied
The Friend I sought; a Man of reverend
   age,
But stout and hale, for travel unimpaired.
There was he seen upon the cottage-
   bench,   35
Recumbent in the shade, as if asleep;
An iron-pointed staff lay at his side.

Him had I marked the day before—
   alone
And stationed in the public way, with
   face
Turned toward the sun then setting,
   while that staff   40
Afforded, to the figure of the man

Detained for contemplation or repose,
Graceful support; his countenance as he
 stood
Was hidden from my view, and he re-
 mained
Unrecognised; but, stricken by the sight,
With slackened footsteps I advanced, and
 soon   46
A glad congratulation we exchanged
At such unthought-of meeting.—For the
 night
We parted, nothing willingly; and now
He by appointment waited for me here, 50
Under the covert of these clustering elms.

We were tried Friends: amid a pleasant
 vale,
In the antique market-village where was
 passed
My school-time, an apartment he had
 owned,
To which at intervals the Wanderer drew,
And found a kind of home or harbour
 there.   56
He loved me; from a swarm of rosy boys
Singled out me, as he in sport would say,
For my grave looks, too thoughtful for
 my years.
As I grew up, it was my best delight   60
To be his chosen comrade. Many a time,
On holidays, we rambled through the
 woods :
We sate—we walked; he pleased me with
 report
Of things which he had seen; and often
 touched
Abstrusest matter, reasonings of the
 mind   65
Turned inward; or at my request would
 sing
Old songs, the product of his native hills;
A skilful distribution of sweet sounds,
Feeding the soul, and eagerly imbibed
As cool refreshing water, by the care 70
Of the industrious husbandman, diffused
Through a parched meadow-ground, in
 time of drought.
Still deeper welcome found his pure
 discourse :
How precious when in riper days I
 learned

To weigh with care his words, and to
 rejoice   75
In the plain presence of his dignity !

Oh! many are the Poets that are
 sown
By Nature; men endowed with highest
 gifts,
The vision and the faculty divine;
Yet wanting the accomplishment of
 verse,   80
(Which, in the docile season of their
 youth,
It was denied them to acquire, through
 lack
Of culture and the inspiring aid of books,
Or haply by a temper too severe,
Or a nice backwardness afraid of shame)
Nor having e'er, as life advanced, been
 led   86
By circumstance to take unto the height
The measure of themselves, these favoured
 Beings,
All but a scattered few, live out their
 time,
Husbanding that which they possess
 within,   90
And go to the grave, unthought of.
 Strongest minds
Are often those of whom the noisy world
Hears least; else surely this Man had not
 left
His graces unrevealed and unproclaimed.
But, as the mind was filled with inward
 light,   95
So not without distinction had he lived,
Beloved and honoured—far as he was
 known.
And some small portion of his eloquent
 speech,
And something that may serve to set in
 view
The feeling pleasures of his loneliness,
His observations, and the thoughts his
 mind   101
Had dealt with—I will here record in
 verse;
Which, if with truth it correspond, and
 sink
Or rise as venerable Nature leads,   104
The high and tender Muses shall accept

With gracious smile, deliberately pleased,
And listening Time reward with sacred
  praise.

  Among the hills of Athol he was born;
Where, on a small hereditary farm,
An unproductive slip of rugged ground,
His Parents, with their numerous off-
  spring, dwelt;   111
A virtuous household, though exceeding
  poor!
Pure livers were they all, austere and
  grave,
And fearing God; the very children
  taught
Stern self-respect, a reverence for God's
  word,   115
And an habitual piety, maintained
With strictness scarcely known on Eng-
  lish ground.

  From his sixth year, the Boy of whom
  I speak,
In summer, tended cattle on the hills;
But, through the inclement and the
  perilous days   120
Of long-continuing winter, he repaired,
Equipped with satchel, to a school, that
  stood
Sole building on a mountain's dreary edge,
Remote from view of city spire, or sound
Of minster clock! From that bleak tene-
  ment   125
He, many an evening, to his distant
  home
In solitude returning, saw the hills
Grow larger in the darkness; all alone
Beheld the stars come out above his head,
And travelled through the wood, with no
  one near   130
To whom he might confess the things he
  saw.

  So the foundations of his mind were
  laid.
In such communion, not from terror free,
While yet a child, and long before his
  time,
Had he perceived the presence and the
  power   135
Of greatness; and deep feelings had
  impressed

So vividly great objects that they lay
Upon his mind like substances, whose
  presence
Perplexed the bodily sense. He had
  received
A precious gift; for, as he grew in years,
With these impressions would he still
  compare   141
All his remembrances, thoughts, shapes,
  and forms;
And, being still unsatisfied with aught
Of dimmer character, he thence attained
An active power to fasten images   145
Upon his brain; and on their pictured
  lines
Intensely brooded, even till they acquired
The liveliness of dreams. Nor did he
  fail,
While yet a child, with a child's eager-
  ness
Incessantly to turn his ear and eye 150
On all things which the moving seasons
  brought
To feed such appetite—nor this alone
Appeased his yearning:—in the after-day
Of boyhood, many an hour in caves
  forlorn,
And 'mid the hollow depths of naked
  crags   155
He sate, and even in their fixed linea-
  ments,
Or from the power of a peculiar eye,
Or by creative feeling overborne,
Or by predominance of thought op-
  pressed,
Even in their fixed and steady linea-
  ments   160
He traced an ebbing and a flowing mind,
Expression ever varying!
                          Thus informed,
He had small need of books; for many a
  tale
Traditionary round the mountains hung,
And many a legend, peopling the dark
  woods,   165
Nourished Imagination in her growth,
And gave the Mind that apprehensive
  power
By which she is made quick to recognise
The moral properties and scope of things.
But eagerly he read, and read again, 170

Whate'er the minister's old shelf sup-
plied;
The life and death of martyrs, who
sustained,
With will inflexible, those fearful pangs
Triumphantly displayed in records left
Of persecution, and the Covenant—times
Whose echo rings through Scotland to
this hour!   176
And there, by lucky hap, had been pre-
served
A straggling volume, torn and incomplete,
That left half-told the preternatural tale,
Romance of giants, chronicle of fiends,
Profuse in garniture of wooden cuts 181
Strange and uncouth; dire faces, figures
dire,
Sharp-kneed, sharp-elbowed, and lean-
ankled too,
With long and ghostly shanks—forms
which once seen
Could never be forgotten!
                              In his heart,
Where Fear sate thus, a cherished visit-
ant,   186
Was wanting yet the pure delight of love
By sound diffused, or by the breathing air,
Or by the silent looks of happy things,
Or flowing from the universal face   190
Of earth and sky. But he had felt the
power
Of Nature, and already was prepared,
By his intense conceptions, to receive
Deeply the lesson deep of love which he,
Whom Nature, by whatever means, has
taught   195
To feel intensely, cannot but receive.

Such was the Boy—but for the growing
Youth
What soul was his, when, from the naked
top
Of some bold headland, he beheld the sun
Rise up, and bathe the world in light!
He looked—   200
Ocean and earth, the solid frame of earth
And ocean's liquid mass, in gladness lay
Beneath him:—Far and wide the clouds
were touched,
And in their silent faces could he read
Unutterable love. Sound needed none,

Nor any voice of joy; his spirit drank
The spectacle: sensation, soul, and form,
All melted into him; they swallowed up
His animal being; in them did he live,
And by them did he live; they were his
life.   210
In such access of mind, in such high hour
Of visitation from the living God,
Thought was not; in enjoyment it ex-
pired.
No thanks he breathed, he proffered no
request;
Rapt into still communion that trans-
cends   215
The imperfect offices of prayer and praise,
His mind was a thanksgiving to the
power
That made him; it was blessedness and
love!

A Herdsman on the lonely mountain-
tops,   219
Such intercourse was his, and in this sort
Was his existence oftentimes *possessed*.
O then how beautiful, how bright, ap-
peared
The written promise! Early had he
learned
To reverence the volume that displays
The mystery, the life which cannot die;
But in the mountains did he *feel* his
faith.   226
All things, responsive to the writing,
there
Breathed immortality, revolving life,
And greatness still revolving; infinite:
There littleness was not; the least of
things   230
Seemed infinite; and there his spirit
shaped
Her prospects, nor did he believe,—he *saw*.
What wonder if his being thus became
Sublime and comprehensive! Low desires,
Low thoughts had there no place; yet
was his heart   235
Lowly; for he was meek in gratitude,
Oft as he called those ecstasies to mind;
And whence they flowed; and from them
he acquired
Wisdom, which works thro' patience;
thence he learned

In oft-recurring hours of sober thought
To look on Nature with a humble heart,
Self-questioned where it did not under-
    stand,
And with a superstitious eye of love.

So passed the time; yet to the nearest
    town
He duly went with what small overplus
His earnings might supply, and brought
    away   246
The book that most had tempted his
    desires
While at the stall he read. Among the
    hills
He gazed upon that mighty orb of song,
The divine Milton. Lore of different kind,
The annual savings of a toilsome life, 251
His Schoolmaster supplied; books that
    explain
The purer elements of truth involved
In lines and numbers, and, by charm
    severe,
(Especially perceived where nature droops
And feeling is suppressed) preserve the
    mind   256
Busy in solitude and poverty.
These occupations oftentimes deceived
The listless hours, while in the hollow
    vale,
Hollow and green, he lay on the green
    turf   260
In pensive idleness. What could he do,
Thus daily thirsting, in that lonesome life,
With blind endeavours? Yet, still upper-
    most,
Nature was at his heart as if he felt,
Though yet he knew not how, a wasting
    power   265
In all things that from her sweet influence
Might tend to wean him. Therefore with
    her hues,
Her forms, and with the spirit of her
    forms,
He clothed the nakedness of austere truth.
While yet he lingered in the rudiments
Of science, and among her simplest laws,
His triangles—they were the stars of
    heaven,
The silent stars! Oft did he take delight
To measure the altitude of some tall crag

That is the eagle's birthplace, or some
    peak   275
Familiar with forgotten years, that shows
Inscribed upon its visionary sides,
The history of many a winter storm,
Or obscure records of the path of fire.

And thus before his eighteenth year
    was told,   280
Accumulated feelings pressed his heart
With still increasing weight; he was o'er-
    powered
By Nature; by the turbulence subdued
Of his own mind; by mystery and hope,
And the first virgin passion of a soul 285
Communing with the glorious universe.
Full often wished he that the winds might
    rage
When they were silent: far more fondly
    now
Than in his earlier season did he love
Tempestuous nights—the conflict and the
    sounds   290
That live in darkness. From his intellect
And from the stillness of abstracted
    thought
He asked repose; and, failing oft to win
The peace required, he scanned the laws
    of light
Amid the roar of torrents, where they
    send   295
From hollow clefts up to the clearer air
A cloud of mist, that smitten by the sun
Varies its rainbow hues. But vainly thus,
And vainly by all other means, he strove
To mitigate the fever of his heart.   300

In dreams, in study, and in ardent
    thought,
Thus was he reared; much wanting to
    assist
The growth of intellect, yet gaining more,
And every moral feeling of his soul
Strengthened and braced, by breathing in
    content   305
The keen, the wholesome, air of poverty,
And drinking from the well of homely life.
—But, from past liberty, and tried re-
    straints,
He now was summoned to select the
    course   309

Of humble industry that promised best
To yield him no unworthy maintenance.
Urged by his Mother, he essayed to teach
A village-school—but wandering thoughts
        were then
A misery to him; and the Youth resigned
A task he was unable to perform.   315

That stern yet kindly Spirit, who con-
        strains
The Savoyard to quit his naked rocks,
The freeborn Swiss to leave his narrow
        vales,
(Spirit attached to regions mountainous
Like their own steadfast clouds) did now
        impel   320
His restless mind to look abroad with
        hope.
—An irksome drudgery seems it to plod on,
Through hot and dusty ways, or pelting
        storm,
A vagrant Merchant under a heavy load
Bent as he moves, and needing frequent
        rest;   325
Yet do such travellers find their own
        delight;
And their hard service, deemed debasing
        now,
Gained merited respect in simpler times;
When squire, and priest, and they who
        round them dwelt
In rustic sequestration—all dependent
Upon the PEDLAR'S toil—supplied their
        wants,   331
Or pleased their fancies, with the wares
        he brought.
Not ignorant was the Youth that still no
        few
Of his adventurous countrymen were led
By perseverance in this track of life   335
To competence and ease:—to him it offered
Attractions manifold;—and this he chose.
—His Parents on the enterprise bestowed
Their farewell benediction, but with hearts
Foreboding evil. From his native hills
He wandered far; much did he see of
        men [1],
Their manners, their enjoyments, and
        pursuits,   342

<hr>

[1] See Note, p. 926.

Their passions and their feelings; chiefly
        those
Essential and eternal in the heart,
That, 'mid the simpler forms of rural life,
Exist more simple in their elements,   346
And speak a plainer language. In the
        woods,
A lone Enthusiast, and among the fields,
Itinerant in this labour, he had passed
The better portion of his time; and there
Spontaneously had his affections thriven
Amid the bounties of the year, the peace
And liberty of nature; there he kept
In solitude and solitary thought
His mind in a just equipoise of love.   355
Serene it was, unclouded by the cares
Of ordinary life; unvexed, unwarped
By partial bondage. In his steady course,
No piteous revolutions had he felt,
No wild varieties of joy and grief.   360
Unoccupied by sorrow of its own,
His heart lay open; and, by nature tuned
And constant disposition of his thoughts
To sympathy with man, he was alive
To all that was enjoyed where'er he
        went,   365
And all that was endured; for, in himself
Happy, and quiet in his cheerfulness,
He had no painful pressure from without
That made him turn aside from wretched-
        ness
With coward fears. He could *afford* to
        suffer   370
With those whom he saw suffer. Hence
        it came
That in our best experience he was rich,
And in the wisdom of our daily life.
For hence, minutely, in his various rounds,
He had observed the progress and decay
Of many minds, of minds and bodies too;
The history of many families;
How they had prospered; how they were
        o'erthrown
By passion or mischance, or such misrule
Among the unthinking masters of the
        earth   380
As makes the nations groan.
                    This active course
He followed till provision for his wants
Had been obtained;—the Wanderer then
        resolved

To pass the remnant of his days, untasked
With needless services, from hardship
 free.   385
His calling laid aside, he lived at ease:
But still he loved to pace the public roads
And the wild paths; and, by the sum-
 mer's warmth
Invited, often would he leave his home
And journey far, revisiting the scenes 390
That to his memory were most endeared.
—Vigorous in health, of hopeful spirits,
 undamped
By worldly-mindedness or anxious care;
Observant, studious, thoughtful, and re-
 freshed
By knowledge gathered up from day to
 day;   395
Thus had he lived a long and innocent
 life.

The Scottish Church, both on himself
 and those
With whom from childhood he grew up,
 had held
The strong hand of her purity; and still
Had watched him with an unrelenting eye.
This he remembered in his riper age   401
With gratitude, and reverential thoughts.
But by the native vigour of his mind,
By his habitual wanderings out of doors,
By loneliness, and goodness, and kind
 works,   405
Whate'er, in docile childhood or in youth,
He had imbibed of fear or darker thought
Was melted all away; so true was this,
That sometimes his religion seemed to me
Self-taught, as of a dreamer in the woods;
Who to the model of his own pure heart
Shaped his belief, as grace divine inspired,
And human reason dictated with awe.
—And surely never did there live on earth
A man of kindlier nature. The rough
 sports   415
And teasing ways of children vexed not
 him;
Indulgent listener was he to the tongue
Of garrulous age; nor did the sick man's
 tale,
To his fraternal sympathy addressed,
Obtain reluctant hearing.
    Plain his garb; 420

Such as might suit a rustic Sire, prepared
For sabbath duties; yet he was a man
Whom no one could have passed without
 remark.
Active and nervous was his gait; his
 limbs
And his whole figure breathed intelli-
 gence.   425
Time had compressed the freshness of his
 cheek
Into a narrower circle of deep red,
But had not tamed his eye; that, under
 brows
Shaggy and grey, had meanings which it
 brought
From years of youth; which, like a Being
 made   430
Of many Beings, he had wondrous skill
To blend with knowledge of the years to
 come,
Human, or such as lie beyond the grave.

So was He framed; and such his course
 of life   434
Who now, with no appendage but a staff,
The prized memorial of relinquished toils,
Upon that cottage-bench reposed his
 limbs,
Screened from the sun. Supine the Wan-
 derer lay,
His eyes as if in drowsiness half shut,
The shadows of the breezy elms above
Dappling his face. He had not heard the
 sound   441
Of my approaching steps, and in the shade
Unnoticed did I stand some minutes'
 space.
At length I hailed him, seeing that his
 hat
Was moist with water-drops, as if the
 brim   445
Had newly scooped a running stream. He
 rose,
And ere our lively greeting into peace
Had settled, "'Tis," said I, "a burning
 day:
My lips are parched with thirst, but you,
 it seems,
Have somewhere found relief." He, at
 the word,   450

Pointing towards a sweet-briar, bade me
  climb
The fence where that aspiring shrub look-
  ed out
Upon the public way. It was a plot
Of garden ground run wild, its matted
  weeds
Marked with the steps of those, whom,
  as they passed,   455
The gooseberry trees that shot in long
  lank slips,
Or currants, hanging from their leafless
  stems,
In scanty strings, had tempted to o'erleap
The broken wall. I looked around, and
  there,
Where two tall hedge-rows of thick alder
  boughs   460
Joined in a cold damp nook, espied a
  well
Shrouded with willow-flowers and plumy
  fern.
My thirst I slaked, and, from the cheer-
  less spot
Withdrawing, straightway to the shade
  returned
Where sate the old Man on the cottage-
  bench;   465
And, while, beside him, with uncovered
  head,
I yet was standing, freely to respire,
And cool my temples in the fanning air,
Thus did he speak. "I see around me
  here
Things which you cannot see: we die, my
  Friend,   470
Nor we alone, but that which each man
  loved
And prized in his peculiar nook of earth
Dies with him, or is changed; and very
  soon
Even of the good is no memorial left. 474
—The Poets, in their elegies and songs
Lamenting the departed, call the groves,
They call upon the hills and streams to
  mourn,
And senseless rocks; nor idly; for they
  speak,
In these their invocations, with a voice
Obedient to the strong creative power 480
Of human passion. Sympathies there are

More tranquil, yet perhaps of kindred
  birth,
That steal upon the meditative mind,
And grow with thought. Beside yon
  spring I stood,
And eyed its waters till we seemed to feel
One sadness, they and I. For them a
  bond   486
Of brotherhood is broken: time has been
When, every day, the touch of human
  hand
Dislodged the natural sleep that binds
  them up
In mortal stillness; and they ministered
To human comfort. Stooping down to
  drink,   491
Upon the slimy foot-stone I espied
The useless fragment of a wooden bowl,
Green with the moss of years, and subject
  only
To the soft handling of the elements: 495
There let it lie—how foolish are such
  thoughts!
Forgive them;—never—never did my
  steps
Approach this door but she who dwelt
  within
A daughter's welcome gave me, and I
  loved her
As my own child. Oh, Sir! the good die
  first,   500
And they whose hearts are dry as summer
  dust
Burn to the socket. Many a passenger
Hath blessed poor Margaret for her gen-
  tle looks,
When she upheld the cool refreshment
  drawn
From that forsaken spring; and no one
  came   505
But he was welcome; no one went away
But that it seemed she loved him. She is
  dead,
The light extinguished of her lonely hut,
The hut itself abandoned to decay,
And she forgotten in the quiet grave. 510

"I speak," continued he, "of One whose
  stock
Of virtues bloomed beneath this lowly
  roof.

She was a Woman of a steady mind,
Tender and deep in her excess of love;
Not speaking much, pleased rather with
the joy   515
Of her own thoughts: by some especial
care
Her temper had been framed, as if to
make
A Being, who by adding love to peace
Might live on earth a life of happiness.
Her wedded Partner lacked not on his
side   520
The humble worth that satisfied her
heart:
Frugal, affectionate, sober, and withal
Keenly industrious. She with pride would
tell
That he was often seated at his loom, 524
In summer, ere the mower was abroad
Among the dewy grass,—in early spring,
Ere the last star had vanished.—They
who passed
At evening, from behind the garden fence
Might hear his busy spade, which he
would ply,
After his daily work, until the light 530
Had failed, and every leaf and flower
were lost
In the dark hedges. So their days were
spent
In peace and comfort; and a pretty boy
Was their best hope, next to the God in
heaven.

"Not twenty years ago, but you I think
Can scarcely bear it now in mind, there
came   536
Two blighting seasons, when the fields
were left
With half a harvest. It pleased Heaven
to add
A worse affliction in the plague of war:
This happy Land was stricken to the
heart!   540
A Wanderer then among the cottages,
I, with my freight of winter raiment,
saw
The hardships of that season: many rich
Sank down, as in a dream, among the
poor;
And of the poor did many cease to be,

And their place knew them not. Mean-
while, abridged   546
Of daily comforts, gladly reconciled
To numerous self-denials, Margaret
Went struggling on through those cala-
mitous years
With cheerful hope, until the second
autumn,   550
When her life's Helpmate on a sick-bed
lay,
Smitten with perilous fever. In disease
He lingered long; and, when his strength
returned,
He found the little he had stored, to meet
The hour of accident or crippling age, 555
Was all consumed. A second infant now
Was added to the troubles of a time
Laden, for them and all of their degree,
With care and sorrow: shoals of artisans
From ill-requited labour turned adrift 560
Sought daily bread from public charity,
They, and their wives and children—hap-
pier far
Could they have lived as do the little
birds
That peck along the hedge-rows, or the
kite
That makes her dwelling on the moun-
tain rocks!   565

"A sad reverse it was for him who long
Had filled with plenty, and possessed in
peace,
This lonely Cottage. At the door he stood,
And whistled many a snatch of merry
tunes
That had no mirth in them; or with his
knife   570
Carved uncouth figures on the heads of
sticks—
Then, not less idly, sought, through every
nook
In house or garden, any casual work
Of use or ornament; and with a strange,
Amusing, yet uneasy, novelty,   575
He mingled, where he might, the various
tasks
Of summer, autumn, winter, and of
spring.
But this endured not; his good humour
soon

Became a weight in which no pleasure
    was:
And poverty brought on a petted mood
And a sore temper: day by day he
    drooped,   581
And he would leave his work—and to the
    town
Would turn without an errand his slack
    steps;
Or wander here and there among the
    fields.
One while he would speak lightly of his
    babes,   585
And with a cruel tongue: at other times
He tossed them with a false unnatural
    joy:
And 'twas a rueful thing to see the looks
Of the poor innocent children. 'Every
    smile,'
Said Margaret to me, here beneath these
    trees,   590
'Made my heart bleed.'"

            At this the Wanderer paused;
And, looking up to those enormous elms,
He said, "'Tis now the hour of deepest
    noon.
At this still season of repose and peace,
This hour when all things which are not
    at rest   595
Are cheerful; while this multitude of flies
With tuneful hum is filling all the air;
Why should a tear . be on an old Man's
    cheek?
Why should we thus, with an untoward
    mind,
And in the weakness of humanity,   600
From natural wisdom turn our hearts
    away;
To natural comfort shut our eyes and
    ears;
And, feeding on disquiet, thus disturb
The calm of nature with our restless
    thoughts?"

HE spake with somewhat of a solemn
    tone: 605
But, when he ended, there was in his face
Such easy cheerfulness, a look so mild,
That for a little time it stole away
All recollection; and that simple tale

Passed from my mind like a forgotten
    sound.   610
A while on trivial things we held dis-
    course,
To me soon tasteless. In my own despite,
I thought of that poor Woman as of one
Whom I had known and loved. He had
    rehearsed   614
Her homely tale with such familiar power,
With such an active countenance, an eye
So busy, that the things of which he
    spake
Seemed present; and, attention now
    relaxed,
A heart-felt chillness crept along my
    veins.
I rose; and, having left the breezy shade,
Stood drinking comfort from the warmer
    sun,   621
That had not cheered me long—ere, look-
    ing round
Upon that tranquil Ruin, I returned,
And begged of the old Man that, for my
    sake,
He would resume his story.

               He replied, 625
"It were a wantonness, and would de-
    mand
Severe reproof, if we were men whose
    hearts
Could hold vain dalliance with the misery
Even of the dead; contented thence to
    draw
A momentary pleasure, never marked
By reason, barren of all future good. 631
But we have known that there is often
    found
In mournful thoughts, and always might
    be found,
A power to virtue friendly; were 't not so,
I am a dreamer among men, indeed   635
An idle dreamer! 'Tis a common tale,
An ordinary sorrow of man's life,
A tale of silent suffering, hardly clothed
In bodily form.—But without further
    bidding
I will proceed.

          While thus it fared with them,
To whom this cottage, till those hapless
    years,   641

Had been a blessèd home, it was my
    chance
To travel in a country far remote;
And when these lofty elms once more
    appeared
What pleasant expectations lured me on
O'er the flat Common!—With quick step
    I reached   646
The threshold, lifted with light hand the
    latch;
But, when I entered, Margaret looked at
    me
A little while; then turned her head
    away
Speechless,—and, sitting down upon a
    chair,   650
Wept bitterly. I wist not what to do,
Nor how to speak to her. Poor Wretch!
    at last
She rose from off her seat, and then,—
    O Sir!
I cannot *tell* how she pronounced my
    name:—
With fervent love, and with a face of
    grief   655
Unutterably helpless, and a look
That seemed to cling upon me, she
    enquired
If I had seen her husband. As she spake
A strange surprise and fear came to my
    heart,
Nor had I power to answer ere she told
That he had disappeared—not two months
    gone.   661
He left his house: two wretched days
    had past,
And on the third, as wistfully she raised
Her head from off her pillow, to look
    forth,   664
Like one in trouble, for returning light,
Within her chamber-casement she espied
A folded paper, lying as if placed
To meet her waking eyes. This trem-
    blingly
She opened—found no writing, but be-
    held
Pieces of money carefully enclosed,   670
Silver and gold. 'I shuddered at the
    sight,'
Said Margaret, 'for I knew it was his
    hand

That must have placed it there; and ere
    that day
Was ended, that long anxious day, I
    learned,
From one who by my husband had been
    sent   675
With the sad news, that he had joined
    a troop
Of soldiers, going to a distant land.
—He left me thus—he could not gather
    heart
To take a farewell of me; for he feared
That I should follow with my babes, and
    sink   680
Beneath the misery of that wandering
    life.'

"This tale did Margaret tell with many
    tears:
And, when she ended, I had little power
To give her comfort, and was glad to take
Such words of hope from her own mouth
    as served   685
To cheer us both. But long we had not
    talked
Ere we built up a pile of better thoughts,
And with a brighter eye she looked around
As if she had been shedding tears of joy.
We parted.—'Twas the time of early
    spring;   690
I left her busy with her garden tools;
And well remember, o'er that fence she
    looked,
And, while I paced along the foot-way
    path,
Called out, and sent a blessing after me,
With tender cheerfulness, and with a
    voice   695
That seemed the very sound of happy
    thoughts.

"I roved o'er many a hill and many
    a dale,
With my accustomed load; in heat and
    cold,
Through many a wood and many an open
    ground,
In sunshine and in shade, in wet and fair,
Drooping or blithe of heart, as might
    befall;   701
My best companions now the driving
    winds,

And now the 'trotting brooks' and whis-
    pering trees,
And now the music of my own sad steps,
With many a short-lived thought that
    passed between,   705
And disappeared.
               I journeyed back this way,
When, in the warmth of midsummer, the
    wheat
Was yellow; and the soft and bladed
    grass,
Springing afresh, had o'er the hay-field
    spread
Its tender verdure. At the door arrived,
I found that she was absent. In the
    shade,   711
Where now we sit, I waited her return.
Her cottage, then a cheerful object, wore
Its customary look,—only, it seemed,
The honeysuckle, crowding round the
    porch,   715
Hung down in heavier tufts; and that
    bright weed,
The yellow stone-crop, suffered to take
    root
Along the window's edge, profusely grew
Blinding the lower panes. I turned
    aside,
And strolled into her garden. It ap-
    peared   720
To lag behind the season, and had lost
Its pride of neatness. Daisy-flowers and
    thrift
Had broken their trim border-lines, and
    straggled
O'er paths they used to deck: carnations,
    once   724
Prized for surpassing beauty, and no less
For the peculiar pains they had required,
Declined their languid heads, wanting
    support.
The cumbrous bind-weed, with its wreaths
    and bells,
Had twined about her two small rows of
    peas,
And dragged them to the earth.
                 Ere this an hour
Was wasted.—Back I turned my restless
    steps;   731
A stranger passed; and, guessing whom
    I sought,

He said that she was used to ramble far.—
The sun was sinking in the west; and now
I sate with sad impatience. From within
Her solitary infant cried aloud;   736
Then, like a blast that dies away self-
    stilled,
The voice was silent. From the bench
    I rose;
But neither could divert nor soothe my
    thoughts.   739
The spot, though fair, was very desolate—
The longer I remained, more desolate:
And, looking round me, now I first
    observed
The corner stones, on either side the
    porch,
With dull red stains discoloured, and
    stuck o'er
With tufts and hairs of wool, as if the
    sheep,   745
That fed upon the Common, thither came
Familiarly, and found a couching-place
Even at her threshold. Deeper shadows
    fell
From these tall elms; the cottage-clock
    struck eight:—
I turned, and saw her distant a few steps.
Her face was pale and thin—her figure,
    too,   751
Was changed. As she unlocked the door,
    she said,
'It grieves me you have waited here so
    long,
But, in good truth, I've wandered much
    of late;
And, sometimes—to my shame I speak—
    have need   755
Of my best prayers to bring me back
    again.'
While on the board she spread our evening
    meal,
She told me—interrupting not the work
Which gave employment to her listless
    hands—
That she had parted with her elder child;
To a kind master on a distant farm   761
Now happily apprenticed.—'I perceive
You look at me, and you have cause;
    to-day
I have been travelling far; and many
    days

About the fields I wander, knowing
    this   765
Only, that what I seek I cannot find;
And so I waste my time: for I am
    changed;
And to myself,' said she, 'have done
    much wrong
And to this helpless infant. I have slept
Weeping, and weeping have I waked; my
    tears   770
Have flowed as if my body were not such
As others are; and I could never die.
But I am now in mind and in my heart
More easy; and I hope,' said she, 'that
    God
Will give me patience to endure the
    things   775
Which I behold at home.'
                It would have grieved
Your very soul to see her. Sir, I feel
The story linger in my heart; I fear
'Tis long and tedious; but my spirit
    clings
To that poor Woman:—so familiarly 780
Do I perceive her manner, and her look,
And presence; and so deeply do I feel
Her goodness, that, not seldom, in my
    walks
A momentary trance comes over me; 784
And to myself I seem to muse on One
By sorrow laid asleep; or borne away,
A human being destined to awake
To human life, or something very near
To human life, when he shall come again
For whom she suffered. Yes, it would
    have grieved   790
Your very soul to see her: evermore
Her eyelids drooped, her eyes downward
    were cast;
And, when she at her table gave me food,
She did not look at me. Her voice was
    low,   794
Her body was subdued. In every act
Pertaining to her house-affairs, appeared
The careless stillness of a thinking mind
Self-occupied; to which all outward
    things
Are like an idle matter. Still she sighed,
But yet no motion of the breast was seen,
No heaving of the heart. While by the
    fire   801

We sate together, sighs came on my ear,
I knew not how, and hardly whence they
    came.

"Ere my departure, to her care I gave,
For her son's use, some tokens of regard,
Which with a look of welcome she re-
    ceived;   806
And I exhorted her to place her trust
In God's good love, and seek his help by
    prayer.
I took my staff, and, when I kissed her
    babe,
The tears stood in her eyes. I left her
    then   810
With the best hope and comfort I could
    give:
She thanked me for my wish;—but for my
    hope
It seemed she did not thank me.
                          I returned,
And took my rounds along this road again
When on its sunny bank the primrose
    flower   815
Peeped forth, to give an earnest of the
    Spring.
I found her sad and drooping: she had
    learned
No tidings of her husband; if he lived,
She knew not that he lived; if he were
    dead,
She knew not he was dead. She seemed
    the same   820
In person and appearance; but her house
Bespake a sleepy hand of negligence;
The floor was neither dry nor neat, the
    hearth
Was comfortless, and her small lot of
    books,
Which, in the cottage-window, heretofore
Had been piled up against the corner
    panes   826
In seemly order, now, with straggling
    leaves
Lay scattered here and there, open or shut,
As they had chanced to fall. Her infant
    Babe
Had from its mother caught the trick of
    grief,   830
And sighed among its playthings. I
    withdrew,

And once again entering the garden saw,
More plainly still, that poverty and grief
Were now come nearer to her: weeds
    defaced
The hardened soil, and knots of withered
    grass: 835
No ridges there appeared of clear black
    mould,
No winter greenness; of her herbs and
    flowers,
It seemed the better part were gnawed
    away
Or trampled into earth; a chain of straw,
Which had been twined about the slender
    stem   840
Of a young apple-tree, lay at its root;
The bark was nibbled round by truant
    sheep.
—Margaret stood near, her infant in her
    arms,
And, noting that my eye was on the tree,
She said, 'I fear it will be dead and gone
Ere Robert come again.' When to the
    House   846
We had returned together, she enquired
If I had any hope:—but for her babe
And for her little orphan boy, she said,
She had no wish to live, that she must die
Of sorrow. Yet I saw the idle loom 851
Still in its place; his Sunday garments
    hung
Upon the self-same nail; his very staff
Stood undisturbed behind the door.
                  And when,
In bleak December, I retraced this way,
She told me that her little babe was dead,
And she was left alone. She now, released
From her maternal cares, had taken up
The employment common through these
    wilds, and gained,
By spinning hemp, a pittance for herself;
And for this end had hired a neighbour's
    boy   861
To give her needful help. That very time
Most willingly she put her work aside,
And walked with me along the miry road,
Heedless how far; and, in such piteous
    sort   865
That any heart had ached to hear her,
    begged
That, wheresoe'er I went, I still would ask

For him whom she had lost. We parted
    then—
Our final parting; for from that time
    forth
Did many seasons pass ere I returned 870
Into this tract again.
                  Nine tedious years;
From their first separation, nine long
    years,
She lingered in unquiet widowhood;
A Wife and Widow. Needs must it have
    been
A sore heart-wasting! I have heard, my
    Friend,   875
That in yon arbour oftentimes she sate
Alone, through half the vacant sabbath
    day;
And, if a dog passed by, she still would
    quit
The shade, and look abroad. On this old
    bench   879
For hours she sate; and evermore her eye
Was busy in the distance, shaping things
That made her heart beat quick. You
    see that path,
Now faint,—the grass has crept o'er its
    grey line;
There, to and fro, she paced through
    many a day
Of the warm summer, from a belt of hemp
That girt her waist, spinning the long-
    drawn thread   886
With backward steps. Yet ever as there
    passed
A man whose garments showed the sol-
    dier's red,
Or crippled mendicant in soldier's garb,
The little child who sate to turn the wheel
Ceased from his task; and she with fal-
    tering voice   891
Made many a fond enquiry; and when
    they,
Whose presence gave no comfort, were
    gone by,
Her heart was still more sad. And by
    yon gate,
That bars the traveller's road, she often
    stood,   895
And when a stranger horseman came, the
    latch
Would lift, and in his face look wistfully:

Most happy, if, from aught discovered
    there
Of tender feeling, she might dare repeat
The same sad question. Meanwhile her
    poor Hut   900
Sank to decay; for he was gone, whose
    hand,
At the first nipping of October frost,
Closed up each chink, and with fresh
    bands of straw
Chequered the green-grown thatch. And
    so she lived
Through the long winter, reckless and
    alone;   905
Until her house by frost, and thaw, and
    rain,
Was sapped; and while she slept, the
    nightly damps
Did chill her breast; and in the stormy
    day
Her tattered clothes were ruffled by the
    wind,
Even at the side of her own fire. Yet
    still   910
She loved this wretched spot, nor would
    for worlds
Have parted hence; and still that length
    of road,
And this rude bench, one torturing hope
    endeared,
Fast rooted at her heart: and here, my
    Friend,—
In sickness she remained; and here she
    died;   915
Last human tenant of these ruined walls!"

The old Man ceased: he saw that I was
    moved;
From that low bench, rising instinctively
I turned aside in weakness, nor had
    power
To thank him for the tale which he had
    told.   920
I stood, and leaning o'er the garden wall
Reviewed that Woman's sufferings; and
    it seemed
To comfort me while with a brother's
    love
I blessed her in the impotence of grief.
Then towards the cottage I returned; and
    traced   925

Fondly, though with an interest more
    mild,
That secret spirit of humanity
Which, 'mid the calm oblivious tenden-
    cies
Of nature, 'mid her plants, and weeds,
    and flowers,
And silent overgrowings, still survived.
The old Man, noting this, resumed, and
    said,   931
"My Friend! enough to sorrow you have
    given,
The purposes of wisdom ask no more:
Nor more would she have craved as due
    to One
Who, in her worst distress, had ofttimes
    felt   935
The unbounded might of prayer; and
    learned, with soul
Fixed on the Cross, that consolation
    springs,
From sources deeper far than deepest
    pain,
For the meek Sufferer. Why then should
    we read
The forms of things with an unworthy
    eye?   940
She sleeps in the calm earth, and peace is
    here.
I well remember that those very plumes,
Those weeds, and the high spear-grass on
    that wall,
By mist and silent rain-drops silvered o'er,
As once I passed, into my heart conveyed
So still an image of tranquillity,   946
So calm and still, and looked so beautiful
Amid the uneasy thoughts which filled
    my mind,
That what we feel of sorrow and despair
From ruin and from change, and all the
    grief   950
That passing shows of Being leave be-
    hind,
Appeared an idle dream, that could main-
    tain,
Nowhere, dominion o'er the enlightened
    spirit
Whose meditative sympathies repose
Upon the breast of Faith. I turned
    away,   955
And walked along my road in happiness."

He ceased.   Ere long the sun declining
    shot
A slant and mellow radiance, which began
To fall upon us, while, beneath the trees,
We sate on that low bench : and now we
    felt,   960
Admonished thus, the sweet hour coming
    on.
A linnet warbled from those lofty elms,
A thrush sang loud, and other melodies,

At distance heard, peopled the milder air.
The old Man rose, and, with a sprightly
    mien   965
Of hopeful preparation, grasped his staff ;
Together casting then a farewell look
Upon those silent walls, we left the
    shade ;
And, ere the stars were visible, had
    reached   969
A village-inn,—our evening resting-place.

BOOK SECOND.

THE SOLITARY.

ARGUMENT.

The Author describes his travels with the Wanderer, whose character is further illustrated.—Morning scene, and view of a Village Wake.—Wanderer's account of a Friend whom he purposes to visit.—View, from an eminence, of the Valley which his Friend had chosen for his retreat.—Sound of singing from below.—A funeral procession.—Descent into the Valley.—Observations drawn from the Wanderer at sight of a book accidentally discovered in a recess in the Valley.—Meeting with the Wanderer's friend, the Solitary.—Wanderer's description of the mode of burial in this mountainous district.—Solitary contrasts with this, that of the individual carried a few minutes before from the cottage.—The cottage entered.—Description of the Solitary's apartment.—Repast there.—View, from the window, of two mountain summits ; and the Solitary's description of the companionship they afford him.—Account of the departed inmate of the cottage.—Description of a grand spectacle upon the mountains, with its effect upon the Solitary's mind.—Leave the house.

In days of yore how fortunately fared
The Minstrel ! wandering on from hall to
    hall,
Baronial court or royal ; cheered with
    gifts
Munificent, and love, and ladies' praise ;
Now meeting on his road an armed
    knight,   5
Now resting with a pilgrim by the side
Of a clear brook ;—beneath an abbey's
    roof
One evening sumptuously lodged ; the
    next,
Humbly in a religious hospital ;
Or with some merry outlaws of the wood ;
Or haply shrouded in a hermit's cell.   11
Him, sleeping or awake, the robber
    spared ;

He walked—protected from the sword of
    war
By virtue of that sacred instrument
His harp, suspended at the traveller's
    side ;   15
His dear companion wheresoe'er he went
Opening from land to land an easy way
By melody, and by the charm of verse.
Yet not the noblest of that honoured
    Race
Drew happier, loftier, more empassioned,
    thoughts   20
From his long journeyings and eventful
    life,
Than this obscure Itinerant had skill
To gather, ranging through the tamer
    ground
Of these our unimaginative days ;

Both while he trod the earth in humblest
    guise   25
Accoutred with his burthen and his staff;
And now, when free to move with lighter
    pace.

What wonder, then, if I, whose favourite
    school
Hath been the fields, the roads, and rural
    lanes,
Looked on this guide with reverential
    love?   30
Each with the other pleased, we now
    pursued
Our journey, under favourable skies.
Turn wheresoe'er we would, he was a
    light
Unfailing: not a hamlet could we pass,
Rarely a house, that did not yield to him
Remembrances; or from his tongue call
    forth   36
Some way-beguiling tale. Nor less regard
Accompanied those strains of apt dis-
    course,
Which nature's various objects might
    inspire;
And in the silence of his face I read   40
Ills overflowing spirit. Birds and beasts,
And the mute fish that glances in the
    stream,
And harmless reptile coiling in the sun,
And gorgeous insect hovering in the air,
The fowl domestic, and the household
    dog—   45
In his capacious mind, he loved them all:
Their rights acknowledging he felt for
    all.
Oft was occasion given me to perceive
How the calm pleasures of the pasturing
    herd
To happy contemplation soothed his
    walk;   50
How the poor brute's condition, forced to
    run
Its course of suffering in the public road,
Sad contrast! all too often smote his heart
With unavailing pity. Rich in love
And sweet humanity, he was, himself,   55
To the degree that he desired, beloved.
Smiles of good-will from faces that he
    knew

Greeted us all day long; we took our
    seats
By many a cottage-hearth, where he re-
    ceived
The welcome of an Inmate from afar,   60
And I at once forgot I was a Stranger.
—Nor was he loth to enter ragged huts,
Huts where his charity was blest; his
    voice
Heard as the voice of an experienced
    friend.
And, sometimes—where the poor man
    held dispute   65
With his own mind, unable to subdue
Impatience through inaptness to perceive
General distress in his particular lot;
Or cherishing resentment, or in vain
Struggling against it; with a soul per-
    plexed,   70
And finding in herself no steady power
To draw the line of comfort that divides
Calamity, the chastisement of Heaven,
From the injustice of our brother men—
To him appeal was made as to a judge;
Who, with an understanding heart, al-
    layed   76
The perturbation; listened to the plea;
Resolved the dubious point; and sentence
    gave
So grounded, so applied, that it was heard
With softened spirit, even when it con-
    demned.   80

Such intercourse I witnessed, while we
    roved,
Now as his choice directed, now as mine;
Or both, with equal readiness of will,
Our course submitting to the changeful
    breeze
Of accident. But when the rising sun   85
Had three times called us to renew our
    walk,
My Fellow-traveller, with earnest voice,
As if the thought were but a moment old,
Claimed absolute dominion for the day.
We started—and he led me toward the
    hills,   90
Up through an ample vale, with higher
    hills
Before us, mountains stern and desolate;
But, in the majesty of distance, now

Set off, and to our ken appearing fair
Of aspect, with aerial softness clad,　95
And beautified with morning's purple
　　beams.

The wealthy, the luxurious, by the stress
Of business roused, or pleasure, ere their
　　time,
May roll in chariots, or provoke the hoofs
Of the fleet coursers they bestride, to raise
From earth the dust of morning, slow to
　　rise ;　101
And they, if blest with health and hearts
　　at ease,
Shall lack not their enjoyment :—but how
　　faint
Compared with ours ! who, pacing side
　　by side,
Could, with an eye of leisure, look on all
That we beheld ; and lend the listening
　　sense　106
To every grateful sound of earth and air ;
Pausing at will—our spirits braced, our
　　thoughts
Pleasant as roses in the thickets blown,
And pure as dew bathing their crimson
　　leaves.　110

Mount slowly, sun ! that we may journey
　　long,
By this dark hill protected from thy
　　beams !
Such is the summer pilgrim's frequent
　　wish ;
But quickly from among our morning
　　thoughts
'Twas chased away : for, toward the
　　western side　115
Of the broad vale, casting a casual glance,
We saw a throng of people ;—wherefore
　　met ?
Blithe notes of music, suddenly let loose
On the thrilled ear, and flags uprising,
　　yield
Prompt answer ; they proclaim the annual
　　Wake,　120
Which the bright season favours.—Tabor
　　and pipe
In purpose join to hasten or reprove
The laggard Rustic ; and repay with
　　boons

Of merriment a party-coloured knot,　124
Already formed upon the village-green.
—Beyond the limits of the shadow cast
By the broad hill, glistened upon our
　　sight
That gay assemblage.　Round them and
　　above,
Glitter, with dark recesses interposed,
Casement, and cottage-roof, and stems of
　　trees　130
Half-veiled in vapoury cloud, the silver
　　steam
Of dews fast melting on their leafy boughs
By the strong sunbeams smitten.　Like
　　a mast
Of gold, the Maypole shines ; as if the
　　rays
Of morning, aided by exhaling dew,　135
With gladsome influence could re-animate
The faded garlands dangling from its
　　sides.

Said I, "The music and.the sprightly
　　scene
Invite us ; shall we quit our road, and
　　join
These festive matins ?"—He replied, "Not
　　loth　140
To linger I would here with you partake,
Not one hour merely, but till evening's
　　close,
The simple pastimes of the day and place.
By the fleet Racers, ere the sun be set,
The turf of yon large pasture will be
　　skimmed ;　145
There, too, the lusty Wrestlers shall con-
　　tend :
But know we not that he, who intermits
The appointed task and duties of the day,
Untunes full oft the pleasures of the day ;
Checking the finer spirits that refuse　150
To flow, when purposes are lightly
　　changed ?
A length of journey yet remains un-
　　traced :
Let us proceed." Then, pointing with his
　　staff
Raised toward those craggy summits, his
　　intent
He thus imparted :—

　　　　　　"In a spot that lies　155

Among yon mountain fastnesses con-
　　cealed,
You will receive, before the hour of noon,
Good recompense, I hope, for this day's
　　toil,
From sight of One who lives secluded
　　there,
Lonesome and lost: of whom, and whose
　　past life,　　　　　　　　　160
(Not to forestall such knowledge as may
　　be
More faithfully collected from himself)
This brief communication shall suffice.

"Though now sojourning there, he, like
　　myself,　　　　　　　　　164
Sprang from a stock of lowly parentage
Among the wilds of Scotland, in a tract
Where many a sheltered and well-tended
　　plant
Bears, on the humblest ground of social life,
Blossoms of piety and innocence.
Such grateful promises his youth dis-
　　played:　　　　　　　　　170
And, having shown in study forward
　　zeal,
He to the Ministry was duly called;
And straight, incited by a curious mind
Filled with vague hopes, he undertook
　　the charge
Of Chaplain to a military troop　175
Cheered by the Highland bagpipe, as they
　　marched
In plaided vest,—his fellow-countrymen.
This office filling, yet by native power
And force of native inclination made
An intellectual ruler in the haunts　180
Of social vanity, he walked the world,
Gay, and affecting graceful gaiety;
Lax, buoyant—less a pastor with his flock
Than a soldier among soldiers—lived and
　　roamed
Where Fortune led:—and·Fortune, who
　　oft proves　　　　　　　185
The careless wanderer's friend, to him
　　made known
A blooming Lady—a conspicuous flower,
Admired for beauty, for her sweetness
　　praised;
Whom he had sensibility to love,
Ambition to attempt, and skill to win. 190

"For this fair Bride, most rich in gifts
　　of mind,
Nor sparingly endowed with worldly
　　wealth,
His office he relinquished; and retired
From the world's notice to a rural home.
Youth's season yet with him was scarcely
　　past,　　　　　　　　　195
And she was in youth's prime. How free
　　their love,
How full their joy! Till, pitiable doom!
In the short course of one undreaded
　　year,
Death blasted all. Death suddenly o'er-
　　threw
Two lovely Children—all that they
　　possessed!　　　　　　200
The Mother followed:—miserably bare
The one Survivor stood; he wept, he
　　prayed
For his dismissal, day and night, com-
　　pelled
To hold communion with the grave, and
　　face
With pain the regions of eternity.　205
An uncomplaining apathy displaced
This anguish; and, indifferent to delight,
To aim and purpose, he consumed his
　　days,
To private interest dead, and public care.
So lived he; so he might have died.
　　　　　　　　　But now,
To the wide world's astonishment, ap-
　　peared　　　　　　　　211
A glorious opening, the unlooked-for
　　dawn,
That promised everlasting joy to France!
Her voice of social transport reached even
　　him!
He broke from his contracted bounds,
　　repaired　　　　　　　215
To the great City, an emporium then
Of golden expectations, and receiving
Freights every day from a new world of
　　hope.
Thither his popular talents he trans-
　　ferred;
And, from the pulpit, zealously main-
　　tained　　　　　　　　220
The cause of Christ and civil liberty,
As one, and moving to one glorious end.

Intoxicating service! I might say
A happy service; for he was sincere
As vanity and fondness for applause, 225
And new and shapeless wishes, would
    allow.

    "That righteous cause (such power
            hath freedom) bound,
For one hostility, in friendly league,
Ethereal natures and the worst of slaves;
Was served by rival advocates that came
From regions opposite as heaven and hell.
One courage seemed to animate them all:
And, from the dazzling conquests daily
    gained
By their united efforts, there arose
A proud and most presumptuous con-
    fidence   235
In the transcendent wisdom of the age,
And her discernment; not alone in rights,
And in the origin and bounds of power
Social and temporal; but in laws divine,
Deduced by reason, or to faith revealed.
An overweening trust was raised; and
    fear   241
Cast out, alike of person and of thing.
Plague from this union spread, whose
    subtle bane
The strongest did not easily escape;
And He, what wonder! took a mortal
    taint.   245
How shall I trace the change, how bear
    to tell
That he broke faith with them whom he
    had laid
In earth's dark chambers, with a Chris-
    tian's hope!
An infidel contempt of holy writ
Stole by degrees upon his mind; and
    hence   250
Life, like that Roman Janus, double-
    faced;
Vilest hypocrisy—the laughing, gay
Hypocrisy, not leagued with fear, but
    pride.
Smooth words he had to wheedle simple
    souls;
But, for disciples of the inner school, 255
Old freedom was old servitude, and they
The wisest whose opinions stooped the
    least

To known restraints; and who most
    boldly drew
Hopeful prognostications from a creed,
That, in the light of false philosophy, 260
Spread like a halo round a misty moon,
Widening its circle as the storms ad-
    vance.

    "His sacred function was at length
            renounced;
And every day and every place enjoyed
The unshackled layman's natural liberty;
Speech, manners, morals, all without dis-
    guise.   266
I do not wish to wrong him; though the
    course
Of private life licentiously displayed
Unhallowed actions—planted like a crown
Upon the insolent aspiring brow   270
Of spurious notions—worn as open signs
Of prejudice subdued—still he retained,
'Mid much abasement, what he had
    received
From nature, an intense and glowing
    mind.
Wherefore, when humbled Liberty grew
    weak,   275
And mortal sickness on her face appeared,
He coloured objects to his own desire
As with a lover's passion. Yet his moods
Of pain were keen as those of better
    men,
Nay keener, as his fortitude was less: 280
And he continued, when worse days were
    come,
To deal about his sparkling eloquence,
Struggling against the strange reverse
    with zeal
That showed like happiness. But, in
    despite
Of all this outside bravery, within,   285
He neither felt encouragement nor hope:
For moral dignity, and strength of mind,
Were wanting; and simplicity of life;
And reverence for himself; and, last and
    best,
Confiding thoughts, through love and fear
    of Him   290
Before whose sight the troubles of this
    world
Are vain, as billows in a tossing sea.

"The glory of the times fading away—
The splendour, which had given a festal
    air
To self-importance, hallowed it, and
    veiled   295
From his own sight—this gone, he for-
    feited
All joy in human nature; was consumed,
And vexed, and chafed, by levity and
    scorn,
And fruitless indignation; galled by
    pride;
Made desperate by contempt of men who
    throve   300
Before his sight in power or fame, and
    won,
Without desert, what he desired; weak
    men,
Too weak even for his envy or his hate!
Tormented thus, after a wandering course
Of discontent, and inwardly opprest 305
With malady—in part, I fear, provoked
By weariness of life—he fixed his home,
Or, rather say, sate down by very chance,
Among these rugged hills; where now he
    dwells,
And wastes the sad remainder of his
    hours,   310
Steeped in a self-indulging spleen, that
    wants not
Its own voluptuousness;—on this re-
    solved,
With this content, that he will live and
    die
Forgotten,—at safe distance from 'a
    world
Not moving to his mind.'"
               These serious words
Closed the preparatory notices   316
That served my Fellow-traveller to be-
    guile
The way, while we advanced up that
    wide vale.
Diverging now (as if his quest had been
Some secret of the mountains, cavern,
    fall   320
Of water, or some lofty eminence,
Renowned for splendid prospect far and
    wide)
We scaled, without a track to ease our
    steps,

A steep ascent; and reached a dreary
    plain,
With a tumultuous waste of huge hill
    tops   325
Before us; savage region! which I paced
Dispirited: when, all at once, behold!
Beneath our feet, a little lowly vale,
A lowly vale, and yet uplifted high
Among the mountains; even as if the
    spot   330
Had been from eldest time by wish of
    theirs
So placed, to be shut out from all the
    world!
Urn-like it was in shape, deep as an urn;
With rocks encompassed, save that to the
    south
Was one small opening, where a heath-
    clad ridge   335
Supplied a boundary less abrupt and
    close;
A quiet treeless nook, with two green
    fields,
A liquid pool that glittered in the sun,
And one bare dwelling; one abode, no
    more!
It seemed the home of poverty and toil,
Though not of want: the little fields,
    made green   341
By husbandry of many thrifty years,
Paid cheerful tribute to the moorland
    house.
—There crows the cock, single in his
    domain:
The small birds find in spring no thicket
    there   345
To shroud them; only from the neigh-
    bouring vales
The cuckoo, straggling up to the hill tops,
Shouteth faint tidings of some gladder
    place.

    Ah! what a sweet Recess, thought I,
    is here!
Instantly throwing down my limbs at
    ease   350
Upon a bed of heath;—full many a spot
Of hidden beauty have I chanced to espy
Among the mountains; never one like
    this;
So lonesome, and so perfectly secure;

Not melancholy—no, for it is green, 355
And bright, and fertile, furnished in itself
With the few needful things that life
    requires.
—In rugged arms how softly does it lie,
How tenderly protected! Far and near
We have an image of the pristine earth,
The planet in its nakedness: were this 361
Man's only dwelling, sole appointed seat,
First, last, and single, in the breathing
    world,
It could not be more quiet: peace is here
Or nowhere; days unruffled by the gale
Of public news or private; years that
    pass   366
Forgetfully; uncalled upon to pay
The common penalties of mortal life,
Sickness, or accident, or grief, or pain.

On these and kindred thoughts intent
    I lay   370
In silence musing by my Comrade's side,
He also silent; when from out the heart
Of that profound abyss a solemn voice,
Or several voices in one solemn sound,
Was heard ascending; mournful, deep,
    and slow   375
The cadence, as of psalms—a funeral
    dirge!
We listened, looking down upon the hut,
But seeing no one: meanwhile from below
The strain continued, spiritual as before;
And now distinctly could I recognise 380
These words:—"*Shall in the grave thy
    love be known,*
In death thy faithfulness?"—"God rest
    his soul!"
Said the old man, abruptly breaking
    silence,—
"He is departed, and finds peace at last!"

This scarcely spoken, and those holy
    strains   385
Not ceasing, forth appeared in view a
    band
Of rustic persons, from behind the hut
Bearing a coffin in the midst, with which
They shaped their course along the
    sloping side
Of that small valley, singing as they
    moved;   390

A sober company and few, the men
Bare-headed, and all decently attired!
Some steps when they had thus advanced,
    the dirge
Ended; and, from the stillness that en-
    sued
Recovering, to my Friend I said, "You
    spake,   395
Methought, with apprehension that these
    rites
Are paid to Him upon whose shy retreat
This day we purposed to intrude."—"I
    did so,
But let us hence, that we may learn the
    truth:
Perhaps it is not he but some one else 400
For whom this pious service is per-
    formed;
Some other tenant of the solitude."

So, to a steep and difficult descent
Trusting ourselves, we wound from crag
    to crag,
Where passage could be won; and, as the
    last   405
Of the mute train, behind the heathy top
Of that off-sloping outlet, disappeared,
I, more impatient in my downward
    course,
Had landed upon easy ground; and there
Stood waiting for my Comrade. When
    behold   410
An object that enticed my steps aside!
A narrow, winding, entry opened out
Into a platform—that lay, sheepfold-wise,
Enclosed between an upright mass of rock
And one old moss-grown wall;—a cool
    recess,   415
And fanciful! For where the rock and
    wall
Met in an angle, hung a penthouse,
    framed
By thrusting two rude staves into the
    wall
And overlaying them with mountain
    sods;
To weather-fend a little turf-built seat 420
Whereon a full-grown man might rest,
    nor dread
The burning sunshine, or a transient
    shower;

But the whole plainly wrought by chil-
  dren's hands!
Whose skill had thronged the floor with
  a proud show
Of baby-houses, curiously arranged;   425
Nor wanting ornament of walks between,
With mimic trees inserted in the turf,
And gardens interposed. Pleased with
  the sight,
I could not choose but beckon to my
  Guide,
Who, entering, round him threw a care-
  less glance   430
Impatient to pass on, when I exclaimed,
"Lo! what is here?" and, stooping down,
  drew forth
A book, that, in the midst of stones and
  moss
And wreck of party-coloured earthen-
  ware,
Aptly disposed, had lent its help to raise
One of those petty structures. "His it
  must be!"   436
Exclaimed the Wanderer, "cannot but be
  his,
And he is gone!" The book, which in
  my hand
Had opened of itself (for it was swoln
With searching damp, and seemingly had
  lain   440
To the injurious elements exposed
From week to week,) I found to be a
  work
In the French tongue, a Novel of
  Voltaire,
His famous Optimist. "Unhappy Man!"
Exclaimed my Friend: "here then has
  been to him   445
Retreat within retreat, a sheltering-place
Within how deep a shelter! He had fits,
Even to the last, of genuine tenderness,
And loved the haunts of children; here,
  no doubt,
Pleasing and pleased, he shared their
  simple sports,   450
Or sate companionless; and here the book,
Left and forgotten in his careless way,
Must by the cottage-children have been
  found:
Heaven bless them, and their inconsiderate
  work!

To what odd purpose have the darlings
  turned   455
This sad memorial of their hapless friend!"

  "Me," said I, "most doth it surprise,
  to find
Such book in such a place!"—"A book
  it is,"
He answered, "to the Person suited well,
Though little suited to surrounding
  things: 460
'Tis strange, I grant; and stranger still
  had been
To see the Man who owned it, dwelling
  here,
With one poor shepherd, far from all the
  world!—
Now, if our errand hath been thrown
  away,
As from these intimations I forebode, 465
Grieved shall I be—less for my sake than
  yours,
And least of all for him who is no more."

  By this, the book was in the old Man's
  hand;
And he continued, glancing on the leaves
An eye of scorn:—"The lover," said he,
  "doomed   470
To love when hope hath failed him—
  whom no depth
Of privacy is deep enough to hide,
Hath yet his bracelet or his lock of hair,
And that is joy to him. When change of
  times
Hath summoned kings to scaffolds, do
  but give   475
The faithful servant, who must hide his
  head
Henceforth in whatsoever nook he may,
A kerchief sprinkled with his master's
  blood,
And he too hath his comforter. How
  poor,
Beyond all poverty how destitute,   480
Must that Man have been left, who,
  hither driven,
Flying or seeking, could yet bring with
  him
No dearer relique, and no better stay,
Than this dull product of a scoffer's pen,

Impure conceits discharging from a heart
Hardened by impious pride !—I did not
    fear   486
To tax you with this journey ; "—mildly
    said
My venerable Friend, as forth we stepped
Into the presence of the cheerful light—
"For I have knowledge that you do not
    shrink   490
From moving spectacles ;—but let us on."

So speaking, on he went, and at the word
I followed, till he made a sudden stand :
For full in view, approaching through
    a gate
That opened from the enclosure of green
    fields   495
Into the rough uncultivated ground,
Behold the Man whom he had fancied
    dead !
I knew from his deportment, mien, and
    dress,
That it could be no other ; a pale face,
A meagre person, tall, and in a garb 500
Not rustic—dull and faded like himself !
He saw us not, though distant but few
    steps ;
For he was busy, dealing, from a store
Upon a broad leaf carried, choicest strings
Of red ripe currants ; gift by which he
    strove,   505
With intermixture of endearing words,
To soothe a Child, who walked beside
    him, weeping
As if disconsolate.—"They to the grave
Are bearing him, my Little-one," he said,
"To the dark pit ; but he will feel no
    pain ;   510
His body is at rest, his soul in heaven."

More might have followed — but my
    honoured Friend
Broke in upon the Speaker with a frank
And cordial greeting.—Vivid was the
    light
That flashed and sparkled from the other's
    eyes ;   515
He was all fire : no shadow on his brow
Remained, nor sign of sickness on his face.
Hands joined he with his Visitant,—a
    grasp,

An eager grasp ; and many moments'
    space—
When the first glow of pleasure was no
    more,   520
And, of the sad appearance which at
    once
Had vanished, much was come and com-
    ing back—
An amicable smile retained the life
Which it had unexpectedly received,
Upon his hollow cheek. "How kind,"
    he said,   525
"Nor could your coming have been better
    timed ;
For this, you see, is in our narrow world
A day of sorrow. I have here a charge"—
And, speaking thus, he patted tenderly
The sun-burnt forehead of the weeping
    child—   530
"A little mourner, whom it is my task
To comfort ;—but how came ye ?—if yon
    track
(Which doth at once befriend us and
    betray)
Conducted hither your most welcome
    feet,
Ye could not miss the funeral train—
    they yet   535
Have scarcely disappeared." "This
    blooming Child,"
Said the old Man, "is of an age to weep
At any grave or solemn spectacle,
Inly distressed or overpowered with awe,
He knows not wherefore ;—but the boy
    to-day,   540
Perhaps is shedding orphan's tears ; you
    also
Must have sustained a loss."—"The hand
    of Death,"
He answered, "has been here ; but could
    not well
Have fallen more lightly, if it had not
    fallen
Upon myself." — The other left these
    words   545
Unnoticed, thus continuing.—
              "From yon crag
Down whose steep sides we dropped into
    the vale,
We heard the hymn they sang—a solemn
    sound

Heard anywhere; but in a place like this
'Tis more than human! Many precious
    rites   550
And customs of our rural ancestry
Are gone, or stealing from us; this, I
    hope,
Will last for ever. Oft on my way have I
Stood still, though but a casual passenger,
So much I felt the awfulness of life,   555
In that one moment when the corse is
    lifted
In silence, with a hush of decency;
Then from the threshold moves with song
    of peace,
And confidential yearnings, tow'rds its
    home,
Its final home on earth. What traveller—
    who—   560
(How far soe'er a stranger) does not own
The bond of brotherhood, when he sees
    them go,
A mute procession on the houseless road;
Or passing by some single tenement
Or clustered dwellings, where again they
    raise   565
The monitory voice? But most of all
It touches, it confirms, and elevates,
Then, when the body, soon to be con-
    signed
Ashes to ashes, dust bequeathed to dust,
Is raised from the church-aisle, and for-
    ward borne   570
Upon the shoulders of the next in love,
The nearest in affection or in blood;
Yea, by the very mourners who had
    knelt
Beside the coffin, resting on its lid
In silent grief their unuplifted heads, 575
And heard meanwhile the Psalmist's
    mournful plaint,
And that most awful scripture which
    declares
We shall not sleep, but we shall all be
    changed!
—Have I not seen—ye likewise may have
    seen—
Son, husband, brothers—brothers side by
    side,   580
And son and father also side by side,
Rise from that posture:—and in concert
    move

On the green turf following the vested
    Priest,
Four dear supporters of one senseless
    weight,
From which they do not shrink, and
    under which   585
They faint not, but advance towards the
    open grave
Step after step—together, with their firm
Unhidden faces: he that suffers most,
He outwardly, and inwardly perhaps,
The most serene, with most undaunted
    eye!—   590
Oh! blest are they who live and die like
    these,
Loved with such love, and with such
    sorrow mourned!"

"That poor Man taken hence to-day,"
    replied
The Solitary, with a faint sarcastic smile
Which did not please me, "must be
    deemed, I fear,   595
Of the unblest; for he will surely sink
Into his mother earth without such pomp
Of grief, depart without occasion given
By him for such array of fortitude.
Full seventy winters hath he lived, and
    mark!   600
This simple Child will mourn his one
    short hour,
And I shall miss him; scanty tribute!
    yet,
This wanting, he would leave the sight of
    men,
If love were his sole claim upon their
    care,
Like a ripe date which in the desert falls
Without a hand to gather it."
                    At this
I interposed, though loth to speak, and
    said,
"Can it be thus among so small a band
As ye must needs be here? in such a
    place
I would not willingly, methinks, lose
    sight   610
Of a departing cloud."—"'Twas not for
    love"—
Answered the sick Man with a careless
    voice—

"That I came hither; neither have I
    found
Among associates who have power of
    speech,
Nor in such other converse as is here, 615
Temptation so prevailing as to change
That mood, or undermine my first re-
    solve."
Then, speaking in like careless sort, he
    said
To my benign Companion,—"Pity 'tis
That fortune did not guide you to this
    house   620
A few days earlier; then would you have
    seen
What stuff the Dwellers in a solitude,
That seems by Nature hollowed out to be
The seat and bosom of pure innocence,
Are made of; an ungracious matter this !
Which, for truth's sake, yet in remem-
    brance too   626
Of past discussions with this zealous
    friend
And advocate of humble life, I now
Will force upon his notice; undeterred
By the example of his own pure course,
And that respect and deference which a
    soul   631
May fairly claim, by niggard age enriched
In what she most doth value, love of God
And his frail creature Man;—but ye
    shall hear.
I talk—and ye are standing in the sun
Without refreshment ! "
                    Quickly had he spoken,
And, with light steps still quicker than
    his words,
Led toward the Cottage. Homely was
    the spot;
And, to my feeling, ere we reached the
    door,
Had almost a forbidding nakedness; 640
Less fair, I grant, even painfully less
    fair,
Than it appeared when from the beetling
    rock
We had looked down upon it. All within,
As left by the departed company,
Was silent; save the solitary clock 645
That on mine ear ticked with a mournful
    sound.—

Following our Guide, we clomb the
    cottage-stairs
And reached a small apartment dark and
    low,
Which was no sooner entered than our
    Host
Said gaily, "This is my domain, my cell,
My hermitage, my cabin, what you will—
I love it better than a snail his house.
But now ye shall be feasted with our
    best."

    So, with more ardour than an unripe girl
Left one day mistress of her mother's
    stores,   655
He went about his hospitable task.
My eyes were busy, and my thoughts no
    less,
And pleased I looked upon my grey-
    haired Friend,
As if to thank him; he returned that
    look,
Cheered, plainly, and yet serious.   What
    a wreck   660
Had we about us ! scattered was the floor,
And, in like sort, chair, window-seat,
    and shelf,
With books, maps, fossils, withered
    plants and flowers,
And tufts of mountain moss.   Mechanic
    tools
Lay intermixed with scraps of paper,
    some   665
Scribbled with verse: a broken angling-
    rod
And shattered telescope, together linked
By cobwebs, stood within a dusty nook;
And instruments of music, some half-
    made,
Some in disgrace, hung dangling from
    the walls.   670
But speedily the promise was fulfilled;
A feast before us, and a courteous Host
Inviting us in glee to sit and eat.
A napkin, white as foam of that rough
    brook
By which it had been bleached, o'erspread
    the board;   675
And was itself half-covered with a store
Of dainties,—oaten bread, curd, cheese,
    and cream;

And cakes of butter curiously embossed,
Butter that had imbibed from meadow-
    flowers
A golden hue, delicate as their own   680
Faintly reflected in a lingering stream.
Nor lacked, for more delight on that
    warm day,
Our table, small parade of garden fruits,
And whortle-berries from the mountain
    side.
The Child, who long ere this had stilled
    his sobs,   685
Was now a help to his late comforter,
And moved, a willing Page, as he was
    bid,
Ministering to our need.
                In genial mood,
While at our pastoral banquet thus we
    sate
Fronting the window of that little cell,
I could not, ever and anon, forbear   691
To glance an upward look on two huge
    Peaks,
That from some other vale peered into
    this.
"Those lusty twins," exclaimed our host,
    "if here
It were your lot to dwell, would soon
    become   695
Your prized companions.—Many are the
    notes
Which, in his tuneful course, the wind
    draws forth
From rocks, woods, caverns, heaths, and
    dashing shores;
And well those lofty brethren bear their
    part
In the wild concert—chiefly when the
    storm   700
Rides high; then all the upper air they
    fill
With roaring sound, that ceases not to
    flow,
Like smoke, along the level of the blast,
In mighty current; theirs, too, is the song
Of stream and headlong flood that seldom
    fails;   705
And, in the grim and breathless hour of
    noon,
Methinks that I have heard them echo
    back

The thunder's greeting. Nor have nature's
    laws
Left them ungifted with a power to yield
Music of finer tone; a harmony,   710
So do I call it, though it be the hand
Of silence, though there be no voice;—
    the clouds,
The mist, the shadows, light of golden
    suns,
Motions of moonlight, all come thither—
    touch,
And have an answer—thither come, and
    shape   715
A language not unwelcome to sick hearts
And idle spirits:—there the sun himself,
At the calm close of summer's longest day,
Rests his substantial orb;—between those
    heights
And on the top of either pinnacle,   720
More keenly than elsewhere in night's
    blue vault,
Sparkle the stars, as of their station
    proud.
Thoughts are not busier in the mind of
    man
Than the mute agents stirring there:—
    alone
Here do I sit and watch."
                A fall of voice,   725
Regretted like the nightingale's last note,
Had scarcely closed this high-wrought
    strain of rapture
Ere with inviting smile the Wanderer
    said:
"Now for the tale with which you threat-
    ened us!"
"In truth the threat escaped me un-
    awares: 730
Should the tale tire you, let this challenge
    stand
For my excuse. Dissevered from man-
    kind,
As to your eyes and thoughts we must
    have seemed
When ye looked down upon us from the
    crag,
Islanders 'mid a stormy mountain sea,
We are not so;—perpetually we touch
Upon the vulgar ordinances of the world;
And he, whom this our cottage hath to-
    day

Relinquished, lived dependent for his
   bread
Upon the laws of public charity.   740
The Housewife, tempted by such slender
   gains
As might from that occasion be distilled,
Opened, as she before had done for me,
Her doors to admit this homeless Pen-
   sioner;
The portion gave of coarse but whole-
   some fare   745
Which appetite required—a blind dull
   nook,
Such as she had, the *kennel* of his rest !
This, in itself not ill, would yet have
   been
Ill borne in earlier life ; but his was now
The still contentedness of seventy years.
Calm did he sit under the wide-spread
   tree   751
Of his old age; and yet less calm and
   meek,
Winningly meek or venerably calm,
Than slow and torpid; paying in this
   wise
A penalty, if penalty it were,   755
For spendthrift feats, excesses of his
   prime.
I loved the old Man, for I pitied him !
A task it was, I own, to hold discourse
With one so slow in gathering up his
   thoughts,
But he was a cheap pleasure to my eyes ;
Mild, inoffensive, ready in *his* way, 761
And helpful to his utmost power: and
   there
Our housewife knew full well what she
   possessed !
He was her vassal of all labour, tilled
Her garden, from the pasture fetched her
   kine;   765
And, one among the orderly array
Of hay-makers, beneath the burning sun
Maintained his place; or heedfully pur-
   sued
His course, on errands bound, to other
   vales,
Leading sometimes an inexperienced child
Too young for any profitable task.   771
So moved he like a shadow that per-
   formed

Substantial service. Mark me now, and
   learn
For what reward !—The moon her month-
   ly round
Hath not completed since our dame, the
   queen   775
Of this one cottage and this lonely dale,
Into my little sanctuary rushed—
Voice to a rueful treble humanised,
And features in deplorable dismay.
I treat the matter lightly, but, alas ! 780
It is most serious : persevering rain
Had fallen in torrents; all the mountain-
   tops
Were hidden, and black vapours coursed
   their sides ;
This had I seen, and saw ; but, till she
   spake,
Was wholly ignorant that my ancient
   Friend—   785
Who at her bidding early and alone,
Had clomb aloft to delve the moorland
   turf
For winter fuel—to his noontide meal
Returned not, and now, haply, on the
   heights
Lay at the mercy of this raging storm.
'Inhuman !'—said I, 'was an old Man's
   life   791
Not worth the trouble of a thought?—
   alas !
This notice comes too late.' With joy I
   saw
Her husband enter—from a distant vale.
We sallied forth together; found the
   tools   795
Which the neglected veteran had dropped,
But through all quarters looked for him
   in vain.
We shouted—but no answer ! Darkness
   fell
Without remission of the blast or shower,
And fears for our own safety drove us
   home.   800

   "I, who weep little, did, I will confess,
The moment I was seated here alone,
Honour my little cell with some few
   tears
Which anger and resentment could not
   dry.

All night the storm endured: and, soon
as help   805
Had been collected from the neighbour-
ing vale,
With morning we renewed our quest:
the wind
Was fallen, the rain abated, but the hills
Lay shrouded in impenetrable mist;
And long and hopelessly we sought in
vain: 810
Till, chancing on that lofty ridge to pass
A heap of ruin—almost without walls
And wholly without roof (the bleached
remains
Of a small chapel, where, in ancient time,
The peasants of these lonely valleys used
To meet for worship on that central
height)—   816
We there espied the object of our search,
Lying full three parts buried among tufts
Of heath-plant, under and above him
strewn,
To baffle, as he might, the watery storm:
And there we found him breathing peace-
ably,   821
Snug as a child that hides itself in sport
'Mid a green hay-cock in a sunny field.
We spake—he made reply, but would not
stir
At our entreaty; less from want of power
Than apprehension and bewildering
thoughts.   826

"So was he lifted gently from the
ground,
And with their freight homeward the
shepherds moved
Through the dull mist, I following—when
a step,
A single step, that freed me from the
skirts   830
Of the blind vapour, opened to my view
Glory beyond all glory ever seen
By waking sense or by the dreaming soul!
The appearance, instantaneously dis-
closed,
Was of a mighty city—boldly say   835
A wilderness of building, sinking far
And self-withdrawn into a boundless
depth,
Far sinking into splendour—without end!

Fabric it seemed of diamond and of gold,
With alabaster domes, and silver spires,
And blazing terrace upon terrace, high
Uplifted; here, serene pavilions bright,
In avenues disposed; there, towers begirt
With battlements that on their restless
fronts
Bore stars—illumination of all gems! 845
By earthly nature had the effect been
wrought
Upon the dark materials of the storm
Now pacified; on them, and on the coves
And mountain-steeps and summits, where-
unto
The vapours had receded, taking there
Their station under a cerulean sky.   851
Oh, 'twas an unimaginable sight!
Clouds, mists, streams, watery rocks and
·   emerald turf,
Clouds of all tincture, rocks and sapphire
sky,
Confused, commingled, mutually in-
flamed,   855
Molten together, and composing thus,
Each lost in each, that marvellous array
Of temple, palace, citadel, and huge
Fantastic pomp of structure without
name,
In fleecy folds voluminous, enwrapped,
Right in the midst, where interspace
appeared   861
Of open court, an object like a throne
Under a shining canopy of state
Stood fixed; and fixed resemblances were
seen
To implements of ordinary use,   865
But vast in size, in substance glorified;
Such as by Hebrew Prophets were beheld
In vision—forms uncouth of mightiest
power
For admiration and mysterious awe. 869
This little Vale, a dwelling-place of Man,
Lay low beneath my feet; 'twas visible—
I saw not, but I felt that it was there.
That which I *saw* was the revealed
abode
Of Spirits in beatitude: my heart
Swelled in my breast.—'I have been
dead,' I cried,   875
'And now I live! Oh! wherefore *do* I
live?'

And with that pang I prayed to be no
    more!—
—But I forget our Charge, as utterly
I then forgot him:—there I stood and
    gazed:
The apparition faded not away,   880
And I descended.
              Having reached the house,
I found its rescued inmate safely lodged,
And in serene possession of himself,
Beside a fire whose genial warmth seemed
    met
By a faint shining from the heart, a gleam
Of comfort, spread over his pallid face.
Great show of joy the housewife made,
    and truly
Was glad to find her conscience set at
    ease;
And not less glad, for sake of her good
    name,
That the poor Sufferer had escaped with
    life.   890
But, though he seemed at first to have
    received

No harm, and uncomplaining as before
Went through his usual tasks, a silent
    change
Soon showed itself: he lingered three
    short weeks;
And from the cottage hath been borne
    to-day.   895

    "So ends my dolorous tale, and glad
    I am
That it is ended." At these words he
    turned—
And, with blithe air of open fellowship,
Brought from the cupboard wine and
    stouter cheer,
Like one who would be merry. Seeing
    this,   900
My grey-haired Friend said courteously—
    "Nay, nay,
You have regaled us as a hermit ought;
Now let us forth into the sun!"—Our
    Host
Rose, though reluctantly, and forth we
    went.

BOOK THIRD.

DESPONDENCY.

ARGUMENT.

Images in the Valley.—Another Recess in it entered and described.—Wanderer's sensations.—Solitary's excited by the same objects.—Contrast between these.—Despondency of the Solitary gently reproved.—Conversation exhibiting the Solitary's past and present opinions and feelings, till he enters upon his own History at length.—His domestic felicity.—Afflictions.—Dejection.—Roused by the French Revolution.—Disappointment and disgust.—Voyage to America.—Disappointment and disgust pursue him.—His return.—His languor and depression of mind, from want of faith in the great truths of Religion, and want of confidence in the virtue of Mankind.

A HUMMING BEE—a little tinkling rill—
A pair of falcons wheeling on the wing,
In clamorous agitation, round the crest
Of a tall rock, their airy citadel—
By each and all of these the pensive ear 5
Was greeted, in the silence that ensued,
When through the cottage-threshold we
    had passed,
And, deep within that lonesome valley,
    stood
Once more beneath the concave of a blue
And cloudless sky.—Anon exclaimed our
    Host,   10
Triumphantly dispersing with the taunt
The shade of discontent which on his
    brow
Had gathered,—"Ye have left my cell,—
    but see
How Nature hems you in with friendly
    arms !
And by her help ye are my prisoners
    still.   15
But which way shall I lead you?—how
    contrive,
In spot so parsimoniously endowed,
That the brief hours, which yet remain,
    may reap
Some recompense of knowledge or de-
    light?"
So saying, round he looked, as if per-
    plexed;   20

And, to remove those doubts, my grey-
    haired Friend
Said—"Shall we take this pathway for
    our guide?—
Upward it winds, as if, in summer heats,
Its line had first been fashioned by the
    flock
Seeking a place of refuge at the root   25
Of yon lilack Yew-tree, whose protruded
    boughs
Darken the silver bosom of the crag,
From which she draws her meagre sus-
    tenance.
There in commodious shelter may we rest.
Or let us trace this streamlet to its
    source ;   30
Feebly it tinkles with an earthy sound,
And a few steps may bring us to the spot
Where, haply, crowned with flowerets
    and green herbs,
The mountain infant to the sun comes
    forth,
Like human life from darkness."—A quick
    turn   35
Through a strait passage of encumbered
    ground,
Proved that such hope was vain:—for now
    we stood
Shut out from prospect of the open vale,
And saw the water, that composed this
    rill,

Descending, disembodied, and diffused 40
O'er the smooth surface of an ample crag,
Lofty, and steep, and naked as a tower.
All further progress here was barred;—
          And who,
Thought I, if master of a vacant hour,
Here would not linger, willingly de-
    tained?   45
Whether to such wild objects he were led
When copious rains have magnified the
    stream
Into a loud and white-robed waterfall,
Or introduced at this more quiet time. 49

Upon a semicirque of turf-clad ground,
The hidden nook discovered to our view
A mass of rock, resembling, as it lay
Right at the foot of that moist precipice,
A stranded ship, with keel upturned, that
    rests
Fearless of winds and waves. Three
    several stones   55
Stood near, of smaller size, and not unlike
To monumental pillars: and, from these
Some little space disjoined, a pair were
    seen,
That with united shoulders bore aloft
A fragment, like an altar, flat and
    smooth: 60
Barren the tablet, yet thereon appeared
A tall and shining holly, that had found
A hospitable chink, and stood upright,
As if inserted by some human hand
In mockery, to wither in the sun,   65
Or lay its beauty flat before a breeze,
The first that entered. But no breeze
    did now
Find entrance;—high or low appeared no
    trace
Of motion, save the water that descended,
Diffused adown that barrier of steep rock,
And softly creeping, like a breath of air,
Such as is sometimes seen, and hardly
    seen,
To brush the still breast of a crystal lake.

"Behold a cabinet for sages built,
Which kings might envy!"—Praise to
    this effect   75
Broke from the happy old Man's reverend
    lip;

Who to the Solitary turned, and said,
"In sooth, with love's familiar privilege,
You have decried the wealth which is
    your own.
Among these rocks and stones, methinks,
    I see   80
More than the heedless impress that
    belongs
To lonely nature's casual work: they bear
A semblance strange of power intelligent,
And of design not wholly worn away.
Boldest of plants that ever faced the
    wind,   85
How gracefully that slender shrub looks
    forth
From its fantastic birthplace! And I
    own,
Some shadowy intimations haunt me here,
That in these shows a chronicle survives
Of purposes akin to those of Man,   90
But wrought with mightier arm than now
    prevails.
—Voiceless the stream descends into the
    gulf
With timid lapse;—and lo! while in this
    strait
I stand—the chasm of sky above my head
Is heaven's profoundest azure; no domain
For fickle, short-lived clouds to occupy,
Or to pass through; but rather an abyss
In which the everlasting stars abide;
And whose soft gloom, and boundless
    depth, might tempt
The curious eye to look for them by day.
—Hail Contemplation! from the stately
    towers,   101
Reared by the industrious hand of human
    art
To lift thee high above the misty air
And turbulence of murmuring cities vast;
From academic groves, that have for thee
Been planted, hither come and find a
    lodge   106
To which thou may'st resort for holier
    peace,—
From whose calm centre thou, through
    height or depth,
May'st penetrate, wherever truth shall
    lead;
Measuring through all degrees, until the
    scale   110

Of time and conscious nature disappear,
Lost in unsearchable eternity [1]!"

A pause ensued; and with minuter care
We scanned the various features of the
 scene: 114
And soon the Tenant of that lonely vale
With courteous voice thus spake—
  "I should have grieved
Hereafter, not escaping self-reproach,
If from my poor retirement ye had gone
Leaving this nook unvisited: but, in sooth,
Your unexpected presence had so roused
My spirits, that they were bent on enter-
 prise;   121
And, like an ardent hunter, I forgot,
Or, shall I say?—disdained, the game that
 lurks
At my own door. The shapes before our eyes
And their arrangement, doubtless must
 be deemed   125
The sport of Nature, aided by blind
 Chance
Rudely to mock the works of toiling Man.
And hence, this upright shaft of unhewn
 stone,
From Fancy, willing to set off her stores
By sounding titles, hath acquired the
 name   130
Of Pompey's pillar; that I gravely style
My Theban obelisk; and, there, behold
A Druid cromlech!—thus I entertain
The antiquarian humour, and am pleased
To skim along the surfaces of things, 135
Beguiling harmlessly the listless hours.
But if the spirit be oppressed by sense
Of instability, revolt, decay,
And change, and emptiness, these freaks
 of Nature
And her blind helper Chance, do *then*
 suffice   140
To quicken, and to aggravate—to feed
Pity and scorn, and melancholy pride,
Not less than that huge Pile (from some
 abyss
Of mortal power unquestionably sprung)
Whose hoary diadem of pendent rocks 145
Confines the shrill-voiced whirlwind,
 round and round

Eddying within its vast circumference,
On Sarum's naked plain—than pyramid
Of Egypt, unsubverted, undissolved—
Or Syria's marble ruins towering high 150
Above the sandy desert, in the light
Of sun or moon.—Forgive me, if I say
That an appearance which hath raised
 your minds
To an exalted pitch (the self-same cause
Different effect producing) is for me 155
Fraught rather with depression than
 delight,
Though shame it were, could I not look
 around,
By the reflection of your pleasure, pleased.
Yet happier in my judgment, even than
 you
With your bright transports fairly may
 be deemed,   160
The wandering Herbalist,—who, clear alike
From vain, and, that worse evil, vexing
 thoughts,
Casts, if he ever chance to enter here,
Upon these uncouth Forms a slight
 regard
Of transitory interest, and peeps round
For some rare floweret of the hills, or
 plant   166
Of craggy fountain; what he hopes for
 wins,
Or learns, at least, that 'tis not to be won:
Then, keen and eager, as a fine-nosed
 hound
By soul-engrossing instinct driven along
Through wood or open field, the harmless
 Man   171
Departs, intent upon his onward quest!—
Nor is that Fellow-wanderer, so deem I,
Less to be envied, (you may trace him oft
By scars which his activity has left 175
Beside our roads and pathways, though,
 thank Heaven!
This covert nook reports not of his hand)
He who with pocket-hammer smites the
 edge
Of luckless rock or prominent stone,
 disguised
In weather-stains or crusted o'er by
 Nature   180
With her first growths, detaching by the
 stroke

---

[1] See Note, p. 926.

A chip or splinter—to resolve his doubts;
And, with that ready answer satisfied,
The substance classes by some barbarous
    name,
And hurries on; or from the fragments
    picks   185
His specimen, if but haply intervened
With sparkling mineral, or should crystal
    cube
Lurk in its cells—and thinks himself
    enriched,
Wealthier, and doubtless wiser, than be-
    fore!
Intrusted safely each to his pursuit,   190
Earnest alike, let both from hill to hill
Range; if it please them, speed from
    clime to clime;
The mind is full—and free from pain their
    pastime."

    "Then," said I, interposing, "One is
    near,
Who cannot but possess in your esteem
Place worthier still of envy. May I
    name,   196
Without offence, that fair-faced cottage-
    boy?
Dame Nature's pupil of the lowest form,
Youngest apprentice in the school of art!
Him, as we entered from the open glen,
You might have noticed, busily engaged,
Heart, soul, and hands,—in mending the
    defects   202
Left in the fabric of a leaky dam
Raised for enabling this penurious stream
To turn a slender mill (that new-made
    plaything)   205
For his delight—the happiest he of all!"

    "Far happiest," answered the despond-
    ing Man,
"If, such as now he is, he might remain!
Ah! what avails imagination high
Or question deep? what profits all that
    earth,   210
Or heaven's blue vault, is suffered to put
    forth
Of impulse or allurement, for the Soul
To quit the beaten track of life, and soar
Far as she finds a yielding element
In past or future; far as she can go   215

Through time or space—if neither in the
    one,
Nor in the other region, nor in aught
That Fancy, dreaming o'er the map of
    things,
Hath placed beyond these penetrable
    bounds,
Words of assurance can be heard; if
    nowhere   220
A habitation, for consummate good,
Or for progressive virtue, by the search
Can be attained,—a better sanctuary
From doubt and sorrow, than the sense-
    less grave?"

    "Is this," the grey-haired Wanderer
    mildly said,   225
"The voice, which we so lately overheard,
To that same child, addressing tenderly
The consolations of a hopeful mind?
'His body is at rest, his soul in heaven.'
These were your words; and, verily,
    methinks   230
Wisdom is ofttimes nearer when we
    stoop
Than when we soar."—
                    The Other, not displeased,
Promptly replied—"My notion is the
    same.
And I, without reluctance, could decline
All act of inquisition whence we rise, 235
And what, when breath hath ceased, we
    may become.
Here are we, in a bright and breathing
    world.
Our origin, what matters it? In lack
Of worthier explanation, say at once
With the American (a thought which
    suits   240
The place where now we stand) that
    certain men
Leapt out together from a rocky cave;
And these were the first parents of man-
    kind:
Or, if a different image be recalled
By the warm sunshine, and the jocund
    voice   245
Of insects chirping out their careless lives
On these soft beds of thyme-besprinkled
    turf,
Choose, with the gay Athenian, a conceit

As sound—blithe race! whose mantles
        were bedecked
With golden grasshoppers, in sign that
        they   250
Had sprung, like those bright creatures,
        from the soil
Whereon their endless generations dwelt.
But stop! these theoretic fancies jar
On serious minds: then, as the Hindoos
        draw   254
Their holy Ganges from a skyey fount,
Even so deduce the stream of human life
From seats of power divine; and hope,
        or trust,
That our existence winds her stately
        course
Beneath the sun, like Ganges, to make part
Of a living ocean; or, to sink engulfed,
Like Niger, in impenetrable sands   261
And utter darkness: thought which may
        be faced,
Though comfortless!—
                Not of myself I speak;
Such acquiescence neither doth imply,
In me, a meekly-bending spirit soothed
By natural piety; nor a lofty mind,   266
By philosophic discipline prepared
For calm subjection to acknowledged law;
Pleased to have been, contented not to be.
Such palms I boast not;—no! to me, who
        find,   270
Reviewing my past way, much to condemn,
Little to praise, and nothing to regret,
(Save some remembrances of dream-like
        joys
That scarcely seem to have belonged to
        me)
If I must take my choice between the
        pair   275
That rule alternately the weary hours,
Night is than day more acceptable; sleep
Doth, in my estimate of good, appear
A better state than waking; death than
        sleep:
Feelingly sweet is stillness after storm,
Though under covert of the wormy
        ground!   281

"Yet be it said, in justice to myself,
That in more genial times, when I was
        free

To explore the destiny of human kind
(Not as an intellectual game pursued 285
With curious subtilty, from wish to cheat
Irksome sensations; but by love of truth
Urged on, or haply by intense delight
In feeding thought, wherever thought
        could feed)
I did not rank with those (too dull or
        nice,   290
For to my judgment such they then ap-
        peared,
Or too aspiring, thankless at the best)
Who, in this frame of human life, perceive
An object whereunto their souls are tied
In discontented wedlock; nor did e'er,
From me, those dark impervious shades,
        that hang   296
Upon the region whither we are bound,
Exclude a power to enjoy the vital beams
Of present sunshine.—Deities that float
On wings, angelic Spirits! I could muse
O'er what from eldest time we have been
        told   301
Of your bright forms and glorious facul-
        ties,
And with the imagination rest content,
Not wishing more; repining not to tread
The little sinuous path of earthly care,
By flowers embellished, and by springs
        refreshed.   306
—'Blow winds of autumn!—let your chill-
        ing breath
Take the live herbage from the mead,
        and strip
The shady forest of its green attire,—
And let the bursting clouds to fury rouse
The gentle brooks!—Your desolating
        sway,   311
Sheds,' I exclaimed, 'no sadness upon me,
And no disorder in your rage I find.
What dignity, what beauty, in this change
From mild to angry, and from sad to gay,
Alternate and revolving! How benign,
How rich in animation and delight,
How bountiful these elements—compared
With aught, as more desirable and fair,
Devised by fancy for the golden age; 320
Or the perpetual warbling that prevails
In Arcady, beneath unaltered skies,
Through the long year in constant quiet
        bound,

Night hushed as night, and day serene as
   day !'
—But why this tedious record?—Age, we
   know,   325
Is garrulous; and solitude is apt
To anticipate the privilege of Age.
From far ye come; and surely with a
   hope
Of better entertainment:—let us hence !"

   Loth to forsake the spot, and still more
   loth   330
To be diverted from our present theme,
I said, "My thoughts, agreeing, Sir, with
   yours,
Would push this censure farther;—for, if
   smiles
Of scornful pity be the just reward
Of Poesy thus courteously employed 335
In framing models to improve the scheme
Of Man's existence, and recast the world,
Why should not grave Philosophy be
   styled,
Herself, a dreamer of a kindred stock,
A dreamer yet more spiritless and dull?
Yes, shall the fine immunities she boasts
Establish sounder titles of esteem
For her, who (all too timid and reserved
For onset, for resistance too inert,
Too weak for suffering, and for hope too
   tame)   345
Placed, among flowery gardens curtained
   round
With world-excluding groves, the brother-
   hood
Of soft Epicureans, taught—if they
The ends of being would secure, and win
The crown of wisdom—to yield up their
   souls   350
To a voluptuous unconcern, preferring
Tranquillity to all things. Or is she,"
I cried, "more worthy of regard, the
   Power,
Who, for the sake of sterner quiet, closed
The Stoic's heart against the vain ap-
   proach   355
Of admiration, and all sense of joy?"

   His countenance gave notice that my
   zeal
Accorded little with his present mind;

I ceased, and he resumed.—"Ah ! gentle
   Sir,
Slight, if you will, the *means;* but spare
   to slight   360
The *end* of those, who did, by system, rank,
As the prime object of a wise man's aim,
Security from shock of accident,
Release from fear; and cherished peace-
   ful days
For their own sakes, as mortal life's chief
   good,   365
And only reasonable felicity.
What motive drew, what impulse, I would
   ask,
Through a long course of later ages, drove,
The hermit to his cell in forest wide;
Or what detained him, till his closing
   eyes   370
Took their last farewell of the sun and
   stars,
Fast anchored in the desert?—Not alone
Dread of the persecuting sword, remorse,
Wrongs unredressed, or insults unavenged
And unavengeable, defeated pride, 375
Prosperity subverted, maddening want,
Friendship betrayed, affection unreturn-
   ed,
Love with despair, or grief in agony;—
Not always from intolerable pangs
He fled; but, compassed round by plea-
   sure, sighed   380
For independent happiness; craving
   peace,
The central feeling of all happiness,
Not as a refuge from distress or pain,
A breathing-time, vacation, or a truce,
But for its absolute self; a life of peace,
Stability without regret or fear;   386
That hath been, is, and shall be ever-
   more !—
Such the reward he sought; and wore
   out life,
There, where on few external things his
   heart
Was set, and those his own; or, if not
   his,   390
Subsisting under nature's steadfast law.

   "What other yearning was the master
   tie
Of the monastic brotherhood, upon rock

Aerial, or in green secluded vale,
One after one, collected from afar,   395
An undissolving fellowship?—What but this,
The universal instinct of repose,
The longing for confirmed tranquillity,
Inward and outward; humble, yet sublime:
The life where hope and memory are as one;   400
Where earth is quiet and her face unchanged
Save by the simplest toil of human hands
Or season's difference; the immortal Soul
Consistent in self-rule; and heaven revealed
To meditation in that quietness!—   405
Such was their scheme: and though the wished-for end
By multitudes was missed, perhaps attained
By none, they for the attempt, and pains employed,
Do, in my present censure, stand redeemed
From the unqualified disdain, that once
Would have been cast upon them by my voice   411
Delivering her decisions from the seat
Of forward youth—that scruples not to solve
Doubts, and determine questions, by the rules   414
Of inexperienced judgment, ever prone
To overweening faith; and is inflamed,
By courage, to demand from real life
The test of act and suffering, to provoke
Hostility—how dreadful when it comes,
Whether affliction be the foe, or guilt!

"A child of earth, I rested, in that stage   421
Of my past course to which these thoughts advert,
Upon earth's native energies; forgetting
That mine was a condition which required
Nor energy, nor fortitude—a calm   425
Without vicissitude; which, if the like
Had been presented to my view elsewhere,
I might have even been tempted to despise.
But no—for the serene was also bright;

Enlivened happiness with joy o'erflowing,
With joy, and—oh! that memory should survive   431
To speak the word—with rapture! Nature's boon,
Life's genuine inspiration, happiness
Above what rules can teach, or fancy feign;
Abused, as all possessions *are* abused   435
That are not prized according to their worth.
And yet, what worth? what good is given to men,
More solid than the gilded clouds of heaven?
What joy more lasting than a vernal flower?—
None! 'tis the general plaint of human kind   440
In solitude: and mutually addressed
From each to all, for wisdom's sake:—
This truth
The priest announces from his holy seat:
And, crowned with garlands in the summer grove,
The poet fits it to his pensive lyre.   445
Yet, ere that final resting-place be gained,
Sharp contradictions may arise, by doom
Of this same life, compelling us to grieve
That the prosperities of love and joy
Should be permitted, ofttimes, to endure
So long, and be at once cast down for ever.   451
Oh! tremble, ye, to whom hath been assigned
A course of days composing happy months,
And they as happy years; the present still
So like the past, and both so firm a pledge
Of a congenial future, that the wheels   456
Of pleasure move without the aid of hope:
For Mutability is Nature's bane;
And slighted Hope *will* be avenged; and, when
Ye need her favours, ye shall find her not;
But in her stead—fear—doubt—and agony!"   461

This was the bitter language of the heart:

But, while he spake, look, gesture, tone
  of voice,
Though discomposed and vehement, were
  such
As skill and graceful nature might sug-
  gest   465
To a proficient of the tragic scene
Standing before the multitude, beset
With dark events. Desirous to divert
Or stem the current of the speaker's
  thoughts,
We signified a wish to leave that place
Of stillness and close privacy, a nook 471
That seemed for self-examination made;
Or, for confession, in the sinner's need,
Hidden from all men's view. To our at-
  tempt
He yielded not; but, pointing to a slope
Of mossy turf defended from the sun, 476
And on that couch inviting us to rest,
Full on that tender-hearted Man he turned
A serious eye, and his speech thus re-
  newed.

"You never saw, your eyes did never
  look   480
On the bright form of Her whom once I
  loved :—
Her silver voice was heard upon the earth,
A sound unknown to you; else, honoured
  Friend !
Your heart had borne a pitiable share
Of what I suffered, when I wept that loss,
And suffer now, not seldom, from the
  thought   486
That I remember, and can weep no more.—
Stripped as I am of all the golden fruit
Of self-esteem; and by the cutting blasts
Of self-reproach familiarly assailed; 490
Yet would I not be of such wintry bare-
  ness
But that some leaf of your regard should
  hang
Upon my naked branches :—lively
  thoughts
Give birth, full often, to unguarded words;
I grieve that, in your presence, from my
  tongue   495
Too much of frailty hath already dropped;
But that too much demands still more.
                  You know,

Revered Compatriot—and to you, kind
  Sir,
(Not to be deemed a stranger, as you come
Following the guidance of these welcome
  feet   500
To our secluded vale) it may be told—
That my demerits did not sue in vain
To One on whose mild radiance many
  gazed
With hope, and all with pleasure. This
  fair Bride—
In the devotedness of youthful love, 505
Preferring me to parents, and the choir
Of gay companions, to the natal roof,
And all known places and familiar sights
(Resigned with sadness gently weighing
  down
Her trembling expectations, but no more
Than did to her due honour, and to me
Yielded, that day, a confidence sublime
In what I had to build upon)—this Bride,
Young, modest, meek, and beautiful, I led
To a low cottage in a sunny bay,   515
Where the salt sea innocuously breaks,
And the sea breeze as innocently breathes,
On Devon's leafy shores;—a sheltered
  hold,
In a soft clime encouraging the soil
To a luxuriant bounty !—As our steps 520
Approach the embowered abode—our
  chosen seat—
See, rooted in the earth, her kindly bed,
The unendangered myrtle, decked with
  flowers,
Before the threshold stands to welcome us !
While, in the flowering myrtle's neigh-
  bourhood,   525
Not overlooked but courting no regard,
Those native plants, the holly and the
  yew,
Gave modest intimation to the mind
How willingly their aid they would unite
With the green myrtle, to endear the
  hours   530
Of winter, and protect that pleasant place.
—Wild were the walks upon those lonely
  Downs,
Track leading into track; how marked,
  how worn
Into bright verdure, between fern and
  gorse,

Winding away its never-ending line   535
On their smooth surface, evidence was
    none:
But, there, lay open to our daily haunt,
A range of unappropriated earth,
Where youth's ambitious feet might move
    at large;
Whence, unmolested wanderers, we be-
    held   540
The shining giver of the day diffuse
His brightness o'er a tract of sea and land
Gay as our spirits, free as our desires;
As our enjoyments, boundless. — From
    those heights
We dropped, at pleasure, into sylvan
    combs;   545
Where arbours of impenetrable shade,
And mossy seats, detained us side by side,
With hearts at ease, and knowledge in
    our hearts
'That all the grove and all the day was
    ours.'

    "O happy time! still happier was at
    hand;   550
For Nature called my Partner to resign
Her share in the pure freedom of that
    life,
Enjoyed by us in common.—To my hope,
To my heart's wish, my tender Mate be-
    came
The thankful captive of maternal bonds;
And those wild paths were left to me
    alone.   556
There could I meditate on follies past;
And, like a weary voyager escaped
From risk and hardship, inwardly retrace
A course of vain delights and thoughtless
    guilt,   560
And self-indulgence—without shame pur-
    sued.
There, undisturbed, could think of and
    could thank
Her whose submissive spirit was to me
Rule and restraint—my guardian—shall
    I say
That earthly Providence, whose guiding
    love   565
Within a port of rest had lodged me safe;
Safe from temptation, and from danger
    far?

Strains followed of acknowledgment ad-
    dressed
To an Authority enthroned above
The reach of sight; from whom, as from
    their source,   570
Proceed all visible ministers of good
That walk the earth—Father of heaven
    and earth,
Father, and king, and judge, adored and
    feared!
These acts of mind, and memory, and
    heart,
And spirit—interrupted and relieved   575
By observations transient as the glance
Of flying sunbeams, or to the outward
    form
Cleaving with power inherent and intense,
As the mute insect fixed upon the plant
On whose soft leaves it hangs, and from
    whose cup   580
It draws its nourishment imperceptibly—
Endeared my wanderings; and the mo-
    ther's kiss
And infant's smile awaited my return.

    "In privacy we dwelt, a wedded pair,
Companions daily, often all day long; 585
Not placed by fortune within easy reach
Of various intercourse, nor wishing aught
Beyond the allowance of our own fire-
    side,
The twain within our happy cottage born,
Inmates, and heirs of our united love; 590
Graced mutually by difference of sex,
And with no wider interval of time
Between their several births than served
    for one
To establish something of a leader's sway;
Yet left them joined by sympathy in
    age;   595
Equals in pleasure, fellows in pursuit.
On these two pillars rested as in air
Our solitude.
         It soothes me to perceive,
Your courtesy withholds not from my
    words
Attentive audience. But, oh! gentle
    Friends,   600
As times of quiet and unbroken peace,
Though, for a nation, times of blessed-
    ness,

Give back faint echoes from the historian's
    page;
So, in the imperfect sounds of this dis-
    course,
Depressed I hear, how faithless is the
    voice   605
Which those most blissful days rever-
    berate.
What special record can, or need, be given
To rules and habits, whereby much was
    done,
But all within the sphere of little things;
Of humble, though, to us, important cares,
And precious interests? Smoothly did
    our life   611
Advance, swerving not from the path
    prescribed;
Her annual, her diurnal, round alike
Maintained with faithful care. And you
    divine
The worst effects that our condition saw
If you imagine changes slowly wrought,
And in their process unperceivable;
Not wished for; sometimes noticed with
    a sigh,
(Whate'er of good or lovely they might
    bring)
Sighs of regret, for the familiar good 620
And loveliness endeared which they re-
    moved.

    "Seven years of occupation undisturbed
Established seemingly a right to hold
That happiness; and use and habit gave
To what an alien spirit had acquired 625
A patrimonial sanctity. And thus,
With thoughts and wishes bounded to
    this world,
I lived and breathed; most grateful—if
    to enjoy
Without repining or desire for more,
For different lot, or change to higher
    sphere,   630
(Only except some impulses of pride
With no determined object, though up-
    held
By theories with suitable support)—
Most grateful, if in such wise to enjoy
Be proof of gratitude for what we have;
Else, I allow, most thankless.—But, at
    once,   636

From some dark seat of fatal power was
    urged
A claim that shattered all.—Our blooming
    girl,
Caught in the gripe of death, with such
    brief time
To struggle in as scarcely would allow 640
Her cheek to change its colour, was
    conveyed
From us to inaccessible worlds, to regions
Where height, or depth, admits not the
    approach
Of living man, though longing to pursue.
—With even as brief a warning—and how
    soon,   645
With what short interval of time between,
I tremble yet to think of—our last prop,
Our happy life's only remaining stay—
The brother followed; and was seen no
    more!

    "Calm as a frozen lake when ruthless
    winds   650
Blow fiercely, agitating earth and sky,
The Mother now remained; as if in her,
Who, to the lowest region of the soul,
Had been erewhile unsettled and dis-
    turbed,
This second visitation had no power 655
To shake; but only to bind up and seal;
And to establish thankfulness of heart
In Heaven's determinations, ever just.
The eminence whereon her spirit stood,
Mine was unable to attain. Immense
The space that severed us! But, as the
    sight   661
Communicates with heaven's ethereal orbs
Incalculably distant; so, I felt
That consolation may descend from far
(And that is intercourse, and union, too,)
While, overcome with speechless grati-
    tude,   666
And, with a holier love inspired, I looked
On her—at once superior to my woes
And partner of my loss.—O heavy change!
Dimness o'er this clear luminary crept 670
Insensibly;—the immortal and divine
Yielded to mortal reflux; her pure glory,
As from the pinnacle of worldly state
Wretched ambition drops astounded, fell
Into a gulf obscure of silent grief, 675

And keen heart-anguish—of itself a-
　　shamed,
Yet obstinately cherishing itself:
And, so consumed, she melted from my
　　arms;
And left me, on this earth, disconsolate!

"What followed cannot be reviewed in
　　thought;　　　　　　　　　680
Much less, retraced in words. If she,
　　of life
Blameless, so intimate with love and joy
And all the tender motions of the soul,
Had been supplanted, could I hope to
　　stand—
Infirm, dependent, and now destitute? 685
I called on dreams and visions, to disclose
That which is veiled from waking thought;
　　conjured
Eternity, as men constrain a ghost
To appear and answer; to the grave I
　　spake
Imploringly;—looked up, and asked the
　　Heavens　　　　　　　　690
If Angels traversed their cerulean floors,
If fixed or wandering star could tidings
　　yield
Of the departed spirit—what abode
It occupies—what consciousness retains
Of former loves and interests. Then my
　　soul　　　　　　　　　695
Turned inward,—to examine of what stuff
Time's fetters are composed; and life was
　　put
To inquisition, long and profitless!
By pain of heart—now checked—and now
　　impelled—
The intellectual power, through words
　　and things,　　　　　　　700
Went sounding on, a dim and perilous
　　way!
And from those transports, and these toils
　　abstruse,
Some trace am I enabled to retain
Of time, else lost;—existing unto me
Only by records in myself not found. 705

"From that abstraction I was roused,—
　　and how?
Even as a thoughtful shepherd by a flash
Of lightning startled in a gloomy cave

Of these wild hills. For, lo! the dread
　　Bastille,
With all the chambers in its horrid
　　towers,　　　　　　　　710
Fell to the ground:—by violence over-
　　thrown
Of indignation; and with shouts that
　　drowned
The crash it made in falling! From the
　　wreck
A golden palace rose, or seemed to rise,
The appointed seat of equitable law　715
And mild paternal sway. The potent
　　shock
I felt: the transformation I perceived,
As marvellously seized as in that moment
When, from the blind mist issuing, I
　　beheld
Glory—beyond all glory ever seen,　720
Confusion infinite of heaven and earth,
Dazzling the soul. Meanwhile, prophetic
　　harps
In every grove were ringing, 'War shall
　　cease;
Did ye not hear that conquest is abjured?
Bring garlands, bring forth choicest
　　flowers, to deck　　　　725
The tree of Liberty.'—My heart re-
　　bounded;
My melancholy voice the chorus joined;
—'Be joyful all ye nations; in all lands,
Ye that are capable of joy be glad!
Henceforth, whate'er is wanting to your-
　　selves　　　　　　　　730
In others ye shall promptly find;—and all,
Enriched by mutual and reflected wealth,
Shall with one heart honour their common
　　kind.'

"Thus was I reconverted to the world;
Society became my glittering bride,　735
And airy hopes my children.—From the
　　depths
Of natural passion, seemingly escaped,
My soul diffused herself in wide embrace
Of institutions, and the forms of things;
As they exist, in mutable array,　　740
Upon life's surface. What, though in my
　　veins
There flowed no Gallic blood, nor had I
　　breathed

The air of France, not less than Gallic
   zeal
Kindled and burnt among the sapless
   twigs
Of my exhausted heart. If busy men 745
In sober conclave met, to weave a web
Of amity, whose living threads should
   stretch
Beyond the seas, and to the farthest pole,
There did I sit, assisting. If, with noise
And acclamation, crowds in open air 750
Expressed the tumult of their minds, my
   voice
There mingled, heard or not. The powers
   of song
I left not uninvoked; and, in still groves,
Where mild enthusiasts tuned a pensive
   lay
Of thanks and expectation, in accord 755
With their belief, I sang Saturnian rule
Returned,—a progeny of golden years
Permitted to descend, and bless mankind.
—With promises the Hebrew Scriptures
   teem:
I felt their invitation; and resumed 760
A long-suspended office in the House
Of public worship, where, the glowing
   phrase
Of ancient inspiration serving me,
I promised also,—with undaunted trust
Foretold, and added prayer to prophecy;
The admiration winning of the crowd; 766
The help desiring of the pure devout.

"Scorn and contempt forbid me to
   proceed!
But History, time's slavish scribe, will tell
How rapidly the zealots of the cause 770
Disbanded—or in hostile ranks appeared;
Some, tired of honest service; these, out-
   done,
Disgusted therefore, or appalled, by aims
Of fiercer zealots—so confusion reigned,
And the more faithful were compelled to
   exclaim, 775
As Brutus did to Virtue, 'Liberty,
I worshipped thee, and find thee but a
   Shade!'

"Such recantation had for me no charm,
Nor would I bend to it; who should have
   grieved

At aught, however fair, that bore the
   mien 780
Of a conclusion, or catastrophe.
Why then conceal, that, when the simply
   good
In timid selfishness withdrew, I sought
Other support, not scrupulous whence it
   came;
And, by what compromise it stood, not
   nice? 785
Enough if notions seemed to be high-
   pitched,
And qualities determined.—Among men
So charactered did I maintain a strife
Hopeless, and still more hopeless every
   hour;
But, in the process, I began to feel 790
That, if the emancipation of the world
Were missed, I should at least secure my
   own,
And be in part compensated. For rights,
Widely—inveterately usurped upon,
I spake with vehemence; and promptly
   seized 795
All that Abstraction furnished for my
   needs
Or purposes; nor scrupled to proclaim,
And propagate, by liberty of life,
Those new persuasions. Not that I re-
   joiced,
Or even found pleasure, in such vagrant
   course, 800
For its own sake; but farthest from the
   walk
Which I had trod in happiness and
   peace,
Was most inviting to a troubled mind;
That, in a struggling and distempered
   world,
Saw a seductive image of herself. 805
Yet, mark the contradictions of which
   Man
Is still the sport! Here Nature was my
   guide,
The Nature of the dissolute; but thee,
O fostering Nature! I rejected—smiled
At others' tears in pity; and in scorn
At those, which thy soft influence some-
   times drew 811
From my unguarded heart.—The tran-
   quil shores

Of Britain circumscribed me; else, per-
haps
I might have been entangled among
deeds,
Which, now, as infamous, I should abhor—
Despise, as senseless: for my spirit re-
lished   816
Strangely the exasperation of that Land,
Which turned an angry beak against the
down
Of her own breast; confounded into hope
Of disencumbering thus her fretful wings.

"But all was quieted by iron bonds
Of military sway. The shifting aims,
The moral interests, the creative might,
The varied functions and high attributes
Of civil action, yielded to a power   825
Formal, and odious, and contemptible.
—In Britain, ruled a panic dread of
change;
The weak were praised, rewarded, and
advanced;
And, from the impulse of a just disdain,
Once more did I retire into myself.   830
There feeling no contentment, I resolved
To fly, for safeguard, to some foreign
shore,
Remote from Europe; from her blasted
hopes;
Her fields of carnage, and polluted air.

"Fresh blew the wind, when o'er the
Atlantic Main   835
The ship went gliding with her thought-
less crew;
And who among them but an Exile, freed
From discontent, indifferent, pleased to
sit
Among the busily-employed, not more
With obligation charged, with service
taxed,   840
Than the loose pendant—to the idle wind
Upon the tall mast streaming. But, ye
Powers
Of soul and sense mysteriously allied,
O, never let the Wretched, if a choice
Be left him, trust the freight of his
distress   845
To a long voyage on the silent deep!
For, like a plague, will memory break out;

And, in the blank and solitude of things,
Upon his spirit, with a fever's strength,
Will conscience prey.—Feebly must they
have felt   850
Who, in old time, attired with snakes and
whips
The vengeful Furies. *Beautiful* regards
Were turned on me—the face of her I
loved;
The Wife and Mother pitifully fixing
Tender reproaches, insupportable!   855
Where now that boasted liberty? No
welcome
From unknown objects I received; and
those,
Known and familiar, which the vaulted
sky
Did, in the placid clearness of the night,
Disclose, had accusations to prefer   860
Against my peace. Within the cabin
stood
That volume—as a compass for the soul—
Revered among the nations. I implored
Its guidance; but the infallible support
Of faith was wanting. Tell me, why
refused   865
To One by storms annoyed and adverse
winds;
Perplexed with currents; of his weak-
ness sick;
Of vain endeavours tired; and by his own,
And by his nature's, ignorance, dismayed!

"Long wished-for sight, the Western
World appeared;   870
And, when the ship was moored, I leaped
ashore
Indignantly—resolved to be a man,
Who, having o'er the past no power,
would live
No longer in subjection to the past,   874
With abject mind—from a tyrannic lord
Inviting penance, fruitlessly endured:
So, like a fugitive, whose feet have cleared
Some boundary, which his followers may
not cross
In prosecution of their deadly chase,
Respiring I looked round.—How bright
the sun,   880
The breeze how soft! Can any thing
produced

In the old World compare, thought I, for
    power
And majesty with this gigantic stream,
Sprung from the desert? And behold
    a city
Fresh, youthful, and aspiring! What are
    these   885
To me, or I to them? As much, at least
As he desires that they should be, whom
    winds
And waves have wafted to this distant
    shore,
In the condition of a damaged seed,
Whose fibres cannot, if they would, take
    root.   890
Here may I roam at large;—my business
    is,
Roaming at large, to observe, and not to
    feel
And, therefore, not to act—convinced
    that all
Which bears the name of action, how-
    soe'er
Beginning, ends in servitude—still pain-
    ful,   895
And mostly profitless. And, sooth to
    say,
On nearer view, a motley spectacle
Appeared, of high pretensions—unre-
    proved
But by the obstreperous voice of higher
    still;
Big passions strutting on a petty stage;
Which a detached spectator may regard
Not unamused.—But ridicule demands
Quick change of objects; and, to laugh
    alone,   903
At a composing distance from the haunts
Of strife and folly, though it be a treat
As choice as musing Leisure can bestow;
Yet, in the very centre of the crowd,
To keep the secret of a poignant scorn,
Howe'er to airy Demons suitable,
Of all unsocial courses, is least fit   910
For the gross spirit of mankind,—the
    one
That soonest fails to please, and quickliest
    turns
Into vexation.
          Let us, then, I said,
Leave this unknit Republic to the scourge

Of her own passions; and to regions haste,
Whose shades have never felt the en-
    croaching axe,   916
Or soil endured a transfer in the mart
Of dire rapacity. There, Man abides,
Primeval Nature's child. A creature weak
In combination, (wherefore else driven
    back   920
So far, and of his old inheritance
So easily deprived?) but, for that cause,
More dignified, and stronger in himself;
Whether to act, judge, suffer, or enjoy.
True, the intelligence of social art   925
Hath overpowered his forefathers, and
    soon
Will sweep the remnant of his line away;
But contemplations, worthier, nobler far
Than her destructive energies, attend 929
His independence, when along the side
Of Mississippi, or that northern stream[1]
That spreads into successive seas, he walks;
Pleased to perceive his own unshackled
    life,
And his innate capacities of soul,
There imaged: or when, having gained
    the top   935
Of some commanding eminence, which yet
Intruder ne'er beheld, he thence surveys
Regions of wood and wide savannah, vast
Expanse of unappropriated earth,
With mind that sheds a light on what he
    sees;   940
Free as the sun, and lonely as the sun,
Pouring above his head its radiance down
Upon a living and rejoicing world!

  "So, westward, tow'rd the unviolated
    woods
I bent my way; and, roaming far and
    wide,   945
Failed not to greet the merry Mocking-
    bird;
And, while the melancholy Muccawiss
(The sportive bird's companion in the
    grove)
Repeated o'er and o'er his plaintive cry,
I sympathised at leisure with the sound;
But that pure archetype of human great-
    ness,   951

---

[1] See Note, p. 927.

I found him not. There, in his stead,
    appeared
A creature, squalid, vengeful, and im-
    pure ;
Remorseless, and submissive to no law
But superstitious fear, and abject sloth.

  "Enough is told ! Here am I—ye have
    heard   956
What evidence I seek, and vainly seek ;
What from my fellow-beings I require,
And either they have not to give, or I
Lack virtue to receive ; what I myself,
Too oft by wilful forfeiture, have lost 961
Nor can regain.   How languidly I look
Upon this visible fabric of the world,
May be divined—perhaps it hath been
    said :—
But spare your pity, if there be in me 965
Aught that deserves respect : for I exist,
Within myself, not comfortless. — The
    tenour
Which my life holds, he readily may con-
    ceive
Whoe'er hath stood to watch a mountain
    brook
In some still passage of its course, and
    seen,   970
Within the depths of its capacious breast,

Inverted trees, rocks, clouds, and azure
    sky ;
And, on its glassy surface, specks of foam,
And conglobated bubbles undissolved,
Numerous as stars ; that, by their onward
    lapse,   975
Betray to sight the motion of the stream,
Else imperceptible.   Meanwhile, is heard
A softened roar, or murmur ; and the
    sound
Though soothing, and the little floating
    isles
Though beautiful, are both by Nature
    charged   980
With the same pensive office ; and make
    known
Through what perplexing labyrinths, ab-
    rupt
Precipitations, and untoward straits,
The earth-born wanderer hath passed ;
    and quickly,   984
That respite o'er, like traverses and toils
Must he again encounter.—Such a stream
Is human Life ; and so the Spirit fares
In the best quiet to her course allowed ;
And such is mine,—save only for a hope
That my particular current soon will reach
The unfathomable gulf, where all is
    still !   991

BOOK FOURTH.

DESPONDENCY CORRECTED.

ARGUMENT.

State of feeling produced by the foregoing Narrative.—A belief in a superintending Providence the only adequate support under affliction.—Wanderer's ejaculation.—Acknowledges the difficulty of a lively faith.—Hence immoderate sorrow.—Exhortations.—How received.—Wanderer applies his discourse to that other cause of dejection in the Solitary's mind.—Disappointment from the French Revolution.—States grounds of hope, and insists on the necessity of patience and fortitude with respect to the course of great revolutions.—Knowledge the source of tranquillity.—Rural Solitude favourable to knowledge of the inferior Creatures; Study of their habits and ways recommended; exhortation to bodily exertion and communion with Nature.—Morbid Solitude pitiable.—Superstition better than apathy.—Apathy and destitution unknown in the infancy of society.—The various modes of Religion prevented it.—Illustrated in the Jewish, Persian, Babylonian, Chaldean, and Grecian modes of belief.—Solitary interposes.—Wanderer points out the influence of religious and imaginative feeling in the humble ranks of society, illustrated from present and past times.—These principles tend to recall exploded superstitions and Popery.—Wanderer rebuts this charge, and contrasts the dignities of the Imagination with the presumptuous littleness of certain modern Philosophers.—Recommends other lights and guides.—Asserts the power of the Soul to regenerate herself; Solitary asks how.—Reply.—Personal appeal.—Exhortation to activity of body renewed.—How to commune with Nature.—Wanderer concludes with a legitimate union of the imagination, affections, understanding, and reason.—Effect of his discourse.—Evening; Return to the Cottage.

HERE closed the Tenant of that lonely
 vale
His mournful narrative—commenced in
 pain,
In pain commenced, and ended without
 peace:
Yet tempered, not unfrequently, with
 strains
Of native feeling, grateful to our minds;
And yielding surely some relief to his, 6
While we sate listening with compassion
 due.
A pause of silence followed; then, with
 voice
That did not falter though the heart was
 moved,
The Wanderer said:—
     "One adequate support 10
For the calamities of mortal life
Exists—one only; an assured belief
That the procession of our fate, howe'er
Sad or disturbed, is ordered by a Being
Of infinite benevolence and power; 15
Whose everlasting purposes embrace
All accidents, converting them to good.
—The darts of anguish *fix* not where the
 seat
Of suffering hath been thoroughly fortified
By acquiescence in the Will supreme 20
For time and for eternity; by faith,
Faith absolute in God, including hope,
And the defence that lies in boundless
 love
Of his perfections; with habitual dread
Of aught unworthily conceived, endured
Impatiently, ill-done, or left undone, 26
To the dishonour of his holy name.
Soul of our Souls, and safeguard of the
 world!
Sustain, thou only canst, the sick of
 heart;
Restore their languid spirits, and recall 30
Their lost affections unto thee and
 thine!"

Then, as we issued from that covert
   nook,
He thus continued, lifting up his eyes
To heaven:—"How beautiful this dome
   of sky;
And the vast hills, in fluctuation fixed 35
At thy command, how awful ! Shall the
   Soul,
Human and rational, report of thee
Even less than these !—Be mute who will,
   who can,
Yet I will praise thee with impassioned
   voice:
My lips, that may forget thee in the
   crowd, 40
Cannot forget thee here; where thou hast
   built,
For thy own glory, in the wilderness !
Me didst thou constitute a priest of thine,
In such a temple as we now behold
Reared for thy presence : therefore am I
   bound 45
To worship, here, and everywhere—as one
Not doomed to ignorance, though forced
   to tread,
From childhood up, the ways of poverty ;
From unreflecting ignorance preserved,
And from debasement rescued.—By thy
   grace 50
The particle divine remained unquenched;
And, 'mid the wild weeds of a rugged soil,
Thy bounty caused to flourish deathless
   flowers,
From paradise transplanted : wintry age
Impends ; the frost will gather round my
   heart ; 55
If the flowers wither, I am worse than
   dead !
—Come, labour, when the worn-out frame
   requires
Perpetual sabbath ; come, disease and
   want ;
And sad exclusion through decay of
   sense ;
But leave me unabated trust in thee— 60
And let thy favour, to the end of life,
Inspire me with ability to seek
Repose and hope among eternal things—
Father of heaven and earth ! and I am
   rich,
And will possess my portion in content !

"And what are things eternal?—powers
   depart," 66
The grey-haired Wanderer steadfastly
   replied,
Answering the question which himself
   had asked,
"Possessions vanish, and opinions change,
And passions hold a fluctuating seat : 70
But, by the storms of circumstance un-
   shaken,
And subject neither to eclipse nor wane,
Duty exists ;—immutably survive,
For our support, the measures and the
   forms,
Which an abstract intelligence supplies ;
Whose kingdom is, where time and space
   are not. 76
Of other converse which mind, soul, and
   heart,
Do, with united urgency, require,
What more that may not perish ?—Thou,
   dread source, 79
Prime, self-existing cause and end of all
That in the scale of being fill their place ;
Above our human region, or below,
Set and sustained ;—thou, who didst wrap
   the cloud
Of infancy around us, that thyself,
Therein, with our simplicity awhile 85
Might'st hold, on earth, communion un-
   disturbed ;
Who from the anarchy of dreaming sleep,
Or from its death-like void, with punctual
   care,
And touch as gentle as the morning light,
Restor'st us, daily, to the powers of sense
And reason's steadfast rule—thou, thou
   alone 91
Art everlasting, and the blessed Spirits,
Which thou includest, as the sea her
   waves :
For adoration thou endur'st ; endure
For consciousness the motions of thy
   will ; 95
For apprehension those transcendent
   truths
Of the pure intellect, that stand as laws
(Submission constituting strength and
   power)
Even to thy Being's infinite majesty !
This universe shall pass away—a work 100

Glorious! because the shadow of thy
    might,
A step, or link, for intercourse with thee.
Ah! if the time must come, in which my
    feet
No more shall stray where meditation
    leads,
By flowing stream, through wood, or
    craggy wild,   105
Loved haunts like these; the unim-
    prisoned Mind
May yet have scope to range among her
    own,
Her thoughts, her images, her high desires.
If the dear faculty of sight should fail, 109
Still, it may be allowed me to remember
What visionary powers of eye and soul
In youth were mine; when, stationed on
    the top
Of some huge hill, expectant, I beheld
The sun rise up, from distant climes
    returned
Darkness to chase, and sleep; and bring
    the day   115
His bounteous gift! or saw him toward
    the deep
Sink, with a retinue of flaming clouds
Attended; then, my spirit was entranced
With joy exalted to beatitude;
The measure of my soul was filled with
    bliss,   120
And holiest love; as earth, sea, air, with
    light,
With pomp, with glory, with magnificence!

"Those fervent raptures are for ever
    flown;
And, since their date, my soul hath under-
    gone   124
Change manifold, for better or for worse:
Yet cease I not to struggle, and aspire
Heavenward; and chide the part of me
    that flags,
Through sinful choice; or dread necessity
On human nature from above imposed.
'Tis, by comparison, an easy task   130
Earth to despise; but, to converse with
    heaven—[1]
This is not easy:—to relinquish all

---

[1] See Note, p. 927

We have, or hope, of happiness and joy,
And stand in freedom loosened from this
    world,
I deem not arduous; but must needs
    confess   135
That 'tis a thing impossible to frame
Conceptions equal to the soul's desires;
And the most difficult of tasks to *keep*
Heights which the soul is competent to
    gain.
—Man is of dust: ethereal hopes are his,
Which, when they should sustain them-
    selves aloft,   141
Want due consistence; like a pillar of
    smoke,
That with majestic energy from earth
Rises; but, having reached the thinner
    air,
Melts, and dissolves, and is no longer seen.
From this infirmity of mortal kind   146
Sorrow proceeds, which else were not; at least,
If grief be something hallowed and or-
    dained,
If, in proportion, it be just and meet,
Yet, through this weakness of the general
    heart,   150
Is it enabled to maintain its hold
In that excess which conscience dis-
    approves.
For who could sink and settle to that
    point
Of selfishness; so senseless who could be
As long and perseveringly to mourn   155
For any object of his love, removed
From this unstable world, if he could fix
A satisfying view upon that state
Of pure, imperishable, blessedness,
Which reason promises, and holy writ   160
Ensures to all believers?—Yet mistrust
Is of such incapacity, methinks,
No natural branch; despondency far less;
And, least of all, is absolute despair.
—And, if there be whose tender frames
    have drooped   165
Even to the dust; apparently, through
    weight
Of anguish unrelieved, and lack of power
An agonizing sorrow to transmute;
Deem not that proof is here of hope with-
    held

When wanted most; a confidence im-
paired   170
So pitiably, that, having ceased to see
With bodily eyes, they are borne down
by love
Of what is lost, and perish through regret.
Oh! no, the innocent Sufferer often sees
Too clearly; feels too vividly; and longs
To realize the vision, with intense   176
And over-constant yearning;—there—
there lies
The excess, by which the balance is de-
stroyed.
Too, too contracted are these walls of
flesh,
This vital warmth too cold, these visual
orbs,   180
Though inconceivably endowed, too dim
For any passion of the soul that leads
To ecstasy; and all the crooked paths
Of time and change disdaining, takes its
course
Along the line of limitless desires.   185
I, speaking now from such disorder free,
Nor rapt, nor craving, but in settled
peace,
I cannot doubt that they whom you de-
plore
Are glorified; or, if they sleep, shall
wake
From sleep, and dwell with God in end-
less love.   190
Hope, below this, consists not with be-
lief
In mercy, carried infinite degrees
Beyond the tenderness of human hearts:
Hope, below this, consists not with belief
In perfect wisdom, guiding mightiest
power,   195
That finds no limits but her own pure will.

"Here then we rest; not fearing for
our creed
The worst that human reasoning can
achieve,
To unsettle or perplex it: yet with pain
Acknowledging, and grievous self-re-
proach,   200
That, though immovably convinced, we
want
Zeal, and the virtue to exist by faith

As soldiers live by courage; as, by
strength
Of heart, the sailor fights with roaring seas.
Alas! the endowment of immortal power
Is matched unequally with custom, time[1],
And domineering faculties of sense
In *all;* in most with superadded foes,
Idle temptations; open vanities,
Ephemeral offspring of the unblushing
world;   210
And, in the private regions of the mind,
Ill-governed passions, ranklings of despite,
Immoderate wishes, pining discontent,
Distress and care. What then remains?—
To seek
Those helps for his occasions ever near
Who lacks not will to use them; vows,
renewed   216
On the first motion of a holy thought;
Vigils of contemplation; praise; and
prayer—
A stream, which, from the fountain of
the heart   219
Issuing, however feebly, nowhere flows
Without access of unexpected strength.
But, above all, the victory is most sure
For him, who, seeking faith by virtue,
strives
To yield entire submission to the law
Of conscience—conscience reverenced and
obeyed,   225
As God's most intimate presence in the
soul,
And his most perfect image in the world.
—Endeavour thus to live; these rules
regard;
These helps solicit; and a steadfast seat
Shall then be yours among the happy few
Who dwell on earth, yet breathe empy-
real air,   231
Sons of the morning. For your nobler
part,
Ere disencumbered of her mortal chains,
Doubt shall be quelled and trouble chased
away;
With only such degree of sadness left   235
As may support longings of pure desire;
And strengthen love, rejoicing secretly
In the sublime attractions of the grave."

---

[1] See Note, p. 927.

While, in this strain, the venerable
    Sage
Poured forth his aspirations, and an-
    nounced   240
His judgments, near that lonely house we
    paced
A plot of green-sward, seemingly pre-
    served
By nature's care from wreck of scattered
    stones,
And from encroachment of encircling
    heath :
Small space ! but, for reiterated steps,
Smooth and commodious; as a stately
    deck   246
Which to and fro the mariner is used
To tread for pastime, talking with his
    mates,
Or haply thinking of far-distant friends,
While the ship glides before a steady
    breeze.   250
Stillness prevailed around us: and the
    voice
That spake was capable to lift the soul
Toward regions yet more tranquil. But,
    methought,
That he, whose fixed despondency had
    given
Impulse and motive to that strong dis-
    course,   255
Was less upraised in spirit than abashed ;
Shrinking from admonition, like a man
Who feels that to exhort is to reproach.
Yet not to be diverted from his aim,
The Sage continued :—
            "For that other loss, 260
The loss of confidence in social man,
By the unexpected transports of our age
Carried so high, that every thought,
    which looked
Beyond the temporal destiny of the Kind,
To many seemed superfluous—as, no
    cause   265
Could e'er for such exalted confidence
Exist ; so, none is now for fixed despair :
The two extremes are equally disowned
By reason : if, with sharp recoil, from one
You have been driven far as its opposite,
Between them seek the point whereon to
    build   271
Sound expectations. So doth he advise

Who shared at first the illusion ; but was
    soon
Cast from the pedestal of pride by shocks
Which Nature gently gave, in woods and
    fields ;   275
Nor unreproved by Providence, thus
    speaking
To the inattentive children of the world :
'Vain-glorious Generation ! what new
    powers
On you have been conferred ? what gifts,
    withheld
From your progenitors, have ye received,
Fit recompense of new desert ? what claim
Are ye prepared to urge, that my decrees
For you should undergo a sudden change ;
And the weak functions of one busy day,
Reclaiming and extirpating, perform 285
What all the slowly-moving years of time,
With their united force, have left undone ?
By nature's gradual processes be taught ;
By story be confounded ! Ye aspire
Rashly, to fall once more ; and that false
    fruit,   290
Which, to your overweening spirits,
    yields
Hope of a flight celestial, will produce
Misery and shame. But Wisdom of her
    sons
Shall not the less, though late, be justi-
    fied.'

    "Such timely warning," said the Wan-
        derer, "gave   295
That visionary voice ; and, at this day,
When a Tartarean darkness overspreads
The groaning nations ; when the impious
    rule,
By will or by established ordinance,
Their own dire agents, and constrain the
    good   300
To acts which they abhor ; though I be-
    wail
This triumph, yet the pity of my heart
Prevents me not from owning, that the
    law,
By which mankind now suffers, is most
    just.
For by superior energies ; more strict 305
Affiance in each other ; faith more firm
In their unhallowed principles ; the bad

Have fairly earned a victory o'er the weak,
The vacillating, inconsistent good.
Therefore, not unconsoled, I wait—in
   hope   310
To see the moment, when the righteous
   cause
Shall gain defenders zealous and devout
As they who have opposed her ; in which
   Virtue
Will, to her efforts, tolerate no bounds
That are not lofty as her rights ; aspiring
By impulse of her own ethereal zeal. 316
That spirit only can redeem mankind ;
And when that sacred spirit shall appear,
Then shall *our* triumph be complete as
   theirs.
Yet, should this confidence prove vain,
   the wise   320
Have still the keeping of their proper
   peace ;
Are guardians of their own tranquillity.
They act, or they recede, observe, and
   feel ;
'Knowing the heart of man is set to be [1]
The centre of this world, about the which
Those revolutions of disturbances   326
Still roll ; where all the aspects of misery
Predominate ; whose strong effects are
   such
As he must bear, being powerless to re-
   dress ;
And that unless above himself he can   330
Erect himself, how poor a thing is man [2] *!'*

"Happy is he who lives to understand,
Not human nature only, but explores
All natures,—to the end that he may find
The law that governs each ; and where
   begins   335
The union, the partition where, that
   makes
Kind and degree, among all visible Beings ;
The constitutions, powers, and faculties,
Which they inherit,—cannot step be-
   yond,—   339
And cannot fall beneath ; that do assign
To every class its station and its office,
Through all the mighty commonwealth of
   things ;

Up from the creeping plant to sovereign
   Man.
Such converse, if directed by a meek,
Sincere, and humble spirit, teaches love :
For knowledge is delight ; and such de-
   light   346
Breeds love : yet, suited as it rather is
To thought and to the climbing intellect,
It teaches less to love, than to adore ;
If that be not indeed the highest love !"

"Yet," said I, tempted here to inter-
   pose,   351
"The dignity of life is not impaired
By aught that innocently satisfies
The humbler cravings of the heart ; and
   he
Is still a happier man, who, for those
   heights   355
Of speculation not unfit, descends ;
And such benign affections cultivates
Among the inferior kinds ; not merely
   those
That he may call his own, and which de-
   pend,
As individual objects of regard,   360
Upon his care, from whom he also looks
For signs and tokens of a mutual bond ;
But others, far beyond this narrow sphere,
Whom, for the very sake of love, he loves.
Nor is it a mean praise of rural life   365
And solitude, that they do favour most,
Most frequently call forth, and best sus-
   tain,
These pure sensations ; that can pene-
   trate
The obstreperous city ; on the barren seas
Are not unfelt ; and much might recom-
   mend,   370
How much they might inspirit and en-
   dear,
The loneliness of this sublime retreat !"

"Yes," said the Sage, resuming the dis-
   course
Again directed to his downcast Friend,
"If, with the froward will and grovelling
   soul   375
Of man, offended, liberty is here,
And invitation every hour renewed,
To mark *their* placid state, who never
   heard

---

[1] See Note, p. 927.   [2] Daniel.

Of a command which they have power to
    break,
Or rule which they are tempted to trans-
    gress: 380
These with a soothed or elevated heart,
May we behold; their knowledge register;
Observe their ways; and, free from envy,
    find
Complacence there:—but wherefore this
    to you?
I guess that, welcome to your lonely
    hearth,   385
The redbreast, ruffled up by winter's cold
Into a 'feathery bunch,' feeds at your
    hand:
A box, perchance, is from your casement
    hung
For the small wren to build in;—not in
    vain,   389
The barriers disregarding that surround
This deep abiding place, before your sight
Mounts on the breeze the butterfly; and
    soars,
Small creature as she is, from earth's
    bright flowers,
Into the dewy clouds. Ambition reigns
In the waste wilderness: the Soul ascends
Drawn towards her native firmament of
    heaven,   396
When the fresh eagle, in the month of May,
Upborne, at evening, on replenished wing,
This shaded valley leaves; and leaves the
    dark
Empurpled hills, conspicuously renewing
A proud communication with the sun 401
Low sunk beneath the horizon!—List!—
    I heard,
From yon huge breast of rock, a voice
    sent forth
As if the visible mountain made the cry.
Again!"—The effect upon the soul was
    such   405
As he expressed: from out the mountain's
    heart
The solemn voice appeared to issue,
    startling
The blank air—for the region all around
Stood empty of all shape of life, and silent
Save for that single cry, the unanswer'd
    bleat   410
Of a poor lamb—left somewhere to itself,

The plaintive spirit of the solitude!
He paused, as if unwilling to proceed,
Through consciousness that silence in such
    place
Was best, the most affecting eloquence.
But soon his thoughts returned upon
    themselves,   416
And, in soft tone of speech, thus he re-
    sumed.

"Ah! if the heart, too confidently
    raised,
Perchance too lightly occupied, or lulled
Too easily, despise or overlook   420
The vassalage that binds her to the earth,
Her sad dependence upon time, and all
The trepidations of mortality,
What place so destitute and void—but
    there
The little flower her vanity shall check;
The trailing worm reprove her thought-
    less pride?   426

"These craggy regions, these chaotic
    wilds,
Does that benignity pervade, that warms
The mole contented with her darksome
    walk
In the cold ground; and to the emmet
    gives   430
Her foresight, and intelligence that makes
The tiny creatures strong by social league;
Supports the generations, multiplies
Their tribes, till we behold a spacious
    plain
Or grassy bottom, all, with little hills—
Their labour, covered, as a lake with
    waves;   436
Thousands of cities, in the desert place
Built up of life, and food, and means of
    life!
Nor wanting here, to entertain the
    thought,
Creatures that in communities exist 440
Less, as might seem, for general guardian-
    ship
Or through dependence upon mutual aid,
Than by participation of delight
And a strict love of fellowship, combined.
What other spirit can it be that prompts
The gilded summer flies to mix and weave

Their sports together in the solar beam,
Or in the gloom of twilight hum their joy?
More obviously the self-same influence
 rules
The feathered kinds; the fieldfare's pen-
 sive flock,   450
The cawing rooks, and sea-mews from
 afar,
Hovering above these inland solitudes,
By the rough wind unscattered, at whose
 call
Up through the trenches of the long-
 drawn vales
Their voyage was begun: nor is its power
Unfelt among the sedentary fowl 456
That seek yon pool, and there prolong
 their stay
In silent congress; or together roused
Take flight; while with their clang the
 air resounds.
And, over all, in that ethereal vault, 460
Is the mute company of changeful clouds;
Bright apparition, suddenly put forth,
The rainbow smiling on the faded storm;
The mild assemblage of the starry hea-
 vens;
And the great sun, earth's universal lord!

"How bountiful is Nature! he shall
 find   466
Who seeks not; and to him, who hath
 not asked,
Large measures shall be dealt. Three
 sabbath-days
Are scarcely told, since, on a service bent
Of mere humanity, you clomb those
 heights;   470
And what a marvellous and heavenly
 show
Was suddenly revealed!—the swains
 moved on,
And heeded not: you lingered, you per-
 ceived
And felt, deeply as living man could feel.
There is a luxury in self-dispraise; 475
And inward self-disparagement affords
To meditative spleen a grateful feast.
Trust me, pronouncing on your own de-
 sert,
You judge unthankfully: distempered
 nerves

Infect the thoughts; the languor of the
 frame   480
Depresses the soul's vigour. Quit your
 couch—
Cleave not so fondly to your moody cell;
Nor let the hallowed powers, that shed
 from heaven
Stillness and rest, with disapproving eye
Look down upon your taper, through
 a watch   485
Of midnight hours, unseasonably twink-
 ling
In this deep Hollow, like a sullen star
Dimly reflected in a lonely pool.
Take courage, and withdraw yourself
 from ways
That run not parallel to nature's course.
Rise with the lark! your matins shall
 obtain   491
Grace, be their composition what it may,
If but with hers performed; climb once
 again,
Climb every day, those ramparts; meet
 the breeze
Upon their tops, adventurous as a bee
That from your garden thither soars, to
 feed   496
On new-blown heath; let yon command-
 ing rock
Be your frequented watch-tower; roll the
 stone
In thunder down the mountains; with all
 your might
Chase the wild goat; and if the bold red
 deer   500
Fly to those harbours, driven by hound
 and horn
Loud echoing, add your speed to the
 pursuit;
So, wearied to your hut shall you return,
And sink at evening into sound repose."

The Solitary lifted toward the hills 505
A kindling eye:—accordant feelings
 rushed
Into my bosom, whence these words
 broke forth:
"Oh! what a joy it were, in vigorous
 health,
To have a body (this our vital frame
With shrinking sensibility endued, 510

And all the nice regards of flesh and
    blood)
And to the elements surrender it
As if it were a spirit !—How divine,
The liberty, for frail, for mortal, man 514
To roam at large among unpeopled glens
And mountainous retirements, only trod
By devious footsteps ; regions consecrate
To oldest time ! and, reckless of the storm
That keeps the raven quiet in her nest,
Be as a presence or a motion—one   520
Among the many there; and while the
    mists
Flying, and rainy vapours, call out shapes
And phantoms from the crags and solid
    earth
As fast as a musician scatters sounds
Out of an instrument; and while the
    streams   525
(As at a first creation and in haste
To exercise their untried faculties)
Descending from the region of the clouds,
And starting from the hollows of the
    earth
More multitudinous every moment, rend
Their way before them—what a joy to
    roam   531
An equal among mightiest energies ;
And haply sometimes with articulate
    voice,
Amid the deafening tumult, scarcely
    heard
By him that utters it, exclaim aloud, 535
'Rage on, ye elements ! let moon and stars
Their aspects lend, and mingle in their
    turn
With this commotion (ruinous though it
    be)
From day to night, from night to day,
    prolonged !'"

"Yes," said the Wanderer, taking from
    my lips   540
The strain of transport, "whosoe'er in
    youth
Has, through ambition of his soul, given
    way
To such desires, and grasped at such
    delight,
Shall feel congenial stirrings late and
    long,

In spite of all the weakness that life
    brings,   545
Its cares and sorrows ; he, though taught
    to own
The tranquillizing power of time, shall
    wake,
Wake sometimes to a noble restlessness—
Loving the sports which once he gloried
    in.

"Compatriot, Friend, remote are Gar-
    ry's hills,   550
The streams far distant of your native
    glen ;
Yet is their form and image here ex-
    pressed
With brotherly resemblance. Turn your
    steps
Wherever fancy leads ; by day, by night,
Are various engines working, not the
    same   555
As those with which your soul in youth
    was moved,
But by the great Artificer endowed
With no inferior power. You dwell
    alone ;
You walk, you live, you speculate alone ;
Yet doth remembrance, like a sovereign
    prince,   560
For you a stately gallery maintain
Of gay or tragic pictures. You have
    seen,
Have acted, suffered, travelled far, ob-
    served
With no incurious eye ; and books are
    yours,
Within whose silent chambers treasure
    lies   565
Preserved from age to age ; more pre-
    cious far
Than that accumulated store of gold
And orient gems, which, for a day of
    need,
The Sultan hides deep in ancestral
    tombs.
These hoards of truth you can unlock at
    will :   570
And music waits upon your skilful
    touch,
Sounds which the wandering shepherd
    from these heights

Hears, and forgets his purpose;—furnished thus,
How can you droop, if willing to be up-
raised?

"A piteous lot it were to flee from
Man— 575
Yet not rejoice in Nature. He, whose
hours
Are by domestic pleasure uncaressed
And unenlivened; who exists whole years
Apart from benefits received or done
'Mid the transactions of the bustling
crowd; 580
Who neither hears, nor feels a wish to hear,
Of the world's interests—such a one hath
need
Of a quick fancy and an active heart,
That, for the day's consumption, books
may yield
Food not unwholesome; earth and air
correct 585
His morbid humour, with delight sup-
plied
Or solace, varying as the seasons change.
—Truth has her pleasure-grounds, her
haunts of ease
And easy contemplation; gay parterres,
And labyrinthine walks, her sunny
glades 590
And shady groves in studied contrast—
each,
For recreation, leading into each:
These may he range, if willing to partake
Their soft indulgences, and in due time
May issue thence, recruited for the tasks
And course of service Truth requires
from those 596
Who tend her altars, wait upon her
throne,
And guard her fortresses. Who thinks,
and feels,
And recognises ever and anon
The breeze of nature stirring in his soul,
Why need such man go desperately
astray, 601
And nurse 'the dreadful appetite of
death?'
If tired with systems, each in its degree
Substantial, and all crumbling in their
turn,

Let him build systems of his own, and
smile 605
At the fond work, demolished with a
touch;
If unreligious, let him be at once,
Among ten thousand innocents, enrolled
A pupil in the many-chambered school,
Where superstition weaves her airy
dreams. 610

"Life's autumn past, I stand on
winter's verge;
And daily lose what I desire to keep:
Yet rather would I instantly decline
To the traditionary sympathies
Of a most rustic ignorance, and take 615
A fearful apprehension from the owl
Or death-watch : and as readily rejoice,
If two auspicious magpies crossed my
way;—
To this would rather bend than see and
hear
The repetitions wearisome of sense, 620
Where soul is dead, and feeling hath no
place;
Where knowledge, ill begun in cold
remark
On outward things, with formal inference
ends;
Or, if the mind turn inward, she recoils
At once—or, not recoiling, is perplexed—
Lost in a gloom of uninspired research;
Meanwhile, the heart within the heart,
the seat 627
Where peace and happy consciousness
should dwell,
On its own axis restlessly revolving,
Seeks, yet can nowhere find, the light of
truth. 630

"Upon the breast of new-created earth
Man walked; and when and wheresoe'er
he moved,
Alone or mated, solitude was not.
He heard, borne on the wind, the articu-
late voice
Of God; and Angels to his sight ap-
peared 635
Crowning the glorious hills of paradise;
Or through the groves gliding like morn-
ing mist

Enkindled by the sun. He sate—and
  talked
With wingèd Messengers; who daily
  brought
To his small island in the ethereal deep
Tidings of joy and love.—From those
  pure heights   641
(Whether of actual vision, sensible
To sight and feeling, or that in this sort
Have condescendingly been shadowed
  forth
Communications spiritually maintained,
And intuitions moral and divine)   646
Fell Human-kind—to banishment con-
  demned
That flowing years repealed not: and
  distress
And grief spread wide; but Man escaped
  the doom
Of destitution;—solitude was not.   650
—Jehovah—shapeless Power above all
  Powers,
Single and one, the omnipresent God,
By vocal utterance, or blaze of light,
Or cloud of darkness, localised in hea-
  ven;
On earth, enshrined within the wander-
  ing ark;   655
Or, out of Sion, thundering from his
  throne
Between the Cherubim—on the chosen
  Race
Showered miracles, and ceased not to
  dispense
Judgments, that filled the land from age
  to age
With hope, and love, and gratitude, and
  fear;   660
And with amazement smote;—thereby
  to assert
His scorned, or unacknowledged, sove-
  reignty.
And when the One, ineffable of name,
Of nature indivisible, withdrew
From mortal adoration or regard,   665
Not then was Deity engulfed; nor Man,
The rational creature, left, to feel the
  weight
Of his own reason, without sense or
  thought
Of higher reason and a purer will,

To benefit and bless, through mightier
  power:—   670
Whether the Persian—zealous to reject
Altar and image, and the inclusive walls
And roofs of temples built by human
  hands—
To loftiest heights ascending, from their
  tops,
With myrtle-wreathed tiara on his brow,
Presented sacrifice to moon and stars, 676
And to the winds and mother elements,
And the whole circle of the heavens, for
  him
A sensitive existence, and a God,
With lifted hands invoked, and songs of
  praise: 680
Or, less reluctantly to bonds of sense
Yielding his soul, the Babylonian framed
For influence undefined a personal shape;
And, from the plain, with toil immense,
  upreared
Tower eight times planted on the top of
  tower,   685
That Belus, nightly to his splendid couch
Descending, there might rest; upon that
  height
Pure and serene, diffused—to overlook
Winding Euphrates, and the city vast
Of his devoted worshippers, far-stretched,
With grove and field and garden inter-
  spersed;   691
Their town, and foodful region for sup-
  port
Against the pressure of beleaguering war.

"Chaldean Shepherds, ranging track-
  less fields,   694
Beneath the concave of unclouded skies
Spread like a sea, in boundless solitude,
Looked on the polar star, as on a guide
And guardian of their course, that never
  closed
His steadfast eye. The planetary Five
With a submissive reverence they be-
  held;   700
Watched, from the centre of their sleep-
  ing flocks,
Those radiant Mercuries, that seemed to
  move
Carrying through ether, in perpetual
  round,

Decrees and resolutions of the Gods;
And, by their aspects, signifying works
Of dim futurity, to Man revealed.   706
—The imaginative faculty was lord
Of observations natural; and, thus
Led on, those shepherds made report of
    stars
In set rotation passing to and fro,   710
Between the orbs of our apparent sphere
And its invisible counterpart, adorned
With answering constellations, under
    earth,
Removed from all approach of living
    sight
But present to the dead; who, so they
    deemed,   715
Like those celestial messengers beheld
All accidents, and judges were of all.

"The lively Grecian, in a land of hills,
Rivers and fertile plains, and sounding
    shores,—
Under a cope of sky more variable,   720
Could find commodious place for every
    God,
Promptly received, as prodigally brought,
From the surrounding countries at the
    choice
Of all adventurers. With unrivalled
    skill,
As nicest observation furnished hints
For studious fancy, his quick hand be-
    stowed   726
On fluent operations a fixed shape;
Metal or stone, idolatrously served.
And yet—triumphant o'er this pompous
    show
Of art, this palpable array of sense,   730
On every side encountered; in despite
Of the gross fictions chanted in the
    streets
By wandering Rhapsodists; and in con-
    tempt
Of doubt and bold denial hourly urged
Amid the wrangling schools—a SPIRIT
    hung,   735
Beautiful region! o'er thy towns and
    farms,
Statues and temples, and memorial
    tombs;
And emanations were perceived; and acts

Of immortality, in Nature's course,   739
Exemplified by mysteries, that were felt
As bonds, on grave philosopher imposed
And armèd warrior; and in every grove
A gay or pensive tenderness prevailed,
When piety more awful had relaxed.
—'Take, running river, take these locks
    of mine'—   745
Thus would the Votary say—'this sever-
    ed hair,
My vow fulfilling, do I here present,
Thankful for my belovèd child's return.
Thy banks, Cephisus, he again hath trod,
Thy murmurs heard; and drunk the
    crystal lymph   750
With which thou dost refresh the thirsty
    lip,
And, all day long, moisten these flowery
    fields!'
And, doubtless, sometimes, when the
    hair was shed
Upon the flowing stream, a thought arose
Of Life continuous, Being unimpaired;
That hath been, is, and where it was
    and is   756
There shall endure,—existence unexposed
To the blind walk of mortal accident;
From diminution safe and weakening
    age;
While man grows old, and dwindles, and
    decays;   760
And countless generations of mankind
Depart; and leave no vestige where they
    trod.

"We live by Admiration, Hope, and
    Love;
And, even as these are well and wisely
    fixed,
In dignity of being we ascend.   765
But what is error?"—"Answer he who
    can!"
The Sceptic somewhat haughtily ex-
    claimed:
"Love, Hope, and Admiration—are they
    not
Mad Fancy's favourite vassals? Does not
    life   769
Use them, full oft, as pioneers to ruin,
Guides to destruction? Is it well to trust
Imagination's light when reason's fails,

The unguarded taper where the guarded
   faints?
—Stoop from those heights, and soberly
   declare
What error is; and, of our errors, which
Doth most debase the mind; the genuine
   seats   776
Of power, where are they? Who shall
   regulate,
With truth, the scale of intellectual rank?"

"Methinks," persuasively the Sage re-
   plied,   779
"That for this arduous office you possess
Some rare advantages. Your early days
A grateful recollection must supply
Of much exalted good by Heaven vouch-
   safed
To dignify the humblest state.—Your
   voice
Hath, in my hearing, often testified 785
That poor men's children, they, and they
   alone,
By their condition taught, can under-
   stand
The wisdom of the prayer that daily asks
For daily bread. A consciousness is
   yours   789
How feelingly religion may be learned
In smoky cabins, from a mother's tongue—
Heard while the dwelling vibrates to the
   din
Of the contiguous torrent, gathering
   strength
At every moment—and, with strength,
   increase   794
Of fury; or, while snow is at the door,
Assaulting and defending, and the wind,
A sightless labourer, whistles at his work—
Fearful; but resignation tempers fear,
And piety is sweet to infant minds.
—The Shepherd-lad, that in the sunshine
   carves,   800
On the green turf, a dial—to divide
The silent hours; and who to that report
Can portion out his pleasures, and adapt,
Throughout a long and lonely summer's
   day
His round of pastoral duties, is not left 805
With less intelligence for *moral* things
Of gravest import. Early he perceives,

Within himself, a measure and a rule,
Which to the sun of truth he can apply,
That shines for him, and shines for all
   mankind.   810
Experience daily fixing his regards
On nature's wants, he knows how few
   they are,
And where they lie, how answered and
   appeased.
This knowledge ample recompense affords
For manifold privations; he refers 815
His notions to this standard; on this rock
Rests his desires; and hence, in after life,
Soul-strengthening patience, and sublime
   content.
Imagination—not permitted here
To waste her powers, as in the worldling's
   mind,   820
On fickle pleasures, and superfluous cares,
And trivial ostentation—is left free
And puissant to range the solemn walks
Of time and nature, girded by a zone
That, while it binds, invigorates and sup-
   ports.   825
Acknowledge, then, that whether by the
   side
Of his poor hut, or on the mountain-top,
Or in the cultured field, a Man so bred
(Take from him what you will upon the
   score
Of ignorance or illusion) lives and breathes
For noble purposes of mind: his heart 831
Beats to the heroic song of ancient days;
His eye distinguishes, his soul creates.
And those illusions, which excite the scorn
Or move the pity of unthinking minds,
Are they not mainly outward ministers
Of inward conscience? with whose service
   charged   837
They came and go, appeared and dis-
   appear,
Diverting evil purposes, remorse
Awakening, chastening an intemperate
   grief,   840
Or pride of heart abating: and, whene'er
For less important ends those phantoms
   move,
Who would forbid them, if their presence
   serve,
On thinly-peopled mountains and wild
   heaths,

Filling a space, else vacant, to exalt 845
The forms of Nature, and enlarge her
    powers ?

"Once more to distant ages of the world
Let us revert, and place before our
    thoughts
The face which rural solitude might wear
To the unenlightened swains of pagan
    Greece. 850
—In that fair clime, the lonely herdsman,
    stretched
On the soft grass through half a summer's
    day,
With music lulled his indolent repose:
And, in some fit of weariness, if he,
When his own breath was silent, chanced
    to hear 855
A distant strain, far sweeter than the
    sounds
Which his poor skill could make, his
    fancy fetched,
Even from the blazing chariot of the sun,
A beardless Youth, who touched a golden
    lute,
And filled the illumined groves with
    ravishment 860
The nightly hunter, lifting a bright eye
Up towards the crescent moon, with
    grateful heart
Called on the lovely wanderer who be-
    stowed
That timely light, to share his joyous
    sport:
And hence, a beaming Goddess with her
    Nymphs, 865
Across the lawn and through the dark-
    some grove,
Not unaccompanied with tuneful notes
By echo multiplied from rock or cave,
Swept in the storm of chase; as moon and
    stars
Glance rapidly along the clouded heaven,
When winds are blowing strong. The
    traveller slaked 871
His thirst from rill or gushing fount, and
    thanked
The Naiad. Sunbeams, upon distant hills
Gliding apace, with shadows in their train,
Might, with small help from fancy, be
    transformed 875

Into fleet Oreads sporting visibly.
The Zephyrs fanning, as they passed,
    their wings,
Lacked not, for love, fair objects whom
    they wooed
With gentle whisper. Withered boughs
    grotesque,
Stripped of their leaves and twigs by
    hoary age, 880
From depth of shaggy covert peeping
    forth
In the low vale, or on steep mountain-side;
And, sometimes, intermixed with stirring
    horns
Of the live deer, or goat's depending
    beard,—
These were the lurking Satyrs, a wild
    brood 885
Of gamesome Deities; or Pan himself,
The simple shepherd's awe - inspiring
    God!"

The strain was aptly chosen; and I
    could mark
Its kindly influence, o'er the yielding
    brow
Of our Companion, gradually diffused;
While listening, he had paced the noise-
    less turf, 891
Like one whose untired ear a murmuring
    stream
Detains; but tempted now to interpose,
He with a smile exclaimed :—
                    "'Tis well you speak
At a safe distance from our native land,
And from the mansions where our youth
    was taught. 896
The true descendants of those godly men
Who swept from Scotland, in a flame of
    zeal,
Shrine, altar, image, and the massy piles
That harboured them,—the souls retaining
    yet 900
The churlish features of that after-race
Who fled to woods, caverns, and jutting
    rocks,
In deadly scorn of superstitious rites,
Or what their scruples construed to be
    such—
How, think you, would they tolerate this
    scheme 905

Of fine propensities, that tends, if urged
Far as it might be urged, to sow afresh
The weeds of Romish phantasy, in vain
Uprooted; would re-consecrate our wells
To good Saint Fillan and to fair Saint
    Anne;   910
And from long banishment recall Saint
    Giles,
To watch again with tutelary love
O'er stately Edinborough throned on
    crags?
A blessed restoration, to behold
The patron, on the shoulders of his priests,
Once more parading through her crowded
    streets   916
Now simply guarded by the sober powers
Of science, and philosophy, and sense!"

  This answer followed.—"You have
    turned my thoughts
Upon our brave Progenitors, who rose
Against idolatry with warlike mind,   921
And shrunk from vain observances, to
    lurk
In woods, and dwell under impending
    rocks
Ill-sheltered, and oft wanting fire and
    food;
Why?—for this very reason that they felt,
And did acknowledge, wheresoe'er they
    moved,   926
A spiritual presence, ofttimes miscon-
    ceived,
But still a high dependence, a divine
Bounty and government, that filled their
    hearts
With joy, and gratitude, and fear, and
    love;   930
And from their fervent lips drew hymns
    of praise,
That through the desert rang. Though
    favoured less,
Far less, than these, yet such, in their de-
    gree,
Were those bewildered Pagans of old
    time.
Beyond their own poor natures and
    above   935
They looked; were humbly thankful for
    the good
Which the warm sun solicited, and earth

Bestowed; were gladsome,—and their
    moral sense
They fortified with reverence for the
    Gods;
And they had hopes that overstepped the
    Grave.   940

  "Now, shall our great Discoverers," he
    exclaimed,
Raising his voice triumphantly, "obtain
From sense and reason less than these
    obtained,
Though far misled? Shall men for whom
    our age
Unbaffled powers of vision hath prepared,
To explore the world without and world
    within,   946
Be joyless as the blind? Ambitious
    spirits—
Whom earth, at this late season, hath
    produced
To regulate the moving spheres, and weigh
The planets in the hollow of their hand;
And they who rather dive than soar,
    whose pains
Have solved the elements, or analysed
The thinking principle—shall they in fact
Prove a degraded Race? and what avails
Renown, if their presumption make them
    such?   955
Oh! there is laughter at their work in
    heaven!
Enquire of ancient Wisdom; go, demand
Of mighty Nature, if 'twas ever meant
That we should pry far off yet be un-
    raised;
That we should pore, and dwindle as we
    pore,   960
Viewing all objects unremittingly
In disconnection dead and spiritless;
And still dividing, and dividing still,
Break down all grandeur, still unsatisfied
With the perverse attempt, while little-
    ness   965
May yet become more little; waging thus
An impious warfare with the very life
Of our own souls!

             And if indeed there be
An all-pervading Spirit, upon whom
Our dark foundations rest, could he de-
    sign   970

That this magnificent effect of power,
The earth we tread, the sky that we be-
    hold
By day, and all the pomp which night
    reveals ;
That these—and that superior mystery
Our vital frame, so fearfully devised, 975
And the dread soul within it—should
    exist
Only to be examined, pondered, searched,
Probed, vexed, and criticised?—Accuse
    me not
Of arrogance, unknown Wanderer as I am,
If, having walked with Nature threescore
    years, 980
And offered, far as frailty would allow,
My heart a daily sacrifice to Truth,
I now affirm of Nature and of Truth,
Whom I have served, that their DIVINITY
Revolts, offended at the ways of men 985
Swayed by such motives, to such ends
    employed ;
Philosophers, who, though the human soul
Be of a thousand faculties composed,
And twice ten thousand interests, do yet
    prize 989
This soul, and the transcendent universe,
No more than as a mirror that reflects
To proud Self-love her own intelligence ;
That one, poor, finite object, in the abyss
Of infinite Being, twinkling restlessly !

"Nor higher place can be assigned to him
And his compeers—the laughing Sage of
    France.— 996
Crowned was he, if my memory do not
    err,
With laurel planted upon hoary hairs,
In sign of conquest by his wit achieved
And benefits his wisdom had conferred ;
His stooping body tottered with wreaths
    of flowers 1001
Opprest, far less becoming ornaments
Than Spring oft twines about a moulder-
    ing tree ;
Yet so it pleased a fond, a vain, old Man,
And a most frivolous people. Him I
    mean 1005
Who penned, to ridicule confiding faith,
This sorry Legend ; which by chance we
    found

Piled in a nook, through malice, as might
    seem,
Among more innocent rubbish."—Speak-
    ing thus,
With a brief notice when, and how, and
    where, 1010
We had espied the book, he drew it forth ;
And courteously, as if the act removed,
At once, all traces from the good Man's
    heart
Of unbenign aversion or contempt,
Restored it to its owner. "Gentle
    Friend," 1015
Herewith he grasped the Solitary's hand,
"You have known lights and guides
    better than these.
Ah ! let not aught amiss within dispose
A noble mind to practise on herself, 1019
And tempt opinion to support the wrongs
Of passion : whatsoe'er be felt or feared,
From higher judgment-seats make no ap-
    peal
To lower : can you question that the soul
Inherits an allegiance, not by choice
To be cast off, upon an oath proposed
By each new upstart notion ? In the
    ports 1026
Of levity no refuge can be found,
No shelter, for a spirit in distress,
He, who by wilful disesteem of life
And proud insensibility to hope, 1030
Affronts the eye of Solitude, shall learn
That her mild nature can be terrible ;
That neither she nor Silence lack the
    power
To avenge their own insulted majesty.

"O blest seclusion ! when the mind
    admits 1035
The law of duty ; and can therefore move
Through each vicissitude of loss and gain,
Linked in entire complacence with her
    choice ;
When youth's presumptuousness is mel-
    lowed down,
And manhood's vain anxiety dismissed ;
When wisdom shows her seasonable
    fruit, 1041
Upon the boughs of sheltering leisure
    hung
In sober plenty ; when the spirit stoops

To drink with gratitude the crystal stream
Of unreproved enjoyment ; and is
    pleased   1045
To muse, and be saluted by the air
Of meek repentance, wafting wallflower
    scents
From out the crumbling ruins of fallen
    pride
And chambers of transgression, now for-
    lorn.
O, calm contented days, and peaceful
    nights !   1050
Who, when such good can be obtained,
    would strive
To reconcile his manhood to a couch
Soft, as may seem, but, under that dis-
    guise,
Stuffed with the thorny substance of the
    past
For fixed annoyance ; and full oft be-
    set   1055
With floating dreams, black and dis-
    consolate,
The vapoury phantoms of futurity ?

"Within the soul a faculty abides,
That with interpositions, which would
    hide
And darken, so can deal that they be-
    come   1060
Contingencies of pomp ; and serve to
    exalt
Her native brightness. As the ample
    moon,
In the deep stillness of a summer even
Rising behind a thick and lofty grove,
Burns, like an unconsuming fire of
    light,   1065
In the green trees ; and, kindling on all
    sides
Their leafy umbrage, turns the dusky
    veil
Into a substance glorious as her own,
Yea, with her own incorporated, by
    power
Capacious and serene. Like power
    abides   1070
In man's celestial spirit ; virtue thus
Sets forth and magnifies herself ; thus
    feeds
A calm, a beautiful, and silent fire,

From the encumbrances of mortal life,
From error, disappointment—nay, from
    guilt ;   1075
And sometimes, so relenting justice wills,
From palpable oppressions of despair."

The Solitary by these words was touched
With manifest emotion, and exclaimed ;
"But how begin ? and whence ?—'The
    Mind is free—   1080
Resolve,' the haughty Moralist would
    say,
'This single act is all that we demand.'
Alas ! such wisdom bids a creature fly
Whose very sorrow is, that time hath
    shorn
His natural wings !—To friendship let
    him turn   1085
For succour ; but perhaps he sits
    alone
On stormy waters, tossed in a little boat
That holds but him, and can contain no
    more !
Religion tells of amity sublime
Which no condition can preclude ; of
    One   1090
Who sees all suffering, comprehends all
    wants,
All weakness fathoms, can supply all
    needs :
But is that bounty absolute ?—His gifts,
Are they not, still, in some degree,
    rewards
For acts of service ? Can his love ex-
    tend   1095
To hearts that own not him ? Will showers
    of grace,
When in the sky no promise may be
    seen,
Fall to refresh a parched and withered
    land ?
Or shall the groaning Spirit cast her load
At the Redeemer's feet ?"
              In rueful tone, 1100
With some impatience in his mien, he
    spake :
Back to my mind rushed all that had
    been urged
To calm the Sufferer when his story
    closed ;
I looked for counsel as unbending now ;

But a discriminating sympathy   1105
Stooped to this apt reply :—
        " As men from men
Do, in the constitution of their souls,
Differ, by mystery not to be explained;
And as we fall by various ways, and sink
One deeper than another, self-con-
   demned   1110
Through manifold degrees of guilt and
   shame ;
So manifold and various are the ways
Of restoration, fashioned to the steps
Of all infirmity, and tending all
To the same point, attainable by all— 1115
Peace in ourselves, and union with our
   God.
For you, assuredly, a hopeful road
Lies open : we have heard from you a
   voice
At every moment softened in its course
By tenderness of heart ; have seen your
   eye,   1120
Even like an altar lit by fire from heaven,
Kindle before us.—Your discourse this
   day,
That, like the fabled Lethe, wished to
   flow
In creeping sadness, through oblivious
   shades
Of death and night, has caught at every
   turn   1125
The colours of the sun. Access for
   you
Is yet preserved to principles of truth,
Which the imaginative Will upholds
In seats of wisdom, not to be approached
By the inferior Faculty that moulds, 1130
With her minute and speculative pains,
Opinion, ever changing !
               I have seen
A curious child, who dwelt upon a tract
Of inland ground, applying to his ear
The convolutions of a smooth-lipped
   shell ;   1135
To which, in silence hushed, his very soul
Listened intensely ; and his countenance
   soon
Brightened with joy ; for from within
   were heard
Murmurings, whereby the monitor ex-
   pressed

Mysterious union with its native sea. 1140
Even such a shell the universe itself
Is to the ear of Faith ; and there are
   times,
I doubt not, when to you it doth impart
Authentic tidings of invisible things ;
Of ebb and flow, and ever - during
   power ;   1145
And central peace, subsisting at the
   heart
Of endless agitation. Here you stand,
Adore, and worship, when you know it
   not ;
Pious beyond the intention of your
   thought ;
Devout above the meaning of your
   will.   1150
—Yes, you have felt, and may not cease
   to feel.
The estate of man would be indeed forlorn
If false conclusions of the reasoning power
Made the eye blind, and closed the
   passages
Through which the ear converses with the
   heart.   1155
Has not the soul, the being of your life,
Received a shock of awful consciousness,
In some calm season, when these lofty
   rocks
At night's approach bring down the un-
   clouded sky,
To rest upon their circumambient
   walls ;   1160
A temple framing of dimensions vast,
And yet not too enormous for the sound
Of human anthems,—choral song, or burst
Sublime of instrumental harmony,
To glorify the Eternal ! What if these 1165
Did never break the stillness that prevails
Here,—if the solemn nightingale be mute,
And the soft woodlark here did never
   chant
Her vespers,—Nature fails not to pro-
   vide
Impulse and utterance. The whispering
   air   1170
Sends inspiration from the shadowy
   heights,
And blind recesses of the caverned rocks ;
The little rills, and waters numberless,
Inaudible by daylight, blend their notes

With the loud streams: and often, at the
hour   1175
When issue forth the first pale stars, is
heard,
Within the circuit of this fabric huge,
One voice—the solitary raven, flying
Athwart the concave of the dark blue
dome,
Unseen, perchance above all power of
sight—   1180
An iron knell! with echoes from afar
Faint—and still fainter—as the cry, with
which
The wanderer accompanies her flight
Through the calm region, fades upon the
ear,
Diminishing by distance till it seemed
To expire; yet from the abyss is caught
again,   1186
And yet again recovered!
                                    But descending
From these imaginative heights, that
yield
Far-stretching views into eternity,
Acknowledge that to Nature's humbler
power   1190
Your cherished sullenness is forced to
bend
Even here, where her amenities are
sown
With sparing hand. Then trust yourself
abroad
To range her blooming bowers, and spa-
cious fields,
Where on the labours of the happy
throng   1195
She smiles, including in her wide em-
brace
City, and town, and tower,—and sea with
ships
Sprinkled;—be our Companion while we
track
Her rivers populous with gliding life;
While, free as air, o'er printless sands we
march,   1200
Or pierce the gloom of her majestic
woods;
Roaming, or resting under grateful shade
In peace and meditative cheerfulness;
Where living things, and things inani-
mate,

Do speak, at Heaven's command, to eye
and ear,   1205
And speak to social reason's inner
sense,
With inarticulate language.
                                    For, the Man—
Who, in this spirit, communes with the
Forms
Of nature, who with understanding heart
Both knows and loves such objects as
excite   1210
No morbid passions, no disquietude,
No vengeance, and no hatred—needs must
feel
The joy of that pure principle of love
So deeply, that, unsatisfied with aught
Less pure and exquisite, he cannot
choose   1215
But seek for objects of a kindred love
In fellow-natures and a kindred joy.
Accordingly he by degrees perceives
His feelings of aversion softened down;
A holy tenderness pervade his frame. 1220
His sanity of reason not impaired,
Say rather, all his thoughts now flowing
clear,
From a clear fountain flowing, he looks
round
And seeks for good; and finds the good
he seeks:
Until abhorrence and contempt are
things   1225
He only knows by name; and, if he
hear,
From other mouths, the language which
they speak,
He is compassionate; and has no thought,
No feeling, which can overcome his love.

"And further; by contemplating these
Forms   1230
In the relations which they bear to
man,
He shall discern, how, through the various
means
Which silently they yield, are multiplied
The spiritual presences of absent things.
Trust me, that for the instructed, time
will come   1235
When they shall meet no object but may
teach

Some acceptable lesson to their minds
Of human suffering, or of human joy.
So shall they learn, while all things speak
   of man,
Their duties from all forms; and general
   laws,   1240
And local accidents, shall tend alike
To rouse, to urge; and, with the will,
   confer
The ability to spread the blessings wide
Of true philanthropy. The light of love
Not failing, perseverance from their
   steps   1245
Departing not, for them shall be con-
   firmed
The glorious habit by which sense is
   made
Subservient still to moral purposes,
Auxiliar to divine. That change shall
   clothe
The naked spirit, ceasing to deplore   1250
The burthen of existence. Science then
Shall be a precious visitant; and then,
And only then, be worthy of her name:
For then her heart shall kindle; her dull
   eye,
Dull and inanimate, no more shall
   hang   1255
Chained to its object in brute slavery;
But taught with patient interest to watch
The processes of things, and serve the
   cause
Of order and distinctness, not for this
Shall it forget that its most noble use,
Its most illustrious province, must be
   found   1261
In furnishing clear guidance, a support
Not treacherous, to the mind's _excursive_
   power.
—So build we up the Being that we are;
Thus deeply drinking-in the soul of
   things,   1265
We shall be wise perforce; and, while
   inspired
By choice, and conscious that the Will is
   free,
Shall move unswerving, even as if im-
   pelled
By strict necessity, along the path
Of order and of good. Whate'er we
   see,   1270

Or feel, shall tend to quicken and refine;
Shall fix, in calmer seats of moral strength,
Earthly desires; and raise, to loftier
   heights
Of divine love, our intellectual soul."

Here closed the Sage that eloquent
   harangue,   1275
Poured forth with fervour in continuous
   stream,
Such as, remote, 'mid savage wilderness,
An Indian Chief discharges from his
   breast
Into the hearing of assembled tribes,
In open circle seated round, and hushed
As the unbreathing air, when not a leaf
Stirs in the mighty woods.—So did he
   speak:
The words he uttered shall not pass
   away
Dispersed, like music that the wind
   takes up
By snatches, and lets fall, to be for-
   gotten;   1285
No—they sank into me, the bounteous gift
Of one whom time and nature had made
   wise.
Gracing his doctrine with authority
Which hostile spirits silently allow;
Of one accustomed to desires that feed
On fruitage gathered from the tree of
   life;   1291
To hopes on knowledge and experience
   built;
Of one in whom persuasion and belief
Had ripened into faith, and faith become
A passionate intuition; whence the
   Soul,   1295
Though bound to earth by ties of pity
   and love,
From all injurious servitude was free.

The Sun, before his place of rest were
   reached,
Had yet to travel far, but unto us,
To us who stood low in that hollow
   dell,   1300
He had become invisible,—a pomp
Leaving behind of yellow radiance spread
Over the mountain-sides, in contrast
   bold

With ample shadows, seemingly, no less
Than those resplendent lights, his rich
 bequest;   1305
A dispensation of his evening power.
—Adown the path that from the glen
 had led
The funeral train, the Shepherd and his
 Mate
Were seen descending:—forth to greet
 them ran
Our little Page: the rustic pair ap-
 proach;   1310
And in the Matron's countenance may be
 read
Plain indication that the words, which
 told
How that neglected Pensioner was sent

Before his time into a quiet grave,
Had done to her humanity no wrong: 1315
But we are kindly welcomed—promptly
 served
With ostentatious zeal.—Along the floor
Of the small Cottage in the lonely Dell
A grateful couch was spread for our
 repose;
Where, in the guise of mountaineers, we
 lay,   1320
Stretched upon fragrant heath, and lulled
 by sound
Of far-off torrents charming the still
 night,
And, to tired limbs and over-busy
 thoughts,
Inviting sleep and soft forgetfulness.

BOOK FIFTH.

THE PASTOR.

ARGUMENT.

"FAREWELL, deep Valley, with thy one rude House,
And its small lot of life-supporting fields,
And guardian rocks!—Farewell, attractive seat !
To the still influx of the morning light
Open, and day's pure cheerfulness, but veiled 5
From human observation, as if yet
Primeval forests wrapped thee round with dark
Impenetrable shade; once more farewell,
Majestic circuit, beautiful abyss,
By Nature destined from the birth of things 10
For quietness profound !"
                                    Upon the side
Of that brown ridge, sole outlet of the vale
Which foot of boldest stranger would attempt,

Lingering behind my comrades, thus I breathed 14
A parting tribute to a spot that seemed
Like the fixed centre of a troubled world.
Again I halted with reverted eyes ;
The chain that would not slacken, was at length
Snapt,—and, pursuing leisurely my way,
How vain, thought I, is it by change of place 20
To seek that comfort which the mind denies ;
Yet trial and temptation oft are shunned
Wisely ; and by such tenure do we hold
Frail life's possessions, that even they whose fate
Yields no peculiar reason of complaint 25
Might, by the promise that is here, be won
To steal from active duties, and embrace

Obscurity, and undisturbed repose.
—Knowledge, methinks, in these disor-
    dered times,
Should be allowed a privilege to have   30
Her anchorites, like piety of old;
Men, who, from faction sacred, and un-
    stained
By war, might, if so minded, turn aside
Uncensured, and subsist, a scattered few
Living to God and nature, and content
With that communion. Consecrated be
The spots where such abide ! But happier
    still
The Man, whom, furthermore, a hope
    attends
That meditation and research may guide
His privacy to principles and powers   40
Discovered or invented ; or set forth,
Through his acquaintance with the ways
    of truth,
In lucid order ; so that, when his course
Is run, some faithful eulogist may say,
He sought not praise, and praise did over-
    look   45
His unobtrusive merit ; but his life,
Sweet to himself, was exercised in good
That shall survive his name and memory.

Acknowledgments of gratitude sincere
Accompanied these musings ; fervent
    thanks   50
For my own peaceful lot and happy
    choice ;
A choice that from the passions of the
    world
Withdrew, and fixed me in a still retreat ;
Sheltered, but not to social duties lost,
Secluded, but not buried ; and with song
Cheering my days, and with industrious
    thought ;   56
With the ever-welcome company of books ;
With virtuous friendship's soul-sustaining
    aid,
And with the blessings of domestic love.

Thus occupied in mind I paced along,
Following the rugged road, by sledge or
    wheel   61
Worn in the moorland, till I overtook
My two Associates, in the morning sun-
    shine

Halting together on a rocky knoll,
Whence the bare road descended rapidly
To the green meadows of another vale.

Here did our pensive Host put forth his
    hand   67
In sign of farewell. "Nay," the old Man
    said,
"The fragrant air its coolness still retains ;
The herds and flocks are yet abroad to
    crop   70
The dewy grass ; you cannot leave us now,
We must not part at this inviting hour."
He yielded, though reluctant ; for his
    mind
Instinctively disposed him to retire   74
To his own covert ; as a billow, heaved
Upon the beach, rolls back into the sea.
—So we descend : and winding round
    a rock
Attain a point that showed the valley—
    stretched
In length before us ; and, not distant far,
Upon a rising ground a grey church-
    tower,   80
Whose battlements were screened by
    tufted trees.
And towards a crystal Mere, that lay
    beyond
Among steep hills and woods embosomed,
    flowed
A copious stream with boldly-winding
    course ;
Here traceable, there hidden—there again
To sight restored, and glittering in the
    sun.   86
On the stream's bank, and everywhere,
    appeared
Fair dwellings, single, or in social knots ;
Some scattered o'er the level, others
    perched
On the hill-sides, a cheerful quiet scene,
Now in its morning purity arrayed.   91

"As 'mid some happy valley of the
    Alps,"
Said I, "once happy, ere tyrannic power,
Wantonly breaking in upon the Swiss,
Destroyed their unoffending common-
    wealth,   95
A popular equality reigns here,

Save for yon stately House beneath whose
    roof
A rural lord might dwell."—"No feudal
    pomp,
Or power," replied the Wanderer, "to
    that House
Belongs, but there in his allotted Home
Abides, from year to year, a genuine
    Priest,   101
The shepherd of his flock; or, as a king
Is styled, when most affectionately praised,
The father of his people. Such is he;
And rich and poor, and young and old,
    rejoice   105
Under his spiritual sway. He hath vouch-
    safed
To me some portion of a kind regard;
And something also of his inner mind
Hath he imparted—but I speak of him
As he is known to all.
              The calm delights   110
Of unambitious piety he chose,
And learning's solid dignity; though born
Of knightly race, nor wanting powerful
    friends.
Hither, in prime of manhood, he with-
    drew
From academic bowers. He loved the
    spot—   115
Who does not love his native soil?—he
    prized
The ancient rural character, composed
Of simple manners, feelings unsupprest
And undisguised, and strong and serious
    thought;
A character reflected in himself,   120
With such embellishment as well beseems
His rank and sacred function. This deep
    vale
Winds far in reaches hidden from our
    sight,
And one a turreted manorial hall
Adorns, in which the good Man's an-
    cestors   125
Have dwelt through ages—Patrons of
    this Cure.
To them, and to his own judicious pains,
The Vicar's dwelling, and the whole do-
    main,
Owes that presiding aspect which might
    well

Attract your notice; statelier than could
    else   130
Have been bestowed, through course of
    common chance,
On an unwealthy mountain Benefice."

    This said, oft pausing, we pursued our
        way;
Nor reached the village-churchyard till
    the sun
Travelling at steadier pace than ours, had
    risen   135
Above the summits of the highest hills,
And round our path darted oppressive
    beams.

    As chanced, the portals of the sacred
        Pile
Stood open; and we entered. On my
    frame,
At such transition from the fervid air,   140
A grateful coolness fell, that seemed to
    strike
The heart, in concert with that temperate
    awe
And natural reverence which the place
    inspired.
Not raised in nice proportions was the
    pile,   144
But large and massy; for duration built;
With pillars crowded, and the roof up-
    held
By naked rafters intricately crossed,
Like leafless underboughs, in some thick
    wood,
All withered by the depth of shade above.
Admonitory texts inscribed the walls,   150
Each, in its ornamental scroll, enclosed;
Each also crowned with wingèd heads—
    a pair
Of rudely-painted Cherubim. The floor
Of nave and aisle, in unpretending guise,
Was occupied by oaken benches ranged
In seemly rows; the chancel only showed
Some vain distinctions, marks of earthly
    state   157
By immemorial privilege allowed;
Though with the Encincture's special
    sanctity
But ill according. An heraldic shield,
Varying its tincture with the changeful
    light,   161

Imbued the altar-window; fixed aloft
A faded hatchment hung, and one by
    time
Yet undiscoloured.   A capacious pew
Of sculptured oak stood here, with drapery
    lined;   165
And marble monuments were here dis-
    played
Thronging the walls; and on the floor
    beneath
Sepulchral stones appeared, with emblems
    graven
And foot-worn epitaphs, and some with
    small
And shining effigies of brass inlaid.   170

   The tribute by these various records
    claimed,
Duly we paid, each after each, and read
The ordinary chronicle of birth,
Office, alliance, and promotion—all
Ending in dust; of upright magistrates,
Grave doctors strenuous for the mother-
    church,   176
And uncorrupted senators, alike
To king and people true. A brazen plate,
Not easily deciphered, told of one
Whose course of earthly honour was be-
    gun   180
In quality of page among the train
Of the eighth Henry, when he crossed the
    seas
His royal state to show, and prove his
    strength
In tournament, upon the fields of France.
Another tablet registered the death,   185
And praised the gallant bearing, of
    a Knight
Tried in the sea-fights of the second
    Charles.
Near this brave Knight his Father lay
    entombed;
And, to the silent language giving voice,
I read,—how in his manhood's earlier
    day   190
He, 'mid the afflictions of intestine war
And rightful government subverted, found
One only solace—that he had espoused
A virtuous Lady tenderly beloved
For her benign perfections; and yet
    more   195

Endeared to him, for this, that, in her
    state
Of wedlock richly crowned with Heaven's
    regard,
She with a numerous issue filled his house,
Who throve, like plants, uninjured by the
    storm
That laid their country waste. No need
    to speak   200
Of less particular notices assigned
To Youth or Maiden gone before their
    time,
And Matrons and unwedded Sisters old;
Whose charity and goodness were re-
    hearsed
In modest panegyric.
                 "These dim lines,   205
What would they tell?" said I,—but,
    from the task
Of puzzling out that faded narrative,
With whisper soft my venerable Friend
Called me; and, looking down the dark-
    some aisle,
I saw the Tenant of the lonely vale   210
Standing apart; with curvèd arm reclined
On the baptismal font; his pallid face
Upturned, as if his mind were rapt, or
    lost
In some abstraction;—gracefully he stood,
The semblance bearing of a sculptured
    form   215
That leans upon a monumental urn
In peace, from morn to night, from year
    to year.

   Him from that posture did the Sexton
    rouse;
Who entered, humming carelessly a tune,
Continuation haply of the notes   220
That had beguiled the work from which
    he came,
With spade and mattock o'er his shoulder
    hung;
To be deposited, for future need,
In their appointed place. The pale Re-
    cluse
Withdrew; and straight we followed,—
    to a spot   225
Where sun and shade were intermixed;
    for there
A broad oak, stretching forth its leafy arms

From an adjoining pasture, overhung
Small space of that green churchyard
  with a light
And pleasant awning. On the moss-
  grown wall   230
My ancient Friend and I together took
Our seats ; and thus the Solitary spake,
Standing before us :—
          "Did you note the mien
Of that self-solaced, easy-hearted churl,
Death's hireling, who scoops out his
  neighbour's grave,   235
Or wraps an old acquaintance up in clay,
All unconcerned as he would bind a sheaf,
Or plant a tree. And did you hear his
  voice?
I was abruptly summoned by the sound
From some affecting images and thoughts,
Which then were silent ; but crave utter-
  ance now.   241

  "Much," he continued, with dejected
    look,
"Much, yesterday, was said in glowing
    phrase
Of our sublime dependencies, and hopes
For future states of being ; and the wings
Of speculation, joyfully outspread,   246
Hovered above our destiny on earth :
But stoop, and place the prospect of the
    soul
In sober contrast with reality,
And man's substantial life. If this mute
    earth   250
Of what it holds could speak, and every
    grave
Were as a volume, shut, yet capable
Of yielding its contents to eye and ear,
We should recoil, stricken with sorrow
    and shame,
To see disclosed, by such dread proof,
    how ill   255
That which is done accords with what
    is known
To reason, and by conscience is enjoined ;
How idly, how perversely, life's whole
    course,
To this conclusion, deviates from the line,
Or of the end stops short, proposed to all
At her aspiring outset.
              Mark the babe 261

Not long accustomed to this breathing
    world ;
One that hath barely learned to shape
    a smile,
Though yet irrational of soul, to grasp
With tiny finger—to let fall a tear ; 265
And, as the heavy cloud of sleep dis-
    solves,
To stretch his limbs, bemocking, as might
    seem,
The outward functions of intelligent
    man ;
A grave proficient in amusive feats
Of puppetry, that from the lap declare
His expectations, and announce his
    claims   271
To that inheritance which millions rue
That they were ever born to ! In due
    time
A day of solemn ceremonial comes ;
When they, who for this Minor hold in
    trust   275
Rights that transcend the loftiest herit-
    age
Of mere humanity, present their Charge,
For this occasion daintily adorned,
At the baptismal font. And when the
    pure
And consecrating element hath cleansed
The original stain, the child is there
    received   281
Into the second ark, Christ's church,
    with trust
That he, from wrath redeemed, therein
    shall float
Over the billows of this troublesome
    world
To the fair land of everlasting life. 285
Corrupt affections, covetous desires,
Are all renounced ; high as the thought
    of man
Can carry virtue, virtue is professed ;
A dedication made, a promise given
For due provision to control and guide,
And unremitting progress to ensure 291
In holiness and truth."
                "You cannot blame,"
Here interposing fervently I said,
"Rites which attest that Man by nature
    lies
Bedded for good and evil in a gulf 295

Fearfully low; nor will your judgment
scorn
Those services, whereby attempt is made
To lift the creature toward that eminence
On which, now fallen, erewhile in ma-
jesty
He stood; or if not so, whose top serene
At least he feels 'tis given him to descry;
Not without aspirations, evermore   302
Returning, and injunctions from within
Doubt to cast off and weariness; in trust
That what the Soul perceives, if glory
lost,   305
May be, through pains and persevering
hope,
Recovered; or, if hitherto unknown,
Lies within reach, and one day shall be
gained."

"I blame them not," he calmly answer-
ed—"no;   309
The outward ritual and established forms
With which communities of men invest
These inward feelings, and the aspiring
vows
To which the lips give public utterance
Are both a natural process; and by me
Shall pass uncensured; though the issue
prove,   315
Bringing from age to age its own re-
proach,
Incongruous, impotent, and blank.—But,
oh!
If to be weak is to be wretched—miser-
able,
As the lost Angel by a human voice
Hath mournfully pronounced, then, in
my mind,   320
Far better not to move at all than move
By impulse sent from such illusive
power,—
That finds and cannot fasten down; that
grasps
And is rejoiced, and loses while it
grasps;
That tempts, emboldens—for a time
sustains,   325
And then betrays; accuses and inflicts
Remorseless punishment; and so re-
treads
The inevitable circle: better far

Than this, to graze the herb in thought-
less peace,
By foresight, or remembrance, undis-
turbed!   330

"Philosophy! and thou more vaunted
name
Religion! with thy statelier retinue,
Faith, Hope, and Charity—from the
visible world
Choose for your emblems whatsoe'er ye
find
Of safest guidance or of firmest trust—
The torch, the star, the anchor; nor
except   336
The cross itself, at whose unconscious
feet
The generations of mankind have knelt
Ruefully seized, and shedding bitter
tears,
And through that conflict seeking rest—
of you,   340
High-titled Powers, am I constrained to
ask,
Here standing, with the unvoyageable
sky
In faint reflection of infinitude
Stretched overhead, and at my pensive
feet
A subterraneous magazine of bones,   345
In whose dark vaults my own shall soon
be laid,
Where are your triumphs? your dominion
where?
And in what age admitted and con-
firmed?
—Not for a happy land do I enquire,
Island or grove, that hides a blessed few
Who, with obedience willing and sin-
cere,   351
To your serene authorities conform;
But whom, I ask, of individual Souls,
Have ye withdrawn from passion's crook-
ed ways,
Inspired, and thoroughly fortified?—If
the heart   355
Could be inspected to its inmost folds
By sight undazzled with the glare of
praise,
Who shall be named—in the resplendent
line

Of sages, martyrs, confessors—the man
Whom the best might of faith, wherever
   fixed,   360
For one day's little compass, has pre-
   served
From painful and discreditable shocks
Of contradiction, from some vague desire
Culpably cherished, or corrupt relapse
To some unsanctioned fear?"
           "If this be so, 365
And Man," said I, "be in his noblest
   shape
Thus pitiably infirm; then, he who
   made,
And who shall judge the creature, will
   forgive.
—Yet, in its general tenor, your com-
   plaint
Is all too true; and surely not mis-
   placed: 370
For, from this pregnant spot of ground,
   such thoughts
Rise to the notice of a serious mind
By natural exhalation. With the dead
In their repose, the living in their mirth,
Who can reflect, unmoved, upon the
   round
Of smooth and solemnized complacencies,
By which, on Christian lands, from age
   to age
Profession mocks performance? Earth is
   sick,
And Heaven is weary, of the hollow
   words
Which States and Kingdoms utter when
   they talk   380
Of truth and justice. Turn to private
   life
And social neighbourhood; look we to
   ourselves;
A light of duty shines on every day
For all; and yet how few are warmed or
   cheered!
How few who mingle with their fellow-
   men   385
And still remain self-governed, and apart,
Like this our honoured Friend; and
   thence acquire
Right to expect his vigorous decline,
That promises to the end a blest old
   age!"

"Yet," with a smile of triumph thus
   exclaimed   390
The Solitary, "in the life of man,
If to the poetry of common speech
Faith may be given, we see as in a glass
A true reflection of the circling year,
With all its seasons. Grant that Spring
   is there,   395
In spite of many a rough untoward blast,
Hopeful and promising with buds and
   flowers;
Yet where is glowing Summer's long rich
   day,
That *ought* to follow faithfully expressed?
And mellow Autumn, charged with
   bounteous fruit,   400
Where is she imaged? in what favoured
   clime
Her lavish pomp, and ripe magnificence?
—Yet, while the better part is missed,
   the worse
In man's autumnal season is set forth
With a resemblance not to be denied, 405
And that contents him; bowers that
   hear no more
The voice of gladness, less and less supply
Of outward sunshine and internal
   warmth;
And, with this change, short air and
   falling leaves,   409
Foretelling aged Winter's desolate sway.

"How gay the habitations that bedeck
This fertile valley! Not a house but
   seems
To give assurance of content within;
Embosomed happiness, and placid love;
As if the sunshine of the day were met
With answering brightness in the hearts
   of all   416
Who walk this favoured ground. But
   chance-regards,
And notice forced upon incurious ears;
These, if these only, acting in despite
Of the encomiums by my Friend pro-
   nounced   420
On humble life, forbid the judging mind
To trust the smiling aspect of this fair
And noiseless commonwealth. The sim-
   ple race
Of mountaineers (by nature's self removed

From foul temptations, and by constant
    care   425
Of a good shepherd tended, as them-
    selves
Do tend their flocks) partake man's
    general lot
With little mitigation. They escape,
Perchance, the heavier woes of guilt;
    feel not
The tedium of fantastic idleness: 430
Yet life, as with the multitude, with
    them
Is fashioned like an ill-constructed tale;
That on the outset wastes its gay desires,
Its fair adventures, its enlivening hopes,
And pleasant interests—for the sequel
    leaving   435
Old things repeated with diminished
    grace;
And all the laboured novelties at best
Imperfect substitutes, whose use and
    power
Evince the want and weakness whence
    they spring."

While in this serious mood we held
    discourse,   440
The reverend Pastor toward the church-
    yard gate
Approached; and, with a mild respectful
    air
Of native cordiality, our Friend
Advanced to greet him. With a gracious
    mien
Was he received, and mutual joy pre-
    vailed.   445
Awhile they stood in conference, and I
    guess
That he, who now upon the mossy wall
Sate by my side, had vanished, if a wish
Could have transferred him to the flying
    clouds,
Or the least penetrable hiding-place   450
In his own valley's rocky guardianship.
—For me, I looked upon the pair, well
    pleased:
Nature had framed them both, and both
    were marked
By circumstance, with intermixture fine
Of contrast and resemblance. To an oak
Hardy and grand, a weather-beaten oak,

Fresh in the strength and majesty of age,
One might be likened: flourishing ap-
    peared,
Though somewhat past the fulness of
    his prime,
The other—like a stately sycamore,   460
That spreads, in gentle pomp, its honied
    shade.

A general greeting was exchanged;
    and soon
The Pastor learned that his approach
    had given
A welcome interruption to discourse
Grave, and in truth too often sad.—"Is
    Man   465
A child of hope? Do generations press
On generations, without progress made?
Halts the individual, ere his hairs be
    grey,
Perforce? Are we a creature in whom
    good
Preponderates, or evil? Doth the will
Acknowledge reason's law? A living
    power   471
Is virtue, or no better than a name,
Fleeting as health or beauty, and un-
    sound?
So that the only substance which remains,
(For thus the tenour of complaint hath
    run)   475
Among so many shadows, are the pains
And penalties of miserable life,
Doomed to decay, and then expire in
    dust!
—Our cogitations this way have been
    drawn,
These are the points," the Wanderer said,
    "on which   480
Our inquest turns.—Accord, good Sir!
    the light
Of your experience to dispel this gloom:
By your persuasive wisdom shall the
    heart
That frets, or languishes, be stilled and
    cheered."

"Our nature," said the Priest, in mild
    reply,   485
"Angels may weigh and fathom: they
    perceive,

With undistempered and unclouded
   spirit,
The object as it is; but, for ourselves,
That speculative height *we* may not reach.
The good and evil are our own; and we
Are that which we would contemplate
   from far.   491
Knowledge, for us, is difficult to gain—
Is difficult to gain, and hard to keep—
As virtue's self; like virtue is beset
With snares; tried, tempted, subject to
   decay.   495
Love, admiration, fear, desire, and hate,
Blind were we without these: through
   these alone
Are capable to notice or discern
Or to record; we judge, but cannot be
Indifferent judges. 'Spite of proudest
   boast,   500
Reason, best reason, is to imperfect man
An effort only, and a noble aim;
A crown, an attribute of sovereign power,
Still to be courted—never to be won.
—Look forth, or each man dive into
   himself;   505
What sees he but a creature too per-
   turbed;
That is transported to excess, that
   yearns,
Regrets, or trembles, wrongly, or too
   much;
Hopes rashly, in disgust as rash recoils;
Battens on spleen, or moulders in de-
   spair?   510
Thus comprehension fails, and truth is
   missed;
Thus darkness and delusion round our
   path
Spread, from disease, whose subtle injury
   lurks
Within the very faculty of sight.   514

"Yet for the general purposes of faith
In Providence, for solace and support,
We may not doubt that who can best
   subject
The will to reason's law, can strictliest
   live
And act in that obedience, he shall gain
The clearest apprehension of those
   truths,   520

Which unassisted reason's utmost power
Is too infirm to reach. But, waiving this,
And our regards confining within bounds
Of less exalted consciousness, through
   which
The very multitude are free to range, 525
We safely may affirm that human life
Is either fair and tempting, a soft scene
Grateful to sight, refreshing to the soul,
Or a forbidding tract of cheerless
   view;
Even as the same is looked at, or ap-
   proached.   530
Thus, when in changeful April fields are
   white
With new-fallen snow, if from the
   sullen north
Your walk conduct you hither, ere the
   sun
Hath gained his noontide height, this
   churchyard, filled
With mounds transversely lying side by
   side   535
From east to west, before you will ap-
   pear
An unillumined, blank, and dreary, plain,
With more than wintry cheerlessness and
   gloom
Saddening the heart. Go forward, and
   look back;
Look, from the quarter whence the lord
   of light,   540
Of life, of love, and gladness doth dis-
   pense
His beams; which, unexcluded in their
   fall,
Upon the southern side of every grave
Have gently exercised a melting power;
Then will a vernal prospect greet your
   eye,   545
All fresh and beautiful, and green and
   bright,
Hopeful and cheerful:—vanished is the
   pall
That overspread and chilled the sacred
   turf,
Vanished or hidden; and the whole
   domain,
To some, too lightly minded, might ap-
   pear   550
A meadow carpet for the dancing hours.

—This contrast, not unsuitable to life,
Is to that other state more apposite,
Death and its two-fold aspect! wintry—
    one,
Cold, sullen, blank, from hope and joy
    shut out;   555
The other, which the ray divine hath
    touched,
Replete with vivid promise, bright as
    spring."

"We see, then, as we feel," the Wan-
    derer thus
With a complacent animation spake,
"And in your judgment, Sir! the mind's
    repose   560
On evidence is not to be ensured
By act of naked reason. Moral truth
Is no mechanic structure, built by rule;
And which, once built, retains a steadfast
    shape
And undisturbed proportions; but a
    thing   565
Subject, you deem, to vital accidents;
And, like the water-lily, lives and thrives,
Whose root is fixed in stable earth, whose
    head
Floats on the tossing waves. With joy
    sincere
I re-salute these sentiments confirmed 570
By your authority. But how acquire
The inward principle that gives effect
To outward argument; the passive will
Meek to admit; the active energy,
Strong and unbounded to embrace, and
    firm   575
To keep and cherish? how shall man
    unite
With self-forgetting tenderness of heart
An earth-despising dignity of soul?
Wise in that union, and without it
    blind!"

  "The way," said I, "to court, if not
    obtain   580
The ingenuous mind, apt to be set
    aright;
This, in the lonely dell discoursing, you
Declared at large; and by what exer-
    cise
From visible nature, or the inner self

Power may be trained, and renovation
    brought   585
To those who need the gift. But, after
    all,
Is aught so certain as that man is
    doomed
To breathe beneath a vault of ignorance?
The natural roof of that dark house in
    which
His soul is pent! How little can be
    known—   590
This is the wise man's sigh; how far we
    err—
This is the good man's not unfrequent
    pang!
And they perhaps err least, the lowly
    class
Whom a benign necessity compels   594
To follow reason's least ambitious course;
Such do I mean who, unperplexed by
    doubt,
And unincited by a wish to look
Into high objects farther than they may,
Pace to and fro, from morn till eventide,
The narrow avenue of daily toil   600
For daily bread."
              "Yes," buoyantly exclaimed
The pale Recluse—"praise to the sturdy
    plough,
And patient spade; praise to the simple
    crook,
And ponderous loom—resounding while
    it holds
Body and mind in one captivity;   605
And let the light mechanic tool be hailed
With honour; which, encasing by the
    power
Of long companionship, the artist's hand,
Cuts off that hand, with all its world of
    nerves,
From a too busy commerce with the
    heart!   610
—Inglorious implements of craft and toil,
Both ye that shape and build, and ye
    that force,
By slow solicitation, earth to yield
Her annual bounty, sparingly dealt forth
With wise reluctance; you would I extol,
Not for gross good alone which ye pro-
    duce,   616
But for the impertinent and ceaseless strife

Of proofs and reasons ye preclude—in
    those
Who to your dull society are born,
And with their humble birthright rest
    content.   620
—Would I had ne'er renounced it!"
                   A slight flush
Of moral anger previously had tinged
The old Man's cheek; but, at this closing
    turn
Of self-reproach, it passed away. Said he,
"That which we feel we utter; as we
    think   625
So have we argued; reaping for our pains
No visible recompense. For our relief
You," to the Pastor turning thus he
    spake,
"Have kindly interposed. May I entreat
Your further help? The mine of real
    life   630
Dig for us; and present us, in the shape
Of virgin ore, that gold which we, by
    pains
Fruitless as those of aery alchemists,
Seek from the torturing crucible. There
    lies
A round us a domain where you have long
Watched both the outward course and
    inner heart: 636
Give us, for our abstractions, solid facts;
For our disputes, plain pictures. Say
    what man
He is who cultivates yon hanging field;
What qualities of mind she bears, who
    comes,   640
For morn and evening service, with her
    pail,
To that green pasture; place before our
    sight
The family who dwell within yon house
Fenced round with glittering laurel; or
    in that
Below, from which the curling smoke
    ascends.   645
Or rather, as we stand on holy earth[1],
And have the dead around us, take from
    them
Your instances; for they are both best
    known,

---

[1] See Note, p. 927.

And by frail man most equitably judged.
Epitomise the life; pronounce, you can,
Authentic epitaphs on some of these 651
Who, from their lowly mansions hither
    brought,
Beneath this turf lie mouldering at our
    feet:
So, by your records, may our doubts be
    solved;
And so, not searching higher, we may learn
*To prize the breath we share with human
    kind;*   656
And look upon the dust of man with awe."

The Priest replied—"An office you
    impose
For which peculiar requisites are mine;
Yet much, I feel, is wanting—else the
    task   660
Would be most grateful. True indeed it is
That they whom death has hidden from
    our sight
Are worthiest of the mind's regard; with
    these
The future cannot contradict the past:
Mortality's last exercise and proof   665
Is undergone; the transit made that shows
The very Soul, revealed as she departs.
Yet, on your first suggestion, will I give,
Ere we descend into these silent vaults,
One picture from the living.
                You behold, 670
High on the breast of yon dark moun-
    tain, dark
With stony barrenness, a shining speck
Bright as a sunbeam sleeping till a shower
Brush it away, or cloud pass over it;
And such it might be deemed—a sleeping
    sunbeam;   675
But 'tis a plot of cultivated ground,
Cut off, an island in the dusky waste;
And that attractive brightness is its own.
The lofty site, by nature framed to
    tempt
Amid a wilderness of rocks and stones
The tiller's hand, a hermit might have
    chosen,   681
For opportunity presented, thence
Far forth to send his wandering eye o'er
    land
And ocean, and look down upon the works,

The habitations, and the ways of men,
Himself unseen! But no tradition tells
That ever hermit dipped his maple dish
In the sweet spring that lurks 'mid yon
    green fields;
And no such visionary views belong   689
To those who occupy and till the ground,
High on that mountain where they long
    have dwelt
A wedded pair in childless solitude.
A house of stones collected on the spot,
By rude hands built, with rocky knolls
    in front,
Backed also by a ledge of rock, whose
    crest   695
Of birch-trees waves over the chimney-
    top;
A rough abode—in colour, shape, and size,
Such as in unsafe times of border-war
Might have been wished for and con-
    trived, to elude
The eye of roving plunderer—for their
    need   700
Suffices; and unshaken bears the assault
Of their most dreaded foe, the strong
    South-west
In anger blowing from the distant sea.
—Alone within her solitary hut;   704
There, or within the compass of her fields,
At any moment may the Dame be found,
True as the stock-dove to her shallow
    nest
And to the grove that holds it. She
    beguiles
By intermingled work of house and field
The summer's day, and winter's; with
    success   710
Not equal, but sufficient to maintain,
Even at the worst, a smooth stream of
    content,
Until the expected hour at which her
    Mate
From the far-distant quarry's vault re-
    turns;
And by his converse crowns a silent day
With evening cheerfulness. In powers of
    mind,   716
In scale of culture, few among my flock
Hold lower rank than this sequestered
    pair:
But true humility descends from heaven;

And that best gift of heaven hath fallen
    on them;   720
Abundant recompense for every want.
—Stoop from your height, ye proud, and
    copy these!
Who, in their noiseless dwelling-place,
    can hear
The voice of wisdom whispering scripture
    texts
For the mind's government, or temper's
    peace;   725
And recommending for their mutual need,
Forgiveness, patience, hope, and charity!"

"Much was I pleased," the grey-haired
    Wanderer said,
"When to those shining fields our notice
    first
You turned; and yet more pleased have
    from your lips   730
Gathered this fair report of them who
    dwell
In that retirement; whither, by such
    course
Of evil hap and good as oft awaits
A tired way-faring man, once *I* was
    brought
While traversing alone yon mountain-pass.
Dark on my road the autumnal evening
    fell,   736
And night succeeded with unusual gloom,
So hazardous that feet and hands be-
    came
Guides better than mine eyes—until a
    light
High in the gloom appeared, too high,
    methought,   740
For human habitation; but I longed
To reach it, destitute of other hope.
I looked with steadiness as sailors look
On the north star, or watch-tower's dis-
    tant lamp,
And saw the light—now fixed—and
    shifting now—   745
Not like a dancing meteor, but in line
Of never-varying motion, to and fro.
It is no night-fire of the naked hills,
Thought I—some friendly covert must be
    near.
With this persuasion thitherward my
    steps   750

I turn, and reach at last the guiding light;
Joy to myself! but to the heart of her
Who there was standing on the open hill,
(The same kind Matron whom your
tongue hath praised)
Alarm and disappointment! The alarm
Ceased, when she learned through what
mishap I came, 756
And by what help had gained those dis-
tant fields.
Drawn from her cottage, on that aery
height,
Bearing a lantern in her hand she stood,
Or paced the ground—to guide her Hus-
band home, 760
By that unwearied signal, kenned afar;
An anxious duty! which the lofty site,
Traversed but by a few irregular paths,
Imposes, whensoe'er untoward chance 764
Detains him after his accustomed hour
Till night lies black upon the ground.
'But come,
Come,' said the Matron, 'to our poor
abode;
Those dark rocks hide it!' Entering, I
beheld
A blazing fire beside a cleanly hearth
Sate down; and to her office, with leave
asked, 770
The Dame returned.
                Or ere that glowing pile
Of mountain turf required the builder's
hand
Its wasted splendour to repair, the door
Opened, and she re-entered with glad
looks,
Her Helpmate following. Hospitable fare,
Frank conversation, made the evening's
treat: 776
Need a bewildered traveller wish for
more?
But more was given; I studied as we sate
By the bright fire, the good Man's form,
and face
Not less than beautiful; an open brow 780
Of undisturbed humanity; a cheek
Suffused with something of a feminine hue;
Eyes beaming courtesy and mild regard;
But, in the quicker turns of the discourse,
Expression slowly varying, that evinced
A tardy apprehension. From a fount 786

Lost, thought I, in the obscurities of time,
But honoured once, those features and
that mien
May have descended, though I see them
here.
In such a man, so gentle and subdued, 790
Withal so graceful in his gentleness,
A race illustrious for heroic deeds,
Humbled, but not degraded, may expire.
This pleasing fancy (cherished and upheld
By sundry recollections of such fall 795
From high to low, ascent from low to high,
As books record, and even the careless
mind
Cannot but notice among men and things)
Went with me to the place of my repose.

"Roused by the crowing cock at dawn
of day, 800
I yet had risen too late to interchange
A morning salutation with my Host,
Gone forth already to the far-off seat
Of his day's work. 'Three dark mid-
winter months
Pass,' said the Matron, 'and I never see,
Save when the sabbath brings its kind
release, 806
My helpmate's face by light of day. He
quits
His door in darkness, nor till dusk returns.
And, through Heaven's blessing, thus we
gain the bread
For which we pray; and for the wants
provide 810
Of sickness, accident, and helpless age.
Companions have I many; many friends,
Dependants, comforters—my wheel, my
fire,
All day the house-clock ticking in mine ear,
The cackling hen, the tender chicken
brood, 815
And the wild birds that gather round my
porch.
This honest sheep-dog's countenance I
read;
With him can talk; nor blush to waste a
word
On creatures less intelligent and shrewd.
And if the blustering wind that drives the
clouds 820
Care not for me, he lingers round my door,

And makes me pastime when our tempers
　　suit;—
But, above all, my thoughts are my
　　support,
My comfort:—would that they were
　　oftener fixed
On what, for guidance in the way that
　　leads　　　　　　　　　　　　825
To heaven, I know, by my Redeemer
　　taught.'.
The Matron ended—nor could I forbear
To exclaim—'O happy! yielding to the
　　law
Of these privations, richer in the main!—
While thankless thousands are opprest
　　and clogged　　　　　　　　830
By ease and leisure; by the very wealth
And pride of opportunity made poor;
While tens of thousands falter in their path,
And sink, through utter want of cheering
　　light;　　　　　　　　　　834
For you the hours of labour do not flag;
For you each evening hath its shining star,
And every sabbath-day its golden sun.'"

"Yes!" said the Solitary with a smile
That seemed to break from an expanding
　　heart,
"The untutored bird may found, and so
　　construct,　　　　　　　　840
And with such soft materials line, her nest
Fixed in the centre of a prickly brake,
That the thorns wound her not; they
　　only guard.
Powers not unjustly likened to those gifts
Of happy instinct which the woodland bird
Shares with her species, nature's grace
　　sometimes　　　　　　　　846
Upon the individual doth confer,
Among her higher creatures born and
　　trained
To use of reason. And, I own that, tired
Of the ostentatious world—a swelling
　　stage　　　　　　　　　　850
With empty actions and vain passions
　　stuffed,
And from the private struggles of man-
　　kind
Hoping far less than I could wish to hope,
Far less than once I trusted and be-
　　lieved—

I love to hear of those, who, not contend-
　　ing　　　　　　　　　　855
Nor summoned to contend for virtue's
　　prize,
Miss not the humbler good at which they
　　aim,
Blest with a kindly faculty to blunt
The edge of adverse circumstance, and turn
Into their contraries the petty plagues
And hindrances with which they stand
　　beset.　　　　　　　　　861
In early youth, among my native hills,
I knew a Scottish Peasant who possessed
A few small crofts of stone-encumbered
　　ground;
Masses of every shape and size, that lay
Scattered about under the mouldering
　　walls　　　　　　　　　866
Of a rough precipice; and some, apart,
In quarters unobnoxious to such chance,
As if the moon had showered them down
　　in spite.
But he repined not. Though the plough
　　was scared　　　　　　　870
By these obstructions, 'round the shady
　　stones
A fertilising moisture,' said the Swain,
'Gathers, and is preserved; and feeding
　　dews
And damps, through all the droughty
　　summer day
From out their substance issuing, main-
　　tain　　　　　　　　　875
Herbage that never fails: no grass springs
　　up
So green, so fresh, so plentiful, as mine!'
But thinly sown these natures; rare, at
　　least,
The mutual aptitude of seed and soil
That yields such kindly product. He,
　　whose bed　　　　　　　880
Perhaps yon loose sods cover, the poor
　　Pensioner
Brought yesterday from our sequestered
　　dell
Here to lie down in lasting quiet, he,
If living now, could otherwise report
Of rustic loneliness: that grey-haired
　　Orphan—　　　　　　　885
So call him, for humanity to him
No parent was—feelingly could have told,

In life, in death, what solitude can breed
Of selfishness, and cruelty, and vice;
Or, if it breed not, hath not power to cure.
—But your compliance, Sir! with our
   request   891
My words too long have hindered."
                Undeterred,
Perhaps incited rather, by these shocks,
In no ungracious opposition given
To the confiding spirit of his own   895
Experienced faith, the reverend Pastor
   said,
Around him looking; "Where shall I
   begin?
Who shall be first selected from my flock
Gathered together in their peaceful fold?"
He paused—and having lifted up his eyes
To the pure heaven, he cast them down
   again   901
Upon the earth beneath his feet; and
   spake :—

"To a mysteriously-united pair
This place is consecrate; to Death and
   Life,
And to the best affections that proceed
From their conjunction; consecrate to
   faith   906
In him who bled for man upon the cross;
Hallowed to revelation; and no less
To reason's mandates; and the hopes
   divine
Of pure imagination;—above all,   910
To charity, and love, that have provided,
Within these precincts, a capacious bed
And receptacle, open to the good
And evil, to the just and the unjust; 914
In which they find an equal resting-place:
Even as the multitude of kindred brooks
And streams, whose murmur fills this
   hollow vale,
Whether their course be turbulent or
   smooth,   918
Their waters clear or sullied, all are lost
Within the bosom of yon crystal Lake,
And end their journey in the same repose!

"And blest are they who sleep; and
   we that know,
While in a spot like this we breathe and
   walk,

That all beneath us by the wings are
   covered
Of motherly humanity, outspread   925
And gathering all within their tender shade,
Though loth and slow to come! A battle-
   field,
In stillness left when slaughter is no more,
With this compared, makes a strange
   spectacle!
A dismal prospect yields the wild shore
   strewn   930
With wrecks, and trod by feet of young
   and old
Wandering about in miserable search
Of friends or kindred, whom the angry sea
Restores not to their prayer! Ah! who
   would think
That all the scattered subjects which
   compose   935
Earth's melancholy vision through the
   space
Of all her climes—these wretched, these
   depraved,
To virtue lost, insensible of peace,
From the delights of charity cut off,   939
To pity dead, the oppressor and the opprest;
Tyrants who utter the destroying word,
And slaves who will consent to be de-
   stroyed—
Were of one species with the sheltered few,
Who, with a dutiful and tender hand,
Lodged, in a dear appropriated spot, 945
This file of infants; some that never
   breathed
The vital air; others, which, though allowed
That privilege, did yet expire too soon,
Or with too brief a warning, to admit
Administration of the holy rite   950
That lovingly consigns the babe to the arms
Of Jesus, and his everlasting care.
These that in trembling hope are laid apart;
And the besprinkled nursling, unrequired
Till he begins to smile upon the breast
That feeds him; and the tottering little-
   one   956
Taken from air and sunshine when the rose
Of infancy first blooms upon his cheek;
The thinking, thoughtless, school-boy;
   the bold youth
Of soul impetuous, and the bashful maid
Smitten while all the promises of life 961

Are opening round her; those of middle age,
Cast down while confident in strength
    they stand,
Like pillars fixed more firmly, as might
    seem,
And more secure, by very weight of all
That, for support, rests on them; the
    decayed   966
And burthensome; and lastly, that poor
    few
Whose light of reason is with age extinct;
The hopeful and the hopeless, first and last,
The earliest summoned and the longest
    spared—   970
Are here deposited, with tribute paid
Various, but unto each some tribute paid;
As if, amid these peaceful hills and groves,
Society were touched with kind concern,
And gentle 'Nature grieved, that one
    should die[1];'   975
Or, if the change demanded no regret,
Observed the liberating stroke—and
    blessed.

"And whence that tribute? wherefore
    these regards[1]?
Not from the naked *Heart* alone of Man
(Though claiming high distinction upon
    earth   980
As the sole spring and fountain-head of
    tears,
His own peculiar utterance for distress
Or gladness)—No," the philosophic Priest
Continued, "'tis not in the vital seat
Of feeling to produce them, without aid
From the pure soul, the soul sublime and
    pure;   986
With her two faculties of eye and ear,

---

[1] See Note, p. 928.

The one by which a creature, whom his sins
Have rendered prone, can upward look
    to heaven;   989
The other that empowers him to perceive
The voice of Deity, on height and plain,
Whispering those truths in stillness, which
    the WORD,
To the four quarters of the winds, pro-
    claims.
Not without such assistance could the use
Of these benign observances prevail: 995
Thus are they born, thus fostered, thus
    maintained;
And by the care prospective of our wise
Forefathers, who, to guard against the
    shocks,
The fluctuation and decay of things,
Embodied and established these high
    truths   1000
In solemn institutions:—men convinced
That life is love and immortality,
The being one, and one the element.
There lies the channel, and original bed,
From the beginning, hollowed out and
    scooped   1005
For Man's affections—else betrayed and
    lost,
And swallowed up 'mid deserts infinite!
This is the genuine course, the aim, and
    end
Of prescient reason; all conclusions else
Are abject, vain, presumptuous, and per-
    verse.   1010
The faith partaking of those holy times,
Life, I repeat, is energy of love
Divine or human; exercised in pain,
In strife, in tribulation; and ordained,
If so approved and sanctified, to pass
Through shades and silent rest, to endless
    joy."   1016

BOOK SIXTH.

THE CHURCHYARD AMONG THE MOUNTAINS.

ARGUMENT.

Poet's Address to the State and Church of England.—The Pastor not inferior to the ancient Worthies of the Church.—He begins his Narratives with an instance of unrequited Love.—Anguish of mind subdued, and how.—The lonely Miner.—An instance of perseverance.—Which leads by contrast to an example of abused talents, irresolution, and weakness.—Solitary, applying this covertly to his own case, asks for an instance of some Stranger, whose dispositions may have led him to end his days here.—Pastor, in answer, gives an account of the harmonising influence of Solitude upon two men of opposite principles, who had encountered agitations in public life.—The rule by which Peace may be obtained expressed, and where.—Solitary hints at an overpowering Fatality.—Answer of the Pastor.—What subjects he will exclude from his Narratives.—Conversation upon this.—Instance of an unamiable character, a Female, and why given.—Contrasted with this, a meek sufferer, from unguarded and betrayed love.—Instance of heavier guilt, and its consequences to the Offender.—With this instance of a Marriage Contract broken is contrasted one of a Widower, evidencing his faithful affection towards his deceased wife by his care of their female Children.

HAIL to the crown by Freedom shaped—to
    gird
An English Sovereign's brow! and to the
    throne
Whereon he sits! Whose deep foundations
    lie
In veneration and the people's love;
Whose steps are equity, whose seat is
    law.
—Hail to the State of England! And
    conjoin   6
With this a salutation as devout,
Made to the spiritual fabric of her
    Church;
Founded in truth; by blood of Martyrdom
Cemented; by the hands of Wisdom
    reared   10
In beauty of holiness, with ordered pomp,
Decent and unreproved. The voice, that
    greets
The majesty of both, shall pray for
    both;
That, mutually protected and sustained,
They may endure long as the sea sur-
    rounds   15
This favoured Land, or sunshine warms
    her soil.

And O, ye swelling hills, and spacious
    plains!

Besprent from shore to shore with steeple-
    towers,
And spires whose "silent finger points to
    heaven[1];"   19
Nor wanting, at wide intervals, the bulk
Of ancient minster lifted above the cloud
Of the dense air, which town or city
    breeds
To intercept the sun's glad beams—may
    ne'er
That true succession fail of English
    hearts,   24
Who, with ancestral feeling, can perceive
What in those holy structures ye possess
Of ornamental interest, and the charm
Of pious sentiment diffused afar,
And human charity, and social love.   29
—Thus never shall the indignities of time
Approach their reverend graces, un-
    opposed;
Nor shall the elements be free to hurt
Their fair proportions; nor the blinder rage
Of bigot zeal madly to overturn;
And, if the desolating hand of war   35
Spare them, they shall continue to bestow,
Upon the thronged abodes of busy men
(Depraved, and ever prone to fill the mind
Exclusively with transitory things)

---

[1] See Note, p. 933.

An air and mien of dignified pursuit;   40
Of sweet civility, on rustic wilds.

The Poet, fostering for his native land
Such hope, entreats that servants may
abound
Of those pure altars worthy; ministers
Detached from pleasure, to the love of
gain   45
Superior, insusceptible of pride,
And by ambitious longings undisturbed;
Men, whose delight is where their duty
leads
Or fixes them; whose least distinguished
day
Shines with some portion of that heavenly
lustre   50
Which makes the sabbath lovely in the
sight
Of blessèd angels, pitying human cares.
—And, as on earth it is the doom of truth
To be perpetually attacked by foes
Open or covert, be that priesthood still,
For her defence, replenished with a band
Of strenuous champions, in scholastic arts
Thoroughly disciplined; nor (if in course
Of the revolving world's disturbances
Cause should recur, which righteous
Heaven avert!   60
To meet such trial) from their spiritual
sires
Degenerate; who, constrained to wield
the sword
Of disputation, shrunk not, though as-
sailed
With hostile din, and combating in sight
Of angry umpires, partial and unjust;   65
And did, thereafter, bathe their hands in
fire,
So to declare the conscience satisfied:
Nor for their bodies would accept release;
But, blessing God and praising him, be-
queathed
With their last breath, from out the
smouldering flame,   70
The faith which they by diligence had
earned,
Or, through illuminating grace, received,
For their dear countrymen, and all man-
kind.
O high example, constancy divine!

Even such a Man (inheriting the zeal
And from the sanctity of elder times   76
Not deviating,—a priest, the like of
whom,
If multiplied, and in their stations set,
Would o'er the bosom of a joyful land
Spread true religion and her genuine
fruits)   80
Before me stood that day; on holy
ground
Fraught with the relics of mortality,
Exalting tender themes, by just degrees
To lofty raised; and to the highest, last;
The head and mighty paramount of
truths,—   85
Immortal life, in never-fading worlds,
For mortal creatures, conquered and se-
cured.

That basis laid, those principles of faith
Announced, as a preparatory act
Of reverence done to the spirit of the
place,   90
The Pastor cast his eyes upon the ground;
Not, as before, like one oppressed with
awe,
But with a mild and social cheerfulness;
Then to the Solitary turned, and spake.

"At morn or eve, in your retired
domain,   95
Perchance you not unfrequently have
marked
A Visitor—in quest of herbs and flowers;
Too delicate employ, as would appear,
For one, who, though of drooping mien,
had yet
From nature's kindliness received a frame
Robust as ever rural labour bred."   101

The Solitary answered: "Such a Form
Full well I recollect. We often crossed
Each other's path; but, as the Intruder
seemed
Fondly to prize the silence which he
kept,   105
And I as willingly did cherish mine,
We met, and passed, like shadows. I
have heard,
From my good Host, that being crazed in
brain

By unrequited love, he scaled the
    rocks,
Dived into caves, and pierced the matted
    woods,   110
In hope to find some virtuous herb of
    power
To cure his malady!"
            The Vicar smiled,—
"Alas! before to-morrow's sun goes down
His habitation will be here: for him
That open grave is destined."
            "Died he then   115
Of pain and grief?" the Solitary asked,
"Do not believe it; never could that be!"

"He loved," the Vicar answered,
    "deeply loved,
Loved fondly, truly, fervently; and dared
At length to tell his love, but sued in
    vain;   120
Rejected, yea repelled; and, if with scorn
Upon the haughty maiden's brow, 'tis
    but
A high-prized plume which female Beauty
    wears
In wantonness of conquest, or puts on
To cheat the world, or from herself to
    hide   125
Humiliation, when no longer free.
That he could brook, and glory in;—but
    when
The tidings came that she whom he had
    wooed
Was wedded to another, and his heart
Was forced to rend away its only
    hope;   130
Then, Pity could have scarcely found on
    earth
An object worthier of regard than he,
In the transition of that bitter hour!
Lost was she, lost; nor could the Sufferer
    say
That in the act of preference he had
    been   135
Unjustly dealt with; but the Maid was
    gone!
Had vanished from his prospects and
    desires;
Not by translation to the heavenly choir
Who have put off their mortal spoils—
    ah no!

She lives another's wishes to com-
    plete,—   140
'Joy be their lot, and happiness,' he cried,
'His lot and hers, as misery must be
    mine!'

"Such was that strong concussion; but
    the Man,
Who trembled, trunk and limbs, like
    some huge oak
By a fierce tempest shaken, soon re-
    sumed   145
The steadfast quiet natural to a mind
Of composition gentle and sedate,
And, in its movements, circumspect and
    slow.
To books, and to the long-forsaken desk,
O'er which enchained by science he had
    loved   150
To bend, he stoutly re-addressed him-
    self,
Resolved to quell his pain, and search for
    truth
With keener appetite (if that might be)
And closer industry. Of what ensued
Within the heart no outward sign ap-
    peared   155
Till a betraying sickliness was seen
To tinge his cheek, and through his frame
    it crept
With slow mutation unconcealable;
Such universal change as autumn makes
In the fair body of a leafy grove   160
Discoloured, then divested.
            'Tis affirmed
By poets skilled in nature's secret ways
That Love will not submit to be controlled
By mastery:—and the good Man lacked
    not friends
Who strove to instil this truth into his
    mind,   165
A mind in all heart-mysteries un-
    versed.
'Go to the hills,' said one, 'remit a while
This baneful diligence:—at early morn
Court the fresh air, explore the heaths
    and woods;
And, leaving it to others to foretell,   170
By calculations sage, the ebb and flow
Of tides, and when the moon will be
    eclipsed,

Do you, for your own benefit, construct
A calendar of flowers, plucked as they
    - blow
Where health abides, and cheerfulness,
    and peace.'   175
The attempt was made;—'tis needless to
    report
How hopelessly; but innocence is strong,
And an entire simplicity of mind
A thing most sacred in the eye of
    Heaven;
That opens, for such sufferers, relief 180
Within the soul, fountains of grace
    divine;
And doth commend their weakness and
    disease
To Nature's care, assisted in her office
By all the elements that round her wait
To generate, to preserve, and to re-
    store;   185
And by her beautiful array of forms
Shedding sweet influence from above; or
    pure
Delight exhaling from the ground they
    tread."

"Impute it not to impatience, if,"
    exclaimed
The Wanderer, "I infer that he was
    healed   190
By perseverance in the course prescribed."

"You do not err: the powers, that had
    been lost
By slow degrees, were gradually regained;
The fluttering nerves composed; the beat-
    ing heart
In rest established; and the jarring
    thoughts   195
To harmony restored.—But yon dark
    mould
Will cover him, in the fulness of his
    strength,
Hastily smitten by a fever's force;
Yet not with stroke so sudden as refused
Time to look back with tenderness on
    her   200
Whom he had loved in passion; and to
    send
Some farewell words—with one, but one,
    request;

That, from his dying hand, she would
    accept
Of his possessions that which most he
    prized;
A book, upon whose leaves some chosen
    plants,   205
By his own hand disposed with nicest care,
In undecaying beauty were preserved;
Mute register, to him, of time and place,
And various fluctuations in the breast;
To her, a monument of faithful love 210
Conquered, and in tranquillity retained!

"Close to his destined habitation, lies
One who achieved a humbler victory,
Though marvellous in its kind. A place
    there is
High in these mountains, that allured a
    band   215
Of keen adventurers to unite their pains
In search of precious ore: they tried, were
    foiled—
And all desisted, all, save him alone.
He, taking counsel of his own clear
    thoughts,
And trusting only to his own weak
    hands,   220
Urged unremittingly the stubborn work,
Unseconded, uncountenanced; then, as
    time
Passed on, while still his lonely efforts
    found
No recompense, derided; and at length,
By many pitied, as insane of mind; 225
By others dreaded as the luckless thrall
Of subterranean Spirits feeding hope
By various mockery of sight and sound;
Hope after hope, encouraged and de-
    stroyed.
—But when the lord of seasons had
    matured   230
The fruits of earth through space of twice
    ten years,
The mountain's entrails offered to his
    view
And trembling grasp the long-deferred
    reward.
Not with more transport did Columbus
    greet
A world, his rich discovery! But our
    Swain,   235

A very hero till his point was gained,
Proved all unable to support the weight
Of prosperous fortune. On the fields he
   looked
With an unsettled liberty of thought,
Wishes and endless schemes; by daylight
   walked   240
Giddy and restless; ever and anon
Quaffed in his gratitude immoderate
   cups;
And truly might be said to die of joy!
He vanished; but conspicuous to this
   day
The path remains that linked his cottage-
   door   245
To the mine's mouth; a long and slanting
   track,
Upon the rugged mountain's stony side,
Worn by his daily visits to and from
The darksome centre of a constant hope.
This vestige, neither force of beating rain,
Nor the vicissitudes of frost and thaw 251
Shall cause to fade, till ages pass away;
And it is named, in memory of the event,
The PATH OF PERSEVERANCE."
          "Thou from whom
Man has his strength," exclaimed the
   Wanderer, "oh!   255
Do thou direct it! To the virtuous grant
The penetrative eye which can perceive
In this blind world the guiding vein of
   hope;
That, like this Labourer, such may dig
   their way,
'Unshaken, unseduced, unterrified;' 260
Grant to the wise *his* firmness of re-
   solve!"

   "That prayer were not superfluous,"
   said the Priest,
"Amid the noblest relics, proudest dust,
That Westminster, for Britain's glory,
   holds
Within the bosom of her awful pile, 265
Ambitiously collected. Yet the sigh,
Which wafts that prayer to heaven, is
   due to all,
Wherever laid, who living fell below
Their virtue's humbler mark; a sigh of
   pain
If to the opposite extreme they sank. 270

How would you pity her who yonder
   rests;
Him, farther off; the pair, who here are
   laid;
But, above all, that mixture of earth's
   mould
Whom sight of this green hillock to my
   mind
Recalls!

        He lived not till his locks were
   nipped   275
By seasonable frost of age; nor died
Before his temples, prematurely forced
To mix the manly brown with silver grey,
Gave obvious instance of the sad effect
Produced, when thoughtless Folly hath
   usurped   280
The natural crown that sage Experience
   wears.
Gay, volatile, ingenious, quick to learn,
And prompt to exhibit all that he pos-
   sessed
Or could perform; a zealous actor, hired
Into the troop of mirth, a soldier, sworn
Into the lists of giddy enterprise— 286
Such was he; yet, as if within his frame
Two several souls alternately had lodged,
Two sets of manners could the Youth
   put on;
And, fraught with antics as the Indian
   bird   290
That writhes and chatters in her wiry cage,
Was graceful, when it pleased him, smooth
   and still
As the mute swan that floats adown the
   stream,
Or, on the waters of the unruffled lake,
Anchors her placid beauty. Not a leaf,
That flutters on the bough, lighter than
   he;   296
And not a flower, that droops in the
   green shade,
More winningly reserved! If ye enquire
How such consummate elegance was bred
Amid these wilds, this answer may suf-
   fice;   300
'Twas Nature's will; who sometimes un-
   dertakes,
For the reproof of human vanity,
Art to outstrip in her peculiar walk.

Hence, for this Favourite—lavishly en-
dowed
With personal gifts, and bright instinctive
wit,   305
While both, embellishing each other,
stood
Yet farther recommended by the charm
Of fine demeanour, and by dance and song,
And skill in letters—every fancy shaped
Fair expectations; nor, when to the
world's   310
Capacious field forth went the Adven-
turer, there
Were he and his attainments overlooked,
Or scantily rewarded; but all hopes,
Cherished for him, he suffered to depart,
Like blighted buds; or clouds that mi-
micked land   315
Before the sailor's eye; or diamond drops
That sparkling decked the morning grass;
or aught
That *was* attractive, and hath ceased to
be !

"Yet, when this Prodigal returned, the
rites
Of joyful greeting were on him bestowed,
Who, by humiliation undeterred,   321
Sought for his weariness a place of rest
Within his Father's gates.—Whence came
he?—clothed
In tattered garb, from hovels where abides
Necessity, the stationary host   325
Of vagrant poverty; from rifted barns
Where no one dwells but the wide-staring
owl
And the owl's prey; from these bare
haunts, to which
He had descended from the proud saloon,
He came, the ghost of beauty and of
health,   330
The wreck of gaiety ! But soon revived
In strength, in power refitted, he renewed
His suit to Fortune; and she smiled again
Upon a fickle Ingrate. Thrice he rose,
Thrice sank as willingly. For he—whose
nerves   335
Were used to thrill with pleasure, while
his voice
Softly accompanied the tuneful harp,
By the nice finger of fair ladies touched

In glittering halls—was able to derive
No less enjoyment from an abject choice.
Who happier for the moment—who more
blithe   341
Than this fallen Spirit? in those dreary
holds
His talents lending to exalt the freaks
Of merry-making beggars,—now, pro-
voked   344
To laughter multiplied in louder peals
By his malicious wit; then, all enchained
With mute astonishment, themselves to
see
In their own arts outdone, their fame
eclipsed,
As by the very presence of the Fiend
Who dictates and inspires illusive feats,
For knavish purposes ! The city, too, 351
(With shame I speak it) to her guilty
bowers
Allured him, sunk so low in self-respect
As there to linger, there to eat his bread,
Hired minstrel of voluptuous blandish-
ment;   355
Charming the air with skill of hand or
voice,
Listen who would, be wrought upon who
might,
Sincerely wretched hearts, or falsely gay.
—Such the too frequent tenour of his
boast
In ears that relished the report;—but all
Was from his Parents happily concealed;
Who saw enough for blame and pitying
love.
They also were permitted to receive
His last, repentant breath; and closed
his eyes,   364
No more to open on that irksome world
Where he had long existed in the state
Of a young fowl beneath one mother
hatched,
Though from another sprung. different in
kind:
Where he had lived, and could not cease
to live,
Distracted in propensity; content   370
With neither element of good or ill;
And yet in both rejoicing; man un-
blest;
Of contradictions infinite the slave,

Till his deliverance, when Mercy made him
One with himself, and one with them
   that sleep."   375

"'Tis strange," observed the Solitary,
   "strange
It seems, and scarcely less than pitiful,
That in a land where charity provides
For all that can no longer feed themselves,
A man like this should choose to bring
   his shame   380
To the parental door; and with his sighs
Infect the air which he had freely breathed
In happy infancy. He could not pine
Through lack of converse; no—he must
   have found
Abundant exercise for thought and speech,
In his dividual being, self-reviewed,   386
Self-catechised, self-punished. —Some
   there are
Who, drawing near their final home, and
   much
And daily longing that the same were
   reached,
Would rather shun than seek the fellow-
   ship   390
Of kindred mould.—Such haply here are
   laid!"

"Yes," said the Priest, "the Genius of
   our hills—
Who seems, by these stupendous barriers
   cast
Round his domain, desirous not alone
To keep his own, but also to exclude   395
All other progeny—doth sometimes lure,
Even by his studied depth of privacy,
The unhappy alien hoping to obtain
Concealment, or seduced by wish to find,
In place from outward molestation free,
Helps to internal ease. Of many such 401
Could I discourse; but as their stay was
   brief,
So their departure only left behind
Fancies, and loose conjectures. Other
   trace
Survives, for worthy mention, of a pair
Who, from the pressure of their several
   fates,   406
Meeting as strangers, in a petty town
Whose blue roofs ornament a distant reach

Of this far-winding vale, remained as
   friends
True to their choice; and gave their
   bones in trust   410
To this loved cemetery, here to lodge
With unescutcheoned privacy interred
Far from the family vault.—A Chieftain
   one
By right of birth; within whose spotless
   breast
The fire of ancient Caledonia burned:
He, with the foremost whose impatience
   hailed   416
The Stuart, landing to resume, by force
Of arms, the crown which bigotry had
   lost,
Aroused his clan; and, fighting at their
   head,
With his brave sword endeavoured to
   prevent   420
Culloden's fatal overthrow. Escaped
From that disastrous rout, to foreign shores
He fled; and when the lenient hand of
   time
Those troubles had appeased, he sought
   and gained,
For his obscured condition, an obscure
Retreat, within this nook of English
   ground.   426

"The other, born in Britain's southern
   tract,
Had fixed his milder loyalty, and placed
His gentler sentiments of love and hate,
There, where *they* placed them who in
   conscience prized   430
The new succession, as a line of kings
Whose oath had virtue to protect the land
Against the dire assaults of papacy
And arbitrary rule. But launch thy bark
On the distempered flood of public life,
And cause for most rare triumph will be
   thine   436
If, spite of keenest eye and steadiest
   hand,
The stream, that bears thee forward,
   prove not, soon
Or late, a perilous master. He—who oft,
Beneath the battlements and stately trees
That round his mansion cast a sober
   gloom,   441

Had moralised on this, and other truths
Of kindred import, pleased and satisfied—
Was forced to vent his wisdom with a
    sigh
Heaved from the heart in fortune's bitter-
    ness,   445
When he had crushed a plentiful estate
By ruinous contest, to obtain a seat
In Britain's senate. Fruitless was the
    attempt:
And while the uproar of that desperate
    strife
Continued yet to vibrate on his ear,   450
The vanquished Whig, under a borrowed
    name,
(For the mere sound and echo of his own
Haunted him with sensations of disgust
That he was glad to lose) slunk from the
    world
To the deep shade of those untravelled
    Wilds;   455
In which the Scottish Laird had long
    possessed
An undisturbed abode. Here, then, they.
    met,
Two doughty champions; flaming Ja-
    cobite
And sullen Hanoverian! You might think
That losses and vexations, less severe   460
Than those which they had severally sus-
    tained,
Would have inclined each to abate his
    zeal
For his ungrateful cause; no,—I have
    heard
My reverend Father tell that, 'mid the
    calm
Of that small town encountering thus,
    they filled,   465
Daily, its bowling-green with harmless
    strife;
Plagued with uncharitable thoughts the
    church;
And vexed the market-place. But in the
    breasts
Of these opponents gradually was wrought,
With little change of general sentiment,
Such leaning towards each other, that
    their days   471
By choice were spent in constant fellow-
    ship;

And if, at times, they fretted with the
    yoke,
Those very bickerings made them love it
    more.

    "A favourite boundary to their length-
        ened walks   475
This Churchyard was. And, whether they
    had come
Treading their path in sympathy and
    linked
In social converse, or by some short space
Discreetly parted to preserve the peace,
One spirit seldom failed to extend its
    sway   480
Over both minds, when they awhile had
    marked
The visible quiet of this holy ground,
And breathed its soothing air;—the spirit
    of hope
And saintly magnanimity; that—spurn-
    ing
The field of selfish difference and dis-
    pute,   485
And every care which transitory things,
Earth and the kingdoms of the earth,
    create—
Doth, by a rapture of forgetfulness,
Preclude forgiveness, from the praise de-
    barred,
Which else the Christian virtue might
    have claimed.   490

    "There live who yet remember here to
        have seen
Their courtly figures, seated on the stump
Of an old yew, their favourite resting-
    place.
But as the remnant of the long-lived tree
Was disappearing by a swift decay,   495
They, with joint care, determined to erect,
Upon its site, a dial, that might stand
For public use preserved, and thus sur-
    vive
As their own private monument: for
    this
Was the particular spot, in which they
    wished   500
(And Heaven was pleased to accomplish
    the desire)
That, undivided, their remains should lie.

So, where the mouldered tree had stood,
  was raised
Yon structure, framing, with the ascent
  of steps
That to the decorated pillar lead,   505
A work of art more sumptuous than
  might seem
To suit this place; yet built in no proud
  scorn
Of rustic homeliness; they only aimed
To ensure for it respectful guardianship.
Around the margin of the plate, whereon
The shadow falls to note the stealthy
  hours,   511
Winds an inscriptive legend."—At these
  words
Thither we turned; and gathered, as we
  read,
The appropriate sense, in Latin numbers
  couched:
"Time flies; it is his melancholy task 515
To bring, and bear away, delusive hopes,
And reproduce the troubles he destroys.
But, while his blindness thus is occupied,
Discerning Mortal! do thou serve the will
Of Time's eternal Master, and that peace,
Which the world wants, shall be for thee
confirmed!"   521

"Smooth verse, inspired by no un-
  lettered Muse,"
Exclaimed the Sceptic, "and the strain
  of thought
Accords with nature's language;—the soft
  voice
Of yon white torrent falling down the
  rocks   525
Speaks, less distinctly, to the same ef-
  fect.
If, then, their blended influence be not
  lost
Upon our hearts, not wholly lost, I grant,
Even upon mine, the more are we re-
  quired   529
To feel for those among our fellow-men,
Who, offering no obeisance to the world,
Are yet made desperate by 'too quick
  a sense
Of constant infelicity,' cut off
From peace like exiles on some barren
  rock,

Their life's appointed prison; not more
  free   535
Than sentinels, between two armies, set,
With nothing better, in the chill night
  air,
Than their own thoughts to comfort them.
  Say why
That ancient story of Prometheus chained
To the bare rock, on frozen Caucasus; 540
The vulture, the inexhaustible repast
Drawn from his vitals? Say what meant
  the woes
By Tantalus entailed upon his race,
And the dark sorrows of the line of
  Thebes?
Fictions in form, but in their substance
  truths,   545
Tremendous truths! familiar to the men
Of long-past times, nor obsolete in ours.
Exchange the shepherd's frock of native
  grey
For robes with regal purple tinged; con-
  vert
The crook into a sceptre; give the pomp
Of circumstance; and here the tragic
  Muse   551
Shall find apt subjects for her highest art.
Amid the groves, under the shadowy
  hills,
The generations are prepared; the pangs,
The internal pangs, are ready; the dread
  strife   555
Of poor humanity's afflicted will
Struggling in vain with ruthless destiny."

"Though," said the Priest in answer,
  "these be terms
Which a divine philosophy rejects,
We, whose established and unfailing
  trust   560
Is in controlling Providence, admit
That, through all stations, human life
  abounds
With mysteries;—for, if Faith were left
  untried,
How could the might, that lurks within
  her, then
Be shown? her glorious excellence—that
  ranks   565
Among the first of Powers and Virtues—
  proved?

Our system is not fashioned to preclude
That sympathy which you for others ask ;
And I could tell, not travelling for my
    theme
Beyond these humble graves, of grievous
    crimes   570
And strange disasters ; but I pass them
    by,
Loth to disturb what Heaven hath hushed
    in peace.
—Still less, far less, am I inclined to treat
Of Man degraded in his Maker's sight
By the deformities of brutish vice :   575
For, in such portraits, though a vulgar
    face
And a coarse outside of repulsive life
And unaffecting manners might at once
Be recognised by all—" " Ah ! do not
    think,"
The Wanderer somewhat eagerly ex-
    claimed,   580
" Wish could be ours that you, for such
    poor gain,
(Gain shall I call it ?—gain of what ?—for
    whom ?)
Should breathe a word tending to violate
Your own pure spirit. Not a step we
    look for
In slight of that forbearance and reserve
Which common human-heartedness in-
    spires,   586
And mortal ignorance and frailty claim,
Upon this sacred ground, if nowhere else."

" True," said the Solitary, " be it far
From us to infringe the laws of charity.
Let judgment here in mercy be pro-
    nounced ;   591
This, self-respecting Nature prompts, and
    this
Wisdom enjoins ; but if the thing we seek
Be genuine knowledge, bear we then in
    mind
How, from his lofty throne, the sun can
    fling   595
Colours as bright on exhalations bred
By weedy pool or pestilential swamp,
As by the rivulet sparkling where it runs,
Or the pellucid lake."
                " Small risk," said I,
" Of such illusion do we here incur ; 600

Temptation here is none to exceed the
    truth ;
No evidence appears that they who rest
Within this ground, were covetous of
    praise,
Or of remembrance even, deserved or not.
Green is the Churchyard, beautiful and
    green,   605
Ridge rising gently by the side of ridge,
A heaving surface, almost wholly free
From interruption of sepulchral stones,
And mantled o'er with aboriginal turf
And everlasting flowers. These Dalesmen
    trust   610
The lingering gleam of their departed
    lives
To oral record, and the silent heart ;
Depositories faithful and more kind
Than fondest epitaph : for, if those fail,
What boots the sculptured tomb ? And
    who can blame,   615
Who rather would not envy, men that
    feel
This mutual confidence ; if, from such
    source,
The practice flow,—if thence, or from
    a deep
And general humility in death ?
Nor should I much condemn it, if it
    spring   620
From disregard of time's destructive
    power,
As only capable to prey on things
Of earth, and human nature's mortal part.

" Yet—in less simple districts, where
    we see
Stone lift its forehead emulous of stone
In courting notice ; and the ground all
    paved   626
With commendations of departed worth ;
Reading, where'er we turn, of innocent
    lives,
Of each domestic charity fulfilled,
And sufferings meekly borne—I, for my
    part,   630
Though with the silence pleased that here
    prevails,
Among those fair recitals also range,
Soothed by the natural spirit which they
    breathe.

And, in the centre of a world whose soil
Is rank with all unkindness, compassed
    round   635
With such memorials, I have sometimes
    felt,
It was no momentary happiness
To have *one* Enclosure where the voice
    that speaks
In envy or detraction is not heard;
Which malice may not enter; where the
    traces   640
Of evil inclinations are unknown;
Where love and pity tenderly unite
With resignation; and no jarring tone
Intrudes, the peaceful concert to disturb
Of amity and gratitude."
           "Thus sanctioned," 645
The Pastor said, "I willingly confine
My narratives to subjects that excite
Feelings with these accordant; love, es-
    teem,
And admiration; lifting up a veil,
A sunbeam introducing among hearts 650
Retired and covert; so that ye shall have
Clear images before your gladdened eyes
Of nature's unambitious underwood,
And flowers that prosper in the shade.
And when
I speak of such among my flock as
    swerved   655
Or fell, those only shall be singled out
Upon whose lapse, or error, something
    more
Than brotherly forgiveness may attend;
To such will we restrict our notice, else
Better my tongue were mute.
              And yet there are,
I feel, good reasons why we should not
    leave   661
Wholly untraced a more forbidding way.
For, strength to persevere and to support,
And energy to conquer and repel—
These elements of virtue, that declare 665
The native grandeur of the human soul—
Are ofttimes not unprofitably shown
In the perverseness of a selfish course:
Truth every day exemplified, no less
In the grey cottage by the murmuring
    stream   670
Than in fantastic conqueror's roving camp,
Or 'mid the factious senate unappalled

Whoe'er may sink, or rise—to sink again,
As merciless proscription ebbs and flows.

"There," said the Vicar, pointing as he
    spake,   675
"A woman rests in peace; surpassed by
    few
In power of mind, and eloquent discourse.
Tall was her stature; her complexion
    dark
And saturnine; her head not raised to
    hold
Converse with heaven, nor yet deprest
    towards earth,   680
But in projection carried, as she walked
For ever musing. Sunken were her eyes;
Wrinkled and furrowed with habitual
    thought
Was her broad forehead; like the brow
    of one
Whose visual nerve shrinks from a pain-
    ful glare   685
Of overpowering light.—While yet a
    child,
She, 'mid the humble flowerets of the vale,
Towered like the imperial thistle, not
    unfurnished
With its appropriate grace, yet rather
    seeking
To be admired, than coveted and loved.
Even at that age she ruled, a sovereign
    queen,   691
Over her comrades; else their simple
    sports,
Wanting all relish for her strenuous
    mind,
Had crossed her only to be shunned with
    scorn.
—Oh! pang of sorrowful regret for those
Whom, in their youth, sweet study has
    enthralled,   696
That they have lived for harsher servi-
    tude,
Whether in soul, in body, or estate!
Such doom was hers; yet nothing could
    subdue   699
Her keen desire of knowledge, nor efface
Those brighter images by books imprest
Upon her memory, faithfully as stars
That occupy their places, and, though
    oft

Hidden by clouds, and oft bedimmed by
haze,
Are not to be extinguished, nor impaired.

"Two passions, both degenerate, for
they both   706
Began in honour, gradually obtained
Rule over her, and vexed her daily life;
An unremitting, avaricious thrift;   709
And a strange thraldom of maternal love,
That held her spirit, in its own despite,
Bound—by vexation, and regret, and
scorn,
Constrained forgiveness, and relenting
vows,
And tears, in pride suppressed, in shame
concealed—
To a poor dissolute Son, her only child.
—Her wedded days had opened with
mishap,   716
Whence dire dependence. What could
she perform
To shake the burthen off? Ah! there
was felt,
Indignantly, the weakness of her sex.
She mused, resolved, adhered to her
resolve;   720
The hand grew slack in alms-giving, the
heart
Closed by degrees to charity; heaven's
blessing
Not seeking from that source, she placed
her trust
In ceaseless pains—and strictest parsimony
Which sternly hoarded all that could be
spared,   725
From each day's need, out of each day's
least gain.

"Thus all was re-established, and a pile
Constructed, that sufficed for every end,
Save the contentment of the builder's
mind;
A mind by nature indisposed to aught
So placid, so inactive, as content;   731
A mind intolerant of lasting peace,
And cherishing the pang her heart deplored.
Dread life of conflict! which I oft compared
To the agitation of a brook that runs   735

Down a rocky mountain, buried now and
lost
In silent pools, now in strong eddies
chained;
But never to be charmed to gentleness:
Its best attainment fits of such repose
As timid eyes might shrink from fathoming.   740

"A sudden illness seized her in the
strength
Of life's autumnal season.—Shall I tell
How on her bed of death the Matron lay,
To Providence submissive, so she thought;
But fretted, vexed, and wrought upon,
almost   745
To anger, by the malady that griped
Her prostrate frame with unrelaxing
power,
As the fierce eagle fastens on the lamb?
She prayed, she moaned;—her husband's
sister watched   749
Her dreary pillow, waited on her needs;
And yet the very sound of that kind foot
Was anguish to her ears! 'And must she
rule,'
This was the death-doomed Woman heard
to say
In bitterness, 'and must she rule and
reign,
Sole Mistress of this house, when I am
gone?   755
Tend what I tended, calling it her own!'
Enough;—I fear, too much.—One vernal
evening,
While she was yet in prime of health and
strength,
I well remember, while I passed her door
Alone, with loitering step, and upward
eye   760
Turned towards the planet Jupiter that
hung
Above the centre of the Vale, a voice
Roused me, her voice; it said, 'That
glorious star
In its untroubled element will shine
As now it shines, when we are laid in
earth   765
And safe from all our sorrows.' With a
sigh
She spake, yet, I believe, not unsustained

By faith in glory that shall far transcend
Aught by these perishable heavens dis-
   closed
To sight or mind. Nor less than care
   divine   770
Is divine mercy. She, who had rebelled,
Was into meekness softened and sub-
   dued ;
Did, after trials not in vain prolonged,
With resignation sink into the grave ;
And her uncharitable acts, I trust,   775
And harsh unkindnesses are all forgiven,
Tho', in this Vale, remembered with deep
   awe."

THE Vicar paused ; and toward a seat
   advanced,
A long stone-seat, fixed in the Church-
   yard wall ;   779
Part shaded by cool sycamore, and part
Offering a sunny resting-place to them
Who seek the House of worship, while
   the bells
Yet ring with all their voices, or before
The last hath ceased its solitary knoll.
Beneath the shade we all sate down ; and
   there   785
His office, uninvited, he resumed.

"As on a sunny bank, a tender lamb
Lurks in safe shelter from the winds of
   March,
Screened by its parent, so that little
   mound
Lies guarded by its neighbour ; the small
   heap   790
Speaks for itself ; an Infant there doth
   rest ;
The sheltering hillock is the Mother's
   grave.
If mild discourse, and manners that con-
   ferred
A natural dignity on humblest rank ;
If gladsome spirits, and benignant looks,
That for a face not beautiful did more
Than beauty for the fairest face can do ;
And if religious tenderness of heart,
Grieving for sin, and penitential tears
Shed when the clouds had gathered and
   distained   800

The spotless ether of a maiden life ;
If these may make a hallowed spot of
   earth
More holy in the sight of God or Man ;
Then, o'er that mould, a sanctity shall
   brood   804
Till the stars sicken at the day of doom.

"Ah ! what a warning for a thoughtless
   man,
Could field or grove, could any spot of
   earth,
Show to his eye an image of the pangs
Which it hath witnessed ; render back
   an echo
Of the sad steps by which it hath been
   trod !   810
There, by her innocent Baby's precious
   grave,
And on the very turf that roofs her own,
The Mother oft was seen to stand, or
   kneel
In the broad day, a weeping Magdalene.
Now she is not ; the swelling turf reports
Of the fresh shower, but of poor Ellen's
   tears   816
Is silent ; nor is any vestige left
Of the path worn by mournful tread of her
Who, at her heart's light bidding, once
   had moved
In virgin fearlessness, with step that
   seemed   820
Caught from the pressure of elastic turf
Upon the mountains gemmed with morn-
   ing dew,
In the prime hour of sweetest scents and
   airs.
—Serious and thoughtful was her mind ;
   and yet,
By reconcilement exquisite and rare, 825
The form, port, motions, of this Cottage-
   girl
Were such as might have quickened and
   inspired
A Titian's hand, addrest to picture forth
Oread or Dryad glancing through the
   shade
What time the hunter's earliest horn is
   heard   830
Startling the golden hills.

          A wide-spread elm

Stands in our valley, named THE JOYFUL
TREE;
From dateless usage which our peasants
hold
Of giving welcome to the first of May
By dances round its trunk.—And if the
sky   835
Permit, like honours, dance and song, are
paid
To the Twelfth Night, beneath the frosty
stars .
Or the clear moon. The queen of these
gay sports,
If not in beauty yet in sprightly air,
Was hapless Ellen.—No one touched the
ground   840
So deftly, and the nicest maiden's locks
Less gracefully were braided;—but this
praise,
Methinks, would better suit another
place.

"She loved, and fondly deemed her-
self beloved.
—The road is dim, the current unper-
ceived,   845
The weakness painful and most pitiful,
By which a virtuous woman, in pure
youth,
May be delivered to distress and shame.
Such fate was hers.—The last time Ellen
danced,
Among her equals, round THE JOYFUL
TREE,   850
She bore a secret burthen; and full soon
Was left to tremble for a breaking vow,—
Then, to bewail a sternly-broken vow,
Alone, within her widowed Mother's
house.
It was the season of unfolding leaves, 855
Of days advancing toward their utmost
length,
And small birds singing happily to mates
Happy as they. With spirit-saddening
power
Winds pipe through fading woods; but
those blithe notes   859
Strike the deserted to the heart; I speak
Of what I know, and what we feel within.
—Beside the cottage in which Ellen
dwelt

Stands a tall ash-tree; to whose topmost
twig
A thrush resorts, and annually chants,
At morn and evening from that naked
perch,   865
While all the undergrove is thick with
leaves,
A time-beguiling ditty, for delight
Of his fond partner, silent in the nest.
—'Ah why,' said Ellen, sighing to her-
self,
'Why do not words, and kiss, and solemn
pledge,   870
And nature that is kind in woman's
breast,
And reason that in man is wise and good,
And fear of him who is a righteous judge;
Why do not these prevail for human life,
To keep two hearts together, that began
Their spring-time with one love, and
that have need   876
Of mutual pity and forgiveness, sweet
To grant, or be received; while that poor
bird—
O come and hear him! Thou who hast to
me
Been faithless, hear him, though a lowly
creature,   880
One of God's simple children that yet
know not
The universal Parent, how he sings
As if he wished the firmament of heaven
Should listen, and give back to him the
voice
Of his triumphant constancy and love;
The proclamation that he makes, how
far   886
His darkness doth transcend our fickle
light!'

"Such was the tender passage, not by
me
Repeated without loss of simple phrase,
Which I perused, even as the words had
been   890
Committed by forsaken Ellen's hand
To the blank margin of a Valentine,
Bedropped with tears. 'Twill please you
to be told
That, studiously withdrawing from the
eye   894

Of all companionship, the Sufferer yet
In lonely reading found a meek resource:
How thankful for the warmth of summer
    days,
When she could slip into the cottage-
    barn,
And find a secret oratory there;
Or, in the garden, under friendly veil 900
Of their long twilight, pore upon her
    book
By the last lingering help of the open sky
Until dark night dismissed her to her
    bed!
Thus did a waking fancy sometimes lose
The unconquerable pang of despised love.

"A kindlier passion opened on her soul
When that poor Child was born. Upon
    its face
She gazed as on a pure and spotless gift
Of unexpected promise, where a grief
Or dread was all that had been thought
    of,—joy   910
Far livelier than bewildered traveller
    feels,
Amid a perilous waste that all night long
Hath harassed him toiling through fear-
    ful storm,
When he beholds the first pale speck
    serene
Of day-spring, in the gloomy east, re-
    vealed,   915
And greets it with thanksgiving. 'Till
    this hour,'
Thus, in her Mother's hearing Ellen
    spake,
'There was a stony region in my heart;
But He, at whose command the parchèd
    rock
Was smitten, and poured forth a quench-
    ing stream,   920
Hath softened that obduracy, and made
Unlooked-for gladness in the desert place,
To save the perishing; and, henceforth, I
    breathe
The air with cheerful spirit, for thy sake,
My Infant! and for that good Mother
    dear,   925
Who bore me; and hath prayed for me
    in vain;—
Yet not in vain; it shall not be in vain.'

She spake, nor was the assurance unful-
    filled;
And if heart-rending thoughts would oft
    return,
They stayed not long.—The blameless
    Infant grew;   930
The Child whom Ellen and her Mother
    loved
They soon were proud of; tended it and
    nursed;
A soothing comforter, although forlorn;
Like a poor singing-bird from distant
    lands;
Or a choice shrub, which he, who passes by
With vacant mind, not seldom may ob-
    serve   936
Fair-flowering in a thinly-peopled house,
Whose window, somewhat sadly, it
    adorns.

"Through four months' space the Infant
    drew its food
From the maternal breast; then scruples
    rose;   940
Thoughts, which the rich are free from,
    came and crossed
The fond affection. She no more could
    bear
By her offence to lay a twofold weight
On a kind parent willing to forget
Their slender means: so, to that parent's
    care   945
Trusting her child, she left their common
    home,
And undertook with dutiful content
A Foster-mother's office.
              'Tis, perchance,
Unknown to you that in these simple
    vales
The natural feeling of equality   950
Is by domestic service unimpaired;
Yet, though such service be, with us,
    removed
From sense of degradation, not the less
The ungentle mind can easily find means
To impose severe restraints and laws
    unjust,   955
Which hapless Ellen now was doomed to
    feel:
For (blinded by an over-anxious dread
Of such excitement and divided thought

As with her office would but ill accord)
The pair, whose infant she was bound to
nurse,   960
Forbad her all communion with her own:
Week after week, the mandate they en-
forced.
—So near! yet not allowed upon that
sight
To fix her eyes—alas! 'twas hard to bear!
But worse affliction must be borne—far
worse;   965
For 'tis Heaven's will—that, after a disease
Begun and ended within three days' space,
Her child should die; as Ellen now ex-
claimed,
Her own—deserted child!—Once, only
once,
She saw it in that mortal malady;   970
And, on the burial-day, could scarcely gain
Permission to attend its obsequies.
She reached the house, last of the funeral
train;
And some one, as she entered, having
chanced
To urge unthinkingly their prompt de-
parture,   975
'Nay,' said she, with commanding look,
a spirit
Of anger never seen in her before,
'Nay, ye must wait my time!' and down
she sate,
And by the unclosed coffin kept her seat
Weeping and looking, looking on and
weeping,   980
Upon the last sweet slumber of her Child,
Until at length her soul was satisfied.

"You see the Infant's Grave; and to
this spot,
The Mother, oft as she was sent abroad,
On whatsoever errand, urged her steps:
Hither she came; here stood, and some-
times knelt   986
In the broad day, a rueful Magdalene!
So call her; for not only she bewailed
A mother's loss, but mourned in bitter-
ness
Her own transgression; penitent sincere
As ever raised to heaven a streaming eye!
—At length the parents of the foster-
child,   992

Noting that in despite of their commands
She still renewed and could not but renew
Those visitations, ceased to send her
forth;   995
Or, to the garden's narrow bounds, con-
fined.
I failed not to remind them that they
erred;
For holy Nature might not thus be
crossed,
Thus wronged in woman's breast: in vain
I pleaded—
But the green stalk of Ellen's life was
snapped,   1000
And the flower drooped; as every eye
could see,
It hung its head in mortal languishment.
—Aided by this appearance, I at length
Prevailed; and, from those bonds released,
she went
Home to her mother's house.
                         The Youth was fled;
The rash betrayer could not face the
shame   1006
Or sorrow which his senseless guilt had
caused;
And little would his presence, or proof
given
Of a relenting soul, have now availed;
For, like a shadow, he was passed away
From Ellen's thoughts; had perished to
her mind   1011
For all concerns of fear, or hope, or love,
Save only those which to their common
shame,
And to his moral being appertained:
Hope from that quarter would, I know,
have brought   1015
A heavenly comfort; there she recognised
An unrelaxing bond, a mutual need;
There, and, as seemed, there only.
                                    She had built,
Her fond maternal heart had built, a nest
In blindness all too near the river's edge;
That work a summer flood with hasty
swell   1021
Had swept away; and now her Spirit
longed
For its last flight to heaven's security.
—The bodily frame wasted from day to
day;

Meanwhile, relinquishing all other cares,
Her mind she strictly tutored to find
　　peace   1026
And pleasure in endurance. Much she
　　thought,
And much she read; and brooded feel-
　　ingly
Upon her own unworthiness. To me,
As to a spiritual comforter and friend,
Her heart she opened; and no pains were
　　spared   1031
To mitigate, as gently as I could,
The sting of self-reproach, with healing
　　words.
Meek Saint! through patience glorified
　　on earth!
In whom, as by her lonely hearth she
　　sate,   1035
The ghastly face of cold decay put on
A sun-like beauty, and appeared divine!
May I not mention—that, within those
　　walls,
In due observance of her pious wish,
The congregation joined with me in
　　prayer   1040
For her soul's good? Nor was that office
　　vain.
—Much did she suffer: but, if any friend,
Beholding her condition, at the sight
Give way to words of pity or complaint,
She stilled them with a prompt reproof,
　　and said,   1045
'He who afflicts me knows what I can
　　bear;
And, when I fail, and can endure no
　　more,
Will mercifully take me to himself.'
So, through the cloud of death, her Spirit
　　passed
Into that pure and unknown world of
　　love   1050
Where injury cannot come:—and here is
　　laid
The mortal Body by her Infant's side."

The Vicar ceased; and downcast looks
　　made known
That each had listened with his inmost
　　heart.
For me, the emotion scarcely was less
　　strong   1055

Or less benign than that which I had felt
When seated near my venerable Friend,
Under those shady elms, from him I
　　heard
The story that retraced the slow decline
Of Margaret, sinking on the lonely heath
With the neglected house to which she
　　clung.   1061
—I noted that the Solitary's cheek
Confessed the power of nature.—Pleased
　　though sad,
More pleased than sad, the grey-haired
　　Wanderer sate;
Thanks to his pure imaginative soul 1065
Capacious and serene; his blameless life,
His knowledge, wisdom, love of truth,
　　and love
Of human kind! He was it who first
　　broke
The pensive silence, saying:—
　　　　　　　　"Blest are they
Whose sorrow rather is to suffer wrong
Than to do wrong, albeit themselves have
　　erred.   1071
This tale gives proof that Heaven most
　　gently deals
With such, in their affliction.—Ellen's
　　fate,
Her tender spirit, and her contrite heart,
Call to my mind dark hints which I have
　　heard   1075
Of one who died within this vale, by doom
Heavier, as his offence was heavier far.
Where, Sir, I pray you, where are laid the
　　bones
Of Wilfred Armathwaite?"
　　　　　　　　The Vicar answered,
"In that green nook, close by the Church-
　　yard wall,   1080
Beneath yon hawthorn, planted by myself
In memory and for warning, and in sign
Of sweetness where dire anguish had been
　　known,
Of reconcilement after deep offence—
There doth he rest. No theme his fate
　　supplies   1085
For the smooth glozings of the indulgent
　　world;
Nor need the windings of his devious
　　course
Be here retraced;—enough that, by mishap

And venial error, robbed of competence,
And her obsequious shadow, peace of mind,
He craved a substitute in troubled joy;
Against his conscience rose in arms, and,
   braving   1092
Divine displeasure, broke the marriage-
   vow.
That which he had been weak enough to do
Was misery in remembrance; he was
   stung,   1095
Stung by his inward thoughts, and by the
   smiles
Of wife and children stung to agony.
Wretched at home, he gained no peace
   abroad;
Ranged through the mountains, slept
   upon the earth,   1099
Asked comfort of the open air, and found
No quiet in the darkness of the night,
No pleasure in the beauty of the day.
His flock he slighted: his paternal fields
Became a clog to him, whose spirit wished
To fly—but whither! And this gracious
   Church,   1105
That wears a look so full of peace and
   hope
And love, benignant mother of the vale,
How fair amid her brood of cottages!
She was to him a sickness and reproach.
Much to the last remained unknown: but
   this   1110
Is sure, that through remorse and grief
   he died;
Though pitied among men, absolved by
   God,
He could not find forgiveness in himself;
Nor could endure the weight of his own
   shame.

   "Here rests a Mother. But from her
   I turn   1115
And from her grave.—Behold—upon that
   ridge,
That, stretching boldly from the moun-
   tain side,
Carries into the centre of the vale
Its rocks and woods—the Cottage where
   she dwelt;
And where yet dwells her faithful Partner,
   left   1120
(Full eight years past) the solitary prop

Of many helpless Children. I begin
With words that might be prelude to
   a tale
Of sorrow and dejection; but I feel
No sadness, when I think of what mine
   eyes   1125
See daily in that happy family.
—Bright garland form they for the pen-
   sive brow
Of their undrooping Father's widowhood,
Those six fair Daughters, budding yet—
   not one,
Not one of all the band, a full-blown
   flower.   1130
Deprest, and desolate of soul, as once
That Father was, and filled with anxious
   fear,
Now, by experience taught, he stands
   assured,
That God, who takes away, yet takes not
   half
Of what he seems to take; or gives it
   back,   1135
Not to our prayer, but far beyond our
   prayer;
He gives it—the boon produce of a soil
Which our endeavours have refused to till,
And hope hath never watered. The Abode,
Whose grateful owner can attest these
   truths,   1140
Even were the object nearer to our sight,
Would seem in no distinction to surpass
The rudest habitations. Ye might think
That it had sprung self-raised from earth,
   or grown
Out of the living rock, to be adorned 1145
By nature only; but, if thither led,
Ye would discover, then, a studious work
Of many fancies, prompting many hands.

   "Brought from the woods the honey-
   suckle twines
Around the porch, and seems, in that
   trim place,   1150
A plant no longer wild; the cultured rose
There blossoms, strong in health, and will
   be soon
Roof-high; the wild pink crowns the
   garden-wall,
And with the flowers are intermingled
   stones

Sparry and bright, rough scatterings of
    the hills. 1155
These ornaments, that fade not with the
    year,
A hardy Girl continues to provide;
Who, mounting fearlessly the rocky
    heights,
Her Father's prompt attendant, does for
    him
All that a boy could do, but with delight
More keen and prouder daring; yet hath
    she, 1161
Within the garden, like the rest, a bed
For her own flowers and favourite herbs,
    a space,
By sacred charter, holden for her use.
—These, and whatever else the garden
    bears 1165
Of fruit or flower, permission asked or not,
I freely gather; and my leisure draws
A not unfrequent pastime from the hum
Of bees around their range of sheltered
    hives
Busy in that enclosure; while the rill,
That sparkling thrids the rocks, attunes
    his voice 1171
To the pure course of human life which
    there
Flows on in solitude. But, when the
    gloom

Of night is falling round my steps, then
    most
This Dwelling charms me; often I stop
    short, 1175
(Who could refrain?) and feed by stealth
    my sight
With prospect of the company within,
Laid open through the blazing window:—
    there
I see the eldest Daughter at her wheel
Spinning amain, as if to overtake 1180
The never-halting time; or, in her turn,
Teaching some Novice of the sisterhood
That skill in this or other household
    work,
Which, from her Father's honoured hand,
    herself,
While she was yet a little-one, had
    learned. 1185
Mild Man! he is not gay, but they are
    gay;
And the whole house seems filled with
    gaiety.
—Thrice happy, then, the Mother may be
    deemed,
The Wife, from whose consolatory grave
I turned, that ye in mind might witness
    where, 1190
And now, her Spirit yet survives on
    earth!"

BOOK SEVENTH.

THE CHURCHYARD AMONG THE MOUNTAINS.—(Continued).

ARGUMENT.

Impression of these Narratives upon the Author's mind.—Pastor invited to give account of certain Graves that lie apart.—Clergyman and his Family.—Fortunate influence of change of situation.—Activity in extreme old age.—Another Clergyman, a character of resolute Virtue.—Lamentations over mis-directed applause.—Instance of less exalted excellence in a deaf man.—Elevated character of a blind man.—Reflection upon Blindness.—Interrupted by a Peasant who passes—his animal cheerfulness and careless vivacity.—He occasions a digression on the fall of beautiful and interesting Trees.—A female Infant's Grave.—Joy at her Birth.—Sorrow at her Departure.—A youthful Peasant—his patriotic enthusiasm and distinguished qualities—his untimely death.—Exultation of the Wanderer, as a patriot, in this Picture.—Solitary how affected.—Monument of a Knight.—Traditions concerning him.—Peroration of the Wanderer on the transitoriness of things and the revolutions of society.—Hints at his own past Calling.—Thanks the Pastor.

WHILE thus from theme to theme the
  Historian passed,
The words he uttered, and the scene that
  lay
Before our eyes, awakened in my mind
Vivid remembrance of those long-past
  hours;
When, in the hollow of some shadowy
  vale,   5
(What time the splendour of the setting
  sun
Lay beautiful on Snowdon's sovereign
  brow,
On Cader Idris, or huge Penmanmaur)
A wandering Youth, I listened with de-
  light
To pastoral melody or warlike air,   10
Drawn from the chords of the ancient
  British harp
By some accomplished Master, while he
  sate
Amid the quiet of the green recess,
And there did inexhaustibly dispense
An interchange of soft or solemn tunes, 15

Tender or blithe; now, as the varying
  mood
Of his own spirit urged,—now, as a voice
From youth or maiden, or some honoured
  chief
Of his compatriot villagers (that hung
Around him, drinking in the impassioned
  notes   20
Of the time-hallowed minstrelsy) required
For their heart's ease or pleasure. Strains
  of power
Were they, to seize and occupy the sense;
But to a higher mark than song can reach
Rose this pure eloquence. And, when the
  stream   25
Which overflowed the soul was passed
  away,
A consciousness remained that it had left,
Deposited upon the silent shore
Of memory, images and precious thoughts,
That shall not die, and cannot be de-
  stroyed.   30

"These grassy heaps lie amicably close,"

Said I, "like surges heaving in the wind
Along the surface of a mountain pool:
Whence comes it, then, that yonder we
　　behold
Five graves, and only five, that rise to-
　　gether　　　　　　　　　　　　35
Unsociably sequestered, and encroaching
On the smooth playground of the village-
　　school?"

The Vicar answered,—"No disdainful
　　pride
In them who rest beneath, nor any course
Of strange or tragic accident, hath helped
To place those hillocks in that lonely
　　guise.　　　　　　　　　　　　　41
—Once more look forth, and follow with
　　your sight
The length of road that from yon moun-
　　tain's base
Through bare enclosures stretches, 'till
　　its line
Is lost within a little tuft of trees;　45
Then, reappearing in a moment, quits
The cultured fields; and up the heathy
　　waste,
Mounts, as you see, in mazes serpentine,
Led towards an easy outlet of the vale:
That little shady spot, that sylvan tuft, 50
By which the road is hidden, also hides
A cottage from our view; though I discern
(Ye scarcely can) amid its sheltering trees
The smokeless chimney-top.—
　　　　　　　　All unembowered
And naked stood that lowly Parsonage 55
(For such in truth it is, and appertains
To a small Chapel in the vale beyond)
When hither came its last Inhabitant.
Rough and forbidding were the choicest
　　roads
By which our northern wilds could then
　　be crossed;　　　　　　　　　　60
And into most of these secluded vales
Was no access for wain, heavy or light.
So, at his dwelling-place the Priest ar-
　　rived
With store of household goods, in pan-
　　niers slung
On sturdy horses graced with jingling
　　bells,　　　　　　　　　　　　65
And on the back of more ignoble beast;

That, with like burthen of effects most
　　prized
Or easiest carried, closed the motley train.
Young was I then, a schoolboy of eight
　　years;
But still, methinks, I see them as they
　　passed　　　　　　　　　　　　70
In order, drawing toward their wished-
　　for home.
—Rocked by the motion of a trusty ass
Two ruddy children hung, a well-poised
　　freight,
Each in his basket nodding drowsily;
Their bonnets, I remember, wreathed with
　　flowers,　　　　　　　　　　　75
Which told it was the pleasant month of
　　June;
And, close behind, the comely Matron
　　rode,
A woman of soft speech and gracious
　　smile,
And with a lady's mien.—From far they
　　came,
Even from Northumbrian hills; yet theirs
　　had been　　　　　　　　　　　80
A merry journey, rich in pastime, cheered
By music, prank, and laughter-stirring
　　jest;
And freak put on, and arch word dropped—
　　to swell
The cloud of fancy and uncouth surmise
That gathered round the slowly-moving
　　train.　　　　　　　　　　　　85
—'Whence do they come? and with what
　　errand charged?'
Belong they to the fortune-telling tribe
Who pitch their tents under the green-
　　wood tree?
Or Strollers are they, furnished to enact
Fair Rosamond, and the Children of the
　　Wood,　　　　　　　　　　　　90
And, by that whiskered tabby's aid, set
　　forth
The lucky venture of sage Whittington,
When the next village hears the show
　　announced
By blast of trumpet?' Plenteous was the
　　growth
Of such conjectures, overheard, or seen 95
On many a staring countenance portrayed
Of boor or burgher, as they marched along.

And more than once their steadiness of
    face
Was put to proof, and exercise supplied
To their inventive humour, by stern looks,
And questions in authoritative tone,   101
From some staid guardian of the public
    peace,
Checking the sober steed on which he
    rode,
In his suspicious wisdom; oftener still,
By notice indirect, or blunt demand   105
From traveller halting in his own despite,
A simple curiosity to ease:
Of which adventures, that beguiled and
    cheered
Their grave migration, the good pair
    would tell,
With undiminished glee, in hoary age. 110

    "A Priest he was by function; but his
      course
From his youth up, and high as man-
    hood's noon,
(The hour of life to which he then was
    brought)
Had been irregular, I might say, wild;
By books unsteadied, by his pastoral care
Too little checked. An active, ardent
    mind;   116
A fancy pregnant with resource and
    scheme
To cheat the sadness of a rainy day;
Hands apt for all ingenious arts and
    games;
A generous spirit, and a body strong 120
To cope with stoutest champions of the
    bowl;
Had earned for him sure welcome, and
    the rights
Of a prized visitant, in the jolly hall
Of country 'squire; or at the statelier
    board
Of duke or earl, from scenes of courtly
    pomp   125
Withdrawn,—to while away the summer
    hours
In condescension among rural guests.

    "With these high comrades he had
      revelled long,
Frolicked industriously, a simple Clerk

By hopes of coming patronage beguiled
Till the heart sickened. So, each loftier
    aim   131
Abandoning and all his showy friends,
For a life's stay (slender it was, but sure)
He turned to this secluded chapelry;
That had been offered to his doubtful
    choice   135
By an unthought-of patron. Bleak and
    bare
They found the cottage, their allotted
    home;
Naked without, and rude within; a spot
With which the Cure not long had been
    endowed:
And far remote the chapel stood,—re-
    mote,   140
And, from his Dwelling, unapproachable,
Save through a gap high in the hills, an
    opening
Shadeless and shelterless, by driving
    showers
Frequented, and beset with howling
    winds.
Yet cause was none, whate'er regret might
    hang   145
On his own mind, to quarrel with the
    choice
Or the necessity that fixed him here;
Apart from old temptations, and con-
    strained
To punctual labour in his sacred charge.
See him a constant preacher to the poor!
And visiting, though not with saintly
    zeal,   151
Yet, when need was, with no reluctant
    will,
The sick in body, or distrest in mind;
And, by as salutary change, compelled
To rise from timely sleep, and meet the
    day   155
With no engagement, in his thoughts,
    more proud
Or splendid than his garden could afford,
His fields, or mountains by the heath-
    cock ranged,
Or the wild brooks; from which he now
    returned
Contented to partake the quiet meal 160
Of his own board, where sat his gentle
    Mate

And three fair Children, plentifully fed
Though simply, from their little house-
　　hold farm;
Nor wanted timely treat of fish or fowl
By nature yielded to his practised
　　hand;—　　　　　　　　　　165
To help the small but certain comings-in
Of that spare benefice. Yet not the less
Theirs was a hospitable board, and theirs
A charitable door.
　　　　　　So days and years
Passed on;—the inside of that rugged
　　house　　　　　　　　　　　170
Was trimmed and brightened by the
　　Matron's care,
And gradually enriched with things of
　　price,
Which might be lacked for use or orna-
　　ment.
What, though no soft and costly sofa
　　there
Insidiously stretched out its lazy length,
And no vain mirror glittered upon the
　　walls,　　　　　　　　　　176
Yet were the windows of the low abode
By shutters weather-fended, which at
　　once
Repelled the storm and deadened its loud
　　roar.
Their snow-white curtains hung in decent
　　folds;　　　　　　　　　　180
Tough moss, and long-enduring mountain-
　　plants,
That creep along the ground with sinuous
　　trail,
Were nicely braided; and composed a
　　work
Like Indian mats, that with appropriate
　　grace
Lay at the threshold and the inner doors;
And a fair carpet, woven of homespun
　　wool　　　　　　　　　　　186
But tinctured daintily with florid hues,
For seemliness and warmth, on festal
　　days,
Covered the smooth blue slabs of moun-
　　tain-stone
With which the parlour-floor, in simplest
　　guise　　　　　　　　　　190
Of pastoral homesteads, had been long
　　inlaid.

"Those pleasing works the Housewife's
　　skill produced:
Meanwhile the unsedentary Master's hand
Was busier with his task—to rid, to plant,
To rear for food, for shelter, and delight;
A thriving covert! And when wishes,
　　formed　　　　　　　　　196
In youth, and sanctioned by the riper
　　mind,
Restored me to my native valley, here
To end my days; well pleased was I to
　　see
The once-bare cottage, on the mountain-
　　side,　　　　　　　　　　200
Screen'd from assault of every bitter
　　blast;
While the dark shadows of the summer
　　leaves
Danced in the breeze, chequering its
　　mossy roof.
Time, which had thus afforded willing
　　help
To beautify with nature's fairest growths
This rustic tenement, had gently shed, 206
Upon its Master's frame, a wintry grace;
The comeliness of unenfeebled age.

"But how could I say, gently? for he
　　still
Retained a flashing eye, a burning palm,
A stirring foot, a head which beat at
　　nights　　　　　　　　　211
Upon its pillow with a thousand schemes.
Few likings had he dropped, few plea-
　　sures lost;
Generous and charitable, prompt to serve;
And still his harsher passions kept their
　　hold—　　　　　　　　　215
Anger and indignation. Still he loved
The sound of titled names, and talked in
　　glee
Of long-past banquetings with high-born
　　friends:
Then, from those lulling fits of vain de-
　　light　　　　　　　　　219
Uproused by recollected injury, railed
At their false ways disdainfully,—and oft
In bitterness, and with a threatening eye
Of fire, incensed beneath its hoary brow.
—Those transports, with staid looks of
　　pure good-will,

And with soft smile, his consort would
reprove.   225
She, far behind him in the race of years,
Yet keeping her first mildness, was ad-
vanced
Far nearer, in the habit of her soul,
To that still region whither all are bound.
Him might we liken to the setting sun 230
As seen not seldom on some gusty day,
Struggling and bold, and shining from
the west
With an inconstant and unmellowed
light;
She was a soft attendant cloud, that hung
As if with wish to veil the restless orb;
From which it did itself imbibe a ray 236
Of pleasing lustre.—But no more of this;
I better love to sprinkle on the sod
That now divides the pair, or rather say,
That still unites them, praises, like hea-
ven's dew,   240
Without reserve descending upon both.

"Our very first in eminence of years
This old Man stood, the patriarch of the
Vale!
And, to his unmolested mansion, death
Had never come, through space of forty
years;   245
Sparing both old and young in that
abode.
Suddenly then they disappeared: not
twice
Had summer scorched the fields; not
twice had fallen,
On those high peaks, the first autumnal
snow,
Before the greedy visiting was closed, 250
And the long-privileged house left empty
—swept
As by a plague. Yet no rapacious plague
Had been among them; all was gentle
death,
One after one, with intervals of peace.
A happy consummation! an accord   255
Sweet, perfect, to be wished for! save
that here
Was something which to mortal sense
might sound
Like harshness,—that the old grey-headed
Sire,

The oldest, he was taken last, survived
When the meek Partner of his age, his Son,
His Daughter, and that late and high-
prized gift,   261
His little smiling Grandchild, were no
more.

"'All gone, all vanished! he deprived
and bare,
How will he face the remnant of his life?
What will become of him?' we said, and
mused   265
In sad conjectures—'Shall we meet him
now
Haunting with rod and line the craggy
brooks?
Or shall we overhear him, as we pass,
Striving to entertain the lonely hours
With music?' (for he had not ceased to
touch   270
The harp or viol which himself had
framed,
For their sweet purposes, with perfect
skill.)
'What titles will he keep? will he remain
Musician, gardener, builder, mechanist,
A planter, and a rearer from the seed? 275
A man of hope and forward-looking mind
Even to the last!'—Such was he, un-
subdued.
But Heaven was gracious; yet a little
while,
And this Survivor, with his cheerful
throng
Of open projects, and his inward hoard
Of unsunned griefs, too many and too
keen,   281
Was overcome by unexpected sleep,
In one blest moment. Like a shadow
thrown
Softly and lightly from a passing cloud,
Death fell upon him, while reclined he
lay   285
For noontide solace on the summer grass,
The warm lap of his mother earth: and so,
Their lenient term of separation past,
That family (whose graves you there
behold)
By yet a higher privilege once more   290
Were gathered to each other.'"
                                    Calm of mind

And silence waited on these closing
    words;
Until the Wanderer (whether moved by
    fear
Lest in those passages of life were some
That might have touched the sick heart
    of his Friend   295
Too nearly, or intent to reinforce
His own firm spirit in degree deprest
By tender sorrow for our mortal state)
Thus silence broke:—"Behold a thought-
    less Man
From vice and premature decay pre-
    served   300
By useful habits, to a fitter soil
Transplanted ere too late.—The hermit,
    lodged
Amid the untrodden desert, tells his
    beads,
With each repeating its allotted prayer,
And thus divides and thus relieves the
    time;   305
Smooth task, with *his* compared, whose
    mind could string,
Not scantily, bright minutes on the
    thread
Of keen domestic anguish; and beguile
A solitude, unsheeen, unprofessed;
Till gentlest death released him.
               Far from us
Be the desire—too curiously to ask   311
How much of this is but the blind
    result
Of cordial spirits and vital temperament,
And what to higher powers is justly
    due.
But you, Sir, know that in a neighbouring
    vale   315
A Priest abides before whose life such
    doubts
Fall to the ground; whose gifts of nature
    lie
Retired from notice, lost in attributes
Of reason, honourably effaced by debts
Which her poor treasure-house is content
    to owe,   320
And conquests over her dominion gained,
To which her frowardness must needs
    submit.
In this one Man is shown a temperance—
    proof

Against all trials; industry severe
And constant as the motion of the day;
Stern self-denial round him spread, with
    shade   326
That might be deemed forbidding, did
    not there
All generous feelings flourish and rejoice;
Forbearance, charity in deed and thought,
And resolution competent to take   330
Out of the bosom of simplicity
All that her holy customs recommend,
And the best ages of the world prescribe.
—Preaching, administering, in every work
Of his sublime vocation, in the walks   335
Of worldly intercourse between man and
    man,
And in his humble dwelling, he appears
A labourer, with moral virtue girt,
With spiritual graces, like a glory,
    crowned."

"Doubt can be none," the Pastor said,
    "for whom   340
This portraiture is sketched. The great,
    the good,
The well-beloved, the fortunate, the
    wise,—
These titles emperors and chiefs have
    borne,
Honour assumed or given: and him, the
    WONDERFUL,
Our simple shepherds, speaking from the
    heart,   345
Deservedly have styled.—From his abode
In a dependent chapelry that lies
Behind yon hill, a poor and rugged wild,
Which in his soul he lovingly embraced,
And, having once espoused, would never
    quit;   350
Into its graveyard will ere long be borne
That lowly, great, good Man. A simple
    stone
May cover him; and by its help, per-
    chance,
A century shall hear his name pro-
    nounced,
With images attendant on the sound; 355
Then, shall the slowly-gathering twilight
    close
In utter night; and of his course remain
No cognizable vestiges, no more

Than of this breath, which shapes itself
    in words
To speak of him, and instantly dis-
    solves."   360

    The Pastor pressed by thoughts which
      round his theme
Still linger'd, after a brief pause, resumed;
"Noise is there not enough in doleful
    war,
But that the heaven-born poet must stand
    forth,
And lend the echoes of his sacred shell,
To multiply and aggravate the din?   366
Pangs are there not enough in hopeless
    love—
And, in requited passion, all too much
Of turbulence, anxiety, and fear—   369
But that the minstrel of the rural shade
Must tune his pipe, insidiously to nurse
The perturbation in the suffering breast,
And propagate its kind, far as he may?
—Ah who (and with such rapture as befits
The hallowed theme) will rise and cele-
    brate   375
The good man's purposes and deeds;
    retrace
His struggles, his discomfitures deplore,
His triumphs hail, and glorify his end;
That virtue, like the fumes and vapoury
    clouds
Through fancy's heat redounding in the
    brain,   380
And like the soft infections of the heart,
By charm of measured words may spread
    o'er field,
Hamlet, and town; and piety survive
Upon the lips of men in hall or bower;
Not for reproof, but high and warm
    delight,   385
And grave encouragement, by song in-
    spired?
—Vain thought! but wherefore murmur
    or repine?
The memory of the just survives in
    heaven:
And, without sorrow, will the ground
    receive   389
That venerable clay. Meanwhile the best
Of what lies here confines us to degrees
In excellence less difficult to reach,

And milder worth: nor need we travel far
From those to whom our last regards
    were paid,
For such example.
              Almost at the root
Of that tall pine, the shadow of whose
    bare   396
And slender stem, while here I sit at eve,
Oft stretches toward me, like a long
    straight path
Traced faintly in the greensward; there,
    beneath
A plain blue stone, a gentle Dalesman
    lies,   400
From whom, in early childhood, was
    withdrawn
The precious gift of hearing. He grew up
From year to year in loneliness of soul;
And this deep mountain-valley was to him
Soundless, with all its streams. The bird
    of dawn   · 405
Did never rouse this Cottager from sleep
With startling summons; not for his
    delight
The vernal cuckoo shouted; not for him
Murmured the labouring bee. When
    stormy winds
Were working the broad bosom of the
    lake   410
Into a thousand thousand sparkling
    waves,
Rocking the trees, or driving cloud on
    cloud
Along the sharp edge of yon lofty crags,
The agitated scene before his eye
Was silent as a picture: evermore   415
Were all things silent, wheresoe'er he
    moved.
Yet, by the solace of his own pure
    thoughts
Upheld, he duteously pursued the round
Of rural labours; the steep mountain-side
Ascended, with his staff and faithful
    dog;   420
The plough he guided, and the scythe he
    swayed;
And the ripe corn before his sickle fell
Among the jocund reapers. For himself,
All watchful and industrious as he was,
He wrought not: neither field nor flock
    he owned: 425

No wish for wealth had place within his
　　mind;
Nor husband's love, nor father's hope or
　　care.

"Though born a younger brother, need
　　was none
That from the floor of his paternal home
He should depart, to plant himself anew.
And when, mature in manhood, he be-
　　held　　　　　　　　　　　　　　431
His parents laid in earth, no loss ensued
Of rights to him; but he remained well
　　pleased,
By the pure bond of independent love,
An inmate of a second family;　　435
The fellow-labourer and friend of him
To whom the small inheritance had fallen.
—Nor deem that his mild presence was a
　　weight
That pressed upon his brother's house;
　　for books
Were ready comrades whom he could not
　　tire;　　　　　　　　　　　　　440
Of whose society the blameless Man
Was never satiate. Their familiar voice,
Even to old age, with unabated charm
Beguiled his leisure hours; refreshed his
　　thoughts;
Beyond its natural elevation raised　445
His introverted spirit; and bestowed
Upon his life an outward dignity
Which all acknowledged. The dark
　　winter night,
The stormy day, each had its own re-
　　source;
Song of the muses, sage historic tale,　450
Science severe, or word of holy Writ
Announcing immortality and joy
To the assembled spirits of just men
Made perfect, and from injury secure.
—Thus soothed at home, thus busy in the
　　field,　　　　　　　　　　　　455
To no perverse suspicion he gave way,
No languor, peevishness, nor vain com-
　　plaint:
And they, who were about him, did not
　　fail
In reverence, or in courtesy; they prized
His gentle manners: and his peaceful
　　smiles,　　　　　　　　　　　460

The gleams of his slow-varying counte-
　　nance,
Were met with answering sympathy and
　　love.

"At length, when sixty years and five
　　were told,
A slow disease insensibly consumed
The powers of nature: and a few short
　　steps　　　　　　　　　　　　465
Of friends and kindred bore him from his
　　home
(Yon cottage shaded by the woody crags)
To the profounder stillness of the grave.
—Nor was his funeral denied the grace
Of many tears, virtuous and thoughtful
　　grief;　　　　　　　　　　　　470
Heart-sorrow rendered sweet by gratitude.
And now that monumental stone pre-
　　serves
His name, and unambitiously relates
How long, and by what kindly outward
　　aids,　　　　　　　　　　　　474
And in what pure contentedness of mind,
The sad privation was by him endured.
—And yon tall pine-tree, whose composing
　　sound
Was wasted on the good Man's living ear,
Hath now its own peculiar sanctity;
And, at the touch of every wandering
　　breeze,　　　　　　　　　　　480
Murmurs, not idly, o'er his peaceful grave.

"Soul-cheering Light, most bountiful
　　of things!
Guide of our way, mysterious comforter!
Whose sacred influence, spread through
　　earth and heaven,
We all too thanklessly participate,　485
Thy gifts were utterly withheld from him
Whose place of rest is near yon ivied
　　porch.
Yet, of the wild brooks ask if he com-
　　plained;
Ask of the channelled rivers if they held
A safer, easier, more determined, course.
What terror doth it strike into the mind
To think of one, blind and alone, ad-
　　vancing　　　　　　　　　　　492
Straight toward some precipice's airy
　　brink!

But, timely warned, *He* would have stayed
　　his steps,
Protected, say enlightened, by his ear;
And on the very edge of vacancy   496
Not more endangered than a man whose
　　eye
Beholds the gulf beneath.—No floweret
　　blooms
Throughout the lofty range of these rough
　　hills,
Nor in the woods, that could from him
　　conceal   500
Its birthplace; none whose figure did
　　not live
Upon his touch. The bowels of the
　　earth
Enriched with knowledge his industrious
　　mind;
The ocean paid him tribute from the
　　stores
Lodged in her bosom; and, by science
　　led,   505
His genius mounted to the plains of
　　heaven.
—Methinks I see him—how his eye-balls
　　rolled,
Beneath his ample brow, in darkness
　　paired,—
But each instinct with spirit; and the
　　frame
Of the whole countenance alive with
　　thought,   510
Fancy, and understanding; while the
　　voice
Discoursed of natural or moral truth
With eloquence, and such authentic
　　power,
That, in his presence, humbler knowledge
　　stood
Abashed, and tender pity overawed."   515

"A noble—and, to unreflecting minds,
A marvellous spectacle," the Wanderer
　　said,
"Beings like these present! But proof
　　abounds
Upon the earth that faculties, which seem
Extinguished, do not, *therefore*, cease
　　to be.   520
And to the mind among her powers of
　　sense

This transfer is permitted,—not alone
That the bereft their recompense may
　　win;
But for remoter purposes of love
And charity; nor last nor least for
　　this,   525
That to the imagination may be given
A type and shadow of an awful truth;
How, likewise, under sufferance divine,
Darkness is banished from the realms of
　　death,
By man's imperishable spirit, quelled.   530
Unto the men who see not as we see
Futurity was thought, in ancient times,
To be laid open, and they prophesied.
And know we not that from the blind
　　have flowed
The highest, holiest, raptures of the
　　lyre: 535
And wisdom married to immortal verse?"

Among the humbler Worthies, at our
　　feet
Lying insensible to human praise,
Love, or regret,—*whose* lineaments would
　　next
Have been portrayed, I guess not; but it
　　chanced   540
That, near the quiet churchyard where
　　we sate,
A team of horses, with a ponderous freight
Pressing behind, adown a rugged slope,
Whose sharp descent confounded their
　　array,
Came at that moment, ringing noisily.   545

"Here," said the Pastor, "do we muse,
　　and mourn
The waste of death; and lo! the giant oak
Stretched on his bier—that massy timber
　　wain;
Nor fail to note the Man who guides the
　　team."

He was a peasant of the lowest class: 550
Grey locks profusely round his temples
　　hung
In clustering curls, like ivy, which the
　　bite
Of winter cannot thin; the fresh air
　　lodged

Within his cheek, as light within a cloud;
And he returned our greeting with a
   smile.   555
When he had passed, the Solitary spake;
"A Man he seems of cheerful yesterdays
And confident to-morrows; with a face
Not worldly-minded, for it bears too much
Of Nature's impress,—gaiety and health,
Freedom and hope; but keen, withal, and
   shrewd.   561
His gestures note,—and hark! his tones
   of voice
Are all vivacious as his mien and looks."

The Pastor answered, "You have read
   him well.
Year after year is added to his store   565
With *silent* increase: summers, winters—
   past,
Past or to come; yea, boldly might I say,
Ten summers and ten winters of a space
That lies beyond life's ordinary bounds,
Upon his sprightly vigour cannot fix   570
The obligation of an anxious mind,
A pride in having, or a fear to lose;
Possessed like outskirts of some large
   domain,
By any one more thought of than by him
Who holds the land in fee, its careless
   lord!   575
Yet is the creature rational, endowed
With foresight; hears, too, every sabbath
   day,
The Christian promise with attentive ear;
Nor will, I trust, the Majesty of Heaven
Reject the incense offered up by him, 580
Though of the kind which beasts and
   birds present
In grove or pasture; cheerfulness of soul,
From trepidation and repining free.
How many scrupulous worshippers fall
   down
Upon their knees, and daily homage
   pay   585
Less worthy, less religious even, than his!

"This qualified respect, the old Man's
   due,
Is paid without reluctance; but in truth,"
(Said the good Vicar with a fond half-
   smile)

"I feel at times a motion of despite   590
Towards one, whose bold contrivances and
   skill,
As you have seen, bear such conspicuous
   part
In works of havoc; taking from these
   vales,
One after one, their proudest ornaments.
Full oft his doings leave me to deplore 595
Tall ash-tree, sown by winds, by vapours
   nursed,
In the dry crannies of the pendent rocks;
Light birch, aloft upon the horizon's edge.
A veil of glory for the ascending moon;
And oak whose roots by noontide dew
   were damped,   600
And on whose forehead inaccessible
The raven lodged in safety.—Many a ship
Launched into Morecambe-bay, to *him*
   hath owed
Her strong knee-timbers, and the mast
   that bears
The loftiest of her pendants; He, from
   park   605
Or forest, fetched the enormous axle-tree
That whirls (how slow itself!) ten thou-
   sand spindles:
And the vast engine labouring in the mine,
Content with meaner prowess, must have
   lacked
The trunk and body of its marvellous
   strength,   610
If his undaunted enterprise had failed
Among the mountain coves.

              Yon household fir,
A guardian planted to fence off the blast,
But towering high the roof above, as if
Its humble destination were forgot— 615
That sycamore, which annually holds
Within its shade, as in a stately tent[1]
On all sides open to the fanning breeze,
A grave assemblage, seated while they
   shear
The fleece-encumbered flock—the JOYFUL
   ELM,   620
Around whose trunk the maidens dance
   in May—
And the LORD'S OAK—would plead their
   several rights

---

[1] See Note, p. 933.

In vain, if he were master of their fate;
His sentence to the axe would doom
them all.
But, green in age and lusty as he is, 625
And promising to keep his hold on earth
Less, as might seem, in rivalship with
men
Than with the forest's more enduring
growth,
His own appointed hour will come at
last;
And, like the haughty Spoilers of the
world, 630
This keen Destroyer, in his turn, must
fall.

"Now from the living pass we once
again:
From Age," the Priest continued, "turn
your thoughts;
From Age, that often unlamented drops,
And mark that daisied hillock, three
spans long! 635
—Seven lusty Sons sate daily round the
board
Of Gold-rill side; and, when the hope
had ceased
Of other progeny, a Daughter then
Was given, the crowning bounty of the
whole;
And so acknowledged with a tremulous
joy 640
Felt to the centre of that heavenly calm
With which by nature every mother's soul
Is stricken in the moment when her throes
Are ended, and her ears have heard the
cry
Which tells her that a living child is
born; 645
And she lies conscious, in a blissful rest,
That the dread storm is weathered by
them both.

"The Father—him at this unlooked-
for gift
A bolder transport seizes. From the side
Of his bright hearth, and from his open
door, 650
Day after day the gladness is diffused
To all that come, almost to all that pass;
Invited, summoned, to partake the cheer

Spread on the never-empty board, and
drink
Health and good wishes to his new-born
girl, 655
From cups replenished by his joyous
hand.
—Those seven fair brothers variously were
moved
Each by the thoughts best suited to his
years:
But most of all and with most thankful
mind
The hoary grandsire felt himself enriched;
A happiness that ebbed not, but remained
To fill the total measure of his soul!
—From the low tenement, his own abode,
Whither, as to a little private cell,
He had withdrawn from bustle, care, and
noise, 665
To spend the sabbath of old age in peace,
Once every day he duteously repaired
To rock the cradle of the slumbering babe:
For in that female infant's name he heard
The silent name of his departed wife;
Heart-stirring music! hourly heard that
name; 671
Full blest he was, 'Another Margaret
Green,'
Oft did he say, 'was come to Gold-rill
side.'

"Oh! pang unthought of, as the pre-
cious boon
Itself had been unlooked-for; oh! dire
stroke 675
Of desolating anguish for them all!
—Just as the Child could totter on the
floor,
And, by some friendly finger's help up-
stayed
Ranged round the garden walk, while she
perchance
Was catching at some novelty of spring,
Ground-flower, or glossy insect from its,
cell 681
Drawn by the sunshine—at that hopeful
season
The winds of March, smiting insidiously,
Raised in the tender passage of the throat
Viewless obstruction; whence, all unfore-
warned, 685

The household lost their pride and soul's
　　delight.
—But time hath power to soften all re-
　　grets,
And prayer and thought can bring to
　　worst distress
Due resignation. Therefore, though some
　　tears
Fail not to spring from either Parent's
　　eye　　　　　　　　　　　　690
Oft as they hear of sorrow like their own,
Yet this departed Little-one, too long
The innocent troubler of their quiet, sleeps
In what may now be called a peaceful
　　bed.

　　"On a bright day—so calm and bright,
　　　it seemed　　　　　　　　695
To us, with our sad spirits, heavenly-
　　fair—
These mountains echoed to an unknown
　　sound ;
A volley, thrice repeated o'er the Corse
Let down into the hollow of that grave,
Whose shelving sides are red with naked
　　mould.　　　　　　　　　　700
Ye rains of April, duly wet this earth !
Spare, burning sun of midsummer, these
　　sods,
That they may knit together, and there-
　　with
Our thoughts unite in kindred quietness !
Nor so the Valley shall forget her loss. 705
Dear Youth, by young and old alike be-
　　loved,
To me as precious as my own !—Green
　　herbs
May creep (I wish that they would softly
　　creep)
Over thy last abode, and we may pass
Reminded less imperiously of thee ;— 710
The ridge itself may sink into the breast
Of earth, the great abyss, and be no more ;
Yet shall not thy remembrance leave our
　　hearts,
Thy image disappear !
　　　　　　　The Mountain-ash 714
No eye can overlook, when 'mid a grove
Of yet unfaded trees she lifts her head
Decked with autumnal berries, that out-
　　shine

Spring's richest blossoms ; and ye may
　　have marked,
By a brook-side or solitary tarn,
How she her station doth adorn : the
　　pool　　　　　　　　　　　　720
Glows at her feet, and all the gloomy
　　rocks
Are brightened round her. In his native
　　vale
Such and so glorious did this Youth
　　appear ;
A sight that kindled pleasure in all hearts
By his ingenuous beauty, by the gleam 725
Of his fair eyes, by his capacious brow,
By all the graces with which nature's hand
Had lavishly arrayed him. As old bards
Tell in their idle songs of wandering gods,
Pan or Apollo, veiled in human form : 730
Yet, like the sweet-breathed violet of the
　　shade,
Discovered in their own despite to sense
Of mortals (if such fables without blame
May find chance-mention on this sacred
　　ground)—
So, through a simple rustic garb's dis-
　　guise,　　　　　　　　　　735
And through the impediment of rural
　　cares,
In him revealed a scholar's genius shone ;
And so, not wholly hidden from men's
　　sight,
In him the spirit of a hero walked
Our unpretending valley.—How the quoit
Whizzed from the Stripling's arm ! If
　　touched by him,　　　　　　741
The inglorious football mounted to the
　　pitch
Of the lark's flight,—or shaped a rainbow
　　curve,
Aloft, in prospect of the shouting field !
The indefatigable fox had learned　745
To dread his perseverance in the chase.
With admiration would he lift his eyes
To the wide-ruling eagle, and his hand
Was loth to assault the majesty he loved :
Else had the strongest fastnesses proved
　　weak　　　　　　　　　　　750
To guard the royal brood. The sailing
　　glead,
The wheeling swallow, and the darting
　　snipe,

The sportive sea-gull dancing with the
    waves,
And cautious water-fowl, from distant
    climes,
Fixed at their seat, the centre of the
    Mere,   755
Were subject to young Oswald's steady
    aim,
And lived by his forbearance.
                 From the coast
Of France a boastful Tyrant hurled his
    threats ;
Our Country marked the preparation vast
Of hostile forces ; and she called—with
    voice   760
That filled her plains, that reached her
    utmost shores,
And in remotest vales was heard—to
    arms !
—Then, for the first time, here you might
    have seen
The shepherd's grey to martial scarlet
    changed,
That flashed uncouthly through the woods
    and fields.   765
Ten hardy Striplings, all in bright attire,
And graced with shining weapons, weekly
    marched,
From this lone valley, to a central spot
Where, in assemblage with the flower and
    choice
Of the surrounding district, they might
    learn   770
The rudiments of war ; ten—hardy,
    strong,
And valiant ; but young Oswald, like a
    chief
And yet a modest comrade, led them
    forth
From their shy solitude, to face the
    world,
With a gay confidence and seemly pride ;
Measuring the soil beneath their happy
    feet   776
Like Youths released from labour, and
    yet bound
To most laborious service, though to them
A festival of unencumbered ease ;
The inner spirit keeping holiday,   780
Like vernal ground to sabbath sunshine
    left.

"Oft have I marked him, at some
    leisure hour,
Stretched on the grass, or seated in the
    shade,
Among his fellows, while an ample map
Before their eyes lay carefully outspread,
From which the gallant teacher would
    discourse,   786
Now pointing this way, and now that.
    —' Here flows,'
Thus would he say, 'the Rhine, that
    famous stream !
Eastward, the Danube toward this in-
    land sea,
A mightier river, winds from realm to
    realm ;   790
And, like a serpent, shows his glittering
    back
Bespotted—with innumerable isles :
Here reigns the Russian, there the Turk ;
    observe
His capital city !' Thence, along a tract
Of livelier interest to his hopes and fears,
His finger moved, distinguishing the
    spots   796
Where wide-spread conflict then most
    fiercely raged ;
Nor left unstigmatized those fatal fields
On which the sons of mighty Germany
Were taught a base submission.—' Here
    behold   800
A nobler race, the Switzers, and their
    land,
Vales deeper far than these of ours, huge
    woods,
And mountains white with everlasting
    snow !'
—And, surely, he, that spake with kind-
    ling brow,
Was a true patriot, hopeful as the best
Of that young peasantry, who, in our
    days,   806
Have fought and perished for Helvetia's
    rights—
Ah, not in vain !—or those who, in old
    time,
For work of happier issue, to the side
Of Tell came trooping from a thousand
    huts,   810
When he had risen alone ! No braver
    Youth

Descended from Judean heights, to march
With righteous Joshua; nor appeared in
    arms
When grove was felled, and altar was cast
    down,
And Gideon blew the trumpet, soul-in-
    flamed,   815
And strong in hatred of idolatry."

The Pastor, even as if by these last
    words
Raised from his seat within the chosen
    shade,
Moved towards the grave;—instinctively
    his steps
We followed; and my voice with joy
    exclaimed: 820
"Power to the Oppressors of the world
    is given,
A might of which they dream not. Oh!
    the curse,
To be the awakener of divinest thoughts,
Father and founder of exalted deeds;
And, to whole nations bound in servile
    straits,   825
The liberal donor of capacities
More than heroic! this to be, nor yet
Have sense of one connatural wish, nor
    yet
Deserve the least return of human thanks;
Winning no recompense but deadly hate
With pity mixed, astonishment with
    scorn!"   831

When this involuntary strain had
    ceased,
The Pastor said: "So Providence is
    served;
The forkèd weapon of the skies can send
Illumination into deep, dark holds,   835
Which the mild sunbeam hath not power
    to pierce.
Ye Thrones that have defied remorse, and
    cast
Pity away, soon shall ye quake with *fear!*
For, not unconscious of the mighty debt
Which to outrageous wrong the sufferer
    owes,   840
Europe, through all her habitable bounds,
Is thirsting for *their* overthrow, who yet
Survive, as pagan temples stood of yore,

By horror of their impious rites, pre-
    served;
Are still permitted to extend their pride,
Like cedars on the top of Lebanon   846
Darkening the sun.
              But less impatient thoughts,
And love 'all hoping and expecting all,'
This hallowed grave demands, where rests
    in peace
A humble champion of the better cause;
A Peasant-youth, so call him, for he
    asked   851
No higher name; in whom our country
    showed,
As in a favourite son, most beautiful.
In spite of vice, and misery, and disease,
Spread with the spreading of her wealthy
    arts,   855
England, the ancient and the free, ap-
    peared
In him to stand before my swimming
    eyes,
Unconquerably virtuous and secure.
—No more of this, lest I offend his dust:
Short was his life, and a brief tale re-
    mains.   860

"One day—a summer's day of annual
    pomp
And solemn chase—from morn to sultry
    noon
His steps had followed, fleetest of the
    fleet,
The red-deer driven along its native
    heights
With cry of hound and horn; and, from
    that toil   865
Returned with sinews weakened and re-
    laxed,
This generous Youth, too negligent of self,
Plunged—'mid a gay and busy throng
    convened
To wash the fleeces of his Father's flock—
Into the chilling flood. Convulsions dire
Seized him, that self-same night; and
    through the space   871
Of twelve ensuing days his frame was
    wrenched,
Till nature rested from her work in death.
To him, thus snatched away, his com-
    rades paid   874

A soldier's honours. At his funeral hour
Bright was the sun, the sky a cloudless
    blue—   876
A golden lustre slept upon the hills;
And if by chance a stranger, wandering
    there,
From some commanding eminence had
    looked
Down on this spot, well pleased would
    he have seen   880
A glittering spectacle; but every face
Was pallid: seldom hath that eye been
    moist
With tears, that wept not then; nor were
    the few,
Who from their dwellings came not forth
    to join
In this sad service, less disturbed than
    we.   885
They started at the tributary peal
Of instantaneous thunder, which an-
    nounced,
Through the still air, the closing of the
    Grave;
And distant mountains echoed with a
    sound
Of lamentation, never heard before!"

The Pastor ceased.—My venerable
    Friend   891
Victoriously upraised his clear bright eye;
And, when that eulogy was ended, stood
Enrapt, as if his inward sense perceived
The prolongation of some still response,
Sent by the ancient Soul of this wide
    land,   896
The Spirit of its mountains and its seas,
Its cities, temples, fields, its awful power,
Its rights and virtues—by that Deity
Descending, and supporting his pure
    heart   900
With patriotic confidence and joy.
And, at the last of those memorial words,
The pining Solitary turned aside;
Whether through manly instinct to con-
    ceal
Tender emotions spreading from the
    heart   905
To his worn cheek; or with uneasy shame
For those cold humours of habitual spleen
That, fondly seeking in dispraise of man

Solace and self-excuse, had sometimes
    urged
To self-abuse a not ineloquent tongue.
·—Right toward the sacred Edifice his
    steps   911
Had been directed; and we saw him now
Intent upon a monumental stone,
Whose uncouth form was grafted on the
    wall,
Or rather seemed to have grown into the
    side   915
Of the rude pile; as ofttimes trunks of
    trees,
Where nature works in wild and craggy
    spots,
Are seen incorporate with the living
    rock—
To endure for aye. The Vicar, taking note
Of his employment, with a courteous
    smile   920
Exclaimed—
      "The sagest Antiquarian's eye
That task would foil;" then, letting fall
    his voice
While he advanced, thus spake: "Tradi-
    tion tells
That, in Eliza's golden days, a Knight
Came on a war-horse sumptuously at-
    tired,   925
And fixed his home in this sequestered
    vale.
'Tis left untold if here he first drew
    breath,
Or as a stranger reached this deep recess,
Unknowing and unknown. A pleasing
    thought
I sometimes entertain, that haply bound
To Scotland's court in service of his
    Queen,   931
Or sent on mission to some northern
    Chief
Of England's realm, this vale he might
    have seen
With transient observation; and thence
    caught
An image fair, which, brightening in his
    soul   935
When joy of war and pride of chivalry
Languished beneath accumulated years,
Had power to draw him from the world,
    resolved

To make that paradise his chosen home
To which his peaceful fancy oft had turned.

"Vague thoughts are these; but, if be-
    lief may rest　　　　　　　　941
Upon unwritten story fondly traced
From sire to son, in this obscure retreat
The Knight arrived, with spear and shield,
    and borne
Upon a Charger gorgeously bedecked 945
With broidered housings.　And the lofty
    Steed—
His sole companion, and his faithful
    friend,
Whom he, in gratitude, let loose to range
In fertile pastures—was beheld with eyes
Of admiration and delightful awe,　　950
By those untravelled Dalesmen.　With
    less pride,
Yet free from touch of envious discontent,
They saw a mansion at his bidding rise,
Like a bright star, amid the lowly band
Of their rude homesteads.　Here the
    Warrior dwelt;　　　　　　955
And, in that mansion, children of his own,
Or kindred, gathered round him.　As a
    tree
That falls and disappears, the house is
    gone;
And, through improvidence or want of
    love
For ancient worth and honourable things,
The spear and shield are vanished, which
    the Knight　　　　　　　961
Hung in his rustic hall.　One ivied arch
Myself have seen, a gateway, last remains
Of that foundation in domestic care
Raised by his hands.　And now no trace
    is left　　　　　　　　　965
Of the mild-hearted Champion, save this
    stone,
Faithless memorial! and his family name
Borne by yon clustering cottages, that
    sprang
From out the ruins of his stately lodge:
These, and the name and title at full
    length,—　　　　　　　970
Sir Alfred Erthing, with appropriate
    words
Accompanied, still extant, in a wreath
Or posy, girding round the several fronts

Of three clear-sounding and harmonious
    bells,
That in the steeple hang, his pious gift."

"So fails, so languishes, grows dim,
    and dies,"　　　　　　　976
The grey-haired Wanderer pensively ex-
    claimed,
"All that this world is proud of.　From
    their spheres
The stars of human glory are cast down;
Perish the roses and the flowers of kings[1],
Princes, and emperors, and the crowns
    and palms　　　　　　　981
Of all the mighty, withered and con-
    sumed!
Nor is power given to lowliest innocence
Long to protect her own.　The man him-
    self
Departs; and soon is spent the line of
    those　　　　　　　　　985
Who, in the bodily image, in the mind,
In heart or soul, in station or pursuit,
Did most resemble him.　Degrees and
    ranks,
Fraternities and orders—heaping high
New wealth upon the burthen of the old,
And placing trust in privilege confirmed
And re-confirmed—are scoffed at with a
    smile
Of greedy foretaste, from the secret stand
Of Desolation, aimed: to slow decline
These yield, and these to sudden over-
    throw:　　　　　　　　　995
Their virtue, service, happiness, and state
Expire; and nature's pleasant robe of
    green,
Humanity's appointed shroud, enwraps
Their monuments and their memory.　The
    vast Frame
Of social nature changes evermore　1000
Her organs and her members, with decay
Restless, and restless generation, powers
And functions dying and produced at
    need,—
And by this law the mighty whole sub-
    sists:
With an ascent and progress in the
    main;　　　　　　　　　1005

---

[1] See Note, p. 933.

Yet, oh! how disproportioned to the
 hopes
And expectations of self-flattering minds!

"The courteous Knight, whose bones
 are here interred,
Lived in an age conspicuous as our own
For strife and ferment in the minds of
 men;   1010
Whence alteration in the forms of things,
Various and vast. A memorable age!
Which did to him assign a pensive lot—
To linger 'mid the last of those bright
 clouds
That, on the steady breeze of honour,
 sailed   1015
In long procession calm and beautiful.
He who had seen his own bright order
 fade,
And its devotion gradually decline,
(While war, relinquishing the lance and
 shield,
Her temper changed, and bowed to other
 laws)   1020
Had also witnessed, in his morn of life,
That violent commotion, which o'erthrew,
In town and city and sequestered glen,
Altar, and cross, and church of solemn
 roof,
And old religious house—pile after pile;
And shook their tenants out into the
 fields,   1026
Like wild beasts without home! Their
 hour was come;
But why no softening thought of grati-
 tude,
No just remembrance, scruple, or wise
 doubt?
Benevolence is mild; nor borrows help,

Save at worst need, from bold impetuous
 force,   1031
Fitliest allied to anger and revenge.
But Human-kind rejoices in the might
Of mutability; and airy hopes,
Dancing around her, hinder and disturb
Those meditations of the soul that feed
The retrospective virtues. Festive songs
Break from the maddened nations at the
 sight
Of sudden overthrow; and cold neglect
Is the sure consequence of slow decay.

"Even," said the Wanderer, "as that
 courteous Knight,   1041
Bound by his vow to labour for redress
Of all who suffer wrong, and to enact
By sword and lance the law of gentle-
 ness,
(If I may venture of myself to speak, 1045
Trusting that not incongruously I blend
Low things with lofty) I too shall be
 doomed
To outlive the kindly use and fair esteem
Of the poor calling which my youth
 embraced
With no unworthy prospect. But enough;
—Thoughts crowd upon me—and 'twere
 seemlier now   1051
To stop, and yield our gracious Teacher
 thanks
For the pathetic records which his voice
Hath here delivered; words of heartfelt
 truth,
Tending to patience when affliction
 strikes;   1055
To hope and love; to confident repose
In God; and reverence for the dust of
 Man."

BOOK EIGHTH.

THE PARSONAGE.

ARGUMENT.

Pastor's apology and apprehensions that he might have detained his Auditors too long, with the Pastor's invitation to his house.—Solitary disinclined to comply—rallies the Wanderer—and playfully draws a comparison between his itinerant profession and that of 'the Knight-errant—which leads to Wanderer's giving an account of changes in the Country from the manufacturing spirit.—Favourable effects.—The other side of the picture, and chiefly as it has affected the humbler classes.—Wanderer asserts the hollowness of all national grandeur if unsupported by moral worth.—Physical science unable to support itself.—Lamentations over an excess of manufacturing industry among the humbler Classes of Society.—Picture of a Child employed in a Cotton-mill.—Ignorance and degradation of Children among the agricultural Population reviewed.—Conversation broken off by a renewed Invitation from the Pastor.—Path leading to his House.—Its appearance described.—His Daughter.—His Wife.—His Son (a Boy) enters with his Companion.—Their happy appearance.—The Wanderer how affected by the sight of them.

THE pensive Sceptic of the lonely vale
To those acknowledgments subscribed his
  own,
With a sedate compliance which the
  Priest
Failed not to notice, inly pleased, and
  said:—
"If ye, by whom invited I began   5
These narratives of calm and humble life,
Be satisfied, 'tis well,—the end is gained;
And in return for sympathy bestowed
And patient listening, thanks accept from
  me.
—Life, death, eternity! momentous
  themes   10
Are they—and might demand a seraph's
  tongue,
Were they not equal to their own support;
And therefore no incompetence of mine
Could do them wrong. The universal
  forms
Of human nature, in a spot like this,   15
Present themselves at once to all men's
  view:
Ye wished for act and circumstance, that
  make
The individual known and understood;

And such as my best judgment could
  select
From what the place afforded, have been
  given;   20
Though apprehensions crossed me that
  my zeal
To his might well be likened, who unlocks
A cabinet stored with gems and pictures—
  draws
His treasures forth, soliciting regard
To this, and this, as worthier than the
  last,   25
Till the spectator, who awhile was pleased
More than the exhibitor himself, becomes
Weary and faint, and longs to be released.
—But let us hence! my dwelling is in
  sight,
And there—"
      At this the Solitary shrunk 30
With backward will; but, wanting not
  address
That inward motion to disguise, he said
To his Compatriot, smiling as he spake;
—"The peaceable remains of this good
  Knight
Would be disturbed, I fear, with wrathful
  scorn,   35

If consciousness could reach him where
   he lies
That one, albeit of these degenerate times,
Deploring changes past, or dreading
   change
Foreseen, had dared to couple, even in
   thought,
The fine vocation of the sword and lance
With the gross aims and body-bending
   toil   41
Of a poor brotherhood who walk the
   earth
Pitied, and, where they are not known,
   despised.

"Yet, by the good Knight's leave, the
   two estates
Are graced with some resemblance.
   Errant those,   45
Exiles and wanderers—and the like are
   these;
Who, with their burthen, traverse hill
   and dale,
Carrying relief for nature's simple wants.
—What though no higher recompense be
   sought
Than honest maintenance, by irksome
   toil   50
Full oft procured, yet may they claim
   respect,
Among the intelligent, for what this
   course
Enables them to be and to perform.
Their tardy steps give leisure to observe,
While solitude permits the mind to feel;
Instructs, and prompts her to supply
   defects   56
By the division of her inward self
For grateful converse: and to these poor
   men
Nature (I but repeat your favourite boast)
Is bountiful—go wheresoe'er they may; 60
Kind nature's various wealth is all their
   own.
Versed in the characters of men; and
   bound,
By ties of daily interest, to maintain
Conciliatory manners and smooth speech;
Such have been, and still are in their
   degree,   65
Examples efficacious to refine

Rude intercourse; apt agents to expel,
By importation of unlooked-for arts,
Barbarian torpor, and blind prejudice;
Raising, through just gradation, savage
   life   70
To rustic, and the rustic to urbane.
—Within their moving magazines is
   lodged
Power that comes forth to quicken and
   exalt
Affections seated in the mother's breast,
And in the lover's fancy; and to feed 75
The sober sympathies of long-tried friends.
—By these Itinerants, as experienced
   men,
Counsel is given; contention they appease
With gentle language; in remotest wilds,
Tears wipe away, and pleasant tidings
   bring;   80
Could the proud quest of chivalry do
   more?"

' Happy," rejoined the Wanderer,
   "they who gain
A panegyric from your generous tongue !
But, if to these Wayfarers once pertained
Aught of romantic interest, it is gone. 85
Their purer service, in this realm at least,
Is past for ever.—An inventive Age
Has wrought, if not with speed of magic,
   yet
To most strange issues. I have lived to
   mark
A new and unforeseen creation rise   90
From out the labours of a peaceful Land
Wielding her potent enginery to frame
And to produce, with appetite as keen
As that of war, which rests not night
   or day,
Industrious to destroy ! With fruitless
   pains   95
Might one like me *now* visit many a tract
Which, in his youth, he trod, and trod
   again,
A lone pedestrian with a scanty freight,
Wished-for, or welcome, wheresoe'er he
   came—
Among the tenantry of thorpe and vill;
Or straggling burgh, of ancient charter
   proud,   101
And dignified by battlements and towers

Of some stern castle, mouldering on the
    brow
Of a green hill or bank of rugged stream.
The foot-path faintly marked, the horse-
    track wild,   105
And formidable length of plashy lane,
(Prized avenues ere others had been
    shaped
Or easier links connecting place with
    place)
Have vanished—swallowed up by stately
    roads
Easy and bold, that penetrate the gloom
Of Britain's farthest glens. The Earth
    has lent   111
Her waters, Air her breezes[1]; and the sail
Of traffic glides with ceaseless intercourse,
Glistening along the low and woody dale;
Or, in its progress, on the lofty side   115
Of some bare hill, with wonder kenned
    from far.

"Meanwhile, at social Industry's com-
    mand,
How quick, how vast an increase! From
    the germ
Of some poor hamlet, rapidly produced
Here a huge town, continuous and com-
    pact,   120
Hiding the face of earth for leagues—and
    there,
Where not a habitation stood before,
Abodes of men irregularly massed
Like trees in forests,—spread through
    spacious tracts,
O'er which the smoke of unremitting fires
Hangs permanent, and plentiful as
    wreaths   126
Of vapour glittering in the morning sun.
And, wheresoe'er the traveller turns his
    steps,
He sees the barren wilderness erased,
Or disappearing; triumph that proclaims
How much the mild Directress of the
    plough   131
Owes to alliance with these new-born
    arts!
—Hence is the wide sea peopled,—hence
    the shores

[1] See Note, p. 933.

Of Britain are resorted to by ships
Freighted from every climate of the
    world   135
With the world's choicest produce.
    Hence that sum
Of keels that rest within her crowded
    ports,
Or ride at anchor in her sounds and bays;
That animating spectacle of sails
That, through her inland regions, to and
    fro   140
Pass with the respirations of the tide,
Perpetual, multitudinous! Finally,
Hence a dread arm of floating power, a
    voice
Of thunder daunting those who would
    approach
With hostile purposes the blessèd Isle, 145
Truth's consecrated residence, the seat
Impregnable of Liberty and Peace.

"And yet, O happy Pastor of a flock
Faithfully watched, and, by that loving
    care
And Heaven's good providence, preserved
    from taint!   150
With you I grieve, when on the darker
    side
Of this great change I look; and there
    behold
Such outrage done to nature as compels
The indignant power to justify herself;
Yea, to avenge her violated rights,   155
For England's bane.—When soothing
    darkness spreads
O'er hill and vale," the Wanderer thus
    expressed
His recollections, "and the punctual
    stars,
While all things else are gathering to
    their homes,   159
Advance, and in the firmament of heaven
Glitter—but undisturbing, undisturbed;
As if their silent company were charged
With peaceful admonitions for the heart
Of all-beholding Man, earth's thoughtful
    lord;
Then, in full many a region, once like
    this   165
The assured domain of calm simplicity
And pensive quiet, an unnatural light

Prepared for never-resting Labour's eyes
Breaks from a many-windowed fabric
　　huge!
And at the appointed hour a bell is
　　heard,　　　　　　　　　　　170
Of harsher import than the curfew-knoll
That spake the Norman Conqueror's stern
　　behest—
A local summons to unceasing toil!
Disgorged are now the ministers of day;
And, as they issue from the illumined
　　pile,　　　　　　　　　　　175
A fresh band meets them, at the crowded
　　door—
And in the courts—and where the rum-
　　bling stream,
That turns the multitude of dizzy wheels,
Glares, like a troubled spirit, in its bed
Among the rocks below.　Men, maidens,
　　youths,　　　　　　　　　　180
Mother and little children, boys and girls,
Enter, and each the wonted task re-
　　sumes
Within this temple, where is offered up
To Gain, the master-idol of the realm,
Perpetual sacrifice.　Even thus of old　185
Our ancestors, within the still domain
Of vast cathedral or conventual church,
Their vigils kept; where tapers day and
　　night
On the dim altar burned continually,
In token that the House was evermore
Watching to God.　Religious men were
　　they;　　　　　　　　　　　191
Nor would their reason, tutored to aspire
Above this transitory world, allow
That there should pass a moment of the
　　year,
When in their land the Almighty's ser-
　　vice ceased.　　　　　　　　195

"Triumph who will in these profaner
　　rites
Which we, a generation self-extolled,
As zealously perform!　I cannot share
His proud complacency:—yet do I exult,
Casting reserve away, exult to see　　200
An intellectual mastery exercised
O'er the blind elements; a purpose given,
A perseverance fed; almost a soul
Imparted—to brute matter.　I rejoice,

Measuring the force of those gigantic
　　powers　　　　　　　　　　205
That, by the thinking mind, have been
　　compelled
To serve the will of feeble-bodied Man.
For with the sense of admiration blends
The animating hope that time may come
When, strengthened, yet not dazzled, by
　　the might　　　　　　　　　210
Of this dominion over nature gained,
Men of all lands shall exercise the same
In due proportion to their country's need;
Learning, though late, that all true glory
　　rests,　　　　　　　　　　214
All praise, all safety, and all happiness,
Upon the moral law.　Egyptian Thebes,
Tyre, by the margin of the sounding
　　waves,
Palmyra, central in the desert, fell;
And the Arts died by which they had
　　been raised.　　　　　　　　219
—Call Archimedes from his buried tomb
Upon the grave of vanished Syracuse,
And feelingly the Sage shall make report
How insecure, how baseless in itself,
Is the Philosophy whose sway depends
On mere material instruments;—how
　　weak　　　　　　　　　　225
Those arts, and high inventions, if un-
　　propped
By virtue.—He, sighing with pensive
　　grief,
Amid his calm abstractions, would admit
That not the slender privilege is theirs
To save themselves from blank forgetful-
　　ness!"　　　　　　　　　　230

When from the Wanderer's lips these
　　words had fallen,
I said, "And, did in truth those vaunted
　　Arts
Possess such privilege, how could we
　　escape
Sadness and keen regret, we who revere,
And would preserve as things above all
　　price,　　　　　　　　　　235
The old domestic morals of the land,
Her simple manners, and the stable worth
That dignified and cheered a low estate?
Oh! where is now the character of peace,
Sobriety, and order, and chaste love,　240

And honest dealing, and untainted speech,
And pure good-will, and hospitable cheer;
That made the very thought of country-
    life
A thought of refuge, for a mind detained
Reluctantly amid the bustling crowd?
Where now the beauty of the sabbath
    kept   246
With conscientious reverence, as a day
By the almighty Lawgiver pronounced
Holy and blest? and where the winning
    grace
Of all the lighter ornaments attached
To time and season, as the year rolled
    round?"   251

"Fled!" was the Wanderer's passion-
    ate response,
"Fled utterly! or only to be traced
In a few fortunate retreats like this;
Which I behold with trembling, when I
    think   255
What lamentable change, a year—a
    month—
May bring; that brook converting as it
    runs
Into an instrument of deadly bane
For those, who, yet untempted to forsake
The simple occupations of their sires, 260
Drink the pure water of its innocent
    stream
With lip almost as pure.—Domestic bliss
(Or call it comfort, by a humbler name,)
How art thou blighted for the poor Man's
    heart!
Lo! in such neighbourhood, from morn
    to eve,   265
The habitations empty! or perchance
The Mother left alone,—no helping hand
To rock the cradle of her peevish babe;
No daughters round her, busy at the
    wheel,   269
Or in dispatch of each day's little growth
Of household occupation; no nice arts
Of needle-work; no bustle at the fire,
Where once the dinner was prepared with
    pride;
Nothing to speed the day, or cheer the
    mind;
Nothing to praise, to teach, or to com-
    mand!   275

"The Father, if perchance he still re-
    tain
His old employments, goes to field or wood,
No longer led or followed by the Sons;
Idlers perchance they were,—but in *his*
    sight;
Breathing fresh air, and treading the
    green earth;   280
Till their short holiday of childhood
    ceased,
Ne'er to return! That birthright now is
    lost.
Economists will tell you that the State
Thrives by the forfeiture — unfeeling
    thought,
And false as monstrous! Can the mother
    thrive   285
By the destruction of her innocent sons
In whom a premature necessity
Blocks out the forms of nature, precon-
    sumes
The reason, famishes the heart, shuts up
The infant Being in itself, and makes
Its very spring a season of decay!   291
The lot is wretched, the condition sad,
Whether a pining discontent survive,
And thirst for change; or habit hath sub-
    dued   294
The soul deprest, dejected—even to love
Of her close tasks, and long captivity.

"Oh, banish far such wisdom as con-
    demns
A native Briton to these inward chains,
Fixed in his soul, so early and so deep;
Without his own consent, or knowledge,
    fixed!   300
He is a slave to whom release comes not,
And cannot come. The boy, where'er he
    turns,
Is still a prisoner; when the wind is up
Among the clouds, and roars through the
    ancient woods;
Or when the sun is shining in the east,
Quiet and calm. Behold him—in the
    school   306
Of his attainments? no; but with the air
Fanning his temples under heaven's blue
    arch.
His raiment, whitened o'er with cotton-
    flakes

Or locks of wool, announces whence he
comes.   310
Creeping his gait and cowering, his lip
pale,
His respiration quick and audible;
And scarcely could you fancy that a
gleam
Could break from out those languid eyes,
or a blush
Mantle upon his cheek.   Is this the form,
Is that the countenance, and such the
port,   316
Of no mean Being?   One who should be
clothed
With dignity befitting his proud hope;
Who, in his very childhood, should ap-
pear
Sublime from present purity and joy! 320
The limbs increase; but liberty of mind
Is gone for ever; and this organic frame,
So joyful in its motions, is become
Dull, to the joy of her own motions dead;
And even the touch, so exquisitely poured
Through the whole body, with a languid
will   326
Performs its functions; rarely competent
To impress a vivid feeling on the mind
Of what there is delightful in the breeze,
The gentle visitations of the sun,   330
Or lapse of liquid element—by hand,
Or foot, or lip, in summer's warmth—per-
ceived.
—Can hope look forward to a manhood
raised
On such foundations?"
                "Hope is none for him!"
The pale Recluse indignantly exclaimed,
"And tens of thousands suffer wrong as
deep.   336
Yet be it asked, in justice to our age,
If there were not, before those arts ap-
peared,
These structures rose, commingling old
and young,
And unripe sex with sex, for mutual
taint;   340
If there were not, then, in our far-famed
Isle,
Multitudes, who from infancy had breathed
Air unimprisoned, and had lived at
large;

Yet walked beneath the sun, in human
shape,
As abject, as degraded?   At this day, 345
Who shall enumerate the crazy huts
And tottering hovels, whence do issue
forth
A ragged Offspring, with their upright hair
Crowned like the image of fantastic Fear;
Or wearing, (shall we say?) in that white
growth   350
An ill-adjusted turban, for defence
Or fierceness, wreathed around their sun-
burnt brows,
By savage Nature?   Shrivelled are their
lips;
Naked, and coloured like the soil, the
feet
On which they stand; as if thereby they
drew   355
Some nourishment, as trees do by their
roots,
From earth, the common mother of us all.
Figure and mien, complexion and attire,
Are leagued to strike dismay; but out-
stretched hand
And whining voice denote them suppli-
cants   360
For the least boon that pity can bestow.
Such on the breast of darksome heaths
are found;
And with their parents occupy the skirts
Of furze-clad commons; such are born
and reared
At the mine's mouth under impending
rocks;   365
Or dwell in chambers of some natural
cave;
Or where their ancestors erected huts,
For the convenience of unlawful gain,
In forest purlieus; and the like are bred,
All England through, where nooks and
slips of ground   370
Purloined, in times less jealous than our
own,
From the green margin of the public way,
A residence afford them, 'mid the bloom
And gaiety of cultivated fields.   374
Such (we will hope the lowest in the scale)
Do I remember ofttimes to have seen
'Mid Buxton's dreary heights.   In earnest
watch,

Till the swift vehicle approach, they
  stand;
Then, following closely with the cloud of
  dust,   379
An uncouth feat exhibit, and are gone
Heels over head, like tumblers on a stage.
—Up from the ground they snatch the
  copper coin,
And, on the freight of merry passengers
Fixing a steady eye, maintain their speed;
And spin—and pant—and overhead again,
Wild pursuivants! until their breath is
  lost,   ·   386
Or bounty tires—and every face, that
  smiled
Encouragement, hath ceased to look that
  way.
—But, like the vagrants of the gipsy
  tribe,
These, bred to little pleasure in them-
  selves,   390
Are profitless to others.
               Turn we then
To Britons born and bred within the pale
Of civil polity, and early trained
To earn, by wholesome labour in the field,
The bread they eat. A sample should I
  give   395
Of what this stock hath long produced to
  enrich
The tender age of life, ye would exclaim,
'Is this the whistling plough-boy whose
  shrill notes
Impart new gladness to the morning air!'
Forgive me if I venture to suspect   400
That many, sweet to hear of in soft verse,
Are of no finer frame. Stiff are his
  joints;
Beneath a cumbrous frock, that to the
  knees
Invests the thriving churl, his legs ap-
  pear,
Fellows to those that lustily upheld   405
The wooden stools for everlasting use,
Whereon our fathers sate. And mark
  his brow!
Under whose shaggy canopy are set
Two eyes—not dim, but of a healthy
  stare—
Wide, sluggish, blank, and ignorant, and
  strange—   410

Proclaiming boldly that they never drew
A look or motion of intelligence
From infant-conning of the Christ-cross-
  row,
Or puzzling through a primer, line by
  line,
Till perfect mastery crown the pains at
  last.   415
—What kindly warmth from touch of
  fostering hand,
What penetrating power of sun or breeze,
Shall e'er dissolve the crust wherein his
  soul
Sleeps, like a caterpillar sheathed in ice?
This torpor is no pitiable work   420
Of modern ingenuity; no town
Nor crowded city can be taxed with
  aught
Of sottish vice or desperate breach of law,
To which (and who can tell where or how
  soon?)
He may be roused. This Boy the fields
  produce: 425
His spade and hoe, mattock and glitter-
  ing scythe,
The carter's whip that on his shoulder
  rests
In air high-towering with a boorish pomp,
The sceptre of his sway; his country's
  name,
Her equal rights, her churches and her
  schools—   430
What have they done for him? And, let
  me ask,
For tens of thousands uninformed as he?
In brief, what liberty of *mind* is here?"

This ardent sally pleased the mild good
  Man,
To whom the appeal couched in its clos-
  ing words   435
Was pointedly addressed; and to the
  thoughts
That, in assent or opposition, rose
Within his mind, he seemed prepared to
  give
Prompt utterance; but the Vicar inter-
  posed
With invitation urgently renewed.   440
—We followed, taking as he led, a path
Along a hedge of hollies dark and tall,

Whose flexile boughs low bending with a
   weight
Of leafy spray, concealed the stems and
   roots
That gave them nourishment. When
   frosty winds   445
Howl from the north, what kindly warmth,
   methought,
Is here—how grateful this impervious
   screen!
—Not shaped by simple wearing of the
   foot
On rural business passing to and fro
Was the commodious walk: a careful
   hand   450
Had marked the line, and strewn its sur-
   face o'er
With pure cerulean gravel, from the
   heights
Fetched by a neighbouring brook.—Across
   the vale
The stately fence accompanied our steps;
And thus the pathway, by perennial
   green   455
Guarded and graced, seemed fashioned
   to unite,
As by a beautiful yet solemn chain,
The Pastor's mansion with the house of
   prayer.

Like image of solemnity, conjoined
With feminine allurement soft and fair,
The mansion's self displayed;—a reverend
   pile   461
With bold projections and recesses deep;
Shadowy, yet gay and lightsome as it
   stood
Fronting the noontide sun. We paused
   to admire
The pillared porch, elaborately embossed;
The low wide windows with their mul-
   lions old;   466
The cornice, richly fretted, of grey stone;
And that smooth slope from which the
   dwelling rose,
By beds and banks Arcadian of gay
   flowers
And flowering shrubs, protected and
   adorned: 470
Profusion bright! and every flower as-
   suming

A more than natural vividness of hue
From unaffected contrast with the gloom
Of sober cypress, and the darker foil
Of yew, in which survived some traces,
   here   475
Not unbecoming, of grotesque device
And uncouth fancy. From behind the
   roof
Rose the slim ash and massy sycamore,
Blending their diverse foliage with the
   green
Of ivy, flourishing and thick, that clasped
The huge round chimneys, harbour of
   delight   481
For wren and redbreast,—where they sit
   and sing
Their slender ditties when the trees are
   bare.
Nor must I leave untouched (the picture
   else
Were incomplete) a relique of old times
Happily spared, a little Gothic niche
Of nicest workmanship; that once had
   held
The sculptured image of some patron-
   saint,
Or of the blessèd Virgin, looking down
On all who entered those religious doors.

But lo! where from the rocky garden-
   mount   491
Crowned by its antique summer-house—
   descends,
Light as the silver fawn, a radiant Girl;
For she hath recognised her honoured
   friend,
The Wanderer ever welcome! A prompt
   kiss   495
The gladsome child bestows at his re-
   quest;
And, up the flowery lawn as we advance,
Hangs on the old Man with a happy
   look,
And with a pretty restless hand of love.
—We enter—by the Lady of the place
Cordially greeted. Graceful was her port:
A lofty stature undepressed by time,
Whose visitation had not wholly spared
The finer lineaments of form and face;
To that complexion brought which pru-
   dence trusts in   505

And wisdom loves.—But when a stately
   ship
Sails in smooth weather by the placid
   coast
On homeward voyage,—what if wind and
   wave,
And hardship undergone in various
   climes,
Have caused her to abate the virgin
   pride,   510
And that full trim of inexperienced hope
With which she left her haven—not for
   this,
Should the sun strike her, and the im-
   partial breeze
Play on her streamers, fails she to as-
   sume
Brightness and touching beauty of her
   own,   515
That charm all eyes. So bright, so fair,
   appeared
This goodly Matron, shining in the
   beams
Of unexpected pleasure.—Soon the board
Was spread, and we partook a plain re-
   past.   519

Here, resting in cool shelter, we beguiled
The mid-day hours with desultory talk;
From trivial themes to general argument
Passing, as accident or fancy led,
Or courtesy prescribed. While question
   rose   524
And answer flowed, the fetters of reserve
Dropping from every mind, the Solitary
Resumed the manners of his happier
   days;
And in the various conversation bore
A willing, nay, at times, a forward part;
Yet with the grace of one who in the
   world   530
Had learned the art of pleasing, and had
   now
Occasion given him to display his skill,
Upon the steadfast 'vantage-ground of
   truth.
He gazed, with admiration unsuppressed,
Upon the landscape of the sun-bright
   vale,   535
Seen, from the shady room in which we
   sate,

In softened perspective; and more than
   once
Praised the consummate harmony serene
Of gravity and elegance, diffused
Around the mansion and its whole do-
   main;   540
Not, doubtless, without help of female
   taste
And female care.—"A blessed lot is
   yours!"
The words escaped his lip, with a tender
   sigh
Breathed over them: but suddenly the door
Flew open, and a pair of lusty Boys   545
Appeared, confusion checking their de-
   light.
—Not brothers they in feature or attire,
But fond companions, so I guessed, in
   field,
And by the river's margin—whence they
   come,   549
Keen anglers with unusual spoil elated.
One bears a willow-pannier on his back,
The boy of plainer garb, whose blush
   survives
More deeply tinged. Twin might the
   other be
To that fair girl who from the garden-
   mount
Bounded:—triumphant entry this for
   him!   555
Between his hands he holds a smooth
   blue stone,
On whose capacious surface see outspread
Large store of gleaming crimson-spotted
   trouts;
Ranged side by side, and lessening by
   degrees
Up to the dwarf that tops the pinnacle.
Upon the board he lays the sky-blue
   stone   561
With its rich freight; their number he
   proclaims;
Tells from what pool the noblest had
   been dragged;
And where the very monarch of the
   brook,
After long struggle, had escaped at last—
Stealing alternately at them and us   566
(As doth his comrade too) a look of pride:
And, verily, the silent creatures made

A splendid sight, together thus exposed;
Dead—but not sullied or deformed by
    death,   570
That seemed to pity what he could not
    spare.

But O, the animation in the mien
Of those two boys! yea in the very words
With which the young narrator was in-
    spired,
When, as our questions led, he told at
    large   575
Of that day's prowess! Him might I
    compare,
His looks, tones, gestures, eager elo-
    quence,
To a bold brook that splits for better
    speed,
And at the self-same moment, works its
    way
Through many channels, ever and anon
Parted and re-united: his compeer   581
To the still lake, whose stillness is to
    sight
As beautiful—as grateful to the mind.
—But to what object shall the lovely
    Girl
Be likened? She whose countenance and
    air   585

Unite the graceful qualities of both,
Even as she shares the pride and joy of
    both.

My grey-haired Friend was moved; his
    vivid eye
Glistened with tenderness; his mind, I
    knew,
Was full; and had, I doubted not, re-
    turned,   590
Upon this impulse, to the theme—ere-
    while
Abruptly broken off. The ruddy boys
Withdrew, on summons to their well-
    earned meal;
And He—to whom all tongues resigned
    their rights
With willingness, to whom the general
    ear   595
Listened with readier patience than to
    strain
Of music, lute or harp, a long delight
That ceased not when his voice had
    ceased—as One
Who from truth's central point serenely
    views
The compass of his argument—began 600
Mildly, and with a clear and steady
    tone.

BOOK NINTH.

DISCOURSE OF THE WANDERER, AND AN EVENING VISIT TO THE LAKE.

"To every Form of being is assigned,"
Thus calmly spake the venerable Sage,
"An *active* Principle:—howe'er removed
From sense and observation, it subsists
In all things, in all natures; in the stars 5
Of azure heaven, the unenduring clouds,
In flower and tree, in every pebbly stone
That paves the brooks, the stationary rocks,
The moving waters, and the invisible air.
Whate'er exists hath properties that spread 10
Beyond itself, communicating good,
A simple blessing, or with evil mixed;
Spirit that knows no insulated spot,
No chasm, no solitude; from link to link
It circulates, the Soul of all the worlds. 15
This is the freedom of the universe;
Unfolded still the more, more visible,
The more we know; and yet is reverenced least,
And least respected in the human Mind,
Its most apparent home. The food of hope 20
Is meditated action; robbed of this
Her sole support, she languishes and dies.
We perish also; for we live by hope
And by desire; we see by the glad light
And breathe the sweet air of futurity; 25
And so we live, or else we have no life.
To-morrow—nay perchance this very hour
(For every moment hath its own to-morrow!)
Those blooming Boys, whose hearts are almost sick
With present triumph, will be sure to find 30
A field before them freshened with the dew
Of other expectations;—in which course
Their happy year spins round. The youth obeys
A like glad impulse; and so moves the man
'Mid all his apprehensions, cares, and fears,— 35
Or so he ought to move. Ah! why in age
Do we revert so fondly to the walks
Of childhood—but that there the Soul discerns
The dear memorial footsteps unimpaired
Of her own native vigour; thence can hear 40

Reverberations; and a choral song,
Commingling with the incense that as-
　　cends,
Undaunted, toward the imperishable hea-
　　vens,
From her own lonely altar?
　　　　　　　　　　　Do not think
That good and wise ever will be allowed,
Though strength decay, to breathe in such
　　estate.　　　　　　　　　　　　46
As shall divide them wholly from the stir
Of hopeful nature. Rightly it is said
That Man descends into the VALE of
　　years;
Yet have I thought that we might also
　　speak,　　　　　　　　　　　　50
And not presumptuously, I trust, of Age,
As of a final EMINENCE; though bare
In aspect and forbidding, yet a point
On which 'tis not impossible to sit
In awful sovereignty; a place of power, 55
A throne, that may be likened unto his,
Who, in some placid day of summer, looks
Down from a mountain-top,—say one of
　　those
High peaks, that bound the vale where
　　now we are.　　　　　　　　　　59
Faint, and diminished to the gazing eye,
Forest and field, and hill and dale appear,
With all the shapes over their surface
　　spread:
But, while the gross and visible frame of
　　things
Relinquishes its hold upon the sense,
Yea almost on the Mind herself, and
　　seems　　　　　　　　　　　　65
All unsubstantialized,—how loud the voice
Of waters, with invigorated peal
From the full river in the vale below,
Ascending! For on that superior height
Who sits, is disencumbered from the press
Of near obstructions, and is privileged 71
To breathe in solitude, above the host
Of ever-humming insects, 'mid thin air
That suits not them. The murmur of the
　　leaves
Many and idle, visits not his ear:　　75
This he is freed from, and from thousand
　　notes
(Not less unceasing, not less vain than
　　these,)

By which the finer passages of sense
Are occupied; and the Soul, that would
　　incline
To listen, is prevented or deterred.　　80

"And may it not be hoped, that, placed
　　by age
In like removal, tranquil though severe,
We are not so removed for utter loss;
But for some favour, suited to our need?
What more than that the severing should
　　confer　　　　　　　　　　　　85
Fresh power to commune with the in-
　　visible world,
And hear the mighty stream of tendency
Uttering, for elevation of our thought,
A clear sonorous voice, inaudible
To the vast multitude; whose doom it is
To run the giddy round of vain delight, 91
Or fret and labour on the Plain below.

"But, if to such sublime ascent the
　　hopes
Of Man may rise, as to a welcome close
And termination of his mortal course; 95
Them only can such hope inspire whose
　　minds
Have not been starved by absolute ne-
　　glect;
Nor bodies crushed by unremitting toil;
To whom kind Nature, therefore, may
　　afford
Proof of the sacred love she bears for all;
Whose birthright Reason, therefore, may
　　ensure.　　　　　　　　　　　101
For me, consulting what I feel within
In times when most existence with herself
Is satisfied, I cannot but believe,
That, far as kindly Nature hath free
　　scope　　　　　　　　　　　105
And Reason's sway predominates; even
　　so far,
Country, society, and time itself,
That saps the individual's bodily frame,
And lays the generations low in dust,
Do, by the almighty Ruler's grace, par-
　　take　　　　　　　　　　　110
Of one maternal spirit, bringing forth
And cherishing with ever-constant love,
That tires not, nor betrays. Our life is
　　turned

Out of her course, wherever man is made
An offering, or a sacrifice, a tool   115
Or implement, a passive thing employed
As a brute mean, without acknowledg-
    ment
Of common right or interest in the end;
Used or abused, as selfishness may prompt.
Say, what can follow for a rational soul
Perverted thus, but weakness in all good,
And strength in evil? Hence an after-call
For chastisement, and custody, and bonds,
And ofttimes Death, avenger of the past,
And the sole guardian in whose hands we
    dare   125
Entrust the future.—Not for these sad
    issues
Was Man created; but to obey the law
Of life, and hope, and action. And 'tis
    known
That when we stand upon our native soil,
Unelbowed by such objects as oppress 130
Our active powers, those powers them-
    selves become
Strong to subvert our noxious qualities:
They sweep distemper from the busy day,
And make the chalice of the big round
    year
Run o'er with gladness; whence the Be-
    ing moves   135
In beauty through the world; and all
    who see
Bless him, rejoicing in his neighbour-
    hood."

"Then," said the Solitary, "by what force
Of language shall a feeling heart express
Her sorrow for that multitude in whom
We look for health from seeds that have
    been sown   141
In sickness, and for increase in a power
That works but by extinction? On them-
    selves
They cannot lean, nor turn to their own
    hearts
To know what they must do; their wis-
    dom is   145
To look into the eyes of others, thence
To be instructed what they must avoid:
Or rather, let us say, how least observed,
How with most quiet and most silent
    death,

With the least taint and injury to the
    air   150
The oppressor breathes, their human form
    divine,
And their immortal soul, may waste
    away."

The Sage rejoined, "I thank you—you
    have spared
My voice the utterance of a keen regret,
A wide compassion which with you I
    share.   155
When, heretofore, I placed before your
    sight
A Little-one, subjected to the arts
Of modern ingenuity, and made
The senseless member of a vast machine,
Serving as doth a spindle or a wheel; 160
Think not, that, pitying him, I could
    forget
The rustic Boy, who walks the fields,
    untaught;
The slave of ignorance, and oft of want,
And miserable hunger. Much, too much,
Of this unhappy lot, in early youth   165
We both have witnessed, lot which I
    myself
Shared, though in mild and merciful
    degree:
Yet was the mind to hinderances exposed,
Through which I struggled, not without
    distress
And sometimes injury, like a lamb en-
    thralled   170
'Mid thorns and brambles; or a bird that
    breaks
Through a strong net, and mounts upon
    the wind,
Though with her plumes impaired. If
    they, whose souls
Should open while they range the richer
    fields   174
Of merry England, are obstructed less
By indigence, their ignorance is not less,
Nor less to be deplored. For who can
    doubt
That tens of thousands at this day exist
Such as the boy you painted, lineal
    heirs
Of those who once were vassals of her
    soil,   180

Following its fortunes like the beasts or
   trees
Which it sustained. But no one takes
   delight
In this oppression; none are proud of it;
It bears no sounding name, nor ever bore;
A standing grievance, an indigenous vice
Of every country under heaven. My
   thoughts   186
Were turned to evils that are new and
   chosen,
A bondage lurking under shape of good,—
Arts, in themselves beneficent and kind,
But all too fondly followed and too far;—
To victims, which the merciful can see
Nor think that they are victims—turned
   to wrongs,
By women, who have children of their
   own,
Beheld without compassion, yea, with
   praise!
I spake of mischief by the wise diffused
With gladness, thinking that the more it
   spreads   196
The healthier, the securer, we become;
Delusion which a moment may destroy!
Lastly I mourned for those whom I had
   seen
Corrupted and cast down, on favoured
   ground,   200
Where circumstance and nature had com-
   bined
To shelter innocence, and cherish love;
Who, but for this intrusion, would have
   lived,
Possessed of health, and strength, and
   peace of mind;
Thus would have lived, or never have
   been born.   205

"Alas! what differs more than man
   from man!
And whence that difference? Whence but
   from himself?
For see the universal Race endowed
With the same upright form! The sun is
   fixed,   209
And the infinite magnificence of heaven
Fixed, within reach of every human eye;
The sleepless ocean murmurs for all ears;
The vernal field infuses fresh delight

Into all hearts. Throughout the world of
   sense,
Even as an object is sublime or fair,   215
That object is laid open to the view
Without reserve or veil; and as a power
Is salutary, or an influence sweet,
Are each and all enabled to perceive
That power, that influence, by impartial
   law.   220
Gifts nobler are vouchsafed alike to all;
Reason, and, with that reason, smiles and
   tears;
Imagination, freedom in the will;
Conscience to guide and check; and death
   to be
Foretasted, immortality conceived   225
By all,—a blissful immortality,
To them whose holiness on earth shall
   make
The Spirit capable of heaven, assured.
Strange, then, nor less than monstrous,
   might be deemed
The failure, if the Almighty, to this
   point   230
Liberal and undistinguishing, should hide
The excellence of moral qualities
From common understanding; leaving
   truth
And virtue, difficult, abstruse, and dark;
Hard to be won, and only by a few;   235
Strange, should He deal herein with nice
   respects,
And frustrate all the rest! Believe it not:
The primal duties shine aloft—like stars;
The charities that soothe, and heal, and
   bless,
Are scattered at the feet of Man—like
   flowers.   240
The generous inclination, the just rule,
Kind wishes, and good actions, and pure
   thoughts—
No mystery is here! Here is no boon
For high—yet not for low; for proudly
   graced—
Yet not for meek of heart. The smoke
   ascends   245
To heaven as lightly from the cottage-
   hearth
As from the haughtiest palace. He, whose
   soul
Ponders this true equality, may walk

The fields of earth with gratitude and
    hope;
Yet, in that meditation, will he find   250
Motive to sadder grief, as we have found;
Lamenting ancient virtues overthrown,
And for the injustice grieving, that hath
    made
So wide a difference between man and
    man.

    "Then let us rather fix our gladdened
        thoughts   255
Upon the brighter scene. How blest that
    pair
Of blooming Boys (whom we beheld even
    now)
Blest in their several and their common
    lot!
A few short hours of each returning day
The thriving prisoners of their village-
    school: 260
And thence let loose, to seek their pleasant
    homes
Or range the grassy lawn in vacancy;
To breathe and to be happy, run and
    shout
Idle,—but no delay, no harm, no loss;
For every genial power of heaven and
    earth,   265
Through all the seasons of the changeful
    year,
Obsequiously doth take upon herself
To labour for them; bringing each in turn
The tribute of enjoyment, knowledge,
    health,
Beauty, or strength! Such privilege is
    theirs,   270
Granted alike in the outset of their
    course
To both; and, if that partnership must
    cease,
I grieve not," to the Pastor here he
    turned,
" Much as I glory in that child of yours,
Repine not for his cottage-comrade,
    whom   275
Belike no higher destiny awaits
Than the old hereditary wish fulfilled;
The wish for liberty to live—content
With what Heaven grants, and die—in
    peace of mind,

Within the bosom of his native vale.   280
At least, whatever fate the noon of life
Reserves for either, sure it is that both
Have been permitted to enjoy the dawn;
Whether regarded as a jocund time,
That in itself may terminate, or lead   285
In course of nature to a sober eve.
Both have been fairly dealt with; looking
    back
They will allow that justice has in them
Been shown, alike to body and to mind."

He paused, as if revolving in his soul
Some weighty matter; then, with fervent
    voice   291
And an impassioned majesty, exclaimed—

    "O for the coming of that glorious
        time
When, prizing knowledge as her noblest
    wealth   294
And best protection, this imperial Realm,
While she exacts allegiance, shall admit
An obligation, on her part, to *teach*
Them who are born to serve her and
    obey;
Binding herself by statute to secure[1]
For all the children whom her soil
    maintains   300
The rudiments of letters, and inform
The mind with moral and religious truth,
Both understood and practised,—so that
    none,
However destitute, be left to droop
By timely culture unsustained; or run   305
Into a wild disorder; or be forced
To drudge through a weary life without
    the help
Of intellectual implements and tools;
A savage horde among the civilised,
A servile band among the lordly free!   310
This sacred right, the lisping babe pro-
    claims
To be inherent in him, by Heaven's will,
For the protection of his innocence;
And the rude boy—who, having overpast
The sinless age, by conscience is en-
    rolled,   315
Yet mutinously knits his angry brow,

---

[1] See Note, p. 933.

And lifts his wilful hand on mischief bent,
Or turns the godlike faculty of speech
To impious use—by process indirect
Declares his due, while he makes known
    his need.   320
—This sacred right is fruitlessly an-
    nounced,
This universal plea in vain addressed,
To eyes and ears of parents who them-
    selves
Did, in the time of their necessity,
Urge it in vain; and, therefore, like a
    prayer   325
That from the humblest floor ascends to
    heaven,
It mounts to reach the State's parental
    ear;
Who, if indeed she own a mother's heart,
And be not most unfeelingly devoid
Of gratitude to Providence, will grant 330
The unquestionable good—which, Eng-
    land, safe
From interference of external force,
May grant at leisure; without risk in-
    curred
That what in wisdom for herself she doth,
Others shall e'er be able to undo.   335

    "Look! and behold, from Calpe's sun-
        burnt cliffs
To the flat margin of the Baltic sea,
Long-reverenced titles cast away as weeds;
Laws overturned; and territory split,
Like fields of ice rent by the polar
    wind,   340
And forced to join in less obnoxious
    shapes
Which, ere they gain consistence, by a
    gust
Of the same breath are shattered and
    destroyed.
Meantime the sovereignty of these fair
    Isles
Remains entire and indivisible: 345
And, if that ignorance were removed,
    which breeds
Within the compass of their several shores
Dark discontent, or loud commotion, each
Might still preserve the beautiful repose
Of heavenly bodies shining in their
    spheres.   350

—The discipline of slavery is unknown
Among us,—hence the more do we re-
    quire
The discipline of virtue; order else
Cannot subsist, nor confidence, nor peace.
Thus, duties rising out of good possest 355
And prudent caution needful to avert
Impending evil, equally require
That the whole people should be taught
    and trained.
So shall licentiousness and black resolve
Be rooted out, and virtuous habits take 360
Their place; and genuine piety descend,
Like an inheritance, from age to age.

    "With such foundations laid, avaunt
        the fear
Of numbers crowded on their native soil,
To the prevention of all healthful
    growth   365
Through mutual injury! Rather in the
    law
Of increase and the mandate from above
Rejoice!—and ye have special cause for
    joy.
—For, as the element of air affords
An easy passage to the industrious
    bees   370
Fraught with their burthens; and a way
    as smooth
For those ordained to take their sounding
    flight
From the thronged hive, and settle where
    they list
In fresh abodes—their labour to renew;
So the wide waters, open to the power, 375
The will, the instincts, and appointed
    needs
Of Britain, do invite her to cast off
Her swarms, and in succession send them
    forth;
Bound to establish new communities
On every shore whose aspect favours
    hope   380
Or bold adventure; promising to skill
And perseverance their deserved reward.

    "Yes," he continued, kindling as he
        spake,
"Change wide, and deep, and silently
    performed,

This Land shall witness; and as days roll
    on,   385
Earth's universal frame shall feel the
    effect;
Even till the smallest habitable rock,
Beaten by lonely billows, hear the songs
Of humanised society; and bloom
With civil arts, that shall breathe forth
    their fragrance,   390
A grateful tribute to all-ruling Heaven.
From culture, unexclusively bestowed
On Albion's noble Race in freedom born,
Expect these mighty issues: from the
    pains   394
And faithful care of unambitious schools
Instructing simple childhood's ready ear:
Thence look for these magnificent results!
—Vast the circumference of hope—and ye
Are at its centre, British Lawgivers;
Ah! sleep not there in shame! Shall Wis-
    dom's voice   400
From out the bosom of these troubled
    times
Repeat the dictates of her calmer mind,
And shall the venerable halls ye fill
Refuse to echo the sublime decree?
Trust not to partial care a general good;
Transfer not to futurity a work   406
Of urgent need. Your Country must
    complete
Her glorious destiny. Begin even now,
Now, when oppression, like the Egyptian
    plague
Of darkness, stretched o'er guilty Europe,
    makes   410
The brightness more conspicuous that in-
    vests
The happy Island where ye think and
    act;
Now, when destruction is a prime pur-
    suit,
Show to the wretched nations for what
    end   414
The powers of civil polity were given."

Abruptly here, but with a graceful air,
The Sage broke off. No sooner had he
    ceased
Than, looking forth, the gentle Lady said,
"Behold the shades of afternoon have
    fallen

Upon this flowery slope; and see—be-
    yond—   420
The silvery lake is streaked with placid
    blue;
As if preparing for the peace of evening.
How temptingly the landscape shines!
    The air
Breathes invitation; easy is the walk
To the lake's margin, where a boat lies
    moored   425
Under a sheltering tree."—Upon this hint
We rose together: all were pleased; but
    most
The beauteous girl, whose cheek was
    flushed with joy.
Light as a sunbeam glides along the hills
She vanished—eager to impart the scheme
To her loved brother and his shy com-
    peer.   431
—Now was there bustle in the Vicar's
    house
And earnest preparation.—Forth we went,
And down the vale along the streamlet's
    edge
Pursued our way, a broken company,   435
Mute or conversing, single or in pairs.
Thus having reached a bridge, that over-
    arched
The hasty rivulet where it lay bespread
In a deep pool, by happy chance we saw
A twofold image; on a grassy bank   440
A snow-white ram, and in the crystal
    flood
Another and the same! Most beautiful,
On the green turf, with his imperial front
Shaggy and bold, and wreathèd horns su-
    perb,
The breathing creature stood; as beauti-
    ful,   445
Beneath him, showed his shadowy coun-
    terpart.
Each had his glowing mountains, each
    his sky,
And each seemed centre of his own fair
    world:
Antipodes unconscious of each other,
Yet, in partition, with their several
    spheres,   450
Blended in perfect stillness, to our sight!

"Ah! what a pity were it to disperse,

Or to disturb, so fair a spectacle,
And yet a breath can do it!"
                           These few words
The Lady whispered, while we stood and
        gazed   455
Gathered together, all in still delight,
Not without awe. Thence passing on,
        she said
In like low voice to my particular ear,
"I love to hear that eloquent old Man
Pour forth his meditations, and descant
On human life from infancy to age.   461
How pure his spirit! in what vivid hues
His mind gives back the various forms
        of things,
Caught in their fairest, happiest, atti-
        tude!
While he is speaking, I have power to
        see   465
Even as he sees; but when his voice hath
        ceased,
Then, with a sigh, sometimes I feel, as
        now,
That combinations so serene and bright
Cannot be lasting in a world like ours,
Whose highest beauty, beautiful as it
        is,   470
Like that reflected in yon quiet pool,
Seems but a fleeting sunbeam's gift, whose
        peace
The sufferance only of a breath of air!"

More had she said—but sportive shouts
        were heard
Sent from the jocund hearts of those two
        Boys,   475
Who, bearing each a basket on his arm,
Down the green field came tripping after
        us.
With caution we embarked; and now the
        pair
For prouder service were addrest; but
        each,
Wishful to leave an opening for my
        choice,   480
Dropped the light oar his eager hand had
        seized.
Thanks given for that becoming courtesy,
Their place I took—and for a grateful
        office
Pregnant with recollections of the time

When, on thy bosom, spacious Winder-
        mere!   485
A Youth, I practised this delightful art;
Tossed · on the waves alone, or 'mid a
        crew
Of joyous comrades. Soon as the reedy
        marge
Was cleared, I dipped, with arms ac-
        cordant, oars
Free from obstruction; and the boat ad-
        vanced   490
Through crystal water, smoothly as a
        hawk,
That, disentangled from the shady boughs
Of some thick wood, her place of covert,
        cleaves
With correspondent wings the abyss of
        air.
—"Observe," the Vicar said, "yon rocky
        isle   495
With birch-trees fringed; my hand shall
        guide the helm,
While thitherward we shape our course;
        or while
We seek that other, on the western shore;
Where the bare columns of those lofty
        firs,
Supporting gracefully a massy dome 500
Of sombre foliage, seem to imitate
A Grecian temple rising from the Deep."

"Turn where we may," said I, "we
        cannot err
In this delicious region."—Cultured slopes,
Wild tracts of forest-ground, and scat-
        tered groves,   505
And mountains bare, or clothed with
        ancient woods,
Surrounded us; and, as we held our way
Along the level of the glassy flood,
They ceased not to surround us; change
        of place,
From kindred features diversely com-
        bined,   510
Producing change of beauty ever new.
—Ah! that such beauty, varying in the
        light
Of living nature, cannot be portrayed
By words, nor by the pencil's silent skill;
But is the property of him alone   515
Who hath beheld it, noted it with care,

And in his mind recorded it with love!
Suffice it, therefore, if the rural Muse
Vouchsafe sweet influence, while her
    Poet speaks
Of trivial occupations well devised,   520
And unsought pleasures springing up by
    chance;
As if some friendly Genius had ordained
That, as the day thus far had been
    enriched
By acquisition of sincere delight,
The same should be continued to its
    close.   525

One spirit animating old and young,
A gipsy-fire we kindled on the shore
Of the fair Isle with birch-trees fringed—
    and there,
Merrily seated in a ring, partook
A choice repast—served by our young
    companions   530
With rival earnestness and kindred glee.
Launched from our hands the smooth
    stone skimmed the lake;
With shouts we raised the echoes;—
    stiller sounds
The lovely Girl supplied—a simple song,
Whose low tones reached not to the
    distant rocks   535
To be repeated thence, but gently sank
Into our hearts; and charmed the peace-
    ful flood.
Rapaciously we gathered flowery spoils
From land and water; lilies of each hue—
Golden and white, that float upon the
    waves,   540
And court the wind; and leaves of that
    shy plant,
(Her flowers were shed) the lily of the
    vale,
That loves the ground, and from the sun
    withholds
Her pensive beauty; from the breeze her
    sweets.

Such product, and such pastime, did
    the place   545
And season yield; but, as we re-
    embarked,
Leaving, in quest of other scenes, the
    shore

Of that wild spot, the Solitary said
In a low voice, yet careless who might
    hear,
"The fire, that burned so brightly to our
    wish,   550
Where is it now?—Deserted on the
    beach—
Dying, or dead! Nor shall the fanning
    breeze
Revive its ashes. What care we for this,
Whose ends are gained? Behold an
    emblem here
Of one day's pleasure, and all mortal
    joys!   555
And, in this unpremeditated slight
Of that which is no longer needed, see
The common course of human gratitude!"

This plaintive note disturbed not the
    repose
Of the still evening. Right across the lake
Our pinnace moves; then, coasting creek
    and bay,   561
Glades we behold, and into thickets peep,
Where couch the spotted deer; or raised
    our eyes
To shaggy steeps on which the careless
    goat
Browsed by the side of dashing water-
    falls;   565
And thus the bark, meandering with the
    shore,
Pursued her voyage, till a natural pier
Of jutting rock invited us to land.

Alert to follow as the Pastor led,
We clomb a green hill's side; and, as we
    clomb,   570
The Valley, opening out her bosom, gave
Fair prospect, intercepted less and less,
O'er the flat meadows and indented coast
Of the smooth lake, in compass seen:—
    far off,
And yet conspicuous, stood the old
    Church-tower,   575
In majesty presiding over fields
And habitations seemingly preserved
From all intrusion of the restless world
By rocks impassable and mountains huge.

Soft heath this elevated spot supplied,

And choice of moss-clad stones, whereon
   we couched   581
Or sate reclined; admiring quietly
The general aspect of the scene; but each
Not seldom over anxious to make known
His own discoveries; or to favourite
   points   585
Directing notice, merely from a wish
To impart a joy, imperfect while un-
   shared.
That rapturous moment never shall I
   forget
When these particular interests were
   effaced
From every mind!—Already had the
   sun,   590
Sinking with less than ordinary state,
Attained his western bound; but rays of
   light—
Now suddenly diverging from the orb
Retired behind the mountain-tops or
   veiled
By the dense air—shot upwards to the
   crown   595
Of the blue firmament—aloft, and wide:
And multitudes of little floating clouds,
Through their ethereal texture pierced—
   ere we,
Who saw, of change were conscious—had
   become
Vivid as fire; clouds separately poised,—
Innumerable multitude of forms   601
Scattered through half the circle of the
   sky;
And giving back, and shedding each on
   each,
With prodigal communion, the bright
   hues
Which from the unapparent fount of
   glory   605
They had imbibed, and ceased not to
   receive.
That which the heavens displayed, the
   liquid deep
Repeated; but with unity sublime!

While from the grassy mountain's open
   side
We gazed, in silence hushed, with eyes
   intent   610
On the refulgent spectacle, diffused

Through earth, sky, water, and all visible
   space,
The Priest in holy transport thus ex-
   claimed:

"Eternal Spirit! universal God!
Power inaccessible to human thought,
Save by degrees and steps which thou
   hast deigned   616
To furnish; for this effluence of thyself,
To the infirmity of mortal sense
Vouchsafed; this local transitory type
Of thy paternal splendours, and the
   pomp   620
Of those who fill thy courts in highest
   heaven,
The radiant Cherubim;—accept the
   thanks
Which we, thy humble Creatures, here
   convened,
Presume to offer; we, who—from the
   breast   624
Of the frail earth, permitted to behold
The faint reflections only of thy face—
Are yet exalted, and in soul adore!
Such as they are who in thy presence
   stand
Unsullied, incorruptible, and drink
Imperishable majesty streamed forth   630
From thy empyreal throne, the elect of
   earth
Shall be—divested at the appointed hour
Of all dishonour, cleansed from mortal
   stain.
—Accomplish, then, their number; and
   conclude
Time's weary course! Or if, by thy decree,
The consummation that will come by
   stealth   636
Be yet far distant, let thy Word prevail,
Oh! let thy Word prevail, to take away
The sting of human nature. Spread the
   law,
As it is written in thy holy book,   640
Throughout all lands: let every nation
   hear
The high behest, and every heart obey;
Both for the love of purity, and hope
Which it affords, to such as do thy will
And persevere in good, that they shall
   rise,   645

To have a nearer view of thee, in heaven.
—Father of good! this prayer in bounty
    grant,
In mercy grant it, to thy wretched sons.
Then, nor till then, shall persecution
    cease,
And cruel wars expire. The way is
    marked,   650
The guide appointed, and the ransom
    paid.
Alas! the nations, who of yore received
These tidings, and in Christian temples
    meet
The sacred truth to acknowledge, linger
    still;
Preferring bonds and darkness to a state
Of holy freedom, by redeeming love 656
Proffered to all, while yet on earth
    detained.

"So fare the many; and the thoughtful
    few,
Who in the anguish of their souls bewail
This dire perverseness, cannot choose but
    ask,   660
Shall it endure?—Shall enmity and strife,
Falsehood and guile, be left to sow their
    seed;
And the kind never perish? Is the hope
Fallacious, or shall righteousness obtain
A peaceable dominion, wide as earth, 665
And ne'er to fail? Shall that blest day
    arrive
When they, whose choice or lot it is to
    dwell
In crowded cities, without fear shall live
Studious of mutual benefit; and he,
Whom Morn awakens, among dews and
    flowers   670
Of every clime, to till the lonely field,
Be happy in himself?—The law of faith
Working through love, such conquest
    shall it gain,
Such triumph over sin and guilt achieve?
Almighty Lord, thy further grace im-
    part!   675
And with that help the wonder shall be
    seen
Fulfilled, the hope accomplished; and thy
    praise
Be sung with transport and unceasing joy.

"Once," and with wild demeanour, as
    he spake,
On us the venerable Pastor turned   680
His beaming eye that had been raised to
    Heaven,
"Once, while the Name, Jehovah, was a
    sound
Within the circuit of this sea-girt isle
Unheard, the savage nations bowed the
    head
To Gods delighting in remorseless deeds;
Gods which themselves had fashioned, to
    promote   686
Ill purposes, and flatter foul desires.
Then, in the bosom of yon mountain-cove,
To those inventions of corrupted man
Mysterious rites were solemnised; and
    there—   690
Amid impending rocks and gloomy
    woods—
Of those terrific Idols some received
Such dismal service, that the loudest voice
Of the swoln cataracts (which now are
    heard
Soft murmuring) was too weak to over-
    come,   695
Though aided by wild winds, the groans
    and shrieks
Of human victims, offered up to appease
Or to propitiate. And, if living eyes
Had visionary faculties to see
The thing that hath been as the thing
    that is,   700
Aghast we might behold this crystal Mere
Bedimmed with smoke, in wreaths volu-
    minous,
Flung from the body of devouring fires,
To Taranis erected on the heights
By priestly hands, for sacrifice performed
Exultingly, in view of open day   706
And full assemblage of a barbarous host;
Or to Andates, female Power! who gave
(For so they fancied) glorious victory.
—A few rude monuments of mountain-
    stone   710
Survive; all else is swept away.—How
    bright
The appearances of things! From such,
    how changed
The existing worship; and with those
    compared,

The worshippers how innocent and blest!
So wide the difference, a willing mind
Might almost think, at this affecting
    hour,   716
That paradise, the lost abode of man,
Was raised again: and to a happy few,
In its original beauty, here restored.

"Whence but from thee, the true and
        only God,   720
And from the faith derived through Him
    who bled
Upon the cross, this marvellous advance
Of good from evil; as if one extreme
Were left, the other gained.—O ye, who
    come   724
To kneel devoutly in yon reverend Pile,
Called to such office by the peaceful sound
Of sabbath bells; and ye, who sleep in
    earth,
All cares forgotten, round its hallowed
    walls!
For you, in presence of this little band
Gathered together on the green hill-side,
Your Pastor is emboldened to prefer 731
Vocal thanksgivings to the eternal King;
Whose love, whose counsel, whose com-
    mands, have made
Your very poorest rich in peace of thought
And in good works; and him, who is
    endowed   735
With scantiest knowledge, master of all
    truth
Which the salvation of his soul requires.
Conscious of that abundant favour show-
    ered
On you, the children of my humble care,
And this dear land, our country, while on
    earth   740
We sojourn, have I lifted up my soul,
Joy giving voice to fervent gratitude.
These barren rocks, your stern inherit-
    ance;
These fertile fields, that recompense your
    pains;
The shadowy vale, the sunny mountain-
    top;   745
Woods waving in the wind their lofty
    heads,
Or hushed; the roaring waters, and the
    still—

They see the offering of my lifted hands,
They hear my lips present their sacrifice,
They know if I be silent, morn or even:
For, though in whispers speaking, the
    full heart   751
Will find a vent; and thought is praise
    to him,
Audible praise, to thee, omniscient Mind,
From whom all gifts descend, all bless-
    ings flow!"

    This vesper-service closed, without de-
        lay,   755
From that exalted station to the plain
Descending, we pursued our homeward
    course,
In mute composure, o'er the shadowy
    lake,
Under a faded sky. No trace remained
Of those celestial splendours; grey the
    vault—   760
Pure, cloudless, ether; and the star of
    eve
Was wanting; but inferior lights appeared
Faintly, too faint almost for sight; and
    some
Above the darkened hills stood boldly
    forth
In twinkling lustre, ere the boat attained
Her mooring-place; where, to the shelter-
    ing tree,   766
Our youthful Voyagers bound fast her
    prow,
With prompt yet careful hands. This
    done, we paced
The dewy fields; but ere the Vicar's door
Was reached, the Solitary checked his
    steps;   770
Then, intermingling thanks, on each be-
    stowed
A farewell salutation; and, the like
Receiving, took the slender path that
    leads
To the one cottage in the lonely dell:
But turned not without welcome promise
    made   775
That he would share the pleasures and
    pursuits
Of yet another summer's day, not loth
To wander with us through the fertile
    vales,

And o'er the mountain-wastes. "An-
other sun,"
Said he, "shall shine upon us, ere we
part;   780
Another sun, and peradventure more;
If time, with free consent, be yours to
give,
And season favours."
          To enfeebled Power,
From this communion with uninjured
Minds,
What renovation had been brought; and
what   785
Degree of healing to a wounded spirit,

Dejected, and habitually disposed
To seek, in degradation of the Kind,
Excuse and solace for her own defects;
How far those erring notions were re-
formed;   790
And whether aught, of tendency as good
And pure, from further intercourse en-
sued;
This—if delightful hopes, as heretofore,
Inspire the serious song, and gentle
Hearts
Cherish, and lofty Minds approve the
past—   795
My future labours may not leave untold.

INDEX OF FIRST LINES.

THE END.